To Sue and Karen

To the memory of Helena G. Piercy
(1911–2001)

Preface

Strategic marketing in companies around the world is confronted with unprecedented challenges and exciting opportunities in the twenty-first century. Driven by demanding customers with complex value requirements, aggressive global competition, turbulent markets, rapid emergence of disruptive new technologies, and global expansion initiatives, marketing strategy has become an enterprise-spanning responsibility with major bottom-line implications. Central to the opportunities generated by these challenges is a critical need to improve executives' understanding of markets and competitive space, customer value delivery, innovation culture and processes, and effective organizational design.

Strategic marketing's demanding role in business performance is demonstrated in the market-driven strategies of successful organizations competing in a wide array of market and competitive situations. Providing superior customer value, leveraging distinctive capabilities, responding rapidly to diversity and change in the marketplace, developing innovation cultures, and recognizing global business challenges are demanding initiatives which require effective marketing strategies for gaining and sustaining a competitive edge. *Strategic Marketing* examines the underlying logic and processes for designing and implementing market-driven strategies.

Market-Driven Strategy

Providing superior value to customers is the core objective of market-driven strategy. Several initiatives are necessary in achieving this objective.

- Marketing strategy provides the guidelines for action that are essential in delivering superior customer value.
- Marketing is a major stakeholder in the essential organizational core processes—new product development, customer relationship management, value/supply-chain management, and business strategy implementation.
- Essential relationship initiatives place new priorities on collaborating with customers, suppliers, value-chain members, and even competitors.
- Understanding customers, competitors, and the market environment requires the active involvement of the entire organization to gain and manage market knowledge decisively.
- Developing methods that enable the organization to continually learn from customers, competitors, and other relevant sources is vital to sustaining a competitive edge.
- The powerful technologies provided by the Internet and the World Wide Web, corporate intranets, and advanced communication and collaboration systems for customer and supplier relationship management underpin effective strategy processes.
- The environmental, ethical, and corporate responsibility aspects of business practice are critical concerns for individual executives as well as their companies, requiring management direction and active involvement by the entire organization.

Customer diversity and new forms of competition create impressive growth and performance opportunities for those firms that successfully apply strategic marketing concepts and analyses in business strategy development and implementation. The challenge to become market-driven is apparent in a wide array of industries around the world. Analyzing market

Strategic Marketing

Ninth Edition

David W. Cravens

M.J. Neeley School of Business
Texas Christian University

Nigel F. Piercy

Warwick Business School
The University of Warwick

Boston   New York   San Francisco   St. Louis
Bangkok   Lisbon   London   Madrid   Mexico City
Milan   Montreal   New Delhi   Santiago   Seoul   Singapore   Sydney   Taipei   Toronto

The McGraw·Hill Companies

STRATEGIC MARKETING
International Edition 2009

Exclusive rights by McGraw-Hill Education (Asia), for manufacture and export. This book cannot be re-exported from the country to which it is sold by McGraw-Hill. This International Edition is not to be sold or purchased in North America and contains content that is different from its North American version.

10 09 08 07 06 05 04 03 02 01
20 09 08
CTF   SLP

Page 16: McGraw-Hill Companies, Inc., Jill Braaten, photographer; page 51; Courtesy of Google; page 88: McGraw-Hill Companies, Inc., Jill Braaten, photographer; page 117: Courtesy of ACCOR; page 135: Courtesy of Best Buy; page 197: ©2007 Keith Eng, photographer; page 227: ©2007 Keith Eng, photographer; page 262: McGraw-Hill Companies, Inc., Jill Braaten, photographer; page 290: McGraw-Hill Companies, Inc., John Flournoy, photographer; page 332: ©2007 Keith Eng, photographer; page 349: Netjets Inc.; page 385: McGraw-Hill Companies, Inc., John Flournoy, photographer; page 404: AP Photo/Ben Margot; page 447: ©2007 Keith Eng, photographer; page 465: McGraw-Hill Companies, Inc., John Flournoy, photographer; page 482: AP Photo/Kathy Willens

When ordering this title, use ISBN: 978-007-126335-1 or MHID: 007-126335-7

Printed in Singapore

www.mhhe.com

behavior and matching strategies to changing conditions require a hands-on approach to marketing strategy development and implementation. Penetrating financial analysis is an important strategic marketing requirement.

Strategic Marketing examines marketing strategy using a combination of concepts, application processes, and cases to develop managers' and professionals' decision making processes and apply them to business situations. The book is intended for use in undergraduate capstone marketing strategy courses and the MBA marketing core and advanced strategy courses.

New and Expanded Scope

Regardless of business size and scope, competing in any market today requires a global perspective. The ninth edition accentuates this global perspective. The author team provides an extensive range of global involvement. The shrinking time-and-access boundaries of global markets establish new competitive requirements. The global dimensions of marketing strategy are integrated throughout the chapters of the book and also considered in several cases. The rapid emergence of powerful new competitive forces throughout the world, often facilitated by new business models, mandates an international viewpoint for executives in most organizations.

Strategic customer relationship management (CRM) is examined in a new chapter, recognizing the escalating importance of this topic in business firms and its essential role in guiding marketing strategy. Customer equity and customer lifetime value are examined along with other relevant aspects of CRM.

Innovation and new product planning and strategic brand management are given increased coverage in this edition. Enhancing brand equity has become a top priority challenge in companies around the world.

Internet initiatives comprise a vital part of the marketing strategies of all companies. Internet strategies are rapidly expanding on a global basis. Because of the nature and scope of the various uses of the Internet, we have integrated this important topic into several chapters rather than developing a separate chapter. Internet Features are included in all chapters.

Special attention and emphasis are given to marketing metrics throughout the book. Improving the measurement of marketing effectiveness is a high priority issue in many companies.

New current applications of business marketing initiatives are included in every chapter. New features examine strategy, innovations, relationship, global ethics and corporate responsibility, Internet, and metrics aspects of business practice.

Teaching and Learning Design

Strategic Marketing uses a decision-making perspective to examine the key concepts and issues involved in analyzing and selecting strategies. It is apparent that many instructors want to examine marketing strategy beyond the traditional emphasis on marketing functions. Marketing strategy is considered from a total business perspective. The length and design of the book offer flexibility in the use of the text material and cases. The feature applications included in each chapter can be used for class discussion and assignments.

The book is designed around the marketing strategy process with a clear emphasis on analysis, planning, and implementation. Part I provides an overview of market-driven strategy and business and marketing strategies. Part II considers markets, segments, and customer value. Part III provides the basis for designing market-driven strategies. Part IV considers market-driven program development. Finally, Part V examines implementing and managing market-driven strategies. Decision process guidelines and applications are provided throughout the book to assist the reader in applying the analysis and strategy development approaches discussed in the text.

The Cases

There are 21 new cases out of a total of 44. Many are well-known companies that students should find both interesting and challenging. Shorter application-focused cases are placed at the end of each part of the book. These cases are useful in applying the concepts and methods discussed in the chapters, and they can be used for class discussion, hand-in assignments, and/or class presentations. The cases consider a wide variety of business environments, both domestic and international. They include goods and services; organizations at different value-chain levels; and small, medium, and large enterprises. The Features in every chapter provide additional illustrations and material for consideration and discussion.

Most of the cases examine the marketing and business strategies of well-known companies. The cases are very timely, offering an interesting and challenging look at contemporary business practice. Importantly, these companies have available extensive financial, product, and corporate information on the Internet, which expands analysis opportunities.

Part VI includes comprehensive cases that offer students a variety of opportunities to apply marketing strategy concepts. Each case considers several important strategy issues. The cases represent different competitive situations for consumer and business goods and services as well as domestic and international markets.

Changes in the Ninth Edition

The ninth edition of *Strategic Marketing* follows the basic design of previous editions. Nevertheless, the revision incorporates many significant changes, topic additions, and updated examples. Every chapter includes new material and expanded treatment of important topics.

Each chapter has been revised to incorporate new concepts and examples, improve readability and flow, and encourage reader interest and involvement. Topical coverage has been expanded (or reduced) where appropriate, to better position the book for teaching and learning in today's rapidly changing business environment. An expanded set of Internet and Feature applications is included at the end of each chapter. Marketing planning guidelines are provided in the Chapter 1 Appendix, financial analysis suggestions are included in the Chapter 2 Appendix, and marketing metrics are discussed in the Chapter 15 Appendix.

Teaching/Learning Resources

A complete and expanded teaching-learning portfolio is available on the Online Learning Center, at www.mhhe.com/cravens9e. It includes an Instructor's Manual with course-planning suggestions, answers to end-of-chapter questions, Internet application guidelines, Feature application guidelines, and extensive instructor's notes for each of the 44 cases. A multiple-choice question test bank and a PowerPoint® presentation for each chapter are also included online. The PowerPoints provide a complete and organized coverage of the chapter topics and application examples.

This edition of the manual has been substantially revised and expanded to improve its effectiveness in supporting course planning, class discussion, and examination preparation. Detailed instructor's notes concerning the use of the cases are provided, including epilogues when available. The text, cases, and Instructor's Manual offer considerable flexibility in course design, depending on the instructor's objectives and the course for which the book is used.

Acknowledgments

The ninth edition has benefited from the contributions and experiences of many people and organizations. Business executives and colleagues at universities in many countries have influenced the development of *Strategic Marketing*. While space does not permit thanking each person, a sincere note of appreciation is extended to all. We shall identify several individuals whose assistance was particularly important.

A special thank you is extended to the reviewers of this and prior editions and to many colleagues who have offered numerous suggestions and ideas. Throughout the development of the ninth edition, several individuals made important suggestions for improving the book.

We are also indebted to the case authors who gave us permission to use their cases. We appreciate the opportunity to include them in the book. Each author or authors are specifically identified with each case.

A special note of thanks is due to the management and professional team of McGraw-Hill/Irwin for their support and encouragement on this and prior editions of *Strategic Marketing:* Paul Ducham, as publisher, has provided an important editorial leadership role; Editor Laura Spell and Editorial Assistant Sara Hunter have been a constant source of valuable assistance and encouragement; Dean Karampelas provided important marketing direction for the project; James Labeots guided the book through the various stages of production while Matthew Baldwin polished the design.

Students have provided various kinds of support that were essential to completing the revision. In particular, we appreciate the excellent contribution to this edition made by Jeremy Lamb, TCU graduate assistant. We also acknowledge the helpful comments and suggestions of many students in our classes.

We appreciate the support and encouragement provided by Dan Short, Dean of the TCU Neeley School of Business, and Howard Thomas, Dean of Warwick Business School. Special thanks are due to Connie Clark at TCU and Sheila Frost at Warwick University for their help on the manuscript and for their assistance in other aspects of the project.

David W. Cravens

Nigel F. Piercy

About the Authors

David W. Cravens

David W. Cravens is Emeritus Professor of Marketing in the M.J. Neeley School of Business at Texas Christian University. He previously held the Eunice and James L. West Chair of American Enterprise Studies and was Professor of Marketing. Formerly, he was the Alcoa Foundation Professor at the University of Tennessee, where he chaired the Department of Marketing and Transportation and the Management Science Program. He has a Doctorate in Business Administration and MBA from Indiana University. He holds a Bachelor of Science in Civil Engineering from Massachusetts Institute of Technology. Before becoming an educator, Dave held various industry and government management positions. He is internationally recognized for his research on marketing strategy and sales management and has contributed over 150 articles and 25 books. Dave is a former editor of the *Journal of Academy of Marketing Science.* He has held various positions in the American Marketing Association and the Academy of Marketing Science. He received the Lifetime Achievement Award from the American Marketing Association in 2002 and was selected as the 1996 Outstanding Marketing Educator by the Academy of Marketing Science. He serves on the editorial boards of several academic journals. He has been a visiting scholar at universities in Austria, Australia, Chile, Czech Republic, England, Ireland, Italy, Germany, Mexico, The Netherlands, New Zealand, Singapore, Switzerland, and Wales. He has conducted management seminars and executive briefings in many countries in Asia, Europe, and South America. He is a frequent speaker at management development seminars and industry conferences.

Nigel F. Piercy

Nigel F. Piercy is Professor of Marketing and Strategic Management at Warwick Business School, in the University of Warwick, United Kingdom, where he also leads the Sales and Account Management Strategy research unit. He was previously Professor of Strategic Marketing and Head of the Marketing Group at Cranfield School of Management, and for a number of years was the Sir Julian Hodge Chair in Marketing and Strategy at Cardiff University. He has been a visiting scholar at Texas Christian University; University of California, Berkeley; Fuqua School of Business, Duke University; Columbia Business School; Athens Laboratory of Business Administration; and Vienna University of Business and Economics. He has extensive experience in executive education and as a management workshop speaker. He has worked with managers and business students in the United States, Europe, the Far East, South Africa, and Zimbabwe. He holds a PhD from the University of Wales, an MA from Durham University Business School, and a BA from Heriot-Watt University, Edinburgh, Scotland. He has been awarded the distinction of a higher doctorate (Doctor of Letters) from Heriot-Watt University for his published research work. Prior to academic life, Nigel was in retail management and latterly in strategic market planning with Nycomed Amersham plc. His research is in the areas of marketing strategy and implementation, and sales management. He has published some 200 articles and chapters and 16 books. He is editor of the *Journal of Strategic Marketing* and serves on the editorial boards of several scholarly journals.

Brief Contents

PART ONE
Strategic Marketing   1

1   Imperatives for Market-Driven
Strategy   2

1A Appendix Strategic Marketing
Planning   27

Cases for Part One   30

PART TWO
**Markets, Segments, and Customer
Value   47**

2   Markets and Competitive Space   48

2A Appendix Financial Analysis for
Marketing Planning and Control   74

3   Strategic Marketing Segmentation   83

4   Strategic Customer Relationship
Management   113

5   Capabilities for Learning About Customers
and Markets   129

Cases for Part Two   156

PART THREE
Designing Market-Driven Strategies   183

6   Market Targeting and Strategic
Positioning   184

7   Strategic Relationships   206

8   Innovation and New Product
Strategy   236

Cases for Part Three   269

PART FOUR
Market-Driven Program Development   289

9   Strategic Brand Management   290

10 Value Chain Strategy   318

11 Pricing Strategy   347

12 Promotion, Advertising, and Sales
Promotion Strategies   372

13 Sales Force, Internet, and Direct
Marketing Strategies   396

Cases for Part Four   418

PART FIVE
**Implementing and Managing Market-Driven
Strategies   443**

14 Designing Market-Driven
Organizations   444

15 Marketing Strategy Implementation
and Control   473

15A Appendix Marketing Metrics   499

Cases for Part Five   502

PART SIX
Comprehensive Cases   525

INDEXES

Name Index   765

Subject Index   772

Table of Contents

PART ONE
STRATEGIC MARKETING   1

Chapter 1
Imperatives for Market-Driven Strategy   2

Market-Driven Strategy   3
  Characteristics of Market-Driven Strategies   4
  Determining Distinctive Capabilities   5
  Classifying Capabilities   6
  Creating Value for Customers   7
  Becoming Market Driven   7
Corporate, Business, and Marketing Strategy   8
  Corporate, Business, and Marketing Strategy   10
  Components of Corporate Strategy   10
  Corporate Strategy Framework   10
  Business and Marketing Strategy   12
  The Marketing Strategy Process   13
Challenges of a New Era for Strategic Marketing   18
  Escalating Globalization   18
  Technology Diversity and Uncertainty   19
  The Web 2.0   20
  Ethical Behavior and Corporate Social Responsiveness   20
Summary   23
Appendix 1A
Strategic Marketing Planning   27

Cases for Part One   30
Case 1-1 Audi   30
Case 1-2 The *New York Times*   34
Case 1-3 Coca-Cola Co. (A)   40

PART TWO
MARKETS, SEGMENTS, AND CUSTOMER VALUE   47

Chapter 2
Markets and Competitive Space   48

Markets and Strategies   49
  Markets and Strategies Are Interlinked   49
  Thinking Outside the Competitive Box   50
  An Array of Challenges   50

Matching Needs with Product Benefits   52
Defining and Analyzing Product-Markets   53
  Forming Product-Markets   55
  Illustrative Product-Market Structure   57
Describing and Analyzing End-Users   57
  Identifying and Describing Buyers   58
  How Buyers Make Choices   59
  Environmental Influences   60
  Building Customer Profiles   60
Analyzing Competition   61
  Defining the Competitive Arena   61
  Key Competitor Analysis   64
  Anticipating Competitors' Actions   66
Market Size Estimation   67
  Market Potential   67
  Sales Forecast   68
  Market Share   68
  Evaluating Market Opportunity   68
Developing a Strategic Vision About the Future   70
  Phases of Competition   70
  Anticipating the Future   70
Summary   71
Appendix 2A
Financial Analysis for Marketing Planning and Control   74

Chapter 3
Strategic Marketing Segmentation   83

Levels and Types of Market Segmentation   84
Market-Driven Strategy and Segmentation   86
  Market Segmentation, Value Opportunities, and New-Market Space   86
  Market Targeting and Strategic Positioning   87
Activities and Decisions in Market Segmentation   89
Defining the Market to Be Segmented   89
Identifying Market Segments   90
  Segmentation Variables   90
  Characteristics of People and Organizations   90
  Product Use Situation Segmentation   91
  Buyers' Needs and Preferences   93
  Purchase Behavior   94
Forming Market Segments   96
  Requirements for Segmentation   96
  Approaches to Segment Identification   98

Customer Group Identification   99
Forming Groups Based on Response Differences   102
Finer Segmentation Strategies   104
Logic of Finer Segments   104
Finer Segmentation Strategies   105
Selecting the Segmentation Strategy   106
Deciding How to Segment   106
Strategic Analysis of Market Segments   106
Summary   109

Chapter 4
Strategic Customer Relationship
Management   113

Pivotal Role of Customer Relationship
Management   114
CRM in Perspective   114
CRM and Database Marketing   114
Customer Lifetime Value   115
Developing a CRM Strategy   116
CRM Levels   116
CRM Strategy Development   118
CRM Implementation   119
Value Creation Process   121
Customer Value   121
Value Received by the Organization   122
CRM and Value Chain Strategy   123
CRM and Strategic Marketing   123
Implementation   123
Performance Metrics   124
Short-Term Versus Long-Term Value   124
Competitive Differentiation   124
Summary   126

Chapter 5
Capabilities for Learning About Customers
and Markets   129

Market-Driven Strategy, Market Sensing,
and Learning Processes   130
Market Sensing Processes   131
Learning Organization   131
Marketing Information and Knowledge Resources   134
Scanning Processes   136
Specific Market Research Studies   138
*Internal and External Marketing Information
Resources*   138
Existing Marketing Information Sources   141
Creating New Marketing Information   143
Marketing and Management Information Systems   146

Marketing Intelligence and Knowledge
Management   147
Marketing Intelligence   147
Knowledge Management   148
Role of the Chief Knowledge Officer   148
Leveraging Customer Knowledge   148
Ethical Issues in Collecting and Using
Information   149
Invasion of Customer Privacy   149
Information and Ethics   150
Summary   151

Cases for Part Two   156

Case 2-1 Pfizer, Inc.   156
Case 2-2 Ikea   162
Case 2-3 China and India: Opportunities
and Challenges   168
Case 2-4 Johnson & Johnson   177

PART THREE
DESIGNING MARKET-DRIVEN
STRATEGIES   183

Chapter 6
Market Targeting and Strategic
Positioning   184

Market Targeting Strategy   185
Targeting Alternatives   185
Factors Influencing Targeting Decisions   186
Targeting in Different Marketing
Environments   187
Emerging Markets   188
Growth Markets   189
Mature Markets   190
Global Markets   192
Positioning Strategy   193
Selecting the Positioning Concept   195
Developing the Positioning Strategy   196
Scope of Positioning Strategy   197
Marketing Program Decisions   197
Determining Positioning Effectiveness   199
Customer and Competitor Research   200
Test Marketing   200
Analytical Positioning Techniques   201
Determining Positioning Effectiveness   201
Positioning and Targeting Strategies   202
Summary   202

Chapter 7
Strategic Relationships   206

The Rationale for Interorganizational
Relationships   207
   Opportunities to Enhance Value   208
   Environmental Complexity   209
   Competitive Strategy   209
   Skills and Resource Gaps   209
   Evaluating the Potential for Collaboration   213
Forms of Organizational Relationships   214
   Supplier Relationships   215
   Intermediate Customer Relationships   216
   End-User Customer Relationships   217
   Strategic Customers   217
   Strategic Alliances   219
   Joint Ventures   221
   Internal Partnering   221
Managing Interorganizational Relationships   223
   Objective of the Relationship   223
   Relationship Management   224
   Partnering Capabilities   225
   Control and Evaluation   226
   Exiting from Alliance   226
Global Relationships Among Organizations   227
   The Strategic Role of Government   228
Summary   231

Chapter 8
Innovation and New Product Strategy   236

Innovation as a Customer-Driven Process   238
   Types of Innovations   239
   Finding Customer Value Opportunities   239
   Finding New Product Opportunities   239
   Initiatives of Successful Innovators   242
   *Recognizing the Realities of Product
   Cannibalization   244*
New-Product Planning   244
   Developing a Culture and Strategy for Innovation   245
   *Developing Effective New-Product Planning
   Processes   247*
   Responsibility for New-Product Planning   248
Idea Generation   249
   Sources of Ideas   249
   Methods of Generating Ideas   251
Screening, Evaluating, and Business Analysis   253
   Screening   253
   Concept Evaluation   254
   Business Analysis   255

Product and Process Development   257
   Product Development Process   257
Marketing Strategy and Market Testing   260
   Market Strategy Decisions   260
   Market Testing   260
Commercialization   263
   The Marketing Plan   263
   Monitoring and Control   263
Variations in the Generic New Product
Planning Process   264
Summary   265

Cases for Part Three   269

Case 3-1 Walt Disney Co.   269
Case 3-2 Intel Corp.   274
Case 3-3 McDonald's Corp.   281
Case 3-4 Tesco Plc.   285

PART FOUR
MARKET-DRIVEN PROGRAM
DEVELOPMENT   289

Chapter 9
Strategic Brand Management   290

Strategic Brand Management   291
   The Strategic Role of Brands   291
   Brand Management Challenges   292
   Brand Management Responsibility   296
   Strategic Brand Management   296
Strategic Brand Analysis   298
   Tracking Brand Performance   299
   Product Life Cycle Analysis   300
   Product Performance Analysis   300
   Brand Positioning Analysis   301
Brand Equity Measurement and Management   301
   Measuring Brand Equity   301
   Brand Health Reports   301
Brand Identity Strategy   302
   Alternatives for Brand Identification   302
   Brand Focus   303
   Identity Implementation   304
Managing Brand Strategy   304
   Strategies for Improving Product Performance   304
Managing the Brand Portfolio   306
   Determining Roles of Brands   307
   Strategies for Brand Strength   307
   Strategic Brand Vulnerabilities   308

Brand Leveraging Strategy   310
  Line Extension   310
  Stretching the Brand Vertically   310
  Brand Extension   311
  Co-Branding   311
  Licensing   311
  Global Branding   311
  Internet Brands   312
  Brand Theft   313
Summary   314

Chapter 10
Value Chain Strategy   318

Strategic Role of Value Chain   319
  Distribution Functions   319
  Channels for Services   321
  Direct Distribution by Manufacturers   321
Channel Strategy   323
  Types of Channels   324
  Distribution Intensity   327
  Channel Configuration   328
  Channel Maps   329
  Selecting the Channel Strategy   330
  Changing Channel Strategy   331
Managing the Channel   333
  Channel Leadership   334
  Management Structure and Systems   334
  Physical Distribution Management   334
  Channel Relationships   336
  Channel Globalization   336
  Multichanneling   337
  Conflict Resolution   337
  Channel Performance   338
  Legal and Ethical Considerations   338
International Channels   340
  Examining International Distribution Patterns   341
  Factors Affecting Global Channel Selection   342
  Global Issues Regarding Multichannel Strategies   342
Summary   343

Chapter 11
Pricing Strategy   347

Strategic Role of Price   348
  Price in the Positioning Strategy   349
  Pricing Situations   350
  Roles of Pricing   350
  Pricing Strategy   351
  Pricing Objectives   352

Analyzing the Pricing Situation   353
  Customer Price Sensitivity   353
  Cost Analysis   356
  Competitor Analysis   357
  Pricing Objectives   359
Selecting the Pricing Strategy   360
  How Much Flexibility Exists?   360
  Price Positioning and Visibility   362
  Illustrative Pricing Strategies   362
  Legal and Ethical Considerations   363
Determining Specific Prices and Policies   365
  Determining Specific Prices   365
  Establishing Pricing Policy and Structure   367
  Pricing Management   367
Summary   369

Chapter 12
Promotion, Advertising, and Sales
Promotion Strategies   372

Promotion Strategy   373
  The Composition of Promotion Strategy   373
  Designing Promotion Strategy   375
  Communication Objectives   376
  Deciding the Role of the Promotion Components   378
  Determining the Promotion Budget   378
  Promotion Component Strategies   380
  Integrating and Implementing the Promotion Strategy   380
  Effectiveness of Promotion Strategy   381
Advertising Strategy   381
  Setting Advertising Objectives and Budgeting   382
  Creative Strategy   384
  Media/Scheduling Decisions   384
  Role of the Advertising Agency   386
  *Implementing the Advertising Strategy and
  Measuring Its Effectiveness   388*
Sales Promotion Strategy   389
  Nature and Scope of Sales Promotion   389
  Sales Promotion Activities   390
  Advantages and Limitations of Sales Promotion   392
  Sales Promotion Strategy   393
Summary   393

Chapter 13
Sales Force, Internet, and Direct
Marketing Strategies   396

Sales Force Strategy   397
  The Role of Selling in Promotion Strategy   398
  Types of Sales Jobs   399

Defining the Selling Process   400
Sales Channels   401
Designing the Sales Organization   402
Sales Force Evaluation and Control   407
Internet Strategy   408
Strategy Development   409
Deciding Internet Objectives   409
E-Commerce Strategy   410
Value Opportunities and Risks   410
Measuring Internet Effectiveness   411
The Future of the Internet   411
Direct Marketing Strategies   412
Reasons for Using Direct Marketing   412
Direct Marketing Methods   413
Advantages of Direct Marketing   414
Direct Marketing Strategy   415
Summary   415

Cases for Part Four   418
Case 4-1 Microsoft Corp.   418
Case 4-2 Nike Inc.   425
Case 4-3 Dell Inc.   433
Case 4-4 Hewlett-Packard Co.   439

PART FIVE
IMPLEMENTING AND MANAGING
MARKET-DRIVEN STRATEGIES   443

Chapter 14
Designing Market-Driven Organizations   444

Trends in Organization Design   445
The New Organization   445
Managing Organizational Process   449
Organizational Agility and Flexibility   451
Employee Motivation   451
Organizing for Market-Driven Strategy   452
Strategic Marketing and Organization Structure   452
Aligning the Organization with the Market   452
Marketing Functions Versus Marketing Processes   453
Marketing as a Cross-Functional Process   454
Marketing Departments   456
Centralization Versus Decentralization   456
Integration or Diffusion   456
Contingencies for Organizing   457
Evaluating Organization Designs   457
Structuring Marketing Resources   459
Structuring Issues   459
Functional Organizational Design   459

Product-Focused Design   459
Market-Focused Design   461
Matrix Design   461
New Marketing Roles   462
Organizing for Global Marketing and Global
Customers   465
Organizing for Global Marketing Strategies   466
Organizing for Global Customers   467
Summary   469

Chapter 15
Marketing Strategy Implementation
and Control   473

The Strategy Marketing Planning Process   474
The Marketing Plan Guides Implementation   474
Contents of the Marketing Plan   475
Managing the Planning Process   475
Implementing the Strategic Marketing Plan   477
Implementation Process   477
Building Implementation Effectiveness   478
Internal Marketing   479
*A Comprehensive Approach to Improving
Implementation   481*
Internal Strategy-Organization Fit   481
Strategic Marketing Evaluation and Control   482
Customer Relationship Management   483
Overview of Control and Evaluation Activities   483
The Strategic Marketing Audit   483
Marketing Performance Measurement   486
The Importance of Marketing Metrics   487
The Use of Marketing Metrics   487
Types of Marketing Metrics   488
Selecting Relevant Metrics   488
Designing a Management Dashboard   489
Interpreting Performance Measurement Results   490
Global Issues for Planning, Implementation,
and Control   493
Global Marketing Planning   493
Implementation Globally   494
Performance Measurement and Control Globally   494
Summary   495
Appendix 15A
Marketing Metrics   499

Cases for Part Five   502
Case 5-1 Verizon Communications Inc.   502
Case 5-2 Home Depot Inc.   507
Case 5-3 Yahoo! Inc.   514
Case 5-4 Nissan Motor Co.   519

PART SIX
COMPREHENSIVE CASES

Cases for Part Six 525

Case 6-1 Microsoft Corp. (B) 525
Case 6-2 Samsung Electronics Co. 533
Case 6-3 General Electric Appliances 539
Case 6-4 Slendertone 548
Case 6-5 Toyota 559
Case 6-6 Coca-Cola Co. (B) 566
Case 6-7 Keurig Inc. 571
Case 6-8 Dura-plast, Inc. 584
Case 6-9 Wal-Mart 595
Case 6-10 Blair Water Purifiers India 600
Case 6-11 Murphy Brewery Ireland, Limited 612
Case 6-12 Dairyland Seed Company 623
Case 6-13 International Business Machines 633

Case 6-14 L'Oréal Nederland B.V. 644
Case 6-15 ESPN 652
Case 6-16 Cowgirl Chocolates 659
Case 6-17 Procter & Gamble Co. 671
Case 6-18 Amazon.com Inc. 679
Case 6-19 Nanophase Technologies Corporation 684
Case 6-20 Cola Wars in China 698
Case 6-21 Smith & Nephew—Innovex 711
Case 6-22 Sun Microsystems 724
Case 6-23 Telus Mobility—What to Do
with Mike 730
Case 6-24 Tri-Cities Community Bank 744
Case 6-25 Cima Mountaineering, Inc. 750

Indexes

Name Index 765
Subject Index 772

Case 6-14 L'Oréal Nederland B.V. 644
Case 6-15 ESPN 647
Case 6-16 Cavinkel Chocolates 659
Case 6-17 Procter & Gamble Co. 671
Case 6-18 Amazon.com Inc. 679
Case 6-19 Nanopure Technologies Corporation 684
Case 6-20 Cola Wars in China 698
Case 6-21 Smith & Nephew—Innovex 711
Case 6-22 Sun Microsystems 724
Case 6-23 Telus Mobility—What to Do with Mike 730
Case 6-24 H-E-B Own Community Bank 740
Case 6-25 Cima Mountaineering Inc. 750

Indexes

Name Index 765
Subject Index 772

PART SIX
COMPREHENSIVE CASES

Cases for Part Six 525
Case 6-1 Microsoft Corp (B) 525
Case 6-2 Samsung Electronics Co. 533
Case 6-3 General Electric Appliances 539
Case 6-4 Steinerhong 545
Case 6-5 Toyota 550
Case 6-6 Coca-Cola Co. (B) 562
Case 6-7 Kemp Inc. 571
Case 6-8 Duro-plast Inc. 584
Case 6-9 Wal-Mart 595
Case 6-10 Hindu Water Purifier India 600
Case 6-11 Murphy Brewery Ireland Limited 612
Case 6-12 Dairyland Seed Company 623
Case 6-13 International Business Machines 635

Strategic Marketing

1

Imperatives for Market-Driven Strategy

Radical market changes, new demands for superior performance, and ever-fiercer competition are rapidly escalating, and pose great challenges to executives around the world. Even market and industry boundaries are no longer easy to define because of the entry of new and disruptive forms of competition. Customers' demands for superior value from the goods and services (products) they purchase are unprecedented, as they become yet more knowledgeable and more perceptive in the judgments they make. New phases of Internet business models—Web 2.0 (the second generation of Internet enterprises after the Web 1.0 dot.com crashes of the early 2000s)—provide wholly new forms of competition.

External influences from diverse pressure groups and lobbyists have escalated dramatically in country after country. The level of searching scrutiny of the ethical standards and corporate responsibility initiatives has never been so high and exerts compelling influence on decision makers in companies. In the face of this turbulence and complexity, companies adopt market-driven strategies guided by the logic that all business strategy decisions should start with a clear understanding of markets, customers, and competitors.[1] Increasingly, it is clear that enhancements in customer value provide a primary route to delivering superior shareholder value.[2]

Nonetheless, while it is important to recognize that the challenges are extreme, there is huge scope for achieving business success. The risks and uncertainties have escalated, and in many ways so have the rewards for developing strategies that deliver superior value. Innovative Web-based businesses like Google and eBay may be prototypes, but in more conventional industries a company like Arcelor Mittal Steel is illustrative.

From acquiring his first steel mill in Indonesia in 1976, Lakshmi Mittal has grown Arcelor Mittal to a dominant force in the global steel business. Mittal supplies more than 30 percent of the steel used by U.S. car companies and is responsible for 10 percent of world steel output—2006 sales were $88.5 billion. Between 1989 and 2004, Mittal made 17 deals across the globe, buying the unwanted assets of bigger steel groups or down-at-heel state-owned plant. Acquisitions have spanned Asia, the Caribbean, the former Eastern Europe, the U.S. (International Steel Group and Ispat Inland), and Europe. Mittal's business turns around failing steel plants through a program of replacing existing management, fixing liquidity by reestablishing credit with suppliers, improving operations, shifting production to higher-value output, forming regional groups to boost purchasing power, and selling off non-core subsidiaries. Importantly, Mittal's long-term strategy was to challenge the existing business model prevalent in the steel industry—conventional industry thinking was dominated by tonnages of steel produced, not profits, and regional supply chains. Mittal's view was that only large steel companies could negotiate advantageously with suppliers of iron ore and coal, and major customers such as automakers. Through a strategy of consolidation, a rigorous program of continuous improvement, and the deployment of a superior knowledge-sharing network across the global business, Mittal has reinvented the steel sector and created new ways to achieve superiority in customer value and competitive strength.[3]

This chapter examines three important market-driven strategy topics:

- *First,* we develop the theme of market-driven strategy and its pivotal role in designing and implementing effective business and marketing strategies. To achieve this, we review the characteristics of market oriented organizations, the development of distinctive capabilities, and the creation of value for customers.

- *Second,* we look at the links between business and marketing strategy and corporate strategy to clarify the scope of strategy and the marketing strategy process. The Appendix discusses Strategic Marketing Planning.

- *Lastly,* to emphasize the turbulent context in which executives make strategic choices, we explore some of the most important challenges in the modern marketplace—escalating globalization, technological change, the Web 2.0, and the imperatives of ethical behavior and corporate social responsibility.

Market-Driven Strategy

The underlying logic of market-driven strategy is that the market and the customers that form the market should be the starting point in business strategy. Importantly, market-driven strategy provides a company-wide perspective, which mandates more effective integration of activities and processes that impact customer value. The development of a market-driven strategy is not a short-term endeavor. A considerable amount of effort is necessary to build a market-driven organizational culture and processes. Also, the methods of measuring progress extend beyond short-term financial performance measures. Certainly, it is important that we recognize that short-term cost savings and profit enhancements may undermine the achievement of strategic goals and the building of superior customer value. Exhibit 1.1 summarizes the characteristics of market-driven strategies.

EXHIBIT 1.1
Characteristics of Market-Driven Strategies

Characteristics of Market-Driven Strategies

Becoming Market Oriented

Market orientation is a business perspective that makes the customer the focal point of a company's total operations. "A business is market-oriented when its culture is systematically and entirely committed to the continuous creation of superior customer value."[4] Importantly, achieving a market orientation involves the use of superior organizational skills in understanding and satisfying customers.[5] Becoming market-oriented requires the involvement and support of the entire workforce. The organization must monitor rapidly changing customer needs and wants, determine the impact of these changes on customer behavior, increase the rate of product innovation, and implement strategies that build the organization's competitive advantage.

A market-oriented organization continuously gathers information about customers, competitors, and markets; views the information from a total business perspective; decides how to deliver superior customer value; and takes actions to provide value to customers.[6] Importantly, these initiatives involve cross-functional participation. Market orientation requires participation by everyone in the organization. An organization that is market oriented has both a culture committed to providing superior customer value and processes for creating value for buyers. Market orientation requires a customer focus, competitor intelligence, and cross-functional cooperation and involvement. This initiative extends beyond the marketing function in an organization.

Customer Focus

The marketing concept has proposed customer focus for half a century, yet until the 1990s this emphasis had limited impact on managers as a basis for managing a business.[7] There are many similarities between the marketing concept and market orientation, although the former implies a functional (marketing) emphasis. The important difference is that market orientation is more than a philosophy since it consists of a process for delivering customer value. The market-oriented organization understands customers' preferences and requirements and effectively deploys the skills and resources of the entire organization to satisfy customers. Becoming customer-oriented requires finding out what values buyers want to help them satisfy their purchasing objectives.

Competitor Intelligence

A market-oriented organization recognizes the importance of understanding its competition as well as the customer:

> The key questions are which competitors, and what technologies, and whether target customers perceive them as alternate satisfiers. Superior value requires that the seller identify and understand the principal competitors' short-term strengths and weaknesses and long-term capabilities and strategies.[8]

Failure to identify and respond to competitive threats can create serious consequences for a company. For example, Polaroid's management did not define its competitive area as all forms of photography, concentrating instead on its instant photo monopoly position, and eventually the company was outflanked by digital photography. Had Polaroid been market oriented its management might have better understood the changes taking place, recognized the competitive threat, and developed strategies to counter the threat. Instead, the company filed for bankruptcy.

Cross-Functional Coordination

Market-oriented companies are effective in getting all business functions working together to provide superior customer value. These organizations are successful in removing the walls between business functions—marketing talks with research and development and finance. Cross-functional teamwork guides the entire organization toward providing superior customer value.

Performance Implications

Companies that are market oriented begin strategic analysis with a penetrating view of the market and competition. Moreover, an expanding body of research findings points to a positive relationship between market orientation and superior performance.[9] Companies that are market oriented display favorable organizational performance, compared to companies that are not market oriented. The positive market orientation/performance relationship has been found in several United States, European, and Asian studies.

Determining Distinctive Capabilities

Identifying an organization's distinctive capabilities (competencies) is a vital part of market-driven strategy. "Capabilities are complex bundles of skills and accumulated knowledge, exercised through organizational processes, that enables firms to coordinate activities and make use of their assets."[10] The major components of distinctive capabilities are shown in Exhibit 1.2, using Southwest Airlines' business model to illustrate each component. The airline's growth and financial performance are impressive. In 2007, Southwest reported its

EXHIBIT 1.2
Distinctive Capabilities at Southwest Airlines

Sources: Wendy Zellner, "Dressed to Kill," *Business-Week*, February 21, 2005, 58–59. Doug Cameron, "Southwest Seeks New Sources of Passenger Revenue," *Financial Times*, Friday, April 20, 2007, 24.

Organizational Processes

Southwest pioneered a point-to-point route system contrasting with the hub-and-spoke design used by many conventional airlines.
The value proposition consists of low fares and limited services (e.g., no in-flight meals).
Major emphasis throughout the organization is on building a loyal customer base.
Operating costs are kept low by using a single aircraft type, minimizing the time between a plane landing and taking off, no assigned seating, and developing strong customer loyalty (lower selling costs).
The business model is characterized by "keeping it simple."

Skills and Accumulated Knowledge

Southwest has developed impressive skills in operating its business model at very low cost.
Accumulated knowledge has guided management in improving its business design over time.
The business model is being leveraged to drive more non-flying revenue, such as hotel booking from its web site and charging for a broader array of services.
Additional directions identified include carrying more cargo, international flights and alliances with other carriers, and in-flight Internet services.

Coordination of Activities

Coordination of activities is facilitated by the point-to-point business model.
High aircraft utilization, simplification of functions, and limited passenger services enable management efficiency, and the provision of on-time, point-to-point services offered on a frequent basis.

Assets

Very low operating costs.
Loyal customer base.
High employee esprit de corps.

64th straight quarter of profitability, a record unmatched in the airline sector. The pioneer of "no frills" flying, the airline now carries more domestic passengers than any other U.S. airline.

An organization's capabilities are not a particular business function, asset, or individual, and instead, consist of core processes of the organization. Michael Porter indicates that "the essence of strategy is in the activities—choosing to perform activities differently or to perform different activities than rivals."[11] His concept of activity networks is consistent with viewing distinctive capabilities as groupings of skills and accumulated knowledge, applied through organizational processes. Mittal Steel's ability to turn around outdated steel mills and to globalize sales is illustrative.

Organizational capabilities and organizational processes are closely related:

> . . . it is the capability that enables the activities in a business process to be carried out. The business will have as many processes as are necessary to carry out the natural business activities defined by the stage in the value chain and the key success factors in the market.[12]

Classifying the organization's capabilities is useful in identifying distinctive capabilities. As shown in Exhibit 1.3, one way of classification is to determine whether processes operate from outside the business to inside, inside out, or spanning processes. The processes shown are illustrative rather than a complete enumeration of processes. Moreover, since a company may have unique capabilities, the intent is not to identify a generic inventory of processes.

Classifying Capabilities

The process capabilities shown in Exhibit 1.3 differ in purpose and focus.[13] The outside-in processes connect the organization to the external environment, providing market feedback and forging external relationships. The inside-out processes are the activities necessary to satisfy customer value requirements (e.g., manufacturing/operations). The outside-in processes play a key role in offering direction for the spanning and inside-out capabilities, which respond to the customer needs and requirements identified by the outside-in processes. Market sensing, customer linking, channel bonding (e.g., producer/retailer relationships), and technology monitoring provide vital information for new product opportunities, service requirements, and competitive threats.

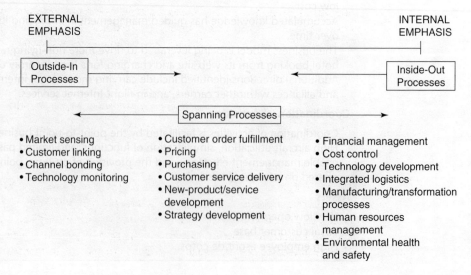

EXHIBIT 1.3
Classifying Capabilities

Source: Chart from George S. Day, "The Capabilities of Market-Driven Organizations," *Journal of Marketing,* October 1994, 41. Reprinted with permission of the American Marketing Association.

EXTERNAL EMPHASIS

INTERNAL EMPHASIS

Outside-In Processes

Inside-Out Processes

Spanning Processes

- Market sensing
- Customer linking
- Channel bonding
- Technology monitoring

- Customer order fulfillment
- Pricing
- Purchasing
- Customer service delivery
- New-product/service development
- Strategy development

- Financial management
- Cost control
- Technology development
- Integrated logistics
- Manufacturing/transformation processes
- Human resources management
- Environmental health and safety

The organizational process view of distinctive capabilities requires shifting away from the traditional specialization of business functions (e.g., operations, marketing, research and development) toward a cross-functional process perspective.[14]

Capabilities and Customer Value

Value for buyers consists of the benefits and costs resulting from the purchase and use of products. Value is perceived by the buyer. Superior value occurs when there are positive net benefits. A company needs to pursue value opportunities that match its distinctive capabilities. A market-oriented company uses its market sensing processes, shared diagnosis, and cross-functional decision making to identify and take advantage of superior value opportunities. Management must determine where and how it can offer superior value, directing these capabilities to customer groups (market segments) that result in a favorable competency/value match.

Creating Value for Customers

Intense global competition and the increasing demands of ever-more sophisticated customers make the creation of customer value an important challenge for managers. We take a closer look at the concept of customer value, and consider how value is generated.

Customer Value

Offering superior customer value is at the core of business design at companies as diverse as Google, Mittal Steel, and Southwest Airlines. Buyers form value expectations and decide to purchase goods and services based on their perceptions of products' benefits less the total costs incurred.[15] Customer satisfaction indicates how well the product use experience compares to the buyer's value expectations. Superior customer value results from a very favorable use experience compared to expectations and the value offerings of competitors.

Providing Value to Customers

As discussed earlier, the organization's distinctive capabilities are used to deliver value by differentiating the product offer, offering lower prices relative to competing brands, or a combination of lower cost and differentiation.[16] Deciding which avenue to follow requires matching capabilities to the best value opportunities. Kodak's innovative approach to pricing the ink cartridges for its latest printers challenges industry conventions. Competitors price printers low, but charge high prices for ink cartridges (in some cases as much for the cartridge as the printer it fits). Kodak EasyShare printers cost more, but the ink cartridges are substantially cheaper than competitors'. Kodak's gamble is to attract high-volume users by offering them better value, leaving low-volume users to the competition.[17]

Nonetheless, there is an important distinction between value and innovation. An *Economist Intelligence Unit Report* included interviews with executives from many leading companies throughout the world: "What counts, conclude the participants, is value innovation. This is defined as creating new value propositions . . . that lead to increased customer satisfaction, loyalty, and—ultimately—sustainable, profitable growth. Market leaders are just that—pioneers."[18]

Becoming Market Driven

The discussion so far points to the importance of becoming market oriented, leveraging distinctive capabilities, and finding a good match between customers' value requirements and the organization's capabilities. The supporting logic for these actions is that they are expected to lead to superior customer value and organizational performance. Research evidence indicates that these characteristics are present in market-driven organizations, which display higher performance than their counterparts that are not market driven. A market-driven organization must identify which capabilities to develop and which investment commitments to make. Market orientation research and evolving business strategy paradigms point to the importance of market sensing and customer linking capabilities in achieving successful market-driven strategies.[19]

Market Sensing Capabilities

Market-driven companies have effective processes for learning about their markets. Sensing involves more than collecting information. It must be shared across functions and interpreted to determine what actions need to be initiated. Mittal's global intranet links managers and generates valuable information for diagnosis and action in performance improvement. Developing an effective market sensing capability is not a simple task. Various information sources must be identified and processes developed to collect and analyze the information. Information technology plays a vital role in market sensing activities. Different business functions have access to useful information and need to be involved in market sensing activities.

Customer Linking Capabilities

There is substantial evidence that creating and maintaining close relationships with customers is important in market-driven strategies.[20] These relationships offer advantages to both buyer and seller through information sharing and collaboration. Customer linking also reduces the possibility of a customer shifting to another supplier. Customers are valuable assets.

Quintiles Transnational has very effective customer linking capabilities.[21] Its drug testing and sales services are available in more than 50 countries. The company has extensive experience in clinical trials and marketing. Quintiles' customers are drug companies located in many countries around the world. Ongoing collaborative relationships are essential to Quintiles' success. It offers specialized expertise, assisting drug producers to reduce the time necessary in developing and testing new drugs. Quintiles helped develop or commercialize every one of the world's top 30 best-selling drugs.

Aligning Structure and Processes

Becoming market driven may require changing the design of the organization, placing more emphasis on cross-functional processes. Market orientation and process capabilities require cross-functional coordination and involvement. Many companies have made changes in organization structures and processes as a part of their customer value initiatives. The changes include improving existing processes as well as redesigning processes. Primary targets for reengineering are sales and marketing, customer relationship management, order fulfillment, and distribution. The objectives of the business process changes are to improve the overall level of product quality, reduce costs, and improve service delivery. Underpinning such changes and initiatives is the importance of what has been called "implementation capabilities," or the ability of an organization to execute and sustain market-driven strategy, and do so on a global basis.[22] In addition to formulating the strategies essential to delivering superior customer value, it is vital to adopt a thorough and detailed approach to strategy implementation.

Corporate, Business, and Marketing Strategy

Business and marketing strategies are being renewed by executives in a wide range of companies, in their efforts to survive and prosper in an increasingly complex and demanding business environment. Choosing high performance strategies in this

Some conventional wisdom suggests that the era of the Personal Computer (PC) is over—it is yesterday's computing platform. Nonetheless, PC sales have grown from 50 million a year to 200 million in the past decade and are still rising.

The real change occupying executives in this sector is more subtle. It is a shift in the "eco-system" of the PC business. The days of the established purchase process of picking your PC from the Dell website, as the one with the most powerful Intel processor you can afford, and then loading Microsoft's Windows XP and Office package may be over.

To establish dominance in the PC world, the Big Three—Dell, Intel, and Microsoft—relied on mutually supportive business models. Microsoft added features to software to encourage upgrades. Intel made faster chips to handle the new software, and Dell used its direct sales model to sell cheaper boxes. This has become a recipe for bloated software, inefficient chips, and poor service.

The result is that Microsoft is being outpaced by Google software, AMD has come up with better chips than Intel, forcing Intel to change course, and Dell is trying to look more like Apple by opening stores and selling Dell computers in Wal-Mart. Dell has ended an exclusive deal with Intel to use AMD chips in some products and to load Google software on Dell PCs. Dell is looking to use acquisitions and partnerships to develop into a computer services business with less dependence on hardware sales.

It is new competitors who have found ways of making more money from the PC platform that was thought to be securely in the hands of the Big Three.

Sources: Adapted from Richard Waters, "Computer Pack Top Dogs Lose Their Bite," *Financial Times,* Monday June 5, 2006, p.19. Kevin Allison and Chris Nuttall, "Dell To Sell Its Computers At Wal-Mart," *Financial Times,* Friday May 25, 2007. Kevin Allison, "Dell To Target Indirect Sales," *Financial Times,* May 17, 2007, p.17. Maija Palmer and Kevin Allison, "Dell Plans More Emphasis on Services," *Financial Times,* Wednesday June 6, 2007, 26.

environment of constant change requires vision, sound strategic logic, and commitment. Market-driven organizations develop closely coordinated business and marketing strategies. Executives in many companies are reinventing their business models with the objective of improving their competitive advantage. These changes include altering market focus, expanding product scope, partnering with other organizations, outsourcing manufacturing, and modifying internal structure. The capacity for continuous reconstruction requires innovation with respect to the organizational values, processes, and behaviors that systematically favor perpetuating the past rather than innovation for renewal.[23]

The transformation of the personal computer marketplace from the dominance of Dell, Intel, and Microsoft by the superior value offered by competitors like AMD in chips and Google in software, and the radical strategic changes required of the established competitors, are illustrative of competitive revolution. This competitive turmoil is described in the STRATEGY FEATURE.

Conventionally, we distinguish between corporate, business, and marketing strategy as shown in Exhibit 1.4. Corporate strategy consists of deciding the scope and purpose of the business, its objectives, and the initiatives and resources necessary to achieve the objectives. Business and marketing strategy is guided by the decisions top management makes about how, when, and where to compete. This should be a two-way relationship—while corporate strategy defines strategic direction, allocates resources, and defines constraints on what cannot be done, executives responsible for marketing strategy have a responsibility to inform corporate strategists about external change in the market that identifies opportunities and threats. We will examine each level or approach to strategy in turn, before describing and illustrating the marketing strategy process in more detail.

EXHIBIT 1.4
Corporate, Business, and Marketing Strategy

Corporate, Business, and Marketing Strategy

Corporate strategy consists of the decisions made by top management and the resulting actions taken to achieve the objectives set for the business. The major corporate strategy components are shown in Exhibit 1.5. *Scope* is concerned with resolving questions about the business the firm should be in, where it should focus, and its enduring strategic purpose. *Corporate objectives* indicate the dimensions of performance upon which to focus and the levels of achievement required. *Corporate strategies* are concerned with how the company can achieve its growth objectives in current or new business areas. *Resource allocation* addresses the division of limited resources across businesses and opportunities. *Synergies* highlight competencies, resources, and capabilities that drive efficiency and effectiveness in the business. Essential to corporate success is matching the capabilities of the organization with opportunities to provide long-term superior customer value.

Components of Corporate Strategy

It is apparent that in the 21st century marketing environments, companies are drastically altering their business and marketing strategies to get closer to their customers, counter competitive threats, and strengthen competitive advantages. Challenges to management include escalating international competition, new types and sources of competition, political and economic upheaval, dominance of the customer, and increasing marketing complexity. These challenges create imperatives for organizational change, which may sometimes be radical.

Corporate Strategy Framework

A useful basis for examining corporate strategy consists of (1) management's long-term vision for the corporation; (2) objectives which serve as milestones toward the vision; (3) resources; (4) businesses in which the corporation competes; (5) structure, systems, and processes; and (6) gaining corporate advantage through multimarket activity.[24]

EXHIBIT 1.5
Components of Corporate Strategy

Deciding Corporate Vision

Management's vision defines what the corporation is and what it does and provides important guidelines for managing and improving the corporation. Strategic choices about where the firm is going in the future—choices that take into account company capabilities, resources, opportunities, and problems—establish the vision of the enterprise. Developing strategies for sustainable competitive advantage, implementing them, and adjusting the strategies to respond to new environmental requirements is a continuing process. Managers monitor the market and competitive environment. Early in the strategy-development process management needs to define the vision of the corporation. It is reviewed and updated as shifts in the strategic direction of the enterprise occur over time.

Top management vision may be radical and sometimes involves risks. While Amazon.com initially promised to revolutionize retailing with its online operations, founder Jeff Bezos wants to transform Amazon into a digital utility—running customers' business logistics and processes using the same state-of-the-art technologies and operations that power Amazon's own online retailing. Amazon is renting out resources it uses to run its own business and has even allowed outside programmers access to its pricing and product data.[25]

Objectives

Objectives need to be set so that the performance of the enterprise can be gauged. Corporate objectives may be established in the following areas: *marketing, innovation, resources, productivity, social responsibility, and finance.*[26] Examples include growth and market-share expectations, product quality improvement, employee training and development, new-product targets, return on invested capital, earnings growth rates, debt limits, energy reduction objectives, and pollution standards. Objectives are set at several levels in an organization beginning with those indicating the enterprise's overall objectives. The time frame necessary for strategic change often goes beyond short-term financial reporting requirements. Companies are using more than financial measures to evaluate longer-term strategic objectives, and non-financial measures for short-term budgets.

Resources

It is important to place a company's strategic focus on its resources—assets, skills, and capabilities.[27] These resources may offer the organization the potential to compete in different markets, provide significant value to end-user customers, and create barriers to competitor duplication. We know that distinctive capabilities are important in shaping the organization's strategy. A key strategy issue is matching capabilities to market opportunities. Capabilities that can be leveraged into different markets and applications are particularly valuable. For example, the GoreTex high performance fabric is used in many applications from apparel to dental floss.

Business Composition

Defining the composition of the business provides direction for both corporate and marketing strategy design. In single-product firms that serve one market, it is easy to determine the composition of the business. In many other firms it is necessary to separate the business into parts to facilitate strategic analyses and planning. When firms are serving multiple markets with different products, grouping similar business areas together aids decision-making.

Business segment, group, or division designations are used to identify the major areas of business of a diversified corporation. Each segment, group, or division often contains a mix of related products (or services), though a single product can be assigned such a designation. Some firms may establish subgroups of related products within a business segment that are targeted to different customer groups.

A business segment, group, or division is often too large in terms of product and market composition to use in strategic analysis and planning, so it is divided into more specific strategic units. A popular name for these units is the *Strategic Business Unit* (SBU). Typically SBUs display product and customer group similarities. A strategic business unit is a single product or brand, a line of products, or a mix of related products that meets a common market need or a group of related needs, and the unit's management is responsible for all (or most) of the basic business functions. Typically, the SBU has a specific strategy rather than a shared strategy with another business area. It is a cohesive organizational unit that is separately managed and produces sales and profit results.

For example, part of the remarkable strategic turnaround at Hewlett-Packard involved restructuring choices made in 2005 by incoming CEO Mark Hurd. He reversed his predecessor's merge of the computer and printer divisions, on the grounds that smaller, more focused business units would perform better than larger, more diffused alternatives, and separated the computer and printer units.[28]

In a business that has two or more strategic business units, decisions must be made at two levels. Corporate management must first decide what business areas to pursue and set priorities for allocating resources to each SBU. The decision makers for each SBU must select the strategies for implementing the corporate strategy and producing the results that corporate management expects. Corporate-level management is often involved in assisting SBUs to achieve their objectives.

Structure, Systems, and Processes

This aspect of strategy considers how the organization controls and coordinates the activities of its various business units and staff functions.[29] Structure determines the composition of the corporation. Systems are the formal policies and procedures that enable the organization to operate. Processes consider the informal aspects of the organization's activities. Strategic choices provide the logic for different structure, systems, and process configurations.

The logic of how the business is designed is receiving considerable attention. "A business design is the totality of how a company selects its customers, defines and differentiates its offerings, defines the tasks it will perform itself and those it will outsource, configures its resources, goes to market, creates utility for customers, and captures profit."[30] The business design (or business model) provides a focus on more than the product and/or technology, instead looking at the processes and relationships that comprise the design.

Business and Marketing Strategy

Many strategy guidelines are offered by consultants, executives, and academics to guide business strategy formulation. These strategy paradigms propose a range of actions including re-engineering the corporation, total quality management, building distinctive competencies, reinventing the organization, supply chain strategy, and strategic partnering. It is not feasible to review the various strategy concepts and methods that are available in many books, seminars, and consulting services. The corporate strategy framework presented here offers a basis for incorporating relevant strategy perspectives and guidelines.

An important issue is whether selecting a successful strategy has a favorable impact on results. Does the uncontrollable environment largely determine business performance or instead, will the organization's strategy have a major impact on its performance? The evidence suggests that strategic choices matter.[31] While environmental factors such as market demand, intensity of competition, government, and social change influence corporate performance, the strategic choices made by specific companies also have a significant impact on their performance. Importantly, the impact may be positive or negative. For example,

Kmart held the leading market position over Wal-Mart in 1980, yet Wal-Mart overtook Kmart by investing heavily in information systems and distribution to develop a powerful customer-driven, low-cost retail network. Kmart declared bankruptcy in early 2002, and was sold for less than $1 billion.

Business and Marketing Strategy Relationships

An understanding of business purpose, scope, objectives, resources, and strategy is essential in designing and implementing marketing strategies that are consistent with the corporate and business unit plan of action. The chief marketing executive's business strategy responsibilities include (1) participating in strategy formulation and (2) developing marketing strategies that are consistent with business strategy priorities and integrated with other functional strategies. Since these two responsibilities are closely interrelated, it is important to examine marketing's role and functions in both areas to gain more insight into marketing's responsibilities and contributions. Peter F. Drucker described this role:

> Marketing is so basic that it cannot be considered a separate function (i.e., a separate skill or work) within the business, on a par with others such as manufacturing or personnel. Marketing requires separate work and a distinct group of activities. But it is, first, a central dimension of the entire business. It is the whole business seen from the point of view of its final result, that is, from the customer's point of view.[32]

Frederick E. Webster describes the role of the marketing manager: "At the corporate level, marketing managers have a critical role to play as advocates for the customer and for a set of values and beliefs that put the customer first in the firm's decision making, and to communicate the value proposition as part of that culture throughout the organization, both internally and in its multiple relationships and alliances."[33] This role includes assessing market attractiveness in the markets available to the firm, providing a customer orientation, and communicating the firm's specific value advantages.

Strategic Marketing

Marketing strategy consists of the analysis, strategy development, and implementation of activities in: developing a vision about the market(s) of interest to the organization, selecting market target strategies, setting objectives, and developing, implementing, and managing the marketing program positioning strategies designed to meet the value requirements of the customers in each market target.

Strategic marketing is a market-driven process of strategy development, taking into account a constantly changing business environment and the need to deliver superior customer value. The focus of strategic marketing is on organizational performance rather than a primary concern about increasing sales. Marketing strategy seeks to deliver superior customer value by combining the customer-influencing strategies of the business into a coordinated set of market-driven actions. Strategic marketing links the organization with the environment and views marketing as a responsibility of the entire business rather than a specialized function.

The Marketing Strategy Process

The marketing strategy analysis, planning, implementation, and management process that we follow is described in Exhibit 1.6. The strategy stages shown are examined and applied through the later parts of this book. *Markets, segments and customer value* consider market and competitor analysis, market segmentation, strategic customer relationship management, and continuous learning about markets. *Designing market-driven strategy* examines customer targeting and positioning strategies, marketing relationship strategies,

EXHIBIT 1.6
Marketing Strategy Process

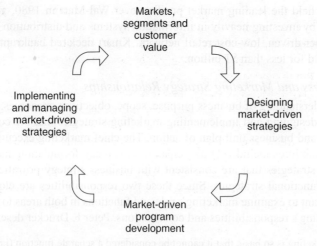

Markets, segments and customer value

Designing market-driven strategies

Market-driven program development

Implementing and managing market-driven strategies

and innovation and new product strategy. *Market-driven program development* consists of brand, value-chain, pricing, and promotion and selling strategies designed and implemented to meet the value requirements of targeted buyers. *Implementing and managing market-driven strategies* considers organizational design and marketing strategy implementation and control.

Markets, Segments, and Customer Value

Marketing management evaluates markets and customers to guide the design of a new strategy or to change an existing strategy. Analysis is conducted on a regular basis after the strategy is underway to evaluate strategy performance and identify needed strategy changes. Activities include:

- **Markets and Competitive Space.** Markets need to be defined so that buyers and competition can be analyzed. A product-market consists of a specific product (or line of related products) that can satisfy a set of needs and wants for the people (or organizations) willing and able to purchase it. The objective is to identify and describe the buyers, understand their preferences for products, estimate the size and rate of growth of the market, and find out what companies and products are competing in the market. Evaluation of competitors' strategies, strengths, limitations, and plans is a key aspect of this analysis.

- **Strategic Market Segmentation.** Market segmentation offers an opportunity for an organization to focus its business capabilities on the requirements of one or more groups of buyers. The objective of segmentation is to examine differences in needs and wants and to identify the segments (subgroups) within the product-market of interest. The segments are described using the various characteristics of people, the reasons that they buy or use certain products, and their preferences for certain brands of products. Likewise, segments of industrial product-markets may be formed according to the type of industry, the uses for the product, frequency of product purchase, and various other factors. The similarities of buyers' needs within a segment enable better targeting of the organization's capabilities to buyers with corresponding value requirements.

- **Strategic Customer Relationship Management.** A strategic perspective on Customer Relationship Management (CRM) emphasizes delivering superior customer value by personalizing the interaction between the customer and the company and achieving the coordination of complex organizational capabilities around the customer. CRM aims to increase the value of a company's customer base by developing better relationships with customers and retaining their business. CRM can play a vital role in market targeting and positioning strategies. Since CRM is an enterprise-spanning initiative, it needs to be carefully integrated with marketing strategy.

- **Capabilities for Continuous Learning About Markets.** Understanding markets and competition has become a necessity in modern business. Sensing what is happening and is likely to occur in the future is complicated by competitive threats that may exist beyond traditional industry boundaries. Managers and professionals in market-driven firms are able to sense what is happening in their markets, develop business and marketing strategies to seize opportunities and counter threats, and anticipate what the market will be like in the future. Several market sensing methods are available to guide the collection and analysis of information.

Designing Market-Driven Strategies

Evaluating markets, segments, and customer value drivers at the outset of the marketing strategy process identifies market opportunities, defines market segments, evaluates competition, and assesses the organization's strengths and weaknesses. Market sensing information plays a key role in designing marketing strategy, which includes market targeting and positioning strategies, building marketing relationships, and developing and introducing new products (goods and services).

- **Market Targeting and Strategic Positioning.** A core issue is deciding how, when, and where to compete, given a firm's market and competitive environment. The purpose of **market targeting strategy** is to select the people (or organizations) that management wishes to serve in the product-market. When buyers' needs and wants vary, the market target is usually one or more segments of the product-market. Once the segments are identified and their relative importance to the firm determined, the targeting strategy is selected. The objective is to find the best match between the value requirements of each segment and the organization's distinctive capabilities. The targeting decision is the focal point of marketing strategy since targeting guides the setting of objectives and developing a positioning strategy. Examples of market target objectives are desired levels of sales, market share, customer retention, profit contribution, and customer satisfaction. **Positioning strategy** is the combination of the product, value chain, price, and promotion strategies a firm uses to position itself against its key competitors in meeting the needs and wants of the market target. The strategies and tactics used to gain a favorable position are called the marketing mix or the marketing program. The positioning strategy seeks to position the brand in the eyes and mind of the buyer and distinguish the product from the competition. The product, distribution, price, and promotion strategy components make up a bundle of actions that are used to influence buyers' positioning of a brand.

- **Strategic Relationships.** Marketing relationship partners may include end-user customers, marketing channel members, suppliers, competitor alliances, and internal teams. The driving force underlying these relationships is that a company may enhance its ability to satisfy customers and cope with a rapidly changing business environment through collaboration of the parties involved. Building long-term relationships with customers and value chain partners offers companies a way to provide superior customer value. Strategic partnering has become an important strategic initiative for many well-known companies and brands. Many firms outsource the manufacturing of their products. Strong relationships with outsourcing partners are vital to the success of these powerful brands.

The Canadian company, Research in Motion Ltd. (RIM), achieved remarkable success with the BlackBerry product range—cell phones with wireless e-mail capabilities. It took RIM from 1997 to early 2004 to sign up the first million users, but by 2007 BlackBerry had 12 millions users worldwide. However, the potential market is estimated at 400–800 million users.

The design and functionality of BlackBerry made RIM the market leader in personal digital assistants (PDAs), overtaking more established players like Palm, Hewlett-Packard and

Dell. BlackBerry software has been licensed to most of the world's largest cell phone handset makers, including Nokia.

RIM achieved an important first-mover advantage with BlackBerry. The brand has become an icon—with its own nickname "The CrackBerry" because of its addictive nature, and its own malady "BlackBerry Thumb" referring to the penalty for over-use of the small keyboard.

While further designs have been launched—the BlackBerry Pearl, for example—the challenge is to stay ahead of aggressive competitors from across the tech industry, including Nokia, Dell, Hewlett-Packard, Good Technology, and Microsoft. There is a danger that e-mail may become standard on all cell phones.

RIM's strategy is to accept that the vast majority of handhelds for e-mail and other services will be made by competitors, and to stake out leadership in software and services:

- Licensing software to phone and handheld manufacturers
- Working with the carriers to push its devices and others using its software
- Offering software and services to allow companies to offer their own services or software applications on a BlackBerry device.

Sources: Heather Green and Cliff Edwards, "The Squeeze on BlackBerry," *BusinessWeek,* December 6, 2004, 74–75. Paul Taylor and Bernard Simon, "RIM Sees Fine BlackBerry Harvest," *Financial Times,* April 12, 2005, 11. Ben Hunt and Stephen Pritchard, "BlackBerries Are Not the Only Fruit," *Financial Times IT Report,* Wednesday June 29, 2005, 1. Jessica E. Vascellaro, "Research in Motion Net, Revenue More Than Double," *The Wall Street Journal,* October 5, 2007, B3.

- **Innovation and New Product Strategy.** New products are needed to replace old products when sales and profit growth decline. Closely coordinated new product planning is essential to satisfy customer requirements and produce products with high quality at competitive prices. New product decisions include finding and evaluating ideas, selecting the most promising for development, designing the products, developing marketing programs, market testing the products, and introducing them to the market. The differences between existing product attributes and those desired by customers offer opportunities for new and improved products. Successful innovation is a major business challenge. An interesting example of a new product achieving remarkable results is the Blackberry handheld device, as described in the INNOVATION FEATURE.

Market-Driven Program Development

Market targeting and positioning strategies for new and existing products guide the choice of strategies for the marketing program components. Product, distribution, price, and promotion strategies are combined to form the positioning strategy selected for each market target. The marketing program (mix) strategies implement the positioning strategy.

- **Strategic Brand Management.** Products (goods and services) often are the focal point of positioning strategy, particularly when companies or business units adopt organizational approaches emphasizing product or brand management. Product strategy includes: (1) developing plans for new products; (2) managing programs for successful products; and (3) deciding what to do about problem products (e.g., reduce costs or improve the product). Strategic brand management consists of building brand value (equity) and managing the organization's system of brands for overall performance.

- **Value-Chain Strategy.** Market target buyers may be contacted on a direct basis using the firm's salesforce or by direct marketing contact (e.g., Internet), or, instead, through a value-added chain (distribution channel) of marketing intermediaries (e.g., wholesalers, retailers, or dealers). Distribution channels are often used in linking producers with end-user household and business markets. Decisions that need to be made include the type of channel organizations to use, the extent of channel management performed by the firm, and the intensity of distribution appropriate for the product or service.

- **Pricing Strategy.** Price also plays an important role in positioning a product or service. Customer reaction to alternative prices, the cost of the product, the prices of the competition, and various legal and ethical factors establish the extent of flexibility management has in setting prices. Price strategy involves choosing the role of price in the positioning strategy, including the desired positioning of the product or brand as well as the margins necessary to satisfy and motivate distribution channel participants.

- **Promotion Strategy.** Advertising, sales promotion, the salesforce, direct marketing, and public relations help the organization to communicate with its customers, value-chain partners, the public, and other target audiences. These activities make up the promotion strategy, which performs an essential role in communicating the positioning strategy to buyers and other relevant influences. Promotion informs, reminds, and persuades buyers and others who influence the purchasing process.

Implementing and Managing Market-Driven Strategy

Selecting the customers to target and the positioning strategy for each target moves marketing strategy development to the action stage (Exhibit 1.6). This stage considers designing the marketing organization and implementing and managing the strategy.

- **Designing Market-Driven Organizations.** An effective organization design matches people and work responsibilities in a way that is best for accomplishing the firm's marketing strategy. Deciding how to assemble people into organizational units and assign responsibility to the various mix components that make up the marketing strategy are important influences on performance. Organizational structures and processes must be matched to the business and marketing strategies that are developed and implemented. Organizational design needs to be evaluated on a regular basis to assess its adequacy and to identify necessary changes. Restructuring and reengineering of organizations has led to many changes in the structures of marketing units.

- **Marketing Strategy Implementation and Control.** Marketing strategy implementation and control consists of: (1) preparing the marketing plan and budget; (2) implementing the plan; and (3) using the plan in managing and controlling the strategy on an ongoing basis. The marketing plan includes details concerning targeting, positioning, and marketing mix activities. The plan spells out what is going to happen over the planning period, who is responsible, how much it will cost, and the expected results (e.g., sales forecasts). The preparation of the marketing plan is discussed in the Appendix to this chapter.

Marketing strategy is an ongoing process of making decisions, implementing them, and tracking their effectiveness over time. In time requirements, strategic evaluation is far more demanding than planning. Evaluation and control are concerned with tracking performance and, when necessary, altering plans to keep performance on track. Evaluation also includes looking for new opportunities and potential threats in the future. It is the connecting link in the strategic marketing planning process shown in Exhibit 1.6. By serving as both the last stage and the first stage (evaluation before taking action) in the planning process, strategic evaluation ensures that strategy is an ongoing activity.

Challenges of a New Era for Strategic Marketing

Nearing the end of the first decade of the 21st century, it is apparent that executives face unprecedented challenges in strategic marketing to cope with turbulent markets, competitive revolution, and escalating customer demands for value superiority. In this chapter we describe the rationale for market-driven strategy and its components, as a business approach relevant to the new challenges of the present and future. Importantly, the personal demands for incisiveness and ingenuity in creating and implementing innovative and robust marketing strategies should not be ignored. In addition to the technical skills of analysis and planning required to implement market-driven strategy, capabilities for understanding new market and competitor phenomena will be at a premium. Societal and global change also mandates high levels of personal integrity in managers and leaders, and the reflection of these qualities in the social responsiveness of organizations.

Escalating Globalization

The internationalization of business is well-recognized in terms of the importance of export/import trade and the growth of international corporations, particularly in the Triad, comprising North America, Europe, and Japan. However, for strategic marketing in the 21st century, such a view of the international marketing issue may be short-sighted. The most intriguing and surprising challenges are likely to come from outside the mature Triad economies. It is important to understand the degree and extent of difference between the developed economies and the new world beyond. The effects may be dramatic. Recall our earlier discussion of the impact of Mittal on the global steel business.

The ability of competitors in emerging countries like China and Korea to produce goods at very low costs and prices was well-documented in the 1990s and early 2000s, and many markets like apparel have been severely affected. It is clear that some major customers may source from countries with massive cost advantages in labor costs. In 2004, Wal-Mart was the world's largest purchaser of Chinese goods, spending $15 billion in China in 2003, making the company China's fifth largest trading partner, ahead of countries like Russia and Britain. Indeed, U.S. consumers are reacting to price differences for medical treatments by traveling abroad. While a heart bypass may cost $25-35,000 in the U.S., the operation is available in Thailand and India for $8-15,000.[34]

The corollary is that emerging markets offer huge opportunities for exporters because of the population size and growing wealth. For example, one of the driving forces in the huge merger of consumer products companies Procter and Gamble and Gillette was to pool expertise in emerging markets—the goal of the combined enterprise is to serve the world's six billion consumers, not just the one billion most affluent. The focus is on the "lower income consumer" in markets like India and China, through the development of affordable products.[35]

India. In 2006, for the first time, the value of India's acquisitions of overseas companies ($22.4 billion) exceeded the value of foreign companies buying into the country ($11.3 billion). The attraction is gaining access to lucrative developed country markets while maintaining the high productivity of the low-cost base in India. High profile deals include:

- Suzlon Energy, manufacturer of wind turbines, pays $521 million for Hansen Transmissions, a gearbox producer in Belgium.
- Tata Steel pays $13.1 billion for Corus, the Anglo-Dutch steelmaker.
- Ranbaxy Laboratories makes acquisitions in Europe and the U.S.A, and targets Germany's Merck in pharmaceuticals.

China. China has foreign exchange reserves exceeding $1000 billion. In 2007, a survey by the Economist Intelligence Unit showed record numbers of Chinese companies are looking to make overseas acquisitions, targeting Asia, Europe and the U.S.A. The highest profile deal is the acquisition by Lenovo of IBM's personal computer business. Other purchases have failed—the attempted acquisition of the U.S. oil group Unocal by the China National Offshore Oil Corporation in 2005 failed. The approach to Maytag, known for its Hoover vacuum cleaners, by Haier, was rejected. Chinese companies want to acquire Western brands and market access. Chinese overseas acquisitions are expected to escalate.

Russia. The value of Russian overseas merger and acquisition deals in 2006 reached $13 billion, compared to $1 billion in 2002. Russia is cash rich on the basis of its exports of oil, gas and metals. Many big Russian companies see expansion into international markets as essential. Energy and metals groups want to move beyond raw materials into higher profit areas such as refining and manufacturing. In 2006, $50 billion of Russian international deals failed. Gas giant Gazprom's interest in Centrica in Britain was rejected for political reasons. Steelmaker Exraz is rumored to be looking at Ipsco Inc, a pipemaker in Illinois. The success rate of international deals is expected to grow rapidly.

Sources: Dan Roberts, Richard McGregor and Stephanie Kirchgaessner, "A New Asian Invasion: China's Champions Bid High for American Brands and Resources," *Financial Times,* Friday June 24, 2005, 17. Joe Leahy, "Unleashed: Why Indian Companies Are Setting Their Sights on Western Rivals," *Financial Times,* Wednesday February 7, 2007, 13. Jason Bush, "Rubles Across the Sea," *BusinessWeek,* April 30, 2007, 43. Sundeep Tucker, "Reluctant Player Prepares to Step On to World Stage," *Financial Times,* May 31, 2007, 7.

Furthermore, the most important exports from countries like India and China may not just be goods and services but new business models, which will impact established ways of doing business in the developed world. For example the GLOBAL FEATURE describes the aggressive expansion and acquisition strategies of companies in several emerging markets.

It is clear that the new breed of multinational company will be from developing nations, like Brazil, China, India, Russia, and even Egypt and South Africa. They are mostly companies that have prevailed in brutally competitive home markets, against local competitors and Western multinationals. They have business models that can generate profits from extremely low prices and survive in very tough environments.[36]

The global marketplace is dynamic and changing in complex ways with fundamental effects on the competitiveness and viability of companies in many sectors. Those who underestimate the rate of change and important shifts in international relationships run the risk of being outmaneuvered.

Technology Diversity and Uncertainty

The skills and vision required to decide which radical innovation opportunities can be successfully commercialized will be extremely demanding, and the risks of failure will be high. Innovations have the potential to revolutionize a range of different industries.

They demand a strategic perspective that accepts the potential for revolution but balances this with commercial imperatives. The danger is that conventional approaches and short-sighted management may miss out on the most important opportunities.

Much innovation will reflect increased globalization. Chinese innovators are on the cutting edge in fields as diverse as autos, energy, semiconductors, and telecommunications.[37] China manufactures the bulk of the world's DVD players, cell phones, shoes, and certain other products. In the past these products have been designed elsewhere and produced in China. Now, some of the most innovative designs are developed in China, for both Chinese and foreign companies.[38] Major organizations like Microsoft and IBM are investing in worldwide innovation networks spanning countries like India, China, Russia, Israel, Singapore, Taiwan, and South Korea to speed development cycles and bring new technologies to market sooner.[39]

The Web 2.0

As the impact of the Web on business became apparent in the 1990s, some authorities argued that the Internet would make conventional strategies obsolete. However, this phase of Internet business (Web 1.0) led to the failure of many Web-based businesses in the early 2000s. A more compelling logic is that the Internet is a powerful complement to traditional business and marketing strategies.[40] Nonetheless, competitive boundaries are likely to be altered and competition will become more intense.

However, discussions of Web 2.0 are dominated by emerging phenomena like social networking sites, such as MySpace—purchased for $580 million by News Corporation in 2005—and video-sharing sites, such as YouTube—purchased by Google for $1.65 billion in 2006. While such sites are highly popular among users—particularly younger consumers—the commercial implications are becoming apparent. It is possible, for example, that a social networking site like MySpace may be a highly effective advertising medium because it can achieve high engagement between individual brands and consumers, displacing traditional advertising spending from some advertisers' budgets.[41]

An interesting example of Web innovations with important marketing opportunities is the virtual reality site Second Life. The site and some of the marketing applications are described in the INTERNET FEATURE.

More generally, file-sharing, blogs, and social networking services have spawned many new services, including the online encyclopedia, Wikipedia, and the free Internet telephone network, Skype. The Web is providing a collaboration mechanism allowing companies to tap into the collective intelligence of employees, customers, and outsiders to solve problems and identify new opportunities. Outcomes range from the new retail marketplace found at eBay to consumer-generated content for advertising.[42] Internet strategy is considered throughout the book as an integral part of thinking about strategic marketing, not as a separate topic.

Ethical Behavior and Corporate Social Responsiveness

The demands on individuals to display high levels of personal integrity will likely increase in the future. Increasing levels of transparency mandate that manager behavior should meet the highest standards. The penalties for failing to meet the highest standards are likely to be severe. Growing emphasis is placed on corporate citizenship and the establishment and protection of secure corporate reputation as an asset with a financial return associated.[43]

While in the past corporate ethics and social responsibility may not have been center-stage in corporate and business strategy, this situation has changed dramatically. Major concerns about fairness and justice, and the impact of business activities on the physical

Virtual reality sites like Second Life provide users with access to an alternative or parallel world, where they can live imaginary lives, and take on the identify of their avatar (the online representation of the person, with the characteristics they choose). Second Life encompasses some 50 virtual square miles, which it would take days to cross (though flying or teleporting are options). There are thousands of eye-catching structures, physical landmarks and interactive objects, as well as virtual businesses, internet-based social groups, and scheduled events ranging from dance parties to yard sales. Residents spend local currency—Linden dollars—available at in-world ATMs. Second Life had 100,000 residents in 2006, but 2.7 million by 2007.

There is already considerable real company involvement in virtual reality worlds:

- Sun Microsystems uses its Second Life presence to develop a better understanding of new communications modes. Sun hosted the first Fortune 500 press conference in the "Sun Pavillion" in Second Life in 2006, attended by 60 avatars including journalists, software developers and Sun customers. Sun can create new products—such as computer hardware—and test it to destruction in Second Life.

- American Apparel Inc became the first real-world clothing retailer to set up shop in Second Life in June 2006. The store sells virtual T-shirts for residents to wear. Adidas has sold 21,000 pairs of virtual shoes in its store.

- Starwood Hotels has built a huge model of its new Aloft hotel on an island, with deluxe pool and designer lounge.

- IBM has bought a large space used for company and industry meetings of IBMers' avatars.

- Crompco Corp., an underground gas tank testing company, has built a virtual gas station for training employees.

- Other businesses have created their own virtual worlds as marketing tools to reach young people who prefer logging on to watching television. Coca-Cola's MyCoke.com envelops fans in everything Coke, with games, music and chat in virtual space. Wells Fargo's Stagecoach Island is a virtual world where people can play games to learn about finance.

Online virtual worlds offer untapped marketing potential for real-world products and services, because they sustain consumer engagement with a brand. Companies may have to think about directing marketing efforts to their customers' online alter egos, as well as their real customers.

Sources: Paul Hemp, "Avatar-Based Marketing," *Harvard Business* Review, June 2006. Allison Enright, "How The Second Half Lives," *Marketing News,* February 15, 2007, 12–14. Robert D. Hof, "My Virtual Life," *BusinessWeek,* May 1, 2006, 72–82.

environment are high on the management agenda. For example, a research study by McKinsey suggests that as many as 70 percent of company managers believe there is room for improvement in the way large companies anticipate social pressure and respond to it. Managers see risks for their businesses in some social challenges—such as, climate change, data privacy, and healthcare—but opportunities in other challenges—such as the growing demand for more ethical, healthier, and safer products.[44] Further indications of the importance of ethical and social responsibility issues are shown in studies of the perceptions of business school students—who will provide the next generations of managers. Business students appear to believe that companies should work more aggressively toward the betterment of society and want to find socially responsible employment in their careers.[45]

However, concern for Corporate Social Responsibility (CSR) extends beyond altruism or corporate philanthropy to a shift in the way that firms develop their business models. Customer pressures on suppliers to evidence higher standards of corporate behavior are considerable. In business-to-business marketing, suppliers unable or unwilling to meet the social responsibilities defined by major customers stand the considerable risk of losing those customers.[46]

In consumer marketing, a recent five-country survey, conducted by market research group GfK NOP, suggests that consumers in five of the world's leading economies believe that business ethics have worsened in the past five years, and they are turning to "ethical consumerism" to make companies more accountable.[47] Respondents believe that brands with "ethical" claims—of environmental policies or treatment of staff or suppliers—would make business more answerable to the public, and that companies should "promote ethical credentials more strongly."[48] The impact of "ethical consumerism" is of escalating significance.

However, while compliance with social demands for more ethical and responsible behavior is an important issue in strategic marketing, exciting new opportunities are being identified by companies in combining social initiatives with their business models and value propositions, to seek new types of competitive advantage. Recently, Porter and Kramer have argued that many prevailing approaches to CSR are fragmented and disconnected from business and strategy, while in fact the real challenge is for companies to analyze their social responsibility prospects using the same frameworks that guide their core business choices. The goal is to establish CSR not simply as corporate altruism, but as a source of opportunity, innovation, and competitive advantage.[49] The most strategic CSR adds a dimension to a company's value proposition, so that social impact is central to strategy. They note that the number of industries and companies whose competitive advantage can involve social value propositions is rapidly growing:

> Organizations that make the right choices and build focused, proactive, and integrated social initiatives in concert with their core strategies will increasingly distance themselves from the pack. . . . Perceiving social responsibility as building shared value rather than as damage control or as a PR campaign will require dramatically different thinking in business. We are convinced, however, that CSR will become increasingly important to competitive success.[50]

Prototypes for the pursuit of social initiatives as a key part of the business model and to achieve competitive strength are illustrated in the ETHICS FEATURE, describing the One Laptop Per Child program and recent high-profile developments at Dell Inc. and Microsoft.

Indeed, environmental initiatives that make business sense are not restricted to high technology business. Remanufacturing at Caterpillar Inc. is one of the company's fastest growing divisions, with sales in excess of $1 billion a year—remanufacturing takes used diesel engines and uses the reclaimed parts to produce "like new" engines that sell for half the cost of a new engine. Similarly, at Xerox reclaimed photocopier parts go straight onto the new-build assembly line.[51] A major interest in the financial services field is the creation of new sustainable financial products, which enable companies like banks to achieve competitive differentiation.[52]

The challenges to executives to develop and implement business models which achieve the goals of both business and society are considerable and span all sectors of industry. While these forces of change describe a challenging yet exciting environment for strategic marketing, across the world marketing professionals are finding new and better ways to respond to the new realities, to deliver superior customer value to their markets, and to enhance shareholder value. Underpinning processes of reinvention and radical innovation are principles of robust marketing strategy. The goal of this book is to identify and illustrate these principles, and provide processes for responding to the challenges.

Ethics Feature

Corporate Social Responsibility for Competitive Advantage

One Laptop Per Child. In 2004 an MIT team said they were going to overcome the digital divide between the rich and poor by making a $100 laptop for the poor children of the world—the One Laptop Per Child (OLPC) project. Initially dismissed as a charitable project, the MIT team's vision has underlined to the commercial IT sector the market power of the poor. The effects on hardware and software companies have been dramatic: Intel has developed low-cost computers aimed at students in third-world countries; AMD has pledged to get half the world's population online by 2015 with its Personal Internet Communicator; Microsoft is supporting the establishment of computer kiosks in villages in developing countries to allowed shared online access; Quanta Computer, the world's largest contract manufacturer of notebook computers, is making OLPC laptops selling for $200. The OLPC project underlines the social benefits and the commercial opportunities of a cheap laptop, which was relatively easy to make using newer technologies, open source software, by stripping out unneeded functions.

Dell Inc. Leading computer supplier, Dell Inc, is leveraging its distinctive competitive competences in initiatives with both business and social benefits—using the strengths of its direct business model to generate collective efforts to reduce energy consumption and protect the environment. The initiative centers on improving the efficiency of IT products, reducing the harmful materials used in them, and cooperating with customers to dispose of old products. Michael Dell's environmental strategy focuses on three areas: creating easy, low-cost ways for businesses to do better in protecting the environment—providing, for example, global recycling and product recovery programs for customers, with participation requiring little effort on their part; taking creative approaches to lessen the environmental impact of products from design to disposal—helping customers to take full advantage of new, energy-saving technology and processes, and advising on upgrades of legacy systems to reduce electricity usage; and looking to partnership with governments to promote environmental stewardship PC. The link between this CSR initiative and the company's business model and value proposition is clear.

Microsoft. In 2007 Microsoft was partnering with governments in less developed countries to offer Microsoft Windows and Office software packages for $3 to governments that subsidize the cost of computers for schoolchildren. The potential business benefit for Microsoft is to double the number of PC users worldwide, and reinforce the company's market growth. The social benefit is the greater investment in technology in some of the poorest countries in the world, with the goal of improving living standards and reducing global inequality.

Sources: Michael Dell, "Everyone Has a Choice," *Financial Times Digital Business—Special Report,* Wednesday April 18, 2007, 1. "Footing the Bill: Gates Offers $3 Software to Poor," *Financial Times,* Friday April 20, 2007, 1.

Summary

The challenges facing business executives are framed by turbulence in the business and competitive environment challenging the resilience of companies to prosper. This chapter aims, first, to examine the nature of market-driven strategy and the market oriented company; second, to explain the links between corporate strategy and business and marketing strategy; and, third, to underline some of the major challenges of the current marketing era, including globalization, technology change, and ethics and corporate social responsibility.

A market-driven strategy requires that the market and customers should be the starting point in business strategy formulation. Market orientation provides the appropriate business perspective that makes the customer the focal point of the company's operations.

A company's distinctive capabilities provide the skills and knowledge that are deployed to create value for customers. Becoming market-driven relies on market sensing and customer linking capabilities, and the alignment of structure and process with market-driven priorities.

Corporate strategy involves management in deciding the long-term vision for the company, setting objectives, focusing on capabilities, choosing the businesses in which the corporation competes, and defining the business design and how it will create value. Business strategy focuses on the strategic plan for each unit. The marketing strategy process involves evaluating markets, segments, and value drivers, designing market-driven strategies, developing market-driven programs, and implementing and managing strategies.

The modern era for market-driven strategy involves many complex and challenging issues for executives. We underline the importance of escalating globalization, emerging Web 2.0 phenomena, technology diversity and uncertainty, and strategic mandates for ethical behavior and corporate social responsibility initiatives linked not simply to compliance but to new sources of competitive advantage.

Questions for Review and Discussion

1. Top management of companies probably devotes more time to reviewing (and sometimes changing) their corporate vision (mission) now than in the past. Discuss the major reasons for this increased concern with the vision for the corporation.

2. Discuss the role of organizational capabilities in corporate strategy.

3. What is the relationship between the corporate strategy and the strategies for the businesses that comprise the corporate portfolio?

4. Discuss the major issues that top management should consider when deciding whether or not to expand business operations into new business areas.

5. Develop an outline of how you would explain the marketing strategy process to an inventor who is forming a new business to develop, produce, and market a new product.

6. Discuss the role of market targeting and positioning in an organization's marketing strategy.

7. Explain the logic of pursuing a market-driven strategy.

8. Examine the relevance of market orientation as a guiding philosophy for a social service organization, giving particular attention to user needs and wants.

9. How do the organization's distinctive capabilities contribute to developing market-driven strategy?

10. How would you explain the concept of superior customer value to a new finance manager?

11. Suppose you have been appointed to the top marketing post of a corporation and the president has asked you to explain market-driven strategy to the board of directors. What will you include in your presentation?

12. Develop a list of the personal challenges confronting the marketing executive, and consider the qualities and capabilities which may be most relevant to meeting these challenges.

Internet Applications

A. Visit the websites of fashion clothing companies Zara (*www.zara.com*) and H&M (*www.hm.com*). What do these sites tell you about the targeting and positioning strategies being pursued by these companies?

B. What does Google's website (*www.Google.com*) tell us about the company's ability to collect information about individuals and businesses? What privacy issues arise, and how can they be resolved?

C. Review the McKinsey & Co. website. Are there indications that the consulting company is market oriented?

Feature Applications

A. Read the ETHICS FEATURE—Corporate Social Responsibility for Competitive Advantage. Summarize the reasons why companies are adopting corporate social responsibility initiatives. What arguments support the pursuit of social initiatives by business organizations, and what arguments suggest that the role of business is primarily to make profits?

B. Review the INTERNET FEATURE—Second Life. What are the marketing opportunities emerging from Web innovations such as virtual reality and social networking sites? How can these opportunities be pursued for gains in competitive strength and position in particular market segments?

Notes

1. George S. Day, "The Capabilities of Market-Driven Organizations," *Journal of Marketing,* October 1994, 37–52.

2. Peter Doyle, *Value-Based Marketing-Marketing Strategies for Corporate Growth and Shareholder Value* (Chichester: John Wiley, 2000).

3. Stanley Reed, "Mittal & Son," *BusinessWeek,* April 16, 2007, 44–50. Stanley Reed, "The Raja of Steel," *BusinessWeek,* December 20, 2004, 18–22.

4. Stanley F. Slater and John C. Narver, "Market Orientation, Customer Value, and Superior Performance," *Business Horizons,* March/April 1994, 22–27.

5. George S. Day, *Market-Driven Strategy: Processes for Creating Value* (New York: Frcc Press, 1990).

6. Slater and Narver, "Market Orientation," 23.

7. Day, "The Capabilities of Market-Driven Organizations," 37.

8. Slater and Narver, "Market Orientation," 23.

9. Rohit Deshpandé and John V. Farley, "Organizational Culture, Market Orientation, Innovativeness, and Firm Performance: An International Research Odyssey," *International Journal of Research in Marketing,* 21, 2004, 3–22.

10. Day, "The Capabilities of Market-Driven Organizations," 38.

11. Michael Porter, "What is Strategy?" *Harvard Business Review,* November/December 1996, 64.

12. Day, "The Capabilities of Market-Driven Organizations," 38.

13. Ibid., 40–43.

14. Frederick E. Webster, Jr., "The Future Role of Marketing in the Organization," *Reflections on the Futures of Marketing,* Donald R. Lehmann and Katherine E. Jocz, eds., Cambridge, MA: *Marketing Science Institute,* 1997, 39–66.

15. Philip Kotler, *Marketing Management,* 9th ed. (Upper Saddle River, N.J.: Prentice-Hall, 1997), Chapter 2.

16. George S. Day and Robin Wensley, "Assessing Advantage: A Framework for Diagnosing Competitive Superiority," *Journal of Marketing,* April 1998, 1–20.

17. Paul Taylor, "The Wicked Price of Print," *Financial Times,* June 1, 2007, 18.

18. Laura Mazur, "Wrong Sort of Innovation," *Marketing Business,* June 1999, 49.

19. Ibid., 43–45.

20. Ibid.

21. David W. Cravens, Gordon Greenley, Nigel F. Piercy, and Stanley Slater, "Mapping the Path to Market Leadership: The Market-Driven Strategy Imperative," *Marketing Management,* Fall 1998.

22. Nigel F. Piercy, "Marketing Implementation: The Implications of Marketing Paradigm Weakness for the Strategy Execution Process," *Journal of the Academy of Marketing Science,* 13(213), 1999, 113–131.

23. Gary Hamel and Liisa Välikangas, "The Quest for Resilience," *Harvard Business Review,* September 2003, 52–63.

24. David J. Collis and Cynthia A. Montgomery, Corporate Strategy, 2nd ed. (Burr Ridge IL: McGraw-Hill/Irwin, 2005), 10–16.

25. Robert D. Hof, "Jeff Bezos' Risky Bet," *BusinessWeek,* November 12, 2006, 52–58.

26. Peter F. Drucker, *Management* (New York: Harper & Row, 1974), 100.

27. Collins and Montgomery, *Corporate Strategy,* 13.

28. Simon London, "The Whole Can Be Less Than the Sum of Its Parts," *Financial Times,* Monday July 4, 2005, 10.

29. Collis and Montgomery, *Corporate Strategy,* 14–15.

30. Adrian J. Slywotzky, *Value Migration* (Boston: Harvard Business School Press, 1996), 4.

31. Shelby D. Hunt and Robert M. Morgan, "The Comparative Advantage Theory of Competition," *Journal of Marketing,* April 1995, 1–15.

32. Peter F. Drucker, *Management: Tasks, Responsibilities, Practices* (New York: Harper & Row, 1974), 63.

33. Frederick E. Webster, "The Changing Role of Marketing in the Organization," *Journal of Marketing,* October 1992, 11.

34. "Over the Sea, Then Under the Knife," *BusinessWeek,* February 16, 2004, 20–22.

35. Jeremy Grant, "Mr Daley's Mission: To Reach Six Billion Shoppers and Make Money," *Financial Times,* Friday, July 15, 2005, 32.

36. Pete Engardio, "Emerging Giants," *BusinessWeek,* July 31, 2006, 39–49.

37. Bruce Einhorn, "A Dragon in R&D," *BusinessWeek,* November 6, 2006, 44–50.

38. Davis Rocks, "China Design," *BusinessWeek,* November 21, 2005, 66–73.

39. Pete Engardio, "Scouring the Planet for Brainiacs," *BusinessWeek,* October 11, 2004, 62–66.

40. Michael E. Porter, "Strategy and the Internet," *Harvard Business Review,* March 2001, 63–78.

41. Matthew Garahan, "A Hunt for Revenue in the Ecosystem," *Financial Times,* Monday, April 30 2007, 24.

42. Robert D. Hof, "The Power of Us," *BusinessWeek,* June 20, 2005, 47–56.

43. Roger L. Martin, "The Virtue Matrix: Calculating the Return on Corporate Responsibility," *Harvard Business Review,* March, 2002, 69–75.

44. Alison Maitland, "The Frustrated Will to Act for Public Good," *Financial Times,* Wednesday January 25 2006, 15.

45. Rebecca Knight, "Business Students Portrayed as Ethically Minded in Study," *Financial Times,* Wednesday, October 25, 2006, 9.

46. Andrew Taylor, "Microsoft Drops Supplier over Diversity Policy," *Financial Times,* March 24/ March 25, 2007, 5.

47. Carlos Grande, "Businesses Behaving Badly, Say Consumers," *Financial Times,* Tuesday February 20, 2007, 24.

48. Carlo Grande, "Ethical Consumption Makes Mark on Branding," *Financial Times,* Tuesday February 20, 2007, 24.

49. Michael E. Porter and Mark R Kramer, "Strategy and Society: The Link Between Competitive Advantage and Corporate Social Responsibility," *Harvard Business Review,* December 2006, 78–92.

50. Ibid., 91–92.

51. Brian Hindo, "Everything Old Is New Again," *BusinessWeek,* September 25, 2006, 63–70.

52. John Willman, "New Way of Gaining Competitive Edge," *Financial Times Special Report: Sustainable Banking,* Thursday, June 7 2007, 1.

Appendix **1A**

Strategic Marketing Planning

Developing the Strategic Plan for Each Business

Strategic analysis is conducted to: (1) diagnose business units' strengths and limitations, and (2) select strategies for maintaining or improving performance. Management decides what priority to place on each business regarding resource allocation and implements a strategy to meet the objectives for the SBU. The strategic plan indicates the action agenda for the business.

The strategic analysis guides establishing the SBU's mission, setting objectives, and determining the strategy to use to meet these objectives. The SBU's strategy indicates market target priorities, available resources, financial constraints, and other strategic guidelines needed to develop marketing plans. Depending on the size and diversity of the SBU, marketing plans may either be included in the SBU plan or developed separately. If combined, the marketing portion of the business plan will represent half or more of the business plan. In a small business (e.g., retail store, restaurant, etc.), the marketing portion of the plan may account for most of the plan. Plans may be developed to obtain financial support for a new venture, or to spell out internal business and marketing strategies.

Preparing the Marketing Plan

Marketing plans vary widely in scope and detail. Nevertheless, all plans need to be based on analyses of the product-market and segments, industry and competitive structure, and the organization's value proposition. We look at several important planning issues that provide a checklist for plan preparation.

Planning Relationships and Frequency

Marketing plans are developed, implemented, evaluated, and adjusted to keep the strategy on target. Since the marketing strategy normally extends beyond one year, it is useful to develop a three-year strategic plan and an annual plan to manage marketing activities during the year. Budgets for marketing activities (e.g., advertising) are set annually. Planning is really a series of annual plans guided by the marketing strategic plan.

The frequency of planning activities varies by company and marketing activity. Market targeting and positioning strategies are not changed significantly during the year. Tactical changes in product, distribution, price, and promotion strategies may be included in the annual plan. For example, the aggressive response of competitors to Healthy Choice's successful market entry required changes in Con Agra's pricing and promotion tactics for the frozen food line.

Planning Considerations

Suppose that you need to develop a plan for a new product to be introduced into the national market next year. The plan for the introduction should include the expected results (objectives), market targets, actions, responsibilities, schedules, and dates. The plan indicates details and deadlines, product plans, a market introduction program, advertising and sales promotion actions, employee training, and other information necessary to launching the product. The plan needs to answer a series of questions—what, when, where, who, how, and why—for each action targeted for completion during the planning period.

Responsibility for Preparing Plans

A marketing executive or team is responsible for preparing the marketing plan. Some companies combine the business plan and the marketing plan into a single planning activity. Regardless of the format used, the marketing plan is developed in close coordination with the strategic plan for the business. There is also much greater emphasis today to involve all business functions in the marketing planning process. A product or marketing manager may draft the formal plan for his/her area of responsibility, coordinating and receiving inputs from advertising, marketing research, sales, and other marketing specialists. Coordination and involvement with other business functions (R&D, finance, operations) is also essential.

Planning Unit

The choice of the planning unit may vary due to the product-market portfolio of the organization. Some firms plan and manage by individual products or brands. Others work with product lines, markets, or specific customers. The planning unit may reflect how marketing activities and responsibilities are organized.

The market target is a useful focus for planning regardless of how the plan is aggregated. Using the target as the basis for planning helps to place the customer in the center of the planning process and keeps the positioning strategy linked to the market target.

Preparing the Marketing Plan

Format and content depend on the size of the organization, managerial responsibility for planning, product and market scope, and other situational factors. An outline for a typical marketing plan is shown in Exhibit 1A-1. We take a brief look at the major parts of the planning outline to illustrate the nature and scope of the planning process. In this discussion the market target serves as the planning unit.

Outline for Preparing an Annual Marketing Plan

The Situation Summary

This part of the plan describes the market and its important characteristics, size estimates, and growth projections. Market segment analysis indicates the segments to be targeted and their relative importance. The competitor analysis indicates the key competitors (actual and potential), their strengths and weaknesses, probable future actions, and the organization's competitive advantage(s) in each segment of interest. The summary should be very brief. Supporting detailed information for the summary can be placed in an appendix or in a separate analysis.

EXHIBIT 1A-1   **Outline for Preparing an Annual Marketing Plan**

Strategic Situation Summary

A summary of the strategic situation for the planning unit (business unit, market segment, product line, etc.).

Market Target(s) Description

Define and describe each market target, including customer profiles, customer preferences and buying habits, size and growth estimates, distribution channels, analysis of key competitors, and guidelines for positioning strategy.

Objectives for the Market Target(s)

Set objectives for the market target (such as market position, sales, and profits). Also state objectives for each component of the marketing program. Indicate how each objective will be measured.

Marketing Program Positioning Strategy

State how management wants the firm to be positioned relative to the competition in the eyes and mind of the buyer.

A. *Product Strategy*

   Set strategy for new products, product improvements, and product deletions.

B. *Distribution Strategy*

   Indicate the strategy to be used for each distribution channel, including the role of channel members, assistance and support provided, and specific activities planned.

C. *Price Strategy*

   Specify the role of price in the marketing strategy and the planned actions regarding price.

D. *Promotion Strategy*

   Indicate the planned strategy and actions for advertising, publicity, Internet, personal selling, and sales promotion.

E. *Marketing Research*

   Identify information needs and planned projects, objectives, estimated costs, and timetable.

F. *Coordination with Other Business Functions*

   Specify the responsibilities and activities of other departments that have an important influence on the planned marketing strategy.

Forecasts and Budgets

Forecast sales and profit for the marketing plan and prepare the budget for accomplishing the forecast.

Describe the Market Target

A description of each market target, size and growth rate, end-users' characteristics, positioning strategy guidelines, and other available information useful in planning and implementation are essential parts of the plan. When two or more targets are involved, it is helpful to indicate priorities for guiding resource allocation.

Objectives for the Market Target(s)

Here we spell out what the marketing strategy is expected to accomplish during the planning period. Objectives are needed for each market target, indicating financial performance, sales, market position, customer satisfaction, and other desired results. Objectives are also usually included for each marketing program component.

Marketing Program Positioning Strategy

The positioning statement indicates how management wants the targeted customers and prospects to perceive the brand. Specific strategies and tactics for product, distribution, price, and promotion are explained in this part of the plan. Actions to be taken, responsibilities, time schedules, and other implementation information are included at this point in the plan.

Planning and implementation responsibilities often involve more than one person or department. One approach is to assign a planning team the responsibility for each market target and marketing mix component. Product and geographical responsibilities are sometimes allocated to individuals or teams. The responsibilities and coordination requirements need to be indicated for marketing units and other business functions. Importantly, the planning process should encourage participation from all of the areas responsible for implementing the plan. Contingency plans may be included in the plan. The contingencies consider possible actions if the anticipated planning environment is different from what actually occurs.

Forecasting and Budgeting

Financial planning includes forecasting revenues and profits and estimating the costs necessary to carry out the marketing plan (see the Appendix to Chapter 2 for financial analysis details). The people responsible for market target, product, geographical area, or other units should prepare the forecasts and budgets. Comparative data on sales, profits, and expenses for prior years is useful to link the plan to previous results.

Cases for Part 1

Case 1-1

Audi

Chef sache. That's German for "the boss's business." And when it's the boss's business at Audi, watch out. Each month, Audi's compulsive chief executive, Martin Winterkorn, rolls up his sleeves and leads a trouble-shooting session with engineers at the company's electronics center, zeroing in on faulty systems and problem parts. Winterkorn's rules: no shifting the blame to anyone else, such as suppliers. No phone calls to subordinates—the brains to remedy the defects better be in the room. And no one leaves until a fix is found.

The boss's business extends way beyond that monthly session. Not even the smallest buttons on the dashboard escape Winterkorn's attention. At the first auto show under his watch, he summarily ordered a gorgeous Audi sedan removed just hours before the opening: The stitching on the upholstery wasn't right. (Audi staffers now bring two of each model to every show.) The 57-year-old PhD in metal physics is obsessed with creating perfect cars. "We want to be the No. 1 premium brand," says Winterkorn.

There's a lot riding on his precision mania. Audi, the $32 billion high-end car unit of Volkswagen, has been striving for two decades to move its cars upmarket. The effort has cost billions in investments in technology, design, and performance. The goal: to match the exclusive image of mighty Mercedes-Benz and BMW. Individual Audi models have been making a splash for years. The 1994 aluminum frame A8 sedan was an industry first. The iconic Audi TT sports roadster and coupe, introduced in 1998, polished Audi's image as a design leader. The A4's cool, minimalist styling and powerful four-cylinder motor created a new generation of popular Audis, including the sizzling Cabriolet. The A4 line accounts for nearly half of all Audi sales.

Now, Winterkorn is presiding over the arrival of Audi into the front ranks. On Feb. 16, Detroit-based *AutoWeek* voted the $41,000 A6 sedan its Car of the Year. Late last year the magazine heralded Audi's flagship luxury model, the A8, as America's best luxury car. In car-crazed Germany, *Auto Motor & Sport* on Feb. 15 elevated Audi to No. 1 in its four key model segments,

from the A3 compact to its flagship A8 sedan. "Audi is on the cusp of its full first turn as an international luxury brand," says James N. Hall, vice-president for industry analysis at researcher Auto-Pacific Inc. in Southfield, Mich.

Avant-Garde Styling

Audi is building up a roster of famous customers, from Spain's King Juan Carlos to musician k.d. lang. It's also luring buyers from rival German auto makers. Bernd Pooch, chief executive of a Berlin machine-tool maker, was a diehard BMW fan. But last November, turned off by the avant-garde styling of the latest 7 Series, the 64-year-old test-drove a $100,000, 275-horsepower Audi Quattro A8. Smitten by the smooth handling and finely crafted interior, he quickly signed a lease. "People just don't know how good Audi really is," he says.

That's especially true in the U.S., where Audi sells less than half the volume of BMW, Mercedes, or Toyota Motor Corp.'s luxury brand Lexus. Audi suffers in the U.S. from an outdated sales and marketing network and a reputation for buggy electronic systems. Reliability "has been our Achilles' heel," admits Marc Trahan, Audi of America's quality director. To ratchet up its global standing, Audi has to smooth out its U.S. kinks.

Still, the numbers track Audi's upward march. Revenue per vehicle is $41,389, up from $25,125 in 1994. Sales have nearly tripled, to more than $32 billion in the same period (Exhibit 1). Profits in 2004 rose 7.4%, to hit a record $1.15 billion. The share price (a small tranche of Audi shares still trade, despite VW's ownership) has soared to $347 from $79 in 2000. In Europe, Audi nearly matched BMW's sales last year, with 559,428 vehicles to BMW's 579,632. Its most powerful versions of the A8 outsell Mercedes and BMW models with comparable engines. "In the last 15 years, Audi has made an incredible advance," says BMW CEO Helmut Panke. "They wanted to be fully accepted as a premium brand, and they made it."

EXHIBIT 1
Audi's Upmarket Drive

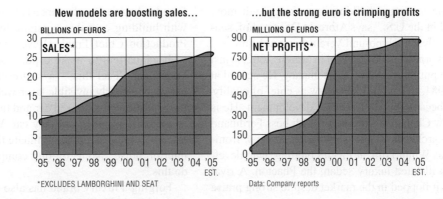

New models are boosting sales...

BILLIONS OF EUROS

SALES*

'95 '96 '97 '98 '99 '00 '01 '02 '03 '04 '05 EST.

*EXCLUDES LAMBORGHINI AND SEAT

...but the strong euro is crimping profits

MILLIONS OF EUROS

NET PROFITS*

'95 '96 '97 '98 '99 '00 '01 '02 '03 '04 '05 EST.

Data: Company reports

Audi, though, is just finishing the first lap of a long race. It now must strengthen global sales outside Europe and add new models to match the depth of BMW and Mercedes offerings. Audi also has a long way to go to match the revenue and profit horsepower of Mercedes and BMW. Last year, Audi clocked sales of 779,000 cars, but Mercedes and BMW sold more than 1.2 million each. By revenues, Audi is still only 55% the size of BMW and 48% that of Mercedes-Benz. Audi's profits are a fraction of its rivals' income, too, since it has fewer expensive models on the market. To remedy that, Winterkorn aims to spend some $15 billion over the next four years, 80% of it on new products.

The son of Hungarian emigrants who moved to Germany in 1945, Winterkorn admits his weakness is impatience. To get workers charged up, he exhorts his troops to take risks and own up to failure quickly. "What he hates is when people cover up mistakes or problems, or shift the blame to someone else," says one manager. The trim and demanding "big boss," as Audi workers refer to Winterkorn, prowls the production line and software labs seeking intelligence from line workers and technicians. A favorite Winterkorn saying: "Don't bore me with the good news. Give me the worst."

In Winterkorn's race to bulk up Audi's size, 2005 is a crucial year. The new models launched in 2004 in Europe have given Audi momentum. It has one of the newest fleets on the market, including the elegant new A6 sedan, redesigned A4 sedan, and the A3 hatchback. A keenly awaited product is the Q7 SUV, costing roughly $40,000, which will hit European showrooms in early 2006, followed by a baby SUV, the Q5, one year later. Under wraps is a sports car in the $100,000 to $200,000 range, dubbed the Le Mans, which is expected to have a 610 hp engine that can accelerate from 0 to 60 mph in just 3.7 seconds. "It would show that anything BMW

and Mercedes can do, Audi can do better," says Garel Rhys, professor of automotive economics at Cardiff Business School in Wales.

But the Audi chief's biggest priority for 2005 is clinching quality gains. Winterkorn is betting his three-year crusade to stamp out glitches, especially in electronics, will boost Audi's rankings above its German rivals in J.D. Power & Associates Inc.'s 2005 quality and reliability rankings, due out in June. "If they make sure they get quality right, they could pick up a lot of dropped straws," says Auto-Pacific's Hall.

Moving Up in the Rankings

Like its German rivals, Audi's cars have been plagued since the late 1990s with electronic snafus as auto makers stuffed more and more microchips into their vehicles. But years of hard work are starting to pay off. In J.D. Power's 2004 ranking of initial quality, Audi moved up three places to rank 11th out of 37 auto brands, one place above BMW and one notch below Mercedes. Chance Parker, Power's quality guru, says Audi still needs to improve its reliability over the long haul—an area where Winterkorn hopes Audi will excel this year. "Some of Audi's [last-generation] launches have been very buggy," Parker says. That's why Audi is 22nd in Power's 2004 ranking of long-term dependability. The good news for Audi is that Mercedes sank to 28th. Audi's ratings should trend upward thanks to the quality of the new models hitting the market.

Audi's other tough goal will be boosting visibility in the U.S. Of Audi's 263 dealerships, 127 share floor space with other brands, and 115 also sell Volkswagen. Johan de Nysschen, Audi of America's boss, is in the middle of a major push to upgrade dealerships. "The cornerstone for brand building is making Audi more successful in the U.S.," says Albrecht Denninghof, senior auto analyst at Hypo-und Vereinsbank in Munich.

Winterkorn, who took control in March, 2002, is just starting to put his stamp on the company. He started at Audi in 1981, moved in 1993 to vw as chief of quality, and then became head of product development. He is close to vw Chairman and former Audi boss Ferdinand Piëch, the architect of Audi's upmarket strategy. Ironically, it was Winterkorn, at Piëch's bidding, who developed vw's ill-fated luxury sedan, the Phaeton. A rival to the A8, it flopped in the market despite strong praise for its engineering.

Now, Audi's growth and profits are increasingly vital to Volkswagen, where high costs and missteps with key models have clouded prospects. Although internal tussles with vw over shared platforms and competing model launches have cost Audi precious time in getting cars to market, the division accounted for nearly 100% of vw Group's net earnings last year. In 2004 the average operating profit per car at Audi was $1,374, while Volkswagen brand cars, suffering from high costs, model mistakes, and an aging fleet, lost an average $13 per vehicle, according to Paris brokerage Exane.

The wholesale parts-sharing of the early 1990s between Audi and vw has given way to a more sophisticated sharing of modules that still saves money but allows Audi cars to look and behave differently. And vw's plummeting profits have dashed Piëch's ill-fated drive to push Volkswagen upmarket. A recent report by Morgan Stanley puts Audi's value at $14 billion—80% of vw Group.

Winterkorn is reaping the payoff of billions of dollars in investments since 1980 when Audi kicked off its upmarket bid with the "Quattro" four-wheel-drive system. To earn its stripes, Audi had to outengineer its rivals, setting industry benchmarks in everything from lightweight aluminum frames, drive systems, and engine performance to the "soft skin" materials covering plastic parts that give Audi's interiors a richer feel. The auto maker's navigation and information system wins high marks as user-friendly and intuitive. "Audi is like the iPod of cars. It's more intelligently designed," says Bill Joy, partner at venture-capital firm Kleiner Perkins Caufield & Byers in Menlo Park, Calif., and former chief scientist at Sun Microsystems Inc.

Audi's 53,000 workers—fiercely proud of the company's engineering heritage, which goes back to founder August Horch—are as obsessed as Winterkorn with building cars that outshine BMW and Mercedes. Production Chief Frank Dreves pauses in the lobby of headquarters to make a point about the latest A3 Sportback. "Feel this," says Dreves, running his fingers over a nearly invisible laser-welded seam between the roof of the tomato red car and the side panel. "This is normally a gutter in every car. We invented a new laser welding process to eliminate the gutter to reduce interior noise. None of our competitors bothers to do this."

Forging a luxury brand has also required stand-out design. In 2002, Piëch lured Italian designer Walter Maria de Silva to Audi from Alfa Romeo. A year later, De Silva unveiled a bold, more sculptured look for the A6 and A8 sedans that started hitting the market last year. The deep front grille, now being extended through most of the model line, gives Audi an edgier look.

But closing the revenue gap with BMW and Mercedes will take another generation of cars at least. Audi has six basic models, compared with 10 at BMW—soon to be 12—and 13 at Mercedes. By selling more top-end cars, BMW and Mercedes generate much greater revenues and higher margins. In 2004, Audi earned an operating margin of 5.5%. "Our goal is to achieve an operating profit margin of 8% within this decade," says Audi Chief Financial Officer Rupert Stadler.

One risk along the way is that a struggling vw shaves capital expenditure, crimping Audi's investments. Winterkorn insists his $15 billion investment plan is secure, but vw Chief Executive Bernd Pischetsrieder has announced he aims to cut spending 6%, or nearly $1 billion, over the next two years.

Audi also needs to invest heavily in marketing and distribution outside Europe to match BMW's and Mercedes' global reach. Although Audi is already a premium-car market leader in China, with a 65% share, rivals are coming on strong, and the market for luxury vehicles has slowed. In Japan, where Audi trails BMW and Mercedes, Winterkorn has canceled a dealership-sharing agreement with Toyota and set up a network of 100 exclusive dealerships. He's also planning to spend $130 million on building a dealer network in Russia over the next five years.

For Winterkorn, the final heat to catch BMW and Mercedes is the challenge of a lifetime. For Piëch, likewise, a victory would crown his life's work as engineer and manager. But getting there will require perfect execution—and a steady hand on the wheel.

Still a Long Way To Go In America

It would be hard to find a more devoted Audi fan than Mark Fullerton. The CEO of a Cincinnati tech-services company and his wife have owned 27 Audis. Fullerton, 53, has toured Audi's factory in Ingolstadt, Germany, six times, and attended its driving school four times. "I believed no one could seduce us away from Audi," he says. So why has Fullerton recently been test-driving cars made by Japanese and other German auto makers?

He fears Audi has lost its edge. Not long ago, he says, "Audi was the only game in town" if you wanted a premium performance car with all-wheel drive at lower prices than its rivals. Now nearly every luxury carmaker offers AWD. And thanks to generous lease terms, Fullerton can lease a $57,620 BMW for $736 a month, about $100 a month less than what he'd pay on a comparable $54,770 Audi. "It pains me," he says.

It pains Audi dealers, too, since leasing accounts for 43% of their sales. Last year, Audi's U.S. sales fell 10%—their first decline in a decade. Management shake-ups rattled dealers. And even as the new A6 sedan was drawing rave reviews, sales got off to a slow start, with little promotion when it hit showrooms last fall. "The good news is that the A8, A6, and new A4 have exceptionally good quality, but in the short term, we're not playing with the full quiver of arrows that the other guys have," says Bill Hoehn, owner of a Carlsbad, Calif., Audi dealership.

Despite a decade on the comeback trail. Audi is still running behind archrivals BMW and Mercedes Benz in the minds of American consumers. The carmaker is hampered by a weak dollar, a shaky U.S. dealer network, and a narrow lineup that includes no sport-utility vehicles. And it still needs to improve its long-term reliability.

That doesn't mean Audi isn't on the upswing. Its U.S. sales jumped 16% in February. Its American executives and engineers are working closely with their German counterparts to eliminate glitches. They're convinced Audi will crack the Top 10 when the latest J.D. Power & Associates' Initial Quality Study is issued this spring. And they are counting on those new models. Says Johan de Nysschen, Audi of America chief: "We will have the newest product lineup in the luxury sector." But de Nysschen is also dead set against raising incentives—and that includes more generous lease deals. Piling on big incentives

effectively lowers a car's pricing, which would hurt both Audi's image and the resale value of its cars. Says de Nysschen: "I don't want to undo all the good that has been done."

Audi Needs an SUV

Its rivals depend on them for a big percentage of U.S. sales

SUV sales as percentage of total*

PORSCHE	58%
LEXUS	53%
BMW	24%
MERCEDES	12%
AUDI	0%

*U.S. sales in 2004
Data: Ward's AutoInfoBank

The problem is the new model that Audi dealers want most—the $40,000 seven-seater Q7 SUV—won't be available until spring 2006, eight years after Mercedes launched the M-Class. With no SUVs, Audi's unit sales in the U.S. are 25% to 30% of rivals. "You only address half the market in the U.S. if you only have cars to sell," de Nysschen admits. Analysts fear that by the time Audi delivers the Q7 and the smaller Q5 in 2007, the trend could be losing momentum. De Nysschen says Audi can sell 50,000 Q7s a year.

It will take more than new models to vault Audi into the top luxury tier in the U.S. Still haunted by memories of the "sudden acceleration" scare of the 1980s, Audi needs to turn out near-perfect cars to build its quality reputation. Audi "has to overcompensate," says Marc Trahan, the company's U.S. quality director. Still, he had to work to convince the Germans to listen to American consumers and move cup holders from the instrument panel, where coffee sloshed onto the stereo controls, to the center console. De Nysschen hopes the efforts will turn customers into goodwill "ambassadors" for the brand. That's essential if Audi doesn't want to lose loyalists like Fullerton.

Source: "Hot Audi," *BusinessWeek,* March 14, 2005, 64–68.

—By Gail Edmondson in Ingolstadt, Germany, with Kathleen Kerwin in Detroit and Karen Nickel Anhalt in Berlin

Case 1-2

The New York Times

Since 1896, four generations of the Ochs-Sulzberger family have guided *The New York Times* through wars, recessions, strikes, and innumerable family crises. In 2003, though, Arthur Ochs Sulzberger Jr., the current proprietor, faced what seemed to be a publisher's ultimate test after a loosely supervised young reporter named Jayson Blair was found to have fabricated dozens of stories. The revelations sparked a newsroom rebellion that humiliated Sulzberger into firing Executive Editor Howell Raines. "My heart is breaking," Sulzberger admitted to his staff on the day he showed Raines the door.

It turns out, though, that fate was not finished with Arthur Sulzberger, who also is chairman of the newspaper's corporate parent, New York Times Co. The strife that convulsed *The New York Times*'s newsroom under the tyrannical Raines has faded under the measured leadership of his successor, Bill Keller, but now its financial performance is lagging. NYT Co.'s stock is trading at about 40, down 25% from its high of 53.80 in mid-2002 and has trailed the shares of many other newspaper companies for a good year and a half. "Their numbers in this recovery are bordering on the abysmal," says Douglas Arthur, Morgan Stanley's senior publishing analyst.

Meanwhile, the once-Olympian authority of the *Times* is being eroded not only by its own journalistic screw-ups—from the Blair scandal to erroneous reports of weapons of mass destruction in Iraq—but also by profound changes in communications technology and in the U.S. political climate. There are those who contend that the paper has been permanently diminished, along with the rest of what now is dismissively known in some circles as "MSM," mainstream media. "The Roman Empire that was mass media is breaking up, and we are entering an almost-feudal period where there will be many more centers of power and influence," says Orville Schell, dean of the University of California at Berkeley's journalism school. "It's a kind of disaggregation of the molecular structure of the media."

The pride that Sulzberger takes in his journalistic legacy is palpable, his knowledge of the *Times*'s august history encyclopedic. Yet "Young Arthur," as he is still known to some at age 53, exudes a wisecracking, live-wire vitality more typical of a founding entrepreneur than of an heir. He began an interview for this article by picking up a big hunk of metal from a conference room table and brandishing it menacingly. "Ask any question you'd like," he growled and then deposited the object in a less obtrusive spot. "It's an award," he added softly.

Sulzberger, who succeeded his father as publisher in 1992 and as chairman in 1997, already rescued *The New York Times* from decline once. With the help of then-CEO Russell T. Lewis, he reinvented the "Gray Lady" by devising a radical solution to the threat of eroding circulation that had imperiled the *Times* and other big-city dailies for years. Sulzberger changed the paper itself by spending big money to add new sections and a profusion of color illustration. At the same time, he made the *Times* the first—and still the only—metro newspaper in America to broaden its distribution beyond its home city to encompass the entire country. Today, nearly 50% of all subscribers to the weekday *Times* live somewhere other than Gotham.

The Sulzbergers who preceded him were newspapermen; Arthur Jr., by his own description, is a "platform-agnostic" multimedia man. In the mid-1990s, NYT Co. became one of the first Old Media companies to move into cyberspace. *Times* reporters also began experimenting with adapting their newspaper stories to another medium new to them—television. Today, NYTimes.com consistently ranks among the 10 most popular Internet news sites, and New York Times Television is one of the largest independent producers of documentary programming in the U.S. "Within our lifetimes, the distribution of news and information is going to shift to broadband," Sulzberger says. "We must enter the broadband world having mastered the three key skill sets—print, Internet, and video—because that's what's going to ensure the future of this news organization in the years ahead."

Sulzberger acknowledges that he and his company are embattled in the present. "These are tough times, and they've been tough times for a while." But he and new CEO Janet L. Robinson (Lewis retired at the end of 2004) are sticking with the long-term plan set nearly a decade ago: enhancing the content of the *Times* and extending its reach into virgin territories west of the Hudson while also building its multimedia capacity. In 2002, NYT Co. added a global dimension to its growth strategy by acquiring full control of the *International Herald Tribune,* which is now being upgraded and expanded.

In essence, Sulzberger is doing what his forebears have always done: sink money into the *Times* in the belief that quality journalism pays in the long run. "The challenge is to remember that our history is to invest during tough times," he says. "And when those times turn—and they do, inevitably—we will be well-positioned for recovery."

Will it work this time? Will toughing it out Sulzberger-style revitalize the *Times* or consign it to creeping irrelevance? "Despite all that has happened, I still think that *The New York Times* has a stature and a position of journalistic authority that is greater than any news organization in the world. Could that be destroyed? I believe that it could be," says Alex S. Jones, a former *Times* media critic who is co-author of *The Trust,* a history of the Sulzbergers and their newspaper. Jones, who now runs the Joan Shorenstein Center on the Press, Politics & Public Policy at Harvard University, hastens to add that he hopes that the paper will thrive again. "I tell you, I hate to think of it not succeeding," he says.

The constancy of their commitment to high-cost journalism has put the Sulzbergers in an increasingly contrarian position. Many of the country's surviving big-city dailies once were owned by similarly high-minded dynastic families that long ago surrendered control to big public corporations that prize earnings per share above all else. Editorial budgets at most newspapers, as well as TV and radio stations, have been squeezed so hard for so long that asphyxiation is a mounting risk. The proliferation of Web sites and cable-TV stations has produced an abundance of commentary and analysis, but the kind of thorough, original reporting in which the *Times* specializes is, if anything, increasingly scarce.

In effect, the Sulzbergers have subsidized the *Times* in valuing good journalism and the prestige it confers over profits and the wealth it creates. In fact, for much of its history, the *Times* barely broke even. Recasting the paper into a publicly held corporation capable of pursuing profit as determinedly as *Times* editors chase Pulitzers was the signal achievement of Arthur Jr.'s father, Arthur O. "Punch" Sulzberger Sr. Still, NYT Co. consistently fails to post the 25% profit margins of such big newspaper combines as Gannett Co. and Knight-Ridder Inc. mainly because of the *Times*'s outsize editorial spending, which the paper does not disclose but which is thought to exceed $300 million a year.

For a time, Arthur Jr. enthralled Wall Street by adding double-digit growth to the Sulzbergian formula. The

value of NYT Co. shares soared 295% from their 1996 low to their 2002 high, boosting the value of the family's 19% holding to $1.5 billion. Like other Old Media families, the Sulzbergers have been able to maintain unquestioned control of their company by creating a new class of voting stock and reserving most of it for themselves. Among them, the various branches of the Sulzberger family control 91% of the Class B voting shares.

The Bancrofts of Dow Jones & Co. and the Grahams of Washington Post Co. share the Sulzbergers' journalism-first philosophy. However the Washington Post has moved beyond newspapering to a greater extent than has NYT Co., which in addition to the *Herald Tribune* owns *The Boston Globe,* 15 small daily newspapers, and eight television stations. Actually, Arthur Jr. has increased his company's financial reliance on the *Times* by selling off magazines and other peripheral properties acquired under his father. In short, NYT Co. is quality journalism's purest traditional play.

In 2004, the company clearly failed to parlay quality into the growth it will need to continue supporting the *Times* franchise. The Wall Street consensus is that the company will report net income of $290 million for 2004, down 4% from the preceding year and a good 35% below the $445 million it netted in the media industry boom year of 2001 (Exhibit 1). Revenues have plateaued at $3 billion, give or take a few hundred million, for five years running.

It wasn't that long ago—Apr. 8, 2002, to be precise—that all seemed right in Arthur Sulzberger Jr.'s rarified world. On that day, most of the *Times*'s 1,200 reporters and editors gathered in its newsroom just off Times Square to celebrate the paper's record haul of Pulitzer Prizes. No newspaper had ever before won more than four Pulitzers in a year; the *Times* won seven in 2002—six of which recognized its Herculean coverage of the September 11 terrorist attacks and their aftermath. Sulzberger was ecstatic, not realizing that he already had made the biggest blunder of his tenure as publisher: naming Howell Raines as executive editor.

Raines, who had joined the paper in 1978 as a national correspondent, had deeply impressed Sulzberger by shaking the stodginess out of the editorial page as its editor during the Clinton years. Raines campaigned hard for the promotion in 2001, vowing to root out complacency and do whatever was needed to raise the staff's "competitive metabolism." By most accounts, Sulzberger saw Raines, then 58, as his journalistic alter ego and collaborator in transforming the *Times* into a fully national, multimedia franchise.

EXHIBIT 1
A Halting Recovery

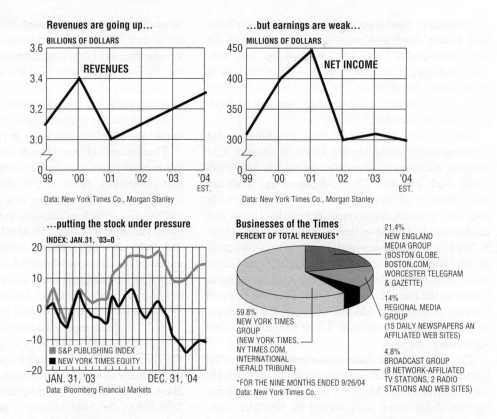

Revenues are going up...
BILLIONS OF DOLLARS
REVENUES
Data: New York Times Co., Morgan Stanley

...but earnings are weak...
MILLIONS OF DOLLARS
NET INCOME
Data: New York Times Co., Morgan Stanley

...putting the stock under pressure
INDEX: JAN.31, '03=0
■ S&P PUBLISHING INDEX
■ NEW YORK TIMES EQUITY
JAN. 31, '03   DEC. 31, '04
Data: Bloomberg Financial Markets

Businesses of the Times
PERCENT OF TOTAL REVENUES*

21.4% NEW ENGLAND MEDIA GROUP (BOSTON GLOBE, BOSTON.COM, WORCESTER TELEGRAM & GAZETTE)

14% REGIONAL MEDIA GROUP (15 DAILY NEWSPAPERS AN AFFILIATED WEB SITES)

4.8% BROADCAST GROUP (8 NETWORK-AFFILIATED TV STATIONS, 2 RADIO STATIONS AND WEB SITES)

59.8% NEW YORK TIMES GROUP (NEW YORK TIMES, NY TIMES.COM, INTERNATIONAL HERALD TRIBUNE)

*FOR THE NINE MONTHS ENDED 9/26/04
Data: New York Times Co.

Just 18 months after self-proclaimed "change agent" Raines had taken charge, the *Times* ran a devastatingly self-critical article recounting how Jayson Blair had plagiarized or made up at least 36 stories. Sulzberger, who has often been accused of lacking gravitas, will be a long time living down his flip initial reaction to Blair's transgressions: "It sucks." Worse, Sulzberger had no feel for how Raines was perceived in the newsroom, where resentment of his arbitrary, self-aggrandizing ways had reached the flash point. Three weeks after Sulzberger had unequivocally affirmed his support for Raines, the publisher fired him and Managing Editor Gerald Boyd.

The Blair-Raines fiasco devastated Sulzberger. But after a long period of introspection, he appears to have regained his confidence if not quite his swagger. "There's no question that the experience changed him," says Steven L. Rattner, a prominent private equity investor who has been one of Sulzberger's closest confidants ever since they worked together as young *Times* reporters in the late 1970s. "It's made him more open to other views and more careful to have a better sense of what's going on," he says. "I think it has been an eye-opening experience for Arthur, and that's never bad for any of us."

Sulzberger swallowed a heaping helping of humble pie in replacing Raines with Keller, a former managing editor whom he had passed over in promoting Raines. Appointed in July, 2003, Keller, 54, has been editor for only as long as Raines was but already has made a number of changes as fundamental as those that his predecessor promulgated yet never implemented. "I cringed every time I read that people thought my job was to come in and calm the place down because it made me sound like the official dispenser of Zoloft," says Keller, whose gracious manner has often been mistaken for passivity. "I saw myself instead as being, in some sense, a change agent without having to wave a revolutionary banner."

Keller has made so many high-level personnel changes that two-thirds of all newsroom workers now report to a new boss. He has also put into practice a string of reforms suggested by several internal committees formed in the wake of the Blair affair. These include the appointment of a standards editor and a public editor, or ombudsman. By most accounts, the *Times* now is much more responsive to outside complaints and criticism than it was.

At considerable expense, the paper also has redesigned a half-dozen of its sections and upgraded its global culture coverage with the addition of 20 writing and editing jobs. "In the last year, there has been more change in a packed period of time than I've seen at this paper ever," says Sulzberger, who also credits Keller with "steadying our culture and lowering the temperature here." It is no mean feat to simultaneously improve morale and shake things up, but Keller is going to have to make certain that a happier newsroom does not again make for a more complacent newsroom. What Raines derided as "the *Times*'s defining myth of effortless superiority" might now be in remission—but has it been eradicated?

While the *Times* appears to be regaining its stride journalistically, it has not been rewarded with circulation gains (see Exhibit 2). In 2004, the paper posted an infinitesimal 0.2% increase in the circulation of both the daily edition, which now stands at about 1.1 million, and the Sunday paper, which is just under 1.7 million. Since the national expansion began in 1998, the *Times* has added 150,000 daily subscribers outside New York but is thought to have lost about 96,000 subscribers in its home market. The net increase of 54,000 represents a 5.1% uptick, which compares with the 3.5% decline in U.S. daily newspaper circulation over this period. What's more, the *Times* posted its gains despite boosting the price of a subscription by more than 25% on average.

New subscribers are increasingly hard to come by for all newspapers as advances in digital communications spur the proliferation of alternative sources of news and information. For the under-30 set in particular, digital accessibility and interactivity tend to trump the familiarity of long-established names like *The New York Times,* CBS, or CNN.

The growing polarization of the body politic along ideological lines also is hurting the *Times* and its big-media brethren. One of the few things on which Bush and Kerry supporters agreed during the Presidential campaign was that the press was unfair in its coverage of their candidate. Keller says the *Times* was deluged with "ferocious letters berating us for either being stooges of the Bush Administration or agents of Michael Moore." Complaints from the Right were far more numerous, even before the newspaper painted a bull's-eye on itself in running a column by public editor Daniel Okrent headlined "Is *The New York Times* a Liberal Newspaper?" Okrent's short answer: "Of course it is."

What a growing, or at least increasingly strident, segment of the population seems to want is not journalism untainted by the personal views of journalists but coverage that affirms their partisan beliefs—in the way that many Fox News shows cater to a conservative constituency. For years, major news organizations have been accused of falling short of the ideal of impartiality that they espouse. Now, the very notion of impartiality is under assault, blurring the line between journalism and propaganda.

For its part, the Bush White House has succeeded to a degree in marginalizing the national or "elite" press by walling off public access to much of the workings of the government and by treating the Fourth Estate

EXHIBIT 2   Circulation by the Numbers

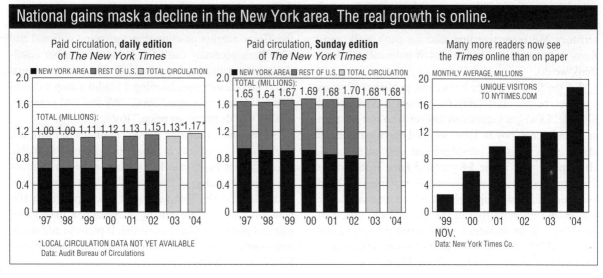

as merely another special interest group that can be safely ignored when it isn't being exploited. The Bushies particularly dislike the *Times,* which, in their view, epitomizes the Eastern liberal Establishment. In his acceptance speech at the Republican convention, George W. Bush mocked the *Times* for what he considered its overly pessimistic coverage of post-World War II Germany. "Maybe that same person is still around, writing editorials," he joked.

The *Times* also is under attack from another branch of the federal government—the judiciary. The paper figures centrally in most of a half-dozen pending court cases that collectively pose a dire threat to the traditional journalistic practice of assuring confidentiality to whistle-blowers and other informants. In October, a federal judge ordered Judith Miller of the *Times* imprisoned for up to 18 months for refusing to testify before a grand jury investigating the leaking of the identity of CIA operative Valerie Plame to conservative columnist Robert Novak. Miller, who researched the Plame affair but never wrote about it, remains free pending a review by the federal Court of Appeals in Washington.

Sulzberger, who spent six years as a reporter, is outraged that journalists are being slapped with contempt charges for refusing to yield confidential sources to prosecutors. "Reporters are going to jail for doing their jobs, and that's just wrong," he says. The publisher has been less outspoken in responding to the paper's political assailants. In an interview with *BusinessWeek,* though, he denied his paper is biased in its coverage of national politics or the war in Iraq or even that it is liberal. The term he prefers is "urban," says Sulzberger. "What we saw play out in this election was urban vs. suburban-rural, not red state vs. blue state," he says. "We are from an urban environment; it comes with the territory. We recognize that, and we can't walk away from it, but neither can we play it politically. I don't think we do."

For the first time since he became publisher 12 years ago, Sulzberger must carry on without Russ Lewis at his side. Lewis, a loquacious lawyer who got his start as a *Times* copy boy in 1966, stepped down on Dec. 26 after seven years as president and CEO of NYT Co. His replacement is the 54-year-old Janet Robinson, a former schoolteacher who joined the company in 1983 and worked her way up through advertising sales. She played an important role in the national expansion of the *Times* as its president and general manager from 1996 into 2004. On the Street, Robinson is known as a formidable manager who relentlessly puts NYT Co.'s

best foot forward. "She's never met a number she couldn't spin positively," one analyst says.

The most pressing business problem the new CEO faces is a paucity of advertising. Through November, the *Times*'s ad revenues were just 2.3% ahead of the previous year—a surprisingly weak performance, considering that the newspaper industry as a whole reported a 9.7% gain in national advertising revenues during the first nine months, according to TNS Media Intelligence/CMR. Expenditures on local newspaper advertising in the industry rose 6.6%.

A strengthening U.S. economy would help the *Times* in 2005 but wouldn't necessarily restore it to competitive parity. The huge runup in advertising rates over the last decade is forcing more U.S. companies to economize, either by shifting into lower-cost media or by homing in more precisely on their target markets. Neither trend bodes well for the *Times,* whose unique status as America's only metro daily with national reach appears to be putting it at a tactical disadvantage in some ways.

The *Times* has many fewer readers outside of New York City than do the two largest national newspapers—*USA Today* and *The Wall Street Journal*—both of which have circulations far in excess of 2 million. "Those two papers tend to be a more cost-effective buy than the *Times* just because their circulation across the country is so much larger," says Jeff Piper, vice-president and general manager of Carat Press, a big media buyer. Even in the New York region, where the *Times* reaches only 14% of all adult readers, the paper's circulation is too diffuse to allow for effective targeting by ZIP Code—a technique that has enriched many other metro dailies with revenue from inserts.

Robinson maintains that there is nothing wrong with the *Times*' market position that a growing national and New York economy can't fix. Underscoring her confidence, the paper just imposed what is now an annual Jan. 1 ad rate increase, layering a 5% hike atop a cumulative 38% increase since 2000. "We feel that premium quality equals premium price," Robinson says.

At the same time, the *Times* continues to move out from the 312 markets in which the paper is available into adjacent precincts. In October, it began printing the national edition in Dayton, Ohio, in a plant owned by the local daily. That enabled it to sell papers in 100 new ZIP Codes while raising its presence in existing markets as far afield as Louisville. It plans to add seven new contract sites to its network of 20 printing plants by the end of 2006.

The reinvention of the *Times* as a national paper has been accompanied by a steady loss of subscribers in the New York metro area. Its dwindling presence at home has been caused in part by forces beyond its control, including a big influx of non-English-speaking immigrants. However, taking the paper further upscale in pursuit of an elite nationwide readership priced it out of some New Yorkers' reach (a seven-day subscription goes for about $480 a year) and constrained its spending on local marketing and promotion. In addition, the *Times* has declined to join in the trend of introducing foreign-language editions or free editions for young adult readers. (It may be rethinking its free-paper aversion, as evidenced by *The Boston Globe*'s recent purchase of a 49% stake in *Metro Boston*, a give-away tabloid.)

The substitution of national for local subscribers benefited the *Times* financially even beyond the sizable premium it earns on national advertising. On average it costs the *Times* about one-third more to produce and deliver a newspaper in its home market (the only place where it owns its printing plants) than in the rest of America. But Sulzberger bristles at the notion that the *Times* is writing off its hometown readers or that a declining New York circulation is the inevitable result of national expansion. "We are not walking away from New York," he says. "But we are growing elsewhere."

The sphere of NYT Co's, ambitions widened to encompass the globe when it muscled Washington Post Co. aside to gain full control of the *International Herald Tribune*, America's broadsheet voice abroad since 1887. The Post reluctantly agreed to relinquish its 50% interest for $65 million after NYT Co. threatened to start a new paper to drive the IHT out of business. "The thing was going sideways and sooner or later was going to die," says Sulzberger, who was harshly criticized by some for lacking the gentlemanliness of his father.

The company considered making the *Tribune* over into a foreign edition of the *Times*, but decided in the end to maintain IHT's separate, international identity. "This needs to be a European paper for Europeans," says Michael Golden, a NYT Co. vice-chairman who was named publisher of IHT in 2003. Actually, the *Trib*'s 240,000 subscribers are concentrated in Europe but spread among 180 countries.

Under Golden, a slightly older first cousin of Sulzberger's, the *Trib* has adopted the *Times*'s playbook, if not its name. The transatlantic flow of copy from the *Times* has increased, but the *Trib* has enlarged its own news staff, too. It has also added

pages, color photos, and new printing sites in Sydney, São Paulo, and Kuwait City. The *Trib* scored impressively in recent reader surveys in Europe and Asia and ad sales are rising, but they still amount to less than $100 million a year. Golden and his cousin yearn to turn the *Trib*'s operating losses into profits, but the general track record of English-language newspapers and magazines abroad is discouraging. Even if the IHT flourishes, it will be a long time before it contributes significantly to its parent company's top or bottom lines.

The same is true of NYT Co.'s investment in television news. The *Times* has built a cadre of television professionals who, in collaboration with a revolving cast of print reporters, have produced much fine work for *Frontline, Nova,* and other programs. In 2003, the *Times* moved beyond production into distribution, laying out $100 million for half-ownership of a digital cable channel, Discovery Times, operated in partnership with Discovery Communications Inc. Discovery Times reaches 35 million homes—an impressive total for a fledgling channel—but its ratings are minuscule: In October, just 27,000 people tuned in during prime time, according to Nielsen//NetRatings.

Online, the *Times* already is making serious money. New York Times Digital (which includes Boston.com as well as NYTimes.com) netted an enviable $17.3 million on revenues of $53.1 million during the first half of 2004, the last period for which its financials have been disclosed. All indications are that the digital unit is continuing to grow at 30% to 40% a year, making it NYT Co.'s fastest-revving growth engine.

Advertising accounts for almost all of the digital operation's revenues, but disagreement rages within the company over whether NYTimes.com should emulate *The Wall Street Journal* and begin charging a subscription fee. Undoubtedly, many of the site's 18 million unique monthly visitors would flee if hit with a $39.95 or even a $9.95 monthly charge. One camp within the NYT Co. argues that such a massive loss of Web traffic would cost the *Times* dearly in the long run, both by shrinking the audience for its journalism and by depriving it of untold millions in ad revenue. The counterargument is that the *Times* would more than make up for lost ad dollars by boosting circulation revenue—both from online fees and new print subscriptions paid for by people who now read for free on the Web.

Sulzberger declines to take a side in this debate, but sounds as if he is leaning toward a pay site. "It gets to

EXHIBIT 3
Strategy Report Card

New York Times Co. aims to deliver top-notch journalism in any form, anyplace.

PRINT Instituted a radical plan to take the flagship paper national. For years, it looked like a masterful stroke as new ads and subscribers poured in. In an effort to build a presence in all markets, the *Times* prints at 20 plants across the nation. Lately, though, circulation growth has hit a wall.

GRADE: B+ (was A last semester)

TELEVISION Has pursued several ventures for translating *Times* stories into documentaries. Two years ago the *Times* spent $100 million for a one-half interest in Discovery Times, a cable channel. Efforts so far have been good for the brand, but not much of a moneymaker.

GRADE: C+

DIGITAL the *Times* was early to see the potential of the Web. Today the *Times* Web site is attracting nearly 18 million visitors each month, and ad sales are growing 30% to 40% a year. The result: a $100 million business in NYT.com with healthy margins and robust growth.

GRADE: A–

INTERNATIONAL Squeezed out *The Washington Post* in 2002 to gain full ownership of the *International Herald Tribune*. The *IHT* has more cachet overseas than the *Times*, so it won't carry the flagship brand for now. But it's getting a *Times*-style makeover. Growth prospects are uncertain.

GRADE: INCOMPLETE

the issue of how comfortable are we training a generation of readers to get quality information for free," he says. "That is troubling."

What's a platform agnostic to do? *The New York Times,* like all print publications, faces a quandary. A majority of the paper's readership now views the paper online, but the company still derives 90% of its revenues from newspapering. "The business model that seems to justify the expense of producing quality journalism is the one that isn't growing, and the one that is growing—the Internet—isn't producing enough revenue to produce journalism of the same quality," says John Battelle, a co-founder of *Wired* and other magazines and Web sites.

Today, Sulzberger faces an even bigger challenge than when he took charge of the *Times* in the mid-1990s (Exhibit 3). Can he find a way to rekindle growth while preserving the primacy of the *Times*'s journalism? The answer will go a long way toward determining not only the fate of America's most important newspaper but also whether traditional, reporting-intensive journalism has a central place in the Digital Age.

–With John Rossant in Paris and Lauren Gard in New York

Source: Anthony Bianco, "The Future of the New York Times," *BusinessWeek,* January 17, 2005, 64–72.

Case 1-3

Coca-Cola Co. (A)

When former Coca-Cola co. executive E. Neville Isdell agreed last May to come out of retirement and become chief executive of the beleaguered soda giant, he brimmed with confidence. No Coke newcomer, Isdell had spent 35 years inside the vast Coke system as the Atlanta company built itself into the world's most recognized global brand, retiring in 2001 after a three-year

stint as head of a large European Coke bottler. "The system isn't broken," Isdell told a *BusinessWeek* reporter at the time. "There's still opportunity for both Coca-Cola and the other brands."

All it took was a tour of Coke's operations in India, China, and 14 other key markets this summer for Isdell to see a different reality: Coca-Cola was a troubled company. Things looked so bad that just 100 days into his new job the 61-year-old Irishman interrupted his fact-finding mission to deliver a surprise warning to Wall Street. Coke, which had been struggling since the death in 1997 of its revered CEO, Roberto C. Goizueta, had made little progress in its efforts to meet the rising challenges of noncarbonated drinks. The soda giant would fall short of the meager 3% growth in earnings that analysts were resigned to for the third and fourth quarters. Moreover, Isdell was clearly prepping Wall Street for perhaps another year—or longer—of underperformance. "We've got a long way to go," a chastened Isdell told analysts. "The last time I checked, there was no silver bullet. That's not the way this business works." Coke later announced that third-quarter earnings had fallen 24%, the worst quarterly drop at Coke in recent history.

As late as the 1990s, Coca-Cola Co. was one of the most respected companies in America, a master of brand-building and management in the dawning global era. Now the Coke machine is badly out of order. The spectacle of Coke's struggles has become almost painful to watch: the battles with its own bottlers; the aged, overbearing board; the failed CEOs and failed attempts to recruit a successor; the dearth of new products; the lackluster marketing. "They've been their own worst enemy, a casualty of their own success," says Emanuel Goldman, who has followed Coke as an analyst since the 1970s (see Exhibit 1).

Yet as grave as those problems are, they only hint at the real dimensions of Coke's woes. The Coca-Cola organization is stuck in a mind-set formed during its heyday in the 1980s and '90s, when Goizueta made Coke into a growth story that captivated the world. An unwillingness to tamper with the structures and beliefs formed during those glory years has left the company unable to adapt to consumer demands for new kinds of beverages, from New Age teas to gourmet coffees, that have eaten into the cola king's market share. "The whole Coke model needs to be rethought," says Tom Pirko, president of BevMark LLC, a Santa Barbara (Calif.) consulting firm. "The carbonated soft-drink model is 30 years old and out of date."

Of all the problems that can beset a corporation, a dysfunctional culture has to be one of the toughest to fix. How do you get thousands of employees suddenly to change their most basic assumptions about their company? After all, the beliefs and attitudes that make up a culture filter into everything else: decisions on basic strategy, management style, staffing, performance expectations, product development. That's why the problems at Coke have proven so intractable. A succession of managers has focused on trying to do what Coke has always done, only better. Meanwhile, rival

---

EXHIBIT 1
Coke's Challenges

Break-Down

Coke today struggles to do the things that once made it great

MORIBUND MARKETING

Once world-class, critics say that today the soda giant has become too conservative, with Norman Rockwell-like ads that don't resonate with the teenagers and young adults that make up its most important audience.

FRICTION WITH BOTTLERS

Over the past decade Coke has often made its profit at the expense of bottlers, pushing aggressive price hikes on the concentrate it sells them. But key bottlers are now fighting back with sharp increases in the price of Coke at retail.

MEDDLING BOARD

Coke's star-studded group of directors, many of whom date back to the Goizueta era, has built a reputation for meddling: Some insiders believe the last CEO, Doug Daft, never recovered after the board unexpectedly vetoed his 2000 deal for Quaker Oats.

LACK OF INNOVATION

In the U.S. market, Coke hasn't created a best-selling new soda since Diet Coke in 1982. In recent years, Coke has been outbid by rival PepsiCo for faster growing noncarb beverages like SoBe and Gatorade.

INTERNATIONAL WORRIES

Coke desperately needs more international growth to offset its flagging U.S. business, but while some markets like Japan remain lucrative, in the large German market Coke's had so many problems it's rebidding all bottling contracts in 2007.

PepsiCo Inc. has a much different view of its mission (hint: it's not just about soda pop)—one that has helped it adapt far more successfully to a changing marketplace. Until Coke can lay the ghost of Goizueta to rest and let go of some long-cherished beliefs, it's unlikely to fix its problems.

Frozen in Time

Is the latest Coke CEO capable of leading Coke out of the valley? It's too early in Isdell's tenure to say for sure, but the early signs are not promising. Although he earned a reputation for bold decision-making as a young executive, Isdell seems to have fallen into lock-step with the reigning Coke orthodoxy. He says the company's salvation lies in simply tuning up the soda operations and capitalizing on existing brands. "We are not talking about radical change in strategy," he told Wall Street analysts in November. "We are talking about a dramatic change in execution."

That was more or less the playbook used by Roberto Goizueta, a charismatic CEO. The Cuban-born executive sold off ancillary businesses and refocused the company on what it did best: selling carbonated soft drinks. At the same time he engaged in some sophisticated reengineering of the company's financial structures. In 1986, Coke spun off a 51% stake in its U.S. bottling operations, a shrewd bit of financial alchemy that let it dump billions of dollars of bottling-related debt off its balance sheet while allowing it to continue pulling the strings at the spin-off. Thanks to near-constant buying and selling of small bottling operations, the deal also helped Coke achieve consistent profit gains, turning the once-stodgy company into—shazam!—a growth stock.

Meanwhile, Coke was able to ride the global boom like few other companies, rushing into once-closed economies such as China, East Germany, and the Soviet Union and sating their pent-up demand for a taste of America. The result: Coke stock soared 3,500% during Goizueta's 16-year reign, helping to make him one of the first supercompensated CEOs and the first professional manager to break the $1 billion pay barrier. After his death from lung cancer in October, 1997, Goizueta was all but deified, his financial structures, his cola-centric philosophy, and even his board of directors frozen in place ever since.

The ensuing years have seen a long and painful descent. After generating average annual earnings growth of 18% between 1990 and 1997, Coke's net income in recent years has grown an average of just 4%. Shares have fallen hard, currently trading at less than half their 1998 peak as more and more investors conclude that Coke's best days may be behind it. "At Coke," says Brian Holland, research director at Boyd Watterson Asset Management LLC, a Cleveland money manager that has cut its Coke holdings by 84% since last December, "there's a lot to fix, and there's no short-term solution."

In the absence of a clear vision, Coke's desire to cling to its past is not hard to understand. After all, in Coke Classic, the company is blessed with a flagship product that remains, for all of the management missteps of the past decade, one of the most powerful brands in the world. And despite the company's problems, it is still a cash cow. Helped by the dollar's decline against other major currencies, Coke is expected to generate roughly $5 billion in operating profits this year, far beyond such companies as Nike, Colgate-Palmolive, and McDonald's that have similar global ambitions. Indeed, part of Coke's paralysis is a fear that nothing else the company enters will ever match the extraordinary margins of soda concentrate.

"Smoke and Mirrors"

Goizueta's most ingenious contribution to Coke, the ingredient that added rocket fuel to the stock price, was a bit of creative though perfectly legal balance-sheet rejiggering that in some ways prefigured the Enron Corp. machinations. Known inside the company as the "49% solution," it was the brainchild of then-Chief Financial Officer M. Douglas Ivester. It worked like this: Coke spun off its U.S. bottling operations in late 1986 into a new company known as Coca-Cola Enterprises Inc., retaining a 49% stake for itself. That was enough to exert de facto control but a hair below the 50% threshold that requires companies to consolidate results of subsidiaries in their financials. At a stroke, Coke erased $2.4 billion of debt from its balance sheet. Just as important, it was able to command six board seats at CCE, which it packed with current or former Coke executives, including then-Coke President Donald R. Keough. With effective control, Coke for years could ensure that CCE was run to Coke's benefit. "Coke was creating a special-purpose entity, like Chewbacca from Enron," marvels one Wall Street analyst, referring to Enron's Chewco Investments limited partnership. Coke disputes any comparison to Enron and says the spin-off was simply a way "to leverage substantial efficiencies and adapt more rapidly to the changing trade landscape in the U.S."

Its behind-the-scenes control of CCE allowed Coke to extract a series of advantages, from pricing to deciding how many vending machines CCE purchased. Coke had tacit control over how much its largest customer—CCE—paid for the concentrate Coke sold it, as well as how much CCE charged retailers for the actual soda. Thus the escalating price wars between Coke and Pepsi came much more out of CCE's margins than Coke's, especially since Coke also required CCE to shoulder a growing portion of its brands' marketing costs.

But that was just one aspect of this unusual relationship. In the '80s and '90s a generation that ran small, family-owned bottlers was looking to retire. Coke had been snapping up these operations as a way to assure quality and to keep them from falling into the hands of leveraged-buyout artists, who would likely bleed them for their cash flow. In CCE it had another so-called anchor bottler, one of roughly a dozen around the world, from which it could exact ever-higher profits as it resold these smaller bottlers to the anchors. There were so many such deals that Coke was able to convince analysts the resulting profits should be considered part of normal operations and not extraordinary income.

For a time, this flurry of dealmaking masked the problems building in Coke's international business. But by the end of the '90s, Coke simply ran out of assets to resell, and its largest bottlers began to sink fast under all the debt-financed acquisitions they had made at Coke's behest. The result: Coke's profits stalled, with operating income falling from $5 billion in 1997 to as low as $3.69 billion in 2000. "In hindsight, a lot of what Coke was doing was smoke and mirrors, stuff that wouldn't pass the accounting standards of today," notes Douglas C. Lane, a private fund manager who now holds 400,000 Coke shares. "And at the time it created expectations of growth that weren't real." Coke notes that all such transactions were fully disclosed at the time.

The next move was inevitable: Coke imposed a crushing 7.6% price hike on its bottlers in the late '90s as Ivester, now CEO, desperately tried to sustain Goizueta's profit streak. Coke's U.S. bottlers, livid over the price increase, burned up the phone lines to some key Coke board members and succeeded in pushing the already embattled Ivester over the ledge. In late 1999, he resigned.

Ivester's successor, Douglas N. Daft, tried to work with bottlers, but relations have steadily deteriorated since. (Daft serves on the board of The McGraw-Hill Cos., which publishes *BusinessWeek*.) In a sign of disunity that would have been unthinkable in the Goizueta era, some bottlers are beginning to push back with price hikes that could boost their own profits—at Coke's expense.

While those hikes could dampen sales—and thus reduce the amount of concentrate bottlers need to purchase from Coke—the bottlers are clearly banking on the belief that they will come out ahead, even if Coke doesn't. At the same time, many bottlers have refused to carry some of the company's new noncarbonated niche offerings that Coke acquired, such as Mad River teas and Planet Java coffee, forcing the company to bury both products last year. While CCE executives maintain that relations have improved under Isdell, Trevor Messinger, a Coke bottler in Rapid City, S.D., readily admits relations between Coke and some bottlers are contentious. "I don't think everybody is on the same page of the playbook," he says.

If the friction between Coke and its bottlers worsens, some analysts believe that Isdell will have no choice but to resort to radical measures to defend Coke's interests—such as reacquiring the 62% of CCE it doesn't own. (Coke's stake has declined to 38% because of dilution.) If CCE continues to raise prices, then reabsorbing the bottler could be the only means left for Coke to ensure that it maintains its share of the pie, reasons Morgan Stanley analyst William P. Pecoriello.

Another scenario swirling inside the Coke system would have Isdell reacquiring CCE and then breaking up its assets and territories for resale to smaller bottlers or even major U.S. beer distributors—which as private companies may be content to work on lower margins than publicly traded CCE. But for now, Coke shows little willingness to tamper with this vestige of the Goizueta era. "I think that there are a number of things that we can do together without having to consider changing the model," Isdell said in an interview.

Nowhere is the Goizueta orthodoxy more apparent than in the company's unwavering focus on its aging group of soda-pop brands, especially the hallowed four: Coca-Cola, Diet Coke, Sprite, and Fanta. Goizueta was fond of discussing Coke's market share in terms of "share of stomach," as though, with the right marketing, people could be induced to give up coffee, milk, and even water in favor of Coke. Seven years after his death, the company remains fixated on making its flagship Coke brand the universal beverage from Stockholm to Sydney. Coke's sodas constitute 82% of its worldwide beverage sales, far more than at Pepsi, which is gaining on Coke's lead in the U.S. beverage market and numbers Tropicana juice, Gatorade sports drinks, and Aquafina water among its billion-dollar beverage brands.

Coke loyalists still believe in the the mantra first coined by legendary Coke Chairman Robert W. Woodruff and often repeated by Goizueta, of putting a Coke within an "arm's reach of desire" of consumers around the globe. But increasingly, consumers are reaching for anything but a soda. The mass market that Coke was so adept at exploiting has splintered. Consumer tastes have shifted from sodas to an array of sports drinks, vitamin-fortified waters, energy drinks, herbal teas, coffee, and other noncarbonated products, some of which are growing as much as nine times faster than cola. After rising steadily during the '80s and '90s, per capita soda consumption in the U.S. has declined every year since 1998. Yet when Daft tried to push Coke to become a "total beverage company," he met with resistance from Coke's board.

In an interview early in the Daft years, investment banker and director Herbert A. Allen dismissed Daft's efforts, declaring: "That's all fine and good, but I still believe that getting the four core [soda] brands right is 85% of the equation." That attitude still seems to dominate. One director, speaking on the condition he not be named, recently dismissed bottled water as "something I guess we have to carry. But the fact is we're still the kings of carbonation—always have been, always will be."

Coke's cultural resistance to diversification has become an enormous liability. South Beach Beverage Co., for example, negotiated with Coke for two years before the soda giant decided against acquiring the New Age juice company. It took Pepsi just two weeks to make an offer. Is SoBe a huge brand? No, but it gives Pepsi access and insight into a market that its soda pop completely bypasses. If you think of yourself as a beverage-and-snack company, as Pepsi does, that's valuable. If you think of yourself as a soda company, as Coke does, it's not.

Pepsi Generation

Its portfolio of beverages and its faster-growing snack foods give Pepsi enormous clout with retailers (see Exhibit 2). Pepsi boasts that it has become the second-largest generator of revenues, after Kraft Foods Inc., for its largest grocer customers. Pepsi isn't shy about using that clout to try to wrest shelf space from Coke and other rivals. "If we were only playing in carbonated soft

EXHIBIT 2 **Coke vs. Pepsi**

Pepsi never quite caught Coke in the cola wars, but its portfolio strategy has made it the long-term winner

COKE	PEPSI
Sales **$21** BILLION	Sales **$27** BILLION
Sales Growth* **2%**	Sales Growth* **4%**
Earnings **$4.3** BILLION	Earnings **$3.6** BILLION
Earnings Growth* **4%**	Earnings Growth* **12%**
Stock** **−40%**	Stock** **38%**
Business Breakdown **100%** BEVERAGE	Business Breakdown **37%** BEVERAGE
	58% FRITO-LAY SNACKS
	5% QUAKER CEREAL

* Five-year average
** Five-years ended 12/3/04
Data: Bloomberg Financial Markets

drinks, competitively we would be disadvantaged in many ways," says PepsiCo CEO Steven S. Reinemund. "Being outside carbonated [soft drinks] makes sure we're growing in the areas where there is growth."

Isdell has said he'll explore new beverage categories. If so, he'll be starting well behind Pepsi. Pepsi got a two-year jump on Coke in bottled water and later outmaneuvered Big Red to acquire both SoBe and Gatorade. As a result, Coke's Powerade has just a 17% share of the fast-growing sports-drink segment in the U.S., vs. 81% for PepsiCo's Gatorade brand. And after garnering just a 2.8% share of the popular energy-drink category—vs. 58.5% for independent rival Red Bull—Coke plans to try again with a second energy drink, Full Throttle, in January.

But in reaching into new categories, Coke may have to figure out how to get these beverages to market using food brokers, since its dedicated bottlers have been loath to handle new products that don't approach the high volumes of soda. Here, too, Pepsi has a head start. Gatorade is already distributed through a well-established system of brokers. Coke also may have to reduce its profit expectations, since the margins on noncarbonated drinks are generally lower. "Even with premium price, they cannot achieve those [soda] margins in the New Age category," warns Lance Collins, founder of New Jersey-based Fuze Beverage LLC, whose products include a diet pomegranate white tea.

The one area at Coke where the thinking has changed since the height of the Goizueta era, though not necessarily for the better, is marketing. At his Atlanta funeral, Goizueta was eulogized to the strains of *I'd Like To Teach the World To Sing* from Coke's syrupy but unforgettable commercials of the '70s. At the height of its powers, the Coke marketing machine could turn even disaster into triumph, as it did when Coke tampered with its historic concentrate formula in 1985. The sweeter new concoction backfired, but Coke seized the opportunity to build intense loyalty for Coca-Cola Classic.

The marketing magic at Coke had begun to fade even before Goizueta's death. In the late '90s, Ivester began shifting resources away from advertising and into blanketing the world with as many vending machines, refrigerated coolers, and delivery trucks as Coke and its bottlers could muster. The goal was simple ubiquity, while the niceties of brand-building were ignored. "There was no vision, no marketing," recalls one former executive. "It was all growth through distribution."

This proved to be a costly shift. For one, vending machines that were put into unconventional locations such as auto-parts stores didn't always pay off. Coke's lackluster advertising didn't help, either. Ivester, who had a deep distrust of Madison Avenue, tended to starve the ad budget, believing that the iconic Coke brand was powerful enough to sell itself. That began to change under Daft, who hired Steven J. Heyer, a former ad exec, and promoted him to president. Then, to evade the stifling Atlanta bureaucracy, he and Heyer pushed decision-making out into the field. But the move went wrong when Coke's local marketers, suddenly unshackled, began producing racy ads, including an Italian spot featuring a couple skinny-dipping. That prompted Coke headquarters to reclaim control and revert to bland Norman Rockwell-type ads. The result, says one former marketing executive, is an erosion of Coke's perceived value as a brand: "Starbucks can charge $2 for a cup of coffee, and they can barely sell a 12-pack of Cokes for $2."

In recent years, Coke showed signs of regaining its footing on the marketing front, thanks in large part to Heyer. But Heyer's departure in June after he was passed over for the top job was viewed as a big loss and is likely to lead to an exodus of the talent he brought to Coke during his three-year tenure. His successor, longtime Coke exec Charles B. "Chuck" Fruit, contends that Coke is producing good ads but has been hurt by a propensity to career from campaign to campaign. "We've suffered from an impatience that we're going to have to overcome," he says. "When we change campaigns and have 11 different looks to a brand at any one time, we're swimming upstream."

"Simple Little Things"

To really break out, Coke could make a transformative acquisition, as Pepsi did in the 1970s when it bought Frito-Lay Inc. But Isdell is downplaying the notion of a big, audacious fix for Coke's troubles. In fact, he readily admits that during one of his European tours he passed on the chance to acquire Red Bull—the independently owned, market-leading energy drink. Rather than a gaudy acquisition, Isdell maintains that Coke's redemption will come from its ability to better perform the "millions of simple little things" that Coke employees do around the globe each day. And Isdell is adamant that there's still growth in carbonated soft drinks. The reason goes back to the bottom line: He says there just aren't many businesses for sale that produce the lush margins—around 30%, some analysts estimate—that Coke makes from selling its proprietary concentrate to bottlers. In the end, Isdell has come around to the view that there's plenty of growth left in soda pop. "Regardless of what the skeptics may think, I know that carbonated soft drinks can grow," he told analysts in mid-September.

That's a remarkably conservative strategy for a man who made his name as a change agent at the soda giant. During his years of helping Coke crack emerging markets in Africa, Asia, and Eastern Europe—assignments that earned him the reputation as the "Indiana Jones of Coke"—the gregarious former rugby player made his mark as the revolutionary who was always willing to challenge the corporate dogma. As a European executive in the late 1980s, Isdell pushed the company into bottled water—a full decade before the cola-centric managers did the same back in the U.S. "He got an awful lot of grief from headquarters," recalls Gavin Darby, a former Coke executive.

And when Coke was poised to reenter India in 1993 after a 17-year absence, Isdell allowed his local managers to establish a beachhead by purchasing the leading India soda maker, Parle, even though Coke had long frowned on acquiring rival soda makers. Coke's former India chief, Jay Raja, recalls Isdell telling him to go for it: "We agreed that we would ask for forgiveness instead of permission." Isdell's instincts were proven right: At a later board meeting, Goizueta hailed Isdell's move, which gave Coke 60% of the Indian soda market almost overnight, as "the deal of the decade," recalls Raja.

Notorious Board

Perhaps the biggest impediment Isdell faces, outsiders say, is Coke's board. More than anyone else, the directors, especially the powerful triumvirate of Warren E. Buffett, Herbert A. Allen, and Donald Keough, are the keepers of the flame at Coke. Over the years they have strictly enforced obedience to the Goizueta Way. This politburo of the Goizueta era (of 14 directors, 10 date back to the late CEO) has chewed through two CEOs in the past five years. Three directors are over the age of 70, but don't look for any departures soon. Earlier this year the board waived Coke's mandatory retirement age, 74, to allow Buffett to remain and Keough to rejoin.

This is a group that believes in getting involved—very involved—in company affairs. Many Coke insiders feel that Daft, Isdell's predecessor who abruptly announced his retirement last February, never recovered from Buffett's 11th-hour veto of his attempt to steal Quaker Oats Co. from Pepsi in November, 2000. The deal was quashed when the legendary financier declared at a special board meeting that Quaker and its powerful Gatorade brand weren't worth giving up 10.5% of the Coca-Cola Co. Daft declined to speak for this article except to say he retired for health reasons. "The board has to challenge management's plan but should not challenge its authority. The Coke board was micro-managing," says John M. Nash, a board consultant and former president of the National Association of Corporate Directors.

So notorious is the Coke board that many blame it for the humiliating rejections Coke received from a string of CEO candidates the board courted before anointing Isdell. Even Buffett's prestige were not enough to persuade James M. "Jim" Kilts, head of Gillette Co., where Buffett was a director for years. Like Robert A. Eckert of Mattel Inc. and Carlos M. Gutierrez of Kellogg Co., Kilts passed on the opportunity to head the world's most powerful brand. (Indeed, one executive that Coke approached for the job was rankled by the way Coke's board leaked the names of people it was pursuing. "It was like the search was playing out on CNN," he says. "One of the greatest legacies that [Isdell] can leave behind is a reshaped board.")

Board members have made clear their opposition to product diversification, as well as their belief that mergers aren't what's needed. At times they've even involved themselves in operations. Keough rankled some marketing staffers when earlier this year he personally killed an edgy TV ad—in which a teen wipes a Coke can under his armpit before handing it to an unwitting friend—that he deemed in poor taste. Isdell maintains that he'll be able to stand his ground with Coke's board. Sonya H. Soutus, a Coke spokeswoman, says it is "presumptuous and unfair" to criticize Coke's board members, who she says have substantial stockholdings, bring a wealth of experience, and have taken steps to address Coke's problems.

Can Isdell return Coke to greatness? In some ways, the clock is working against him. At 61, he may be only a transitional CEO. Still, long-timers can sometimes bring special skills to rejuvenating a tired corporate culture. "A.G. Lafley was a product of Procter & Gamble, and William Johnson was a product of [H.J.] Heinz," notes Gary M. Stibel, a management guru at Westport (Conn.)-based New England Consulting Group. "They remembered what it was like when their companies were great, and they returned them to that greatness." There are plenty of other examples, though, such as Eastman Kodak Co., where a succession of CEOs was unable to break from the past and continued to ride outdated models and product lineups nearly into oblivion. As two CEOs have already discovered at Coke, it isn't easy following in the footsteps of a legend.

Source: Dean Foust, "Gone Flat," *BusinessWeek,* December 20, 2004, 76–82.

Part

Markets, Segments, and Customer Value

2

2

Markets and
Competitive Space

Markets are increasingly complex, turbulent, and interrelated, creating challenges for managers in understanding market structure and identifying opportunities for growth. The traditional view assumes that the market and competitive space are stable and changes are predictable. Importantly, this perspective may be misleading and even dangerous when market boundaries reconfigure because of new technologies and competition and the emergence of new business designs (such as Google, Inc., the world's leading Internet search engine). Sustaining and building competitive advantage increasingly requires altered strategic thinking about market boundaries and structure. Rapid technological change, market convergence, Internet access, global competition, and the diversity of buyers' preferences in many markets require continuous monitoring to identify promising business opportunities, assess the shifting requirements of buyers, evaluate changes in competitive positioning, and guide managers' decisions about which buyers to target and how to position brands to appeal to targeted buyers. A complete view of the market is important, even when management's interest centers on one or a few market segments within a particular market. Understanding the scope and structure of the entire market is necessary to develop strategy and anticipate market changes and competitive threats. Understanding markets and how they are likely to change in the future are vital inputs to market-driven strategies.

Illustrative of the challenges of transformation in markets and competitive space are Eastman Kodak's delayed responses to the potential disruptive impact of digital photography on traditional film and camera markets. The pervasive impact of digital imaging technology demanded a rapid change in Kodak's business design and understanding of the market.[1] Kodak's revenues from its traditional products and services declined from $10 billion in 2001 to an estimated $5 billion in 2007, when total revenues were expected to exceed $10 billion. The consequences of Kodak's delayed responses to the changing markets include major financial losses, extensive layoffs, expensive plant closures, and escalating debt. Kodak's prior management (new CEO in June 2005) had underestimated the speed and rate of decline of purchases in film markets around the world. The 25 percent annual declines in Kodak's film sales were more than three times greater than estimated by management. While Kodak holds a strong position in the U.S. digital camera market, adding to the firm's financial problems are the very small margins on digital cameras. Management decided to stop building digital market share in late 2006 at the expense of profitability and halted production of digital cameras, outsourcing manufacturing to a Singapore-based supplier. The company was expected to reach breakeven on digital camera sales at the end of 2006.

Kodak's competitive threats are not unique. Leica, the luxury traditional camera producer, was close to collapse in 2005 but management forecast better performance in 2006 with the introduction of its M8 digital rangefinder model. Many companies and industries are experiencing major changes in their core markets. Strategic thinking in changing markets confronts executives with complex challenges but also exciting opportunities. These new challenges are driven by demanding customers with changing value requirements, aggressive global competition, market turbulence, rapid emergence of new and increasingly turbulent technologies, and the escalating globalization initiatives of many companies.

The Kodak illustration highlights several important issues concerning markets and competitive space. The changes described show how competitive threats may develop from new competition (electronics firms). Importantly, the rapid growth of digital photography points to the importance of market sensing and strategic vision in assessing the nature and scope of new competitive threats and guiding strategic initiatives to counter the threats.

The chapter begins with a discussion of how markets and strategies are interrelated, followed by an approach to determining product-market scope and structure. Next, we look at how buyers are described and analyzed, and examine the important process of competitor analysis. Guidelines follow for developing a strategic vision about the scope and composition of markets in the future. Finally, we consider how to estimate market size. Financial Analysis guidelines are included in the Appendix.

Markets and Strategies

Knowledge about markets and competitive space is essential in guiding business and marketing strategies. First, we look at how markets impact strategy and discuss the importance of thinking outside the competitive box. Next, we examine several forces that are creating changes in market boundaries and structure, and consider the need to define markets in terms of buyers' needs and product benefits.

Markets and Strategies Are Interlinked

Market changes often require altering business and marketing strategies. Managers who do not understand their markets and how they will change in the future may find their strategies inadequate as buyers' value requirements change and new products become available which better satisfy buyers' requirements. Many forces are causing the transformation of industries and are changing the structure of markets and nature of competition. These influences create both market opportunities and threats by altering the nature and scope of products, markets, and competitive space. Market-driven companies proactively alter their strategies to deliver superior value to existing and new customers. For example, PepsiCo shows impressive performance in understanding and catering to changing tastes in the beverage and snacks market, rather than trying to change them.[2] The company faces the facts about market change and adapts products to them. To capitalize on the growing market for New Age herbally enhanced beverages, PepsiCo acquired SoBe Beverages in 2001, and extended the brand into an energy drink for the school age market—SoBe No Fear—and SoBe Fuerte, aimed at the Hispanic market. Sabritas chips were brought in from PepsiCo's Mexican subsidiary targeting the foreign-born segment of the large and escalating U.S. Hispanic market. PepsiCo defines its mission as serving the consumer, not protecting its existing brands.

Thinking Outside the Competitive Box[3]

Not surprisingly there is a tendency for executives to think in terms of a stable "competitive box" around their businesses—defined by technology, geography, competitors, and the existing customer base. This frame of reference enables analytical tools to be successfully applied, research to be carried out, and plans to be made. This traditional perspective is logical in stable markets but fails to address the reality that the real threats as well as exciting opportunities may be present outside the conventional competitive box shown in Exhibit 2.1. Increasingly, new markets, new types of competition, and new business designs are emerging which fuel market growth and cannibalize the existing customer base of incumbents' markets. Importantly, effective processes for understanding markets and competitive space and guiding the strategic initiatives appropriate for the markets require strategic thinking outside the competitive box.

An Array of Challenges

Changes in markets are drastically altering opportunities and competitive space and increasing the importance of strategic thinking in these changing markets. Disruptive innovation, commoditization of product designs, creation of new market space, and fast changing markets are challenges that underline the need to identify changes in the market(s) and diagnose the strategic implications of the changes.

Disruptive Innovation

These innovations provide simpler and less costly ways to match the value requirements offered by the products (goods and services) of incumbent firms serving the market.[4] Examples of disruptive innovations and new business models are illustrated by Amazon.com on traditional bookstores, digital photography on cameras and film, and steel mini-mills on integrated mills. The opportunity for market access by disruptive innovations is created by the products of incumbent firms in the market which are exceeding the value requirements of buyers. Disruptive innovations may meet the needs of new segments or entire markets.

EXHIBIT 2.1
Opportunities Outside the Competitive Box

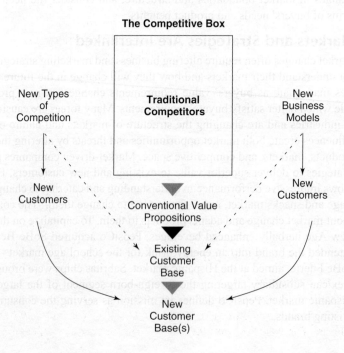

Google is renowned as the leading Internet search engine. Established in 1998, Google was valued at $23 billion when it was floated on the stock market in 2004, and made annual profits of nearly $3 billion in 2006. The company's strategy initiatives reveal ambitions beyond search:

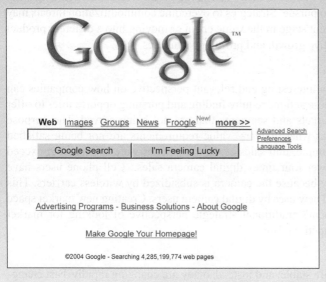

- Initial income was from search-related advertising—Google had online advertising income of $11 billion in 2007.

- The company's strategy is expressed as "100 percent relevant beyond search," indicating its intention to leverage capabilities in areas other than simply Web searching.

- Google is targeting the global advertising industry—online and off-line. Recent developments include a move into video (through the purchase of YouTube as an outlet for video advertising); audio (by the acquisition of dMarc, an automated network selling radio advertising, and a deal with ClearChannel, the world's largest radio company); and print (with an agreement to sell advertising on behalf of 66 U.S. newspapers).

- Google is partnering with media companies to supply video content to affiliated websites—including MTV. It has formed an alliance with News Corporation's MySpace to access social networking.

- Google is now positioning itself as a rival to Microsoft—Google Apps allows users to off-load their e-mail systems to Google, while keeping their own e-mail addresses, as well as providing an online office productivity suite to compete directly with Microsoft's Office package. Google offers a free e-mail service—Gmail—challenging Microsoft's Hotmail; Picasa to allow online photo storage; Google Earth and Google Maps; free Web publishing; and is working on computer security products.

- Plans for e-book digitization—scanning books and making them online searchable—aims to do the same for books as the iPod did for music.

- Google's mission is to "organize the world's information" and not simply to personalize advertising, but to organize people's daily lives.

Sources: Tony Allen-Mills, "Search Me?," *The Sunday Times,* May 27, 2007, 1–13; Robert D. Hof, "Google Steps into Microsoft's Office," *BusinessWeek,* February 12, 2007, 62–64; Richard Waters, "Act Two: How Google Is Muscling Its Way into the Advertising Mainstream," *Financial Times,* January 19, 2007, 13; Richard Waters, "All Eyes on Google Advertising," *Financial Times,* April 17, 2007, 22.

Disruptive innovations may impact various technologies and industries. Indications of these new threats to existing firms can often be identified through perceptive market sensing outside the competitive box. Complacency and management's hesitancy to consider options beyond the core business focus are potential problems. When indications are found that markets are changing, strategic thinking initiatives need to be pursued. The strategic development of Google is illustrative of the disruptive changes that can be created by an able competitor. This is described in the STRATEGY FEATURE.

Commoditization Threats

When modularization (products comprised of standardized components) occurs products become commodities, making it difficult to earn anything more than subsistence returns.[5] For example, when the personal computer (PC) market became commoditized the opportunity for profits shifted to microprocessors (Intel) and operating system software (Microsoft). Commoditization was a key factor for IBM's management in deciding to move out of the PC market. The business was sold to Lenovo, the leading Chinese PC company.

The potential effect of commoditization in markets highlights the importance of developing a vision about how the market is likely to change in the future, and deciding what business strategy initiatives to pursue. Strategies to overcome commoditization threats may involve competing at a different stage in the value chain or moving into a different product category that provides attractive growth and profit opportunities.

Creating New Market Space

Kim and Mauborgne offer an interesting and relevant perspective on how companies can create new market space.[6] These actions require finding and pursuing opportunities to offer potential buyers value in markets and segments that are not being served. The purpose is to target new opportunities where buyers' value requirements are not being satisfied by existing products. For example, unit sales of camera phones were estimated to exceed 400 million units in 2006, over four times digital camera sales.[7] Cell phone users have access to digital photography because the camera is subsidized by wireless carriers. This creates new market space and new uses by digital camera users. Creating new market space requires changing management's traditional strategic perspective of looking for market opportunities inside the Competitive Box.

Fast Changing Markets

Increasingly, fewer markets are stable, and instead, many are changing rapidly. Fast changing markets require modifications in management's strategic thinking. Indications of changes are signaled by shifting customer value requirements, new technologies, changes in competitive space, and new business models. Fast changing markets may sometimes be difficult to predict and strategy initiatives may necessitate trial and error adjustments guided by market responses. Not acknowledging or responding to the threats and requirements of fast changing markets is the real danger. Importantly, even in markets assumed to be comparatively stable, innovation can quickly alter market space.

Matching Needs with Product Benefits

The term *product-market* recognizes that a market exists only when there are buyers with needs who have the ability to purchase goods and services and products are available to satisfy the needs. There is a compelling logic that competitive strength comes from putting customer needs at the center of a company's operations; that this perspective should guide strategic thinking for markets. For example, Progressive Insurance shows remarkable sales growth and shareholder value creation by its focus on the most important needs of its customers. The INNOVATION FEATURE describes how the company has adapted its operations to effectively meet customer needs.

Markets are comprised of groups of people who have the *ability* and *willingness* to buy something because they have a need (value requirement) for it.[8] The ability to buy and willingness to buy indicate that there is demand for a particular product. People with needs and wants buy the benefits provided by a good or service to satisfy either a household or organizational use situation. A product-market matches people with needs—needs that lead to a demand for a good or service—to the product benefits that satisfy those needs. Thus, a product-market combines the benefits of a product with the needs that motivate people to express a demand for that product.

Accordingly, markets are defined in terms of needs substitutability among different products and brands and by the different ways in which people choose to satisfy their

- In the period 1994 to 2004, Progressive Insurance increased sales from $1.3 billion to $9.5 billion, and ranks high in the *BusinessWeek* Top 50 U.S. companies for shareholder value creation.
- The company invents new ways of providing services to save customers time, money, and irritation, while often lowering costs at the same time.
- Loss adjusters are sent to the road accidents rather than working at the head office, and they have the power to write checks on the spot.
- Progressive reduced the time needed to see a damaged automobile from seven days to nine hours.
- Policyholders' cars are repaired quicker, and the focus on this central customer need has won much auto insurance business for Progressive.
- These initiatives also enable Progressive to reduce its own costs—the cost of storing a damaged automobile for a day is $28, about the same as the profit from a six-month policy.

Source: Adapted from Adrian Mitchell, "Heart of the Matter," *The Marketer,* June 12, 2004, 14.

needs. "A product-market is the set of products judged to be substitutes within those usage situations in which similar patterns of benefits are sought by groups of customers."[9] The influence of competing brands becomes stronger the closer the substitutability and the more direct the competition. The Ford Taurus competes directly with the Toyota Camry, whereas in a less direct yet relevant way, other major purchases (e.g., vacation travel) compete with automobile expenditures due to the buyer's budget constraints.

As an example, a financial services product-market for short-term investments may include money market accounts, mutual funds, U.S. Treasury bills, bank certificates of deposit, and other short-term investment alternatives. If one type of product is a substitute for another, then both should be included in the product-market.

By determining how a firm's specific product or brand is positioned within the product-market, management can monitor and evaluate changes in the product-market to decide whether alternate targeting and positioning strategies and product offerings are needed. When defining a product-market, it is essential to establish boundaries that are broad enough to contain all of the relevant product categories which are competing for the same buyer needs.

Defining and Analyzing Product-Markets

In the remainder of the chapter we discuss the activities involved in defining and analyzing product-markets. The steps are shown in Exhibit 2.2, beginning with determining product-market boundaries and structure.

Determining Product-Market Boundaries and Structure

Product-market boundaries and structure provide managers with important information for developing business and marketing strategies, and alert management to new competition. Considering only a company's brands and the direct competitors may mask potential competitive threats or opportunities.

Product-Market Structure

A company's brand competes with other companies' brands in generic, product-type, and product-variant product-markets. The **generic product-market** includes a broad group of

EXHIBIT 2.2

Defining and Analyzing Product-Markets

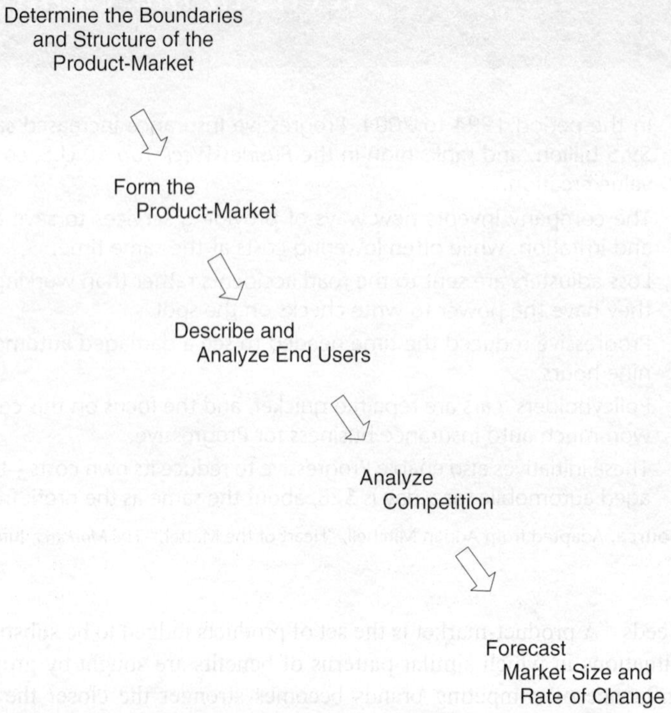

Determine the Boundaries and Structure of the Product-Market

⇩

Form the Product-Market

⇩

Describe and Analyze End Users

⇩

Analyze Competition

⇩

Forecast Market Size and Rate of Change

products that satisfy a general, yet similar, need. For example, several classes or types of products can be combined to form the generic product-market for kitchen appliances. The starting point in determining product-market boundaries is to identify the particular need or want that a group of products satisfies, such as performing kitchen functions. Since people with a similar need may not satisfy the need in the same manner, generic product-markets are often heterogeneous, containing different end-user groups and several types of related products (e.g., kitchen appliances).

The **product-type product-market** includes all brands of a particular product type, such as ovens for use in food preparation by consumers. The product type is a product category or product classification that offers a specific set of benefits intended to satisfy a customer's need or want in a specific way. Differences in the products within a product-type product-market may exist, creating **product-variants.**[10] For example, electric, gas, and microwave ovens all provide heating functions but employ different technologies.

Guidelines for Definition

In defining the product-market, it is helpful to indicate (1) the basis for identifying buyers in the product-market of interest (geographical area, consumer/business, etc.); (2) the market size and characteristics; and (3) the brand and/or product categories competing for the needs and wants of the buyers included in the product-market.

The composition of a product-market can be determined by following the steps shown in Exhibit 2.3. We illustrate how this process can be used to determine the composition of the kitchen appliance product-market. Suppose top management of a kitchen appliance firm is considering expanding its mix of products. The company's present line of laundry and dishwashing products meets a generic need for the kitchen functions of cleaning. Other kitchen use situations include heating and cooling of foods. In this example the generic need is performing various kitchen functions. The products that provide kitchen functions are ways of satisfying the generic need. The break out of products into specific product-markets (e.g., A, B, C, and D) would include equipment for washing and drying

EXHIBIT 2.3
Determining the Composition of a Product-Market

Start with the generic need satisfied by the product category of interest to management

Identify the product categories (types) that can satisfy the generic need

Identify the specific product-markets within the generic product-market

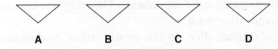

A   **B**   **C**   **D**

clothing, appliances for cooling food, cooking appliances, and dishwashers. The buyers in various specific product-markets and the different brands competing in these product-markets can be identified and analyzed. The process of mapping the product-market structure begins by identifying the generic need (function) satisfied by the product of interest to management. Need identification is the basis for selecting the products that fit into the product market.

An example of the product-market structure to meet people's needs for food is shown in Exhibit 2.4. A fast-food restaurant chain such as McDonald's should consider more than its regular customers and direct competitors in its market opportunity analysis. The consumption need being satisfied is fast and convenient preparation of food. The buyer has several ways of meeting the need such as purchasing fast foods, preparing food in the microwave in the home, patronizing supermarket delis, buying prepared foods in convenience stores, and ordering take outs from traditional restaurants. The relevant competitive space includes all of these fast-food sources. It is essential to analyze market behavior and trends in the product-markets shown in Exhibit 2.4, since competition may come from any of the alternative services.

Forming Product-Markets

The factors that influence how product-market boundaries should be determined include the purpose for analyzing the product-market, the rate of changes in market composition over time, and the extent of market complexity.

Purpose of Analysis

If management is deciding whether or not to exit from a business, primary emphasis may be on financial performance and competitive position. Detailed analysis of the product-market may not be necessary. In contrast, if the objective is finding one or more attractive

EXHIBIT 2.4
Illustrative Fast-Food Product-Market Structure

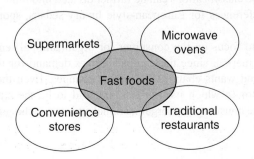

market segments to target in the product-market, a much more penetrating analysis is necessary. When different products satisfy the same need, the product-market boundaries should contain all relevant products and brands. For example, the photography product-market should include digital cameras, related equipment and services, and conventional cameras, film, and services. Product-market boundaries should be determined in a manner that will facilitate strategic thinking, enabling management to capitalize on existing and potential opportunities and to avoid possible threats.

Changing Composition of Markets

As discussed earlier product-markets may change as new technologies become available and new competition emerges. New technologies offer buyers different ways of meeting their needs. For example, fax technology gave people in need of overnight letter delivery an alternative way to transmit the information. The entry into the market by new competitors also alters competitive space.

Industry classifications often do not clearly define product-market boundaries. For example, people may meet their needs for food with products from several industries as shown in Exhibit 2.4. Industry-based definitions do not consider alternative ways of meeting needs. Industry classifications typically have a product supply rather than a customer demand orientation. Of course, since industry associations, trade publications, and government agencies generate a lot of information about products and markets, information from these sources should be included in market analysis. However, market analysis activities should not be constrained by industry boundaries.

Extent of Market Complexity

Three characteristics of markets capture a large portion of the variation in their complexity: (1) the *functions* or uses of the product needed by the customer, (2) the *technology* used in the product to provide the desired function, and (3) the different *customer segments* using the product to perform a particular function.[11]

Customer function considers the role or purpose of the good or service. It is the value provided to the customer. Thus, the function provides the capability to satisfy the value requirements of the customer. In the case of the personal computer, the function performed may be entertainment for the household, information search, Internet purchasing, or the performance of various business functions.

Different *technologies* may satisfy the use situation of the customer. Steel and aluminum materials meet a similar need in various use situations. The technology consists of the materials and designs incorporated into products. In the case of a service, technology relates to how the service is rendered. For example, voice calls can be sent via the Internet, traditional phone lines, and wireless phones.

Customer segment recognizes the diversity of the needs of customers in a particular product-market such as automobiles. A specific brand and model won't satisfy all buyers' needs and wants. Two broad market segments for automobile use are households and organizations. These classifications can be further divided into more specific customer segments, such as preferences for European-style luxury sedans, sport utility vehicles, and sports cars.

It is important to focus on the consumer (or organizational) end-user of the product when defining the market, since the end-user drives demand for the product. When the end-users' needs and wants change, the market changes. Even though a producer considers the distributor to which its products are sold to be the customer, the market is really defined by the consumer and organizational end-users who purchase the product for consumption.

Illustrative Product-Market Structure

Suppose you are a brand manager for a cereal producer. You know that brands like Life, Product 19, and Special K compete for sales to people that want nutritional benefits from cereal. Nonetheless, our earlier discussion highlights the value of considering a more complete picture of how competing brands like Life, Product 19, and Special K also may experience competition from other ways of meeting the needs satisfied by these brands. For example, a person may decide to eat a Kellogg's Nutri-Grain cereal bar instead of a bowl of cereal, and the consumer may want to vary the type of cereal, eating a natural or regular type of cereal. Because of the different product types and variants competing for the same needs and wants, the cereal brand manager should develop a picture of the product-market structure within which her/his brand is positioned. Exhibit 2.5 provides an illustrative product-market structure for cereals. The diagram can be expanded to portray other relevant product types (e.g., breakfast bars) in the generic product-market for food and beverages.

Describing and Analyzing End-Users

After determining the product-market structure it is useful to develop profiles of end-user buyers for the generic, product-type, and product-variant levels of the product-market

EXHIBIT 2.5
Illustrative Product-Market Structure

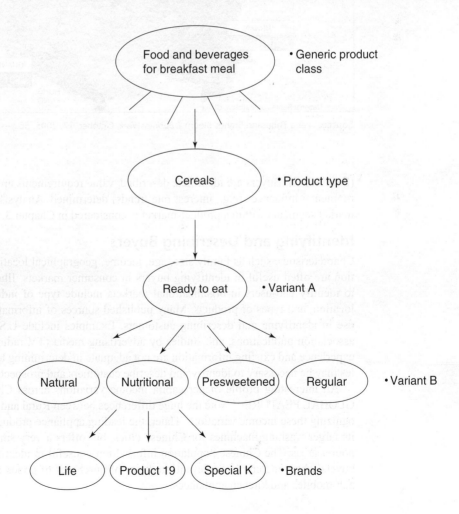

RICH CHINA, POOR CHINA
Incomes vary hugely across the mainland

☐ RURAL PER CAPITA INCOME, 2003
■ URBAN PER CAPITA INCOME, 2003
IN U.S. DOLLARS

HEILONGJIANG

JILIN

XINJIANG

INNER MONGOLIA

BEIJING $691 $1,714

LIAONING $362 $894

TIANJIN

HEBEI

QINGHAI

SHANXI

NINGXIA

SHANDONG

JIANGSU $523 $1,144

GANSU

SHAANXI

HENAN

SHANGHAI $821 $1,835

TIBET

HUBEI $317 $904

ANHUI

SHANGHAI

SICHUAN $275 $869

ZHEJIANG

HUNAN

JIANGXI

FUJIAN

GUIZHOU

YUNNAN $210 $944

GUANGXI

GUANGDONG $501 $1,528

HONG KONG

Data: National Bureau of Statistics, China

Source: "Let a Thousand Brands Bloom," *BusinessWeek,* October, 17, 2005, 58.

(Exhibit 2.2). Buyers are identified, described, value requirements are indicated, and environmental influences (e.g., interest rate trends) determined. Analysis of the buyers in the market segments within a product-market is considered in Chapter 3.

Identifying and Describing Buyers

Characteristics, such as family size, age, income, geographical location, sex, and occupation are often useful in identifying buyers in consumer markets. Illustrative factors used to identify end-users in organizational markets include type of industry, company size, location, and types of products. Many published sources of information are available for use in identifying and describing customers. Examples include U.S. Census data, trade association publications, and studies by advertising media (TV, radio, magazines). When experience and existing information are not adequate in determining buyers, research studies may be necessary to identify and describe customers and prospects.

An interesting profile of per capita income variations across China is shown in the GLOBAL FEATURE.[12] Note the huge differences between Rural and Urban income. Recognizing these income variations, Haier, the leading appliance producer in China, designs its larger washing machines for Chinese cities, but offers a very small model at $37 for poorer areas. The Chinese population information is useful in identifying and describing buyers where income is a relevant predictor of purchases of goods and services such as automobiles and kitchen appliances.

How Buyers Make Choices

Often, simply describing buyers does not provide enough information to guide market targeting and positioning decisions. We also need to try to find out *why* people buy products and specific product brands. In considering how customers decide what to buy, it is useful to analyze how they move through the sequence of steps leading to a decision to purchase a particular brand. Buyers normally follow a decision process. They begin by recognizing a need (problem recognition); next, they seek information; then, they identify and evaluate alternative products; and finally, they purchase a brand. Of course, the length and complexity of this process varies by product and purchasing situation. Decisions for frequently purchased products with which a buyer has past experience tend to be routine. One part of studying buyer decision processes is finding out what criteria people use in making decisions. For example, how important is the brand name of a product in the purchase decision?

Illustrations of the buying decision process stages for a consumer purchase and an organizational purchase are shown in Exhibit 2.6. The consumer purchase involves a portable CD player purchased by a student, whereas the organizational purchase is for a portable CD player component from an outside supplier. Both processes move through the major stages in the buying decision process, but the issues and activities are quite different.

EXHIBIT 2.6   **Comparing the Stages in Consumer and Organizational Purchases**

Source: Roger A. Kerin, Steve W. Hartley, and William Rudelius, *Marketing The Core* (Burr Ridge, IL: McGraw-Hill/Irwin, 2004), 129.

STAGE IN THE BUYING DECISION PROCESS	CONSUMER PURCHASE: PORTABLE CD PLAYER FOR A STUDENT	ORGANIZATIONAL PURCHASE: EARPHONES FOR A PORTABLE CD PLAYER
Problem recognition	Student doesn't like the features of the portable CD player now owned and desires a new portable CD player.	Marketing research and sales departments observe that competitors are improving the earphones on their portable CD models. The firm decides to improve the earphones on their own new models, which will be purchased from an outside supplier.
Information search	Student uses past experience, that of friends, ads, the Internet, and *Consumer Reports* to collect information and uncover alternatives.	Design and production engineers draft specifications for earphones. The purchasing department identifies suppliers of portable CD player earphones.
Alternative evaluation	Alternative portable CD players are evaluated on the basis of important attributes desired in a portable CD player, and several stores are visited.	Purchasing and engineering personnel visit with suppliers and assess (1) facilities, (2) capacity, (3) quality control, and (4) financial status. They drop any suppliers not satisfactory on these factors.
Purchase decision	A specific brand of portable CD player is selected, the price is paid, and the student leaves the store.	They use (1) quality, (2) price, (3) delivery, and (4) technical capability as key buying criteria to select a supplier. Then they negotiate terms and award a contract.
Postpurchase behavior	Student reevaluates the purchase decision, may return the portable CD player to the store if it is unsatisfactory.	They evaluate suppliers using a formal vendor rating system and notify a supplier if earphones do not meet their quality standard. If the problem is not corrected, they drop the firm as a future supplier.

EXHIBIT 2.7
Population Trends for the 50 States in the United States: 1995 to 2025

Source: U.S. Bureau of the Census, Population Division, PPL-47.

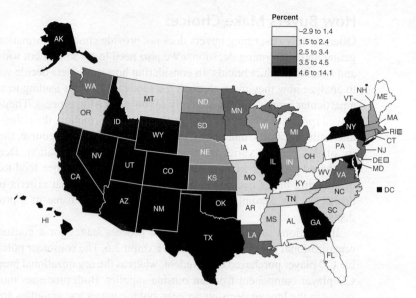

Percent
-2.9 to 1.4
1.5 to 2.4
2.5 to 3.4
3.5 to 4.5
4.6 to 14.1

Environmental Influences

The final step in building customer profiles is to identify the external environmental factors that influence buyers and thus impact the size and composition of the market over time. These influences include government actions (e.g., tax cuts), social change, economic shifts, technology, and other factors that may alter buyers' needs and wants. Typically, these factors are not controlled by the buyer or the firms that market the product, and substantial changes in environmental influences can have a major impact on customers' purchasing activities. Therefore, it is important to identify the relevant external influences on a product-market and to estimate their future impact. During the past decade various changes in market opportunities occurred as a result of uncontrollable environmental factors. Illustrations include the shifts in population age-group composition, changes in tax laws affecting investments, and variations in interest rates. Consider, for example, the population trends for the 50 states in the United States from 1995 to 2025. Note that some states (Exhibit 2.7) display high growth rates while others are declining in size. Residential construction rates and various other product-markets will be impacted by differences in population growth across regions and states in the U.S.

Building Customer Profiles

Describing customers begins with the generic product-market. At this level customer profiles are likely to describe the size and general composition of the customer base. For example, the commercial air travel customer profile for a specified geographical area (e.g., South America) would include market size, growth rates, mix of business and pleasure travelers, and other general characteristics. The product-type and variant profiles are more specific about customer characteristics such as needs and wants, use situations, activities and interests, opinions, purchase processes and choice criteria, and environmental influences on buying decisions. Normally, product-type analysis considers the organization's product and closely related product types.

In developing marketing strategy, management is concerned with deciding which buyers to target within the product-market of interest and how to position to each target. The customer profiles help to guide these decisions. The profile information is also useful in deciding how to segment the market. More comprehensive customer analyses are necessary in market segmentation analysis, which we discuss in Chapter 3.

Analyzing Competition

Competitor analysis considers the companies and brands that compete in the product-market of interest. Analyzing the competition follows the five steps shown in Exhibit 2.8. In Step 1 we determine the competitive arena in which an organization competes and describe the characteristics of the competitive space. Steps 2 and 3 identify, describe, and evaluate the organization's key competitors. Steps 4 and 5 anticipate competitors' future actions and identify potential competitors that may enter the market.

Defining the Competitive Arena

Competition often includes more than the firms that are direct competitors, like Coke and Pepsi. For example, the different levels of competition for diet colas are shown in Exhibit 2.9. The product variant is the most direct type of competition. Nevertheless, other product categories of soft drinks also compete for buyers, as do other beverages. A complete understanding of the competitive arena helps to guide strategy design and implementation. Since competition often occurs within specific industries, study of the industry structure is useful in defining the competitive arena, recognizing that more than one industry may be competing in the same product-market, depending on the complexity of the product-market structure. For example, the digital photography product-market includes traditional camera and film competitors and electronics industry competitors.

Industry Analysis

Competitor analysis is conducted from the point of view of a particular firm. For example, a soft drink firm such as Coca-Cola should include other beverage brands in its industry analysis. Two kinds of information are needed: (1) a descriptive profile of the industry; and (2) an analysis of the value chain (distribution) channels that link together the various organizations in the value-added system from suppliers to end-users. Thus, the industry analysis is horizontal and covers similar types of firms (e.g., soft drink producers), whereas the value chain analysis considers the vertical network of firms that supply materials and/or parts, produce products (and services), and distribute the products to end-users.

The industry analysis includes: (1) industry characteristics and trends, such as sales, number of firms, and growth rates; and (2) operating practices of the firms in the industry, including product mix, service provided, barriers to entry, and geographical scope. Many industries provide information in publications and websites that is useful in the analysis. Industry associations also publish research reports which typically include growth forecasts.

EXHIBIT 2.8
Analyzing the Competition

1 ▷ Define the competitive arena for the generic, specific, and variant product-markets.

2 ▷ Identify key competitors.

3 ▷ Evaluate key competitors.

4 ▷ Anticipate actions by competitors.

5 ▷ Identify and evaluate potential competitors.

EXHIBIT 2.9
Examples of Levels of Competition

Source: Donald R. Lehmann and Russell S. Winer, *Analysis for Marketing Planning*, 4th ed. (Burr Ridge, IL: Richard D. Irwin, 1997), 22. Copyright © The McGraw-Hill Companies. Used with permission.

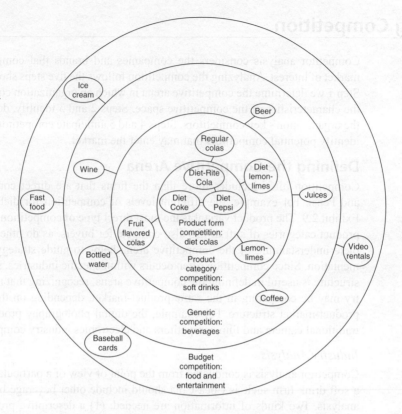

First, we need to identify the companies that comprise the industry and develop descriptive information on the industry and its members. It is important to examine industry structure beyond domestic market boundaries, since international industry developments often affect regional, national, and international markets. It is also necessary to include all relevant industries in the analysis. For example, as shown in Exhibit 2.10, including only the firms providing traditional long distance phone services would provide an incomplete assessment of the industries and firms that provide services. The traditional boundaries between phone companies, cable providers, and other tech firms are changing rapidly. Note the large differences in revenue growth.

The industry identification is based on product similarity, location at the same level in the value chain (e.g., manufacturer, distributor, retailer) and geographical scope. The industry analysis considers:

- Industry size, growth, and composition.
- Typical marketing practices.
- Industry changes that are anticipated (e.g., consolidation trends).
- Industry strengths and weaknesses.
- Strategic alliances and potential mergers/acquisitions among competitors.

Analysis of the Value-Added Chain

The study of supplier and distribution channels is important in understanding and serving product-markets. While some producers may go directly to their end-users, many work with other organizations through distribution channels. The extent of vertical integration by competitor backward (supply) and forward toward end-users is also useful information.

EXHIBIT 2.10 **The Shifting Telecom Landscape**

Source: "The Shifting Telecom Landscape," *BusinessWeek,* February 28, 2005, 36.

	Revenue in Billions						
	2003	**2004**	**2005**	**2006**	**2007**	**2008**	**Compound Annual Growth Rate**
• Video	$ 0.2	$ 0.3	$ 0.5	$ 1.0	$ 1.6	$ 2.5	65.7%
• Consumer broadband	2.8	3.5	4.0	4.2	4.6	4.8	11.4
• Consumer long distance	20.7	18.2	16.0	13.6	11.3	9.2	−15.0
• Business local	26.3	26.7	26.4	26.1	25.8	25.5	−0.6
• Business long distance	26.1	24.5	23.0	21.3	19.7	18.2	−7.0
• Business data*	44.8	45.6	46.6	47.1	46.8	45.4	0.3
• Consumer local	46.9	42.2	39.0	36.2	34.0	32.3	−7.25
• Wireless	91.5	108.7	119.2	132.8	144.5	153.6	10.9
Total	$260.7	$271.5	$277.0	$285.0	$291.3	$294.9	2.5%

*Includes Internet access, private data lines, ATM traffic, and frame relay data: In-Stat/MDR

The types of relationships (collaborative or transactional) in the distribution channel should be identified and evaluated. The extent of outsourcing activities in the value chain is also of interest. Different channels that access end-user customers should be included in the channel analysis. By looking at the distribution approaches of industry members, we can identify important patterns and trends in serving end-users. Value chain analysis may also uncover new market opportunities that are not served by present channels of distribution. Finally, information from various value chain levels can help in forecasting end-user sales.

The use of outsourcing manufacturing and other business functions expanded rapidly in the United States and Europe during the last decade. By outsourcing an organization may gain strategic advantage by focusing on its core competencies, while outsourcing other necessary business functions to independent partners. Thus, analysis of outsourcing activities may be an important aspect of competitor analysis.

Competitive Forces

Different competitive forces are present in the value-added chain. The traditional view of competition is expanded by recognizing Michael Porter's five competitive forces that impact industry performance:

1. Rivalry among existing firms.
2. Threat of new entrants.
3. Threat of substitute products.
4. Bargaining power of suppliers.
5. Bargaining power of buyers.[13]

The first force recognizes that active competition among industry members helps determine industry performance, and it is the most direct and intense form of competition. The aggressive competition between General Motors and Toyota is illustrative. Rivalry may occur within a market segment or across an entire product-market. The nature and scope of competition may vary according to the maturity of the industry.

The second force highlights the possibility of new competitors entering the market. Existing firms may try to discourage new competition by aggressive expansion and other types of market entry barriers. The entry of Wal-Mart into the supermarket business has substantially expanded and intensified the competitive arena in this market.

The third force considers the potential impact of substitutes. New technologies that satisfy the same customer value requirement are important sources of competition. Including alternative technologies (e.g., disruptive innovations) in the definition of product-market structure identifies substitute forms of competition.

The fourth force is the power that suppliers may be able to exert on the producers in an industry. For example, the high costs of labor exert major pressures on the commercial airline industry. Coke and Pepsi exert important influences on their independent bottlers and encourage collaboration. Companies may pursue vertical integration strategies to reduce the bargaining power of suppliers. Collaborative relationships are useful to respond to the needs of both partners.

Finally, buyers may use their purchasing power to influence their suppliers. Wal-Mart, for example, has a strong influence on the suppliers of its many products. Understanding which organizations have power and influence in the value chain provides important insights into the structure of competition.

Key Competitor Analysis

Competitor analysis is conducted for the firms directly competing with each other (e.g., Nike and Reebok) and other companies that management may consider important in strategy analysis (for example, potential market entrants). The rapid expansion of competitor intelligence activities by many companies in the last decade highlights the high priority executives place on monitoring competitors' activities. Many companies around the world have developed very effective intelligence units. Nonetheless, there are important ethical and legal issues to consider in competitive intelligence gathering. These issues are illustrated in the ETHICS FEATURE.

We now look at two major aspects of competitor analysis: (1) preparing a descriptive profile for each competitor; and (2) evaluating the competitor's strengths and weaknesses (Steps 2 and 3 of Exhibit 2.8).

Describing and Evaluating the Competitor

A *key competitor* is any organization going after the same market target as the firm conducting the analysis. American and Southwest Airlines are key competitors on many U.S. routes. Key competitors are brands that compete in the same product-market or segment(s) within the market (Motorola, Nokia, and Samsung cell phones). Different product types that satisfy the same need or want may also actively compete against each other. Thus, microwave dinners may compete with fast-food operators.

Information which is typically included in the competitor profile is shown in Exhibit 2.11. Sources of information include annual reports, industry studies by government and private organizations, business magazines and newspapers, industry trade publications and websites, reports by financial analysts (e.g., *Value Line Investment Survey*), government reports, standardized data services (e.g., Information Resources, Inc. and Nielsen), databases, suppliers, customers, company personnel, and salespeople. Direct contact with the research directors of trade publications is often a useful source of information about the industry and key competitors.

It is important to gain as much knowledge as possible about the background, experience, qualifications, and tenure of key executives for each major competitor. This information

Ethics Feature   *Competitor Intelligence Gathering*

Most competitive intelligence gathering relies on publicly available information and the views of distributors and customers. However, there are important limits to the behavior of intelligence gatherers. The Society of Competitive Intelligence Professionals outlaws misrepresentation by intelligence gatherers in its code of ethics. Nonetheless, there are grey areas, which raise serious ethical dilemmas:

- What if intelligence researchers pose as something else—conference organizers, headhunters, students, or journalists to tease information out of intelligence targets?
- Is it acceptable if competitor staff members are interviewed for phantom jobs which do not exist, to see what they reveal when questioned?
- Is it reasonable for researchers to pose as customers to collect competitor information?

Unethical intelligence gathering practices carry substantial risks if discovered, and are completely unacceptable to reputable companies. Many organizations now operate ethics compliance systems, and report corporate citizenship actions to shareholders and investors.

Direct contact with competitors to gather intelligence may be interpreted as "inappropriate conversations" associated with anti-competitive behavior, and attract investigation and punishment by regulatory bodies.

Source: Stephen Overell, "Agents Who Shed Light on Hidden Corporate Life," *Financial Times,* Monday, March 19, 2001, p. 14; Joseph Weber, "The New Ethics Enforcers," *BusinessWeek,* February 13, 2006, 76–77.

EXHIBIT 2.11
Describing and Evaluating Key Competitors

- Business scope and objectives
- Management experience, capabilities, and weaknesses
- Market position and trends
- Market target(s) and customer base
- Positioning strategy for each target
- Distinctive capabilities
- Financial performance (current and historical)

---

includes the executives' performance records, their particular areas of expertise, and the firms where they were previously employed. These analyses may suggest the future strategic initiatives of a key competitor.

Market targets and customer base analyses center on the market segments targeted by the competitor and the competitor's actual and relative market-share position. Relative market position is measured by comparing the share of the firm against the competitor with the highest market share in the segment. All segments in the product-market that could be targeted by the firm should be included in the competitor evaluation.

The competitor's past performance offers a useful basis for comparing competitors. The customer value proposition offered by the competitor for each segment is important information. This may indicate competitive opportunities as well as a possible threat. The competitor's distinctive capabilities need to be identified and evaluated.

An analysis of each competitor's past sales and financial performance indicates how well the competitor has performed on a historical basis. Competitor ratings are also useful in the comparisons (e.g., *Consumer Reports*). A typical period of analysis is three to five years or longer depending on the rate of change in the market. Performance information may include sales, market share, net profit, net profit margin, cash flow, and debt.

Additionally, for specific types of businesses other performance information may be useful. For example, sales-per-square-foot is often used to compare the performance of retail stores. Operating cost per passenger mile is a relevant measure for airline performance comparisons.

Assessing how well competitors meet customer value requirements requires finding out what criteria buyers use to rate each supplier. Customer-focused assessments are more useful than relying only on management judgments of value delivery. Measurement methods include customer comparisons of value attributes of the firm versus its competitors, customer surveys, loyalty measures, and the relative market share of end-use segments.[14] Customer value assessment is further considered in Chapter 4.

Using the competitor information, we can develop an overall evaluation of the key competitor's current strengths and weaknesses. Additionally, the summary assessment of distinctive capabilities includes information on the competitor's management capabilities and limitations, technical and operating advantages and weaknesses, marketing strategy, and other key strengths and limitations. Since competitors often display different capabilities, it is important to highlight these differences.

Anticipating Competitors' Actions

Steps 4 and 5 in competitor analysis (Exhibit 2.8) consider what each key competitor may do in the future, and identify potential new competitors. The information obtained in the previous steps of the analysis should be helpful in estimating future trends, although possible strategy shifts by competitors may occur.

Estimating Competitors' Future Strategies

Competitors' future strategies may continue the directions that they have established in the past, particularly if no major external influences require changing their strategies. Nevertheless, assuming an existing strategy will continue is not wise. Competitors' current actions may signal probable strategy shifts that may create future threats.

An interesting development in the telecommunication market is the growth in the use of Internet calling. First introduced in 1995, Voice-Over Internet Protocol (VOIP) experienced start-up problems but by 2003, the technology was a rapidly growing share of home and business markets.[15] Industry authorities expect the technology to become a significant competitive threat. VOIP subscribers are estimated to increase to over five times the 2003 level by 2006.

Relatedly, the acquisition strategy at eBay is a strong indicator of the company's goal to move from being an online auction site to an e-commerce engine that sells Web tools to small businesses. Current developments at eBay are illustrated in the INTERNET FEATURE, and are indicative of the areas in which eBay will be a competitor in the future.

Identifying New Competitors

New competitors may come from four major sources: (1) companies competing in a related product-market; (2) companies with related technologies; (3) companies already targeting similar customer groups with other products; and/or (4) companies competing in other geographical regions with similar products. Market entry by a new competitor is likely under one or more of these conditions:

- High profit margins are being achieved by market incumbents.
- Future growth opportunities in the market are attractive.
- No major market-entry barriers are present.

The online auction site eBay.com has become one of the Web's most successful sites with 233 million registered users. The impact on many areas of conventional retailing has been substantial.

EBay executives believe future growth depends on evolving the company beyond a destination site into a provider of tools and services that power e-commerce across the Web. The company is making considerable efforts to break out of its current business model, and has spent $6 billion in five years. Key acquisitions include:

- PayPal—payment processor for eBay and other websites - $1.5 billion (July 2002).
- Rent.com provides property rental and roommate search services—$415 million (December 2004).
- Kurant/Pro—helps sellers set up online storefronts separate from eBay (January 2005).
- Shopping.com runs a comparison-shopping website—$620 million (June 2005).
- Skype—its Internet telephone service can connect sellers with shoppers—$2.5 billion (September 2005).
- Stubhub—a ticket reselling site that is promoted on eBay—$310 million (January 2007).
- Stumbleupon—recommends websites based on user interests - $75 million (May 2007).

Source: Catherine Holahan, "Going, Going . . . Everywhere," *BusinessWeek,* June 18, 2007, 62–64.

- Competition is limited to one or a few competitors.
- Gaining an equivalent (or better) competitive advantage over the existing firm(s) serving the market is feasible.

If one or more of these conditions are present in a competitive situation, new competition will probably appear.

Market Size Estimation

An important part of market opportunity analysis is estimating the present and potential size of the market. Market size is usually measured by dollar sales and/or unit sales for a defined product-market and specified time period. Other size measures include the number of buyers, average purchase quantity, and frequency of purchase. Three key measures of market size are: *market potential, sales forecast,* and *market share.*

Market Potential

Market potential is the maximum amount of product sales that can be obtained from a defined product-market during a specified time period. It includes the total opportunity for sales by all firms serving the product-market. Market potential is the upper limit of sales that can be achieved by all firms for a specified product-market over an indicated time period. Often, actual industry sales in a specified year fall somewhat below market potential because the production and distribution systems are unable to completely meet the needs of all buyers who are both *willing* and *able* to purchase the product during the period of interest.

Useful information for considering market potential and growth rates for various product categories in Russia is shown in Exhibit 2.12. The share of household ownership percentages and share increases provide an indication of where the market potential appears promising. Not surprisingly, cell phone and computer penetration is expanding rapidly. Household income is increasing fast and 70 percent of all income is disposable in Russia compared to 40 percent in Western countries.[16] Market potential is exploding for many product categories including tourism and financial services.

EXHIBIT 2.12
Market Penetration and Growth Rates for Selected Consumer Product Categories in Russia

Source: Jason Bush, "Shoppers Gone Wild," *BusinessWeek,* February 20, 2006, 46.

Ownership by Share of Households		
	2001	2005
Mobile phone	6%	50%
Computer	5	20
Washing machine	16	35
Stereo	15	31
Video recorder	39	50
Car	25	31
Imported TV	58	71
Apartment or house	71	82
August 2001 vs. August 2005		Data: GfK Rus.

Sales Forecast

The sales forecast indicates the expected sales for a defined product-market during a specified time period. The industry sales forecast is the total volume of sales expected by all firms serving the product market. The sales forecast can be no greater than market potential and typically falls short of potential as discussed above. A forecast can be made for total sales at any product-market level (generic, product type, variant) and for specific subsets of the product-market (e.g., market segments). A company sales forecast can also be made for sales expected by a particular firm.

Several sales forecasting methods are described in Exhibit 2.13. The advantages of each technique are indicated. Time-series analysis is popular for projecting future sales but is very dependent on the stability of historical trends.

Market Share

Company sales divided by the total sales of all firms for a specified product-market determines the market share of a particular firm. Market share may be calculated on the basis of actual sales or forecasted sales. Market share can be used to forecast future company sales and to compare actual market position among competing brands of a product. Market share may vary depending on the use of dollar sales or unit sales due to price differences across competitors.

It is essential in preparing forecasts to specify exactly what is being forecast (defined product-market), the time period involved, and the geographical area. Otherwise, comparisons of sales and market share with those of competing firms will not be meaningful.

Evaluating Market Opportunity

Since a company's sales depend, in part, on its marketing plans, management's forecasts and marketing strategy are closely interrelated. Forecasting involves "what if" analyses. Alternative positioning strategies (product, distribution, price, and promotion) need to be evaluated for their estimated effects on sales. Because of the marketing effort/sales relationship, it is important to consider both market potential (opportunity) and planned marketing expenditures in determining the forecast. The impact of different sales forecasts must be evaluated from a total business perspective, since these forecasts affect production planning, human resource needs, and financial requirements.

Sales forecasts of target markets are needed so that management can estimate the financial attractiveness of both new and existing market opportunities. The market potential and growth estimates gauge the overall attractiveness of the market. The sales forecast for the company's brand in combination with cost estimates provide a basis for profit projections. The decision to enter a new market or to exit from an existing market depends heavily on

EXHIBIT 2.13   Summary of Advantages and Disadvantages of Various Forecasting Techniques

Source: Mark W. Johnston and Greg W. Marshall, *Sales Force Management,* 7th ed. (New York: McGraw-Hill/Irwin, 2003), 131.

Sales Forecasting Method	Advantages	Disadvantages
User expectations	1. Forecast estimates obtained directly from buyers 2. Projected product usage information can be highly detailed 3. Insightful method aids planning marketing strategy 4. Useful for new product forecasting	1. Potential customers must be few and well defined 2. Does not work well for consumer goods 3. Depends on the accuracy of user's estimates 4. Expensive, time-consuming, labor-intensive
Sales force composite	1. Involves the people (sales personnel) who will be held responsible for the results 2. Is fairly accurate 3. Aids in controlling and directing sales effort 4. Forecast is available for individual sales territories	1. Estimators (sales personnel) have a vested interest and therefore may be biased 2. Elaborate schemes sometimes are necessary to counteract bias 3. If estimates are biased, process to correct the data can be expensive
Jury of executive opinion	1. Easily done, very quick 2. Does not require elaborate statistics 3. Utilizes "collected wisdom" of the top people 4. Useful for new or innovative products	1. Produces aggregate forecasts 2. Expensive 3. Disperses responsibility for the forecast 4. Group dynamics operate
Delphi technique	1. Minimizes effects of group dynamics	1. Can be expensive and time-consuming
Market test	1. Provides ultimate test of consumers' reactions to the product 2. Allows assessment of the effectiveness of the total marketing program 3. Useful for new and innovative products	1. Lets competitors know what firm is doing 2. Invites competitive reaction 3. Expensive and time-consuming to set up 4. Often takes a long time to accurately assess level of initial and repeat demand
Time-series analysis	1. Utilizes historical data 2. Objective, inexpensive	1. Not useful for new or innovative products 2. Factors for trend, cyclical, seasonal, or product life-cycle phase must be accurately assessed and included 3. Technical skill and good judgment required
Statistical demand analysis	1. Great intuitive appeal 2. Requires quantification of assumptions underlying the estimates 3. Allows management to check results 4. Uncovers hidden factors affecting sales 5. Method is objective	1. Factors affecting sales must remain constant and be identified accurately to produce an accurate estimate 2. Requires technical skill and expertise 3. Some managers reluctant to use method due to the sophistication

financial analyses and projections. Alternate market targets under consideration can be compared using sales and profit projections. Similar projections of key competitors are also useful in evaluating market opportunities.

Developing a Strategic Vision About the Future

Market development and competitive space may not follow clearly defined and predictable paths. Nonetheless, signals can be identified that are useful in pointing to possible market changes. Answers to the questions shown in Exhibit 2.14 are needed in Developing a Strategic Vision concerning the firm's market(s). These issues need to be addressed for each product-market.

Phases of Competition

It is useful to distinguish between different phases in the development of competition. In the initial stage, companies compete in identifying product concepts, technology choices, and building competencies.[17] This phase involves experimentation with ideas, and the path to market leadership is not clearly defined. Phase 2 may involve partnering of companies with the objective of controlling industry standards, though these firms eventually become competitors. Finally, as the market becomes clearly defined and the competitive space established, the competitors concentrate on market share for end products and profits. The personal computer market is currently in this stage.

Anticipating the Future

Increasingly, we find that change and turbulence, rather than stability, characterize many product-markets. Moreover, as discussed above, it is often possible to determine the forces underway that will alter product-market structure. Though these influences are not easily identified and analyzed, the organizations that choose to invest substantial time and effort in anticipating the future create an opportunity for competitive advantage. Fuji appears to have done a better job of anticipating the future of digital photography than did Kodak. Executives in market-driven companies recognize the importance of developing these capabilities.

Hamel and Prahalad offer a compelling blueprint for analyzing the forces of change. While the details of their process cannot be captured in a few pages of discussion, the following questions are examples of the information needed to anticipate the future:[18]

- What are the influences (discontinuities) present in the product-market that have the potential to profoundly transform market/competitor structure?
- Investigate each discontinuity in substantial depth.

EXHIBIT 2.14
Developing a
Strategic Vision

- Are product-market boundaries and composition of the product-market undergoing transformation?
- How and to what extent is the end-user customer base changing?
- Are the scope and structure of competitor space changing due to market and industry transformation and entry/exit of competitors?
- Are there potential threats from disruptive technologies and/or commoditization?
- Are the composition and structure of the value chain(s) serving the end-user market(s) changing?
- Do other influences operating in the product-market have the potential to significantly transform the product?
- At what life-cycle stage is the product-market (new, growth, maturity, decline), and how fast is the life cycle advancing?

- How will the trend impact customers?
- What is the likely economic impact?
- How fast is the trend developing?
- Who is exploiting this trend?
- Who has the most to gain/lose?
- What new product opportunities will be created by this discontinuity?
- How can we learn more about this trend?

Following the blueprint requires looking in depth at the relevant forces of change in a product-market and other markets that are interrelated. Anticipating the future requires searching beyond the existing competitive arena for influences that promise to impact product-market boundaries. The process requires the involvement of the entire organization and it demands a substantial amount of time. A company with a market orientation and cross-functional processes should be able to utilize these processes for anticipating the future. Importantly, developing a vision about the future needs to be an ongoing process.

Summary

Analyzing markets and competition is essential to making sound business and marketing decisions. The uses of product-market analyses are many and varied. An important aspect of market definition and analysis is moving beyond a product or industry focus by incorporating market needs into the analysts' viewpoint.

Business strategies and markets are interrelated and companies which do not understand their markets and how they are likely to change in the future are at a competitive disadvantage. Effective market sensing is essential in guiding business and marketing strategies. Disruptive innovation, the process of customers shifting their purchases to new products that better meet their needs, should be anticipated and counterstrategies developed. An essential part of becoming market-oriented is identifying future directions of market change.

This chapter examines the nature and scope of defining and analyzing product-market structure. By using different levels of aggregation (generic, product-type, and product-variant), products and brands are positioned within more aggregate categories, thus helping to better understand customers, product interrelationships, industry structure, distribution approaches, and key competitors. This approach to product-market analysis offers a consistent guide to needed information, regardless of the type of product-market being analyzed. Analyzing market opportunity includes (1) determining product-market boundaries and structure; (2) forming the product-market; (3) describing and analyzing end-users; (4) analyzing competition; and (5) estimating market size and growth rates.

After determining the product-market boundaries and structure, information on various aspects of the market is collected and examined. First, it is useful to study the people or organizations who are the end-users in the product-market at each level (generic, product type, and variant). These market profiles of customers help to evaluate opportunities and guide market targeting and positioning strategies. Next, we identify and analyze the firms that market products and services at each product-market level to aid strategy development. Industry and key competitor analysis considers the firms that compete with the company performing the market opportunity analysis. Thus, industry analysis for a personal computer producer would include the producers that make up the industry. The analysis should also include firms operating at all stages (levels) in the value-added chain, such as suppliers, manufacturers, distributors, and retailers.

The next step is a comprehensive assessment of the major competitors. The competitor analysis should include both actual and potential competitors that management considers important. Competitor analysis includes: (1) describing the company; (2) evaluating the competitor; and (3) anticipating the future actions of competitors. It is also important to identify possible new competitors. Competitor analysis is an ongoing activity and requires coordinated information collection and analysis.

An important part of product-market analysis is estimating potential and forecasting sales. The forecasts often used in product-market analysis include estimates of market potential, sales forecasts of total sales by firms competing in the product-market, and the sales forecast for the firm of interest. This information is needed for various purposes and is prepared for different units of analysis, such as product category, brands, and geographical areas. The forecasting approach and techniques should be matched to the organization's needs.

The mounting evidence about markets points to the critical importance of understanding and anticipating changes in markets by developing a strategic vision about the future. In gaining these insights, it is useful to view competition as a three-stage process of experimentation, partnering to set industry standards, and then pursuing market share and profits. Analyzing the forces of change provides a basis for anticipating how product-markets will change in the future.

Questions for Review and Discussion

1. Discuss the important issues that should be considered in defining the product-market for a totally new product.

2. Under what product and market conditions is the end-user customer more likely to make an important contribution to product-market definition?

3. What recommendations can you make to the management of a company competing in a rapid growth market to help it identify new competitive threats early enough so that counterstrategies can be developed?

4. There are some dangers in concentrating product-market analysis only on a firm's specific brand and those brands that compete directly with a firm's brand. Discuss.

5. Using the approach to product-market definition and analysis discussed in the chapter, select a brand and describe the generic, product type, and brand product-markets of which the brand is a part.

6. For the brand you selected in Question 5, indicate the kinds of information needed to conduct a complete product-market analysis. Also suggest sources for obtaining each type of information.

7. Select an industry and describe its characteristics, participants, and structure.

8. A competitor analysis of the 7UP soft drink brand is being conducted. Management plans to position the brand against its key competitors. Should the competitors consist of only other non-cola drinks?

9. Outline an approach to competitor evaluation, assuming you are preparing the analysis for a regional bank holding company.

10. Discuss how a small company (less than $1 million in sales) should analyze its competition.

11. Many popular forecasting techniques draw from past experience and historical data. Discuss some of the more important problems that may occur in using these methods.

12. What are the relevant issues a cross-functional team should consider in developing a strategic vision about the future for the organization's product-market(s)?

Internet Applications

A. Visit the website of Project 2000 (www2000.ogsm.Vanderbilt.edu), founded at the Owen Graduate School of Vanderbilt University to determine if the Web provides useful information for market and competitor analysis. Describe the various types of market information available on the Web.

B. Visit Hoover's website (www.hoovers.com). Investigate the different options for competitive and market analysis provided. How can these online tools best be utilized? What limitations apply?

C. Johnson & Johnson is currently competitive in the surgical stent market (a device inserted surgically in an artery to enable blood flow). Perform an Internet analysis of the stent market indicating past and current unit sales levels and forecasts for 2006–2010.

D. Samsung Electronics is one of the top producers of cell phones. Draw from Internet sources to prepare an analysis of the global cell phone market.

Feature Applications

A. Select a product-market where new types of competition and/or new business models are developing. Discuss how and to what extent "opportunities outside the competitive box are developing."

B. Review the GLOBAL FEATURE concerning China's geographical income distributions. Discuss how this information could be useful to a company planning to enter the Chinese market with water purification treatment units for use in residences.

Notes

1. This illustration is based on William M. Bulkeley, "Kodak's Loss Widens as Revenue Declines 8.8%," *The Wall Street Journal,* August 2, 2006, B10; "A Tense Kodak Moment," *BusinessWeek,* October 17, 2005, 84–85; "Another Kodak Moment," *The Economist,* May 14, 2005, 69.

2. Diane Brady, "A Thousand and One Noshes," *BusinessWeek,* June 14, 2004, 44.

3. This discussion is based on David W. Cravens, Nigel F. Piercy, and Artur Baldauf, "Strategic Thinking for Changing Markets," Working Paper, October 15, 2007.

4. Clayton M. Christensen and Michael E. Raynor, *The Innovator's Solution* (Boston: Harvard Business School Press, 2003), Chapter 1.

5. Ibid., Chapter 6.

6. W.C. Kim and R. Mauborgne, *Blue Ocean Strategy* (Boston: Harvard Business School Press, 2005).

7. Pui-Wing Tam, "Entreaty to Camera-Phone Photographers: Please Print," *The Wall Street Journal,* December 28, 2004, B1 and B3.

8. This discussion is based upon suggestions provided by Professor Robert B. Woodruff of the University of Tennessee, Knoxville.

9. Rajendra K. Srivastava, Mark I. Alpert, and Allan D. Shocker, "A Customer-Oriented Approach for Determining Market Structures," *Journal of Marketing,* Spring 1984, 32.

10. George S. Day, *Strategic Marketing Planning: The Pursuit of Competitive Advantage* (St. Paul, MN: West Publishing, 1984), 72.

11. Derek F. Abell, *Defining the Business: The Starting Point of Strategic Planning* (Englewood Cliffs, NY: Prentice Hall, 1980).

12. "Let a Thousand Brands Bloom," *BusinessWeek,* October 17, 2005, 58 and 60.

13. Michael E. Porter, *Competitive Advantage* (New York: Free Press, 1985), 5.

14. George S. Day and Robin Wensley, "Assessing Advantage: A Framework for Diagnosing Competitive Superiority," *Journal of Marketing,* April, 1988, 12–16.

15. Peter Grant and Almar Latour, "Circuit Breaker," *The Wall Street Journal,* October 9, 2003, A1 and A9; "Net Phones Start Ringing Up Customers," *BusinessWeek,* December 29, 2003, 45–46.

16. Jason Bush, "Shoppers Gone Wild," *BusinessWeek,* February 20, 2006, 46.

17. C. K. Prahalad, "Weak Signals Versus Strong Paradigms," *Journal of Marketing Research,* August 1995, iii–vi.

18. Gary Hamel and C. K. Prahalad, *Competing for the Future* (Boston: Harvard Business School Press, 1994), 101.

Appendix **2A**

Financial Analysis for Marketing Planning and Control

Several kinds of financial analyses are needed for marketing analysis, planning, and control activities. Such analyses represent an important part of case preparation activities. In some instances it will be necessary to review and interpret the financial information provided in the cases. In other instances, analyses may be prepared to support specific recommendations. The methods covered in this appendix represent a group of tools and techniques for use in marketing financial analysis. Throughout the discussion, it is assumed that accounting and finance fundamentals are understood.

Unit of Financial Analysis

Various units of analysis that can be used in marketing financial analysis are shown in Exhibit 2A.1. Two factors often influence the choice of a unit of analysis: (1) the purpose of the analysis and (2) the costs and availability of the information needed to perform the analysis.

Financial Situation Analysis

Financial measures can be used to help assess the present situation. One of the most common and best ways to quantify the financial situation of a firm is through ratio analysis. These ratios should be analyzed over a period of at least three years to discern trends.

Key Financial Ratios

Financial information will be more useful to management if it is prepared so that comparisons can be made. James Van Horne comments upon this need.

To evaluate a firm's financial condition and performance, the financial analyst needs certain yardsticks. The yardstick frequently used is a ratio or index, relating two pieces of financial data to each other. Analysis and interpretation of various ratios should give an experienced and skilled analyst a better understanding of the financial condition and performance of the firm than he would obtain from analysis of the financial data alone.[1]

As we examine the financial analysis model in the next section, note how the ratio or index provides a useful frame of reference. Typically, ratios are used to compare historical and/or future trends within the firm or to compare a firm or business unit with an industry or other firms.

Several financial ratios often used to measure business performance are shown in Exhibit 2A.2. Note that these ratios are primarily useful as a means of comparing:

1. Ratio values for several time periods for a particular business.

2. A firm to its key competitors.

3. A firm to an industry or business standard.

There are several sources of ratio data. These include data services such as Dun & Bradstreet, *The Value Line Investment Survey,* industry and trade associations, government agencies, and investment advisory services.

Other ways to gauge the productivity of marketing activities include sales per square feet of retail floor space, occupancy rates of hotels and office buildings, and sales per salesperson.

[1]James C. Van Horne, *Fundamentals of Financial Management,* 4th ed. (Englewood Cliffs, NJ: Prentice-Hall, 1980), 103–4.

EXHIBIT 2A.1
Alternative Units for Financial Analysis

Market	Product/Service	Organization
Market	Industry	Company
Market niche(s)	Product mix	Segment/division/unit
Geographic area(s)	Product line	Marketing department
Customer groups	Specific product	Sales unit:
Individual customers	Brand	Region
	Model	District branch
		Office/store

EXHIBIT 2A.2   Summary of Key Financial Ratios

Source: Adapted from Arthur A. Thompson, Jr., and A. J. Strickland III, *Strategy and Policy*, 4th ed. (Homewood, IL: Richard D. Irwin, 1987), 270–1.

Ratio	How Calculated	What It Shows
Profitability ratios:		
1. Gross profit margin	$$\frac{\text{Sales} - \text{Cost of goods sold}}{\text{Sales}}$$	An indication of the total margin available to cover operating expenses and yield a profit.
2. Operating profit margin	$$\frac{\text{Profits before taxes and before interest}}{\text{Sales}}$$	An indication of the firm's profitability from current operations without regard to the interest charges accruing from the capital structure.
3. Net profit margin (or return on sales)	$$\frac{\text{Profits after taxes}}{\text{Sales}}$$	Shows after-tax profits per dollar of sales. Subpar profit margins indicate that the firm's relatively low, its costs are relatively high, or both.
4. Return on total assets	$$\frac{\text{Profits after taxes}}{\text{Total assets}} \quad \text{or}$$ $$\frac{\text{Profits after taxes} + \text{Interest}}{\text{Total assets}}$$	A measure of the return on total investment in the enterprise. It is sometimes desirable to add interest to after-tax profits to form the numerator of the ratio, since total assets are financed by creditors as well as by stockholders; hence, it is accurate to measure the productivity of assets by the returns provided to both classes of investors.
5. Return on stockholders' equity (or return on net worth)	$$\frac{\text{Profits after taxes}}{\text{Total stockholders' equity}}$$	A measure of the rate on stockholders' investment in the enterprise.
6. Return on common equity	$$\frac{\text{Profits after taxes} - \text{Preferred stock dividends}}{\text{Total stockholders' equity} - \text{Par value of preferred stock}}$$	A measure of the rate of return on the investment which the owners of common stock have made in the enterprise.
7. Earnings per share	$$\frac{\text{Profits after taxes} - \text{Preferred stock dividends}}{\text{Number of shares of common stock outstanding}}$$	Shows the earnings available to the owners of common stock.
Liquidity ratios:		
1. Current ratio	$$\frac{\text{Current assets}}{\text{Current liabilities}}$$	Indicates the extent to which the claims of short-term creditors are covered by assets that are expected to be converted to cash in a period roughly corresponding to the maturity of the liabilities.
2. Quick ratio (or acid-test ratio)	$$\frac{\text{Current assets} - \text{Inventory}}{\text{Current liabilities}}$$	A measure of the firm's ability to pay off short-term obligations without relying on the sale of its inventories.
3. Cash ratio	$$\frac{\text{Cash \& Marketable securities}}{\text{Current liabilities}}$$	An indicator of how long the company can go without further inflow of funds.

(continued)

EXHIBIT 2A.2—(concluded)

Ratio	Formula	What It Shows
4. Inventory to net working capital	$\dfrac{\text{Inventory}}{\text{Current assets} - \text{Current liabilities}}$	A measure of the extent to which the firm's working capital is tied up in inventory.
Leverage ratios:		
1. Debt to assets ratio	$\dfrac{\text{Total debt}}{\text{Total assets}}$	Measures the extent to which borrowed funds have been used to finance the firm's operations.
2. Debt to equity ratio	$\dfrac{\text{Total debt}}{\text{Total stockholders' equity}}$	Provides another measure of the funds provided the creditors versus the funds provided by owners.
3. Long-term debt to equity ratio	$\dfrac{\text{Long-term debt}}{\text{Total stockholders' equity}}$	A widely used measure of the balance between debt and equity in the firm's overall capital structure.
4. Times-interest-earned (or coverage ratios)	$\dfrac{\text{Profits before interest and taxes}}{\text{Total interest charges}}$	Measures the extent to which earnings can decline without the firm's becoming unable to meet its annual interest costs.
5. Fixed-charge coverage	$\dfrac{\text{Profits before taxes and interest} + \text{Lease obligations}}{\text{Total interest charges} + \text{Lease obligations}}$	A more inclusive indication of the firm's ability to meet all of its fixed-charge obligations.
Activity ratios:		
1. Inventory turnover	$\dfrac{\text{Cost of goods sold}}{\text{Inventory}}$	When compared to industry averages, it provides an indication of whether a company has excessive inventory or perhaps inadequate inventory.
2. Fixed-assets turnover*	$\dfrac{\text{Sales}}{\text{Fixed assets}}$	A measure of the sales productivity and utilization of plant and equipment.
3. Total-assets turnover	$\dfrac{\text{Sales}}{\text{Total assets}}$	A measure of the utilization of all the firm's assets; a ratio below the industry average indicates the company is not generating a sufficient volume of business given the size of its asset investment.
4. Accounts receivable turnover	$\dfrac{\text{Annual credit sales}}{\text{Accounts receivable}}$	A measure of the average length of time it takes the firm to collect on the sales made on credit.
5. Average collection period	$\dfrac{\text{Accounts receivable}}{\text{Total sales} \div 365}$ or $\dfrac{\text{Accounts receivable}}{\text{Average daily sales}}$	Indicates the average length of time the firm must wait after making a sale before it receives payment.

*The manager should also keep in mind the fixed charges associated with noncapitalized lease obligations.

EXHIBIT 2A.3 **Illustrative Contribution Margin Analysis for Product X ($000)**

Sales	$300
Less: Variable manufacturing costs	100
Other variable costs traceable to product X	50
Equals: Contribution margin	150
Less: Fixed costs directly traceable to product X	100
Equals: Product net income	$ 50

Contribution Analysis

When the performance of products, market segments, and other marketing units is being analyzed, management should examine the unit's profit contribution. Contribution margin is equal to sales (revenue) less variable costs. Thus, contribution margin represents the amount of money available to cover fixed costs, and contribution margin less fixed costs is net income. An illustration of contribution margin analysis is given in Exhibit 2A.3. In this example, product X is generating a positive contribution margin. If product X were eliminated, $50,000 of product net income would be lost, and the remaining products would have to cover fixed costs not directly traceable to them. If the product is retained, the $50,000 can be used to contribute to other fixed costs and/or net income.

Financial Analysis Model

The model shown in Exhibit 2A.4 provides a useful guide for examining financial performance and identifying possible problem areas. The model combines several important financial ratios into one equation. Let's examine the model, moving from left to right. Profit margin multiplied by asset turnover yields return on assets. Moreover, assuming that the performance target is return on net worth (or return on equity), the product of return on assets and financial leverage determines

performance. Increasing either ratio will increase net worth. The values of these ratios will vary considerably from one industry to another. For example, in grocery wholesaling, profit margins are typically very low, whereas asset turnover is very high. Through efficient management and high turnover, a wholesaler can stack up impressive returns on net worth. Furthermore, space productivity measures are obtained for individual departments in retail stores that offer more than one line, such as department stores. The measures selected depend on the particular characteristics of the business.

Evaluating Alternatives

As we move through the discussion of financial analysis, it is important to recognize the type of costs being used in the analysis. Using accounting terminology, costs can be designated as fixed or variable. A cost is *fixed* if it remains constant over the observation period, even though the volume of activity varies. In contrast, a *variable* cost is an expense that varies with sales over the observation period. Costs are designated as mixed or semivariable in instances when they contain both fixed and variable components.

Break-Even Analysis

This technique is used to examine the relationship between sales and costs. An illustration is given in Exhibit 2A.5. Using sales and cost information, it is easy to determine from a break-even analysis how many units of a product must be sold in order to break even, or cover total costs. In this example 65,000 units at sales of $120,000 are equal to total costs of $120,000. Any additional units sold will produce a profit. The break-even point can be calculated in this manner:

$$\text{Break-even units} = \frac{\text{Fixed costs}}{\text{Price per unit} - \text{Variable cost per unit}}$$

EXHIBIT 2A.4 **Financial Analysis Model**

Profit margin		Asset turnover		Return on assets		Financial leverage		Return on net worth
↓		↓		↓		↓		↓
Net profits (after taxes)	×	Net sales	→	Net profits (after taxes)	×	Total assets	=	Net profits (after taxes)
Net sales		Total assets		Total assets		Net worth		Net worth

Price in the illustration shown in Exhibit 2A.5 is $1.846 per unit, and variable cost is $0.769 per unit. With fixed costs of $70,000, this results in the break-even calculation:

$$\text{BE units} = \frac{\$70,000}{\$1.846 - \$0.769} = 65,000 \text{ units}$$

To determine how many units must be sold to achieve a target profit (expressed in before-tax dollars), the formula is amended as follows:

$$\text{Target profit units} = \frac{\text{Fixed costs} + \text{Target profit (before tax)}}{\text{Price per unit} - \text{Variable cost per unit}}$$

Using the same illustration as above and including a target before-tax profit of $37,700, the target profit calculation becomes:

$$\text{Target profit units} = \frac{\$70,000 + \$37,700}{\$1.846 - \$0.769}$$
$$= 100,000 \text{ units}$$

Break-even analysis is not a forecast. It indicates how many units of a product at a given price and cost must be sold in order to break even or achieve a target profit. Some important assumptions that underlie the above break-even analysis include the use of constant fixed and variable costs, a constant price, and a single product.

In addition to break-even analysis, several other financial tools are used to evaluate alternatives. Net present value of cash flow analysis and return on investment are among the most useful. For example, assume there are two projects with the cash flows shown in Exhibit 2A.6.

Though return on investment is widely used, it is limited by its inability to consider the time value of money. This is shown in Exhibit 2A.7. Return on investment for *both* projects X and Y is 10 percent. However, a dollar today is worth more than a dollar given in three years. Therefore, in assessing cash flows of a project or investment, future cash flows must be discounted back to the present at a rate comparable to the risk of the project.

EXHIBIT 2A.6   Cash Flow Comparison ($000s)

	Project X	Project Y
Start-Up Costs	<1,000 >	<1,000 >
Year 1	500	300
Year 2	500	400
Year 3	300	600

EXHIBIT 2A.5
Illustrative Break-Even Analysis

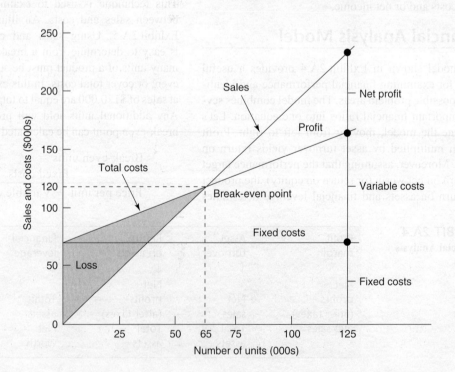

EXHIBIT 2A.7
Present Value of Cash Flows

Time	Cash Flow	PV Factor	NPV of Cash Flow
Project X			
0	<1,000>	$1/(1 + .12)^0 = 1$	<1,000>
1	500	$1/(1 + .12)^1 = 0.8929$	= 446.45
2	500	$1/(1 + .12)^2 = 0.7972$	= 398.60
3	300	$1/(1 + .12)^3 = 0.7118$	= 213.54
		Present value	+ 58.59
Project Y			
0	<1,000>	$1/(1 + .12)^0 = 1$	<1,000>
1	300	$1/(1 + .12)^1 = 0.8929$	= 267.87
2	400	$1/(1 + .12)^2 = 0.7972$	= 318.88
3	600	$1/(1 + .12)^3 = 0.7118$	= 427.08
		Net present value	+ 13.83

Discounting cash flows is a simple process. Assume that the firm is considering projects X and Y and that its cost of capital is 12 percent. Additionally, assume that both projects carry risk comparable to the normal business risk. Under these circumstances, the analyst should discount the cash flows back to the present at the cost of capital, 12 percent. Present value factors can be looked up or computed using the formula $1/(1 + i)^n$, where i equals our discounting rate per time period and n equals the number of compounding periods. In this example, the present value of cash flows would be as shown in Exhibit 2A.7.

Because both projects have a positive net present value, both are good. However, if they are mutually exclusive, the project with the highest net present value should be selected.

Financial Planning

Financial planning involves two major activities: (1) forecasting revenues and (2) budgeting (estimating future expenses). The actual financial analyses and forecasts included in the strategic marketing plan vary considerably from firm to firm. In addition, internal financial reporting and budgeting procedures vary widely among companies. Therefore, consider this approach as one example rather than the norm.

The choice of the financial information to be used for marketing planning and control will depend on its relationship with the corporate or business unit strategic plan. Another important consideration is the selection of performance measures to be used in gauging marketing performance. The objective is to indicate the range of possibilities and suggest some of the more frequently used financial analysis.

Pro forma income statements can be very useful when one is projecting performance and budgeting. Usually, this is done on a spreadsheet so that assumptions can be altered rapidly. Usually, only a few assumptions need be made. For example, sales growth rates can be projected from past trends and adjusted for new information. From this starting point, cost of goods can be determined as a percentage of sales. Operating expenses can also be determined as a percentage of sales based on past relationships, and the effective tax rate as a percentage of earnings before taxes. However, past relationships may not hold in the future. It may be necessary to analyze possible divergence from past relationships.

In addition, pro forma income statements can be used to generate pro forma cash flow statements. It is then possible to compare alternative courses of action by employing a uniformly comparable standard cash flow.

Supplemental Financial Analyses

The preceding sections of this appendix detailed the various forms of traditional financial analysis useful in marketing decision making. There are supplemental forms of analysis that can also be helpful in different types of marketing decisions. These supplemental techniques draw mainly from the management accounting discipline and rely on data that are available only to internal decision makers. Many of the financial analyses in the earlier sections employed data from published financial statements.

Only recently have marketing decision makers been able to look to management accounting to provide an additional set of quantitative tools to aid in the decision process.[2] These tools may be referred to collectively as strategic management accounting practices. Simmonds is generally credited with originating the term *strategic management accounting,* which he defines as "the provision and analysis of management accounting data about a business and its competitors for use in developing and monitoring the business strategy."[3] Although academic researchers may disagree about the specific techniques which constitute strategic management accounting, a wide selection of management accounting practices available for use in marketing decision making. These practices are described in Exhibit 2A.8

[2]George Foster and Mahendra Gupta, "Marketing, Cost Management and Management Accounting," *Journal of Management Accounting Research* 6 (1994), 43–77.

[3]K. Simmonds, "Strategic Management Accounting," *Management Accounting* (UK) 59, no. 4 (1981), 26–29.

and include activity-based costing, attribute costing, benchmarking, brand valuation budgeting and monitoring, competitor cost assessment, competitive position monitoring, competitor performance appraisal, integrated performance measurement, life cycle costing, quality costing, strategic costing, strategic pricing, target costing, and value-chain costing.[4]

Exhibit 2A.8 also provides a description of the various marketing applications of strategic management accounting practices in terms of specific decision-making situations. Most of these practices require the marketing decision maker to gather information additional to that normally used for the preparation of external financial statements. In most cases, this information is already available in the accounting information system of the firm. However, it may be necessary to compile data from outside the firm in a more formalized manner to perform analysis using some of these strategic management accounting practices.

[4]For a comprehensive description of strategic management accounting techniques and differences in attitudes toward the use of these techniques between accounting and marketing managers, see Karen S. Cravens and Chris Guilding, "An Empirical Study of the Application of Strategic Management Accounting Techniques," *Advances in Management Accounting* 10 (2001), 95–124.

EXHIBIT 2A.8 Supplemental Financial Analyses Using Management Accounting Practices

Strategic Management Accounting Practice	Description of the Practice	Description of Marketing Application
Activity-based costing	Indirect costs are assigned to a product or service in relation to the activities used to produce the product or provide the service. Decision making focuses on the collection of activities necessary to produce the product or service rather than the costs in a specific category.	This technique is particularly useful in determining the costs of customization or the provision of additional services to customers. Since the activities are the central focus for costing, decision makers can evaluate customers and markets in terms of the activities required to serve their needs.
Attribute costing	Products or services are costed in terms of attributes that appeal to customers. Thus, the cost object is not the entire product but a collection of features that respond to customer needs.	The nature of the cost object can be modified to support different strategic decision-making situations. As customers modify their preferences, decision makers can consider how particular product attributes satisfy their needs relative to marketing positioning strategies.
Benchmarking	Benchmarking is improving existing processes by looking to an ideal standard. The standard may be established from an external source such as a competitor, a partner, or an unrelated industry or company or by another area of the same firm.	Benchmarking provides an opportunity to assess processes for improvement and strategic advantage in terms of operational effectiveness. Critical lapses in customer service or customer contact situations can be remedied.
Brand valuation—budgeting and monitoring	Brand valuation assesses the current and future potential of a brand in quantitative terms. A "capitalized" value for internally developed brands can be created even though in the United States this value may not be included on a balance sheet.	Current spending on brand promotion activities can be evaluated in terms of future benefits. This can assist with budgeting decisions relative to a portfolio of brands or products and in monitoring the mix and potential of existing products.
Competitive position monitoring	This type of analysis is used in evaluating the market strategy of a competitor. Overall competitor positions in the market and industry are assessed, including sales and trend information, along with market share and cost estimates.	Since this technique requires an external focus, it allows decision makers to assess the position of a product in terms of existing and future strategy relative to competitors. Situations allowing a firm to improve competitive position can be identified and acted upon.
Competitor performance appraisal	This form of analysis is a detailed part of competitive position monitoring and focuses on preparing a quantitative analysis of the competitor's external financial statements.	Decision makers can identify the key areas of a competitor's market advantage and relate areas of advantage to strategic decisions.

(continued)

EXHIBIT 2A.8—*(concluded)*

Integrated performance measurement	This form of analysis uses performance appraisal based on measures that are developed in terms of a customer focus. Integrated measures may be linked to customer satisfaction and may include nonfinancial measures monitored at the individual and departmental levels.	Measures focusing on the customer can be linked to overall strategic objectives throughout the organization. Decision makers can get a clear picture of how their decisions (and performance) affect overall corporate performance.
Life cycle costing	A product or service is costed based on stages in the life of a product rather than financial reporting periods.	Decision makers can adopt a longer-term perspective to evaluate the performance of a product without the constraints of annual reporting periods.
Quality costing	Accounting measures support determining the cost of quality and the cost of a quality failure.	Decision makers can evaluate the impact on customers and market position when choices are made regarding quality issues.
Strategic costing	Strategic costing involves recognizing that the ultimate objective of expenditures related to a product or service may be more long-term in perspective. Thus, cost minimization is not the prime objective. Choices involving costs are evaluated in terms of long-term issues and the future potential of strategies.	Long-term strategy and strategic objectives considering product positioning and market penetration can be evaluated more completely. The long-term implications of a decision receive precedence over the short-term effect.
Strategic pricing	Strategic pricing adopts a more long-term and demand-focused approach to pricing rather than considering a cost-based and historical foundation.	Pricing decisions can be evaluated more in terms of competitive and market choices.
Target costing	A market-based approach is used to determine the target cost for a future product. The target cost is the remainder after a desired profit margin is subtracted from the estimated market price of a new product.	Since the product is designed to meet the target cost, decision makers know that the product will be able to enter the market at a price that allows an adequate level of profits. External rather than internal factors determine the price.
Value-chain costing	The cost of a product is evaluated over the entire value chain of production from research and development to customer service. This value chain may include multiple functional areas within the organization and cover different financial accounting reporting periods.	Operational efficiencies and competitive positioning can be evaluated at all stages of the value chain, not merely from the costs incurred during production. Links to suppliers, customers, and competitors can be considered at all points of the value chain.

Chapter 3

Strategic Market Segmentation

Segmenting markets is a foundation for superior performance. Understanding how buyers' needs and wants vary is essential in designing effective marketing strategies. Effective approaches to segmenting markets may be one of the most critical factors in developing and implementing market-driven strategy. The need to improve an organization's understanding of buyers is escalating because of buyers' demands for uniqueness and an array of technologies available to generate products to satisfy these demands. Companies are responding to the opportunities to provide unique customer value with products ranging from customized phone pagers for business users to self-designed greeting cards for consumers, and even postage stamps with customers' own photographs incorporated.

Best Buy provides an interesting illustration of strategic market segmentation. While accounting for around 17 percent of the U.S. and Canada consumer electronics market, nonetheless 2003 saw the piloting of Best Buy's "customer-centricity" strategy, radically shifting the company's strategic emphasis from products and technology to customers. The goal is to focus on the most attractive customers based on the important differences between them in their purchasing and preferences in consumer electronics. The customer base has been segmented into basic lifestyle groups. High priority target groups are described as:

- **Jill**—the "soccer mom," who is the main shopper for the family, but often avoids electronics stores, she is well-educated and confident, and wants to enrich her children's lives with technology, yet she is intimidated by technology and jargon.
- **Barry**—the wealthy professional man, who demands the latest technology and best service.
- **Buzz**—the young "tech enthusiast," who wants technology and entertainment.
- **Ray**—the family man, who wants technology that improves his and his family's life.
- **Mr Storefront**—the small business customer who can use Best Buy's product solutions and services.

Other interesting segments are the **Carrie's** (young, single females) and the **Helen and Charlie's** (older couples whose children have left home). Stores are being adapted to serve at least one dominant customer segment shopping at each store—though Jill and Barry stores are a frequent combination of segments in the same store. At the store level, employees are trained to recognize and focus on the needs and preferences of the target segments for that store. Indications are that stores converted to focus on the target segments perform substantially better than other stores.[1]

Buyers vary according to how they use products, the needs and preferences that the products satisfy, and their consumption patterns. These differences create market segments. Market segmentation is the process of identifying and analyzing subgroups of buyers in a product-market with similar response characteristics (e.g., frequency of purchases). Recognizing differences between market segments, and how they change better and faster than competitors is an increasingly important source of competitive advantage.

Indeed, even for companies producing consumer products, the concept of a "one-size-fits-all mass market" is increasingly less relevant. Many consumer markets show signs of fragmentation into "microsegments" driven by diverse product preferences and media usage and demanding "right for me" in products purchased.[2] This is why Nike offers more than 300 varieties of sport shoe, not just one.

The most specific form of market segmentation is to consider each buyer as a market segment. This is the basis for "one-to-one marketing."[3] Such fine-tuned segmentation is possible for an expanding array of products due to mass customization techniques. It offers an exciting new approach to serving the unique needs and wants of individual buyers. Custom designed products satisfy the individual buyer's needs and wants at prices comparable to mass produced products. The growing adoption of Customer Relationship Management systems that integrate all information about each individual customer into a single location provides unprecedented opportunities to learn about customer needs from their actual behavior. This is discussed in Chapter 4.

The worldwide apparel industry is increasingly adopting mass customization technologies to allow clothing to be designed and produced for the individual consumer. Pioneered by Levi Strauss & Co with Personal Pair jeans (later Original Spin), stores as diverse as Brooks Brothers, Harrods in London, Bon Marché in Paris, and many other retailers use body scanning to measure dimensions and produce clothes customized for the individual consumer. For Levi's the goal is to reduce the traditional struggle to locate jeans that fit well, into a ten-second shopping experience—when the consumer steps out of the "measure me up" kiosk, personal stylists are available to help choose the best styles. At Harrods, customized apparel by designers like Vivienne Westwood and Nick Holland is produced based on body scanning information. Internet-based companies offer mass-customized clothing, including IC3D (Interactive Custom Clothes Company Designs), American Fit, and Beyond Fleece.[4]

We begin the chapter with a discussion of the different purposes that segmentation models can fulfill and the role of market segmentation in marketing strategy, followed by a discussion of the variables used to identify segments. Next, we look at the methods for forming segments followed by a review of high-variety strategies. Finally, we consider the issues and guidelines involved in selecting the segmentation strategy and in its implementation.

Levels and Types of Market Segmentation

Segmentation is an important capability in strategic marketing, which is linked to choosing market targets and positioning against alternatives to build competitive advantage. Importantly, we recognize that segmentation may serve several purposes at levels which range from the strategic to the operational. The Best Buy analysis of its customer base and realignment of its stores and employee behaviors around segments illustrates an interesting approach to strategic market segmentation. Many traditional views emphasize segmentation as an operational tool—for example, to aim advertising effectively at different types of customers.

However, segmentation models appropriate to developing advertising programs may be quite different from those used to develop marketing strategy. While advertising-oriented segmentation aims to identify targets that differ in their responses to a given message, strategic segmentation has the goal of identifying market segments that differ in their purchasing power, goals, aspirations and behavior, in ways relevant to identifying new product and value opportunities.[5]

It is useful to examine segmentation as operating at several decision making levels in the way suggested by Exhibit 3.1. Strategic segmentation links to the management vision and strategic intent of corporate strategy and emphasizes product benefits that different types of buyers seek. Managerial segmentation is concerned with allocating resources around segment targets, including them in marketing plans and aligning organizational processes around them. Operational segmentation issues are concerned with the marketing program changes needed to reach segment targets with advertising and promotions, and with distribution systems. The Best Buy example illustrates these levels of segmentation approach: the strategic issues are concerned with consumer lifestyles and the benefits that different types of consumers seek in choosing and purchasing consumer electronics. The managerial issues are concerned with identifying target segment members, redesigning stores to serve chosen segments, and providing employees with the training and power to focus on the segment targets. Operational segmentation issues are concerned with delivering relevant messages to targets and supporting the segmentation strategy at the store level.

In considering the role of segmentation, the deepest decisions are whether to revise the business model in response to how social forces are changing the lives of different types of customer, how to position a brand, which segments to pursue, and whether to make fundamental changes to the product or to develop an entirely new product. The shallowest decisions are concerned with issues like whether to make small improvements in existing products, how to select targets of a media campaign, or whether to adjust prices.[6]

It is important to effective market-driven strategy that these different aspects of segmentation should be aligned and integrated. The goal of strategic marketing segmentation is to support the processes whereby products are designed and developed around the needs of different types of purchasers to offer superior customer value, and then to identify the mechanisms by which that value can be delivered. This requires segmenting markets in ways that reflect how customers actually live their lives and the jobs that they need to get done.[7]

EXHIBIT 3.1
Levels of Market Segmentation

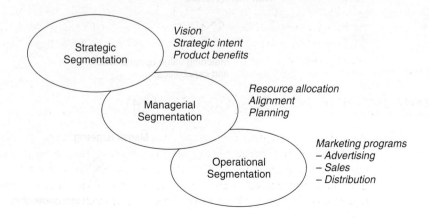

Market-Driven Strategy and Segmentation

Market segmentation needs to be considered early in the development of market-driven strategy. Segments are identified, customer value opportunities and new market spaces are explored in each segment, organizational capabilities are matched to promising segment opportunities, market target(s) are selected from the segment(s) of interest, and a positioning strategy is developed and implemented for each market target (Exhibit 3.2). We examine each of these activities to indicate the role of segmentation in the marketing strategy process.

Market Segmentation, Value Opportunities, and New Market Space

Market segmentation is the process of placing the buyers in a product-market into subgroups so that the members of each segment display similar responsiveness to a particular positioning strategy. Buyer similarities are indicated by the amount and frequency of purchase, loyalty to a particular brand, how the product is used, and other measures of responsiveness. So, segmentation is an identification process aimed at finding subgroups of buyers within a total market. The opportunity for segmentation occurs when differences in buyers' demand (response) functions allow market demand to be divided into segments, each with a distinct demand function.[8] The term "market niche" is sometimes used to refer to a market segment that represents a relatively small portion of the buyers in the total market. We consider a niche and a segment to be the same.

Segmentation identifies customer groups within a product-market, each containing buyers with similar value requirements concerning specific product/brand attributes. A segment is a possible market target for an organization competing in the market. Segmentation offers a company an opportunity to better match its products and capabilities

EXHIBIT 3.2
Segmentation in the Market-Driven Strategy Process

Segments

Value opportunities

New market space

Matching value opportunities and capabilities

Market targeting

Strategic positioning

The airline sector is a mature marketplace, which has been dominated by the financial difficulties of the large, full-service carriers, and the moves towards industry consolidation. Major successes have been achieved by the "no frills" budget carriers—Southwest in the U.S., Ryanair in Europe, AirAsia in Malaysia, Air Deccan in India, Gol in Brazil—with very low fares.

However, the newest niche strategy is the all-business-class airline, aimed at the premium cabin traveler on a budget. The new carriers offer gourmet food, beds that are bed-like and cashmere blankets, but at transatlantic fares in the $1,000–$3,500 range, compared to as much as $8,000 at the established airlines. The target is business travelers, corporate customers, and leisure travelers prepared to upgrade.

Eos, the first all-business-class start-up, started flying between the U.S. and the U.K. in 2005. Maxjet and Silverjet (U.K.-based) were in operation by 2007. They threaten the business class services of the major transatlantic carriers—British Airways, Virgin Atlantic, American Airlines and United Airlines. By 2007, the three all-business-class carriers accounted for more than 20 percent of the premium seat capacity in the London/New York market.

British Airways and Virgin Atlantic are rushing to launch their own transatlantic all-business-class services, to defend the premium traveler segment.

Sources: Kerry Capell, "Business Class at Bargain Prices," *BusinessWeek,* February 5, 2007, 46. Chris Bryant and Maggie Urry, "Virgin Atlantic Set to Launch Business-Only Service," *Financial Times,* June 5, 2007, 24. Kevin Done, "Maxjet in £ 50.5 Million AIM Listing, *Financial Times,* June 14, 2007, 21.

to buyers' value requirements. Customer satisfaction can be improved by providing a value offering that matches the value proposition considered important by the buyer in a segment.

Importantly, market analysis may identify segments not recognized or served effectively by competitors. There may be opportunities to tap into new areas of value and create a unique space in the market. For example, while the global airline business is highly competitive, low-cost airlines like Southwest have been able to develop profitable opportunities. Interestingly, the newest entrants to the sector are all-business-class airlines, providing premium air travel at fares very competitive against the conventional airlines. This development is described in the INNOVATION FEATURE.

While broad competitive comparisons can be made for an entire product-market, more penetrating insights about competitive advantage and market opportunity result from market segment analyses. Examining specific market segments helps to identify how to (1) attain a closer match between buyers' value preferences and the organization's capabilities, and (2) compare the organization's strengths (and weaknesses) to the key competitors in each segment.

Market Targeting and Strategic Positioning

Market targeting consists of evaluating and selecting one or more segments whose value requirements provide a good match with the organization's capabilities. Companies typically appeal to only a portion of the people or organizations in a product-market, regardless of how many segments are targeted. Management may decide to target one, a few, or several segments to gain the strength and advantage of specialization. Alternatively, while a specific segment strategy is not used, the marketing program selected by management is likely to appeal to a particular subgroup of buyers within the market. Segment identification and targeting are obviously preferred. Finding a segment by chance does not give management the opportunity of evaluating different segments in terms of the financial and competitive advantage implications of each segment. When segmentation is employed, it should be by design, and the underlying analyses should lead to the selection of one or more promising segments to target.

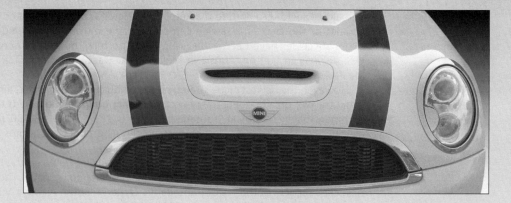

- Notwithstanding depressed car markets in the U.S. and Europe, BMW's remake of the 1959 classic is one of the most successful model overhauls ever. Sales of 176,000 cars in 2003 were up 22.4 percent from 2002, and the Oxford, England factory is running at capacity. In 2007, the plant produced the millionth Mini.
- The new Mini look is a cute snout and bull-dog like stance offering an appealing contrast to boxy sports utility vehicles. While based on the original Mini, this is a premium priced vehicle, packed with technology.
- The car is positioned to be "quintessentially cool." Its biggest selling point is its individualistic appeal.
- Budget for the U.S. launch was only $13 million, so BMW used event-focused "guerrilla tactics," unconventional stunts, and irreverent humor to spark an infectious buzz.
- One of the first Mini-sightings in the U.S. was a Mini strapped to the roof of a sports utility vehicle with the sign "What are you doing for fun this weekend?" The Mini also appeared seated in football stadiums like a fan watching the game.
- The cool status of the Mini was cemented in place when it was used in the 2003 remake of the movie *The Italian Job*. The 2006 launch of the Mini-Cooper used an internet-only campaign in homage to *The Matrix*.
- When the Mini convertible came to the U.S. and European markets in 2004, the cars were delivered with the top down and a seal to be broken when the roof was raised for the first time. Buyers were asked to sign a mock contract committing them to keep the roof down as long as they could—to stay true to the Mini convertible's open-minded spirit.
- BMW nurtured Mini mania by keeping supply just short of demand. More than half of buyers custom-order the Mini and wait three months for delivery.

Source: Gail Edmondson and Michael Eidam, "The Mini Just Keeps Getting Mightier," *BusinessWeek,* April 5, 2004, 26; John Reed, "Millionth Mini Marks Milestone for BMW," *Financial Times,* April 16, 2007, 4.

Recall the Chapter 1 description of positioning strategy as the combination of the actions management takes to meet the needs and wants of each market target. The strategy consists of product(s) and supporting services, distribution, pricing, and promotion components. Management's choices about how to influence target buyers by favorably positioning the product in their eyes and minds help in designing the positioning strategy.

The GLOBAL FEATURE describes the positioning strategy chosen by BMW for the new Mini, as a lifestyle vehicle, and the innovative marketing program choices that fit with buyer characteristics in this niche of the automobile market.

Market segmentation lays the groundwork for market targeting and positioning strategies. The skills and insights used in segmenting a product-market may give a company

EXHIBIT 3.3
Activities and Decisions in Market Segmentation

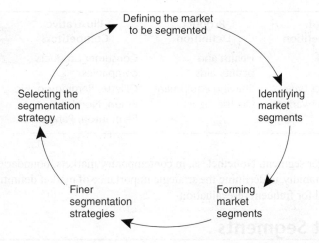

important competitive advantages by identifying buyer groups that will respond favorably to the firm's marketing efforts. The previous Best Buy example is illustrative. Faulty segmentation reduces the effectiveness of targeting and positioning decisions. For example, in 2000 General Motors made the decision to axe the Oldsmobile brand—the oldest auto brand in the U.S. Although sometimes a symbol of innovation and style, Oldsmobile failed to establish a strong position in a long-term market niche or segment—it did not deliver the "class" of Cadillac and Buick, nor the wider market appeal of Chevrolet.[9]

Activities and Decisions in Market Segmentation

The process of segmenting a market involves several interrelated activities and decisions beginning with defining the market to be segmented (Exhibit 3.3). It is necessary to decide how to segment the market, identifying segments, which involves selecting the variable(s) to use as the basis for identifying segments. For example, frequency of use of a product (e.g., frequent, moderate, and occasional) may be a possible basis for segmentation. Next, the method of forming market segments is decided. This may consist of managers using judgment and experience to divide the market into segments. Alternatively, segments may be formed using statistical analysis. The availability of customer purchase behavior information in CRM systems, for example, provides a growing base for this analysis. Part of forming segments is deciding whether finer (smaller) segments should be used. Finally, strategic analysis is conducted on each segment to assist management in deciding which segment(s) to target.

Defining the Market to Be Segmented

Market segmentation may occur at any of the product-market levels shown in Exhibit 3.4. Generic-level segmentation is illustrated by segmenting supermarket buyers based on shopper types (e.g., on the basis of available shopping time). Product-type segmentation is shown by the differences in price, quality, and features of shaving equipment. Product variant-segmentation considers the segments within a category such as electric razors.

An important consideration in defining the market to be segmented is estimating the variation in buyers' needs and requirements at the different product-market levels and identifying the types of buyers included in the market. The all-business-class airline discussed in the earlier INNOVATION FEATURE illustrates a strategy focused on a specific

EXHIBIT 3.4
Segmentation in the
Health and Beauty
Supplies Market

Level of Competition	Product Definition	Illustrative Competitors	Need/Want Satisfied
Generic	Health and beauty aids	Consumer products companies	Enhancement of health and beauty
Product type	Shaving equipment	Gillette, Remington, Bic	Shaving
Product variant	Electric razors	Braun, Norelco, Remington, Panasonic	Electric shaving

passenger segment. Nonetheless, in contemporary markets, boundaries and definitions can change rapidly, underlining the strategic importance of market definition and selection, and the need for frequent re-evaluation.

Identifying Market Segments

After the market to be segmented is defined, one or more variables are selected to identify segments. For example, the United States Automobile Association (USAA) segments by type of employment. Although unknown to many people, USAA has built a successful business serving the financial services needs of U.S. military personnel located throughout the world. USAA has close relationships with its 5.6 million members using powerful information technology. The USAA service representative has immediate access to the client's consolidated file, the one-to-one service encounter is highly personalized, and USAA achieves a 98 percent retention rate in its chosen market segment.[10] In 2007, USAA was "#1 Customer Service Champ" in a BusinessWeek survey.[11]

First, we discuss segmentation variables, followed by a review of the variables that are used in segmentation analyses.

Segmentation Variables

One or more variables (e.g., frequency of use) may be used to divide the product-market into segments. *Demographic* and *psychographic* (lifestyle and personality) characteristics of buyers are of interest, since this information is available from the U.S. Census reports and many other sources including electronic databases. The *use situation* variables consider how the buyer uses the product, such as purchasing a meal away from home for the purpose of entertainment. Variables measuring buyers' *needs* and *preferences* include attitudes, brand awareness, and brand preference. *Purchase-behavior* variables describe brand-use and consumption (e.g., size and frequency of purchase). We examine these variables to highlight their uses, features, and other considerations important in segmenting markets.

Characteristics of People and Organizations

Consumer Markets

The characteristics of people fall into two major categories: (1) geographic and demographic, and (2) psychographic (lifestyle and personality). Demographics are often more useful to describe consumer segments after they have been formed rather than to identify them. Nonetheless, these variables are popular because available data often relate demographics to the other segmentation variables. Geographic location maybe useful for segmenting product-markets. For example, there are regional differences in the popularity of transportation vehicles. In several U.S. states the most popular vehicle is a pickup truck. The "truck belt" runs from the upper Midwest south through Texas and the Gulf coast states. The Ford brand is dominant in the northern half of the truck belt while Chevrolet leads in the southern half.

Demographic variables describe buyers according to their age, income, education, occupation, and many other characteristics. Demographic information helps to describe groups of buyers such as heavy users of a product or brand. Demographics used in combination with buyer behavior information are useful in segmenting markets, selecting distribution channels, designing promotion strategies, and other decisions on marketing strategy.

Lifestyle variables indicate what people do (activities), their interests, their opinions, and their buying behavior. Lifestyle characteristics extend beyond demographics and offer a more penetrating description of the consumer.[12] Profiles can be developed using lifestyle characteristics. This information is used to segment markets, help position products, and guide the design of advertising messages.

For example, consumer goods companies in many personal care and beauty product areas are looking for sales growth with male purchasers, rather than females. The male shopper is conventionally not well understood by companies in these product fields. Lifestyle and product choice differences between different types of males are shown in the STRATEGY FEATURE. While crude, this model provides an initial basis for examining product development opportunities for different segments of the male personal care product market.

Organizational Markets

Several characteristics help in segmenting business markets. The type of industry (sometimes called a vertical market) is related to purchase behavior for certain types of products. For example, automobile producers purchase steel, paint, and other raw materials. Since automobile firms' needs may vary from companies in other industries, this form of segmentation enables suppliers to specialize their efforts and satisfy customer needs. Other variables for segmenting organizational markets include size of the company, the stage of industry development, and the stage of the value-added system (e.g., producer, distribution, retailer).

Organizational segmentation is aided by first examining (1) the extent of market concentration, and (2) the degree of product customization.[13] Concentration considers the number of customers and their relative buying power. Product customization determines the extent to which the supplier must tailor the product to each organizational buyer. If one or both of these factors indicate quite a bit of diversity, segmentation opportunities may exist.

For example, Boeing caters to the specific needs of each air carrier purchasing commercial aircraft, adapting designs to meet customer priorities. Nonetheless, the costs of customization are high and Boeing has had to evaluate the value/cost relationships of its attempts to satisfy the needs of single airline segments.

Product Use Situation Segmentation

Markets can be segmented based on how the product is used. As an illustration, Nikon, the Japanese camera company, offers a line of high performance sunglasses designed for activities and light conditions when skiing, snowboarding, skating, and driving. Nikon competes in the premium portion of the market with prices somewhat higher than Ray-Ban, the market leader. Timex uses a use situation basis of segmentation for its watches.

Needs and preferences vary according to different use situations. Consider, for example, segmenting the market for prescription drugs. Astra/Merck identifies the following segments based on the type of physician/patient drug use situation:

- **Health care as a business**—customers such as managed care administrators who consider economic factors of drug use foremost.
- **Traditional**—physicians with standard patient needs centered around the treatment of disease.

Consumer products companies in fields like personal care and cosmetics are focusing more attention on the male consumer. They are having to re-think the characteristics of the male purchaser. Male shopper stereotypes or segments include:

The Metrosexual

- The affluent, urban sophisticate, who adds deeper meaning, quality and beauty to consumption. Thinks of loafers as objets d'art.
- P&G, Beiersdorf and Polo Ralph Lauren do good business with the metro.

The Maturiteen

- More savvy, responsible, mature and pragmatic than previous cohorts, with poise attributed to baby boomer parents who treat kids as equals.
- A technology master, adept at online research, often acting as an inhouse shopping consultant. Never knew a time without the Web, and its interactivity has nurtured in them a radical view of brands—they own them.
- Adidas, Sony and Unilever are skillful at playing along with them.

The Modern Man

- Neither retro nor metro, he's something in the middle. A sophisticated consumer in his 20s and 30s—a bigger shopper than his Dad, but still a sports fan.
- Comfortable with women but doesn't like shopping with them. Moisturizer and hair gel are perfectly ordinary to him.
- Philips Norelco used locker room humor to get the modern man comfortable with the below-the-neck shaver, Bodygroom.

The Dad

- Largely ignored, but in their peak earning years.
- Smart companies like Dyson and Patek Philippe are reaching out to them.

The Retrosexual

- If the metrosexual champions the female ethos with a "go Girl," the retrosexual is screaming "Stop!" Has lived through the same cultural turmoil and consumerism, but rejects feminism and happily wallows in traditional male behavior. Nostalgic for the good old days before moisturizers for men.
- Burger King and P&G's Old Spice have this dude nailed.

Source: Nanette Byrnes, "Secrets of the Male Shopper," *BusinessWeek,* September 4, 2006, 45–54.

- **Cost sensitive**—physicians for whom cost is paramount, such as those with a sizable number of indigent patients.
- **Medical thought leaders**—people on the leading edge, often at teaching hospitals, who champion the newest therapies.[14]

A sales representative provides the medical thought leader with cutting-edge clinical studies, whereas the cost-sensitive doctor is provided information related to costs of treatments.

Mass customization offers a promising means of responding to different use situations at competitive prices. Recall the earlier clothing industry example.

Buyers' Needs and Preferences

Needs and preferences that are specific to products and brands can be used as segmentation bases and segment descriptors. Examples include brand loyalty status, benefits sought, and proneness to make a deal. Buyers may be attracted to different brands because of the benefits they offer. For example, the "fair trade" branding of products as diverse as coffee and clothing, with goals of benefiting producers in developing countries, has shown remarkable growth in the 2000s. The segment consists of consumers who are prepared to pay a higher price for staple products, if their actions benefit people in poorer countries. This is an example of "ethical branding" aimed at a new and growing segment of ethically-motivated consumers.[15]

Consumer Needs

Needs motivate people to act. Understanding how buyers satisfy their needs provides guidelines for marketing actions. Consumers attempt to match their needs with the products that satisfy their needs. People have a variety of needs, including basic physiological needs (food, rest, and sex); the need for safety; the need for relationships with other people (friendship); and personal satisfaction needs.[16] Understanding the nature and intensity of these needs is important in (1) determining how well a particular brand may satisfy the need; and/or (2) indicating what change(s) in the brand may be necessary to provide a better solution to the buyer's needs.

Attitudes

Buyers' attitudes toward brands are important because experience and research findings indicate that attitudes influence behavior. Attitudes are enduring systems of favorable or unfavorable evaluations about brands.[17] They reflect the buyer's overall liking or preference for a brand. Attitudes may develop from personal experience, interactions with other buyers, or by marketing efforts, such as advertising and personal selling.

Attitude information is useful in marketing strategy development. A strategy may be designed either to respond to established attitudes or, instead, to attempt to change an attitude. In a given situation, relevant attitudes should be identified and measured to indicate how brands compare. If important attitude influences on buyer behavior are identified and a firm's brand is measured against these attitudes, management may be able to improve the brand's position by using this information. Attitudes are often difficult to change, but firms may be able to do so if buyers' perceptions about the brand are incorrect. For example, if the trade-in value of an automobile is important to buyers in a targeted segment and a company learns through market research that its brand (which actually has a high trade-in value) is perceived as having a low trade-in value, advertising can communicate this information to buyers.

Perceptions

Perception is defined as "the process by which an individual selects, organizes, and interprets information inputs to create a meaningful picture of the world."[18] Perceptions are how buyers select, organize, and interpret marketing stimuli, such as advertising, personal selling, price, and the product. Perceptions form attitudes. Buyers are selective in the information they process. As an illustration of selective perception, some advertising messages may not be received by viewers because of the large number of messages vying for their attention. For example, Exhibit 3.5 lists products where substantial proportions of TV advertisements are actively ignored or skipped using a personal video recorder. Negative attitudes and perceptions may be a major barrier to communicating with consumers.

EXHIBIT 3.5
Television Viewers Watch Fewer Ads

Source: Survey of the 15 largest U.S. television markets in 2003 by CNW Marketing Research Inc. reported in Anthony Bianco, "The Vanishing Mass Market," *BusinessWeek,* July 12, 2004, 65.

	Ads Actively Ignored on Television	Ads Skipped Using Personal Video Recorder
Beer	4.8%	31.9%
Movie trailers	11.6	44.1
Soft drinks	21.6	82.7
Drug	32.3	45.6
Specialty clothing	33.4	62.4
Home products	41.6	90.3
Fast food	45.1	95.7
Cars (national)	52.8	68.8
Pet-related	55.5	81.5
Credit cards	62.7	94.2
Mortgage financing	74.1	94.7
Upcoming program	75.3	94.4
Unweighted average	43.1	71.6

Or, more simply, for example, a salesperson's conversation may be misunderstood or not understood because the buyer is trying to decide if the purchase is necessary while the salesperson is talking.

People often perceive things differently. Business executives are interested in how their products, salespeople, stores, and companies are perceived. Perception is important strategically in helping management to evaluate the current positioning strategy and in making changes in this positioning strategy. Perception mapping is a useful research technique for showing how brands are perceived by buyers according to various criteria. We discuss how preference mapping is used to form segments later in the chapter.

Purchase Behavior

Consumption variables such as the size and frequency of purchases are useful in segmenting consumer and business markets. Marketers of industrial products often classify customers and prospects into categories on the basis of the volume of the purchase. For example, a specialty chemical producer concentrates its marketing efforts on chemical users that purchase at least $100,000 of chemicals each year. The firm further segments the market on the basis of how the customer uses the chemical. The development of CRM systems offers fast access to records of actual customer purchase behavior and characteristics. CRM and loyalty programs are generating insights into customer behavior and segment differences, and providing the ability to respond more precisely to the needs of customers in different segments. We discuss the impact of CRM on analyzing customer characteristics in Chapter 4.

Since buying decisions vary in importance and complexity, it is useful to classify them to better understand their characteristics, the products to which they apply, and the marketing strategy implications of each type of purchase behavior. Buyer decisions can be classified according to the extent to which the buyer is involved in the decision.[19] A high-involvement decision may be an expensive purchase, have important personal consequences, and impact the consumer's ego and social needs. The decision situation

EXHIBIT 3.6
Consumer Involvement in Purchase Decisions

Source: Eric N. Berkowitz, Roger A. Kerin, Steven W. Hartley, and William Rudelius, *Marketing,* 5th ed. (Chicago: Richard D. Irwin, 1997), 156. Copyright © The McGraw-Hill Companies. Used with permission.

| | Consumer Involvement | | |
| | High | | Low |
Characteristics of Purchase Decision Process	Extended Problem Solving	Limited Problem Solving	Routine Problem Solving
Number of brands examined	Many	Several	One
Number of sellers considered	Many	Several	Few
Number of product attributes evaluated	Many	Moderate	One
Number of external information sources used	Many	Few	None
Time spent searching	Considerable	Little	Minimal

may consist of extended problem solving (high involvement), limited problem solving, or routine problem solving (low involvement). The characteristics of these situations are illustrated in Exhibit 3.6.

These categories are very broad since the range of involvement covers various buying situations. Even so, the classifications provide a useful way to compare and contrast buying situations. Also, involvement may vary from individual to individual. For example, a high-involvement purchase for one person may not be such for another person, since perceptions of expense, personal consequences, and social impact may vary across individuals. Exhibit 3.7 summarizes the various segmentation variables and shows examples of segmentation bases and descriptors for consumer and organizational markets. As we examine the methods used to form segments, the role of these variables in segment determination and analysis is illustrated.

EXHIBIT 3.7
Illustrative Segmentation Variables

Source: Eric N. Berkowitz, Steven W. Hartley, William Rudelius, and Roger A. Kerin, *Marketing,* 7th ed. (Burr Ridge, IL: McGraw-Hill/Irwin, 2003).

	Consumer Markets	Industrial/Organizational Markets
Characteristics of people/organizations	Age, gender, race Income Family size Lifecycle stage Geographic location Lifestyle	Type of industry Size Geographic location Corporate culture Stage of development Producer/intermediary
Use situation	Occasion Importance of purchase Prior experience with product User status	Application Purchasing procedure New task, modified rebuy, straight rebuy
Buyers' needs/preferences	Brand loyalty status Brand preference Benefits sought Quality Proneness to make a deal	Performance requirements Brand preferences Desired features Service requirements
Purchase behavior	Size of purchase Frequency of purchase	Volume Frequency of purchase

Forming Market Segments

Turning around the performance of Miller Brewing's business was in part based on developing new segment targets for Miller's beer brands. Targets for some of the biggest brands are:

- **Miller Genuine Draft**—aiming at "mainstream sophisticates," males aged 25–35 attracted by the tag line "Beer. Grown Up."
- **Milwaukee's Best Light**—targeting "hardworking men" with a beer to be picked up after a long day at work, sponsors the World Series of Poker on ESPN to get the attention of these poker-playing consumers.
- **Pilsner Urquell**—for "beer aficionados," or more discerning drinkers. Select salespeople—"beer merchants"—educate bar staff and retailers on the special character of the Czech beer, the original golden pilsner.
- **Miller Icehouse**—for "drinking buddies," hanging out, playing Xbox, or getting ready to go out, targeting the modern young male.[20]

The requirements for segmentation are discussed first, and then the methods of segment formation are described and illustrated.

Requirements for Segmentation

An important question is deciding if it is worthwhile to segment a product-market. For example, for many years Gillette successfully adopted a "one product for all" strategy in the razor market. While in many instances segmentation is a sound strategy, its feasibility and value need to be evaluated. Nonetheless, the growing fragmentation of mature mass markets into segments with different needs and responsiveness to marketing actions may mandate segmentation strategy. Correspondingly, the growth of narrowcast media—cable-television and radio; specialized magazines; cell-phone and personal digital assistant screens; and the Internet—has made major changes in the costs of reaching market segments. Segment targets which could not traditionally be reached with communications and product variants to match their needs at reasonable costs to the seller may now be accessible targets.[21] For example, the INTERNET FEATURE illustrates some of the ways in which the Web is changing the ability of companies both to identify segments in the marketplace, but as importantly to reach them more precisely with targeted communications.

It is important to decide if it is worthwhile to segment a product market. Five criteria are useful for evaluating a potential segmentation strategy.

Response Differences

Determining differences in the responsiveness of the buyers in the product-market to positioning strategies is a key segment identification requirement. Suppose the customers in a product-market are placed into four groups, each a potential segment, using a variable such as income (affluent, high, medium, and low). If each group responds (e.g., amount of purchase) in the same way as all other groups to a marketing mix strategy, then the four groups are not market segments. If segments actually exist in this illustration, there must be differences in the responsiveness of the groups to marketing actions, such as pricing, product features, and promotion. The presence of real segments requires actual response differences. Simply finding differences in buyers' characteristics such as income is not enough.

For example, income is useful in finding response differences in emerging markets. In Russia, average income per person in 2006 was just $300 a month. Nonetheless, a surprising number of Russians live as well or better than their Western counterparts—in

The attractiveness of market segments is influenced by the ability to reach targets with marketing communications. The Internet is rapidly changing the ability of companies to reach both narrow and broad target segments:

- Young adults are low users of print media and television, making them difficult to target using conventional methods. However, of American teens (12–17 years old), 87 percent use the Internet, 65 percent use instant messaging, and 44 percent go online everyday. The "MySpace generation" is found in social networking websites like MySpace and Facebook.com and blogging sites like Xanga.com.

- One of the strengths for Google as the Internet's most used search engine is the ability to analyze individuals' search patterns to identify interests and behaviors, allowing personalized advertising to be developed and delivered around those interests.

- Dogster.com is a social networking site for dog owners. Users can create free Web pages to share photos and tell stories about their pets. After two years in operation, in 2006 Dogster.com was attracting 10 million paid advertisements a month.

- Jaman is an Internet start-up online art house for movie downloads—such as Bollywood and martial arts movies. Its target is individuals interested in world movies and the works of independent filmmakers, and includes a social networking element. Users are likely to be sophisticated consumers with international interests, and the site provides access to this otherwise difficult to locate consumer.

Sources: Kevin Allinson, "Web Brings New Breed of Ads," *Financial Times,* Wednesday, August 30, 2006, 21. Jessi Hempel, "The MySpace Generation," *BusinessWeek,* December 12/19, 2005, 64–72. Richard Waters, "Google's Buried Treasure," *Financial Times,* Wednesday, July 23, 2003, 11. Stephen H. Wildstrom, "At Last, An Online Art House," *BusinessWeek,* April 30, 2007, 22.

fact, the richest tenth of Russia's population earns around fifteen times as much as the poorest tenth. In 2006, Russia was home to 88,000 millionaires. Importantly, some 70 percent of Russians' income is disposable, compared to around 40 percent for the typical Western consumer—the result of low flat-rate income tax and subsidized housing and utilities. The emergence of a Russian middle class with substantial spending power provides a promising target for luxury goods brands like Mercedes-Benz, Cartier, and Christian Dior.[22]

Identifiable Segments

It must be possible to identify the customer groups that exhibit response differences, and sometimes finding the correct groups may be difficult. For example, even though variations in the amount of purchase by customers occur in a market, it may not be possible to identify which people correspond to the different response groups in the market. While it is usually feasible to find descriptive differences among the buyers in a product-market, these variations must be matched to response differences. The impact of the Internet is important to identifying segments (INTERNET FEATURE).

Actionable Segments

A business must be able to aim a marketing program strategy at each segment selected as a market target. As discussed earlier, specialty magazines offer one means of selective targeting. Ideally, the marketing effort should focus on the segment of interest and not be wasted on non-segment buyers. Cable television, magazine, and radio media are able to provide coverage of narrowly defined market segments. The Internet offers great potential for direct marketing channels to reach specialized segments. Similarly, databases offer very focused access to buyers.

Cost/Benefits of Segmentation

Segmentation must be financially attractive in terms of revenues generated and costs incurred. It is important to evaluate the benefits of segmentation. While segmentation may cost more in terms of research and added marketing expenses, it should also generate more sales and higher margins. The objective is to use a segmentation approach that offers a favorable revenue and cost combination. Interestingly, Bain & Co research suggests that in their studies over a five-year period, companies that successfully tailor product offerings to desirable customer segments show annual profit growth of around 15 percent—compared to only 5 percent annual growth in other companies in their sectors.[23]

Stability over Time

Finally, the segments must show adequate stability over time so that the firm's marketing efforts will have enough time to produce favorable results. If buyers' needs change too fast, a group with similar response patterns at one point may display quite different patterns several months later. The time period may be too short to justify using a segmentation strategy. However, this question is also one where the impact of narrowcast media and advanced production technology may drastically reduce the time over which a segment targets needs to be stable for it to be an attractive target.

Product Differentiation and Market Segmentation

The distinction between product differentiation and market segmentation is not always clear. *Product differentiation* occurs when a product offering is perceived by the buyer as different from the competition on any physical or nonphysical product characteristic, including price.[24] Using a product differentiation strategy, a firm may target an entire market or one (or more) segments. Competing firms may differentiate their product offerings in trying to gain competitive advantage with the same group of targeted buyers. Market targeting using a differentiation strategy is considered further in Chapter 6.

Approaches to Segment Identification

Segments are formed by: (A) grouping customers using descriptive characteristics and then comparing response differences across the groups; or (B) forming groups based on response differences (e.g., frequency of purchase) and determining if the groups can be identified based on differences in their characteristics. Exhibit 3.8 illustrates the two approaches. Approach A uses a characteristic such as income or family size believed to be

EXHIBIT 3.8
Approaches
to Segment
Identification

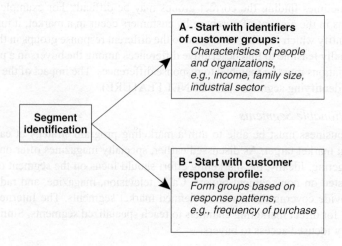

Segment identification

A - Start with identifiers of customer groups:
Characteristics of people and organizations, e.g., income, family size, industrial sector

B - Start with customer response profile:
Form groups based on response patterns, e.g., frequency of purchase

related to buyer response. After forming the groups, they are examined to see if response varies across groups. Approach B places buyers with similar response patterns into groups and then develops buyer profiles using buyer characteristics. We describe each approach to show how it is used to identify segments.

Customer Group Identification

After the product-market of interest is defined, promising segments may be identified, using management judgment in combination with analysis of available information and/or marketing research studies. Consider, for example, hotel lodging services. Exhibit 3.9 illustrates ways to segment the hotel lodging product-market. An additional breakdown can be made according to business and leisure travelers. These categories may be further refined by individual customer and group customer segments. Groups may include conventions, corporate meetings, and tour groups. Several possible segments can be distinguished. Consider, for example, Marriott's Courtyard hotel chain. These hotels fall into the midpriced category and are targeted primarily to frequent business travelers who fly to destinations, are in the 40-plus age range, and have relatively high incomes.

When using the customer group identification approach, it is necessary to select one or more of the characteristics of people or organizations as the basis of segmentation. Using these variables, segments are formed by (1) management judgment and experience; or (2) supporting statistical analyses. The objective is to find differences in responsiveness among the customer groups. We look at some of the customer grouping methods to show how segments are formed.

Management Insight and Available Information

Management's knowledge of customer needs is often a useful guide to segmentation. For example, both experience and analysis of published information are often helpful in segmenting business markets. Business segment variables include type of industry, size of purchase, and product application. Company records often contain information for analyzing the existing customer base. Published data such as industry mailing lists can be used to identify potential market segments. These groups are then analyzed to determine if they

EXHIBIT 3.9
Product-Market Segmentation Dimensions for Hotel Lodging Services

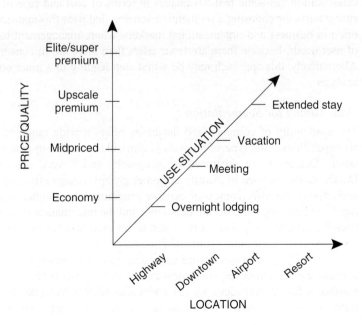

display different levels of response. Effective segmentation may sometimes be achieved through insight and creativity, but it is important to avoid stereotyped thinking based on industry norms. A distinctive segmentation strategy which does not mirror those of competitors may be an important source of advantage.

Segmenting using management judgment and experience underpins the success of Coach in serving both fashion-conscious consumers and factory outlet customers. The luxury positioning of the Coach brand places it on a par with Gucci, Versace, and Dior, although Coach prices are much lower. Flagship Coach stores are located on Beverley Hills' Rodeo Drive and New York's Madison Avenue. Nonetheless, the fastest-growing part of Coach's business is the factory outlets where the previous season's products are sold at discounted prices. Although an unconventional approach to segmentation in the luxury goods market, Coach carefully manages its brand position with upscale shoppers, but also builds sales with older bargain-hunters in factory outlets.[25]

Cross Classification Analyses

Another method of forming segments is to identify customer groups using descriptive characteristics and compare response rates (e.g., sales) by placing the information in a table. Customer groups form the rows and response categories form the columns. Review of industry publications and other published information may identify ways to break up a product-market into segments. Standardized information services such as Information Resources Inc. collect and publish consumer panel data on a regular basis. These data provide a wide range of consumer characteristics, advertising media usage, and other information which is analyzed by product and brand sales and market share. The data are obtained from a large sample of households through the United States. Similar statistical data are available in many overseas countries.

Information is available for use in forming population subgroups within product-markets. The analyst can use many sources, as well as management's insights and hunches regarding the market. The essential concern is whether a segmentation scheme identifies customer groups that display different product and brand responsiveness. The more evidence of meaningful differences, the better chance that useful segments exist. Cross-classification has some real advantages in terms of cost and ease of use. There may be a strong basis for choosing a segmenting scheme that uses this approach. This occurs more often in business and organizational markets, where management has a good knowledge of user needs, because there are fewer users than there are in consumer product-markets. Alternatively, this approach may be a first step leading to a more comprehensive type of analysis.

Data Mining for Segmentation

The availability of computerized databases offers a wide range of segmentation analysis capabilities. This type of analysis is particularly useful in consumer market segmentation. Databases are organized by geography and buyers' descriptive characteristics. Databases can be used to identify customer groups, design effective marketing programs, and improve the effectiveness of existing programs. The number of available databases is rapidly expanding, the costs are declining, and the information systems are becoming user friendly. Several marketing research and direct mail firms offer database services. Further discussion on data mining is provided in Chapter 4.

By identifying customer groups using descriptive characteristics and comparing them to a measure of customer responsiveness to a marketing mix such as product usage rate (e.g., number of fax ink cartridges per year), potential segments can be identified. If the response rates are similar within a segment, and differences in response exist between segments, then promising segments are identified. Segments do not always emerge from these analyses, because in some product-markets distinct segments may not exist, or the segment interrelationships may be so complex that an analysis of these predetermined groupings will not identify useful segments. Product differentiation strategies may be used in these situations.

Segmentation Illustrations

A now-classic study for Mobil examines buyers in the gasoline market to identify segments. The findings, including information obtained from over 2,000 motorists, are summarized in Exhibit 3.10. The research identified five primary purchasing groups.[26] Interestingly, the study found that the Price Shopper spent an average of $700 annually, compared to $1,200 for the Road Warriors and True Blues. Mobil's marketing strategy was to offer gasoline buyers a quality buying experience, including upgraded facilities, more lighting for safety, responsive attendants, and quality convenience products. The target segments are Road Warriors and Generation F3, involving a major effort on convenience stores and reduced time at the gas pump based on the Mobil *Speed Pass*. The test results from the new strategy raised revenues by 25 percent over previous sales for the same retail sites.

As shown by the profiles described in Exhibit 3.10, needs and preferences vary quite a bit within a market. Trying to satisfy all of the buyers in the market with the same marketing approach is difficult. Analyzing both the customer and the competition is important. Specific competitors may be better (or worse) at meeting the needs of specific customer groups (e.g., Mobil's Road Warriors). Finding gaps between buyers' needs and competitors' offerings provides opportunities for improving customer satisfaction. Also, companies study competitors' products to identify ways to improve their own.

In a different sector, one European bank employed a psychologist to examine customers' monthly statements to search for clues to lifestyle and personality profiles. The study identified three customer groups:

- **Hedonistic Grazers**—impulsive and spontaneous people, with a tendency to live for the moment; Bridget Jones characters who are instant pleasure seekers and do not like to postpone fun and extravagance any longer than is absolutely necessary.

EXHIBIT 3.10   Diversity of Gasoline Buyers

Source: Alanna Sullivan, "Mobil Bets Drivers Pick Cappuccino over Low Prices," *The Wall Street Journal*, January 30, 1995, B1. Wall Street Journal. Central Edition [Staff Produced Copy Only] by Alanna Sullivan. Copyright 1995 by Dow Jones & Co Inc. Reproduced with permission of Dow Jones & Co Inc. in the format Textbook via Copyright Clearance Center.

Road Warriors:	True Blues:	Generation F3:	Homebodies:	Price Shoppers:
Generally higher-income, middle-aged men, who drive 25,000 to 50,000 miles a year . . . buy premium with a credit card . . . purchase sandwiches and drinks from the convenience store . . . will sometimes wash their cars at the carwash.	Usually men and women with moderate to high incomes who are loyal to a brand and sometimes to a particular station . . . frequently buy premium gasoline and pay in cash.	(for fuel, food, and fast): Upwardly mobile men and women—half under 25 years of age—who are constantly on the go . . . drive a lot and snack heavily from the convenience store.	Usually housewives who shuttle their children around during the day and use whatever gasoline station is based in town or along their route of travel.	Generally aren't loyal to either brand or a particular station; and rarely buy the premium line . . . frequently on tight budgets . . . efforts to woo them have been the basis of marketing strategies for years.
16% of buyers	**16% of buyers**	**27% of buyers**	**21% of buyers**	**20% of buyers**

- **Material Martyrs**—masters of time management and efficiency; control freaks who plan their weekly meals in advance and prefer to buy furniture than to go out; introverted and home loving; careful and frugal.
- **Steady Builders**—mature, settled, stable people, with a strong sense of responsibility, who debate a big expense rather than spend spontaneously.[27]

Understanding lifestyle differences is critical to providing financial services tailored to the differences between these groups, since there is a link between lifestyle and the needs for financial services, as well as responsiveness to different offers.

In an era of increased globalization, it is also important to recognize that segmentation has an international dimension in many markets. At the simplest level, country differences will dictate the need for variations in the sizes of products like apparel and household furniture based on ethnic identity in overseas countries. However, a strategic approach to segmentation internationally requires deeper analysis. For example, global brands may be judged on quality, global and social responsibility characteristics by consumers. An international research study suggests segments relating to how consumers relate to global brands are:

- **Global Citizens** (55%)—rely on the global success of a company to indicate quality and innovation, but concerned about social responsibility issues. The U.S. and U.K. have relatively few global citizens, but they are more common in Brazil, China, and Indonesia.
- **Global Dreamers** (23%)—less discerning about and more fervent in their admiration of transnational companies. They see global brands as quality products and accept the cultural symbols they provide, and are less concerned with social responsibility issues.
- **Antiglobals** (13%)—skeptical that transnational companies deliver higher quality goods, and dislike brands that preach American values. Do not trust global companies to behave responsibly, and their brand preferences indicate they try to avoid doing business with transnational firms.
- **Global Agnostics** (9%)—do not base purchase decisions on a brand's global attributes, and judge them on the same criteria they use for local brands. Higher numbers in the US, but lower in Japan, Indonesia, and China.[28]

Forming Groups Based on Response Differences

The alternative to selecting customer groups based on descriptive characteristics is to identify groups of buyers by using response differences to form the segments. A look at a segmentation analysis for the packaging division of Signode Corporation illustrates how this method is used.[29] The products consist of steel strappings for various packaging applications. An analysis of the customer base identified the following segments: programmed buyers (limited service needs), relationship buyers, transaction buyers, and bargain hunters (low price, high service). Statistical (cluster) analysis formed the segments using twelve variables concerning price and service trade-offs and buying power. The study included 161 of Signode's national accounts. Measures of the variables were obtained from sales records, sales managers, and sales representatives. The segments vary in responsiveness based on relative price and relative service.

The widespread adoption of CRM systems offers greater opportunity for timely and detailed analysis of response differences between customers. The "data warehouse," by integrating transactional data around customer types, makes possible complex analyses to understand differences in the behavior of different customer groups, to observe customer lifecycles, and to predict behavior.[30] We discuss CRM in Chapter 4. Response difference approaches draw more extensively from buyer behavior information than the customer group identification methods discussed earlier. Note, for example, the information on Signode's customer responsiveness to price and service. We now look at additional applications to more fully explore the potential of the customer response approaches.

Cluster Analysis

Cluster analysis (a statistical technique) groups people according to the similarity of their answers to questions such as brand preferences or product attributes. This method was used to form segments for Signode Corporation. The objective of cluster analysis is to identify groupings in which the similarity within a group is high and the variation among groups is as great as possible. Each cluster is a potential segment.

Perceptual Maps

Another segmentation method uses consumer research data to construct perceptual maps of buyers' perceptions of products and brands. The information helps select market-target strategies, and decide how to position a product for a market target.

While the end result of perceptual mapping is simple to understand, its execution is demanding in terms of research skills. Although there are variations in approach, the following steps are illustrative:

1. Select the product-market area to be segmented.
2. Decide which brands compete in the product-market.
3. Collect buyers' perceptions about attributes for the available brands (and an ideal brand) obtained from a sample of people.
4. Analyze the data to form one, two, or more composite attribute dimensions, each independent of the other.
5. Prepare a map (two-dimensional X and Y grid) of attributes on which are positioned consumer perceptions of competing brands.
6. Plot consumers with similar ideal preferences to see if subgroups (potential segments) will form.
7. Evaluate how well the solution corresponds to the data that are analyzed.
8. Interpret the results as to market-target and product-positioning strategies.

An example of a perception map is shown in Exhibit 3.11. Each Group (I–V) contains people from a survey sample with similar preferences concerning expensiveness and quality for the product category. The Brands (A–E) are positioned using the preference data obtained from the survey participants. Assuming you are product manager for Brand C, what does the information indicate concerning possible targeting? Group V is a logical market target and III may represent a secondary market target. To appeal most effectively to Group V, we will probably need to change somewhat Group V consumers' price perceptions of Brand C. Offering a second brand less expensive than C to appeal to Group IV is another possible action. Of course, it is necessary to study the research results in much greater depth than this brief examination of Exhibit 3.11. Our intent is to illustrate the method of segmenting and show how the results might be used.

Perceptual mapping, like many of the research methods used for segment identification, is expensive and represents a technical challenge. When used and interpreted properly, these methods are useful tools for analyzing product-market structure to identify possible market targets and positioning concepts. Of course, there are many issues to be considered in specific applications such as choosing the attributes, identifying relevant products and brands, selecting the sample, and evaluating the strength of results.

EXHIBIT 3.11
Consumer Perception Mapping Illustration

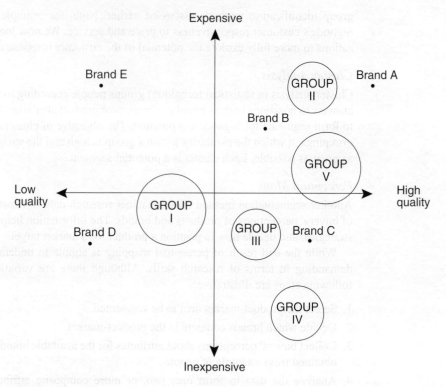

Finer Segmentation Strategies

A combination of factors may help a company utilize finer segmentation strategies. Technology may be available to produce customized product offerings. Furthermore, highly sophisticated databases for accessing buyers can be used, and buyers' escalating preferences for unique products encourage consideration of increasingly smaller segments. In some situations, an individual buyer may comprise a market segment. Thus, an important segmentation issue is deciding how small segments should be. We consider the logic of finer segments followed by a discussion of the available finer segmentation strategies.

Logic of Finer Segments

Several factors working together point to the benefits of considering very small segments—in some cases, segments of one. These include (1) the capabilities of companies to offer cost effective, customized offerings; (2) the desires of buyers for highly customized products; and (3) the organizational advantages of close customer relationships.

Customized Offerings

The capabilities of organizations to offer customized products is feasible because of extensive information flow and comprehensive data bases, computerized manufacturing systems, and integrated value chains.[31] Database knowledge, computer-aided product design and manufacturing, and distribution technology (e.g., just-in-time inventory) offer promising opportunities for serving the needs and preferences of very small market segments. This technology combined with the Internet has led to the emergence of "sliver" companies or "micro-multinationals"—small, flexible organizations selling highly-specialized products across the world. For example, with products which can be digitized and delivered online, such as computer software, music collections, financial services like travel and auto insurance, and e-books, there is already capacity for almost infinite customization.

Diverse Customer Base

The requirements of an increasingly diverse customer base for many products are apparent. For example, the international automobile industry is facing the challenge of the Three Day Car Program—allowing the buyer to specify the detail and design choices of a vehicle online, the order stimulates production, with delivery three days later. This Program has been designed because of the diversity in customer preferences in autos, and the sheer number of variants included in modern vehicles.

Close Customer Relationships

Companies recognize the benefits of close relationships with their customers. By identifying customer value opportunities and developing cost effective customized offerings, relationships can be profitable and effective in creating competitive barriers.

Finer Segmentation Strategies

We examine three approaches for finer segmentation opportunities: micro-segmentation, mass customization, and variety seeking.[32]

Micro-segmentation

This form of segmentation seeks to identify narrowly defined segments using one or more of the previously discussed segmentation variables (Exhibit 3.7). It differs from more aggregate segment formation in that micro-segmentation results in a large number of very small segments. Each segment of interest to the organization receives a marketing mix designed to meet the value requirements of the segment.

Mass Customization

Providing customized products at prices not much higher than mass produced items is feasible using mass customization concepts and methods. Achieving mass customization objectives is possible through computer-aided design and manufacturing software, flexible manufacturing techniques, and flexible supply systems.

Variety-Seeking Strategy

This product strategy is intended to offer buyers opportunities to vary their choices in contrast to making unique choices.[33] The logic is that buyers who are offered alternatives may increase their total purchases of a brand. Mass customization methods also enable companies to offer an extensive variety at relatively low prices, thus gaining the advantages of customized and variety offerings.

Finer Segmentation Issues

While the benefits of customization are apparent, there are several issues that need to be examined when considering finer segmentation strategies:[34]

1. How much variety should be offered to buyers? What attributes are important in buyers choices and to what extent do they need to be varied?
2. Will too much variety have negative effects on buyers? It is possible that buyers will become confused and frustrated when offered too many choices?
3. Is it possible to increase buyers' desire for variety, creating a competitive advantage?
4. What processes should be used to learn about customer preferences? This may involve indirect methods (e.g., database analysis), or involving buyers in the process.

High variety strategies, properly conceived and executed, offer powerful opportunities for competitive advantage by providing superior value to customers. As highlighted by the above issues, pursuing these finer segmentation strategies involves major decisions including which strategy to pursue and how to implement the strategy. Estimating the value and cost tradeoffs of the relevant alternatives is important in deciding how fine the segmentation should be.

Selecting the Segmentation Strategy

We have considered several approaches to market segmentation, ranging from forming segments via experience and judgment to finer segmentation strategies. We now discuss deciding how to segment the market and strategic analysis of the segments that have been identified.

Deciding How to Segment

The choice of a segmentation method depends on such factors as the maturity of market, the competitive structure, and the organization's experience in the market. The more comprehensive the segmentation process, the higher the costs of segment identification will be, reaching the highest level when field research studies are involved and finer segmentation strategies are considered. It is important to maximize the available knowledge about the product-market. An essential first step in segmentation is analyzing the existing customer base to identify groups of buyers with different response behavior (e.g., frequent purchase versus occasional purchase). Developing a view of how to segment the market by managers may be helpful. In some instances this information will provide a sufficient basis for segment formation. If not, experience and existing information are often helpful in guiding the design of customer research studies.

The five segmentation criteria discussed earlier help to evaluate potential segments. Deciding if the criteria are satisfied rests with management after examining response differences among the segments. The segmentation plan should satisfy the responsiveness criterion plus the other criteria (end users are identifiable, they are accessible via a marketing program, the segment(s) is economically viable, and the segment is stable over time). The latter criterion may be less of an issue with mass customization since changes can be accommodated. Segmentation strategy should not be static. The competitive advantage gained by finding (or developing) a new market segment can be very important.

Strategic Analysis of Market Segments

Each market segment of interest needs to be studied to determine its potential attractiveness as a market target. The major areas of analysis include customers, competitors, positioning strategy, and financial and market attractiveness.

Customer Analysis

When forming segments, it is useful to find out as much as possible about the customers in each segment. Variables such as those used in dividing product-markets into segments are also helpful in describing the people in the same segments. The objective is to find descriptive characteristics that are highly correlated to the variables used to form the segments. Standardized information services are available for some product-markets including foods, health and beauty aids, and pharmaceuticals. Large markets involving many competitors make it profitable for research firms to collect and analyze data that are useful to the firms serving the market. We discuss marketing information resources in Chapter 5.

An essential part of customer analysis is determining how well the buyers in the segment are satisfied. Customer satisfaction depends on the perceived performance of a product and supporting services and the standards that customers use to evaluate that performance.[35] The customer's standards complicate the relationship between organizational product specifications (e.g., product attribute tolerances) and satisfaction. Standards may involve something other than prepurchase expectations such as the perceived performance of competing products. Importantly, the standards are likely to vary across market segments.

Competitor Analysis

Market segment analysis considers the set of key competitors currently active in the market in which the segment is located plus any potential segment entrants. In complex market structures, mapping the competitive arena requires detailed analysis. The competing firms are described and evaluated to highlight their strengths and weaknesses. Information useful in the competitor analysis includes business scope and objectives; market position; market target(s) and customer base; positioning strategy; financial, technical, and operating strengths; management experience and capabilities, and special competitive advantages (e.g., patents). It is also important to anticipate the future strategies of key competitors.

Value chain analysis can be used to examine competitive advantage at the segment level. A complete assessment of the nature and intensity of competition in the segment is important in determining whether to enter (or exit from) the segment and how to compete in the segment. Competitor and value chain analysis are discussed in Chapter 2.

Positioning Analysis

We consider positioning strategy in Chapter 6. Segment analysis involves some preliminary choices about positioning strategy. One objective of segment analysis is to obtain guidelines for developing a positioning strategy. Flexibility exists in selecting how to position the firm (or brand) with its customers and against its competition in a segment. Positioning analysis shows how to combine product, distribution, pricing, and promotion strategies to favorably position the brand with buyers in the segment. Information from positioning maps like Exhibit 3.11 is useful in guiding positioning strategy. The positioning strategy should meet the needs and requirements of the targeted buyers at a cost that yields a profitable margin for the organization.

Estimating Segment Attractiveness

The financial and market attractiveness of each segment needs to be evaluated. Included are specific estimates of revenue, cost, and segment profit contribution over the planning horizon. Market attractiveness can be measured by market growth rate projections and attractiveness assessments made by management.

Financial analysis obtains sales, cost, and profit contribution estimates for each segment of interest. Since accurate forecasting is difficult if the projections are too far into the future, detailed projections typically extend two to five years ahead. Both the segment's competitive position evaluation and the financial forecasts are used in comparing segments. In all instances the risks and returns associated with serving a particular segment need to be considered. Flows of revenues and costs can be weighted to take into account risks and the time value of revenues and expenditures.

It should be recognized that as information availability grows, for example through the data warehouses associated with CRM systems, the evaluation of segment attractiveness also has the potential for identifying unattractive market segments, and even individual customers which may be candidates for deletion. There may also be ethical considerations which limit the attractiveness of certain segments. The ETHICS FEATURE describes some

Segmentation studies for many markets identify children as a high value opportunity. Confectionery, fast food, music, and toys are examples. Children exhibit great "pester power" influencing their own consumption and that of the family.

Parents and health advisors across the world warn of the dangers of childhood obesity. For food firms, an ethical dilemma targeting this segment concerns the impact of their marketing actions on the young.

If they are accepted as proper market targets, ethical questions surround the ways in which advertisers reach young consumers with promotional messages, in ways which get around parental controls and conventional media:

- Reports in Europe suggest some advertising agencies use Internet chatrooms to place commercial messages to reach young consumers, getting around strict rules concerning advertising to children.

- Food companies have been accused of using text messaging (SMS), websites and viral marketing campaigns to sell products to children.

- Some advertising agencies run focus group research with consumers as young as three years old, to establish ways to channel "pester power" onto family purchasing.

Sources: Glen Owen, "Scandal of the Advertisers Who Pose as Young Girls on Internet Chatrooms," *Daily Mail*, April 2, 2006, 27. Jenny Wiggins, "Food Industry Criticised over Tactics to Tempt Children," *Financial Times*, January 31, 2006, 5. Gill Swain, "Pester Power," *The Sunday Times*, December 29, 2002, 1–16.

of the issues surrounding targeting children (or some groups of children), and some of the undesirable practices that have emerged. The potential for damage to brand and corporate reputation in such situations is considerable.

Segmentation "Fit" and Implementation

One important aspect of evaluating segment attractiveness is how well the segments match company capabilities and the ability to implement marketing strategies around those segments.[36] There are many organizational barriers to the effective use of segmentation strategies. New segment targets which do not fit into conventional information reporting, planning processes, and budget systems in the company may be ignored or not adequately resourced. Innovative models of customer segments and market opportunities may be rejected by managers or the culture of the organization.

There are dangers that managers may prefer to retain traditional views of the market and structure information in that way, or that segmentation strategy will be driven by existing organizational structures and competitive norms.[37] It is important to be realistic in balancing the attractiveness of segments against the ability of the organization to implement appropriate marketing strategies to take advantage of the opportunities identified. Building effective marketing strategy around market segmentation mandates an emphasis on action-ability as well as technique and analysis.[38]

Many of the issues we consider in later chapters impact on the operational capabilities of a company to implement segmentation strategies, for example, strength in cross-functional relationships may be a prerequisite to delivering value to new segments; the ability to work with partners may be needed to develop new products to build a strong position in a key market segment. The existence of these capabilities, or the ability to develop them, should be considered in making segmentation decisions.

Segment Attractiveness Analysis

An illustrative market segment analysis is shown in Exhibit 3.12. A two-year period is used for estimating sales, costs, contribution margin, and market share. Depending on the

EXHIBIT 3.12
Segment
Attractiveness
Analysis

Estimated ($ millions)	Segment		
	X	Y	Z
Sales*	10	16	5
Variable costs*	4	9	3
Contribution margin*	6	7	2
Market share†	60%	30%	10%
Total segment sales	17	53	50
Segment position:			
Business strength	High	Medium	Low
Attractiveness‡	Medium	Low	High

*For a two-year period.
†Percent of total sales in the segment.
‡Based on a five-year projection.

forecasting difficulty, estimates for a longer time period can be used. When appropriate, estimates can be expressed as present values of future revenues and costs. Business strength in Exhibit 3.12 refers to the present position of the firm relative to the competition in the segment. Alternatively, it can be expressed as the present position and an estimated future position, based upon plans for increasing business strength. Attractiveness is typically evaluated for some future time period. In the illustration a five-year projection is used.

The example shows how segment opportunities are ranked according to their overall attractiveness. The analysis can be expanded to include additional information such as profiles of key competitors. The rankings are admittedly subjective since decision makers will vary in their weighting of estimated financial position, business strength, and segment attractiveness. Place yourself in the role of a manager evaluating the segments. Using the information in Exhibit 3.12, rank segments X, Y, and Z as to their overall importance as market targets. Unless management is ready to allocate a major portion of resources to segment Z to build business strength, it is a candidate for the last-place position. Yet Z has some attractive characteristics. The segment has the most favorable market attractiveness of the three, and its estimated total sales are nearly equal to Y's for the next two years. The big problem with Z is its business strength. The key question is whether Z's market share can be increased. If not, X looks like a good prospect for top rating, followed by Y, and by Z. Of course, management may decide to go after all three segments.

Summary

Because buyers differ in their preferences for products, finding out what these preferences are and grouping buyers with similar needs is an essential part of business and marketing strategy development. Effective segmentation is key to market-driven strategy, linking strategic issues with the management of resources and operations around segment targets. Segmentation links value opportunities in the market and new market spaces to a company's capabilities to achieve a strong strategic positioning.

Segmentation demands close attention to market definition, identifying market segments and forming segment targets, which are described, analyzed, and evaluated. Segmentation of a product-market requires that response differences exist between segments and that the segments are identifiable and stable over time. Also, the benefits of segmentation should exceed the costs. The variables useful as bases for forming and describing segments include the characteristics of people and organizations, use situation, buyers' needs and preferences, and purchase behavior.

Segments can be formed by identifying customer groups using the characteristics of people or organizations. The groups are analyzed to determine if the response profiles are different across the candidate segments. Alternatively, customer response information can be used to form customer groupings and then the descriptive characteristics of the groups analyzed to find out if segments can be identified. Several examples of segment formation are discussed to illustrate the methods that are available for this purpose.

Finer segmenting strategies present attractive options for moving toward small segments and responding to buyers' unique value requirements. Technology, buyer diversity, and relationship opportunities are the drivers of finer segmentation strategies. These strategies include microsegmentation, mass customization, and variety seeking. While potentially attractive, finer segmentation strategies are more complex than other forms of segmentation and require comprehensive benefit and cost evaluations.

Segment analysis and evaluation consider the strengths and limitations of each segment as a potential market target for the organization. Segment analysis includes customer descriptions and satisfaction analysis, evaluating existing and potential competitors and competitive advantage, marketing program positioning analysis, and financial and market attractiveness. Segment analysis is important in evaluating customer satisfaction, finding new-product opportunities, selecting market targets, and designing positioning strategies. Nonetheless, it is also important to understand the organizational barriers to implementing segmentation strategy which may exist in a company, and to evaluate the "fit" of segmentation with company capabilities. Effectively implemented, a good segmentation strategy creates an important competitive edge for an organization.

Questions for Review and Discussion

1. Competing in the single European market raises some interesting market segment questions. Discuss the segmentation issues regarding this multiple-country market.

2. Why are there marketing strategy advantages in using demographic characteristics to break out product-markets into segments?

3. The real test of a segment formation scheme occurs after it has been tried and the results evaluated. Are there ways to evaluate alternative segmenting schemes without actually trying them?

4. Suggest ways of obtaining the information needed to conduct a market segment analysis.

5. Why may it become necessary for companies to change their market segmentation identification over time?

6. Is considering segments of one buyer a reality or a myth? Discuss.

7. Is it necessary to use a unique positioning strategy for each market segment targeted by an organization?

8. Under what circumstances may it not be possible to break up a product-market into segments? What are the dangers of using an incorrect segment formation scheme?

9. What are some of the advantages in using mass customization technology to satisfy the needs of buyers?

10. Does the use of mass customization eliminate the need to segment a market?

Internet Applications

A. Explore several of the following websites:

www.adquest.com

www.americanet.com

www.autosite.com

www.mlm2000.com

www.sidewalk.com

www.monster.com

www.realtor.com

How does the information from these sites affect our traditional concept of market segmentation? How is the segmentation process altered by such Internet providers?

B. Evaluate the following site for additional ideas and material concerned with market segmentation and the types of support that can be provided for companies:

www.marketsegmentation.co.uk

Feature Applications

A. Review the material in the INNOVATION FEATURE "All-Business-Class Airlines." Do these new ventures represent a robust segmentation strategy? What other segment opportunities can be identified in the airline business? How could these be exploited?

B. Review the BMW Mini case in the GLOBAL FEATURE "The BMW Mini." Do you believe that BMW has built a robust niche or segment strategy, or is the car a fashion item with limited lasting appeal to car buyers, like other "retro" attempts?

Notes

1. This illustration is based on Ariana Eunjung Cha, "In Retail, Profiling for Profit," *Washington Post,* Wednesday, August 17, 2005, A01. Matthew Boyle, "Best Buy's Giant Gamble," *Fortune,* April 3, 2006.

2. Anthony Bianco, "The Vanishing Mass Market," *BusinessWeek,* July 12, 2004, 62–68.

3. Don Peppers and Martha Rogers, *Enterprise One-to-One* (New York: Doubleday, 1997).

4. Hadley Freeman, "Nothing in Your Size? Stores Seek to Measure Up," *The Guardian,* Saturday, September 6, 2006. "Levi's Extends Its '10 Second Fitting Kiosk Market Tour," *TheWise Marketer.com,* Tuesday, September 6, 2006.

5. Daniel Yankelovich and David Meer, "Rediscovering Market Segmentation," *Harvard Business Review,* February 2006, 122–131.

6. Ibid.

7. Clayton M. Christensen, Scott Cook, and Taddy Hall, "Marketing Malpractice: The Cause and the Cure," *Harvard Business Review,* December 2005, 74–83.

8. Peter R. Dickson and James L. Ginter, "Market Segmentation, Product Differentiation, and Marketing Strategy," *Journal of Marketing,* April 1987, 1–10.

9. Nikki Tait, "Mixed Emotions as Olds Guard Bows Out," *Financial Times,* December 20, 2000, 27.

10. Leonard L. Berry, "Relationship Marketing of Services—Growing Interest, Emerging Perspectives," *Journal of the Academy of Marketing Science,* Fall 1995, 238–240.

11. *BusinessWeek,* March 5, 2007.

12. Henry Assael, *Consumer Behavior and Marketing Action,* 2nd ed. (Boston: PWS-Kent Publishing, 1984), 225.

13. Jay L. Laughlin and Charles R. Taylor, "An Approach to Industrial Market Segmentation," *Industrial Marketing Management,* 20 (1991), 127–136.

14. Daniel S. Levine, "Justice Served," *Sales & Marketing Management,* May, 1995, 53–61.

15. Meg Carter, "Big Business Pitches Itself on Fair Trade Territory," *Financial Times,* Tuesday, October 25, 2005, 13.

16. A. H. Maslow, "Theory of Human Motivation," *Psychology Review,* July 1943, 43–45.

17. Assael, *Consumer Behavior and Marketing Action,* 650.

18. Bernard Berelson and Gary A. Steiner, *Human Behavior: An Inventory of Scientific Findings* (New York: Harcourt Brace Jovanovich, 1964), 88.

19. Eric N. Berkowitz, Steven W. Hartley, William Rudelius, and Roger A. Kerin, *Marketing,* 7th ed. (Burr Ridge, IL: McGraw-Hill/Irwin, 2003).

20. Adrienne Carter, "It's Norman Time," *BusinessWeek,* May 29 2006, 64–68.

21. Anthony Bianco, "The Vanishing Mass Market."

22. Neil Buckley, "From Shock Therapy to Retail Therapy: Russia's Middle Class Starts Spending," *Financial Times,* October 31, 2006, 17. Jason Bush, "Russia: Shoppers Gone Wild," *Business-Week,* February 20, 2006, 46–47.

23. Rob Markey, John Ott and Gerard du Toit, "Winning New Customers Using Loyalty-Based Segmentation," *Strategy and Leadership,* Vol. 35 No. 3 2007, 32–37.

24. Peter R. Dickson and James L. Ginter, "Market Segmentation, Product Differentiation, and Marketing Strategy," *Journal of Marketing,* April 1987, 1–10.

25. Diane Brady, "Coach's Split Personality," *BusinessWeek,* November 7, 2005, 36.

26. Allanna Sullivan, "Mobil Bets Drivers Pick Cappuccino over Low Prices," *The Wall Street Journal,* January 30, 1995, B1 and B4.

27. "Bank Asks Lying Expert to Study Accounts," *The Sunday Times,* November 19 2000, 1.

28. Douglas B. Holt, John A. Quelch, and Earl L. Taylor, "How Global Brands Compete," *Harvard Business Review,* September 2004, 68–75.

29. V. Kasturi Ranga, Rowland T. Moriarity, and Gordon S. Swartz, "Segmenting Customers in Mature Industrial Markets," *Journal of Marketing,* October 1992, 72–82.

30. Financial Times, Understanding Customer Relationship Management, London: *Financial Times,* Spring 2000.

31. Ali Kara and Erdener Kaynak, "Markets of a Single Customer: Exploiting Conceptual Developments in Market Segmentation," *European Journal of Marketing,* No. 11/12, 1997, 873–895.

32. Barbara E. Kahn, "Dynamic Relationships with Customers: High-Variety Strategies," *Journal of the Academy of Marketing Science,* Winter 1998, 45–53.

33. Kahn, "Dynamic Relationships."

34. Ibid.

35. The following discussion of customer satisfaction is based on discussions with Robert B. Woodruff, The University of Tennessee, Knoxville.

36. Nigel F. Piercy and Neil A. Morgan, "Strategic and Operational Segmentation," *Journal of Strategic Marketing,* Vol. 1 No. 2 1993, 123–140.

37. Noel Capon and James M. Hulbert, *Marketing Management in the 21st Century* (New Jersey: Prentice-Hall, 2001), 185–186.

38. D. Young, "The Politics Behind Market Segmentation," *Marketing News,* October 21, 1996, 17.

Chapter 4

Strategic Customer Relationship Management

Building effective customer relationships is widely recognized by executives as a high priority business initiative.[1] A study of 960 international executives rated customer relationship management (CRM) and strategic planning highest among ten priority strategic initiatives for improving organizational performance.[2] CRM is a cross-functional core business process concerned with achieving improved shareholder value through the development of effective relationships with key customers and customer segments.[3]

Forming and sustaining valuable customer relationships is the most prized strategic outcome of correctly visualized and implemented CRM programs.[4] A Mercer consultant survey of top executives found developing and sustaining customer relationships to be the most important source of competitive advantage in the twenty-first century. One of the primary conclusions of research concerning CRM failures is that achieving desired customer outcomes requires the alignment of the entire organization, while avoiding the narrow and incomplete perspective of viewing CRM as a technology initiative. Moreover, a fragmented or functional focus is not sufficient.

Successful CRM initiatives are guided by a carefully formulated and implemented organizational strategy. CRM offers sellers the opportunity to gather customer information rapidly, identify the most valuable customers over the relevant time horizon, and increase customer loyalty by providing customized products and services. This is described as "tying in an asset" when the asset is the customer. CRM supports a customer-responsive strategy, which gains competitive advantage when it:

- Delivers superior customer value by personalizing the interaction between the customer and the company.
- Demonstrates the company's trustworthiness and reliability to the customer.
- Tightens connections with the customer.
- Achieves the coordination of complex organizational capabilities around the customer.[5]

CRM encourages a focus on customer loyalty and retention, with the goal of winning a larger share of the total lifetime value of each profitable customer.

We begin by taking a more detailed look at CRM and its pivotal role in contributing to bottom-line enterprise performance. Next, developing a CRM strategy and building customer lifetime value are examined. Finally, we discuss the value creation process and consider the relationship between CRM and market segmentation, targeting, and strategic positioning.

Pivotal Role of Customer Relationship Management

The term CRM means very different things in different circumstances, a consequence of the rapid evolution and development of this approach to managing customer relationships. CRM may be used to identify an array of initiatives including automated customer contact systems, salesforce productivity, customer service and automated call centers, and enterprise-wide systems designed to integrate information about customers into a single access point.

CRM in Perspective

CRM may refer to little more than building relationships with customers to match a company's product and service offer better with customer needs. Others see CRM as developing a unified and cohesive view of the customer, without regard to how the customer chooses to communicate with the organization (in person, by mail, Internet, or telephone). Emphasis is placed on enhanced customer service and the use of call centers to provide consistency in how the company interacts with customers. Alternatively, CRM may focus only on the creation and use of a customer database to support decision makers.

It is important to shift attention from the technology and hardware of CRM to the continuing process of "making managerial decisions with the end goal of increasing the value of the customer base through better relationships with customers, usually on an individual basis."[6] The emphasis on strategy built around profitable customers as the primary concern of CRM is emphasized by Bain & Co. Bain's view is that CRM must combine business processes with customer strategies to develop customer loyalty and enhance financial performance.[7] Another useful viewpoint suggests that CRM consists of three main elements:

* Identifying, satisfying, retaining, and maximizing the value of a firm's best customers.
* Wrapping the firm around the customer to ensure that each contact with the customer is appropriate and based upon extensive knowledge of both the customer's needs and profitability.
* Creating a full picture of the customer.[8]

Advances in technology are highly supportive to the implementation of CRM at all levels of the business. One interesting development is described in the INNOVATION FEATURE.

CRM and Database Marketing

Information technology has enabled companies to develop extensive databases concerning existing and potential customers. This information is useful in segmentation, account management, and many other marketing applications. Technology can be used by companies to interact with the customer and develop flexible customer-level responses. Databases are an important part of CRM. "However, the overarching framework of CRM includes much more than just databases and IT systems."[9] CRM enables the use of database applications at very disaggregated levels including individual customers.

Pay by Touch is a rapidly growing company operating a biometric network. To pay, customers press a finger on a scanner and enter a personal number to have the goods charged to a credit card or bank account. From a pilot scheme at Piggly Wiggly supermarkets in South Carolina, Pay By Touch has expanded to more than 3,000 locations in the U.S. Supervalu, the second largest traditional U.S. grocer, is the largest user. Aside from payment efficiency, purchases can be tied to the biometric identity of the customer.

Beyond simplifying payments, Pay By Touch can use its SmartShop technology to direct weekly incentives and special price cuts to an individual customer based on shopping habits and preferences. For retailers, this system offers a way to direct offers effectively to their most loyal customers, rather than supporting the "cherry picking" on bargains by customers who only buy the offers.

Source: Adapted from Jonathan Birchall, "Pay By Touch Puts Its Finger on Loyalty," *Financial Times,* Friday, June 22, 2007, 19.

A database created through CRM technology should contain information about the following:

- *Transactions*—should include a complete purchase history for each customer with accompanying details (date, price paid, products purchased).
- *Customer Contacts*—with multiple channels of distribution and communication the database should record all customer contacts with the company and its distributors, including sales calls, service requests, complaints, inquiries, and loyalty program participation.
- *Descriptive Information*—for each individual customer, relevant descriptive data that provide the basis for market segmentation and targeted marketing communications.
- *Response to Marketing Stimuli*—whether the customer responded to specific advertising, a price offer, a direct marketing initiative, or a sales call, or any other direct contact.[10]

Increasingly sophisticated software is available to undertake data mining and model data from the CRM database.

Customer Lifetime Value

While traditional approaches to market segmentation identify groups of customers by their purchase behavior and/or descriptive data, CRM offers the opportunity to examine individual customers or narrowly defined groups, and to calculate what each customer offers the company in profits. The metric *customer lifetime value* (CLV) calculates past profit produced by the customer for the firm—the sum of all the margins of all the products purchased over time, *less* the cost of reaching that customer. To this is added a forecast of margins on future purchases (under different assumptions for different customers), discounted back to their present value. This process provides an estimate of the profitability of a customer during the time span of the relationship. The CLV calculation is a powerful tool for focusing marketing and promotional efforts where they will be most productive.

Thus, CLV provides the estimated profitability of a customer (business or consumer) during the time span of the relationship. A study conducted by Deloitte Consulting found that companies which recognize the importance of understanding CLV are 60 percent more profitable than firms that do not consider CLV.[11] The familiar Pareto Rule

In 1998, Joe Simpson, a British mountain climber, wrote a book called *Touching the Void*, an account of his near-death climbing experience in the Andes. It sold only modestly. Ten years later, Jon Krakauer wrote *Into Thin Air,* another book about a mountain climbing tragedy, which became a best-seller. Suddenly, *Touching the Void* began to sell again. Random House rushed out a new edition to meet demand. Booksellers promoted *Touching the Void* in their *Into Thin Air* displays. A paperback of the older book spent fourteen weeks on the New York Times best-seller list. *Touching the Void* now outsells *Into Thin Air* more than two to one. The decisive factor was Amazon.com recommendations, suggesting that readers who liked *Into Thin Air* would also like *Touching the Void*.

The theory of "The Long Tail" reflects Internet economics. Selling products like music or film downloads can be done with extremely low inventory and distribution costs, which means that a company can capture the entire market, including the long tail of non-hits, which is often where the real value is. The biggest money may be in the smallest sales. The basis of a long tail strategy is to make everything available and to assist buyers in the search.

Non-hits may be a bigger market than hits. In 2004 in the U.S. books selling more than 250,000 copies sold 53 million copies in total. Books selling under 1,000 copies totaled 84 million. Hits are only what appeals to the largest available middle ground of the population. Music companies and publishers are actively repackaging products from their back catalogs to exploit the "long tail."

"Long Tail" strategies have become attractive because of enhanced customer knowledge and insight into the existence of very small niches in markets, driven by CRM and Internet technology.

Sources: Chris Anderson, *The Long Tail: How Endless Choice Is Creating Unlimited Demand* (London: Random House Business Books, 2007). Dominic Rushe, "Retailers Start to Climb the Long Tail Tail," *The Sunday Times,* October 29, 2006, 3–13. Tony Jackson, "The Freedom in Selection," *Financial Times,* Wednesday, July 12, 2006, 11.

suggests that 20 percent of customers yield 80 percent of the profits, so it is very important to find the high value customers, which are typically a small part of the total customer base.

Nonetheless, the power of CRM to enhance a company's depth of customer knowledge and to allow access to individuals and small groups of customers is having profound effects on strategic thinking. The STRATEGY FEATURE discusses the "Long Tail" issue as an example of new strategies being driven by the combination of CRM and Internet technology.

Developing a CRM Strategy

We discuss alternative levels of an organization's focus toward CRM, followed by strategy development guidelines and the CRM implementation process.

CRM Levels

CRM can be viewed from companywide, customer-facing, and functional levels.[12] Each level has important but different implications for strategic marketing. All three perspectives are important, although the companywide or strategic level provides the most complete view of CRM. The functional perspective considers the processes that are needed to fulfill required marketing functions. The customer-facing level offers a single view of the customer across all of the organization's access channels to the customer. This level of CRM is concerned with coordinating information across all contact channels on a continuing basis. The RELATIONSHIP FEATURE describes hotel group Accor's customer-facing activities.

The France-based hotel group Accor links CRM data to guest survey information in its U.S. Sofitel and Novatel hotels, to anticipate the preferences of frequent users. The VP for sales and marketing for Accor North America notes "It takes us back to the time when there were small inns and the owner knew every customer and treated them as an individual. It should help streamline check-in and accommodate preferences for guests who, for example, request the same room every time. The group will be able to market with a microscope instead of a telescope."

Source: Marian Edmunds, "Your Wish Is on My Database," *Financial Times,* February 28, 2000, 16.

The company-wide level provides a strategic focus for CRM.[13] It considers the implications of knowledge about customers and their preferences across the entire company. The intent is to guide the interactions between the organization and its customers in seeking to maximize the lifetime value of customers for the firm. Importantly, the strategic perspective acknowledges that: (1) customers vary in their economic value to the company; and (2) customers differ in their expectations toward the firm.

The strategic use of CRM resources reflects the shift in focus by marketing executives to the customer who delivers long-term profits, that is, an emphasis on customer retention rather than acquisition. Well-known metrics suggest that as little as a 5 percent increase in customer retention can have an impact as high as 95 percent on the net present value delivered by the customer.[14] Other studies by McKinsey consultants find that repeat customers generate over twice as much gross income as new customers.[15] CRM emphasizes that executives should focus the organization's strategy on customer profitability and the gains from reducing customer "churn."

Interestingly, as CRM evolves and offers executives deeper insights into their customer base, the new information may challenge strategic assumptions in important ways. For example, the points made above suggest a powerful linkage between enhanced customer loyalty and higher customer profitability. However, companies are discovering through CRM database analysis that this is not always true. Some groups of customers may not justify the costs required to retain them, because the real fit between their needs and the company's products is weak. Just because a group of customers was profitable in the past, it may be dangerous to assume this will always be true. For example, many non-loyal customers are initially profitable, causing the company to chase them for further profits—but once these customers have ceased buying they become increasingly unprofitable if the company continues to invest in them. CRM data provides executives with a unique basis to address such issues as loyalty and profitability on the basis of fact instead of assumption, and to focus on individual customers, rather than groups containing many dissimilar buyers.[16]

CRM Strategy Development

The major steps in developing a CRM strategy are shown in Exhibit 4.1. We provide an overview of each step.

Organizational Commitment to CRM

Everyone in the firm needs to be supportive of the CRM initiative, beginning with top management. This commitment is consistent with the characteristics of a market-oriented culture. All functions in the firm are likely to have an involvement with certain of the CRM processes and activities. These parts of the business need to be involved at the beginning of strategy development. Ongoing cooperation and acceptance are essential to success. The customer is the unifying basis for employee and functional involvement.

The Project Team

The cross-functional team is the center of decision analysis and action for the CRM process. The team will need to become familiar with the CRM process before pursuing analysis and action initiatives. All relevant functions and departments should be involved. Initially, external consulting capabilities may be needed. Major financial commitments will be required as well as management and professional time commitments. Value chain representation may also be needed depending on the firm's position in the value chain (supplier, producer, or marketing intermediary). For example, a CRM strategy by PepsiCo would need to include independent bottler representation.

EXHIBIT 4.1   **The Steps in Developing a CRM Strategy**

Source: V. Kumar and Werner J. Reinartz, *Customer Relationship Management* (Hoboken, NJ: John Wiley & Sons, Inc.), 2006, 39.

1. Gain an organization-wide commitment to CRM strategy.
2. Form a cross-functional CRM project team for decision analysis and actions.
3. Conduct a business needs analysis concerning customer relationships.
4. Develop and define the CRM strategy to guide management process.

Business Needs Analysis

Each company's requirements concerning customer relationships need to be examined. These analyses are critical in providing direction to CRM initiatives, which must be integrated into the business strategy. The departments and individuals unitizing the CRM system (e.g., managers from sales, marketing, customer service and value chain) should clearly indicate what is needed from the strategy and agreement must be reached concerning CRM expectations and performance metrics.

The CRM Strategy

The components of the CRM strategy are shown in Exhibit 4.2.[17] The value proposition spells out what the organization must provide in order to satisfy customer expectations. Understanding customers' value requirements is essential. The business case is an assessment which indicates the shareholder value and financial return of delivery of the required customer value. CRM initiatives require substantial resources and return needs to be carefully evaluated. The customer strategy indicates how different customer segments will be formed and managed. In business-to-business markets, firms may need to target individual customers. The enterprise transformation plan indicates the necessary initiatives to launch the CRM strategy—the changes which are required throughout the enterprise. Finally, all relevant stakeholders must be familiar with the plan, to assure that the necessary value propositions are determined and provided to the targeted customer segments.

CRM Implementation

Gartner Inc. estimated worldwide CRM expenditures at $76 billion in 2005 and expanding at rapid growth rates.[18] Other estimates place expenditures at much higher levels. However, the evidence of the performance of CRM systems has been disappointing for many companies. The Gartner Group concluded that 55 percent of all CRM projects do not produce results. A Bain & Co. 2001 survey of management tools ranked CRM at the bottom for satisfaction—indeed, one in five users in the Bain survey reported their CRM initiatives had not only failed to deliver profitable growth, but had also damaged long-term customer relationships.[19]

Successful Implementation

One recommendation proposes that the major components of the successful implementation of CRM are:

- A front office that integrates sales, marketing, and service functions across all media (call centers, people, retail outlets, value chain members, Internet).

EXHIBIT 4.2
Develop and Define the CRM Strategy to Guide the Management Process

Source: V. Kumar and Werner J. Reinartz, *Customer Relationship Management* (Hoboken, NJ: John Wiley & Sons, Inc., 2006), 42.

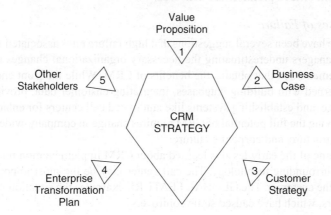

Call centers provide support and service to customers, though some sell as well. They are used predominantly in mass-market consumer industries. The centers exist to improve the quality of customer service.

There are many attractions in outsourcing call center operations to low-pay countries like India and Taiwan—an in-house call center agent in the U.S. is likely to be paid around $29,000, while the agent in India receives $2,667. The majority of call centers in India use college-educated employees. The better Indian call center operators train staff in the accent and dialect of their customers' regions, and staff adapt sleeping patterns to align with working hours in the customers' country. The intent is that consumers contacting the call center will not even be aware that they are speaking to someone in a foreign country.

Nonetheless, some major companies are pulling back from overseas call center operations for several reasons:

- Customer complaints about service received and language difficulties.
- Survey data suggest 60 percent of Americans say they are less likely to do business with a company after a bad call center experience, and 62 percent say their most recent experience with an overseas call center was disappointing. The dissatisfaction level is twice that shown by calls to centers that they believe are in the U.S.
- Technology difficulties leave call center agents with no information about customers, giving the impression they do not know what the customer is talking about.
- Media coverage has become increasingly critical of companies off-shoring call center jobs.

While sometimes attractive economically, there is a risk that overseas call centers may undermine the quality of customer relationships and pose a threat to corporate and brand reputation for those who employ them.

Sources: Kerry Miller, "Hello India? Er, Des Moines," *BusinessWeek,* June 25, 2007, 14. Pete Encardio, "Making Bangalore Sound Like Boston," *BusinessWeek,* April 10, 2006, 48.

- A data warehouse that stores customer information and the appropriate analytical tools with which to analyze that data and learn about customer behavior.
- Business rules developed from the data analysis to ensure the front office benefits from the firm's learning about its customers.
- Measures of performance that enable customer relationships to continually improve.
- Integration into the firm's operational support (or "back office") systems, ensuring the front office's promises are delivered.[20]

Causes of Failure

There have been several suggestions that high failure rates associated with CRM are caused by managers underestimating the necessary organizational changes required for effective implementation that obtains the benefits of CRM. While the front end of CRM systems is concerned with building databases, integrating customer data, providing better customer service, and establishing systems like automated call centers for enhanced responsiveness, achieving the full potential of CRM requires change in company-wide processes, organization structure, and corporate culture.

Some of the early lessons learned about CRM implementation relate to the call centers and surrounding technology. The call center may be the most important point of contact with the customer. The GLOBAL FEATURE examines the situation with international call centers, which have caused some controversy.

EXHIBIT 4.3
Useful Websites for
Additional CRM
Material

www.dbmarketing.com

The website of the Database Marketing Institute, with a number of articles and speeches concerning recent developments in database marketing, available to be downloaded.

www.thearling.com

A site with extensive information about developments in data mining, and articles and papers on this topic for download.

www.1to1.com

The website of the Peppers & Rogers Group features the work and consultancy of Don Peppers and Martha Rogers. White Papers are available for download. A free subscription to the inside 1 to 1 newsletter is also available.

www.teradata.com

The website of the Teradata Division of NCR. It contains an interesting technical library on data warehousing and data mining as well as customer case studies.

www.crmdaily.com

This website provides new headline material on a daily basis concerning various CRM applications and management issues on a free subscription basis.

Bain & Co. research suggests that there are four significant pitfalls to avoid in CRM initiatives:

1. Implementing CRM before creating a customer strategy—success relies on making strategic customer and positioning choices, and this outweighs the importance of the computer systems, software, call centers, and other technologies.

2. Putting CRM in place before changing the organization to match—CRM affects more than customer-facing processes: it impacts internal structures and systems that may have to change.

3. Assuming that more CRM technology is necessarily better, rather than matching the technology to the customer strategy.

4. Investing in building relationships with disinterested customers, instead of those customers who value them.[21]

Websites giving additional information on various aspects of CRM are shown in Exhibit 4.3. There is also extensive literature on the topic and several recent books have been published.

Value Creation Process

Payne and Frow define the value creation process in CRM as (1) the value the customer receives; and (2) the value the organization receives.[22] Successfully managing the value exchange between the customer and the firm is essential in effective CRM.

Customer Value

The benefits the customer receives are expressed by the value proposition. The objective of the organization is to provide a superior customer experience. The value proposition "explains the relationship among the performance of the product, the fulfillment of the customer's needs, and the total cost to the customer over the customer relationship life cycle."[23]

Metrics Feature *How General Electric Co. Measures Customers' Experience*

Assessing whether a superior customer experience is accomplished requires determining the relative importance placed by customers on different attributes of the product. Market segmentation may be useful in analyses to find the extent of correspondence between customer value requirements and value provided by the firm. Conjoint analysis and other techniques can be used in these assessments. An interesting approach to measuring customers' experience used by General Electric Co. is described in the METRICS FEATURE.

Value Received by the Organization

Determining value received from CRM requires the following information:

> First, it is necessary to determine how existing and potential customer profitability varies across different customers and customer segments. Second, the economics of customer acquisition and customer retention and opportunity for selling, up-selling, and building customer advocacy must be understood.[24]

As discussed earlier a key concept associated with the value received by the organization via CRM is customer lifetime value (CLV). CLV is the expected profitability of a customer over the time-span of the relationship with the customer. The sum of CLV for all of a firm's customers is termed customer equity. CLV provides useful information in selecting valuable customers for targeting.

Value received by the customer is also relevant. It is important to recognize the potential negative impact of issues regarding consumer trust on CRM activities.[25] If buyers believe that the information collected by their suppliers may be used to exploit them, their trust in the relationship may be jeopardized. Accordingly, executives need to recognize trust and privacy implications of CRM initiatives.

CRM approaches may also be valuable in identifying less attractive customers and developing effective ways to handle this issue—what Larry Selden calls separating the "angel customers" and the "demon customers."[25] For example, the INTERNET FEATURE describes an approach adopted by retailers to manage the problem of excessive product returns by some customers.

Some consumers cost retailers a lot of money because of such practices as: "wardrobing"—buying expensive clothes, wearing them once, and then returning them; "pack attacks"—damaging a package on display to buy it later at a discount; and excessive returning. Excessive or fraudulent returning is estimated to cost U.S. retailers $16 billion annually. Some consumers buy hundreds of items and return them all (or all but one).

The Return Exchange is a California-based data warehouse which can analyze customers return behavior from retail companies. When products are returned to stores, customer ID and product details are sent to The Return Exchange. If analysis suggests the individual is an excessive returner, the customer's pattern of returns—the number, frequency, and value—are displayed at the store when returns are made. The retailer can decide whether the customer should be given a warning or refused a return.

Source: Adapted from Paul Rubens, "How to Get Rid of 'Devil Customers,'" ft.com, June 13, 2007.

CRM and Value Chain Strategy

It is important that CRM be integrated with the different channels that access end-user customers. "The multi-channel integration process is arguably one of the most important processes in CRM because it takes the outputs of the business strategy and value creation processes and translates them into value-adding activities with customers."[26] Many companies interact with customers using multiple channels including salespeople, value chain partners, email and Internet, telephoning, and direct marketing. The concept of the "perfect customer experience," an example of integrated channel management, is described in Exhibit 4.4.

CRM and Strategic Marketing

From the perspective of strategic marketing, there are several reasons why CRM is important and why there should be extensive marketing involvement in decisions about CRM. Importantly, an organizational perspective is needed in guiding the CRM strategy.

Implementation

It is critical that the adoption and implementation of CRM be seen as more than technology focused on efficiency. There are significant implications for the strategic positioning of a company and its customer relationships, where the voice of marketing should be heard. Our earlier discussion of CRM implementation highlights several relevant issues.

EXHIBIT 4.4
The Perfect Customer Experience

Source: Adrian Payne and Pennie Frow, "A Strategic Framework for Customer Relationship Management," *Journal of Marketing* (October 2005), 173.

"The perfect customer experience," which must be affordable for the company in the context of the segments in which it operates and its competition, is a relatively new concept. This concept is now being embraced in industry by companies such as TNT, Toyota's Lexus, Oce, and Guinness Breweries. Therefore, multi-channel integration is a critical process in CRM because it represents the point of cocreation of customer value. However, a company's ability to execute multi-channel integration successfully is heavily dependent on the organization's ability to gather and deploy customer information from all channels and to integrate it with other relevant information.

Operationally it is important not to assume that the drivers of value for all customers are the same, or that CRM is the key to all important customer relationships. For example, there are signs that many customers are weary of call centers and automated responses.

Performance Metrics

The availability of CRM data provides the opportunity to update the measures used by managers to assess the success of their brands in the marketplace. Traditional financial and market-based indicators like sales, profitability, and market share will continue to be important. However, CRM allows the development of measures that are customer-centric and more insightful concerning marketing strategy effectiveness. CRM-based measures of performance (both online and offline) may include: customer acquisition cost, conversion rates (from lookers to buyers), retention/churn rates, same customer sales rates, loyalty measures, and customer "share of wallet."[27]

The client-satisfaction measure discussed in the earlier METRICS FEATURE is used in all of GE's business units from homeowners to hospitals. The CEO highlights the net-prompter score as a key part of GE's growth formula.[28] Respondents are categorized as promoters, passives, and detractors relative to how likely they are to recommend GE to a friend. Perhaps most important, the metric indicates the firm's commitment to CRM.

Short-Term Versus Long-Term Value

It is important that when decisions are made about a company's customer priorities using historical customer profitability, long-term issues should be considered. Customers who are currently unprofitable may be attractive long-term prospects for suppliers who maintain loyalty through the hard times until the customers become profitable, and customers who are currently profitable may not be the best prospects for the future. The simple availability of CRM information should not be allowed to override strategic choices of customers to be retained where a long-term relationship may be highly attractive. This is why the active participation of marketing executives in CRM initiatives is important.

Customer lifetime value is an attractive measure to use to examine long-term customer attractiveness. For example, in many countries retail banks aggressively recruit young people as customers when they are undergraduate and graduate students (and likely to be unprofitable to the bank) with the goal of retaining the customer with a better than average chance of becoming a high-net-worth individual (and offering profitable opportunities to the bank).

Competitive Differentiation

If certain customers are unprofitable, then rather than "firing" the customer, the competitive issue may be how to change the route to market to make them profitable to the company. For example, when British Airways made the decision to focus only on its profitable business-class passengers at the expense of economy travelers, Virgin Airways gained the economy-class passengers by offering a better value proposition than BA. CRM data may provide one of the most powerful tools for identifying different customers on the basis of their behavior and other characteristics, to locate those whose needs have good fit with a company's capabilities. As one-to-one marketing expert Don Peppers has noted: "For every credit card company that wants to concentrate on higher income customers, there's another credit card company that wants to concentrate on lower income customers, and they do it by streamlining their service and making it more cost-efficient."[29] It is important that decisions about customer choices reflect strategic priorities.

Ethics Feature

Using CRM Tools to De-Select Customers

The logic of CRM as a source of customer knowledge suggests that some customers will be more attractive than others—they are more profitable, they buy more, or they are better prospects. In retailing, the "devil customers" who cost retailers money may be as much as 20 percent of the customer base. The dilemma is the stance to take with less profitable customers.

With unattractive customers we can . . .

Stop doing business with them, or do less business with them . . .

- Turn their business away.
- Less attractive customers can be charged for services that are free to others.
- More attractive customers are offered better deals if they threaten to defect, but these offers are not available to less attractive customers.

Offer them a lower level of service or added value . . .

- Call center technology can "recognize" customers and direct calls to different sales and service teams, based on the prospects with that customer. The most attractive prospects can be dealt with quicker and offered special deals and discounts.
- More attractive customers can be offered special deals through loyalty or frequent user programs.

Work to make them more attractive and profitable . . .

- Focus on factors that can make the less profitable customer more attractive—a higher share of their spending spent, cross-selling, promoting higher margin products.

However, there may be a moral dilemma regarding the fairness of treating some customers differently than others. When Express clothing stores stopped accepting returns from "serial returners" and Filene's Basement banned a few customers from its stores because of excessive returns and complaints, both received much adverse publicity. European banks which have tried to restrict access of poorer customers to bank branches and services have been similarly criticized. The logic of favoring some customers over others may be weakened by potential damage to the brand.

Sources: Ariana Eunjung Cha, "In Retail, Profiling for Profit," *Washington Post,* August 17, 2005, A01; Paul Rubens, How to Get Rid of 'Devil Customers,'" ft.com, June 13, 2007.

Nonetheless, there are issues of social responsibility and ethics which surround the ways in which CRM technology can be used to differentiate between attractive and less attractive customers. If handled insensitively this differentiation may be damaging to corporate and brand reputation. The ETHICS FEATURE highlights some of these dilemmas.

Lack of Competitive Advantage

Investment in CRM to build competitive advantage may be an illusion if a company focuses only on automated call centers and customer complaint systems. The level of expenditure on CRM suggests that most competitors in most markets will have similar resources, and may be quicker to get to the real competitive strengths in aligning resources and capabilities around customers. Competitive advantage requires more than just investment in CRM technology, particularly if it is poorly implemented. Our earlier discussion indicated the danger of allowing technology to drive the CRM strategy. Similar CRM technology is available to most companies in most markets, and the issue for competitive advantage enhancement is not having the technology but how it is used.

Information-Based Competitive Advantage

One of the most important aspects of CRM from a strategic marketing perspective is the creation of a major new source of knowledge about customers. Used appropriately the databases and information resources and capabilities created through CRM technology may be one of the most valuable resources a company has for uncovering new value-creating opportunities for customers and for developing market understanding and insights ahead of the competition. As a further resource for developing and exploiting market sensing capabilities, CRM systems have enormous potential, which many organizations are beginning to exploit to build competitive advantage.

Summary

To some, CRM means little more than building relationships with customers to match the product offer better with customer needs. Others see CRM as concerned with developing a unified and cohesive view of the customer, no matter how the customer chooses to communicate with the organization (in person, by mail, Internet, or telephone), and emphasizing enhanced customer service and the use of call centers to provide consistency in how the company interacts with customers. To others, CRM focuses on the creation and use of a customer database to support decision makers.

Understanding customer relationship management begins with recognizing that CRM seeks to increase the value of an organization's customer base by developing and retaining better relationships with customers. CRM may involve the use of databases but includes much more than technology. CRM makes it possible to examine individual customers or narrowly defined groups (micro segments) and calculate what each offers the company in potential profits. The resulting customer lifetime value (CLV) can be used to focus marketing and promotional efforts.

CRM strategy can be viewed from companywide, customer-facing, and functional perspectives. The companywide or strategic perspective provides the most complete view of CRM. Designing the CRM strategy follows a sequence of initiatives: gaining organizational commitment to CRM, forming the project team, analyzing business needs, and determining the CRM strategy to be pursued by the organization.

CRM strategy includes the value proposition to be offered, the business case, the customer strategy, the enterprise transformation plan, and responsibilities to other stakeholders. CRM strategy implementation involves integration of sales, marketing, and service functions across all media and value chain members, creation of a data warehouse, decision guidelines for use of CRM analyses, determination of performance benchmarks, and integration of cross-functional operations.

Several hurdles to successful CRM implementation include implementing before creating a customer strategy, launching CRM before making essential organizational changes, assuming that more CRM technology is necessarily better, and investing time and resources with disinterested customers. CRM is a major undertaking that is complex and demanding.

CRM is a value creation process consisting of the value the customer receives and the value the organization receives. The benefits the customer receives are expressed in the value proposition. The value the organization receives is determined by a penetrating analysis of the profitability of the customer base. Customer lifetime value is the basis of the assessment.

CRM is an important aspect of strategic marketing, recognizing that CRM is an enterprise spanning initiative. It is essential that CRM be carefully integrated with marketing strategy. CRM has a vital role to play in market targeting and marketing program positioning strategies.

Questions for Review and Discussion

1. How should CRM be defined to provide a complete strategy perspective?
2. Discuss the value of considering CRM at different organizational levels.
3. What is involved in estimating customer lifetime value (CLV)?
4. Discuss the process of developing a CRM strategy.
5. What are the important issues in CRM implementation?
6. Discuss how CRM creates value for the firm's stakeholders.
7. What is the relationship between CRM and market segmentation?
8. Discuss the role of the cross-functional CRM team.

Internet Applications

A. Visit the website of SalesForce.com. Based on the information provided discuss how SalesForce.com can contribute to a company's CRM.
B. Visit one of the websites discussed in Exhibit 4.3. Discuss how the website may be useful to a company in its CRM activities.

Feature Applications

A. Critically evaluate the "Net Promoter" concept of customer satisfaction used by the General Electric Co. What role does customer experience information play in GE's CRM?

Notes

1. Sridhar N. Ramaswami, Mukesh Bhargava, and Rajendra Srivastava, "Market-based Assets and Capabilities, Business Process, and Financial Performance," MSI Working Paper Series, No. 04–001, 2004.
2. "The Cart Pulling the Horse," *The Economist,* April 9, 2005.
3. Adrian Payne and Pennie Frow, "A Strategic Framework for Customer Relationship Management," *Journal of Marketing,* 69, October 2005, 167–176.
4. Sudhir Kale, "CRM Failure and the Seven Deadly Sins," *Marketing Management* 13, April 2004, 42–46.
5. George Day, "Tying on an Asset," in Understanding CRM (London: *Financial Times,* 2000).
6. Don Peppers and Martha Rogers, *Managing Customer Relationships* (Hobroken, NJ: Wiley, 2004), 33.
7. Darrell K. Rigby, Frederick F. Reichheld, and Phil Schafter, "Avoid the Four Perils of CRM," *Harvard Business Review,* February 2002, 101–109.
8. Lynette Ryals, Simon D. Knox, and Stan Maklan, *Customer Relationship Management: The Business Case for CRM,* Financial Times Report (London: Prentice Hall, 2000).

9. V. Kumar and Werner J. Reinartz, *Customer Relationship Management* (Hobroken, NJ: John Wiley & Sons, Inc. 2006), 4.

10. Russell S. Winer, "A Framework for Customer Relationship Management," *California Management Review* 43, No. 4, Summer 2001, 89–105, 92.

11. Kale, "CRM Failure and the Seven Deadly Sins."

12. The following discussion is based on Kumar and Reinartz, *Customer Relationship Management,* 33–47.

13. Ibid.

14. Frederick F. Reichheld, *The Loyalty Effect* (Cambridge, MA: Harvard Business School Press, 1996).

15. Winer, "A Framework for Customer Relationship Management."

16. Werner Reinartz and V. Kumar, "The Mismanagement of Customer Loyalty," *Harvard Business Review,* July 2002, 86–94.

17. Kumar and Reinartz, *Customer Relationship Management,* 42–44.

18. Wendy S. Close, "The Need for a Multi-vendor Strategy in Achieving Outstanding CRM," *Gartner Inc. CRM Project Volume 2* (June 2001).

19. Rigby, Reichheld, and Schafter, "Avoid the Four Perils of CRM."

20. Simon Knox, Stan Maklan, Adrian Payne, Joe Peppard, and Lynette Ryals, *Customer Relationship Management: Perspectives from the Marketplace* (Oxford: Butterworth-Heinemann, 2003).

21. Rigby, Reichheld, and Schafter, "Avoid the Four Perils of CRM."

22. Payne and Frow, "A Strategic Framework for Customer Relationship Management," 170–172.

23. Ibid., 172.

24. Ibid., 172.

25. Selden, Larry and G. Colvin, *Angel Customers and Demon Customers: Discover Which Is Which and Turbo-Charge Your Stock* (Knoxville, TN: Portfolio Hardcover, 2003).

26. Payne and Frow, "A Strategic Framework for Customer Relationship Management," 172.

27. Winer, "A Framework for Customer Relationship Management."

28. Kathryn Kranhold, "Client-Satisfaction Tool Takes Root," *The Wall Street Journal,* July 10, 2006, B3.

29. Richard Tomkins, "Goodbye to Small Spenders," *Financial Times,* February 4, 2000, 13.

Chapter 5

Capabilities for Learning About Customers and Markets

Market-oriented companies display superiority in understanding customers, markets, and competitors. "Every discussion of market orientation emphasizes the ability of the firm to learn about customers, competitors, and channel members in order to continually sense and act on events and trends in present and prospective markets."[1] Market-driven companies display innovative skills in gathering, interpreting, and using information to guide their business and marketing strategies and to achieve competitive advantage.

Increasingly, learning about markets is more about interpreting information than finding it. With resources like online Internet searches, in-company information and intelligence systems, marketing research agency reports and surveys, ethnographical research techniques, and burgeoning technical literature in most fields, executives may be in danger of being overwhelmed by information. Research suggests that how accurate executives are about the competitive environment may be less important for strategy, and the organizational changes that follow strategy, than the way they interpret and understand information about their environments. This suggests that investments in enhancing and shaping those interpretations may create a more durable competitive advantage then investments in obtaining more information.[2] The imperative in market-led strategy is the quest for superior interpretation and market understanding.

Industry-based research by the Business Performance Management Forum suggests that companies fail to respond to fast-changing markets because they are unable to understand and adjust to what their customers want. The failure of executives to "read" their markets means their companies struggle to meet the demands of increasingly competitive international markets and sophisticated customers.[3]

Procter and Gamble illustrates the competitive strength that comes from superior customer knowledge. A.G. Lafley has managed a transformation at P&G since he arrived in 2000, pushing the company up-market in the West and down-market in developing countries, concentrating resources in the top brands, and, in the merger with Gillette, creating the world's biggest consumer goods company which is outperforming rivals Colgate and Unilever.[4] Lafley has made the old P&G more innovative and outward-looking;

his mantra is "The customer is boss" and he believes that P&G must deliver more than brands—it must deliver a consumer experience. The new P&G invests less in formal marketing research and more in talking to people one-to-one in their homes, or in facilities that replicate the home environment—like the Consumer Village, where P&G meets consumers and works to identify desired consumer experiences with products. For example, research teams spent time in homes across the U.S., watching people clean baths, resulting in the Mr Clean Magic Reach—an extendible tool with changeable cleaning pads to reach high areas and tight corners in bathrooms. Researchers have spent weeks in the homes of low-income consumers to understand what it is like to live on $50 a month—resulting, for example, in Tide Clean White in China for hand-washing of clothes. P&G's virtual reality Cave is a walk-in three-dimensional room where computer-generated imagery allows P&G researchers to test alternative retail concepts and experiences. In addition, P&G has launched two new social networking sites to gain insight into consumer habits and preferences in online forums for women. Impressive innovation and responsiveness at P&G is built on processes for continuous learning and knowledge-generation.

A theme linking companies in many sectors is their capabilities in superior market sensing and their ability to develop competitive advantage from their learning processes. Boeing, for example, has been running an online naming contest—the "Name Your Plane" program—to connect not with airlines but with airline passengers, and to better understand their preferences.[5] At leading global steel producer, Arcelor Mittall, competitive advantage has been built over other global steel groups by a knowledge-sharing program in key activities, that encourages internationally-located operations to trade knowledge to benefit the network. At General Electric, top employees receive bigger bonuses and better promotion opportunities based on their knowledge sharing effectiveness.[6]

The challenge is increasingly one of knowledge management to build company-wide understanding of the marketplace and responsiveness, rather than simply collecting information. Market sensing and learning are required core competencies underpinning market-driven strategy.

In this chapter we examine how continuous learning about markets improves competitive advantage. First, we look at the relationship between market-driven strategy, market sensing, and learning processes. Then, we overview marketing information and knowledge development resources, including marketing research and information systems. Next, we look at marketing intelligence and knowledge management. Finally, several important issues are highlighted concerning the ethical issues which surround the collection and use of information in strategic marketing.

Market-Driven Strategy, Market Sensing, and Learning Processes

The ability to learn from customers underpins market-driven strategy. Market-driven firms are characterized by their ability to sense and respond to events and trends in their markets.[7] Market sensing is a key capability of the market-driven organization, concerned with the ability of organizations to continuously learn about their markets, and acts as an antecedent to market orientation.[8] Companies like P&G illustrate the close relationship between a market-oriented culture and organizational learning. Market orientation is both a culture and also a process committed to achieving superior customer value (Chapter 1). The process consists of information acquisition, broad information dissemination, and shared diagnosis and coordinated action.[9]

Market Sensing Processes

There are many approaches used by market-driven companies to understand the opportunities and threats emerging in their markets, and to predict how customers will react to changes in marketing strategy. They include:

- **Building open-minded inquiry processes**—market-driven organizations show an openness to studying change, to avoid complacency.
- **Analyzing competitors' actions**—detailed attention to rivals' tactics and strategies to develop understanding of their plans and capabilities.
- **Listening to front-line employees**—motivating the involvement of staff who are in contact with customers in building understanding of change and new opportunities and threats.
- **Searching for latent customer needs**—finding unserved needs through dialogue, observation and engagement with customers.
- **Scanning the periphery of the market**—actively looking for new opportunities in the market.
- **Encouraging experimentation**—building culture and process around continuous curiosity and new ideas.[10]

Companies like Toyota, Coach and Samsung demonstrate how the risk in markets can be shaped by paying continuous attention to how customers are changing, and evaluating more deeply how markets are developing. They have a "knowledge-intensity," in which revealing and relevant data are gathered and studied frequently. Knowledge intensity identifies both market risk and new opportunities for growth:

> It's answering the question: what do we know about customers that others don't? And then using that knowledge to make and keep profitable customers for life.[11]

Many of the characteristics of robust market sensing strategy and market knowledge intensity are illustrated in the preparations of Tesco, the British retailer, for entry to the U.S. market. This is described in the GLOBAL FEATURE. Sensing activities and the generation of market knowledge are important learning processes, often associated with the learning organization.

Learning Organization

Our understanding of the learning organization is not complete. The processes used by successful organizations continue to be studied and interpreted. However, it is clear that these organizations share several important characteristics, relevant to superior market sensing capabilities:

> Learning organizations are guided by a shared vision that focuses the energies of organizational members on creating superior value for customers. These organizations continuously acquire, process, and disseminate throughout the organization knowledge about markets, products, technologies, and business processes. They do not hesitate to question long held assumptions and beliefs regarding their business. Their knowledge is based on experience, experimentation, and information from customers, suppliers, competitors, and other sources. Through complex communication, coordination, and conflict resolution processes, these organizations reach a shared interpretation of the information, which enables them to act swiftly and decisively to exploit opportunities and defuse problems. Learning organizations are exceptional in their ability to anticipate and act on opportunities in turbulent and fragmenting markets.[12]

Additional research promises to further expand our knowledge about these complex and relevant organizational processes.

Tesco is the leading British supermarket retailer. The company has impressive international growth achievements. International developments are carefully tailored to local customer preferences and shopping behavior.

The United States is a difficult market for European retailers and many have failed to adapt to the demands of the American consumer or meet the intense competition.

Tesco is entering the U.S. market with Fresh & Easy, a new neighborhood store chain, focused on selling fresh food. Initial store openings are in Los Angeles, Las Vegas, Phoenix, and San Diego.

In planning the new venture, a Tesco team spent thousands of hours trying to discover what the American consumer wants:

- For two weeks 50 senior Tesco directors and managers lived the "American dream"— shopping and eating with U.S. families on the West Coast, even sharing their leisure activities.

- Hiring researchers to probe the refrigerator contents and lifestyles of sixty American families—checking what time they get up, what they eat for breakfast, when they shop, and preparing meals for them to try.

- A prototype store was built in secrecy in Los Angeles—the cover story was that they were making a movie, and executives used plastic bags of cash rather than corporate charge cards to buy things for the mock store, rather than tip off rivals to what they were doing. Consumers were flown in to test new ideas and products. More than 200 focus groups toured the store and gave feedback.

The goal is not to transfer the Tesco format from Britain to America, but to design an American store for American consumers.

While most Tesco U.S. stores will be located in prosperous suburbs surrounding Los Angeles, Phoenix, San Diego, and Las Vegas, others will be situated in poor, inner-city areas to address the "grocery gap"—the lack of supermarkets in inner city areas like South Central Los Angeles. Wal-Mart has been unable to establish inner city stores because of union opposition, but the new Tesco small retail formats do not need the environmental and planning approvals that have provided trade unions with the opportunity to block Wal-Mart's expansion.

Sources: Kerry Capell, "Tesco: California Dreaming?" *BusinessWeek,* February 27, 2006, 38. Richard Fletcher and John Harlow, "Tesco's Leahy Is Wild About the West," *Sunday Times,* September 3, 2006, 3–7. Jenny Davey, "Tesco Drives into America," *SundayTimes,* June 10, 2007, 3–1. Jonathan Birchall, "Tesco Aims to Fill 'Grocery Gap," *Financial Times,* Thursday, June 28, 2007, 20.

Learning and Competitive Advantage

The advantage gained from learning is that the organization is able to quickly and effectively respond to opportunities and threats, and to satisfy customers' needs with new products and improved services.[13] Learning capabilities and skills are central to business agility. Learning drastically reduces the time necessary to accomplish projects such as new product development. For example, fashion retailer H&M can get new designs into its stores in as little as three weeks, compared to the six months needed by traditional clothing retailers. H&M's designers carefully watch fashion trends—for example the worldwide sales reports. Identifying a new trend leads to immediate action—sketches and patterns which go electronically to fabrics buyers and production units worldwide. Executives in charge can conceive and produce new fashions on their own authority.[14] Superior learning capabilities and speed of learning create a new competitive advantage, which may be extremely difficult for competitors to imitate or equal.

Interestingly, market sensing capabilities and knowledge-generation may directly create competitive advantage. United Parcel Service (UPS) has a joint venture with the largest domestic marketing research agency in China. UPS used this relationship to sponsor two major studies of urban, middle-class China consumers, to identify the demand in different market segments for U.S. consumer products. The research reports were made available to U.S. small and medium-sized exporting firms identifying new business opportunities. The goal is to gain recognition of UPS as the knowledge leader on the subject, and the premier carrier flying to more points in China than any other U.S. airline.[15] Indeed, it is increasingly common with large customers that suppliers are required to identify end-use market opportunities for their buyers, and market learning and knowledge developments are key elements of competing.

Learning About Markets

Learning about markets requires developing processes throughout the organization for obtaining, interpreting, and acting on information from sensing activities. The learning processes of market-oriented companies include a sequence of activities beginning with open-minded inquiry.[16]

- **Objective Inquiry.** One danger to be avoided is not exploring new views about markets and competition, because they are not taken seriously. Search for information is of little value if management already has a fixed view on which new information will have no influence whatever it indicates. Not all companies see the value in continuous learning about markets. Managers who are not part of market-driven cultures may be unwilling to invest in information to improve their decision-making results. The same companies often encounter problems because of faulty or incomplete market sensing. Developing processes for continuous learning allows firms to capture more information about customers, suppliers, and competitors.[17] This capability provides the potential for growth based on informed decisions and a more complete mapping and analysis of the competitive environment. Firms can respond much more quickly to competitors' actions and take advantage of situations in the marketplace. Open-minded inquiry also helps to anticipate value migration threats, which are frequently initiated by competitors from outside the traditional market or industry.[18]

- **Information Distribution for Synergy.** The widespread distribution of information within the organization can leverage the value of the information by cutting across business functions to share information on customers, channels of distribution, suppliers, and competitors. Synergistic distribution works to remove functional hurdles and practices. Cross-functional teams are useful to encourage transfer of information across functions. The explosion in information connectivity (access) facilitates widespread information distribution.[19] Unbundling information from its physical carrier such as salespeople will provide access as well as speed in organizations. This will help cross-functional teams and alter hierarchical structures and proprietary information systems. Expanded information connectivity promises to encourage cooperation among functions and enhance organizational learning.

- **Mutually Informed Interpretations.** The mental model of the market guides managers' interpretation of information. The intent is to reach a shared vision about the market and about the impact that new information has on this vision. The market-oriented culture encourages market sensing. But the process requires more than gathering and studying information. "This interpretation is facilitated by the mental models of managers, which contain decision rules for deciding how to act on the information in light of anticipated outcomes."[20] The model reflects the executives' vision about the forces influencing the market and likely future directions of change. Learning occurs as members of the organization evaluate the results of their decisions based on their vision at the time the decisions were made. Deciding to take the high risk of cutting-edge ventures requires managers to reach a shared vision about uncertain future market opportunities.

- **Accessible Memory.** This part of the learning process emphasizes the importance of keeping and gaining access to prior learning. The objective is not to lose valuable information that can continue to be used. Doing this involves integrating the information into the organizational memory, and not losing information when people leave the organization. Information storage technology is an important facilitator, but the human factor remains critical.

Barriers to Market Learning Processes

In some situations learning processes may be ineffective. If managers do not understand or accept the value of new information and insight from the marketplace, they are likely to maintain existing perspectives and reject new ones. Rigid organizational structures and inflexible information systems may stand in the way of learning and knowledge-sharing in an organization. Political interests may defend the status quo, or the pressure of existing business operations may block the capacity of managers to take on new ideas. For example, Donald Sull describes companies falling prey to "active inertia"—responding to market shifts by accelerating activities that succeeded in the past—with the result that the market changes but the company does not and performance declines.[21] While investment in market sensing and learning process is mandated by both market orientation and the speed of market change, it is important to recognize that making these processes effective may require decisive management action to address organizational barriers.

The development of effective market-driven strategy is closely related to market sensing capabilities and market learning processes. Learning is increasingly proving to be a core capability of successful organizations. Nonetheless, it is important to recognize that learning and knowledge-creation disrupt existing business models and open the way to new ones. Consider, for example, the powerful customer-knowledge-based strategy at Best Buy, which is examined in the INNOVATION FEATURE.

Next, we examine the various methods of acquiring and processing information for use in marketing decision making. The objective is to show how the various information capabilities assist decision makers in strategic and operating decisions. A good marketing information management strategy takes into account the interrelationship of these capabilities.

Marketing Information and Knowledge Resources

Some marketing information resource development activity is concerned with creating processes for continuous scanning of markets for rapid noting of significant trends, events, and changes, while some may be undertaking specific focused studies to answer management questions—such as the effectiveness of an advertising campaign in a market. Marketing information resources can be generated internally—for example, in analyzing company records, or conducting market research studies—or externally—using marketing research agencies and consultants. Enhancing the marketing information resources available to executives may involve using information sources which are already in existence—for example, a Google search for competitor offerings—or the development of

Best Buy is the leading consumer electronics retailer in the U.S. and Canada. At the company's Minneapolis headquarters there is a mock retail hospital—a row of truncated beds containing effigies of stricken retailers like Kmart and Woolworths, with their corporate logos propped on the pillows and their weak financial results on bedside charts. A nearby sign declares: "This Is Where Companies Go When Their Strategies Get Sick."

To stay up with agile rivals like Wal-Mart and Costco, Best Buy has shifted its focus from products to consumers, in a new business model aimed at building a strong position with the most attractive consumer groups. The Best Buy strategy emphasizes treating each customer as a unique individual, developing solutions to meet their needs, and engaging employees to serve them.

New ideas come from listening to customers and employees more closely—ideas which previously would never have reached corporate headquarters. More than 120,000 employees act as agents of the customer, not the product manufacturer. Employees closely engaged with consumers identify new growth opportunities. Those with the highest potential have included small business customers, new services offerings and international growth—worth $230 billion in revenue in 2007.

Importantly, Best Buy actively shares its customer knowledge with manufacturers and product developers. The company has assembled a team of engineers, technologists and product experts from Apple, Xerox, Kodak and other leading R&D companies, focused on meeting new customer needs.

A core competency for innovation at Best Buy is gathering and synthesizing customer intelligence. This advances collaboration with suppliers, while building Best Buy's private label business in consumer electronics.

Sources: Devendra Mishra, "How Best Buy Uses Customer Input to Develop Private Label Line," www.dealerscope.com/story, June 14, 2006. Matthew Boyle, "Best Buy's Giant Gamble," *Fortune*, April 3, 2006.

Traditional Xerox product development involved building a prototype and then getting customer feedback. The company has lost business to Canon, IBM, Kodak, and other manufacturers.

However, new approaches focus on "customer-led innovation" or "dreaming with the customer." The goal is "Involving experts who know the technology with customers who know the pain points":

- For a new commercial printer idea—focus groups with customers were the first step. They found that customers were enthusiastic about the idea of a high-speed printer that could operate at half-speed if a problem arose, instead of shutting down. The result was Xerox's first two-engine model—the Nuvera 288 Digital Perfecting System.
- The research team had thought customers would want to use the second engine for fancy inks or special colors—not to help the broken machine to limp along until help arrived. Talking to customers changed their minds.
- Xerox's Group Technology Officer is investing more energy in finding out what customers think about Xerox's bright ideas: scientists and engineers are encouraged to meet face-to-face with the 1,500–2,000 customers who visit showrooms at the company's four global research facilities each year; others work on-site with a customer for a week or two each year to observe products in use; a team of ethnographers is charting customer behavior.

Source: Nanette Byrnes, "Xerox' New Design Team: Customers," *BusinessWeek,* May 7, 2007, 72.

new information resources through observation studies, or survey work. There is a wide variety of potential information sources in enhancing market learning processes, and the marketing information system provides a way of integrating these.

Importantly, marketing research and information resources should be seen as a model for innovation and change, rather than simply supporting the incremental administration of brands.[22] Marketing information may challenge the assumptions managers make about customers and provide them with new insights to guide strategy choices. An illustration is provided by Xerox's new product development approaches, described in the STRATEGY FEATURE.

Scanning Processes

Some information resource development is concerned with building processes for continuous monitoring of customers and markets to quickly identify and explain changes, new trends, and important events to which executives should respond. Effective scanning must balance the need to provide executives with relevant intelligence, while at the same time not attempting to report everything that happens in a market and overloading executives with information. Nonetheless, scanning may require watching for new opportunities outside the existing core markets.[23] The strategic challenge is to watch for the signals of disruptive change in the marketplace, which predict competitive battles to come, or highlight major strategic choices that executives must make about marketing strategy.[24] Scanning activities will vary across companies—from fashion trend spotting at H&M and Zara, to daily monitoring of steel prices in different markets at Arcelor Mittall.

Recent advances in monitoring center on Internet-based conversations. Public Services Broadcasting (PBS) uses the brand monitoring services of Umbria Inc. to analyze Web log (blog) conversations that include references to at least six of its top programs. The goal is to understand better and to watch continuously who is watching, talking about, promoting, and criticizing its programming online.[25] Relatedly, a number of major U.S. retailers have launched online review facilities to get rapid customer feedback through analyzing consumer opinion about products—purchasers of washing machines at Sears can post online reviews directly on the sears.com site. Sears judges that the opening of a dialogue with customers, from which they can learn, far outweighs any risks to the company's reputation.[26]

Organizing scanning effectively as a component of market sensing and learning may involve a number of initiatives or approaches:[27]

- Making **existing functional groups** responsible for scanning—though with the risk they will focus only on the familiar, not the periphery.
- **Create ad hoc issue groups**—identify important questions to address and assign them to task forces.
- **A high-level lookout**—IBM has a facility called the "Crow's Nest," a team scanning specific topics at the periphery of the organization and sharing insights with top management.
- **New initiatives**—Shell created its GameChanger Program in 1996, to encourage managers to envision and test new opportunities beyond the core business: in its first six years it commercialized thirty technologies and created three new businesses.
- **Investing in start-ups**—modest investments which may build a clear view of emerging technologies and markets.
- **Outsource**—use consultants for fresh perspectives on the business to be incorporated in strategic decision making.

One approach to presenting the result of scanning to executives is shown in Exhibit 5.1. The market sensing grid can be used as a participative, cross-functional structure for capturing insights from scanning (and other marketing information resources as they

EXHIBIT 5.1
A Grid for Market Sensing

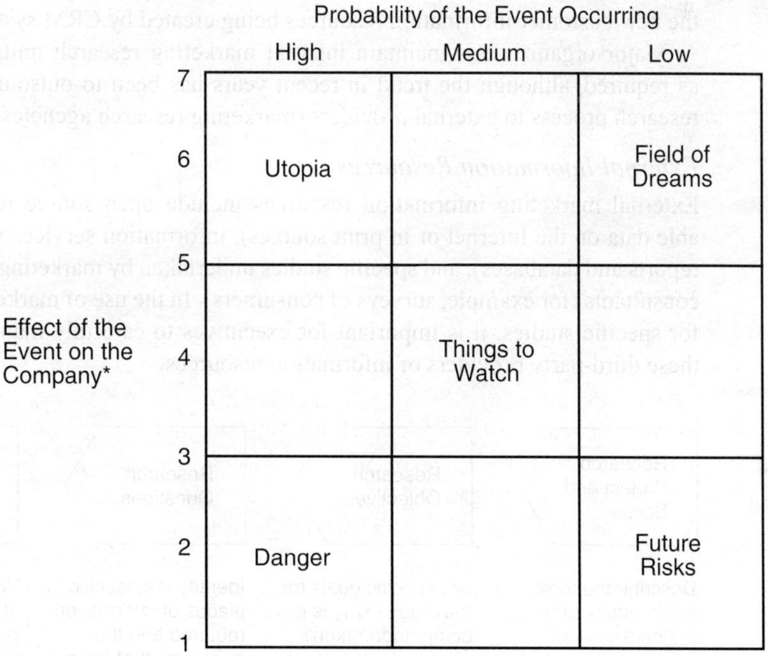

* 1 = Disaster, 2 = Very bad, 3 = Bad, 4 = Neutral, 5 = Good, 6 = Very good, 7 = Ideal.

become available). The process is to identify significant market events impacting on the business (or part of it) over a three to five year period, and to position events by estimated probability and impact. By including external views, such as these from suppliers, technology experts, distributors, and customers, it is possible to build a picture of the marketplace that may challenge existing company beliefs and management assumptions, and identify the highest priorities for further scanning and other information collection activities.[28]

Specific Marketing Research Studies

Marketing research is "the systematic gathering, recording, processing, and analyzing of marketing data, which—when interpreted—will help the marketing executive to uncover opportunities and to reduce risks in decision making."[29] Strategies for obtaining marketing research information include collecting existing information, using standardized research services, and conducting special research studies.

The starting point in undertaking specific marketing research studies is carefully defining the problem to be studied, indicating specific objectives, and determining what information is needed to help solve the problem. A problem definition framework to guide marketing research studies is shown in Exhibit 5.2.

Internal and External Marketing Information Resources

Marketing information resources exist internal to the company, as well as being collected from external sources.

Internal Information Resources

The internal information system of the firm affects the extent and ease of the collection of existing information. The nature and scope of the information and the information system network will vary greatly from firm to firm and among industries. Even simple information systems are able to generate analyses of sales and cost data. Many firms have extensive internal information systems, or at least the capability to implement such systems. Recall the new customer information resources being created by CRM systems (Chapter 4).

Major organizations maintain internal marketing research units to undertake studies as required, although the trend in recent years has been to outsource at least part of the research process to external providers (marketing research agencies).

External Information Resources

External marketing information resources include open source resources (freely available data on the Internet or in print sources), information services (paid-for, standardized reports and databases), and specific studies undertaken by marketing research agencies and consultants (for example, surveys of consumers). In the use of marketing research agencies for specific studies, it is important for executives to carefully manage relationships with these third-party providers of information resources.

EXHIBIT 5.2
Problem Definition to Guide Marketing Research Studies

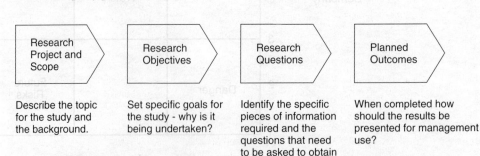

Research Project and Scope	Research Objectives	Research Questions	Planned Outcomes
Describe the topic for the study and the background.	Set specific goals for the study - why is it being undertaken?	Identify the specific pieces of information required and the questions that need to be asked to obtain that information	When completed how should the results be presented for management use?

Relationships with External Marketing Research Providers

Marketing information providers are likely to be marketing research firms. In the global marketing research industry in 2005, the top twenty-five marketing research firms had revenues of $14.4 billion.[30] These twenty-five organizations account for approximately two-thirds of world expenditures through commercial firms for research purposes. Exhibit 5.3 shows the top ten agencies in 2005. Agency research is predominantly market measurement studies, media audience research, and customer satisfaction measurement. Research into the impact of the Internet on markets is growing rapidly.

With the increasing globalization of brands and international competition, growing emphasis is being placed on a global perspective on marketing research. Particular interest is being shown in research in China and India, but also Latin America and parts of Africa, as well as eastern Europe and Russia. Particular problems in global research relate to cross-cultural differences that impact on information quality and characteristics. For example, an industry rule of thumb is that in the Americas the further North you go, the more reserved consumers are in what they express. The same consumer perception of the quality of a product might receive high scores in Latin America, average marks in the U.S. and less favorable reviews in Canada, because of cultural differences. For companies in international markets, making allowances for such cultural differences in examining global marketing research is an important challenge.[31]

Research studies follow a step-by-step process beginning with defining the problem to be investigated and the objectives of the research. A project proposal should indicate the objectives, research method, sampling plan, method of analysis, and cost. In deciding whether to undertake a special marketing research study and when interpreting the results, several considerations are important:

- **Defining the Problem.** Care must be exercised in formulating the research problem. It is essential to spell out exactly what information is needed to solve the problem. If this cannot be done, exploratory research should be conducted to help define the research

EXHIBIT 5.3   Top Ten Global Marketing Research Firms in 2005

Source: Extracted from "Honomichl Global Top 25" Special Section of Marketing News, August 15, 2006, p. H4.

Global Rank 2005	Organization	Headquarters	Web site	Global research revenue ($ millions)	Research-only full-time employees
1	VNU NV	Haarlem, Netherlands	vnu.com	3,537.9	37,884
2	Taylor Nelson Sofres plc	London, UK	tns-global.com	1,802.7	13,580
3	IMS Health Inc	Fairfield, Conn.	imshealth.com	1,754.8	6,900
4	GfK AG	Nuremburg, Germany	gfk.com	1,311.3	7,515
5	The Kantar Group	Fairfield, Conn.	kantargroup.com	1,237.2	6,600
6	Ipos Group SA	Paris, France	ipos.com	964.6	6,100
7	Information Resources Inc	Chicago	infores.com	624.0	3,604
8	Synovate	London, UK	synovate.com	602.9	5,559
9	Westat Inc	Rockville, Md	westat.com	420.4	1,835
10	Arbitron Inc	New York	arbitron.com	310.0	1,057

problem and determine the objectives of the project. Caution should be exercised to avoid defining a symptom rather than the underlying problem—do falling sales reflect declining market size, new competitive activity, or ineffective promotion? It is useful to prepare a written statement of the research problem, specific objectives, the information that is needed, information sources, and when the information is needed. When companies contract with research firms to do the research, it is important that the supplier be as familiar as possible with the problem to be studied. Management needs to clearly define the intended project and may choose to involve the research supplier in defining the problem. Failure to adequately define and clarify the problem to be studied may undermine relationships between client and research agency.

- **Understanding the Limitations of the Research.** Most studies are unable to do everything that the user wishes to accomplish and also stay within the available budget. Priorities for the information that is needed should be indicated. Also, obtaining certain information may not be feasible. For example, measuring the impact of advertising on profits may not be possible due to the influence of many other factors on profits. Research suppliers should be able to indicate the limitations that may exist for a particular project. Discussions with a potential supplier are advisable before making a final commitment to the project. This will be useful in finalizing information need priorities.

- **Quality of the Research.** There are many challenges to obtaining sound research results. The available evidence indicates that some studies are not well-designed and implemented and may contain misleading results. Factors that affect the quality of study results include the experience of the research personnel, skills in carefully managing and controlling the data collection process, the size of the sample, the wording of questions, and how the data are analyzed.

- **Costs.** Customized research studies are frequently expensive. The factors that affect study costs include sample size, the length of the questionnaire, and how the information will be obtained. The complexity of the study objectives and the analysis methods also increase the professional capabilities required in research personnel. Costs must be compared carefully to the likely benefits of the research to executives in making decisions.

- **Evaluating and Selecting Suppliers.** When selecting a marketing research supplier, it is useful to talk with prior clients to determine their satisfaction with the research firm. It is also important to identify consultants who are experienced in conducting the particular type of research needed by the user. Familiarity with the industry may also be important. Spending some time in evaluating a potential research supplier is very worthwhile. Experience and qualifications are important in selecting the supplier. Several useful screening questions are shown in Exhibit 5.4. These could be used to evaluate possible suppliers before asking for a detailed research proposal from the supplier.

- **Research Methods.** It is important to recognize that the research problem to be addressed indicates the appropriateness of different research methods. Large-scale consumer/company surveys may not be the most appropriate approach. Qualitative research methods, rather than surveys and other quantitative methods may be more appropriate in some circumstances. The use of focus groups is a typical way of collecting rich qualitative data, as compared to the more representative information from a survey or market test. For example, companies like Nokia use customer focus groups for several purposes. Testing a new messaging product for the U.S. market involved small groups giving individual feedback on product features, which were changed before the product launch. The global positioning statement for the Nokia 3390 phone—"You Make It You"—was created from unfavorable focus group reactions to company attempts to describe positioning.[32]

EXHIBIT 5.4
Screening Potential
Marketing Research
Suppliers

Research agency screening issues:

- Recommendations from other clients.
- Industry and manager opinions about the agency.
- Agency size and resources.
- Agency experience in this type of marketing research.
- Agency online capabilities.
- Sub-contracting arrangements at the agency.
- Interviewer training and supervision.
- Arrangements for validating data collected, e.g., by interviewers.
- Quality of research instruments for the project, e.g., questionnaires.
- Adequate arrangements for sampling.
- Quality of reports produced for other clients (if not confidential).
- Warranties and guarantees provided.

Existing Marketing Information Sources

In-Company Resources

There is considerable value and potential in using the information in the organization's current system. This is essential for the strategic mission of the firm, as well as for efficient utilization of assets. Information is a resource that needs to be consciously managed.[33] Management should structure the information system to capture this resource and control its use. Information is not a by-product of activities of the firm. It is a scarce, valuable resource that affects the future success or failure of the firm. Management may not have control over the actions of competitors or consumers, but an effective information system provides a way to anticipate and react.

The product mix and the nature of business operations influence what type of internal marketing information system is appropriate in a particular firm. Nonetheless, electronic information systems are necessary in all kinds of companies. The system needs to be designed to meet the information needs of the organization. Manufacturers have different information requirements from retailers or wholesalers. The size and complexity of the firm also influence the composition of the information system.

The costs and benefits of the information must be evaluated for both short-term and long-term planning. Incremental efforts and expenditures in the early stages of creating an internal information system may avoid future costly modifications. Achieving long-term performance may require temporary losses to finance a system. It is critical to consider a long-term perspective in evaluating information system decisions.

Harrah's Entertainment is an example of a company developing market-led strategy on the basis of existing information. Harrah's operates twenty-six casinos in thirteen states and in 2006 had more than $7 billion in revenue. In a sector known for fickle customers, Harrah's built a strategy based on customer loyalty. Harrah's has used the data in their customer loyalty program—the Total Gold card—to uncover consumer preferences based on tracking the millions of individual transactions conducted. Harrah's found that 26 percent of their customers generated 82 percent of their revenues. These were not the high-rollers targeted by competitors, they were former teachers, doctors, bankers and machinists—middle-aged and senior adults with discretionary time and income who enjoy gambling. They typically do not stay in casino hotels, but visit a casino on the way home from work or on a weekend night out. They respond differently to marketing and promotions because they enjoy the anticipation and excitement of gambling itself. Harrah's strategy is one of providing visibly higher levels of service to the customers with greatest value to the company. The transactional data can even be used to see which particular customers are playing which slot machines and to identify what it was about the particular machine that appealed to them. Harrah's successful strategy is driven by leveraging an existing information source to build competitive differentiation.[34]

Open Source Resources

A wide variety of information resources exist in the form of published information which can be accessed freely or at low cost. Government and international agencies provide valuable statistical sources in such areas as population trends, economic development, household purchasing, and international market differences. Universities, private research firms, industry and trade organizations, and consultants often publish useful information. Frequently these resources can be accessed online. For example, the World Bank (www.worldbank.com) and the U.S. Central Intelligence Agency publication *The World Factbook* (www.cia.gov/library) both provide concise and high quality data on the economic performance, governmental characteristics, communications, and infrastructure for the majority of countries in the world.

The Internet also provides a more general search facility, using Google or Yahoo, to identify sources of information on topics of interest, and online databases like Wikipedia, the online encyclopedia, can indicate prior research conducted on the topic of interest and further sources of information. While charges may apply to access some proprietary databases, many are available for no cost.

Some care is needed to evaluate the quality and objectivity of Internet information sources, but they should not be ignored as a marketing information resource.

Research Agency Resources

A wide variety of marketing information is available for purchase in special publications and on a subscription basis. A key advantage to the standardized information in these resources is that the costs of collection and analysis are shared by many users. The major limitation is that the information may not correspond well with the user's individual needs. Many services allow online access to data, enabling subscribers to automatically input external information into their own information systems.

Many standardized information services are available to meet a wide range of decision making needs. Some examples follow:[35]

Nielsen Media Research (www.nielsenmedia.com), part of the VNU Group, collects information on television audience measurement, with measurement meters in 10,000 U.S. homes assessing the viewing habits of 26,000 individuals. Measurement is provided through People Meters, set-tuning meters and diaries. More specialized measurements include Hispanic TV viewing in the U.S. Similar services are provided in other countries.

HIS Energy supplies information on drilling and production for firms interested in oil and gas exploration activities around the world (energy.his.com).

VNU Marketing Information group (including ACNielsen) provides retail measurement services (tracking product sales instore), consumer panel data (tracking the purchase behavior of more than 265,000 households in twenty-seven countries, mainly through the use of in-home scanners), and retailer services relating to instore effectiveness (www.vnu.com).

Using the large data banks collected and organized by these services, many different analyses can be made, depending on a company's information needs. The cost of gathering the information for use by one company would be prohibitive. By sharing the databases, a wide range of company information needs can be met.

Creating New Marketing Information

When existing marketing information resources do not address executives' research needs, then it may be necessary to collect new information. Approaches may include observation and ethnographic studies, quantitative research surveys, or Internet-based data collection. These data collection methods may require marketing research agency resources or be carried out by analysts inside the company.

Observation and Ethnographic Studies

Studies involving observation include, for example, counting customer traffic flows in a retail store, measuring waiting times for service in a shop, or the reaction of exhibition visitors to display stands.

Considerable attention is being given to the use of ethnographic approaches in collecting marketing information. Research suggests that it may be mistaken for executives to assume that consumers think in a well-reasoned or rational way, or that they can readily explain their thinking and behavior.[36] Accordingly, asking customers direct questions may give misleading results, and observational techniques like ethnography may be more insightful.

Ethnography is a social science based on anthropology, and its use in marketing studies is based on the idea that richer information and insight can be generated by immersion in the consumer's life. For example, a Henley Center project for a radio station called Modal Targeting highlighted the different modes that listeners go through during the day, to establish when they would be most receptive to different types of messages. Another ethnography project examined the behavior of parents and children shopping together by observing them in stores and recording basic information such as what they said to each other.[37]

When WD-40 wanted to reposition a product line as essential bathroom cleaners, the company undertook open-ended research to try to understand how consumers clean and how they shop. In-home ethnographies and focus groups examined consumer cleaning habits and product usage. They found consumers engage in two types of cleaning: weekly deep cleans and quick daily cleaning, and liked the idea of a brand focused on the bathroom. The brand's new positioning—X14 as The Bathroom Expert—and its competitive differentiation, come directly from insights into how people clean.[38]

There are a growing number of cases where traditional research approaches have failed to identify the insights important to new marketing strategy initiatives, but where qualitative, ethnographic research has proved effective:

Marriott used an ethnographic research agency to rethink the hotel experience for an increasingly important customer segment: the young, technology sophisticated "road warrior." A team including a designer, an anthropologist, a writer, and an architect spend six weeks touring hotels in twelve cities. They loitered in hotel lobbies, cafes, and bars, and asked guests to graph what they were doing hour by hour. The findings were: hotels are generally good at serving large parties, but not small groups of business travelers; hotel lobbies tend to be dark and poorly designed for doing business; Marriott lacked places where guests could comfortably combine work with pleasure outside their rooms. The result was the reinvention of the lobbies of Marriott and Renaissance Hotels, creating for each a social zone, with small tables, brighter lights and wireless Web access. Another area allows solo travelers to work in larger, quiet, semiprivate spaces.

General Electric used ethnographic research to develop its competitive positioning in the plastic fibers business—providing material for high value products like fire-retardant jackets and bulletproof vests. Researchers interviewed presidents, managers, and engineers at textile makers, touring their offices and photographing their plants. One major insight caused GE to rethink their strategy: GE thought that the fibers industry was a commodity business based on obtaining the cheapest materials. What it found instead was an artisan-based industry where customers wanted to collaborate from the earliest stages to develop high-performance materials—these are people with curiosity who like to get their hands dirty. GE now shares prototypes with customers, by-passing executives and working closely with engineers on technical questions. A considerable advantage has been achieved in access to a new market.[39]

Intel used ethnographic research to examine the use of computers by children in China. The work involved a two-and-a-half year study of Asian families in seven countries, examining their lives and values. In the U.S. the conventional parents' belief is that a child should be bought a computer in the early stage of his/her development—exposing the child to computing at the earliest age. In China, parents believe the opposite—they want children to learn Mandarin, and the computer is a distraction from this. This insight led Intel designers to launch a PC aimed at the Chinese home educational market, which has a touch-sensitive screen that allows users to write in Mandarin, tracing the order in which the character is being written (correct stroke order being an important part of the learning process). Chinese parents also had misgivings about allowing children unlimited Internet access. Locks and keys are important symbols of authority in China. Instead of installing a software-based key on the PC, Intel included a physical locking mechanism, visible elsewhere in the room, and reassuring to parents.[40]

The strength of qualitative research, such as ethnography, is in the richness of the data, which can create important insights into the market. The weakness is that the small numbers of subjects studied means that it is difficult to know if the results are representative of the wider market. Qualitative approaches of this kind may be followed by more conventional, quantitative studies to confirm and validate findings.

Research Surveys

Research surveys are initiated in response to problems or special information needs. Examples include market segmentation, new-product concept tests, product use tests, brand-name research, and advertising recall tests. Studies use field surveys involving personal, phone, or mail interviews with respondents who represent target populations.

For example, the mid-2000s saw Wal-Mart advertising its new Metro 7 fashion range in *Vogue* magazine and participating in the New York Fashion Week. The Metro 7 initiative reflects the findings of a survey of 6,000 consumers. The research survey established that a significant number of customers wanted more from their Wal-Mart store—they wanted more fashionable, contemporary style clothes. The opportunity was with the 25 to 45 year old Wal-Mart shopper, who was not necessarily more affluent than others, but who spent more on trendy fashion. After years of relying on its "Always Low Prices—Always" strategy, and leaving consumer research to suppliers, weak sales growth is driving Wal-Mart to build a new market research and consumer insights competency within the business to enhance the ability to adapt to market change and identify new opportunities.[41]

Internet-Based Research

The impact of Internet resources on the ability to collect new market information is considerable. New and speedy ways of conducting studies using electronic questionnaires, e-mail questionnaires, and electronic panels are expanding rapidly. Expenditure on Internet-based marketing research now exceeds $1.2 billion annually.[42] The ability to evaluate customer feedback and monitor customer Web-based behavior can also provide insights and identify new opportunities (scanning). The INTERNET FEATURE summarizes some major impacts of the Internet on marketing information collection.

Online market research services offer less expensive and more rapidly available market research surveys. For example, InsightExpress provides clients with a survey template to build an online questionnaire, allowing them to sample from a panel of 100 million

Online Surveys

- Surveys based on the Internet are a fast and inexpensive way to generate feedback on products and marketing communications. Limitations are that only online customers can participate and there is growing resistance to unsolicited marketing messages and spam among Web users.
- They may use tools companies already have at hand—the Web site, targeted e-mails, e-mail blasts, or other formats like Personal Digital Assistants.
- The only cost for the research may be employee time in writing the survey and posting it. Cheaply available self-service Web tools like Zoomerang or SurveyMonkey allow users to type in questions and click on the survey report.
- Companies unable to fund traditional marketing research can now afford to survey customers and uncover new business opportunities at low cost.

Customer Feedback and Peer-to-Peer Web Communication

- Some companies have designed online systems to allow consumers to voice opinions and describe experiences and evaluations of products and services.
- Online customer feedback is a form of digitized word-of-mouth communication.
- Channels for online feedback include message boards, discussion forums, opinion forums, newsgroups, and chat rooms.
- There are a growing number of independent online goods and service review forums, such as Epinions.com and Rateitall.com, where buyers pool product assessments on a peer-to-peer basis.

Monitoring Customer Web Behavior

- Controversially, there has been a major increase in the use of spyware and adware among Internet companies. Many have ethical reservations about this technology and some user reactions are hostile.
- Spyware and adware are cookies that users download from the Internet—some say often unwittingly and without intention—that hide themselves on the user's hard drive.
- Spyware collects personal data and tracks the user's Web site use, while adware observes Web visits and provides relevant pop-up ads based on the user's Internet use.

Sources: Ben Elgin, "Guess What—You Asked for Those Pop-Up Ads," *BusinessWeek,* June 28, 2004, 88–90; Catherine Arnold, "Cast Your Net," *Marketing News,* Nov. 24, 2003, 15–19; Robin T. Peterson and Zhilin Yang, "Web Product Reviews Help Strategy," *Marketing News,* April 1, 2004, 18–20.

with a patented sampling methodology, pay by credit card, and download results within a few days. An online research project may cost a small fraction of a traditional research project. Ice cream company Ben & Jerry's is an Insight Express client which transferred to online research because traditional data collection was too slow. An in-house database of Ben & Jerry's loyal customers is sampled alongside an Insight Express panel to test new flavors and new products. Reservations exist regarding the quality of the data produced by online services, but they provide a cheap route to sensing the market quickly.

Useful insights can also be built by examining customer online behavior. The key words entered into search engines like Google, MSN, and Yahoo provide an insight into competitive preferences and purchase intentions, bearing in mind that nearly 80 percent of all online purchases start at a major search engine. User clicks on a company's website can be counted to identify successful promotions and cross-sells between products. The website can be used as a platform for experimentation—comparing the impact of alternate content on site visitors. The importance of online research of this kind is underlined by customer multiple channel behavior—it is estimated that almost 90 percent of online shoppers actually complete their purchase by buying offline at the store.[43]

For example, Anglo-Dutch food and personal products company Unilever spends around $400 million a year on marketing research. It now conducts more than 80 percent of its U.S. research online. The policy is to exploit the speed and low cost of the Web to research consumer behavior. Unilever's estimate is that the Web is 10 to 20 percent cheaper than traditional data collection methods. The company expects increasingly to shift to Internet projects in other countries—the trigger is when a minimum of half the population has Internet access. Unilever data testing suggests Internet responses were more honest than those produced by traditional methods, and the company is moving from brand research into more strategic work in Internet research projects.[44]

Marketing and Management Information Systems

Enhanced technology capabilities have led many companies to invest in formalized information systems to exploit their data resources. Important issues include the establishment of specialized marketing information systems, as well as more general management information systems and the potentials for marketing decision support systems and expert systems.

Marketing Information Systems

The marketing information system provides a mechanism for integrating marketing information and intelligence resources. A marketing information system "consists of people, equipment, and procedures to gather sort, analyze, evaluate and distribute needed, timely, and accurate information to marketing decision makers." It is developed from internal company records, marketing intelligence activities, and marketing research.[45]

Importantly, while companies have invested heavily in developing information systems, inward-oriented firms emphasize enhanced operating efficiency and reduced costs through automating information processing. The market-oriented firm, however, looks for ways in which information systems can make the firm more effective in the marketplace.[46]

Databases are a particularly relevant form of information resource, frequently supported by CRM systems. For example, in its European retail operation, supermarket Tesco uses its loyalty club data to indicate demographic, income, and housing characteristics of consumers in the catchment area of a store to design appropriate product assortments—stores near large universities may concentrate on high-value ready-meal replacements from pizzas to take-away, pre-cooked curries, while stores in family residential areas emphasize extensive food choices, cooking ingredients and products for babies and children. Recall the growing role of Customer Relationship Management (CRM) technology in building new databases (Chapter 4)—or data warehouses—from the company's own customer contacts. These new data sources are the focus of many data mining exercises and can create new insights into customer behavior.

Companies vary considerably in the degree and way to which they have formalized marketing information systems. It is useful to consider the nature of more general management information systems and moves towards the development of marketing decision-support systems for additional insight. The marketing information system may operate as an independent entity, or as a component of the more general management information system.

Management Information Systems

Management information systems (MIS) provide raw data to decision makers throughout a firm. The system collects data on the transactions and operations of the firm and may include competitor and environmental information. The decision makers (and systems analysts) are responsible for extracting the data relevant for a decision and in the appropriate format to facilitate the process. The system can provide information for decisions at all levels of the organization. Lower and middle-level managers are likely to use the system most often for operating decisions. The system may generate routine reports for frequent operating decisions, such as weekly sales by product, or may be queried for special analyses on an as-needed basis. Non-routine decisions may consist of tracking the sales performance of a sales district over several months, determining the number of customer returns for a particular good, or listing all customers or suppliers within a given geographic area. The basic MIS collects data and allows for retrieval and manipulation of format in an organized manner. Typically, the MIS does not interact in the decision making process. More advanced MIS capabilities provide important decision analysis capabilities.

Marketing Decision-Support Systems

A decision-support system (DSS) assists in the decision making process using the information captured by the MIS. A marketing decision-support system (MDSS) integrates data that are not easily found, assimilated, formatted, or readily manipulated with software and hardware into a decision making process that provides the marketing decision maker with assistance when needed.[47] The MDSS allows the user flexibility in applications and in format. A MDSS can be used for various levels of decision making ranging from determining reorder points for inventory to launching a new product.

MDSSs may operate autonomously or instead may require interaction with the decision maker during the process. There may be several stages before a recommendation is formed where the decision maker responds to queries to refine the scenario. Thus, an interactive MDSS requires more assistance from the decision maker and has more room for variation than an autonomous MDSS. The system is dependent on the quality and accuracy of the information and assumptions that are used in designing the system. The process should be viewed as a tool to assist in decision making and is not a final product in itself.

Expert systems are an extension of decision support systems and apply a variety of sophisticated models to make inferences from a knowledge base, which are significant to marketing decisions.[48] These tools have considerable potential for leveraging the value of marketing information.

Marketing Intelligence and Knowledge Management

Extracting the maximum sensing and learning value from marketing information resources is enhanced by efforts to develop formal information systems. However, in the pursuit of this goal, increasing attention is also being given to active marketing intelligence gathering and knowledge management approaches. The potential for a chief knowledge officer to manage learning processes is a relevant development, with the goal of leveraging customer knowledge for competitive advantage.

Marketing Intelligence

Importantly, we have shown that the emphasis on market sensing in market-driven companies does not rely on hard data alone. For example, many companies have invested in in-company intelligence units to co-ordinate and disseminate "soft" or qualitative data and improve shared corporate knowledge.[49] Intelligence may come from published materials in trade and scientific journals, salesperson visit reports, programs of customer visits by executives, social contacts, feedback from trade exhibitions and personal contacts, or even rumor in the marketplace. Formal marketing intelligence gathering activities may be an important element of the scanning processes we discussed earlier.

Knowledge Management

There is increasing recognition that knowledge about customers should be managed as a strategic asset, because competitive advantage can be created by not merely possessing current market information but by knowing how to use it. Market knowledge is inextricably linked to organizational learning and market orientation in the market-driven company.[50]

Peter Drucker argues, for example, that often 90 percent of the information that companies collect is internal—market research and management reports that only tell executives about their own company—while the real challenge is to build knowledge about new markets they do not yet serve and new technologies they do not yet possess.[51] Knowledge that builds competitive advantage involves major emphasis on rigorous customer perspectives and competitor comparisons.[52]

Role of the Chief Knowledge Officer

To meet this challenge, some companies have established positions with titles such as chief knowledge officer or chief learning officer. While the titles and the job responsibilities vary, all appear linked to improving an organization's knowledge management and learning processes. The chief knowledge/learning manager role may be a staff position with only a small number of personnel involved, or a broader role with responsibility for building infrastructure and related knowledge management functions.[53] The position may report to the chief executive officer, information officer or other high level executive. Companies that have these positions include Ernst & Young, IBM, and the World Bank.

Other organizations have developed a management role described as a chief learning officer, with a more general role in developing and enhancing company-wide learning processes. For example, Shell Oil has appointed a head of global learning to stimulate individual and organizational skills in learning focused on business improvement.[54] Interestingly, the Shell initiative underlines the cross-functional nature of organizational learning processes, and the potential role of human resource development functions in working with departments like marketing to enhance learning processes.

While there appear to be differences between the role and functions of knowledge and learning officers, both positions do not occur in the same company.[55] Knowledge management is concerned with knowledge (information) collection and linking information within the organization. While the future of the position is not clear, as it develops there is likely to be a relationship between knowledge management and the discussion in this chapter of continuous learning about markets.

For example, Xerox claims a saving of $200 million from a single project that uncovered and shared expertise across the group. Internal benchmarking found its Austrian subsidiary was unusually successful at persuading customers to renew contracts. Sharing the Austrian approach with other groups brought 70 percent up to the Austrian standard in three months.[56]

Leveraging Customer Knowledge

One study is illustrative of methods being employed by companies to improve the availability and use of customer knowledge in impacting strategic decisions.[57]

Creating "Customer Knowledge Development Dialogues"

For example, Chrysler's Jeep division runs customer events called "Jeep Jamborees," attracting enthusiasts for the vehicle. Jeep employees connect with customers through informal conversations and semi-formal round-tables. Engineers and ethnographic researchers focus on the Jeep owner's relationship with the vehicle, driving changes to existing models and plans for new models.

Operating Enterprise-Wide "Customer Knowledge Communities"

IBM, for example, uses collaborative Internet workspace called the *CustomerRoom* with major accounts, where individuals throughout its divisions and functions can exchange knowledge with each other and with the customer.

Capturing Customer Knowledge at the Point of Customer Contact

Customer Relationship Management systems capture customer behavior and response information which offers rich potential for better insights into issues like customer defection and competitors' strengths, as well as emerging customer needs and perceptions.

Management Commitment to Customer Knowledge

Management responsibility includes investing resources, time, and attention in maintaining customer dialogs and communities as a commitment to enhanced organizational understanding of the customer. For example, the Vice President of Marketing at Ford's LincolnMercury division actively participates in customer-related chatrooms on the Internet and encourages other employees to follow this lead. Other approaches include planned programs of customer visits for cross-functional teams of executives as a systematic way of acquiring customer information, but also building superior understanding and responsiveness to customer perspectives.[58]

Ethical Issues in Collecting and Using Information

Lastly, important privacy and ethical issues concerning the role of information in the organization need to be assessed by managers and professionals. Questions regarding ethical and socially responsible behavior are escalating in importance for individual executives and organizations. These questions may impact particularly on approaches to collecting customer information, and the uses made of that information.

Invasion of Customer Privacy

The dramatic increase in use of databases has generated concerns about the invasion of privacy of individuals. Companies have responded to the issue by asking customers to indicate their preferences concerning mailing lists and other uses of the information. Nonetheless, concerns about this issue will undoubtedly continue as the sophistication of communications technology and software continues to develop.

Consider, for example, the use of patient information in the drug industry. Database marketing by pharmaceutical companies is guided by information obtained from toll-free number calls, subscription to magazines, and pharmacy questionnaires.[59] This information can be used to guide database marketing programs, targeting people with specific health concerns such as depression, arthritis, and other problems. Some patients are objecting about the use of their prescription data to guide direct mail and other promotional efforts. Yet further objections relate to the possible sharing of medical information databases of this kind with other parties, such as insurance companies who may want to determine premiums on the basis of health data for existing patients and their children.

Indeed, public concern about identity theft abuses surrounding companies holding and selling personal information is leading to greater regulatory control of individual information use.[60] Further privacy dilemmas are raised, for example, by the potential for using Radio Frequency Identification (RFID) tags to monitor consumer products throughout their life—RFID tags in clothes could be used to track the wearer's movements and activities throughout the life of the apparel. While the data possibilities are rich, concerns exist over invasion of privacy and inappropriate use of the data collected.[61] Although the Google search engine generates rich and valuable data about individuals' Web behavior of considerable relevance to advertising and marketing decisions, critics are concerned that Google has unwittingly created a form of privatized surveillance well suited to government use in countries like China.[62] Companies have responded to the mood of the public concerning environmentalism and ethical consumerism, and individual privacy rights may also be a leading issue.

Information and Ethics

Related to the issue of invasion of privacy is the issue of how companies and research suppliers should respond to ethical issues. For example, should a prospective client share a supplier's detailed project proposal with a competing supplier? A central issue concerns which organization pays for the cost of preparing the proposal. If the proposal is prepared at the expense of the supplier, then the proposal is the property of the supplier.[63] Sharing the proposal with its competition would be an issue of questionable ethics.

Other issues relate to the ways in which information is collected and from whom it is collected. There are major professional restrictions, for example, on collecting marketing information from children. The possible use of Internet chat-rooms to create dialogues with child consumers avoids conventional restrictions, but poses a substantial ethical dilemma for executives presented with such data, as well as risks to corporate reputation.

In terms of the dilemmas which may emerge in how information is collected, consider the use of medical brain scanning technology to capture clues as to consumer product preferences and reactions to marketing messages described in the ETHICS FEATURE. The use of brain scanning technology promises very useful marketing information. Brain scanning studies have examined: predicting memory recall based on the amount of memory encoding taking place when a person scans a product or package; comparing brain responses to new products compared to existing versions; providing quantitative evaluation of the memorability and comprehensibility of advertisements placed in different media; providing flavor and fragrance houses with physiological evidence that their flavors and fragrances really do induce the mood swings they claim.[64] Executives face difficult issues in deciding if "neuromarketing" is an acceptable use of medical technology or whether it breaches the individual's right to privacy.

Information sharing with research suppliers, other external contractors, strategic alliance partners, and acquisition/merger prospects often involves highly confidential information. There are many possible situations that present ethical questions and concerns. Companies normally sign confidentiality agreements. Nonetheless, revealing trade secrets is a risk that relies primarily on the ethical behavior of the participants. Moreover, these situations offer excellent opportunities for learning.

Importantly, the generation, collection, and application of intelligence and information resources in strategic marketing must be conducted within a framework provided by corporate ethical guidelines and social responsibility initiatives, as well as the individual ethical standards of executives, and the expectations of stakeholder groups like shareholders and employees. Attention to the appropriateness of behavior in this area is a growing concern.

- Medical research has created the magnetic resonance imaging (MRI) scanner to detect injury and disease associated with the brain. Some suggest these should be redefined as "market research imaging" machines.
- More recent MRI technology and software allows the machine to picture the flow of blood in the brain in response to visual stimuli—almost a picture of thoughts pinpointing what part of the brain recognizes things, enabling researchers to understand better the very essence of the mind and how it thinks, decides and feels. This is "functional" MRI technology (fMRI).
- A controversial use of fMRI is probing customer preferences—sometimes called "neuromarketing"—researchers at Harvard, Emory, Caltech and Baylor are studying how consumer preferences for different kinds of products track with activity in different parts of the brain, as well as reactions to marketing messages.
- A new company in California offers a service to Hollywood studios to test audiences as they watch movie trailers to see which generate the most "brain buzz."
- Consumer watchdog Gary Ruskin complains "it's wrong to use a medical technology for marketing, not healing."
- Other ethical concerns include the issue of privacy.
- Prominent neurobiologist Donald Kennedy, former head of the U.S. Food and Drug Administration, urges caution in collecting brain data: "Our brains are us, marking out the special character of our personal capacities, emotions and convictions . . . As to my brainome, I don't want anyone to know it for any purpose whatsoever."
- A further issue is whether brain scan data should be made available to insurers, employers, and even law enforcement agencies.

Source: Joan O'C. Hamilton, "Journey to the Center of the Mind," *BusinessWeek,* April 19, 2004, 66–67. Aili McConnon, "If Only I Had a Brain to Scan," *BusinessWeek,* January 22, 2007, 19.

Summary

Developing and enhancing market learning processes are critical activities in the market oriented company and underpin the development of effective market-driven strategies. Responding effectively to fast-changing markets and intense competition demands deep customer knowledge and insight. Market knowledge management is a core capability for companies pursuing a market-driven approach to strategy.

Market sensing processes are the foundation of the learning organization for developing competitive advantage from superior customer understanding. The basis for superior customer knowledge is a range of marketing information and knowledge resources. These resources include active scanning processes, as well as specific marketing research studies. Information and intelligence resources are both internal to the company and external in the marketplace, and both require management attention. Where external information resources are accessed through the use of a marketing research agency, careful attention needs to be paid to managing the relationship with the information provider.

A useful distinction is between existing and new information resources. Existing resources include in-company records, open source resources like online databases, and published research agency studies. Creating new marketing information may involve observation and ethnographic studies, research surveys, and Internet-based research. Marketing and management information systems provide frameworks for integrating information resources and displaying them to decision makers.

Underpinning the effective management of market learning processes are active approaches to marketing intelligence gathering and to knowledge management. The role of the chief knowledge officer or the chief learning officer is becoming increasingly relevant to developments in developing a company's learning capabilities. The goal is leveraging customer knowledge effectively.

There is growing attention to the ethical issues surrounding the collection and use of market and customer information. Individual rights to privacy, information sharing, collecting data from the vulnerable, and invasive data collection approaches are illustrative. Corporate ethical frameworks and the ethical standards of individual executives are important in ensuring responsible behavior in this area.

Questions for Review and Discussion

1. Discuss how an organization's marketing information skills and resources contribute to its distinctive capabilities.

2. How would you explain to a group of top-level executives the relationship between market-orientation and continuous learning about markets?

3. Outline an approach to developing an effective market sensing capability for a regional full-service bank.

4. Compare and contrast the use of standardized information services as an alternative to special research studies for tracking the performance of a new packaged food product.

5. Suppose the management of a retail floor covering (carpet, tile, wood) chain is considering a research study to measure household awareness of the retail chain, reactions to various aspects of wallpaper purchase and use, and identification of competing firms. How could management estimate the benefits of such a study in order to determine if the study should be conducted?

6. Are there similarities between marketing intelligence and the operations of the U.S. Central Intelligence Agency? Do companies ever employ business spies?

7. What obstacles may be faced in enhancing a company's ability to learn more and better about its customers, and how should they be addressed?

8. Why would a company consider observational or ethnographic research in preference to conventional surveys?

9. Data mining from databases is receiving increased attention in many companies. Discuss the underlying logic of data mining.

10. What are the relevant issues that need to be considered when obtaining the services of an outside supplier for a marketing research project?

11. What do you consider to be the proper ethical limits on the collection and use of customer information by companies?

Internet Applications

A. Revisit the list of major marketing research agencies in Exhibit 5.3. Visit several of the websites listed. Examine the major types of information provided both as standardized services and special study capabilities. List these and identify the ways in which such resources can impact on marketing decisions.

B. Select a well-known company or brand and use a search engine to find Web pages that include its name. Review the content of blogs and online reviews, and examine the lessons that the company should learn from this feedback. Discuss the impact of Internet-based information on traditional ideas about confidentiality and privacy.

Feature Applications

A. Revisit the INTERNET FEATURE "The Web and Marketing Information." What are the major advantages of the Web in developing marketing information resources, and what are the potential disadvantages? How do these two lists balance against each other?

B. Examine the marketing information example described in the ETHICS FEATURE "Neuromarketing." Should limits be placed on the ability of commercial organizations to capture and exploit information about individuals for reasons of privacy? Why should such issues concern marketing executives?

Notes

1. George S. Day, "The Capabilities of Market-Driven Organizations," *Journal of Marketing,* October 1994, 43.

2. Kathleen M. Sutcliffe and Klaus Weber, "The High Cost of Accurate Knowledge," *Harvard Business Review,* May 2003, 74–82.

3. Francesco Guerrera, "US Groups 'Fail to Understand Customer Needs,'" *Financial Times,* Monday, June 5, 2006, 27.

4. This illustration is adapted from: Andrew Davidson, "The Razor-Sharp P&G Boss," *The Sunday Times,* December 3, 2006, 3–6. Neil Buckley, "The Power of Original Thinking," *Financial Times,* Friday, January 14, 2005, 11. Alan Mitchell, "P&G Takes Hoppers to Another World in the War of the Brands," *Financial Times,* Wednesday, October 18, 2006, 10. Lisa Cornwell, "P&G Launches Two Social Networking Sites," *Marketing News,* February 1, 2007, 21.

5. Allison Enright, "Boeing by Design," *Marketing News,* October 1, 2005, 10.

6. Peter Marsh, "Skills Sharing Fires Up Performance," *Financial Times,* Thursday, September 15, 2005, 19.

7. George S. Day, "Managing the Market Learning Process," *Journal of Business and Industrial Marketing,* Vol. 17 No. 4 2002, 240–252.

8. George S. Day, "The Capabilities of Market-Driven Organizations," *Journal of Marketing,* Vol. 56 October 1994, 37–52.

9. Stanley F. Slater and John C. Narver, "Market Orientation, Customer Value, and Superior Performance," *Business Horizons,* March/April 1994, 22–27.

10. George S. Day, "Managing the Market Learning Process," *Journal of Business and Industrial Marketing,* Vol. 17 No. 4 2002, 240–252.

11. This illustration is based on Adrian Slywotsky and Karl Weber, *The Upside: From Risk Taking to Risk Shaping* (New York: Crown Business, 2007).

12. Ibid., 71.

13. Ibid.

14. Steve Hamm, "Speed Demons," *BusinessWeek,* March 27, 2006, 67–76.

15. Michael Fielding, "Special Delivery: UPS Conducts Surveys to Help Customers Export to China," *Marketing News,* February 1, 2007, 13.

16. The following discussion is based on Day, "The Capabilities of Market-Driven Organizations." See also Stanley F. Slater and John C. Narver, "Market-Oriented Isn't Enough: Build a Learning Organization," Report No. 94–103, Cambridge, MA: Marketing Science Institute, 1994.

17. Nigel F. Piercy and Nikala Lane, "Marketing Implementation: Building and Sustaining a Real Market Understanding," *Journal of Marketing Practice: Applied Marketing Science,* Vol. 2 No. 3 1996, 15–28.

18. Adrian J. Slywotzky, *Value Migration* (Boston: Harvard Business School Press, 1996).

19. Philip B. Evans and Thomas S. Wurster, "Strategy and the New Economics of Information," *Harvard Business Review,* September–October 1997, 70–82. See also, Philip Evans and Thomas S. Wurster, *Blown To Bits: How the New Economics of Information Transforms Strategy* (Boston, MA: Harvard Business School Press, 2000).

20. Day, "The Capabilities of Market-Driven Organizations," 43.

21. Donald Sull, *Why Good Companies Go Bad and How Great Managers Remake Them* (Cambridge MA: Harvard Business School Press, 2005).

22. Peter Lorange, "Memo to Marketing," *Sloan Management Review,* Winter 2005, 16–20.

23. George S. Day and Paul J. H. Shoemaker, "Scanning the Periphery," *Harvard Business Review,* November 2005, 135–148.

24. Clayton M. Christensen, Scott D. Anthony and Erik A. Roth, "Seeing What's Next: Using the Theories of Innovation to Predict Industry Change" (Boston MA: Harvard Business School Press, 2004).

25. Allison Enright, "Listen Learn: Net Chatter Coverage Yields Valuable Insight," *Marketing News,* April 1, 2007, 25.

26. Jonathan Birchall, "Retailers Give Customers the Final Word," *Financial Times,* Friday, October 6, 2006, 13.

27. This illustration is adapted from George S. Day and Paul J. H. Shoemaker, "Scanning the Periphery," *Harvard Business Review,* November 2005, 135–148.

28. Nigel F. Piercy and Nikala Lane, "Marketing Implementation: Building and Sustaining a Real Market Understanding," *Journal of Marketing Practice: Applied Marketing Science,* Vol. 2 No. 3 2006, 15–28.

29. William R. Dillon, Thomas J. Madden, and Neil H. Firtle, *Marketing Research in a Marketing Environment,* 3rd ed. (Homewood, IL: Richard D. Irwin, 1994), 737.

30. Jack Honomichl, "No Great Gains," *Marketing News,* August 15, 2006, H54.

31. Catherine Arnold, "Global Perspective," *Marketing News,* May 15, 2004, 43.

32. Deborah L. Vence, "Turned on a Dime," *Marketing News,* March 15, 2004.

33. Kenneth C. Laudon and Jane Price Laudon, *Management Information Systems* (New York: Macmillan, 1988), 235.

34. Gary Loveman, "Diamonds in the Data Mine," *Harvard Business Review,* May 2003, 109–113.

35. A description of the top twenty-five companies in the global marketing research industry can be found in the "Honomichl Global 25" Special Section of the *Marketing News,* August 15, 2005, H1–H62.

36. Gerald Zaltman, *How Customers Think: Essential Insights into the Mind of the Market* (Boston MA: Harvard Business School Press, 2003).

37. Rupert Steiner, "Homing In on Consumers," *Sunday Times,* August 25, 2002, 3–8.

38. Michael Fielding, "A Clean Slate," *Marketing News,* May 1, 2007, 9.

39. Spencer E. Ante, "The Science of Desire," *Business Week,* June 5, 2006, 98–106.

40. Kim Thomas, "Anthropologists Get to the Bottom of Customers' Needs," *Financial Times,* Wednesday, August 24, 2005, 9.

41. Jonathan Birchall, "What Wal-Mart Women Really Really Want," *Financial Times,* Monday, October 10, 2005, 11.

42. Allison Enright, "Web Consumer Habits Yield Real-World Results," *Marketing News,* November 1, 2006, 20.

43. Eric J Hansen, "Apply Online Market Data for Offline Insights," *Marketing News,* April 1, 2007, 30.

44. Carlos Grande, "Unilever to Cash In on Benefits of Web Research," *Financial Times,* Tuesday, April 17, 2007, 18.

45. Philip Kotler and Kevin Lane Keller, *A Framework for Marketing Management,* 3rd ed. (Upper Saddle River NJ: Pearson/Prentice-Hall, 2007), 41.

46. Noel Capon and James M. Hulbert, *Marketing Management in the 21st Century* (Upper Saddle River, NJ: Prentice-Hall, 2001).

47. Nikolaos F. Matsatsinis and Y. Siskos, *Intelligent Support Systems for Marketing Decisions* (New York: Springer, 2002). Berend Wierenga and Gerrit van Bruggen, *Marketing Management Support Systems: Principles, Tools and Implementation* (New York: Springer, 2000).

48. Arvind Rangaswamy, Raymond R. Burke, Jerry Wind and Jehoshua Eliashberg, *Expert Systems for Marketing,* Marketing Science Institute Working Paper 87–107, Cambridge MS: Marketing Science Institute, 1987. Luiz Moutinho, Bruce Curry, Fiona Davies and Paulo Rita, *Computer Modelling and Expert Systems in Marketing* (London: Routledge, 1995).

49. Thomas A. Stewart, "Getting Real About Brainpower," *Fortune,* November 27, 1995.

50. Rohit Deshpande, "From Market Research Use to Market Knowledge Management," in Rohit Deshpande (ed.), *Using Market Knowledge* (Thousand Oaks, CA: Sage, 2001), 1–8.

51. Peter Drucker, *Peter Drucker on the Profession of Management.* (Boston, MA: Harvard Business School Press, 1998).

52. George S. Day, "Learning About Markets," in Rohit Deshpande (ed.), *Using Market Knowledge* (Thousand Oaks, CA: Sage, 2001), 9–30.

53. Thomas A. Stewart, "Is This Job Really Necessary?" *Fortune,* January 12, 1998, 154–155.

54. See http://sww-learn.sshel.com.

55. Thomas Stewart, *Fortune,* ibid.

56. Vanessa Houlder, "Xerox Makes Copies," *Financial Times,* July 14, 1997, 10.

57. Eric Lesser, David Mundel and Charles Wiecha, "Managing Customer Knowledge," *Journal of Business Strategy,* November/December 2000, 35–37.

58. Edward F. McQuarrie and Shelby H. McIntyre, "Implementing the Marketing Concept Through a Program of Customer Visits," in Rohit Deshpande (ed.), *Using Market Knowledge* (Thousand Oaks, CA: Sage, 2001), 163–190.

59. William M. Bulkeley, "Prescriptions, Toll-Free Numbers Yield a Gold Mine for Marketers," *The Wall Street Journal,* April 17, 1998, B1 and B3.

60. Stephanie Kirchgaessner, "Access Denied: The Data Industry May Face New Restrictions After Privacy Breaches," *Financial Times,* Friday, May 20, 2005.

61. Jon Ungoed-Thomas, "Hidden Surveillance Chips Can Keep Tabs on Shoppers," *Sunday Times,* February 5, 2006, 1–7.

62. John Lanchester, "Big Google Is Watching You," *Sunday Times,* January 29, 2006, 5–3.

63. Dillon, Madden, and Firtle, *Marketing Research in a Marketing Environment,* 48. Elizabeth MacDonald and Joanne S. Lublin, "In the Debris of a Failed Merger: Trade Secrets," *The Wall Street Journal,* March 10, 1998, B1 and B10.

64. Gemma Calvert, "It's a No-Brainer," *The Marketer,* December 2006, 19–21.

Cases for Part 2

Case 2-1

Pfizer, Inc.

Every weekday, some 38,000 Pfizer Inc. sales reps fan out around the globe. Armed with briefcases full of free drug samples, reams of clinical data, and lavish expense accounts for wining and dining their quarry, the reps infiltrate doctors' offices and hospitals. Their goal: to persuade medical professionals the world over to make Pfizer drugs the treatment of choice for their patients' aches and pains.

This massive sales force—roughly the size of three army divisions—is just the advance guard in Pfizer's quest for world drug domination. Equally important is the drugmaker's $3 billion annual ad budget. A pricey array of prime-time commercials and glossy magazine ads show vibrant people freed from the threats of heart disease, hay fever, and a dismal sex life. Sure, consumers can't just go out and buy this stuff: It has to be prescribed by a doctor. But Pfizer and the industry have learned that stoking demand among consumers puts irresistible pressure on doctors. That's why Pfizer is now the fourth-largest advertiser in the land.

Efforts such as these impose huge fixed costs. Pfizer, for example, now spends twice as much on sales and administrative expenses—$16.9 billion last year—as it does on research and development. And it employs 15,000 scientists and support staff in seven major labs around world. As long as those labs are churning out a steady stream of blockbuster drugs for Pfizer's gargantuan sales force to promote, this mass-market approach is extremely profitable. Pfizer, which has more than its share of megasellers, including such familiar names as Lipitor, Viagra, and Zoloft, earned $16 billion last year, not counting discontinued operations and onetime items, on sales of $52 billion.

There's only one problem: The blockbuster model doesn't really work anymore. Pharmaceutical companies, Pfizer being the leader, have sent so many sales reps into the field that they're tripping over one another. The company's once-vaunted labs, along with those of most of the industry, have hit a dry patch, with introductions of promising new treatments slowing alarmingly. Some of Pfizer's recent launches have been duds. (Ever heard of Caduet or Inspra?) The diseases Pfizer and others now chase are harder to defeat with a one-pill, mass-market solution. HMOs and the like are putting the brakes on skyrocketing drug spending.

End of an Era

It could get much worse. As *BusinessWeek* went to press, the Food & Drug Administration was holding contentious hearings about the fate of some of the biggest-selling and most lavishly promoted drugs— painkillers that include Pfizer's $3.3 billion Celebrex and $1.3 billion Bextra. Evidence is mounting that all these so-called Cox 2's—and not just Merck & Co.'s withdrawn Vioxx—may be linked to cardiovascular problems. Critics go further, though, arguing that Pfizer has not aggressively tried to answer that question—and in at least one case has not publicized important safety data on Celebrex. Even if the drugs survive, they are almost surely irreparably damaged.

Add it up, and it looks an awful lot like the end of an era. Big Pharma's sales are expected to grow by a sluggish 2.2% annual average through 2010, according to Datamonitor PLC. Pfizer's top line over that period will actually decline, by an estimated 1.5% a year (see Exhibit 1). While Pfizer has posted strong earnings growth during Chairman and Chief Executive Officer Henry A. "Hank" McKinnell Jr.'s four-year tenure, much of that has come from cost-cutting in the wake of big acquistions. That has caused investors to flee the stock, which has dropped 45% since he became CEO. "The pharmaceutical industry is in the process of transformation," says longtime Pfizer board member Stanley O. Ikenberry. "We have to reexamine all the assumptions that pharmaceutical companies have made for as long as I can remember."

That's why Pfizer has quietly circulated a memo telling its employees to brace for a restructuring that analysts expect will slash billions from the company's cost base. That's not to say McKinnell, 62, has accepted the end of the blockbuster era. While he acknowledges that Pfizer is heading into rough times, he also argues that the company is primed for a resurgence. And he

EXHIBIT 1 The Pfizer Formula Loses Its Punch

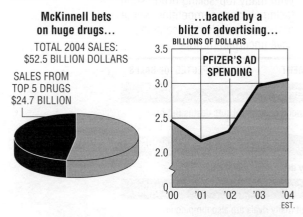

McKinnell bets on huge drugs...

TOTAL 2004 SALES: $52.5 BILLION DOLLARS

SALES FROM TOP 5 DRUGS $24.7 BILLION

...backed by a blitz of advertising...

BILLIONS OF DOLLARS

PFIZER'S AD SPENDING

'00 '01 '02 '03 '04 EST.

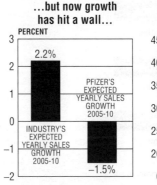

...but now growth has hit a wall...

PERCENT

2.2%

PFIZER'S EXPECTED YEARLY SALES GROWTH 2005-10

INDUSTRY'S EXPECTED YEARLY SALES GROWTH 2005-10

−1.5%

...pushing down Pfizer's stock price

DOLLARS

MONTHLY CLOSE

JAN. '01   FEB. 15, '05

Data: Pfizer Inc., SG Cowen Securities, Datamonitor PLC, Bloomberg Financial Markets

has become the public face of an industry that these days seems only one step above the tobacco business in public opinion. That's him on C-SPAN for an hour, trying to soothe callers irate over the high price of drugs. That's him calmly looking into the camera in TV ads as he explains how Pfizer's scientists are pushing for cures for the greatest of human scourges. He simply won't cotton to the notion that his company's go-go years are gone-gone.

Quite the opposite. McKinnell argues that there are a host of untreated diseases that represent huge potential markets. He says Pfizer's internal research is presenting more great opportunities than ever before—indeed, the company is on track to file 20 new drug applications in the five-year period ending in 2006. And he boasts that a number of those are potential blockbusters.

Size, McKinnell believes, is especially advantageous as clinical trials become more complex and expensive. Who else but Pfizer, McKinnell asks, could afford to wager $2.1 billion on what he thinks is the

next megablockbuster, a heart disease-fighting compound that goes by the chemical name torcetrapib? Pfizer is testing the drug in a combo pill with its current cholesterol fighter, Lipitor. And while this product is still three years away from the market, if tests show that it causes major reductions of plaque in arteries of the heart, McKinnell believes it could eventually surpass Lipitor's $11 billion in annual sales. "If it works, it will be the biggest blockbuster ever," says McKinnell. As for those who argue that the blockbuster model is a bust, he has sharp words: "People who advocate that don't understand our business."

Niche Marketing

Still, the signs are all around him. He has seen the Age of Viagra pass as rivals crowded into the erectile-dysfunction field; sales of that signature Pfizer product slid 11% last year, to $1.7 billion, far below initial projections. Nonetheless, Pfizer and its competitors keep anteing up more advertising dollars (see Feature at end of the case). Viagra is the leader, but the companies behind Cialis and Levitra are ceding nothing, making erectile-dysfunction drugs one of the most heavily advertised categories on TV. McKinnell is left scratching his head: "Normally a new entry creates new interest in the market. That doesn't seem to be happening here. We certainly have the Viagra team trying to figure that out."

That's not to say there won't be blockbuster drugs in the future. McKinnell is right that there are some huge opportunities, such as an anti-smoking drug his labs are working on. But by and large, the diseases that remain without satisfactory treatments either represent smaller markets or are so complex that they defy one-size-fits-all solutions. Pfizer has a number of exciting cancer drugs in development, for example. While those may be decent-size products, cancer therapies typically aren't multibillion-dollar products sold by your neighborhood general practitioner. And as medicine moves toward more personalized treatments linked to an individual's genetic makeup, marketing will need to become even more sophisticated. What all this means is that there will be fewer $1 billion-plus sellers that lend themselves to being marketed through the existing blockbuster sales machine that has sustained Big Pharma over the past decade.

This drying up of the pipeline exposes another challenge that drug companies face: They enjoy patent protection only for a limited time—10 years typically

EXHIBIT 2

Source: *BusinessWeek*

Pfizer's Pipeline Problem

With many top-selling drugs soon facing cheaper competition, some of the company's replacements have uncertain futures.

DRUG	TREATMENT	EXPECTED '09 SALES
torcetrapib/Lipitor	Cholesterol	$1.5 billion
Huge potential if data show that raising good cholesterol cuts deaths.But how many years will it take to get the data?		
Exubera*	Diabetes	$1.4 billion
Analysts worry that safety concerns may delay its introduction.		
indiplon*	Insomnia	$1.4 billion
Sleep drugs should be a big market—but many rivals are also jumping in.		
Macugen*	Macular degeneration	$815 million
Launching this quarter. Pfizer has a head start but may see competition in the next few years.		
varenicline	Smoking	$400 million
Strong demand for drugs that help you quit, but smokers tend to prefer them over the counter, not by prescription.		
Lyrica	Neuropathic pain	$250 million
Sales may be limited because it has been deemed a controlled substance by regulators.		

*Pfizer shares revenues or profits from sales with partners Data: SG Cowen, Banc of America Securities

(see Exhibit 2). After that they face an onslaught of cheap generic competition. Pfizer will see blockbuster drugs worth $14 billion in sales per year lose their patent protection in the next three years. Even with the drug applications McKinnell has in mind, most analysts agree that there's not enough in Pfizer's labs to keep the company growing in the face of those losses. And many of the drugs it's pursuing are the results of partnerships that will ultimately make them less profitable to the company.

The thing about the blockbuster model is that it gives you great leverage. But it cuts both ways. Each of Pfizer's sales reps costs close to $170,000 per year including car, computer, and benefits, estimates Credit Suisse First Boston analyst Catherine J. Arnold. That figure doesn't change a lot if the company's sales are soaring or falling. So a big-selling drug can generate fantastic margins as sales ramp up. Pfizer generated an astonishing $45 billion in gross profits last year. That works out to $1.2 million per sales rep. Celebrex, with rich 90% gross margins, according to analysts, contributed some $3 billion of that.

But watch what happens if those blockbusters fizzle. If Celebrex gets yanked from the market, profits per sales rep immediately drop to $1.1 million—a 7% decline in productivity. If several drugs fall dramatically, which will inevitably happen as patents run out, and if others fail to take off quickly, that massive sales force could quickly become a massive millstone. Even without the unexpected loss of one of the blockbusters, Pfizer's net income is expected to fall nearly 9% this year, to $14.7 billion, as generics begin to launch and big franchises such as the Cox-2 drugs take hits.

Clearly, McKinnell needs to do something. The Stanford University PhD in business, who blows off steam shooting his Sig Sauer handgun as a guest at the FBI firing range in Quantico, Va., will soon take aim at a major restructuring. According to the late-January memo obtained by *BusinessWeek,* McKinnell has ordered a top-to-bottom review intended to make the drug giant more flexible and less bureaucratic. But don't expect him to make big cuts in his sales machine. Sources say Pfizer's overhaul will entail having salespeople call on fewer doctors and talk about fewer products—with the goals of cutting down on the repetitive pitches doctors get and making it easier to determine who's most productive. And the sales force will shrink, though largely through attrition and selective cuts. Employees have been told that decisions on cost reductions and the like will be announced to Wall Street around the April analyst meeting. Friedman, Billings, Ramsey & Co. analyst David Moskowitz figures McKinnell may slash as much as $3 billion in expenses over the next several years.

Radical Restructuring?

Pfizer, though, may require more radical surgery. One smart move would be to inject the sort of bottom-up decision-making into Pfizer that has worked so well at companies such as Johnson & Johnson. Decentralization might be a better match for a company that figures to have a more diverse portfolio of products requiring more targeted sales strategies. That would be a huge shift for famously top-down Pfizer. McKinnell says Pfizer has begun using a similar approach for product planning, linking managers from drug discovery through licensing focused around specific disease categories, such as cardiovascular or metabolic disorders. He says that sort of structure eventually could be pushed across the entire company, in effect creating a series of smaller, more focused businesses. In the memo to employees, Karen L. Katen, president of global drugs, and Chief Financial Officer David L. Shedlarz wrote: "Many of you have expressed frustration with processes that are getting increasingly cumbersome, and with decision-making that seems to be slowing down. We share those frustrations."

Even bolder would be a diversification into other health-care businesses to reduce the reliance on pharmaceuticals. Pfizer was just such a beast not that long ago—in the early '90s it sold everything from heart valves to perfume. Former Chairman and CEO William C. Steere Jr. divested most of those businesses to focus on the high-growth drug operation. That set the stage for Pfizer's hot run. These days, though, medical devices are a hot growth business. The problem is, if Pfizer bought a device business today, it would pay a stiff price, since many device makers have seen their shares bid up. Buying another big drug company would be tough, too, since it would make Pfizer's revenue base even larger, compounding the challenge it now faces in expanding that top line.

A more likely path is for McKinnell to go shopping for drugs to shore up Pfizer's portfolio. He certainly has the financial muscle—Pfizer is expected to generate $10 billion in free cash flow in 2005 and may repatriate as much as $38 billion in overseas profits to take advantage of a one-time tax break. That's money McKinnell can put to work licensing drugs or buying up smaller companies.

One way or another, though, Pfizer has to address its dearth of new blockbusters. Like others in the industry, Pfizer has been plagued by declining productivity in its labs. According to SG Cowen Securities Corp. analyst Stephen M. Scala, Pfizer spent about $70 million on each product in its pipeline in 2004, up from $53 million just two years earlier. That is slightly higher than the $65 million average for the companies Scala follows. And a number of the most exciting products in the pipeline were either acquired or licensed—a sign of the weakness in Pfizer's early-discovery operations. Its last blockbuster that was discovered in its own labs, Viagra, launched in 1998.

That's why investors are so skeptical that McKinnell can get Pfizer back to its teens-plus revenue growth of the 1990s. Says portfolio manager Edwin C. Ciskowski at money-management firm Broadview Advisors: "It's a mature company with modest growth prospects."

Even Pfizer's potential hits won't help as much as you would think. To understand why the company is essentially running in place, look at its huge gamble on torcetrapib. The compound, which is supposed to raise HDL, or "good" cholesterol, is being tested at a cost of $800 million, with Pfizer spending $1.3 billion more to acquire a biotech company that is developing another HDL-raising drug. No product is more critical to Pfizer, since it will take a big hit when Lipitor, which contributes 30% of current earnings, loses patent protection. But even if the new drug is a home run and trials show the combo reduces heart attacks and death, ultimately it is a replacement, not a driver of new growth.

Patent Challenge

The launch of the pill, expected in 2008, could become a lot more difficult if Pfizer loses a critical patent challenge. If Indian drugmaker Ranbaxy Laboratories Ltd. succeeds in knocking down both Lipitor patents—which is seen as a long shot—a generic Lipitor could hit in 2006. If Ranbaxy wins on one of them, which some observers expect, generics could arrive in March, 2010. Either way the loss would make it much tougher to get people to switch from a cheap generic Lipitor to a much more expensive combination of Lipitor and torcetrapib. Credit Suisse's Arnold figures if Pfizer loses on both challenges, the stock, now at $25, would be worth $18. McKinnell says he's confident Pfizer will win on both decisions.

Clearly, all this is hard for McKinnell to swallow. He is, after all, the architect of the bigger-is-better strategy. He played a key role in the acquisition of Warner-Lambert Co. in 2000 and led the Pharmacia Corp. purchase in 2003. McKinnell, widely known as a quick study, has no shortage of confidence in both Pfizer and his own abilities. In a recent interview, he explained how working with an executive coach helped him learn to stop jumping in with an answer before someone has finished talking. "My mind works pretty fast, and I tend to know your question before you ask it," McKinnell says matter-of-factly. He says he now listens to the full question, pauses, and then answers.

McKinnell's faith in the Pfizer way is well known. Anthony H. Wild, former president of Warner-Lambert's drug operation and now head of a small drugmaker called Medpointe Inc., recalls working with McKinnell on the integration of their companies in early 2000. During a dinner in a Paris restaurant, Wild says, McKinnell observed that as he toured and met with Pfizer and Warner managers, he became more convinced that Pfizer managers might be the best choice for key positions in the combined company. Wild says the Warner executives in attendance were stunned, taking the comment as an indication that they had no future with Pfizer. "I saw a few jaws dropping," Wild adds. McKinnell says he doesn't recall the incident. But in the end, most of the Warner managers left or were let go.

That blunt style is well known within Pfizer. Shortly after taking over as CEO in early 2001, McKinnell made clear his concerns about the R&D productivity problem in a meeting in San Juan with Pfizer's top 300 scientists, including R&D chief John L. LaMattina. Known inside Pfizer as the "Houston, we have a problem" speech, McKinnell used that line to make it clear that the labs weren't delivering as they should. He says he meant it as a wake-up call: "They were busy congratulating themselves on opening new buildings."

The group, which had already created a task force to see what it could learn from previous drug-development flops, responded with a system to ensure that when it came to compounds in development, they had a good balance between totally novel approaches and less

risky ones. They also came up with a series of tests that might help identify duds earlier.

But that solves only part of the problem. Since many of the drugs that do succeed are apt to be smaller and more targeted, they will force a big shift in the way Pfizer sells those drugs. While the company does have salespeople selling to specialists today, that sales force is dominated by reps who pitch a lot of drugs to a wide swath of practitioners. In the future, Pfizer will need more in the way of small, highly trained SWAT teams to target doctors focused on a particular disease. That approach will undermine a lot of the economies of scale Pfizer has enjoyed in the past.

Wide Sales, More Risk

Even now, Pfizer's mass approach to the market is taking some major hits. For one thing, rivals have caught on. Pfizer was one of the most aggressive drugmakers in building up its army of reps in the 1990s. But with an explosion in numbers across the industry, it's getting harder for any one salesperson to get face time with physicians. The number of U.S. reps grew nearly 8% from 2002 to 2004, according to research firm Verispan LLC.

With so many sales reps on the prowl, doctors have been absolutely besieged—and they're starting to push back. Dr. Edward L. Langston, a physician in Lafayette, Ind., says his practice had to institute a policy last year to restrict when salespeople could visit and where in the office they could talk to doctors. "We've had multiple times where we'd see three reps from Pfizer in one day," he says. Pfizer's Katen says she hasn't seen a drop in productivity. But Sanford C. Bernstein & Co. analyst Richard T. Evans says: "They are all committing death-by-salesperson."

As Pfizer evolves into a company with a bigger portfolio and a greater number of targeted or niche products, its massive marketing arm could weaken. In 2003, Pfizer shelled out $2.96 billion—behind only General Motors, Procter & Gamble, and Time Warner, according to *Advertising Age*. But many of the new medical advances are in areas such as oncology, ophthalmology, or virology, where treatments vary from patient to patient and don't lend themselves to a cutesy 30-second sales pitch.

The dangers of mixing glib advertising and medicine are now more obvious than ever. Consider Pfizer's Celebrex and Merck's Vioxx, two next-generation painkillers. The much-ballyhooed benefit of the drugs when they were launched in the late '90s was that they were safer on the stomach. But according to a recent paper published in the *Archives of Internal Medicine,* more than half of the growth in the market for these Cox-2 drugs from 1999 to 2002 was sales to patients who were not at risk for stomach problems and who could have taken older, cheaper drugs safely. No doubt some of that sales growth was driven by the drugmakers' heavy promotion and advertising.

Now it's clear that broadening the market carries with it grave risks—legal as well as medical. With Vioxx pulled from the market and Celebrex also showing evidence of a link to heart attacks, plaintiffs' lawyers are gunning for Merck and Pfizer. Merck's legal bill could approach $20 billion. Pfizer's liability is less clear. The Justice Dept. and a group of state attorneys general have requested information on the safety and marketing of Celebrex and Bextra. If the evidence suggests that Pfizer knew more about heart risks than the company has admitted, it could lead to hefty penalties. In fact some critics have argued that the company did not publicize an earlier study looking at the use of Celebrex in Alzheimer's disease that showed more cardiovascular problems in patients getting the drug than in those taking a placebo. Pfizer says the data were shared with the FDA and that the higher rates for Celebrex may have been the result of differences in cardiac health between the Celebrex group and the placebo group. Even McKinnell is critical of pharmaceutical ads. "Somehow we created an image that these products are totally safe," he says. "We need to communicate in the advertising that no drug is absolutely safe."

Overly aggressive marketing also has made drug companies easier targets politically. And that pressure will only grow—particularly after the government starts paying for prescription drugs for seniors in 2006. McKinnell speaks passionately about trying to educate politicians on the cost-effectiveness of drugs. But it's a hard sell. The company invested nearly $20 million in a program in Florida that was intended to show that better utilization of drugs would actually save the state money. It did—but not enough to deter lawmakers, who are demanding big Medicaid price cuts.

Big Pharma's blockbuster business model may be wobbly, but McKinnell remains defiant, insisting that he will find some way to snap Pfizer out of its malaise. "We are willing to run experiments. Things that don't work, we stop, and things that do work, we press on,"

he says. "And we are exceptional in execution." Maybe so, but this is one ailing patient whose condition defies a simple cure.

Feature: The Little Blue Pill—And Pals—Have the Blues

Judging by the tons of TV and print ads that pitch erectile dysfunction drugs, you would think the big three—Viagra, Cialis, and Levitra—were selling as briskly as beer at a football game. After all, what could be more marketable than a pill that helps aging men perform better in bed?

It's not working out that way. Despite gargantuan ad budgets, sales are trailing expectations for all three contenders. Viagra's worldwide sales fell 11% last year and, at $1.7 billion, were less than half what was projected by Wall Street firms a few years ago. Cialis and Levitra drove the category up 10% in the U.S. But Wall Street analysts—some of whom had speculated years ago that Viagra alone would be a $4.5 billion brand by 2004—aren't impressed. Cialis, marketed through a joint venture between Eli Lilly & Co. and Icos Corp., rang up U.S. sales of $203 million in its first full year and spent $165 million on ads. And GlaxoSmithKline PLC's Levitra, co-marketed until recently with Bayer, sold just $128 million worth of pills, well below what the companies spent on TV, print, and other media. Combined, the three spent 37% of their sales on ads, according to TNS Media Intelligence. Compare that with Ford Motor Co., which spent about 7% of U.S. automotive revenue on media last year.

Viagra's drop has been much steeper than anyone predicted. When it came on the scene back in 1998, Viagra was a textbook case in how to market a prescription drug as a consumer product. In less than two years, Pfizer Inc. cemented the name into the popular lexicon in a way that marketers only dream about. "I've hardly ever seen a brand franchise in any category take off so fast," says Los Angeles marketing consultant Dennis Keene.

The reality today is much different. Less than 15% of the estimated 30 million men suffering from erectile dysfunction (ED) have tried one of the drugs. Matthew G. Beebe, brand team leader for Cialis at Lilly, says that many are still embarrassed to ask their doctor about the drugs. Another problem is that too many patients are disappointed when they take the pill and nothing happens. Dr. Timothy Schuster, assistant professor of urology at the University of Michigan Medical Center, says many patients don't use the right dosage. He adds: "A lot of doctors don't make the connection between ED and underlying disease like cardiovascular disease and don't engage patients."

But drugmakers can also blame themselves for lagging sales. In their rush to grab more of the market, they flooded doctors with free samples. Last year, up to 40% of the pills taken by men were free, says pharmaceutical research firm ImpactRx. And clearly, the ad-fueled hype stoked some early demand from those who were more curious than afflicted.

Much of that hype has now faded—but don't expect pillmakers to back off. Viagra's latest ads have men playfully sprouting blue horns the same color as a Viagra pill. The Food & Drug Administration slapped Pfizer's wrist last fall, making it withdraw some ads that the agency said overpromised and failed to give adequate warning about side effects. Cialis has taken a more romantic approach, with middle-aged couples

canoodling, to emphasize the drug's 36-hour working time (compared with Viagra's and Levitra's four-hour windows of opportunity). Levitra has the steepest hill to climb because it works about the same as Viagra but has less brand recognition. Bayer passed U.S. marketing control last year to GlaxoSmithKline and Schering-Plough Corp. In January, Glaxo and new partner Schering-Plough tapped Saatchi & Saatchi to scope out a different direction.

So far, the passion pills haven't had to worry much about decency standards on TV networks. NBC says it won't run the ads on "family" shows, but the drug companies aren't interested in those programs anyway. "We aim where the men are," says Lilly's Beebe. But hitting them with Cupid's arrow is proving to be anything but a sure thing.

–By David Kiley in New York

Source: Amy Barrett, "Pfizer's Funk," *BusinessWeek,* February 28, 2005, 72–82.

Case 2-2

Ikea

When Roger Penguino heard Ikea was offering $4,000 in gift certificates to the first person in line at the opening of its new Atlanta store, he had no choice. He threw a tent in the back of his car and sped down to the site. There, the 24-year-old Mac specialist with Apple Computer Inc. pitched camp, hunkered down, and waited. And waited. Seven broiling days later, by the time the store opened on June 29, more than 2,000 Ikea fanatics had joined him. Some were lured by the promise of lesser prizes for the first 100. Others were just there for the carnival atmosphere (somebody even brought a grill). The newly wed Penguino got his certificates and bagged a $799 Karlanda sofa and a $179 Malm bed, among other items. He also achieved celebrity status: "Whenever I go back, employees recognize me and show me the new stuff."

Penguino is a citizen of Ikea World, a state of mind that revolves around contemporary design, low prices, wacky promotions, and an enthusiasm that few institutions in or out of business can muster. Perhaps more than any other company in the world, Ikea has become a curator of people's lifestyles, if not their lives. At a time when consumers face so many choices for everything they buy, Ikea provides a one-stop sanctuary for

coolness. It is a trusted safe zone that people can enter and immediately be part of a like-minded cost/design/environmentally-sensitive global tribe. There are other would-be curators around—Starbucks and Virgin do a good job—but Ikea does it best.

If the Swedish retailer has its way, you too will live in a BoKlok home and sleep in a Leksvik bed under a Brunskära quilt. (Beds are named for Norwegian cities; bedding after flowers and plants. One disaster: a child's bed called Gutvik, which sounds like "good f***" in German.) Ikea wants to supply the food in your fridge (it also sells the fridge) and the soap in your shower.

The Ikea concept has plenty of room to run: The retailer accounts for just 5% to 10% of the furniture market in each country in which it operates. More important, says CEO Anders Dahlvig, is that "awareness of our brand is much bigger than the size of our company." That's because Ikea is far more than a furniture merchant. It sells a lifestyle that customers around the world embrace as a signal that they've arrived, that they have good taste and recognize value. "If it wasn't for Ikea," writes British design magazine *Icon,* "most people would have no access to affordable contemporary design." The magazine even voted Ikea founder Ingvar Kamprad the most influential tastemaker in the world today.

As long as consumers from Moscow to Beijing and beyond keep striving to enter the middle class, there will be a need for Ikea. Think about it: What mass-market retailer has had more success globally? Not Wal-Mart Stores Inc., which despite vast strengths has stumbled in Brazil, Germany, and Japan. Not France's Carrefour, which has never made it in the U.S. Ikea has had its slip-ups, too. But right now its 226 stores in Europe, Asia, Australia, and the U.S. are thriving, hosting 410 million shoppers a year. The emotional response is unparalleled. The promise of store vouchers for the first 50 shoppers drew thousands to an Ikea store in the Saudi Arabian city of Jeddah in September, 2004. In the ensuing melee, two people died and 16 were injured. A February opening in London attracted up to 6,000 before police were called in.

Why the uproar? Ikea is the quintessential global cult brand. Just take those stunts. Before the Atlanta opening, Ikea managers invited locals to apply for the post of Ambassador of Kul (Swedish for fun). The five winners wrote an essay on why they deserved $2,000 in vouchers. There was one catch: They would have to live in the store for three days before the opening, take part in contests, and sleep in the bedding department. "I got about eight hours of sleep total because of all the drilling and banging going on," says winner Jordan Leopold, a manager at Costco Wholesale.

Leopold got his bedroom set. And Ikea got to craft another story about itself—a story picked up in the press that drew even more shoppers. More shoppers, more traffic. More traffic, more sales. More sales, more buzz. A new store in Bolingbrook, Ill., near Chicago is expected to generate some $2.5 million in tax revenues, so the town is paying down debt and doing away with some local levies.

Such buzz has kept Ikea's sales growing at a healthy clip: For the fiscal year ended Aug. 31, revenues rose 15%, to $17.7 billion (see Exhibit 1). And although

privately held Ikea guards profit figures as jealously as its recipe for Swedish meatballs, analyst Mattias Karlkjell of Stockholm's ABG Sundal Collier conservatively estimates Ikea's pretax operating profits at $1.7 billion. Ikea maintains these profits even while it cuts prices steadily. "Ikea's operating margins of approximately 10% are among the best in home furnishing," Karlkjell says. They also compare well with margins of 5% at Pier 1 Imports and 7.7% at Target, both competitors of Ikea in the U.S.

To keep growing at that pace, Ikea is accelerating store rollouts. Nineteen new outlets are set to open worldwide in the fiscal year ending Aug. 31, 2006, at a cost of $66 million per store, on average. CEO Dahlvig is keen to boost Ikea's profile in three of its fastest-growing markets: the U.S., Russia (Ikea is already a huge hit in Moscow), and China (now worth $120 million in sales). In the U.S. he figures the field is wide open: "We have 25 stores in a market the size of Europe, where we have more than 160 stores." The goal is 50 U.S. outlets by 2010: Five are opening this year, up from just one in 2000.

The key to these rollouts is to preserve the strong enthusiasm Ikea evokes, an enthusiasm that has inspired two case studies from Harvard Business School and endless shopper comment on the Net. Examples: "Ikea makes me free to become what I want to be" (from Romania). Or this: "Half my house is from Ikea—and the nearest store is six hours away" (the U.S.). Or this: "Every time, it's trendy for less money" (Germany).

What enthralls shoppers and scholars alike is the store visit—a similar experience the world over. The blue-and-yellow buildings average 300,000 square feet in size, about equal to five football fields. The sheer number of items—7,000, from kitchen cabinets to

EXHIBIT 1

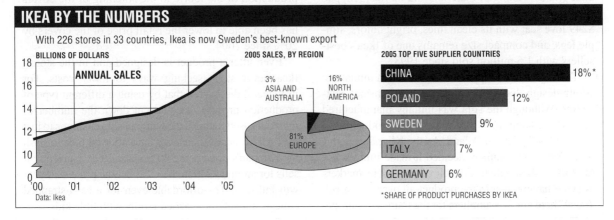

candlesticks—is a decisive advantage. "Others offer affordable furniture," says Bryan Roberts, research manager at Planet Retail, a consultancy in London. "But there's no one else who offers the whole concept in the big shed."

The global middle class that Ikea targets shares buying habits. The $120 Billy bookcase, $13 Lack side table, and $190 Ivar storage system are best-sellers worldwide. (U.S. prices are used throughout this case.) Spending per customer is even similar. According to Ikea, the figure in Russia is $85 per store visit—exactly the same as in affluent Sweden.

Wherever they are, customers tend to think of the store visit as more of an outing than a chore. That's intentional: As one of the Harvard B-school studies states, Ikea practices a form of "gentle coercion" to keep you as long as possible. Right at the entrance, for example, you can drop off your kids at the playroom, an amenity that encourages more leisurely shopping.

Then, clutching your dog-eared catalog (the print run for the 2006 edition was 160 million—more than the Bible, Ikea claims), you proceed along a marked path through the warren of showrooms. "Because the store is designed as a circle, I can see everything as long as I keep walking in one direction," says Krystyna Gavora, an architect who frequents Ikea in Schaumburg, Ill. Wide aisles let you inspect merchandise without holding up traffic. The furniture itself is arranged in fully accessorized displays, down to the picture frames on the nightstand, to inspire customers and get them to spend more. The settings are so lifelike that one writer is staging a play at Ikea in Renton, Wash (Exhibit 2).

Along the way, one touch after another seduces the shopper, from the paper measuring tapes and pencils to strategically placed bins with items like pink plastic watering cans, scented candles, and picture frames. These are things you never knew you needed but at less than $2 each you load up on them anyway. You set out

EXHIBIT 2   What a Sweetheart of a Love Seat

Lars Engman learned the hard way that furniture needs to do more that just look good. After his 6-year-old daughter and her rambunctious pals destroyed his expensive Italian-made sofa in three months in the 1970s, the Ikea product developer was inspired to create an equally stylish but kidproof alternative. "I wanted it to be hard-wearing and kid-friendly without compromising on design," says Engman, now Ikea's design manager, based in Almhult, Sweden. It would have to be soft around the edges yet sturdy enough to withstand years of wear and tear, and have machine-washable slipcovers to make it easy to keep clean. More important, it would have to meet the Ikea challenge of good looks at a low price. A tall order. But after endless testing of materials and fabrics, Klippan was born in 1980. More than two decades later, the $249 love seat with its clean lines, bright colors, simple legs, and compact size remains one of Ikea's best-sellers with 1.5 million sold since 1998.

The saga of the Klippan is that of Ikea in miniature: strong design, logistical efficiency, and constant cost-cutting. Although the sofa was initially manufactured in Sweden, soon after Ikea outsourced production to lowercost suppliers in Poland. As the Klippan's popularity grew, the company decided it made more sense to work with suppliers in each of Ikea's big markets to avoid having to ship the product all over the world. Today, there are five suppliers for the frames in Europe,

plus three in the U.S. and two in China, each of which is guaranteed a minimum volume.

After much experimenting with different materials, the frames are now made from a combination of particleboard, fiberboard, and polyurethane foam, a mix that is cheaper and lighter in weight than solid wood. It wasn't until last year, though, that Ikea finally figured out how to break down the Klippan so it could be flat-packed. Now the frame comes in four separate pieces: The armrests and back slip into slots in the seating base. The new system saves 50% on shipping costs and also frees up room at Ikea's warehouses.

The cotton slipcovers for the Klippan have also gotten cheaper. By centralizing everything from the production of the fabric to the stitching of the covers to just four core suppliers in China and Europe, Ikea has been able to lower the retail price of the covers by 20% since 2004.

Even after a product is designed and in the stores, Ikea never stops seeking ways to lower costs. For instance, it discovered that by using a different type of production process, it could cut down the number of materials used to make the Klippan sofa cushions to just two. All of these efficiencies have allowed Ikea to slash the Klippan's price some 40% since 1999. Currently it sells for around $249 in the U.S., but the price next year will fall to $202—affordable even for a cash-strapped college student, or a harried family with little kids.

to buy a $40 coffee table but end up dropping $500 on everything from storage units to glassware. "They have this way of making you believe nothing is expensive," says Bertille Faroult, a shopper at Ikea on the outskirts of Paris. The bins and shelves constantly hold surprises: Ikea replaces a third of its product line every year.

Then there's the stop at the restaurant, usually placed at the center of the store, to provide shoppers a breather and encourage them to keep going. You proceed to the warehouse, where the full genius of founder Kamprad is on display. Nearly all the big items are flat-packed, which not only saves Ikea millions in shipping costs from suppliers but also enables shoppers to haul their own stuff home—another savings. Finally you have the fun (or agony) of assembling at home, equipped with nothing but an Allen wrench and those cryptic instructions.

A vocal minority rails at Ikea for its long lines, crowded parking lots, exasperating assembly experiences, and furniture that's hardly built for the ages (the running joke is that Ikea is Swedish for particle board). But the converts outnumber the critics. And for every fan who shops at Ikea, there seems to be one working at the store itself. The fanaticism stems from founder Kamprad, 79, a figure as important to global retailing as Wal-Mart's Sam Walton. Kamprad started the company in 1943 at the age of 17, selling pens, Christmas cards, and seeds from a shed on his family's farm in southern Sweden. In 1951, the first catalog appeared (Kamprad penned all the text himself until 1963). His credo of creating "a better life for many" is enshrined in his almost evangelical 1976 tract, *A Furniture Dealer's Testament.* Peppered with folksy tidbits—"divide your life into 10-minute units and sacrifice as few as possible in meaningless activity," "wasting resources is a mortal sin" (that's for sure: employees are the catalog models), or the more revealing "it is our duty to expand"—the pamphlet is given to all employees the day they start.

Kamprad, though officially retired, is still the cheerleader for the practices that define Ikea culture. One is egalitarianism. Ikea regularly stages Antibureaucracy Weeks, during which executives work on the shop floor or tend the registers. "In February," says CEO Dahlvig, "I was unloading trucks and selling beds and mattresses." (Exhibit 3).

Another is a steely competitiveness. You get a sense of that at one of Ikea's main offices, in Helsingborg, Sweden. At the door-way, a massive bulletin board tracks weekly sales growth, names the best-performing country markets, and identifies the best-selling furniture. The other message that comes across loud and clear: Cut prices. At the far end of the Helsingborg foyer is a row of best-selling Klippan sofas, displaying

---

EXHIBIT 3

Source: *BusinessWeek*

How to Build a Cult Brand

Ikea sells a lifestyle that signifies hip design, thrift, and simplicity. For the aspiring global middle class, buying Ikea is a sign of success. Here's how the Swades do it.

CREATE THE STORY

The retailer is a master at building buzz, which creates evangelists for its brand, who then spread the story by phone, word of mouth, and even blogs from Shanghai to Chicago. The Ambassador of Kul promotion, for example, gives essay contest winners the chance to camp out in a store before it opens. That excites shoppers and generates huge publicity.

INSPIRE THE STAFF

Employees won't get rich, but they do get to enjoy autonomy, very little hierarchy, and a family-friendly culture. In return they buy into the philosophy of frugality and style that drives the whole company.

SEDUCE THE SHOPPER

Customer focus is so intense that even senior management must work behind cash registers and in the warehouse for brief stints every year. The stores are laid out to promote fun: Restaurants and play centers encourage shoppers to spend the day. Simple touches, from free pencils to paper measuring-tapes, make it easy to shop.

SURPRISE ON VALUE

Ikea mandates price cuts every year, but designers also deliver on looks and quality. Every year designers must meet stretch goals, like designing a bedroom set for $130.

models from 1999 to 2006 with their euro price tags. In 1999 the Klippan was $354. In 2006 it will be $202.

The montage vividly illustrates Ikea's relentless cost-cutting. The retailer aims to lower prices across its entire offering by an average of 2% to 3% each year. It goes deeper when it wants to hit rivals in certain segments. "We look at the competition, take their price, and then slash it in half," says Mark McCaslin, manager of Ikea Long Island, in Hicksville, N.Y.

It helps that frugality is as deeply ingrained in the corporate DNA as the obsession with design. Managers fly economy, even top brass. Steen Kanter, who left Ikea in 1994 and now heads his own retail consultancy in Philadelphia, Kanter International, recalls that while flying with Kamprad once, the boss handed him a coupon for a car rental he had ripped out from an in-flight magazine.

This cost obsession fuses with the design culture. "Designing beautiful-but-expensive products is easy," says Josephine Rydberg-Dumont, president of Ikea of Sweden. "Designing beautiful products that are inexpensive and functional is a huge challenge."

No design—no matter how inspired—finds its way into the showroom if it cannot be made affordable. To achieve that goal, the company's 12 full-time designers at Almhult, Sweden, along with 80 freelancers, work hand in hand with in-house production teams to identify the appropriate materials and least costly suppliers, a trial-and-error process that can take as long as three years. Example: For the PS Ellan, a $39.99 dining chair that can rock back on its hind legs without tipping over, designer Chris Martin worked with production staff for a year and a half to adapt a wood-fiber composite, an inexpensive blend of wood chips and plastic resin used in highway noise barriers, for use in furnishings. Martin also had to design the chair to break down into six pieces, so it could be flat-packed and snapped together without screws (Exhibit 4).

With a network of 1,300 suppliers in 53 countries, Ikea works overtime to find the right manufacturer for the right product. It once contracted with ski makers—experts in bent wood—to manufacture its Poang armchairs, and it has tapped makers of supermarket carts to turn out durable sofas. Simplicity, a tenet of Swedish design, helps keep costs down. The 50¢ Trofé mug comes only in blue and white, the least expensive pigments. Ikea's conservation drive extends naturally from this cost-cutting. For its new PS line, it challenged 28 designers to find innovative uses for discarded and unusual materials. The results: a table fashioned from reddish-brown birch heartwood (furniture makers prefer the pale exterior wood) and a storage system made from recycled milk cartons.

If sales keep growing at their historical average, by 2010 Ikea will need to source twice as much material as today. "We can't increase by more than 20 stores a year because supply is the bottleneck," says Lennart Dahlgren, country manager for Russia. Since Russia is a source of timber, Ikea aims to turn it into a major supplier of finished products.

Adding to the challenge, the suppliers and designers have to customize some Ikea products to make them sell better in local markets. In China, the 250,000 plastic placemats Ikea produced to commemorate the year of the rooster sold out in just three weeks. Julie Desrosiers, the bedroom-line manager at Ikea of Sweden, visited people's houses in the U.S. and Europe to peek into their closets, learning that "Americans prefer to store most of their clothes folded, and Italians like to hang." The result was a wardrobe that features deeper drawers for U.S. customers.

The American market poses special challenges for Ikea because of the huge differences inside the U.S. "It's so easy to forget the reality of how people live," says Ikea's U.S. interior design director, Mats Nilsson. In the spring of 2004, Ikea realized it might not be reaching California's Hispanics. So its designers visited the homes of Hispanic staff. They soon realized they had set up the store's displays all wrong. Large Hispanic families need dining tables and sofas that fit more than two people, the Swedish norm. They prefer bold colors to the more subdued Scandinavian palette and display tons of pictures in elaborate frames. Nilsson warmed up the showrooms' colors, adding more seating and throwing in numerous picture frames.

Ikea is particularly concerned about the U.S. since it's key to expansion—and since Ikea came close to blowing it. "We got our clocks cleaned in the early 1990s because we really didn't listen to the consumer," says Kanter. Stores weren't big enough to offer the full Ikea experience, and many were in poor locations. Prices were too high. Beds were measured in centimeters, not king, queen, and twin. Sofas weren't deep enough, curtains were too short, and kitchens didn't fit U.S.-size appliances. "American customers were buying vases to drink from because the glasses were too small," recalls Goran Carstedt, the former head of Ikea North America, who helped engineer a turnaround. Parts of the product line were adapted (no more metric

EXHIBIT 4   **Need a Home to Go with That Sofa?**

Like many young couples, artist Nina Leth Jensen, 32, and her husband, Jakob, 33, a manager with the Copenhagen metro, feared they would never be able to afford their own home. With a four-year-old child and another on the way, the family was desperate to move to a bigger space but found themselves priced out of the market.

Then in June, 2004, Nina spotted an ad for BoKlok (Swedish for "smart living"), a line of affordable pre-fab homes marketed by Ikea. "I told my husband, 'this is the house for us,' " says Nina. "We already had a lot of Ikea furniture, so why not have a total Ikea home?"

Today, the Jensens live in a BoKlok development in Hillerod, Denmark, just outside of Copenhagen. For $45,000, some 25% less than comparable homes in the area, the family got an airy 800-square-foot, three-bedroom apartment with an open-plan living area, small garden, and garage. Ikea also threw in $500 in gift certificates and the free services of an Ikea designer.

Aimed largely at first-time buyers, BoKlok is proving a big hit, with more than 2,500 units sold in Sweden, Finland, Norway, and Denmark since the program was launched in 1997. In a new development outside Oslo, the 60 homes sold out in 45 minutes. Next up: Southampton, England, where the first BoKloks will go on sale in January. BoKlok, a stand-alone company that is jointly controlled by Ikea and Swedish developer Skanska, also is eyeing France, Poland, the Netherlands, and the U.S. "There is a global need for affordable housing," says BoKlok managing director Anders Larsson. "We want to fill that gap."

To come up with the right price tag, Ikea enlisted well-known Swedish economist Pia Nilsson. In-store customer surveys then revealed what the market wanted: a safe, low-rise apartment in a small-scale development with outside space, open-plan living, and lots of light.

A BoKlok development consists of several timber-framed buildings, each containing five to six apartments. Putting the units together is a snap. Most of the work takes place on the factory floor. The assembly line starts with carpenters, who erect the walls and windows. Then a fully equipped Ikea kitchen and bathroom are added. Floors, shelving units, and electrical wiring are installed before painters add the final touches. The modular units are then delivered to the construction site on 18-wheel trucks. A crane drops them in place, and builders complete the last fittings, a process that typically takes just one day.

CEO Anders Dahlvig acknowledges BoKlok "generates a lot of buzz for the brand," but adds, "we are not a house builder ourselves, so we have to be cautious." Yet with more and more people clamoring for the total Ikea lifestyle, Ikea may have to change its tune.

---

measurements), new and bigger store locations chosen, prices slashed, and service improved. Now U.S. managers are paying close attention to the tiniest details. "Americans want more comfortable sofas, higher-quality textiles, bigger glasses, more spacious entertainment units," says Pernille Spiers-Lopez, head of Ikea North America.

Can the cult keep thriving? Ikea has stumbled badly before. A foray into Japan 30 years ago was a disaster (the Japanese wanted high quality and great materials, not low price and particle board). The company is just now gearing up for a return to Japan next year. Ikea is also seeing more competition than ever. In the U.S., Target Corp. has recruited top designer Thomas O'Brien to develop a range of low-priced furnishings, which were launched in October. Kmart has been collaborating with Martha Stewart on its own furniture line. An Ikea-like chain called Fly is popular in France. In Japan Nitori Co. has a lock on low-cost furniture.

Perhaps the bigger issue is what happens inside Ikea. "The great challenge of any organization as it becomes larger and more diverse is how to keep the core founding values alive," says Harvard Business School Professor Christopher A. Bartlett, author of a 1996 case study. Ikea is still run by managers who were trained and groomed by Kamprad himself—and who are personally devoted to the founder. As the direct links with Kamprad disappear, the culture may start to fade.

For now, the founder's legacy is alive and well. The Klippan couches are selling briskly. New lines of foods, travel gear, and toiletries are due soon. Ikea is gearing up for its Christmas tree promotion—you buy a live tree, then return it for a rebate (and end up shopping at Ikea in the slow month of January).

And the fans keep clamoring for more. At least once a year, Jen Segrest, a 36-year-old freelance Web designer, and her husband travel 10 hours round-trip from their home in Middletown, Ohio, to Ikea in Schaumburg, Ill., near Chicago. "Every piece of furniture in my living room is Ikea—except for an end table, which I hate. And next time I go to Ikea I'll replace it," says Segrest. To lure the retailer to Ohio, Segrest has

even started a blog called OH! IKEA. The banner on the home page reads "Ikea in Ohio—Because man cannot live on Target alone."

Source: Kerry Capell, "IKEA," *BusinessWeek,* November 14, 2005, 97–106.

Case 2-3
China and India: Opportunities and Challenges

It may not top the must-see list of many tourists. But to appreciate Shanghai's ambitious view of its future, there is no better place than the Urban Planning Exhibition Hall, a glass-and-metal structure across from People's Square. The highlight is a scale model bigger than a basketball court of the entire metropolis—every skyscraper, house, lane, factory, dock, and patch of green space—in the year 2020.

There are white plastic showpiece towers designed by architects such as I.M. Pei and Sir Norman Foster. There are immense new industrial parks for autos and petrochemicals, along with new subway lines, airport runways, ribbons of expressway, and an elaborate riverfront development, site of the 2010 World Expo. Nine futuristic planned communities for 800,000 residents each, with generous parks, retail districts, man-made lakes, and nearby college campuses, rise in the suburbs. The message is clear. Shanghai already is looking well past its industrial age to its expected emergence as a global mecca of knowledge workers. "In an information economy, it is very important to have urban space with a better natural and social environment," explains Architectural Society of Shanghai President Zheng Shiling, a key city adviser.

It is easy to dismiss such dreams as bubble-economy hubris—until you take into account the audacious goals Shanghai already has achieved. Since 1990, when the city still seemed caught in a socialist time warp, Shanghai has erected enough high-rises to fill Manhattan. The once-rundown Pudong district boasts a space-age skyline, some of the world's biggest industrial zones, dozens of research centers, and a bullet train. This is the story of China, where an extraordinary ability to mobilize workers and capital has tripled per capita income in a generation, and has eased 300 million out of poverty. Leaders now are frenetically laying the groundwork for decades of new growth.

Invaluable Role

Now hop a plane to India. It is hard to tell this is the world's other emerging superpower. Jolting sights of extreme poverty abound even in the business capitals. A lack of subways and a dearth of expressways result in nightmarish traffic.

But visit the office towers and research and development centers sprouting everywhere, and you see the miracle. Here, Indians are playing invaluable roles in the global innovation chain. Motorola, Hewlett-Packard, Cisco Systems, and other tech giants now rely on their Indian teams to devise software platforms and dazzling multimedia features for next-generation devices. Google principal scientist Krishna Bharat is setting up a Bangalore lab complete with colorful furniture, exercise balls, and a Yamaha organ—like Google's Mountain View (Calif.) headquarters—to work on core search-engine technology. Indian engineering houses use 3-D computer simulations to tweak designs of everything from car engines and forklifts to aircraft wings for such clients as General Motors Corp. and Boeing Co. Financial and market-research experts at outfits like B2K, OfficeTiger, and Iris crunch the latest disclosures of blue-chip companies for Wall Street. By 2010 such outsourcing work is expected to quadruple, to $56 billion a year.

Even more exhilarating is the pace of innovation, as tech hubs like Bangalore spawn companies producing their own chip designs, software, and pharmaceuticals. "I find Bangalore to be one of the most exciting places in the world," says Dan Scheinman, Cisco Systems Inc.'s senior vice-president for corporate development. "It is Silicon Valley in 1999." Beyond Bangalore, Indian companies are showing a flair for producing high-quality goods and services at ridiculously low prices (page 64), from $50 air flights and crystal-clear 2¢-a-minute cell-phone service to $2,200 cars and cardiac operations by top surgeons at a fraction of U.S. costs. Some analysts see the beginnings of hypercompetitive multinationals. "Once they learn to sell at Indian prices with world quality, they can compete anywhere," predicts University of Michigan management guru C.K.

Prahalad. Adds A. T. Kearney high-tech consultant John Ciacchella: "I don't think U.S. companies realize India is building next-generation service companies."

Simultaneous Takeoffs

China and India. Rarely has the economic ascent of two still relatively poor nations been watched with such a mixture of awe, opportunism, and trepidation. The postwar era witnessed economic miracles in Japan and South Korea. But neither was populous enough to power worldwide growth or change the game in a complete spectrum of industries. China and India, by contrast, possess the weight and dynamism to transform the 21st-century global economy. The closest parallel

to their emergence is the saga of 19th-century America, a huge continental economy with a young, driven workforce that grabbed the lead in agriculture, apparel, and the high technologies of the era, such as steam engines, the telegraph, and electric lights.

But in a way, even America's rise falls short in comparison to what's happening now. Never has the world seen the simultaneous, sustained takeoffs of two nations that together account for one-third of the planet's population. For the past two decades, China has been growing at an astounding 9.5% a year, and India by 6%. Given their young populations, high savings, and the sheer amount of catching up they still have to do, most economists figure China and India possess the fundamentals to keep growing in the 7%-to-8% range for decades (Exhibit 1).

EXHIBIT 1

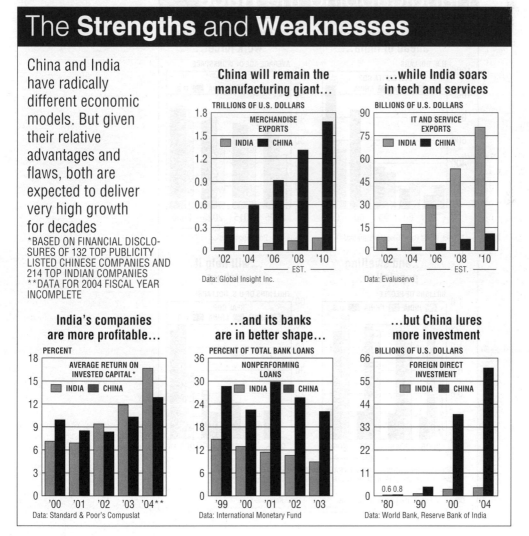

Barring cataclysm, within three decades India should have vaulted over Germany as the world's third-biggest economy. By mid-century, China should have overtaken the U.S. as No.1. By then, China and India could account for half of global output. Indeed, the troika of China, India, and the U.S.—the only industrialized nation with significant population growth—by most projections will dwarf every other economy (Exhibit 2).

What makes the two giants especially powerful is that they complement each other's strengths. An accelerating trend is that technical and managerial skills in both China and India are becoming more important than cheap assembly labor. China will stay dominant in mass manufacturing, and is one of the few nations building multibillion-dollar electronics and heavy industrial plants. India is a rising power in software, design, services, and precision industry. This raises a provocative question: What if the two nations merge into one giant "Chindia?" Rival political and economic ambitions make that unlikely. But if their industries truly collaborate, "they would take over the world tech industry," predicts Forrester Research Inc. analyst Navi Radjou.

In a practical sense, the yin and yang of these immense workforces already are converging. True, annual trade between the two economies is just $14 billion. But thanks to the Internet and plunging telecom

EXHIBIT 2

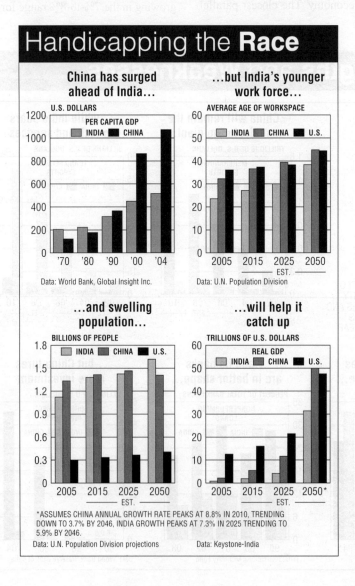

costs, multinationals are having their goods built in China with software and circuitry designed in India. As interactive design technology makes it easier to perfect virtual 3-D prototypes of everything from telecom routers to turbine generators on PCs, the distance between India's low-cost laboratories and China's low-cost factories shrinks by the month. Managers in the vanguard of globalization's new wave say the impact will be nothing less than explosive. "In a few years you'll see most companies unleashing this massive productivity surge," predicts Infosys Technologies CEO Nandan M. Nilekani.

To globalization's skeptics, however, what's good for Corporate America translates into layoffs and lower pay for workers. Little wonder the West is suffering from future shock. Each new Chinese corporate take-over bid or revelation of a major Indian outsourcing deal elicits howls of protest by U.S. politicians. Washington think tanks are publishing thick white papers charting China's rapid progress in microelectronics, nanotech, and aerospace—and painting dark scenarios about what it means for America's global leadership.

Such alarmism is understandable. But the U.S. and other established powers will have to learn to make room for China and India. For in almost every dimension—as consumer markets, investors, producers, and users of energy and commodities—they will be 21st-century heavyweights (Exhibit 3). The growing economic might will carry into geopolitics as well. China and India are more assertively pressing their interests in the Middle East and Africa, and China's military will likely challenge U.S. dominance in the Pacific.

One implication is that the balance of power in many technologies will likely move from West to East (Exhibit 4). An obvious reason is that China and India graduate a combined half a million engineers and scientists a year, vs. 60,000 in the U.S. In life sciences, projects the McKinsey Global Institute, the total number of young researchers in both nations will rise by 35%, to 1.6 million by 2008. The U.S. supply will drop by 11%, to 760,000. As most Western scientists will tell you, China and India already are making important contributions in medicine and materials that will help everyone. Because these nations can throw more brains at technical problems at a fraction of the cost, their contributions to innovation will grow (Exhibit 5).

Consumers Rising

American business isn't just shifting research work because Indian and Chinese brains are young, cheap, and plentiful. In many cases, these engineers combine skills—mastery of the latest software tools, a knack for complex mathematical algorithms, and fluency in new multimedia technologies—that often surpass those of their American counterparts. As Cisco's Scheinman puts it: "We came to India for the costs, we stayed for the quality, and we're now investing for the innovation."

EXHIBIT 3

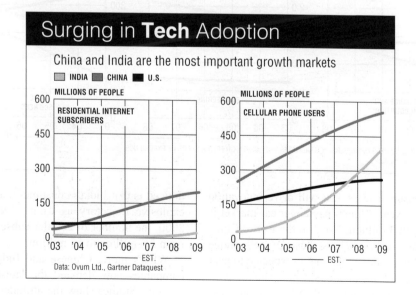

Surging in **Tech** Adoption

China and India are the most important growth markets

■ INDIA   ■ CHINA   ■ U.S.

RESIDENTIAL INTERNET SUBSCRIBERS (MILLIONS OF PEOPLE)

CELLULAR PHONE USERS (MILLIONS OF PEOPLE)

Data: Ovum Ltd., Gartner Dataquest

EXHIBIT 4

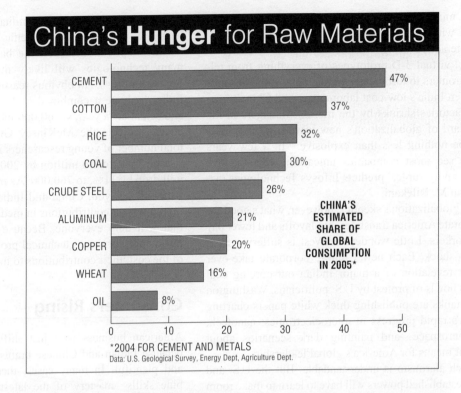

China's **Hunger** for Raw Materials

CHINA'S ESTIMATED SHARE OF GLOBAL CONSUMPTION IN 2005*

CEMENT	47%
COTTON	37%
RICE	32%
COAL	30%
CRUDE STEEL	26%
ALUMINUM	21%
COPPER	20%
WHEAT	16%
OIL	8%

*2004 FOR CEMENT AND METALS
Data: U.S. Geological Survey, Energy Dept, Agriculture Dept.

EXHIBIT 5

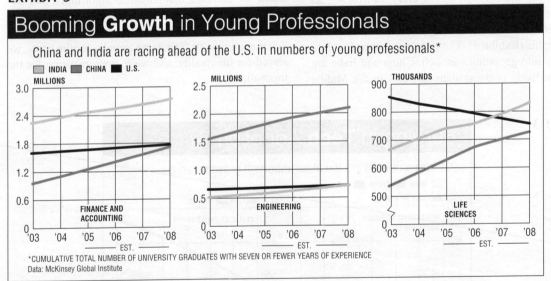

Booming **Growth** in Young Professionals

China and India are racing ahead of the U.S. in numbers of young professionals*

INDIA   CHINA   U.S.

FINANCE AND ACCOUNTING (MILLIONS): '03 – '08 EST.

ENGINEERING (MILLIONS): '03 – '08 EST.

LIFE SCIENCES (THOUSANDS): '03 – '08 EST.

*CUMULATIVE TOTAL NUMBER OF UNIVERSITY GRADUATES WITH SEVEN OR FEWER YEARS OF EXPERIENCE
Data: McKinsey Global Institute

A rising consumer class also will drive innovation (Exhibit 6). This year, China's passenger car market is expected to reach 3 million, No. 3 in the world. China already has the world's biggest base of cell phone subscribers—350 million—and that is expected to near 600 million by 2009. In two years, China should overtake the U.S. in homes connected to broadband. Less

noticed is that India's consumer market is on the same explosive trajectory as China five years ago. Since 2000, the number of cellular subscribers has rocketed from 5.6 million to 55 million.

What's more, Chinese and Indian consumers and companies now demand the latest technologies and features. Studies show the attitudes and aspirations of

EXHIBIT 6

Source: *BusinessWeek*

A Profile of **Youth** in India and China

CHINA	INDIA
66% OF YOUNG CHINESE ADULTS REGARD THEMSELVES AS INDIVIDUALISTS	**62%** OF YOUNG SINGLE WOMEN SAY IT IS O.K. TO HAVE FAULTS THAT OTHERS CAN SEE
23% OF YOUNG CHINESE ADULTS SAY IT IS NOT IMPORTANT TO HAVE A CHILD	**76%** OF YOUNG SINGLE WOMEN SAY THEY SHOULD DECIDE WHEN TO HAVE A CHILD
64% OF YOUNG ADULTS SAY MARRIED MEN SHOULD DO HOUSEWORK	**51%** OF YOUNG URBAN WOMEN SAY A BIG HOUSE AND CAR ARE KEY TO HAPPINESS

Data: Grey Global Group

today's young Chinese and Indians resemble those of Americans a few decades ago. Surveys of thousands of young adults in both nations by marketing firm Grey Global Group found they are overwhelmingly optimistic about the future, believe success is in their hands, and view products as status symbols. In China, it's fashionable for the upwardly mobile to switch high-end cell phones every three months, says Josh Li, managing director of Grey's Beijing office, because an old model suggests "you are not getting ahead and updated." That means these nations will be huge proving grounds for next-generation multimedia gizmos, networking equipment, and wireless Web services, and will play a greater role in setting global standards. In consumer electronics, "we will see China in a few years going from being a follower to a leader in defining consumer-electronics trends," predicts Philips Semiconductors Executive Vice-President Leon Husson.

For all the huge advantages they now enjoy, India and China cannot assume their role as new superpowers is assured. Today, China and India account for a

mere 6% of global gross domestic product—half that of Japan. They must keep growing rapidly just to provide jobs for tens of millions entering the workforce annually, and to keep many millions more from crashing back into poverty. Both nations must confront ecological degradation that's as obvious as the smog shrouding Shanghai and Bombay, and face real risks of social strife, war, and financial crisis. Increasingly, such problems will be the world's problems. Also, with wages rising fast, especially in many skilled areas, the cheap labor edge won't last forever. Both nations will go through many boom and harrowing bust cycles. And neither country is yet producing companies like Samsung, Nokia, or Toyota that put it all together, developing, making, and marketing world-beating products.

Both countries, however, have survived earlier crises and possess immense untapped potential. In China, serious development only now is reaching the 800 million people in rural areas, where per capita annual income is just $354. In areas outside major cities, wages are as little as 45¢ an hour. "This is why China can have another 20 years of high-speed growth," contends Beijing University economist Hai Wen.

Very impressive. But India's long-term potential may be even higher. Due to its one-child policy, China's working-age population will peak at 1 billion in 2015 and then shrink steadily. China then will have to provide for a graying population that has limited retirement benefits. India has nearly 500 million people under age 19 and higher fertility rates. By mid-century, India is expected to have 1.6 billion people—and 220 million more workers than China. That could be a source for instability, but a great advantage for growth if the government can provide education and opportunity for India's masses. New Delhi just now is pushing to open its power, telecom, commercial real estate and retail sectors to foreigners. These industries could lure big capital inflows. "The pace of institutional changes and industries being liberalized is phenomenal," says Chief Economist William T. Wilson of consultancy Keystone Business Intelligence India. "I believe India has a better model than China, and over time will surpass it in growth."

For its part, China has yet to prove it can go beyond forced-march industrialization. China directs massive investment into public works and factories, a wildly successful formula for rapid growth and job creation. But considering its massive manufacturing output, China is surprisingly weak in innovation. A full 57% of exports are from foreign-invested factories, and China underachieves in software, even with 35 software colleges and plans to graduate 200,000 software engineers a year. It's not for lack of genius. Microsoft Corp.'s 180-engineer R&D lab in Beijing, for example, is one of the world's most productive sources of innovation in computer graphics and language simulation.

While China's big state-run R&D institutes are close to the cutting edge at the theoretical level, they have yet to yield many commercial breakthroughs. "China has a lot of capability," says Microsoft Chief Technology Officer Craig Mundie. "But when you look under the covers, there is not a lot of collaboration with industry." The lack of intellectual property protection, and Beijing's heavy role in building up its own tech companies, make many other multinationals leery of doing serious R&D in China.

China also is hugely wasteful. Its 9.5% growth rate in 2004 is less impressive when you consider that $850 billion—half of GDP—was plowed into already-glutted sectors like crude steel, vehicles, and office buildings. Its factories burn fuel five times less efficiently than in the West, and more than 20% of bank loans are bad. Two-thirds of China's 13,000 listed companies don't earn back their true cost of capital, estimates Beijing National Accounting Institute President Chen Xiaoyue. "We build the roads and industrial parks, but we sacrifice a lot," Chen says.

India, by contrast, has had to develop with scarcity. It gets scant foreign investment, and has no room to waste fuel and materials like China. India also has Western legal institutions, a modern stock market, and private banks and corporations. As a result, it is far more capital-efficient. A *BusinessWeek* analysis of Standard & Poor's Compustat data on 346 top listed companies in both nations shows Indian corporations have achieved higher returns on equity and invested capital in the past five years in industries from autos to food products. The average Indian company posted a 16.7% return on capital in 2004, vs. 12.8% in China.

Small-Batch Expertise

The burning question is whether India can replicate China's mass manufacturing achievement. India's info-tech services industry, successful as it is, employs fewer than 1 million people. But 200 million Indians subsist on $1 a day or less. Export manufacturing is one of India's best hopes of generating millions of new jobs.

India has sophisticated manufacturing knowhow. Tata Steel is among the world's most-efficient producers. The country boasts several top precision auto parts companies, such as Bharat Forge Ltd. The world's biggest supplier of chassis parts to major auto makers, it employs 1,200 engineers at its heavily automated Pune plant. India's forte is small-batch production of high-value goods requiring lots of engineering, such as power generators for Cummins Inc. and core components for General Electric Co. CAT scanners.

What holds India back are bureaucratic red tape, rigid labor laws, and its inability to build infrastructure fast enough. There are hopeful signs. Nokia Corp. is building a major campus to make cell phones in Madras, and South Korea's Pohang Iron & Steel Co. plans a $12 billion complex by 2016 in Orissa state. But it will take India many years to build the highways, power plants, and airports needed to rival China in mass manufacturing. With Beijing now pushing software and pledging intellectual property rights protection, some Indians fret design work will shift to China to be closer to factories. "The question is whether China can move from manufacturing to services faster than we can solve our infrastructure bottlenecks," says President Aravind Melligeri of Bangalore-based QuEST, whose 700 engineers design gas turbines, aircraft engines, and medical gear for GE and other clients.

However the race plays out, Corporate America has little choice but to be engaged—heavily. Motorola illustrates the value of leveraging both nations to lower costs and speed up development. Most of its hardware is assembled and partly designed in China. Its R&D center in Bangalore devises about 40% of the software in its new phones. The Bangalore team developed the multimedia software and user interfaces in the hot Razr cell phone. Now, they are working on phones that display and send live video, stream movies from the Web, or route incoming calls to voicemail when you are shifting gears in a car. "This is a very, very critical, state-of-the-art resource for Motorola," says Motorola South Asia President Amit Sharma.

Companies like Motorola realize they must succeed in China and India at many levels simultaneously to stay competitive. That requires strategies for winning consumers, recruiting and managing R&D and professional talent, and skillfully sourcing from factories. "Over the next few years, you will see a dramatic gap opening between companies," predicts Jim Hemerling, who runs Boston Consulting Group's Shanghai practice.

EXHIBIT 7

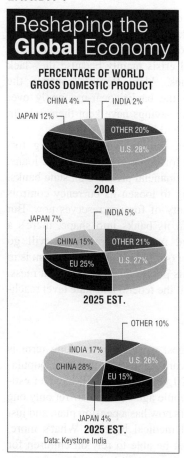

Reshaping the **Global** Economy

PERCENTAGE OF WORLD GROSS DOMESTIC PRODUCT

CHINA 4% — INDIA 2%
JAPAN 12%
OTHER 20%
U.S. 28%
2004

JAPAN 7% — INDIA 5%
CHINA 15% — OTHER 21%
EU 25% — U.S. 27%
2025 EST.

OTHER 10%
INDIA 17% — U.S. 26%
CHINA 28% — EU 15%
JAPAN 4%
2025 EST.
Data: Keystone India

"It will be between those who get it and are fully mobilized in China and India, and those that are still pondering."

In the coming decades, China and India will disrupt workforces, industries, companies, and markets in ways that we can barely begin to imagine (Exhibit 7). The upheaval will test America's commitment to the global trade system, and shake its confidence. In the 19th century, Europe went through a similar trauma when it realized a new giant—the U.S.—had arrived. "It is up to America to manage its own expectation of China and India as either a threat or opportunity," says corporate strategist Kenichi Ohmae. "America should be as open-minded as Europe was 100 years ago." How these Asian giants integrate with the rest of the world will largely shape the 21st-century global economy.

Growth Obstacles

Plenty of forces can still throw the Chinese and Indian economies far off course. The economic fundamentals of both nations, with their enormous populations of young workers and consumers, point to strong growth for decades under almost every forecast. But it is instructive to remember that financial crashes, coups, political strife, and plain bad management have derailed many other miracle economies from Southeast Asia to Latin America. And the same huge populations that can translate into economic power for China and India also could prove to be a double-edged sword if social, political, and environmental challenges are not deftly managed. Indeed, growth doesn't have to slow all that much to pose serious social problems. Both China and India need annual growth of at least 8% just to provide jobs for the tens of millions joining the workforce each year. Fear of worker unrest is a big reason Beijing has kept stoking its boom with massive lending and growth in the money supply, despite economists' warnings that it is setting the stage for a nasty bust. If India grows only 6.5% a year, which seems a respectable rate, its jobless rate would still jump, resulting in another 70 million unemployed by 2012, forecasts India's Planning Commission.

Slower growth also could keep China and India from fulfilling the widespread predictions that they will become superpowers. For example, in forecasting that India will rank just behind the U.S. as the world's No. 3 economy by mid-century, with a gross domestic product of $30 trillion, Goldman, Sachs & Co. assumes 8.5% average annual growth. But what if India grows at less than 6%, its average for the past 20 years? By 2050, it would have only a $7.3 trillion economy—smaller than Taiwan's even then and just 2.6% of global GDP, notes Stephen Howes, the World Bank's former chief India economist. Worse, India's masses would remain extremely poor. "If you don't grow fast enough, will you have social forces that bring everything to a stalemate?" asks Infosys Technologies Ltd. CEO Nandan M. Nilekani. "That's the worry."

To achieve the high growth predictions, China and India will have to overcome formidable challenges. Some of the biggest:

Environment

Both countries have paid a steep ecological price for rapid industrial and population growth, with millions of deaths attributed to air and water pollution each year.

Air quality in big cities like New Delhi, Chongqing, and Bombay is among the world's worst. And forests are vanishing at alarming rates.

Enforcement of environmental laws in both nations is poor. Many power plants and factories depend on coal and don't invest in clean technologies. China is one of the world's most wasteful users of oil. If it does not act quickly, the long-term costs of health problems linked to the environment and the required cleanup will skyrocket. A growing scarcity of water in both nations could slow industry within two decades.

Political Backlash

China's Communist Party harshly represses dissent. But virtually each week brings new reports of big protests in cities and villages over corruption, pollution, or worker abuse. They underscore China's lack of democratic institutions and the widening gap between rich and poor. Serious challenges to Communist rule can still erupt, especially if the economy stalls. Judging from history, the process could be tumultuous.

India has a democracy, but it also has extremely unbalanced growth and rampant corruption. The surprise electoral defeat of the ruling Bharatiya Janata Party by a more populist coalition led by Sonia Gandhi's Congress Party in 2004 served as a warning of mass discontent. The new government also is reform minded, but the pace of economic liberalization has slowed. Further electoral setbacks for reformers are possible if the poor don't see the benefits of growth. Tensions between Hindus and Muslims have eased after bloody riots in 2003 and 2004. But communal violence remains a threat.

Financial Crisis

Debt and currency crises have derailed many high-flying emerging markets. India needed an International Monetary Fund bailout in 1991. China withstood the 1997 Asian financial crisis mainly because they lack convertible currencies. Also, Beijing controls the banks. Bailouts and the banks' near-monopoly over China's vast domestic savings have kept them solvent despite mountains of bad loans to state firms.

In 2006, however, Beijing will start letting foreign banks compete for deposits and domestic loans. That could put more financial pressure on state banks. China also is starting to loosen its currency controls a bit. China has plenty of foreign reserves now. But if Beijing can't whip its banks into shape, there's a danger that financial market liberalization will go wrong, leading to a crash. India's financial system is in stronger shape, but its public finances remain a mess, with budget deficits at the federal and state level reaching 10% of GDP.

Health

Perhaps China's biggest worry over the long term is inadequate medical care for its rapidly aging population (Exhibit 8). In 20 years, China will have an estimated 300 million people age 60 or older. Yet only one in six Chinese workers now has a pension plan, and just 5% have guaranteed medical benefits. What's more, many retirees will not be able to rely on children for support. Beijing promises to build a broader safety net, but adequate health care and pensions could consume a huge portion of GDP and deplete China's economic strength in the future.

EXHIBIT 8

Source: *BusinessWeek*

The **Numbers** Are Ominous

1 Million	**30** Million	**203** Million
PREMATURE DEATHS EACH YEAR IN CHINA AND INDIA ATTRIBUTED TO AIR POLLUTION	INDIANS AND CHINESE PROJECTED TO BE INFECTED WITH THE HIV/AIDS VIRUS BY 2010	WORKERS WITHOUT FULL-TIME EMPLOYMENT BASED ON UNOFFICIAL ESTIMATES
Data: World Bank	Data: National Intelligence Council of India, U.N. Program on AIDS	Data: CIA World Factbook Based on a 9.2% unemployment rate in India and 20% in China

Both nations also could face full-blown crises with AIDS, tuberculosis, avian flu, and other infectious diseases, and their health systems have been slow to mobilize. At least 5 million Indian adults are infected with HIV, one of the world's highest rates outside sub-Saharan Africa. India's National Intelligence Council predicts the number could pass 20 million in 2010. The U.N. estimates the number of Chinese with HIV could hit 10 million in five years. Some 200,000 Chinese also die annually of TB. And a serious flu epidemic could kill millions. "Many investors don't appreciate the economic damage a serious outbreak would cause in our crowded cities," says Subroto Bagchi, chief operating officer of Bangalore info-tech services firm MindTree Consulting Ltd.

War

India and neighboring Pakistan have fought three times since their independence in 1947—and have had many border skirmishes over Kashmir. Now, both nations possess nuclear weapons, so a war could be catastrophic. New Delhi and Islamabad have recently eased tensions and begun peace talks. But the rise to power of a radical Islamic regime in Pakistan, or election of a stridently Hindu nationalist government in India, could easily reignite tensions. China's biggest flash point remains Taiwan. Beijing has cooled its fiery rhetoric lately, but still vows to invade should the island declare independence. Any war in the Taiwan Strait would likely involve the U.S. and possibly Japan—China's two biggest trade partners—and paralyze shipping in and out of China's southern ports. It also would likely result in long-term Sino-U.S. tensions that would spill into trade.

It's too much to expect for any developing nation to avoid military, financial, environmental, and health crises for decades. But the test for a great power is how well it manages a great crisis.

Source: Pete Engardio, "Crouching Tigers, Hidden Dragons," *BusinessWeek,* August 22/29, 2005, 52–61.

Case 2-4

Johnson & Johnson

Lots of executives at Johnson & Johnson have stories about William C. Weldon's powers of persuasion. The onetime drug salesman who now leads the health-care giant is famed for his ability to convince, cajole, or sometimes just sweet-talk colleagues into seeing things his way. A couple of years ago, Dr. Per A. Peterson, the chief of pharmaceutical research and development, was fed up with personnel headaches and told Weldon he was thinking of leaving the company. The next morning, Peterson, who lives minutes from Weldon in central New Jersey, got a call from the boss at 5:30, inviting him over for breakfast. As Weldon tended to the skillet, the two men discussed Peterson's concerns. And then they talked some more: Their conversation lasted well into the afternoon. Eventually, Peterson agreed to stay, and within a week Weldon had made the changes Peterson sought. "What else can you say to a guy who cooks you an omelette at six in the morning?" says Peterson with a laugh. "You say yes."

Weldon, 54, and one year into the job, will need those skills in spades as he guides J&J in the new century. The 117-year-old company is an astonishingly complex enterprise, made up of 204 different businesses organized into three divisions: drugs, medical devices and diagnostics, and consumer products. Much of the company's growth in recent years has come from pharmaceuticals; they accounted for almost half of J&J's sales and 61% of its operating profits last year. With revenue of $36 billion, J&J is one of the largest health-care companies in the U.S. That allows it to take bigger risks: When a surgical device business lost some $500 million between 1992 and 1995, J&J hardly felt it.

Consumers know Johnson & Johnson for its Band-Aids and baby powder. But competitors know the company as a fierce rival that boasts a rare combination of scientific expertise and marketing savvy. It regularly develops or acquires innovative products and then sells them more aggressively than almost anyone around. Even if a hospital might prefer to purchase its surgical tools from one company and its sutures from another, it could likely end up buying both from J&J because J&J offers favorable prices to hospitals that buy the whole package. J&J can also trade on its "heritage," as Weldon calls it, when it comes to persuading doctors to try its new drugs and devices. Or when it comes to persuading consumers: When J&J launched anemia drug Procrit in 1991, few expected it to make much of a difference to the company's performance. Not only did J&J spend millions to educate physicians about the condition, it also ran a series of ads on television—an unusual move considering that the drug is marketed specifically to treat anemia in chemotherapy patients. But it worked: Procrit is now J&J's best-selling drug.

The company Weldon inherited from his predecessor, Ralph S. Larsen, has been one of the most consistent, most successful health-care companies for years. Others around it are suffering as patents for important drugs expire with little of real consequence to replace them. That's expected in an industry so dependent on the unpredictable pace of scientific innovation. But not at J&J. The company is famed for delivering at least 10% earnings growth year in and year out going back nearly two decades. In the first quarter, it reported a 13% rise. Its stock price, meanwhile, has increased from less than $3, split-adjusted, in the mid-1980s to almost 20 times that now. Over the past two years, as the Standard & Poor's 500-stock index has fallen 28.1%, J&J stock has increased 19.4%. And in 2002, J&J earned $6.8 billion (excluding special charges), compared with $5.9 billion the previous year.

Maintaining that record could be Weldon's biggest challenge: Just to keep up, he must in essence create a new $4 billion business every year. But J&J's crucial drug business is finally succumbing to the pressures slowing down the rest of the industry. Procrit sales were nearly flat in the first quarter because of a new rival, news that sent the stock down 3% in one day. And like its peers, J&J doesn't have much coming out of its labs now. Meanwhile, its new drug-coated stent has been held up at the Food & Drug Administration. Approval still seems highly likely. But if the device does not get the O.K., it would be a huge blow to J&J.

What makes matters worse for Weldon is that the other component of J&J's growth—acquisitions—could become more problematic, too. Over the past decade, J&J has bought 52 businesses for $30 billion; 10% to 15% of its top-line growth each year comes from such investments. But to buy something that really affects overall performance is a different proposition for a $36 billion company than it is for a $10 billion company. "You get to a point where finding acquisitions that fit the mold and make a contribution becomes increasingly difficult," warns UBS Warburg analyst David Lothson. "This puts pressure on the sustainability of this strategy, and ultimately it could break down."

J&J's success has hinged on its unique culture and structure. But for the company to thrive in the future, that system has to change. Each of its far-flung units operates pretty much as an independent enterprise. Businesses set their own strategies; they have their own finance and human resources departments, for example. While this degree of decentralization makes for relatively high overhead costs, no chief executive, Weldon included, has thought that too high a price to pay. Johnson & Johnson has been able to turn itself into a powerhouse precisely because the businesses it buys, and the ones it starts, are given near-total autonomy. That independence fosters an entrepreneurial attitude that has kept J&J intensely competitive as others around it have faltered.

Now, though, the various enterprises at J&J can no longer operate in near isolation. Weldon believes, as do most others in the industry, that some of the most important breakthroughs in 21st century medicine will come from the ability to apply scientific advances in one discipline to another. The treatment of many diseases is becoming vastly more sophisticated: Sutures are coated with drugs to prevent infections; tests based on genomic research could determine who will respond to a certain cancer drug; defibrillators may be linked to computers that alert doctors when patients have abnormal heart rhythms.

The company should be perfectly positioned to profit from this shift toward combining drugs, devices, and diagnostics, claims Weldon, since few companies will be able to match its reach and strength in those three basic areas (Exhibit 1). "There is a convergence that will allow us to do things we haven't done before," he says. Indeed, J&J has top-notch products in each of those categories. It has been boosting its research and development budget by more than 10% annually for the past few years, which puts it among the top spenders, and now employs 9,300 scientists in 40 labs around the world.

But J&J can cash in only if its fiercely independent businesses can work together. In effect, Weldon wants J&J to be one of the few companies to make good on that often-promised, rarely delivered idea of synergy. To do so, he has to decide if he's willing to put J&J's famed autonomy at risk. For now, Weldon is creating new systems to foster better communication and more frequent collaboration among J&J's disparate operations.

Already J&J has been inching toward this more cohesive approach: Its new drug-coated stent, which could revolutionize the field of cardiology, grew out of a discussion in the mid-1990s between a drug researcher and one in J&J's stent business. Now Weldon has to promote this kind of cooperation throughout the company without quashing the entrepreneurial

EXHIBIT 1 It's Not Really about Baby Powder

Pharmaceuticals
The most profitable and fastest-growing of J&J's businesses, but expected to slow considerably as competition for its key drugs increases. The company wants to use drug-delivery technology to come up with new formulations of existing products.

SHARE OF SALES	47.2%
SHARE OF OPERATING PROFITS	60.9%

Devices & Diagnostics
Its drug-coated stent could be a multibillion-dollar blockbuster. But with the FDA approval process dragging on, J&J could also face a competing product before year end. The diagnostic group hopes to develop gene-based tests linked to promising new treatments.

SHARE OF SALES	34.7%
SHARE OF OPERATING PROFITS	26.2%

Consumer
It's the least profitable and slowest-growing of J&J's businesses, but with widely known products such as Johnson's Baby Shampoo and Band-Aids, the operation cloaks the company in an image of decency that indirectly benefits every J&J sales rep. A key opportunity: over-the-counter versions of drugs that lose their patents.

SHARE OF SALES	18.1%
SHARE OF OPERATING PROFITS	12.9%

spirit that has made J&J what it is today. Cultivating those alliances "would be challenging in any organization, but particularly in an organization that has been so successful because of its decentralized culture," says Jerry Cacciotti, managing director at consulting firm Strategic Decisions Group. Weldon, like every other leader in the company's history, worked his way up through the ranks. Among other things, it made him a true believer in the J&J system. Whatever he hopes to achieve, he doesn't expect to undermine that.

In many ways, Weldon personifies the Johnson & Johnson ethos. Though he was one of the first J&J executives to go casual in the 1990s and sometimes schedules business lunches at his favorite burger joint in Manhattan, Weldon is compulsively competitive. As he says, "it's no fun to be second." One of his first bosses recalls how Weldon badgered him to release sales figures early because Weldon was desperate to know if he had won a company competition. Weldon

is such an intense athlete that he was just a sprint away from ruining his knee altogether when he finally gave up playing basketball. It's not easy for him to keep a respectable distance from his managers now. "It's like a barroom brawl [where] you are outside looking in when you want to be in the middle of it," he says.

Weldon became famous for setting near-impossible goals for his people and holding them to it. "There was rarely an empty suit around Bill," says one former J&Jer. "If you weren't pulling your weight, you were gone." In the 1990s, when Weldon ran a business that sold surgical tools, executives back at headquarters in New Brunswick, N.J., used to systematically upgrade the reviews he gave his employees.

With that in mind, consider what Weldon is willing to do so that his changes don't threaten J&J's ecosystem: restrain himself. Although he talks incessantly about synergy and convergence, the steps he's actually taking to make sure his units cross-fertilize are measured ones. He isn't pushing specific deals on his managers. For example, industry sources say J&J has held on-and-off talks with Guidant Corp., which makes implantable defibrillators. That field of cardiovascular medicine is a growing market that's perfectly suited for some of these emerging combination therapies. But Weldon isn't leading the way in those talks. And he's delegating crucial decisions about how to spend R&D dollars.

Weldon is subtly turning up the heat on cooperation between his different units, however. J&J experts in various diseases have been meeting quarterly for the past five years to share information. Weldon and James T. Lenehan, vice-chairman and president of J&J, are now setting up two groups, focused on two diseases (they won't say which), that will work together more formally. After six months, each group will report on potential strategies and projects.

To understand Weldon's vision for the new J&J, it's useful to look at how he reshaped the pharmaceutical operation when he took it over in 1998. At the time, J&J's drug business was posting solid growth thanks to popular products such as the anemia drug Procrit and the anti-psychotic medication Risperdal. But the drug R&D operation was sputtering after several potential treatments had failed in late-stage testing. Weldon's solution was to create a new committee comprised of R&D executives and senior managers from the sales and marketing operations to decide which projects to green-light. Previously, those decisions were made largely by scientists in the company's two major R&D operations; there was no such thing as setting common priorities. Weldon also created a new post to oversee R&D and gave the job to Peterson. "Some people may have thought Bill curtailed their freedom," says Peterson. "But we've improved the decision-making to eliminate compounds that just won't make it."

Although most of the changes Weldon instituted in the pharmaceutical business won't yield real results for years, there is some evidence that this new collaboration is working (Exhibit 2). Shortly after taking charge of the drug unit, Weldon visited J&J's research facility in La Jolla, Calif., to learn about the company's genomic studies. Researchers were focused on building a massive database using gene patterns that correlate to a certain disease or to someone's likely response to a particular drug. When they told Weldon how useful the database could be for J&J's diagnostic business, he in turn urged Lenehan, who oversees the unit, to send his people out. Now, Peterson says, the diagnostics team is developing a test that the drug R&D folks could use to predict which patients will benefit from an experimental cancer therapy. If the test works, it could significantly cut J&J's drug-development costs.

Even the company's fabled consumer brands are starting to take on a scientific edge. Its new liquid Band-Aid is based on a material used in a wound-closing product sold by one of J&J's hospital-supply businesses. And a few years ago, J&J turned its prescription

EXHIBIT 2 **What Synergy Could Look Like at J&J**

Improved Drugs
J&J's pharmaceutical operation is working with the company's drug-delivery operation, Alza, to come up with a new formulation of the epilepsy drug Topamax. The drug has been shown to also promote weight loss, and this would make it a more tolerable obesity treatment.

New Medical Tests
A new diagnostic unit is working with data generated by drug researchers; they could, for example, develop a gene-based test to identify patients most likely to respond to experimental cancer treatments.

Cutting-Edge Consumer Products
In 2002, J&J rolled out the new Band-Aid Brand Liquid Bandage, a liquid coating that is applied to cuts on hard-to-cover areas like fingers and knuckles. The product is based on a material used in a wound-closing product sold by J&J's hospital-products company, Ethicon.

antifungal treatment, Nizoral, into a dandruff shampoo. Indeed, these kinds of products are one reason operating margins for the consumer business have increased from 13.8% in 2000 to 18.7% in 2002.

But perhaps the most promising result of this approach is J&J's drug-coated stent, called Cypher (Exhibit 3). A few years after that first meeting between researchers, J&J created teams from the drug business and the device operation to collaborate on manufacturing the stent, which props open arteries after angioplasty. "If we didn't have all this [expertise]," Weldon says, "we'd probably still be negotiating with [outside] companies to put this together." And to show that he is letting managers mind their own businesses, Weldon says that he only gets briefed about the stent's progress every month (though he does invite Robert W. Croce, the division head, to dinner for more casual updates). "They are the experts who know the marketplace, know the hospitals, and know the cardiologists," Weldon says of the Cypher team. "I have the utmost confidence in them."

With that empowerment, though, comes the clear expectation that J&J's experts will go after their markets with the same tenacity Weldon displayed in his climb to the top. Before heading up the drug division, Weldon made his reputation at J&J in the early '90s as head of a new unit, Ethicon Endo-Surgery Inc. Ethicon Endo was supposed to establish itself in the emerging field of endoscopic surgery. J&J did what only a company of its resources can: It poured hundreds of millions into building a full line of tools for surgeons. And Weldon did what he does best: He went after the leading company, United States Surgical Corp., as if it were a mortal threat.

Weldon spent much of his time on the road, traveling the country from his base in Cincinnati to meet with surgeons and hospital executives. Once he canceled a flight home from San Diego after hearing that a potential customer was wavering. He went back the following morning to nail down the deal. Weldon often set more ambitious goals than headquarters did. Nick Valeriani, who was then vice-president of sales and marketing, recalls: "We'd have a great year and Bill would say, 'Nice job. Why couldn't it have been 25% higher?'" By 1996, J&J surpassed U.S. Surgical, which was later bought by Tyco International Ltd.

That's not to say that Weldon doesn't understand the power of positive reinforcement. Twice he wheedled higher bonuses for his managers out of New Brunswick. Another time at Ethicon Endo, he closed up shop for a day of rest after a particularly harried couple of months.

EXHIBIT 3   The Race to Keep Arteries Clear—and Rivals at Bay

There are a lot of "ifs" when it comes to Johnson & Johnson's new drug-coated stent, called Cypher. The biggest question is timing: The stent could be a billion-dollar product this year if the Food & Drug Administration approves it in time to give J&J a head start against rivals. A stent is used to prop open arteries after angioplasty; the new device is coated with a drug that prevents those arteries from re-clogging. The agency has held off giving its O.K. over a number of issues, including the shelf life of the stent. A short shelf life could hinder J&J's ability to meet initial market demand, since it wouldn't be able to sell all the stents it has manufactured already. The company says it has addressed all FDA concerns.

Even if the stent hits the market soon, as J&J has said, rivals won't be far behind. Boston Scientific Corp. is developing a stent coated with a different drug that it could launch by year's end. And if the two devices are equally effective, doctors may not favor J&J's version. That's because analysts say Boston Scientific's metal stent itself, as well as the system for inserting it into the body, is more flexible and easier to use.

Then there's the risk of a backlash against the cost of J&J's new stent. In 1994, when J&J introduced the first widely used one, the company irked cardiologists with the stent's steep price: $1,600. Nor had J&J gotten additional Medicare reimbursement for hospitals. To make matters worse, it took the company three years to develop a meaningful improvement on the original. The result is that J&J lost its dominance in a crucial market it helped to create. Robert W. Croce, company group chairman for Cordis, the unit developing the stent, says J&J has successfully lobbied for increased Medicare reimbursement in advance this time (good thing, since the stent might go for as much as $3,000) and plans to roll out a new and better version every 15 months.

But Brue Chandler, executive vice-president at St. Joseph's Health System in Atlanta, says he has already heard Cordis sales representatives mention the possibility of discounts on other company products to help offset the price of the stent. "I find that objectionable, because it doesn't go to the core issue of introducing a product at a [reasonable] price," says Chandler. He adds: "They've already begun alienating the purchasing market." J&J's Croce says the company will work with hospitals to deal with their concerns about the stent's cost. And it won't do so by offering selective discounts on other products. Still, if J&J isn't careful, history could repeat itself.

By Amy Barrett in New Brunswick, N.J.

How Cypher Works

1. A catheter, with a balloon at the tip, is threaded into the patient through the femoral artery in the groin until it reaches the clogged artery. The balloon is expanded, opens the artery, and is removed.

2. A catheter, now with a stent at the end with a balloon inside, is inserted. When it reaches the artery, the balloon is inflated, propping open the stent. The catheter and balloon are removed, leaving the stent in place.

3. Over time, the drug sirolimus, which is coated onto the stent, is released into the blood vessel wall. It acts to block the creation of excessive amounts of scar tissue that could reclog the artery.

He never told anyone at headquarters. And no one in New Brunswick ever said a word about it. "Hell, you are the goddamn boss," he says. "Sometimes it is better to beg forgiveness than to ask permission."

And for those executives who fell short, Weldon made it clear he didn't like to be disappointed. When a new J&J drug business, Centocor Inc., failed to meet the aggressive sales goals it set for 2000, Weldon was at the offices in Malvern, Pa., before the week was out. David P. Holveck, former company group chairman of Centocor who now runs J&J's venture-capital arm, says of Weldon: "He is a man of few words. But his body language was very clear: In this game there are two strikes. In 2001, we were expected to get it right." They did.

Not everybody appreciated Weldon's demands. None would speak for attribution, but several former executives at Ethicon Endo say Weldon alienated those he felt weren't part of the team. "He is an intimidator and a dominator," says one former executive who claims Weldon turned on him after he opposed an acquisition.

Weldon hasn't really ever taken much for granted. His father was a stagehand on Broadway for several years. While his mother, a seamstress, worked on costumes for the ballet and theater, Weldon would watch the shows from backstage. She handled Marilyn Monroe's wardrobe the night the actress sang *Happy Birthday* to President John F. Kennedy in 1962, and she retired last year at the age of 80. "My parents were very hardworking, union people," Weldon says. "It's a tough life."

When Weldon was in elementary school, the family moved to Ridgewood, N.J., which former classmates describe as a wealthy and somewhat socially competitive town. There, Weldon grew up in one of the less prosperous neighborhoods. He was an indifferent student but a determined athlete who played on both the basketball and football teams.

Weldon put himself through Quinnipiac University in Hamden, Conn., by working as a mover in Newark, N.J., on weekends and holidays. He says he got serious about his studies after he married his high school sweetheart, Barbara Dearborn, midway through college. Shortly after graduating with a major in biology, Weldon had his one and only interview at J&J. Howard Klick, who hired him as a sales rep at the McNeil Pharmaceutical unit, recalls asking him for a sales pitch on a pen. Weldon took the pen apart, then gave Klick the hard sell. "He was hungry," Klick says. "He had fire in the belly."

He'll need that drive if he's to maintain J&J's growth trajectory. At this point, most of J&J's important drugs are under assault from competitors. Growth of the company's biggest-selling product, the $4.3 billion Procrit franchise, has stalled in the face of Aranesp, a drug from archrival Amgen Inc. And side-effect problems have plagued the European version, called Eprex. As a result, Procrit, which grew at a 20%-plus rate over the past few years, may actually post a 2% decline in worldwide sales in 2003, according to J.P. Morgan Securities analyst Michael Weinstein. Meanwhile, J&J's $1.3 billion rheumatoid arthritis drug Remicade faces competing products from Amgen and Abbott Laboratories.

Weldon downplays the threat. He argues that Remicade has tremendous potential because it can be used to treat other conditions, including Crohn's disease, and that Procrit will continue to dominate the anemia market. And J&J does have 56 drugs in late-stage testing (though only eight are truly new).

With J&J's blockbusters slowing, Weldon may expect his successor at the drug unit to do something dramatic. That's what he did two years ago when he completed the company's biggest acquisition ever: buying drug-delivery player Alza Corp. for $13.2 billion to shore up the business. There are supposed synergies here too, he says. Alza's technology could help J&J devise safer and more effective formulations of existing drugs. Among them: a new sustained-release version of the epilepsy drug Topamax that could be used to treat obesity.

But buying growth is likely to be more of a challenge for J&J these days. For one thing, nearly every pharmaceutical operation around is looking to make deals. And there are relatively few companies with products that are far enough along and important enough to make a real difference to J&J.

Of course, the drug business' problems now fall to its new boss, Christine A. Poon, whom Weldon helped recruit from Bristol-Myers Squibb Co. But Weldon still jumps in every now and then. One weekend earlier this year, several senior executives were hammering out details on the $2.4 billion acquisition of Scios Inc., a biotech company that has a drug for congestive heart failure. They called Weldon at home to ask for his input on one point. Weldon decided to go to the office to give his answer. And he stayed until well after midnight. Weldon says he wanted to make an appearance because it was Poon's first major acquisition. "I wanted to be there, if nothing else, to give her some moral support," he says.

But you know he got a thrill from being back in the thick of things. As Weldon leads the company into a new era, he'll have to be careful not to cross the line between supporting his executives and encroaching on their territory. Their autonomy has been central to Johnson & Johnson's success. To refine the J&J way, Weldon will have to be among the most disciplined and restrained of executives. Keeping a company on top can be just as hard as getting it there.

Source: Amy Barrett, "Staying on Top," *BusinessWeek*, May 5, 2003, 60–68.

Part 3

Designing Market-Driven Strategies

Chapter

6

Market Targeting and Strategic Positioning

Deciding which buyers in the market to target and how to position a company's products for each market target are core decisions of market-driven strategy, guiding the entire organization in its efforts to deliver superior value to customers. Effective targeting and positioning strategies are critical in gaining and sustaining superior business performance. When these decisions are faulty, they weaken business and marketing performance.

Whole Foods Market Inc. is an interesting example of successful market targeting and positioning in the very competitive retail grocery market in the United States.[1] The retailer specializes in natural and organic foods, although the prepared foods and many other products it sells are not organic. The high end grocer targets middle class buyers who have strong value preferences for natural foods and are willing to pay premium prices for the products that are not often available from other grocery retailers. Whole Foods offers its foods in stores with appealing earth-toned hues and soft lighting. The corporate culture encourages a strong commitment to environmental issues.

Many well known food brands are not offered in Whole Foods' 186 health food-oriented U.S. supermarkets in early 2007, with 20 store openings scheduled. Whole Foods sales and profit performance is impressive in the tight profit margin retail grocery market. The retailer has grown from $1.84 billion in sales in 2000 to an estimated $6.57 billion in 2007. Management's growth target is $12 billion by 2010. Net profit increased from $29 million in 2000 to $210 million in 2007. However, Whole Foods has some major future challenges including conventional supermarkets aggressively moving into the specialty foods market and questions as to whether buyers will sustain their preferences for natural foods.

In analyzing successful marketing strategies of companies like Whole Foods, one feature stands out. Each has market targeting and positioning strategies that are positive contributors to gaining a strong market and financial position for the firm. Examples of effective targeting and positioning strategies are found in all kinds and sizes of businesses, including companies marketing industrial and consumer goods and services in domestic and international markets.

We first examine market targeting strategy and discuss how targets are selected. A discussion of targeting in different market environments follows. Next, we consider strategic positioning and look at what is involved in determining a positioning strategy for each market target. We conclude with a discussion of evaluating positioning effectiveness.

Market Targeting Strategy

The market targeting decision identifies the people or organizations in a product-market toward which an organization directs its positioning strategy initiatives. Selecting one or more promising market targets is a very demanding management challenge. For example, should the organization attempt to serve all buyers who are willing and able to buy a particular good or service, or instead selectively focus on one or more subgroups (segments)? Whole Foods management adopted a selective market targeting strategy.

Consider, for example, the development of Intel's marketing strategy of progressively targeting new product-markets in addition to the existing PC and servers' core business. Intel's market initiatives are described in the STRATEGY FEATURE. In 2006 Intel's new CEO began moving Intel into several new fields including consumer electronics, wireless communications, and health care, based on management's strategic vision of how Intel's markets and competitive space are changing (see Intel Case 3–2). This is an interesting example of the challenges of competing in rapidly changing markets.

Targeting and positioning strategies consist of: (1) identifying and analyzing the segments in a product-market; (2) deciding which segment(s) to target; and (3) designing and implementing a positioning strategy for each target.

Many companies use some form of market segmentation, since buyers have become increasingly differentiated regarding their value requirements. Micro-segmentation (finer segmentation) is becoming popular, aided by effective segmentation and targeting methods based on customer relationship management. The Internet offers an opportunity for direct access to individual customers. In the following discussion we assume that the market of interest is segmented on some basis.

Targeting Alternatives

The targeting decision determines which customer group(s) the organization will serve. A specific marketing effort (positioning strategy) is directed toward each target that management decides to serve. For example, Pfizer's targeting strategy for the launch of its new prescription pain relief product Relpax was as follows:

> Pfizer for the first time launched a new product—Relpax—without any TV advertising at all. Relpax is a prescription medicine for migraine headache relief. Pfizer identified **active young mothers as the prime target group** for Relpax and adjusted its media mix accordingly. "They are listening to the radio in the car, [going] on the Internet late at night, or reading a magazine in a quiet moment," says Dorothy L. Weitzer, a Pfizer marketing vice-president. "They are not watching TV."[2]

Market targeting approaches fall into two major categories: (1) segment targeting when segments are clearly defined; and (2) targeting based on product differentiation. As shown by Exhibit 6.1, segment targeting ranges from a single segment to targeting all or most of the segments in the market. American Airlines uses extensive targeting in air travel services, as does General Motors with its different brands and styles of automobiles. An example of selective targeting is Autodesk's targeting of architects with its line of computer-aided design software.

While segment targeting is used more extensively than product differentiation, the latter may be appropriate in certain situations. When segments are difficult to identify, even though diversity in preferences may exist, companies may appeal to buyers through product specialization or product variety. While differences may exist in needs and wants, buyers' preferences are diffused, making it difficult to define segments.[3] Specialization

Part of CEO Craig R. Barrett's strategy at Intel was to invest $28 billion in cutting-edge plants and new technologies, notwithstanding the longest downturn in the computer chip industry's history.

His goal was to have Intel chips at the heart of products in several new markets in addition to personal computers and servers. Intel is branching out from computer chips to semiconductors for a range of new products, which will in turn boost Intel's core personal computer and server business.

Intel's primary product-markets are:

- **PCs and Servers**—The core business, where Intel has an 83 percent market share of a $27 billion market.
- **Flat-Panel Televisions**—A $10 billion market where Intel's processors for decoding TV signals could halve the cost of flat-panel screens.
- **Handhelds**—Intel's chips power half of all handheld computers in a market worth $2 billion.
- **Personal Media Players**—Intel is positioned to become a leading producer of processors and memory chips in the emerging market for portable video players.
- **WiMax**—Intel's new technology should deliver high-speed Net access to a PC within thirty miles of a transmission point.
- **Cellular phones**—Intel currently holds 20 percent of a $9 billion market for memory chips and digital signal processors.

Source: Cliff Edwards, "Intel," *BusinessWeek*, March 8, 2004, 42–50.

involves offering buyers a product differentiated from competitors' products and designed to appeal to customer needs and wants not satisfied by competitors. Using a product variety strategy, the Vanguard Group offers a wide range of mutual funds to investors, which are not targeted to particular investor segments.

Factors Influencing Targeting Decisions

Market segment analysis discussed in Chapter 3 helps to evaluate and rank the relative attractiveness of the segments under consideration as market targets. These evaluations include customer information, competitor strengths and positioning, and the financial and market attractiveness of the segments. An important guide in targeting is determining the value requirements of the buyers in each segment. Market segment analysis is essential in evaluating both existing and potential market targets.

EXHIBIT 6.1
Market Targeting Approaches

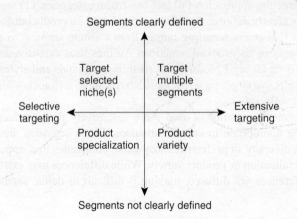

Management needs to decide if it will target a single segment, selectively target a few segments, or target all or most of the segments in the product-market. Several factors may influence the choice of the targeting strategy:

- Stage of product-market maturity.
- Extent of diversity in buyer value requirements.
- Industry structure.
- The firm's capabilities and resources.
- Opportunities for gaining competitive advantage.

Since the relevance and importance of these factors is likely to vary according to stage of product-market maturity, we use maturity as the basis for considering different targeting situations. The objective is to look at how each factor affects the market target strategy.

Targeting in Different Market Environments

The product-market environment is influenced by the extent of concentration of competing firms, the stage of maturity, and exposure to international competition. Four life cycle stages illustrate the range of product-market structures:

Emerging. Product-markets which are newly formed are categorized as emerging, and are created by factors such as a new technology, the changing needs of buyers, and the identification of unmet needs by suppliers. The satellite radio service market is illustrative of an advanced emerging product-market.

Growing. These product-markets are experiencing rapid growth. Flat-panel TVs are in an advanced stage of growth, accounting for world-wide sales in 2006 of 44 million units out of a total of 185 million TVs.[4] Competition consists of several firms and one or more may be gaining a leading market position.

Mature. These product-markets are shifting from growth to maturity, as indicated by the product life cycles of the products. Growing rapidly until reaching high levels of household penetration, microwave ovens are now in the maturity stage.

Declining. A declining product-market is actually fading away instead of experiencing a temporary decline or cyclical changes. Camera and film photography products have reached the declining stage as digital photography dominates the product-market.

The four product-market stages of evolution are neither exhaustive nor mutually exclusive. Moreover, changing environmental and industry conditions may alter a product-market classification. Also, rapid growth may occur in some countries while growth is mature or declining in other countries or regions. Because of these variations a global perspective concerning product-markets is important.

The four different market environments discussed above are closely related to the product life cycle (PLC) stages. Looking at competition during the stages of the product life cycle and at different product-market levels (generic, product type, and variant) provides insights into different types and intensities of competition. We know that products, like people, move through life cycles, and products' life cycles are increasingly shorter due to the rapid pace of technological change in the twenty-first century.

The life cycle of a typical product is shown in Exhibit 6.2. Sales begin at the time of introduction and increase over the pattern shown. Profits initially lag sales, since expenses often exceed sales during the initial stage of the product life cycle as a result of heavy introductory expenses. Total sales and profits decline after the product reaches the maturity stage. Typically, profits fall off before sales.

EXHIBIT 6.2

Life Cycle of a Typical Product

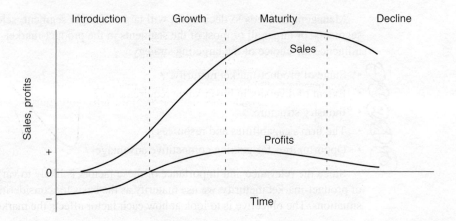

Emerging, growth, and mature market environments are discussed to illustrate different targeting situations. Also, several targeting and positioning issues in global markets are considered.

Emerging Markets

Knowledge about an emerging market is very limited. The market is new and is relatively small. The number of competitors initially consists of the first market entrant and one or two other firms. Growth patterns are uncertain and the emerging market may eventually disappear. Market definition and analysis are rather general in the early stages of product-market development. Buyers' needs and wants are not highly differentiated because they do not have experience with the product. Determining the future scope and direction of growth of product-market development may be difficult, as will forecasting the size of market growth.

There are two types of emerging markets: (1) a totally new product-market; and (2) a new product technology entering an existing product-market. In the first situation, the emerging market is formed by people/organizations whose needs and wants have not been satisfied by available products. A cure for the AIDS virus is an example. In the second situation, the market entry provides an alternative value proposition to buyers in an existing market. The entry of digital photography into the traditional camera and film market is an example of the second entry situation.

Buyer Diversity

The similarity of buyers' preferences in the emerging market often limits segmentation efforts. It may be possible to identify a few broad segments. If segmentation is not feasible, an alternative is to define and describe an average or typical user, directing marketing efforts toward these potential buyers.

Product-Market Structure

New enterprises are more likely to enter a new product-market than are large, well-established companies. The exception is a major innovation in a large company coupled with strong entry barriers. The pioneers developing a new product-market "are typically small new organizations set up specifically to exploit first-mover advantages in the new resource space."[5] These entrepreneurs often have limited resources and must pursue product-market opportunities that require low levels of investment. Industry development is influenced by various factors, including attractiveness of the market, rate of acceptance of the product by buyers, entry barriers, performance of firms serving the market, and future expectations.

Capabilities and Resources

A firm entering an existing product-market with a new product is more likely to achieve a competitive edge by offering buyers unique benefits rather than lower prices for equivalent benefits, though cost may be the basis of superior value when the new product is a lower-cost alternate technology to an existing product. For example, Voiceover Internet Protocol is a potential threat to the pricing models of the telecommunications industry.

Entry of disruptive technologies into existing product-markets may present competitive threats to the incumbent firms, because the value proposition of the new technology (e.g., digital photography) may eventually attract buyers away from incumbent firms.[6] We discuss disruptive technology in Chapter 8.

Targeting Strategy

Targeting in an emerging market is likely to focus on a preference or use situation that corresponds to the value proposition offered by the new product. The targeting decision will depend, in part, on whether a totally new product-market or new product technology is involved. Targeting in the former situation is likely to focus on an average or typical user. Targeting for a new technology in an existing market may require trying to link the value offered by the technology to buyers expected to benefit from the value offered. Market entry experimentation may be needed to refine the targeting strategy.

Growth Markets

Segments are likely to be found in the growth stage of the market. Identifying customer groups with similar value requirements improves targeting, and "experience with the product, process, and materials technologies leads to greater efficiency and increased standardization."[7] During the growth stage the market environment moves from highly uncertain to moderately uncertain. Further change in the market is likely, but there is a level of awareness about the forces that influence the size and composition of the product-market.

Patterns of use can be identified and the characteristics of buyers and their use patterns can be determined. Segmentation by type of industry (use situation) may be feasible in industrial markets. Demographic characteristics such as age, income, and family size may identify broad segments for consumer products such as food and drugs. Analysis of the characteristics and preferences of existing buyers yields useful guidelines for estimating market potential.

Product-Market Structure

We often assume that high growth markets are very attractive, and that early entry offers important competitive advantages. Nevertheless, there are some warnings for industry participants:

> First, a visible growth market can attract too many competitors—the market and its distribution channel cannot support them. The intensity of competition is accentuated when growth fails to match expectations or eventually slows. Second, the early entrant is unable to cope when key success factors or technologies change, in part because it lacks the financial skills or organizational skills.[8]

For example, the fiber-optic cable network market in the U.S. attracted far too many competitors (some 1500). Most of the networks were not being used in the early 2000s due to significant overbuilding.

Existing companies are likely to enter new product-markets at the growth stage. They have the resources to support market entry, and if there is a good capabilities/customer value requirements match, and the growth market offers high potential, entry is likely.

Recall, for example, the various existing firms that entered the digital photography market at the growth stage. Later entrants also have the advantage of evaluating the attractiveness of the product-market during its initial development.

Capabilities and Resources

The firms competing in growth markets are likely to follow one of these strategies: (1) pursuit of a market leadership strategy; or (2) follow very selective targeting and positioning strategies. Eastman Kodak is following the leadership strategy in the digital photography market, whereas, Pentax is using a more focused strategy.

Targeting Strategy

There are at least three possible targeting strategies in growth markets: (1) extensive market coverage by firms with established businesses in related markets; (2) selective targeting by firms with diversified product portfolios; and (3) very focused targeting strategies by small organizations serving one or a few market segments.[9]

A selective targeting strategy is feasible when buyers' needs are differentiated or when products are differentiated. The segments that are not served by large competitors provide an opportunity for a small firm to gain competitive advantage. The market leader(s) may not find a small segment attractive enough to seek a position in the segment. If the buyers in the market have similar needs, a small organization may gain advantage through specialization, concentrating on a specific product or component.

Mature Markets

Not all firms which enter the emerging and growth stages of the market survive in the maturity stage. The needs and characteristics of buyers also change over time. Market entry at the maturity stage is less likely than in previous life cycle stages, although firms with disruptive technologies are likely to enter at this stage.

Buyer Diversity

Segmentation is often essential at the maturity stage of the life cycle. The product-market is clearly defined, indicating buyers' preferences and the competitive structure. The factors that drive market growth are recognized, and the market is not likely to expand or decline rapidly. Nonetheless, eventual decline may occur unless actions are taken to extend the product life cycle through product innovations.

Identification and evaluation of market segments are necessary to select targets that offer each firm a competitive advantage. Since the mature market has a history, information should be available concerning how buyers respond to the marketing efforts of the firms competing in the product-market. Knowledge of the competitive and environmental influences on the segments in the market helps to obtain accurate forecasts and guide positioning strategies.

The maturity of the product-market may reduce its attractiveness to the companies serving the market, so a market-driven organization may benefit from (1) scanning the external environment for new opportunities that are consistent with the organization's skills and resources (core competencies); (2) identifying potential disruptive technology threats to the current technologies for meeting customer needs; and (3) identifying opportunities within specific segments for new and improved products. These initiatives become even more urgent when market growth shifts to decline.

Wal-Mart, the world's largest retailer, altered its targeting and positioning strategies in 2006 to target six groups of buyers in the mature U.S. retail market.[10] The six demographic groups are affluent buyers, empty-nesters, African-Americans, Hispanics, suburbanites, and rural residents. Management is grouping its 3,400 stores into six different models. Products and other positioning efforts are matched to each target group.

Buyers in mature markets are experienced and increasingly demanding. They are familiar with competing brands and display preferences for particular brands. The key marketing issue is developing and sustaining brand preference, since buyers are aware of the product type and its features. Many top brands like Coca-Cola, Gillette, and Wrigley's have held their leading positions for more than half a century. This highlights the importance of obtaining and protecting a lead position at an early stage in the development of a market.

Product-Market Structure

Mature product-markets typically experience intense competition for market share, emphasis on cost reduction, continuing needs for new products, international competition, tight profit margins, and increases in the role and importance of value chain strategies. Deciding how to compete successfully in a mature product-market is a demanding challenge.

The typical mature industry structure consists of a few companies that dominate the industry and several other firms that pursue market selectivity strategies. The larger firms may include a market leader and two or three competitors with relatively large market positions compared to the remaining competitors. Acquisition may be the best way of market entry rather than trying to develop products and marketing capabilities. Mature industries are increasingly experiencing pressures for global consolidation. Examples include automobiles, foods, household appliances, prescription drugs, and consumer electronics.

Capabilities and Resources

Depending on the firm's position in the mature market, management's objective may be cost reduction, selective targeting, or product differentiation. Poor performance may lead to restructuring the corporation to try to improve financial performance. If improvement is not feasible, the decision may be to exit from the business.

Audi AG implemented a major turnaround strategy in the mid-1990s designed to appeal to more automobile buyers with an exciting image. The midrange Audi A4 introduced in 1995 attracted new buyers and was part of a major new product strategy to increase sales and profits. Leveraging Audi's capabilities and resources, the A4's initial entry was very successful. Supported by a major advertising campaign, the new model attracted younger buyers. Appealing to this target was a major objective of the new marketing strategy. Audi's A6 and A8 models were targeted to additional market segments.

Targeting

Both targeting and positioning strategies may change in moving from the growth to maturity stages of the product-market. Targeting may be altered to reflect changes in priorities among market targets. Wal-Mart's U.S. targeting and positioning changes discussed above are illustrative. Positioning within a targeted market may be adjusted to improve customer satisfaction and operating performance.

Targeting segments is appropriate for all firms competing in a mature product-market. The strategic issue is deciding which segments to serve. Market maturity may create new opportunities and threats in a company's market target(s). The STRATEGY FEATURE describes Levi Strauss' challenges in the mature jeans market.

Firms pursuing extensive targeting strategies may decide to exit from certain segments. General Motors dropped the Oldsmobile automotive brand in the early 2000s because of

Levi Strauss experienced major sales and profit declines after the mid-1990s. Revenues fell from $7 billion in 1996 to $4 billion in fiscal 2003.

For years the Levi brand targeted the middle price and quality market, avoiding discounters like Wal-Mart, Target, and Kohl's. Management also failed to recognize the significance of the boom in high-fashion denim. In a surprising turnaround initiative Levi has expanded its jeans market coverage to target both price and fashion-conscious buyers.

The new Levi Signature brand is available at Wal-Mart, Target, and other discounters. The more expensive Premium Red Tab is targeted to up-scale customers of retailers like Nordstrom and Neiman-Marcus.

Attempting to appeal to a wide range of market targets with a variety of poorly differentiated Levi jeans brands is risky. A potential consequence is damage to the Levi brand, and the initiative may not have a major impact on Levi's sales and profits.

Levi Strauss' failure to respond to changes in its core jeans market is illustrative of the challenges of competing in highly competitive mature markets. Recognizing the seriousness of the problem, management hired a turnaround consulting firm in late 2003.

Source: Wendy Zellner, "Lessons from a Faded Levi Strauss," *BusinessWeek,* December 15, 2003, 44.

---

the targeting overlap with its Buick brand. The targets that are retained in the portfolio can be prioritized to help guide new product planning, value chain strategy, pricing strategy, and promotion strategy and expenditures.

Global Markets

Understanding global markets is important regardless of where an organization decides to compete, since domestic markets often attract international competitors. The increasingly smaller world linked by instant communications, global supply networks, and international finance markets mandates evaluating global opportunities and threats. In selecting strategies for global markets, there are two primary options for consideration: (1) the advantages of global integration; and (2) the advantages of local responsiveness.[11]

Global Integration

This strategy considers the extent to which standardized products and other strategy elements can be designed to compete on a global basis. The world is the market arena and buyers are targeted without regard to national boundaries and regional preferences. The objective is to identify market segments that span global markets and to serve these opportunities with global positioning strategies.

Local Responsiveness

While local responsiveness is a relevant issue, the central consideration is how to segment global markets. Increasingly, the basis for global segmentation is not by country.[12] Instead, other segmentation variables are often more important. Examples include climate, language group, media habits, and income. Nestlé's skills in local responsiveness have been very important in generating strong revenue and profit performance.

Targeting

Strategies for competing in international markets range from targeting a single country, regional (multinational) targeting, or targeting on a global basis. The strategic issue is

The global success of Harry Potter books—stories of a schoolboy wizard—is based on high levels of reader enthusiasm and unconventional marketing approaches.

- Harry Potter's publishers (Scholastic Corp in the U.S., and Bloomsbury in the U.K. covering the rest of the world) have sold more than 350 million Potter books worldwide. Scholastic had a 12 million print run for the sixth Potter book.

- The seventh Potter book was launched in 2007, with the fifth movie out a few weeks later, and plans for a Harry Potter attraction in Orlando, Florida, expected to cost half a billion dollars.

- Escalating worldwide sales have been driven by Warner's massive marketing spend for the Potter movies, but especially the word-of-mouth reader recommendations to families and children.

- Sales in the U.S. and U.K. have seen deep price cutting by retailers like Amazon.com, Wal-Mart and Tesco—each seeking to get consumers into the store or onto the web site to sell other products. Amazon alone pre-ordered a million copies of the final book.

- Sales in China and other non-English speaking countries have been supported by growing numbers of people learning to read and speak English—and using the Harry Potter books as a way to get children to learn.

- The author—J. K. Rowling—hardly promotes the books, and has withdrawn more from promotional efforts with each new book.

- Strict embargos prevent fans anywhere in the world from gaining access to the book before the official publication date. Scholastic's book launch campaigns to "tease" fans in the U.S. have involved: a complete blackout on advance information, no review copies, and no author interviews allowed, while juicy plot details were "leaked" to the press. Some booksellers were allowed to display the volume before the publication day—but in locked cages.

The Harry Potter books and movies (as well as merchandise) have succeeded with crossing international boundaries in reaching the market target of child readers, and boys in particular.

Sources: Diane Brady, "The Twisted Economics of Harry Potter," *BusinessWeek,* July 2, 2007, 38–39. Ben Fenton, "Potter Sets Another Bloomsbury Record," *Financial Times,* Friday, June 29, 2007, 23. Stephen Brown, "Torment Your Customers (They'll Love It)," *Harvard Business Review,* October 2001, 83–88.

deciding whether to compete internationally, and, if so, how to compete. Also, the choice of a domestic focus requires an understanding of relevant global influences on the domestic strategy.

The GLOBAL FEATURE describes the remarkable success of the Harry Potter books in competing in global markets in an unconventional way and crossing national boundaries to reach the target market.

Positioning Strategy

Positioning strategy is discussed in the rest of the chapter. First, we provide an overview of strategic positioning and consider selection of the positioning concept. Next, we examine the composition of positioning strategy and how the positioning components are combined into an integrated strategy. Finally, we look at how positioning effectiveness is evaluated.

Positioning may focus on an entire company, a mix of products, a specific line of products, or a particular brand, although positioning is often centered on the brand. Positioning initiatives are closely linked to business strategy because strategic positioning comprises

EXHIBIT 6.3
Strategic Positioning Initiatives

POSITIONING CONCEPT

How management wants buyers in the market target to position the product (brand)

MARKET TARGET

POSITIONING EFFECTIVENESS

How well management's positioning objectives are achieved for the market target

POSITIONING STRATEGY

The combination of marketing actions used to communicate the positioning concept to targeted buyers

the efforts of the business to deliver superior value to its customers. The major initiatives necessary in strategic positioning are described in Exhibit 6.3. The buyers in the market target are the focus of the positioning strategy designed for the target. The *positioning concept* indicates management's desired positioning of the product (brand) in the eyes and minds of the targeted buyers. It is a statement of what the product (brand) means guided by the value requirements of the buyers in the market target.[13] Positioning is intended to deliver the value requirements appropriate for each market target pursued by the organization. For example, Gatorade is targeted to active people experiencing hot and thirsty use situations. The drink is positioned as the best thirst quencher and replenisher, backed by scientific tests, and Gatorade's 80 percent market share attests to effective positioning of the brand. Selecting the desired positioning requires an understanding of buyers' value requirements and their perceptions of competing brands.

The *positioning strategy* is the combination of marketing program (mix) strategies used to portray the positioning desired by management to the targeted buyers. This strategy includes the product, supporting services, distribution channels, price, and promotion actions taken by the organization. *Positioning effectiveness* considers how well management's positioning objectives are being achieved in the market target. This includes determining the metrics to be used in assessing effectiveness.

As shown in Exhibit 6.4 the positioning objective is to have each targeted customer perceive the brand distinctly from other competing brands and favorably compared to the other brands. Of course, the actual positioning of the brand is determined by the buyer's perceptions of the firm's positioning strategy (and perceptions of competitors' strategies). The desired result is to gain a relevant, distinct, and enduring position that is considered

EXHIBIT 6.4
How Positioning Works

Objective	Match the organization's distinctive capabilities with the customer value requirements for the market target. (How do we want to be perceived by targeted buyers?)
Desired Result	Gain a relevant, distinct, and enduring position by the targeted buyers that they consider important.
Actions by the Organization	Design and implement the positioning strategy (marketing program) for the market target.

Innovation Feature

Spotting Shifts in Demand in Designing Hennes & Mauritz (H&M) Apparel

It's 1:30 p.m. on a Monday in the bustling H&M store on Manhattan's Fifth Avenue, and Alma Saldana, a 28-year-old makeup artist from Houston, is stuffing three tiny vests into her black H&M shopping bag. That's on top of blouses, jackets, and pants. Saldana is in a buying frenzy. This is her first visit to H&M, the Stockholm-based fashion retailer, and it's everything she had hoped for. "Somebody told me you find great fashion at a very cheap price, and it's true!" she exclaims.

Such enthusiasm has made H&M one of the hottest fashion companies around. Central to its success is its ability to spot shifts in demand and respond with lightning speed. While traditional clothing retailers design their wares at least six months ahead of time, H&M can rush items into stores in as little as three weeks. Most of the work is done ahead, too. But when it sees consumers scooping up something like vests, it speeds a slew of new variations into stores within the same season, to the delight of shoppers like Saldana. "Speed is important. You need to have a system where you can react in a short lead time with the right products," says Chief Executive Rolf Eriksen.

How does it work? H&M designers had included a couple of cropped vests in their autumn/winter collections. In August, shortly after the vests went on sale, they started "flying out of the stores," says Margareta van den Bosch, H&M's head of design. H&M's designers in Stockholm (it has more than 100) spotted the trend in the company's worldwide sales reports, published internally every Monday. About half of them immediately started sketching new styles. As quickly as designs came off their desks, pattern makers snipped and pinned, pressing employees into service as live models. At the same time, buyers ordered fabrics. The designs were zoomed electronically to workers at H&M's production offices in Europe and Asia, which then selected manufacturers that could handle the jobs quickly. In less than two months most H&M stores had five to ten new vest styles in stock.

One of the secrets to H&M's speed is decisiveness. The people in charge of each collection can dream up and produce new fashions on their own authority. Only huge orders require approval from higher ups. "We have a flat organization. We have a shorter way to a decision," says Sanna Lindberg, president of H&M Hennes & Mauritz USA. That makes H&M fashionable in more ways than one.

Source: Steve Hamm, "SPEEDDEMONS," *BusinessWeek*, March 27, 2006, 70–71.

important by the buyers that are targeted. Management must design and implement the positioning strategy to achieve this result. A company's positioning strategy (marketing program) works to persuade buyers to favorably position the brand.

Achieving a distinct and valued position with targeted buyers is a pivotal initiative for the Stockholm based fashion retailer, Hennes & Mauritz (H&M), as described in the INNOVATION FEATURE. The specialty retailer's effectiveness in getting different functions of the business to work together in designing products is impressive. H & M's positioning strategy also benefits from effective market sensing and speed of response. H & M is a formidable competitor for Gap and other specialty retailers.

Selecting the Positioning Concept

The positioning concept indicates how management wants buyers to perceive the company's brand. Selecting the positioning concept is a key marketing and business strategy decision:

> The position can be central to customers' perception and choice decisions. Further, since all elements of the marketing program can potentially affect the position, it is usually necessary to use a positioning strategy as a focus for the development of the marketing program. A clear positioning strategy can insure that the elements of the marketing program are consistent and supportive.[14]

Choosing the positioning concept is an important first step in designing the positioning strategy. The positioning concept of the brand is "the general meaning that is understood by customers in terms of its relevance to their needs and preferences."[15] The positioning strategy is the combination of marketing mix actions that is intended to implement the desired positioning of the brand concept to achieve a specific position with targeted buyers.

Positioning Concepts[16]

The positioning concept should be linked to buyers' value requirements. The focus of the concept may be *functional, symbolic,* or *experiential.* A *functional* concept applies to products that solve consumption-related problems for externally-generated consumption needs. Examples of brands using this basis of positioning include Crest toothpaste (cavity prevention), Clorox liquid cleaner (effective cleaning), and a checking account with ABC Bank (convenient services). *Symbolic positioning* relates to the buyer's internally generated need for self-enhancement, role position, group membership, or ego-identification. Examples of symbolic positioning are Rolex watches and Louis Vuitton luxury goods. Finally, the *experiential* concept is used to position products that provide sensory pleasure, variety, and/or cognitive stimulation. BMW's automobile brands are positioned using an experiential concept that emphasizes the driving experience.

Three aspects of positioning concept selection are important.[17] First, the positioning concept applies to a specific brand rather than all of the competing brands in a product classification such as toothpaste. Second, the concept is used to guide positioning (marketing program) decisions over the life of the brand, recognizing that the brand's specific position may change over time. However, consistency over time is important. Third, if two or more positioning concepts, for example, functional and experiential, are used to guide positioning strategy, the multiple concepts are likely to confuse buyers and perhaps weaken the effectiveness of positioning actions. Of course, the specific concept selected may not fall clearly into one of the three classifications.

The Positioning Decision

In deciding how to position a brand, it is useful to study the positioning of competing brands using attributes that are important to existing and potential buyers of the competing brands. The objective is to try to determine the preferred (ideal) position of the buyers in each market segment of interest and then compare this preferred position with the actual positions of competing brands. Marketing research (e.g., preference maps) may be necessary in identifying customers' ideal positioning. Management then seeks a distinct position that matches the firm's distinctive capabilities with buyers' preferred position in the target of interest.

Determining the existing positioning of a brand by targeted buyers and deciding whether the position satisfies management's objectives are considered later in the chapter. First, we discuss developing the positioning strategy.

Developing the Positioning Strategy

The positioning strategy integrates the marketing program (mix) components into a coordinated set of initiatives designed to achieve the firm's positioning objective(s). Developing the positioning strategy includes determining the activities and results for which each marketing program component (product, distribution, price, promotion) will be responsible, choosing the amount to spend on each program component, and deciding how much to spend on the entire program.

Selecting the positioning strategy may be guided by a combination of management judgment and experience, analysis of prior activities and results, trial (e.g., test marketing), and field research. We consider several issues regarding targeting and supporting activities, followed by deciding how to develop the positioning strategy.

Scope of Positioning Strategy

The positioning strategy is usually centered on a single brand (Colgate's Total toothpaste) or a line of related products (kitchen appliances) for a specific market target. Whether the strategy is brand-specific or greater in scope depends on such factors as the size of the product-market, characteristics of the good or service, the number of products involved, and product interrelationships in the consumer's use situation. For example, the marketing programs of Johnson & Johnson, Procter & Gamble, and Sara Lee focus on positioning each of their various brands, whereas firms such as General Electric Company, Caterpillar, NIKE, and Samsung use the corporate name to position the product-line or product-portfolio. When serving several market targets, an umbrella strategy covering multiple targets may be used for certain of the marketing program components. For example, advertising may be designed to appeal to more than a single target, or the same product (coach airline seats) may be targeted to different buyers through different distribution channels, pricing, and promotion activities.

Marketing Program Decisions

A look at Nokia Corporation's positioning strategy illustrates how the Finland based global cellular phone producer combines its marketing mix components into a coordinated strategy.[18] Nokia is the world's largest producer of cell phones, with 2007 estimated sales of $59 billion, up from nearly $30 billion in 2001. Profits during the same period grew from $2.8 billion to $5.8 billion. Nokia's positioning strategy includes aggressive innovation initiatives, a very effective global value chain network, competitive pricing, and effective promotion strategies matched to its major global markets in Asia, Europe, Middle East, Africa, and the Americas. Nokia encountered intense competitive pressures and slower growth in 2004 and 2005, but overcame these problems by 2006. Motorola's clamshell phone was a particularly tough challenge. Nokia is selling nearly double the number of handsets of its largest competitor (Motorola).

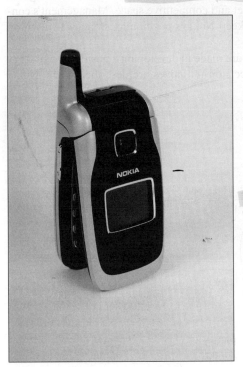

Product Strategy

In addition to cell phones, Nokia develops and produces infrastructure equipment and systems for wireless and fixed networks. It has a very active new product development program designed to excel over competition. Nokia is emphasizing radio technology and mobile-phone software in R&D efforts. Cell phones account for 63 percent of Nokia's revenues and nearly 90 percent of profits. In 2007 Nokia launched Ovi—an online music service to compete with Apple's iTunes, allowing music downloads to cell phones.

Value Chain Strategy

Nokia manages the value chain from supplier to end-user, integrating its global supply network with phone company partners. The network is very efficient although complex due to the numerous components that are part of each cell phone. The value chain has over 60 billion components moving through it each year. Nokia has been particularly effective in connecting with end-user consumers in China.

Pricing Strategy

Nokia's pricing strategy was rigid in the early 2000s but became more flexible as intense competition developed. The company's market share dropped from 35 percent which it held for several years to a low of 29 percent in 2004. It has since regained its lost market share through innovative products and competitive pricing.

Promotion Strategy

Nokia has two important customers—end-users of cell phones and service providers. The company made some mistakes with providers who wanted their phones to be identified as a provider brand. Nokia resisted while smaller competitors responded to gain market share so Nokia eventually adopted a more flexible position with its partners. Nokia had to decentralize its distribution to end-users in China, going from three sales offices to seventy to counter the sales efforts of local phone producers. It also introduced China-specific phone models with special software. These initiatives gained Nokia a strong preference over Motorola and Samsung.

Competitive Advantage

Nokia is strong on all of its positioning components. Management made some mistakes but responded with change initiatives after gaining feedback from the marketplace. Offering an innovative array of fashionable and functional cell phones is a continuing challenge. Most impressive are the firm's skills in managing a global value chain network. Nonetheless, Nokia faces tough global competition. Its positioning strategy for each market target will be an important competitive advantage that management must continue to strengthen and adapt in the complex and dynamic market and competitive space. Management's continual investment in market sensing should keep Nokia's positioning strategy focused on customer's value requirements.

An overview of the various decisions that are made in developing a positioning strategy is shown in Exhibit 6.5. Several of these decision initiatives are described in the Nokia

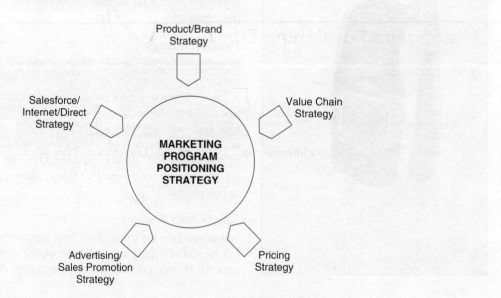

EXHIBIT 6.5
Positioning Strategy Overview

illustration. We examine each positioning component in Chapters 9–13. The present objective is to show how the components fit into the positioning strategy. The positioning concept is the core focus for designing an integrated strategy, which indicates how (and why) the product mix, line, or brand is to be positioned for each market target. This strategy includes:

- The product (good or service) strategy, including how the product/brand will be positioned against the competition in the market target.
- The value chain (distribution) strategy to be used.
- The pricing strategy, including the role and positioning of price relative to competition.
- The advertising and sales promotion strategy and the objectives which these promotion components are expected to achieve.
- The sales force strategy, direct marketing strategy, and Internet strategy, indicating how they are used in the positioning strategy.

Designing the Positioning Strategy

It is necessary to determine the major strategy guidelines for each marketing program component. What is the role of each positioning component and the objective(s) for each? What are the major strategy initiatives and which organizational unit(s) will be responsible? What are the estimated costs? Typically, the positioning strategy will be a continuation of the existing strategy, although as discussed in the Nokia illustration, changes may be necessary (e.g., shifting to more competitive pricing).

Cross-Functional Relationships

Responsibilities for the positioning strategy components (product, distribution, price, and promotion) are often assigned to various functional units within a company or business unit. This separation of responsibilities (and budgets) highlights the importance of coordinating the positioning strategy. Responsibility should be assigned for coordinating and managing all aspects of the positioning strategy. Some companies use strategy teams for this purpose. Recall in the INNOVATION FEATURE the close inter-functional coordination by H&M in identifying new apparel designs and quickly moving them into the retailer's stores. Product and brand managers may be given responsibility for coordinating the positioning strategy across functional units.

Determining Positioning Effectiveness

Estimating how the market target will respond to a proposed marketing program, and, after implementation, determining program effectiveness are essential in selecting and managing positioning strategies. Positioning evaluation should include *customer analysis, competitor analysis,* and *internal analysis.*[19] Importantly, these analyses need to be conducted on a continuing basis to determine how well the positioning strategy is performing. Positioning shows how the company or brand is differentiated from its competitors. The objective is to appeal to the value requirements of the targeted buyers. Buyers position companies and brands in responding to specific attributes or dimensions about products or corporate values. Management's objective is to gain (or sustain) a distinct position that corresponds to customers' value preferences for the brand or company being positioned in the market target of interest.

Several methods and metrics are available for analyzing positioning alternatives and determining positioning effectiveness. These include customer and competitor research, market testing of proposed strategies, and the use of analytical techniques (Exhibit 6.6).

EXHIBIT 6.6
Determining Positioning Effectiveness

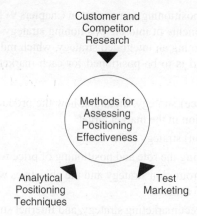

Customer and Competitor Research

Methods for Assessing Positioning Effectiveness

Analytical Positioning Techniques

Test Marketing

Customer and Competitor Research

Research studies provide customer and competitor information which may be helpful in designing positioning strategy and evaluating strategy results. Several of the research methods discussed in Part II can be used to determine the position of a brand. For example, preference maps can guide analysis in considering alternative marketing program strategies by mapping customer preferences for various competing brands compared to customers' ideal preferences.

Methods are available for considering the effects on sales of different marketing program components. For example, using multivariate testing (MVT), a screening experiment can be conducted to identify important causal factors affecting market response.[20] The advantage of MVT is examining the effects of several factors at the same time. For example, a medical equipment producer identified seven factors considered to be possible influences on the sales of a new product for use by surgeons in the operating room.

The effect of each factor can be measured using field tests to vary the amount (level) of the factor exposed to targeted buyers. For example, the high level of training consisted of a training initiative whereas the low level was no training. A fractional factorial experimental design was used to evaluate the effects of the seven factors. Different factor combinations were tested. One factor combination included no training, a monetary incentive, no vacation incentive, no mailing to physicians, mailing to operating room supervisors, letter from the president, and offering the standard product (rather than a customized version). A sample of sixty-four salespeople was randomly selected, and groups of eight were randomly assigned to each of the eight treatment combinations which were intended to enable testing the effects of each factor plus the influence of various combinations of factors.

One useful finding from the tests was that several of the factors had no impact on sales. For example, the customized product did not sell as well as the standard product. This information saved the firm an estimated $1 million in expenses by eliminating the need to offer customized product designs. Before conducting the tests, management had planned to customize the product for surgeons' use. The other results of the screening experiment were useful in designing the positioning strategy for the product. Interestingly, the vacation incentive for the salespeople had the largest effect on sales of all of the factors, surpassing even a financial incentive.

Test Marketing

Test marketing generates information about the commercial feasibility of a promising new product or about new positioning strategies for new products. The research method can also be used to test possible changes in the marketing program components (e.g., different amounts of advertising expenditures). Conventional test marketing is conducted in one or more cities where the product is marketed and data are collected to determine probable sales and/or profitability. In addition to the standard test market there are other types of market tests including controlled, electronic, simulated, and virtual tests.[21] The alternative forms of tests provide different options concerning test reality and costs. Electronic technology offers some attractive options to standard tests.

While usually less costly than a national market introduction, conventional test marketing is very expensive. Market tests of packaged consumer products often cost $2 million or more depending on the scope of the tests and locations involved. The competitive risks of revealing one's plans must also be weighed against the value of test market information. The major benefits of testing are risk reduction through better demand forecasts and the opportunity to fine-tune a marketing program strategy. We continue the discussion of test marketing of new products in Chapter 8.

Analytical Positioning Techniques

Obtaining information about customers and prospects, analyzing it, and then developing strategies based on the information coupled with management judgment is the crux of positioning analysis. Some promising results have been achieved by incorporating research data into formal models for decision analysis. These models are developed using historical sales and marketing program data. A wide range of software is available for marketing model applications (e.g., advertising media allocation models).[22]

Determining Positioning Effectiveness

How do we know if we have a good positioning strategy? Information is needed as to whether the strategy yields the results which are expected concerning sales, market share, profit contribution, growth rates, customer satisfaction, and other competitive advantage outcomes. Developing a positioning strategy that cannot be easily copied is an essential consideration. For example, a competitor would need considerable resources—not to mention a long time period—to duplicate the powerful Revenue Management decision support system developed by American Airlines. In contrast, an airline can respond immediately with a price cut to meet the price offered by a competitor.

Companies do not alter their positioning strategies on a frequent basis, although adjustments are made at different stages of product-market maturity and in response to environmental, market, and competitive forces. Recall the changes made by Nokia to gain market share. Even though frequent changes are not made, a successful positioning strategy should be evaluated on a one-to-three year basis to identify shifting buyer preferences, changes in competitor's strategies, and positioning weaknesses.

Faulty positioning can subvert a company's marketing strategy. Positioning errors include:

- *Underpositioning*—when customers have only vague ideas about the company and its products and do not perceive anything distinctive about them.
- *Overpositioning*—when customers have too narrow an understanding of the company, product, or brand. For example, Mont Blanc sells pens for several thousand dollars, but it is important to the company that the consumer is aware that Mont Blanc pens are available in much cheaper models.
- *Confused positioning*—when frequent changes and contradictory messages confuse customers regarding the positioning of the brand.
- *Doubtful positioning*—when the claims made for the product or brand are not regarded as credible by the customer.[23]

- Motorcycle icon Harley-Davidson is world renowned for its sale of distinctive "dream machines"—high price, high performance motorcycles. It sells more than 300,000 machines a year, and in many locations demand outstrips supply so dealers can charge a price premium.
- The core market for the hogs is middle-aged male baby-boomers. The CEO once stated: "What we sell is the ability for a 43-year-old accountant to dress up in black leather, ride a motorcycle through town, and make people instantly afraid of him." However, this is an aging customer base.
- The challenge for the company is to broaden its market and attract female customers and younger users of the bikes, without undermining its positioning in its core market.
- The gamble is that new product features and services aimed to attract new types of customer will not alienate existing customers.
- Product features on new Harleys to appeal to the broader market targets include: smaller handlebar grips, an easier-pulling clutch, and lower seats; new materials and engine technology will make the bikes more powerful but easier to handle; Harley dealers are providing riders' education classes to help novices learn to ride and get licensed.

Source: Michael L. Abramson, "Hurdles on the Road to Hog Heaven," *BusinessWeek,* November 10, 2003, 60–62.

Positioning and Targeting Strategies

Positioning strategies become particularly challenging when management decides to target several segments. The objective is to develop an effective positioning strategy for each targeted segment. The use of a different brand for each targeted segment is one way of focusing a positioning strategy. The Gap employs this strategy with its Gap, Banana Republic, and Old Navy brands.

It is a challenge for a company with a clear positioning and segment choice in place to also target additional segments which may undermine the strength of positioning in the existing segment. This issue may be particularly important to maintaining growth in mature markets. The STRATEGY FEATURE describing the targeting and positioning dilemma confronting Harley-Davidson is illustrative.

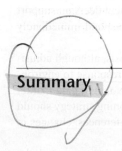

Summary

Choosing the right market target strategy can affect the performance of the enterprise. The targeting decision is critical to guiding the positioning strategy of a brand or company in the marketplace. Moreover, locating the firm's best match between its distinctive capabilities and a market segment's value requirements may require a detailed analysis of several segments. Targeting decisions establish key guidelines for business and marketing strategies.

The market targeting options include a single segment, selective segments, or extensive segments. Choosing among these options involves consideration of the stage of product-market maturity, buyer diversity, product-market structure, and the organization's distinctive capabilities. When segments cannot be clearly defined, product specialization or product variety strategies may be used.

Market targeting decisions need to take into account the product-market life cycle stage. Risk and uncertainty are high in the emerging market stage because of the lack of experience in the new market. Targeting in the growth stage benefits from prior experience, although competition is likely to be more intense than in the emerging market stage. Targeting approaches may be narrow or broad in scope based on the firm's resources and competitive advantage. Targeting in mature markets often involves multiple targeting (or product variety) strategies by a few major competitors and single/selective (or product specialization) strategies by firms with small market shares. Global targeting ranges from local adaptation to global reach.

The positioning concept describes how management wants buyers to position the brand, and is based on targeted buyers' value requirements. The concept used to position the brand may be based on the functions provided by the product, the experience it offers, or the symbol it conveys. Importantly, buyers position brands whereas companies seek to influence how buyers position brands. Success depends on how well the organization's distinctive capabilities match the value requirements of each targeted segment.

Developing the positioning strategy requires integrating the product, value chain, price, and promotion strategies to focus them on the market target. The result is an integrated strategy designed to achieve management's positioning objectives while gaining the largest possible competitive advantage. Shaping this bundle of strategies into an integrated set of initiatives is a major challenge for marketing decision makers. Since the strategies span different functional areas and responsibilities, close cross-functional coordination is essential.

Building on an understanding of the market target and the objectives to be accomplished by the marketing program, the positioning strategy matches the firm's capabilities to buyers' value preferences. These programming decisions include selecting the amount of expenditure, deciding how to allocate these resources to the marketing program components, and making the most effective use of resources within each mix component. The factors that affect marketing program strategy include the market target, competition, resource constraints, management's priorities, and the stage of the product life cycle. The positioning strategy consists of the initiatives that will be pursued to achieve the desired positioning relative to the competition.

Central to the positioning decision is examining the relationship between the marketing effort and market response. Positioning analysis is useful in estimating the market response as well as in evaluating competition and buyer preferences. The analysis methods include customer/competitor research, market testing, and positioning models. Analysis information, combined with management judgment and experience, are the basis for evaluating the positioning strategy.

Questions for Review and Discussion

1. Discuss why it may be necessary for an organization to alter its targeting strategy over time.
2. What factors are important in selecting a market target?
3. Discuss the considerations that should be evaluated in targeting a macro-market segment whose buyers' needs vary versus targeting three micro-segments within the macro segment.
4. How might a medium-sized bank determine the major market targets served by the bank?
5. Select a product and discuss how the size and composition of the marketing program might require adjustment as the product moves through its life cycle.
6. Suggest an approach that can be used by a regional family restaurant chain to determine the firm's strengths over its competitors.
7. Describe a positioning concept for three different brands/products that corresponds to functional, experiential, and symbolic positioning.
8. Discuss some of the more important reasons why test market results may *not* be a good gauge of how well a new product will perform when it is launched in the national market.

9. "Evaluating marketing performance by using return-on-investment (ROI) measures is not appropriate because marketing is only one of several influences upon ROI." Develop an argument against this statement.

10. Two factors complicate the problem of making future projections as to the financial performance of marketing programs. First, the flow of revenues and costs is likely to be uneven over the planning horizon. Second, sales may not develop as forecasted. How should we handle these factors in financial projections?

11. Discuss the relationship between the positioning concept and positioning strategy.

12. Select a product type product-market (e.g., ice cream). Discuss the use of functional, symbolic, and experiential positioning concepts in this product category.

13. Discuss the conditions that might enable a new competitor to enter a mature product-market.

14. Competing in the mature market for air travel promises to be a demanding challenge in the twenty-first century. Discuss the marketing strategy issues facing American Airlines during the next decade.

15. Assume you are assisting Nokia in determining information needs for monitoring its cell phone targeting and positioning strategies. What are your recommendations?

Internet Applications

A. PepsiCo competes in the United States and many other countries. Consider how Pepsi may utilize maps in analyzing and selecting market targets (see tiger.census.gov and www.nationalgeographic.com).

B. Go to www.johnsandjohnson.com and click on "Background" and then on "Principal Global Operations." Identify the positioning strategies of the different companies.

C. Go to www.mcdonalds.com and analyze McDonald's positioning initiatives and discuss important positioning issues for McDonalds.

D. Based on information available at www.cisco.com describe Cisco Systems' positioning strategy.

Feature Applications

A. Examine the issues described in the STRATEGY FEATURE—Harley-Davidson, and identify the problem Harley faces concerning positioning in its core market segment while trying to gain business from new segments with different needs. How can the company resolve this dilemma?

B. H&M's initiatives described in the INNOVATION FEATURE could be accomplished by competitors like Gap. Why have competitors failed to recognize these opportunities?

Notes

1. This example is based on "Eating Too Fast at Whole Foods," *BusinessWeek,* October 24, 2005, 82, 84; financial data from, *The Value Line Investment Survey, Ratings and Reports,* February 2, 2007, 15–23.

2. Anthony Bianco, "The Vanishing Mass Market," *BusinessWeek,* July 12, 2004, 63.

3. Ravi S. Achrol, "Evolution of the Marketing Organization: New Forms for Turbulent Environments," *Journal of Marketing,* October 1991, 82–83.

4. Evan Ramstad, "Flat-Panel TVs, Long Touted, Finally are Becoming the Norm," *The Wall Street Journal,* April 15–16, 2006, A1.

5. Mary Lambkin and George S. Day, "Evolutionary Processes in Competitive Markets: Beyond the Product Life Cycle," *Journal of Marketing,* July 1989, 4.

6. Clayton M. Christensen and Michael E. Raynor, *The Innovator's Solution* (Boston: Harvard Business School Press, 2003), Chapter 1.

7. Lambkin and Day, "Evolutionary Processes in Competitive Markets," 14.

8. Elaine Romanelli, "New Venture Strategies in the Minicomputer Industry," *California Management Review,* Fall 1987, 161.

9. Lambkin and Day, "Evolutionary Processes in Competitive Markets," 12.

10. Ann Zimmerman, "To Boost Sales, Wal-Mart Drops One-Size-Fits-All Approach," *The Wall Street Journal,* September 7, 2006, A1, A7.

11. Philip R. Cateora and John L. Graham, *International Marketing,* 12th ed. (Burr Ridge, IL: McGraw-Hill Irwin, 2005), Chapter 11.

12. Ibid., 22–23.

13. C. Whan Park, Bernard J. Jaworski, and Deborah J. Macinnis, "Strategic Brand Concept-Image Management," *Journal of Marketing,* October 1986, 135–145.

14. David A. Aaker and J. Gary Shansby, "Positioning Your Product," *Business Horizons,* May-June 1982, 56–62.

15. C. W. Park and Gerald Zaltman, *Marketing Management* (Chicago: The Dryden Press, 1987), 248.

16. This discussion is based on Park, Jaworski, and Macinnis, "Strategic Brand Concept-Image Management," 136–137; and David A. Aaker, *Building Strong Brands* (New York: The Free Press, 1996), 95–101.

17. Ibid.

18. This illustration is based on Bruce Einhorn and Nandini Lakshman, "Nokia Connects," *BusinessWeek,* March 27, 2006, 44–45, "Will Rewiring Nokia Spark Growth?" *BusinessWeek,* February 14, 2005, 46–47; and "The Giant in the Palm of Your Hand," *The Economist,* February 12, 2005, 67–69.

19. Aaker, *Building Strong Brands,* Chapter 6.

20. Rita Koselka, "The New Mantra: MVT," *Forbes,* March 11, 1996, 114–116; David W. Cravens, Charles H. Holland, Charles W. Lamb, Jr., and William C. Moncrief III, "Marketing's Role in Product and Service Quality," *Industrial Marketing Management,* November 1988, 301.

21. Donald R. Cooper and Pamela S. Schindler, *Marketing Research* (Burr Ridge, IL: McGraw-Hill/ Irwin, 2006), 321–327.

22. Gary L. Lilien and Arvind Rangaswamy, *Marketing Engineering: Computer Assisted Marketing Analysis and Planning* (Reading, MA: Addison-Wesley, 1998).

23. Graham J. Hooley, John A. Saunders, and Nigel F. Piercy, *Marketing Strategy and Competitive Positioning,* 3rd ed. (London Prentice-Hall Europe, 2003), 269.

Chapter 7

Strategic Relationships

The formation of strategic relationships among suppliers, producers, distribution channel organizations, and customers (intermediate customers and end-users) occurs for several reasons. The goal may be gaining access to markets, enhancing value offerings, reducing the risks caused by rapid environmental change, sharing complementary skills, acquiring new knowledge, building sustained close relationships with major customers, or obtaining resources beyond those available to a single company. Strategic relationships of these kinds are escalating in importance because of realities such as the environmental complexity and risks of a global economy, the skill and resource limitations of a single organization, and the power of major customers to insist on collaborative relationships with their strategic suppliers. Strategic alliances, joint ventures, and strategic account collaborations are examples of cooperative relationships between independent firms.

One of the key elements of IBM's business services strategy in the 2000s has been to multiply collaborative projects across all the major parts of the business: top U.S. science and engineering universities are funded to create a new academic discipline called Services Science; a partnership with Sony and Toshiba produced the new Cell processor that is in Sony's Playstation 3 and Toshiba's TVs, and will be the foundation for IBM's next generation of computers; computer code is given to the Apache free open-source Web server, and Apache is then incorporated into its commercial software; 600 IBM programmers are paid to work on the Linux open source operating system and key patents have been given to Linux. Other parts of the business have been grown through key acquisitions. Collaborating with customers and even competitors to invent new technologies is part of IBM's new strategy of openness. Sharing intellectual property in the form of software, patents and ideas should stimulate industry growth and create opportunities for IBM to sell high-value products and services that meet the new demand.[1]

Increasingly, business and marketing strategies involve more than a single organization. In this chapter we examine the nature and scope of the strategic relationships among various types of partners. We consider the full range of strategic relationships shown in Exhibit 7.1. First, we examine the rationale for interorganizational relationships and discuss the logic underlying collaborative relationships. Next, we look at different kinds of organizational relationships, followed by a discussion of several considerations that are important in developing effective interorganizational relationships. We emphasize the risks and strategic vulnerabilities that new types of business relationship strategy may create. Finally, we examine several issues that are important concerning global relationships.

EXHIBIT 7.1
Strategic
Relationships

The Rationale for Interorganizational Relationships

At one time companies mainly established relationships with other organizations to achieve tactical objectives, such as selling in smaller overseas markets. However, the modern reality is that strategic relationships among organizations relate to the key elements of overall competitive strength—technology, costs, and marketing. Unlike tactical relationships, the effectiveness of these strategic agreements among companies can affect their long-term performance and even survival.

Several factors create a need to establish cooperative strategic relationships with other organizations. These influences include the opportunities to enhance value offerings to customers; the diversity, turbulence, and riskiness of the global business environment; the escalating complexity of technology; the existence of large resource requirements; the need to gain access to global markets; and the availability of an impressive array of information technology for coordinating intercompany operations. As shown in Exhibit 7.2, the various drivers of relationships fall into four broad categories: (1) opportunities to enhance value by combining the competencies of two or more organizations; (2) environmental complexity; (3) competitive strategy; and (4) skills and resource gaps.

EXHIBIT 7.2
Drivers of
Interorganizational
Relationships

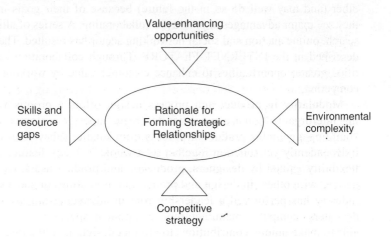

A network of grand alliances has taken shape between major Internet companies, as they prepare for the new business models of Web 2.0 and 3.0:

- Google and eBay—the alliance involves exclusive rights for Google to provide text-based advertising on eBay sites outside the U.S., and a worldwide "click to call" advertising agreement under which they will carry their respective voice services—eBay's Skype and Google Talk—on each other's shopping and search pages.
- Google and MySpace—Google has a deal with News Corporation to provide all the search and text-advertising technology on News Corp's web sites, including the very popular social networking site, MySpace.
- Yahoo and eBay—an online deal makes Yahoo the exclusive provider of branded advertising on eBay's U.S. site, while Yahoo will use eBay's payment system—PayPal—to permit customers to pay for Yahoo services. Together Yahoo and eBay reach more than 80 percent of the U.S. Internet audience.
- Google and AOL—an alliance for a global online advertising partnership, making AOL content available to Google users, with a $1 billion investment in AOL by Google. Google supplies search technology to AOL sites.
- Yahoo and Microsoft—a partnership in connecting instant messaging systems and voice chat.

While Internet search and auction companies appeared to be on a collision course, they see more benefit in collaborating than in all-out war.

Interestingly, the alliances formed emphasize the degree to which Microsoft has been shut out from the dominant online advertising partnerships. Forecasts are that Microsoft will have to acquire a company like eBay or Yahoo to rebuild its position.

Sources: Richard Waters, "Grand Alliances Shaping Web 2.0," *Financial Times,* Tuesday, August 29, 2006, 21. "The Alliance Against Google," Economist.com, August 10, 2006, www.economist.com/business.

Opportunities to Enhance Value

The opportunity present in many markets today is that organizations can couple their competencies to offer superior customer value. Even when partnering is not required, a relationship strategy may result in a much more attractive value offering.

Interestingly, the development of Internet alliances emphasizes that while major players like Google and eBay could adopt aggressive competitive positioning against each other (and may well do so in the future) because of their goals in online advertising, they see major advantages at present in collaborating. A series of alliances in the Internet search, online auction and social networking sector has resulted. These developments are described in the INTERNET FEATURE. Through collaboration companies have identified greater opportunities to enhance customer value by working together rather than competing.

Modularity in product and process design offers a promising basis for leveraging interorganizational capabilities to create superior customer value. It consists of "building a complex product or process from smaller subsystems that can be designed independently yet function together as a whole."[2] A key feature of modularity is the flexibility gained by designers, producers, and product users. Companies are able to partner with others in design and production of modules or subsystems. The computer industry has performed a leadership role in advancing the use of modularity. Chip designers, computer manufacturers, component specialists, and software firms are able to make unique contributions to product design, manufacture, and use by working within the framework of an integrated architecture which indicates how the modules fit together and the functions each will perform. Modularity can be applied to processes as well as products.[3]

Environmental Complexity

The theme of the changing and turbulent global business environment is examined in several chapters, so the present discussion is brief. Environments display escalating turbulence and diversity. Diversity refers to differences between the elements in the environment, including people, organizations, and social forces affecting resources.[4] Interlinked global markets create important challenges for companies. Coping with diversity involves both the internal organization and its relationships with other organizations. Environmental diversity reduces the capacity of an organization to respond quickly to customer needs and new product development.[5] Organizations meet this challenge by: (1) altering their internal organization structures; and (2) establishing strategic relationships with other organizations.

Procter and Gamble has reconfigured itself from being an inward-facing company to an outward facing organization that is open to collaboration. More than 50 percent of its innovation output comes from outside the company. When a revolutionary food wrapping technology was developed, P&G chose not to follow the old model of launching its own brand. The CEO took the view that this would not maximize value for the company, and instead entered a joint venture with a key competitor, who had brand, sales and distribution strengths in this market.[6]

Environmental diversity makes it difficult to link buyers and the goods and services that meet buyers' needs and wants in the marketplace. Because of this, companies are teaming up to meet the requirements of fragmented markets and complex technologies. These strategies may involve supplier and producer collaboration, strategic alliances between competitors, joint ventures between industry members, and network organizations that coordinate partnerships and alliances with many other organizations.[7]

Competitive Strategy

In some cases, working with other organizations may be a key element of how an organization competes. There are several examples suggesting this factor is of increasing importance. The "hollow organization" competes primarily through its relationships with other organizations to deliver value to end-users. The "hollow" airline, for example, is one where the airline itself owns little more than its brand, network and Internet site—engineering and maintenance services are outsourced; aircraft are leased by the hour from the manufacturer; airport services are provided by third party suppliers; food and catering services are outsourced; sales and distribution channels are online; and alliances with other airlines provide access to a network of destinations. The entirely hollow airline does not exist, but many companies in this sector already display several of its characteristics. This strategy relies on the ability to manage an array of strategic relationships with outsourcers, suppliers and alliances.

An interesting example of the use of interorganizational relationships to impact competitive strategy is provided by IBM's moves in the computer software market. Together with Sun Microsystems, IBM has been an aggressive and active supporter for suppliers of opensource software like Linux. Through sharing technology and partnerships in technology development, IBM is rebuilding the technology "ecosystem" and importantly changing its dependence on Microsoft. The INNOVATION FEATURE describes these developments.

Skills and Resource Gaps

The skills and resource requirements of technologies in many industries often surpass the capabilities of a single organization. Even those companies that can develop the capabilities

IBM collects about $1 billion a year in licensing fees from its 40,000 patents. Nonetheless, in January 2005, IBM pledged to make 500 of its software patents, valued at about $10 million, freely available to open-source software projects, such as the Linux operating system and the Apache web page server software.

The move was central to IBM's efforts to counter Microsoft and its Windows operating system monopoly. IBM's strategy is "collaborative innovation"—sharing some of its intellectual property bolsters open-source alternatives to Windows, such as Linux. IBM wants to see a non-Microsoft ecosystem in which its software and services will fit with the open-source programs it helped to develop.

IBM is also building "innovation networks"—partnerships in technology development.

Other technology companies have also donated key pieces of technology for open-source projects—Sun Microsystems handed over a suite of desktop applications, now called OpenOffice, which is a free alternative to Microsoft's Office suite.

Microsoft's response was to build a legal team to attempt to enforce intellectual property claims, and help protect its monopoly.

Sources: Steve Hamm, "One Way to Hammer at Windows," *BusinessWeek,* January 24, 2005, 34. Roger Parloff, "Microsoft Tales On the Free World," *Fortune,* May 28, 2007, 45–51.

---

may do so faster via partnering. Thus, the sharing of complementary technologies and risks are important drivers for strategic partnerships.

An interesting and unusual illustration is provided by the Anglo-German alliance between Warren Kade, a small British clothing company, and Siemens, the German engineering and electronics conglomerate. The alliance helps position Siemens' mobile phones as fashion accessories associated with designer clothing on the Paris catwalk, but with the potentials for new design concepts to be incorporated in the phones, and advanced electronics to be designed into fashion clothing. The alliance unusually brings fashion and technology closer together.[8]

Technology Constraints

Technology constraints impact industry giants as well as smaller firms. Small companies with specialized competitive strengths are able to achieve impressive bargaining power with larger firms because of their high levels of competence in specialized technology areas, and their ability to substantially compress development time. The partnerships between large and small pharmaceutical companies are illustrative. The small firm gains financial support, while the large firm gets access to specialized technology.

Access to technology and other skills, specialization advantages, and the opportunity to enhance product value are important motivations for establishing relationships among organizations. These relationships may be vertical between suppliers and producers or horizontal across industry members.

Financial Constraints

The financial needs for competing in global markets are often greater than the capacity of a single organization. As a result, companies must seek partners in order to obtain the resources essential for competing in many industries, or to spread the risks of financial loss with another firm.

Astron Clinica is a small British technology company with twenty-eight employees. It developed the Siascope machine—a device that scans the skin for melanomas. Scientists from P&G's beauty products division recognized the potential for the machine to evaluate skin conditions in the choice of beauty care products. The device was developed into the Siascope hand-held scanner branded under the Olay name (P&G's first ever co-branding). The companies now have a research collaboration as well as a commercial agreement. Alone Astron Clinton could not have taken the product to market—nor afforded the costly one-page U.S. national newspaper advertisements provided by P&G for their machines.[9]

Market Access

Interorganizational relationships are also important in gaining access to markets. Products have traditionally been distributed through marketing intermediaries such as wholesalers and retailers in order to access end-user markets. These vertical channels of distribution are important in linking supply and demand. Horizontal relationships have often been established between competing firms to access global markets and domestic market segments not served by the cooperating firms. These cooperative marketing agreements expand the traditional channel of distribution coverage and gain the advantage of market knowledge in international markets.

Standard Chartered Bank is an interesting example of a company establishing a strong competitive position in emerging markets through a combination of internal growth, strategic alliances and acquisitions. Standard Chartered was formed by the 1969 merger of The Standard Bank of British South Africa and the Chartered Bank of India, Australia and China. It derives 90 percent of its profits from Asia, Africa and the Middle East. It is expanding aggressively in India and China. The unique network built by the bank combines deep local knowledge with global capability to offer innovative products and services in the consumer and wholesale banking markets. Standard Chartered has outmaneuvered and outperformed larger rivals in building its position in emerging markets.[10]

International strategic alliances are used by many companies competing throughout the world. Commercial air travel is one of the more active industries involving overseas partners and competing through strategic alliances. This sector provides an interesting example also of the creation of new corporate brands through strategic alliances, where the alliance becomes the brand, such as the **one**world alliance revolving around British Airways and American Airlines.[11] The GLOBAL FEATURE demonstrates how essential these strategic relationships have become to competing in this industry. In effect, competition is between alliances rather than between individual organizations.

Information Technology

Information technology makes establishing interorganizational relationships feasible in terms of time, cost, and effectiveness. Advances in information technology provide an important resource for improving the effectiveness of both internal and interorganizational communications.

Information systems enable organizations to communicate effectively even though the collaborating firms are widely dispersed geographically. In particular, the Internet provides a powerful means to reduce product development times by sharing designs for components and subassemblies with suppliers, customers, and collaborators throughout the world. Internet collaboration tools allow unified communications (combining information systems with voice and text messaging), the development of global virtual teams, video and Web conferencing, and asynchronous communication (where people interact over a period of time rather than responding instantly to questions). These tools facilitate working across traditional corporate boundaries.[12]

In their short history, airline alliances have seen numerous airlines switching alliances and some alliances have disappeared: the Qualifyer alliance failed after defections by members to other alliances; the Wings alliance (KLM and Northwest) merged into SkyTeam with the KLM/Air France merger.

The three main airline alliances (**one**world, Star and SkyTeam) account for some 60 percent of the total world airline capacity, with eighteen of the world's twenty biggest airlines signed up. Unaligned legacy carriers account for 30 percent of world capacity, with low cost carriers accounting for the remaining 10 percent.

Source: www.oneworld.com.

Oneworld (10 member airlines): "**One**world revolves around you"	*Founding members:* American Airlines, British Airways, Canadian Airlines, Cathay Pacific Airways and Qantas Airways (1 February 1999).
	Additional members: Finnair and Iberia (September 1999), Aer Lingus and LAN Airlines (May 2000), Malev, Japan Airlines and Royal Jordanian (April 2007).
	Former members: Canadian Airlines, after being purchased by Air Canada, withdrew from the alliance in June 2000. Aer Lingus (joined May 2000, left April 2007).
	Future members: Dragonair is joining in late-2007.
SkyTeam (10 member airlines): "Caring more about you"	*Founding members:* Air France, Delta, AeroMexico and Korean Airlines (June 2000).
	Additional members: CSA Czech Airlines (March 2001), Alitalia (July 2001), KLM, Continental Airlines and Northwest Airlines (September 2004), Aeroflot (April 2006).
	Future members: China Southern Airlines has signed a Global Airline Alliance Adherence Agreement. MEA, Air Europa, Copa Airlines, Kenya Airways, Tarom and Portugalia Airlines have begun the process of attaining Associate status.
Star Alliance (17 member airlines, 3 regional members): "The way the Earth connects"	*Founding members:* United Airlines, Air Canada, Lufthansa, Thai Airways International and SAS-Scandinavian Airlines (14 May 1997).
	Additional members: VARIG Brazilian Airlines (October 1997), Air New Zealand (March 1999), All Nippon Airways (October 1999), Austrian Airlines Group (March 2000), Singapore Airlines (April 2000), bmi British Midland, (July 2000), Asiana Airlines (March 2003), Spanair (April 2003), LOT Polish Airlines (October 2003), US Airways (May 2004), Blue1 (October 2004, regional member), Adria Airways and Croatia Airlines (December 2004, regional members), TAP Air Portugal (March 2005), South African Airways and Swiss International Airlines (April 2006).
	Former members: Ansett Airlines (joined March 1999, failed in 2001), Mexicana Airlines (joined July 2000, ended March 2004), VARIG Brazilian Airlines (joined October 1997, ended January 2007).
	Future members: Air China Limited has signed a Memorandum of Understanding; Shanghai Airlines and Turkish Airlines have been invited to join.

Source: www.tourismfuturesintl.com.

Evaluating the Potential for Collaboration

Collaborative relations may include shared activities such as product and process design, cooperative marketing programs, applications assistance, long-term supply contracts, and just-in-time inventory programs. The amount of collaboration may vary substantially across industries and individual companies. Moreover, in a given competitive situation a firm may pursue different degrees of collaboration across its customer base. For example, some customer relationships are transactional, but the same supplier may seek collaborative relationships with other customers.

Several criteria are relevant when considering possible collaborative relationships with other organizations. We examine each factor, indicating important issues concerning how the factor may impact a strategic relationship.

What Is the Strategy?

Partnering is the result of two organizations working together toward a common objective such as sharing technologies, market access, or compressing new product development time. For example, a supplier may benefit from a customer's leading-edge application of the supplier's product. The key issue is that there should be a strong underlying strategic logic for collaboration. The alignment between alliance strategy and business strategy is crucial to success in partnering.[13] Many alliance failures show a management concern for the alliance as an end in itself, rather than as a means toward achieving a broader strategic goal.[14]

For example, in the early 1990s there were several alliances between computer and telecommunications companies like Apple, AT&T, and Hewlett-Packard to develop hand-held computers. None of the products generated survived and the alliances disappeared. Nonetheless, this does not signal failure. The alliances allowed participants to conduct market experiments quickly and at relatively low cost.[15] Indeed, research by Accenture on alliance issues and trends finds that for nearly half the companies involved in strategic alliances, learning was seen as the critical goal. Achieving learning goals through alliances is highly associated with successful alliances.[16]

Consider the strategic rationale for the alliance between Boeing and Lockheed Martin to promote the advancement of the future of air transportation in the United States. Rapid expansion of air traffic in the U.S. identifies an opportunity in developing new generations of air traffic control systems to enable this growth. The collaboration brings together Lockheed Martin's air traffic management experience with Boeing's strengths in aircraft systems, avionics, aviation operations and airspace simulation and modeling.[17] While the challenges in meeting the goals of the alliance are considerable, there is a clear and compelling strategic logic from the outset.

The Costs of Collaboration

This factor considers the costs as well as the benefits of partnering with customers, suppliers, and competitors. Strategic relationships are demanding in terms of both time and resources. The relationship may require substantial investments by the partners, which may not easily be transferred to other business relationships. Accordingly, the benefits need to be candidly assessed and compared to the costs. This requires careful planning of the relationship to spell out activities, participants, and costs.

Opportunity costs should form part of this calculation—participation in an alliance may restrict a company's freedom to pursue other strategies. Alliance partners may object to strategic moves by other alliance members, even though they are outside the scope of the alliance agreement. British supermarket leader Tesco had a joint venture in the U.S. with Safeway to operate Grocery Works for online home shopping. Tesco's plans to enter the U.S. market with its new convenience store format have led Safeway to reevaluate the joint venture, and to end the collaboration by making Grocery Works a wholly owned subsidiary.[18]

Is Relationship Strategy Essential?

Normally, relationships are formed because the partners believe that combining their efforts is essential, and that pursuing the project alone is not feasible. However, experience indicates that strategic relationships are more likely to succeed when dependence is important and equivalent between the collaborating organizations.

Are Good Candidates Available?

Promising partners may be unwilling to collaborate or already involved with other organizations. For example, many of the desirable global airline alliance partners have established relationships (see the GLOBAL FEATURE on Airline Strategic Alliances), and partnering with weaker companies is increasingly undesirable in this sector.

Do Relationships Fit Our Culture?

The corporate cultures of the partners should be adaptable to the partnership. This issue is particularly important for partners from countries with substantial national cultural differences. The partners' approach to business activities and priorities should be compatible.

For example, the global alliance between British Telecom (BT) and AT&T aimed to combine resources around "Concert"—a product to provide multinational corporations with a single, global telecoms source based on "virtual private networks," with target sales of $10 billion. BT had a record of failed partnerships in its globalization history. AT&T lacked experience in collaborative situations, and its earlier global alliance—Unisource— had broken down over AT&T's reluctance to cooperate with foreign partners or commit to common investment with them. After a relationship of persistent squabbling between BT and AT&T, the Concert alliance collapsed after only two years. Costs to BT of unwinding from the alliance are estimated at $2.1 billion, with charges of $5.5 billion to AT&T from Concert's demise.[19]

We will discuss shortly the related question of partnering capabilities. It is becoming clear that the ability to operate effective relationship strategies between organizations relies on skills and capabilities which vary considerably between organizations.

Forms of Organizational Relationships

The types of organizational relationships that may be formed by a firm are shown in Exhibit 7.3. Included are supplier and customer partnerships (vertical relationships), lateral (horizontal) relationships, and internal relationships. Relationships are both interorganizational (between organizations) and intraorganizational (internal relationships). Supplier relationships include those companies providing goods and services, some of which may be regarded as strategic suppliers or outsources, because they impact on the focal firm's ability to deliver value to its customers. Customer partnerships include both intermediate customers (e.g., distributors) and end-use customers (consumers of the product). Lateral relationships may be with competitors, unrelated companies at the same stage of the value chain, or governmental organizations. Internal partnerships include relationships with strategic business units, functional departments and employees within the business.

A useful way to examine organizational relationships is to consider whether the tie between firms is *vertical* or *horizontal*. The focal firm may participate in both vertical and horizontal relationships. We first look at vertical relationships among organizations, and

EXHIBIT 7.3
**Vertical and Lateral
Organizational
Relationships**

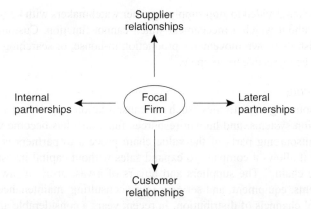

then, strategic alliances and joint ventures, followed by internal relationships. Evolving global relationships among organizations are examined in a subsequent section.

Supplier Relationships

Moving products through various stages in the value-added process often involves linking suppliers, manufacturers, distributors, and consumer and business end-users of goods and services into vertical channels. Functional specialization and efficiency create the need for different types of organizations. For example, wholesalers stock products in inventory and deploy them when needed to retailers, thus reducing the delays of ordering direct from manufacturers.

Over recent years the use of collaborative relationships with suppliers has expanded in many industries. While problems such as industrial secrets, labor objections, and loss of control occurred, the benefits of leveraging of distinctive capabilities of partners are substantial in developing new products and production processes. These relationships are extensively used in the automotive and computer industries.

Strategic Suppliers

Relationships with suppliers are often managed by a company's procurement function. However, when a supplier has a major impact on the company's value offering and its relationships with its own customers, the supplier may be regarded as strategic. In some situations, managing supplier relationship management systems closely linked to customer relationship management systems may be mandated. In such cases, the involvement of marketing executives in supplier relationships may be vital.[20] The depth of supplier relationships characterizes the business strategy of successful automakers Toyota and Honda.[21]

Dell Inc. and EMC have a successful strategic relationship in the information storage business. EMC manufactures storage products and Dell is a re-seller. The alliance pairs a leading computer systems company (Dell) with the leader in networked information storage systems (EMC). Dell is able to address a broader range of customer needs for storage products, while EMC increases its presence in the rapidly growing Windows-based storage markets. Dell is the major re-seller of EMC storage products in several areas. The co-branded EMC products are Dell's standard offer for storage area networks and high-end network-attached storage solutions. The companies work together in technical design of systems and selling to Dell's enterprise customers.[22]

High levels of dependence on a strategic supplier are an important concern. Swatch in Switzerland has a dominant position in mechanical watch movements—supplying movements for around three-quarters of the mechanical watches produced in Switzerland. To be called "Swiss-made," watches have to have movements manufactured in Switzerland. In

2005, Swatch decided to stop supplying other watchmakers with key components of movements, without which a mechanical watch cannot function. Customers are left investing to establish their own movements production in-house, or searching for other supplies, or they risk being unable to compete.[23]

Outsourcing

The outsourcing of activities, such as transportation, repair and maintenance services, information systems, and human resources functions, has become widely used in recent years. Outsourcing parts of the value chain process to partners is a form of leveraged growth—it allows a company to expand sales without capital investment at all stages of the value chain.[24] The suppliers and buyers of a vast array of raw materials, parts and components, equipment, and services (e.g., consulting, maintenance) are linked together in vertical channels of distribution. In recent years a considerable amount of outsourcing activity has located manufacturing and systems like call centers in emerging markets with very low costs. In many cases outsourcing operations has been followed by outsourcing R&D and design—for example, Taiwanese companies design and manufacture most laptop computers sold worldwide; India's HCL is co-developing systems and controls for Boeing's Dreamliner; and GlaxoSmithKline and Eli Lilly are teaming up with Asian biotechnology companies to cut the $500 million cost of bringing a new pharmaceutical to market.[25]

An interesting illustration is provided by BMW. For the first time in its history, luxury automobile manufacturer BMW has outsourced production of its vehicles. The company has outsourced engineering and production of the X3 compact SUV to Magna Steyr in Austria. Magna had previously produced cars for Mercedes-Benz, Audi, Volkswagen, Jeep and Chrysler, and leveraged this experience to get the X3 from concept to production in 28 months—several months faster than BMW's normal in-house performance. The new manufacturing model offers major benefits, but also carries substantial risks. A growing number of auto manufacturers around the world are using the new manufacturing model for niche market vehicles.[26]

Nonetheless, there are strategic risks in outsourcing key activities like manufacturing to third parties. While there are attractions in reducing manufacturing costs by outsourcing, and focusing on R&D, product design and marketing, contract manufacturers may become competitors or share information with rivals. It may be difficult to quickly replace contract manufacturers under these conditions.[27] A particular concern is the "third shift," when an overseas contractor makes unauthorized products based on the customer's designs, which are then sold as counterfeits, threatening the position of the genuine brand.[28]

Intermediate Customer Relationships

Intermediate customers may include marketing intermediaries (e.g., wholesalers and retailers) and producers assembling products for the end-use market. Vertical relationships also occur between producers and marketing intermediaries. Value chain relationships provide access to consumer and organizational end-users. Interorganizational relationships vary from highly collaborative to transactional ties. We discuss value chain relationships in Chapter 10.

Value chain considerations may motivate new strategic relationships. The Gap is facing considerable sales problems in its traditional markets in North America and Europe. Gap Inc. has developed its first ever franchise arrangements to open stores in Singapore and Malaysia, partnering with local retailer F J Benjamin Holdings. The move is based on the logic that Gap has a strong following among consumers from these markets who shop at Gap when they are abroad, who can now shop in local franchised Gap outlets.[29]

End-User Customer Relationships

The driving force underlying strategic relationships is that a company may enhance its ability to satisfy customers and cope with a rapidly changing business environment through partnering. For example, Boeing involves airlines and even passengers in design choices for its airframes; Marriott partners with corporate customers to add value to corporate travel; and Harley-Davidson has a Harley Owners Group with more than 100,000 members.

Some believe that the future of competition lies in co-creation initiatives with customers—only by letting individual corporate customers and consumers shape products can real fit with customer needs be achieved.[30] For example, Sumerset Houseboats Inc. in Kentucky custom builds boats, engaging each individual customer in a dialogue throughout design and construction. Through the Internet, it also connects to a community of Sumerset houseboat owners so they can compare notes, which boosts customer satisfaction but also provides Sumerset with unique design insights for future products.[31]

Although building collaborative relationships may not always be the best course of action, this avenue for gaining a competitive edge is increasing in popularity. However, an important issue is selecting the customers with which to develop relationships since some may not want to partner and others may not offer enough potential to justify partnering with them. A look at Marriott's partnering strategy is illustrative.

Building customer relationships is the core sales strategy of Marriott International, Inc.'s Business Travel Sales Organization. The travel manager is the target for the selling activities of the 2,500 person sales organization. The key features of the major account sales strategy are: (1) choose customers wisely (Marriott follows a comprehensive customer evaluation process); (2) build customer research into the value proposition (understanding what drives customer value and satisfaction); (3) lead with learning by following a step-by-step sales process; (4) invest in the customer's goal setting process, rather than Marriott's; and (5) develop a relationship strategy with a sense of purpose, trust, open access, shared leadership, and continuous learning. Marriott's management recognizes that customers who regularly purchase the company's services are valuable assets who demand continuous attention by high-performance teams. Rapidly changing markets and customer diversity add to the importance of developing strong ties with valuable customers to stay in touch with their changing requirements.[32]

Relationship strategies need to recognize differences in the value of customers to the seller as well as the specific requirements of customers.[33] Marriott's emphasis on carefully selecting customers with whom to partner illustrates the importance of prioritizing sales strategies by segmenting accounts for corporate influence and profit. Relationship building is appropriate when large differences exist in the value of customers. Valuable customers may want close collaboration from their suppliers concerning product design, inventory planning, and order processing, and they may proactively pursue collaboration. The objective is to develop buyer and seller relationships so that both partners benefit from the relationship.

Frequent flyer programs have been very successful in building long-term relationships with customers. The Advantage program pioneered by American Airlines attracted other airlines as well as hotel chains, credit card companies, and rental car companies. In many different business situations, a small percent of customers account for a very large percentage of purchases. The 80/20 rule is illustrative, which states that 20 percent of customers are the source of 80 percent of sales.

Strategic Customers[34]

Similarly, in the management of relationships with large corporate customers, many organizations have moved to the adoption of Strategic/Key Account Management structures and Global Account Management approaches as ways of building teams dedicated to managing the relationship with the most valuable customers.[35] Procter and Gamble's 200 person team to manage its relationship with Wal-Mart, its biggest retailer customer, is illustrative. Strategic, key, and global accounts (customers) are increasingly considered strategic partners.

Dominant Customers

Importantly, some customers may dominate a supplier's customer portfolio. These customers may pose considerable challenges because of their ability to exert considerable influence and control over suppliers. For example, more than 450 suppliers have established offices in Wal-Mart's home town of Bentonville, Arkansas, in order to be close to their largest customer.[36] Inventory reduction moves at Wal-Mart led P&G to reduce its organic sales growth forecast by 12 percent in 2006, with a subsequent fall in share price.[37] Frequently it is mistaken to regard dominant customers as strategic relationships or partners; they are simply very large accounts with a conventional, though possibly imbalanced, buyer-seller relationship with suppliers. These sales relationships are examined in Chapter 13.

Nonetheless, the strategic significance of dominant customers should not be underestimated. The merger of Gillette with Procter and Gamble in 2006 created the world's largest consumer brands group, with a combined portfolio of brands that gives the company a much stronger bargaining position with major retailers like Wal-Mart, Carrefour, and Tesco. However, the merger also represents a significant change to P&G's business model with a new focus on lower-income consumers in markets like India and China. In positioning in these emerging markets, P&G is deliberately not partnering with powerful global retailers. In China, Gillette offers P&G access to a huge distribution system staffed by individual Chinese entrepreneurs—what P&G calls a "down the trade" system ending up with a one-person kiosk in a small village selling shampoo and toothpaste. The result of P&G's strategy should be to achieve growth in Asian markets and reduce dependence on mature markets dominated by powerful retailers.[38]

Strategic Account Management

Strategic customers are those with which the relationship is based on collaboration and joint decision making, where both buyer and seller invest time and resources in the strategic relationship. For a growing number of companies strategic account management (SAM) provides an innovative model for managing relationships with their most important customers. For example, the published strategy statement of IMI plc, a global engineering company based in the U.K., identifies strategic account management (SAM) as a key theme in achieving its goal of "leading global niche markets." The company is investing heavily "to enhance our ability to create and manage close customer relationships with our clients [and] provide IMI business managers with the skills to create and develop close and successful relationships with major customers . . . which places key account management among the central elements of IMI's business approach."[39]

The importance of these developments is underlined when customers actively promote concentration in their supply base and attempt to restrict supplier numbers. For example, in September 2005, Ford Motor announced its intention to reduce its supply base of 2,000 by around half to reduce its $90 billion purchasing budget and to improve quality. Ford announced seven "key suppliers" covering about half its parts purchasing, which get enhanced access to Ford's engineering and product planning. Ford will work more closely with selected suppliers, consulting them earlier in the design process and giving them access to key business plans on future vehicles, and committing to giving them business to allow the suppliers to plan their own investments.[40]

The rationale for SAM is that a supplier's most important customers require dedicated resources and special value-adding activities (such as joint product development, business planning, and consulting services) in the value offering. SAM is seen as a new business model that goes beyond conventional buyer-seller relationships to establish partnership and joint decision making between the customer and supplier. Nonetheless, there are substantial risks in high levels of dependence on strategic customers. Investments should be weighed against the risks of customer disloyalty and strategic change, as well as the perception of strategic customer privileges by the rest of the customer base. The attraction of SAM may rest on a degree of market and relationship stability which may not exist.

For example, in 2005 Apple Computer announced an end to its long-term strategic relationship with IBM as supplier of microprocessors for Apple desktop computers, and named Intel as the replacement. Apple believes that Intel can provide components for the products of the future, with higher performance and lower prices. Supplier switch is increasingly viewed as a strategic move by companies like Apple to leverage their competitive position, which takes higher priority than loyalty to existing strategic suppliers. Indeed, supplier switch of this kind may be an inevitable consequence of strategic change.[41]

Strategic Alliances

A strategic alliance between two organizations is an agreement to cooperate to achieve one or more common strategic objectives. Strategic alliances play a major role in almost every industry, and the typical corporation relies on alliances for 15–20 percent of its total revenues, assets, or income.[42] The relationship is horizontal in scope, between companies at the same level in the value chain. While the term *alliance* is sometimes used to designate customer partnerships, it is used here to identify collaborative relationships between companies that are competitors or in related industries. The alliance relationship is intended to be long-term and strategically important to both parties. The following discussion assumes an alliance between two parties, though recognizing that a company may have several alliance partners.

Each organization's contribution to the alliance is intended to complement the partner's contribution. The alliance requires each participant to yield some of its independence. The rationale for the relationship may be to gain access to markets, utilize existing distribution channels, share technology development costs, or obtain specific skills or resources. The alliance is not a merger between two independent organizations, although the termination of an alliance may eventually lead to an acquisition of one partner by the other partner. It is different from a joint venture launched by two firms or a formal contractual relationship between organizations. Moreover, the alliance involves more than purchasing stock in another company. Instead, it is a commitment to actively participate on a common project or program that is strategic in scope.

Some lateral relationships in strategic alliances may involve partners from wholly different sectors with a common interest in particular end customers. Honda is in a strategic alliance with Hong Kong Disneyland. Honda is sponsoring the park's Autopia attraction, which allows guests to drive to the future on electric cars, and Honda has exclusive rights to feature the park's images to promote its products. The companies see the alliance as creating opportunities for both brands.[43]

Alliance Success

The competitive realities of surviving and prospering in the complex and rapidly changing business environment encourage companies to form strategic alliances in many different industries. Some strategic partnerships have endured for substantial periods—an ongoing Fuji-Xerox joint venture was established in 1962, and Samsung and Corning have been working together since 1973.[44]

Nonetheless, the record of success of alliances is not favorable, and success rates of less than 50 percent have often been found by researchers.[45] While the alliance is a promising strategy for enhancing the competitive advantage of the partners, several failures have occurred due to the complexity of managing these relationships.

Alliance Weaknesses

Weaknesses in alliances may come from several causes. For example, collaborations suffer from the potential threat of opportunistic behavior by one of the partnering organizations. AT&T and Yahoo have a successful partnership in their venture to offer a fully integrated, high-speed broadband connection to AT&T subscribers. Yahoo receives a monthly fee for every AT&T customer using the service. Having been approached by other Internet companies, AT&T now wants Yahoo to accept only a share of revenue from products Yahoo provides. AT&T planted a story in *Wall Street Journal* to indicate that the deal was up for renegotiation at a time when Yahoo's stock was weak. It is likely that the scope of the partnership and the terms will change to Yahoo's disadvantage.[46]

Weak alignment of objectives, performance metrics, and clashes of corporate cultures can all undermine alliance effectiveness. Poorly structured partnerships may be extremely damaging to all concerned.

Types of Alliances

An alliance typically involves marketing, research and development, operations (manufacturing), and/or financial relationships between the partners. Capabilities may be exchanged or shared. In addition to functions performed by the partners, other aspects of alliances may include market coverage and effectively matching the specific characteristics of the partners.

The alliance helps each partner to obtain business and technical skills and experience that are not available internally. One partner contributes unique capabilities to the other organization in return for needed skills and experience. The intent of the alliance is that both parties benefit from sharing complementary functional responsibilities rather than independently performing them.

Requirements for Alliance Success

The success of the alliance may depend heavily on effectively matching the capabilities of the participating organizations and on achieving the full commitment of each partner to the alliance. The benefits and the trade-offs in the alliance must be favorable for each of the partners. The contribution of one partner should fill a gap in the other partner's capabilities.

One important concern in the alliance relationship is that the partner may gain access to confidential technology and other proprietary information. While this issue is important, the essential consideration is assessing the relationship's risks and rewards and the integrity of the alliance partner. A strong bond of trust between the partners exists in most successful relationships. The purpose of the alliance is for each partner to contribute something distinctive rather than to transfer core skills to the other partner. It is important for the managers in each organization to evaluate the advisability and risks concerning the transfer of skills and technologies to the partner.

Alliance Vulnerabilities

Relatedly, it is important to recognize that alliance relationships may be fragile and difficult to sustain effectively, particularly if there is a lack of trust or mutuality of interest between partners. Moreover, careful analysis is required of the impact of a failed alliance on a company's remaining ability to compete and survive. The higher the level of dependence on a partner organization, the greater the strategic vulnerability created if the alliance fails.

Joint Ventures

Joint ventures are agreements between two or more firms to establish a separate entity. These relationships may be used in several ways: to develop a new market opportunity; to access an international market; to share costs and financial risks; to gain a share of local manufacturing profits; or, to acquire knowledge or technology for the core business. For example, Coca-Cola has a longstanding joint venture with Nestlé—Beverage Partners Worldwide (formerly Coca-Cola and Nestlé Refreshments)—to take its tea and coffee brands into global markets alongside Nestlé products. In 2007, this venture was refocused on the ready-to-drink tea market—Nestle tea brands are licensed to Coca-Cola, but Nestle and Coca-Cola compete in coffee and non-tea beverages worldwide. In some cases, joint ventures can grow valuable assets—in 2001 Xerox was able to sell half its stake in Fuji Xerox Co. to Fuji for $1.3 billion, to counter liquidity problems.[47]

While joint ventures are similar to strategic alliances, a venture results in the creation of a new organization. Environmental turbulence and risk set the rationale for the venture more so than a major skill/resource gap, although both pressures may be present. Lack of success in the management of joint ventures often reflects a lack of adequate attention to planning and executing the launch of the venture, leading to strategic conflicts between partners, governance problems and missed operational synergies. A dedicated team focused on managing alignment of strategic interests of the partners and creating a shared governance system improves the chances of building a high-performing joint venture.[48]

Internal Partnering

Internal partnerships may occur between business units, functional departments, and individual employees (Exhibit 7.3). The intent is to encourage and facilitate cross-functional cooperation rather than specialization. Key internal processes such as new product development benefit from cross-functional cooperation in areas such as research and development, marketing, purchasing, finance, and operations working together to identify, evaluate, develop, and commercialize new product concepts.

The success of internal relationship strategies requires developing strong internal collaboration that cuts across functional boundaries. As noted in earlier chapters, many companies are using teams of people from various functions to manage processes such as new-product development, customer relationships, order processing, and delivery of products.

As we discussed in Chapter 1, a market-oriented organization is committed to delivering superior customer value through market sensing, interfunctional cooperation, and shared decision making. The relationship strategy requires attention to the internal structure. The starting point is building a collaborative customer-driven internal culture. Research suggests that organizations which collaborate well internally perform better in meeting customer needs, accommodating special customer requests, and introducing new products. As a result, they are perceived more favorably by customers.[49]

Four steps may be important to evaluating internal partnering: (1) a cost benefit analysis of the potential gains from improved internal synergies; (2) investigation of why collaboration is not happening—personal relationship difficulties, competing priorities, resource constraints, skills gaps; (3) assessment of what is needed to unblock the problem—restructuring,

Relationship Feature

Costco Versus Wal-Mart People Costs

Costco has achieved a major position in the U.S. warehouse club business, against major competitors Sam's Club, owned by Wal-Mart, and BJ's Wholesale Club.

- Costco's success is underpinned by selling a mix of higher margin products to more affluent customers—catering better than competitors to small shop owners and high income consumers.
- Costco searches constantly for innovation and higher productivity—new ways to repackage goods into bulk items, saving labor and increasing supply chain efficiency. It was the first wholesale club to offer fresh meat, pharmacies and photo labs.
- Remarkably, Costco compensates its employees more generously to motivate and retain good workers—one fifth of whom are unionized—and gets lower staff turnover and higher productivity. *BusinessWeek* comparisons show how Costco pays its people more but gets higher productivity in return:

It Pays a Lot More Than Wal-Mart. . .	Costco	Wal-Mart's Sam's Club	But Gets More Out of Its Workers. . .	Costco	Walmart's Sam's Club
Average hourly wage	$15.97	$11.52	Employee turnover	6% a year	21% a year
Annual health costs per worker	$5,735	$3,500	Labor and overhead costs	9.8% of sales	17% of sales
Covered by health plan	82%	47%	Sales per square foot	$795	$516
Annual retirement costs per worker	$1,330	$747	Profits per employee	$13,647	$11,037
Covered by retirement plans	91%	64%	Yearly operating income growth	10.1%	9.8%

- The 102,000 Sam's Club employees in the U.S. generated $35 billion in sales in 2003, while Costco did $34 billion with one-third fewer employees.
- Costco has one of retailing's most productive and loyal workforces.

Source: Stanley Holmes and Wendy Zellner, "The Costco Way," *BusinessWeek*, April 12, 2004, 56–57.

personnel changes, senior management intervention; and (4) consideration of the possible downside of efforts to enhance internal collaboration before acting—distraction costs and loss of accountability, initiative, and motivation.[50]

The importance of effective internal partnering to support market-driven strategy is underlined by the remarkable performance of warehouse club Costco compared to arch rival Sam's Club, owned by Wal-Mart. Costco combines higher compensation and more generous employment terms for its employees with higher productivity than Sam's Club can achieve. The RELATIONSHIP FEATURE describes CostCo's clever marketing strategy supported by strong employee relationships driving competitive advantage.

Managing Interorganizational Relationships

We know that forming and managing effective collaborative partnerships between independent organizations is complex, so we need to look further into the process of developing effective relationships. Key elements of this process are indicated in Exhibit 7.4. The objective of the relationship is first considered, followed by a discussion of several relationship management guidelines.

Objective of the Relationship

In some situations collaborative action may be an option rather than a requirement. Several possible strategic objectives of relationships are discussed below.

New Technologies and Competencies

This objective is a continuing challenge for many companies because of the increasing complexity of technology and the short time span between identifying and commercializing new technologies. Alliances with others may provide a rapid approach to learning about new technologies and their potentials.

Developing New Markets and Building Market Position

Alliances and other collaborative relationships may be promising alternatives for a single company interested in developing a market or entering a global market. This strategy requires finding potential partners that have strong marketing capabilities, and/or market position. Collaboration may be used to enter a new product market or to geographically expand a position in a market already served.

Market Selectivity

Competing in mature markets often involves either market domination or market selectivity strategies. Competition in these markets is characterized by a small core of major firms and several smaller competitors that concentrate their efforts in market segments. Firms with small market position need to adopt strategies that enable them to compete in market segments where they have unique strengths and/or the segments are not of interest to large competitors. Cooperative relationships may be appropriate for these firms. The possible avenues for relationships include purchasing components to be processed and marketed to one or a few market segments, subcontracting to industry leaders, and providing distribution services to industry leaders.

EXHIBIT 7.4
Managing
Organizational
Relationships

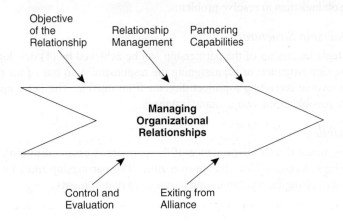

Restructuring and Cost-Reduction

Competing in international markets often requires companies to restructure and/or reduce product costs. Restructuring may result in forming cooperative relationships with other organizations. Cost reduction requirements may encourage the firm to locate low-cost sources of supply. Many producers in Europe, Japan, and the United States establish relationships with companies in newly industrialized countries such as Korea and Taiwan. These collaborative relationships enable companies to reduce plant investment and product costs.

Relationship Management

While collaborative relationships are increasingly necessary, the available concepts and methods for managing these partnerships are limited. Contemporary business management skills and experience apply primarily to a single organization rather than offering guidelines for managing interorganizational relationships. However, the experience that companies have gained in managing distribution-channel relationships provides a useful, although incomplete, set of guidelines.

Planning

Comprehensive planning is critical when combining the skills and resources of two independent organizations to achieve one or more strategic objectives. The objectives must be specified, alternative strategies for achieving the objectives evaluated, and decisions must be made concerning how the relationship will be structured and managed. To determine the feasibility and attractiveness of the proposed relationship, the initiating partner may want to evaluate several potential partners before selecting one.

Trust and Self-Interest

Successful partnerships involve trust and respect between the partners and a willingness to share with each other on various self-interest issues. Confrontational relationships are not likely to be successful. Prior informal experience may be useful in showing whether participants can cooperate on a more formalized strategic project.

Conflicts

Realizing that conflicts will occur is an important aspect of the relationship. The partners must respond when conflicts occur and work proactively to resolve the issues. Mechanisms for conflict resolution include training the personnel who are involved in relationships, establishing a council or interorganizational committee, and appointing a mutually acceptable ombudsman to resolve problems.

Leadership Structure

Strategic leadership of the partnership can be achieved by (1) developing an independent leadership structure; or (2) assigning the responsibility to one of the partners. The former may involve recruiting a project director from outside. The latter option is probably the more feasible of the two in many instances.

Flexibility

Recognizing the interdependence of the partners is essential in building successful relationships. Relationships change over time. The partnership must be flexible in order to adjust to changing conditions and partnership requirements.

Cultural Differences

Strategic relationships among companies from different nations are influenced by cultural differences. Both partners must accept these realities. If partners fail to respond to the cultural variations, the relationship may be adversely affected. These differences may be related to stage of industrial development, political system, religion, economic issues, and corporate culture.

For example, the joining of U.S. automaker Chrysler with Daimler-Benz in Germany had a compelling strategic logic—combining Daimler's luxury auto skills with Chrysler's volume manufacturing abilities. Nonetheless, the relationship was terminated in 2007 with the sale of Chrysler to the private equity company Cerberus. Chrysler held a large public celebration to mark the end of its relationship with Daimler. The DaimlerChrysler relationship was dogged by poor collaboration and in-fighting between the partnered companies. Difficulties stemmed in part from the national cultural differences and traditions between German and U.S. managers. Collaboration barriers were associated with culture differences in individualism (high for U.S. managers and much lower for Germans) and uncertainty avoidance (high for German executives and much lower for Americans).[51]

Similarly, an alliance between the Swedish pharmaceutical company Pharmacia and U.S. firm Upjohn developed serious problems because of culture differences between managers. The Swedes practiced a gradualist style of management, favoring consensus, which clashed with the U.S. style emphasizing decisive action and results. The Americans could not understand why the Swedes went on holiday for the entire month of August, and the Swedes could not understand why the Americans banned alcohol at lunch. Small disagreements escalated in major ones.[52]

Technology Transfer

When the partnership involves both developing technology and transferring the technology into commercial applications, special attention must be given to implementation. Important issues include organizational problems, identifying a commercial sponsor, appointing a team to achieve the transfer, and building transfer mechanisms into the plan. Planners, marketers, and production people are important participants in the transfer process.

Learning From Partner's Strengths

Finally, the opportunity for an organization to expand its skills and experience should be exploited. Japanese companies have been particularly effective in taking advantage of this opportunity.

Partnering Capabilities

In addition to establishing a sound process for designing and managing interorganizational relationships, it is important to consider what is necessary to build an organizational competence in strategic collaboration. The capability to manage effectively through partnerships does not exist in all organizations. Recall the collapse of the BT and AT&T strategic alliance for global telecommunications described earlier. Partnering effectively with other organizations is a key core competence, which may need to be developed. Eli Lilly is recognized as a company that generates value from its alliances, and this company addresses the skills gap by running partnership training classes for its managers and for its partners. Other successful collaborative strategies are operated by companies like Hewlett-Packard and Oracle by establishing a dedicated strategic alliance function in the company.[53]

Control and Evaluation[54]

Many conventional approaches to control and evaluation are inappropriate and ineffective in managing interorganizational collaborations. Alliance performance evaluation is a critical success factor, which requires the development and implementation of a formal evaluation process that reflects the unique differences between alliances and more traditional organizational forms. A "balanced scorecard" approach allows evaluation criteria to be specified in financial, customer focus, internal business process, and learning and growth dimensions. The goal is to have measurement metrics with both short- and long-term importance, and to incorporate both quantitative measures (e.g., sales, growth, costs) but also important qualitative measures which speak to the strength and sustainability of the alliance (e.g., trust, communications flows, conflicts, culture gaps). Importantly, particularly in the early stages of a collaborative relationship, qualitative metrics may be the most important predictors of success.

The challenge of developing appropriate ways to assess interorganizational performance and strength is considerable. It is useful to consider measures and metrics against the following principles:

- Metrics should be comparable across alliances.
- Metrics should be defined and discussed with alliance partners.
- There should be clarity about the implications of alliance performance.
- A process for auditing alliance performance should be implemented.
- Alliance performance should be linked to individual performance review.
- A forum should be created for reviewing and acting on alliance performance data.[55]

Poorly constructed relationships may show up in a variety of alliance difficulties: a lack of learning and innovation; project delays; dissatisfaction with the partner's performance; missed milestones; lack of responsiveness to changes in the marketplace; perceptions that the alliance is not adding value. These indications of problems may reflect poor relationship quality.[56]

There is a strong argument that the performance of alliances should be subject to regular review to establish where problems exist and where restructuring arrangements may be advantageous. Companies may miss opportunities to reduce costs and generate additional income by failing to: (1) *Launch a process*—scan major alliances for signs they need restructuring; (2) *Diagnose performance*—assess the venture's strategic fit and the attractiveness of continuing the alliance; (3) *Generate restructuring options*—decide whether to fix, grow, or exit the alliance; (4) *Execute the changes*—assign accountability for making changes.[57]

Exiting from Alliance

Specific collaborations and alliances may come to the end of their useful lives when the relationship fails to deliver value or the market opportunity declines. One attraction of strategic alliances is that they can be fluid and temporary arrangements to take advantage of opportunities when they occur. Effective management of strategic relationships should pay attention to managing the termination of alliances when necessary. Research suggests that executives often persist with alliances, even though measures indicate the collaboration is no longer attractive.[58] This may reflect the sunk costs in the alliance, the desire to imitate competitors' alliance successes, and the high external visibility of the alliance.

Early preparations for the eventual end of the alliance are recommended. The lack of agreement about how the alliance should be ended when appropriate suggests that when tensions arise between partners, alliance managers are reluctant to alert their superiors and risk being blamed for the failure, and instead focus their tensions on alliance counterparts. The outcome is likely to be a dysfunctional strategic alliance marked by deep animosity between alliance managers. Discussions about alliance termination are likely to be emotionally charged and ineffective.[59]

The assignment of responsibility for disengagement from strategic partnerships may usefully be given to senior executives not linked to establishing the original alliance. A successful disengagement plan, agreed between partners at the establishment of the alliance should consider:

- Identifying and agreeing to the events that will trigger exit from the alliance.
- Detailed description of the rights of each partner to alliance assets and products on disengagement.
- Design of the disengagement process.
- A communication plan for continuous flow of information to alliance partners, customers, suppliers, and other involved parties during the alliance dissolution.[60]

Failure risks in alliances and potential losses from failures mandate careful attention to the costs and processes of ending strategic relationships when this becomes a more attractive option than continuing.

Global Relationships Among Organizations

Several kinds of organizations compete in global markets. One form is the multinational corporation that may operate in several countries, using a separate organization in each country. Examples of joint ventures and strategic alliances competing in international markets are discussed throughout the chapter. The use of cooperative agreements by companies in the United States, Japan, and the European Union expanded during the 1990s and 2000s. Global relationships offer significant advantages in gaining market access and leveraging the capabilities of individual firms. Nonetheless, it is important to recognize that global relationships may operate in significantly different ways to those in the domestic marketplace.

The Global Integrated Enterprise

IBM is a highly internationalized business. It has over 50,000 employees in India—IBM's second biggest operation outside the U.S. The company has moved its head of procurement from New York to Shenzen in China.[61]

Samuel Palmisano, IBM's Chairman and CEO, has defined a vision for the globally integrated enterprise (GIE), as the twenty-first century successor to the multinational corporation.[62] Palmisano argues that businesses are changing in fundamental ways—structurally, operationally, and culturally—in response to imperatives for globalization and the impact of new technology. The emerging GIE is a company that shapes its strategy, management, and operations in pursuit of a new goal: the integration of production and value delivery worldwide. Shared business practices and connected business activities make it possible for companies to transfer work from in-house operations to outside specialists. Global integration forces companies to choose where they want work performed geographically, and whether they want it performed in-house or by an external partner. The center of the GIE is global collaboration both with commercial partners and governments. Palmisano's vision at IBM provides substantial support for the emphasis we have placed on the development of strategic relationships to deliver superior value to customers. Importantly, he places this imperative in a global or worldwide context.

Similarly, John Hagel and John Seely-Brown argue that lowered barriers to international trade and technological developments suggest companies must concentrate their areas of expertise, while collaborating globally with others specializing in different activities. The goal is to find ways of working with suppliers not simply to cut costs but to collaborate on product innovation. Li & Fung is a Hong Kong-based clothing supplier that Hagel and Seely-Brown describe as a "process orchestrator." The company produces goods for Western companies drawing on a network of 7,500 partners—yarn from Korea, dyed in Thailand, woven in Taiwan, cut in Bangladesh, assembled in Mexico, with a zipper from Japan. Importantly, these companies are partners to Li & Fung rather than simply suppliers. By operating as a network, the partners help each other innovate in both design and manufacture.[63]

Inter-Nation Collaborations

Inter-nation partnerships may create significant market change and shifts in international trading patterns. Consider the relationship between Korea and China. In the 1990s Korea's focus was on the U.S. market and its foreign relations were centered on Washington D.C. Increasingly in the twenty-first century, Korea looks at China as the regional leader in diplomacy and statecraft. In 2003, South Korean businesses invested more in China—$4.4 billion—than U.S. companies who put $4.2 billion into China. Some 25,000 Korean companies manufacture in China. Companies like Samsung and LG are using China as a major manufacturing base to produce goods more cheaply and increase global market share for their electronics products and appliances. While some fear the effects of the export of Korean jobs and technology to China, the relationship between the two countries has major global implications for the future.[64]

Interestingly, the Airbus Industrie A380 airliner project—creating the largest passenger airliner ever built—was based on an innovative cross-national alliance, greatly favored by European governments, with jobs spread over Germany, France, Britain, and Spain. The alliance has been plagued by defections—British Aerospace sold its stake in 2006—senior management losses, cross-border wrangles, and weak governance. The project has received large government subsidies, leaving Boeing in the U.S. feeling substantially disadvantaged. However, it appears that the price of government subsidy has been constant political meddling reducing efficiency and leading to huge production mistakes.[65] Technical problems, which should have been avoided, and production delays to the A380 look likely to lead to lost earnings of at least $6 billion, as customers like FedEx cancel orders and transfer the business to Boeing.[66] The coupling of cross-national difficulties and government interference may offset much of the advantage achieved through public subsidy.

The Strategic Role of Government

While the role of the government in the United States is largely one of facilitating and regulating free enterprise, governments in several other countries play a proactive role with business organizations.

Government Interventions

Government interventions range from indicating preferred strategies to companies to the full subsidy of commercial enterprises to achieve political ends. For example, in Japan the aerospace industry has been reduced over several years to the role of licensees

The flat-screen industry is highly competitive. Long-term rivals South Korea's Samsung and LG Group agreed to join forces to stave off increasing competition from Japan and Taiwan (after some prodding by the government).

The alliance between the leading South Korean flat-screen producers includes R&D, patent sharing, procurement, cross-purchasing and adopting common industry standards.

The key members of the alliance see the benefits of collaboration as increased cost competitiveness as protection against established Japanese firms and fast-rising rivals in Taiwan and China.

Samsung Electronics and LG Philips compete with Japan's Sharp and Taiwan's AU Electronics and Chi Mei optoelectronics in the liquid crystal display panel market, while LG Electronics and Samsung SDI trail Japan's Matsushita Electric Industrial in the plasma-display panel market.

South Korea is the world's biggest flat-screen maker. Its market leadership is threatened by increasing cross-border collaboration to combine Japan's technology with Taiwan and China's production capacity.

Source: Song Jung-a, "Korea's Flat-Screen Makers Put Rivalry on Hold," *Financial Times,* Tuesday, June 5, 2007, 30.

and parts suppliers. To re-build the sector for the benefit of Japan economically and politically, the government is supporting a regional jet project with Mitsubishi Heavy Industries—the MRJ will be the first jet-powered commercial passenger aircraft designed and built in Japan. The government's role is to provide a third of the development cost. Analysts suggest it is unlikely that the project will break even.[67]

The STRATEGY FEATURE describes developments in Korea surrounding the flat-screen business of Samsung and LG. It is interesting to consider the relative impact of market forces and government pressures on the companies involved.

Competing With State-Owned Enterprises

Nations may operate government-owned corporations, though in recent years a trend toward privatization of these corporations occurred in the United Kingdom, Australia, Mexico, and other countries. Nevertheless, government-supported corporations continue to compete in various global industries, including air transportation, chemicals, computers, and consumer electronics. Not surprisingly, competitors often are critical of government organizations because of their unfair advantage resulting from government financial support.

The impact of state involvement in enterprise may be considerable. In the petrochemicals/energy market, the term "the seven sisters" was once used to describe the Western companies that controlled oil supplies in the Middle East. By the 2000s only four of the original seven sisters remained: ExxonMobil and Chevron in the U.S. and BP and Royal Dutch Shell in Europe. These companies control around 10 percent of the world's oil and gas and hold 3 percent of reserves. As oil prices have risen, these companies have been sidelined by a new "seven sisters." The new players are largely state-owned and they control almost one-third of the world's oil and gas production, and more than one-third of oil and gas reserves. The new "seven sisters" are Saudi Aramco, Russia's Gazprom, CNPC of China, BIOC of Iran, Venezuala's PDVSA, Brazil's Petrobas, and Petronas of Malasia. In effect, control of this sector has changed hands.[68]

Collaborating With State-Owned Enterprises

Internationalization imperatives will place many companies in the position where they consider potentials for developing strategic relationships with enterprises actually owned

229

Corporate social responsibility initiatives have led to several industry-based alliances to tackle environmental and social risks—Hewlett-Packard, Dell, IBM and others have launched an industry code of conduct for suppliers; big brands like Mattel and Hasbro have said their suppliers must meet the jointly agreed standards of the International Council of Toy Industries.

The idea is to pool experience and to reduce the inefficiencies when all companies in a sector attempt to individually audit suppliers' environmental and employment practices.

Nonetheless, the collaborative nature of these arrangements means participants must pay attention to competition legislation. If companies are regarded as too deeply entwined, regulators may find that competition between them has weakened and take action.

Industry alliances for any purpose must avoid certain behaviors:

- **Market manipulation**—corporate alliances must demonstrate that their joint activities do not lead to price fixing or other forms of market limitation.
- **Boycotts**—codes of conduct must be voluntary and individual companies must address issues of breach of the code by suppliers.
- **Benefits**—an alliance should demonstrate the low risk of anti-competitive harm and pro-competitive benefits and efficiencies to be gained.
- **"Comfort letters"**—alliances can seek an official letter from bodies like the U.S. Justice Department stating the authority does not intend to challenge the activities of the alliance.

Sources: Sarah Murray, "Alliances Heed Anti-Trust Traps," *Financial Times,* Thursday, January 5, 2006, 10. Robert Wright, "Competition Spotlight Could Fall on 'Partners,'" *Financial Times,* April 22/23, 2006, 21.

by foreign governments, or which have recently been taken out of state ownership. Considerable care is required in evaluating the potential gains from such relationships, and in understanding the different requirements for managing them.

For example, the Chinese government has relaxed regulations to allow foreign market entrants to form joint ventures, and to allow foreigners to acquire state-owned enterprises (SOEs). Research suggests that several factors are important in developing strategic relationships with Chinese enterprises of this kind: (1) Chinese SOEs tend to have substantial organizational slack which may indicate either inefficiencies or potential for improved performance; (2) many Chinese SOEs maintain three sets of books: one set exaggerates performance to impress administrative superiors, one underreports performance for tax purposes, and one set is fairly accurate for use by managers themselves. Foreign negotiators are likely to be shown the "bragging books"; (3) the belief that ethnic Chinese managers from overseas Chinese economies will be the best choice for managing joint ventures is misplaced—local staff are quite capable of responding well to Western managers, while Chinese managers may struggle with an ambiguous managerial identity.[69]

Government Regulation

There have been notable advances in recent decades in slackening government control of business. Nonetheless, antitrust laws in the United States and Europe prohibit certain kinds of cooperation among direct competitors in an industry. The intense global competition and loss of competitiveness in many industries seem to be changing the traditional view of lone-wolf competition among companies. While the antitrust laws continue to be in place, there may be more flexibility by government agencies in interpreting whether collaboration among firms in an industry is an antitrust issue. For example, even the pursuit of corporate social responsibility initiatives on a collaborative basis raises several antitrust issues. This situation is described in the ETHICS FEATURE.

Summary

The competitive realities of surviving and prospering in the complex and rapidly changing business environment encourage teaming up with other companies, so cooperative strategic relationships among independent companies are escalating in importance. The major drivers of interorganizational relationships are value opportunities, environmental complexity, competitive strategy, and skills and resource gaps. Enhanced value offers to customers may be achieved more effectively through collaboration with other organizations than independently. Complex environments mandate altering internal organizational structures and establishing strategic relationships with other organizations. Alliance and collaboration may be a key part of how an organization differentiates itself and competes. Technology and financial constraints, the need to access markets, and the availability of information technology all contribute to skill and resource gaps, which may be filled through collaboration.

In examining the potential for collaborative relationships several criteria need to be evaluated. Important criteria include determining the underlying strategic logic of the proposed relationship, deciding whether partnering is the best way to achieve the strategic objective in the light of the real costs of collaboration, assessing how essential the relationship is, determining if good candidates are available, and considering whether collaborative relationships are compatible with the corporate culture.

Relationships between organizations range from transactional exchanges to collaborative partnerships. These relationships may be vertical in the value-added chain or horizontal within or across industries. Vertical relationships involve collaboration between customers and suppliers and distribution channel linkages among firms. Dominant customers and differences between customers in prospects for the future encourage the development of strategic account management approaches. Horizontal partnerships may include competitors and other industry members. The horizontal or lateral relationships include strategic alliances and joint ventures.

Collaborative relationships are complex, and, not surprisingly, generate conflicts. Many horizontal relationships have not been particularly successful, even though the number of these partnerships is escalating throughout the world. Trust and commitment between the partners are critical to building a successful relationship. Planning helps to improve the chances of success. The capability to manage effectively through partnerships requires distinct skills and new approaches, not available in all organizations.

Several objectives may be achieved through strategic relationships, including gaining access to new technologies, developing new markets, building market position, implementing market segmentation strategies, and pursuing restructuring and cost-reduction strategies. The requirements for successfully managing interorganizational relationships include planning, balancing trust and self-interest, recognizing conflicts, defining leadership structure, achieving flexibility, adjusting to cultural differences, facilitating technology transfers, and learning from partners' strengths. The development of appropriate control and evaluation approaches, and the design of appropriate exit paths for these new business forms have become priorities.

Global relationships among organizations may include conventional organizational forms, alliances, joint ventures, network corporations, and trading companies. The global integrated enterprise describes a new organizational form, which may replace the conventional multinational company model. A strategy of developing global relationships internationally needs to account for the complexities of inter-nation collaborations and the role of overseas governments in facilitating and encouraging these developments. Important issues also relate to the role of interventionist governments overseas and the challenges of competing with, or collaborating with, state-owned enterprises. Anti-trust regulation is also a relevant concern in developing strategic relationships internationally.

Questions for Review and Discussion

1. Discuss the major factors that encourage the formation of strategic partnerships between companies.

2. Compare and contrast vertical and horizontal strategic relationships between independent companies.

3. Discuss the similarities and differences between strategic alliances and joint ventures.

4. A German electronics company and a Japanese electronics company are discussing the formation of a strategic alliance for each to market the other firm's products in their respective countries. What are the important issues in making this relationship successful for both partners?

5. What are the attractions and possible problems in developing a strategic relationship with a major customer in the form of strategic account management?

6. To what extent is it reasonable for a partner organization to attempt to exert control over your strategic choices in areas not part of the alliance or joint venture?

7. Establishing successful interorganizational relationships is difficult, according to authorities. Will the success record improve in the future as more companies pursue this strategy?

8. Are vertical relationships more likely to be successful than horizontal relationships? Discuss.

9. Suppose you are seeking a Japanese strategic alliance partner to market your French pharmaceutical products in Asia. What characteristics are important in selecting a good partner?

10. Discuss how alliances may enable foreign companies to reduce the negative reaction that is anticipated if they tried to purchase companies in other countries.

11. Discuss how government may participate in helping domestic companies develop their competitive advantages in an industry such as aerospace products.

12. Identify and discuss important issues in deciding whether to create internal cross-functional relationships.

Internet Applications

A. Visit the website www.alliancestrategy.com and review the presentations and material available at the site. Summarize what factors should be considered in making alliances between organizations effective.

B. Go to the investor information and company history information on www.amazon.com. Identify the evolving network of strategic relationships with customers, suppliers, and collaborators both on the Web and with conventional organizations. Which of these relationships are the most important to Amazon?

Feature Applications

A. Review the airline alliance lists, statistics, and news in the GLOBAL FEATURE in this chapter. Examine the changes happening and predicted in airline alliances by searching "airline alliances" on the Internet. What conclusions can be drawn about the strategic vulnerabilities of alliances?

B. Examine the material presented in the RELATIONSHIP FEATURE. How can it be possible for Costco to perform well against competitors when it carries a burden of higher labor costs? Are there issues in this case which may be worth considering in other situations where a company faces strong low-cost, low-price competition?

Notes

1. David Kirkpatrick, "IBM Shares Its Secrets," *Fortune,* September 5, 2005, 60–67. Steve Hamm, "Big Blue Shift," *BusinessWeek,* June 5, 2006, 108–110.

2. Carliss Y. Baldwin and Kim B. Clark, "Managing in an Age of Modularity," *Harvard Business Review,* September-October 1997, 84–93 at 84.

3. Ron Sanchez, "Fitting Together a Modular Approach," *Financial Times,* Thursday, August 15, 2002, 14.

4. Ravi S. Achrol, "Evolution of the Marketing Organization: New Forms for the Turbulent Environments," *Journal of Marketing,* October 1991, 78–79.

5. Ibid.

6. Rod Newing, "From Inward to Outward," *Financial Times Report: Understanding the Culture of Collaboration,* Friday, June 29, 2007, 14.

7. Frederick E. Webster, Jr., "The Changing Role of Marketing in the Organization," *Journal of Marketing,* October 1992, 1–17.

8. Gill South, "Upwardly Mobile," *The Business,* September 2, 2000, 26–29.

9. Jenny Wiggins, "Why Little and Large Teamed Up on Skincare," *Financial Times,* Wednesday, November 8, 2006, 14.

10. Peter Thal Larsen, "One-Time 'Banana-Skin' Bank Blossoms," *Financial Times,* Friday, May 25, 2007, 19.

11. Hong-Wei He and John M. T. Balmer, "Alliance Brands: Building Corporate Brands Through Strategic Alliances," *Journal of Brand Management,* Vol. 13 No. 4/5 2006, 242–256.

12. Rod Newing, "The Great Enabler," *Financial Times Report: Understanding the Culture of Collaboration,* Friday, June 29, 2007, 18–19.

13. Salvatore Parise and John C. Henderson, "Knowledge Resource Exchange in Strategic Alliances," *IBM Systems Journal,* Vol. 40 No. 4, 2001, 908–924.

14. James D. Bamford, Benjamin Gomes-Casseres and Michael S. Robinson, *Mastering Alliance Strategy: A Comprehensive Guide to Design, Management and Organization* (Somerset NJ: Jossey-Bass, 2002).

15. Benjamin Gomes-Casseres, "Strategy Must Lie at the Heart of Alliance," *Financial Times,* October 16, 2000, 14–15.

16. Nick Palmer, "Alliances: Learning to Change," www.accenture.com, January 2003.

17. "Boeing and Lockheed Martin Form Strategic Alliance," *Airline Industry Information,* January 23, 2007, 1.

18. Teena Lyons, "Expansion Riles Tesco's US Partners: West Coast Store Plan Puts Deals in Danger," *Mail on Sunday,* April 2, 2006, 7.

19. "Concertina'd," *Financial Times,* October 17, 2001, 28.

20. Frederick E. Webster, Jr., "The Changing Role of Marketing in the Organization," *Journal of Marketing,* October 1992, 1–17.

21. Jeffrey K. Liker and Thomas Y. Choi, "Building Deep Supplier Relationships," *Harvard Business Review,* December 2004, 104–113.

22. "Dell/EMC Extend Multi-Billion Dollar Strategic Alliance Until 2011," *Al Bawaba,* September 18, 2006, 1.

23. Peter Marsh, "Swatch Decision Throws a Spanner in Swiss Watch Industry's Works," *Financial Times,* Wednesday, August 10, 2005, 10.

24. John Hagel, "Leveraged Growth: Expanding Sales Without Sacrificing Profits," *Harvard Business Review,* October 2002, 69–77.

25. Pete Encardio and Bruce Einhorn, "Outsourcing Innovation," *BusinessWeek,* March 21, 2005, 46–53.

26. Gail Edmondson, "Look Who's Building Bimmers," *BusinessWeek,* December 8, 2003, 18–19.

27. Benito Arruñada and Xosé H Vásquez, "When Your Contract Manufacturer Becomes Your Competitor," *Harvard Business Review,* September 2006, 135–144.

28. Roger Parloff, "Not Exactly Counterfeit," *Fortune,* May 15, 2006, 64–70.

29. Kevin Lim, "Gap to Open First Stores in Asia Outside Japan," *Wall Street Journal,* August 2, 2006.

30. C.K. Prahalad and Venkat Ramaswamy, *The Future of Competition: Co-Creating Unique Value with Customers* (Cambridge, MA: Harvard Business School Press, 2004).

31. Prahalad and Ramaswamy, ibid.

32. David W. Cravens, "The Changing Role of the Salesforce in the Corporation," *Marketing Management,* Fall 1995, 50.

33. Ibid.

34. This section is based on: Nigel Piercy, "The Strategic Sales Organization," *The Marketing Review,* Vol. 6 2006, 3–28. Nigel F Piercy and Nikala Lane, "The Underlying Vulnerabilities in Key Account Management Strategies," *European Management Journal,* Vol. 24 No. 3 2006, 151–182. Nigel F. Piercy and Nikala Lane, "Ethical and Moral Dilemmas Associated with Strategic Relationships Between Business-to-Business Buyers and Sellers," *Journal of Business Ethics,* Vol. 72 2007, 87–102.

35. Noel Capon, *Key Account Management and Planning* (New York: Free Press, 2001).

36. Jenny Wiggins and Elizabeth Rigby, "New Neighbour Disney Knocks at Tesco's Door," *Financial Times,* December9/10 2006, 3.

37. Jonathan Birchall, "Wal-Mart Aims for Further Inventory Cuts," *Financial Times,* April 20, 2006, 25.

38. Jeremy Grant, "Mr Daley's Mission: To Reach 6Bn Shoppers and Make Money," *Financial Times,* July 15, 2005, 32.

39. Quotation from "IMI plc—Key Themes," www.imi.plc/about

40. James Mackintosh and Bernard Simon, "Ford to Focus on Business from 'Key Suppliers'," *Financial Times,* Friday, September 30, 2005, 32.

41. Scott Morrison and Richard Waters, "Time Comes to 'Think Different'," *Financial Times,* Tuesday, June 7, 2005, 25.

42. David Ernst and James Bamford, "Your Alliances Are Too Stable," *Harvard Business Review,* June 2005, 133–141.

43. "Honda and Hong Kong Disneyland Form Strategic Alliance," *JCN Newswire,* July 12, 2006, 1.

44. Loren Gary, "A Growing Reliance on Alliance," *Harvard Management Update,* April 2004, 3–4.

45. Salvatore Parise and John C. Henderson, "Knowledge Resource Exchange in Strategic Alliances," *IBM Systems Journal,* 40 (4), 2001, 908–924.

46. "AT&T, Yahoo Hit 5-Year Mark with Broadband Partnership," *FinancialWire,* November 22 2006, 1. Michael Arrington, "AT&T Piles on Yahoo," www.techcrunch.com, March 9, 2007.

47. Matthew Schifrin, "Partner or Perish," *Forbes,* May 21, 2001, 26–28.

48. James Bamford, David Ernst and David G. Fubrini, "Launching a World-Class Joint Venture," *Harvard Business Review,* February 2004, 90–100.

49. Richard Wilding, "Playing to the Tune of Shared Success," *Financial Times Report: Understanding Collaboration,* November 10, 2006, 2–3.

50. Andrew Campbell, "Why In-House Collaboration Is So Difficult," *Financial Times,* Monday, February 13, 2006, 14.

51. Tom Lester, "Masters of Collaboration," *Financial Times Report: Understanding the Culture of Collaboration,* Friday, June 29, 2007, 8.

52. Morgan Witzel, "The Power of Difference," *Financial Times Report: Understanding Collaboration,* November 10, 2006, 13.

53. Jeffrey H. Dyer, Prashant Kale and Harbir Singh, "How to Make Strategic Alliances Work," *Sloan Management Review,* Summer 2001, 37–43.

54. This discussion is based on: Karen Cravens, Nigel Piercy and David Cravens, "Assessing the Performance of Strategic Alliances," *European Management Journal,* Vol. 18 No. 5 2000, 529–541.

55. Jonathan Hughes, *Implementing Alliance Metrics: Six Basic Principles,* Vantage Partners' White Paper, www.vantagepartners.com/publications, 2002.

56. Stuart Kliman and Christopher Hiserman, *Creating an Alliance Management Capability* (Boston MA: Vantage Partners, 2005).

57. David Ernst and James Bamford, "Your Alliances Are Too Stable," *Harvard Business Review,* June 2005, 133–141.

58. Andrew Delios, Andrew C. Inkpen and Jerry Ross, "Escalation in Strategic Alliances," *Management International Review,* Vol. 44 No. 4 2004, 457–479.

59. Ranjay Gulati, Maxim Sytch and Parth Mehrotra, "Preparing for the Exit: When Forming a Business Alliance, Don't Ignore One of the Most Crucial Ingredients—How to Break Up," *Wall Street Journal,* March 3 2007, R–1.

60. Gulati et al. (2007), ibid.

61. "Globalization's Offspring," Economist.com, April 4, 2007.

62. Samuel J Palmisamo, "The Globally Integrated Enterprise," *Foreign Affairs,* Vol. 85 No. 3, 127–138.

63. John Hagel III and John Seely-Brown, *The Only Sustainable Edge: Why Business Strategy Depends on Productive Friction and Dynamic Specialization* (Boston MA: Harvard Business School Press, 2005).

64. Moon Ihlwan and Dexter Roberts, "Korea's China Play," *BusinessWeek,* March 29, 2004, 48–52.

65. Carol Matlock, "Snafus: Wayward Airbus," *BusinessWeek,* October 23, 2006, 46–48.

66. Nelson D Schwartz, "Big Plane, Big Problems," *Fortune,* March 5, 2007, 53–55.

67. Jonathan Soble, "Japanese Aerospace Makes Ready for Take-Off," *Financial Times,* Thursday, July 5, 2007, 7.

68. Carola Hoyas, "The New Seven Sisters: Oil and Gas Giants That Dwarf the West's Top Producers," *Financial Times,* Monday, March 12, 2007, 15.

69. Mike W Peng, "Making M&A Fly in China," *Harvard Business Review,* March 2006, 26–27.

Chapter 8

Innovation and New Product Strategy

Creativity and innovation are essential to all organizations' growth and performance in the global marketplace. Among the best according to The Boston Consulting Group are Apple, Google, Nokia, Toyota, and Procter & Gamble.[1] The survey of over 1000 senior executives in 63 countries identified the 25 most innovative companies shown in the INNOVATION FEATURE. Innovation takes many forms including new goods and services, organizational processes, and business models. Importantly, even when the critical role of innovation is recognized by managers, deciding which innovation opportunities to pursue is a demanding challenge. Companies must create a culture of innovation and develop effective processes to identify innovation opportunities and transform ideas into new-product successes.

The economic pressures and market turbulence that impacted companies in a wide range of industries during the early years of the twenty-first century shifted many executives' strategic priorities away from the development of cutting edge new products.[2] The innovation processes of companies like Boeing, Kodak, and Motorola, were not meeting the challenges of aggressive development of new products. Instead, short-term, bottom-line performance was the center of attention. These short term cost initiatives may sometimes be necessary, but it is essential to also pursue long-term innovation strategies. Innovation creates competitive advantage for the organization and value for customers.

Based on a survey of CEOs and government leaders on the topic of innovation, IBM Chairman Samuel J. Polmisano highlights the following innovation initiatives as important success factors:[3]

- Innovation is a mandatory avenue to successful business performance due to the intense pressures of global competition and commoditization of products and processes.
- Business model innovation plays a critical role in gaining a unique position in markets and competitive space. Product differentiation is only a short-term competitive advantage.
- Collaboration relationships within the organization and among value chain members, competition, government, and other relevant groups are essential in achieving successful innovation results.
- The Chief Executive Officer must personally lead the organization's innovation culture initiatives.

In this chapter we consider the planning of new products beginning with a discussion of innovation as a customer-driven process. Next, we discuss the steps in new-product

Innovation Feature

The World's Most Innovative Companies

Ranking 2007	Ranking 2006		Why
1	1	**Apple**	Our first-place innovator for the third year in a row. Apple is a master of product and store design. Now that it's invading the cell-phone market, will it continue its winning streak?
2	2	**Google**	It didn't invent search advertising but lifted it to its current heights. Google's famously chaotic innovation process has plunged it into everything from radio ads to online office software.
3	4	**Toyota Motor**	Toyota's dominance in hybrids could lead to the first plug-in electric auto in the next four years. Now the No. 1 carmaker, its continuous improvement process is copied worldwide.
4	6	**General Electric**	CEO Jeff Immelt's push for "imagination breakthroughs," or growth opportunities of $50 million to $100 million, is increasingly leading GE into emerging markets and green tech.
5	5	**Microsoft**	To some, Microsoft is more fast follower than leading innovator. Still, the software giant's massive R&D budget generates creations that help ensure Windows' and Office's hegemony.
6	7	**Procter & Gamble**	After years of scouting for new products outside its walls, P&G has mapped the innovation strengths of global regions. CEO A.G. Lafley is pushing for more disruptive new ideas.
7	3	**3M**	The legendary Post-it Note is just one of 3M's many creations, which include everything from dental fillings to roofing shingles. Next on its list: diagnostic tests for infectious diseases.
8	43	**Walt Disney**	CEO Bob Iger is refueling Disney's creative culture, quashing bureaucracy. Moves such as putting ABC shows on iTunes and acquiring Pixar helped move Disney up our list.
9	10	**IBM**	Last year the tech services behemoth held an online brainstorm with 150,000 people to dream up new ideas. It hosts annual symposia with outsiders to collaborate on forecasting.
10	13	**Sony**	This traditional tech hardware maker is devoting more resources to software. To turn its PlayStation 3 console from living-room box to virtual gateway, it created a 3D online world.
11	20	**Wal-Mart Stores**	Wal-Mart is struggling with growth. But its "green" actions, such as using its leverage as the world's largest retailer to cut suppliers' packaging waste, helped move it up our list.
12	23	**Honda Motor**	Headed by a former R&D chief, Honda has been known for its fuel-efficient cars. But its environmental approach isn't limited to autos. Next up: solar panels and a fuel-sipping jet.
13	8	**Nokia**	To build sales in emerging markets, managers spend time in the homes of local customers. That has led to features for illiterate users such as an icon-driven handset directory.
14	9	**Starbucks**	The coffee chain's 50-person R&D group created eight new flavors last year. It also started its own music label and partnered with outsiders to publish books and produce movies.

(continued)

(concluded)

15	22	Target	Target stands out from its discount rivals by selling designer-inspired products. Innovative marketing, such as buying all the ads in one issue of *The New Yorker*, has also set it apart.
16	16	BMW	BMW is flat, flexible, and fast-reacting. Employees are urged to "break the rules" to cut costs or push through winning ideas, such as the Z4 coupe, which higher-ups initially nixed.
17	12	Samsung Electronics	Samsung stays ahead with intensive investment in new facilities and production systems. These days, it's focusing on the convergence of technologies and phone features.
18	11	Virgin Group	Most of its businesses, such as credit card or mobile virtual networks, are collaborative: Virgin supplies the branding and customer service while partners put up much of the cash.
19	17	Intel	The world's largest chipmaker, Intel is making big headway in health care. It recently previewed its most powerful chip to date and is planning a $2.5 billion plant in China.
20	21	Amazon	The online retailer is now innovating its business model, turning its backroom operations into a digital utility that rents out computer power and warehouse space to other firms.
21	70	Boeing	With the game-changing 787, Boeing is innovating how planes are designed, financed, and built. Designed by engineers on three continents, the new jet is setting sales records.
22	14	Dell	Dell made its name with a model built around direct selling and efficient PC assembly. But today the action is mostly in retail stores and laptops, and Dell is groping for ways to adapt.
23	27	Genentech	Genentech created the biotech industry and has set a high bar ever since. Success comes from taking risks on unproven drug technologies and then turning them into blockbusters.
24	18	eBay	It pioneered person-to-person e-commerce. When eBay's core business slowed, it bought Net-phone phenom Skype. The big unanswered question: Can you buy innovation?
25	28	Cisco Systems	Long known for its M&A chops. Cisco's innovation reputation is gaining as it grows beyond network equipment and into such areas as high-def, high-cost videoconferencing systems.

Source: Jena McGregor, "Most Innovative Companies," May 14, 2007, 55.

planning, including generating ideas, screening and evaluating the ideas, business analysis, product development and testing, designing the market entry strategy, market testing, and new-product introduction. The chapter concludes with a discussion of variations in the generic new product planning process.

Innovation as a Customer-Driven Process

New product opportunities that offer superior value to customers range from totally new innovations to incremental improvements in existing products. We discuss the different types of innovations, the importance of finding customer value opportunities, and essential drivers of successful innovations.

Types of Innovations

Innovations can be classified according to (1) newness to the market; and (2) the extent of customer value created, resulting in the following types of innovations:[4]

- *Transformational Innovation:* Products that are radically new and the value created is substantial. Examples include CNN News Channel, automatic teller machines, and digital cameras.
- *Substantial Innovation:* Products that are significantly new and create important value for customers. Examples include Kimberly Clark Huggies/Nappies and Diet Coke.
- *Incremental Innovations:* New products that provide improved performance or greater perceived value (or lower cost), include new flavor Coca-Cola.

A company's new-product initiatives may include innovation in one or more of the three categories. The reality is that many new products are extensions of existing product lines and incremental improvements of existing products rather than totally new products. These extensions and improvements account for as much as 70 to 80 percent of all innovations. The new product planning process we discuss in this chapter applies to any of the three categories and is used in planning new services as well as tangible goods.

The INNOVATION FEATURE describes several interesting innovation initiatives pursued by Google, the Internet search leader. Google is an impressive success story driven by innovative people like Marissa Mayer. Not surprisingly, in 2007 Google was No. 1 on *Fortune* magazine's 100 Best Companies to Work For list.

New-product initiatives are guided by customer needs analysis. Even transformational innovations should have some relationship to needs that are not being met by existing products. However, as we discuss shortly, potential customers may not be good sounding boards for radically new innovations. Importantly, these transformational innovations may have a disruptive impact on existing products.

Finding Customer Value Opportunities

Customer value requirements provide important information for determining where opportunities exist to develop new products. Market segment identification and analysis help find segments which offer new-product opportunities to the organization. Extensive study of existing and potential customers and the competition are vital in guiding effective new-product planning.

We know that customer value is the combination of benefits provided by a product minus all of the costs incurred by the buyer (Chapter 1). Customer satisfaction indicates how well the product-use experience compares to the value expected by the buyer. The closer the match between expectations and the use experience, the better the resulting value delivery.

Customer Value

The objective of customer value analysis is to identify needs for: (1) new products; (2) improvements in existing products; (3) improvements in the processes that produce the products; and (4) improvements in supporting services. The intent is to find gaps (opportunities) between buyers' expectations and the extent to which they are being met (Exhibit 8.1). Everyone in the organization needs to be involved in this process. Google's innovation initiatives are illustrative. This market-driven approach to product planning helps to avoid a mismatch between technologies and customer needs.

Finding New Product Opportunities

A difference between expectations and use experience may indicate a new product opportunity. For example, an alert U.S. Surgical Corporation (USS) salesperson saw an opportunity to

Marissa Mayer joined Google in early 1999 as a programmer when the workforce totaled 20. By 2007 Google had 5,700 employees and expected sales of $16 billion.

As Director of Consumer Web Products Marissa is a champion of innovation, and she favors new product launches that are early and often.

HOW GOOGLE INNOVATES

The search leader has earned a reputation as one of the most innovative companies in the world of technology. These are illustrative of the ways Google hatches new ideas:

FREE (THINKING) TIME

Google gives all engineers one day a week to develop their own pet projects, no matter how far these projects are from the company's central mission. If work gets in the way of free days for a few weeks, they accumulate. Google News came out of this process.

THE IDEA LIST

Anyone at Google can post thoughts for new technologies of businesses on an ideas mailing list, available companywide for input and vetting. But beware: Newbies who suggest familiar or poorly thought-out ideas can face an intellectual pummeling.

OPEN OFFICE HOURS

Think back to your professors' office hours in college. That's pretty much what key managers, including Mayer, do two or three times a week, to discuss new ideas. One success born of this approach was Google's personalized home page.

BIG BRAINSTORMS

As it has grown, Google has cut back on brainstorming sessions. Mayer still holds them eight times a year, but limits hers to 100 engineers. Six concepts are pitched and discussed for ten minutes each. The goal: To build on the initial idea with at least one complementary idea per minute.

ACQUIRE GOOD IDEAS

Although Google strongly prefers to develop technology in-house, it has also been willing to snap up small companies with interesting initiatives. In 2004 it bought Keyhole, including the technology that let Google offer sophisticated maps with satellite imagery.

Source: "Managing Google's Idea Factory," *BusinessWeek,* October 3, 2005, 88–90.

---

satisfy a surgical need that was not being met with existing products. USS is a unit of Tyco Healthcare Group L.P. Its products include wound closure products and advanced surgical devices. The close working relationship of USS sales representatives with surgeons in operating rooms, nurses, and administrators gives USS a critical competitive advantage.[5] The salesperson identified the new product opportunity by observing surgeons' early use of self-developed instruments to perform experiments in laparoscopy. Using this procedure, the surgeon inserts a tiny TV camera into the body with very thin surgical instruments. USS responded quickly to this need by designing and introducing a laparoscopic stapler. The product is used in gall bladder removal and other internal surgical applications.

Matching Capabilities to Value Opportunities

Each value opportunity should be considered in terms of whether the organization has the capabilities to deliver superior customer value. Organizations will normally have the

EXHIBIT 8.1
Finding New Product Opportunities

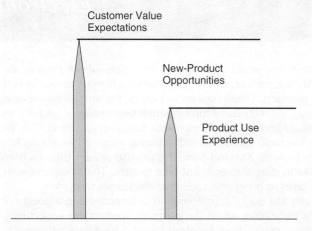

capabilities needed for product line extensions and incremental improvements. Developing products for a new product category requires realistic assessment of the organization's capabilities concerning the new category. Partnering with a company that has the needed capabilities is an option concerning the addition of a new product category. For example, XM Satellite Radio partnered with Samsung Electronics Co. to produce the first portable satellite radio combined with a digital music player as described in the STRATEGY FEATURE.

Transformational Innovations

Customers may not be good guides to totally new product ideas that may be called radical or breakthrough innovations since they create new families of products and businesses.[6] When such ideas are under consideration, potential customers may not understand how the new product will replace an existing product. The problem is that customers may not anticipate a preference for a revolutionary new product.[7] For example, initial response from potential users of optical fibers, video cassette recorders, Federal Express, and CNN was not encouraging. In these situations, management must form a vision about the innovation and be willing to make the commitment to develop the technology as Corning Inc. did with optical fiber technology. The risk, of course, is that management's vision may be faulty.

Incremental product improvements are guided by analyzing customer value opportunities (Exhibit 8.1), whereas these approaches to finding new product opportunities are not very useful in evaluating potential transformational innovations:

> The familiar admonition to be customer-driven is of little value when it is not at all clear who the customer is—when the market has never experienced the features created by the new technology. Likewise, analytic methods for evaluating new product opportunities (e.g., discounted cash flow and market diffusion analyses) appear to be much more appropriate for incremental than for discontinuous innovation.[8]

Radical innovations have the potential of disrupting existing (sustaining) technologies and creating negative impacts on the leading firms that pursue new product strategies using existing technologies.[9] Examples of disruptive innovations include Amazon.com., jetBlue (airline), Salesforce.com (customer management software), and steel minimills. Disruptive technologies are often not considered to be threats by firms pursuing sustaining technologies. Clayton Christensen and Michael E. Raynor in *The Innovator's Solution* offer a compelling analysis of these threats and provide important guidelines for managing disruptive innovations.[10] The challenge for companies confronted with potential

In the white-hot world of digital convergence, where services are increasingly packaged with hardware, partnerships are essential to being first to market with the best blend of services and products. "From now on this will be the normal way of doing business in consumer electronics," predicts Dan Murphy, senior vice-president for sales and marketing at XM.

He should know. XM's alliance with Samsung Electronics Co. to produce the first portable satellite radio combined with a digital music player shows how this sort of thing can be done. In April, XM and Samsung plan to release their co-branded Helix, going from handshake to store shelves in just nine months. That compares with the 12 to 18 months it typically takes to bring new consumer electronics to market.

How did XM do it? A combination of foresight and a good eye for allies. The journey started in early 2005, when the company spotted the opportunity to meld satellite radio with a music player. Even before it found a hardware partner, XM started designing the building blocks for the machine—including chips, an antenna, and a tiny circuit board. Last May it approached Samsung and discovered that the Korean electronics giant had fixed on the same idea.

The two companies created a virtual product-development team jointly headed by one manager from each company. Samsung engineers focused on industrial design and manufacturing, while XM focused on the antenna, the user interface, and delivering one-of-a-kind features. Consumers will be able to "bookmark" a song they're listening to on the radio and later buy it on the Napster Inc. Website with just a few clicks of their computer mouse.

This collaboration marks a sea change at Samsung. The company used to be a go-it-alone outfit. No more. Now it's on the lookout for more partners. "We have to find other companies that are leaders in their field who can move as quickly as we can," says Peter Weedfald, a senior vice-president at Samsung Electronics America Inc.

Source: Steve Hamm, "SPEEDDEMONS," *BusinessWeek,* March 27, 2006, 74.

---

disruptive opportunities and threats is recognizing that product planning processes differ for sustaining and disruptive innovations. Executives must manage both processes. It may be necessary to position the disruptive technology in a separate organization independent from the core business.

Commoditization and intense global competition are creating pressures for change. The evolution of a creative company toward a new corporate model might logically follow the steps shown in Exhibit 8.2.[11] When products become commodities, profit margins decline and differentiated advantages are difficult to achieve.

Unless proactive initiatives are taken, the existing technology in the core business is likely to dominate innovation activities. A good market/technology match is important in being successful with radical technologies. Priority should be given to market niches that the traditional technology does not serve well. Christensen and Raynor also propose that products developed from disruptive technologies which are not currently valued by customers may match future value requirements very well. The eventual strong preference for digital photography displayed by buyers is illustrative.

Initiatives of Successful Innovators

Certain companies seem to consistently excel over others in developing successful new products. Importantly, successful innovators often pursue similar initiatives. The strategic initiatives shown in Exhibit 8.3 have consistently been good predictors of successful

EXHIBIT 8.2
The Evolution of the Creative Company
A new corporate model is taking shape—focusing on creativity and innovation

Source: Bruce Nussbaum, "How to Build Innovative Companies,"*BusinessWeek,* August 1, 2005, 62–63.

STEP 1

Technology and information become commoditized and globalized. Suddenly, the advantage of making things "faster, cheaper, better" diminishes, and profit margins decline.

STEP 2

With commoditization, core advantages can be shipped abroad. Outsourcing to India, China, and Eastern Europe sends a growing share of manufacturing and even the Knowledge Economy overseas.

STEP 3

Design Strategy begins to replace Six Sigma as a key organizing principle. Design plays key role in product differentiation, decision-making, and understanding the consumer experience.

STEP 4

Creative innovation becomes the key driver of growth. Companies master new design thinking and metrics and create products that address consumers' unmet, and often unarticulated, desires.

STEP 5

The successful Creative Corporation emerges, with new Innovation DNA. Winners build a fast-moving culture that routinely beats competitors because of a high success rate for innovation.

innovative organizations based on research studies, management judgment and experience, and analysis of specific companies' innovation experience.

Creating an innovative culture is essential to generating successful new products. Research findings constantly point to the importance of an innovative organizational climate and culture.[12] This requires top management to position innovation as a distinct

EXHIBIT 8.3
Characteristics of Successful Innovators

Creating an Innovative Culture

Leveraging Capabilities

Selecting the Right Innovation Strategy

STRATEGIC INITIATIVES

Making Resource Commitments

Developing and Implementing Effective New Product Processes

organizational priority and communicate the importance of innovation to all employees. Moreover, deciding the right innovation strategy involves defining the product, market, and technology scope of the organization. This requires determining corporate purpose and scope which set important guidelines and boundaries for new product planning. High quality new product planning processes are essential to operationalize the organization's innovation strategy. Importantly, achieving successful new product outcomes requires allocating adequate resources to new product initiatives. Finally, the extent to which the organization can leverage its capabilities into promising new product and market opportunities enhances innovation performance (if the leveraging efforts are successful). Procter and Gamble has been particularly effective in getting its different businesses to collaborate in leveraging their capabilities to develop new products.

Recognizing the Realities of Product Cannibalization

Cannibalization occurs when a new product attracts sales from an existing product. Executives may be hesitant to develop improved products because of their successful existing products. Instead, proactive cannibalization is often a viable strategy. Proactive cannibalization consists of the pursuit of a deliberate, ongoing strategy of developing and introducing new products that attract the buyers of a company's existing products. The strategic logic of this concept is offering buyers a better solution to a need currently being satisfied. Executive resistance to cannibalization is driven by the belief that it is unproductive for a company to compete with its own products and services. Nonetheless, the reality is that changes in market requirements and customer value opportunities will result in competitor threats for existing products and technologies.

There are various examples of the negative consequences of avoiding cannibalization initiatives in the communications, financial services, retailing, and other sectors. Illustrative is Sony's continued support of its Trinitron TVs even though it was apparent that consumers favored flat-panel TVs. Proactive cannibalization may be essential to many firms to sustain a competitive advantage and achieve financial performance and growth objectives. In support of the logic of proactive cannibalization, research sponsored by the Marketing Science Institute indicates that managers of successful firms proactively resist the instinct to retain the value of past investments in product development.[13] They pursue proactive cannibalization initiatives.

New-Product Planning

A new product does not have to be a high-technology breakthrough to be successful but it must deliver superior customer value. Post-it Notes has been a big winner for 3M Company.[14] The familiar notepaper pads come in various sizes and each page has a thin strip of adhesive which can be attached to reports, telephones, walls, and other places. The idea came from a 3M researcher. He had used slips of paper to mark songs in his hymnbook, but the paper kept falling out. To eliminate the problem, the employee applied an adhesive that had been developed in 3M's research laboratory which failed to provide the adhesive strength needed in the original application. The adhesive worked fine for marking songs in the book. Interestingly, office-supply vendors initially saw no market for the sticky-back notepaper. The 3M Company employed extensive sampling to show the value of the product. Over the signature of the CEO's administrative assistant, samples were sent to executive assistants at all Fortune 500 companies. After using the supply of samples, the executive assistants wanted more. Post-it-Notes quickly became indispensable in both offices and homes.

Creating an innovative culture is an important foundation for successful innovation (Exhibit 8.3). It is also necessary to set some boundaries concerning the types of new products to be considered for possible development. We examine these issues followed by a discussion of the activities that comprise the new product planning process.

Developing a Culture and Strategy for Innovation

Open communications throughout the organization and high levels of employee involvement and interest are characteristic of innovative cultures. Recognizing the importance of developing a culture and innovation strategy, Google has pursued several actions intended to encourage innovation initiatives (see earlier INNOVATION FEATURE). Evidence of innovative cultures may be found in corporate mission statements, advertising messages, presentations by top executives, and case studies in business publications.

Innovation Culture

Creating (and strengthening) an innovation culture can be encouraged by several interrelated management initiatives:[15]

- Plan and implement a two-day innovation workshop of top executives to develop an innovation plan. This would involve use of cross-functional teams, resource allocations, rewards, and innovation performance metrics.
- Develop an innovation statement highlighting the company's objectives and senior management's roles and responsibilities.
- Conduct innovation training programs for employees and managers to encourage commitment and involvement.
- Communicate the priority of innovation via articles, newsletters, and presentations to employees, shareholders, and customers.
- Schedule innovation speakers on a regular basis to expose employees to innovation authorities.

Strategy for Innovation

The organization's innovation strategy spells out management's choice of the organization's most promising opportunities for new products. This strategy should take into account the organization's distinctive capabilities, relevant technologies, and the market opportunities that provide a good customer value match with the organization's capabilities.

A major benchmarking study of 161 business units across a broad range of industries in the U.S., Germany, Denmark, and Canada indicates that a carefully formulated and communicated new product innovation strategy is a cornerstone of superior new product performance.[16] A successful new product strategy includes:

1. Setting specific, written new product objectives (sales, profit contribution, market, share, etc.).
2. Communicating throughout the organization the role of new products in contributing to the goals of the business.
3. Defining the areas of strategic focus for the corporation in terms of product scope, markets, and technologies.
4. Including longer term, transformational projects in the portfolio along with incremental projects.

Adopting these strategy guidelines should assist management in selecting the right innovation strategy.

The STRATEGY FEATURE on balancing innovation initiatives discusses the importance of considering innovation projects that include search into three domains for organic

The aversion to "Big I" growth strategies is rooted in the belief that potential rewards will be accrued too far in the future at too high a risk. This belief imposes costs that need to be understood. Even though the actual rewards may be realized far in the future, the equity markets account for them in their expectations of (suitably discounted) earnings. If the firm is viewed as mired in slow-growth markets, vulnerable to emerging technologies, and lacking a compelling story about its future growth thrust, the stock price will surely suffer.

Balancing Risk and Reward along the Growth Path

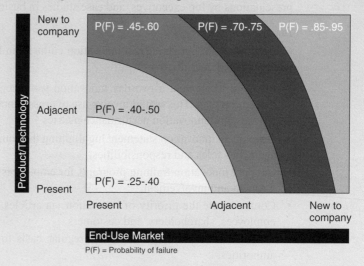

P(F) = Probability of failure

As the risk matrix shows, it is far less risky for a business to launch a new product or technology into a familiar served market than to adapt a current product to a new end-use market. Market risks are much greater than product risks because there are more dimensions of uncertainty, including competitors, channels, and consumers. If the market is entirely unfamiliar, the firm doesn't even know what it doesn't know—and the knowledge is hard to acquire. Market risks also tend to arise much later in the product development process, and are harder to resolve. A further complication is that an existing brand name may have no meaning in a "new to the company" market. Because prospective buyers lack any experience, they view the new entrant as risky and need special inducements to try the new product.

Some firms have been able to overcome the centripetal pull of innovation resources toward cautious, lower-yield "small i" growth initiatives and improve their organic growth rate. This requires visible and vocal top management commitment, supported with resources and incentives. A disciplined organic growth process is also needed to deliberately shift the balance of the portfolio of growth initiatives toward opportunities with higher risk-adjusted returns.

Many steps were taken to encourage fresh thinking at General Electric including diversifying the top ranks with outsiders (in a break from their "promote-from-within" history), keeping executives in their positions longer so they become deeply immersed in their industries, and tying executive compensation to new ideas, improved customer satisfaction, and top-line growth. The leaders of each GE business were required to submit at least three "Imagination Break-Through" proposals per year promising at least $100 million in additional growth.

Source: George S. Day, "Closing the Growth Gap: Balancing 'Big I' and 'Small i' Innovation," Report No. 06–121, *Marketing Science Institute*, 2006, pp. 5–7.

growth: deeper market penetration, expansion into adjacent markets, and exploration beyond adjacencies as shown by the risk matrix. Support for the matrix logic is provided by many sources.

Developing Effective New Product Planning Processes

Creating the right culture and selecting the right innovation strategy are essential but not sufficient initiatives in pursuing successful innovation initiatives (Exhibit 8.3). Innovation is achieved through the processes put in place by the organization. The previously discussed benchmarking study found that having a high quality new product development process in place is the most important cornerstone of new product planning performance.

Developing successful new products requires systematic planning to coordinate the many decisions, activities, and functions necessary to identify and move a new-product idea to commercial success. A basic (generic) planning process can be used in planning a wide range of new products. There may be necessary modifications in the process in certain situations and these issues are discussed in the last section of the chapter. The major stages in the planning process are shown in Exhibit 8.4. Later in the chapter we examine each stage to see what activities are involved, how the stages depend on each other, and why cross-functional participation and coordination of new product planning are very important.

Successful new product planning requires: (1) generating a continuing stream of new-product ideas that will satisfy the organization's requirements for new products; and (2) putting in place people, processes, and methods conducting activities and evaluating new-product ideas as they move through each of the planning stages.

The following initiatives are important in effectively applying the planning process to develop and introduce new products. First, the process involves different business functions, so it is necessary to develop ways of coordinating and integrating cross-functional activities in the planning process. Second, compressing the time span for product development creates an important competitive advantage. For example, U.S. Surgical's quick response to laparoscopy equipment development enabled the company to establish first position in the market. Third, the product planning activities require resources and must be managed so that the results deliver high levels of customer satisfaction at acceptable costs. Finally, the planning process can be used for new service development as well as physical products.

EXHIBIT 8.4
New Product Planning Process

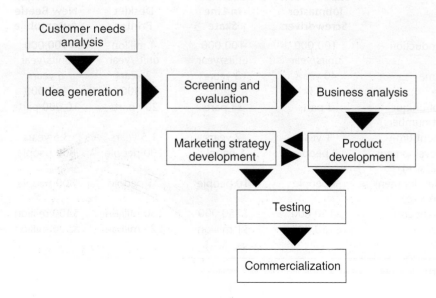

Responsibility for New-Product Planning

Since new-product development involves different business functions such as marketing, finance, operations, human resources, and research and development (R&D), ways of encouraging cross-functional interaction and coordination are essential. Various organizational designs may be employed to coordinate interfunctional interactions that are necessary in developing successful new products, including:[17]

- Coordination of new product activities by a high-level business manager.
- Cross-functional coordination by a new product planning team.
- Creation of a cross-functional project task force responsible for new-product planning.
- Designation of a new-products manager to coordinate planning among departments.
- Formation of a matrix organizational structure for integrating new-product planning with business functions.
- Creation of a design center which is similar in concept to a new product team, except the center is a permanent part of the organization.

The design team and design center are more recent new-product coordination mechanisms. Though cross-functional teams are widely cited as promising new-product planning mechanisms, research findings suggest that they may be most appropriate for planning truly new and innovative products.[18] The more traditional bureaucratic structures (e.g., new products manager) may be better in planning line extensions and product improvements. The danger of the traditional structure is failing to identify new product opportunities outside the scope of existing new product planning, and not identifying potential disruptive threats.

The nature and scope of new product projects may influence how the responsibilities are allocated. Illustrative characteristics of various new product development efforts are described in Exhibit 8.5. An interesting example of how XM Satellite Radio and Samsung

EXHIBIT 8.5
Attributes of Different Products and Their Associated Development Efforts*

Source: Karl T. Ulrich and Stephen D. Eppinger, *Product Design and Development,* 3rd Ed. (Burr Ridge, IL: Irwin/McGraw-Hill, 2004), 5

	Stanley Tools Jobmaster Screwdriver	Rollerblade In-Line Skate	Hewlett-Packard DeskJet Printer	Volkswagen New Beetle Automobile	Boeing 777 Airplane
Annual production volume	100,000 units/year	100,000 units/year	4 million units/year	100,000 units/year	50 units/year
Sales lifetime	40 years	3 years	2 years	6 years	30 years
Sales price	$3	$200	$300	$17,000	$130 million
Number of unique parts (part numbers)	3 parts	35 parts	200 parts	10,000 parts	130,000
Development time	1 year	2 years	1.5 years	3.5 years	4.5 years
Internal development team (peak size)	3 people	5 people	100 people	800 people	6,800 people
External development team (peak size)	3 people	10 people	75 people	800 people	10,000 people
Development cost	$150,000	$750,000	$50 million	$400 million	$3 billion
Production investment	$150,000	$1 million	$25 million	$500 million	$3 billion

*All figures are approximate, based on publicly available information and company sources.

Electronics partnered to develop the first portable satellite radio combined with a digital music player in only nine months is described in the earlier STRATEGY FEATURE. The co-branded Helix was scheduled for introduction in April 2006.

Idea Generation

Guided by the new product innovation strategy, finding promising new ideas is the starting point in the new-product development process (Exhibit 8.4). Idea generation ranges from incremental improvements of existing products to transformational products. As discussed earlier encouraging a commitment to innovation throughout the organization is an important catalyst for new idea generation. Exhibit 8.6 describes how General Electric's innovation champion is pursuing this objective.

Sources of Ideas

New-product ideas come from many sources. Limiting the search for ideas to those generated by internal research and development activities is far too narrow an approach for most firms. Sources of new-product ideas include R&D laboratories, employees, customers, competitors, outside inventors, acquisition, and value chain members. Both solicited and spontaneous ideas may emerge from these sources. Increasingly, companies are developing "open-market innovation" approaches to generating ideas using licensing, joint ventures, and strategic alliances.[19] By opening their boundaries to suppliers, customers, outside researchers, even competitors, businesses are increasing the import and

EXHIBIT 8.6
An Innovation Champion in Action at GE

Source: Bruce Hussbaum, "How to Build Creative Companies," *BusinessWeek,* August 1, 2005, 77.

Beth Comstock calls herself "a little bit of the crazy, wacky one" at corporate headquarters. And it's an apt description when you realize she works at General Electric Co. Comstock, 44, is charged with transforming GE's culture, famously devoted to process, engineering, and financial controls, to one that's more agile and creative. Chairman and CEO Jeffrey R. Immelt tapped the former communications chief to become GE's first-ever chief marketing officer almost three years ago. The job came with a critical twist: the goal of driving innovation through the company's 300,000-plus ranks.

"Creativity is still a word we're wrestling with," Comstock concedes. "It seems a bit undisciplined, a bit chaotic for a place like GE." More comfortable territory is the term "imaginative problem-solving"—encouraging people to think "what if"—yet always with the aim of driving growth. One of Comstock's first moves was to bring in anthropologists to audit GE's culture. They came back with praise for GE's famous work ethic but noted that employees wanted more "wow"—more discoveries from the company founded by Thomas Edison.

Comstock has a role whose importance is spreading throughout Big Business—that of innovation champion. She began by studying the best practices at companies such as Procter & Gamble, FedEx, and 3M. She brought in a raft of creativity consultants, futurists, and design gurus to lead sessions with different operations. Their names were jolting for GE types: Play, a Richmond (VA.) group that helps execs think differently, and Jump, based in San Mateo, CA., which researches how people use things. GE is expanding its army of designers to bring businesses closer to customers. And Comstock is staging "dreaming sessions" where Immelt, senior execs, and customers debate future market trends. Comstock concedes some managers view the workshops as a waste of time. "We have a long way to go," she says. But for GE, there's no turning back.

By Diane Brady in New York

export of new ideas to improve the speed, cost, and quality of innovation. For example, when Pitney-Bowes was challenged with protecting consumers and postal workers from envelopes tainted with anthrax spores by terrorists, they had no in-house response—their expertise is in secure metering systems to protect postal revenues. They collected ideas from fields as diverse as food handling and military security, before working with outside inventors to introduce new products and services to secure mail against bioterrorism—specialized scanners and imaging systems to identify suspicious letters and packages.

Importantly, generating new product ideas and developing them into new products involves many companies in developing international collaborations and networks. The GLOBAL FEATURE illustrates this globalization of innovation efforts.

The Search Process

It is essential to establish a pro-active idea-generation and evaluation process that meets the needs of the enterprise. Answering these questions is helpful in developing the idea-generation program:

- Should idea search activities be targeted or open-ended? Should the search for new-product ideas be restricted to ideas that correspond to the firm's new product strategy?
- How extensive and aggressive should new-product idea search activities be?
- What specific sources are best for generating a regular flow of new-product ideas?
- How can new ideas be obtained from customers?
- Where will responsibility for new-product idea search be placed? How will new-product idea generation activities be directed and coordinated?
- What are potential threats from disruptive technologies that may satisfy customers better than our products?

For most companies, the idea search process should be targeted within a range of product and market involvement that is consistent with corporate mission and objectives and business unit strategies. While some far-out new-product idea may occasionally change the future of a company, more often open-ended idea search dissipates resources and misdirects efforts. However, management should be pro-active in monitoring potential disruptive innovations and opportunities beyond the core product and market focus.

Idea Sources

Identifying the best sources of ideas depends on many factors including the size and type of firm, technologies involved, new-product needs, resources, management's preferences, and the organization's capabilities. Management needs to consider these factors and develop a proactive strategy for idea generation that will satisfy the firm's requirements. Creating an innovative culture should encourage generating new product ideas. The innovation strategy provides idea generation guidelines.

Many new-product ideas originate from the users of products and services. Lead user analyses offer promising potential for the development of new products.[20] The objective is to identify the companies and product users that pioneer new applications and to study their requirements to guide new-product development in product-markets that change rapidly. Lead users identify gaps between their value expectations and available products and then pursue initiatives to meet their needs. Implementing this approach to idea generation requires major internal and external initiatives. The benefits can be significant for an organization's idea generating activities. The intent is to satisfy the lead users' needs, thus accelerating new product adoption by other companies.

Innovation is an increasingly global game. It can involve a worldwide research and development operation like Microsoft's Advanced Technology Center outside Beijing, or IBM's labs in China, Israel, Switzerland, Japan, and India.

Or innovation can be the product of a much more amorphous structure—global innovation networks—bringing together in-house engineers, contract designers and manufacturers, university scientists and technology suppliers for a particular project.

Because technology crosses borders faster than ever, thanks to the Internet, inexpensive telecom links, and advances in interactive design software, the location of R&D facilities matters far less than who controls these networks and where the benefits accrue. By mobilizing scattered R&D teams, companies can speed development cycles, and more rapidly bring technologies to market.

Procter & Gamble uses online networks to get in touch with thousands of experts worldwide to support its rapid new product innovation process. It found a professor in Bologna, Italy, who had invented an ink-jet method for printing edible images on cakes. P&G used this method to create Pringles potato chips with jokes and pictures printed on them—boosting the product's growth. The new product came out in one year rather than the usual three or four.

In 2006, IBM organized its online Innovation Jam—trying to get the opinions of 100,000 minds—clients, consultants, and employee family members across the world—to tinker with its technology in the pursuit of new ideas.

Sources: Pete Engardio, "Scouring the Plant for Brainiacs," *BusinessWeek,* October 11, 2004, 62–66. Jessi Hempel, "Big Blue Brainstorm," *BusinessWeek,* August 7, 2006, p.79. Steve Hamm, "Speed Demons," *BusinessWeek,* March 27, 2006, 67–76.

Web-search inquiries represent a relatively new source of information concerning buyers' product preferences. For example, analysis of search terms may indicate product characteristics and features that are of interest to buyers. Search research may be useful in generating ideas and providing new product design information.

Involving customers in the innovation process goes beyond obtaining direct customer feedback. Some companies have gone to the extent of equipping customers with the tools to develop and design their own products—ranging from minor modifications to major innovations. For example, Bush Boake Allen (BBA) is a global supplier of specialty flavors to food companies like Nestlé.[21] BBA has developed a toolkit which enables customers to create their own flavors, which BBA then manufactures.

Methods of Generating Ideas

There are several ways of obtaining ideas for new products. Typically, a company considers multiple options in generating product ideas.

Search

Utilizing several information sources may be helpful in identifying new-product ideas. New-product idea publications are available from companies that wish to sell or license ideas they do not wish to commercialize. New technology information is available from commercial and government computerized search services. News sources may also yield information about the new-product activities of competitors. Many trade publications contain new-product announcements. Companies need to identify the relevant search areas and assign responsibility for idea search to an individual or team.

Marketing Research

Surveys of product users help to identify needs that can be satisfied by new products. The focus group is a useful technique to identify and evaluate new-product concepts, and this research method can be used for both consumer and industrial products. The focus group consists of eight to twelve people invited to meet with an experienced moderator to discuss a product-use situation. Idea generation may occur in the focus group discussion of user requirements for a particular product-use situation. Group members are asked to suggest new-product ideas. Later, focus group sessions may be used to evaluate alternative product concepts intended to satisfy the needs identified in the initial session. More than one focus group can be used at each stage in the process. Ethnographic research approaches are also relevant to the search for unsatisfied customer needs (Chapter 5).

Another research technique which is used to generate new-product ideas is the advisory panel. The panel members are selected to represent the firm's target market. For example, such a panel for a producer of mechanics' hand tools would include mechanics. Companies in various industries, including telecommunications, fast foods, and pharmaceuticals use customer advisory groups.

Internal and External Development

Research and development laboratories continue to generate many new product ideas. The United States is the leading spender on industrial research and development in the world and, with the exception of countries like Japan and Korea, very few countries allocate a higher percentage of Gross Domestic Product to R&D. Escalating R&D costs are driving innovative companies to explore new ways of matching R&D resources to value opportunities—through "open source innovation," strategic alliances, joint ventures, and the global search for promising innovation prospects.

Pharmaceutical, semi-conductor, software, and biotech companies spend significantly more percentage-wise on R&D than other industries.[22] For example, in 2004 Microsoft's R&D was 21 percent of sales compared to 3 percent by General Motors. Microsoft spent $7,779 million on R&D in 2004. Also relevant is the amount of R&D expenditures allocated to longer-term projects.

New-product ideas may originate from development efforts outside the firm. Sources include inventors, government and private laboratories, and small high-technology firms. Strategic alliances between companies may result in identifying new-product ideas, as well as sharing responsibility for other activities in new-product development.

Other Idea-Generation Methods

Incentives may be useful to get new-product ideas from employees, marketing partners, and customers. Management should also guard against employees leaving the company and developing a promising idea elsewhere. For this reason many firms require employees to sign secrecy agreements.

Finally, acquiring another firm offers a way to obtain new-product ideas. This strategy may be more cost-effective than internal development and can substantially reduce the lead-time required for developing new products. Procter and Gamble's purchase of the battery powered Crest SpinBrush from the inventor and Glide dental floss from the Gore Company are examples.

Idea-generation identifies one or more new product opportunities that are screened and evaluated. Before comprehensive evaluation, the idea must be transformed into a defined concept, which states what the product will do (anticipated attributes) and the benefits that are superior to available products.[23] The product concept expresses the idea in operational terms so that it can be evaluated as a potential candidate for development into a new product.

Screening, Evaluating, and Business Analysis

Management needs a screening and evaluation process that will eliminate unpromising ideas as soon as possible while keeping the risks of rejecting good ideas at acceptable levels. Moving too many ideas through too many stages in the new product planning process is expensive. Costs build up from the idea stage to the commercialization stage, whereas the risks of developing a bad new product decline as information accumulates about product performance and market acceptance. The objective is to eliminate the least promising ideas before too much time and money are invested in them. However, the tighter the screening procedure, the higher the risk of rejecting a good idea. Based on the specific factors involved, it is necessary to establish a level of risk that is acceptable to management.

Evaluation occurs regularly as an idea moves through the new-product planning stages. Since the objective is to eliminate the poor risks as early as possible, evaluation is necessary at each stage in the planning process. We discuss several evaluation techniques. Typically, evaluation begins by screening new product ideas to identify those that are considered to be most promising. These ideas become concepts and are subjected to more comprehensive evaluation. Finally, business analysis determines whether to move the concept into the new product development stage (Exhibit 8.4).

Screening

A new-product idea receives an initial screening to determine its strategic fit in the company or business unit. Two questions need to be answered: (1) is the idea compatible with the organization's mission and objectives; and (2) is the product initiative commercially feasible? The compatibility of the idea considers factors such as internal capabilities (e.g., development, production, and marketing), financial needs, and competitive factors. Commercial feasibility considers market attractiveness, technical feasibility, financial attractiveness, and social and environmental concerns. The number of ideas generated by an organization is likely to influence the approach utilized in screening the ideas. A large number of ideas call for a formal screening process.

Screening eliminates ideas that are not compatible or feasible for the business. Management must establish how narrow or wide the screening boundaries should be. For example, managers from two similar firms may have very different missions and objectives as well as different propensities toward risk, so an idea could be strategically compatible in one firm and not in another. Also, new product strategies and priorities may be revised when top management changes. For example, when Vice-Chairman Robert A. Lutz joined General Motors in 2001 his primary charge was to build collaborative relationships with design and engineering managers with the objective of developing exciting new styling concepts.[24] Collaboration initiatives were a departure from past practices at GM.

After identifying relevant screening criteria, scoring and importance weighting techniques may be used to make a composite evaluation of the factors considered in the screening process. By summing the weighted scores, an evaluation is obtained for each idea being screened. Management can set ranges for passing and rejecting. The effectiveness of these methods is highly dependent on including all of the relevant criteria and gaining agreement on the relative importance of the screening factors from the people involved in the evaluation process.

Concept Evaluation

The boundaries concerning idea screening, concept evaluation, and business analysis are often not clearly drawn. These evaluation stages may be combined, particularly when only a few ideas are involved. After completing initial screening, each idea that survives becomes a new product concept and receives a more comprehensive evaluation. Several of the same factors used in screening may be evaluated in greater depth, including buyers' reactions to the proposed concept. A team representing different business functions should participate in concept evaluation.

Importance of Concept Evaluation

Extensive research on companies' new product planning activities highlights the critical role of extensive market and technical assessments *before* beginning the development of a new product concept.[25] These "up-front" evaluations should result in a clearly defined new product concept indicating its market target(s), customer value offering, and positioning strategy. Research concerning product failures strongly suggests that many companies do not devote enough attention to "up-front" evaluation of product concepts.

The failure of the handheld CueCat scanner offers compelling evidence of the value and importance of concept evaluation. The purpose of CueCat was to read a bar code and when attached to a personal computer, provide a direct access to a Web page for the product. The founder of Digital Convergence Corp. raised $185 million from investors to commercially launch CueCat.[26] Large investors included Belo Corp. ($37.5 million), Radio Shack ($30 million), and Young & Rubicam ($28 million). The business plan was to give away 50 million CueCats ($ 6.50 cost) and obtain revenues from advertisers and licensing fees. Four million CueCats were distributed but few were used. People did not want to carry the scanner around and could quickly access Web sites by typing the address. CueCat did not fill a consumer need. Importantly, this weakness could have been identified by concept evaluation before large expenditures were made to produce and distribute the product.

Several concept evaluation issues are highlighted in Exhibit 8.7. Evaluation includes more than concept tests. For example, the new product team may perform competitor analyses, market forecasts, and technical feasibility evaluations. The questions indicated in Exhibit 8.7 are helpful in deciding how to evaluate the new product concept.

Concept Tests

Concept tests are useful in evaluation and refinement of the characteristics of proposed new products. The purpose of concept testing is to obtain a reaction to the new-product concept from a sample of potential buyers before the product is developed. More than one concept test may be used during the evaluation process. The technique supplies important information for reshaping, redefining and coalescing new-product ideas.[27] Concept tests help to evaluate the relative appeal of ideas or alternative product positionings, supply information for developing the product and marketing strategy, and identify potential

EXHIBIT 8.7
Concept Evaluation Issues

- What is the objective (purpose) of concept evaluation?
- How much time/resources should be allocated to evaluation?
- What are the risks?
- Who will perform the evaluation?
- Who decides the outcomes?
- What evaluation techniques are most useful?

market segments. An example of a proposal to conduct a concept test for evaluating alternative investment products is described in Exhibit 8.8.

The concept test is a useful way to evaluate a product idea very early in the development process. The costs of these tests are reasonable, given the information that can be obtained. Since the actual product and a commercial setting are not present, the evaluation is somewhat artificial. The concept test is probably most useful in identifying very favorable or unfavorable product concepts. The research method also offers a basis for comparing two or more concepts. An important requirement of concept testing is that the product (good or service) can be described in words and visually, and the participant must have the experience and capability to evaluate the concept. The respondent must be able to visualize the proposed product and its features based on a verbal or written description and/or picture.

Computer technology offers very promising capabilities for visual testing of new product concepts. Potential customers can be provided with multimedia virtual buying environment. For example, virtual methodology was used to evaluate the potential of new electric cars: "Respondents viewed multimedia presentations, read on-line articles about the new product, talked with users of the vehicle, visited a showroom, and were able to virtually get into the vehicle and talk with salespeople."[28]

Business Analysis

Business analysis estimates the commercial feasibility of the new-product concept. Obtaining an accurate financial projection depends on the quality of the revenue and cost forecasts. Business analysis is normally accomplished at several stages in the new-product planning process, beginning at the business analysis stage before the product concept moves into the development stage. Financial projections are refined at later stages.

Revenue Forecasts

The newness of the product, the size of the market, and the competing products all influence the accuracy of revenue projections. In the case of an established market such as breakfast cereals, snack foods, and toothpaste, estimates of total market size are usually available from industry information. Industry associations often publish forecasts and government agencies such as the U.S. Commerce Department forecast sales for various industries. The more difficult task is estimating the market share that is feasible for a new-product entry.[29] A range of feasible share positions can be forecast at the concept stage and used as a basis for preliminary financial projections. Managers may have success norms based on prior experience.

In certain situations major difficulties may exist in forecasting the demand for new products. Consider, for example, the dilemma that faced telecom companies with third-generation (3G) mobile phone services. European carriers spent some $250 billion buying 3G rights and new networks. Notwithstanding efficient data connections at broadband speeds, cheaper voice calls, Internet access, photo messaging, games, streaming video clips, and videoconferencing on 3G phones, consumers have shown limited interest in buying mobile multimedia. There is a possible risk that levels of business achieved may never pay back the cost of the 3G licenses acquired in 2001 and 2002.[30] After a very slow start-up the forecasts in 2004 became cautiously optimistic, indicating an evolution rather than revolution.

Preliminary Marketing Plan

An initial marketing strategy should be developed as a part of the business analysis. Included are market target(s), positioning strategy, and marketing program plans. While this plan is

EXHIBIT 8.8   Project Proposal: New Product Concept Screening Test

Source: Adapted from William R. Dillon, Thomas J. Madden, and Neil H. Firtle, *Marketing Research in a Marketing Environment,* 3rd ed. (Burr Ridge, IL: Richard D. Irwin, 1994), 562. Copyright © The McGraw-Hill Companies. Used with permission.

Brand:	New products.
Project:	Concept screening.
Background and objectives:	The New York banking group has developed 12 new-product ideas for investment products (services). The objectives of this research are to assess consumer interest in the concepts and to establish priorities for further development.
Research method:	Concept testing will be conducted in four geographically dispersed, central location facilities within the New York metropolitan area.
	Each of the 12 concepts plus 1 retest control concept will be evaluated by a total of 100 men and 100 women with household incomes of $25,000. The following age quotas will be used for both male and female groups within the sample:
	18–34 = 50 percent
	35–49 = 25 percent
	50 and over = 25 percent
	Each respondent will evaluate a maximum of eight concepts. Order of presentation will be rotated throughout to avoid position bias.
	Because some of the concepts are in low-incidence product categories, user groups will be defined both broadly and narrowly in an attempt to assess potential among target audiences.
Information to be obtained:	This study will provide the following information to assist in concept evaluation:
	Investment ownership.
	Purchase interest (likelihood of subscription).
	Uniqueness of new service.
	Believability.
	Importance of main point.
	Demographics.
Action standard:	To identify concepts warranting further development, top-box purchase intent scores will be compared to the top-box purchase intent scores achieved by the top 10 percent of the concepts tested in earlier concept screening studies.
	Rank order of purchase intent scores on the *uniqueness, believability,* and *importance* ratings will also be considered in the evaluation and prioritization of concepts for further development.
Material requirements:	Fifty copies of each concept.
Cost and timing:	The cost of this research will be $15,000 ± 10%
	This research will adhere to the following schedule:
	Field work 1 week
	Top-line 2 weeks
	Final report 3 weeks
Supplier:	Burke Marketing Research.

preliminary, it is an early guide to strategy development and coordination among marketing, design, operations, and other business functions. The choice of the marketing strategy is necessary in developing the revenue forecast.

Cost Estimation

Several different costs occur in the planning and commercialization of new products. One way to categorize the costs is to estimate them for each stage in the new-product planning process (Exhibit 8.4). The costs increase rapidly as the product concept moves through the development process. Expenditures for each planning stage can be further divided into functional categories (e.g., marketing, research and development, and operations).

Profit Projections

Analyses appropriate for new-product evaluation include break-even, cash flow, return on investment, and profit contribution. Management can use break-even analysis as a basis for assessing whether it is feasible to reach and exceed break-even. Business analysis estimates should take into consideration the probable flow of revenues and costs over the time span used in the analysis. Typically, new products incur heavy costs before they start to generate revenues.

Product and Process Development

After completing the business analysis, management must decide either to begin product development or abort the project. During the development stage the concept may be transformed into one or more prototypes. The prototype is the actual product, but may be custom produced rather than by an established manufacturing process. Use testing of the product may occur during the development stage.

Our earlier discussion of customer-guided new-product planning emphasizes the importance of transforming customer preferences into internal product design guidelines. Product design decisions need to be guided by customer preferences and analysis of competitor advantages and weaknesses. Product development should involve the entire new-product planning team.

Product Development Process

The development of the new product includes product design, industrial design (ease-of-use and style), process (manufacturing) design, packaging design, and decisions to make or outsource various product components. Development typically consists of various technical activities, but also requires continuing interaction among R&D, marketing, operations, finance, and legal functions. The relative importance of the activities differs according to the product involved. For example, product and process design are extensive for complex products like large commercial aircraft. In contrast line extensions (e.g., new flavors and package sizes) of food products do not require extensive design activities.

Importantly, the effective management of lean product development processes that take products to market more rapidly has become a competitive imperative. In many sectors the time taken to bring a product to market has been halved. At Nissan Motor Co. the development of new cars used to take twenty-one months, now the process is completed in ten and a half months. In cell phones, Nokia, Motorola, and others used to take twelve to eighteen months to develop basic models, now this takes six to nine months. Faster product development processes are mandated in many markets.[31]

When the new product is a service there are similarities in the development process and also some differences. New financial services must be designed and processes developed for making them available to customers. However, the service is not tangible so its design must take this into account. Use testing may be particularly important for services such as software. The reality is that many products today are combinations of goods and services. Starbucks, the world's largest coffee chain, is illustrative. The Starbucks experience is more than drinking a cup of expensive coffee.

Product Specifications

Product specifications describe what the product will do rather than how it should be designed. This information indicates the product planners' expectations regarding the benefits provided by the product based on customer analysis, including essential physical and operating characteristics.[32] These guidelines help the technical team determine the best design strategy for delivering the benefits. The more complete the specifications for the product, the better the designers can incorporate the requirements into the design. The specifications also provide a basis for assessing design feasibility. In some situations benefit/cost assessments may require changing the specifications.

Industrial Design

Many companies are placing increasing emphasis on the ease-of-use and style of products. Design consultants assist companies on various design initiatives. Industrial design has become a major part of the new product development process for many products. Design was an important contributor to Apple's success in the early 2000s. The design process of the consultant IDEO, the industry leader, is described in the RELATIONSHIP FEATURE.

Prototype

The technical team uses the product specifications to guide the design of one or more physical products. Similar information is needed to guide software design and design of new services. At this stage the product is called a prototype since it is not ready for commercial production and marketing. Many of the parts may be custom built, and materials, packaging, and other details may differ from the commercial version. Nevertheless, the prototype needs to be capable of delivering the benefits spelled out in the specifications. Scale models are used for some products such as commercial aircraft, which can be tested in wind tunnels to evaluate their performance characteristics. Computer technology is also used in testing and evaluation of new products such as automobiles and aircraft.

Use Tests

When testing of the prototype is feasible, designers can obtain important feedback from users concerning how well the product meets the needs that are spelled out in the product specifications. A standard approach to use testing is to distribute the product to a sample of users, asking them to try the product. Follow-up occurs after the test participant has had sufficient time to evaluate the product. The design of new industrial products may include the active involvement of users in testing and evaluating the product at various stages in the development process. The relatively small number of users in industrial markets compared to consumer markets makes use testing very feasible. Use tests are also popular for gaining reactions to new consumer products such as foods, drinks, and health and beauty aids. Clinical trials may also be conducted to support performance claims of products such as foods offering therapeutic benefits.

Relationship Feature   *IDEO Redefines Good Design by Creating Experiences, Not Just Products*

A company goes to IDEO with a problem. Management wants a better product, service, or space—no matter. IDEO puts together an eclectic team composed of members from the client company and its own experts who go out to observe and document the consumer experience. Often, IDEO will have top executives play the roles of their own customers. Execs from food and clothing companies show off their own stuff in different retail stores and on the Web. Health-care managers get care in different hospitals. Wireless providers use their own—and competing—services.

The next stage is brainstorming. IDEO mixes designers, engineers, and social scientists with its clients in a room where they intensely scrutinize a given problem and suggest possible solutions. It is managed chaos: a dozen or so very smart people examining data, throwing out ideas, writing potential solutions on big Post-its that are ripped off and attached to the wall.

IDEO designers then mock up working models of the best concepts that emerge. Rapid prototyping has always been a hallmark of the company. Seeing ideas in working, tangible form is a far more powerful mode of explanation than simply reading about them off a page. IDEO uses inexpensive prototyping tools—Apple-based iMovies to portray consumer experiences and cheap cardboard to mock up examination rooms or fitting rooms. "IDEO's passion is about making stuff work, not about being artists," says design guru Tucker Viemeister, CEO of Dutch-based designer Springtime USA. "Their corporate customers really buy into it."

Source: Bruce Nussbaum, "The Power of Design," *BusinessWeek,* May 17, 2004, 91.

Unlike a market test, the use test normally does not identify the brand name of the product or the company name. While it is less accurate in gauging market success compared to the market test, the use test yields important information such as preferences, ratings, likes/dislikes, advantages/limitations, unique features, usage and users, and comparisons with competing products.

Process Development

The process for producing the product in commercial quantities must be developed. Manufacturing (producing) the product at the desired quality level and cost is a critical determinant of profitability. The new product may be feasible to produce in the laboratory but not on a full-scale basis because of costs, production rates, and other considerations. Initial production delays can also jeopardize the success of a new product. Airbus experienced delays in producing its new A-380 super-jumbo jet and this created concerns for several customers.

The feasibility to *mass customize* and *modularize* may have a major impact on product and process design.[33] Mass customization enables customizing product offerings at relatively low costs. Modularity involves developing and producing a product using interrelated modules, thus facilitating mass customization. The system architecture for the product links the modules together, but each part can be designed and produced independently within the organization or by outsourcing. Modularity was pioneered by the computer industry, but is applicable to many other products.

Marketing Strategy and Market Testing

Developing the marketing strategy for a new product varies depending on whether it is an incremental improvement or new to the market and/or the company. The latter requires complete targeting and positioning strategies (Chapter 6). The incremental product improvement may only need a revised promotion strategy to convey to target buyers information about the benefits offered by the improved product. It is also important to consider how the new product will relate to the firm's existing products. Regardless of the newness of the product, reviewing the proposed marketing strategy helps to avoid market introduction problems.

Marketing Strategy Decisions

Evaluation efforts (e.g., concept and use tests) conducted during concept evaluation and product development supply information that may be helpful in designing the marketing strategy. Examples of useful planning guidelines include user characteristics, product features, advantages over competing products, types of use situations, feasible price range, and potential buyer profiles. Marketing strategy planning begins at the concept evaluation stage and continues during product development. Activities such as packaging, name selection, environmental considerations, product information, colors, materials, and product safety must also be decided between design, operations, and marketing.

Market Targeting

Selection of the market target(s) for the new product range from offering a new product to an existing target, to identifying an entirely new group of potential users. Examining available marketing research information for the new product may yield useful insights as to targeting opportunities. It may also be necessary to conduct additional research such as market testing before finalizing the market targeting strategy.

Positioning Strategy

The core of this strategy is how management wants the new product to be positioned in the eyes and minds of the targeted buyers. Several positioning decisions are made during marketing strategy development. Issues such as packaging, name selection, sizes, and other aspects of the product must be decided. The value chain strategy determines the customer access channels to be used. It is also necessary to select a price strategy and to develop the advertising and sales promotion strategy. Testing of ads may occur at this stage. Decisions must be made concerning use of the Internet. Finally, sales management must design a personal selling strategy including deciding about sales force additions and training and allocation of selling effort to the new product.

The market introduction of the new high definition digital video disk players in 2006 presented some interesting targeting and positioning challenges. Sony offers its Blu-ray format while Toshiba has the HD-DVD format, selling at $499 compared to Sony players at $1,000.[34] A key positioning challenge is whether one format will eventually become the market standard. Blu-ray has some superior features but will they be valued by buyers at double the price of Toshiba's players? The situation is similar to the battle between VHS and Beta technologies in the 1980s. VHS became the standard even though the Beta technology was considered superior.

Market Testing

"A test market is a controlled experiment conducted in a carefully chosen marketplace (e.g., website, store, town, or other geographical location) to measure marketplace response and predict sales or profitability of a product".[35] Market testing can be considered after the product is fully developed, assuming the product is suitable for market testing. Market tests gauge buyer response to the new product and evaluate one or more positioning strategies. Test marketing is used for consumer products such as foods, beverages, and health and beauty aids. Market tests can also be conducted for business-to-business goods and services. Several methods of testing are available including simulated test marketing, scanner based tests, and conventional tests.

A description of the different new product evaluation methods is shown in Exhibit 8.9. The testing tools for each of the stages are indicated. Note how market testing fits into the planning process. The exhibit also provides an overview of the marketing plan development.

Simulated Tests

The distinguishing feature of simulated tests is that they are conducted in a simulated shopping environment and may be used in place of or before a full-scale market test.[36] Typically, a research facility is used to provide a simulated shopping experience in order to obtain feedback from the participants. Not surprisingly, the findings are not as accurate as actual market tests.

Simulated tests offer several advantages including speed, low costs ($50,000 to $150,000 compared to $1 million or more for traditional market tests), and the tests yield relatively accurate forecasts of market response. The tests also eliminate the risk present in conventional testing of competitor exposure.

Scanner Based Tests

These tests are conducted in an actual market environment. The test product must be made available in each test city. Information Resources Inc.'s BehaviorScan system pioneered the use of cable television and a computerized database to track new products during these tests. The system uses information and responses from recruited panel members in each test city. Each member has an identification card to show to participating store cashiers. Purchases are electronically recorded and transmitted to a central data bank. Cable television enables BehaviorScan to use controlled advertisement testing. Some viewers can be exposed to ads while the ads are being withheld from other viewers.

EXHIBIT 8.9
How Market Testing Relates to the Other Testing Steps

Source: Chart from C. Merle Crawford and C. Anthony Di Benedetto, *New Products Management,* 7th ed. (Burr Ridge, IL: Irwin/McGraw-Hill, 2003), 435. Copyright © The McGraw-Hill Companies. Used with permission.

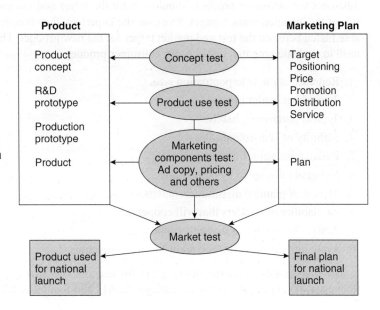

Traditional Tests

This method of market testing introduces the product under actual market conditions in one or more test cities.[37] It is typically used for frequently purchased consumer products. The time required for the tests ranges from a year to 18 months or more. Test marketing employs a complete marketing program including advertising and personal selling. Product sampling is often an important factor in launching the new product in the test market. The product is marketed on a commercial basis in each city, and test results are then projected to the national or regional target market. Because of its high cost, conventional test marketing represents the final evaluation before full-scale market introduction. Management may decide not to test market in order to avoid competitor awareness and high testing costs, and to speed up the new product introduction.

Web-Enabled Tests

While these tests offer less control than other tests, they are increasingly used due to speed and relatively low costs. Procter and Gamble initially offered Crest Whitestrips via the product's dedicated website.[38] The research information obtained during an 8-month campaign was valuable in guiding P&G's full-scale market introduction of the successful product. The Internet will be an important basis for market testing in the future.

Testing Industrial Products

Market testing can be used for industrial products. Selection of test sites may need to extend beyond one or two cities to include sufficient market coverage. For example, a region of a country might be used for testing. The test firm has substantial control of an industrial products test through the use of direct mail, the Internet, and personal selling. The relatively small number of customers also aids targeting of marketing efforts.

Selecting Test Sites

Test sites for consumer products should exhibit the buyer and environmental characteristics of the intended market target. Since no site is perfect, the objective is to find a reasonable match between the test and market target for the new product. These criteria are often used to evaluate potential test sites for consumer products.

1. Representation as to population size.
2. Typical per capita income.
3. Typical purchasing habits.
4. Stability of year-round sales.
5. Relative isolation from other cities.
6. Not easily disrupted by competitors.
7. Typical of planned distribution outlets.
8. Availability of retailers that will cooperate.
9. Availability of media that will cooperate.
10. Availability of research and audit service companies.[39]

The highest-ranked metropolitan areas for test markets in the U.S. are Albany, NY; Rochester, NY; Greensboro, NC; Birmingham, AL; and Syracuse, NY.[40]

External Influences

Probably the most troublesome external factor that may affect test market results is competition that does not compete on a normal basis. Competitors may attempt to drive test market results awry by increasing or decreasing their marketing efforts and making other changes in their marketing actions. It is also important to monitor the test market environment to identify other unusual influences such as major shifts in economic conditions.

Commercialization

Introducing new products into the market requires finalizing the marketing plan, coordinating market entry activities across business functions, implementing the marketing strategy, and monitoring and controlling the product launch. Procter & Gamble's entry into Japan's dish soap market in 1995 is an interesting example of an international new product venture.[41] P & G's Joy brand gained a leading 20 percent share of the $400 million dish-soap market by 1997. The successful strategy included offering new technology, packaging that retailers liked, attractive margins for retailers, and heavy spending on innovative commercials that got consumers' attention. At the time of market entry, Kao and Lion (Japanese companies) together had nearly 40 percent of the market. P & G developed a highly concentrated formula for Joy to eliminate consumers' concerns about Joy's strengths compared to other brands. Encouraged by commercials to try the new product, Japanese home-makers were pleased with Joy's performance.

The Marketing Plan

Market introduction requires a complete marketing strategy that is spelled out in the marketing plan. The plan should be coordinated with the people and business functions responsible for the introduction, including salespeople, sales and marketing managers, and managers from other functional areas such as operations, distribution, finance, and human resources. Responsibility for the new-product launch is normally assigned to a marketing or product manager. Alternatively, companies may assign responsibility to product planning and market introduction teams.

The timing and geographical scope of the launch are important decisions. The options range from a national market introduction to an area-by-area rollout. In some instances the scope of the introduction may extend to international markets. The national introduction is a major endeavor, requiring a comprehensive implementation effort. A rollout reduces the scope of the introduction and enables management to adjust marketing strategy based on experience gained in the early stages of the launch. Of course, the rollout approach, like market testing, gives competition more time to react.

Monitoring and Control

Real-time tracking of new-product performance at the market entry stage is extremely important. Standardized information services (e.g., Information Resources Inc.) are available for monitoring sales of products such as foods, health and beauty aids, and prescription drugs. Information for these services is collected through store audits, consumer diary panels, and scanner services. Special tracking studies may be necessary for products that are not included in standardized information services. The Internet is rapidly becoming an essential new product information gathering and monitoring capability. These activities include private online communities and research panels that provide companies with shoppers' feedback.

- Ecoimagination was launched in 2005 by Jeffrey Immelt, GE's Chief Executive Officer, to highlight GE's focus on green issues—placing green technology products under a single brand.

- By 2007, GE had doubled its sales of environmentally-friendly products to $12 billion over the previous two years—this includes wind-turbines, water-purification systems, and energy-efficient appliances.

- Immelt has $50 billion of projects in the pipeline and is on track to meet its target of $20 billion in "green" sales by 2010.

- In 2006, GE invested $900 million of its $3.7 billion R&D budget on green projects.

- The focus on green products is part of Immelt's priority to reduce GE's exposure to low growth industries and move to more profitable areas.

- In managing the Ecoimagination initiative, GE is rigorous in selecting projects that are wanted by customers and are financially viable, but that also meet the criterion that they must significantly and measurably improve customers' environmental and operating performance.

Sources: Francesco Guerra, "Turning Green Requires a Lot of Imagination," *Financial Times,* Friday, May 24, 2007, 28. Fiona Harvey, "GE Looks Out for a Cleaner Profit," *Financial Times,* Friday, July 1, 2005, 13.

It is important to include product performance metrics and performance targets in the new-product plan to track how well the product is performing. Often included are profit contribution, sales, market share, and return on investment objectives—including the time horizon for reaching objectives. It is also important to establish benchmarks for objectives that indicate minimum acceptable performance. For example, market share threshold levels are sometimes used to gauge new-product performance. Repeat purchase data are essential for tracking frequently purchased products. Regular measures of customer satisfaction are also relevant in tracking market performance

Management vision for the strategic direction to be taken by the business is also a significant influence on innovation. The ETHICS FEATURE describes the pursuit of sustainable product development at General Electric, as part of its Ecoimagination corporate responsibility initiative. Many companies now include sustainability goals in their product development and innovation strategy.

Variations in the Generic New Product Planning Process

The new product planning process (Exhibit 8.4) is based on the logic of being market driven and focused on customer needs. While a market-oriented focus is always important, some variations in the generic process may be necessary due to the new product strategy of a particular company. The major impact of the variants is on the types of ideas that are considered by the firm. Several variations from the generic process are described in Exhibit 8.10.

The variants set some boundaries on the types of ideas considered by a company. For example, PepsiCo's beverage division has a focus on drinks in its idea seeking activities. Pepsi's introduction of Sierra Mist carbonated beverage is an example of a process-intensive new product. The generic new product planning process (Exhibit 8.4) is relevant to all of the product variants other than limiting to some extent the types of ideas to be considered.

EXHIBIT 8.10   **Summary of Variants of the Generic Development Process**

Source: Karl T. Ulrich and Stephen D. Eppinger, *Product Design and Development,* 3rd ed. (Burr Ridge, IL: Irwin/McGraw-Hill, 2004), 19.

Process Type	Description	Distinct Features	Examples
Generic (Market-Pull) Products	The team begins with a market opportunity and selects appropriate technologies to meet customer needs.	Process generally includes distinct planning, concept development, system-level design, detail design, testing and refinement, and production ramp-up phases.	Sporting goods, furniture, tools.
Technology-Push Products	The team begins with a new technology, then finds an appropriate market.	Planning phase involves matching technology and market. Concept development assumes a given technology.	Gore-Tex rainwear, Tyvek envelopes.
Platform Products	The team assumes that the new product will be built around an established technological subsystem.	Concept development assumes a proven technology platform.	Consumer electronics, computers, printers.
Process-Intensive Products	Characteristics of the product are highly constrained by the production process.	Either an existing production process must be specified from the start, or both product and process must be developed together from the start.	Snack foods, breakfast cereals, chemicals, semiconductors.
Customized Products	New products are slight variations of existing configurations.	Similarity of projects allows for a streamlined and highly structured development process.	Motors, switches, batteries, containers.
High-Risk Products	Technical or market uncertainties create high risks of failure.	Risks are identified early and tracked throughout the process. Analysis and testing activities take place as early as possible.	Pharmaceuticals, space systems.
Quick-Build Products	Rapid modeling and prototyping enables many design-build-test cycles.	Detail design and testing phases are repeated a number of times until the product is completed or time/budget runs out.	Software, cellular phones.
Complex Systems	System must be decomposed into several subsystems and many components.	Subsystems and components are developed by many teams working in parallel, followed by system integration and validation.	Airplanes, jet engines, automobiles.

Summary   New product planning is a vital activity in every company, and it applies to services as well as physical products. Companies that are successful in new product planning follow a step-by-step process of new product planning combined with effective organization designs for managing new products. Experience and learning help these firms to improve product planning over time.

Several key initiatives are pursued by companies which are successful innovators. These include: (1) creating an innovative culture; (2) selecting the right innovation strategy; (3) developing and implementing effective new product processes; (4) making resource commitments; and (5) leveraging distinctive capabilities.

Top management often defines the product, market, and technology scope of new product ideas to be considered by an organization. The steps in new product planning include customer needs analysis, idea generation and screening, concept evaluation, business analysis, product development and testing, marketing strategy development, market testing, and commercialization (Exhibit 8.4).

Idea generation starts the process of planning for a new product. There are various internal and external sources of new-product ideas. Ideas are identified by information search, marketing research, research and development, incentives, and acquisition. Screening, evaluation, and business analysis help determine if the new-product concept is sufficiently attractive to justify proceeding with development.

Design of the product and use testing transform the product from a concept into a prototype. Product development creates one or more prototypes. Product testing obtains user's reactions to the new product. Production development determines how to produce the product in commercial quantities at costs that will enable the firm to price the product at a level attractive to buyers. Marketing strategy development begins early in the product planning process. A new marketing strategy is needed for a totally new product. Product line additions, modifications, and other changes require a less extensive strategy development.

Completion of the product design and marketing strategy moves the process to the market testing stage. At this point management may decide to obtain some form of market reaction to the new product before full-scale market entry. Testing options include simulated test marketing, scanner-based test marketing, and conventional test marketing. Industrial products are not market tested as much as consumer products. Instead, use tests of product prototypes are more typical for industrial products. Commercialization completes the planning process, moving the product into the marketplace to pursue sales and profit performance objectives.

The market-driven, customer focused generic planning process provides the basic guide to developing new products. Nonetheless, some variations may be necessary in applying the process when technology, production processes, and other limiting factors define the scope of ideas considered by a particular firm.

Questions for Review and Discussion

1. Explain the relationship between customer satisfaction and customer value.
2. In many consumer products companies, marketing executives seem to play the lead role in new-product planning, whereas research and development executives occupy this position in firms with very complex products such as electronics. Why do these differences exist? Do you agree that such differences should occur?
3. Discuss the features and limitations of focus group interviews for use in new-product planning.
4. Identify and discuss the important issues in deciding how to organize for new-product planning.
5. Discuss the issues and trade-offs of using tight evaluation versus loose evaluation procedures as a product concept moves through the planning process to the commercialization stage.
6. What factors may affect the length of the new-product planning process?
7. Compare and contrast the use of scanner tests and conventional market tests.
8. Is the use of a single city test market appropriate? Discuss.

9. Examine the new product planning process assuming a platform strategy is being used by the organization (Exhibit 8.10). How does the use of a platform strategy alter the planning process?

10. Discuss the potential role of the Internet in the new product planning process. Which stages of the process may benefit most from Internet initiatives?

Internet Applications

A. Visit the website of the Gap (www.gap.com). Discuss how the Web can be used in new product planning for a bricks-and-mortar retailer such as the Gap.

B. Virgin Group Ltd. is an interesting corporate conglomerate headed by British tycoon, Richard C.N. Branson. Visit Virgin.com and develop a critical analysis of Virgin's new product strategy of launching a portfolio of online businesses.

C. Dell, Inc. is expanding its product portfolio. Go to www.dell.com and describe the product categories in which Dell competes.

D. Visit the Hennes & Mauritz website and compare H&M's product offerings with those offered by Gap (www.gap.com).

Feature Applications

A. The Google INNOVATION FEATURE describes how the company manages its idea factory. Are there risks of expanding too far beyond the core search business? How should new product planners avoid this problem without disregarding all potential opportunities beyond the core business?

B. The STRATEGY FEATURE indicates how XMSatellite Radio and Samsung Electronics collaborated on developing a new product. Discuss the advantages and limitations of using this approach to new product development.

C. The RELATIONSHIP FEATURE describes how the design consultant IDEO assists companies in new product design. Discuss the advantages and limitations of having this activity performed by a consultant rather than internally.

Notes

1. Jena McGregor, "Most Innovative Companies," *BusinessWeek,* May 14, 2007, 52.

2. Thomas D. Kuczmarski, Erica B. Seamon, Kathryn W. Spilotro, and Zachary T. Johnston, "The Breakthrough Mindset," *Marketing Management,* March/April 2003, 38–43.

3. "Innovation: The View from the Top," *BusinessWeek,* April 3, 2006, 52 and 54.

4. Suzanne Treville, "Improving the Innovation Process," *OR/MS Today,* December 1994, 29.

5. "Getting Hot Ideas from Customers," *Fortune,* May 18, 1992, 86–87.

6. Gary S. Lynn, Joseph G. Morone, and Albert S. Paulson, "Marketing and Discontinuous Innovation: The Probe and Learn Process," *California Management Review,* Spring 1996, 8–37.

7. Ibid.

8. Ibid., 11.

9. Clayton M. Christensen and Michael E. Raynor, *The Innovator's Solution* (Boston: Harvard Business School Press, 2003).

10. Ibid.

11. Bruce Nussbaum, "How to Build Innovative Companies," *BusinessWeek,* August 1, 2005, 62–63.

12. Robert Cooper, "Benchmarking New Product Performance: Results of the Best Practices Study," *European Management Journal,* February 1998, 1–7; "Producer Power," *The Economist,* March 4, 1995, 70; Kuczmarski, et al. "The Breakthrough Mindset."

13. Chandy, Rajesh K. and Gerald J. Tellis, "Organizing for Radical Product Innovation," *MSI Report No. 98–102,* Cambridge, MA: Marketing Science Institute, 1998.

14. Lawrence Ingrassia, "By Improving Scratch Paper, 3M Gets New-Product Winner," *The Wall Street Journal,* March 31, 1983, 27.2.

15. Kuczmarski, et al. "The Breakthrough Mindset," 43.

16. Cooper, "Benchmarking New Product Performance."

17. Eric M. Olsen, Orville C. Walker, Jr., and Robert W. Ruekert, "Organizing for Effective New-Product Development: The Moderating Role of Product Innovativeness," *Journal of Marketing,* January 1995, 48–62.

18. Ibid.

19. Darrell Rigby and Chris Zook, "Open-Market Innovation," *Harvard Business Review,* October 2002, 80–89.

20. Stefan H. Thomke, *Managing Product and Service Development* (Burr Ridge, IL: McGraw-Hill/Irwin, 2007), 189–198. Eric von Hippell, *Democratizing Innovation* (Cambridge, MA, The MIT Press, 2005).

21. Ibid., 359–381.

22. "R & D 2005," *Technology Review,* September 2005, 50–52.

23. C. Merle Crawford and C. Anthony Di Benedetto, *New Products Management,* 7th ed. (Burr Ridge, IL: Irwin/McGraw-Hill, 2003), Chapter 4.

24. "GM's Design Push Picks Up Speed," *BusinessWeek,* July 18, 2005, 40–42.

25. Cooper, "Benchmarking New Product Performance."

26. Elliot Spagat, "A Web Gadget Fizzles Despite a Salesman's Dazzle," *The Wall Street Journal,* June 27, 2001, B1, B4.

27. William R. Dillon, Thomas J. Madden, and Neil H. Firtle, *Marketing Research in a Marketing Environment,* 3rd ed. (Burr Ridge, IL: Richard D. Irwin, Inc., 1994).

28. Glen L. Urban, *Digital Marketing Strategy* (Pearson Prentice Hall, 2004), 96.

29. David Welch, "Why Hybrids Are Such a Hard Sell," *BusinessWeek,* March 19, 2007, 45.

30. Almar Latour, "Disconnected," *The Wall Street Journal,* June 5, 2001, A1, A8; "Vision Meet Reality," *The Economist,* September 4, 2004 63–65.

31. Steve Hamm, "Speed Demons," *BusinessWeek,* March 27, 2006, 67–76.

32. Crawford and Di Benedetto, *New Products Management,* Chapter 12.

33. See, for example, James H. Gilmore and B. Joseph Pine II, "The Four Faces of Mass Customization," *Harvard Business Review,* January-February 1997, 91–101; and Kathleen M. Eisenhardt and Shona L. Brown, "Time Pacing: Competing in Markets That Won't Stand Still," *Harvard Business Review,* March-April 1998, 67.

34. Andrew Simons, "HD-DVD Takes an Early Lead-In Sales Race Against Blu-ray," *The Wall Street Journal,* April 26, 2006, B3B.

35. Donald R. Cooper and Pamela S. Schindler, *Marketing Research* (Burr Ridge, IL: McGraw-Hill/Irwin, 2006), 321.

36. Ibid., 325–326.

37. Ibid., 323–324.

38. Ibid., 327.

39. Dillon, Madden, and Firtle, *Marketing Research,* 582–584.

40. Acxiom Corporation, www.acxiom.com/testmarkets, 2005.

41. Norhiko Shirouzu, "P & G's Joy Makes an Unlikely Splash in Japan," *The Wall Street Journal,* December 19, 1997, B1 and B8.

Cases for Part 3

Case 3-1

Walt Disney Co.

Early on a July workday in 1997, Jim McCluney, then head of Apple's worldwide operations got the call. McCluney was summoned with other top brass of the beleaguered company to Apple Computer Inc.'s boardroom on its Cupertino (Calif.) campus. Embattled Chief Executive Gil Amelio wasted no time. With an air of barely concealed relief, he said: "Well, I'm sad to report that it's time for me to move on. Take care," McCluney recalls. And he left.

A few minutes later, in walked Steve Jobs. The co-founder of the once proud company had been fired by Apple 12 years before. He had returned seven months earlier as a consultant, when Amelio acquired his NEXT Software Inc. And now Jobs was back in charge. Wearing shorts, sneakers, and a few days' growth of beard, he sat down in a swivel chair and spun slowly, says McCluney, now president of storage provider Emulex Corp. "O.K., tell me what's wrong with this place," Jobs said. After some mumbled replies, he jumped in: "It's the products! So what's wrong with the products?" Again, executives began offering some answers. Jobs cut them off. "The products SUCK!" he roared. "There's no sex in them anymore!"

The one-time *enfant terrible* of the technology world has calmed down considerably en route to becoming a 50-year-old billionaire. But what hasn't changed is his passion for doing, and saying, just about anything to help create the kinds of products that consumers love. In the nine years since Jobs returned to Apple, his unique modus operandi has sparked broad changes in the world of music, movies, and technology.

Now Jobs is stepping into the Magic Kingdom. On Jan. 24, Walt Disney Co. agreed to pay $7.4 billion in stock to acquire Pixar Animation Studios, where Jobs is chairman, CEO, and 50.6% owner. As part of the deal, Jobs will become the largest shareholder at Disney and take a seat on the entertainment giant's board. His top creative executive at Pixar, John A. Lasseter, will oversee the movies at both Pixar's and Disney's animation studios. Pixar's president, Edwin Catmull, will run the business side for the two studios.

The alliance between Jobs and Disney is full of promise. If he can bring to Disney the same kind of industry-shaking, boundary-busting energy that has lifted Apple and Pixar sky-high, he could help the staid company become the leading laboratory for media convergence. It's not hard to imagine a day when you could fire up your Apple TV and watch Net-only spin-offs of popular TV shows from Disney's ABC Inc. Or use your Apple iPhone to watch Los Angeles Lakers superstar Kobe Bryant's video blog, delivered via Disney's ESPN Inc. "We've been talking about a lot of things," says Jobs. "It's going to be a pretty exciting world looking ahead over the next five years."

One reason for the rich possibilities is that Disney CEO Robert A. Iger is a kindred spirit. The 54-year-old Iger, who succeeded longtime Disney chief Michael D. Eisner on Oct. 1, is a self-avowed early adopter who listens to a 120-channel Sirius satellite radio in his car. He travels with a pair of iPods, bopping along to the new nano during his 5 a.m. workouts. Jobs seems to know it: Iger says the first call that he got in March when he was named to the top job came from the Apple CEO. "He wished me well and hoped we could work together soon," recalled Iger in an interview two months ago.

Lightning fast is more like it. Two weeks after Iger took office, the Disney CEO was on stage at a San Jose movie theater with Jobs as the two men introduced Apple's new video iPod and the availability of such ABC shows as *Lost* and *Desperate Housewives*. The deal came together on Internet time, in just three days. Iger wanted to show that Disney can be a nimble company, willing to embrace the latest digital technologies to deliver its content. "I think we impressed [Jobs and other Apple execs] with how quickly we could make a decision," said Iger in the earlier interview.

Vindication

Yet the Alliance has plenty of risks, too. Jobs will have to navigate a minefield of conflicts as he runs Apple and sits on Disney's board. He'll also have to demonstrate he can take on the unfamiliar role of supporting player. The same perfectionism that allows him to help create great products has made it difficult for him to stand by if someone is going in what he considers the wrong direction. When he returned to Apple as part of the NEXT acquisition, he insisted he didn't want Amelio's job, and then quickly took charge. Already, there's speculation in Silicon Valley that Disney's chief could get "Amelioed."

Iger isn't in the most secure spot. He has revamped Disney's management style and has improved some operations. Still, the company's stock is at about the same level it was a decade ago. And Iger has only been CEO a few months, so he's on new footing with Disney's directors. One management expert calls the Jobs move "courageous" but says "Iger just put a gun to his head," predicting that Jobs' influence in the boardroom would be so pervasive that Iger could be gone within a year.

Particularly ticklish will be Disney's animation business. While Iger has stressed that it's crucial to the company's future, Jobs may have closer ties, since his two lieutenants will be running the show. Even during the conference call announcing the Disney-Pixar deal, there were hints of differences. One analyst asked whether Lasseter would have authority to decide whether Pixar movies such as *Toy Story* will be made into Broadway plays. Jobs began by acknowledging that Lasseter works for Iger, then added, "[Lasseter] has always had strong feelings about the exploitation of stories and characters." So if Lasseter and Iger disagree, who would Jobs back?

Jobs declined to be interviewed for this article. But some executives who know him well insist that Iger has nothing to fear. "People are misreading Steve Jobs," says Edgar S. Woolard Jr., the former chairman of Apple and former chairman and CEO of chemical giant DuPont. "If he has a good relationship with you, there is nobody better in the world to work with. Iger made a very wise move, and two years from now everyone will be saying that."

Jobs certainly has much to offer. The past few years have been a thorough vindication of his ideas and leadership. Just a decade ago he was considered a temperamental micromanager whose insistence on total control and stylish innovation had doomed his company to irrelevance. While Apple tried to develop both the hardware and software for its computers, Microsoft, Intel, and a flock of PC makers slashed the onetime industry leader to bits by separating the two. Asked in late 1997 what Jobs should do as head of Apple, Dell Inc.'s then-CEO Michael S. Dell said at an investor conference: "I'd shut it down and give the money back to the shareholders."

Fighting words that Dell may regret today. Apple shares have soared from $7 a share three years ago to $74, and the company's market cap of $62 billion is just shy of Dell's. Why? Jobs has applied his old strategy to the new digital world (Exhibit 1). With absolute control, breakout innovation, and stellar marketing, he has created products that consumers lust after. The smooth melding of Apple's iPod with the iTunes software has helped make it an icon of the Digital Age. Rivals from Microsoft to Dell to Sony Corp. have been left in the dust. "He has set the basic model for any digital business from now on," says Toshiba Corp. CEO Atsutoshi Nishida. Microsoft is even considering making its own digital music player, since providing its software to Dell and other hardware developers has failed to slow Apple.

Jobs' success at Pixar is no less remarkable. He bought the business from director George Lucas 20 years ago for $10 million. Catmull and Lasseter believed they could use computer animation to create full-length movies, even though many in Hollywood and at Disney thought computers could never deliver the nuance and emotion of hand-drawn animation. Jobs bought into the vision. The result: Pixar has knocked out six blockbusters, from *Toy Story* in 1995 to *Finding Nemo* and *The Incredibles* in recent years. "The great thing about Steve is that he knows that great business comes from great product," says Peter Schneider, the former chairman of Disney's studio. "First you have to get the product right, whether it's the iPod or an animated movie."

Of course the trick isn't in wanting to make great products. It's being able to do it. So what is Jobs' secret? There are many, but it starts with focus and a near-religious faith in his strategy. For years, Jobs plugged away at Apple with his more proprietary approach, not worrying much about Wall Street's complaints. In fact, one of his first moves was to take an ax to Apple's product line, lopping off dozens of products to focus on just four. "Our jaws dropped when we heard that one," recalls former Apple chairman Woolard. Time and again since, Apple has eschewed calls to boost market share by making lower-end products or expanding into adjacent markets where the company wouldn't be the leader. "I'm as proud of what we don't do as I am of what we do," Jobs often says.

EXHIBIT 1   Redefining The CEO

Just over a decade ago, Steve Jobs was considered a has-been whose singular achievement was cofounding Apple Computer back in the 1970s. Now, given the astounding success of Apple and Pixar, he's setting a new bar for how to manage a Digital Age corporation:

Strategy

Jobs is an obsessive perfectionist who insists on having total control over the most minute product details. That was considered hopelessly idealistic in the lean years as Microsoft and its partners trounced Apple with cheaper PCs. Now, as music, movies, and photography go digital, **consumers want elegant simple devices.** And Jobs insistence on controlling all aspects of a product—from hardware and software to the service that comes with them—is the new blueprint.

Leadership

At Apple, micromanagement is not a dirty word. While Jobs relies heavily on his execs, he's astonishingly hands-on in his areas of expertise. He can demand minuscule changes to product designs, **rehearse for hours to perfect his famous product intro presentations** and work at length with reporters on stories he choose to be involved with. The downside: Apple won't discuss his succession planning much. This despite the fact that Jobs has much more impact on his company than most CEOs and underwent cancer surgery in 2004.

Culture

Elitism has its advantages. Since founding Apple with engineer Stephen Wozniak, Jobs has believed that small teams of top talent will outperform better-funded big ones. He has used the same approach at Pixar, where **creative chief John Lasseter has led the way in creating blockbusters like** *Toy Story and*

Finding Nemo. Jobs also outsources far more selectively than his rivals. He'd rather have all his creatives working together than save a few bucks by outsourcing such work overseas.

Innovation

Other CEOs may focus on finance or sales. Jobs spends most of his time trying to come up with the next blockbuster product. Think **iPod and iTunes.** As a tech pioneer, he doesn't have to depend on lieutenants for technology smarts or product taste. To keep on top of the latest technologies, he personally meets not only with suppliers but also sometimes with suppliers' suppliers.

Marketing

Tech companies have long been ham-handed marketers. Their best is usually utilitarian or cute (remember "Dude, you're getting a Dell"?). Yet Apple has consistently stood out for aspirational ads with a heavy dose of counterculture rebellion. **The "Think Different" series** featured John Lennon, Rosa Parks, and Pablo Picasso. The message isn't about trimming costs by 10%. It's this. If you dream of changing the world, we want to help you do it. Jobs even had a hand in writing the copy.

Partnering

Jobs chooses his partners carefully. He burnishes his image by associating with artists like U2. Yet he can be a brutal negotiator. **His personal clash with ex-Disney CEO Michael Eisner** destroyed negotiations over distributing Pixar movies and contributed to Eisner stepping down. And Jobs never told Motorola that on the same day Motorola and Apple unveiled their Rokr iTunes phone, he was going to announce the iPod nano. Sources say Moto execs fumed that the nano stole its thunder.

It's all based on a fundamental belief that a killer product will bring killer profits. That's certainly the case at Pixar. While analysts have often urged the company to crank up its movie machine and pump out more releases, the company is only now reaching the point that it can make one a year. And at least until the Disney deal was

struck, the plan was to stay there for good. The reason: Pixar's executives focus on making sure there are no "B teams," that every movie gets the best efforts of Pixar's brainy staff of animators, storytellers, and technologists.

Indeed, Jobs says with pride that Pixar has made the tough call to stop production at some point on every one of its movies to fix a problem with a storyline or character. "Quality is more important than quantity, and in the end, it's a better financial decision anyway," Jobs told *BusinessWeek* last year. "One home run is much better than two doubles," he said, explaining that then there's only one marketing and production budget rather than two.

The fixation on quality over quantity refers to personnel as much as production. Ever since the days when he marveled at Stephen G. Wozniak's engineering skill while building the first Apple computer, Jobs believed that a small team of top talent can run circles around far larger but less talented groups. He spends a lot of energy working the phones, trying to recruit people he has heard are the best at a certain job.

"Benevolent Benefactor"

This is one reason that Jobs, while a micromanager at Apple, plays a very different role at Pixar. He handles many of the business duties. But he's very hands-off on the creative side. Sources say he typically spends less than a day a week at the company's picturesque campus in Emeryville, across the San Francisco Bay from Apple's Cupertino headquarters. "Steve doesn't tell us what to do," says one Pixar employee. "Steve's our benevolent benefactor."

Jobs may be a multibillionaire, but that hasn't cut into his work ethic. He brings an entrepreneur's energy to tasks many CEOs would see as beneath them, whether it's personally checking the fine print on partnership agreements or calling reporters late in the evening to talk over a story he thinks is important. And Jobs seems perfectly willing to forgo some aspects of the executive life to focus on his own priorities. For example, unlike most CEOs he rarely participates in Wall Street analyst conferences.

His famous keynote speeches are maybe the best example of his intensity. In trademark jeans and mock-turtleneck, Jobs unveils Apple's latest products as if he were a particularly hip and plugged-in friend showing off inventions in your living room. Truth is, the sense of informality comes only after grueling hours of practice. One retail executive recalls going to a Macworld rehearsal at Jobs' behest, then waiting four hours before Jobs came off the stage to acknowledge his presence. Rude, perhaps, but the keynotes are a competitive weapon. Marissa Mayer, a Google Inc. executive who plays a central role in launching the search giant's innovations, insists that up-and-coming product

marketers attend Jobs' keynotes. "Steve Jobs is the best at launching new products," she says. "They have to see how he does it."

Of course, that entrepreneurial zeal is there for a reason: He's one of a shrinking collection of tech chieftains who are actually entrepreneurs. "I was very lucky to have grown up with this industry," Jobs told *BusinessWeek* in 2004. "I did everything coming up—shipping, sales, supply chain, sweeping the floors, buying chips, you name it. I put computers together with my own two hands. As the industry grew up, I kept on doing it."

The same can be said of his role as a movie mogul. Following Pixar's hit with *Toy Story* in 1995, Jobs and then-chief financial officer Lawrence B. Levy gave themselves a crash course in movie business economics. That helped Jobs persuade Disney to agree to a far more lucrative distribution deal than Pixar had had in the past. Former Disney executive Schneider, who negotiated that deal with Jobs, says he applies equal parts industry knowledge, intensity, and sheer charisma. Jobs prefers to negotiate one-on-one, and let lawyers tie up the details after the handshake is done. "He says 'Fine, we have a deal,' and you're saying, 'Wait, wait, I need to check with Michael [Eisner],' and he's saying, 'No, it's done.'"

That's not to say Jobs is an easy partner. Unlike every other electronics maker, Apple refuses to let even the biggest retailers know what new products are coming until Jobs unveils them. That means the retailers can't get a jump on arranging ad campaigns or switching out inventory. But Jobs would rather have the surge of publicity that comes with his dramatic product intros. Indeed, Motorola executives were furious when Apple surprised them by announcing the iPod nano last October, stealing the thunder from the iTunes phone that Apple and Moto had developed together.

In the final analysis, Jobs' true secret weapon is his ability to meld technical vision with a gut feel for what regular consumers want and then market it in ways that make consumers want to be part of tech's cool club. Says a leading tech CEO who requested anonymity: "God usually makes us either left brain people or right brain people. Steve seems to have both sides, so he can make extraordinary experiences."

Polarizing Figure

In the wake of the Disney-Pixar deal, the question is how Jobs can apply his unique skills to the media industry. From record labels to music studios, many execs are only reluctantly experimenting with technological change. Besides being concerned that piracy protections aren't strong enough, they're petrified of losing control since it's unclear how they'll make money in the new world. And Jobs is a polarizing figure. While the major music labels were excited by the possibilities opened up by Apple's iPod, they're now leery that Jobs has pulled a fast one. Apple reaps billions from selling its hit music player, but there are sparse profits from the songs being sold over the Net.

The Disney deal may help give Jobs some additional credibility in the media world. While he had a major stake in Pixar in the past, he now sits on the board of one of the biggest media companies in the country. That means he has a fiduciary responsibility to protect the company's assets, from *Desperate Housewives* to Mickey Mouse.

Iger's assets and Jobs' vision could prove a potent combination. They've already shown how they can experiment in new areas and then create enough consumer excitement that others are compelled to follow. After Iger agreed to put ABC's shows on iTunes for downloading to video iPods, the other major networks followed suit. The same day as the Disney-Pixar agreement, iTunes began offering short films from the early days of Mickey and Goofy. How long before protective movie studio chiefs are digging through back catalogs in hopes of bringing in extra revenues?

It's one more way in which iTunes is evolving into something much more powerful than a simple music store. Besides songs, TV shows, and short films, it offers music videos and podcasts from National Public Radio and independents like Brian Ibbott, creator of the cover song show *Coverville*. In December alone, 20 million people visited the site, triple the number the year before.

What could the future according to Jobs look like? (Exhibit 2). For starters, no radical changes will occur

EXHIBIT 2   **The Revolution Will Be Podcast**

The Internet and digital technologies are remaking the world of media. With Apple's Jobs taking a seat on Disney's board, the two companies could lead the way.

Unlimited TV Channels

Big and small producers alike are turning to the Web as an alternative TV channel, creating new series online and dishing up blogs and podcasts around TV characters and news. Disney's ABC could jump in and use Apple's iTunes to promote **Net-only spin-offs of shows like the 1970s' *Charlie's Angels.***

Movies on Demand

iTunes now sells one-hour TV shows. Movies, perhaps even **Pixar's upcoming *Cars,*** will likely follow. The Net is becoming a massive video-on-demand service, giving Disney a way to reach film audiences directly. CEO Iger, already one of the most tech-savvy media execs, is pushing the company to adapt to changing movie viewing habits.

Micro Audiences Rule

To reach fragmenting audiences, more **targeted programming will appear online, on cell phones, and through digital videorecorders.** Expect channels featuring hours of footage about deep sea diving or behind-the-scenes shots of the filming of Pixar and Disney movies.

Polish Less, Release More

With plummeting production and distribution costs, content isn't as expensive to make and has a shorter life span. Unpolished snippets of interviews, backstage filming, and animated shorts are released more quickly. One sure hit: ESPN could partner with **Los Angeles Lakers superstar Kobe Bryant** to do a video blog after each game.

DIY Programming

The concepts of prime time or show lineups are becoming antiquated as people pick and choose when they watch or listen to programming. At the same time, **do-it-yourself entertainment is on the rise.** Many viewers want video tidbits they can play with or the ability to influence shows by posting their thoughts on blogs.

overnight. Given Apple's powerful branding, it's easy to forget that Jobs hasn't typically been the first to pioneer new areas. Many MP3 players existed before the iPod, and Microsoft has been slogging away for years on PCs fit for entertainment in the living room. Apple has taken the first steps in this direction by adding the ability to control a Mac from the couch via the Apple Remote and FrontRow software.

Speculation is rife that Jobs will move Apple fully into the living room, and there's little reason he wouldn't. The most likely scenario is that Apple would build a version of its Mac mini that could be attached to a TV and entertainment center so the mini could store family photographs and home videos along with music and videos downloaded from iTunes. Taken to the extreme, the living room of 2010 may no longer need to have a CD-rack, DVD player, TiVo, set-top box, or stereo. All those capabilities could be built into a single box, an Apple TV, or an Apple-branded home entertainment center.

IGER, The Peacemaker

Then there's the wireless-phone realm. Apple purchased the domain name iPhone.org years ago and in December trademarked the name Mobile Me. That may suggest it will introduce a mobile phone or personal digital assistant to download songs over the air or sync up with a Mac or PC.

The Disney-Pixar deal could open up all sorts of strategic options for Disney and Iger if they can capitalize on Jobs' skills. For example, Disney could decide to push hard toward distributing more of its content directly over the Internet rather than relying on cable companies or movie theaters. Iger has been the most vocal voice in Hollywood on this score of late, even suggesting that new Disney movies should be released on the Internet the same day they hit the cinemas.

Since taking over from Eisner, Iger has shown himself willing to move quickly and take bold steps to remake the bureaucratic company he inherited. Among

Iger's first decisions was dismantling the corporate strategic planning operation Eisner often used to scuttle risky new plans. Iger patched things up with dissident former board members Roy E. Disney and Stanley P. Gold, who incited a shareholder revolt that kept large investors away. And while Eisner warred with Jobs, Iger worked hard to improve Disney's relationship. A key part of the reason for the Disney-Pixar deal, says Jobs, was "we got to know Bob."

Still, Jobs will be joining a Disney in short supply of its old pixie dust. As a board member, Jobs may argue for fast-tracking some of the digital distribution experiments Eisner discarded. Yet that could clash with Iger's ideas about how or how quickly Disney should proceed. A board showdown could prove difficult. Not only is Iger a new CEO, but he also was the second choice among at least some of Disney's 13 board members. (Some favored Meg Whitman, eBay Inc.'s CEO and a former Disney executive.)

Iger's worst nightmare may be that Jobs could sway so many Disney board members that he would win a wide-open race to become Disney chairman. Last year, with the board reportedly split between directors Gary L. Wilson and Robert W. Matschullat, former Senator George J. Mitchell was named interim chairman. He will remain as chairman until he retires at the end of 2006.

Jobs has said he doesn't want the Disney top board job. Plus, that would complicate the potential conflicts of interest with Apple, as Disney makes more high-tech deals to distribute its content. Still, the mercurial new Disney board member could make a play to become chairman, say those with knowledge of Disney's board. "The problem then is that Bob would have a larger-than-life chairman to deal with only a year after a larger-than-life CEO was running his life," says one source close to Disney. "I can't imagine he's thrilled over that." Steve Jobs' arrival at the Magic Kingdom could have more thrills than a trip to Disneyland.

Source: Peter Burrows and Ronald Grover, "Steve Jobs Magic Kingdom," *BusinessWeek*, February 6, 2006, 63–69.

Case 3-2

Intel Corp.

Even the gentle clinking of silverware stopped dead. Andrew S. Grove, the revered former Intel Corp. chief executive and now a senior adviser, had stepped up to the microphone in a hotel ballroom down the

street from Intel's Santa Clara (Calif.) headquarters, preparing to respond to a startling presentation by new Chief Marketing Officer Eric B. Kim. All too familiar with Grove's legendary wrath, many of the 300 top managers at the Oct. 20 gathering tensed in their seats as they waited for a tongue-lashing of epic proportions. "No one knew what to think," recalls one attendee.

The reason? Kim's plan, cooked up with new CEO Paul S. Otellini, was a sharp departure from the company Grove had built. Essentially, they were proposing to blow up Intel's brand, the fifth-best-known in the world. As Otellini looked on from a front table, Kim declared that Intel must "clear out the cobwebs" and kill off many Grove-era creations. Intel Inside? Dump it, he said. The Pentium brand? Stale. The widely recognized dropped "e" in Intel's corporate logo? A relic.

Grove's deep baritone, sharpened by the accent of his native Hungary, pierced the expectant silence. But instead of smiting the Philistines, Intel's patriarch sprinkled holy water on Otellini's plan. He understood that it was no repudiation of him, but rather a recognition that times had changed—and that Intel needed to change with them. "I want to say," he boomed, "that this program strikes me as one of the best manifestations incorporating Intel values of risk-taking, discipline, and results orientation I have ever seen here. I, for one, fully support it."

As executives rose to greet him with relieved applause, the moment signaled an historic shift for one of the world's most powerful technology companies. The iconic Intel would leave the Grove era behind and head into uncharted territory. Otellini will unveil the new strategy and new products on Jan. 5, at the Consumer Electronics Show in Las Vegas. Central to the effort will be the first new corporate logo in more than three decades and a $2.5 billion advertising and marketing blitz, *BusinessWeek* has learned.

The changes go far deeper than the company's brand. Under Grove and successor Craig R. Barrett, Intel thrived by concentrating on the microprocessors that power personal computers. By narrowing the company's focus, the duo buried the competition. They invested billions in hyperproductive plants that could crank out more processors in a day than some rivals did in a year. Meanwhile, they helped give life to the Information Age, with ever-faster, more powerful chips.

Otellini is tossing out the old model. Instead of remaining focused on PCs, he's pushing Intel to play a key technological role in a half-dozen fields, including consumer electronics, wireless communications, and health care. And rather than just microprocessors, he wants Intel to create all kinds of chips, as well as software, and then meld them together into what he calls "platforms." The idea is to power innovation from the living room to the emergency room. "This is the right thing for our company, and to some extent the industry," he says. "All of us want [technology] to be more

powerful and to be simpler, to do stuff for us without us having to think about it."

Why the shift? Stark necessity. PC growth is slowing, even as cell phones and handheld devices compete for the *numero uno* spot in people's lives. Otellini must reinvent Intel—or face a future of creaky maturity. Revenue growth has averaged 13% for the past three years, but analysts figure Intel will see only 7% growth in 2006, to $42.2 billion. Meantime, profits, which have surged an average 40% annually over the past three years, are expected to rise a measly 5%, to $9.5 billion. "It's a race for Intel and other companies to figure out how fast is revenue going to come from emerging areas before PC margins begin to come down sharply," says Ragu Gurumurthy, head of technology practice for Boston tech consultancy Adventis Corp.

20,000 New Faces

Intel has tried entering new markets in the past, particularly under Barrett. Yet it always treated them as tangential and never let them detract from the core processor effort. Not anymore. Otellini, who took over as CEO in May, has reorganized the company top to bottom, putting most of its 98,000 employees into new jobs. He created business units for each product area, including mobility and digital health, and scattered the processor experts among them. He has also added 20,000 people in the past year. The result? Intel is poised to launch more new products in 2006 than at any time in its history.

Intel's culture is changing, too. Under the charismatic Grove, who was CEO from 1987 to 1998 and then chairman until 2005, the company was a rough-and-tumble place. Grove's motto was "Only the paranoid survive," and managers frequently engaged in "constructive confrontation," which any outsider would call shouting. Engineers ruled the roost. Grove and Barrett also instituted the practice of doling out cash to PC makers for joint advertising, which Intel rivals have alleged blocks them from some markets.

Otellini is more diplomatic, partly by nature, partly by necessity. The intensely private 55-year-old rarely reveals irritation—and then, with a slight frown. His management mantra: "Praise in public, criticize in private."

He's also the first non-engineer to run the company. Otellini studied economics in college at the University of San Francisco and then joined Intel in 1974, straight out of B-school at the University of California at

Berkeley. Many of the new employees he's bringing on aren't typical Intel hires either. They include software developers, sociologists, ethnographers, even doctors to help develop products. He lays particular emphasis on marketing expertise because he thinks the only way Intel can succeed in new markets is by communicating more clearly what the technology can do for customers. "To sell technology now, you have to do it in a way where it's much more simple," says Otellini. "You can't talk about the bits and the bytes."

The changes have created some angst among employees. In particular, many high-level engineers working on PC products feel they've been stripped of their star status. "The desktop group used to rule the company, and we liked it that way," says one former chip designer, adding that some engineers now feel "directionless." Other employees are simply uncomfortable with the new emphasis on marketing. "There definitely are people who are highly skeptical, who think this is all fluff, all just gloss—that if you make good technology, you don't need the glitz," says Genevieve Bell, an in-house ethnographer who researches how people in emerging markets like China and India use technology.

Yet Intel and Otellini aren't shying away from glitz these days. For its bash at the Consumer Electronics Show, the company has booked the hip-hop band Black Eyed Peas, with its hit *Let's Get It Started.* Beforehand, Otellini will unveil the new Intel during his keynote speech. It starts with a whole new look for the 37-year-old company. The Intel Inside logo will disappear, replaced by an updated Intel logo with a swirl around it to signify movement. For the first time since the early 1990s, the company will add a tagline: "Leap ahead." (Exhibit 1).

Meantime, the famous Pentium brand will be slowly phased out. In its place: a troika of brands, two of them freshly minted. Viiv (rhymes with "alive") is the name of a new chip for home PCs, designed to replace your TiVo, stereo, and, potentially, cable or satellite set-top box. It will be able to download first-run movies, music, and games, and shift them around the home. Intel also will launch a set of notebook PC chips under the three-year-old Centrino brand, as well as so-called dual-core chips, which will put two processor cores on one silver of silicon. The new brand "Core" will be put on products that don't meet the specifications of the Viiv or Centrino platforms. The effort is winning high-profile

EXHIBIT 1

REMAKING INTEL FROM TOP TO BOTTOM

Marketing is becoming as important as engineering, a big shift for the company Grove founded

	ANDY GROVE'S INTEL	PAUL OTELLINI'S INTEL
MOTTO	"Only the paranoid survive"	"Praise in public, criticize in private"
STRATEGY	CEO from 1987 to 1998, Grove is best known for the high-stakes decision to leave the money-losing memory-chip business and focus on developing microprocessors for PCs and servers. That helped Intel bury its competition, with ever-faster processors.	Otellini says that Intel has to move beyond microprocessors and that speed alone is no longer enough. Instead, he wants to create "platforms" of microprocessors combining silicon and software that lead to new devices and technologies.
BRANDING	Created the Pentium and "Intel Inside" branding that highlighted the computer's guts for first time. intel®	Created the "Leap ahead" logo, Intel's first new corporate logo in more than 30 years. (intel) Leap ahead™
MANAGEMENT STYLE	Direct and confrontational. His shouts echoed down company halls.	Direct, with encyclopedic knowledge, but so soft-spoken you sometimes strain to hear him.
PARTNERS	Working closely with Microsoft, Intel concentrated on wooing PC industry giants such as Dell, Compaq, IBM, and HP.	Everyone and everything, from Cisco in networking to Motorola for mobile devices to hospitals for digital health.
HOW EMPLOYEES GOT AHEAD	Engineers ruled, based largely on their skills running divisions within the core PC business.	Marketers and even ethnographers are on equal footing with chip engineers
FOOTS	A Hungarian Jew whose family narrowly escaped the Holocaust and later fled the Iron Curtain.	Son of Italian immigrants who initially wanted him to become a priest in San Francisco.
THE OFFICE	Instituted "signing sheet" for people who were more than five minutes late for work.	A decentralized organization where BlackBerrys and e-mail are the primary ways to reach employees.
VITTLES	Headquaters cafeteria offered stale sandwiches, bland food.	A revamped canteen, which now serves up sushi and made-to-order lunches.

support. On Jan. 10, Apple Computer Inc., which has never used Intel's chips before, is expected to be one of the first companies to offer products with the dual-core chips.

One of Otellini's key steps in all this was hiring Kim away from Samsung Group a year ago. Kim had led Samsung's marketing since 1999 and helped build the Korean maker of consumer electronics, cell phones, and computer chips into a hot global brand. But Otellini didn't just swipe a major talent away from the company that's increasingly seen as Intel's prime competitor. By hiring an outsider who reports directly to the CEO for the first time in Intel's history, Otellini also got someone who could play bad cop and push through unpopular changes when necessary. Rank-and-file employees do grumble about Kim and what they consider his autocratic style, but he makes no apologies. "I tell people they're not just about making silicon. They're helping people's lives improve, and we need to let the world know that," says Kim.

Yet it's a daunting task, especially for a company that has never had much success outside the computer industry. Companies that have been good at transforming themselves, from Nissan and Apple to Texas Instruments, typically need a crisis to precipitate change, says management expert Jay R. Galbraith of Galbraith Associates. And although Intel is facing a possible slowdown, it's still pulling in nearly $1 billion a month in profits. "Change is really hard when you're solidly on top," says Galbraith. "He'll have to bring in new people who have new skill sets."

A Mean Pack

Competitors keep nipping at Intel's flanks. Longtime rival Advanced Micro Devices Inc. in 2003 launched its Opteron and Athlon 64 chips, outgunning Intel in both raw power and lower power consumption. AMD's market share rose to 17.8% last quarter, up from 16.6% in early 2003, and some analysts predict it will gain more until Intel fields competitive chips in late 2007. AMD CEO Hector J. de Ruiz equates Intel's position with that of American auto makers, scrambling to find innovation even as consumers flock to Japanese rivals. "People are smart enough to pick quality when given a choice, and calling something a platform doesn't guarantee quality," Ruiz says.

In the cell phone market, Texas Instruments and Qualcomm Inc. have held fast against Intel's incursions. Intel Executive Vice-President Sean M. Maloney

once wore snowshoes to a company sales conference to illustrate the deep slog. In 2006, AMD and TI plan to field their own chip platforms aimed at capturing some real estate in the digital home.

So Otellini is shaking things up throughout the company. In addition to the reorg, he's making big changes in the way products are developed. While in the past engineers worked on ever faster chips and then let marketers try to sell them, there are now teams of people with a cross-section of skills. Chip engineers, software developers, marketers, and market specialists all work together to come up with compelling products.

One example of the new approach is Bern Shen. A doctor who practiced internal medicine for 15 years, he joined Intel three months ago to help develop technologies for digital health. He works with Intel's ethnographers to figure out which technologies might help in monitoring the vital signs of the elderly or tracking the diet of people with Alzheimer's. "The fact that they hired me is an indication of the new Intel," he says.

Otellini is convinced such collaboration will lead to breakthrough innovations. He imagines a day when people will use Centrino laptops to watch live TV on the subway or when kids will be able to download *Spider-Man 3* to their home theater on the same day it's released worldwide. Shen's work could lead to Intel technology that allows the elderly to keep living at home, even as data on their vital signs are zapped to doctors several times a day. "This is the right model," Otellini says. "Now it's just a matter of playing it out."

If the world buys Otellini's ideas, industries from Hollywood to health care could be turned upside down. Media and entertainment may be forced to rethink their business models. The health industry could be transformed, as doctors diagnose or even treat patients remotely. "The most important thing about Intel is that they've got the vision," says Russ Bodoff, executive director of the Center for Aging Services Technologies (CAST), a coalition of 400 companies, universities, and hospitals. "They are pushing some very innovative approaches, in areas that relate to dementia, Alzheimer's care, and Parkinson's disease."

The ultimate goal: to provide the manufacturers of everything from laptops and entertainment PCs to cell phones and hospital gear with complete packages of chips and software. The template is Centrino. When Otellini was leading product planning in the core PC business from 1998 to 2002, he decided that rather than roll out just another fast processor, he would bundle it with a relatively new wireless Internet technology called Wi-Fi. The combo made it a breeze for people to connect to the Net from airport lounges and coffee shops. Backed with an initial $300 million marketing campaign, Centrino notebooks became an instant hit, revitalizing the PC market and persuading consumers to snap up the higher-margin products.

Now, a Giant Step

Still, Intel's first big success in diversification was only a half-step away from the core PC market. Will it be able to do as well in other areas? (Exhibit 2). Consider Viiv. In the consumer electronics market where Viiv devices will be positioned as an all-in-one DVD player, game console, TiVo, and music jukebox, it faces plenty of big-name competitors. Meanwhile, brand-new challengers are appearing on the horizon. Sony Corp., with its PlayStation 3 due out in just a few months, aims to offer games, movies, and music on the device, which uses chips from IBM. Cable and satellite providers such as Comcast Corp. and DirecTV Group Inc. are adding more features and services to their set-top boxes, such as on-demand television shows and XM satellite radio.

Cutting through the clutter of competitive activity is why Otellini and Kim have lifted branding to new heights at Intel (Exhibit 3). But for a huge company like Intel, it will be especially tough. "In many ways, it's like trying to change the engines on an airplane when you're flying it," says Russ Meyer, chief strategy officer for branding consultancy Landor Associates.

EXHIBIT 2

INTEL'S BIGBANG

This year, Intel will roll out more new products than ever before. Here's what to expect.

NOTEBOOKS

Intel plans to introduce three new chips for laptops, One, called **Core Duo**, consumes less power—so notebooks can run for 5 to 10 hours, instead of the typical three or four. Another chip will offer consumers the ability to communicate wirelessly at longer ranges.

Prognosis: Excellent. Intel should continue to dominate the laptop market. Already, its January launch of the Core Duo has the support of three times as many times PC makers as the preceding chip.

PCs

Intel's looking to win a place in your living room, with its new **Viiv** chips. One Viiv entertainment PC will mimic a TV, complete with remote control and surround–sound technology. Another Viiv computer, expected by yearend, will let consumers connect PCs to DVD players, TVs, and stereo tuners so they can shift digital content around the home.

Prognosis: Good. Viiv has won early buzz, with Sony, Philips, and Creating snazzy new PCs with the technology. Consumer electronics maker Onkyo is launching its first-ever PC with Viiv.

SERVERS

Intel will introduce a new chip that promises to lower the bills for electricity consumption, a primary problem for corporate customers that maintain thousands of servers in data centers.

Prognosis: Mixed. Rival AMD continues to gain share in servers with its 64-bit Opteron chips and likely to extend those gains until at least 2008, when Intel launches a totally revamped server platform.

WIRELESS

Intel will roll out chips to power cell phones and devices such as BlackBerrys, plus new memory chips for high-end cell phones and Apple's iPod. Longer term, the company plans to use wireless to move into the digital health market. One example: It's developing sensors that can communicate with computer networks, so caregivers can monitor the health of senior citizens remotely.

Prognosis: Difficult. Qualcomm and Texas Instruments are expected to continue to lead the market for cell-phone chips. Also, it's early yet for its digital health efforts. Intel should gain some ground in memory chips, however, given its strong technology.

EXHIBIT 3

LESSONS FOR BLOWING UP YOUR BRAND

Intel, like Coca-Cola and Sony is struggling to redefine its brands in an age of increasing media clutter. Here are some guidelines for how to manage such an overhaul:

PRIME THE PUMP First, make sure the leaders of the company understand the new brand. They will be key to explaining the brand message to the rank and file.

DO YOUR HOME WORK It's critical to stay on top of consumer habits as you evolve. Focus groups work, up to a point, but think about using new research techniques such as ethnography to watch how consumers use your products—and those of rivals.

TREAD CAREFULLY Don't change your brand unless you can clearly and concisely highlight the differences from competitors. Otherwise, you risk losing your core customers.

THINK GLOBALLY What works in one geographical area may not work in another. Identify the emotional attachment people may have to your brand in a particular region, and consider whether it translates to others.

Companies must try not only to differentiate themselves from competitors but also to align internally to make sure the same message is clear to employees. For an "ingredient" brand like Intel with no products that a consumer actually can pick up from the local Best Buy or Wal-Mart, the trick also is to convince new customers of the value of using its products.

With that in mind, Otellini's Digital Home team has struck some of the biggest content deals to date with major Hollywood players and music services to entice both customers and consumers to the Viiv platform. The hundreds of millions it will dole out for marketing Viiv has partners like Sony and Philips Electronics salivating. They also seem to be genuinely impressed with the new attitude at Otellini's Intel. "I have seen more flexibility, more of an open mindset than in years past," says Sony Vice-President Mike Abary, who heads the company's Vaio PC business. "They realize that times have changed, that they don't have all the answers. So it has been much more collaborative working with them."

Otellini also has gone to great lengths to win over marketing maestro Steve Jobs. It's quite a reversal. For years, Grove and Barrett pooh-poohed Apple as a niche company whose products had sleek form, but nowhere near the function of computers with Intel's chips. Yet Otellini set about wooing Jobs almost from the start. In June, a month after Otellini took over, the two companies announced Apple would begin shipping Macs and other products with Intel chips inside in 2006. Otellini aims to use the Apple relationship to force PC makers to step up their innovation. "They've always been a front-runner in design," he says. "As they start taking advantage of some of our lower-power products, that form factor will improve significantly. I think it will help drive a trend toward smaller, cheaper, cooler."

Jobs's influence extends beyond design. At Otellini's urging, Apple's "Think Different" vernacular is beginning to take root inside Intel. The two chief executives also appear to be developing a real friendship. Intel insiders say they talk regularly. And when Prince Charles and his wife, Camilla, visited Silicon Valley in late November, Jobs and Otellini were side by side, hobnobbing with the royals.

The Apple relationship could create some strain with Intel's two old *compadres* in the PC business, Dell and Microsoft. Dell has been one of Intel's most loyal customers: It's the only major U.S. maker of PCs that hasn't come out with boxes powered by AMD chips. So if Intel provides strong support for Apple in the PC business,

it could prompt Dell to do business with AMD's Ruiz. Dell is going after more consumer business, Apple's primary turf. In late 2005, Dell introduced a higher-end XPS line and it plans to ship Viiv PCs.

Meantime, Intel execs seem open to easing their once ironclad ties to Microsoft. At the start, PC makers will have to use Microsoft's Windows Media Center Edition operating system to earn the Viiv brand—and Intel's co-marketing dollars. But Intel says this may not continue, opening the door to Viiv machines with the Linux open source operating system or even Apple's. Indeed, Kim says he expects some PC companies to ship Viiv boxes, without Windows.

Another budding relationship in Intel's march on new markets is with Google. Otellini joined the search company's board in April, 2004, and has found a few areas of joint interest. For one, Otellini heard that Google's energy bill for its servers now exceeds the cost of the equipment. (With 100,000 servers, Google's electricity bill probably tops $50 million a year.) That prompted Otellini to explore the prospects for energy-efficient chips. In August, Intel announced it would dump its old architecture in favor of lower-power chips in 2006.

The two companies also have a shared interest in wireless broadband. Google is exploring whether to set up free Wi-Fi "hot spots" in San Francisco and other cities. Footing the bill for Net access may make sense for Google since it allows the company to show digital ads to any Web surfers who use the service. Intel would benefit because free Wi-Fi could further sales of Centrino laptops. Google execs have also said they're interested in WiMax, another wireless technology Intel is backing. Intel plans to imbed WiMax, which is similar to Wi-Fi but works over greater distances, into PC chips late this year.

Outsiders Welcome

To bolster the push, Otellini is looking to recruit more execs from outside the company. In the past year, Maloney hired Nokia Corp. veteran Steven Gray as a key member of the cellular team. And Maloney is turning more often to Intel Vice-President Sam Arditi, a cellular industry veteran with experience in radio chips and processors—key ingredients in handsets.

The result: closer ties with Nokia and Samsung, which are both collaborating with Intel on WiMax. In September, Maloney also announced a deal with Research In Motion Ltd., making it the first major name to use its cellular platform of radio, processors, and memory. "The relationship is going to be very important to RIM," says co-CEO Jim Basillie.

For all that, Otellini's internal challenges may prove more daunting than the external ones. For one, PC chip development still casts a long shadow at the company. During Grove's and Barrett's tenures, anyone not producing for the core PC business was considered a second-class citizen. Barrett described the problem as akin to the creosote bush, a tall desert plant that drips poisonous oil, killing off all vegetation that tries to grow nearby. Microprocessors so dominated the company's strategy, he says, that other businesses could not sprout around it. That was one reason Otellini reorganized into product areas.

The shake-up hasn't helped company morale, though. Especially hard-hit were the engineering teams in California and Texas, which had been working on the Pentium 4 until Otellini canceled it. Some of the design specialists have quit for new jobs, often with AMD or TI. To smooth over the troubles, Otellini has toured the chipmaker's outposts, talking with engineers and others without their managers around. "A lot of what he heard was pent-up frustration, no doubt," says one engineer. "But you appreciate the fact that he's listening." Intel's attrition in 2005 was 4%, about average for the tech industry.

Sniping about the rise of marketers such as Kim continues. Says Schmuel "Mooly" Eden, an Israeli engineer who helped spearhead the Centrino launch and now heads marketing for the Mobility Group: "When I went back to Israel to talk to some of the engineers, they said: 'You're only one year in marketing, and already you're brain-damaged.'"

As Intel gears up for its big bang of product launches, there's no doubt the mantle of leadership has shifted. This year, Otellini, for the first time, will write a performance review for Grove. In his advisory role, Grove sits in on important meetings, particularly in digital health, and gives his thoughts. Asked about the prospects of critiquing the company legend, Otellini just laughs. Reviewing Grove will be a breeze next to the challenge of remaking the world's largest chipmaker.

Of Apples and BlackBerrys

In early December, Paul S. Otellini outlined for the first time some of the historic changes—and challenges—he faces in remaking Intel. After a speech at a conference in San Francisco, he spoke with technology correspondent Cliff Edwards.

On exiting the PC era:
The era we're going into now is one where as computing becomes more ubiquitous, and as it becomes more pervasive and has more uses, computers are going to become tailored to the needs. Whether you call an iPod a computer or not, or you call my BlackBerry a computer, it doesn't matter. They're going to be devices you can program, and they'll do something. The product lines that we are addressing today . . . are all focused on where we think computing is headed in the next four, five years.

On dropping the Pentium brand:
Pentium was the quintessential product of the era of megahertz. It stood for "faster is better." I wanted to signal a shift. Going forward, the paradigm is going to be increasingly portable machines, increasingly energy-efficient machines, increasingly smaller . . . Changing the name of our products goes a long way to putting an exclamation point on the design change behind them. Is it orthodox to walk away from one of the most recognized brand names in the world? Probably not. I don't think we'll walk away from it overnight.

On its plans for health care:
In digital health, we're just trying to play catch-up. [Health care takes up] 15% of GDP in the U.S. and [there are predictions] of going beyond 25% by 2015. To think that a quarter of this country's GDP would be dedicated to health care is a scary proposition. That 10 points has to come out of something: the education system or military. By applying productivity, I think we can really drive service up and costs down. Just like any other industry.

On Apple, which will use Intel chips in its PCs for the first time in 2006:
At the end of the day, we live to sell chips. First and foremost, it's market-expanding for us. Secondly, the thing that Apple really brings to the Intel family of customers is their innovation. They are a hugely innovative company and really push the envelope in terms of feature sets. Their ability to not just mix hardware and software, which is unique, but also to drop software upgrades rather frequently to take advantage of hardware changes, that alone is very appealing. The hardware will have the receptacle for software.

On whether to pay out more dividends:
We have the luxury of being a company that generates a lot of cash. To the extent we don't use it for expansion, I think we have an obligation to give it back to shareholders. On the other hand, if we have an opportunity to use cash, we'll certainly grab it.

Will Intel go out and make acquisitions?
We actually bought a lot of companies this year. I
don't know the exact number, but it's north of 20.
They're all kind of $10–$250 million, maybe a couple of ones at $300 million. They're small enough to
integrate nicely and easily. They often fill technology
holes or gaps . . . I wouldn't rule out buying a large
company if the price and opportunity were right.

**On his role in the new look and feel for the head-
quarters lobby and cafeteria:**
I was talking to [architect] Art Gensler at a social thing.
He was complaining about how drab our buildings

were. He said good taste doesn't cost any more. But
when his guys gave me an estimate, I was like, "Whoa,
Art told me good taste doesn't cost any more." So we're
going to have to do some trimming.

**Will he have a motto, like Andy Grove's "Only the
paranoid survive"?**
He wrote that after he was in the job five or six years.
[Laughs] Come back to me then.

Source: Cliff Edwards, "Inside Intel," *BusinessWeek,* January 9,
2006, 47–54.

Case 3-3

McDonald's Corp.

Richard Steinig remembers beaming as if he had won
the lottery. There he was all of 27 when he became a
junior partner with a McDonald's Corp, franchisee in
1973, just a year after starting as a $115-a-week man-
ager trainee in Miami. "It was an incredible feeling,"
says Steinig. His two stores each generated $80,000 in
annual sales, and he pocketed more than 15% of that as
profit. Not bad at a time when the minimum wage was
still under $2 an hour and a McDonald's hamburger
and fries set you back less than a dollar, even with a
regular Coke.

Fast-forward 30 years. Franchise owner Steinig's
four restaurants average annual sales of $1.56 million,
but his face is creased with worry. Instead of living the
American Dream, Steinig says he's barely scraping by.
Sales haven't budged since 1999, but costs keep rising.
So when McDonald's began advertising its $1 menu
featuring the Big N' Tasty burger, Steinig rebelled.
The popular item cost him $1.07 to make—so he sells
it for $2.25 unless a customer asks for the $1 promotion price. No wonder profit margins are no more than
half of what they were when he started out. "We have
become our worst enemy," Steinig says.

Welcome to Hamburger Hell. For decades, McDonald's
was a juggernaut. It gave millions of Americans their
first jobs while changing the way a nation ate. It rose
from a single outlet in a nondescript Chicago suburb to
become an American icon. But today, McDonald's is a
reeling giant that teeters from one mess to another.

Consider the events of just the past three months:
On Dec. 5, after watching McDonald's stock slide 60%

in three years, the board ousted Chief Executive Jack
M. Greenberg, 60. His tenure was marked by the introduction of 40 new menu items, none of which caught
on big, and the purchase of a handful of non-burger
chains, none of which were rolled out widely enough
to make much difference. Indeed, his critics say that by
trying so many different things—and executing them
poorly—Greenberg let the burger business deteriorate.
Consumer surveys show that service and quality now
lag far behind those of rivals.

The company's solution was to bring back retired
Vice-Chairman James R. Cantalupo, 59, who had overseen McDonald's successful international expansion in
the '80s and '90s. Unfortunately, seven weeks later, the
company reported the first quarterly loss in its 47-year
history. Then it revealed that January sales at outlets
open at least a year skidded 2.4%, after sliding 2.1%
in 2002.

Can Cantalupo reverse the long slide at McDonald's?
When he and his new team lay out their plan to analysts
in early April, they are expected to concentrate on getting the basics of service and quality right, in part by
reinstituting a tough "up or out" grading system that
will kick out underperforming franchisees. "We have
to rebuild the foundation. It's fruitless to add growth if
the foundation is weak," says Cantalupo. He gives himself 18 months to do that with help from Australian-
bred chief operating officer, Charles Bell, 42, whom
Cantalupo has designated his successor, and Mats
Lederhausen, a 39-year-old Swede in charge of global
strategy (Exhibit 1).

But the problems at McDonald's go way beyond
cleaning up restaurants and freshening the menu.
The chain is being squeezed by long-term trends that
threaten to leave it marginalized. It faces a rapidly

EXHIBIT 1

Out of the Frying Pan. . .

New CEO Cantalupo is giving himself 18 months to get McDonald's back on track. He faces a daunting to-do list:

Improve the Basics	Rekindle the Flame with Franchisees	Whip up Something New	Stop Eating Your Own Lunch
McDonald's lags in consumer surveys. Using mystery shoppers and unannounced inspections, it will give special help to laggard franchisees. But if they flunk again, Cantalupo vows, they'll lose their shops.	Franchisees, who own 85% of all U.S. McDonald's, face stagnant sales. So any added costs from new equipment or programs cut into margins. Cantalupo has to get them to buy into his plan.	McDonald's last big hit was Chicken McNuggets in 1983. Rather than trying to do too much in his test kitchens, Cantalupo may encourage franchisees—who created the Big Mac and Egg McMuffin—to be more creative.	Even with cutbacks, McDonald's plans to add 1,230 hamburger outlets worldwide in 2003. Some analysts say that to avoid cannibalization, Cantalupo needs to shutter more than the 500 sites he plans on closing this year.

fragmenting market, where America's recent immigrants have made once-exotic foods like sushi and burritos everyday options, and quick meals of all sorts can be found in supermarkets, convenience stores, even vending machines. One of the fastest-growing restaurant categories is the "fast-casual" segment—those places with slightly more expensive menus, such as Cosi, a sandwich shop, or Quizno's, a gourmet sub sandwich chain, where customers find the food healthier and better-tasting. As Lederhausen succinctly puts it: "We are clearly living through the death of the mass market."

If so, it may well mark the end of McDonald's long run as a growth company. Cantalupo seemed to acknowledge as much when he slashed sales growth estimates in the near term to only 2% annually, down from 15%. No one at Oak Brook (Ill.) headquarters blames the strong dollar or mad cow disease anymore for the company's problems—a big change from the Greenberg era. Perhaps most telling is that the chain plans to add only 250 new outlets in the U.S. this year, 40% fewer than in 2002. Sales in Europe rose only 1%, and the chain this year will add only 200 units to the 6,070 it has there—30% fewer new openings than last year. Meanwhile, it is closing 176 of its 2,800 stores in Japan because of the economic doldrums there.

Up until a few years ago, franchisees clamored to jump on board. But last year, in an exodus that was unheard of in Mickey D's heyday, 126 franchisees left the system, with 68, representing 169 restaurants, forced out for poor performance. The others left

seeking greener pastures. The company buys back franchises if they cannot be sold, so forcing out a franchisee is not cheap. McDonald's took a pretax charge of $292 million last quarter to close 719 restaurants—200 in 2002 and the rest expected this year.

For their part, investors have already accepted that the growth days are over. Those who remain will happily settle for steady dividends. Last Oct. 22, when McDonald's announced a 1¢ hike in its annual dividend, to 23½¢, its stock rose 9%, to $18.95—even though the company said third-quarter profits would decline. It was the biggest one-day gain for McDonald's on the New York Stock Exchange in at least two years. Today, though, the stock is near an eight-year low of $13.50, off 48% in the past year (Exhibit 2). One of the few money managers willing to give McDonald's a chance, Wendell L. Perkins at Johnson Asset Management in Racine, Wis.,

EXHIBIT 2   **For Investors, Only Heartburn**

Data: Bloomberg Financial Markets

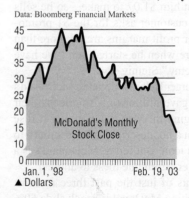

McDonald's Monthly Stock Close

Jan. 1, '98   Feb. 19, '03

▲ Dollars

says: "McDonald's needs to understand that it is a different company from 10 years ago and increase its dividend to return some of that cash flow to shareholders to reflect its mature market position."

The company has the cash to boost shareholder pay outs. It recently canceled an expensive stock buyback program. Cantalupo won praise on Wall Street for killing an expensive revamp of the company's technology that would have cost $1 billion. But if increasing the dividend would make Wall Street happy, it would raise problems with its 2,461 franchisees. That would be essentially an admission that McDonald's is giving up on the kind of growth for which they signed up.

Already, franchisees who see the chain as stuck in a rut are jumping ship to faster-growing rivals. Paul Saber, a McDonald's franchisee for 17 years, sold his 14 restaurants back to the company in 2000 when he realized that eating habits were shifting away from McDonald's burgers to fresher, better-tasting food. So he moved to rival Panera Bread Co., a fast-growing national bakery café chain. "The McDonald's-type fast food isn't relevant to today's consumer," says Saber, who will open 15 Paneras in San Diego.

In the past, owner-operators were McDonald's evangelists. Prospective franchisees were once so eager to get into the two-year training program that they would wait in line for hours when applications were handed out at the chain's offices around the country. But there aren't any lines today, and many existing franchisees feel alienated. They have seen their margins dip to a paltry 4%, from 15% at the peak. Richard Adams, a former franchisee and a food consultant, claims that as many as 20 franchisees are currently leaving McDonald's every month. Why? "Because it's so hard to survive these days," he says.

One of the biggest sore points for franchisees is the top-down manner in which Greenberg and other past CEOs attempted to fix pricing and menu problems. Many owner-operators still grumble over the $18,000 to $100,000 they had to spend in the late 1990s to install company-mandated "Made for You" kitchen upgrades in each restaurant. The new kitchens were supposed to speed up orders and accommodate new menu items. But in the end, they actually slowed service. Reggie Webb, who operates 11 McDonald's restaurants in Los Angeles, says his sales have dipped by an average of $50,000 at each of his outlets over the past 15 years. "From my perspective, I am working harder than ever

and making less than I ever had on an average-store basis," says Webb. He'll have to open his wallet again if McDonald's includes his units in the next 200 restaurants it selects for refurbishing. Franchisees pay 70% of that $150,000 cost.

Franchisees also beef about McDonald's addiction to discounting. When McDonald's cut prices in a 1997 price war, sales fell over the next four months. The lesson should have been obvious. "Pulling hard on the price lever is dangerous. It risks cheapening the brand," says Sam Rovit, a partner at Chicago consultant Bain & Co. Yet Cantalupo is sticking with the $1 menu program introduced last year. "We like to wear out our competitors with our price," he says. Burger King and Wendy's International Inc. admit that the tactic is squeezing their sales. But in the five months since its debut, the $1 menu has done nothing to improve McDonald's results.

As a last resort, McDonald's is getting rid of the weakest franchises. Continuous growth can no longer bail out underperformers, so Cantalupo is enforcing a "tough love" program that Greenberg reinstated last year after the company gave it up in 1990. Owners that flunk the rating and inspection system will get a chance to clean up their act. But if they don't improve, they'll be booted.

The decline in McDonald's once-vaunted service and quality can be traced to its expansion of the 1990s, when headquarters stopped grading franchises for cleanliness, speed, and service. Training declined as restaurants fought for workers in a tight labor market. That led to a falloff in kitchen and counter skills— according to a 2002 survey by Columbus (Ohio) market researcher Global Growth Group. McDonald's came in third in average service time behind Wendy's and sandwich shop Chick-fil-A Inc. Wendy's took an average 127 seconds to place and fill an order, vs. 151 seconds at Chick-fil-A and 163 at McDonald's. That may not seem like much, but Greenberg has said that saving six seconds at a drive-through brings a 1% increase in sales.

Trouble is, it's tough to sell franchisees on a new quality gauge at the same time the company is asking them to do everything from offering cheap burgers to shouldering renovation costs. Franchising works best when a market is expanding and owners can be rewarded for meeting incentives. In the past, franchisees who beat McDonald's national sales average were typically rewarded with the chance to open or buy more stores. The largest franchisees now operate upwards of 50 stores. But with falling sales, those incentives don't cut it. "Any company today has to be very vigilant about their business model and willing to break it, even if it's successful, to make sure they stay on top of the changing trends," says Alan Feldman, CEO of Midas Inc., who was COO for domestic operations at McDonald's until January, 2002. "You can't just go on cloning your business into the future."

By the late 1990s, it was clear that the system was losing traction. New menu items like the low-fat McLean Deluxe and Arch Deluxe burgers, meant to appeal to adults, bombed. Non-burger offerings did no better, often because of poor planning. Consultant Michael Seid, who manages a franchise consulting firm in West Hartford, Conn., points out that McDonald's offered a pizza that didn't fit through the drive-through window and salad shakers that were packed so tightly that dressing couldn't flow through them. By 1998, McDonald's posted its first-ever decline in annual earnings and then-CEO Michael R. Quinlan was out, replaced by Greenberg, a 16-year McDonald's veteran.

Greenberg won points for braking the chain's runaway U.S. expansion. He also broadened its portfolio, acquiring Chipotle Mexican Grill and Boston Market Corp. But he was unable to focus on the new ventures while also improving quality, getting the new kitchens rolled out, and developing new menu items. Says Los Angeles franchisee Webb: "We would have been better off trying fewer things and making them work." Greenberg was unable to reverse skidding sales and profits, and after last year's disastrous fourth quarter, he offered his resignation at the Dec. 5 board meeting. There were no angry words from directors. But there were no objections, either.

Insiders say Cantalupo, who had retired only a year earlier, was the only candidate seriously considered to take over, despite shareholder sentiment for an outsider. The board felt that it needed someone who knew the company and could move quickly. Cantalupo has chosen to work with younger McDonald's executives, whom he feels will bring energy and fresh ideas to the table. Bell, formerly president of McDonald's Europe, became a store manager in his native Australia at 19 and rose through the ranks. There, he launched a coffeehouse concept called McCafe, which is now being introduced around the globe. He later achieved success in France, where he abandoned McDonald's

cookie-cutter orange-and-yellow stores for individualized ones that offer local fare like the ham-and-cheese Croque McDo.

The second top executive Cantalupo has recruited is a bonafide outsider—at least by company standards. Lederhausen holds an MBA from the Stockholm School of Economics and worked with Boston Consulting Group Inc. for two years. However, he jokes that he grew up in a french-fry vat because his father introduced McDonald's to Sweden in 1973. Lederhausen is in charge of growth and menu development.

Getting the recipe right will be tougher now that consumers have tasted better burgers. While McDonald's says it may start toasting its buns longer to get the flavor right, rivals go even further. Industry experts point to 160-store In-N-Out, a profitable California burger chain. Its burgers are grilled when ordered—no heat lamps to warm up precooked food. Today, In-N-Out is rated No. 1 by fast-food consumers tracked by consultant Sandelman & Associates Inc. in San Diego. "The burger category has great strength," adds David C. Novak, chairman and CEO of Yum! Brands Inc., parent of KFC and Taco Bell. "That's America's food. People love hamburgers."

McDonald's best hope to recapture that love might be to turn to its most innovative franchisees. Take Irwin Kruger in New York, who recently opened a 17,000-square-foot showcase unit in Times Square with video monitors showing movie trailers, brick walls, theatrical lighting—and strong profits. "We're slated to have sales of over $5 million this year and profits exceeding 10%," says Kruger. Rejuvenated marketing would help, too: McDonald's called its top ad agencies together in February to draw up a plan that would go beyond the ubiquitous Disney movie tie-ins.

It will take nothing short of a marketing miracle, though, to return McDonald's to its youthful vigor. "They are at a critical juncture and what they do today will shape whether they just fade away or recapture some of the magic and greatness again," says Robert S. Goldin, executive vice-president at food consultant Technomic Inc. As McDonald's settles into middle age, Cantalupo and his team may have to settle for stable and reliable.

By Pallavi Gogoi and Michael Arndt in Oak Brook, IL.

Source: "Hamburger Hell," *BusinessWeek*, March 3, 2003, 104–108.

Case 3-4

Tesco Plc.

Cheshunt, England–When Wal-Mart Stores Inc. entered the British market in 1999 by buying a chain of stores here, many expected it to dominate. Instead, Wal-Mart's largest non-American operation has been struggling recently, and its top local rival is thriving.

That rival is Tesco PLC, Britain's largest retailer. Its big weapon is information about its customers. Tesco has signed up 12 million Britons for its Clubcard program, giving cardholders discounts in exchange for their name, address and other personal information. The Clubcard has helped boost Tesco's market share in groceries to 31%, nearly double the 16% held by Wal-Mart's Asda chain, according to market-research firm Taylor Nelson Sofres.

The data let Tesco tailor promotions to individual shoppers and figure out quickly how new initiatives are working. After Tesco introduced Asian herbs, cooking oil and other ethnic foods in neighborhoods with many Indians and Pakistanis, the data showed the new products were also popular with affluent white customers. The company quickly expanded the rollout.

Tesco's computers often turn up counterintuitive results. Shoppers who buy diapers for the first time at a Tesco store can expect to receive coupons by mail for baby wipes, toys—and beer. Tesco's analysis showed that new fathers tend to buy more beer because they are home with the baby and can't go to the pub.

The data-driven strategy puts Tesco at the vanguard in retailing as traditional advertising loses effectiveness. Procter & Gamble Co., Coca-Cola Co. and Kimberly-Clark Corp. are among the consumer-products companies that buy analyses based on Tesco data.

The British retailer is increasingly battling Wal-Mart around the globe. It plans to open a chain of small stores on the West Coast of the U.S. next year, its first foray onto Wal-Mart's home turf. Wal-Mart wants to expand in Central Europe, where Tesco has a firm foothold.

As the U.S. market becomes saturated, Wal-Mart is looking overseas for growth. It has had some successes, including Mexico and Canada, but many of its overseas ventures are hurting. Its Japanese unit has suffered losses. Last month, Wal-Mart abandoned an eight year effort in South Korea by selling its 16 outlets there

to a local competitor for $872 million. Tesco says its 39 Korean stores are successful.

Asda in the U.K. accounts for about 10% of Wal-Mart's overall business and 45% of its international sales. The unit thrived under Wal-Mart's ownership for several years but Wal-Mart says sales were "slightly negative" last year and profits were "below plan." (It doesn't report exact figures.)

Tesco has used its knowledge of shoppers to fight Wal-Mart's core appeal: low prices. After Wal-Mart bought Asda, Tesco searched its database and singled out shoppers who buy the cheapest available item. They were most likely to be tempted by Asda, Tesco figured.

Tesco then identified 300 items that these price-sensitive shoppers bought regularly. One was Tesco Value Brand Margarine. Tesco lowered the price of the margarine, along with other products with similar profiles. As a result, shoppers didn't defect to Asda, says Clive Humby, chairman of Dunnhumby, a British research firm that is majority-owned by Tesco and analyzes customer data for the retailer. Tesco's sales jumped 17% to $79 billion in the year ended Feb. 25, and net income rose 17% to $2.96 billion (see Exhibit 1).

Founded in 1919 as a grocery stand in East London, Tesco grew into a supermarket chain after World War II and opened its first superstore in 1968. The company's name comes from its first private-label product, Tesco Tea, which founder Jack Cohen named by combining the initials of a tea supplier, T.E. Stockwell, with the first two letters of his own last name.

In the 1990s, as space for new big stores became scarcer, the retailer refined its strategy. Today it operates

EXHIBIT 1

Upper Class

Tesco's net income, in billions of dollars converted from pounds at current year.

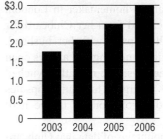

Note: Year ending in February
Source: the company

2,306 stores in Britain in four sizes: huge supercenters stocking everything from lawn furniture to apples; large stores that have a limited range of nonfood items; regular supermarkets; and "Tesco Express" convenience stores with merchandise tailored to neighborhood tastes.

Tesco's size is raising antitrust concerns in the U.K. Last month, the British government ordered an investigation into the power of the country's four biggest supermarket chains. Tesco Chief Executive Terry Leahy said the company isn't doing anything improper to block competition. He said Tesco is successful because "millions of ordinary consumers vote with their feet when they go shopping."

As Wal-Mart is increasingly doing in the U.S., Tesco tries to appeal to both affluent and bargain shoppers. It has several private labels, ranging from the "Tesco Finest" line that includes duck pâté and cashmere sweaters to the "Tesco Value" brand, which offers baked beans and the like. The idea for the Finest line came a few years ago when Clubcard data showed that higher-spending customers weren't buying wine, cheese and fruit from Tesco. The retailer upgraded its offerings in those categories.

In 1995, Tesco introduced the Clubcard under Mr. Leahy, then head of marketing. Today, about 80% of Tesco shoppers are Clubcard members. They join by filling out an application form at a store, which includes optional questions about the size of their household, the ages of their children and dietary preferences.

Members receive a plastic card in the mail, which they use at the checkout to receive a point for every pound they spend. (They must spend at least £150, about $280, to begin getting points.) Each point is a penny off future purchases, or it can be converted into miles in frequent flier programs. On top of the points, big spenders get discount coupons every three months on particular products, keyed to their buying profile in Tesco's database.

Adele Fiala, a 36-year-old homemaker in London, recently used air miles earned from her Clubcard for a weekend trip to Seville, Spain, with her husband. While she tosses promotional mailings, "I always open the mail from Tesco," she says. She recently switched from powdered laundry detergent to liquid capsules after receiving a one-pound-off coupon in the mail from Tesco.

To help analyze the mountains of data that Clubcard generates, Tesco turns to consultancy Dunnhumby, named for its two founders—Mr. Humby and his wife, Edwina Dunn. Dunnhumby is also active in the U.S. as an adviser to supermarket chain Kroger Inc., analyzing customer data and running its loyalty-card program. Dunnhumby's offices in Ealing, just outside London, receive data on 15 million Tesco shopping baskets every week.

Each product is scored on 50 dimensions such as price and the size of the package. The computer looks for customers whose shopping baskets have similar combinations of scores. Dunnhumby classifies shoppers in six segments. The "Finer Foods" segment, for example, is made up of affluent, time-strapped shoppers who buy upscale products. "Traditional" shoppers are homemakers with time to buy ingredients and cook a meal.

Many retailers consider loyalty programs expensive to manage and think they slow down the checkout line. Neither Wal-Mart nor its Asda unit has a frequent-shopper card, though Asda tried one for four years before dropping it in early 1999. Asda argues that it can get nearly the same information for less money by combining Wal-Mart's powerful sales-tracking computers with targeted market research such as focus groups.

"There clearly are benefits to having loyalty-card information but there are costs as well," says Jon Owen, head of research and pricing at Asda. "We prefer to give our customers the value in different ways."

Asda executives believe Tesco's databases have little to do with its success. Instead, they say Asda fell behind because it failed to reach out to higher-end shoppers with products such as better produce and gourmet ready-to-eat meals. It also lost its crown as the low-price leader. Andy Bond, Asda's chief executive, said this March in a conference call with analysts that Tesco and other supermarkets were matching Asda's prices.

Mr. Bond said last December that the unit is "operationally failing." Mike Duke, the chief executive of Wal-Mart's international division, says: "We took our eye off the customer." Recently, Asda has upgraded its foods and, in a shift from Wal-Mart's supercenter strategy, opened small discount stores like those Tesco operates.

Tesco doesn't disclose its investment in Clubcard but spokesman Jonathan Church says it is "worth every penny."

A typical quarterly coupon package Tesco sends to customers includes three coupons for products they regularly buy and three for goods that they might like, or that Tesco wants them to try. While industry adage says that only 1% or 2% of all coupons ever get redeemed, about 15% to 20% of all Tesco coupons are redeemed.

The package also includes vouchers through which Clubcard members can redeem their accumulated points. If a member has spent £300, she will get a voucher for £3 off any purchase. Tesco says 95% of these vouchers are redeemed, suggesting that they help entice shoppers to return to the store.

Tesco statements mailed to Karen Masek, an actor and mother of two in London, reflect her preference for fresh produce, environment-friendly cleaning products and organic meat. "They definitely know your shopping habits," she says. "They've never sent me anything totally off the mark."

Recent mailings to Ms. Masek, 43, have included coupons for new vegetables, cooking sauces, and nuts or seeds. Ms. Masek, who made sure her nanny had a Tesco loyalty card as well, says she often redeems the coupons and uses Clubcard points to pay for video rentals.

Martin Hayward, director of consumer strategy at Dunnhumby, says such cases show why loyalty cards are worth the trouble. "You couldn't do that just with data" from checkout receipts, he says.

The data are also useful for consumer-product makers. Five years ago, Kimberly-Clark introduced a premium version of its Andrex toilet paper in Britain infused with aloe vera. Clubcard records helped the Irving, Texas, company track who was buying the toilet paper and whether shoppers stayed loyal to it. Dunnhumby also found that regular buyers of Andrex Aloe Vera were also big buyers of skin-care products. Kimberly-Clark then sent direct mail to 500,000 customers, offering them free beauty treatments if they could show that they bought the toilet paper twice.

Tesco's recent rollout of an ethnic food line called "World Foods" shows how customer data can shape decision-making at almost every step of the way. The idea got its start when Clubcard records showed shoppers at a small store in the town of Slough weren't buying full meals. Many people in the town have South Asian or Arab roots.

Tesco decided to replace the store with a supercenter. Focus groups confirmed that people in Slough were buying some products at Tesco but turning to smaller markets for many staples—large stacks of rice, big canisters of cooking oil and Asian brands. Many criticized the small plastic packages of herbs at Tesco and said they wanted loose bunches that they could touch and smell.

When the new Slough store opened in August 2005, it offered more than 800 foreign products, up from 150 in the previous store. It has a large halal butcher shop, the latest movies from India, newspapers in Arabic, Urdu, Punjabi and Bengali, and a jewelry counter with bangles in yellow 22-karat gold popular in India. The shopping carts are lower and flatter to fit big sacks of rice and flour.

Tesco wanted to know if the strategy was working, so it turned to Dunnhumby. The analysis found that 36% of Slough shoppers were buying goods from the World Foods line. That figure roughly matched the proportion of Slough's nonwhite population.

Dunnhumby then checked addresses of World Foods buyers against government census data that identify immigrant neighborhoods. It turned out that more than a quarter of the World Foods customers were coming from largely white neighborhoods. By examining the shopping baskets of these customers, Dunnhumby concluded that upscale white shoppers with an interest in non-European food were responsible for some of the success of the World Food line.

In the following days, executives huddled over big maps showing Britain's ethnic makeup. They outlined a plan to roll out the World Foods line to 300 stores in immigrant areas as well as to 25 stores in mostly white parts of the country.

A few weeks later, Tesco stores in places like Holland Park, a leafy part of west London, and Bar Hill, an affluent town near Cambridge, were stocking fragrant herbs and frozen samosas. Tesco says the Bar Hill store is selling World Foods better than any of its other stores. Dunnhumby is running numbers to get the details.

Source: Cecilie Rohwedder, "No.1 Retailer in Britain Uses 'Clubcard' to Thwart Wal-Mart," *The Wall Street Journal,* June 6, 2006, A1, A16. Reprinted by permission of The Wall Street Journal, Copyright © 2006 Dow Jones & Company, Inc. All Rights Reserved Worldwide. License number 1674400826205.

Part

Market-Driven Program Development

4

Chapter

9

Strategic Brand Management

Products play an important role in generating sales and profits and creating growth opportunities for all companies. Moreover, management initiatives for new and existing products are closely interrelated. Many companies have several products and/or brands in their portfolios. The objective is to achieve the highest overall performance from the portfolio of products offered by the firm. This requires successful new product introductions, effective targeting and positioning of existing products, selecting metrics and tracking performance of the portfolio, and improving or eliminating poor performing products. Strategic brand management of the portfolio is an ongoing challenge, involving executives from all business functions.

PepsiCo has been very successful in its strategic brand management in recent years, displaying much stronger performance than Coca-Cola in an extremely competitive environment. At the core of Pepsi's brand management initiatives is an impressive array of beverage and snack products. One of Pepsi's strengths is not being dependent on only beverages for profits and growth. It has sixteen brands that each accounts for $1 billion in annual sales. Pepsi's competitive advantage is a carefully formulated and executed brand management strategy.[1] Pepsi's acquisition of Quaker Oats and Gatorade (80% market share) enhanced its portfolio. Coke had the lead opportunity to acquire Quaker but declined due to lack of the board of directors' support. Pepsi's strategic brand management initiatives, guided by excellent market sensing capabilities, established Aquafina in the lead position in the bottled water market. Interestingly, snacks account for 47 percent of Pepsi's profits (generated by Frito Lay and Quaker Oats) compared to 31 percent for beverages. Remaining profit is contributed by Pepsi's very successful overseas operations. One of Pepsi's major brand management challenges is getting its brand managers to collaborate on sales and marketing programs. This initiative is designated the "Power of One," and is considered as a key strategic growth initiative.

Strategic brand management requires several interrelated initiatives designed to build strong brands and a powerful portfolio. First, we examine the challenges of brand management, and discuss the importance and scope of strategic brand analysis. Next, we look at brand identity strategies, and consider what is involved in managing each brand over time and managing the portfolio of brands. The chapter is concluded with a discussion of brand leveraging initiatives.

Strategic Brand Management

It is important to distinguish between the terms *product* and *brand*. In practice they are often used interchangeably, although there are differences in meaning. A *product* is intended to meet the needs of buyers in the product-market. It may consist of objects, services, organizations, places, people, and ideas. This view of the product covers a wide range of situations, including tangible goods and intangible services. Thus, political candidates are products, as are travel services, medical services, refrigerators, gas turbines, and computers.

A *brand* is the product offered by a specific company. The American Marketing Association defines a brand as follows (www.marketingpower.com):

> A name, term, design, symbol, or any other feature that identifies one seller's good or service as distinct from those of other sellers. The legal term for brand is *trademark*. A brand may identify one item, a family of items, or all items of that seller. If used for the firm as a whole, the preferred term is *trade name*.

While the products of some companies are not identified as brands, most have some form of brand designation. Throughout the chapter when discussing a company's product, product line, or product mix (portfolio) we assume that the products have a brand identity.

In the past differences between goods and intangible services have been emphasized by highlighting how services are different (e.g., intangible, consumed when they are produced, and variable consistency). However, a compelling logic has been proposed that the distinction between goods and services should be replaced by a view that services are the dominant perspective in the twenty-first century, consisting of both tangible and intangible components.[2] The service-centered logic integrates goods with services and these offerings deliver value to customers. Thus, the important issue is understanding the composition of the value offering being made to buyers by a brand.

First, we look at the strategic role of brands. A discussion follows of brand management challenges. Next, we consider where responsibility for brand management is placed in an organization. Finally, the initiatives involved in strategic brand management are examined.

The Strategic Role of Brands

Strategic brand management is a key issue in many organizations and is not the domain only of consumer packaged goods companies. General Motors' Saab brand is facing a challenging brand management question: How to revive a struggling brand?[3] Interestingly, the company was founded as an aircraft maker in Sweden in 1937. Saab experienced losses in twelve of the past fourteen years. Saab is a well-engineered automobile but does not have a strong image in the marketplace. People don't really know what it stands for. In 2005, management decided to link the Saab name with its jet aircraft heritage and launched a major promotion program designed around this theme. Emphasis was placed on performance, design, and safety. Also, major model design initiatives were underway. Given GM's overall performance challenges, unless Saab's performance improves, its future may be uncertain.

A strategic brand perspective requires executives to decide what role brands play for the company in creating customer value and shareholder value. This role should be the basis for directing and sustaining brand investments into the most productive areas. It is important to distinguish between the functions of brands for buyers and sellers.[4] For buyers, brands reduce:

- Customer search costs, by identifying products quickly and accurately.
- The buyer's perceived risk, by providing an assurance of quality and consistency (which may then be transferred to new products).

- The social and psychological risks associated with owning and using the "wrong" product, by providing psychological rewards for purchasing brands that symbolize status and prestige.

For sellers, brands play a function of facilitation, by making easier some of the tasks the seller has to perform. Brands facilitate:

- Repeat purchases that enhance the company's financial performance, because the brand enables the customer to identify and re-identify the product compared to alternatives.
- The introduction of new products, because the customer is familiar with the brand from previous buying experience.
- Promotional effectiveness, by providing a point of focus.
- Premium pricing by creating a basic level of differentiation compared to competitors.
- Market segmentation, by communicating a coherent message to the target audience, telling them for whom the brand is intended and for whom it is not.
- Brand loyalty, of particular importance in product categories where loyal buying is an important feature of buying behavior.

The opportunity for using brand strength to build customer value and competitive advantage has encouraged managers to focus attention on global estimates of the value of brands and the concept of brand equity. The financial value of brands is an important indication of how well a brand is being managed by a company.[5] Exhibit 9.1 shows the top ranked twenty-five brands from the 2006 Interbrand (branding consultant) valuations of global brands with a value greater than $1 billion. Interbrand calculates brand value as the net present value of the earnings the brand is expected to generate in the future. The Interbrand model bases brand earnings on forecasts of brand revenues, allowing for risk and the role of the brand in stimulating customer demand. The Interbrand measure of brand strength includes: leadership (ability to influence the market); stability (survival ability based on customer loyalty); market (security from change of technology and fashion); geography (ability to cross geographic borders); support (consistency and effectiveness of brand support); and, protection (legal title).

Strong brands are major contributors to the distinctive capabilities of companies like BMW, Google, Hewlett-Packard, General Electric, Nokia, and Toyota. Sustaining and building brand strengths is a continuing challenge for managers. The GLOBAL FEATURE describes several of BMW's brand-building initiatives. BMW's management launched a major effort in the late 1990s to develop a whole spectrum of upscale cars in response to changing lifestyles identified through extensive market sensing initiatives.[6] The new styles involved billions of dollars of expenditures. By early 2005 BMW had completed about half of the style changes and sales were up 34 percent over the previous four years, but sales of the new-look 5 and 7 series were not doing well in the U.S. The new 3 series was launched in 2005. BMW has a powerful brand but observers were beginning to question the success of the initiatives to broaden the company's offerings.

Brand Management Challenges

Several internal and external forces create hurdles for product and brand managers in their efforts to build strong brands:[7]

- **Intense Price and Other Competitive Pressures.** Deciding how to respond to these pressures shifts managers' attention away from brand management responsibilities.
- **Fragmentation of Markets and Media.** Many markets have become highly differentiated in terms of customer needs. Similarly, the media (advertising and

EXHIBIT 9.1 The Global Brand Scoreboard

Source: "The 100 Top Brands," *BusinessWeek*, August 7, 2006, 60–61.

Rank 2006/2005			2006 Brand Value $Millions	2005 Brand Value $Millions	Percent Change	Country of Ownership	Description
1	1	Coca-Cola	67,000	67,525	−1%	U.S.	Flagging appetite for soda has cut demand for Coke, but the beverage giant has a raft of new products in the pipeline that could reverse its recent slide.
2	2	Microsoft	56,926	59,941	−5%	U.S.	Threats from Google and Apple haven't yet offset the power of its Windows and Office monopolies.
3	3	IBM	56,201	53,376	5%	U.S.	Having off-loaded its low-profit PC business to Lenovo, IBM is marketing on the strategic level to corporate leaders.
4	4	GE	48,907	46,996	4%	U.S.	The brand Edison built has extended its reach from ovens to credit cards, and the "Ecoimagination" push is making GE look like a protector of the planet.
5	5	Intel	32,319	35,588	−9%	U.S.	Profits and market share weren't the only things slammed by rival AMD. Intel's brand value tumbled 9%, as it lost business from high-profile customers.
6	6	Nokia	30,131	26,452	14%	Finland	Fashionable designs and low-cost models for the developing world enabled the mobile phone maker to regain ground against competitors.
7	9	Toyota	27,941	24,837	12%	Japan	Toyota is closing in on GM to become the world's biggest automaker. A slated 10% increase in U.S. sales this year will help even more.
8	7	Disney	27,848	26,441	5%	U.S.	New CEO Robert Iger expanded the brand by buying animation hit-maker Pixar and beefing up digital distribution of TV shows through the Internet and iPods.
9	8	McDonald's	27,501	26,014	6%	U.S.	A new healthy-living marketing campaign—and the premium-priced sandwiches and salads that came with it—have led to a fourth year of sales gains.
10	11	Mercedes-Benz	21,795	20,006	9%	Germany	The new S-Class sedan and M-Class SUV are helping repair a tarnished quality reputation. High costs and weak margins will take longer to fix.
11	12	Citi	21,458	19,967	7%	U.S.	Already the biggest U.S. bank, Citigroup's quest to generate more revenue from world markets has it introducing its brand to new emerging markets.

(continued)

EXHIBIT 9.1—*(concluded)*

12	10	Marlboro	21,350	21,189	1%	U.S.	Marlboro remains firmly in the saddle, particularly outside the U.S., as it expands into developing markets.
13	13	Hewlett-Packard	20,458	18,866	8%	U.S.	Under CEO Mark Hurd, HP is skipping glitzy image ads to push specific products. Improving profits and a 40% stock price increase haven't hurt.
14	14	American Express	19,641	18,559	6%	U.S.	A preeminent financial-services brand among high-end customers, the company is recasting itself as hip to broaden its appeal to a younger set.
15	16	BMW	19,617	17,126	15%	Germany	BMW continues to churn out hot models that buyers love to drive and Japanese automakers can't seem to replicate.
16	15	Gillette	19,579	17,534	12%	U.S.	Gillette's new six-bladed Fusion razor met with ridicule when it was introduced. But with Fusion sales soaring, Gillette is still king.
17	18	Louis Vuitton	17,606	16,077	10%	France	With a glitzy new flagship on the Champs Elysées, the world's richest luxury brand celebrates yet another year of robust growth.
18	17	Cisco	17,532	16,592	6%	U.S.	Cisco's decision to lead with its Linksys brand for consumers hasn't made the company a household name yet, but it's helping.
19	19	Honda	17,049	15,788	8%	Japan	As gas prices rise, Honda's gas sippers are helping the Japanese carmaker gnaw into the Big Three's market share.
20	20	Samsung	16,169	14,956	8%	S. Korea	Samsung is rolling out hot LCD TVs and ever more powerful memory chips. But it is missing in action with low-end handsets, hurting market share.
21	25	Merrill Lynch	13,001	12,018	8%	U.S.	Merrill Lynch has made a dramatic transformation from a sleepy, stable brokerage to a lean and mean investment bank.
22	23	Pepsi	12,690	12,399	2%	U.S.	It tapped a growing obsession with obesity by shifting marketing dollars to Diet Pepsi. Another boost? Rival Coke's move to copy Pepsi Max with Coke Zero.
23	24	Nescafe	12,507	12,241	2%	Switzerland	Sales of instant coffee are piping hot in emerging markets, while flavored coffees and new products have boosted appeal in the U.S. and Europe.
24	38	Google	12,376	8,461	46%	U.S.	Its recent inclusion as a verb in the *Oxford English Dictionary* confirms what competitors feared: Google means search to an army of Web users.
25	21	Dell	12,256	13,231	−7%	U.S.	The king of the inexpensive PC is trying to regain trust with a campaign to bolster customer service and technical support.

THE BIG THREE: BMW'S CORE MODELS

3 SERIES
Sporty compact that sells upwards of 530,000 units a year.
Starting price: $28,495

5 SERIES
BMW's linchpin model and profit-driver accounts for 30% of sales.
Starting price: $38,295

7 SERIES
Flagship luxury sedan offers wealthy buyers a more dynamic drive than rivals.
Starting price: $69,195

1 SERIES
A premium subcompact car arriving in 2005 aimed at younger buyers.
Starting price: NA

6 SERIES
Coupe to hit market in late 2003 and convertible in 2004. Both will revive a former 6 model last produced in 1989.
Starting price: NA

NEW MODELS ON THE MARKET OR IN THE WORKS

X3
Baby SUV with 6-cylinder engine set to launch in late 2003. Development and production entirely outsourced to Austria's Magna Steyr.
Starting price: NA

X5
Powerful sport-utility off-roader launched in 2001 ranked among the top-selling luxury SUVs in the U.S.
Starting Price: $40,195

Z4
Sleek new roadster hit showrooms in 2003 replacing the Z3 with improved suspension and bigger engine range.
Starting price: $33,795

MINI
BMW remade this British icon into a hot-selling premium small car that fetches $37,000 fully loaded.
Starting Price: $16,425

ROLLS ROYCE
Super luxury limousine revamped using BMW's 12-cylinder engine.
Starting Price: $320,000

Source: "BMW," *BusinessWeek*, June 19, 2003, 58–59

sales promotion) available to access market segments have become very fragmented and specialized. The Internet has compounded market targeting and access complexity.

- **Complex Brand Strategies and Relationships.** Multiple additions to core brands such as BMW's initiatives have created complex brand management situations. These complexities may encourage managers to alter strategies rather than building on the existing strategies.

- **Bias Against Innovation.** Brand complacency may result in a failure to innovate. Innovation may be avoided to prevent cannibalism of existing products.

- **Pressure to Invest Elsewhere.** A strong brand may generate complacency and cause management to shift resources to new initiatives.

- **Short-Term Pressures.** Managers encounter many short-term pressures that shift their attention and resources away from important brand-building programs. Top management's need to achieve quarterly financial targets is illustrative.

The key to reducing these negative impacts on brand-building strategies is developing brand strategy guidelines, tracking initiatives on a regular basis, and critically assessing potential challenges that shift management attention away from core strategies.

Brand Management Responsibility

Responsibility for strategic brand management extends to several organizational levels. Three management levels often are found in companies that have strategic business units, different product lines, and specific brands within lines.

Product/Brand Management

Responsibilities for these positions consist of planning, managing, and coordinating the strategy for a specific product or brand. Management activities include market analysis, targeting, positioning strategy, performance analysis and strategy adjustment, identification of new product needs, and management and coordination of product/brand marketing activities. Marketing plans for specific brands are often developed at this level. Product or brand managers typically do not have authority over all brand management activities, but they have responsibility for the performance of their brands. These managers are sponsors or advocates of specific products, negotiating and collaborating on behalf of their product/brand strategies with the salesforce, research and development, operations, marketing research, and advertising and sales promotion managers.

Product Group/Marketing Management

A business which has several product categories and/or brands may assign responsibility for coordinating the initiatives of product or brand managers to a product director, group manager, or marketing manager. This person coordinates and monitors the activities and approves the recommendations of a group of product or brand managers. The executive's responsibilities are to manage the brand portfolio. Additionally, the product group manager coordinates product management activities and decisions with the business unit management.

Product Portfolio Management

This responsibility is normally assigned to the chief executive of the strategic business unit (SBU), the corporate level of an organization, or a team of top executives. Illustrative decisions include product acquisitions, research and development priorities, new-product decisions, product drop decisions, and resource allocation. Evaluation of brand/product portfolio performance may also be centered at this level. In a corporation with two or more SBUs, top management may coordinate and establish product management guidelines for the SBU management. We look further into the organization of marketing activities in Chapter 14.

Market-Driven Management

Increasingly, changes are being made by companies to integrate sales, marketing, and other business functions into cross-functional teams.[8] A study by the Boston Consulting Group indicated that 90 percent of the responding companies have restructured their marketing departments. It is apparent that traditional product and brand-based organizations will increasingly evolve into customer and market-based approaches to implement more effectively the mandate for customer focus.

Strategic Brand Management

Strategic brand management decisions are relevant to all businesses, including suppliers, producers, wholesalers, distributors, and retailers. While many of these decisions involve the evaluation, selection, and dropping of products from suppliers, retailers may

Sir Howard Stringer, a Welsh-born American citizen, was appointed CEO of Sony, the troubled Japanese electronics giant, in 2005. Sony's past strategic brand management initiatives had failed to close the digital gap between software/services/content/devices. During the CEO's first year several cost reduction and portfolio initiatives were implemented to launch the turnaround strategy:

> The Aibo, a beloved robotic pet, was put to sleep. They shut down the Qualia line of boutique electronics that included a $4,000 digital camera and a $13,000 70-inch television. They eliminated 5,700 jobs and closed nine factories, including one in south Wales. (He took some flak back home for that.) They have sold $705 million worth of assets. You probably didn't know that Sony owned a chain of 1,221 cosmetics salons and the 18 Japanese outlets of the Maxim's de Paris restaurant chain. They're gone. Gone, too, is a group of salary-men in their 60s, 70s, and 80s who, after retiring from senior management positions, were given the title of "advisor," a tradition established by Sony's founders. "That was very symbolic," says Hideki (Dick) Komivama, a Sony executive and key ally of Stringer's. The 45 advisors each had a secretary, a car and driver, and worst of all, the ability to gum up decision-making and second-guess people doing real jobs. No more.

Source: Marc Gunther, "The Welshman, the Walkman, and the Salary Men," *Fortune,* June 12, 2006, 72.

also develop new goods and services, such as Gap and Target have done. These retailers are involved in designing some of their own products. Moreover, suppliers are faced with important brand management decisions.

The importance of strategic brand management is illustrated by Sony, the troubled Japanese electronics giant. The GLOBAL FEATURE describes how Sony's new management is launching its turnaround strategy. The core challenge is customer value driven innovation.

Strategic brand management consists of several interrelated initiatives as shown in Exhibit 9.2.[9] We briefly describe each activity, examining it in greater depth in the following sections of the chapter.

Strategic Brand Analysis

Analysis provides essential information for decision making for each of the brand management activities shown in Exhibit 9.2. Analysis includes market/customer, competitor, and brand information.

EXHIBIT 9.2
Strategic Brand Management

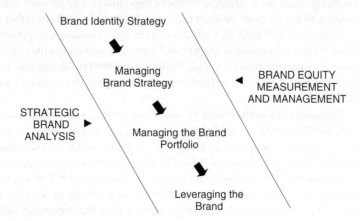

Brand Equity Measurement and Management

Each of the strategic brand management initiatives shown in Exhibit 9.2 may have a positive or negative impact on the value of the brands in the portfolio. Brand equity recognizes the importance of brand value and identifies the key dimensions of equity. The objective is to build brand equity over time.

Brand Identity Strategy

The intent of brand identity is to determine "a unique set of brand associations that the brand strategist aspires to create or maintain."[10] The identity may be associated with the product, the organization, a person, or a symbol. Identity implementation determines what part of the identity is to be communicated to the target audience and how this will be achieved. The brand positioning statement describes the identity information to be used to position the brand in the eyes and minds of targeted buyers.

Managing Brand Strategy

A brand must be managed from its initial launch throughout the brand's life cycle. While the brand strategy may be altered over time, the intent is to pursue consistent initiatives, build the strength of the brand, and avoid damaging the brand. Target's management has been very successful in managing the retailer's brand, whereas Kmart's faulty brand management eventually contributed to its bankruptcy.

Managing the Brand Portfolio

This initiative consists of coordinating the organization's portfolio or system of brands with the objective of achieving optimal system performance. The focus is on the performance of the portfolio and its brand interrelations rather than an individual brand. Procter and Gamble has been particularly impressive in managing its very successful brand portfolio.

Leveraging the Brand

Leveraging involves extending the core brand identity to a new addition to the product line, or to a new product category. Nike's leveraging the core footwear brand into apparel and sports equipment is illustrative of extending the brand to new product categories.

Strategic Brand Analysis

A company may have a single product, a product line, or a portfolio of product lines. In our discussion of managing existing products, we assume that product/brand strategy decisions are being made for a strategic business unit (SBU). The product composition of the SBU consists of one or more product lines and the specific product(s) that make up each line.

Strategic brand analysis includes market and customer, competitor, and brand analysis. Since Chapter 2 considers market and customer and competitor analysis, the present discussion centers on brand analysis. Various aspects of the brand may be examined including performance, portfolio interrelationships, leveraging strengths and weaknesses, and brand values.

Evaluating the performance of the brand portfolio helps guide decisions on new products, modified products, and eliminating products. Consider, for example, Apple's decision to drop the Newton handheld computer.[11] Apple invested an estimated $500 million in the brand extension beginning in 1987. The core concept was a computer that could convert the user's handwriting into electronic format. Introduced in 1993 at around $1,000, the Newton was too expensive for many users and there were problems with the handwriting recognition feature. Competition eventually emerged from the successful Palm Pilot introduced in

EXHIBIT 9.3
Tracking Brand
Performance

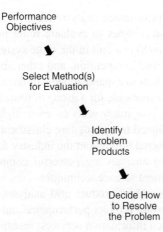

Performance
Objectives

Select Method(s)
for Evaluation

Identify
Problem
Products

Decide How
to Resolve
the Problem

1996. Over 1 million units were sold in a two-year period. The designers created a handheld unit that could do a few things well. Apple's Message Pad was never profitable, although some industry observers suggest that Apple could have been the market leader by continuing product improvement. The Personal Digital Assistant units were a disruptive technology that required time to develop a position in the mainstream market (see Chapter 8).

Tracking Brand Performance

Evaluating the products in the brand portfolio requires tracking the performance of each brand as shown in Exhibit 9.3. Management needs to establish the performance objectives and benchmarks for tracking performance. We discuss brand metrics in Chapter 15. Objectives may include both financial and non-financial factors. Because of the demand and cost interrelationships among products, it is necessary to sort out the sales and costs attributable to each product to show how well it is doing. Activity-based cost analysis is useful for this purpose.[12]

The next step in tracking performance is selecting one or more methods to evaluate product performance. Several useful techniques are shown in Exhibit 9.4. The results of the analyses should identify problem products as well as those performing at or above management's expectations. Finally, management must decide how to resolve the problem.

EXHIBIT 9.4
Methods for
Analyzing
Product Portfolio
Performance

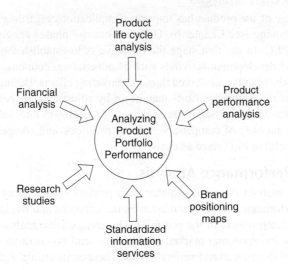

Product
life cycle
analysis

Product
performance
analysis

Analyzing
Product
Portfolio
Performance

Financial
analysis

Research
studies

Brand
positioning
maps

Standardized
information
services

An interesting application of performance analysis for a service is the revenue management system used by American Airlines to evaluate route performance. Each route (e.g., Los Angeles—Dallas/Fort Worth) is a unit in the route system or network. Based on performance, forecasts of demand and competition, and other strategic and tactical considerations, the airline makes decisions to expand, reduce, or terminate service throughout the route network. Each analyst is responsible for a group of routes. Based on management guidelines, the analyst determines how many seats on each flight are to be allocated to AA advantage miles and those assigned to various fare classifications. American Airlines pioneered this system and is recognized throughout the industry for its distinctive revenue management capabilities. Assisting analysts are powerful computer models developed using experience data and management science techniques.

We look at product life cycle analysis, product grid analysis, and positioning analysis to illustrate methods for diagnosing product performance and identifying alternatives for resolving problems. Standardized information services, research studies, and financial analysis are discussed in previous chapters.

Product Life Cycle Analysis

As discussed in Chapter 6 the major stages of the product life cycle (PLC) are: introduction, growth, maturity, and decline. Relevant issues in PLC analysis include:

- Determining the length and rate of change of the product life cycle.
- Identifying the current PLC stage and selecting the product strategy that is appropriate for this stage.
- Anticipating threats and finding opportunities for altering and extending the PLC.

Rate of Change

Product life cycles are becoming shorter for many products due to new technology, rapidly changing preferences of buyers, and intense competition. Cycles also vary for different products. A clothing style may last only one season, whereas a new commercial aircraft may be produced for many years after introduction. Determining the rate of change of the PLC is important because of the need to adjust the marketing strategy to correspond to the changing conditions.

Product Life Cycle Strategies

The PLC stage of the product has important implications regarding all aspects of targeting and positioning (see Chapter 6). Different strategy phases are encountered in moving through the PLC. In the first stage the objective is to establish the brand in the market through brand development activities such as advertising, coupons, and sampling. In the growth stage the brand is reinforced through marketing efforts. During the maturity/decline stage, product repositioning efforts may occur by adjusting size, color, and packaging to appeal to different market segments. Analysis of the growth rate, sales trends, time since introduction, intensity of competition, pricing practices, and competitor entry/exit information are useful in PLC stage analysis.

Product Performance Analysis

Performance analysis considers whether each product is measuring up to management's minimum performance criteria, and assesses the strengths and weaknesses of the product relative to other products in the portfolio. The comparative analysis of products can be performed by incorporating market attractiveness and competitive strength assessments using two-way (horizontal and vertical) grids. These analyses highlight differences among products. After identifying the relative market attractiveness and competitive strength of the products in the portfolio, more comprehensive analysis of specific performance factors may also be useful.

Brand Positioning Analysis

Perceptual maps are useful in comparing brands. Recall our discussion of these methods in earlier chapters. Preference mapping offers useful guidelines for strategic targeting and product positioning. The analyses can relate buyer preferences to different brands and indicate possible brand repositioning options. New-product opportunities may also be identified in the analysis of preference maps. Positioning studies over time can measure the impact of repositioning strategies.

Toyota faced an interesting brand positioning problem which led to the introduction of the Scion brand in 2002. The problem was that Toyota and Lexus buyers had an average age of fifty-four, and Toyota needed to attract younger auto consumers, many of whom perceived Toyotas as autos for older people. Scion, based in California, sees its "funky" cars as the first stepping stone in a young auto buyer's journey. Scion sees itself as a "guerrilla brand" linked to the lifestyle of younger buyers. Scion has established its own record label and designer clothing range. The average age of Scion buyers is thirty-one years, but the dilemma for Toyota is how many Scion buyers will migrate in time to Toyota and Lexus.[13]

Brand Equity Measurement and Management

Measuring Brand Equity

Aaker proposes several measures to capture all relevant aspects of brand equity:[14]

- Loyalty (price premium, satisfaction/loyalty).
- Perceived quality and leadership/popularity measures.
- Associations/differentiation (perceived value, brand personality, organizational associations).
- Awareness (brand awareness).
- Market behavior (market share, price and distribution indices).

These components provide the basis for developing operational measures of brand equity.

Several methods for brand valuation have been proposed. Interbrand's approach was used in the Exhibit 9.1 brand value estimates. Young & Rubicam (Y&R) has developed a brand evaluation tool, Brand Asset Valuator (BAV).[15] The technique uses the brand's vitality (relevance and differentiation) and brand stature (esteem and familiarity) to gauge the health of the brand. Y&R has conducted studies with 30,000 consumers and 6,000 brands in 19 countries.

Brand Health Reports

It is important to consider absolute brand values and investments, and the change in brand value over time, in the evaluation of brand health. Several major companies have adopted brand health report cards which provide indicators to monitor the direction of change in brand equity and identify the key issues to be addressed. Brand health reports can be compiled for individual brands or the entire brand portfolio.[16] The brand report card can assess the brand against the characteristics of the strongest brands by scoring against the following key criteria of brand strength:

- The brand excels at delivering the benefits customers truly desire.
- The brand stays relevant.

- The pricing strategy is based on consumers' perceptions of value.
- The brand is properly positioned.
- The brand is consistent.
- The brand portfolio and hierarchy make sense.
- The brand makes use of and coordinates a full repertoire of marketing activities to build brand equity.
- The brand's managers understand what the brand means to consumers.
- The brand is given proper support and that support is sustained over the long run.
- The company monitors sources of brand equity.[17]

Others suggest that brand health assessment measures should include: market position (e.g., market share and repeat purchase behavior), perception (e.g., awareness, differentiation), marketing support (e.g., share of advertising spending in the sector compared to market share), and profitability.[18] Brand health reports need to be produced on a regular and systematic basis to alert managers to necessary changes in strategy and new market opportunities.

Brand Identity Strategy

Determining the most promising brand identity strategy for an organization's products is a very important strategic initiative (Exhibit 9.2). Brand identification should span a long time horizon, providing a foundation for building brand equity:

> Brand identity is a unique set of brand associations that the brand strategist aspires to create or maintain. These associations represent what the brand stands for and imply a promise to customers from the organization members.[19]

We first discuss alternatives for brand identification and consider the role of the value proposition in brand identity. Next, options for focusing brand identity are described. Finally, we look at how brand identity is implemented.

Alternatives for Brand Identification

In addition to identifying the brand based on the product or the organization, David Aaker extends brand identification options to the brand as a person and the brand as a symbol.[20] The brand as a person (brand personality) perspective recognizes that strong brands may have an identity beyond the product or the company, which has positive impacts on the customer relationship and perception of value. The brand as a symbol underlines the role in brand building of visual imagery, metaphors, and brand heritage. For example, consider Nike's "swoosh" visual symbolism, the Energizer bunny metaphor for long battery life, and Starbuck's Seattle coffee house tradition. This involves "getting to the heart of the brand" to understand the promise that the brand makes to the customer and the brand's value proposition.[21] A clear and effective brand identification strategy is a foundation for building brand strength.

While employing all four brand identity perspectives may not be appropriate for an organization, it is important to consider identity options beyond only a product focus. Moreover, it is essential to recognize that brand identity articulates how management would like the brand to be perceived.

The value proposition conveys the benefit(s) offered by the brand. These benefits may be functional, emotional, or self-expressive.[22] Recall our discussion of these alternative positioning concepts in Chapter 6. The intent is to consider the benefits that distinguish the brand from its competition. The value proposition expresses the underlying logic of the relationship between the brand and the customer.

Brand Focus

One of several options as to where to focus the brand identity may be appropriate for a company. We look at the features of each. The major alternatives include product line, corporate, and combination bonding.

Product Line Branding

This strategy places a brand name on one or more lines of related products representing different product categories (e.g., Crest toothpaste, brushes, and floss). This option provides focus and offers cost advantages by promoting the entire line rather than each product. One advantage of product line branding is that additional items (line extensions) can be introduced utilizing the established brand name.

Corporate Branding

This strategy builds brand identity using the corporate name to identify the entire product offering. Examples include IBM in computers, BMW in automobiles, and Victoria's Secret in intimate apparel. Corporate branding has the advantage of using one advertising and sales promotion program to support all of the firm's products. It also facilitates the introduction and promotion of new products. The shortcomings of corporate branding include a lack of focus on specific products and possible adverse effects on the product portfolio if the company encounters negative publicity for one of its products.

Combination Branding

A company may use a combination of product line and corporate branding. Sears, for example, employs both product-line and corporate branding (e.g., the Kenmore appliance and Craftsman tool lines). Combination branding benefits from the buyer's association of the corporate name with the product or line brand name.

Private Branding

Retailers with established brand names, such as Costco, Krogers, Target, and Wal-Mart Stores, Inc., contract with producers to manufacture and place the retailer's brand name on products sold by the retailer. Called private branding, the major advantage to the producer is eliminating the costs of marketing to end-users, although a private-label arrangement may make the manufacturer dependent on the firm using the private brand. Nevertheless, the arrangement can yield benefits to both the producer and the value chain member. The retailer uses its private brand to build store loyalty, since the private brand is associated with the retailer's stores.

Indeed, the power of retailers to challenge traditional leading brands is growing. AC Nielson research confirms that two-thirds of customers around the world believe that supermarkets' own brands are a good alternative to other brands.[23] Kumar and Steenkamp identify private labels as: (1) *"value"* or generic at a basic level; (2) *copycat brands,* which imitate the qualities of premium brands at a lower price; (3) *premium store brands,* which sell at the same or higher price as manufacturers' premium bands; or (4) *value innovators,* like IKEA, offering their unique value for money proposition.[24] Retailer market sensing in positioning different types of private labels and opening up new markets underlines an important challenge to traditional brand owners.

Identity Implementation

Identity implementation involves deciding the components of the brand identity and value proposition to be included in the brand position statement. These questions should be answered in formulating the identity implementation strategy:[25]

1. Select a brand position that will be favorably recognized by customers and will differentiate the brand from its competitors.
2. Determine the primary and secondary target audiences.
3. Select the primary communication objectives.
4. Determine the points of advantage.

Determination of the brand position is the core of the implementation strategy. This decision involves selecting the part of the core identity to be communicated to the target audiences, including points of leverage and key benefits.[26]

Managing Brand Strategy

Proactive efforts should be devoted to managing each brand over time. Analyzing performance shows how well the existing brand strategy is performing, helps management to identify new product needs, and points to where the existing strategy should be altered.

The challenging and dynamic process of successfully managing brand strategy is illustrated by Procter and Gamble and the lessons apparent in P&G strategy after the Gillette merger. These lessons are described in the INNOVATION FEATURE.

Brands that have been successful over a long time period offer useful insights about brand strategy management. Established brands like Budweiser, Hershey, IBM, and Intel continue to build strong market positions. The performance records of powerful brands are the result of: (1) marketing skills; (2) product quality; and (3) strong brand preference developed through years of successful advertising.[27] The brand equity that has been built for a company's brands is a valuable asset. A common characteristic of many enduring brands is that the targeting and positioning strategy initially selected has generally been followed during the life of each brand. Consistency in the marketing strategy over time is very important.[28]

Burberry PLC is an interesting example of the challenges of managing a brand over time. The Burberry plaid is one of the most recognized logos throughout the world.[29] The tan plaid performed a key role in transforming Burberry from a raincoat producer to a luxury fashion brand offering everything from dresses to dog collars. A new CEO joined the company in 2006, and quickly decided plaid overexposure was a major brand symbol problem. Part of a series of initiatives, Burberry is strategically diversifying into new icons. For example, an equestrian knight and the signature of founder Thomas Burberry are being added to handbags, shoes, and scarves. Importantly, the intent is to surpass rather than replace Burberry's trademark tartan.

Strategies for Improving Product Performance

Product improvement strategies include decisions for each product in the product line as shown in Exhibit 9.5. Product line actions may consist of adding a new product, reducing costs, improving the existing product, altering the marketing strategy, or dropping the product.

Additions to the Product Line

Management may decide to add a new product to the line to improve performance. As discussed in Chapter 8 the new product concept should be carefully evaluated before it is developed and introduced in the market.

Innovation Feature

P&G/Gillette's Branding Lessons

The P&G purchase of Gillette shows that innovation is key to branding and marketing is more diffuse and personal. Five new lessons for branding:

- **Innovate, Innovate, Innovate**—Why tinker with Tide? To build a widening family of detergents and cleaners including everything from Tide Coldwater for cold water washing to Tide Kick, a combination measuring cup and stain penetrator.
- **Move Fast or Lose Out**—Customers are hooked on innovation and demanding it faster.
- **Minimize Exposure to Wal-Mart**—Wal-Mart is the key customer for any consumer brand, but balancing those sales with plenty of others is vital to a brand's health—P&G has shifted business away from basic products like paper towels to higher-margin products like Olay skin care products.
- **The New Media Message**—P&G has mastered "surround-sound marketing"—using everything from in-store demos to pitches on Wal-Mart TV, to online innovations, to target specific customers and to fit the medium to the message.
- **Think Broadly**—P&G is a solver of problems in the home, and doesn't define itself by products. While toothpaste rival Colgate-Palmolive was focusing on the toothpaste tube, P&G grabbed greater "share of mouth" with innovations such as the inexpensive spin toothbrush and premium-priced Whitestrips teeth-whitening kits.

Source: Nanette Byrnes, Robert Berner, Wendy Zellner and William C. Symonds, "Branding: Five New Lessons," *BusinessWeek*, February 14, 2005, 26–28.

Cost Reduction

We know that lower costs give a company a major advantage over the competition. A product's cost may be reduced by changes in its design, manufacturing improvements, reduction of the cost of supplies, and improvements in marketing productivity. Costco, the warehouse retailer, is continually working to lower the costs of its products through inventory management, operating improvements, and other initiatives. Interestingly, Costco's average store sales are about double that of competing Sam's Club.

Product Improvement

Products are often improved by changing their features, quality, and styling. Automobile features and styles are modified on an annual basis. Many companies allocate substantial resources to the regular improvement of their products. Compared to a decade ago, today's products, such as disposable diapers, cameras, computers, and consumer electronics show vast improvements in performance and features. For example, the Skoda automobile brand was associated with low mechanical standards and reliability, until acquired by Volkswagen whose engineering and production expertise has transformed the Skoda product into one of the leading European brands.

EXHIBIT 9.5
Strategies for Improving Product Performance

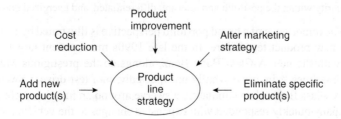

305

One way to differentiate a brand against competition is with unique *features*. Another option is to let the buyer customize the features desired in a product. Optional features offer the buyer more flexibility in selecting a brand. The capability to produce products with varied features that appeal to market diversity is an important competitive advantage.

Style may offer an important competitive edge for certain product categories. The impact of intangibles like style should not be underestimated. Trackers of trends have been surprised by the influence of Japanese design and culture in the 2000s. Japanese designs are impacting fields as diverse as toys (e.g., small dolls); cars (e.g., Toyota's gas-electric Prius); and fashion (e.g., Louis Vuitton's Murakami bags). Japanese-style comics called *manga,* as thick as paperback books, selling for $10 in Target and Borders, are at the center of pop culture, along with *anime,* the distinctive Japanese-style cartoons.[30]

Marketing Strategy Alteration

Changes in market targeting and positioning may be necessary as a product moves through its life cycle. However, the changes should be consistent with the core strategies. Problems or opportunities may point to adjusting the marketing strategy during a PLC stage. Tylenol's marketing strategy over its life cycle has been altered while maintaining a consistent positioning on its strong association with doctors and hospitals.

Product Elimination

Dropping a problem product may be necessary when cost reduction, product improvement, or marketing strategy initiatives are not feasible for improving poor performance of the product. In deciding to drop a product, management may consider a variety of performance criteria in addition to the product's sales and profit contribution. Elimination may occur at any PLC stage, although it is more likely to occur in either the introduction or decline stages. Risks are involved in eliminating products that have loyal buyers, so the exit strategy should be carefully planned and implemented.

Environmental Effects of Products

Environmental issues concerning product labeling, packaging, use, and disposal need to be considered. Protection of the environment involves a complex set of trade-offs among social, economic, political, and technology factors.

Managing the Brand Portfolio

Portfolio management is concerned with enhancing the performance of all the brands and product lines offered by a company. Initiatives include changing brand and product line priorities, adding new product lines or brands, and deleting product lines or brands. Companies that have several different brands and product categories should manage them as a portfolio rather than pursuing independent brand strategies:

> The brand portfolio strategy specifies the structure of the brand portfolio and the scope, roles, and interrelationships of the portfolio brands. The goals are to create synergy, leverage, clarity within the portfolio and relevant, differentiated, and energized brands.[31]

The importance of a brand portfolio perspective is illustrated by DaimlerBenz's response to a new product test failure. In the late 1990s management targeted the small car market with the new A-Class Baby Benz, alongside the prestigious Mercedes-Benz C- and E-Class lines.[32] In 1997, wholly unexpectedly, in a test drive a Swedish journalist rolled the A-Class Benz when simulating a swerve around an imaginary elk (the "Elk Test"). The company quickly responded with expensive changes to the vehicle including new tires and electronic stabilizing as standard. Nonetheless, after 3000 cancelled orders the car was taken off the market for three months to undertake chassis modifications. Rumors spread that the company had stretched itself too far too quickly to get into the mass car market. Nonetheless, the company survived the crisis and its responsive and careful approach protected the brand portfolio from long-term damage.

Determining Roles of Brands

A brand portfolio perspective encourages the use of brands to support the entire portfolio as well as the support of each brand:

> A key to managing brands in an environment of complexity is to consider them as not only individual performers, but members of a system of brands that must work to support one another. A brand system can serve as a launching platform for new products or brands and as a foundation for all brands in the system.[33]

The major objectives of brand portfolio management are shown in Exhibit 9.6. Importantly, the focus is the entire portfolio rather than specific brands.

Strategies for Brand Strength

A cohesive and clearly defined brand portfolio is essential to achieving strong portfolio performance. The importance of a strategic brand management perspective is described:

> Brand portfolio strategy becomes especially critical as brand contexts are complicated by multiple segments, multiple products, varied competitor types, complex distribution channels, multiple brand extensions, and the wider use of endorsed brands and sub-brands.[34]

Nestlē, the world's largest food company, has over 8,000 brands.[35] Starting in 2001 management pursued initiatives to streamline operations to reduce cost, strengthen key product groups via acquisitions, outsource activities such as tomato canning and pasta production, and develop new products. By 2003, $1.5 billion in cost reductions had been achieved. Some critics observe that significantly expanded marketing expenditures may offset the cost reductions.

Strategies for building brand strength and sustaining that strength for the brand portfolio require attention to the implementation of brand identification, revitalizing brands in the later stages of their life cycles, and recognizing the strategic vulnerabilities of core brands to competitive attack or changing market conditions.

EXHIBIT 9.6
Brand Portfolio Management Objectives

Source: David A. Aaker, *Building Strong Brands,* New York: The Free Press, 1996, 241–242.

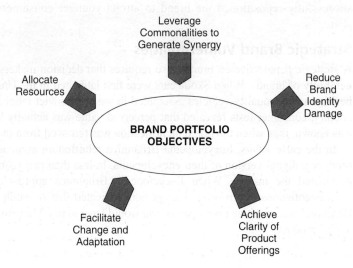

Leverage Commonalities to Generate Synergy

Allocate Resources

Reduce Brand Identity Damage

BRAND PORTFOLIO OBJECTIVES

Facilitate Change and Adaptation

Achieve Clarity of Product Offerings

Adding a New Line

The motivation for adding a new product line may be to:

- Increase the growth rate of the business.
- Offer a more complete range of products to wholesalers and retailers.
- Gain marketing strength and economies in distribution, advertising, and personal selling.
- Leverage an existing brand position.
- Avoid dependence on one product line or category.

The product portfolio may be expanded through internal development or by purchase of an entire company or a line of products. Purchase may be a favorable option compared to the costs of internal development. Acquisition is also a faster means of expanding the product mix. Strategic alliances may also be used to expand product lines.

Brand Building Strategies

The essence of strategies for brand strength is that management should actively "build, maintain, and manage the four assets that underlie brand equity—awareness, perceived quality, brand loyalty, and brand association."[36] Critical to this process is developing the brand identification strategy and implementing that identity throughout the company and the marketplace.

Attention is frequently needed in coordinating the brand identity across the organization, the various media it uses, and the different markets and segments it serves.[37] For example, IBM's corporate brand identifies a great number of products and company divisions in diverse end-user markets. The challenge is to implement the brand identification consistently across these different situations. The risk of failing to do so is customer confusion and reduced brand equity.

Brand Revitalization

Mature brands that are important in the company's overall strategy may require rejuvenation. For example, Procter & Gamble's Oil of Olay has a fifty-three-year-old brand history and retains a strong position in the skin care market by adding products that link to the brand heritage.[38] Similarly, when P&G acquired the mature Old Spice men's fragrance brand, it was underperforming in its target market of older consumers. P&G successfully repositioned the brand to attract younger consumers and rebuilt market share.[39]

Strategic Brand Vulnerabilities

A strategic perspective on brands also requires that decision makers be aware of the vulnerability of brands. When Skoda cars were first launched in the United Kingdom, with a heritage of low quality vehicles assembled in part by convict labor in a then-Communist country, consumer tests revealed that perceived value was actually lower when the brand was known, than when the brand identification was removed from the cars.

In the early 1990s, Encyclopedia Britannica rebuffed an approach from Microsoft to produce a digital version of their encyclopedia. In less than two years Microsoft's Encarta dominated the market. When Encyclopedia Britannica approached Microsoft to re-open negotiations, Microsoft's management indicated that research findings showed that Britannica had negative brand equity and would have to pay Microsoft to have its name on a joint product.[40]

Strategy Feature
Limited Brands Shifts its Focus from Apparel to Accessories

- Ten years ago apparel represented 70 percent of Limited's sales. By 2005, 70 percent of sales were from skin-care products, cosmetics, and lingerie.
- Clothes are increasingly out of fashion—after declines for three years, U.S. apparel sales increased only 4 percent in 2004 to $172.8 billion.
- Apparel dollar sales declines are due to discount pricing and households spending more on electronics, home improvement, and spa services.
- Limited is trying to make itself over as a high-end Procter & Gamble.
- Victoria's Secret is adding hair and cosmetics lines to its beauty business (has three of the top ten selling fragrances in the U.S.).
- One new product is "Tutti Dolci" (all sweets), food-inspired scents—lotion and lip gloss in fragrances like lemon meringue, angel-food cake, and chocolate fondue.
- Victoria's Secret has also accelerated new product development.
- From 2003 through 2005 Intimate Brands (lingerie and beauty products) accounted for all the corporation's operating income.
- Limited is also partnering with other companies to sell its brands and develop new products.
- Limited has three business groups:
  - Beauty and Personal Care
  - Lingerie
  - Apparel
- Apparel is a continuing challenge with 2004 operating margins at 1.4 percent compared to over 19 percent for Bath & Body Works and Victoria's Secret.
- Limited has about 3,700 stores. 2005 sales were nearly $9.7 billion with net profits at $51 million.

Sources: Limited Brands 2005 Annual Report; Value Line Investment Survey; and Amy Merrick, "For Limited Brands Clothes Become the Accessories," *The Wall Street Journal*, March 8, 2005, A1 and A14.

Proactive market sensing efforts by a company are essential in identifying and responding to strategic brand vulnerabilities. For example, in the mid-1990s Limited Brands, the specialty apparel retailer, determined that the apparel market was becoming very competitive and unprofitable. Management perceptively recognized that Limited's brand emphasis should shift from apparel to accessories as described in the STRATEGY FEATURE. Interestingly, in early 2007 there was speculation that the retailer was considering the sale of its apparel brands.

An important issue in managing brand portfolios is deciding how many brands should comprise the system. Four questions are relevant in deciding whether to introduce a new brand name:

1. Is the brand sufficiently different to merit a new name?
2. Will a new name really add value?
3. Will the existing brand be placed at risk if it is used on a new product?
4. Will the business support a new brand name?[41]

Brand Leveraging Strategy

Established brand names may be useful to introduce other products by linking the new product to an existing brand name. The primary advantage is immediate name recognition for the new product. Methods of capitalizing on an existing brand name include line extension, stretching the brand vertically, brand extension, co-branding, and licensing.

Line Extension

This leveraging strategy consists of offering additional items in the same product class or category as the core brand. Extensions may include new flavors, forms, colors, and package sizes. Coca-Cola Blak (Coffee Coke) is an example. The primary danger is overextending the line and weakening the brand equity. Many new products are line extensions.

Line extensions are attractive options for many companies. They help expand the market opportunity for the product line by offering more variety. The extensions are useful in countering competitors' efforts. Some extensions may encourage cannibalization as illustrated by Gillette's introduction of its Fusion razor in 2006. It will attract sales from the Mach3 razor although Fusion's higher price may discourage purchases. Soundly conceived and well-executed extensions strengthen the brand's position in the marketplace. However, relying on line extensions as the primary basis for innovation may be risky.

Stretching the Brand Vertically[42]

This form of line extension may include moving up or down in price/quality from the core brand. It may involve sub-brands that vary in price and features. The same name may be used (e.g., BMW 300, 500, 700), or the brand name linked less directly (Courtyard by Marriott). The advantages of this strategy include expanded market opportunities, shared costs, and leveraging distinctive capabilities. The primary limitations are damage to the core brand when moving lower (e.g., lower price/quality versions of a premium brand) or difficulty in moving the brand to a higher price/quality level.

Moving the brand down is more likely to affect buyers' perceptions than other brand management options. It is an attractive option because of the size of the lower price/quality market, and this initiative is relatively easy to pursue since it benefits from the image of the higher level brand. Gap tried it with its discount Gap but quickly recognized the risks exceeded the benefits and instead launched Old Navy. Several risks of moving down are shown in Exhibit 9.7.

Moving the brand up is also risky. Pursuing a questionable vertical move upward in price and quality, Volkswagen introduced its luxury $75,000 sedan in the U.S. in late 2003, investing $1 billion to develop the Phaeton. VW has a strong brand image but not the right logo for a luxury automobile. Moreover, Phaeton was competing with VW's Audi A8 luxury sedan. In late 2005 management announced plans to withdraw the Phaeton from the U.S. market, and its future in Europe was questionable.

EXHIBIT 9.7
Moving Down Is Easy but Risky

Source: Aaker, *Building Strong Brands* (New York: The Free Press, 1996), 279–281.

- Affects perceptions of the brand—perhaps even more significantly than other brand management options.
  We are influenced more by unfavorable information than by favorable information.
- The brand's ability to deliver self-expressive benefits may be reduced.
- Potential cannibalization problem.
- Potential failure risk.
- Problem when the line extension is perceived to be inconsistent with the quality expected from the brand.

Brand Extension

This form of leveraging benefits from buyers' familiarity with an existing brand name in a product class to launch a new product line in another product class.[43] The new line may or may not be closely related to the brand from which it is being extended. Examples of related extensions include Ivory shampoo and conditioner, Nike apparel, and Swiss Army watches. Critics of brand extensions indicate that these initiatives often do not succeed and may damage the core brand. There are several potential risks associated with brand extensions: (1) diluting existing brand associations; (2) creating undesirable attribute associations; (3) failure of the new brand to deliver on its promise; (4) an unexpected incident (e.g., product recall); and (5) cannibalization of the brand franchise.[44] Among the more successful brand extensions of the 1990s were the various lines of Healthy Choice foods.

Regardless of the possible dangers of brand extension, it continues to be very popular. Two considerations are important. There should be a logical tie between the core brand and the extension. It may be a different product type while having some relationship to the core brand. The extension also needs to be carefully evaluated as to any negative impact on the brand equity of the core brand.

An interesting example of how the Virgin Group in the United Kingdom is extending the brand into new industries is described in the RELATIONSHIP FEATURE. Sir Richard Branson, CEO of Virgin Group, launched Virgin USA, a discount airline, in 2007.

Co-Branding

This strategy consists of two well-known brands working together in promoting their products. The brand names are used in various promotional efforts. Airline co-branding alliances with credit card companies are illustrative. The advantage is leveraging the customer bases of the two brands. Joint products may be involved or instead a composite product may be co-branded.

Co-branding may involve business-to-business partners although, more commonly co-branding is used to link consumer brands. Disney, for example, is co-branding breakfast cereals, toaster pastries and waffles with Kellogg, as well as Disney Xtreme! Coolers with Minute Maid.[45]

"Co-branding occurs when brands from different organizations (or distinctly different businesses within the same organization) combine to create an offering in which brands from each play a driver role."[46] Promotional budgets can be shared and new product introductions facilitated. The important challenge is selecting the right brand combination and coordinating the implementation between two independent companies. An effective co-branding arrangement is a strong competitive strategy.

Licensing

Another popular method of using the core brand name is licensing. The sale of a firm's brand name to another company for use on a non-competing product is a major business activity. The firm granting the license obtains additional revenue with only limited costs. It also gains free publicity for the core brand name. The main limitation to licensing is that the licensee may create an unfavorable image for the brand. Licensing may be used for corporate, product line, or specific brands.

Global Branding

Companies operating in international markets face various strategic branding challenges. For example, European multinational Unilever reduced its brand portfolio from 1,600 to 400, to focus on its strong global brands like Lipton, while acquiring more global brands for its portfolio: SlimFast, Ben & Jerry's Homemade, and Bestfoods (Knorr, Hellmans). The company's global brand strategy is intended to position it favorably with international retailers.[47]

An Experienced Virgin

Virgin Group is one of the greatest examples of extending a brand into new industries without diverging from its core values—irreverent, unconventional, creative, entertaining, active. "Each time Virgin entered a new business," explains John Mathers, director, Sampson Tyrrell Enterprise, "all the commercial pundits suggested it was stretching the brand too far. They reasoned that few people would want to buy financial services, for example, from a youth brand with a rock and roll image." But ever since its inception in the early 1970s, Virgin has been racking up an impressive number of notches on its corporate bedpost.

Virgin's businesses now include book publishing, radio and television broadcasting, hotel management, entertainment retail, trading and investments, and an airline—"a highly successful migration of core values that are very much the product of an ideology," says Interbrand's Tom Blackett.

Andrew Welch of Landor cites an example of how the Virgin megastore in Paris has been able to transcend its boundaries of being purely a retailer: "It has become a temple for young consumers and youth culture. Paris youth place their trust in Virgin for guidance on what is contemporary culture. As such, Virgin is considered the consummate specialist in all things for youth fashion and fashionability."

"Virgin has succeeded in many markets in creating a new reality that its competitors have been compelled to follow because it touches the consumer in a fundamental way," summarizes Blackett, "which may actually be the key to shaking up mature environments in the future."

Source: Excerpt from Stephen J. Garone, *Managing Reputation with Image and Brands* (New York: The Conference Board, 1998), 11. Reprinted with permission from The Conference Board.

Increasingly cosmopolitan consumers in many countries with similar tastes drawn from exposure to similar media and the economies of scale of global brand identification and communications, encourage the development of global brands. However, global brand identity may also create barriers to building strong identification with local markets, so both a global and local perspective may be important.

Aaker and Joachimsthaler argue that global brand strategy is often misguided, and the priority should not be building global brands (although they may result). Instead, the priority should be working for global brand leadership—strong brands in all markets supported by effective, strategic global brand management.[48] Nonetheless, this may involve different approaches to those successful in the domestic market.

Multinational operations increasingly face the challenge of managing brand portfolios containing global, regional and national brands. For example, Nestlé manages a four-level brand portfolio: ten worldwide corporate brands (e.g., Nestlé, Carnation, Buitoni); forty-five worldwide strategic brands (e.g., KitKat, Polo, Coffee-Mate) which are the responsibility of general management at the strategic business unit level; 140 regional strategic brands (e.g., Stouffers, Contadina, Findus) which are the responsibility of strategic business units and regional management; and 7,500 local brands (e.g., Texicana, Brigadeiro, Rocky) which are the responsibility of managers in local markets.[49] While some observers believe Nestlé's brand strategy may be overly complex, the performance of the world's largest food company has been favorable.

Internet Brands

Some controversy surrounds the issue of branding on the Internet, relating mainly to the sustainability of brands that exist only on the Internet, but extending to how the Web can

The Web provides those hostile to a company or a brand an international distribution system, no barriers to entry, and little censorship or accountability. Unofficial websites and blogs are set up to scrutinize individual companies, creating online communities where customers and employees can share information and vent opinions. The dilemma for companies is if, and how, to respond.

- Companies like Lenovo, Southwest Airlines and Dell have specialists dedicated to engaging or co-opting online critics.
- Dell has made blogger outreach such a discipline, the company's team sat down in Austin, Texas for drinks with the blogger who ignited the Dell Hell customer-service crusade with his rants about the company.
- Companies like BuzzLogic use algorithms to analyze which bloggers and social media are driving the conversation around issues that matter to brand owners.
- Home Depot found itself being accused of being a "consistent abuser" of peoples' time by an MSN columnist, which sparked 10,000 angry e-mails and 4,000 Web posts. A heartfelt and repentant online apology letter was sent to all Home Depot customers.

Sources: Michell Conlin, "Web Attack," *BusinessWeek,* April 16, 2007, 54–56; Allison Enright, "Knock, Knock: Who's There?" *Marketing News,* June 1, 2007, 11–12.

impact the brand equity of conventional brands. It is all but impossible for the decision maker to ignore the linkage between the brand and the Internet. Interestingly, successful online brands may be those adopting brand strategies that rely on traditional, offline forms of communications. For example, the career website Monster.com makes successful use of sponsoring the halftime report at the Super Bowl backed by advertising spots in the pre-game and during the game. Monster's target is men and women aged 18 to 49, and the Super Bowl event gives excellent coverage, which coincides with the time of the year when many people are thinking of changing their jobs.[50]

The Internet can play a pivotal role in enhancing brand relationships and corporate reputation, by offering customers a new degree of interactivity with the brand, and speed and adaptability in the relationship-building process.[51] Nonetheless, interactivity also brings threats to the brand to which brand managers may need to respond. The INTERNET FEATURE describes some of the attributes of blogs in relation to brands.

While much remains to be learned about the requirements for effective brand building on the Internet, these initiatives should be included in strategic brand management responsibilities.

Brand Theft

Counterfeit brands represent a huge global business that negatively impacts authentic brands. The fakes negatively impact brand equity and attract sales from the real brands. A wide range of fake brands are sold including software, apparel, electronics, watches, and many other products. Much of the counterfeit merchandise is produced in China, although other Asian countries are also involved in the value chain. Microsoft estimates it loses $10 billion a year from pirated software, and that around half its branded products used in businesses and homes are illegal.

Counterfeiting is as profitable as selling drugs and much less likely to result in major jail terms if participants are arrested. Software is a very attractive product since it is easy to copy for fake sales. Law enforcement officials are far more interested in drug trafficking than fake goods. The high margins and lower law enforcement concerns have attracted organized crime to distribution of counterfeit brands.

Passing off counterfeits as genuine is easier on the Internet because customers cannot physically inspect the goods, and they are often sold under the image of the genuine product. Internet counterfeiters are hard to trace.

- The Internet is estimated to account for 14 percent ($90 billion) of the annual $624 billion global counterfeit trade.
- There is a booming trade in online sales of counterfeit medicines and pharmaceuticals, particularly "lifestyle" drugs like Viagra to treat impotence.
- World Wrestling Entertainments (WWE) is one of many brand owners struggling to stem the tide of counterfeit goods sold over the Internet.
- Every morning WWE goes online to find about 3,500 auctions selling fake WWE t-shirts, DVDs and other accessories.
- Estimates suggest 90 percent of Louis Vuitton and Christian Dior items listed on eBay are fakes. The brand owners are suing eBay.
- The "brand new" Vuitton holdall bag listed at $188 on eBay is certainly cheap compared to the genuine article which retails at $885 in select stores like Neiman Marcus.
- A French court in 2005 ordered Google Inc. to pay nearly $400,000 in damages to Vuitton/Dior owner LVMH because the search engine had displayed advertising from merchants selling fake Vuitton goods.

Sources: Maija Palmer, "Cyberspace Fakes Make Brands Truly Worried," *Financial Times,* Wednesday, April 11, 2007, 10. Eric Schine, "Faking Out the Fakers," *BusinessWeek,* June 4, 2007, 76–80. Carol Matlack, "Fed Up With Fakes," *BusinessWeek,* October 9, 2006, 56–57.

Brand counterfeiting has been fueled by the ease with which counterfeit products can be sold on the Internet—it is estimated that counterfeit trade on the Internet is worth $90 billion a year. The ETHICS FEATURE describes some aspects of the online counterfeit brand threat.

Summary

Strategic brand management provides guidelines in selecting strategies for each of the components of the positioning strategy, forming the leading edge of efforts to influence buyers' positioning of the company's brands. Brand strategy needs to be matched to the right value chain, pricing, and promotion strategies. Product decisions shape both corporate and marketing strategies, and are made within the guidelines of the corporate mission and objectives. The major product decisions for a strategic business unit include selecting the mix of products to be offered, deciding how to position a SBU's product offering, developing and implementing strategies for the products in the portfolio, selecting the branding strategy for each product, and managing the brand portfolio.

Most successful corporations assign an individual or organizational unit responsibility for strategic brand management. Product managers for planning and coordinating product activities are used by many companies, although new customer- and market-based structures are increasing in popularity.

Brand equity is a valuable asset that requires continuous attention to build and protect the brand's value. The equity of a brand includes both its assets and liabilities, including brand loyalty, name awareness, perceived quality, brand associations, and proprietary brand assets. Increasingly, companies are measuring brand equity to help guide product portfolio strategies, and adopting regular brand health checks. Mature brands may require specific revitalization approaches. Managers must be aware also of existing and emerging strategic brand vulnerabilities.

Analysis of a company's brand strategy helps to establish priorities and guidelines for managing the product portfolio. The analysis methods include portfolio screening, analysis of the product life cycle, product performance analysis, positioning analysis, and financial analysis. It is necessary to decide for each product if: (1) a new product should be developed to replace or complement the product; (2) the product should be improved (and, if so, how); or (3) the product should be eliminated. Strategy alternatives for the existing products include cost reduction, product alteration, marketing strategy changes, and product elimination. Product mix modification may also occur.

Strategic brand management is guided by brand equity value and brand strategy analysis. The strategy consists of: (1) brand identity strategy; (2) managing each brand over time; (3) managing the brand portfolio; and (4) leveraging the brand. These interrelated initiatives need to be managed as a process.

Brand identity may focus on the product, the organization, a person, or a symbol. The brand identification used by a firm involves deciding among corporate branding, product-line branding, specific product branding, and combination branding. Brand identification in the marketplace offers a firm an opportunity to gain a strategic advantage through brand equity building and brand leveraging opportunities.

Each brand needs to be managed over time but coordinated and integrated with the brands in the portfolio. Management is concerned with the combination and effectiveness of brands in the portfolio. Each brand should contribute to the portfolio as well as benefiting from it. The objective should be to coordinate strategies across the portfolio rather than managing each brand on an independent basis.

Opportunities for leveraging brands include line extensions in the existing product class, extending the line vertically up or down, extending the brand to different product classes, co-branding with other brands, and licensing the brand name. Line extensions are widely used alongside the other forms of leveraging. For companies with international operations, additional concerns relate to global branding issues. Increasingly, attention is also required to the role of the Internet in implementing brand identification. Brand theft is an escalating challenge on a global basis.

Questions for Review and Discussion

1. Eli Lilly & Company manufactures a broad line of pharmaceuticals with strong brand positions in the marketplace. Lilly is also a manufacturer of generic drug products. Is this combination branding strategy a logical one? If so, why?

2. Discuss the advantages and limitations of following a branding strategy of using brand names for specific products.

3. What is the role of strategic brand analysis in building strong brands?

4. To what extent are the SBU strategy and the product strategy interrelated?

5. Suppose that a top administrator of a university wants to establish a product-management function covering both new and existing services. Develop a plan for establishing a product planning program.

6. Many products like Jell-O reach maturity. Discuss several ways to give mature products new vigor. How can management determine whether it is worthwhile to attempt to salvage products that are performing poorly?

7. How does improving product quality lower the cost of producing a product?

8. Why do some products experience long successful lives while others have very short life cycles?

9. How can a company combine the strengths of global brands with the need to adapt to local market requirements in a multinational operation?

10. Discuss the underlying logic of managing brand portfolios.

11. What are the strengths and limitations in moving the Marriott brand vertically upward and downward in terms of price and quality?

Internet Applications

A. Examine the Fortune Brands website (www.fortunebrands.com). Analyze and evaluate the strategic initiatives used by Fortune Brands in their strategic brand management.

B. Visit the website of lastminute.com (www.lastminute.com). Map the business model used by this Web brand. Review the strengths and weaknesses of the model, and consider how the brand has been established and how it may be extended.

C. Go to www.e4m.biz, operated by the UK's Marketing Council. Register at the site and choose the Business-to-Consumer area, and the Brand Consistency option under Strategy Area. Review several of the short cases describing how major companies are striving for consistency in their brand identification while using multiple channels including the Internet. What conclusions can you draw regarding the requirements for brand consistency across multiple channels?

D. Visit the Yahoo Inc. website. Describe Yahoo's brand portfolio.

Feature Applications

A. Review the BMW GLOBAL FEATURE. What are the important issues confronting BMW's management in managing the company's brand portfolio? How can a brand portfolio perspective assist in meeting these challenges?

B. The RELATIONSHIP FEATURE describing the brand extension initiatives of Virgin Group indicates entry into many new markets, several of which are unrelated. Have the different markets created any problems for the extension initiatives?

Notes

1. This illustration is based in part on Katrina Brooker, "The Pepsi Machine," *Fortune,* February 6, 2006, 68–72

2. Stephen L. Vargo and Robert F. Lusch, "Evolving to a New Dominant Logic for Marketing," *Journal of Marketing,* January 2004, 1–17.

3. Gina Chon, "Ailing Saab Seeks Turnaround by Touting Aviation Roots," *The Wall Street Journal,* October 21, 2005, B1 and B6.

4. The discussion in this section is based on Pierre Berthon, James M. Hulbert and Leyland F. Pitt, *Brands, Brand Managers, and the Management of Brands: Where to Next?* Boston, MA: *Marketing Science Institute,* Report No. 97–122, 1997.

5. "The 100 Top Brands," *BusinessWeek,* August 7, 2006, 60–61.

6. Neal E. Boudette, "BMW's Push to Broaden Line Hits Some Bumps in the Road," *The Wall Street Journal,* January 10, 2005, A1 and A7.

7. David A. Aaker, *Building Strong Brands* (New York: The Free Press, 1996), 26–35.

8. Berthon et al. *Brand Managers and the Management of Brands.*

9. David A. Aaker, *Building Strong Brands* (New York: The Free Press, 1996), 26–35.

10. Ibid., 68.

11. Jim Carlton, "Apple Drops Newton, An Idea Ahead of Its Time," *The Wall Street Journal,* March 2, 1998, B1 and B8.

12. Robert Cooper and Robert S. Kaplan, "Measure Costs Right: Make the Right Decisions," *Harvard Business Review,* September-October 1998, 96–103.

13. Bernard Simon, "Scion Brand Greases the Wheels for Toyota," *Financial Times,* Wednesday, April 26, 2006, 10.

14. David A. Aaker, *Managing Brand Equity* (New York: The Free Press, 1991), 15.

15. Kevin L. Keller, *Strategic Brand Management,* 2nd ed. (Upper Saddle River, NJ: Prentice Hall, 2003), 509–511.

16. Kevin Lane Keller, "The Brand Report Card," *Harvard Business Review,* January/February 2000, 147–157.

17. Ibid., 148–149.

18. Noel Capon and James M. Hulbert, *Marketing Management in the 21st Century* (Upper Saddle River, NJ: Prentice-Hall, 2001).

19. Aaker, *Building Strong Brands,* 68.

20. This discussion is based on Aaker, *Building Strong Brands,* Chapter 3.

21. Don E. Schultz, "Getting to the Heart of the Brand," *Marketing Management* September/October 2000, 8–9.

22. Aaker, *Building Strong Brands,* 102.

23. Stefan Stern, "Quality Becomes Commodity in Brand Battle," *Financial Times,* Wednesday, March 14, 2007, 12.

24. Nirmalya Kumar, Jan-Benedict, and E. M. Steenkamp, *Private Label Strategy* (Cambridge, MA: Harvard Business School Press, 2007).

25. Aaker, *Building Strong Brands,* 183.

26. Ibid., Chapter 6.

27. Ronald Alsop, "Enduring Brands Hold Their Allure by Sticking Close to Their Roots," *The Wall Street Journal,* Centennial Edition.

28. Ibid.

29. Cecilie Rohwedder, "Burberry's New CEO Seeks Alternate Brand Symbols as Famed Tartan Grows Trite," *The Wall Street Journal,* July 7, 2006, B1, B3.

30. Christopher Palmeri and Nanette Byrnes, "Is Japanese Style Taking Over the World?" *BusinessWeek,* July 26, 2004, 96–98.

31. David A. Aaker, *Brand Portfolio Strategy* (New York: The Free Press, 2004), 13.

32. David Woodruff, "A-Class Damage Control at DaimlerBenz," *BusinessWeek,* November 24, 1997, 62. Rufus Olins and Matthew Lynn, "A-Class Disaster," *Sunday Times,* November 16, 1997, 54.

33. Aaker, *Building Strong Brands,* 241.

34. Aaker, *Brand Portfolio Strategy,* 13.

35. "Nestle Is Starting to Slim Down at Last," *BusinessWeek,* October 27, 2003, 56–57.

36. Aaker, *Building Strong Brands,* 35.

37. Ibid., 340.

38. Dana James, "Rejuvenating Mature Brands Can Be a Stimulating Exercise," *Marketing News,* August 16, 1999, 16–17.

39. James Heckman, "Don't Let the Fat Lady Sing: Smart Strategies Revive Dead Brands," *Marketing News,* January 4, 1999, 1.

40. L. Downes and C. Mui, *Unleashing the Killer App: Digital Strategies for Market Dominance* (Boston, MA: Harvard Business School Press, 1998).

41. Aaker, *Building Strong Brands,* 264–266.

42. Aaker, *Brand Portfolio Strategy,* Chapter 7.

43. Ibid.

44. Ibid., 210–213.

45. Stephanie Thompson, "The Mouse in the Food Aisle," *Advertising Age,* September 10, 2001, 73.

46. Aaker, *Brand Portfolio Strategy,* 20.

47. Richard Tomkins, "Manufacturers Strike Back," *Financial Times,* June 16, 2000, 14.

48. David A. Aaker and Erich Joachimsthaler, *Brand Leadership* (New York, The Free Press, 2000).

49. "A Dedicated Enemy of Fashion," *The Economist,* August 31, 2002, 47–48; A. J. Parsons, "Nestle: The Visions of Local Managers," *The McKinsey Quarterly,* No. 2 1996, 5–29

50. Michael Krauss, "Monster.com Exec Shares Vision for Brand," *Marketing News,* May 1, 2004, 6.

51. Larry Chiagouris and Brant Wansley, "Branding on the Internet," *Marketing Management,* Summer 2000, 34–38.

Chapter 10

Value Chain Strategy

The group of vertically aligned organizations that add value to a good or service in moving from basic supplies to finished products for consumer and organizational end users is the value chain. Strategic choices in value chain options are an important part of market-driven strategy. We use the term *value chain* in preference to others, which describe distribution activities from other perspectives (such as that of manufacturing or operations functions) to underline the central purpose of superior customer value. Terms such as physical distribution management, logistics, distribution, and supply chain management are all used to identify certain aspects of the value chain and its management, as well as new organizational units found in many companies. The term value chain focuses attention on the whole system of processes, activities, organizations, and structures that combine to create value for customers as products move from their point of origin to the end-user.

The value chain (or network) is the configuration of distribution channels linking value chain members with end-users. We examine the decisions faced by a company in developing a channel of distribution strategy. Channels of distribution are a central issue in managing the value chain. An effective and efficient distribution channel provides the member organizations with an important strategic edge over competitors. Distribution strategy concerns how a firm reaches its market targets. We also emphasize the need for marketing decision makers to incorporate into their thinking the impact of innovations in supply chain strategy and digital channels. An important goal is maintaining the ability of the market-driven company to realign its value chain, when this is necessary to meet the changing needs of its customers and markets.

The strategic importance of value chain decisions and realignment is illustrated by developments at Dell Inc. in the computer business. Throughout the 1990s and early 2000s, Dell was renowned for the power of the "Dell direct business model." Leveraging outstanding supply chain efficiency, Dell delivered superior value to (mainly corporate) customers through a flow model, in which customer orders generate the production and assembly of the product. The direct business model allows customers more choices in specifying products to their precise needs, and reduces stocks held in the value chain to an absolute minimum—Dell can run its global operation on five or six days' stock. The Internet provides Dell with direct access to the supply base for computers and components and links to major customers that promote superior learning and responsiveness to customer needs.

Nonetheless, Dell now faces slowing sales growth, loss of market share to Hewlett-Packard, and new competitive imperatives. In key target markets like China, the direct model is not favored by customers who prefer personal service—and unofficial re-sellers have developed. Low levels of service associated with the direct model have attracted increasing criticism, particularly in the consumer market. Faced with these challenges,

Dell is broadening its business model to target computer re-sellers—specialty vendors who design and install computer systems for corporate customers. In addition, Dell is developing a global retail strategy that includes selling computers in Wal-Mart stores. Experimental Dell own-branded stores are expected to expand, along with the kiosks located inside shopping malls. Redesigning its value chain strategy is critical to Dell achieving its strategic goals, particularly in overseas markets, and rebuilding its competitive position.[1]

We look at the role of the value chain in marketing strategy and discuss several channel strategy issues. Next, we examine the process of selecting the type of channel, determining the intensity of distribution, and choosing the channel configuration of organizations. A discussion of managing the distribution channel follows. We then look at distributing through international channels.

Strategic Role of Value Chain

A good distribution network creates a strong competitive advantage for an organization. In Chapter 7 we discussed partnering between international airlines to gain market access. However, the airlines example also underlines the impact of the Internet on distribution channels. For example, for a growing number of airlines, an e-mailed reservation number has replaced the multi-part ticket that the traveler had to collect from a travel agent or receive through the mail. Significantly, European no-frills airlines like easyJet and Ryanair are working to achieve 100 percent direct Internet booking and ticketing, replacing the traditional functions of the travel agent. Channels are a major element of how airlines compete. We consider the impact of digital channels as part of the choice executives face in developing distribution strategy.

We describe the distribution functions in the channel and then look at the distribution of services. We also examine several factors affecting the choice of whether to use distribution intermediaries or go direct to end users.

Distribution Functions

The *channel of distribution* is a network of value chain organizations performing functions that connect goods and services with end-users. The distribution channel consists of *interdependent* and *interrelated* institutions and agencies, functioning as a system or network, cooperating in their efforts to produce and distribute a product to end-users. Examples of channels of distribution for consumer and industrial products are shown in Exhibit 10.1. Direct and indirect channels may both have digital or Internet-based elements. Commonly, a company may use several channel links to reach different types of customers. In addition to the intermediaries that are shown, many facilitating organizations perform services, such as financial institutions, transportation firms, advertising agencies, and insurance firms.

Several value-added activities are necessary in moving products from producers to end-users. *Buying and selling* activities by marketing intermediaries reduce the number of transactions for producers and end-users. *Assembly* of products into inventory helps to meet buyers' time-of-purchase and variety preferences. *Transportation* eliminates the locational gap between buyers and sellers, thus accomplishing the physical distribution function. *Financing* facilitates the exchange function. *Processing and storage* of goods involves breaking large quantities into individual orders, maintaining inventory, and assembling orders for shipment. *Advertising and sales promotion* communicate product availability, location, and features. *Pricing* sets the basis of exchange between buyer and seller. *Reduction of risk* is accomplished through mechanisms such as insurance, return policies,

EXHIBIT 10.1
Value Chain
Structures

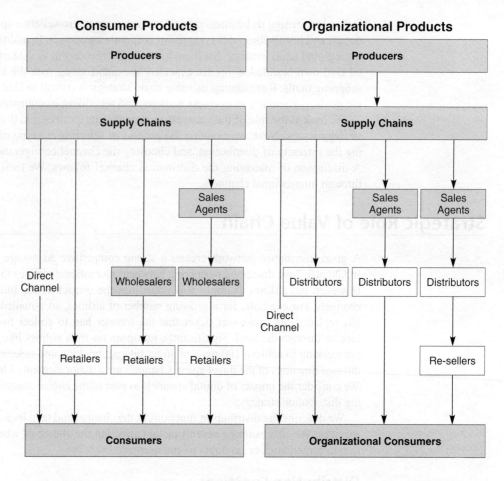

and futures trading. *Personal selling* provides sales, information, and supporting services. *Communications* between buyers and sellers include personal selling contacts, written orders and confirmations, and other information flows. Finally, *servicing and repairs* are essential for many types of products. Increasingly, the Internet provides an enabling and information-sharing technology, changing the way in which these value-adding functions are carried out.

Developing the channel strategy includes determining the functions that are needed and which organizations will be responsible for each function. Middlemen offer important cost and time advantages in the distribution of a wide range of products.

When first selecting a channel of distribution for a new product, the pricing strategy and desired positioning of the product may influence the choice of the channel. For example, a decision to use a premium price and a symbolic positioning concept calls for retail stores that buyers will associate with this image. For example, while the consumer can view and configure alternative models on the company's Web page, it is not possible to buy a new Rolex watch on the Internet.

Once the channel-of-distribution design is complete and responsibilities for performing the various marketing functions are assigned, these decisions establish guidelines for pricing, advertising, and personal selling strategies. For example, the manufacturers' prices must take into account the requirements and functions of middlemen as well as pricing practices in the channel. Likewise, promotional efforts must be matched to the various channel participants' requirements and capabilities. Consumer-products manufacturers often direct advertising to consumers to help *pull* products through distribution channels. Alternatively, promotion may be concentrated on middlemen to help *push* the product through the channel. Intermediaries may also need help in planning their marketing efforts and other supporting activities.

Channels for Services

Services such as air travel, banking, entertainment, health care, and insurance often involve distribution channels. The service provider renders the service to the end-users rather than it being produced like a good and moved through marketing intermediaries to the end-user. Because of this the distribution networks for services differ somewhat from those used for goods. While channels for services may not require as many levels (e.g., producer, distributor, retailer), the network may actually be more complex.

The objectives of channels for services are similar to those for goods, although the functions performed in channels differ somewhat from those for goods. Services are normally rendered when needed rather than placed into inventory. Similarly, services may not be transported although the service provider may go to the user's location to render the service. Processing and storage are normally not involved with services. Servicing and repair functions may not apply to many services. The other functions previously discussed apply to both goods and services (e.g., buying and selling, financing, advertising and sales promotion, pricing, reduction of risk (e.g., lost baggage insurance), and communications).

Direct Distribution by Manufacturers

We consider channel of distribution strategy from a manufacturer's point of view, although many of the strategic issues apply to firms at any level in the value chain—supplier, wholesale, or retail. Manufacturers are unique because they may have the option of going directly to end-users through a company salesforce or serving end-users through marketing intermediaries. Manufacturers have three distribution alternatives: (1) direct distribution; (2) use of intermediaries; or (3) situations in which both (1) and (2) are feasible. The Internet direct channel makes alternative (1) open to many more companies. The factors that influence the distribution decision include buyer and competitive considerations, product characteristics, and financial and control factors.

Buyer Considerations

Manufacturers look at the amount and frequency of purchases by buyers, as well as the margins over manufacturing costs that are available to pay for direct selling costs. Customers' needs for product information and applications assistance may determine whether a company sales force or independent marketing intermediaries can best satisfy buyers' needs.

Competitive Considerations

Distribution channels may be an important aspect of how a company differentiates itself and its products from others, and this may impel decision makers towards increased emphasis on direct channels. The Internet can change the economics of distribution in favor of direct marketing.

For example, the 2000s have shown substantial growth in custom online ordering, a form of mass customization. On its website www.mymms.com , Masterfoods USA (the division of Mars that makes M&M's), offers consumers a palette of 21 colors to coat M&M's—for example in their school colors—and to add printed messages. The cost is nearly three times that of regular M&M's, but it provides a growing niche business. On the other hand, Nike's custom online ordering at Nikeid.com was constrained by the need for consumers to try on the sneaker—so they have moved to Web kiosks in Niketown stores to combine regular retail with the custom product.[2]

Product Characteristics

Companies often consider product characteristics in deciding whether to use a direct or distribution-channel strategy. Complex goods and services often require close contact between customers and the producer, who may have to provide application assistance, service, and other supporting activities. For example, chemical-processing equipment, mainframe computer systems, pollution-control equipment, and engineering-design services are often marketed directly to end-users via company salesforces. Another factor is the range of products offered by the manufacturer. A complete line may make distribution by the manufacturer economically feasible, whereas the cost of direct sales for a single product may be prohibitive. High-volume purchases may make direct distribution feasible for a single product. Companies whose product designs change because of rapidly changing technology often adopt direct sales approaches. Also qualified marketing intermediaries may not be available, given the complexity of the product and the requirements of the customer. Direct contact with the end-user provides feedback to the manufacturer about new product needs, problem areas, and other concerns. Many supporting services may be Web-based.

Financial and Control Considerations

It is necessary to decide if resources are available for direct distribution, and, if they are, whether selling direct to end-users is the best use of the resources. Both the costs and benefits need to be evaluated. Direct distribution gives the manufacturer control over distribution, since independent organizations cannot be managed in the same manner as company employees. This may be an important factor to the manufacturer.

For example, in the early 2000s several high technology manufacturers opened retail outlets. By 2007, Apple Computer had opened more than 180 stores—spanning the U.S., Europe, and Japan. The goal is to educate consumers about the company's computers, music players, and other product innovations. It is a response to the threat of commoditization in electronics—the consumer with little brand loyalty who buys the cheapest possible product. Similar motives underpin the opening of retail outlets by Sony Electronics and palmOne—the aim is to reinforce their brands with affluent consumers and gain better insight into fast-changing trends in consumer electronics. These moves underline the importance of market access and market learning in sustaining competitive differentiation.[3]

Other reasons for manufacturers entering the retail marketplace may focus on the need to manage the brand experience more closely than could be achieved through independent retailers. The STRATEGY FEATURE examines novel ventures by Nestlé and Heineken in building their own retail operations.

Exhibit 10.2 highlights several factors favoring distribution by the manufacturer. A firm's financial resources and capabilities are also important considerations. The producers of business and industrial products are more likely than producers of consumer products to utilize company distribution to end-users. This is achieved by a direct to the end-user network of company sales offices and a field sales force or by a vertically integrated distribution system (distribution centers and retail outlets) owned by the manufacturer. Companies with superior Internet capabilities may also favor the direct channel more than others.

Strategy Feature

Branded Manufacturers Enter the Retail Market

Several brand-owners are extending their channel strategy from reliance on conventional retailers to establish a position at the retail level of the value chain:

- Nespresso, a subsidiary of Nestlé, is establishing "coffee boutiques." Located at prestigious addresses like New York's Madison Avenue and London's Beauchamp Place, the boutiques are lined with dark wood paneling, discreetly lit, with plush interiors. Nespresso previously sold coffee capsules for espresso machine by mail-order (and online) to members of the "Nespresso Club," and then started selling branded coffee machines.

- Nespresso plans further retail expansion—taking the brand into hotels, restaurants, offices, and first-class airline lounges. The goal is to enable an increasing number of people to experience the brand first-hand. The brand experience is hoped to lead to purchase of the coffee machines and accessories.

- In a similar move, Heineken, the premium beer company, has opened a restaurant on the Champs Elysée in Paris, to link beer with food. It plans Heineken bars at international airports, to follow the model it has established at Hong Kong airport—the first branded beer bar developed for an airport.

The strategic logic for such moves is that branded consumer goods companies are often at the mercy of third-party retailers when it comes to the marketing and placement of their products. The goal is to move beyond selling a "product in a box" to offering a superior "service experience."

Nespresso's objective is to become a lifestyle brand and this is reflected in its new channel strategy.

Sources: Jenny Wiggins and Haig Simonian, "How To Serve a Bespoke Cup of Coffee," *Financial Times,* Tuesday, April 3, 2007, p. 10.

Channel Strategy

We now consider the decisions that are necessary in developing a channel of distribution strategy. They include (1) determining the type of channel arrangement; (2) deciding the intensity of distribution; (3) selecting the channel configuration (Exhibit 10.3).

EXHIBIT 10.2
Factors Favoring Distribution by the Manufacturer

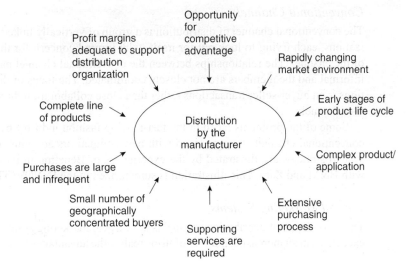

EXHIBIT 10.3
Channel Strategy
Selection

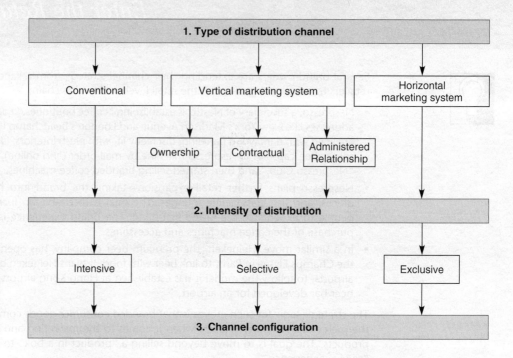

Management may seek to achieve one or more objectives using the channel of distribution strategy. While the primary objective is gaining access to end-user buyers, other related objectives may also be important. These include providing promotional and personal selling support, offering customer service, obtaining market information, and gaining favorable revenue/cost performance. Recall the moves into retail by Apple, Sony, and palmOne to build brand values with consumers.

Types of Channels

The major types of channels are conventional channels and vertical marketing systems (VMS), although horizontal marketing systems are important in some situations, along with emerging digital channels.

Conventional Channel

The conventional channel of distribution is a group of vertically linked independent organizations, each trying to look out for itself, with limited concern for the total performance of the channel. The relationships between the conventional channel participants are rather informal and the members are not closely coordinated. The focus of the channel organizations is on buyer-seller transactions rather than close collaboration throughout the distribution channel.

Some of the problems faced in the fast-moving fashion industry by a company using a conventional channel strategy, faced with new competitors adopting a vertical marketing system strategy, are illustrated by the experiences of Benetton in its struggle to compete with H&M and Zara. This illustration is summarized in the INNOVATION FEATURE.

Vertical Marketing Systems

The second type of distribution channel is the vertical marketing system (VMS). Marketing executives in an increasing number of firms realize the advantages to be gained by managing

- Italian fashion company Benetton became one of the world's best known brands in the 1980s, based on distinctive casual wear and provocative advertising.
- The company saw itself as a manufacturer, not a retailer, with a traditional business model based on the wholesale distribution of clothes to franchisees.
- The channel strategy was based on regional agents—regarded as strategic partners—which manage the franchisees selling Benetton products, while Benetton avoided the risks of running or owning retail outlets. The model worked well in Italy but not in other markets like the U.S.
- In the 1990s, Benetton was left behind by new competitors like Zara from Spain and H&M from Sweden, getting new fashion design into their own stores in a matter of weeks and at bargain prices.
- With Benetton falling out of fashion, store owners who sold the brand began to cut back on orders rather than risk steep markdowns. Benetton closed stores in the U.S., where it struggled to compete on price.
- In the 2000s, under a new CEO, Benetton has worked to improve its relationships with store owners by selling them products at lower wholesale prices so they could make higher profits, which hurt Benetton's own profits—management considered it worthwhile to get longer-term loyalty.
- Investments have been made in supply chain efficiency—some production outsourced to China and inventory broken into smaller shipments to be sent to stores in line with changes in consumer demand.
- New designs to make Benetton "hip" again are fueled by a network of trend-spotters across Europe and Asia, and the high-end cat walks of Paris, Milan, and London.
- Faster fashion is helping Benetton get back on track, though the brand that once set trends must now follow them.

Sources: Gail Edmonson, Jack Ewing and Christina Passariello, "Has Benetton Stopped Unraveling?" *BusinessWeek,* June 23, 2003, 22–23. Stacy Meichtry, "Benetton Picks Up the Fashion Pace," *Wall Street Journal,* April 10, 2007, p. B-1.

the channel as a coordinated or programmed system of participating organizations. We consider later the influence of supply chain management approaches and the Internet on the operations of channels. Vertical marketing systems dominate the U.S. retailing sector and are significant factors in the business and industrial products and services sectors.

A primary feature of a VMS is the management (or coordination) of the distribution channel by one organization. Programming and coordination of channel activities and functions are directed by the firm that is the channel manager. Operating rules and guidelines indicate the functions and responsibilities of each participant. Management assistance and services are supplied to the participating organizations by the firm that is the channel leader.

Three types of vertical marketing systems may be used: *ownership, contractual,* and *administered.* During recent years, a fourth form of VMS has developed in which the channel organizations form collaborative relationships rather than control by one organization. We consider this as a *relationship* VMS.

Ownership VMS

Ownership of distribution channels from source of supply to end-user involves a substantial capital investment by the channel coordinator. This kind of VMS is also less adaptable to change compared to the other VMS forms. For these reasons a more popular alternative may be to develop collaborative relationships with channel members (e.g., supplier/manufacturer alliances). Such arrangements tend to reduce the coordinator's control over the channel but overcome the disadvantages of control through ownership. Nonetheless, in highly competitive markets, the need for control of distribution may make channel ownership more attractive. Globally, many auto manufacturers are establishing their own retail outlets and establishing Internet sales, and buying out independent franchisees and distributors to regain channel control to build an ownership VMS, replacing conventional channels.

Contractual VMS

The contractual form of the VMS may include various formal arrangements between channel participants including franchising and voluntary chains of independent retailers. Franchising is popular in fast foods, lodging, and many other retail lines. Traditional automobile dealerships are another example of a contractual VMS. Wholesaler-sponsored retail chains are used by food and drug wholesalers to establish networks of independent retailers. Contractual programs may be initiated by manufacturers, wholesalers, and retailers.

Administered VMS

The administered VMS exists because one of the channel members has the capacity to influence other channel members. This influence may be the result of financial strengths, brand image, specialized skills (e.g., marketing, product innovation), and assistance and support to channel members. For example, DeBeers has managed the worldwide distribution of rough diamonds through its marketing cartel for over a century, acting as "buyer of last resort" to achieve market stability and steady price appreciation for diamonds. De Beers controls about 60 percent of global diamond production. In 2007, De Beers cut the number of clients (distributors, cutters, and traders) to which it sells diamonds by around 20 percent, to concentrate the product on the distributors De Beers judged best able to stimulate demand for diamond jewelry.[4]

Relationship VMS

This type of channel shares certain characteristics of the administered VMS, but differs in that a single firm does not exert substantial control over other channel members. Instead, the relationship involves close collaboration and sharing of information. The relationship VMS may be more logical in channels with only two or three levels.

The economic performance of vertical marketing systems is likely to be higher than that in conventional channels, if the channel network is properly designed and managed. However, the participating firms in the channel must make certain concessions and be willing to work toward overall channel performance. There are rules to be followed, control is exercised in various ways, and generally there is less flexibility for the channel members. Also, some of the requirements of the total VMS may not be in the best interests of a particular participant. Nonetheless, competing in a conventional distribution channel against a VMS is a major competitive challenge, so a channel member may find membership in a VMS to be beneficial.

Horizontal Marketing Systems

The horizontal marketing system exists when two or more unrelated companies put together resources or programs to exploit a marketing opportunity.[5] For example, Kroger, the largest U.S. supermarket, has introduced an extended range of financial services—home loans, pet insurance, identity theft products—in partnership with the U.S. subsidiaries of Royal Bank of Scotland. The horizontal marketing system is a relevant issue in reviewing channel strategy, but is close in its characteristics to the partnering, joint venture, and strategic alliance arrangements considered as strategic relationships in Chapter 7, and is not discussed further in this chapter.

Digital Channels

A further relevant development is the digital—or Internet-based—distribution channel. While online selling has become commonplace, there are several emerging issues meriting attention.

First, product digitization is important in many markets. Where a traditional product can be converted to digital format, then it can be constructed and delivered to the user directly through the Internet, and conventional distribution may be avoided. Examples include music and software downloads, where the need for a conventional CD to be physically handled by distributors or retailers is reduced or removed. Similar developments include business and consumer information services, insurance and other financial services, e-books, education and training, computer games, television services, and movie rental and purchase. Interestingly, after some years of hesitation, video content creators like Hollywood studios are moving into digital distribution channels, creating services allowing consumers to watch films when and where they want. These moves are stimulated by the goal of new revenue streams and concern that traditional distribution models are declining.[6] Similarly, Sony is cutting U.S. jobs and reviewing its business model to react to the shift of the computer games industry from sales of packaged software in retail stores to networking and online distribution.[7]

Second, while product digitization goes hand in hand with the digitization of channel functions, it is not a prerequisite. Consider the airline ticket example. While the airline still provides a seat on the aircraft, many of the traditional distribution functions carried out by travel agents or airline retail outlets are replaced by an online reservation number and an online, pre-printed boarding card, and online choice of seats, food, and entertainments. Opportunities exist more broadly to digitize certain channel functions for both products and services. The idea of "lean consumption" underlines the emergence of these opportunities to minimize customer time and effort and to deliver exactly what they want, when and where they want it.[8]

The digitization of products and channel functions is not necessarily associated with the process of disintermediation—replacing distributors with direct manufacturer-owned channels. Rather, companies like iTunes and online insurance brokers are creating new types of online distributor—a process of reintermediation. Indeed, digitization of distribution functions can work closely with conventional channel arrangements—in-store online ordering of out-of-stock products, or collecting online purchases from retail outlets are illustrative developments.

Distribution Intensity

The second step in channel strategy is selecting distribution intensity (Exhibit 10.3). Distribution intensity is best examined in reference to how many retail stores (or industrial product dealers) carry a particular brand in a geographical area. If a company decides to distribute its products in many of the retail outlets in a trading area that might normally carry such a product, it is using an *intensive* distribution approach. Typical examples would be consumer food or beverage products. A trading area may be a portion of a city, the entire metropolitan area, or a larger geographical area. If one retailer or dealer in the trading area distributes the product, then management is following an *exclusive* distribution strategy. Examples include Lexus automobiles and Caterpillar industrial equipment. *Selective* distribution falls between the two extremes. Rolex watches and Louis Vuitton fashion goods are distributed on a selective basis.

Choosing the right distribution intensity depends on management's targeting and positioning strategies and product and market characteristics. The major issues in deciding distribution intensity are:

- Identifying which distribution intensities are feasible, taking into account the size and characteristics of the market target, the product, and the requirements likely to be imposed by prospective intermediaries (e.g., they may want exclusive sales territories).
- Selecting the alternatives that are compatible with the proposed market target and marketing program positioning strategy.
- Choosing the alternative that (1) offers the best strategic fit; (2) meets management's financial performance expectations; and (3) is attractive enough to intermediaries so that they will be motivated to perform their assigned functions.

The characteristics of the product and the market target to be served often suggest a particular distribution intensity. For example, an expensive product, such as a Toyota Lexus luxury automobile, does not require intensive distribution to make contact with potential buyers. Moreover, several dealers in a trading area could not generate enough sales and profits to be successful due to the luxury car's limited sales potential.

The distribution intensity should correspond to the marketing strategy selected. For example, Estée Lauder distributes cosmetics through selected department stores that carry quality products. Management decided not to meet Revlon head-on in the marketplace, and instead concentrates its efforts on a small number of retail outlets. In doing this, Estée Lauder avoids huge national advertising expenditures and uses promotional tactics to help attract its customers to retail outlets. Buyers are frequently offered free items when purchasing other specified items.

Strategic requirements, management's preferences, and other constraints help determine the distribution intensity that offers the best strategic fit and performance potential. The requirements of intermediaries need to be considered, along with management's desire to coordinate and motivate them. For example, exclusive distribution is a powerful incentive to intermediaries and also simplifies management activities for the channel leader. But if the company granted exclusive distribution rights is unable (or unwilling) to fully serve the needs of target customers, the manufacturer will not gain the sales and profit opportunities that could be obtained by using more intermediaries.

Channel Configuration

The third step in selecting the distribution strategy is deciding: (1) how many levels of organizations to include in the vertical channel; and (2) the specific kinds of intermediaries to be selected at each level (Exhibit 10.3). The type (conventional or VMS) of channel and the distribution intensity selected help in deciding how many channel levels to use and what types of intermediaries to select. Different channel levels are shown in Exhibit 10.1. As an example, an industrial products producer might choose between distributors and sales agents (independent organizations that receive commissions on sales) to contact industrial buyers, or some combination of these intermediaries. Several factors may influence the choice of one of the channel configurations shown in Exhibit 10.1.

End-User Considerations

It is important to know *where* the targeted end-users might expect to purchase the products of interest. The intermediaries that are selected should provide an avenue to the market segments(s) targeted by the producer. Analysis of buyer characteristics and preferences provides important information for selecting firms patronized by end-users. This, in turn, guides decisions concerning additional channel levels, such as the middlemen selling to the retailers that contact the market target customers.

Product Characteristics

The complexity of the product, special application requirements, and servicing needs are useful in guiding the choice of intermediaries. Looking at how competing products are distributed may suggest possible types of intermediaries, although adopting competitors' strategies may not be the most promising channel configuration. The breadth and depth of the products to be distributed are also important considerations since intermediaries may want full lines of products.

Carbonated beverages like Coke and Pepsi have very interesting channels of distribution. For example, Pepsi sells syrup to independent bottlers. They bottle the beverage and sell and distribute to retailers. Pepsi also promotes its brands with retailers and consumers. Strong relationships between Pepsi and its bottlers are essential to the success of the channel network.

Manufacturer's Capabilities and Resources

Large producers with extensive capabilities and resources have a lot of flexibility in choosing intermediaries. These producers also have a great deal of bargaining power with the intermediary, and, the producer may be able (and willing) to perform certain of the distribution functions. Such options are more limited for small producers with limited capabilities and resource constraints.

Required Functions

The functions that need to be performed in moving products from producer to end-user include various channel activities such as storage, servicing, and transportation. Studying these functions is useful in choosing the types of intermediary that are appropriate for a particular product or service. For example, if the producer needs only the direct-selling function, then independent manufacturers' agents may be the right intermediary to use. Alternatively, if inventory stocking and after-sales service are needed, then a full-service wholesaler may be essential.

Availability and Skills of Intermediaries

Evaluation of the experience, capabilities, and motivation of the intermediaries which are under consideration for channel membership is also important. Firms within the same industry often vary in skills and experience. Also, qualified channel members may not be available. For example, some types of intermediary will not distribute competing products. The more complex the channel network, the more challenging it is to complete various distribution functions. Nevertheless, using specialists at two (or more) levels (e.g., brokers, wholesalers, dealers) may offer substantial economies of scale through the specialization of functions. The channel configuration that is selected typically takes into account several important trade-offs.

Channel Maps

It is often useful to produce a map of existing or planned channel strategy, to allow comparison with competitors and to identify new opportunities. For example, Exhibit 10.4 shows an illustrative channels map for one region's annual use of central heating units. There are two customer groups: construction companies using heating units in new buildings, and domestic customers upgrading their residences. The customers are reached through independent distributors, small hardware retailers, large retail hardware chains, construction sub-contractors, and direct sales by the manufacturers. A well-constructed channel map indicates clearly the end-user customers, and shows the relative roles of distributors, construction sub-contractors, retailers, and other marketing intermediaries in reaching end-users. Channel map analysis should emphasize end-users.

EXHIBIT 10.4
Illustrative Channel Map for all Producers of Heating Units

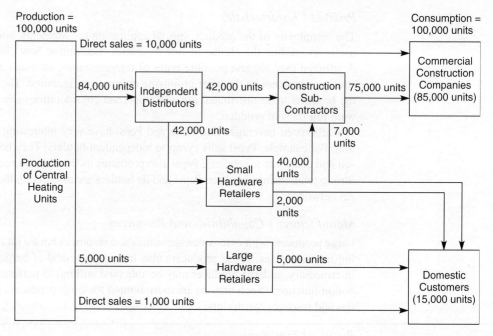

The figures shown in the channel map are for all suppliers to the market in the region. They can be compared to existing and planned sales of an individual company through each channel link to identify areas of weakness and strength against competitors—for example, by calculating market share for each channel link—and to aid establishing channel priorities. Profitability data will highlight differences between channels, from an industry and an individual company perspective. Trend and forecasts can be incorporated to highlight shifts in channel importance and necessary changes in channel strategy. Anticipated changes in product use by different customers will also impact channel configuration choices.

Selecting the Channel Strategy

The major channel-strategy decisions we have examined are summarized in Exhibit 10.3. Management: (1) chooses the type(s) of channel to be used; (2) determines the desired intensity of distribution; and (3) selects the channel configuration. One of the first issues to be resolved is deciding whether to manage the channel, partner with other members, or instead to be a participant. This choice often rests on the bargaining power a company can exert in negotiating with other organizations in the channel system and the value (and costs) of performing the channel management role. The options include deciding to manage or coordinate operations in the channel of distribution, becoming a member of a vertically coordinated channel, or becoming a member of a conventional channel system. The following factors need to be assessed in the choice of the channel strategy.

Market Access

As emphasized throughout the chapter the market target decision needs to be closely coordinated with channel strategy, since the channel connects products and end-users. The market target decision is not finalized until the channel strategy is selected. Information about the customers in the market target can help eliminate unsuitable channel-strategy alternatives. Multiple market targets may require more than a single channel of distribution. One advantage of intermediaries is that they have an established customer base. When this customer base matches the producer's choice of market target(s), market access is achieved very rapidly.

Value-Added Competencies

The channel selected should offer the most favorable combination of value-added competencies. Making this assessment requires looking at the competencies of each participant and the trade-offs concerning financial and flexibility and control considerations.

Financial Considerations

Two financial issues affect the channel strategy. First, are the resources available for launching the proposed strategy? For example, a small producer may not have the money to build a distribution network. Second, the revenue-cost impact of alternative channel strategies needs to be evaluated. These analyses include cash flow, income, return on investment, and operating capital requirements (see Appendix to Chapter 2).

Flexibility and Control Considerations

Management should decide how much flexibility it wants in the channel network and how much control it would like to have over other channel participants. An example of flexibility is how easily channel members can be added (or eliminated). A conventional channel offers little opportunity for control by a member firm, yet there is a lot of flexibility in entering and exiting from the channel. The VMS offers more control than the conventional channel. Legal and regulatory constraints also affect channel strategies in such areas as pricing, exclusive dealing, and allocation of market coverage.

Channel Strategy Evaluation

Suppose a producer of industrial controls for fluid processing (e.g., valves, regulators) is considering two channel strategy alternatives: (1) using independent manufacturer's representatives (agents) versus (2) recruiting a company sales force to sell its products to industrial customers. The representatives receive a commission of 8 percent on their dollar sales volume and have to be trained. Salespeople will cost an estimated $150,000 in annual salary and expenses. Salespeople must be recruited, trained, and supervised.

An illustrative channel strategy evaluation is shown in Exhibit 10.5. The company sales force alternative is more expensive (using a two-year time frame) than the use of independent sales agents. Assuming both options generate contributions to profit, the trade-off of higher expenses needs to be evaluated against flexibility and control considerations, and the higher quality of selling efforts with the direct sales force option. One possibility that is often used by manufacturers seeking access to a new market is to initially utilize manufacturer's representatives with a longer-term strategy of converting to a company sales force. This offers an opportunity to gain market knowledge while keeping selling expenses in line with actual sales.

Changing Channel Strategy

The issue of flexibility in channel strategy has been a considerably higher priority for many companies in recent years. The Dell example discussed at the beginning of this chapter is illustrative of the need to change channel strategy in response to new marketing strategy requirements, competitive pressures, and customer change.

EXHIBIT 10.5
Illustrative Channel
Strategy Evaluation

Evaluation Criteria	Strategy 1:** Manufacturer's Representatives	Strategy 2:** Company Sales Force
Market Access	Rapid market coverage	One- to three-year development time
Value-added Competencies	Medium	High
Sales Forecast (2 years)	$20 million	$30 million
Forecast Accuracy	High	Medium/Low
Estimated Costs	$2 million*	$3.6 million#
Selling Expenses (Costs/Sales)	10%	12%
Flexibility	Good	Limited
Control	Limited	Good

* Includes 8 percent commission plus management time in recruiting and training representatives.
# Includes $150,000 each for ten salespeople (including salary and costs) plus management time.
** Two-year time span.

Channel Strategy Modification

Channel strategy should be reviewed regularly, since modifications may be required when: marketing strategy has changed market targets and priorities; distribution is not working as planned; new channel possibilities have developed; customer buying patterns have changed; market structure or segmentation changes; new competitors have entered; or the product moves into a later product life cycle stage. It is unlikely that any channel will remain effective through the product life cycle—early buyers may be prepared to pay for high added-value channels, but later buyers are likely to favor low-cost channels. The optimal channel strategy will almost certainly change over time. Modifications may encompass: adding or dropping channel members; adding or dropping specific channels; or, adopting new channels and sales approaches.[9]

Avon Cosmetics is the world's leading direct selling company, operating in 143 countries. Channel strategy is dominated by part-time, mainly female, salespeople selling cosmetics from a catalogue direct to consumers in their homes. Nonetheless, faced with

intense competition and the impact of greater female participation in the workforce (meaning they are not home for the direct sell), Avon has made significant changes to its channel strategy. While the direct selling operation remains dominant, Avon products can be purchased online, and depending on geographic location they can be bought in kiosks in shopping malls, beauty centers and beauty boutiques, and in outlets and department stores.[10]

Channel Migration

Channel migration refers to the strategic shift from one channel to another (for example, the move in low-cost airlines like Ryanair away from selling tickets through travel agents to selling only on the Internet—98 percent of Ryanair tickets are now sold online).[11] Companies face a challenge in responding to opportunities for channel migration when a new channel possibility opens up.[12] New possibilities range from Internet channels to direct selling opportunities to working with new types of marketing intermediaries. Essential questions to consider are (1) whether the new channel complements or replaces existing distribution channels;

and (2) if the new channel enhances or undermines the company's existing capabilities and value chain. The answers to these questions should indicate the necessary channel migration strategy.

For example, the emergence of an Internet channel may have one of several effects: it may be complementary to existing channels and fit with existing capabilities (Dell's transition from conventional direct selling to the Internet is illustrative); it may be complementary to new channels, but require new capabilities (such as the transition from branch-based retail banking to online banking); it may replace existing channels but still enhance existing capabilities (as the case with online travel booking/agencies); or, it may replace existing channels and require new capabilities (the situation faced by traditional music production companies and retailers).[13]

Channel migration indicates the need to add or drop channels, reinforce or develop new channel capabilities, and the resistance or conflict to be faced with existing channel members.

Importantly, channel migration decisions are not restricted to the online and off-line channel balance. Liz Claiborne, the clothing and accessories company, operates a portfolio of forty-four brands and the business is divided between direct retail and wholesale channels. The wholesale business has been hit by shifts in the U.S. department store landscape, including the merger of Federated and May's stores, and increased private label competition from stores like Target, JCPenney, and Kohl's. In 2007, the company decided to dispose of its sixteen wholesale brands, sold through department stores and other outlets, and to focus on developing its own retail businesses through its four leading brands—Mexx, Juicy Culture, Lucky Brand denim, and Kate Spade. The goal is to operate as a specialty retailer with no wholesale channel.[14]

Channel Audit

Channel modification and migration decisions require careful analysis. The channels map discussed earlier (Exhibit 10.4) is a starting point. The map provides a tool for monitoring the amount of business going through different channels to different customer types, and to include new channel possibilities in the model. Developing trends and new channels provide a trigger for considering channel strategy change. Nonetheless, channel strategy change needs to make sense in the context of overall marketing strategy, and implementation must be achievable even if there are conflicts with existing channels.

For example, direct Internet sales compete with distributors and salespeople in the value chain. One of Dell Inc.'s key advantages in growing the computer business with its direct business model was that it was very difficult for existing market leaders like IBM and H-P to operate a direct business model—they were tied to traditional distribution channels and were reluctant to compete with their own distributors. There was a considerable delay before competitors migrated their own channels to incorporate Internet sales and distribution.

Managing the Channel

After deciding on the channel design, the actual channel participants are identified, evaluated, and recruited. Finding competent and motivated intermediaries is critical to successfully implementing the channel strategy. Channel management activities include choosing how to assist and support intermediaries, developing operating policies, providing incentives, selecting promotional programs, and evaluating channel results. To gain a better insight into channel management, we discuss channel leadership, management structure and systems, physical distribution and supply chain management, channel relationships, conflict resolution, channel performance, and legal and ethical considerations.

Channel Leadership

Some form of interorganization management is needed to ensure that the channel has satisfactory performance as a competitive entity.[15] One firm may gain power over other channel organizations because of its specific characteristics (e.g., size), experience, and environmental factors, and its ability to capitalize on such factors. Gaining this advantage is more feasible in a VMS than in a conventional channel. Performing the leadership role may also lead to conflicts arising from differences in the objectives and priorities of channel members. Conflicts with retailers created by the channel strategy changes are illustrative. The organization with the most power may make decisions that are not considered favorable by other channel members.

Management Structure and Systems

Channel coordination and management are often the responsibility of the sales organization (Chapter 13). For example, a manufacturer's salespeople develop buyer-seller relationships with wholesalers and/or retailers. The management structure and systems may vary from informal arrangements to highly structured operating systems. Conventional channel management is more informal, whereas the management of VMS is more structured and programmed. The VMS management systems may include operating policies and procedures, information system linkages, various supporting services to channel participants, and setting performance targets.

Physical Distribution Management

Physical distribution (logistics) management has received considerable attention from distribution, marketing, manufacturing, and transportation professionals. The objective is improving the distribution of supplies, goods in process, and finished products. Physical distribution is a key channel function and thus an important part of channel strategy and management. Management needs to first select the appropriate channel strategy. Once the strategy is selected, physical distribution management alternatives can be examined for the value chain network. Many organizations now address physical distribution issues as part of a supply chain strategy.

Supply Chain Strategy[16]

The impact of supply chain strategies has extended beyond issues of transportation, storage, and stock-holding issues to influence relationships between channel members and customer value. For example, the Efficient Consumer Response (ECR) program is a cooperative partnership between retailers and manufacturers to reduce supply chain costs—lower stock levels; fewer damaged goods; simpler transaction management. ECR approaches have achieved impressive cost savings, particularly for retailers. Collaboration and information sharing have become central to supply chain design. Integrating processes across organizational boundaries is essential to building the seamless supply chain, where "it is supply chains that compete not companies."[17]

A major development in supply chain management comes from Japanese management approaches and the example of Toyota in the automotive field in particular.[18] This focuses on the application of lean thinking to create the *lean supply chain*.[19] The foundation of the lean supply chain is defining value from the perspective of the end-customer, to identify the value stream of activities in the supply chain that are needed to place the correctly specified product with the customer. All non-value creating activities are "muda" or waste and should be eliminated. Attention is given to continuous flow of products in the supply chain, instead of traditional "batch and queue" approaches, to eliminate time wasting, storage, and scrap. Products are not produced upstream in the supply chain until ordered by the downstream customer, i.e., pulled through the supply chain, removing the need for large inventories and customer waiting time. The goal is to remove demand instability through collaboration between suppliers and distributors, and ultimately to allow customers to order directly from the production system.[20] The ECR initiative is an example of a lean supply chain model.

Nonetheless, in response to the impact of turbulent volatile markets, some emphasis has been placed on creating *agile supply chains* which are not lengthy and slow-moving "pipelines," but agile and responsive to market change.[21] Supply chain agility means using market knowledge and a virtual corporation to respond to marketplace volatility, as opposed to the lean approach which seeks to remove waste and manage volatility out of the supply chain by leveling demand.[22] The agile supply chain reserves capacity to cope with unpredictable demand.[23] While lean supply chains require long-term partnership with suppliers, the agile model mandates fluid and market-based relationships to enhance responsiveness to the market and capacity for rapid change.[24] Agile supply chain models emphasize customer satisfaction rather than meeting a more limited set of value criteria based on reduced costs.

The Impact of Supply Chain Management on Marketing

Supply chain strategies impact on several critical issues for marketing strategy and the value chain: product availability in the market, speed to market with innovations, the range of product choices offered to customers, product deletion decisions, prices, and competitive positioning. In the market-driven company, a strategic value chain perspective requires collaboration and integration between marketing and supply chain management. Important issues to consider are that:

1. Supply chain decisions are made with an understanding of the real drivers of customer value in different market segments, and the forces for value migration, not simply on the basis of measurable quality and technical product specifications.

2. Supply chain decisions do not create inflexibility and inability to respond to marketplace change.

3. Supply chain decisions should be made in the light of strategic marketing questions, such as brand identification, product choice for customers, product promotion, and building sustainable competitive advantage, not only short-term cost savings.

4. Supply chain strategy may not be a source of competitive advantage, if all players in the market have similar technology and designs.

E-Procurement

The development of Internet-based supply chain management highlights the growing role of e-procurement—where customers search and buy online, accessing a far greater choice of suppliers. The major impact is with business-to-business customers, including retailers and purchasers of industrial products. Industry portals and complex e-procurement systems offer very specific supplier search facilities. E-procurement is associated with supplier base reduction and the use of devices like online auctions and exchanges. The impact of e-procurement is being felt both in direct and indirect channels and is an increasingly significant factor in managing channels.

Channel Relationships

Chapter 7 considers various forms of strategic relationships between organizations, examining the degree of collaboration between companies, the extent of commitment of the participating organizations, and the power and dependence ties between the organizations. We now look at how these issues relate to channel relationships.

Degree of Collaboration

Channel relationships are often transactional in conventional channels but may become more collaborative in VMS's. The extent of collaboration is influenced by the complexity of the product, the potential benefits of collaboration, and the willingness of channel members to work together as partners. Supply chain models encourage collaboration and information-sharing between suppliers and producers.

Commitment and Trust Among Channel Members

The commitment and trust of channel organizations is likely to be higher in VMS's compared to conventional channels. For example, a contractual arrangement (e.g., franchise agreement) is a commitment to work together. Yet the strength of the commitment may vary depending on the contract terms. For example, contracts between manufacturers and their independent representatives or agents typically allow either party to terminate the relationship with a thirty-day notification.

Highly collaborative relationships among channel members call for a considerable degree of commitment and trust between the partners. The cooperating organizations provide access to confidential product plans, market data, and other trade secrets. Trust normally develops as the partners learn to work with each other and find the relationship to be favorable to each partner's objectives.

Power and Dependence

In VMS's, power is concentrated with one organization and the other channel members are dependent on the channel manager. This concentration of power does not exist with the Relationship VMS. Power in conventional channels is less concentrated than in VMS's, and channel members are less dependent on each other. Conventional channel relationships may, nevertheless, result in some channel members possessing more bargaining power than others.

In many sectors, suppliers face unprecedented pressure from powerful channel members. New merchandizing strategies with this effect include house branding and category killers[25] House branding includes retailers who have established the retail store network as the brand, such as Gap, Banana Republic, and Victoria's Secret. These retailers rely on contract manufacturers to produce their brands. Category killers are companies like Toys 'R' Us, Home Depot, Staples, and Linens 'n Things that attempt to dominate one segment of the market, often with very low prices. Suppliers may have substantially less control over these channels than in the past. Responses may include suppliers reclaiming important value-added services from distributors to build stronger relationships with end-users; eliminating layers in the conventional channel; or creating new channels.

Channel Globalization

Significantly for consumer goods suppliers, many major retail chains have expanded internationally. The globalization of distribution channels is underlined by the launch of Internet-based online exchanges. With the ability to source and merchandise globally, efficient supply chains, and powerful information technology, major retailers have more bargaining power than many of their suppliers. Domestic suppliers face global competition.

Agentrics (a merger of the Global Exchange Network and Worldwide Retail Exchange) brings together fifty of the world's largest retailers and over 80,000 suppliers, with a goal of streamlining and automating sourcing globally, and supporting collaboration between retailers and suppliers. Although facing problems of technology integration as well as anti-trust questions, it is estimated that Internet-based procurement systems may cut 30 percent off costs.[26] In business-to-business marketing, it is telling that by the early 2000s, major purchasers like Boeing and Motorola were warning that suppliers unable or unwilling to make the transition to Web-based commerce would be locked out of their businesses.[27]

Suppliers face competition at a global level even in what would previously have been seen as domestic business. Buyers able to access online exchanges or participate in online reverse auctions have in effect globalized the distribution channel.

Multichanneling

An important trend in distribution is the use of multiple channels to gain greater access to end-user customers. Increasingly, suppliers face the challenge of managing relationships between the multiple channels used in the same market. The problem is to define innovative channel combinations that best meet customer needs. However, in many situations the way channels are used is defined by customer choice. Customers may "channel surf"—Forrester Research estimates that as many as half of all customers shop for information in one channel, then defect from that channel to make the purchase in another medium. Where customers have become more adversarial, buy more strategically, and have the information and technology to make more informed decisions, it may be risky to assume that discrete channels serving static market segments is a sustainable option. Channel decisions must be informed by understanding the various paths buyers follow as they move through the purchase process.[28]

Williams Sonoma, for instance has a cross-channel selling strategy with sales split 60/40 between retail outlets and online/catalog sales. The company continues to find ways of improving each channel so it drives results in the others—catalogs do not simply sell products; by acting as in-home advertising they bring the company to the attention of new customers who are encouraged to use the stores.[29] The INTERNET FEATURE describes the channel hopping behavior of consumers, to which retailers like Circuit City are successfully responding and building new value offers for consumers.

Care is required in managing channels which may in part compete with each other—the website, the salesperson, and the distributor may all share the same target customer. Attention is required to ensure that incentives and rewards are aligned with the channel strategy. For example, should salespeople be incentivized to put business onto the direct Internet channel; should prices be varied across channels to reflect costs or customer expectations; should customer choice of channel option be actively managed?

Conflict Resolution

Conflicts are certain to occur between the channel members, and in multi-channeling between channels, because of differences in objectives, priorities, and corporate cultures. Looking at a proposed channel relationship by each participating organization may identify areas (e.g., incompatible objectives) that are likely to lead to major conflicts. In such situations, management may decide to seek another channel partner. Effective communications before and after establishing the channel relationships can also help to eliminate or reduce conflicts.

Several methods are used to resolve actual and potential conflicts.[30] One useful approach is to involve channel members in the decisions that will affect the organizations. Another helpful method of resolving or reducing conflict is developing effective communications

- Channel hopping is where customers flit between Internet and phone shopping, home deliveries or call and collect, or use the conventional store.

- Research suggests that people use the technology at home to find the right products at attractive prices in the most time-efficient way, and then decide how to purchase.

- At Circuit City managers have been surprised by the success of the "go-get" transactions—the customer orders a product online, the in-store sales clerk goes gets it, and the customer collects it from the store. In-store pick-ups account for 62 percent of the company's online sales. Notwithstanding the convenience of home delivery, many customers prefer to go to the store. Now Circuit City customers get a $24 gift card if the item they ordered is not available for pick-up within 24 minutes.

- Apple's retail outlets emphasize a "high touch" customer service. Nonetheless, at busy times, there are not enough experts in-store (at the Genius Bar) to deal with customer service issues. Now customers are offered an in-store, live, interactive Internet link to an expert sales agent located in another store or call centre.

- At Mothercare, a British mother-and-baby retailer, customers use an in-store computer to order on the Internet items not in stock at the store, not available in smaller stores, or that they simply do not want to carry home (but do want to see in the store before purchasing).

Sources: Lauren Mills, "The Woman Who Wants to Change the Way We Shop," *Mail on Sunday,* October 8, 2006, 6. Jonathan Birchall, "Are You Being e-Served?" *Financial Times,* January 3, 2007, 8. Lucy Killgren and Tom Braithwaite, "Mothercare's Growth Continues," *Financial Times,* April 5, 2007, 21. Jonathan Birchall, "The New Profit Pick-Me-Up," *Financial Times,* June 21, 2006, 15.

channels between channel members. Pursuing objectives that are important to all channel members also helps to reduce conflict. Finally, it may be necessary to establish methods for mediation and arbitration.

Channel Performance

The performance of the channel is important from two points of view. First, each member is interested in how well the channel is meeting the member's objectives. Second, the organization that is managing or coordinating the channel is concerned with its performance and the overall performance of the channel. Tracking performance for the individual channel members includes various financial and market measures such as profit contribution, revenues, costs, market share, customer satisfaction, and rate of growth. Several criteria for evaluating the overall performance of the channel are shown in the METRICS FEATURE.

Companies gain a strategic advantage by improving distribution productivity. Reducing distribution costs and the time in moving products to end-users are high-priority action areas in many companies. Much of the impact of Toyota's successful strategy in the auto market is from huge cost and time savings in the value chain—from operations through supply chain to distribution.

Monitoring the changes that are taking place in distribution and incorporating distribution strategy considerations into the strategic planning process are essential strategic marketing activities. Market turbulence, global competition, and information technology create a rapidly changing distribution environment. Furthermore, multi-channeling creates new challenges in measuring channel effectiveness.[31]

Legal and Ethical Considerations

Various legal and ethical considerations may impact channel relationships. Legal concerns to the federal government include arrangements between channel members that

Performance Objective	Possible Measures	Applicable Product and Channel Level
Product Availability		
• Coverage of relevant retailers	• Percent of effective distribution	• Consumer products (particularly convenience goods) at retail level
• In-store positioning	• Percent of shelf-facings or display space gained by product, weighted by importance of store	• Consumer products at retail level
• Coverage of geographic markets	• Frequency of sales calls by customer type; average delivery time	• Industrial products; consumer goods at wholesale level
Promotional Effort		
• Effective point-of-purchase (POP) promotion	• Percent of stores using special displays and POP materials, weighted by importance of store	• Consumer products at retail level
• Effective personal selling support	• Percent of salespeople's time devoted to product; number of salespeople receiving training on product's characteristics and applications	• Industrial products; consumer durables at all channel levels; consumer convenience goods at wholesale level
Customer Service		
• Installation, training, repair	• Number of service technicians receiving technical training; monitoring of customer complaints	• Industrial products, particularly those involving high technology; consumer durables at retail level
Market Information		
• Monitoring sales trends, inventory levels, competitors' actions	• Quality and timeliness of information obtained	• All levels of distribution
Cost-Effectiveness		
• Cost of channel functions relative to sales volume	• Middlemen margins and marketing costs as percent of sales	• All levels of distribution

Source: Harper W. Boyd, Jr., Orville C. Walker, Jr., and Jean-Claude Larréché, *Marketing Management,* 3rd ed. (New York: Irwin/McGraw-Hill, 1998), 317. Copyright © The McGraw-Hill Companies, Used with permission.

Ethical and social responsibility imperatives are migrating through many value chains, when a pressure to comply affects value chain partners.

- The world's largest retailers—Wal-Mart, Tesco, Carrefour, and Metro—with more than $500 billion in aggregate annual sales, are working together to develop a code of standards called the Global Social Compliance Program. The new code covers both food and non-food production and focuses on the employment and working conditions of suppliers, and labor abuse.

- Growing "green consumer" pressure on supermarkets to reduce environmental impact is reflected in mandates to suppliers to reduce packaging and the choice of local and regional suppliers to reduce the "carbon footprint" of transporting food over long distances.

- Microsoft drops suppliers who do not meet the software company's standards on employee diversity. Suppliers have been told that the supplier base has to represent all the peoples of the world: male, female, different ethnicities, different cultures, different backgrounds. Vendors who fail to heed the request are being reduced or terminated.

- Wal-Mart has written to its top 100 law firms gathering statistics on hiring and retention of women and ethnic minorities. The company says it will end or limit relationships with law firms failing to achieve diversity targets.

Sources: Jonathan Birchall and Elizabeth Rigby, "Big Retailers Join Forces in an Effort to Fight Labour Abuses," *Financial Times,* January 11, 2007, 1. Andrew Taylor, "Microsoft Drops Suppliers over Diversity Policy," *Financial Times,* March 24/25, 2007, 5. Jonathan Birchall, "Wal-Mart Lays Down the Law," *Financial Times,* February 21, 2007, 11.

substantially lessen competition, restrictive contracts concerning products and/or geographical coverage, promotional allowances and incentives, and pricing practices.[32] State and local laws and regulations may also impact channel members.

The importance of ethical standards and the emergence of corporate social responsibility initiatives was underlined in Chapter 1 as one of the major challenges facing executives in the twenty-first century. Escalating demands for accountability from external stakeholders, the goals of managers themselves, and the aspirations of entrants to management professions, all support close attention to standards of behavior and the impact of societal demands on business practices. Many organizations have formal statements of ethical positioning and many have appointed executives with responsibility for monitoring compliance and reporting performance against these standards to shareholders.[33]

Channel decisions that impact other channel members may create ethical situations. Complexity increases in international channels crossing different cultures. The ETHICS FEATURE describes the migration of ethical and moral imperatives through the value chains in several sectors.

International Channels

Distribution channels available in international markets are not totally different from the channels in a country like the United States. Uniqueness is less a function of structural alternatives and more related to the vast range of operational and market variables that influence channel strategy.[34] Several channel of distribution alternatives are shown in Exhibit 10.6. The arrows show the many possible channel networks linking producers, middlemen, and end-users.

EXHIBIT 10.6
International Channel of Distribution Alternatives

Source: Phillip R. Cateora, and John L. Graham, *International Marketing,* 12th ed. (Burr Ridge, IL: McGraw-Hill/Irwin, 2005), 414, Copyright © The McGraw-Hill Companies. Used with permission.

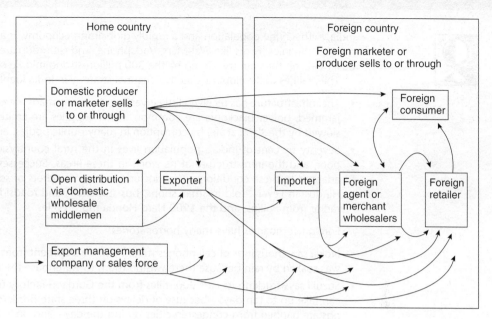

Examining International Distribution Patterns

While the basic channel structure (e.g., agents, wholesalers, retailer) is similar across countries, there are many important differences in distribution patterns among countries. Examining actual distribution patterns indicates the complexity of the international distribution task.[35] Generalization about distribution practices throughout the world is obviously not possible.

Studying the distribution patterns in the nation(s) of interest is important in obtaining guidelines for distribution strategy. Various global trends such as satellite communications, the Internet, regional cooperative arrangements (e.g., European Union), and transportation networks (e.g., inter-modal services) impact distribution systems in various ways reflecting globalization. Global market turbulence and corporate restructuring create additional influences on distribution strategies and practices. Channel maps for overseas markets can be insightful (Exhibit 10.4).

Importantly, market structures may be significantly different in global markets. For example, in the food market, notwithstanding the strong position of Wal-Mart and up-market innovations like Whole Foods Market and Trader Joe's, many U.S. retail chains are relatively weak and fragmented and lack the scale to bargain with food companies or to produce their own labels. Many have in effect rented out their shelves to food companies such as Heinz and Kraft.[36] This market structure gives food product manufacturers considerable scope to manage channels and channel members, for example in a VMS arrangement. By contrast, in Europe, each country market is relatively small, and retail concentration is extremely high. In the United Kingdom, for example, one retailer (Tesco) controls more than 30 percent of the national grocery market, and the top five firms (Tesco, Asda Sainsbury and Morrisons) control 75 percent of the market.[37] Similar concentration is seen in other European countries with the impact of French retailers like Carrefour. The ability for manufacturers to control channel members is quite different when powerful retailing companies control such high shares of the market, and different channel strategy choices are necessary.

Furthermore, some of the most attractive prospects are in emerging markets, where local market conditions are substantially different from those in developed countries. The

India, with a huge population and a rapidly globalizing economy, is a key target market for many companies. Firms like Wal-Mart, Vodaphone, and Citigroup are placing multi-million dollar bets on the country—lured by the 300 million-strong middle class.

The realities of developing effective channel strategy in India identify challenges:

- The infrastructure has received little investment—many roads are crumbling, airports are jammed, power blackouts are common, water supplies are limited. Improvements are slowed by the sheer scale, by corruption in many public bodies, and by cost.

- Seventy percent of India's population lives in the rural countryside. The population is poor, and the infrastructure at its worst in these areas. Successes have been products adapted to these conditions. They include four-cent sachets of soap, salt and tea from Hindustan Lever—sold in small shops, bus-stop staffs and roadside cafes; $20 wind-up radios from Philips; and the $900 Hero-Honda motorcycle.

Foreign companies have many horror stories:

- Nokia saw thousands of cell phones ruined when a shipment from its factory in Chennai was soaked by rain because there was no room to warehouse the crates at the airport.

- Suzuki says trucking its cars 900 miles from the Gurgaon factory to the port in Mumbia can take up to ten days—because of delays on three state borders on the way, and big rigs are banned from congested cities during the day—and once at the port, the autos can wait weeks for the next outbound ship, because there is not enough dock space for cargo carriers to load and unload.

- When GE sent executives to survey a potential site for a factory to manufacture locomotives in partnership with India Railways, they returned discouraged—it took five hours to drive the fifty miles from the airport to the site, and when they got there they found nothing—no roads, no power, no schools, no water, no hospitals, no housing.

Source: Steve Hamm, "The Trouble with India," *BusinessWeek,* March 19, 2007, 49–58. Manjeet Kripalani, "Rural India, Have a Coke," *BusinessWeek,* May 27, 2002, 30–31.

importance of channel strategy in adapting to these local conditions may be a critical factor for success. The GLOBAL FEATURE illustrates some of the problems faced by companies entering the India market, relating to the lack of infrastructure and other barriers.

Factors Affecting Global Channel Selection

The channel strategy analysis and selection process presented in the chapter can be used for developing or evaluating international channel strategy, recognizing that many situational factors affect channel decisions in specific countries. The factors affecting the choice of international channels include cost, capital requirements, control, coverage, strategic product-market fit, and the likelihood that the middlemen will remain in business over a reasonable time horizon.[38] The political and economic stability of the country is, of course, very important. Stability needs to be evaluated early in the decision to enter the country. Increasingly, global security considerations have become important factors in choosing the route to market.[39]

Global Issues Regarding Multichannel Strategies

The impact of the Internet and efficient global communications systems highlight the need to consider the relationship between domestic channels and global channels. The international company is automatically multichanneling. Problems may occur when there are differences between domestic and global channels in prices and product availability. If the product is cheaper in the domestic market than overseas, then overseas customers may seek to access the lower priced product through online sales. Correspondingly, if the product is cheaper through global channels, then domestic buyers may attempt to access the product online from the global channel, or even import the product back into the domestic market if price differences are large enough. It may be very difficult to prevent customers from pursuing these practices. Similar issues arise if product availability varies between domestic and global channels. It is increasingly challenging to differentiate the value offers between domestic and global channels, and there may be considerable risks to customer relationships in maintaining this channel strategy.

Summary

The value chain consists of the organizations, systems, and processes that add to customer value in moving products to end users. A strategic value chain perspective aims to align a company's value chain with changing customer and competitive requirements. The core of the value chain is the channel of distribution. A strong channel network is an important way to gain competitive advantage. The choice between company distribution to end-users and the use of intermediaries is guided by end-user needs and characteristics, product characteristics, and financial and control considerations.

Manufacturers select the type of channel to be used, determine distribution intensity, design the channel configuration, and manage various aspects of channel operations. These channels are either conventional or vertical marketing systems (VMS). The VMS, the dominant channel for consumer products, is increasing in importance for business and industrial products. In a VMS, one firm owns all organizations in the channel, a contractual arrangement exists between organizations, one channel member is in charge of channel administration, or members develop collaborative relationships. Digital channels are of growing importance in many sectors. Channel decisions also include deciding on intensity of distribution and the channel configuration.

The choice of a channel strategy begins when management decides whether to manage the channel or to assume a participant role. Strategic analysis identifies and evaluates the channel alternatives. Several factors are evaluated, including access to the market target, channel functions to be performed, financial considerations, and legal and control constraints. The channel strategy adopted establishes guidelines for price and promotion strategies. Channel modification or migration strategies mandate regular review of channel strategy.

International channels of distribution may be similar in structure to those found in the United States and other developed countries. Nevertheless, important variations exist in the channels of different countries because of the stage of economic development, government influence, and industry practices. The Internet has a dramatic impact on the globalization of channels of distribution.

Questions for Review and Discussion

1. In the late 1990s several airlines started selling tickets using the Internet. Discuss the implications of this method of distribution for travel agencies.
2. Distribution analysts indicate that costs for supermarkets equal about 98 percent of sales. What influence does this high break-even level have on supermarkets' diversification into delis, cheese shops, seafood shops, and flowers?
3. Why do some large, financially strong manufacturers choose not to own their dealers but instead establish contractual relationships with them?

4. What are the advantages and limitations of the use of multiple channels of distribution by a manufacturer?

5. Discuss some likely trends in the distribution of automobiles in the twenty-first century, including the shift away from exclusive distribution arrangements.

6. In the late 1990s Radio Shack initiated co-branding strategies with Compaq Computer and SPRINT. Discuss the logic of this strategy, pointing out its strengths and shortcomings.

7. Identify and discuss some of the factors that should increase the trend toward collaborative relationships in vertical marketing systems.

8. Why might a manufacturer choose to enter a conventional channel of distribution?

9. Discuss what is meant by channel migration and the issues that a manufacturer faces in dealing with migration issues.

10. Suppose the management of a raw material supplier is interested in performing a financial analysis of a distribution channel comprised of manufacturers, distributors, and retailers. Outline an approach for doing the analysis.

11. Discuss some of the important strategic issues facing a drug manufacturer in deciding whether to distribute veterinary prescriptions and over-the-counter products through veterinarians or distributors.

12. Consider the differences in retail concentration between the U.S. and Europe. How do those differences impact on manufacturers' channel strategies?

Internet Applications

A. Examine the websites of Aveda (www.aveda.com) and The Body Shop (www.bodyshop.com). Compare and contrast the distribution networks of these two retailers.

B. Go the site of Agentrix (www.agentrix.com), and review the public pages describing the history, membership, and operation of this international online exchange for retailers (combining the earlier online exchanges the Global Exchange Network and the Worldwide Retail Exchange). Identify and list the ways in which the exchange alters distribution strategy for suppliers, and the impact on consumers.

Feature Applications

A. The STRATEGY FEATURE describes retail ventures being started by manufacturers. Consider what motivates such ventures. Are there other examples that you can identify? Develop a list of the market and customer factors which may cause manufacturers to add direct channels.

B. The GLOBAL FEATURE describes certain local market conditions in India, particularly rural India. What adaptations should international marketers review when planning channel strategy in developing countries, and how can they find out what is required?

Notes

1. Nanette Byrnes and Peter Burrows, "Where Dell Went Wrong," *BusinessWeek,* February 19, 2007, 62–63. Kevin Allison, "Dell to Target Indirect Sales," *Financial Times,* May 17, 2007, 27. Kevin Allison and Chris Nuttall, "Dell to Sell Its Computers at Wal-Mart," *Financial Times,* May 25, 2007, 24. Maija Palmer and Kevin Allison, "Dell Plans More Emphasis on Services," *Financial Times,* June 6, 2007, 26.

2. Faith Keenan, Stanley Holmes, Jay Greene and Roger O. Crockett, "A Mass Market of One," *BusinessWeek,* December 2, 2002, 62–65.

3. Cliff Edwards, "Boutiques for the Flagging Brand," *BusinessWeek,* May 24, 2004, 68.

4. James Lamont, "De Beers to Reduce Its Client List," *Financial Times,* June 9, 2007, 23.

5. Philip Kotler and Kevin Lane Keller, *A Framework for Marketing Management,* 3rd ed. (Upper Saddle River NJ: Pearson/Prentice Hall, 2007).

6. Paul Taylor, "Coming Soon: Films on File," *Financial Times,* Wednesday, May 31, 2006, 12.

7. Mariko Sanchanta, "Sony to Cut U.S. Jobs to Prop Up PS3," *Financial Times,* Friday, June 8, 2007, 28.

8. James P Womack and Daniel T Jones, "Lean Consumption," *Harvard Business Review,* March 2005, 59–68.

9. Philip Kotler and Kevin Lane Keller, *A Framework for Marketing Management,* 3rd ed. (Upper Saddle River NJ: Pearson/Prentice Hall, 2007).

10. Dominic Rushe, "Avon Calling," *Sunday Times,* January 15 2006, 3–5. Nanette Byrnes, "Avon: More Than Cosmetic Changes," *BusinessWeek,* March 12, 2007, 62–63.

11. Kerry Capell, "Wal-Mart with Wings," *BusinessWeek,* November 27, 2006, 44–46.

12. Nirmalya Kumar, *Marketing as Strategy: Understanding the CEO's Agenda for Driving Growth and Innovation* (Boston MA: Harvard Business School Press, 2004).

13. Nirmalya Kumar (2004) Ibid., p. 89.

14. Jonathan Birchall, "Liz Claiborne to Cut Brands and Focus on Retail Business," *Financial Times,* Thursday, July 12, 2007, 26.

15. For a complete discussion of channel management see Anne Coughlin, Erin Anderson, Louis W. Stern and Adel I. El-Ansary, *Marketing Channels,* 7th ed. (Englewood Cliffs, NJ: Prentice Hall, Inc., 2006).

16. This section of the chapter benefited from the advice and insightful contributions of Niall C. Piercy, School of Management, University of Bath, U.K.

17. Martin Christopher, *Marketing Logistics,* 2nd ed. (Oxford: Butterworth-Heinemann, 2003).

18. This section is based on Nigel F. Piercy, "Marketing Implementation: The Implications of Marketing Paradigm Weakness for the Strategy Execution Process," *Journal of the Academy of Marketing Science,* Vol. 26 No. 3, 1998, 222–236.

19. James P. Womack and Daniel T. Jones, *Lean Thinking: Banish Waste and Create Wealth in Your Corporation* (New York: Simon and Schuster, 1996).

20. Daniel T. Jones, "The Route to the Future," *Manufacturing Engineer,* February 2001, 33–37.

21. Martin Christopher, "The Agile Supply Chain," *Industrial Marketing Management,* Vol. 29 No. 1, 2000, 37–44.

22. J.B. Naylor, M.M. Naim, and D. Berry, "Leagility: Interfacing the Lean and Agile Manufacturing Paradigm in the Total Supply Chain," *International Journal of Production Economics,* Vol. 62, 1999, 107–118.

23. Martin Christopher and Denis R. Towill, "Supply Chain Migration from Lean to Functional to Agile and Customized," *Supply Chain Management,* Vol. 5 No. 4, 2000, 206–221.

24. B. Evans and M. Powell, "Synergistic Thinking: A Pragmatic View of 'Lean' and 'Agile'," *Logistics and Transport Focus,* Vol. 2 No. 10, December 2000. Mark Whitehead, "Flexible: Friend or Foe," *Supply Management,* January 6, 2000, 24–27.

25. Robert Meehan, "Create, Revise Channels for Customers," *Marketing News,* October 23, 2000, 48.

26. Jonathan Fenby, "B2B, Or Not to Be?," *Sunday Business,* March 26, 2000.

27. Weld Royal, "Death of a Salesman," www.industryweek.com, May 17, 1999, 59–60.

28. Paul F. Nunes and Frank V. Cespedes, "The Customer Has Escaped," *Harvard Business Review,* November 2003, 96–105.

29. Ibid.

30. James A. Narus and James C. Anderson, "Turn Your Industrial Distributors into Partners," *Harvard Business Review,* March-April 1986, 66–71.

31. Matt Hobbs and Hugh Wilson, "The Multi-Channel Challenge," *Marketing Business,* February 2004, 12–15.

32. An expanded discussion of these issues is available in Anne Coughlin, Erin Anderson, Louis W. Stern and Adel I. El-Ansary, *Marketing Channels,* 7th ed. (Englewood Cliffs, NJ: Prentice Hall, Inc., 2006). Chapter 12.

33. Alison Maitland, "GE to Release Audit of Ethical Violations," *Financial Times,* Thursday, May 19, 2005, 29. Joseph Weber, "The New Ethics Enforcers," *BusinessWeek,* February 13 2006, 76–77.

34. Philip R. Cateora and John Graham, *International Marketing*, 13th ed. (Burr Ridge IL: McGraw-Hill/Irwin, 2006).

35. Cateora and Graham (2006), ibid.

36. John Gapper, "America's Time-Warp Supermarkets," *Financial Times*, Monday, June 11, 2007, 11.

37. Elizabeth Rigby, "Food Retailing Recovery on Special Offer," *Financial Times*, Thursday, November 16, 2006, 21.

38. Cateora and Graham (2006), ibid.

39. Stephen Fidler, "Appetite for Risk Drives Industry," *Financial Times Special Report: Corporate Security*, June 27, 2007, 1.

Chapter 11

Pricing Strategy

Determining appropriate pricing strategies for products is challenging and dynamic in many firms because of deregulation, informed buyers, intense global competition, slow growth in many markets, and the opportunity for firms to strengthen market position. Price impacts financial performance and is an important influence on buyers' positioning of brands. Price may become a proxy measure for product quality when buyers have difficulty in evaluating the quality of complex products.

Developing a global perspective concerning the pricing strategies for many products is increasingly important. This is dramatically illustrated by the impact on developed country markets of products produced in China. This huge country can effectively compete with very low wages coupled with high technology capabilities. Moreover, China produces a wide range of consumer and business products. Prices range from 30 to 50 percent below the prices of the U.S. and other industrialized nations. China's competitive edge is further strengthened by an enormous domestic market. The GLOBAL FEATURE highlights several aspects of the China Challenge.

Nonetheless, it should be recognised that in some cases very low product prices from countries like China may be associated with undesirable employment conditions for local workers, unattractive levels of environmental pollution by production units, and compromised standards in product safety and quality.[1] Consumer criticisms of the social responsibility stance of fashion retailers sourcing products in very low cost markets have emerged. Major product recalls, like those implemented by Mattel in the toys industry in 2007 because of lead paint contaminating Barbie doll accessories, and the recall of household textiles contaminated with cancer-causing chemicals are illustrative of the problems which may be faced. However, the demand from consumers for very low price products remains strong.

Pricing decisions have substantial consequences for many companies as illustrated by the effects of price competition from China. Once implemented, it may be difficult to alter price strategy—particularly if the change calls for a significant increase in prices. Pricing actions that violate laws can land managers in jail. Price has many possible uses as a strategic instrument in business strategy.

First, we examine the strategic role of price in marketing strategy and discuss several pricing situations. Next, we describe and illustrate the steps to developing or modifying pricing strategy. We then examine situation analysis for pricing decisions, using several application situations to highlight the nature and scope of pricing analysis and consider deciding which pricing strategy to adopt. Finally, we discuss pricing policies and look at several special pricing issues.

Why should U.S. manufacturers worry when they have weathered decades of competition from Japan, Korea, and Europe? Because China is different. Here's why:

SPEED
Earlier rivals usually took years to build up an American presence. Chinese competition often arrives en masse and seizes share rapidly with unbeatable prices, leaving little time for the U.S. companies to adjust.

BREADTH
Other Asian nations shed labor-intensive work as they industrialized, but China is gaining share in low-end work such as garments and simple assembly at the same time its advancing into higher-value areas such as digital electronics.

COMPETITION
Japan and Korea are limited players in many industries. But in China, dozens of manufacturers battle for share in the domestic markets for appliances, cell phones, cars, and more, keeping everyone lean.

ALLIANCES
Unlike Japan or Korea, China welcomes foreign investment in key industries. Foreign ventures account for 60 percent of exports and a big share of local sales, so it's tough to complain that China is closed.

SIZE
China is both an export power and is itself becoming the world's biggest market for cars, appliances, cell phones, and more. That gives China unparalleled economies of scale.

ACCESS
Retail giants such as Wal-Mart that import directly help Chinese electronics makers build U.S. market share without the need to spend as much on distribution and ads as Sony, Sharp, and Samsung did.

U.S. POLICY
When imbalances got out of hand in the 1980s and 1990s the U.S. threatened sanctions to prod Japan and China to address trade grievances. China's entry into the WTO limits U.S. ability to act unilaterally.

Source: Pete Engardio and Dexter Roberts, "The China Price," *BusinessWeek,* December 6, 2004, 104–105.

Strategic Role of Price

In some companies, price plays a dominant role in marketing strategy, whereas, in other situations, price may perform a more passive role. Nevertheless, the strategic role of price is too often not recognized. "Part of the reason that pricing is misused and poorly understood is the common practice of making it the last marketing decision. We think that we must design products, communication plans, and a method of distribution before we have something to price. We then use pricing tactically to capture whatever value we can."[2] This practice should be avoided. Pricing plays an important strategic role in marketing strategy. Strategic choices about market targets, positioning strategies, and products and distribution strategies set guidelines for both price and promotion strategies. Product quality and features, type of distribution channel, end-users served, and the functions performed by value chain members all help establish a feasible price range. When an organization forms a new distribution network, selection of the channel and intermediaries may be driven by price strategy.

An illustration of the competitive advantage that may be achieved by strategic pricing decisions that focus on the value offered through fractional jet ownership is provided by Berkshire Hathaway's NetJets. The company is the market leader with a market share of 70 percent based on net value of aircraft sold and leased. In the fall of 2007, NetJets' worldwide fractionally managed fleet consisted of 612 aircraft. Fractional ownership enables individuals and companies to enjoy all of the benefits and more of owning their own jet at a fraction of the cost. Moreover, the responsibility of hiring and training flight crews, scheduling, and maintenance is handled by NetJets. Management identified a private air travel market opportunity for individuals and companies preferring the cachet and convenience of private air travel whose needs may not require the purchase of an aircraft. By buying a fractional interest in a corporate jet, customers also avoid purchasing a full interest corporate aircraft that would spend much of the time sitting on the ground.[3]

Price in the Positioning Strategy

Price is an important part of positioning strategy, and pricing decisions need to be coordinated with decisions for all of the positioning components. Importantly, this pricing perspective mandates understanding how pricing is viewed and understood by customers.

Product Strategy

Pricing decisions require analysis of the product mix, branding strategy, and product quality and features to determine the effects of these factors on price strategy. When a single product is involved, the pricing decision is simplified. Yet, in many instances, a line or mix of products must be priced. The prices for products in a line do not necessarily correspond to the cost of each item. For example, prices in supermarkets are based on a total mix strategy rather than individual item pricing. Understanding the composition of the mix and the interrelationships among products is important in determining pricing strategy, particularly when the brand identity is built around a line or mix of products rather than on a brand-by-brand basis. Consider a situation involving a product and consumable supplies for the product. One popular strategy is to price the product at competitive levels and set higher margins for supplies. Examples include parts for automobiles and cartridge refills for laser printers.

Product quality and features affect price strategy. A high-quality product may benefit from a high price to help establish a prestige position in the marketplace and satisfy management's profit performance requirements. Alternatively, a manufacturer supplying private-branded products to a retailer like Wal-Mart or Target must price competitively in order to obtain sales.

Distribution Strategy

Type of channel, distribution intensity, and channel configuration also influence pricing decisions. The functions performed and the motivation of intermediaries need to be considered in setting prices. Value-added resellers require price margins to pay for their activities and provide incentives to obtain their cooperation. Pricing is equally important when distribution is performed by the producer. Pricing in coordinated and managed channels reflects total channel considerations more so than in conventional channels. Intensive distribution is likely to call for more competitive pricing than selective or exclusive distribution. In multi-channel situations, pricing may pose a particular challenge. For example, if the website offers a lower price than conventional channels, how will members of those channels react? Pricing decisions must take into account these issues.

Responsibility for Pricing Decisions?

Responsibility for pricing decisions varies across organizations. Marketing executives determine pricing strategy in many companies. Pricing decisions may be made by the chief executive officer in some firms such as aircraft producers and construction firms. Manufacturing and engineering executives may be assigned pricing responsibility in companies that produce custom-designed industrial equipment. The vital importance of pricing decisions argues strongly for cross-functional participation. Pricing impacts all business functions. Operations, engineering, finance, and marketing executives should participate in strategic pricing decisions, regardless of where responsibility is assigned. Coordination of strategic and tactical pricing decisions with other aspects of marketing strategy is also critical because of the marketing program interrelationships involved.

Pricing Situations

Pricing strategy requires continuous monitoring because of changing external conditions, the actions of competitors, and the opportunities to gain a competitive edge through pricing actions. Our earlier look at the competitive impact of low priced Chinese products is illustrative. Various situations require pricing actions such as:

- Deciding how to price a new product, or line of products.
- Evaluating the need to adjust price as the product moves through the product life cycle.
- Changing a positioning strategy that calls for modifying the current pricing strategy.
- Deciding how to respond to the pressures of competitive threats.

Decisions about pricing for existing products may include increasing, decreasing, or holding prices at current levels. Understanding the competitive situation and possible actions by competitors is important in deciding if and when to alter prices. Demand and cost information are strong influences on new-product pricing. Deciding how to price a new product also should include considering competing substitutes, since few new products occupy a unique position in the market.

Dell Inc. has encountered a challenging pricing strategy situation in its consumer computer business.[4] In 2002 Dell experienced over 25 percent revenue growth in the important consumer growth segment. By 2005 growth had declined to 10 percent, and less than 8 percent growth was expected in 2007. The problem was aggressive price competition from Hewlett-Packard Co. and Gateway Inc. Offering value to consumer buyers requires low prices but also new features, help desks, and extensive retail distribution networks. Dell has exhausted its cost-cutting advantages in the consumer market, yet competition is offering even lower prices. Dell spends less on research and development than Apple Computer Inc., yet Dell's revenues are four times larger. Innovation has become critical for Dell in the consumer segment. Moreover, access by competitors to buyers through thousands of retail stores provides Dell's competition with important advantages. Dell's strategy options are to follow the consumer market down in pricing or continue to concentrate on only the business market which offers limited growth opportunities.

Roles of Pricing

Prices perform various roles in the marketing program—as a signal to the buyer, an instrument of competition, a means to improve financial performance, and a substitute for other marketing program functions (e.g., promotional pricing).

Signal to the Buyer

Price offers a fast and direct way of communicating with the buyer. The price is visible to the buyer and provides a basis of comparison between brands. Price may be used to position the brand as a high-quality product or instead to pursue head-on competition with another brand, as illustrated by Hewlett-Packard's aggressive competition with Dell on personal computers in the consumer segment.

Instrument of Competition

Price offers a way to quickly attack competitors or, alternatively, to position a firm away from direct competition. For example, off-price retailers use a low-price strategy against department stores and other retailers. Price strategy is always related to competition whether firms use a higher, lower, or equal price.

Improving Financial Performance

Since prices and costs determine financial performance, pricing strategies need to be assessed as to their estimated impact on the firm's financial performance, both in the short and long run. Global competition has forced many firms to adopt pricing approaches that will generate revenues in line with forecasts. Importantly, both revenues and costs need to be taken into account in selecting pricing strategies.

Marketing Program Considerations

Prices may substitute for selling effort, advertising, and sales promotion. Alternatively, price may be used to reinforce these promotion activities in the marketing program. The role of pricing often depends on how other components in the marketing program are used. For example, prices can be used as an incentive to channel members, as the focus of promotional strategy, and as a signal of value. In deciding the role of pricing in marketing strategy, management evaluates the importance of prices to competitive positioning, probable buyers' reactions, financial requirements, and interrelationships with other components in the marketing program.

Pricing Strategy

The major steps in selecting a pricing strategy for a new product or altering an existing strategy are shown in Exhibit 11.1. Strategy formulation begins by determining pricing objectives, which guide strategy development. Next, it is necessary to analyze the pricing situation, taking into account demand, cost, competition, and pricing objectives. These

EXHIBIT 11.1
**Steps in Selecting a
Pricing Strategy**

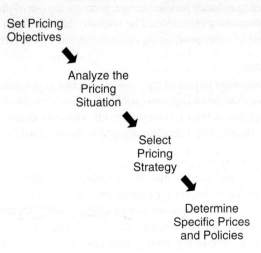

analyses indicate how much flexibility there is in pricing a new product or changing the pricing strategy for an existing product. Interestingly, Gillette's consumer tests of the MACH 3 razor indicated that there was little buyer resistance to a price 45 percent above Gillette's SensorExcel.[5] This information indicated that management had a lot of flexibility in deciding how to price the MACH 3. Based on the situation analysis and the pricing objectives, the pricing strategy is selected. Finally, specific prices and operating policies are determined to implement the strategy. Each step in the pricing strategy that is shown in Exhibit 11.1 is discussed in more detail in the rest of the chapter.

Pricing Objectives

Pricing strategies are expected to achieve specific objectives. More than one pricing objective is usually involved, and sometimes the objectives may conflict with each other. If so, adjustments may be needed on one of the conflicting objectives. For example, if one objective is to increase market share by 30 percent and the second objective is to obtain a high profit margin, management should decide if both objectives are feasible. If not, one must be adjusted. Objectives set essential guidelines for pricing strategy.

Pricing objectives vary according to the situational factors (e.g., intensity of competition, economic conditions, etc.) present and management's preferences. A high price may be set to recover investment in a new product. This practice is typical in the pricing of new prescription drugs. A low price may be used to gain market position, discourage new competition, or attract new buyers. Several examples of pricing objectives follow:

Gain Market Position

Low prices may be used to gain sales and market share. Limitations include encouraging price wars and reduction (or elimination) of profit contributions. Even though buyers may have been responsive to a price for MACH 3 that was 45 percent above SensorExcel, Gillette's management used a 35 percent price increase that was more likely to gain market position.

Achieve Financial Performance

Prices are selected to contribute to financial objectives such as profit contribution and cash flow. Prices that are too high may not be acceptable to buyers. A key objective for Dell Inc. in the consumer market segment was pricing to achieve financial performance in combination with holding market position.

Product Positioning

Prices may be used to enhance product image, promote the use of the product, create awareness, and other positioning objectives. The visibility of price (high or low) may contribute to the effectiveness of other positioning components such as advertising.

Stimulate Demand

Price is used to encourage buyers to try a new product or to purchase existing brands during periods when sales slow down (e.g., recession). A potential problem is that buyers may balk at purchasing when prices return to normal levels. Discount coupons for new products like Colgate's Total toothpaste help stimulate demand without actually lowering listed prices.

Influence Competition

The objective of pricing actions may be to influence existing or potential competitors. Management may want to discourage market entry or price cutting by current competitors. Alternatively, a price leader may want to encourage industry members to raise prices. One problem is that competitors may not respond as predicted.

Intel employed an interesting strategy for competing with inexpensive semiconductors which offered rapid graphics processing and posed a threat to Intel's flagship Pentium chip.[6] Rather than lowering the Pentium price to appeal to the price-sensitive market segment, Intel developed the Cirrus chip based on the Pentium platform which eliminated additional design and tooling costs. Some of the Pentium capabilities were not activated in the new chip, which was priced to compete with competitors' products. Intel stimulated demand without lowering the price of its premium chip.

Analyzing the Pricing Situation

Pricing analysis is essential in evaluating new product concepts, developing test marketing strategy, and designing a new product introduction strategy. Pricing analysis is also important for existing products because of changes in the market and competitive environment, unsatisfactory market performance, and modifications in marketing strategy over the product's life cycle. Intel's analysis of pricing in the price-sensitive chip market segment is illustrative. The factors influencing the pricing situation include: (1) customer price sensitivity; (2) product costs; (3) current and potential competitive actions; and (4) pricing objectives (Exhibit 11.2). We examine each factor and illustrate what is involved in the analyses.

Customer Price Sensitivity

One of the challenges in pricing analysis is estimating how buyers will respond to different prices. The pricing of Procter & Gamble Company's analgesic brand, Aleve, illustrates this situation. The product was introduced in a highly-competitive $2.38 billion market in 1994.[7] Aleve is the over-the-counter version of Naprosyn (developed by Syntex Corporation). P&G estimated first year sales of $200 million. A $100 million marketing effort spearheaded Aleve's market entry. The pricing was the same as Advil though Aleve lasts eight to twelve hours compared to Advil's eight hours. Aggressive promotional pricing (coupons) was anticipated from the leading competitors, Tylenol ($700 million sales) and Advil ($330 million). Some industry authorities expected Aleve to pose a greater threat to the weaker brands (Bayer, Bufferin, and Nuprin) rather than the two leading competitors.

Analysis of buyers' price sensitivity should answer the following questions:

1. Size of the product-market in terms of buying potential.
2. The market segments and market targeting strategy to be used.
3. Sensitivity of demand in each segment to changes in price.
4. Importance of non-price factors, such as features and performance.
5. The estimated sales at different price levels.

Let's examine these questions for Aleve. The analgesic market was growing at about a 3 percent annual rate. Aleve offers extended relief benefits to arthritis sufferers and people

EXHIBIT 11.2
Factors Impacting the Pricing Situation

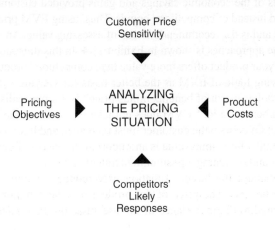

with sore muscles. P&G apparently wanted to stress the brand's performance (value proposition) rather than encourage price competition. Management's $200 million sales estimate would position Aleve in third place behind Tylenol and Advil.

The core issue in pricing is finding out what value requirements (benefits-costs) the buyer places on the product or brand.[8] Pricing decision makers need this information in order to determine the pricing strategy. Basing price only on cost may lead to pricing too high or too low compared to the value perceived by the buyer. Buyers see different values depending on their use situation so market segment analysis is essential. For example, people who want an analgesic that lasts longer are likely to perceive a high value provided by Aleve.

Price Elasticity

Price elasticity is the percentage change in the quantity sold of a brand when the price changes, divided by the percentage change in price. Elasticity is measured for changes in price from some specific price level so elasticity is not necessarily constant over the range of prices under consideration. Surprisingly, research indicates that in some situations people will buy more of certain products at *higher* prices, thus displaying a price-quantity relationship that slopes upward to the right, rather than the typical downward sloping volume and price relationship. In these instances, buyers seem to be using price as a measure of quality because they are unable to evaluate the product. Estimating the exact shape of the demand curve (price-quantity relationship) is probably impossible in most instances. Even so, there are ways to estimate the sensitivity of customers to alternative prices. Test marketing can be used for this purpose. Study of historical price and quantity data may be helpful. End-user research studies, such as consumer evaluations of price, are also used. These approaches, coupled with management judgment, help indicate the responsiveness of sales to different prices in the range of prices that is under consideration.

An interesting discussion of the challenges in obtaining information from potential buyers about their willingness to purchase a product at different prices is provided in Exhibit 11.3. The differences in people's responses based on how price questions are presented highlight the importance of experience and research skills in customer pricing research.

Nonprice Factors

Factors other than price may be important in analyzing buying situations. For example, buyers may be willing to pay a premium price to gain other advantages or, instead, be willing to forgo certain advantages for lower prices. Factors other than price which may be important are quality, uniqueness, availability, convenience, service, and warranty.

The value offered to the buyer by a brand is relevant information in setting price and determining pricing strategy.[9] Customer value mapping (CVM) estimates value as the perceived quality buyers obtain per unit of price. In contrast, value using economic value modeling (EVM) consists of the economic savings and gains provided customers due to purchase of the firm's brand instead of competitors' brands. Thus, using EVM price is determined by the value provided and is the recommended basis of assessing value. An illustrative comparison of the two value approaches is shown in Exhibit 11.4. In this illustration using the preferred EVM method, your product offers more value than competitors' products.

The underlying logic of EVM as the better basis for viewing value offered to the customer is that "dollar worth of benefits minus price" is a more realistic view of value than using the price/benefit ratio.[10] CVM does not take into account the differentiated benefits that are offered. Of course, the customer must recognize and have a preference for the differentiated benefits. Economic value is an important frame of reference in communicating with customers and designing a positioning strategy.

In some instances the buying situation may reduce the importance of price in the buyer's choice process. The price of the product may be a minor factor when the cost is small compared to the importance of the use situation. Examples include infrequently

EXHIBIT 11.3
Effects of Price Presentation

Source: Kent B. Monroe, *Pricing.* 3rd ed. (Burr Ridge, IL: McGraw-Hill/ Irwin, 2003), 223. Copyright © The McGraw-Hill Companies. Used with permission.

One problem in conducting price research is how to get information from respondents about their willingness to purchase a product at different prices. Ideally, we would like to know how the individual would respond to different prices. However, once they realize that we are trying to estimate their demand curve individuals may provide answers that reflect their understanding of the traditional demand curve—that they buy more at lower prices and less or none at higher prices. The problem is that price is presented as a cost or sacrifice to potential buyers, not as an attribute. To present price as an attribute means that other product or service information must be presented to the respondents.

One research study looked at a range of prices, but the researchers varied whether only one price was presented to respondents or whether multiple prices were presented. In the multiple price situation, prices were presented sequentially, either high to low or low to high. As the graph indicates, substantial differences occurred in the estimates. Presenting multiple prices produced downward sloping demand curves, but a single price presentation revealed increasing estimated usage between $3 and $9, declining thereafter.

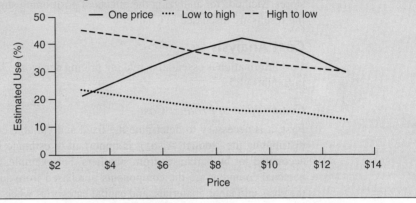

purchased electric parts for home entertainment equipment, batteries for appliances, and health and beauty aids during a vacation. The need for important but relatively inexpensive parts for industrial equipment is another situation that reduces the role of price in the buyer's purchase decision. Quick Metal, an adhesive produced by Loctite Corporation, is used by maintenance personnel to repair production equipment such as a broken gear tooth. At less than $20 a tube, the price is not a major concern since one tube will keep an expensive production line operating until a new part is installed.

Other examples of non-price factors that affect the buying situation include: (1) purchases of products that are essential to physical health, such as pain relief; (2) choices

EXHIBIT 11.4
Comparison of Approaches to Value Determination

Source: Gerald E. Smith and Thomas T. Nagle, "A Question of Value," *Marketing Management,* July/August 2005, 40.

Suppose your firm's differentiated product provides $15,000 in value for customers and costs $6,000, whereas competitors' commodity products offer $10,000 in value and cost $3,000.

EVM Value	CVM Price/Benefit Ratio
Your Product:	Your Product:
$15,000 − $6,000 = $9,000	$\dfrac{\$6,000}{\$15,000} = 0.40$
Competitors' Products:	Competitors' Products:
$10,000 − $3,000 = $7,000	$\dfrac{\$3,000}{\$10,000} = 0.30$
Your product offers higher value than competitors' products	Competitors' products offer the most favorable price/benefit

among brands of complex products that are difficult to evaluate, such as DVD equipment (a high price may be used as a gauge of quality); and (3) image-enhancement situations such as serving prestige brands of drinks to socially important guests.

Forecasts

Forecasts of sales are needed for the price alternatives that management is considering. In planning the introduction of Aleve, P&G's management could look at alternative sales forecasts based on different prices and other marketing program variations. These forecasts, when combined with cost estimates, indicate the financial impact of different price strategies. The objective is to estimate sales in units for each product (or brand) at the prices under consideration.

Controlled tests can be used to forecast the effects of price changes. For example, a fast-food chain can evaluate the effects of different prices on demand using tests in a sample of stores. Methods for analyzing the effects of positioning strategy components and positioning results are discussed in Chapter 6.

Cost Analysis

Cost information is essential in making pricing decisions. A guide to cost analysis is shown in Exhibit 11.5.

Composition of Product Cost

First, it is necessary to determine the fixed and variable costs involved in producing and distributing the product. Also, it is important to estimate the amount of the product cost accounted for by purchases from suppliers. For example, a large portion of the cost of a personal computer are the components purchased from suppliers. It is useful to separate the costs into labor, materials, and capital categories when studying cost structure.

Activity based costing (ABC) is a technique which provides information for pricing strategy. Many firms have adopted ABC as a costing mechanism to more appropriately assign indirect costs to goods and services. The key component of ABC is to assign costs based upon the activities that are performed to create the good or provide the service being examined. With ABC, decision makers obtain a much more accurate representation of product costs. This information is useful in pricing decisions and comparisons across product lines and customer groups. Since ABC estimates the cost of the product in terms of a collection of activities, it is much easier to evaluate pricing for particular attributes or service levels. Similarly, it is possible to make comparisons to competitors by evaluating the costs of activities necessary to offer product enhancements.

Firms that successfully implement ABC do so initially as an accounting technique, yet the ultimate objective is to facilitate activity based management (ABM). In this manner, the cost data become an integral part of the product strategy in terms of considering the entire value chain, encompassing suppliers, customers, and competitors. For example, products that may require packaging or delivery modifications incur additional costs. With ABM, decision makers have a better understanding of these additional costs, can price accordingly, and can consider these costs in conjunction with the offerings of competitors.

EXHIBIT 11.5
Cost Analysis for Pricing Decisions

- Determine the components of the cost of the product.
- Estimate how cost varies with the volume of sales.
- Analyze the cost competitive advantage of the product.
- Decide how experience in producing the product affects costs.
- Estimate how much control management has over costs.

Volume Effect on Cost

The next part of cost analysis examines how costs vary at different levels of production or quantities purchased. Can economies of scale be gained over the volume range that is under consideration, given the target market and positioning strategy? At what volume levels are significant cost reductions possible? Volume effect analysis determines the extent to which the volume produced or distributed should be taken into account in estimating costs.

Competitive Advantage

Comparing key competitors' costs is often valuable. Are their costs higher, lower, or about the same? Although such information may be difficult to obtain, experienced managers can often make accurate estimates. In some industries such as commercial airlines cost information is available. It is useful to place key competitors into relative product cost categories (e.g., higher, lower, same). Analysts may be able to estimate competitive cost information from knowledge of types of costs, wage rates, material costs, production facilities, and related information.

Experience Effect

It is important to consider the effect of experience on costs. Experience or learning-curve analysis (using historical data) indicates whether costs and prices for various products decline by a given amount each time the number of units produced doubles. However, price declines may be uneven because of competitive influences. When unit costs (vertical axis) are plotted against total accumulated volume (horizontal axis), costs decline with volume if an experience effect is present.[11] This occurs when experience over time increases the efficiency of production operations.

Control over Costs

Finally, it is useful to consider how much influence an organization may have over its product costs in the future. To what extent can research and development, bargaining power with suppliers, process innovation, and other improvements help to reduce costs over the planning horizon? These considerations are interrelated with experience-curve analysis, yet may operate over a shorter time range. The bargaining power of an organization in its channels of distribution, for example, can have a major effect on costs, and the effects can be immediate.

Competitor Analysis

Each competitor's pricing strategy needs to be evaluated to determine: (1) which firms represent the most direct competition (actual and potential) for buyers in the market targets that are under consideration; (2) how competing firms are positioned on a relative price basis and the extent to which price is used as an active part of their marketing strategies; (3) how successful each firm's price strategy has been; and (4) the key competitors' probable responses to alternative price strategies.

The discussion in Chapter 2 considers guidelines for competitor identification. It is important to determine both potential and current competitors. The fiber-optic cable network industry is an interesting competitor analysis situation. In 2001, an estimated 39 million miles of fiber networks covered the United States, while less than 3 percent of this capacity was actually in use.[12] The anticipated escalating demand for telecommunications bandwidth encouraged many firms like Quest Communications International Inc. and Level 3 Communications Inc. to rapidly build underground fiber-optic networks. Barriers to entry were low. Nearly 1500 firms had developed cable networks by 2001. Global Crossing Ltd., losing money on over $1 billion in revenues, spent $20 billion to build a

Strategy Feature

Extended Warranty Warfare in Retailing

In late 2005 Wal-Mart Inc. launched extended warranties on TVs and computers selling above $300: Wal-Mart warranty prices are creating challenges for Best Buy and Circuit City profit margins. Here are service contract price comparisons on a per-year basis (for the same or similar items).

SERVICE CONTRACT PRICE

PRODUCT		Wal-Mart	Best Buy	Circuit City
RCA 52-inch HDTV projection TV	About $1000	$29.44	$62.49	$100.00
Toshiba notebook computer	$996 to $1,250	$34.44	$83.33	$92.50
Hewlett-Packard desktop computer package	$629 to $748, including rebates	$29.44	$69.99	$82.49

(Data: Wal-Mart, Best Buy, and Circuit City websites)

The pricing options for Best Buy and Circuit City are to: (1) not change their prices and face possible sales losses; or (2) reduce warranty prices and negatively impact profits.

Source: Robert Berner, "Watch Out, Best Buy and Circuit City," *BusinessWeek,* November 21, 2005, 46 and 48.

100,000 mile global network. The excess capacity was expected to cause prices for network space to fall more than 60 percent in 2001. An industry shakeout was likely since there is not enough demand to support the large number of competitors. In 2006 rising Internet usage was beginning to expand fiber-optic cable usage although extensive excess capacity remained.

The success of a competitor's price strategy is usually gauged by financial performance. One problem with using this metric to gauge pricing success is accounting for influences other than price on profits.

The most difficult of the four questions about competition is predicting what rivals will do in response to alternative price actions. No changes are likely unless one firm's price is viewed as threatening (low) or greedy (high). Competitive pressures, actual and potential, often narrow the range of feasible prices and rule out the use of extremely high or low prices relative to competition. In new-product markets, competitive factors may be insignificant, although very high prices may attract potential competitors.

The retail consumer electronics market offers an interesting look at the effects of intense competition. Wal-Mart Inc. launched a competitive battle against Best Buy Co. and Circuit City Stores Inc. in 2005 using much lower prices for TV and computer service contract warranties.[13] The initiative is part of Wal-Mart's strategy to up-scale its merchandise, including the interiors of many of its electronics departments and addition of high-end products. The extended warranty on electronics products is a retailer's most profitable line of business. As shown in the STRATEGY FEATURE Wal-Mart's warranty prices are on the average 50 percent lower than Best Buy and Circuit City.

358

A popular exercise in seminars and executive briefings we hold is to ask executives to participate in a prisoner's dilemma pricing game. Each team must decide whether to price its products high or low compared to those of another team in 10 rounds of competition. The objective is to earn the most money; results are determined by the decision that two competitors make in comparison with each other.

The game fairly accurately simulates a typical profit/loss scenario for price competition in mature markets. The objective is to impart several lessons in pricing competition, the first being that pricing is more like playing poker than solitaire. Success depends not just on a combination of luck and how the hand is played but also on how well competitors play their hands. In real markets, outcomes depend not only on how customers respond but, perhaps more important, on how competitors respond to changes in price.

If a competitor matches a price decrease, neither the initiator nor the follower will achieve a significant increase in sales and both are likely to have a significant decrease in profits. In developing pricing strategy, managers need to anticipate the moves of their competitors and attempt to influence those moves by selectively communicating information to influence competitive behavior.

The second lesson is that managers must adopt a very long time horizon when considering changes in price. Once started, price wars are difficult to stop. A simple decision to drop price often becomes the first shot in a war that no competitor wins. Before initiating a price decrease, managers must consider how it will affect the competitive stability of markets.

The third lesson from the prisoner's dilemma is that careful use of a value-based marketing approach can reverse a trend toward price-based marketing. This is accomplished through signaling, a nonprice competitive tactic that involves selectively disclosing information to competitors to influence their behavior. The steel and airline industries provide prominent examples of the signaling strategy's use. They often rely on announcements that conveniently appear on the front pages of the *Wall Street Journal* to signal competitors of pending price moves and provide them with opportunities to follow. The strategy takes time to implement, but it provides a far better long-term competitive position for marketers who employ it.

Source: Excerpt from Reed Holden and Thomas T. Nagle, "Kamikaze Pricing," *Marketing Management,* Summer 1998, 34. Reprinted with permission of the American Marketing Association.

Game theory is a promising method for analyzing competitors' pricing strategy options. The technique became very popular in the 1990s. An interesting application of game theory is discussed in the STRATEGY FEATURE. Game theory was used to design the auction process for the simultaneous sale of several third generation (3G) wireless phone licenses in Britain.[14] The process was very successful for the government. After 150 rounds of bidding, final bidders for five licenses paid a total of $34 billion, more than seven times the amount initially anticipated by the government.

Pricing Objectives

Management's objectives may affect the extent of pricing flexibility and should be included as the last part of analyzing the pricing situation. For example, an objective of gaining market position where low prices are used to increase sales and market share would narrow the range of pricing options even if the demand-cost gap is wide. Similar assessments are needed depending on the pricing objectives set by management. Importantly, if one or more of the pricing objectives cannot be achieved based on the assessments of customer price sensitivity, costs, and competitors' likely responses (Exhibit 11.2), the feasibility of the objective(s) may need to be evaluated.

Selecting the Pricing Strategy

Analysis of the pricing situation provides essential information for selecting the pricing strategy. Using this information management needs to: (1) determine extent of pricing flexibility; and (2) decide how to position price relative to costs and how visible to make the price of the product. The pricing strategy needs to be coordinated with the development of the entire marketing program since in most, if not all, instances there are other important marketing program component influences on buyers' purchasing behavior.

How Much Flexibility Exists?

Demand and cost factors determine the extent of pricing flexibility. Within these upper and lower boundaries, competition and pricing objectives also influence the choice of a specific pricing strategy. Exhibit 11.6 illustrates how these factors influence flexibility. The price gap between demand and cost may be narrow or wide. A narrow gap simplifies the decision; a wide gap provides a greater range of feasible pricing options. Choice of the pricing strategy is influenced by competitors' strategies, present and future, and by management's pricing objectives. Management must determine where to position price within the flexibility band shown in Exhibit 11.6. In competitive markets the feasibility range may be very narrow. Recall, for example, P&Gs pricing of Aleve, which was priced the same as a key competitor's brand. New markets or emerging market segments in established markets may allow management more flexibility in strategy selection.

A pricing strategy situation is described in the RELATIONSHIP FEATURE. Several important pricing issues are highlighted. Before reading the next paragraph identify the issues that you believe need to be considered in deciding what action to take concerning the pricing of Novaton. Also decide whether you agree or disagree with the decision made by Novet's pricing team.

The Novaton illustration highlights several issues to consider in analyzing the pricing situation (Exhibit 11.2). A key question is why Novaton is not selling well in the market.[15] The problem may be price but it could also be very low customer awareness (25 percent). Surprisingly, the team's pricing analyses did not consider customers' perceptions of Novaton. Depending on how customers position the brand, a price cut may not be effective. The information about Holycon's plans may be correct but the team is basing a very important pricing decision on extremely limited intelligence. Similarly, the competitor's manufacturing capacity information came from only one person. Finally, the competitor's costs were estimated by assuming Holycon had similar operations to Novaton's. This premise may be faulty.

EXHIBIT 11.6
Determinants of Pricing Flexibility

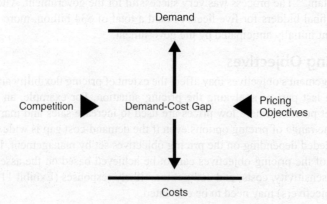

Demand

Competition ▶ Demand-Cost Gap ◀ Pricing Objectives

Costs

The meeting was held on a snowy day in January. Novet's corporate offices, located in a large midwestern city, were quiet as people arrived late because of the new snowstorm. Mary Fritz, a marketing manager, started the discussion: "Let me review our progress on Novaton. We introduced it 18 months ago to a marketplace containing no competitive products, and we knew this product would be really valuable to our customers. We set our initial price at $250 per unit, expecting to sell 5,000 units in our first year, an additional 20,000 units this year, and 40,000 units next year. We just knew that as customers started to use the product, they would tell others. And word of mouth would be our best advertisement.

"We know this new product is really great," Fritz said, "and the customers who bought it like it a lot. But we've only sold 492 units so far. Now we're hearing Holycon Inc. is about to introduce a competing unit called the H-200. Some of our distributors have seen the H-200 and say it's just as good. Holycon has told the distributors they will price at 15 percent below us. In other markets where we've faced Holycon, we've had to be really aggressive in cutting prices in order to keep share. This time, we would like to get ahead of them, and use a preemptive strategy."

Fritz's group manager, Nina Pacofsky, responded: "OK, what do you suggest? And don't forget, we've committed to some very hefty profit goals this year. I'm not ready to tell Division we're not going to make it—especially this early in the year."

"Well, here's what we propose," said Fritz. "Since Holycon has always cut prices in the past, we're going to cut prices first this time and make it hard for them to compete. We propose to cut prices by 30 percent. In order to keep our profitability level, we're going to cut back on advertising. And, we figure that the lower price will not only discourage Holycon, but be so attractive when combined with our features that volume will go way up. We'll actually exceed our projected profit level for the year."

John Fine, the product manager, asked what the awareness level was for Novaton. Fritz didn't know, but Sally Olson found a note in a market research report indicating that awareness was about 25 percent.

Pacofsky hesitated. "Does anyone know if Holycon has actually built manufacturing facilities for their product?"

James Busky, the manufacturing manager, responded: "I heard from an extruder salesman that he had sold two extruders to Holycon. The salesman told me what the extruders were and said they were for a secret project. But, based on the type of extruders, they could only be used to compete with us. And, given the size of the extruders, Holycon's capacity will probably be about 40,000 units per year, almost 60 percent of our capacity."

Pacofsky wanted to know what Holycon's costs were likely to be and also wondered whether Holycon would be able to make any money if Novaton's prices were 30 percent lower.

"Based on our costs, and the fact that Holycon invested two years after us, we believe Holycon will have a margin of 3 percent on sales," said Tom Jeffries, the group competitive intelligence and market research specialist. "Because we were first to market, and customers know us better, we think Holycon will not get enough share to justify its entry. We think they'll drop out of the market if we cut our prices."

"OK," Pacofsky said. "Go ahead with the price cut. We know Holycon always cuts prices, and it's clear we're not getting customers to buy because our prices are too high. Keep me up-to-date on sales. And we've got to keep our profits up."

The meeting adjourned. Mary Fritz headed off to draft new price lists and announcements to the sales force. Heading to her office, she dropped into the advertising manager's office, and asked him to stop all advertising on Novaton.

Source: George E. Cressman Jr., "Snatching Defeat from the Jaws of Victory," *Marketing Management*, Summer 1997, 10. Reprinted with permission of the American Marketing Association.

Thus, there are several serious questions about Fritz's pricing strategy.[16] It was later determined after Holycon entered the market that the underlying problem causing the low sales was low awareness. Interestingly, customers actually considered Novaton to be better than Holycon. Novet's market sensing information was faulty. Holycon's costs were 60 percent less than Novet's costs for Novaton. Holycon came into the market at prices 40 percent below Novaton's original price. After two years of tough price competition Novet dropped out of the market. This might have been avoided if the pricing team had recognized that a better pricing strategy would have been to position Novaton as offering superior value worth its original price and aggressively communicated the value proposition to build awareness with potential buyers.

Price Positioning and Visibility

A key decision is how far above cost to price a new product within the flexibility band (Exhibit 11.6). A relatively low market entry price may be used with the objective of building volume and market position, or instead, a high price may be selected to generate large margins. The former is a "penetration" strategy whereas the latter is a "skimming" strategy. Analysis of the results of low price strategies in highly competitive markets indicates that while the strategies are sometimes necessary, they should be used with considerable caution.[17] Recall our earlier discussion of the consequences of game theory in the STRATEGY FEATURE.

Lack of knowledge about the probable market response of buyers to the new product complicates the pricing decision. Several factors may affect the choice of a pricing approach for a new product, including the cost and life span of the product, the estimated responsiveness of buyers to alternative prices, and assessment of competitive reaction. The dangers of faulty assessment of these factors are illustrated by the RELATIONSHIP FEATURE about the Novaton product.

A decision should also be made about how visible price will be in the promotion of the new product. The use of a low entry price requires active promotion of the price to gain market position. When firms use a high price relative to cost, price often assumes a passive role in the marketing mix, and performance in combination with other attributes of the product are stressed in the marketing program.

Illustrative Pricing Strategies

The pricing strategy selected depends on how management decides to position the product relative to competition, and whether price will perform an active or passive role in the marketing program. The use of price as an active (or passive) factor refers to whether price is highlighted in advertising, personal selling, and other promotional efforts. Many firms choose neutral pricing strategies (at or near the prices of key competitors), emphasizing non-pricing factors in their marketing strategies.[18] The neutral pricing strategy seeks to remove price as the basis of choosing among competing brands. We examine the four illustrative strategies shown in Exhibit 11.7, describing their characteristics and features.

High-Active Strategy

Emphasizing a high price in promotional activities is intended to convey to the buyer that the expensive brand offers superior value. While used on a very limited basis, this pricing strategy has been employed to symbolically position products such as high-end alcoholic beverages. Making price visible and active can appeal to the buyer's perceptions of

EXHIBIT 11.7
Role of Price

Role of Price

	Active	Passive
High	High-Active e.g. value superiority	High-Passive e.g. emphasize non-price competitive factors
Low	Low-Active e.g. discounters	Low-Passive e.g. avoid price comparisons

Price Level

quality, image, and dependability of products and services. A firm using a high-price strategy is also less subject to retaliation by competitors, particularly if its brand is differentiated from other brands.

High-Passive Strategy

High prices may be essential to gain the margins necessary to serve small target markets, produce high-quality products, or pay for the development of new products. Relatively high-priced brands are often marketed by featuring non-price factors rather than using high-active strategies. Product features and performance can be stressed when the people in the target market are concerned with product quality and performance. Expensive Swiss watches are marketed using the high-passive pricing strategy.

Low-Active Strategy

Several retailers use this pricing strategy, including Home Depot (home improvement), Dollar General Stores (apparel), Office Depot (office supplies), and Southwest Airlines (air travel). The low-active strategy is also popular with discount stock brokers. When price is an important factor for a large segment of buyers, a low-active price strategy is very effective, as indicated by the rapid growth of retailers like Wal-Mart. It is a more attractive option when competition for the market target is not heavy or when a company has cost advantages and a strong position in the product-market. Southwest Airlines has performed very well using the low-active pricing strategy for its city-to-city route network.

Low-Passive Strategy

This strategy may be used by small producers whose brands are not familiar to buyers and have lower-cost features than other suppliers. By not emphasizing a low price, the firm runs less danger that potential buyers will assume the brand is inferior to other brands. Some firms participating in conventional distribution channels may not spend much on marketing their products and, thus, can offer low prices because of lower costs.

Legal and Ethical Considerations

A wide variety of laws and regulations affect pricing actions. Legal constraints are important influences on the pricing of goods and services in many different national and cooperative regional trade environments. Pricing practices in the United States that have received the most attention from government include:

Price Fixing

A conspiracy among firms to set prices for a product is termed price fixing. Pricing fixing is illegal under the Sherman Act. When two or more competitors collude to explicitly or implicitly set prices, this practice is called *horizontal price fixing.* For example, six foreign vitamin companies recently pled guilty to price fixing in the human and animal vitamin industry and paid the largest fine in U.S. history: $335 million. *Vertical price fixing* involves controlling agreements between independent buyers and sellers (a manufacturer and a retailer) whereby sellers are required to not sell products below a minimum retail price. This practice, called *resale price maintenance,* was declared illegal in 1975 under provisions of the Consumer Goods Pricing Act.

Price Discrimination

The Clayton Act as amended by the Robinson-Patman Act prohibits price discrimination—the practice of charging different prices to different buyers for goods of like grade and quality. However, not all price differences are illegal; only those that substantially lessen competition or create a monopoly are deemed unlawful.

Deceptive Pricing

Price deals that mislead consumers fall into the category of deceptive pricing. Deceptive pricing is outlawed by the Federal Trade Commission. *Bait and switch* is an example of deceptive pricing. This occurs when a firm offers a very low price on a product (the bait) to attract customers to a store. Once in the store, the customer is persuaded to purchase a higher-priced item (the switch) using a variety of tricks, including (1) degrading the promoted item and (2) not having the promised item in stock or refusing to take orders for it.

Predatory Pricing

Predatory pricing is charging a very low price for a product with the intent of driving competitors out of business. Once competitors have been driven out, the firm raises its prices. Proving the presence of this practice has been difficult and expensive because it must be shown that the predator explicitly attempted to destroy a competitor and the predatory price was below the defendant's average cost.[19]

Ethical issues in pricing are more subjective and difficult to evaluate than legal factors. Companies may include ethical guidelines in their pricing policies. Deciding what is or is not ethical is often difficult. Possible ethical issues should be evaluated when developing a pricing strategy.

Ethics concerning the pricing of prescription drugs are a continuing challenge for the industry. The drug producers are under continuing pressure from consumers, elected officials, and special interest groups concerning high drug prices. Drug pricing raises possible ethical issues, although the companies indicate their prices are necessary due to large research and development expenses. Nonetheless, one study reported that the average price of fifty drugs most used by the elderly increased 3.9 percent in 1999 compared to the 2.2 percent inflation rate.[20] Price controls have been proposed by consumer groups. The pharmaceutical industry was criticized for spending $14 billion in 1999 on promotion, public relations, advertising, and drug samples to doctors.

Consider the dilemma, for example, facing executives in the tobacco industry and those associated with it, regarding the low pricing of cigarettes in the developing world described in the ETHICS FEATURE.

- The global tobacco industry supports about 100,000 jobs worldwide and duties on tobacco products provide huge tax revenues for governments throughout the developed world.
- Tobacco companies describe their product as "a legal and widely enjoyed consumer product," while also recognizing that cigarette smoking poses a severe health risk for both users and "passive smokers."
- Cigarette smoking is declining in many developed countries, but remains at high levels in the developing world.
- The industry is implementing several important initiatives in the developing world: campaigns against child labor in tobacco cultivation; is involved in programs to alleviate indigenous diseases in developing countries; encourages environmental protection.
- The dilemma is whether tobacco companies should be actively supporting cigarette smoking in developing countries, and the role of low-priced brands in developing these markets, compared to the effects of tobacco cultivation industry of declining demand.
- These dilemmas are shared with companies who transport and retail tobacco products.

Determining Specific Prices and Policies

The last step in pricing strategy (Exhibit 11.1) is selecting specific prices and formulating policies to help manage the pricing strategy. Pricing methods are first examined, followed by a discussion of pricing policy.

Determining Specific Prices

It is necessary to either assign a specific price to each product item or to provide a method for computing price for a particular buyer-seller transaction. Many methods and techniques are available for calculating price.

Price determination is normally based on *cost, demand, competition,* or a combination of these factors. Cost-oriented methods use the cost of producing and marketing the product as the basis for determining price. Demand-oriented pricing methods consider estimated market response to alternative prices. The most profitable combination of price and market response level is selected. Competition-oriented methods use competitors' prices as a reference point in setting prices. The price selected may be above, below, or equal to competitors' prices. Typically, one method (cost, demand, or competition) provides the primary basis for pricing, although the other factors are also considered.

Cost-Oriented Approaches

Break-even pricing is a cost-oriented approach that may be used to determine prices. The initial computation is as follows:

Break-even (units) = Total fixed costs divided by Unit price − Unit variable cost

When using this method, we select a price and calculate the number of units that must be sold at that price to cover all fixed and variable costs. Management must assess the feasibility of exceeding the break-even level of sales to generate a profit. One or more possible prices may be evaluated. Break-even analysis is not a complete basis for determining price, since both demand and competition are important considerations in the pricing decision. With break-even price as a frame of reference, demand and competition can be evaluated. The price selected is at some level higher than the break-even price.

Another popular cost-oriented pricing method is cost-plus pricing. This technique uses cost as the basis of calculating the selling price. Costco uses this method to determine its warehouse prices. A percentage amount of the cost is added to cost to determine price. A similar method, popular in retailing, markup pricing, calculates markups as a percentage of the selling price. When using markup pricing, this formula determines the selling price.

$$\text{Price} = \text{average unit cost divided by } 1 - \text{markup percent*}$$

*Percent expressed in decimal form

Competition-Oriented Approaches

Pricing decisions are always affected by competitors' prices and their potential actions. Pricing methods that use competitors' prices in calculating actual prices include setting prices equal to or at some specified increment above or below the competition's prices. In industries such as air travel, one of the firms may be viewed by others as the price leader. When the leader changes its prices, other firms follow with similar prices. American Airlines has attempted to perform such a leadership role in the United States, although its pricing changes are not always adopted by competing airlines. Another form of competition-oriented pricing is competitive bidding where firms submit sealed bids to the purchaser. This method is used in the purchase of various industrial products and supplies.

Reverse auction pricing is an interesting competitive form of Internet pricing. Buyers benefit through savings and suppliers expand their market coverage. This method of determining price involves sellers bidding for organizational buyers' purchases:

> Many times, supplier performance is rated, and these ratings are presented by the site as a benefit to current and prospective buyers. Freemarkets.com conducts online auctions of industrial parts, raw materials, commodities, and services. Suppliers bid lower prices in real time until the auction is closed to fill the purchase orders of large buying organizations.[21]

The sharing of information benefits both buyers and sellers although the buyer controls the process. The underlying logic is that prices continue to fall due to declining bids until a stable market price is reached.

Demand-Oriented Approaches

The buyer is the frame of reference for these methods. One popular method is estimating the value of the product to the buyer. The objective is to determine how much the buyer is willing to pay for the product based on its contribution to the buyer's needs or wants. Recall our earlier discussion of estimating value provided to the customer (EVM). This approach is used for both consumer and business products. Information on demand and price relationships is needed in guiding demand-oriented pricing decisions. Internet auction pricing is a demand-oriented method of pricing.

Many pricing methods are in use, so it is important to select specific prices within the guidelines provided by price strategy and to incorporate demand, cost, and competition considerations. Other sources provide extensive coverage of pricing decisions.[22]

Establishing Pricing Policy and Structure

Determining price flexibility, positioning price against competition, and deciding how active price will be in the marketing program do not provide the operating guidelines necessary for implementing the pricing strategy. Policy guidelines must be determined for use in guiding pricing decisions and pricing structure.

Pricing Policy

A pricing policy may include consideration of discounts, allowances, returns, and other operating guidelines. The policy serves as the basis for implementing and managing the pricing strategy. The policy may be in written form, although many companies operate without formal pricing policies.

Pricing Structure

When more than one product item is involved, management must determine product mix and line-pricing interrelationships in order to establish price structure. Pricing structure concerns how individual items in the line are priced in relation to one another: The items may be aimed at the same market target or different end-user groups. For example, department stores often offer lower priced store brands and premium national brands. In the case of a single product category, price differences among the product items typically reflect more than variations in costs. For example, commercial airlines must work with an array of fares in the pricing structure.

The pricing of the Toyota Camry and the Lexus ES 330 is an interesting example of pricing products in relation to each other. The ES 330 is targeted to the semi-luxury automobile market. The ES 330 has essentially the same body as the Camry, but the Lexus sells for substantially more than the Camry. Of course, the Lexus offers certain unique features, but some of the price difference has to be image rather than substance. Interestingly, the performance of both brands is impressive.

Once product relationships are established, some basis for determining the price structure must be selected. Many firms base price structure on market and competitive factors as well as differences in the costs of producing each item. Some use multiple criteria for determining price structure and have sophisticated computer models to examine alternate pricing schemes. American Airlines' revenue management system is illustrative. Other companies use rules of thumb developed from experience.

Most product line pricing approaches include both cost considerations and demand and competitive concerns. For example, industrial-equipment manufacturers sometimes price new products at or close to cost and depend on sales of high-margin items such as supplies, parts, and replacement items to generate profits. The important consideration is to price the entire mix and line of products to achieve pricing objectives.

Pricing Management

Pricing strategy is an ongoing process rather than a once-a-year budgeting activity. Several principles of pricing management are outlined in Exhibit 11.8. Importantly, pricing strategy is an interrelated process requiring central management direction and control.

Special pricing situations may occur in particular industries, markets, and competitive environments. Some examples follow.

Price Segmentation

Price may be used to appeal to different market segments. For example, airline prices vary depending on the conditions of purchase. Different versions of the same basic product may be offered at different prices to reflect differences in materials and product features. Recall

EXHIBIT 11.8
Managing Pricing Strategy

Source: Adapted from Kent B. Monroe, *Pricing*, 3rd ed. (Burr Ridge, IL: McGraw-Hill/Irwin, 2003) 624–626.

1. The more that competitors and customers know about your pricing, the better off you are. In an information age, it is necessary to be transparent about prices and the value of a firm's offerings.
2. In highly competitive markets, the focus should be on those market segments that provide opportunities to gain competitive advantage. Such a focus leads to a value-oriented pricing approach.
3. Pricing decisions should be made within the context of an overall marketing strategy that is embedded within a business or corporate strategy.
4. Successful pricing decisions are profit oriented, not sales volume or market share oriented.
5. Prices should be set according to customers' perceptions of value.
6. Pricing for new products should start as soon as product development begins.
7. The relevant costs for pricing are the incremental avoidable costs.
8. A price may be profitable when it provides for incremental revenues in excess of incremental costs.
9. A central organizing unit should administer the pricing function. Generally, it is better to avoid letting salespeople set price, especially without access to profitability information and specific training in pricing and revenue management.
10. Pricing management should be viewed as a process and price setting as a daily management activity, not a once-a-year activity.

our earlier discussion of Intel's PC chip strategy. Industrial-products firms may use quantity discounts to respond to differences in the quantities purchased by customers. Price elasticity differences make it feasible to appeal to different segments.

Value Chain Pricing

The pricing strategies of sellers in the value chain should include consideration of the pricing needs (e.g., flexibility and incentives) of producers and facilitating firms (e.g., wholesalers). These decisions require analysis of cost and pricing at all value chain levels. If producer prices to intermediaries are too high, inadequate margins may discourage intermediaries from actively promoting the producer's brand. Margins vary based on the nature and importance of the added value that intermediaries in the channel are expected to provide. For example, margins between costs and selling prices must be large enough to compensate a wholesaler for carrying a complete stock of replacement parts. When a firm uses more than one distribution channel, the question of price differences between channels also has to be considered.

Price Flexibility

Will prices be firm, or will they be negotiated between buyer and seller? Perhaps most important, firms should make price flexibility a policy decision rather than a tactical response. Some companies' price lists are very rigid while others have list prices that give no indication of actual selling prices. It is also important to recognize the legal and ethical issues in pricing products when using flexible pricing policies.

When considering reducing prices it is important to estimate how operating profits will be impacted. Estimates of how operating profits will be reduced for a one percent price cut provided by Mc Kinsey & Co. consultants are 24 percent for food stores and drugstores, 13 percent for airlines, and 11 percent for computers and office equipment.[23] Smaller operating profit decreases are estimated for tobacco (5 percent) and diversified financials (2.4 percent).

Product Life Cycle Pricing

Some companies have policies to guide pricing decisions over the life cycle of the product. Depending on its stage in the product life cycle, the price of a particular product or an entire line may be based on market share, profitability, cash flow, or other objectives. In many product-markets, price declines (in constant dollars) as the product moves through its life cycle. Because of life-cycle considerations, different objectives and policies may apply to particular products within a mix or line. Price becomes a more active element of strategy as products move through the life cycle and competitive pressures build, costs decline, and volume increases. Life-cycle pricing strategy should be consistent with the overall marketing program positioning strategy used.

Summary

The challenging role of pricing strategies is underlined by pressures from global competition, as well as difficulties in altering prices once they are established and regulatory restrictions on executives' pricing actions. However, price plays a very important role in business strategy. The strategic role of price is underlined by its impact on positioning strategy—particularly relating to product strategy choices and distribution channels. An important question relates to the location of responsibility for pricing decisions, and the need to coordinate tactical and strategic pricing decisions with other aspects of marketing strategy. Pricing requires continuous review because of changing external conditions, competitive moves, and the emergence of opportunities to gain competitive advantage through pricing actions.

Importantly, price plays a number of roles in the market-driven program, acting as a signal to the buyer, providing a competitive mechanism, offering a means to impact financial performance, and acting as a substitute for other marketing program functions. Major steps in constructing a pricing strategy are: determining pricing objectives, analyzing the pricing situation, selecting the pricing strategy, and determining specific prices and policies.

Pricing objectives vary according to company priorities and other situational factors, such as intensity of competition and economic conditions, and may address different goals. Analysis of the pricing situation examines the level of customer price sensitivity, product costs, existing and anticipated competitive actions, and pricing objectives. The selection of a pricing strategy must be based on the degree of pricing flexibility that exists for the company with the product and the market being targeted, and the positioning impact of price on the product. Several opportunities exist for combining the role of price visibility in strategy with price level. An extremely important context for selecting pricing strategy is the legal and ethical issues surrounding price. Regulation in most countries prohibits competitors from setting price levels, price discrimination between different buyers, deceptive pricing, and predatory pricing to drive competitors from business. In addition to legal considerations, ethical and moral questions also confront executives in choosing prices.

The determination of specific prices may be based on costs, competition, and/or demand influences. Implementing and managing the pricing strategy also includes establishing pricing policy and structure. Finally, management of pricing strategy is an interrelated process that must be managed on a continuing basis. Several special pricing considerations include price segmentation, distribution channel pricing, price flexibility, and product life-cycle pricing.

Questions for Review and Discussion

1. Discuss the role of price in the marketing strategy for Rolex watches. Contrast Timex's price strategy with Rolex's strategy.

2. The Toyota Camry and the Lexus ES 330 are very similar but the ES 330 is priced substantially higher than the Camry. Discuss the features and limitations of this pricing strategy.

3. Indicate how a fast-food chain can estimate the price elasticity of a proposed new product such as a new chicken sandwich.

4. Real estate brokers typically charge a fixed percentage of a home's sales price. Advertising agencies follow a similar price strategy. Discuss why this may be sound price strategy. What are the arguments against it from the buyer's point of view?

5. Cite examples of businesses to which the experience-curve effect may not be applicable. What influence may this have on price determination?

6. In some industries prices are set low, subsidies are provided, and other price-reducing mechanisms are used to establish a long-term relationship with the buyer. Utilities, for example, sometimes use incentives to encourage contractors to install electric- or gas-powered appliances. Manufacturers may price equipment low, then depend on service and parts for profit contribution. What are the advantages and limitations of this pricing strategy?

7. Discuss why it is important to consider pricing from a strategic rather than a tactical perspective.

8. Discuss some of the ways that estimates of the costs of competitors' products can be determined.

9. Discuss how a pricing strategy should be developed by a software firm to price its business-analysis software line.

10. Suppose a firm is considering changing from a low-active price strategy to a high-active strategy. Discuss the implications of this proposed change.

11. Describe and evaluate the price strategy used for the Lexus 430 European-style luxury sedan.

Internet Applications

A. Explore the website of American Airlines (www.aa.com). Consider how the website can facilitate price discrimination.

B. Visit the website of Amazon.com. Evaluate Amazon's pricing strategy. How do its prices compare to those of "brick and mortar" retailers? Critically evaluate the company's product offering and identify potential market segments.

C. Visit the Oracle.com website. Discuss how Oracle considers price in the information provided for its business process software suite.

D. Study the information available from Starbucks' website (www.starbucks.com). Discuss how the Web site enhances the firm's ability to obtain premium prices.

Feature Applications

A. From the RELATIONSHIP FEATURE, develop a list of the pricing issues faced by the executives at Novet. What are the arguments that can be made for avoiding the price cutting option?

B. Consider "The China Challenge" described in the GLOBAL FEATURE. What are the pricing implications for developed countries in competing against Chinese brands? What actions do you recommend?

Notes

1. Tom Braithwaite, "Delays in Toyshops as Chinese Retest Stocks," *Financial Times,* Thursday August 30 2007. Peter Smith, "Scare Spurs Australian Crackdown on Clothing and Textiles," *Financial Times,* Friday August 24 2007, 7. Claire Newell and Robert Winnett, "Revealed: Topshop Clothes Made with 'Slave Labour,'" *Sunday Times,* August 12 2007, 1–3.

2. Thomas Nagle, "Making Pricing a Key Driver of Your Marketing Strategy," *Marketing News,* November 9, 1998, 4.

3. W. Chan Kim and Renee Maugorgne, "Now Name a Price That's Hard to Refuse," *Financial Times,* January 24, 2001; "Netjets, Fast Facts," Netjets Inc., Woodbridge, NJ: August 2007.

4. Louise Lee, "It's Dell vs. The Dell Way," *BusinessWeek,* March 6, 2006, 62; Louise Lee and Peter Burrows, "Dell's Edge Is Getting Duller," *BusinessWeek,* November 14, 2005, 48.

5. Mark Maremont, "How Gillette Brought Its MACH 3 to Market," *The Wall Street Journal,* April 15, 1998, B1, B8.

6. This illustration is based on George E. Cressman, Jr. and Thomas T. Nagle, "How to Manage an Aggressive Competitor," *Business Horizons,* March-April 2002, 26.

7. Laura Bird, "P & G's New Analgesic Promises Pain for Over-the-Counter Rivals," *The Wall Street Journal,* June 16, 1994, B9.

8. Robert J. Dolan, "How Do You Know When the Price Is Right," *Harvard Business Review,* September-October 1995, 174–183.

9. This discussion is based on Gerald E. Smith and Thomas T. Nagle, "A Question of Value," *Marketing Management,* July/August 2005, 39–43.

10. Ibid.

11. A guide to determining experience curves is provided in Kent B. Monroe, *Pricing: Making Profitable Decisions,* 3rd ed. (McGraw-Hill/Irwin, Burr Ridge, IL, 2003), Chapter 13.

12. Rebecca Blumenstein, "Overbuilt Web," *The Wall Street Journal,* June 16, 2001, A1 and A8; Deborah Solomon, "Global Crossing Finds That the Race Has Just Begun," *The Wall Street Journal,* June 22, 2001, B4; Mark Heinzl and Shawn Young, "With Rising Internet Traffic, Spare Fiber-Optic Lines Fill Up," *The Wall Street Journal,* April 27, 2006, B1, B4.

13. Robert Berner, "Watch Out, Best Buy and Circuit City," *BusinessWeek,* November 21, 2005, 46 and 48.

14. Almar Latour, "Disconnected," *The Wall Street Journal,* June 5, 2001, A1 and A8.

15. The following issues are based on Cressman, "Snatching Defeat from the Jaws of Victory," *Marketing Management,* Summer 1997, 10–11.

16. Ibid.

17. Reed K. Holden and Thomas T. Nagle, "Kamikaze Pricing," *Marketing Management,* Summer 1998, 31–39.

18. Ibid.

19. Robert A. Kerin, Stephen W. Hartley, and William Rudelius, *Marketing: The Core* (Burr Ridge, IL: McGraw-Hill/Irwin, 2004), 272.

20. Shailagh Murry and Lucette Lagnado, "Drug Companies Face Assault on Prices, *The Wall Street Journal,* May 11, 2000, B1 and B4.

21. Jeffrey F. Rayport and Bernard J. Jaworski, *e-Commerce* (New York: McGraw-Hill/Irwin, 2001), 157.

22. See, for example, Monroe, *Pricing;* and Thomas T. Nagle and Reed K. Holden, *The Strategy and Tactics of Pricing,* 3rd ed. (Englewood Cliffs, NJ: Prentice Hall, 2002).

23. Janice Revall, "The Price Is Not Always Right," *Fortune,* May 14, 2001, 240.

Chapter 12

Promotion, Advertising, and Sales Promotion Strategies

The purpose of promotion strategy is to manage the organization's communications initiatives, coordinating and integrating advertising, personal selling, sales promotion, interactive/Internet marketing, direct marketing, and public relations to communicate with buyers and others who influence purchasing decisions. The promotion strategies of many companies are encountering rapid changes and challenges due to the availability of alternative communications channels, rapidly changing markets and competitive space, customer relationship management initiatives, and global expansion of markets. Billions are spent every week around the world on the various promotion activities. Effective management of these expensive resources is essential to gain the optimum return from the promotion expenditures. Integrating the promotion components into a consistent overall strategy requires close coordination across the responsible units in the organization.

Google provides an interesting perspective on how promotion strategy is changing.[1] The search engine has transformed itself into a media octopus, generating $10.6 billion in advertising revenues in 2006. Google has a 31 percent share of online advertising revenue. Initially Google linked keywords to advertisers' text ads, and then expanded into print advertising, purchasing print ad space in magazines and selling the space to its ad customers. The company has moved into radio ad buying and is testing TV ads. Google's Click-to-Call enables people with Internet phone service to connect to an advertiser's call center. Driving these initiatives is a 2,500 person sales and marketing organization. Google's popularity with advertisers is based on cost and accountability of expenditures.

The communications activities that make up promotion strategy inform people about products and persuade the company's buyers, value-chain organizations, and the public at large to purchase brands. The objective is to combine the promotion components into an integrated strategy for communicating with buyers and others who influence purchasing decisions. Since each component has certain strengths and shortcomings, an integrated strategy incorporates the advantages of each component into a cost-effective promotion mix.

First, we review promotion strategy and examine the decisions that are involved in designing the strategy. The intent is to develop an integrated view of communications strategy to which each of the promotion components contributes. Next, we discuss each component beginning with the major decisions that comprise advertising strategy and the factors affecting advertising decisions. The final section considers the design and implementation of sales promotion strategies. Personal selling, direct marketing, and Internet strategies are discussed in Chapter 13.

Promotion Strategy

Promotion strategy consists of planning, implementing, and controlling an organization's communications to its customers and other target audiences. The purpose of promotion in the marketing program is to achieve management's desired communications objectives with each audience. An important marketing responsibility is planning and coordinating the integrated promotion strategy and selecting the specific strategies for each of the promotion components. Word-of-mouth communications among buyers and the communications activities of other organizations may also influence the firm's target audience(s).

The Composition of Promotion Strategy

Advertising

Advertising consists of any form of non-personal communication concerning an organization, product, or idea that is paid for by a specific sponsor. The sponsor makes payment for the communication via one or more forms of media (e.g., television, radio, magazine, newspaper, online). Advertising expenditures in the U.S. were expected to total $238 billion in 2008.[2] Online advertising should exceed $20 billion in 2008. Network and cable TV and Internet advertising are expected to experience the highest growth rates (10-12 percent) compared to single digit growth for radio, magazines, and newspapers. The U.S. accounts for about 53 percent of world-wide advertising. Advertising expenditures of companies are shifting away from prime-time TV. For example, McDonald's spent only half of its advertising budget on prime-time in 2005 compared to 80 percent in 2001.[3] The company has shifted heavily to the Internet, placing television ads online.

Among the advantages of using advertising to communicate with buyers are the low cost per exposure, the variety of media (newspapers, magazines, television, radio, Internet, direct mail, and outdoor advertising), control of exposure, consistent message content, and the opportunity for creative message design. In addition, the appeal and message can be adjusted when communications objectives change. Internet advertising enables advertisers to target their communications to specific buyers with more focus than other media options. Advertising also has some disadvantages. It cannot interact with the buyer and may not be able to hold viewers' attention. Moreover, the message is fixed for the duration of an exposure.

Personal Selling

Personal selling consists of verbal communication between a salesperson (or selling team) and one or more prospective purchasers with the objective of making or influencing a sale. Annual expenditures on personal selling are much larger than on advertising, perhaps twice as much. Importantly, both promotion components share some common features, including creating awareness of the brand, transmitting information, and persuading people to buy. Personal selling is expensive. Business-to-business salespeople's compensation and supervision are likely to cost $125,000 or more per person each year. The cost of a sales call may be $400 or more for industrial goods and services, and, typically, multiple calls are necessary to sell the product.[4] Personal selling has several unique strengths:

salespeople can interact with buyers to answer questions and overcome objections, they can target buyers, and they have access to market and competitor knowledge and provide feedback.

Sales Promotion

Sales promotion consists of various promotional activities including trade shows, contests, samples, point-of-purchase displays, product placement in films and other media, trade incentives, and coupons. Sales promotion expenditures are much greater than spending on advertising, and as large as sales force expenditures. This array of special communications techniques and incentives offers several advantages: sales promotion can be used to target buyers, respond to special occasions, and create an incentive for purchase. Sales promotion activities may be targeted to consumers, value chain members, or employees (e.g., salespeople). An active sales promotion initiative is the placement of branded products in films, magazines, videogames and music, and TV.[5] A CBS TV executive estimates that three-fourths of all scripted prime-time network programs will include paid product placement. Expenditures for product placement were less than $5 billion in 2006 but are growing. The expanded use of product placement is because of its appeal to advertisers and television firms' interest in supplementing revenues lost to internet advertising. Pricing and other operating guidelines are fragmented.

Direct Marketing

Direct marketing includes the various communications channels that enable companies to make direct contact with individual buyers. Examples are catalogs, direct mail, telemarketing, television selling, radio/magazine/newspaper selling, and electronic shopping. The distinguishing feature of direct marketing is the opportunity for the marketer to gain direct access to the buyer. Direct marketing expenditures account for an increasingly large portion of promotion expenditures.

Interactive/Internet Marketing

Included in this promotion component are the Internet, CD-ROM, kiosks, and interactive television. Interactive media enable buyers and sellers to communicate with each other. The Internet performs an important and rapidly escalating role in promotion strategy. In addition to providing a direct sales channel, the Internet may be used to identify sales leads, conduct Web-based surveys, provide product information, and display advertisements. The Internet is the platform for a complete business strategy in the case of Internet business models. Marketing strategies are increasingly linked to Internet initiatives.

Interestingly, while Internet ad spending is much less than TV spending, U.S. households spend about the same amount of time viewing each medium.[6] This points to the strong interest of advertisers concerning Internet advertising. The INTERNET FEATURE highlights several reasons for advertisers' strong interest in the Internet.

Public Relations

Public relations for a company and its products consist of communications placed in the commercial media at no charge to the company receiving the publicity. For example, a news release on a new product may be published in a trade magazine. The media coverage is an article or news item. The objective of the public relations department is to encourage relevant media to include company-released information in media communications. Public relations activities can make an important contribution to promotion strategy when the activity is planned and implemented to achieve specific promotion objectives. (Public relations activities are also used for publicity purposes such as communicating with financial

Brand Advertising On-Line Has Taken Off

SEARCH WORKS

Google and Yahoo! have demonstrated the power of the Web by using customers' search queries to connect them with advertisers.

CUSTOMERS ARE ONLINE

More than half of American households have always-on Net connections. And the Web reaches millions at the office. The Big Three portals—Yahoo, AOL, and MSN—reach a combined 50 million a day—twice the TV audience of a World Series game.

VIDEO ROCKS

The adoption of broadband, which can handle videos, lets advertisers put TV-like ads online. Longer spots by BMW and Adidas have reached cult status. As demand for video soars, portals sell choice slots in advance, much like TV's up-front sales.

FEEDBACK IS INSTANT

Marketers and online publishers have tools to track an ad's performance in real time allowing them to make quick adjustments if customers aren't clicking. This turns the Net into a vast marketing lab. And as video grows, it becomes a test bed for TV ads.

CUSTOMERS LEAVE TRAILS

It was an empty promise during the dot-com days, but now advertisers have the technology to follow customers, click by click, and to hit them with relevant ads. The upshot? No wasted money peddling dog food to cat owners.

Source: Stephen Baker, "The On-line Ad Surge," *BusinessWeek,* November 22, 2004, 79.

analysts.) Publicity in the media can be negative as well as positive and cannot be controlled by the organization to the same extent as other promotion components. Since a company does not purchase the media coverage, public relations is a cost-effective method of communication. The media are usually willing to cover topics of public interest. Many companies retain public relations consultants who proactively pursue opportunities to feature their companies and brands. For many companies the active management of "corporate reputation" is a public relations priority because reputation impacts on many of the stakeholders in the company.

Designing Promotion Strategy

Market target and positioning strategies guide promotion decisions as shown in Exhibit 12.1. Several activities are involved in designing an organization's promotion strategy including: (1) setting communication objectives; (2) deciding the role of each of the components make in the promotion program; (3) estimating the promotion budget; (4) selecting the strategy for each promotion component; (5) integrating and implementing the promotion component strategies; and (6) evaluating the effectiveness of the integrated promotion strategies. Specific strategies must be determined for advertising, personal selling, sales promotion, direct marketing, Internet, and public relations, and these promotion components need to be carefully integrated and coordinated to achieve communication objectives.

Market targets and product, distribution, and price decisions provide a frame of reference for: (1) deciding the role of promotion strategy in the total marketing program; and (2) identifying the specific communications tasks of the promotion activities. One important

375

EXHIBIT 12.1
Designing Promotion Strategy

MARKET TARGETING AND
POSITIONING STRATEGIES
▽
COMMUNICATION
OBJECTIVES
▽
ROLE OF PROMOTION
COMPONENTS
▽

| Advertising | Sales Promotion | Public Relations | Personal Selling | Direct Marketing | Interactive/ Internet Marketing |

PROMOTION BUDGET
▽
PROMOTION COMPONENT   ◁   Coordination
STRATEGIES   with Product,
                                  Value Chain, and
                                  Pricing Strategies
▽
INTEGRATE AND IMPLEMENT STRATEGIES
FOR THE COMPONENTS
▽
EVALUATE EFFECTIVENESS OF
PROMOTION STRATEGY

question is deciding the role that the promotion strategy will play in marketing strategy. Advertising and personal selling are often a major part of a firm's marketing strategy. In consumer package goods firms, sales promotion and advertising comprise a large portion of the promotion program. In industrial firms, personal selling often dominates the promotion strategy, with advertising and sales promotion playing a supporting role. The use of sales promotion and public relations varies considerably among companies. The role of direct marketing also differs across companies and industries.

Interestingly, Singapore Airlines performs an important promotion role in marketing the nation. The airline is consistently one of the more profitable global airlines, although much smaller than the major carriers.[7] The airline's favorable brand position helps to position the country with executives, government officials, and tourists who experience Singapore Airline's renowned services. The tiny city-state with a small population has a strong brand image, enhanced by the airline's favorable reputation with customers and competitors throughout the world. The airline's advertising in business and travel magazines is designed to favorably position its distinctive bundle of values. Global air travel is expected to double in 2010 compared to 1990, and much of the growth is in Asia.

Communication Objectives

Communication objectives help determine how the promotion strategy components are used in the marketing program. Several illustrative communication objectives follow.

Need Recognition

A communication objective, which is important for new-product introductions, is to trigger a need. Need recognition may also be important for existing products and services, particularly when the buyer can postpone purchasing or choose not to purchase (such as life insurance). For example, P&G emphasized the need to control dandruff in its advertising of Head & Shoulders shampoo in China. The ads focused attention on how dandruff is very visible on people with black hair.

Finding Buyers

Promotion activities can be used to identify buyers. The message seeks to get the prospective buyer to respond. Recall, for example, the use of the Internet to obtain instant feedback as discussed in the earlier INTERNET FEATURE. Salespeople may be given responsibility for identifying and screening prospects. The use of toll-free numbers is often helpful in identifying customers as well as issues and problems of interest to the callers.

Brand Building

Promotion can aid a buyer's search for information. One of the objectives of new product promotional activities is to help buyers learn about the product. Prescription drug companies advertise to the public to make people aware of diseases and the brand names of products used for treatment. In the past, they targeted only doctors through ads in medical journals and contacts by salespeople. Advertising is often a more cost-effective way to disseminate information than personal selling, particularly when the information can be exposed to targeted buyers by electronic or printed media.

Evaluation of Alternatives

Promotion helps buyers evaluate alternative brands, and such evaluations may be a primary objective of promotion activities. Both comparative advertising and personal selling are effective in demonstrating a brand's strengths over competing brands. An illustration of this form of advertising is to analyze competing brands of a product, showing a favorable comparison for the brand of the firm placing the ad. For example, Procter & Gamble Co. is pursuing company-wide initiatives to reestablish relationship bonds between customers and its core brands.[8] The intent is to position brands like Tide as offering more value than a commodity detergent. P&G in its promotion activities is seeking to differentiate Tide to avoid comparisons by buyers with competitors based on price and habit. P&G managers and strategists from its advertising agency, Saatchi and Saatchi, went out into the field to talk with and observe women buyers to guide the development of a relationship positioning message for Tide. P&G's brand building initiatives are described in the RELATIONSHIP FEATURE.

Decision to Purchase

Influencing the buyer's decision to purchase a brand is an important promotion objective. Several of the promotion components may be used to encourage the buyer to purchase a brand. Personal selling is often effective in obtaining a purchase commitment from the buyers of consumer durable goods and industrial products. Direct selling organizations such as Avon (cosmetics) and Cutco (knives) use highly programmed selling approaches to encourage buyers to purchase their products. Communication objectives in these firms include making a target number of contacts each day. Point-of-purchase sales promotions, such as displays in retail stores, are intended to influence the purchase decision, as are discount coupons. One of the advantages of personal selling over advertising is its flexibility in responding to the buyer's objections and questions at the time the decision to purchase is being made.

Customer Retention

Communicating with buyers after they purchase a product is an important objective of promotion for many brands. Follow-up by salespeople, advertisements stressing a firm's service capabilities, and toll-free numbers placed on packages to encourage users to seek information or report problems are illustrations of post-purchase communications. Hotels leave questionnaires in rooms for occupants to use in evaluating hotel services.

Procter & Gamble aims to inspire meaningful relationships with even the most mundane products:

TIDE Ads convey that women can focus on other things in their lives because Tide is taking care of the laundry.

ALWAYS P & G is using design and wit to elevate the image of the sanitary napkin. One ad bends an Always into a chaise lounge. The copy: "If you're going to sit all day, it better be comfortable."

PAMPERS No longer is pitched as just the most absorbent diaper; Pampers now is sold as helping the development of your baby.

Source: Robert Berner, "Detergent Can Be So Much More," *BusinessWeek,* May 1, 2006, 68.

As illustrated, various communication objectives may be assigned to promotion strategy. The uses of promotion vary according to the type of purchase, the stage of the buyer's decision process, the maturity of the product-market, and the role of promotion in the marketing program. Objectives need to be developed for the entire promotion program and for each promotion component. Certain objectives, such as sales and market share targets, are shared with other marketing program components. In the following sections and the next chapter we discuss and provide examples of objectives for each promotion component.

Deciding the Role of the Promotion Components

Early in the process of developing the promotion strategy, it is useful to set guidelines as to the expected contribution for each of the promotion components. These guidelines help determine the strategy for each promotion component. It is necessary to decide which communication objective(s) will be the responsibility of each component. For example, advertising may be responsible for creating awareness of a new product. Sales promotion (e.g., coupons and samples) may encourage trial of the new product. Personal selling may be assigned responsibility for getting wholesalers and/or retailers to stock the new product. It is also important to decide how large the contribution of each promotion component will be, which will help to determine the promotion budget.

Determining the Promotion Budget

Isolating the specific effects of promotion may be difficult due to pursuit of multiple promotion objectives, lags in the impact of promotion on sales, effects of other marketing program components (e.g., retailers' cooperation), and the influences of uncontrollable factors (e.g., competition, economic conditions). Realistically, budgeting in practice is likely to emphasize improving promotion effectiveness rather than seeking the optimal size of the budget. Because of this, more practical budgeting techniques are normally used, such as: (1) objective and task; (2) percent of sales; (3) competitive parity; or (4) all you can afford. These same approaches are used to determine advertising and sales promotion budgets. The personal-selling budget is largely determined by the number of people in the sales force and their qualifications. Direct marketing budgets are guided by the unit costs of customer contact such as cost per catalog mailed.

In many companies, the promotion budget may include only planned expenditures for advertising and sales promotion. Typically a separate budget is developed for the sales organization, which may include sales promotion activities such as incentives for sales-people and value-chain members. Public relations budgets also are likely to be separate from promotion budgeting. Even so, it is important to consider the size and allocation of total promotion expenses when formulating the promotion strategy. Unless this is done, the integration of the components is likely to be fragmented. Internet budgets may be separate or included with the promotion component that utilizes Internet capabilities.

An example of a promotion budget (excluding sales force and public relations) for a phar-maceutical product is shown in Exhibit 12.2. Note the relative size of advertising and sam-ple expenditures. The sampling of drugs to doctors by salespeople is a substantial amount of the promotion budget. Sampling is an important promotion component in this industry.

Objective and Task

This logical and cost-effective method is probably the most widely used budgeting approach. Management sets the communication objectives, determines the tasks (activities) neces-sary to achieve the objectives, and adds up costs. This method also guides determining the role of the promotion components by selecting which component(s) is appropriate for attaining each objective. Marketing management must carefully evaluate how the promo-tion objectives are to be achieved and choose the most cost-effective promotion compo-nents. The effectiveness of the objective and task method depends on the judgment and experience of the marketing team. The budget shown in Exhibit 12.2 was determined using the objective and task method. The pharmaceutical firm executives involved in the budgeting process include product managers, the division manager, sales management, and the chief marketing executive.

Percent of Sales

Using this method, the budget is calculated as a percent of sales and is, therefore, quite arbitrary. The percentage figure is often based on past expenditure patterns. The method fails to recognize that promotion efforts and results are related. For example, repeating a 10-percent-of-sales budget from the previous year may be too much or not enough promotion expenditures to achieve sales and other promotion objectives. Budgeting by percent of sales can result in too much spending on promotion when sales are high and not enough when sales are low. In a cyclical industry where sales follow up-and-down trends, a strategy of increasing promotion expenditures during low sales periods may be more appropriate.

Competitive Parity

Promotion expenditures for this budgeting method are guided by how much competitors spend. Yet competitors may be spending too much (or not enough) on promotion. Another key shortcoming of the competitive parity method is that differences in marketing strategy between competing firms may require different promotion strategies. A comparison of promotional strategies of these firms is not very meaningful, since their market targets,

EXHIBIT 12.2
Illustrative Promotion Budget for a Pharmaceutical Product

Promotional Activity	2009 Budget
Promotional material	$ 305,000
Samples	610,000
Direct Mail	459,000
Journal advertising	533,000
Total Budget	**$1,907,000**

promotion objectives, and use of promotion components are different. Interestingly, Louis Vuitton, the largest and most profitable luxury brand in the world, spends only 5 percent of its revenues on advertising which is only half of the industry average.[9]

All You Can Afford

Since budget limits are a reality in most companies, this method is likely to influence all budget decisions. Top management may specify how much can be spent on promotion. For example, the guideline may be to increase the budget to 110 percent of last year's actual promotion expenditures. The objective and task method can be combined with the "all-you-can-afford" method by setting task priorities and allocating the budget to the higher priority tasks.

Determining the promotion budget is typically an interactive process among budgeting team members. Trade-offs must be evaluated concerning the expenditure needs of promotion components, priorities among the components, and total budget limits. These discussions by the budgeting team and top management play an important role in promotion strategy integration.

Promotion Component Strategies

The strategies for the promotion components need to be consistent with market targeting strategy and contribute to the desired positioning of the brand. Determining the strategy for each promotion component includes setting objectives and budget, selecting the strategy, and determining the promotion activities (and timing) to be pursued. For example, advertising activities include choosing the creative strategy, formulating the message(s), and selecting the media to carry the ads.

In this chapter we consider advertising and sales promotion strategy determination. Public relations strategy involves similar initiatives to advertising strategy determination and is not discussed. The following chapter examines sales force, Internet, and direct marketing strategies.

Integrating and Implementing the Promotion Strategy

Several factors may affect the composition of the promotion program as shown by Exhibit 12.3. Advertising, public relations, personal selling, direct marketing, Internet, and sales promotion strategies have the potential to be fragmented when responsibility is

EXHIBIT 12.3
Illustrative Factors That Influence the Design of Promotion Strategy

assigned across several departments. There are differences in priorities, and determining the productivity of each promotion component is difficult. For example, coordination between personal selling and advertising is complicated since each of these promotion components has specific objectives, a separate budget and management, and different measures of effectiveness. Coordinating the activities of the two functions is an important responsibility of higher-level management. The separation of selling and advertising strategies also prevails in a variety of consumer and industrial products firms. An important marketing management issue is how to integrate the promotion strategy components.

Developing and implementing integrated communications strategies are essential for manufacturers as well as retailers, and for both consumer and business products. Effective management of these strategies has a positive impact on revenues and the productivity of promotion strategy:

> The move toward Integrated Marketing Communications is one of the most significant marketing developments that occurred during the 1990s, and the shift toward this approach is continuing as we begin the new century. The IMC approach to marketing communications planning and strategy is being adopted by both large and small companies and has become popular among firms marketing consumer products and services as well as business-to-business marketers. There are a number of reasons why marketers are adopting the IMC approach. A fundamental reason is that they understand the value of strategically integrating the various communications functions rather than having them operate autonomously. By coordinating their marketing communications efforts, companies can avoid duplication, take advantage of synergy among promotional tools, and develop more efficient and effective marketing communications programs.[10]

Effectiveness of Promotion Strategy

Tracking the performance of promotion strategy involves: (1) evaluating the effectiveness of each promotion component, and (2) assessing the overall effectiveness of the integrated promotion strategy. In this and the next chapter we discuss measurement of effectiveness of the individual promotion components. Cross-functional teams can be used to assess overall promotion strategy effectiveness. Comparisons of actual results to objectives can be employed in the evaluation of each promotion component and the effectiveness of the integrated promotion strategy.

Advertising Strategy

Management's perception of how advertising can contribute to the communication objectives has an important influence in deciding advertising's role. Estimating the impact on buyers helps to decide advertising's role and scope in the marketing program and to choose specific objectives for advertising.

The nature and scope of advertising is changing as suggested by our lead-in example concerning Google. The CEO of Ogilvy & Mather, one of the world's largest advertising agencies comments on the past and the present:

> Advertising was a straightforward business: agencies had to devise a good idea for an ad and then choose the right publication or broadcast slot in order to catch consumers' attention. Today, advertising is far more complex, thanks to technological advances, social shifts and the far greater sophistication of both the advertisers and audiences. Modern consumers demand to be wooed, not berated.[11]

Identifying and describing the target audiences is the first step in developing advertising strategy. Next, it is important to set specific objectives and estimate the advertising budget. There may be an adjustment (up or down) of this initial budget as the specific advertising activities and media choices are determined. The selection of the creative strategy follows. Specific messages need to be designed for each ad. Ads may be pre-tested. Choices of the advertising media and programming schedules implement the creative strategy. The final step is implementing the advertising strategy and evaluating its effectiveness. Each of these activities is examined, highlighting important features and strategy issues. In the discussion we assume that the target audience(s) has been selected.

Setting Advertising Objectives and Budgeting

Advertising Objectives

Our earlier discussion of promotion strategy objectives identified various objectives that may be relevant for advertising. These include need recognition, identifying buyers, brand building, evaluation of alternatives, decision to purchase, and customer retention. More than one objective may be applicable for a particular advertising strategy.

Exhibit 12.4 shows alternative levels for setting advertising objectives. In moving from the most general level (exposure) to the most specific level (profit contribution) the objectives are increasingly more closely linked to buyers' purchase decisions. For example, knowing that advertising causes a measurable increase in sales is much more useful to management than knowing that a specific number of people are exposed to an advertising message. The key issue is whether objectives such as exposure and awareness are related to purchase behavior. For example, how much will exposure to the advertising increase the chances that people will purchase a product? Objectives such as exposure and awareness often can be measured, whereas determining the sales and profit impact of advertising may be more difficult due to the impact of other factors on sales and profits. Because of the ease of measurement, exposure and awareness objectives are used more often than attitude change, sales, and profit objectives.

Several questions that are useful in determining advertising objectives are presented in Exhibit 12.5. The questions consider different uses of advertising ranging from generating immediate sales to brand building. Specific objectives are shown for each of the nine questions.

Budget Determination

The budgeting methods for promotion discussed earlier in the chapter are also used in advertising budgeting. The objective and task method has a stronger supporting logic than the other methods. Consider, for example, the Italian government's advertising program

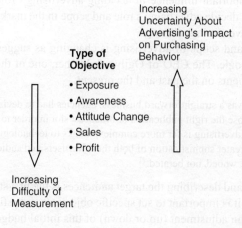

EXHIBIT 12.4
Alternative Levels for Setting Advertising Objectives

Increasing Uncertainty About Advertising's Impact on Purchasing Behavior

Type of Objective

• Exposure
• Awareness
• Attitude Change
• Sales
• Profit

Increasing Difficulty of Measurement

EXHIBIT 12.5   Determining Advertising Objectives

Source: William Arens, *Contemporary Advertising*, 7th ed. (Burr Ridge, IL: Irwin/McGraw-Hill, 1999), R18. Copyright © The McGraw-Hill Companies. Used with permission.

1. Does the advertising aim at *immediate sales?* If so, objectives might be:

   - Perform the complete selling function.
   - Close sales to prospects already partly sold.
   - Announce a special reason for buying now (price, premium, and so forth).
   - Remind people to buy.
   - Tie in with special buying event.
   - Stimulate impulse sales.

2. Does the advertising aim at *near-term sales?* If so, objectives might be:

   - Create awareness.
   - Enhance brand image.
   - Implant information or attitude.
   - Combat or offset competitive claims.
   - Correct false impressions, misinformation.
   - Build familiarity and easy recognition.

3. Does the advertising aim at building a *long-range consumer franchise?* If so, objectives might be:

   - Build confidence in company and brand.
   - Build customer demand.
   - Select preferred distributors and dealers.
   - Secure universal distribution.
   - Establish a "reputation platform" for launching new brands or product lines.

4. Does the advertising aim at helping increase sales? If so, objectives would be:

   - Hold present customers.
   - Convert other users to advertiser's brand.
   - Cause people to specify advertiser's brand.
   - Convert nonusers to users.
   - Make steady customers out of occasional ones.
   - Advertise new uses.
   - Persuade customers to buy larger sizes or multiple units.
   - Remind users to buy.
   - Encourage greater frequency or quantity of use.

5. Does the advertising aim at some specific step that leads to a sale? If so, objectives might be:

   - Persuade prospect to write for descriptive literature, return a coupon, enter a contest.
   - Persuade prospect to visit a showroom, ask for a demonstration.
   - Induce prospect to sample the product (trial offer).

6. How important are supplementary benefits of advertising? Objectives would be:

   - Help salespeople open new accounts.
   - Help salespeople get larger orders from wholesalers and retailers.
   - Help salespeople get preferred display space.
   - Give salespeople an entrée.
   - Build morale of sales force.
   - Impress the trade.

7. Should the advertising impart information needed to consummate sales and build customer satisfaction? If so, objectives may be to use:

   - "Where to buy it" advertising.
   - "How to use it" advertising.
   - New models, features, package.
   - New prices.
   - Special terms, trade-in offers, and so forth.
   - New policies (such as guarantees).

8. Should advertising build confidence and goodwill for the corporation? Targets may include:

   - Customers and potential customers.
   - The trade (distributors, dealers, retail people).
   - Employees and potential employees.
   - The financial community.
   - The public at large.

9. What kind of images does the company wish to build?

   - Product quality, dependability.
   - Service.
   - Family resemblance of diversified products.
   - Corporate citizenship.
   - Growth, progressiveness, technical leadership.

intended to favorably position Italian fashion designers and craftsmen as the world's finest.[12] The objectives were to increase Italy's share of U.S. imports and enhance the prestige of its brands. The Italian Trade Commission budgeted $25 million on advertising and other promotion activities in the five-year period through 1997 to achieve these objectives. The aggressive campaign generated positive results with an increase in Italy's U.S. imported apparel share from 4.5 to 5.9 percent. Much larger increases in apparel share were obtained by the more expensive imports like Versace and Giorgio Armani.

Budget determination, creative strategy, and media/programming strategy are closely interrelated, so these decisions need to be closely coordinated. A preliminary budget may be set, subject to review after the creative and media/programming strategies are determined. Using objective and task budgeting, creative plans and media alternatives should be examined in the budgeting process.

Creative Strategy

The range of advertising objectives shown in Exhibit 12.5 indicates the possible focus of the creative strategy. For example, if the objective is to enhance the image of a brand, then the message conveyed by the ad would seek to strengthen the brand image. This theme is illustrated by one of BMW's magazine ads introducing the new X5 4.8 which stated: "No matter how we disguise it, its heritage keeps showing through."

The creative strategy is guided by the market target and the desired positioning for the product or brand. Recall, in Chapter 6, we discuss positioning according to the *functions* performed by the brand, the *symbol* to be conveyed by the brand, or the *experience* provided by the brand. The creative theme seeks to effectively communicate the intended positioning to buyers and others influencing the purchase of the brand.

There are several successful advertising campaign themes that have been used for many years. Examples include Nike's "Just Do It" and "You are in good hands with Allstate."[13] Interestingly, some of the highest-rated and lowest-rated ads have been created by the same advertising agency (we discuss the agency's role later in the chapter).

Creative advertising designs enhance the effectiveness of advertising by providing a unifying concept that binds together the various parts of an advertising campaign. Advertising agencies are experts in designing creative strategies. The agency professionals may design unique themes to position a product or firm in some particular way or use comparisons with competition to enhance the firms' brands. Choosing the right creative theme for the marketing situation can make a major contribution to the success of an advertising program. While tests are used to evaluate creative approaches, the task is more of an art than a science. Perhaps the best guide to its creativity is an agency's track record and the success of its tests of creative approaches.

Several challenges are impacting the creative process and changing the design of creative strategies:

> The new generation of advertising creatives will face a world of ever-growing complexity. They must handle many challenges of integrated marketing communications (IMC) as they help their clients build relationships with highly fragmented target markets. They will need to understand the wide range of new technologies affecting advertising (computer hardware and software, electronic networking, high-definition television, and more). And they have to learn how to advertise in emerging international markets.[14]

The earlier illustration describing P&G's initiatives to develop creative strategies for the firm's core brands highlights the importance of this part of advertising strategy.[15] In their field studies of buyers, executives followed buyers as they shopped and sat in on sessions to listen to them talk about their lives. This information was very useful in designing creative ads.

Media/Scheduling Decisions

A company's advertising agency or media placement organization normally guides media selection and scheduling decisions. These professionals have the experience and technical ability to match media and scheduling to the target audience(s) specified by the firm. The media, timing, and programming decisions are influenced largely by two factors: (1) access to the target audience(s); and (2) the costs of reaching the target group(s). A comparison of advertising rates for several media is shown below:[16]

Medium	Vehicle	Cost	Reach	CPM*
TV	30 seconds network prime time	$120,000	10 million households	$12
Consumer Magazine	Page, 4-color in Cosmopolitan	$ 86,155	2.5 million paid readers	35
Online service	Banner on CompuServe major-topic page	$ 10,000 per month	750,000 visitors	13
Website	Banner on Infoseek	$ 10,000 per month	500,000 page views per month	20

*CPM = Cost per thousand exposures.

The audience coverage varies considerably so the access provided to the target audience is also important. The various media provide extensive profile information on their viewers. *Standard Rates and Data Services* publishes advertising costs for various media. The costs are determined by circulation levels and the type of publication. In deciding which medium to use, it is important to evaluate the cost per exposure and the match of the characteristics of the subscribers to market targets. The medium should provide coverage of the buyers in the market target for the product or brand being advertised. High media costs help explain why companies may transfer resources to online advertising, such as banners and click-throughs, where production and media costs are much lower.

Media models are available to analyze allocations and decide which media mix best achieves one or more objectives. These models typically use an exposure measure (Exhibit 12.4) as the basis for media allocation. For example, cost per thousand exposures can be used to compare alternative media. The models also consider audience characteristics (e.g., age group composition) and other factors. The models are useful in selecting media when many advertising programs and a wide range of media are used.

The fragmentation of many consumer markets is driving significant amounts of advertising spending from traditional mass media to more focused narrowcast media. The INNOVATION FEATURE describes some of these changes.

New types of Internet-based media are becoming very significant to media scheduling choices. Social networking websites like MySpace, Facebook, and YouTube are becoming important media for reaching audiences not easily accessed through conventional print and TV approaches. Publisher Random House, for example, created a Web page on MySpace for Hannibal, to promote the publication of Thomas Harris' novel *Hannibal Rising* about Hannibal Lector. The aim was to reach young readers who are resistant to traditional advertising media and even official websites. Social networking sites provide options for branded viral marketing campaigns to be pasted on personal pages and passed around within the social networking community. Viral marketing—distributing promotional video clips across the Internet— is increasingly used by advertisers, for example Unilever's Axe deodorant, Volkswagen, Diageo's Smirnoff Raw Tea, and Virgin Money. Viral marketing

- The decline in prime-time television audience ratings and newspaper circulation since the 1970s has been accompanied by the development of a proliferation of digital and wireless communication channels: hundreds of narrowcast cable TV and radio channels; thousands of specialized magazines; millions of computer terminals, video game consoles, personal digital assistants and cell phone screens.

- In the 1960s an advertiser could reach 80 percent of U.S. women with a spot aired simultaneously on CBS, NBC, and ABC, while now an ad would have to run on 100 TV channels to get near this feat.

- Mass media's share of advertising is declining as marketers boost spending on more targetable, narrowcast media.

- The fastest form of online advertising is "paid search"—the search engine used displays paid advertisements or "sponsored links" with the search results. Internet users can be targeted by region and city.

- Online media are interactive, so advertisers can gather invaluable personal information from consumers and get a more precise measurement of advertising impact.

- A recent study by Sanford C. Bernstein & Co. predicts by 2010 marketers will spend more for advertising on cable and the Internet, than on network TV or on magazines.

Source: Anthony Bianco, "The Vanishing Mass Market," *BusinessWeek,* July 12, 2004, 58–62.

is also known as "word-of-mouse" or "buzz" marketing and involves releasing a compelling, but branded, video-clip or computer game, hoping that Internet users will distribute it widely to friends and contacts.[17]

Role of the Advertising Agency

Advertising agencies perform various functions for clients including developing creative designs and selecting media. In addition to creative skills and media selection, full service agencies offer a range of services including marketing research, sales promotion, marketing planning. The traditional basis of compensation is a 15 percent fee on media expenditures. For example, $1 million of advertising provides a commission of $150,000. The agency pays the $850,000 for the media space and bills the client $1,000,000.

Agency Relationship

The relationship between a corporate client and an agency is a cooperative effort. The client briefs the agency on the marketing strategy and the role of advertising in the marketing program. In some instances agency executives may be involved in the design of marketing strategy. The better the agency understands the company's targeting and positioning strategies, the more effective the agency can be in providing advertising services. The agency may assign one or more professionals full-time to a client with a large advertising budget.

Choosing an advertising agency is an important decision. It is also necessary to evaluate the relationship over time, since a company's advertising requirements change. Good agency relationships are usually the result of collaboration with an agency that has the capabilities and commitment needed by the client. Several factors that should be considered in evaluating an agency are shown in Exhibit 12.6.

The increasing demands for integrated marketing communications strategies, and the development of complex multi-media campaigns, may require re-evaluation of the traditional client/agency relationship. Traditional agencies may not be strong in areas like

EXHIBIT 12.6 **Checklist for Evaluating Advertising Agencies**

Source: William F. Arens, *Contemporary Advertising,* 6th ed. (Burr Ridge, IL: Richard D. Irwin, 1996), 93. Copyright The McGraw-Hill Companies. Used with permission.

Rate each agency on a scale from 1 (strongly negative) to 10 (strongly positive).

General Information
☐ Size compatible with our needs.
☐ Strength of management.
☐ Financial stability.
☐ Compatibility with other clients.
☐ Range of services.
☐ Cost of services; billing policies.

Marketing Information
☐ Ability to offer marketing counsel.
☐ Understanding of the markets we serve.
☐ Experience dealing in our market.
☐ Success record; case histories.

Creative Abilities
☐ Well-thought-out creativity; relevance to strategy.
☐ Art strength.
☐ Copy strength.
☐ Overall creative quality.
☐ Effectiveness compared to work of competitors.

Production
☐ Faithfulness to creative concept and execution.
☐ Diligence to schedules and budgets.
☐ Ability to control outside services.

Media
☐ Existence and soundness of media research.
☐ Effective and efficient media strategy.
☐ Ability to achieve objectives within budget.
☐ Strength at negotiating and executing schedules.

Personality
☐ Overall personality, philosophy, or position.
☐ Compatibility with client staff and management.
☐ Willingness to assign top people to account.

References
☐ Rating by current clients.
☐ Rating by past clients.
☐ Rating by media and financial sources.

online advertising. The consumer goods company Unilever, for example, has established internal teams to cope with rapid changes in advertising media—in the form of communications planning and digital advertising operations units. As the use of TV advertising declines—down from 85 percent of the global advertising spent in 2000 to 65 percent in 2006—Unilever is developing "holistic" campaigns that make use of a wider range of marketing tools.[18]

Agency Compensation

Most agencies operate on some type of commission arrangement, though the arrangement may involve a commission for media placement and a separate arrangement for other services. For example, media placement would receive a 5 percent commission, whereas other services associated with the advertising would yield an additional 10 percent. These changes in the original 15 percent commission are because advertising specialists are available (e.g., media buying) and offer reduced fees for specific services. Projects such as research studies are priced on an individual basis.

Clients may work out flexible payment arrangements with their agency. The agency may keep a record of its costs and the client will pay for the services it requires. The resulting compensation may be greater or less than the traditional 15 percent commission. In some situations agencies may share cost savings with the client.

Industry Composition

Large, full service agencies like Dentsu in Tokyo and Young and Rubicam in New York account for the dominant portion of billings. Nonetheless, several local and regional agencies have created pressures for change throughout the industry. Concerns of clients about arbitrary commission rates and lack of flexibility in client services have led to placing business with small specialty agencies that provide media buying, creative design, and other services. There are many local and regional agencies that serve small and medium-size clients.

Ad agencies are experiencing major changes driven by clients' shifting media priorities and the emergence of new competitors like Google. Ad-skipping technology provided by TiVo and other firms helps TV viewers skip commercials. Internet advertising is experiencing huge growth trends. Some critics indicate that clients and their agencies have lost contact with consumers. Turbulence and change are likely to continue to impact traditional agencies in the future.

Implementing the Advertising Strategy and Measuring Its Effectiveness

Before an advertising strategy is implemented, it is advisable to establish the criteria that will be used for measuring advertising effectiveness. Advertising expenditures are wasted if firms spend too much or allocate expenditures improperly. Measuring effectiveness provides necessary feedback for future advertising decisions. Importantly, the quality of advertising can be as critical to getting results as the amount of advertising.

Tracking Advertising Performance

As previously discussed advertising's impact on sales may be difficult to measure because other factors also influence sales and profits. Most efforts to measure effectiveness consider objectives such as attitude change, awareness, or exposure (Exhibit 12.4), although Internet advertising is changing performance measurement opportunities. Comparing objectives and results helps managers decide when to alter or stop advertising campaigns. Services such as Nielsen's TV ratings are available for the major media. These ratings have a critical impact on the allocation of advertising dollars, although recent research findings question the accuracy of the ratings. Various measurement concerns are causing several changes in the rating process.

Methods of Measuring Effectiveness

Major emphasis by several companies is being placed on developing better methods of measuring the effectiveness of advertising. Companies are seeking ways for choosing between alternative methods of promotion such as displays in supermarkets versus radio advertising. Examples of some new methods of advertising effectiveness measurement are described in the METRICS FEATURE.

Several methods are used to evaluate advertising results. Analysis of historical data identifies relationships between advertising expenditures and sales using statistical techniques such as regression analysis. Recall tests measure consumers' awareness of specific ads and campaigns by asking questions to determine if a sample of people remembers an ad. Longitudinal studies track advertising expenditures and sales results before, during, and after an advertising campaign. Controlled tests are a form of longitudinal study in which extraneous effects are measured and/or controlled during the test. Test marketing can be used to evaluate advertising effectiveness. Effort/results models use empirical data to build a mathematical relationship between sales and advertising effort.

Interestingly, one of the leading full-service global advertising companies, WPP Group, is applying statistical analysis (econometric models) to measure the effectiveness of advertising expenditures.[19] The search for more effective measurement techniques is driven by concerns about the effectiveness of TV advertising, pressures on costs, and changing media technologies.

Frustrated over their inability to measure the bang they get for their marketing bucks, advertisers are trying new methods of gauging advertising effectiveness:

GENERAL MOTORS	GM is shifting more dollars into "addressable" media: direct marketing, online, and events through which it can collect names, profiles, and e-mail addresses. This gives a clearer sense of which messages inspire people to actually buy a car.
PROCTER & GAMBLE	P&G is an early subscriber to Apollo, a joint Arbitron/VNU project that will track the media habits of 70,000 people. Apollo should yield ad effectiveness using that data plus home scanning of groceries, Internet usage, and frequent surveys.
HOME DEPOT	Sophisticated computer modeling matches media plans to sales. The data allow smarter, more localized spending decisions: Newspaper ads may drive paint sales in one region, for instance, while radio works better in another.

Source: "Making Marketing Measure Up," *BusinessWeek*, December 13, 2004, 113.

Sales Promotion Strategy

Sales promotion expenditures are increasing more rapidly than advertising in many companies. Both advertising and sales promotion initiatives are receiving major attention by companies in their attempts to boost productivity and reduce costs. Sales promotion activities provide extra value or incentives to consumers and value chain participants.[20] The intent is to encourage sales. Sales promotion is some form of inducement (e.g., coupon, contest, rebate, etc.). Importantly, sales promotion activities can be targeted to various points of influence in the value chain.

To pursue its goal of doubling its market share to 10 percent of light trucks in the U.S. Toyota has favored sales promotion strategy over conventional advertising. The head of marketing at Toyota claims "We can have the most beautiful advertising but that's not going to change people's minds. The only way you can do that is in person." [21] Rides in the Tundra are offered at fishing shows and tournaments, and at dirt-bike races. Test-drives can also be arranged at a big chain of building materials stores. The market targets for the Tundra are people with outdoor interests and owners of building and construction businesses. Specially trained "truck champions" are available at dealerships. Additionally, negative perceptions of the truck as an import are being countered with sponsorship of Brooks and Dunn, a top country music act, and sponsorship of the Texas Football Classic, a high school tournament.

We look at the nature and scope of sales promotion, the types of sales promotion activities, their advantages and limitations, and the decisions involved in determining sales promotion strategy.

Nature and Scope of Sales Promotion

Purchase rebates are one of the most active forms of sales promotion. Rebates are popular with companies, although consumers dislike the hassles of submitting rebate forms, providing proof of purchase, and delays in obtaining the rebates. The STRATEGY FEATURE examines the realities of mail-in rebates.

- Consumers hate the hassles, companies love unredeemed rebates, and regulators are investigating the consumer complaints.
- As much as 40 percent of rebates never get redeemed.
- Some 400 million rebates are offered each year with a total value of $6 billion.
- Unclaimed rebates translate into more than $2 billion of *extra* revenue for retailers and their suppliers each year.
- Complex filing rules and long delays discourage consumers.
- Companies emphasize the filing processes that are intended to discourage fraud.
- The largest rebate processor monitors 10,000 addresses suspected of submitting bogus rebates.
- Rebates offer companies an opportunity to promote small discounts without marking the products down.
- Rebates have become very popular with computer and consumer-electronics companies.
- The value of rebates has also increased.
- Regulators are intensifying their scrutiny of the companies offering rebates.
- The developing back-lash against rebates is pushing some companies to halt rebate strategies.
- Others are encouraging online filing.
- Fulfillment houses are revising their processing systems, using computer technology to validate claims.
- Consumers would like mail-in-rebates to go away but want the best price they can get.

Source: Brian Grow, "The Great Rebate Runaround," *BusinessWeek,* December 5, 2005, 34, 36, and 37.

The responsibility for sales promotion activities often spans several marketing functions, such as advertising, merchandising, product planning, and sales. For example, a sales contest for salespeople is typically designed and administered by sales managers, and the costs of the contest are included in the sales department budget. Similarly, planning and coordinating a new product sampling or coupon refund program may be assigned to a product manager. Point-of-purchase promotion displays in retail stores may be the responsibility of the field sales organization.

Total expenditures for sales promotion by business and industry in the United States are likely more than double advertising expenditures. The complete scope of sales promotion is often difficult to identify because the activities are included in various departments and budgets. Unlike advertising, sales promotion expenditures are not published in business publications or on the Internet.

A relevant issue is deciding how to manage the various sales promotion activities. While these programs are used to support advertising, pricing, channel of distribution, and personal selling strategies, the size and scope of sales promotion suggest that the responsibility for managing sales promotion should be assigned to one or a team of executives. Otherwise, sales promotion activities become fragmented, and may not be properly integrated with other promotion components. The chief marketing executive should assign responsibility for coordination and evaluation of sales promotion activities.

Sales Promotion Activities

Many activities may be part of the total promotion program, including trade shows, specialty advertising (e.g., imprinted calendars), contests, point-of-purchase displays, coupons, recognition programs (e.g., awards to top suppliers), and free samples. Companies may direct their sales promotion activities to consumer buyers, industrial buyers, value chain members, and salespeople, as shown in Exhibit 12.7. Sales promotion programs fall into three major categories: incentives, promotional pricing, and informational activities.

Promotion to Consumer Targets

Sales promotion is used in the marketing of many consumer goods and services, and includes a wide variety of activities, as illustrated in Exhibit 12.7. A key management concern is evaluating the effectiveness of promotions such as coupons, rebates, contests, and other awards. The large expenditures necessary to support these programs require that the results and costs be objectively assessed.

The sponsoring of sports events and individuals is a major initiative by various companies and brands. Sales promotion results from the association of the brand with the event or person. An example is PepsiCo's sponsorship of the Pepsi 400 NASCAR race. Similarly, sports celebrities may be sponsored. The strategy issue is determining the benefits versus costs of these sales promotion activities.

Product-placement activities are expanding in popularity with product sponsors. Viewing a product on a TV show provides interesting use exposure if the placement is in a realistic setting. Companies may be interested in positioning the product in a typical use setting rather than the immediate generation of sales. General Motors obtained an impressive product placement opportunity in the movie *Transformers*.[22] Interestingly the stars of the movie are GM cars which are transformed into robots fighting evil. Leveraging the sales promotion opportunity, movie fans are able to create their own transformers at Chevyautobot.com.

EXHIBIT 12.7
Sales Promotion Activities Targeted to Various Groups

Sales Promotion Activity	Targeted to:			
	Consumer Buyers	Industrial Buyers	Channel Members	Salespeople
Incentives				
Contests	X	X	X	X
Trips	X	X	X	X
Bonuses			X	X
Prizes	X	X	X	X
Advertising support			X	
Free items	X	X		
Recognition			X	X
Promotional Pricing				
Coupons	X			
Allowances		X	X	
Rebates	X	X	X	
Cash	X			
Informational Activities				
Displays	X			
Demonstrations	X	X	X	
Selling aids			X	X
Specialty advertising (e.g., pens)	X	X	X	
Trade shows	X	X	X	

Promotion to Industrial Targets

Many of the sales promotion methods that are used for consumer products also apply to industrial products, although the role and scope of the methods may vary. For example, trade shows perform a key role in small and medium-sized companies' marketing strategies. The advantage of the trade show is the heavy concentration of potential buyers at one location during a very short time period. The cost per contact is much less than a salesperson calling on prospects at their offices. While people attending trade shows also spend their time viewing competitors' products, an effective display and buyer/seller interactions offer a unique opportunity to hold the prospects' attention.

The Internet has many of the features of trade shows while eliminating certain of their limitations. For example, the Web enables the French woolens manufacturer, Carreman, to provide its customers fabric samples in one day.[23] The company posted its top fabrics on the Etexx website for online sample ordering. Management is optimistic that its customers will respond favorably to the initiative. Etexx, a start up based in Nice, France, created an e-marketplace for buyers and sellers of fabrics.

Sales promotion programs that target industrial buyers may consume a greater portion of the marketing budget than advertising. Many of these activities support personal selling strategies. They include catalogs, brochures, product information reports, samples, trade shows, application guides, and promotional items such as calendars, pens, and calculators.

Promotion to Value Chain Members

Sales promotion is an important part of manufacturers' marketing efforts to wholesalers and retailers for such products as foods, beverages, and appliances. Catalogs and other product information are essential promotional components for many lines. The Internet offers an alternative way to make catalog information available. Promotional pricing is often used to push new products through channels of distribution. Various incentives are popular in marketing to value chain members. Specialty advertising items such as calendars and memo pads are used in maintaining buyer awareness of brands and company names.

Promotion to the Sales Force

Incentives and informational activities are the primary forms of promotion used to assist and motivate company salespeople. Sales contests and prizes are popular. Companies also make wide use of recognition programs like the "salesperson of the year." Promotional information is vital to salespeople. Presentation kits help salespeople describe new products and the features of existing products to customers.

A high-tech promotion tool with exciting potential is the automated sales presentation created with integrated use of sound, graphics, and video briefcase computers. These multimedia or interactive techniques give salespeople powerful presentation capabilities, allowing them access to a complete product information system available on the notebook computer.

Advantages and Limitations of Sales Promotion

Because of its wide array of incentive, pricing, and communication capabilities, sales promotion has the flexibility to contribute to various marketing objectives. A marketing manager can target buyers, value chain members, and salespeople, and the sales response of the sales promotion activities can be measured to determine their effectiveness. For example, a company can track its coupon redemption or rebate success. Many of the incentive and price promotion techniques trigger the purchase of other products.

Sales promotion is not without its disadvantages. In most instances, rather than substituting for advertising and personal selling, sales promotion supports other promotional efforts. Control is essential to prevent some people from taking advantage of free offers, coupons, and other incentives as illustrated in the STRATEGY FEATURE. Value-added resellers may build inventories on products that receive manufacturers' trade discounts. Incentives and price-promotional activities need to be monitored. An effective advertisement can be run thousands of times, but promotional campaigns are usually not reusable. Thus, the costs of development must be considered in evaluating benefits and costs.

Sales Promotion Strategy

The steps in developing the sales promotion strategy are similar to the design of advertising strategy. First, it is necessary to define the communications task(s) that the sales promotion program is expected to accomplish. Next, specific promotion objectives are set for awareness levels and purchase intentions. It is important to evaluate the relative cost-effectiveness of feasible sales promotion methods and to select those that offer the best results/cost combination. Both the content of the sales promotion and its timing should be coordinated with other promotion activities. Finally, the program is implemented and is evaluated on a continuing basis. Evaluation examines the extent to which objectives are achieved. For example, trade show results can be evaluated to determine how many show contacts are converted to purchases.

Summary

Promotion strategy is a vital part of the marketing positioning strategy. The components—advertising, sales promotion, public relations, personal selling, direct marketing, and interactive/Internet marketing—offer an impressive array of capabilities for communicating with market targets and other relevant audiences. However, promotion activities are expensive. Management must decide the size of the promotion budget and allocate it to the promotion components. Each promotion activity offers certain unique advantages and also shares several characteristics with the other components.

Promotion strategy is guided by the market targeting and positioning strategies. Communication objectives must be determined and the role of each promotion component selected by marketing management. Budgeting indicates the amount and allocation of resources to the promotion strategy components. The major budgeting methods are objective and task, percent of sales, competitive parity, and all you can afford. Objective and task is the recommended method. Several product and market factors affect whether the promotion strategy will emphasize advertising, sales promotion, personal selling, or seek a balance between the forms of promotion. The effective integration of the communications program is a major challenge for many firms. Finally, the effectiveness of the promotion strategy is evaluated.

The steps in developing advertising strategy include identifying the target audience, deciding the role of advertising in the promotional mix, indicating advertising objectives and budget size, selecting the creative strategy, determining the media and programming schedule, and implementing the program and measuring its effectiveness. Advertising objectives may range from audience exposure to profit contribution. Advertising agencies offer specialized services for developing creative strategies, designing messages, and selecting media and programming strategies. Measuring advertising effectiveness is essential in managing this expensive resource.

Our discussion of sales promotion highlights several methods that are available for use as incentives, advertising support, and informational activities. Typically, firms use sales promotion activities in conjunction with advertising and personal selling rather than as a primary component of promotion strategy. Sales promotion programs may target consumer buyers, industrial buyers, value chain organizations, and salespeople. Sales-promotion strategy should determine the methods that provide the best results/cost combinations for achieving the communications objectives.

Questions for Review and Discussion

1. Compare and contrast the role of promotion in an international public accounting firm with promotion by American Airlines.

2. Identify and discuss the factors that are important in determining the promotion program for the following products:

   a. Video tape recorder/player.

   b. Personal computer.

   c. Boeing 7E7 Dreamliner commercial aircraft.

   d. Residential homes.

3. What are the important considerations in determining a promotion budget?

4. Under what conditions is a firm's promotion strategy more likely to be advertising/sales promotion-driven rather than personal selling-driven?

5. Discuss the advantages and limitations of using awareness as an advertising objective. When may this objective be appropriate?

6. Identify and discuss the important differences between advertising and sales promotion strategies in promotion strategy.

7. Coordination of advertising and personal selling strategies is a major challenge in large companies. Outline a plan for integrating these strategies.

8. Discuss the role of sales promotion methods in the promotion strategy of a major airline.

9. How and to what extent is the Internet likely to be useful in companies' promotion strategies?

Internet Applications

A. Discuss how Godiva Chocolatier's website (www.godiva.com) corresponds to the brand image portrayed by its retail stores. What are the promotion objectives that Godiva's management seems to be pursuing on the website?

B. Go to the websites of NBC and the BBC (www.nbc.com and www.bbc.co.uk). Contrast the ways NBC and the BBC promote their daily TV programs online. Which similarities and differences do you detect? Suggest ways of improvement considering the respective cultural frame of reference and target market for NBC and BBC.

C. Discuss how Apple's (www.apple.com) marketing strategy for iPod Mini is enhanced by a Web-based approach.

Feature Applications

A. Consider the online promotion activities described in the INTERNET FEATURE. Discuss how these initiatives offer compelling advantages over traditional promotion strategies.

B. Review the RELATIONSHIP FEATURE concerning Procter & Gamble's advertising efforts designed to avoid its core brands such as Tide detergent becoming commodity products. Consider whether it is possible for consumers to genuinely engage with products of this kind.

Notes

1. This illustration is based on Robert D. Hof, "Is Google Too Powerful?" *BusinessWeek,* April 19, 2007, 47–55; David Kiley, "Google: Searching for an Edge in Ads," *BusinessWeek,* January 30, 2006, 80–92.

2. *Marketing News,* "Marketing Fact Book," July 15, 2007, 29.

3. Ronald Grover, "Mad Ave is Starry-Eyed over Met Video," *BusinessWeek,* May 23, 2005, 38.

4. Mark W. Johnston and Greg W. Marshall, *Sales Force Management,* 7th ed. (Burr Ridge, IL: McGraw-Hill Irwin, 2003), 48.

5. "Lights, Camera, Brands," *The Economist,* October 29, 2005, 61–62.

6. "Target Practice," *The Economist,* April 2, 2005, 13.

7. "SIA Presses for Higher Yields with New Aircraft, IFE Systems," *Aviation Week & Space Technology,* June 4, 2001, 69–70.

8. Robert Berner, "Detergent Can Be So Much More," *BusinessWeek,* May 1, 2006, 68.

9. "The Vuitton Machine," *BusinessWeek,* March 22, 2004, 98–100, 102.

10. George E. Belch and Michael A. Belch, *Advertising and Promotion,* 6th ed. (Burr Ridge, IL: McGraw-Hill/Irwin, 2004), 11.

11. "Queen of Madison Avenue," *The Economist,* February 24, 2007, 80.

12. Wendy Bounds and Deborah Ball, "Italy Knits Support for Fashion Industry," *The Wall Street Journal,* December 15, 1997, B8.

13. George E. Belch and Michael A. Belch, *Advertising and Promotion,* 5th ed. (New York: McGraw-Hill/Irwin, 2001), 262.

14. William F. Arens, *Advertising,* 9th ed. (Burr Ridge, IL: McGraw-Hill/Irwin, 2004), 384.

15. Berner, "Detergent Can Be So Much More," 66, 68.

16. Belch and Belch, *Advertising and Promotion,* 5th ed., 517.

17. Allison Enright, "Viral Campaign Hooks Potential Users," *Marketing News,* May 15, 2007, 9–10; Matthew Garahan, "A Hunt for Revenue in the Ecosystem," *Financial Times,* Monday, April 30, 2007, 24; Danuta Kean, "Vampires and Cannibals Find Prey Online," *Financial Times,* Tuesday, November 7, 2006, 12.

18. Gary Silverman, "Unilever in Advertising Shake-Up," *Financial Times,* Tuesday, March 14, 2006, 23.

19. Aaron O. Patrick, "Econometrics Buzzes Ad World as a Way of Measuring Results," *The Wall Street Journal,* August 16, 2005, B8.

20. Belch and Belch, *Advertising and Promotion,* Chapter 16.

21. Bernard Simon, "Consumers Get to Meet the New Toyota Pick-Up," *Financial Times,* Friday, September 15, 2006, 12.

22. Dorothy Pomerantz, "Best Ad Ever," *Forbes,* June 18, 2007, 44.

23. "Streamlining," *BusinessWeek,* E.Biz, September 18, 2000, EB70.

Chapter

13

Sales Force, Internet, and Direct Marketing Strategies

Sales organizations in many companies around the world have experienced significant changes in how the selling function is being performed over the last decade. Many transactional selling activities are handled by the Internet, while salespeople are more focused on collaborative and consulting relationships with customers. Contrary to some forecasts the role of selling has not deteriorated. More than a few companies and business units have shifted resources from marketing to sales because management considers the sales organization is vital in attaining marketing and business strategy objectives.[1] Personal selling, the Internet, and direct marketing initiatives are being impacted by many changes in the twenty-first century. The Internet has become an important and expanding avenue of direct contact between customers and companies selling goods and services. Management may use a combination of salespeople, direct marketing, and the Internet to perform selling and sales support functions. Coordinating an organization's activities across multiple customer contact initiatives is essential to avoid conflicts and enhance overall results.

Hewlett-Packard Co.'s (H-P) sales force organizational changes are illustrative of the market-driven initiatives underway in many companies.[2] In 2006 H-P's new CEO had received feedback from 400 customers and internal executives which caused a major overhaul of H-P's sales force strategy and structure. Before the changes H-P had eleven layers of managers between the CEO and customers; sales team efforts were fragmented and duplicative. Seventy percent of H-P's revenues are from companies, yet salespeople were not actively seeking their business. New initiatives included product specialization by salespeople, salesperson customer responsibility assignment and reduction of the number of accounts, and standardization of account management software. H-P's performance is improving and greater gains are expected from the sales strategy and structure changes.

In this chapter we first discuss developing and implementing sales force strategy. Next, we consider the issues and initiatives concerning Internet strategy. Finally, we describe and illustrate the various methods used in direct marketing to customers.

Sales Force Strategy

Sales force strategy requires deciding how to use personal selling to contact sales prospects, generate sales, and develop the types of customer relationships that management considers necessary to accomplish the organization's sales force objectives. Personal selling activities vary considerably across companies based on how personal selling contributes to marketing positioning strategy and promotion strategy. For example, a Pfizer pharmaceutical salesperson maintains regular contact with doctors and other professionals, but actual purchases are made at retail outlets where the prescriptions are filled. Nonetheless, Pfizer's salespeople play a vital role in the company's marketing strategy. The drug salesperson provides information on new products, distributes samples, and works toward building long-term relationships.

Sales force strategy includes six major initiatives as shown in Exhibit 13.1. First, the role of the sales force in the promotion strategy is determined. This requires deciding how personal selling is expected to contribute to the marketing program. Second, the selling process must be determined, indicating how selling will be accomplished with targeted customers. Third, in selecting sales channels, management decides how the sales organization, major account management, telemarketing, and the Internet will contribute to the selling process. Fourth, the design of the sales organization must be determined and assessed over time to determine its effectiveness. Recall H-P's redesign initiatives discussed in the lead-in illustration. Fifth, salespeople are recruited, trained, and managed. Finally, the results of the selling strategy are evaluated and adjustments are made to narrow the gap between actual and desired results.

Salespeople's interactions with many customers and the geographical dispersion of salespeople are likely to create more ethical issues than are experienced in other types of jobs. Sales managers may encounter a wide range of ethical situations as discussed in the ETHICS FEATURE.

EXHIBIT 13.1
Sales Force Strategy

Determine the Role
of the Sales Force in
the Promotion Strategy

⇩

Select the Selling
Process (how selling
will be accomplished)

⇩

Decide if and How
Alternative Sales
Channels Will be
Utilized

⇩

Design the Sales
Organization

⇩

Recruit, Train, and
Manage Salespeople

⇩

Evaluate Performance
and Make Adjustments
Where Necessary

Ethics Feature

Challenges in Selling and Sales Management

Two sets of ethical dilemmas are of particular concern to sales managers. The first set is embedded in the manager's dealings with the salespeople. Ethical issues involved in relationships between a sales manager and the sales force include such things as fairness and equal treatment of all social groups in hiring and promotion, respect for the individual in supervisory practices and training programs, and fairness and integrity in the design of sales territories, assignment of quotas, and determination of compensation and incentive rewards. Ethical issues pervade nearly all aspects of sales force management.

The second set of ethical issues arises from the interactions between salespeople and their customers. These issues only indirectly involve the sales manager because the manager cannot always directly observe or control the actions of every member of the sales force. But managers have a responsibility to establish standards of ethical behavior for their subordinates, communicate them clearly, and enforce them vigorously.

Source: Mark W. Johnston and Greg W. Marshall, *Sales Force Management.* 7th ed. (Burr Ridge, IL: McGraw-Hill/Irwin, 2003), 21. Copyright © The McGraw-Hill Companies. Used with permission.

The Role of Selling in Promotion Strategy

Salespeople's responsibilities may range from taking orders from customers to extensive collaboration as consultants to customers. While management has some flexibility in choosing the role and objectives of the sales force in the marketing program, several factors often guide the role of selling in a firm's integrated marketing communications strategy, as shown in Exhibit 13.2. Recall our discussion of IMC in Chapter 12. Considerable direction

EXHIBIT 13.2

Factors Influencing the Role of Personal Selling in a Firm's IMC Strategy

Source: Mark W. Johnston and Greg W. Marshall, *Sales Force Management.* 7th ed. (Burr Ridge, IL: McGraw-Hill/Irwin, 2003), 87. Copyright © The McGraw-Hill Companies. Used with permission.

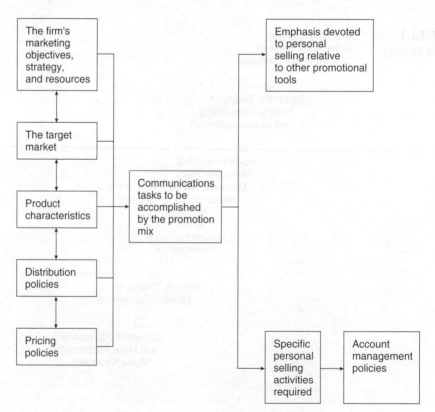

as to how personal selling will be used is provided by the target market, product characteristics, distribution policies, and pricing policies. The selling effort needs to be positioned into the integrated communications program. It is also useful to indicate how the other promotion-mix components, such as advertising, support and relate to the sales force. Sales management needs to be aware of the plans and activities of other promotion components.

The objectives assigned to salespeople frequently involve management's expected sales results. Sales quotas are used to state these expectations. Companies may give incentives to salespeople who achieve their quotas. Team selling incentives may also be used. Objectives other than sales are important in many organizations. These include increasing the number of new accounts, providing services to customers and channel organizations, retaining customers, selecting and evaluating value chain intermediaries, and obtaining market information. The objectives selected need to be consistent with marketing strategy and promotion objectives and measurable so that salesperson performance can be evaluated.

Selling roles range from transactional selling to consulting-type relationships. The Internet is replacing salespeople in transactional selling, whereas it may be used to provide support for relationship-type selling roles. Transactional selling is not restricted to small, low volume buyers. The important issue is how much direct contact with the salesperson is needed by the buyer. For example, physicians may need detailed assistance on new drugs from salespeople, whereas transactional selling via the Internet is preferred for older and less complex products prescribed by doctors. Importantly, companies may need to utilize different types of selling for the same customer.

Types of Sales Jobs

The salespeople who sell to ultimate consumers (door-to-door sales, insurance sales, real estate brokers, retail store sales, etc.) comprise a major portion of the number of salespeople, but a much greater volume of sales is accounted for by business-to-business salespeople.[3] B2B sales may be to resellers (e.g., retail chains), business users, and institutions. Consumer and organizational sales are similar in several respects, but B2B sales may involve more complex products, more extensive purchasing processes, different selling skills, and more collaborative management processes (e.g., training, coaching, directing, and evaluating).

Illustrative sales positions for salespeople include new business selling, trade selling, missionary selling, and consultative/technical selling.[4]

New Business Selling

This selling job involves obtaining sales from new buyers. The buyers may be one-time purchasers or repeat buyers. For example, recruiting a new online business customer by an Office Depot salesperson is an illustration of a one-time selling situation. Alternatively, the selling strategy may be concerned with obtaining new buyers on a continuing basis. Commercial insurance and real estate sales firms use this strategy.

Trade Selling

This form of selling provides assistance and support to value chain members rather than obtaining sales. A producer marketing through wholesalers, retailers, or other intermediaries may provide merchandising, logistical, promotional, and product information assistance. For example, PepsiCo's field sales organization assists retailers in merchandising and support activities, works closely with bottlers, and builds relationships with fast food and other retailers selling drinks on premises.

Missionary Selling

A strategy similar to trade selling is missionary selling. In these selling situations a producer's salespeople work with the customers of a channel member to encourage them to purchase the producer's product from the channel member. For example, commercial airline sales representatives contact travel agencies, providing them with schedule information on new routes and encouraging agencies to book flights on their airline.

Consultative/Technical Selling

Firms that use this strategy sell to an existing customer base and provide technical and application assistance. These positions may involve the sales of complex equipment or services such as management consulting. Importantly, consultative selling requires giving sales professionals authority in negotiating sales as illustrated by sales of Boeing's large commercial aircraft.[5] These sales relationships involve high-level consultative selling strategies as described in the RELATIONSHIP FEATURE.

An organization may use more than one of the selling strategies. For example, a transportation services company might use a new business strategy for expanding its customer base and a missionary selling strategy for servicing existing customers. The skills needed by the salesperson vary according to the selling strategy used.

Several changes are underway in many sales organizations. These initiatives require redesigning the traditional sales organization, leveraging information technology to lower costs and provide quick response, designing the sales strategy to meet different customer needs, building long-term relationships with customers and business partners, and responding proactively to global competitive opportunities and challenges. The sales force continues to be essential in many organizations, although salespeople are being asked to assume new responsibilities and the methods for keeping score are changing.

Defining the Selling Process

Several selling and sales support activities are involved in moving from identifying a buyer's needs to completing the sale and managing the post-sale relationships between buyer and seller. This selling process includes: (1) prospecting for customers; (2) opening the relationship; (3) qualifying the prospect; (4) presenting the sales message; (5) closing the sale; and (6) servicing the account.[6] The process may be very simple, consisting of a routine set of actions designed to close the sale, such as supermarket purchases. Alternatively, the process may extend over a long time period, with many contacts and interactions between the buyers, other people influencing the purchase, the salesperson assigned to the account, and technical specialists in the seller's organization. The selling process for Boeing aircraft is illustrative.

Sales management guides the selling process by indicating the customers and prospects the firm is targeting and providing guidelines for developing customer relationships and obtaining sales results. This process is management's strategy for achieving the sales force objectives in the selling environment of interest. Salespeople implement the process following the guidelines set by management, such as the product strategy (relative emphasis on different products), customer targeting and priorities, and the desired selling activities and outcomes.

The selling process is normally managed by the salesperson who has responsibility for a customer account, although an increasing number of companies are assigning this responsibility to customer relationship management teams. Account management includes planning and execution of the selling activities between the salesperson and the customer or prospect. Some organizations analyze this process and set guidelines for use by salespeople to plan their selling activities. Selling process analysis may result in programmed selling steps or alternatively, may lead to highly customized selling approaches where the salesperson develops specific strategies for each account. A company may also use team selling (e.g., product specialists and salesperson), major account management, telemarketing, and Internet support systems.

During the 2000s Boeing experienced an intense competitive battle against Airbus for control of the commercial jetliner market. Airbus was winning the battle until 2005 when Boeing's Asia-Pacific jet sales were $26 billion compared to Airbus' $9 billion.

Under a new CEO management gave salespeople much more control over selling strategy compared to previous tight and rigid control by top management. Boeing lost many sales to Airbus because of top management's unwillingness to give competent sales professionals flexibility in negotiating sales. Larry Dickenson, Boeing's top salesman who covers the Asia-Pacific market, builds on over eighteen years of relationships with airlines like Cathay Pacific, Quantas Airways Ltd., and Singapore Airlines Ltd., to negotiate winning contracts.

Importantly, Dickenson carefully plans and executes each sales campaign, overseeing every detail in the process that may span several years. The strategy is a combination of attractive pricing, financing, and leasing arrangements in combination with training and service packages.

Source: Stanley Holmes, "Boeing's Jet Propellant," *BusinessWeek,* December 26, 2005, 40.

Indications of a possible need for a change in the sales process include faulty forecasting, sales declines, lost customers, new customers from acquisitions, drops in profit margins, and price wars. The changes made by FedEx Corp. are illustrative.[7] Management combined its air and ground freight sales forces in 2000. Rather than deploying separate sales forces, customers are now contacted by salespeople representing both air and ground services. The changes provided more uniform coverage and eliminated costly duplicated customer contacts. FedEx has experienced strong sales and profit growth, moving to an estimated $36 billion in sales for 2007 and more than $2 billion in net profit. These changes are illustrative of customer management initiatives being implemented by several companies.

The selling process provides guidelines for sales force recruiting, training, allocation of effort, organizational design, and the use of selling support activities such as telemarketing and the Internet. Understanding the selling process is essential in coordinating all elements of the marketing program.

Sales Channels

An important part of deciding the personal selling strategy is choice of the alternative channels to end-user customers. Management must decide: (1) which channel(s) to use in contacting value chain members and end users; and (2) how telemarketing, Internet, and direct marketing will be used to support the field sales force. For example, management may decide to contact major accounts using national or global account managers, manage regular accounts using the field sales force, and service small accounts via telemarketing or the Internet. The reality is that direct contact by face-to-face salespeople is very expensive and the need for this resource should be evaluated in terms of benefits and costs.

The choice of a particular sales channel is influenced by the buying power of customers, the selling channel threshold levels, and the complexity of buyer-seller relationships. The buying power of a supplier's total customer base may range from several major accounts to a large number of very low volume purchasers. Customers and prospects can be classified into: (1) major accounts; (2) other customers requiring face-to-face contact; and (3) accounts whose purchases (or potential) do not justify regular contact by field salespeople. Many companies are serving these accounts using the Internet.

The number of customers in each buying power category influences the selection of selling channels. The need for a multiple selling channel strategy should be determined. For example, the amount of telemarketing effort that is needed determines whether a telemarketing or electronic support unit should be considered. Similarly, enough major accounts should exist in order to develop and implement a major account program. If the customer base does not display substantial differences in purchasing power and servicing requirements, then the use of a single sales force channel may be appropriate.

There is a trend toward greater use of customer management strategies by many companies. For example, Newell Rubbermaid Inc., producer of a range of consumer household products, has a major sales force initiative underway to introduce new products and build relationships with retailers.[8] The nearly 900 salespeople work with stores in spotlighting Newell Rubbermaid products and conducting product comparisons in the stores for end users. Hundreds of college graduates have been recruited to strengthen relationships with retailers.

Designing the Sales Organization

Designing the sales organization includes selecting an organizational structure and deciding the number and deployment of salespeople to geographical areas and/or customers and prospects.

Organizational Design

The organizational design adopted should support the firm's sales force strategy. As companies adjust their selling strategies, organizational structure may also require changes. FedEx's shift to a single sales force for its air and ground services is illustrative. There is a significant trend toward a greater focus on customers' (market-driven) designs rather than products or geography as the basis for the design of the sales organization.

The characteristics and requirements of the customer base, the product(s), and the geographic location of buyers are the more important influences on the design of the sales organization. The answers to several questions are helpful in narrowing the choice of an organizational design.

1. What is the selling job? What activities are to be performed by salespeople?
2. Is specialization of selling effort necessary according to type of customer, different products, or salesperson activities (e.g., sales and service)?
3. Are channel of distribution relationships important in the organizational design?
4. How many and what kinds of sales management levels are needed to provide the proper amount of supervision, assistance, and control?
5. Will sales teams be used, and if so, what will be their composition?
6. How and to what extent will sales channels other than the field sales force be used to contact and serve customers?

The sales force organizational design needs to be compatible with the selling strategy and other marketing program strategies. Several illustrative types of organization designs are shown in Exhibit 13.3. These designs should take into account the scope of the product portfolio and differences in customer needs. Whenever the customer base is widely dispersed, geography is likely to be relevant in the organizational design. The market-driven design is heavily influenced by the customer base, although geographical location may also influence the design. The product/market design takes both factors into account in determining how the organization is structured. Similar customer needs and a complex range of products point to the product-driven design. If the product or the customer base does not

EXHIBIT 13.3
Sales Organization Designs

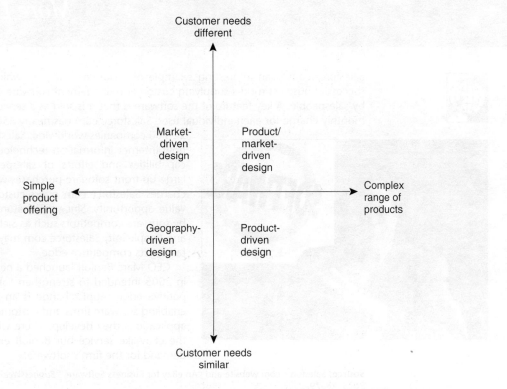

dominate design considerations, a geographical organization is used. The assigned geographical area and (or) accounts that are the responsibility of each salesperson comprise the sales territory or work unit.

Sales Force Deployment

Sales management must decide how many salespeople are needed and how to deploy them to customers and prospects. Several factors outside the salesperson's control often affect his/her sales results, such as market potential, number and location of customers, intensity of competition, and market (brand) position of the company. Sales force deployment analysis should consider both salesperson factors and the relevant uncontrollable factors.

There is a compelling amount of evidence indicating that sales unit design has a strong impact on sales unit performance. The better the sales unit is designed, the higher the performance of the unit assigned to a manager and the assigned salespeople (typically ten or less). Studies conducted involving over 1,000 field sales managers in eight countries around the world support the strong role of sales unit design.[9]

Salesforce.com is an interesting example of a software service designed to help salespeople manage their customer relationships. The software can easily be implemented in large and small organizations as described in the INTERNET FEATURE.

Several methods are available for analyzing sales force size and the deployment of selling effort including: (1) revenue/cost analysis; (2) single-factor models; (3) sales and effort response models; and (4) portfolio deployment models. Normally, sales and/or costs are the basis for determining sales force size and allocation.

Revenue/Cost Analysis techniques require information on each salesperson's sales and/or costs. One approach compares each salesperson to an average break-even sales level, thus helping management to spot unprofitable territories. Another approach analyzes the

Salesforce.com is an interesting example of a dot-com start-up which has developed a successful business model supplying customer management software over the Net for use by salespeople. A key feature of the software is that it is sold as a service to customers at a monthly charge for each individual user. Salesforce.com has nearly 450,000 subscribers @ 22,700 companies worldwide. Salesforce.com illustrates how Internet information technology can enhance the capabilities and efforts of salespeople. By replacing large up-front software purchases with monthly service charges Salesforce.com offers customers a compelling value opportunity. Since this feature can be duplicated by software competitors such as Siebel Systems, Oracle, and PeopleSoft, Salesforce.com may have difficulty sustaining its competitive edge.

CEO Marc Benioff launched a new product initiative in 2005 intended to strengthen Salesforce.com's competitive edge. AppExchange is an online marketplace enabling software firms and customers to trade and sell applications they develop. There will be no charge for the eBay-like service but Benioff expects it to expand demand for the firm's software.

Source: Salesforce.com website and "An eBay for Business Software," *BusinessWeek,* September 19, 2005, 78–79.

profit performance of accounts or trading areas, to estimate the profit impact of adding more salespeople, or to determine how many people a new sales organization needs. These techniques are very useful in locating high- and low-performance territories.

Single-Factor Models assume that size of the salesforce and/or effort deployment are determined by one factor, such as market potential or workload (e.g., number of calls required), whose values can be used to determine required selling effort. Suppose there are two territories, X and Y. Territory X has double the market potential (opportunity for business) of territory Y. If selling effort is deployed according to market potential, X should get double the selling effort of Y.

Consideration of multiple influences (e.g., market potential, intensity of competition, and workload) on market response can improve salesperson deployment decisions. Several promising *sales and effort response models* are available to assist management on sales force size and deployment decisions.[10] Exhibit 13.4 shows the information provided by one of these models. The analysis indicates that Jones' territory requires only about 36 percent of a person whereas Smith's territory can support about 2.36 people. The inadequate sales coverage in Smith's territory is risky in terms of dissatisfaction and loss of customers, whereas, expensive salesperson effort is being wasted in Jones' territory. Also, too much contact may irritate customers. The allocations are determined by incrementally increasing selling effort in high-response areas and reducing effort where sales response is low. Note that Exhibit 13.4 includes only two territories of a large sales organization. Sales response is determined from a computer analysis of the selling effort-to-sales response relationship.

We know that salespeople differ in ability, motivation, and performance. Managers are involved in selecting, training, monitoring, directing, evaluating, and rewarding salespeople. A brief look at each activity illustrates the responsibilities and functions of a sales manager.

EXHIBIT 13.4
Sales Force
Deployment Analysis
Illustration for
Jones's and Smith's
Territories

Trading Area†	Present Effort (percent)	Recommended Effort (percent)	Estimated Sales* Present Effort	Estimated Sales* Recommended Effort
Jones:				
1	10%	4%	$ 19	$ 13
2	60	20	153	120
3	15	7	57	50
4	5	2	10	7
5	10	3	21	16
Total	100%	36%	$ 260	$ 206
Smith:				
1	18%	81%	$ 370	$ 520
2	7	21	100	130
3	5	11	55	65
4	35	35	225	225
5	5	11	60	70
6	30	77	400	500
Total	100%	236%	$ 1,210	$ 1,510

*In $000.
†Each territory is made up of several trading areas.

Finding and Selecting Salespeople

In a major study, the chief sales executives in over 100 firms selling business-to-business products indicated on a 1 to 10 scale how important twenty-nine salesperson characteristics are to the success of their salespeople.[11] The executives indicated that the three most significant success characteristics are (1) being customer-driven and highly committed to the job; (2) accepting direction and cooperating as a team player; and (3) and being motivated by one's peers, financial incentives, and oneself.

Exhibit 13.5 describes several salesperson characteristics that are often important for different types of selling situations. The characteristics vary based on the type of selling

EXHIBIT 13.5
Characteristics
Related to Sales
Performance in
Different Types of
Sales Jobs

Source: Mark Johnston and
Greg Marshall, *Sales Force
Management.* 7th ed. (Burr
Ridge, IL: McGraw-Hill/ Irwin,
2003), 312. Copyright © The
McGraw-Hill Companies. Used
with permission.

Type of Sales Job	Characteristics That Are Relatively Important	Characteristics That Are Relatively Less Important
Trade selling	Age, maturity, empathy, knowledge of customer needs and business methods	Aggressiveness, technical ability, product knowledge, persuasiveness
Missionary selling	Youth, high energy and stamina, verbal skill, persuasiveness	Empathy, knowledge of customers, maturity, previous sales experience
Technical selling	Education, product and customer knowledge—usually gained through training, intelligence	Empathy, persuasiveness, aggressiveness, age
New business selling	Experience, age and maturity, aggressiveness, persuasiveness, persistence	Customer knowledge, product knowledge, education, empathy

strategy being employed, so we must first define the job that is to be performed. Managers use application forms, personal interviews, rating forms, reference checks, physical examinations, and various kinds of tests to assist them in making hiring decisions. The personal interview is widely acknowledged as the most important part of the selection process for salespeople.

Training

Some firms use formal programs to train their salespeople, while others use informal on-the-job training. Factors that affect the type and duration of training include type of sales job, product complexity, prior experience of new salespeople, and management's commitment to training. Training topics may include selling concepts and techniques, product knowledge, territory management, and company policies and operating procedures.

In training salespeople, companies may seek to: (1) increase productivity; (2) improve morale; (3) lower turnover; (4) improve customer relations; and (5) enable better management of time and territory.[12] These objectives are concerned with increasing the results from the salesperson's effort and/or reducing selling costs. Sales training should be evaluated concerning its benefits and costs. Evaluations may include before-and-after training results, participant critiques, and comparison of salespeople receiving training to those that have not been trained. Product knowledge training is probably more frequently used than any other type of training.

Supervising and Motivating Salespeople

The manager who supervises salespeople has a key role in implementing a firm's selling strategy. She or he faces several important management issues. Coordinating the activities of a field sales force is difficult due to lack of regular contact, although Internet access overcomes to some extent the lack of face-to-face contact. Compensation incentives are often used to encourage salespeople to obtain sales. However, salespeople need to be self-motivated. As discussed earlier, sales executives want salespeople who are customer-driven, committed to the company and to team relationships, and motivated by peers, incentives, and themselves.

The most widely used basis of compensation is a combination of salary and incentive pay. In situations where sales management wants to exercise control over salesperson activities, 75 percent salary and 25 percent incentive pay is a typical arrangement. The compensation plan should be fair to all participants and create an appropriate incentive. Salespeople also respond favorably to recognition programs and special promotions such as vacation travel awards.

Managers assist and encourage salespeople, and incentives highlight the importance of results, but the salesperson is the driving force in selling situations. Sales management must match promising selling opportunities with competent and self-motivated professional salespeople while providing the proper company environment, leadership, and collaborative support. Although most sales management professionals consider financial compensation the most important motivating force, research findings indicate that personal characteristics, environmental conditions, and company policies and procedures are also important motivating factors.[13]

A major study involving a large (1,000 +) sample of business-to-business salespeople found that salespeople who experienced higher levels of management monitoring and directing by managers displayed higher performance, job satisfaction, and organizational commitment.[14] Importantly, the management control efforts are collaborative and appear to be favorably received by many salespeople. These findings suggest that higher levels of management control are associated with favorable salesperson attitudes and behavior.

Sales Force Evaluation and Control

Sales management is continually working to improve the productivity of selling efforts. During the last decade personal selling costs increased much faster than advertising costs, so achieving high sales force performance is important. The evaluation of sales force performance considers sales results, costs, salesperson activities, and customer satisfaction. Several issues are important in evaluation, including where to focus the analysis, measures of performance, performance standards, and taking into account factors that the sales organization and individual salespeople cannot control.

During the last several years many pharmaceutical companies expanded their salesforces, reaching over 100,000 salespeople worldwide in 2004.[15] However, several of these companies began re-evaluating the productivity of their sales forces. The STRATEGY FEATURE describes how Wyeth is changing its selling strategy and reducing the size of its sales force.

Where to Focus the Analysis

Evaluation extends beyond the salesperson to include other organizational units, such as districts and branches. Selling teams are used in some types of selling. Companies that use teams focus evaluations on team results. Product performance evaluation by geographical area and across organization units is relevant in the firms that produce more than one product. Individual account sales and cost analyses are useful for customers such as national accounts and accounts assigned to salespeople.

Performance Measures

Management needs yardsticks for measuring salesperson performance. For example, the sales force of a regional food processor that distributes through grocery wholesalers and large retail chains devotes most of its selling effort to calling on retailers. Since the firm does not have information on sales of its products by each individual retail outlet, evaluations are based on the activities of salespeople rather than sales outcomes. This type of control system focuses on "behavior" rather than "outcomes."

Sales managers may use both activity (behavior) and outcome measures of salesperson performance. Research indicates that multiple item measures of several activities and outcomes are useful in performance evaluation.[16] Illustrative areas include sales planning, expense control, sales presentation, technical knowledge, information feedback, and sales results. Achievement of the sales quota (actual sales/quota sales) is a widely used outcome measure of sales performance. Other outcome measures include new business generated, market share gains, new product sales, and profit contributions.

Performance evaluation is influenced by the sales management control system used by the organization. Emphasis may be placed on salesperson activities, on outcomes, or a combination of activities and outcomes. The objective is to use the type of control that is most effective for the selling situation. Direct selling organizations like Avon and Mary Kay focus more on outcome control. Companies like American Airlines and Pfizer include both activity and outcome control. An important aspect of management control is the compensation plan. When salespeople are compensated primarily by commission earnings on sales results, pay becomes the primary management control mechanism.

Setting Performance Standards

Although internal comparisons of performance are frequently used, they are not very helpful if the performance of the entire sales force is unacceptable. A major problem in setting sales performance standards is determining how to adjust them for factors that are not under the salesperson's control (i.e., market potential, intensity of competition, differences in customer needs, and quality of supervision). A competent salesperson may not appear to be

- Wyeth's changes in the sales organization are driven by concerns of physicians about duplicated sales coverage and the need to improve sales force productivity.
- The prior approach of multiple salespeople calling on doctors to market the same drugs is being changed.
- Out of Wyeth's sales force of 5,000, about half call on primary-care doctors. As many as 750 may be cut or re-assigned.
- The selling strategy is to reduce the frequency of sales calls, while making each more worthwhile.
- Initiatives include assigning each salesperson responsibility for more drugs, reducing sales calls on the doctors who write the fewest prescriptions, and utilizing a part-time sales force for coverage of selected accounts, and use of Internet-based seminars.
- Other pharmaceutical companies are expected to follow Wyeth's sales force strategy initiatives.

Source: Scott Hensley, "Wyeth to Revamp, Cut Its Sales Force," *The Wall Street Journal,* June 20, 2005, A3, A6.

performing well if assigned to a poor sales territory (e.g., salesperson Jones Exhibit 13.4), when, the low performance may not be due to the salesperson. Such differences need to be included in the evaluation process since territories often are not equal in terms of opportunity and other uncontrollable factors.

We know that evaluating performance is one of sales management's more difficult tasks. Typically, performance tracking involves assessing a combination of outcome and behavioral factors. In compensation plans other than straight commission, performance evaluation may affect the salesperson's pay, so obtaining a fair evaluation is important.

By evaluating the organization's personal selling strategy, management may identify various problems requiring corrective action as illustrated by the Wyeth example. Problems may be linked to individual salespeople or to decisions that impact the entire organization. A well-designed information system helps in the diagnosis of performance and guides corrective actions when necessary.

Internet Strategy

We now consider Internet strategy, examining the alternatives, integration of Internet initiatives with marketing and promotion strategies, options for measuring effectiveness, and the Internet's expanding role in business and marketing strategies. Also, recall our discussion of the topic in earlier chapters.

The Internet is a worldwide means of exchanging information and communicating through a series of interconnected computers.[17] It offers a fast and versatile communications capability. Internet initiatives span a wide range of global industries and companies, and there have been successes but also many failures, stimulated by over-optimistic expectations and faulty implementation. Initiatives have been pursued by both traditional enterprises and new business designs. One of the more visible Internet enterprises is Amazon.com Inc., the online retailer with estimated sales of over $12 billion in 2007. Business-to-business use of the Internet is far more extensive than consumer adoption of the Internet, although consumer use of the Internet for information on products and actual purchase is expanding rapidly. The impacts of the Internet on business organizations in the future are expected to be both transformational as well as incremental in scope.

Strategy Development

The first step in Internet strategy development is to determine the role of the Internet in the organization's business and marketing strategies. This role may involve a separate business model, a value chain channel, a marketing communications tool, or an advertising medium:

> Marketers lured by the Internet's promise of immediacy, interactivity, availability, customization, and global reach need to evaluate when it really pays to reach customers through the Internet and how the Internet best fits into overall marketing strategy. To do so, they need to pay even closer attention to customers and rethink how to evaluate market opportunities, set marketing strategy, and deploy marketing programs.[18]

Several examples of how U.S. retailing is being impacted by the Internet are described in Exhibit 13.6. Online shopping is gaining popularity and is impacting the operations of all retailers. Industry observers indicate that the Web has reached adolescence.[19]

Deciding Internet Objectives

The capabilities of the Internet fall into two broad categories: a communications medium, and a direct response medium enabling users to purchase and sell products. The communications features of the Internet include the following.[20]

Creating Awareness and Interest

Advertising on the Internet offers important advantages to many companies. The opportunity for global exposure provides a compelling brand building capability.

Disseminating Information

Providing product, application, and company information via the Internet is essential in the competitive marketplace. This capability offers an opportunity for direct one-on-one contact.

EXHIBIT 13.6
E-Tailing Finally Hits Its Stride

Source: "E-Tailing Finally Hits Its Stride," *BusinessWeek*, December 20, 2004, 36–37.

The E-Tail Effect

How e-commerce is shaking up the retail landscape:

The Big Guns Arrive

After early struggles, online sales at brick-and-mortar giants such as Wal-Mart, Sears, and Gap are soaring. These chains are also using the Web to test new products and move into new markets.

Niches Go National

More and more niche players are succeeding by offering variety rivals can't match. Luggage seller eBags, for example, is able to stock 12,000 styles, compared with 250 in a typical store.

Search Lends a Hand

Using Google and similar websites, consumers can search far and wide for specialized products – say, stainless-steel farm sinks. That's creating markets for lesser known brands and new merchants.

More Pricing Pressures

Shoppers are increasingly using price-comparison sites such as Shopping.com and Shopzilla. The result: Ever more cutthroat competition for brick-and-mortar and online stores alike.

Obtaining Research Information

The Internet offers a very cost-effective means of obtaining information, such as user profiles. However, concerns have been voiced about invasion of consumer privacy.

Brand Building

Access to users provides an opportunity to build a brand that is unique compared to other media. This highlights the importance of developing effective designs for websites.

Improving Customer Service

The Internet provides an important avenue of after-the-sale customer contact. Dell Inc. offers a wide range of services to its corporate customers via the Internet.

We now consider what is involved in developing an e-commerce capability. This initiative may be pursued by an existing company such as Avon Products Corp. or a new Web-based business model.

E-Commerce Strategy

Designing and launching a new e-commerce business that enables buyers to purchase products is a major initiative. Moreover, faulty evaluation of market opportunities and inadequate planning have resulted in many Web-based business failures. Several interrelated decisions must be made:

1. Which customer groups should I serve?
2. How do I provide a compelling set of benefits to my targeted customer? How do I differentiate my "value proposition" versus online and offline competitors?
3. How do I communicate with customers?
4. What is the content, "look-and-feel," level of community, and degree of personalization of the website?
5. How should I structure my organization? What business services and applications software choices do I need to consider?
6. Who are my potential partners? Whose capabilities complement ours?
7. How will this business provide value to shareholders?
8. What metrics should I use to judge the progress of the business? How do I value the business?[21]

The intent of the present discussion is to describe what is involved in an e-business initiative; an extensive coverage of the topic is provided by several other sources.[22]

Value Opportunities and Risks

The earlier discussion highlights several unique features of the Internet as a communications medium. Properly designed and managed, Web-based initiatives provide important opportunities for offering superior customer value. These include:[23]

1. Very focused targeting is possible via the Web.
2. Messages can be designed to address the needs and preferences of the target audience.
3. The Web offers a compelling opportunity for interaction and feedback.
4. A core value offering of the Internet is access to a wide range of information.
5. The sales potential offered by the Internet is substantial.

6. The Internet provides an exciting opportunity for communications innovation.
7. The exposure opportunities of the Internet are significant, enabling many small companies and professionals to attain cost-effective access to customers and prospects.
8. The speed of response via the Internet is impressive.

The extensive value opportunities offered by the Web explain the many initiatives pursued by companies. Nonetheless, there are some risks associated with the use of the Internet as a communications medium.[24] These include difficulties in effectiveness measurement, changes in audience characteristics, access and response delays, multiple-ad exposure, potential for deception, and costs that may be higher than traditional media.

Measuring Internet Effectiveness

Measurement of effectiveness problems associated with the Internet are particularly challenging. This is not surprising given the explosive growth of Web-based initiatives and the limited experience with the medium. Nonetheless, there are many sources of measurement data. Evaluating the quality and relevance of alternative measurement sources requires careful assessment by the organization pursuing Internet strategies.

In an attempt to provide guidelines for Internet effectiveness measurement an industry study was undertaken that resulted in a 2002 report.[25] The voluntary guidelines included five recommended measures for independent auditing and verification. The metrics proposed were ad impressions, clicks, unique visitors, total visits, and page impressions.

The Future of the Internet

Perhaps the Internet shakeout was inevitable because of the race to develop Internet capabilities and business designs. Acknowledging the setbacks, it is apparent that Internet initiatives will expand significantly in the future. Internet technology and applications will experience an exciting future:

> Although the specific details are unpredictable and unimportant, digital technology will inevitably accelerate, intensify, and reduce the cost of marketing activities. What is important is that marketing managers will help guide the company's customers toward better utilization of the company's products and services.[26]

The reality is that the Internet will not result in a massive transformation of business practices.[27] Its impact is expected to be much greater for companies and organizations that are very dependent on the flow of information. The impact of the Internet in the future promises to be revolutionary for certain industries and incremental for others. We have experienced the impact of the Internet on sales of books, music, and air travel. Internet evolutions forecast for the future include jewelry, payments, telecom, hotels, real estate, and software.[28] For example, while Internet jewelry sales account for only $2 billion of the $45 billion total industry sales, rapid growth is expected.

The Internet has encouraged the development of "consumer-generated content" for some advertising. For example, The Hub is a Wal-Mart site, jointly sponsored by Sony, aiming to reach out to fashion-conscious young consumers. High school students are invited to create their own Web pages and videos, the winners to be used in Wal-Mart's cable TV and cinema advertising. Targeting young males as consumers of Doritos, Frito-Lay invited consumers online to create Doritos ads, with the winners broadcast on CBS during the NFL Superbowl in 2006. The advertising spot they filled is estimated to cost more than $2 million. The goal is to tap into the creativity and engagement of consumers, though the approach carries some risks.[29]

Direct Marketing Strategies

The purpose of direct marketing is to make direct contact with end-user customers through alternative media (e.g., computer, telephone, mail, and kiosk). Many direct marketing methods are available, each offering certain advantages and limitations. The rapid growth of direct marketing during the last decade indicates the importance placed by many companies on these direct avenues to customers. For example, Williams-Sonoma, the kitchenware retailer, generates over 40 percent of its annual revenues from catalog and Internet sales. The company first builds a catalog customer base in a metro-area. Williams-Sonoma may open a retail store when sufficient catalog shoppers are identified, targeting catalog buyers with store promotion mailings.

First, we look at several considerations in the use of direct marketing. Next, the major direct marketing methods are discussed. Finally, we consider at how direct marketing strategies are developed and implemented.

Reasons for Using Direct Marketing

The expanding popularity of direct marketing methods is driven by a combination of factors such as socioeconomic trends, low costs, databases, and buyers' demands for value. We examine how these influences affect companies' use of mail, phone, media, and computers to contact individual buyers.

Socioeconomic Trends

Several trends make the availability of direct marketing purchases attractive to many buyers. Having two working spouses imposes major time constraints on households, so purchase via direct channels is a useful way of saving time as well as making contact at the convenience of the customer. Many single person households also favor direct marketing purchases. Buyers can shop at home, save time, and avoid shopping congestion. Rapid response to order processing and shipping enables buyers to obtain their purchases in a few days. Liberal exchange policies reduce the risks of direct purchases.

Low Access Costs

While the cost per contact varies according to the method of direct contact, costs are much lower than face-to-face sales contact. The availability of databases that can target specific customer groups enables companies to selectively target buyers. Companies like American Express can market products to their credit card users. Similarly, airline frequent flyer mailing lists provide cost-effective access to buyers. The availability of credit cards simplifies the payment process.

Database Management

The availability of computerized databases is an important determinant of successful direct marketing.[30] The information in the systems includes internal data on customers and purchased data on customers and prospects. The customer and prospect information contained in databases can be used to generate mailing lists and prospect lists and to identify market segments. These segments offer a direct communications channel with customers and prospects.

Value

The shopping information provided via direct marketing, convenience, reduced shopping time, rapid response, and competitive prices gives buyers an attractive bundle of value in many buying situations. Effective database management enables direct marketing to identify buyers who purchase on a continuing basis.

The differentiated needs and wants of buyers can be addressed through direct marketing, thus enhancing the value offered by the direct marketer. Offerings may be mass-customized when the direct marketer has the capability to modularize the product offering. For example, kiosks can be linked to information networks that transmit customized orders to customers.

Direct Marketing Methods

The major direct marketing methods are shown in Exhibit 13.7. We briefly examine each method to highlight its features and limitations.

Catalogs and Direct Mail

Contact by mail with potential buyers may generate orders by phone or mail, or instead to encourage buyers to visit retail outlets to view goods and make purchases. Examples of companies using catalogs and other printed matter to encourage direct response include L.L. Bean (outdoor apparel and equipment) and the American Marketing Association (marketing seminars and conferences).

Notwithstanding the importance of Internet initiatives, the rate at which catalogs are sent out by companies continues to rise. Victoria's Secret alone dispatches around 400 million catalogs a year. Companies are using catalogs alongside websites to provide tangibility to consumers—L.L. Bean's 2006 catalog included a fabric swatch to demonstrate the softness of its fleece fabric. Catalogs may be about brand building and attracting customers, while the website is the ideal place to place orders.[31]

Telemarketing

This form of direct marketing consists of the use of telephone contact between the buyer and seller to perform all or some of the selling function. Telemarketing offers two key advantages—low contact cost and quick access by both buyer and seller. It may be used as the primary method of customer contact or as a way to support the field sales force. Telemarketing escalated in importance during the last decade and is a vital part of the selling activities of many companies. Telemarketing, like the Internet, is a potential avenue of conflict with an organization's face-to-face sales force, and may be an annoyance for consumers. Legal restrictions exist in the U.S.

Direct Response Media

Many companies use television, radio, magazines, and newspapers to obtain sales from buyers. Direct response from the advertising is obtained by mail, telephone, and fax. People see the ads, decide to buy, and order the item from the organization promoting the product.

EXHIBIT 13.7
Direct Marketing Methods

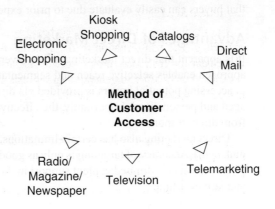

Magazines, newspapers, and radio offer a wide range of direct marketing advertisements. The intent of the direct response communications is to persuade the person reading or hearing the ad to order the product. The advantage of using these media is the very low cost of exposure. While the percent of response is also low, the returns can be substantial for products that buyers are willing to purchase through these media.

Electronic Shopping

The computer age has created two major methods of direct marketing: computer ordering by companies from their supplier and consumer and business shopping via the Internet as discussed earlier in the chapter. Electronic shopping by business buyers is appropriate when the customer's requirements involve routine repurchase of standard items, and direct access to the buyer is not necessary. Electronic capabilities may be used to support a field sales force rather than as the sole method of customer contact. Computer ordering helps the seller establish a close link to customers and reduces order cycles (time from order placement to receipt) and inventory stocks. Computer ordering enables the buyer to reduce inventory levels, cut costs, and monitor customer preferences. For example, Wal-Mart's computerized scanning equipment in its stores informs the retailer about what (and where) customers are buying and meeting their needs, via the computerized ordering system. While some customers may resist becoming dependent on suppliers through electronic linkages, there is a strong trend toward closer ties between suppliers and organizational buyers.

As discussed earlier in the chapter virtual shopping on the Internet has developed rapidly during the last few years. Many companies are taking advantage of the potential opportunities of direct marketing to computer users. The business-to-business sector accounts for the largest portion of total Internet sales. There are three types of networks: (1) The Internet is a global interlink of computer networks that have a common software standard; (2) The Intranet is a company internal capability using Internet software standards; and (3) The Extranet consists of providing external partners access to the Intranet.[32] For example, a retail chain may serve customers via the Internet, coordinate store operations via the Intranet, and utilize the Extranet to interact with freelance product designers and other external partners.

Kiosk Shopping

Similar in concept to vending machines, kiosks offer buyers the opportunity to purchase from a facility (stand) located in a retail complex or other public area (e.g., airport). Kiosks may have Internet linkages. Airline tickets and flight insurance are examples of products sold using kiosks. In some instances the order may be placed at the kiosk but delivered to the customer's address. The advantage to the seller is exposure to many people, and the buyer benefits from the shopping convenience. Kiosks are best suited for selling products that buyers can easily evaluate due to prior experience.

Advantages of Direct Marketing

It is apparent that direct marketing offers several advantages for sellers.[33] This marketing approach enables selective reach and segmentation opportunities. Considerable flexibility in accessing potential buyers is provided via direct marketing. Timing contact can be managed and personalized. Importantly, the effectiveness of direct marketing can be measured from direct response.

Direct marketing also has certain limitations.[34] It may have negative image factors (e.g., junk mail). Accuracy of targeting is only as good as the lists used to access potential buyers. There may also be limited content support in direct-response advertising. Also, postal rates increase over time.

Direct Marketing Strategy

As highlighted in our discussion, direct marketing promotion has the primary objective of obtaining a purchase response from individual buyers. While the methods differ in nature and scope, all require the development of a strategy. Market target(s) must be identified, objectives set, positioning strategy developed, communication strategy formulated, programs implemented and managed, and results evaluated against performance expectations.

The direct marketing strategy should be guided by the organization's marketing strategy. Direct marketing provides the way of reaching the customer on a one-to-one basis. Product strategy must be determined, prices set, and distribution arranged. Direct marketing may be the primary avenue to the customer as in the case of L.L. Bean, Inc. in its targeting of outdoor apparel buyers using catalog marketing. Other companies may use direct marketing as one of several ways of communicating with their market targets. Dell Inc. employs direct sales contact with business customers, telephone sales, and Internet sales. The Internet may also be used by Dell's customers to obtain information before placing an order by phone.

Summary

Management analyzes the firm's marketing strategy, the target market, product characteristics, distribution strategy, and pricing strategy to identify the role of personal selling in the promotion mix. New business, trade selling, missionary selling, and consultative/technical selling strategies illustrate the possible roles that may be assigned to selling in various firms. The selling process indicates the selling activities necessary to move the buyer from need awareness to a purchase decision. Various sales channels are used in conjunction with the field sales force to accomplish the selling process activities.

Sales force organizational design decisions include the type of organizational structure to be used, the size of the sales force, and the allocation of selling effort. Deployment involves decisions regarding sales force size and effort allocation. Managing the sales force includes recruiting, training, supervising, and motivating salespeople. Evaluation and control determine the extent to which objectives are achieved and determine where adjustments are needed in selling strategy and tactics.

 The Internet provides a unique and compelling means of electronic contact between buyers and sellers. The core capability of the Internet is communicating with buyers and prospects via an interactive process. The Internet is a relatively new medium and companies are learning how to obtain its advantages and avoid its risks. The key organizational decision is deciding what role the Internet will play in the business and marketing strategies. The options range from a separate business model to a promotional medium.

The Internet offers several communications features including disseminating information, creating awareness, obtaining research information, brand building, encouraging trials, improving customer service, and expanding distribution. Developing an Internet business model is a major initiative involving the design of a new business. Faulty evaluation of market opportunities and inadequate planning have resulted in many Web-based failures.

The Internet's unique features offer important opportunities for providing superior customer value. It also has some potential risks in its use as a communications medium. A major challenge is measuring the effectiveness of Internet initiatives.

The purpose of direct marketing is to obtain a sales response from buyers by making direct contact using mail, telephone, advertising media, or computer. The rapidly expanding adoption of direct marketing methods that occurred in the last decade is the consequence of several influences including socio-economic trends, low costs of exposure, computer technology, and buyers' demands for value. Direct marketing is used by many companies to contact organizational and consumer buyers.

Direct marketing offers several advantages including selective reach, segmentation opportunities, flexibility, timing control, and effectiveness measurement. However, certain direct methods may convey a negative image.

Companies have many options available for direct marketing to buyers. The methods include catalogs, direct mail, telemarketing, television, radio magazines/newspapers, electronic shopping, and kiosk shopping. Developing a strategy for using each method includes selecting the market target(s), setting objectives, selecting positioning strategy, developing the communications strategy, implementing and managing the strategy, and evaluating results.

Questions for Review and Discussion

1. What information does management require to analyze the selling situation?
2. Suppose an analysis of sales force size and selling effort deployment indicates that a company has a sales force of the right size but that the allocation of selling effort requires substantial adjustment in several territories. How should such deployment changes be implemented?
3. What questions would you want answered if you were trying to evaluate the effectiveness of a business unit's sales force strategy?
4. Discuss some of the advantages and limitations of recruiting salespeople by hiring the employees of companies with excellent training programs.
5. Is incentive compensation more important for salespeople than for product managers? Why?
6. Select a company and discuss how sales management should define the selling process.
7. What are the unique capabilities offered by the Internet to business users of the communications medium?
8. Discuss whether the Internet may replace conventional catalogs and direct mail methods of promotion.
9. Direct marketing is similar in many ways to advertising. Why is it important to view direct marketing as a specific group of promotion methods?
10. Discuss the reasons why many companies are interested in the marketing potential of the Internet.
11. Select one of the direct marketing methods and discuss the decisions that are necessary in developing a strategy for using the method.
12. Suppose you have been asked to evaluate whether a regional camera and consumer electronics retailer should obtain Internet space. What criteria should be used in the evaluation?

Internet Applications

A. Examine the website of Salesforce.com. Discuss how the Internet service provider can assist sales managers in their sales force management activities.
B. Visit Nokia's US website (www.nokiausa.com). Evaluate Nokia's sales approach online. How does Nokia enhance its direct marketing strategy through Web-based offerings? How could the company increase traffic to its online sales platform without creating channel conflict?
C. Review the website of Merrill Lynch (www.ml.com). How does Merrill Lynch leverage its global position to adjust to local markets through the Internet? Why is the Internet particularly relevant for firms in the financial services industry?

Feature Applications

A. Review the STRATEGY FEATURE concerning Wyeth's sales force initiatives. Discuss how these changes should be integrated with the drug company's promotion and marketing strategies.
B. The ETHICS FEATURE highlights several aspects of ethics that are relevant to salespeople. Discuss why salespeople are more likely to be confronted with ethical situations than manufacturing employees.

Notes

1. Frederick E. Webster, Alan J. Malter, and Shankar Ganesan, "The Decline and Dispersal of Marketing Competence," *MIT Sloan Management Review,* 46 (4) 2005, 35–43.
2. Pui-Wing Tam, "Hurd's Big Challenge at H-P: Overhauling Corporate Sales," *The Wall Street Journal,* April 3, 2006, A1, A13.

3. The following discussion is based on Mark W. Johnston and Greg W. Marshall, *Sales Force Management,* 7th ed. (Burr Ridge, IL: McGraw-Hill/Irwin, 2003), 49–50.

4. Ibid.

5. Stanley Holmes, "Boeing's Jet Propellant," *BusinessWeek,* December 26, 2005, 40.

6. Johnson and Marshall, *Sales Force Management,* 51–56.

7. Rick Brooks, "FedEx Fiscal Fourth-Quarter Profit Rose by 11%, Surpassing Expectations," *The Wall Street Journal,* June 29, 2000, B2.

8. Erik Ahlberg, "Newell Rubbermaid Rebirth Is a Work in Progress," *The Wall Street Journal,* November 27, 2002, B3A.

9. David W. Cravens, Nigel F. Piercy, and George S. Low, "Globalization of the Sales Organization: Management Control and Its Consequences," *Organizational Dynamics,* (3), 2006, 1–14.

10. Johnston and Marshall, *Sales Force Management,* Chapter 5.

11. David W. Cravens, Thomas M. Ingram, Raymond W. LaForge, and Clifford E. Young, "Hallmarks of Effective Sales Organizations," *Marketing Management,* Winter 1992, 56–67.

12. Johnston and Marshall, *Sales Force Management,* Chapter 5.

13. Ibid., Chapter 7.

14. David W. Cravens, Greg W. Marshall, Felicia G. Lassk, and George S. Low, "The Control Factor," *Marketing Management,* Vol. 13, No. 1, January-February 2004, 39–44.

15. Scott Hensley, "Wyeth to Revamp, Cut Its Sales Force," *The Wall Street Journal,* June 20, 2005, A3, A6.

16. Cravens, et al., "The Control Factor."

17. George E. Belch and Michael A. Belch, *Advertising and Promotion,* 6th ed. (New York: McGraw-Hill Irwin, 2004), 486.

18. Bernard Jaworski and Katherine Jocz, "Rediscovering the Customer," *Marketing Management,* September/October 2002, 24.

19. "E-Tailing Finally Hits Its Stride," *BusinessWeek,* December 20, 2004, 36–37.

20. The following is based on Belch and Belch, *Advertising and Promotion,* 492–493.

21. Jeffrey F. Rayport and Bernard J. Jaworski, *e-Commerce* (New York: McGraw-Hill/Irwin, 2001), 12.

22. See, for example, Glen L. Urban, *Digital Marketing Strategy* (Upper Saddle River, NJ: Pearson Prentice Hall), 2004.

23. Belch and Belch, *Advertising and Promotion,* 504–505.

24. Ibid., 505–506.

25. Ibid., 502–503.

26. Glen L. Urban, *Digital Marketing Strategy,* 180.

27. Michael J. Mandel and Robert D. Hof, "Rethinking the Internet," *BusinessWeek,* March 26, 2001, 117–122.

28. Timothy J. Mullaney, "E-Biz Strikes Again," *BusinessWeek,* May 10, 2004, 80–90.

29. Jon Fine, "What Makes 'Citizen Ads' Work?" *BusinessWeek,* February 19, 2007, 24; Aline van Duyn and Jonathan Birchall, "Wall-Mart's Amateur Advertisers," *Financial Times,* Friday, July 21, 2006, 8.

30. William J. McDonald, *Direct Marketing* (Burr Ridge, IL: McGraw-Hill/Irwin, 1998), 93.

31. Louise Lee, "Catalogs, Catalogs Everywhere," *BusinessWeek,* December 4, 2006, 32–34.

32. "Log On, Link Up, Save Big," *BusinessWeek,* June 22, 1998, 136.

33. Belch and Belch, *Advertising and Promotion,* 480–481.

34. Ibid.

Cases for Part 4

Case 4-1

Microsoft Corp.

Would you invest your hard-earned dollars in a company like this? Its revenues soared an average of 36% through the 1990s, but now it's heading into miserly single-digit growth. It has long been a powerful engine fueled by major updates of its products, yet the next major one, an unprecedented five years in the making, isn't expected until 2006. The company hasn't made much headway in newer, promising markets. And its share price is stuck exactly where it was in mid-1998. Not buying, huh? Well, tough luck: You probably already own a piece of this rock.

The company is Microsoft Corp., one of the most widely held stocks on the planet. And sure, for all its challenges, this icon of American capitalism still has a lot going for it. With a market cap of $279 billion, its valuation is the second highest in the world after General Electric Co. And it remains the most profitable company in the $1 trillion tech industry, pumping out $1 billion a month in cash.

But Microsoft just isn't the phenom it used to be. After 29 years, the software giant is starting to look like a star athlete who's past his prime. Growth is tepid. Expansion is stymied. Bureaucracy is a concern. And a company that used to be so intimidating it attracted antitrust suits on two continents seems, well, vulnerable (Exhibit 1).

The threats it faces are among the most serious in Microsoft's history (Exhibit 2) For starters, there's Linux, the software dubbed "open source" because the code is shared freely by developers around the world. With grass-roots and government support from Finland to China, Linux has become so popular that it's challenging Microsoft's core business as no rival ever has. Europe's trustbusters are coming down hard, too. On Mar. 24, they smacked the company with a ruling aimed at preventing Microsoft from leveraging Windows to gain ground in new markets, which could keep the giant tied up in court for years.

"Long Wait"

But most worrisome are delays of the new operating system, the very heart of Microsoft's business empire. Code-named Longhorn, the next version of Windows is an ambitious attempt to fundamentally change how people use computers. But critics have taken to calling it Long Wait. Already, execs concede that it won't debut until 2006, three years after researcher Gartner Inc. originally expected it to ship. That means Longhorn will come out five years after the last operating system, the longest gap ever between major Windows updates. And *BusinessWeek* has learned that to hit even that target, Microsoft is lowering its sights for the product, cutting back on key features such as an innovative way to store and search information on PCs. "Schedule is a priority for the release," wrote Microsoft Vice-President Joe Peterson in a Mar. 19 e-mail to employees on the project. "[We] expect teams to scale back features to meet target dates."

All this has Wall Street's best and brightest penciling in estimates for Microsoft that would have been an insult a few years back. Never mind 30%, or even 20% revenue growth. The optimistic forecast is for 11% growth over the next few years, shown here as the best-case scenario (charts). The Wall Street consensus is that the company will boost revenues 8% a year through 2006, according to Thomson First Call. That's right in line with the rate Gartner expects for the overall software industry. In other words, after nearly three decades of outracing the market, Microsoft is expected to be a middle-of-the-pack performer. "Microsoft is doing what large companies do—invest in new segments while maintaining the core," says David B. Yoffie, a professor at Harvard Business School. "So far, though, they're not doing it successfully."

The significance of this goes way beyond Microsoft's growth rate. For almost two decades, Gates & Co. have set the agenda for the tech industry, the most dynamic slice of the U.S. economy. Where Microsoft

EXHIBIT 1 Where's the Growth?

Data: Sanford C. Bernstein

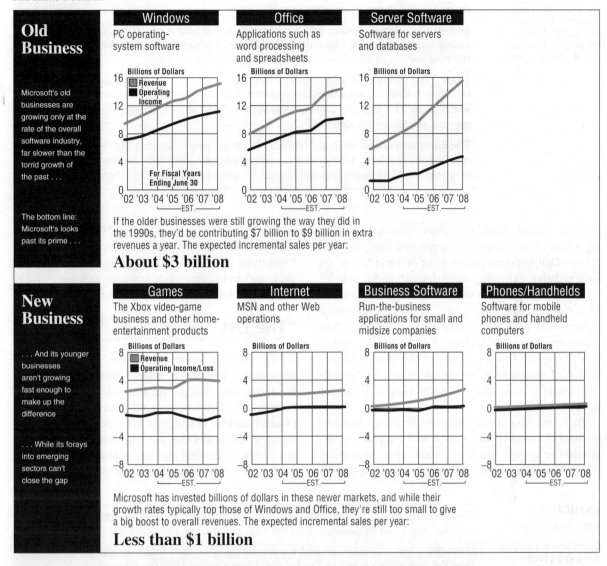

Old Business

Microsoft's old businesses are growing only at the rate of the overall software industry, far slower than the torrid growth of the past . . .

The bottom line: Microsoft's looks past its prime . . .

Windows
PC operating-system software

Billions of Dollars
■ Revenue
■ Operating Income

For Fiscal Years Ending June 30
'02 '03 '04 '05 '06 '07 '08
—EST.—

Office
Applications such as word processing and spreadsheets

Billions of Dollars
'02 '03 '04 '05 '06 '07 '08
—EST.—

Server Software
Software for servers and databases

Billions of Dollars
'02 '03 '04 '05 '06 '07 '08
—EST.—

If the older businesses were still growing the way they did in the 1990s, they'd be contributing $7 billion to $9 billion in extra revenues a year. The expected incremental sales per year:

About $3 billion

New Business

. . . And its younger businesses aren't growing fast enough to make up the difference

. . . While its forays into emerging sectors can't close the gap

Games
The Xbox video-game business and other home-entertainment products

Billions of Dollars
■ Revenue
■ Operating Income/Loss
'02 '03 '04 '05 '06 '07 '08
—EST.—

Internet
MSN and other Web operations

Billions of Dollars
'02 '03 '04 '05 '06 '07 '08
—EST.—

Business Software
Run-the-business applications for small and midsize companies

Billions of Dollars
'02 '03 '04 '05 '06 '07 '08
—EST.—

Phones/Handhelds
Software for mobile phones and handheld computers

Billions of Dollars
'02 '03 '04 '05 '06 '07 '08
—EST.—

Microsoft has invested billions of dollars in these newer markets, and while their growth rates typically top those of Windows and Office, they're still too small to give a big boost to overall revenues. The expected incremental sales per year:

Less than $1 billion

led, everyone from partners and rivals to Corporate America followed. The question now is whether Microsoft is losing the dynamism it needs to retain that leadership. Is mighty Microsoft becoming IBM in the 1980s—profitable but lumbering? Big but irrelevant? A giant but toothless? "They are already less relevant now than they were 10 years ago." says Michael A. Cusamano, professor at Massachusetts Institute of Technology's Sloan School of Management and co-author of *Microsoft's Secrets,* a book on the company's success.

But ask CEO Steven A. Ballmer if Microsoft is past its prime, and he bristles. "No—in no sense do I feel like we're past our prime," he says during an interview in his windowless conference room. "The thing that I think is fair to say is we are past adolescence. Isn't adolescence when you grow really fast and you can sometimes be a little raucous? And then when you get into your prime, you're just hitting on every cylinder, you're having a great life, you're creating a family, you're rising to new responsibilities. We're in our prime, baby. We're post-adolescent. We are in our prime." He pulls

Slowing PC Sales   Worldwide PC sales are expected to grow 11% this year but trail off to 8% in 2008, according to researcher IDC. Since Microsoft dominates desktop software, that puts a drag on its growth.

Security Problems   Viruses and worms have forced cashstrapped corporate customers to buy security software, slowing Windows sales. Microsoft pulled workers off Longhorn, the next version of Windows, to focus on security improvements.

Linux   The free operating-system software is all the rage for corporate server computers, retarding Microsoft's growth in this crucial market. Researcher Gartner says Linux' share will grow to 21% in 2007, while Windows' will slip to 68%. Overseas, Linux also is gaining momentum in desktop PCs.

The European Union Ruling   If the EU decision prevents Microsoft from bundling new applications such as Web search and Net phone-calling with Windows, demand for upgrades could be depressed and Microsoft's attempts to enter new markets stymied.

out color-coded charts that show Microsoft outpacing a host of well-respected companies: Intel, GE, SAP. "Here's Dell, the great growth story of our industry," he says, pointing. "Growing more slowly than Microsoft."

Ballmer's right. Microsoft has boosted revenues 13% over the past three years, a stellar performance during tech's darkest days. But analysts are predicting a slow-mo future, and Ballmer declines to say whether they're wrong. "I'm not going to make some bold prediction of what a good growth rate is or a bad growth rate. I want to make sure that we're doing well relative to our industry."

Ballmer's boss of more than two decades, Chairman William H. Gates III, takes issue with the entire measurement of growth. He says it's naive to compare the $32 billion Microsoft with smaller players. "If growth

is your metric, we're not your guy," Gates says, jumping out of his seat. Instead, the company's focus is on innovation, says Gates, who gave up the CEO title four years ago to become chief software architect. "We're doing more new things than any other company."

"The List"

While Ballmer drives day-to-day operations, the 48-year-old founder is taking personal control of the technology charge. He has put together what is now called "The List" around Microsoft's Redmond (Wash.) campus (Exhibit 3). It's a priority ranking of 50 or so initiatives that cut across product lines and are critical to making the next generation of products successful—everything from security software and

Search.   Look out, Google. Microsoft plans to put search technology into the operating system. And it will let people search the Web and their PCs all at once.

Security.   Spam and viruses and worms, oh my. Windows draws attacks like no other, and the company has drawn fire for not doing enough to plug security holes. Gates vows to do better.

Telephony.   Forget old-fashioned phone calls. Gates wants to bring computer innovation to telecom. Think video voice mails. Or instant messaging with talk, not text.

Voice Recognition.   Who wants to type? Microsoft is developing voice recognition so you won't have to. It's also developing software to read you your e-mail or Word documents.

FileSystem.   Finding things on a PC is too cumbersome. New software will let you find not just digital photos but, for example, e-mails from the people in them.

Digital-Rights Management.   Photos, music, and video are going digital. Microsoft is developing software to let people use that content without violating intellectual-property rights.

the user interface to Web search and telephony. The List is so important that each item has been assigned to one top executive, who is responsible for driving it throughout the company. "We're using a lot of IQ to go after these things," says Gates.

A look down The List provides intriguing insight into Microsoft's concept of innovation. The company pours about $6 billion a year into research and development, and the vast majority of that goes to improve its monopoly businesses, Windows and Office. In the past, it developed ClearType technology for high-resolution text displays and grammar checking that identifies errors as people write with its word-processing software. Gates's work now on security and search also will be baked into Microsoft's most popular software. This approach, which he calls "integrated innovation," is the reason people continue to buy new versions of Windows. "I don't know if people really get what I'm saying or if they just think I'm being cute when I say our biggest competitor is our installed base," he says. "You can sit on the existing [products]—that's a perfectly legitimate choice. This is not a soft drink where you get thirsty and say, 'I drank my word processor. Let's have another.' "

Microsoft's success in making people thirsty has been critical in the development of the entire personal-computer industry. From the biggest PC makers to the smallest software-application developers, almost all built their companies on top of Microsoft's creations. Critics may carp, but each time Microsoft gives users another reason to buy Windows or Office, it gives its partners another opportunity to sell their wares as well. That's why Ballmer bridles at criticism that Microsoft doesn't pioneer new markets. Important innovation, he says, is not simply dreaming up a new idea but also refining it enough to get people clamoring for it. "The thing that is most important is to be the guy who can come up with the innovation that gets the category to explode," he says. "The guy I really want to be is the category exploder." Perhaps more than any other company, Microsoft exploded the markets for PCs and for productivity software, such as Office's word processing and spreadsheets.

Now, however, the company seems to have misplaced its dynamite. The U.S. PC market is largely mature, so Microsoft has moved into new businesses. But these categories, such as online services and video-game consoles, already are dominated by large rivals—and they know Microsoft's tactics. So instead of opening new frontiers, Microsoft finds itself in pitched battles for existing territory. "Microsoft is the only company in the world that can afford to take fortified hills—and that's almost a disadvantage," says Richard E. Belluzzo, ex-Microsoft president and now CEO of data-storage player Quantum Corp. "They have too much money, too many good people, too much time—all of which can hurt [them] in some ways."

To bust out of this rut, Microsoft may need to put more focus on creating something altogether new. The company has spent a total of $32.6 billion on R&D since 1990, more than the next five largest software companies combined. Yet tech-industry observers marvel that it has produced so few breakthroughs. After all, it was Apple Computer Inc. that stole the show in digital music with its sleek iPod. And two Stanford University grad students came up with the search technology behind blockbuster Google Inc. "Plowing millions of dollars into me-too technology because you think there's indirect money you can make [through Windows and Office] is pure foolishness," says Cusamano.

Executive Squeeze

Some question whether Ballmer is doing enough to encourage innovation. In April, 2002, the chief divided the company into seven business units and gave each leader profit-and-loss responsibility (Exhibit 4). But he didn't give them complete independence. As part of integrated innovation, they're all supposed to coordinate their activities and align with the core Windows strategy. "They don't own 100% of their own destiny," says recently retired treasurer and deputy CFO Jean-Francois Heitz. Autonomy isn't the only issue. Ballmer's intense focus on financial details forced managers to spend untold hours boning up on the minutiae of their businesses. He backed off after they complained, but some former execs think the planning process is still too much. "In the past, the system was optimized for people who could get [stuff] done," says a former exec. Now, "everybody is always preparing for a meeting."

Microsoft says these frustrations are just part of the growing pains of becoming a mature organization. Ballmer gives the new management system an A-. "I know it's absolutely the right thing for the long-term health of the company," he says.

Gates and Ballmer have led Microsoft through minefields before. In the 1990s, Gates engineered the company's powerful response to the Internet challenge, while Ballmer built a sales operation that penetrated corporations worldwide and ended the company's over-dependence on desktop computing. Today, Microsoft is

EXHIBIT 4   **Gates and Ballmer on 'Making the Transition'**

In separate interviews, *Business Week's* Seattle bureau chief, Jay Greene, sat down with William H. Gates III, Microsoft's chairman, and CEO Steven A. Ballmer to discuss innovation, competition, and the company's future.

GATES

On Microsoft's growth prospects: If you want growth, don't go to the big guy. Go to the small guy. If growth is your story, you're looking in the wrong place. Now, if you're looking for innovation. . . we're more of a change agent for the way business is done, the way people work, the way people do things at home. We're 100 times more interested in [change] than we are [in] growth percentages or something like that.

On the company's innovation: With our $6 billion a year [in research and development], we're doing more new things than anyone else. Because of our high-volume approach, we can do a lot of new things that strengthen and maintain our profit pool and in some ways grow it. Percentage-wise it's not all that dramatic, and yet it's the most important work in the world.

On how its seven business units cooperate: We use this structure [profit and loss for each unit] to make sure that things are delegated and measured and fairly autonomous, and then we have various mechanisms that keep these P&Ls working together. The most interesting story for us is how we said: "O.K., give the P&Ls default autonomy, but then be very explicit about the things they need to work together on."

[These are] initiatives that I'm driving where many of the really big breakthrough things, like getting people to take advantage of [the new operating system] Longhorn, cut across the P&L structure. And that's just natural because it's integrated innovation.

We tried one approach, and it was just mediocre. Now we've got this new one that we put in place [last year], and it looks like this approach is really going to work well.

On the new approach: Gates's to-do list: So there's this list of [about 50] things. You see things on there like telephony. [These are technologies that cut across business units], where many P&Ls are involved, and it's so important to a scenario that we've got to get it right. They'd better be huge things, where if we get them right people go: "Wow, that's cool." They'd better be big-impact things. We're using a lot of IQ to go after these things. These are the things that, as they get into the products, define the excellence of the products.

This is the first time that we've really had a structure to formally deal with it. So it's not just "Hey, if you're confused, send mail to Bill"—something extremely ad hoc like that. This is very structured and very necessary for the breadth of things we're trying to do.

On Microsoft's real competition: I don't know if people really get what I'm saying or if they just think I'm being cute when I say our biggest competitor is our installed base. Yes, we have other competitors—Sony, Linux, Nokia, Oracle, and IBM. But the fact that you can sit on the existing [products]—that's a perfectly legitimate choice. This is not a soft drink where you get thirsty and say: "I drank my word processor, let's have another." No. Some people actually say to us: "There are no new things you can do." I know at least for the next decade that is just wrong. It's just wrong, and it will be fun to surprise them.

BALLMER

On Microsoft's growth prospects: we'll outperform the rest of our industry. The real issue isn't what's your growth rate. It's always got to be what's your growth rate relatively. Will there be startups that will be able to get a nice little boost early? Sure. Those same startups, if they were part of Microsoft, might not move our overall meter. We've grown a billion-dollar advertising business [in MSN] over the last several years. If that was a startup, it would look awfully darned good. So we sit here and look at the opportunities, and I couldn't be more excited.

On revenue growth vs. profit growth: We'll focus on both. In a sense, we have had the luxury of being able to have great profit growth without putting much of our IQ on the cost and efficiency side. We're putting more of our IQ on the cost and efficiency side. But, hey, the basic way all companies grow is with innovation. If we don't innovate, we don't grow. Yes, we'll apply more IQ on the efficiency and cost side. But still, the future to our growth will be innovation.

On innovation: Like all great companies, we have a mix of *de novo* innovation—that is, things that started here. And we have a mix of things where we provide a better innovation, better integration, better synthesis than somebody else may have done with a basic concept that they had come up with. But if you take a look at where we are today with TV software, we really pioneered the work. Smart phones, we really pioneered the work. Now the truth is, those categories are still nascent.

EXHIBIT 4—*(concluded)*

The thing that is most important is to be the guy who can come up with the innovation that sets the category to explode, not the one that did the *de novo* innovation. Sometimes we're the category exploder. Sometimes we're the *de novo* guys. The guy I really want to be is the category exploder.

On his restructuring the company into seven business units: I know we did absolutely the right thing. I'm so excited about what we did two years ago. Everybody is kind of having to grow and get to the next level. It's really exciting to see, and I know it's absolutely the right thing for the long-term health of the company.

On giving more authority to execs: I think we are still really making the transition from the world in which we could think of ourselves, in a sense, as being in one or two businesses that could be run in a very centralized fashion to a business where we need to have strong business leadership really shepherding those businesses . . . I think really letting those talents grow, building the talents underneath them, that will be a critical part for us to realize our potential.

On comparisons of Longhorn to Cairo, an ill-fated Windows attempt in the 1990s: [Longhorn] will ship. It's got our best brain-power on it. The fact that we'll ship, of course, makes it dissimilar to the old Cairo project. But it's a firm project with a firm schedule with a team working on it. I think we pushed it back appropriately because of the need to focus in on security. But it is a very ambitious piece of work. It will be in the pantheon of most ambitious Windows releases of all times.

On whether the decision of European Commission trust-busters will force Microsoft to change Longhorn: I don't think so. We're now studying the 300-page document. At the last press conference, the commissioner went out of his way to say that he was acting consistently . . . with the precedent set in the U.S. courts and in the U.S. consent decree. In the U.S. consent decree, it's quite clear we can continue to innovate, to integrate new capabilities into Windows. So if in fact they are consistent, we should be able to continue down the path we've been on with Longhorn.

On whether Microsoft is having a midlife crisis: No, we're not having a midlife crisis. We're in a great mode. I don't know if you remember this old TV show, *The Mary Tyler Moore Show.* At the end she throws her hat up and says, "We're going to make it." That is kind of the spirit [we have]. We've got a lot to do, great opportunities, let's go, go, go, go, go, go, go.

pushing hard on many fronts. Among them: applications for small and midsize businesses, the Xbox game console. Web-surfing cell phones, software for wristwatches that can get news updates, and most recently, speech-recognition systems. In each case, prospects for meaningful revenue growth are modest—at least for the next four years, for which analysts have done projections.

Cash Back?

With $53 billion in the bank, Microsoft could buy its way to faster growth. Indeed, it already has made a move in that direction, spending $2.5 billion over the past three years to move into the market for business applications for small to midsize companies. It could follow that up with acquisitions in a host of promising areas, such as security, collaboration, and game software.

But many analysts expect Microsoft to shy away from large deals and dole out more cash to shareholders— just like a mature company. It started paying a dividend last year and now spends $1.73 billion annually on it. While shareholders have clamored for more, the company has said it needs the cash as an insurance policy against the European Commission antitrust probe and an antitrust suit brought by Sun Microsystems Inc. On Apr. 2, Microsoft settled the Sun case, paying its longtime nemesis nearly $2 billion. Now analysts expect Microsoft to start forking more cash over to shareholders, either in the form of a higher dividend or a big stock buyback. "Microsoft is growing up," says John Linehan, portfolio manager for the T. Rowe Price Value Fund, which recently became one of the company's top 10 shareholders. "It's a very attractive investment in the value camp."

Without acquisitions, however, Microsoft may struggle in new markets, given the shortcomings of its me-too approach. Consider Web access. Microsoft poured more than $10 billion into its MSN business in the past eight years, estimates Sanford C. Bernstein & Co. analyst Charles DiBona, much of it trying to catch America Online in attracting dial-up Net subscribers.

While Microsoft succeeded in becoming AOL's most ferocious rival, the market has begun to evaporate as consumers migrate to broadband Net connections. Now, the money-losing business is dragging down the rest of MSN's numbers. "Some of that investment in MSN was not the best use of cash," says DiBona.

In some cases, Microsoft's track record of gobbling up profits has made potential partners leery. That's what's happening in the market for souped-up cell phones that can handle Web-surfing, e-mail, and photo-swapping. After four years of effort, Microsoft has persuaded a handful of mobile-phone makers to use its software, including Motorola Inc. But market leader Nokia Corp. and other major players are determined to thwart Microsoft's attempts to dominate their business the way it has the PC industry. Nokia and Sony Ericsson Mobile Communications use competing software from Symbian and have even taken equity stakes in the London company. "The name for this in the industry is ABM—anybody but Microsoft," says David Nagel, CEO of PalmSource, another maker of mobile-phone software.

Microsoft does better in markets adjacent to businesses it dominates. An example: Its foray into applications for small and midsize businesses. These companies typically own its Windows and Office products. Microsoft jumped in three years ago, buying two accounting-software companies, Great Plains Software and Navision. The business is growing at a healthy 20% a year, hitting $567 million in revenues in fiscal 2003.

That's little more than a rounding error at Microsoft today, but the plan is to keep offering ever-more-powerful software to these smaller businesses. Last year, Microsoft released its first homegrown application: customer-relationship management software for handling sales forces and customer-service staff. "It's all green fields," says Douglas J. Burgum, senior vice-president for Business Solutions Group. To stimulate demand, Microsoft is offering a promotion through June. It's selling its year-old CRM package for $99 per user for the first five users—a nearly $300 discount per user—if customers also buy Microsoft's $1,500 server product. It's classic Microsoft—and a tactic its rivals can't match, since they don't sell server software.

Logjam

Even here, though, Microsoft probably won't be able to add to overall revenue growth in a major way. Gartner expects the CRM market to rise an average of 5.5% a year through 2007, to $966 million. To add to Burgum's challenges, the next major version of his products, code-named Project Green, which meld the Great Plains and Navision products, won't be out until Longhorn debuts.

Indeed, Longhorn is becoming something of a logjam. Its delay is holding up the other products Microsoft usually debuts with a new operating system. A new version of Office often is released about the same time, with its applications fine-tuned to the new system's capabilities. Windows chief James E. Allchin pulled engineers off Longhorn to address security concerns in current products. That delayed what is already the most complex operating system Microsoft has ever built. The giant is debuting a new user interface, overhauling the way people store and retrieve files, and adding technology to let traditional applications interact with a new generation of programs called Web services. "Longhorn is an extremely ambitious project," says Gates.

The most important change is to the file system—the way information is stored on the PC. Microsoft is creating a new design not just for Windows but for all of its products that makes it easier to retrieve photos, documents, songs, and e-mail. That's important as users stash more and more files on their computers. If Microsoft gets it right, it will be simple, for example, for users to zip through thousands of pictures and sort them by date or by the people in them.

But Longhorn won't do everything Gates first envisioned. *BusinessWeek* has obtained copies of two internal e-mails showing that Microsoft is cutting some of the most ambitious technologies to get the product out the door. For example, Longhorn will now ship with a scaled-back version of the file system. The current plan, in practical terms, means people will be able to search their PCs for documents and information related to each other, but they won't be able to reach into corporate servers for similar files.

What's more, Microsoft is retreating from trying to link its two monopolies even more closely. *BusinessWeek* has learned that the company intended to develop the next version of Office so it would work only on Longhorn, not earlier versions of Windows. But in a videoconference with employees on Apr. 1, Microsoft's Peterson said such tight integration won't be possible given Longhorn's changes. "The great big version of Office that really takes advantage of the platform is something we're pushing out further in time," he said. "That's one big trade-off we've already made."

While Microsoft has been publicly vague on timing, Peterson wasn't. One e-mail said the company will ship the first beta version of the software next February and plans Longhorn's debut for the first six months of 2006. Microsoft confirmed the content of the e-mails and videoconference but declined to elaborate.

Getting Longhorn finished is critical because the delay is starting to take a toll. Customers who planned their software upgrades based on timing guidance from Microsoft must rejigger their plans. Those who can't wait for improved security and reliability will turn to alternatives, says Tony Yustein, a former Microsoft employee who now runs SoftCom Technology Consulting Inc., a Web-hosting company in Toronto. Yustein is adding Linux systems because of his growing frustration with his old company. "Microsoft has lost its perspective, concentration, and vision in operating systems," he says.

Viable Option

Linux poses the biggest threat to Microsoft since the Web burst on the scene in the mid-'90s. The 13-year-old operating system is attractive to tech companies and corporations alike because it gives them a viable alternative to Microsoft's products that they can modify at will. Also, since Linux computers run on the same processors as Windows and the software is available for free, for the first time Microsoft is confronted with competition that is cheaper to buy. Until now, Linux' momentum has come primarily at the expense of the Unix software in server computers.

But corporations increasingly are adopting Linux as a viable option to Windows. Robert W. Egan, vice-president for information technology at Boise Cascade Corp., is using Linux to run his company's internal Web site and network-maintenance programs—things he used to run on Windows. Other companies may follow suit: In a recent survey of corporate tech purchasers by Merrill Lynch & Co., 48% said they plan to boost their use of open-source software this year, and 34% of that subgroup are targeting applications that traditionally ran on Windows.

The place where Linux will likely have the most profound impact is in developing nations. Tech companies are staring hungrily at China and India as their next growth markets. Yet Microsoft likely won't dominate there, as it has in the U.S. Last November, China Standard Software Co., a consortium of government-funded companies, agreed to deploy a million computers in the next year using Linux on the desktop and Office rival StarOffice, made by Sun. "There are places, particularly in government, where people are making political decisions instead of right-minded decisions," says Ballmer.

The threat has Microsoft focused on Linux as Enemy No. 1. In the past two years, to win favor in China, Microsoft has pledged to spend more than $750 million on cooperative research, technology for schools, and other investments.

From Linux in China to Longhorn in waiting, Microsoft is increasingly stymied as it goes after new opportunities. But riding out the old businesses won't be enough. "The biggest challenge is to remain as tremendously successful as they have been in the past. That's a curse," says Hasso Plattner, chairman of the supervisory board at German software giant SAP. A lot of CEOs would probably accept Microsoft's curse and call it a blessing. But that's not good enough for Gates and Ballmer. "Some people actually say to us, 'There are no new things you can do,'" Gates says. "I know, at least for the next decade, that is just wrong. It's just wrong, and it will be fun to surprise them." There's no denying he has the will. Now he has to make it so.

With Jim Kerstetter and Peter Burrows in San Mateo, Calif., and Steve Hamm and Spencer E. Ante in New York

Source: Jay Greene, "Microsoft's Midlife Crisis," *BusinessWeek*, April 19, 2004, 88, 90–92, 94, 96–98.

Case 4-2

Nike Inc.

In many ways, the sleek, four-story building that houses Nike Inc.'s Innovation Kitchen is a throwback to the company's earliest days. Located on the ground floor of the Mia Hamm building on Nike's 175-acre headquarters campus in Beaverton, Ore., the Kitchen is where Nike cooked up the shoes that made it the star of the $35 billion athletic footwear industry. In this think tank for sneakers, designers find inspiration in everything from Irish architecture to the curving lines of a Stradivarius violin. One wall displays models of every Air Jordan ever made, while low-rise cubicles are littered with sketches of new shoes. The Kitchen is off limits to most visitors and even to most Nike employees. The sign on the door says, only half in jest: "Nobody gets in to see the cooks. Not nobody. Not no how."

This is where, nearly 20 years ago, Nike star designer Tinker Hatfield came up with the Air Jordan—the best-selling sports shoe of all time. Right now, Hatfield and his team are tallying the results of the Athens 2004 Olympic Games. Hatfield and his design geeks produced an array of superfast sneakers for the Games, including the sleek track spike called Monsterfly for sprinters and the Air Zoom Miler for distance runners. As befits a global company, Nike's sponsored athletes hailed from all over the world. They took home a lot of hardware from Athens, including 50 gold medals and dozens more silver and bronze. In the men's 1,500-meter run, for instance, Hicham El Guerrouj of Morocco grabbed gold, Bernard Lagat of Kenya took the silver, and Rui Silva of Portugal won the bronze. All wore the Air Zoom Miler, while U.S. sprinter Shawn Crawford won the 200-meter gold in a pair of Monsterflys. And Nike apparel had its day in the sun, too. The top four finishers in the men's 100-meter race all wore the sign of the Swoosh.

Going Establishment

The most telling events for Nike didn't take place on the track, however. The brash guerrilla marketer, famous for thumbing its nose at big-time sporting events, was showing a new restraint. Eight years ago in Atlanta, Nike ambushed basketball sponsor Champion (a brand of Sara Lee Corp.) by sneaking giant Swoosh signs into the arena. When the cameras panned the stands, TV audiences saw the Nike logo loud and clear, while Champion had nothing. Nike has even signed up to become an official U.S. Olympic sponsor in four years in Beijing, and it has toned down its anti-Establishment attitude. For good reason: These days, Nike *is* the Establishment when it comes to global sports marketing. With revenues exceeding $12 billion in fiscal 2004, the company that Philip H. Knight started three decades ago by selling sneakers out of the back of a car at track meets has finally grown up (Exhibit 1).

EXHIBIT 1

Nike
Through The Years
The company that made sports marketing hip was co-founded by an accountant

1964
Phil Knight, a CPA at Price Waterhouse, and college track coach Bill Bowerman chip in $500 each to start Blue Ribbon Sports.

1970
Bowerman, inspired by his wife's **waffle iron**, dreams up new shoe treads. The Waffle Trainer becomes the best-selling U.S. training shoe.

1971
Blue Ribbon changes its name to Nike and adopts the **Swoosh.** The original logo was designed by a college student for $35. She later got an undisclosed amount of stock.

1973
Long-distance runner **Steve Prefontaine** becomes the first major track athlete to wear Nikes in competition.

1980
Nike goes public, selling 2.4 million shares at $11 apiece. After several splits, Nike's stock now trades around $78 a share.

1985
The **Air Jordan**, best-selling athletic shoe of all time, makes its debut.

1987
Nike scores its first memorable ad campaign. *Revolution*, built around the **Beatles** song, disgusts some rock 'n' roll purists—but it puts Nike on the map.

1992
When picking up their Olympic medals, Nike-sponsored players like Magic Johnson use U.S. flags to hide Reebok jackets. The first Nike town opens.

1994
Nike begins its move into soccer, signing top players. Current endorsers include soccer star **Freddy Adu**, 15.

1999
Co-founder Bowerman dies, Knight reasserts control at Nike, now reeling from allegations of sweatshop conditions overseas.

2003
For the first time, more than half of Nike's sales come from outside the U.S. New products like the **Mercurial Vapor** have helped lift Nike past Adidas as the No.1 European soccer shoe.

The kind of creativity that led Bill Bowerman, the University of Oregon track coach who co-founded the company with Knight, to dream up a new kind of sneaker tread after studying the pattern on his wife's waffle iron, is still revered at Nike. When it comes to the rest of the business, however, it's a whole new ball game. Gone are the days when Nike execs, working on little more than hunches, would do just about anything and spend just about any amount in the quest for publicity and market share. Scott Bedbury, a former Nike marketing chief, recalls pitching his advertising budget to Knight back in 1987. He was asking for a huge increase, from $8 million to $34 million and was prepared to make his case. Instead, Knight asked him the one question he hadn't prepped for: "How do we know you're asking for enough?" That year, Nike spent a jaw-dropping $48 million. The brash innovator of sports marketing may still open the checkbook wide—as it did when it signed basketball phenom LeBron James to a $90 million endorsement contract last year, but those grand gestures are far fewer at the new Nike.

In the past few years, the company has devoted as much energy to the mundane details of running a business—such as developing top-flight information systems, logistics, and (yawn) supply-chain management—as it does to marketing coups and cutting-edge sneaker design. More and more, Nike is searching for the right balance between its creative and its business sides, relying on a newfound financial and managerial discipline to drive growth. "Senior management now has a clear understanding of managing the creative process and bringing it to the bottom line.

That's the big difference compared to the past," says Robert Toomey, an equity analyst at RBC Dain Rauscher Inc. in Seattle (Exhibit 2).

Businesslike—and Uncool?

In the old days, Nike operated pretty much on instinct. It took a guess as to how many pairs of shoes to churn out and hoped it could cram them all onto retailers' shelves. Not anymore. Nike has overhauled its computer systems to get the right number of sneakers to more places in the world more quickly. By methodically studying new markets, it has become a powerhouse overseas—and in new market segments that it once scorned, such as soccer and fashion. It has also beefed up its management team. And after stumbling with its acquisitions, Nike has learned to manage those brands—Cole Haan dress shoes, Converse retro-style sneakers, Hurley International skateboard gear, and Bauer in-line and hockey skates—more efficiently. Indeed, part of Nike's growth strategy is to add to its portfolio of brands.

To many of the Nike faithful, those sorts of changes smacked of heresy. Lebron James is cool. Matrix organization and corporate acquisitions aren't. But cool or not, the new approach is working. In fiscal 2004, ended May 31, Nike showed just how far it had elevated its financial game. It turned in a record year, earning almost $1 billion, 27% more than the year before, on sales that climbed 15%, to $12.3 billion. What's more, orders worldwide were up a healthy 10.7%. In North America orders rose 10% following eight stagnant quarters (Exhibit 3).

EXHIBIT 2

All **Grown Up**
NO LONGER DOES NIKE DEPEND JUST ON HIGH-PERFORMANCE SHOES.

FINANCIAL DISCIPLINE	IMPROVED OPERATIONS	NEW VENTURES	EXPANDING BRAND NIKE
For a time in the late 1990s, Nike didn't even have a chief financial officer. Expenses sometimes spiraled out of control. The arrival of Don Blair from PepsiCo in 1999, who became CFO, and the creation of a new management team brought order and discipline.	For years Nike's antiquated supply-chain system struggled to move goods efficiently from factory to retailer. Nike spent $500 million modernizing its technology. The result: Nike gets products to customers faster and cheaper.	Nike is committed to owning brands that complement its core Nike brand and help insulate the company from the volatile market for sporting goods.	The Beaverton (Ore.) outfit is not just a sneaker company anymore. These days, Nike is big in sports fashion and has become a powerful player in the world's most popular sport, soccer.

EXHIBIT 3

Source: Stanley Holmes, "The New Nike," BusinessWeek, September 20, 2004, 78–86.

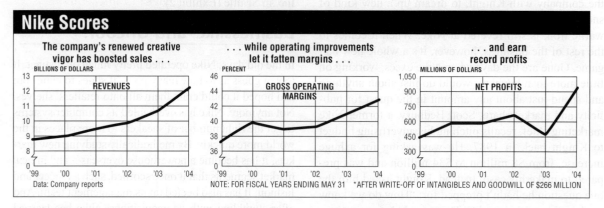

Nike Scores

The company's renewed creative vigor has boosted sales . . . (BILLIONS OF DOLLARS — REVENUES) | . . . while operating improvements let it fatten margins . . . (PERCENT — GROSS OPERATING MARGINS) | . . . and earn record profits (MILLIONS OF DOLLARS — NET PROFITS)

Data: Company reports

NOTE: FOR FISCAL YEARS ENDING MAY 31   *AFTER WRITE-OFF OF INTANGIBLES AND GOODWILL OF $266 MILLION

That performance has pleased investors, who now see a company where earnings are less volatile and less fad-driven, yet still growing rapidly enough to spin off lots of cash. In the past fiscal year, Nike's free cash flow totaled $1.2 billion, and its return on invested capital was 22%, up from only 14% four years ago. The company boosted its dividend by 43% last fall and completed a $1 billion share repurchase. It plans to buy back $1.5 billion more in shares over the next four years. The result: Nike stock recently traded at about 78, up 37% in the past year vs. a 9% rise in the Standard & Poor's 500-stock index. The truth is, the onetime corporate rebel is edging toward blue-chip respectability. Who'd have figured?

Nike believes its newfound discipline will enable it to meet its targets of 15% average annual profit growth and revenue growth in the high single digits. Wall Street shares that optimism. Says John J. Shanley, an analyst at Susquehanna Financial Group, an institutional broker in Bala Cynwyd, Pa.: "Nike is probably in the best financial position it has been in in a decade." In fact, some analysts believe Nike is poised to become a $20 billion company by the end of the decade.

That would have seemed laughable just a few years ago—sales started falling after hitting the $9.6 billion mark in 1998. Even before Nike's superstar endorser and basketball great Michael Jordan retired from the game in 2003, Nike's creative juices seemed to have run dry. Air Jordans at $200 were collecting dust on store shelves as buyers seeking a different look began switching to Skechers, K-Swiss, and New Balance shoes. Nike wrestled with accusations that it exploited Asian factory workers. Ho-hum new sneakers and troubled acquisitions didn't help. Nike, eager to regain its

old momentum, bumped up production—only to end up pushing more sneakers into the market than the customers wanted to buy. As for financial discipline? Well, just consider this: From 1997 to 1999, Nike didn't even have a chief financial officer. "We had a bit of a burning platform," says Donald W. Blair, the executive whom Knight recruited from PepsiCo Inc. to fill the position.

It was during those tough times that Phil Knight, who had disengaged from Nike in order to travel and pursue other interests, came back to the company. The year was 1999. Co-founder Bowerman had died, and Nike was floundering. Knight, now 66, needed to set things straight. Standing before thousands of employees at a company meeting, he admitted that the managers who were running the place had failed. And he went on to blame himself. "He said he wasn't as engaged as he should be, and he said there were things he could do better," recalls Steve Miller, Nike's former global sports marketing director, who was there. "I was personally stunned he would be so open about his failings." Knight, whose son died in a scuba diving accident earlier this summer, declined to speak to *BusinessWeek*.

Knight has been hailed as a visionary for his company's breakthrough design, technology, and marketing prowess. In the 1980s and '90s, Knight forever changed the rules of sports marketing with Nike's huge endorsement contracts and in-your-face advertising. Mixing marketing and pop music is common-place now. But Nike created a small furor in 1987 when it used the Beatles' *Revolution* in ads to sell cross-training sneakers.

Still, when his iconoclastic company faltered, Knight looked beyond the technology and marketing antics that had served it well in the past. Upon his return to the company five years ago, his first order of business was to put together a new executive team. Knight drew on some Nike veterans, executives who carry the heritage and culture of Nike's early years. But he also recruited some key players from far outside Nike and its industry. CFO Blair, who came aboard in 1999, was lured from Pepsi, while Mindy F. Grossman was plucked from Polo Ralph Lauren Corp. the next year with the mission of redefining Nike's $3.5 billion global apparel business. The-day-to-day boss, Chief Operating Officer Thomas E. Clarke, now runs Nike's new business ventures division.

Knight made his boldest management move in 2001, when he named two longtime Nike insiders, creative brand and design wonk Mark G. Parker and operations maven Charles D. Denson, as co-presidents. With Grossman and Blair providing an outsider's perspective and with Parker and Denson steeped in the company's culture, Knight hoped to achieve a balance between the old and the new, the creative and the financially responsible. The unusual co-president structure was hardly Business 101, and many observers figured the new team wouldn't last. Few believed co-presidents could survive the inevitable political maneuvering and clash of egos.

Succession Sweepstakes?

No matter what else Knight intended, it also looked very much as if he had set up a horse race among those most likely to succeed him. Knight, who owns 80% of Nike's voting stock, and about 36% of the common shares, has never said when or even if he will retire or what will happen to his voting stock on his death. Speculating on his eventual departure has been the topic of water-cooler conversations for nearly a decade. The succession issue remains the single biggest question at the company, although the new management structure has gone a long way toward assuring investors that the bench is deep.

Possibly because there was little time for politicking or back-stabbing, given Nike's plight, Parker, Denson, and the rest have mostly steered clear of those pitfalls and focused on shoring up Nike's weaknesses. "There are aspects of this culture that are incredibly powerful and strong," says Parker, citing design and marketing. "But we needed to get after the basic pieces of the business: operating principles, financial management, supply-chain renovation, and inventory management."

In the old days at Nike, the culture encouraged local managers to spend big and to go flat-out for market share instead of profitability. In Paris, for instance, the company spent lavishly for a soccer park at the 1998 World Cup to promote itself. Analysts estimate, conservatively, that it was more than $10 million over budget. The cost, which Nike never disclosed, caused Wall Street to start asking whether anyone was in charge.

So Parker and Denson engineered a matrix structure that breaks down managerial responsibility both by region and product. Because the company pumps out 120,000 products every year in four different launch cycles, local managers always had plenty of choice—but also plenty of ways to screw up. Under the matrix, Nike headquarters establishes which products to push and how to do it, but regional managers are allowed some leeway to modify those edicts. The matrix won't guarantee that another fiasco like the Paris soccer park cannot occur, but it makes it a lot less likely.

Filling the Orders

Nike also overhauled its supply-chain system, which often left retailers either desperately awaiting delivery of hot shoes or struggling to get rid of the duds. The old jerry-built compilation strung together 27 different computer systems worldwide, most of which couldn't talk with the others. Under Denson's direction, Nike has spent $500 million to build a new system. Almost complete, it is already contributing to quicker design and manufacturing times, and fatter gross margins—42.9% last year, up from 39.9% five years ago. Nike says that the percentage of shoes it makes without a firm order from a retailer has fallen from 30% to 3%, while the lead time for getting new sneaker styles to market has been cut to six months from nine.

Meanwhile, Nike has started paying serious attention to its handful of acquisitions, once treated as more of an after-thought. After buying up Cole Haan almost 15 years ago, Nike struggled to add any real value at the dress-shoe outfit. But lately, Nike managers have figured out that by giving their acquired brands some independence, rather than forcing Nike's testosterone-laced corporate culture on them, they can achieve better results (Exhibit 4). "We've learned to let those brands pull resources and expertise out of the mother ship as opposed to pushing the mother ship onto the brands," Blair says. Nike doesn't break out results for each

EXHIBIT 4

Nike's Company Portfolio

There's more to Nike than just the iconic sneaker brand

HURLEY INTERNATIONAL

This skateboard-equipment maker helps Nike crack the youth market. Nike helps Hurley overseas, but it is otherwise taking a hands-off approach. Bought for an estimated $95 million in 2002.

COLE HAAN

Nike's first-ever acquisition, this maker of dress and casual shoes has only recently got on its feet, mainly by incorporating athletic-shoe technology while becoming more fashion-conscious. Bought for $80 million in1988.

BAUER

Makes ice hockey skates and related sports gear. Bauer also manufactures in-line skates. The consensus on Wall Street: Nike overpaid by buying at the height of the fad. Purchased for $409 million in 1995.

CONVERSE

Its retro-style sneakers have made it the most successful sub-brand. Nike is concerned with how to keep the brand fresh, but is letting Converse answer that question. Bought for $305 million in 2003.

sub-brand, but the group's sales grew 51%, to $1.4 billion last year. With nearly a quarter of the sales growth, Converse was the star.

That still-modest portfolio of different brands helps to lessen the company's dependence on hit shoes and could help Nike turn in a more consistent performance. That's why Nike is eager to snap up complementary brands as they become available. In mid-August it paid $43 million for Official Starter Properties, licensors of sneakers and athletic apparel whose brands include the budget-level Shaq label. "What we're trying to do is move toward more of a consumer, noncyclical model," says Blair. "The key is trying to find the right balance of discipline, innovation, creativity, and structure."

Nike has also had to grapple with the touchy topic of sweatshop labor at the 900-odd independent overseas factories that make its clothes and sneakers. When Nike was getting pummeled on the subject in the 1990s, it typically had only two responses: anger and panic. Executives would issue denials, lash out at critics, and then rush someone to the offending supplier to put out the fire. But since 2002, Nike has built an elaborate program to deal with charges of labor exploitation. It allows random factory inspections by the Fair Labor Assn., a monitoring outfit it founded with human rights groups and other big companies, such as Reebok International Ltd. and Liz Claiborne Inc., that use overseas contractors. Nike also has an inhouse staff of 97 which has inspected 600 factories in the past two years,

grading them on labor standards. "You haven't heard about us recently because we have had our head down doing it the hard way. Now we have a system to deal with the labor issue, not a crisis mentality," says Maria S. Eitel, Nike vice-president for corporate responsibility.

It's overseas, in fact, where most of Nike's sales now come from. Last year, for the first time, international sales exceeded U.S. sales—still the company's single largest market. Under Grossman, Nike is making sports fashion a core business, something unthinkable until recently inside Nike's male-dominated culture. Thanks to stylish athletic wear—think tennis star Serena Williams at the U.S. Open—Nike's worldwide apparel sales climbed 30% in three years, to $3.5 billion in fiscal 2004.

Of course, Nike still faces challenges. After several years of red-hot growth, European sales of higher-priced shoes have started to slide. In the U.S., retro-sneaker makers like K-Swiss, Diesel, and Puma are filling a rising demand. And Adidas-Salomon has redoubled efforts to attack the North America basketball market, where Nike has a 60% share. Taking a leaf from Nike's book, Adidas just signed three NBA all-stars: Tracy McGrady, Tim Duncan, and Kevin Garnett, each of whom will have his own sneaker. On the technology front, Adidas has unveiled the Adidas 1, a $250 shoe slated for December that has a computer chip that automatically adjusts the fit as the wearer runs.

Nike aims to keep pace in the techno-battle with Nike Free, a shoe still being tested, that makes runners feel as if they were barefoot. It's inspired by the barefoot runners of Kenya, who have proved that shoeless training builds strength and improves performance. Meanwhile the company continues to refine its Shox technology—a special cushioning system first developed for runners, which is now becoming a top seller in categories from running to basketball to cross training. The shoes, which sell for up to $135 a pair, helped put to rest the idea that high-priced sneakers no longer sell well in the U.S.

Swiftest Kick

Nike has also shown it can grow by expanding into new markets. When the U.S. hosted the World Cup in 1994, Nike's global soccer sales were $45 million. But a team of executives persuaded Knight that soccer was the company's future. Today, soccer sales are nearly $1 billion, or 25% of the global market. This year, for the first time, Nike's share of the soccer shoe market in Europe, 35%, exceeded Adidas, at 31%. Nike has achieved that fast growth in part by using the same outsize marketing tactics that made it big in the U.S. It paid the prestigious Manchester United club an unprecedented $450 million over 14 years to run its merchandising and uniform operation.

Just before this summer's European soccer championships, Nike launched its Total 90 III, a sleek shoe that draws inspiration from cars used in the Le Mans 24-hour road race. Nike realized that millions of kids around the globe play casual pickup soccer games in the street and developed the shoe especially for them. That insight does not impress soccer purists. "Nike is selling a lot of the Total 90 street shoes and is including them in the soccer category," huffs Adidas CEO Herbert Hainer. "They are trying to turn the business model into a lifestyle." He's right, of course. Just as Nike made basketball shoes into an off-the-court fashion statement, its Total 90s have become fashion accessories for folks who may never get closer to a soccer pitch than the stands.

What's the lesson? Let other companies worry about the traditional boundaries between sport and fashion. Nike has built its empire by transforming the technology and design of its high performance sports gear into high fashion, vastly expanding its pool of potential customers. If competitors want to get hung up on what exactly Nike's selling, that's O.K. with the folks in Beaverton. It's all Nike to them.

EPILOGUE

From the time Nike founder and Chairman Philip H. Knight anointed William D. Perez as his successor in November, 2004, the two men had a regularly scheduled meeting on Monday mornings at 9. The get-togethers had been Knight's idea. They gave CEO Perez, a surprise choice who had previously held the top post at S.C. Johnson & Son Inc., the manufacturer of Glade air fresheners and Drano, an informal forum for bouncing ideas off the legendary figure who all but personified the company.

When Knight took a seat at the round conference table in Perez' office on Jan. 9, it seemed like any other mundane Monday meeting. The discussion methodically progressed through several unremarkable issues, Perez says. But Knight was saving a bombshell for last. Abruptly declaring that Perez had failed to mesh with the rest of the Nike team, Knight told him it was time to go. Perez was stunned. "He caught me off guard," he said in an extensive interview with *BusinessWeek*. Knight declined to comment on the details of Perez's account. "I and the Board decided that the company could be better managed with a proven, seasoned industry veteran," he said.

Bad Chapter

Perez says he asked Knight for a few days to absorb the news and prepare his family for upheaval. He also asked the board for an opportunity to appeal the decision and was granted a 15-minute audience on Jan. 18. But on Jan. 20 the board sided with the company's largest shareholder and approved Knight's recommendation to name Nike veteran and co-President Mark Parker as chief executive. "He will become the best CEO this company has ever had," Knight crowed in a Jan. 23 conference call.

No amount of corporate spin can conceal one of the worst chapters in the history of Nike Inc. It marks the third time the mercurial Knight, 67, has tried giving up his throne. Nike's leader and board members have long acknowledged that the company's top strategic priority is managing succession. But despite the company's hip image and record performance this year, it's hard to imagine they'll have much luck enticing strong outside candidates to consider joining the company in the near future. "It's almost like a death wish coming into that company from outside," says Stephanie R. Joseph, president of the Directors' Network Inc., which runs workshops and seminars for board members.

EXHIBIT 5

Perez vs. Knight: The Issues That Drove Them Apart

In the 13 months since William Perez was tapped as founder Phil Knight's successor, basic differences in their approach to the business became clear—and led to Perez' ouster

STRATEGY	AUTONOMY	COSTS	CULTURE
PEREZ: Proposed increasing direct sales to consumers through Web and Nike stores.	**PEREZ:** Thought he would have free rein to make over the company	**PEREZ:** Wanted to take an ax to Nike's lavish operating expenses	**PEREZ:** Believed that Nike was far too resistant to outside ideas
KNIGHT: Favored current practice of selling through third-party retailers	**KNIGHT:** Continued to give strong input on even seemingly minor issues	**KNIGHT:** Supported the goal but differed with Perez on how to achieve it	**KNIGHT:** Didn't think Perez really understood Nike's creative mind-set

---

That perception could become problematic because Knight and the board, when they hired Perez, acknowledged the insular company's need for fresh blood. Knight also recognized Nike's reputation as a difficult place for transplants to thrive and promised to go out of his way to make Perez feel at home. "There will be a little bit of a bumpy period," Knight told *BusinessWeek* a month after he hired Perez, but "I'm committed to making it work."

The fact that Perez failed, despite Knight's stated intentions, underscores how hard it is for new CEOs to fill the shoes of charismatic corporate founders whose personality and ego are closely tied to their companies. History is full of examples of legendary leaders who, because of their own shortcomings or problems with their successors (below), had trouble handing over the reins. In Perez' view, Knight's name belongs near the top of this list. "From virtually the day I arrived, Phil was as engaged in the company as he ever was," Perez said. "He was talking to my direct reports. It was confusing for the people and frustrating for me" (Exhibit 5).

Deft Juggler

The wounds are still raw for the man who just got dumped from one of the most glamorous jobs in American business. He retreated to his second home in Naples, Fla., immediately after the dismissal. "It's been very tough on my family," said Perez, 58, noting that his wife had left a job she loved as a high school Spanish teacher in Racine, Wis., when he took the Nike post. He added that Knight "piled it on in the media" after the news was announced.

So why did Knight even hire Perez? Because he wanted someone with strong financial and managerial discipline and a track record overseeing the growth of a profitable consumer-products company. In running S.C. Johnson, Perez had deftly juggled the managing of multiple brands in multiple countries. Knight and the board took more than a year searching for the right candidate. After reading 75 résumés, conducting 15 interviews, and meeting extensively with three or four final candidates, Knight picked Perez, a self-described introvert with a quiet, analytic bearing.

Hoping to give his successor sufficient time to understand Nike's $11 billion global sneaker and apparel business, Knight put nothing on Perez' plate during the first six months. His sole job was to travel, listen to employees, and meet business partners. The honeymoon ended, says Perez, as soon as he began to assert his leadership. He triggered a wide-spread staff revolt, one that he was never able to overcome, with his first big move: hiring Boston Consulting Group to help him conduct a sweeping review of the company's strategies and practices.

The study required managers to spend two hours responding to a detailed survey. "Perez started asking questions of 20- to-30-year veterans that have never been asked before," says one Nike manager. "Surveys are not Nike's specialty. It's not Nike's culture."

The consultants had two goals: figuring out how to control the double-digit rise in operating expenses and examining whether Nike had the right growth strategy in place. Almost all of their ultimate recommendations hit longtime staffers, quite a few of whom came from rival firms McKinsey & Co. and Bain & Co., like bombshells. Boston Consulting proposed boosting sales by, among other things, opening outlet stores—a move that the image-obsessed Nike team feared would degrade the value of the brand. The firm wanted to cut costs by outsourcing day care, janitorial, and security services. "The intent was to raise awareness in the company to control operating expenses," Perez said. "I was trying to accelerate the pace, but most of my resistance came from Phil."

Knight and Perez also clashed over a highly charged political battle between the company and the city of Beaverton, Ore., which was trying to annex the Nike campus against the company's wishes. This summer, a friendly state legislature stopped the city from its annexation claim and gave Nike its independence for another 35 years before the issue would be reviewed again. "I thought that was fine," Perez says. "But not Phil. He wanted to sue Beaverton. I thought that was a bad idea because it would have created ill will with the public and with the lawmakers that had helped us out." But what rankled Perez even more was the larger question: Why was Knight even devoting any time to such a minor issue?

Perez, who came from a consumer-product marketing background, says he sometimes wondered if Nike's famously creative, irreverent advertising was actually conveying relevant messages about the product. The first commercial he saw was a 30-second spot aimed at last year's NCAA basketball tournament. The commercial showed ants crawling onto the basketball court. After 28 seconds, a voice would say "Nike basketball." His concern: The ad explained nothing about the product, and it had minimal brand presence. "I came from a rational world of communications," Perez said.

Nike insiders, meanwhile, were developing a parallel set of concerns about Perez. "He didn't have an intuitive sense of Nike as a brand," said one of them. "He relied more on the spreadsheet, analytical approach as opposed to having a good creative marketing sense."

In the end, Knight said that he could tolerate only so much friction. "I think the failure to really kind of get his arms around this company and this industry led to confusion on behalf of the management team," he said at the Jan. 23 press conference. In a later interview with *BusinessWeek,* Knight claimed to have learned from the misadventure. "Communication is huge, and I didn't know that would be as big of an issue with Bill," Knight said. "There is no question communication between Mark Parker and me will be better than between me and Bill." That's probably true. It's hard to see how the dialogue between Knight and Perez could have been much worse.

Source: Stanley Holmes, "Inside the Coup at Nike," *Business-Week,* February 6, 2006, 34–37.

Case 4-3

Dell Inc.

When Dell CEO Michael S. Dell and President Kevin B. Rollins met privately in the fall of 2001, they felt confident that the company was recovering from the global crash in PC sales. Their own personal performance, however, was another matter. Internal interviews revealed that subordinates thought Dell, 38, was impersonal and emotionally detached, while Rollins, 50, was seen as autocratic and antagonistic. Few felt strong loyalty to the company's leaders. Worse, the discontent was spreading: A survey taken over the summer, following the company's first-ever mass layoffs, found that half of Dell Inc.'s employees would leave if they got the chance.

What happened next says much about why Dell is the best-managed company in technology. At other industry giants, the CEO and his chief sidekick might have shrugged off the criticism or let the issue slide. Not at Dell. Fearing an exodus of talent, the two execs focused on the gripes. Within a week, Dell faced his top 20 managers and offered a frank self-critique, acknowledging that he is hugely shy and that it sometimes made him seem aloof and unapproachable. He vowed to forge tighter bonds with his team. Some in the room were shocked. They knew personality tests given to key execs had repeatedly shown Dell to be an "off-the-charts introvert," and such an admission from him had to have been painful. "It was powerful stuff," says Brian Wood, the head of public-sector sales for the Americas. "You could tell it wasn't easy for him."

Michael Dell didn't stop there. Days later, they began showing a videotape of his talk to every manager in the company—several thousand people. Then Dell and Rollins adopted desktop props to help them do what didn't come naturally. A plastic bulldozer cautioned Dell not to ram through ideas without including others, and a Curious George doll encouraged Rollins to listen to his team before making up his mind.

Walking Databases

To some, the way Michael Dell handled sagging morale might seem like another tale of feel-good management. But to those inside the company, it epitomizes how this Round Rock (Tex.) computer maker has transformed itself from a no-name PC player into a powerhouse brand (Exhibit 1). Sure, Dell is the master at selling direct, bypassing middlemen to deliver PCs cheaper than any of its rivals. And few would quarrel that it's the model of efficiency, with a far-flung supply chain knitted together so tightly that it's like one electrical wire, humming 24/7. Yet all this has been true for more than a decade. And although the entire computer industry has tried to replicate Dell's tactics, none can hold a candle to the company's results. Today, Dell's stock is valued at a price-earnings multiple of 40, loftier than IBM, Microsoft, Wal-Mart Stores, or General Electric.

As it turns out, it's how Michael Dell manages the company that has elevated it far above its sell-direct business model. What's Dell's secret? At its heart is his belief that the status quo is never good enough, even if it means painful changes for the man with his name on the door. When success is achieved, it's greeted with five seconds of praise followed by five hours of postmortem on what could have been done better. Says Michael Dell: "Celebrate for a nanosecond. Then move on." After the outfit opened its first Asian factory, in Malaysia, the CEO sent the manager heading the job one of his old running shoes to congratulate him. The message: This is only the first step in a marathon.

Just as crucial is Michael Dell's belief that once a problem is uncovered, it should be dealt with quickly and directly, without excuses. "There's no 'The dog ate my homework' here," says Dell. No, indeed. After Randall D. Groves, then head of the server business, delivered 16% higher sales last year, he was demoted. Never mind that none of its rivals came close to that. It could have been better, say two former Dell

EXHIBIT 1 Managing the Dell Way

Michael Dell revolutionized the PC biz with a direct-sales model that keeps costs low and customer satisfaction high. That was 19 years ago, yet Dell is still outdistancing rivals. Credit his management principles:

Be Direct

It's an attitude, not just a business model. When the CEO talks, he doesn't mince words, and workers shouldn't either. They're supposed to question everything and **challenge their bosses.** And no one is exempt. In Dell's own annual 360-degree review, workers complained of his detached style, so he has pledged to be more emotionally engaged.

Leave the Ego at the Door

The company favors "two-in-a-box" management, in which two executives share responsibility for a product, a region, or a company function. That forces them to **work as a team,** playing off each other's strengths and watching out for each other's weaknesses.

No Excuses

Dell believes in accountability above all else: "There's no 'The dog ate my homework' at Dell," he warns. A manager must quickly **admit a problem, confront it,** and never be defensive. Dell ruthlessly exposes weak spots during grueling quarterly reviews. And execs know they had better fix the problem before the next meeting.

No Easy Targets

It's not enough to rack up profits or turbocharge growth—execs must **do both.** Miss a profit goal, and you're not cutting costs fast enough, Overshoot it, and you're leaving sales on the table. In the past year, the server, storage, and networking chiefs were reassigned, despite solid results. "Pity the folks who didn't use all the bullets in their gun," says a former exec.

No Victory Laps

To Dell, **celebration breeds complacency.** He once rejected an idea to display Dell artifacts in the company's lobby because "museums are looking at the past." When they succeed, managers must make due with a short e-mail or a quick pat on the back. The founder's mantra: "Celebrate for a nanosecond, then move on."

Worry about Saving Money, Not Saving Face

Unlike its rivals. Dell is quick to **pull the plug** on disappointing new ventures. The latest: Despite a year of work and extensive news coverage, Michael Dell spiked a plan to put e-commerce kiosks in Sears stores after just four were installed. Instead, kiosks are going into public areas in malls.

executives. Groves referred calls to a Dell spokesman, who says Groves's job change was part of a broader reorganization.

Above all, Michael Dell expects everyone to watch each dime—and turn it into at least a quarter. Unlike most tech bosses, Dell believes every product should be profitable from Day One. To ensure that, he expects his managers to be walking databases, able to cough up information on everything from top-line growth to the average number of times a part has to be replaced in the first 30 days after a computer is sold.

But there's one number he cares about most: operating margin. To Dell, it's not enough to rack up profits or grow fast. Execs must do both to maximize long-term profitability. That means products need to be priced low enough to induce shoppers to buy, but not so low that they cut unnecessarily into profits. When Dell's top managers in Europe lost out on profits in 1999 because they hadn't cut costs far enough, they were replaced. "There are some organizations where people think they're a hero if they invent a new thing," says Rollins. "Being a hero at Dell means saving money."

It's this combination—reaching for the heights of perfection while burrowing down into every last data point—that no rival has been able to imitate. "It's like watching Michael Jordan stuff the basketball," says Merrill Lynch & Co. technology strategist Steven Milunovich. "I see it. I understand it. But I can't do it."

How did this Mike come by his management philosophy? It started 19 years ago, when he was ditching classes to sell homemade PCs out of his University of Texas dorm room. Dell was the scrappy underdog, fighting for his company's life against the likes of IBM and Compaq Computer Corp. with a direct-sales model that people thought was plain nuts. Now, Michael Dell is worth $17 billion, while his 40,000-employee company is about to top $40 billion in sales. Yet he continues to manage Dell with the urgency and determination of a college kid with his back to the wall. "I still think of us as a challenger," he says. "I still think of us attacking."

It's not that Michael Dell leads by force of personality. He's blessed with neither the tough-guy charisma of Jack Welch nor the folksy charm of the late Sam Walton. Once, after hearing about the exploits of flamboyant Oracle Corp. CEO Lawrence J. Ellison, he held up a piece of paper and deadpanned to an aide: "See this? It's vanilla and square, and so am I." This egoless demeanor permeates the company. Everyone is expected to sacrifice their own interests for the good of the business, and no one gets to be a star. If Michael Dell is willing to modify the personality traits he was born with, other top execs are expected to be just as self-sacrificing. Frequently, Dell pairs execs to run an important business, an approach called "two-in-a-box." That way, they work together, checking each others' weaknesses and sharing the blame when something goes wrong. One such executive calls Dell's senior leadership "the no-name management team."

All this has kept Dell on track as rivals have gone off the rails. Since 2000, the company has been adding market share at a faster pace than at any time in its history—nearly three percentage points in 2002. A renewed effort to control costs sliced overhead expenses to just 9.6% of revenue in the most recent quarter and boosted productivity to nearly $1 million in revenue per employee. That's three times the revenue per employee at IBM and almost twice Hewlett-Packard Co.'s rate.

Still, for the restless Michael Dell, that's not nearly enough. He wants to make sure the company he has spent half his life building can endure after he's gone. So he and Rollins have sketched out an ambitious financial target: $60 billion in revenues by 2006 (Exhibit 2).

EXHIBIT 2
Building a Behemoth

Data: Merrill Lynch & Co., Dell Inc.

Dell is gunning for $60 billion in revenue by 2006, an ambitious goal that requires it to grow 15% a year for the next four years. Here's how it plans to get there:

	2001	2002	2003*	2004*	2005*	2006*
PCs	$20	$23	$26	$27	$29	$30
Servers/Storage	5	5	7	8	9	10
Services	3	4	4	5	7	9
Software/Peripherals**	3	4	4	7	10	13
Total***	$31	$36	$41	$47	$54	$62

All figures are revenues in billions
*Estimated
**Including printers
***May not add up because of rounding

That's twice what the company did in 2001 and enough to put it in league with the largest, most powerful companies in the world. Getting there will require the same kind of success that the company achieved in PCs—but in altogether new markets. Already, Michael Dell is moving the company into printers, networking, handheld computers, and tech services. His latest foray: Dell is entering the cutthroat $95 billion consumer-electronics market with a portable digital-music player, an online music store, and a flat-panel television set slated to go on sale Oct. 28 (Exhibit 3).

Can Dell graduate from PC prodigy to corporate icon? Driving for nonstop growth will require grooming a new generation of leaders, which Rollins concedes is a major challenge given the company's pressure-cooker atmosphere. In the 1990s, after seasoned execs recruited from titans such as Intel and IBM quickly jumped ship, Dell learned that outsiders don't adapt easily to its demanding culture. And unlike in the

past, Dell won't be able to count on stock options to make up for the discomfort. Some 32% of its outstanding options are priced above the current share price of $35, and the company has sliced grants to about 40 million shares this year, one-third the 2001 level. Little wonder that so far, Dell has achieved only a modest improvement in morale, according to its internal surveys. "They need to work a lot on appreciating people," says Kate Ludeman, an executive coach who has worked with Dell since 1995.

"One-Trick Pony"

Dell also faces an innovation dilemma. Its penny-pinching ways leave little room for investments in product development and future technologies, especially compared with rivals. Even in the midst of the recession, IBM spent $4.75 billion, or 5.9% of its revenues, on research and development in 2002, while

EXHIBIT 3 Beyond the PC

Data: Dell, Merrill Lynch. Consumer Electronics Assn.

With 80% of its sales coming from the maturing PC market, Dell wants to apply its low-cost ways to new markets. If successful, it could maintain a brisk 15% annual growth rate.

TOTAL 2003 MARKET

Consumer Electronics	PC Peripherals	Printers	Storage	Networking	Services
$95 Billion	$65 Billion	$50 Billion	$19.2 Billion	$11 Billion	$368 Billion

ESTIMATED DELL SALES FOR 2003

Negligible	$3.8 Billion	$500 Million	$1.5 Billion	$127 Million	$4.1 Billion
Dell is dipping its toe into the cutthroat industry with flat-panel TVs, digital music players, and an online music service to appeal to its home PC customers. Dell spent $361 million on advertising last year, much of it to build its consumer brand.	Dell has sold its own monitors and digital projectors for years, and introduced its Axim personal digital assistant in late 2002. While it now sells wireless e-mail devices made by other companies, Dell is looking at going solo.	Rather than only resell other company's printers, this year Dell debuted six of its own models. Merrill Lynch thinks Dell's printer sales could rise to $1.4 billion in 2006—good, but not enough to undercut printer king Hewlett-Packard.	For the past two years, Dell has teamed with EMC to develop versions of the storage giant's low-cost models. That has helped Dell nab 5,400 new customers. Look for Dell to build the pricier models in the future.	Attracted by networking giant Cisco Systems' 70% gross margins, Dell sees a chance to take significant share with low-end switches that cost 50% less. The major challenge: Developing more sophisticated products.	Besides offering basic repair services, Dell now helps customers make better use of Dell gear–for instance, when a company needs guidance on setting up a corporate network. Dell hopes this will boost hardware sales—and margins.

HP ponied up $3.3 billion, or 5.8% of revenues. And Dell? Just a paltry $455 million, or 1.3%. Rivals say that handicaps Dell's ability to move much beyond PCs, particularly in such promising markets as digital imaging and utility computing. "Dell is a great company, but they are a one-trick pony," says HP CEO Carleton S. Fiorina. What's more, Dell has shown little patience for the costs of entering new markets, killing off products—like its high-end server—when they didn't produce quick profits, rather than staying committed to a long-term investment. "They're the best in the world at what they do," says IBM server chief William M. Zeitler. "The question is, will they be best at the Next Big Thing?"

For Michael Dell, inventing the Next Big Thing is not the goal. His mission is to build the Current Big Thing better than anyone else. He doesn't plan on becoming IBM or HP. Rather, he wants to focus on his strength as a superefficient manufacturer and distributor. That's why Dell continues to hone the efficiency of its operations. The company has won 550 business-process patents, for everything from a method of using wireless networks in factories to a configuration of manufacturing stations that's four times as productive as a standard assembly line. "They're inventing business processes. It's an asset that Dell has that its competitors don't," says Erik Brynjolfsson, director of the Center for eBusiness at the Massachusetts Institute of Technology's Sloan School of Management.

Dell's expansion strategy is carefully calibrated to capitalize on that asset. The game plan is to move into commodity markets—with standardized technology that's widely available—where Dell can apply its skills in discipline, speed, and efficiency. Then Dell can drop prices faster than any other company and prompt demand to soar. In markets that Dell thinks are becoming commoditized but still require R&D, the company is taking on partners to get in the door. In the printer market, for example, Dell is slapping its own brand on products from Lexmark International Inc. And in storage, Dell has paired up with EMC Corp. to sell co-branded storage machines. Dell plans to take over manufacturing in segments of those markets as they become commoditized. It recently took on low-end storage production from EMC, cutting its cost of goods 25%.

Dell's track record suggests the CEO will meet his $60 billion revenue goal by 2006. Already, Dell has grabbed large chunks of the markets for inexpensive servers and data-storage gear. After just two quarters, its

first handheld computer has captured 37% of the U.S. market for such devices. And Rollins says initial sales of Dell printers are double its internal targets. With the potential growth in PCs and new markets, few analysts doubt that Dell can generate the 15% annual growth needed to reach the mark. The company has averaged better than 19% growth over the past four quarters, and on Oct. 8 Rollins assured investors that everything was on track. "It's almost machine-like," says Goldman, Sachs & Co. analyst Laura Conigliaro. For the year, analysts expect Dell to boost revenues 16%, to $41 billion, and profits 24%, to $2.6 billion, according to a survey of Wall Street estimates by First Call.

What should help Dell as it plunges into so many new markets is the founder's level-headed realism. A student of business history, he has paid close attention to how some of tech's legendary figures lost their way by refusing to admit mistakes. He cites Digital Equipment Corp.'s Ken Olsen as one who stuck with his strategy until the market passed him by and hints that Sun Microsystems Inc.'s Scott G. McNealy could be next.

Dell, on the other hand, has reversed course so fast he's lucky he didn't get whiplash. In 2001, he scrapped a plan to enter the mobile-phone market six months after hiring a top exec from Motorola Inc. to head it up. He decided the prospects weren't bright enough to offset the costs of entry. The next year, Dell wrote off its only major acquisition, a storage-technology company bought in 1999 for $340 million. Dell backed out of the high-end storage business because it decided its technology wasn't ready for market. "It's amazing how a guy who was so young when he founded the company could evolve as he has," says Edward J. Zander, former president of Sun Microsystems. "Guys that have been in the saddle for 15 and 20 years tend to get too religious. He's the exception to the rule."

Michael Dell, in fact, has one of the longest tenures of any founder who remains CEO. At 19 years and counting, he's second in the tech industry only to Oracle's Ellison. "This sounds strange coming from me," says William H. Gates III, who was CEO of Microsoft Corp. for 25 years before giving it up to be chairman and chief software architect, "but very few business leaders go from the early stage of extremely hands-on stuff to have a leadership style and management process that works for a company that's an absolutely huge and superimportant company."

One way Dell has done it is through his power-sharing arrangement with Rollins, à la his "two-in-a-box" philosophy. Brought on as a consultant in 1993 to help plot the company's first long-range plan, Rollins helped it recover from a series of miscues, including the bungled launch of its notebook business and a disastrous go at trading currencies. Three years later, Dell hired Rollins away from Bain & Co. to run North American sales.

Now, Rollins is the day-to-day general. He and Dell sit in adjoining offices separated by only a glass wall. During a pivotal meeting in the fall of 2001, Dell proposed they agree not to make a major move without the other's approval. Working in tandem helps avoid mistakes that the more entrepreneurial Dell or the more rigid Rollins might make alone. Says Dell: "This company is much stronger when the two of us are doing it together." And there's no question that Rollins is the successor. "If I get hit by a truck, he's the CEO. Everyone knows that."

The Gauntlet

Not that the current CEO is letting up. He maintains pinpoint control over the company's vast operations by constantly monitoring sales information, production data, and his competitors' activities. He keeps a BlackBerry strapped to his hip at all times. In the office, he reserves an hour in the morning and one each afternoon to do nothing but read and respond to e-mail, according to one former executive. "Michael can be a visionary, and he can tell you how many units were shipped from Singapore yesterday," says General Electric Co. CEO Jeffrey R. Immelt, a top Dell customer.

Dell's penchant for tracking every last detail can land him in hot water. On Oct. 10, during the trial of former Credit Suisse First Boston tech banker Frank P. Quattrone for allegedly obstructing an investigation into the bank's handling of hot initial public offerings, prosecutors revealed e-mails between Dell and Quattrone. In one July, 2000, exchange, Dell requested 250,000 shares in Corvis Corp., a promising networking company that was preparing to go public, for his corporate venture-capital fund. Dell suggested the allocation "would certainly help" the relationship between his company and CSFB. Dell declined to comment. But his spokesperson says he was merely trying to assist the fund and noted that the company did not do any investment-banking business with CSFB before or after the exchange. In a separate e-mail on which Michael Dell was copied, the manager of Dell's personal venture fund requested Corvis shares for the fund. A spokesperson for that fund says it had invested in Corvis in 1999 and there was nothing improper about the request.

Rollins has the same attention to detail as Michael Dell. He is overseeing a Six Sigma transformation of everything from manufacturing to marketing that is expected to help cut expenses $1.5 billion this year. The emphasis is on small surgical strikes on defects and waste, not massive restructurings. Consider a Six Sigma meeting one balmy July afternoon. Rollins listened to John Holland, a technician in Dell's server factory, describe how his team replaced the colored paper it used to print out parts lists with plain white paper, saving $23,000. "Where else do you get a supervisor making $40,000 a year presenting to the president of a $40 billion company?" says Americas Operations Vice-President Dick Hunter, Holland's boss.

The discipline in Michael Dell's management style is most apparent in how the company approaches new markets. Take Dell's plunge into the $50 billion printer business. Beginning in 2001, a team of Dell strategists spent more than a year researching the market. Dell only started serious planning after finding that nearly two-thirds of its customers said they would buy a Dell printer if they could get the same kind of service they got when they bought a PC or server. In the summer of 2002, Vice-President Tim Peters, a veteran of Dell's handheld launch, was tapped to lead the effort. But like any exec planning to put out a new product, he had to face the gauntlet of Dell and Rollins. After thinking up a strategy, he had to sit by while it was picked apart.

Nothing was left to chance. Dell prodded Peters to think about product features and the buying experience, while Rollins pushed him to keep costs low without sacrificing quality. Both bosses wanted to make sure the timing was right. That required intense discussions about how standardized printer technologies were and the state of the supply chain that Dell would use. One key challenge: ink. Customers typically buy replacement cartridges at a nearby retailer. It didn't seem likely that they would wait for days for an Internet order from Dell to arrive.

The toughest task in any product launch is the math. At Dell, a new line of PCs, which is good for $2 billion to $3 billion in annual revenue, costs roughly $10 million to launch. Any new idea must have a comparable return says G. Carl Everett, a Dell senior vice-president who retired in 2001, and turn a profit from the get-go. That's what Peters had to promise in printers. The rare exceptions occur only when Dell senses an opportunity that's critical to the company's future. Dell's server business, for instance, took 18 months to reach profitability, says former Vice-President Michael D. Lambert.

In the printer business, it took seven months for Peters to work everything out. The products debuted in March and were profitable immediately. Peters' proposed solution to the ink riddle: Every Dell printer comes loaded with software directing users to Dell. com, where they can order a new cartridge and have it delivered the next day. Still, Michael Dell never let up: The night before the launch, he sat up until 2 a.m. to watch the printers debut online and then zipped e-mails to Peters with suggestions for improvement. When initial sales came in at double the internal target, Peters' team got a very Dell-like reward: a quick trip to see *Terminator 3.*

That flick may turn out to have more than therapeutic value, considering that rival HP is determined to wipe out Dell's printer ambitions. HP's strategy is to leave Dell in the dust with a burst of innovation. It spends $1 billion a year on printer research—more than twice Dell's entire R&D budget. HP is using that money to develop products like high-end photo ink, which will last 73 years, nearly 10 times as long as what Dell offers. "Dell is going to hit a wall," says Jeff Clarke, HP's executive vice-president for global operations. "We view them as low-tech and low-cost. They're the Kmart of the industry." And some experts say Dell won't threaten HP's 60% market share anytime soon. Gartner Inc. estimates that Dell claimed less than 1% of the printer market in the second quarter, mostly at the low end of the business.

Attacking from Below

If past experience is any guide, Dell may struggle as it tries to move upmarket. With its bare-bones R&D budget, it had to kill off high-end servers that go head-to-head with fancy gear from Sun, saying the soft demand didn't merit its attention. And after two and a half years selling net-working gear, Dell has failed to deliver products powerful enough to threaten Cisco Systems Inc.'s dominant market share. Yet Dell is betting that as technology improves, the low-end products it sells so deftly will become more than good enough for most customers, leaving rivals scrambling to find their next high-end innovation. "The history of the industry is [that] the attack from below works," says Merrill Lynch's Milunovich.

Indeed, Dell has had no trouble gobbling up sales as markets mature. In storage, its sales now account for 10% of EMC's revenue, some $600 million annually. In the low-margin home-PC market, which Dell long avoided, unit sales have grown an average of 46% in the past four quarters.

Michael Dell certainly would take exception to HP's jabs about his company being the Kmart of tech. But there are some striking similarities between Dell and another giant retailer: Wal-Mart. Like the behemoth from Bentonville, Ark., Dell has built a business as a super-efficient distributor, with the tightly run operations and thrifty management to enter any number of new markets quickly and easily. "We've always toyed with the idea that we could distribute anything," says Morton L. Topfer, a former Dell vice-chairman who now sits on the company's board. Maybe not anything. But Dell is striving to greatly expand his reach in the tech world. With his management philosophy of constant improvement, he seems well on his way.

By Andrew Park in Round Rock, Tex., with Peter Burrows in San Mateo, Calif., and bureau reports

Source: "What You Don't Know about Dell," *BusinessWeek,* November 3, 2003, 77–84.

Case 4-4
Hewlett-Packard Co.

Just weeks after arriving at Hewlett-Packard Co. as chief executive a year ago, Mark Hurd began hearing the complaints about H-P's corporate sales force.

At an Arizona retreat with 25 top corporate customers, several of them told Mr. Hurd they didn't know whom to call at H-P because of the company's confusing management layers. Others complained they got different price quotes from H-P salespeople in Europe and the U.S.

Mr. Hurd, who had previously run ATM and electronic cash-register maker NCR Corp., heard similar gripes from within H-P. Ann Livermore, head of enterprise, or corporate, technology, told Mr. Hurd it once took her three months to get approval to hire 100 sales specialists. H-P salespeople complained to Mr. Hurd that they spent just a third of their time with customers because they were often burdened with administrative tasks.

Sensing a fundamental problem, Mr. Hurd dug into H-P's sales structure. He found that there were 11 layers of management between him and a customer—far too many, he thought. In Europe, H-P assigned four people from different departments to chase a sales deal, while rivals such as Dell Inc. and International Business Machines Corp. typically assigned three people. That meant H-P was slower to cut a deal—and thus lost many bids. And of the 17,000 people working in H-P's corporate sales, only around 10,000 directly sold to customers. The rest were support staff or in management.

Among consumers, H-P has gained a reputation as a top supplier of high technology from personal computers to printers to cameras. But the $87 billion-a-year company had a problem selling to its best customers—companies, which account for 70% of its revenue. Mr. Hurd concluded that H-P salespeople appeared to expect corporate clients to seek them out. "To win a deal, you have to show up," Mr. Hurd says. "We had to get out of the simplistic mode of just inventing something and expecting people to show up to buy it."

Problems in corporate sales were one reason H-P delivered inconsistent earnings and lack-luster growth under Mr. Hurd's predecessor, Carly Fiorina, who was ousted from the company in February last year. While Ms. Fiorina tinkered with the corporate sales structure several times during her tenure, H-P's net income of $3.5 billion at the end of its fiscal 2004 was roughly similar to what the company achieved in 1999. H-P's stock sank more than 50% during her 5½ years in power. A spokeswoman for Ms. Fiorina, who is planning a book tour for her just-completed memoir, said she declined to comment.

Thus began one of Mr. Hurd's biggest management challenges: overhauling H-P's vast corporate sales force. Last July, Mr. Hurd eliminated a sales group that sold a broad portfolio of H-P's products. He divvied up the workers among H-P's PC, printing and corporate-technology businesses to give the salespeople a chance to master the specific products they sell. He cut hundreds of underperforming workers and did away with three layers of sales management. One of his top sales lieutenants pared back meetings to give salespeople more time to spend with customers. And Mr. Hurd is assigning just one salesperson to many top customers so they'll always know whom to contact.

As recently as four years ago, H-P made all of its profits from consumer products such as ink cartridges and essentially used those profits to subsidize its flailing corporate business. Now, a year after Mr. Hurd succeeded Ms. Fiorina, revamping the corporate sales force has become the centerpiece of the 49-year-old CEO's high-stakes effort to revive the lumbering tech giant.

Under Ms. Fiorina, the corporate sales force had gotten unwieldy, particularly after she engineered H-P's purchase of rival Compaq Computer Corp. in 2002, H-P executives have said. Many salespeople felt little sense of urgency to sell, says H-P's senior vice president of enterprise sales in the Americas, Jack Novia.

H-P's predicament is the reverse of what it faced in the 1970s and 1980s, when it was a pro at selling to corporations but was behind the times in selling tech to individual consumers. In the 1990s, H-P struck many deals with big electronics retailers and gained prominent shelf space in consumer stores and online.

Changing H-P's sales culture isn't easy. H-P's earnings have improved during the past few quarters and its shares are up more than 60% since Mr. Hurd's arrival last March. But the CEO has set a modest target for revenue growth of 4% to 6% for H-P's 2007 fiscal year (Exhibit 1). He says work in transforming sales is in its initial stages. There are still too many internal layers of bureaucracy weighing down salespeople, he says. Once all those hurdles are removed, he says he expects the sales force to be twice as productive as it was.

John Crary, vice president of information technology at automotive-parts supplier Lear Corp., says he hasn't seen much change in H-P's sales so far. He says his H-P salesperson was reassigned last year, and he hasn't yet found out who his main sales representative will be. While H-P has told him big changes will be coming this month, "they haven't manifested themselves yet," he says.

EXHIBIT 1

Aiming for Growth
H-P's quarterly revenue since Mark Hurd joined the company in late March 2005:

	REVENUE, IN BILLIONS	% INCREASE FROM YEAR-EARLIER PERIOD
1Q 2006	$22.7	6%
4Q 2005	22.9	7
3Q 2005	20.8	10
2Q 2005	21.6	7

Note: Fiscal years end October 31.
Source: the company

Other customers say they see improvement. James E. Farris, a senior technology executive at Staples Inc., says H-P has freed up his salesman to drop by Staples at least twice a month instead of about once a month before. The extra face time enabled the H-P salesman to create more valuable collaborations, such as arranging a workshop recently for Staples to explain H-P's technology to the retailer's executives. As a result, Mr. Farris says he is planning to send more business H-P's way.

Mr. Hurd spent 25 years at NCR, working up from a sales job in Texas to CEO. In his first 60 days at H-P, he says he talked to 400 corporate customers and got an earful about how difficult it was for many of them to deal with the company. Mr. Hurd also heard firsthand from salespeople about their frustrations. Simply getting a price quote or a sample product to a customer had become a lengthy ordeal, he found. Some wags had renamed the sales process, known internally as the "soar process"—for solution, opportunity, approval and review—as the "sore process."

Over lunch with Mr. Hurd at the Cincinnati Bankers Club last May, Bill Weaver, an H-P vice president of enterprise sales, said that his team of 700 salespeople typically spent 33% to 36% of its time with customers. The rest of the time was spent negotiating internal H-P bureaucracy, he told Mr. Hurd, making his team less productive than he wanted. "The customer focus was lacking," Mr. Weaver says. "Trying to navigate inside H-P was difficult. It was unacceptable."

Late last May, Mr. Hurd took Memorial Day weekend to mull what to do about sales. He returned to Dayton, Ohio, where his family was still living at the time. Inside his study, the CEO holed up with his spreadsheets and slide presentations, eventually deciding to duplicate the sales structure he had overseen at NCR.

H-P's corporate salespeople were responsible for hawking a broad portfolio of products and typically didn't specialize in any one product area. They reported to a group that operated independently of H-P's product-based business units. As a result, the three units also had little control of the sales process–even though a big part of their budget went to the sales group. And after years of acquisitions, the corporate sales team had grown inefficient. One example: Salespeople used 30 different types of software, left over from the various acquisitions, to track pending sales deals.

At NCR, the sales force had once been organized by country, which prevented one salesman from dealing with all the needs of a multinational customer. In the late 1990s, like many other companies, NCR reorganized the sales team, breaking it up and placing the salespeople under the business units. Mr. Hurd wanted to do the same thing now at H-P. The move would make the business units king, reclaiming control of the sales process, he figured. Each salesperson would also be responsible for selling a smaller selection of products, and so could develop an expertise in a particular product area.

In mid-July, Mr. Hurd publicly announced the restructuring, including the layoffs of more than 14,500 employees, or around 10% of H-P's work force. The switch gives the business units direct control of 70% of their budgeted costs, up from 30%. With the layoffs, H-P has cut to eight from 11 the layers of management between Mr. Hurd and the corporate customer.

Other changes quickly followed. H-P narrowed the number of sales accounts that each salesperson was tied to, with the goal that each person would call on three or fewer accounts. H-P is now reshuffling its ranks to repopulate its top 2,000 corporate accounts with just one salesperson to act as the single contact for each customer.

In November, Mr. Hurd changed how H-P salespeople are compensated. Sales commissions were linked to how much revenue the sales teams generated. But, with his eye on the bottom line, Mr. Hurd also linked commissions to the profitability of the products sold. At the same time, H-P directed salespeople to use just one type of software from Oracle Corp. to track the sales pipeline. That move enabled Mr. Hurd and other executives to get an uncluttered view into the sales deals being chased at any one time.

Mr. Novia, the senior vice president of enterprise sales in the Americas, soon organized what had been a haphazard policy on conference calls with the sales staff. Mr. Novia asked that they occur every Monday, so salespeople could be on the road meeting customers the rest of the week. H-P also began rolling out new laptop computers and other technology to the sales force for the first time in several years.

H-P salesman Richard Ditucci began noticing some of the changes late last year. At the time, Mr. Ditucci was trying to sell computer servers to Staples. As part of the process, Staples had asked Mr. Ditucci to provide a sample server for the company to evaluate. In the past, such requests typically took two to three weeks to fulfill because of H-P's bureaucracy.

This time, Mr. Ditucci got the server he needed within three days. The quick turnaround helped him win the contract, valued at several million dollars. (H-P and Staples's Mr. Farris declined to specify the amount.)

Now H-P is installing the 1,000 servers that will run critical information and data for the retailer 24 hours a day, seven days a week. The new H-P servers replace Staples' previous servers from IBM.

Keith Morrow, chief information officer of convenience-store chain 7-Eleven Inc., says his H-P sales representative is now "here all the time," and has been pitching more products tailored to his business. Last October, 7-Eleven began deploying in its U.S. stores 10,000 H-P pen pads—a mobile device that helps 7-Eleven workers on the sales floor.

Top H-P executives say they are also able to make speedier decisions because of the new sales structure. Earlier this year, Ms. Livermore, H-P's head of enterprise technology, decided to add 50 salespeople

specializing in data storage to H-P's corporate sales force. While it had once taken her three months to get the approval and funding for such a task, she says it took her 30 minutes this time because she now has direct control over the sales process.

But the gains are incremental. H-P says salespeople now spend slightly more than 40% of their time in front of customers, up from around 30% a year ago, but the majority of time is still taken up dealing with others at H-P. H-P also says it is winning 10% more corporate sales deals than before, but declined to elaborate on underlying numbers. Mr. Hurd says the company faces "more work ahead."

Source: Pul-Wing Tam, "Hurd's Big Challange at H-P: Overhauling Corporate Sales," *The Wall Street Journal,* April 3, 2006, A1, A13. Reprinted by permission of The Wall Street Journal, Copyright © 2006 Dow Jones & Company, Inc. All Rights Reserved Worldwide. License number 1674400826205.

Part

5

Implementing and Managing Market-Driven Strategies

14

Designing Market-Driven Organizations

Aligning the strategy and capabilities of the organization with the market, in order to provide superior customer value, is a priority in companies across different industrial sectors.[1] Organizational change is essential in many companies to achieve this objective. The market-driven organization must reflect customer value requirements in its design, roles, and activities.

Recent decades have seen a period of unprecedented organizational change, and this activity promises to continue. Companies have realigned their organizations to establish closer contact with customers, improve customer service, bring the Internet into operations and marketing, reduce unnecessary layers of management, decrease the time span between decisions and results, and improve organizational effectiveness in other ways. Organizational changes include the use of information systems to reduce organizational layers and response time, use of multi-functional teams to design and produce new products, development of new roles and structures, and creation of flexible networks of organizations to compete in turbulent business environments.

Closely associated with Procter & Gamble's market-driven business and marketing strategy initiatives were critically important organizational changes.[2] P&G is widely recognized for its powerful marketing capabilities, but at the end of the 1990s faced intense competition throughout the world and loss of position in several key product markets. To turn the business around, P&G implemented a massive global restructuring plan aimed to improve the company's innovation and competitiveness. The reorganization cost an estimated $2 billion.

Previously organized into four business units covering the regions of the world, in 1998 seven new executives reporting to the P&G CEO were given profit responsibility for global product units such as baby care, beauty, and fabric and home care (Global Business Units). Several of the Global Business Units are headquartered overseas. The Global Business Units have the authority to develop new products and marketing programs. The new design concept also includes eight Market Development Units intended to tackle local market issues (e.g., supermarket retailing in South America), as well as Global Business Services and corporate functions. The regional units can leverage P&G's scale through a single sales force, multibrand marketing efforts, and consolidated media and communications planning and buying. Key objectives were to increase the speed of decision making and move new products into commercialization faster, as well as managing the business on a global basis.

"Change agents" have been appointed to work across the P&G Global Business Units to lead cultural and business change by helping teams to work together more effectively by using real-time collaboration tools. Virtual innovation teams are linked by intranets, which can be accessed by senior executives to keep up with developments. The program involves considerable downsizing in personnel, and substantial change—25 percent of P&G brand managers left the company in eighteen months. The sales organization is being designed to focus salesperson attention more directly on individual brands. The organization design supports distinct strategies articulated clearly so all business disciplines—from product supply to purchasing—can work together. P&G is working to develop more career marketing experts.

With its new organization design in place, P&G shows solid sales growth across all its major businesses and geographies. Competitors complain about P&G's renewed aggression in pricing and promotion. P&G is targeting profitable market segments throughout the world, where previously competitors were virtually unchallenged. The considerable savings from restructuring have been plowed back into market development. The company is focused on big brands in big categories (laundry, hair care, diapers and feminine protection); big developed markets; emerging, developing markets; and, partnerships with big retailers.

P&G's innovations in organizational design underline the nature of the fundamental changes facing many companies in realigning their structures and processes with the requirements of a turbulent and intensely competitive environment.

First, we examine several important trends in organization design and then consider major issues impacting on organizing for market-driven strategy. We discuss changing roles for the marketing function/department in companies and alternative organization designs. Finally, we look at several organizing issues related to global marketing and global customers.

Trends in Organization Design

Organizational requirements to create and implement effective market-driven strategy should be considered in the context of broader shifts in the way in which organizations are being shaped and managed. Organization design is increasingly recognized as an imperative for senior management and a key element of corporate strategy. There is major concern that traditional approaches to organizational structure—usually vertically oriented with *ad hoc* changes and overlays—make critical aspects of organizational working more complex and less efficient. If organizing models lag behind the demands of new strategies, there are limits on how well a company can perform in implementing strategy.[3]

While flatter organizations (fewer management levels) are expected, together with more disaggregated organizations (more functions outsourced to partners), and traditional hierarchies will be broken down,[4] the debate about the characteristics of the new organization and the shape it will take continues. Several relevant themes are considered before examining the organizational imperatives for market-driven strategy.

The New Organization[5]

Traditional Structures

Conventional approaches to organizing consist of business units, operating similarly but separately, controlled by a central authority (head office) which determines strategy and watches over implementation. This is a system of "command and control," made visible in organization charts that lay down organizational hierarchy. Boston Consulting Group reports that "the imperialist corporate center" remains the commonest type of headquarters/business unit relationship. Even when companies decentralize decision making and accountability, they often recentralize when they run into trouble.

The main failing of the traditional approach is that it creates barriers to the spread of knowledge and to achievement of economies of scale. Ideas and commands flow vertically between the center and the business unit, creating "silos" with little communication across the business units (or silos). Globalization frequently leads to attempts to add a "matrix overlay." For example, Philips established both national geographic organizations and product divisions, held together with coordinating committees designed to resolve conflicts between the two lines of command. The matrix overlay has proved problematic, and Philips is pulling back to a more conventional structure. Effective organization design requires more than *ad hoc* structural changes.

In traditional organizational structures, units were either within the organization and closely connected to other units, or they were outside the organization and not connected at all. Transactions with external suppliers were at arm's length. The line between what was inside and outside the organization has become blurred with the rapid growth in joint ventures, alliances, and other strategic relationships (Chapter 7). Partnering underlines the need for new organizational approaches.

Organizational Design Shifts

Many organizations have implemented major changes in the way they manage and organize, and others are examining their needs for re-thinking their policies. IBM has, for example, changed from a company once dominated by lifetime employees selling computer products, to a "conglomeration of transient suppliers"—in the modern IBM, 50 percent of employees have worked for the company for less than five years; 40 percent of the 320,000 employees are "mobile" meaning they do not report daily to an IBM site; and about 30 percent are women.

Change in the ways in which companies are organized are driven by communications technology, the globalization of production and sales, and the transfer of responsibility to outsiders for core business functions, through outsourcing, joint ventures, and alliances. Change is also mandated by the way in which individuals work to carry out their job responsibilities, and the emergence of the "networked worker"—working electronically from a knowledge-base and constantly communicating.

Organizational change appears more easily achieved also when there are major strategic shifts in response to weakening business performance. The radical reshaping of the Cadbury Schweppes' confectionery and beverages business is illustrative. Reducing organization costs may be a major part of recovering competitiveness. The Cadbury organization strategy is described in the METRICS FEATURE.

Innovation

Key in shaping the new organizational form is the imperative for enhanced rates and effectiveness in innovation to achieve organic growth. Increasingly, innovation is achieved by companies looking outside their boundaries for knowledge and expertise, rather than relying on internal R&D or marketing initiatives. We noted earlier how companies like IBM and P&G have opened their organizations up to partner with innovation drivers from outside their companies. The management of cross-boundary relationships requires new approaches to organizing.

- Cadbury Schweppes is the world's largest confectionery business. Under competitive pressure and the attentions of activist shareholder Nelson Peltz, Cadbury Schweppes is radically reshaping its business.
- The restructuring is to cost around $900 million.
- The U.S. beverages business—Dr Pepper, 7-Up, and Snapple—is to be sold.

- The goal is to find savings of around $500 million a year from the remaining confectionery business, including closing some global manufacturing operations.
- Cadbury has relatively low profit margins compared to competitors—Cadbury averages 10 percent, compared to 18 percent at Wrigley and Hershey. The low margins are linked to Cadbury's complex operating structure, with many brands and manufacturing sites.
- The biggest focus is on overheads—sales, general, and administrative costs. Some administrative functions are to be outsourced.
- The organizational structure has become too complex with too many overlaps. Organizational costs account for 20 percent of turnover, as compared to 12 percent for Cadbury's rivals.

Sources: Ben Laurence, "Cadbury Sheds 5,000 Jobs in Drastic Revamp," *Sunday Times*, June 17, 2007, 3–1. Jenny Wiggins, "Cadbury Sweet Talk on Confectionery Revival Fails to Move Skeptics," *Financial Times*, Wednesday June 20, 2007, 22.

The Knowledge-Based Worker

Innovation and growth depend increasingly on knowledge workers or professionals. Knowledge workers have "thinking-intensive" jobs.[6] They represent a growing proportion of the employees of large companies—possibly as much as 25 percent of employees in financial services, media, and pharmaceuticals.[7] Knowledge workers may operate more effectively as "internal partners" rather than conventional employees (Chapter 7). Knowledge workers have been identified as the source of future wealth for companies, but a resource that requires different organizational approaches to achieve effectiveness. The management of knowledge workers may put less emphasis on formal structure and reporting lines, and more emphasis on: (1) leadership, concerned with the individual, the team, and goals; (2) talent management, to provide career development paths in flattened organizations and to retain talent in the organization; and (3) a culture of innovation and creativity. "Talent marketplaces" inside the organization allow capable employees to plot their own career paths internally.[8]

Managing Culture

The active management of the culture of an organization may be a key element of achieving and sustaining competitive advantage. Toyota aims to have employees who are self-motivating and to a high degree self-directing, and the "Toyota Way" embodies the values and culture that guide decision making. Toyota's progression to becoming the number

Toyota's distinct business beliefs and methods have origins in the five principles laid down in 1935 by the founder, Sakichi Toyoda, though not formally documented until 2001, when the company recognized that the growing number of Toyota employees outside Japan needed to be trained in their use.

PILLAR I

Challenge—we form long-term vision, meeting challenges with courage and creativity to realize our dreams.

Kaizen: Continuous improvement—we improve our business operations continuously, always driving for innovation and evolution.

Genchi Genbutsu: "Go and see for yourself"—we go to the source to find the facts to make correct decisions, build consensus, and achieve our goals.

PILLAR II

Respect—we respect others, make every effort to understand each other, take responsibility, and do our best to build mutual trust.

Teamwork—we stimulate personal and professional growth, share the opportunities for development, and maximize individual and team performance.

EVERYTHING MATTERS EXPONENTIALLY

Having overtaken General Motors as the world's biggest carmaker, within two months, Toyota launched a far-reaching initiative called EM^2—"Everything Matters Exponentially" in the U.S. EM^2 is a total re-examination of product planning, customer service, sales and marketing, and involves retraining all U.S. factory workers. The key is a relentless reinforcement of a culture that avoids the "big company disease" of complacency, and letting bad habits set in.

Sources: Thomas A. Stewart and Anand P. Raman, "Lessons from Toyota's Long Drive," *Harvard Business Review*, July–August 2007, 74–83. David Welch, "Staying Paranoid at Toyota," *BusinessWeek*, July 2, 2007, 80–82.

one automaker in the world has been characterized by initiatives that focus on avoiding complacency and emphasizing change. The Toyota Way and a recent culture initiative are described in the STRATEGY FEATURE.

Collaborative Working

Many companies emphasize the importance of organizing around teams. Executives are increasingly expected to work as team members, but also to be skilled at constructing effective teams. Boston Consulting Group explains how at Linux, the open-source software "community," teamwork managed to deal with a virus that had breached a vulnerable spot in the operating system—some twenty people, many of whom had never met, employed by a dozen different companies, living in many different time zones, and stepping outside their job descriptions, accomplished in twenty-nine hours what would otherwise have taken weeks or months. Linux emphasizes community not structure and work principles that energize teams and reduce costs.

IBM has worked to get rid of the command and control structure of the past and to build a culture of connection and collaboration—within the company as well as outside. Resolving a technical problem in the wake of Hurricane Katrina meant using the company's Blue Pages Plus expertise locator on the corporate intranet, locating the right people, establishing a Web page that can be edited by anyone with access, to act as a virtual meeting room, and a team of IBM staff in the U.S., Germany, and the U.K., designing a solution to the problem.

Informal Networks

Culture change and effective teamwork require insight into the informal networks that employees create outside their company's formal structure. Mapping networks shows most people combine with clusters of eight to ten people with whom they communicate most, and with whom they feel "safe." Some influential individuals move across network clusters—they are "knowledge mules" who carry ideas from one corporate silo to another and thereby generate new ideas. Knowledge "mules," or brokers, are critical to innovation. Higher levels of interaction among employees is associated with the ability to solve complex organizational problems.

Organizational Diversity and External Relationships

New organizations are likely to contain contradictions—some parts centralized, others not; close and loose relationships between business units will co-exist in the same company. Organization structures in the future may consist of some strategically aligned businesses linked closely where there are opportunities to create value from leveraging shared capabilities, but other business units with loose relationships because greater value lies in a differentiated focus.

Outsourcing core business functions to partner organizations poses another collaborative working challenge. Some organizations have insourced back functions which had been outsourced—for example, some banks are bringing payment processing back into their companies to leverage the data for insights that will provide new business platforms. Dependence among businesses creates new sources of uncertainty and risk. Companies may develop extended organizational forms to cope. One type of structure may manage outsourced operations, and another structure may work better for internal activities. Boeing's partners' "council meetings" are illustrative of new approaches to managing and organizing relationships with external partners. We have examined several relevant partnering issues in Chapter 7.

Managing Organizational Process

A key characteristic of the new organization is an emphasis on managing organizational process, rather than a primary emphasis on structure. Exhibit 14.1 shows possible new structures as companies move away from traditional hierarchical structures. At the time of this

EXHIBIT 14.1
Alternative Organizational Structures

Source: George S. Day, "Aligning the Organization to the Market," in *Reflections on the Future of Marketing,* Donald R. Lehmann and Katherine E. Jocz, eds. (Cambridge, MA: Marketing Science Institute, 1997), 69–73.

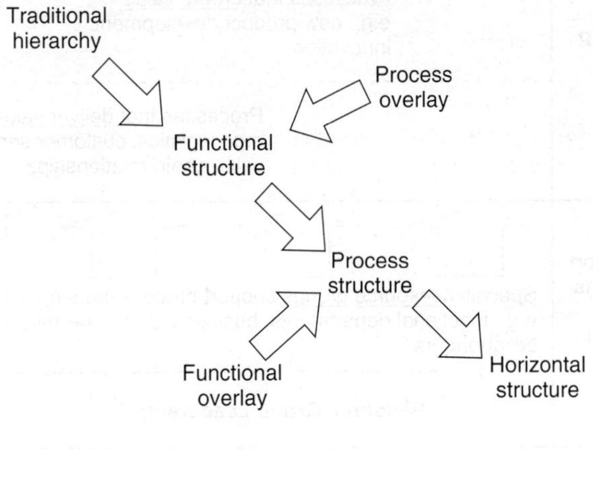

Traditional hierarchy

Functional structure

Process overlay

Process structure

Functional overlay

Horizontal structure

research, a study of 73 companies by the Boston Consulting Group placed 32 percent in the hierarchy, 38 percent in the process overlay, and 30 percent in the functional overlay form. No horizontal structures were reported.[9] The prevailing organizational forms appeared to be the hybrid overlay structures.

As shown in Exhibit 14.1 the structures of large established companies are moving toward horizontal business processes while retaining integrating functions (marketing, human resources) and specialist functions (research and development, marketing).[10] The processes are major clusters of strategically important activities such as new product development, order generation and fulfillment, and value/supply chain management. As companies adopt process structures, various organizational changes occur including fewer levels and fewer managers, greater emphasis on building distinctive capabilities using multifunctional teams, customer value driven processes and capabilities, and continuously changing organizations that reflect market and competitive environment changes.[11]

This hybrid organizational form may take the form shown in Exhibit 14.2, which is based on observation of several major companies moving their organizations in this direction. The names given to major processes vary but are concerned with defining, creating, and delivering value. Processes are led by senior executives. Support for processes comes from resource groups, which may be conventional functional departments or business units, or external collaborators. Coordination mechanisms link process management with resource group management, such as business plans and planning groups or cross-functional teams.

Consumer packaged goods companies such as Kraft Foods have pioneered the move toward hybrid structures, and away from traditional product and brand management approaches in order to place greater emphasis on customer management:

> Teams are organized around three core processes: the consumer management team, replacing the brand management function, is responsible for customer segments; customer process teams, replacing the sales function, serve the retail accounts; and the supply management team, absorbing the logistics function, ensures on-time delivery to retailers. There is also a strategic integration team, to develop effective overall strategies and coordinate the teams. Although this team relies on deep understanding of the market, it might not be in the marketing function.

EXHIBIT 14.2
An Illustration of a Process-based Organization Structure

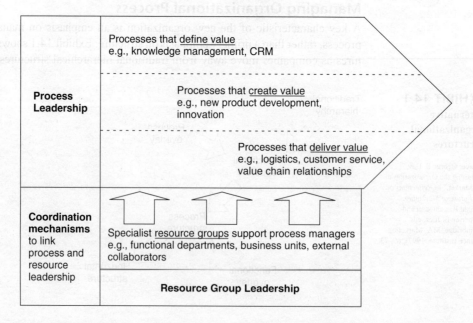

While functions remain, their roles are to coordinate activities across teams to ensure that shared learning takes place, to acquire and nurture specialized skills, to deploy specialists to the cross-functional process teams, and to achieve scale economies.[12]

Organizational Agility and Flexibility

Considerable emphasis is placed on flexibility and agility in the new organization. Markets and competitive scenarios that change rapidly place a priority on speed and responsiveness. Traditional organizational forms may be too slow in response to exploit new opportunities as they occur and respond effectively to competitive threats. Speed may require finding new ways to identify opportunities, launching initiatives with agile teams, breaking the unwritten rules of the organization, outsourcing tasks to specialists, and using the same business model again to exploit further opportunities.[13]

Toyota, for example, emphasizes "the criticality of speed," constantly focusing on flexibility and market responsiveness, and the organization is designed to be faster than that of competitors. The design of an organization affects its ability (and willingness) to respond quickly. The advantage of doing things faster than the competition is clearly established in various kinds of business. Zara's skill in moving women's apparel from design to the store in weeks instead of months enables the retailer to market new designs ahead of its competitors. At Toyota, teams of designers, engineers, product planners, workers, and suppliers are required to work face-to-face, in the process Toyota calls *obeya*—literally "big room." This dramatically cuts the time it takes to get from drawing board to showroom. It took only nineteen months to develop the 2003 Solara—well below the industry average of about three years.[14]

Organizations that set themselves up to do things faster have a competitive advantage. Business agility provides a competitive strength based on flexible technology and structures, and new working practices that allow organizations to remove bottlenecks and points of rigidity. Recall the earlier discussion of agile supply chains (Chapter 10). Increasingly organizations are being designed for agility and responsiveness.[15] In the past, organizations were designed with stability in mind. The priority now is to build organizations which are capable of changing. One of the strengths of self-managing teams and small, close-to-the-customer business units, is greater organizational responsiveness and speed in adapting to changed circumstances.[16]

Employee Motivation

The effective design of new organizations is, in part, related to the motivation and aspirations of the people who work at all levels in the company. Booz, Allen & Hamilton research underlines that for talented people in Western companies today, financial incentives matter far less than non-financial factors—esteem, a challenging and varied job, the chance to work in teams, the opportunity to interact with interesting people. It is dangerous to assume that people are motivated only by money and to design organizations and processes on that basis. Instead, IBM has shifted the emphasis in annual bonus schemes from the performance of the employee's individual unit and toward that of the company as a whole. At Toyota, most of a manager's bonus is linked to the performance of the business in the whole of his/her region, and only a small part to individual performance.

The life aspirations of individuals entering professional and management roles are also significant. Designing organizations in which the most talented individuals cannot work productively is a danger with conventional approaches. The RELATIONSHIP FEATURE describes some of the issues faced in working with and managing employees from the "MySpace Generation."

The MySpace Generation lives, buys, plays, and socializes online. Social networking websites are a way of life. Currently in their teen years, the MySpace Generation will be the staff of our major organizations within a few years.

The children of the baby-boomers—twentysomethings or Generation Y—are already marching into the workplace.

They are ambitious, demanding, and question everything. They are different. They have tattoos and piercings. When it comes to loyalty, the company is the last on the list. They are never far from rock music. They always seem to be at the gym. The idea of a "work ethic" doesn't work. Home is the only safe place to be (so many continue living with their parents). If they don't like the job—they quit (because the worst that can happen is moving back home).

Work/life balance is very important. They want interesting work from the first day, and for people to notice and react to their performance.

They are expected to be the most high-maintenance workforce in the history of the world, but also the most high-performing.

Sources: Jessi Hempel, "The MySpace Generation," *BusinessWeek,* December 12/19 2005, 63–70. Nadira A. Hira, "You Raised Them, Now Manage Them," *Fortune,* May 28 2007, 26–33.

Organizing for Market-Driven Strategy

Trends in organizational strategy provide the context for examining the organizational conditions favorable to market-driven strategy. We consider the link between strategic marketing and organization structure, moves to enhance the alignment of organizations with their markets, the role of marketing as an organizational process owner as well as a functional specialization, and particularly the cross-functional role of marketing in achieving internal partnerships and integration of company resources around customer value.

Strategic Marketing and Organization Structure

As strategies change and evolve in a company, it is increasingly important to examine organizational issues in the implementation of marketing strategy. Across many business sectors, several factors lead companies to re-think how they organize for effective marketing—to counter performance shortfalls by better integration; to globalize products and brands effectively; to bring sales and marketing closer together; to focus on brands and products.

Organizational change is a continuing process in many companies. We have described the trend away from vertical structures toward flat horizontal structures with greater emphasis on managing processes (for example, new product development) and less emphasis on functional specialization. These observations are highly relevant to implementing market-driven strategy effectively.

Aligning the Organization with the Market[17]

Organizations are evolving toward closer alignment with their markets as a result of new marketing strategies and increasingly assertive customers demanding more accountability and responsiveness. Market change is reinforcing the customer dimension of organization, and companies are structuring operations around customer groups. Research suggests three stages of evolution: (1) improving alignment through informal lateral integration; (2) using integrating mechanisms such as key account or segment managers; (3) full customer alignment with customer-based units at the front of the organization or matrix structures around segments. Many organizations will stop short of the third phase.

In stage 1, the functional or product organization is retained, but sales or product management takes informal steps to cross silos and solve customer problems. Stage 2 gains partial alignment with customers through integrating functions like global account coordinators and market segment specialists breaking away from a focus on products. The third stage involves comprehensive approaches to get full structural alignment with the market, using customer-based front-end units or matrix structures with segment champions. The customer-based front-end unit structure is illustrated in Exhibit 14.3. Fidelity Investment developed this model to cope with the challenges of selling to discount brokers and independent financial advisers—dedicated groups were created to provide personalized service and services to key customer segments, while product groups continued to develop and manage an array of funds and financial services that could be easily bundled.

Market alignment by matrix structures is illustrated by Sony in the U.S. consumer electronics market. With five product divisions operating largely independently, Sony overlaid a market segment structure onto the existing product structure. The head of each product business unit was given added responsibility for one of the market segments—the head of digital imaging products became the champion for the "double income, no kids" segment and the head of personal mobile products was champion for the "Generation Y" consumer segment. The dual focus for these executives was supported through the reward system.

Structural alignment around markets is likely to be disruptive and add organizational costs, and executives should consider the imperatives to:

- Have a strategic rationale for realignment, such as providing better solutions to customers or gaining deeper knowledge of their needs.
- Keep everyone focused on the customer experience, with clear accountabilities for the quality of relationships with major customers, integration, and tracking lost customers.
- Adjust the pace of alignment to allow for anticipated obstacles and ways to overcome them.
- Keep realigning in response to market change and advances in technology.

Marketing Functions Versus Marketing Processes

While the existence of conventional marketing functions or departments remains important to achieve efficiency in carrying out operational marketing tasks, there is increasing evidence

EXHIBIT 14.3
Customer-Based Front-End Organization

Source: Adapted from George S. Day, *Aligning the Organization with the Market,* Marketing Science Institute Report 05–003 (Cambridge MA: Marketing Science Institute, 2005).

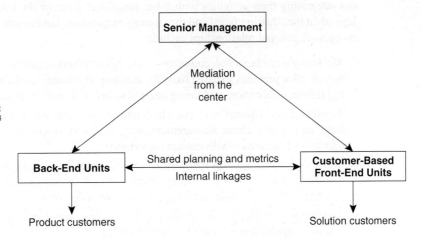

that when considering marketing strategy, marketing should be seen as a set of processes that work across the organization and its partners to shape and implement strategy.[18] Indeed, some of the most admired firms in the world underline the strategic importance of marketing processes. At GE, marketing was a "lost function" under Jack Welch, while incoming CEO Jeff Immelt has revitalized the marketing organization as a driver of growth. At Microsoft, Steve Balmer emphasizes the marketing organization's lead role in making Microsoft "value propositions shine through for customers." At Intel the transition is from an engineering mind-set of relentlessly increasing microprocessor speed, to a marketing-led approach of designing microprocessors for specific customer end-use applications like mobility and entertainment.[19] A process perspective underlines the cross-functional role of marketing.

Marketing as a Cross-Functional Process

In providing leadership in market-driven strategy, marketing is increasingly seen as a cross-functional activity working across traditional organizational boundaries to develop and implement strategy. Challenges of internal partnership between functional specialists and achieving integration of organizational capabilities around customer value creation are highly relevant.

The Challenge of Integration

There have been several problems related to integration between marketing and other activities in companies. Effectiveness depends on developing strong linkages between marketing and other functional units. This may involve a variety of approaches.

Many traditional approaches to organization design have hindered the ability of companies to coordinate and integrate activities around customer needs. In some organizations there are major barriers to effective communication between marketing and other units, leading to misunderstanding and conflict, such as poor use of market information by R&D departments for reasons of rivalry and political behavior.[20] Additionally, the integration problem may be exacerbated by "ownership" of key activities by other functions: (1) Customer Relationship Management systems span departments and systems to integrate customer knowledge; (2) critical new product "pipelines" may place priority on leveraging R&D capabilities faster than the competitor; (3) the implementation of electronic commerce may leave traditional marketing behind; and (4) many of the people and processes that impact on customer value are outside the control of the marketing area.[21]

Marketing's Links to Other Functional Units

Increasingly, marketing and sales professionals must display superior skills in coordinating and integrating their activities with other functional areas of the business. Priorities will depend on the situation faced and the strategy in question, but illustrative examples of critical cross-functional relationships include:

- *Marketing and Finance/Accounting*—viewing customers as assets which impact on shareholder value provides a shared basis for avoiding traditional conflicts dialogue on marketing resource allocation, and lining internal systems up with customer value imperatives.
- *Marketing and Operations*—the challenge is matching internal capabilities in operations and supply chain management, e.g., in speed, flexibility, quality management, operational systems—with market opportunities.
- *Marketing and Sales*—in many situations the sales force represents the ability of the company to implement marketing strategy, which is constrained by lack of "buy-in," and traditional sales management practices which do not support strategic change.
- *Marketing and R&D*—the challenge is building structures to link innovation and research capabilities with market opportunities.

- *Marketing and Customer Service*—customer service operations may represent the most important point of contact between a customer and the company and impact directly on customer perceptions of value, mandating alignment with strategic initiatives.
- *Marketing and Human Resource Management*—the key issue may be building competitive advantage through the quality of the people in the company, with major implications for aligning processes of recruitment, selection, training, development, evaluation, and reward with business strategy requirements.[22]

Effective cross-functional working is the key to many of the examples we have discussed. Many successful companies display characteristics of cross-functional effectiveness: Costco, Zara, and Toyota are illustrative. This capability may be a key attribute of the market-led company of the future. The move towards process-based organizations further underlines this requirement.

Approaches to Achieving Effective Integration

Organizational mechanisms for enhancing the quality of marketing's links with other functional units include: effective cross-functional teams, shared goals, superior internal communications, high levels of top management support, and attention to resolving internal disputes and conflicts.[23] Several approaches to building effective integration may be considered as part of organization design. Formal mechanisms for integration include:

- Relocation and design of facilities to encourage communication and exchange of information.
- Personnel movement using joint training and job rotation to facilitate managers' understanding of other functions.
- Reward systems that prioritize higher levels goals (e.g., company profits from a cross-functional project) not just functional objectives.
- Formal procedures, for example, requiring coordinated input from marketing, finance, operations, and IT to complete project documentation.
- Social orientation facilitating non-work interaction between personnel from different functions.
- Project budgeting to centralize control over financial resources so they are channeled, for example, to a project or process team not to a functional department.[24]

Evidence relating to the effectiveness of these approaches is mixed. Nonetheless, the initiatives emphasize the need to examine more than simple structural choices in designing the effective market-driven organization. Interestingly, several routes to enhanced integration, for example, increased personal communication, spatial proximity, or social interaction, will become progressively more difficult in the intranet-based, hollow organization. In such cases, integration issues may become a high priority for management attention.

Interestingly, a number of companies adopt inclusion organization approaches to leveraging integration. JetBlue, the low-cost airline, has changed its chain of command so that technology reports to the marketing department. Similarly, chemicals giant DuPont has moved its technology department from its operations and services division to marketing and sales, and toy-maker Mattel has long had IT reporting to marketing. The logic is that locating IT within marketing removes an integration barrier and ensures that technology will be used to solve customer problems.[25]

Building the "customer-engaged" organization may be one of the most formidable challenges facing marketing executives. Approaches to addressing the need to build customer focus throughout a company may include creating a Customer Value Guide that conveys the essence of what represents value to customers, for the benefit of decision-makers in the organization, and conducting "customer engagement" workshops with all employees to focus thinking on customer value.[26]

Marketing Departments

Marketing capabilities and competencies in an organization are important resources that create value in a company. One topical issue is whether those resources should be grouped into a formal marketing function and where this should be located in the organization. The existence of a marketing department does not necessarily indicate that a company displays high levels of market orientation. Nor does the absence of a formal marketing department indicate that a company is not market oriented. Conventionally, we expect that a market-driven company will have some formal marketing organization, but there are some indications that forward-thinking companies are revisiting this issue. P&G, for example, has moved from conventional marketing departments to its customer business development structure to focus marketing and selling resources on major retailer customers.

Important organization design choices relate to the centralization or decentralization of marketing tasks and activities, the integration or diffusion of marketing responsibilities, organizing contingencies, and the role to be played by marketing in the organization.[27]

Centralization Versus Decentralization

Companies with two or more business units may have corporate marketing organizations as well as business unit marketing organizations. Corporate involvement may range from a coordinating role to one in which the corporate staff has considerable influence on business unit marketing operations. Also, the chief marketing executive and staff may participate in varying degrees in strategic planning for the enterprise and the business unit. The corporate role of marketing is influenced by top management's approach to organizing the corporation, as well as the nature and complexity of business operations. Marketing strategy decisions are typically centered at the business-unit and product-market levels. Even so, it is very important for the top management team to include strategic marketing professionals. The market-driven nature of business strategy requires the active participation of marketing professionals.

A major organizational design issue is whether marketing tasks and activities should be centralized (at the corporate level) or decentralized (at the business unit level) in a multi-business organization.

Research suggests that when marketing tasks across business units are highly related, the marketing function tends to be centralized at the corporate level.[28] Nonetheless, there are also signs that organizations are increasingly structuring marketing activities around customer-centric arrangements, such as key account teams and segment managers in a less centralized format.[29] Influenced by the general trend in organizations toward decentralized management approaches, many corporations are moving marketing functions away from the corporate level to the business unit level. Decentralization is a better way to cope with growing product and market complexity, and to enhance speed of response to market changes.[30] The available evidence suggests that there is no one best way to structure marketing activities and that managers should consider strategic requirements as well as the capabilities and cultural requirements for the two approaches.[31]

Integration or Diffusion

Another major issue concerns whether marketing tasks and activities should be diffused (performed by people in different departments/functions) or focused (performed by individuals belonging to the marketing department/function). Research suggests that in practice there are signs that in many organizations marketing activities are moving from the marketing function to cross-functional teams and other functions (such as R&D or sales).[32] The integration of marketing functions associated with becoming market oriented, may be followed by the *dis*integration of marketing functions to achieve greater cross-functional effectiveness in delivering superior value to customers. The diffusion of marketing activities across multiple functions is more common in market-oriented businesses serving business customers, and operating in uncertain markets with uncertain technologies.[33]

There are attractions in achieving a "customer mind-set" among all employees in a firm, not just marketing employees, suggesting that marketing tasks and activities should be the responsibility of multiple functions, not just the marketing department.[34]

Contingencies for Organizing

The formalization of marketing as an organizational function and the centralization/decentralization and diffusion/focused possibilities underline the need to consider organizational and market contingencies to guide decisions. For example, a classic view of four organizing concepts is shown in Exhibit 14.4. Note the usage context and performance characteristics of each structure. Since strategy implementation may involve a usage context that combines two of the structures, trade-offs are involved. The adopted organization structure may facilitate the implementation of certain activities and tasks. For example, the bureaucratic form should facilitate the implementation of repetitive activities such as telephone processing of air travel reservations and ticketing. Once management analyzes the task(s) to be performed and the environment in which they will be done, it must determine its priorities. For example, is the objective performance and short-run efficiency or adaptability and longer-term effectiveness:

> Activities in different categories should be structured differently whenever feasible. Some firms appear to be moving in this direction, as shown by reports of cuts in corporate staff departments, the shifting of more planning and decision-making authority to individual business unit and product-market managers, and the increased use of ad hoc task forces to deal with specific markets or problems—all of which indicate a shift toward more decentralized and flexible structures.[35]

Corporate culture may also have an important influence on implementation. For example, implementing new strategies may be more difficult in highly structured, bureaucratic organizations. General Motors' difficulty in responding to the global competitive pressures during the last decade is illustrative. Management should consider its own management style, accepted practices, specific performance of executives, and other unique characteristics in deciding how to design the organization.

Evaluating Organization Designs

The design of the marketing organization is influenced by several contingencies: market and environmental factors, the characteristics and capabilities of the organization, and the marketing strategy followed by the firm. In evaluating the adequacy of an organization's design, the following factors provide guidelines:

- The organization should correspond to the strategic marketing plan. For example, if the plan is structured around markets or products, then the marketing organizational structure should reflect this same emphasis.
- Coordination of activities is essential to successful implementation of plans, both within the marketing function and with other company and business unit functions. The more highly specialized that marketing functions become, the more likely coordination and communications will be hampered.
- Specialization of marketing activities leads to greater efficiency in performing the functions. As an illustration, a central advertising department may be more cost-efficient than establishing an advertising unit for each product category. Specialization can also provide technical depth. For example, product or application specialization in a field sales force will enable salespeople to provide consultative-type assistance to customers.

EXHIBIT 14.4 Four Archetypical Marketing Organizational Forms

Source: Robert W. Ruekert, Orville C. Walker Jr., and Kenneth J. Roering, "The Organization of Marketing Activities: A Contingency Theory of Structure and Performance," *Journal of Marketing,* Winter 1985, 20. Reprinted with permission of the American Marketing Assocation.

	Market versus Hierarchical Organization	
	Internal Organization of Activity	**External Organization of Activity**
	Bureaucratic Form	Transactional Form
Centralized Formalized Nonspecialized	*Appropriate usage context* • Conditions of market failure • Low environmental uncertainty • Tasks that are repetitive, easily assessed, requiring specialized assets *Performance characteristics* • Highly effective and efficient • Less adaptive *Examples in marketing* • Functional organization • Company or division sales force • Corporate research staffs	*Appropriate usage context* • Under competitive market conditions • Low environmental uncertainty • Tasks that are repetitive, easily assessed, with no specialized investment *Performance characteristics* • Most efficient form • Highly effective for appropriate tasks • Less adaptive *Examples in marketing* • Contract purchase of advertising space • Contract purchase of transportation of product • Contract purchase of research field work
Structural Characteristics	Organic Form	Relational Form
Decentralized Nonformalized Specialized	*Appropriate usage context* • Conditions of market failure • High environmental uncertainty • Tasks that are infrequent, difficult to assess, requiring highly specialized investment *Performance characteristics* • Highly adaptive • Less efficient *Examples in marketing* • Product management organization • Specialized sales force organization • Research staffs organized by product groups	*Appropriate usage context* • Under competitive market conditions • High environmental uncertainty • Tasks that are nonroutine, difficult to assess, requiring little specialized investment *Performance characteristics* • Highly adaptive • Highly effective for nonroutine, specialized tasks • Less efficient *Examples in marketing* • Long-term retainer contract with advertising agency • Ongoing relationship with consulting firm

- The organization should be structured so that responsibility for results will correspond to a manager's influence on results. While this objective is often difficult to fully achieve, it is an important consideration in designing the marketing organization.

- Finally, one of the real dangers in a highly structured and complex organization is the loss of flexibility. The organization should be adaptable to changing conditions. The rationale for the venture marketing organization, considered later in the chapter, is illustrative.

Since some of these characteristics conflict with others, organizational design requires looking at priorities and balancing conflicting consequences.

Structuring Marketing Resources

Whether marketing activities are centralized or decentralized, and whether they involve a fully integrated marketing department or a marketing unit with more limited responsibilities, structuring the array of marketing resources in a formal organization design involves important management choices. We consider several structuring issues, before discussing traditional organization designs available, and several of the newer marketing roles being identified in some companies.

Structuring Issues

Functional specialization is often the first consideration in selecting an organizational design for marketing resources. Specialist functions are attractive because they develop expertise, resources, and skills in a particular activity. Emphasis on functions may be less appropriate when trying to direct activities toward market targets, products, and customers. Market targets and product scope also influence organizational design. When two or more targets and/or a mix of products are involved, companies often depart from functional organizational designs that place advertising, selling, research, and other supporting services into functional units. Similarly, distribution channels and sales force considerations may influence the organizational structure adopted by a firm. For example, the marketing of home entertainment products targeted to business buyers of employee incentives and promotional gifts might be placed in a unit separate from a unit marketing the same products to consumer end-users. Geographical factors have a heavy influence on organization design because of the need to make the field supervisory structure correspond to how the sales force is assigned to customers.

The major forms of marketing organizational designs are *functional, product, market,* and *matrix* designs.

Functional Organizational Design

This design assigns departments, groups, or individuals, responsibility for specific activities, such as advertising and sales promotion, pricing, sales, marketing research, and marketing planning and services. Depending on the size and scope of its operations, the marketing organization may include some or all of these activities. The functional approach is often used when a single product or a closely related line is marketed to one market target.

Product-Focused Design

The product mix may require special consideration in the organizational design. New products often do not receive the attention they need unless specific responsibility is assigned to the planning and coordination of the new-product activities. This problem may also occur with existing products when a business unit has several products and there are technical and/or application differences. We examine several approaches to organizing using a product focus.

Product/brand management

The product or brand manager, sometimes assisted by one or a few additional people, is responsible for planning and coordinating various business functions for the assigned products. Typically, the product manager does not have authority over all product-planning activities but may coordinate various product-related activities. The manager usually has background and experience in research and development, engineering, or marketing and is normally assigned to one of these departments. Product managers' titles and responsibilities vary widely across companies.

Product management structures continue to be used in many organizations even though there is a trend toward process designs.[36] The product management system assigns clear responsibility for product performance, and the system encourages coordination across business functions. Nonetheless, the product focus may take emphasis away from the market. Also, there may be a short-term focus on financial performance. An example of a product-focused structure is shown in Exhibit 14.5.

Category Management

Associated with the Efficient Consumer Response approach to supply chain management (Chapter 10), one development in product-focused organization is the adoption of category management structures. Categories are groups of products defined by consumer purchase behavior patterns. For example, Nestle and Interbrew are working with retailers to develop categories structures within which their brands can be developed and restructuring their organizations around the categories.[37]

Venture Teams

The venture team requires the creation of an organizational unit to perform some or all of the new-product-planning functions. This unit may be a separate division or company created specifically for new product or new business ideas and initiatives. Venture teams offer several advantages, including flexibility and quick response. They provide functional involvement and full-time commitment, and they can be disbanded when appropriate. Team members may be motivated to participate on a project that offers possible job advancement opportunities.

New Product Teams

The new product team is similar to a venture team in that it is comprised of functional specialists working on a specific new product development project. The product team has a high degree of autonomy with the authority to select leaders, establish operating procedures, and resolve conflicts. The team is formed for a specific project, although it may be assigned subsequent projects. Successful innovation at 3M is based on cross-functional new product teams.[38]

Factors that often influence the choice of a product organization design are the kinds and scope of products offered, the amount of new-product development, the extent of coordination necessary among functional areas, and the management and technical problems previously encountered with new products and existing products. For example, a firm with an existing functional organizational structure may create a temporary team to manage and coordinate

EXHIBIT 14.5
Product-Focused Structure

Source: Donald R. Lehmann and Russell S. Winer, *Product Management.* 2nd ed. (Chicago: Richard D. Irwin, 1997), 4. Copyright © The McGraw-Hill Companies. Used with permission.

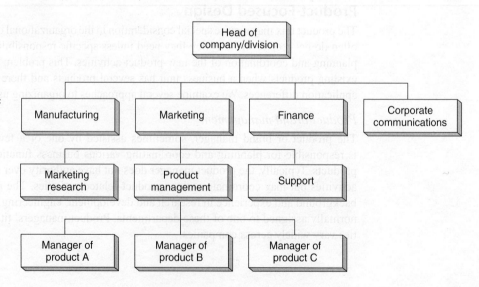

the development of a major new product. Before or soon after commercial introduction, the firm will shift responsibility for the product to the functional organization. The team's purpose is to allocate initial direction and effort to the new product so that it is properly launched.

Market-Focused Design

This approach is used when a business unit serves more than one market target (e.g., multiple market segments) and customer considerations are an important factor in the design of the marketing organization. For example, the customer base often affects the structuring of the field sales organization. A key advantage of this design is its customer focus.[39] Greater use of organization designs that focus on customer groups is predicted.[40] A potential conflict may exist if a company also has in place a product management system. Some firms appoint market managers and have a field sales force that is specialized by type of customer. The market manager operates much like a product manager, with responsibility for market planning, research, advertising, and sales force coordination. Market-oriented field organizations may be deployed according to industry, customer size, type of product application, or in other ways to achieve specialization to end-user groups. Conditions that suggest a market-oriented design are: (1) multiple market targets being served within a strategic business unit; (2) substantial differences in the customer requirements in a given target market; and/or (3) each customer or prospect purchasing the product in large volume or dollar amounts.

Matrix Design

This design utilizes a cross-classification approach to emphasize two different factors, such as products and marketing functions (Exhibit 14.6). Field sales coverage is determined by geography, whereas product emphasis is obtained using product managers. In addition to working with salespeople, product managers coordinate other marketing functions such

EXHIBIT 14.6
A Marketing Organization Based on a Combination of Functions and Products

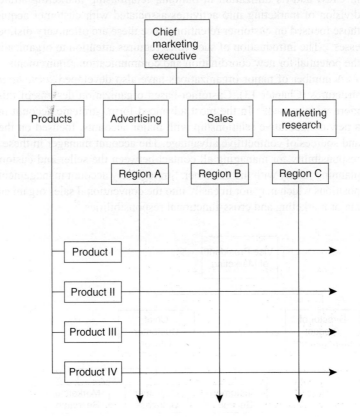

as advertising and marketing research. Of course, other matrix schemes are possible. For example, within the sales regions shown in Exhibit 14.6, salespeople may be organized by product type or customer group. Also, marketing functions may be broken down by product category, such as appointing an advertising supervisor for Product II.

Combination approaches are effective in that they respond to important influences on the organization and offer more flexibility than the other traditional approaches. A major difficulty with these designs is establishing lines of responsibility and authority. Product and market managers frequently complain that they lack control over all marketing functions even though they are held accountable for results. Nevertheless, matrix approaches are popular, so their operational advantages must exceed their limitations.

New Marketing Roles

As we discussed early in the chapter, the use of self-managing employee teams, emphasis on business processes rather than activities, and the application of information technology are creating major changes in organization design. There are several new roles and organizing approaches relevant to structuring marketing resources.

New Marketing Specializations

The identification of *new specialist roles* in marketing processes raises the question of appropriate location in the organization structure (within the marketing function or more broadly in the business unit). Examples include the chief knowledge or information officer in marketing, and the possible role of the chief relationship officer. Some companies have, for example, appointed a chief customer officer, whose job focuses only on customer interactions and the customer experience. One possible structure for the marketing organization of the future reflecting these concerns is illustrated in Exhibit 14.7. Large investment in CRM and its utilization in building relationship marketing strategy, may lead to the division of marketing into activities associated with customer acquisition processes and those focused on customer retention, since these are often very distinct and different processes.[41] The introduction of such roles requires attention to organizational positioning and the potential for new coordination and communication requirements.

A number of major organizations have also developed *strategic account management* structures (Chapter 13). Customer-based organization designs of this kind are becoming more widely used.[42] In the most advanced form, strategic account management involves a new collaborative relationship with major accounts, focused on the customer's strategy and sources of competitive advantage. The account manager in these cases has a strategic responsibility for managing all contact between the seller and customer organization and planning jointly with the customer. Strategic key account management positions are senior positions which may not fit easily into the conventional sales organization and which carry major marketing and cross-functional responsibilities.[43]

EXHIBIT 14.7
Illustration of a New Organization Structure for Marketing

Source: Adapted from Russell S. Winer, "A Framework for Customer Relationship Management," *California Management Review* Vol. 43, no. 4, 2001, 89–105.

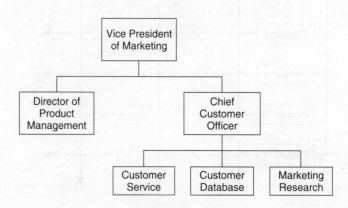

In many companies an additional issue is where and how to position *Internet-based channels* in the marketing organization and the business unit. Early approaches isolated Internet channels from the rest of the business, while the real challenge for most companies is how to integrate the Internet into the core business.[44] Major "bricks and clicks" companies like Staples are rethinking the policy of separating their dot.com operations from the rest of the business, and bringing them back into the main operation.[45] The Web operations of successful retailers like Walgreens in the U.S. and Tesco in the U.K. are closely integrated with their retail stores. Several important organizational issues are involved in achieving that integration. Some illustrations of the impact of the Internet on marketing organization designs are shown in the INTERNET FEATURE.

Venture Marketing Organizations

An interesting approach adopted by some companies extends the idea of venture teams, as a way of responding to high priority opportunities faster than conventional organizational approaches allow. The Venture Marketing Organization (VMO) adopts the principles of venture capitalism: they aggressively seek new opportunities, allocate resources to the best, but cut their losses as they go. The VMO has a number of defining characteristics:

- Fluidity—to keep pace with the market, the VMO continually reconfigures, with little formal structure or fixed membership in opportunity teams.
- People are allocated roles not jobs—the issue is managing talent within the organization and applying it to promising opportunities.
- Fast decision making is made from the top.
- Opportunity identification is everyone's job.

Resources are focused on the highest payback opportunities and losers are quickly pruned.[46]

The impressive impact of a VMO-style approach to new market opportunities at Starbucks is described in the INNOVATION FEATURE.

Partnering with Other Organizations

Selecting or modifying marketing organization design should take into consideration the trade-offs between performing marketing functions within the organization and having external organizations perform the functions. For example, many organizations are outsourcing all or some of their sales functions to third parties. In 1999, Intel broke with its tradition of employee salespeople, and committed a segment of its market to outsourced sales organizations. By 2003, Intel was using twenty-five outsourcers to generate $800 million in sales on four continents.[47]

The discussion of relationship strategies in Chapter 7 examines the use of partnering to perform various business functions. Contractual arrangements are often made for advertising and sales promotion services, marketing research, and telemarketing. Services are also available to perform marketing functions in international markets. Outsourcing various business functions is an active initiative in may companies due to cost reduction pressures, availability of competent services, increased flexibility, and shared risk. There are various marketing functions that may be provided by independent suppliers. Examples include telemarketing, database marketing, field sales, logistics, website design and management, and information services.

Internal units provide more control of activities, easier access to other departments, and greater familiarity with company operations. The commitment of the people to the organization is often higher since they are part of the corporate culture. The limitations of internal units include difficulty in quickly expanding or contracting size, lack of experience in other business environments, and limited skills in specialized areas such as advertising, marketing research, Web design, and database management.

External organizations offer specialized skills, experience, and flexibility in adapting to changing conditions. These firms may have lower costs than an organization that performs the

Internet Feature

Impacts of the Internet on Organization Designs

- The Internet requires attention to revision of the whole of the organization's structure, systems and processes, and new managerial roles and practices may be mandated by the Web.
- Forrester Inc. research suggests that companies have made little progress in building the organizational structures needed to manage Internet-based business, and for many this remains an important challenge to be addressed.

Organizational issues reflecting the impact of the Internet on company processes will include:

- Fast access to information from any location in the organization and remote access from distributed locations for salespeople, distributors, customers and partner organizations.
- Accelerated trends towards flatter organizations with whole levels of management removed to achieve faster response to market change.
- Virtual teams working on projects across geographical and traditional organizational boundaries.
- New integrated approaches to Supplier Relationship Management (SRM) and Customer Relationship Management (CRM) systems.
- Managing and controlling the outsourcing of more business processes and activities to specialist third party suppliers.

Sources: Jill Kickul and Lisa Gundry, "Breaking Through Boundaries for Organizational Innovation: New Managerial Roles and Practices in E-Commerce Firms," *Journal of Management,* Vol. 27 No. 3, 2001, 347–361. Nicole Lewis, "E-Biz Goals Thwarted By Lack of Structure, Skills," *Ebn,* January 22, 2001, 64.

function(s) internally. Obtaining services outside the firm also has limitations, including loss of control, longer execution time, greater coordination requirements, and lack of familiarity with the organization's products and markets. Identifying core competencies, coordinating relationships, defining operating responsibilities, establishing good communications, and monitoring and evaluating performance are essential to gaining effective use of external organizations.

Networked Organizations

The marketing coalition company has been proposed as another new organization form for marketing.[48] The marketing coalition company is an horizontally aligned organization acting as the control center for organizing a network of specialist firms. The core of this organization is a functionally specialized marketing capability that coordinates a network of independent functional units. They perform such functions as product technology, engineering, and manufacturing. No pure forms of the marketing coalition company are known to exist, although several Japanese companies have certain characteristics of the coalition company.

The marketing coalition design is an example of a network organization. Networks are groups of independent organizations that are linked together to achieve a common objective.[49] They are comprised of a network coordinator and several network members who typically are specialists. Network organizations occur in new ventures and reformed traditional organizations. The underlying rationale for network formation is leveraging the skills and resources of the participating organizations. Many of the aspects of strategic alliances discussed in Chapter 7 are highly relevant to considering networked organizations.

Venture Marketing Organization at Starbucks

The Venture Marketing Organization (VMO) is a fluid approach to identifying new opportunities and concentrating resources on the best. Starbucks has a VMO-style approach to innovation.

- Starbucks approaches new opportunities by assembling teams whose leaders often come from the functional areas most critical to success. The originator of the idea may take the lead role only if qualified.

- If teams need skills that are not available internally they look outside. To lead the "Store of the Future" project, Starbucks hired a top executive with retail experience away from Universal Studios; and to develop its lunch service concept, it chose a manager from Marriott.

- After the new product is launched, some team members may stay to manage the venture, while others are redeployed to new-opportunity teams or return to line management. Success on a team is vital for promotion or a bigger role on another project.

- Teamwork extends to partner organizations. When pursuing a new ice cream project, Starbucks quickly realized they lacked the in-house packaging and channel management skills to move quickly. Teaming up with Dreyer's Grand Ice Cream got the product to market in half the normal time, and within four months it was the top-selling brand of coffee ice cream.

- Starbucks emphasizes the importance of identifying new opportunities throughout its organization. Anyone in the company with a new idea for an opportunity uses a one-page form to pass it to a senior executive team. If the company pursues the idea, the originator, regardless of tenure or title, is usually invited onto the launch team as a full-time member.

- In its first year, Starbucks' Frappuccino, a cold coffee drink, contributed 11 percent of company sales. The idea originated with a frontline manager in May 1994, gaining high-priority status from a five-person senior executive team in June. The new team developed marketing, packaging and channel approaches in July. A joint venture arrangement with PepsiCo was in place by August. The first wave of rollout was in October 1994, with national launch in May 1995.

- A high-level steering committee meets every two weeks to rate new opportunities against two simple criteria: impact on company revenue growth, and effects on the complexity of the retail store. The committee uses a one-page template to assess each idea, relying on a full-time process manager to ensure the information is presented consistently.

Sources: Nora A. Aufreiter, Teri L. Lawver, Candance D. Lun, "A New Way to Market," *The McKinsey Quarterly,* Issue 2, 2000, 52–61. Nora Aufreiter and Teri Lawver, "Winning the Race for New Market Opportunities," *Ivey Business Journal,* September/October 2000, 14–16.

Organizing for Global Marketing and Global Customers

Implementing the global strategies of companies creates several important organizational issues. A key issue is the degree to which products and marketing strategies and programs are standardized across domestic and international markets, as compared to being adapted to local market requirements. Of critical importance is the development of global customers—for example, in retailing and in the IT and automotive sectors.

Many strategic alliances involve global relationships (Chapter 7). Expanded use of various types of alliances is expected to continue, particularly as a way of competing internationally. The effectiveness of the alliance depends on how well operating relationships are established and managed on an ongoing basis, and how well the partners can work together. These principles are highly relevant to the organizational change involved in globalizing.

Indeed, it is clear that international experience and proven capabilities will increasingly be required for executive advancement in the twenty-first century.[50] The global marketing strategy context underlines the importance for the market-driven company of nurturing and retaining superior management talent. International experience promises to become increasingly important to marketing executives' career development.

Organizing for global marketing strategies is examined followed by a discussion of the importance of appropriate organizational designs for managing relationships with global customers. Much of the earlier material in the chapter applies to international operations. This discussion highlights several additional considerations.

Organizing for Global Marketing Strategies

The important distinction in marketing throughout the world is that buyers differ in their needs, preferences, and priorities. Since such differences exist *within* a national market, the variations between countries are likely to be greater. Brands like Budweiser beer and Levi's jeans have significantly different market positions in international markets compared to those they occupy in the U.S. Global market targeting and positioning strategies create several marketing organizational issues.

Business Functions

Global decisions concerning production, finance, and research and development are often more feasible than making the marketing decisions that span these markets. Marketing strategies often require sensitivity to cultural and linguistic differences. Foreign currencies, government regulations, and different product standards further complicate buyer-seller relationships. The important issue is recognizing when standardized marketing strategies can be used and when they must be modified.

Organizational Issues

The marketing organization selected for competing in national markets is influenced by the market *scope* (e.g., single-country, multinational, or global strategy), and by the market *entry strategy* (export, licensing, joint venture, strategic alliance, or complete ownership). The adoption of a global strategy using joint ventures, alliances, and/or complete ownership presents the most complex organizational challenge.

The marketing organization design in international operations may take one of three possible forms: (1) a global product division; (2) geographical divisions, each with product and functional responsibilities; or (3) matrix design incorporating (1) or (2) in combination with centralized functional support or instead a combination of area operations and global product management.[51] The global form corresponds to rapid growth situations for firms that have a broad product portfolio. The geographic form is used to obtain a close relationship with national and local governments. The matrix form is utilized by companies reorganizing for global competition. An example of a combination organization design is shown in Exhibit 14.8.

Coordination and Communication

Organizing marketing activities to serve international markets creates important coordination and communication requirements. Language and distance barriers complicate

EXHIBIT 14.8
**Marketing
Organization Plan
Combining Product,
Geographic, and
Functional Features**

Source: Philip R. Cateora and John L. Graham, *International Marketing,* 12th ed. (Burr Ridge, IL: McGraw-Hill/Irwin, 2005), 336. Copyright © The McGraw-Hill Companies. Used with permission.

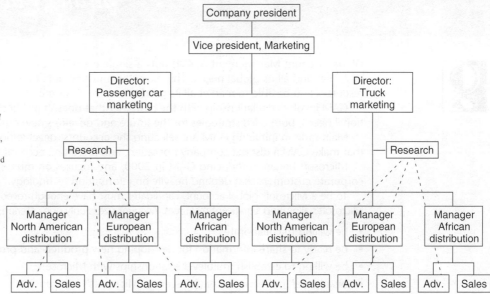

organizational relationships. For many companies, growing emphasis on effective global teamwork is replacing traditional concepts of domestic versus international divisions. Many of the constraints to organizing globally have lessened, even for companies with a limited international involvement. Enabling technology provided by the Internet and collaboration software facilitates the operation and management of global teams.

Organizing for Global Customers

A major challenge for many companies is the growing importance of global customers, which expect to buy on a global basis and to receive favorable treatment across all their worldwide locations. This challenge is illustrated by the growth of global retailing businesses and the development of global account management organizations.

The Growth of Global Customers

In the consumer goods sector, the growth of global retailers has been substantial. In consumer packaged goods, Ahold (Netherlands), Carrefour (France) and METRO (Germany) each operate in more than twenty-five countries. Aldi (Germany), Auchan (France), Rewe (Switzerland), Tesco (United Kingdom), and Wal-Mart each operate in ten or more countries. Similar trends are appararent in industries as diverse as apparel, chemicals, entertainment, financial services, and personal computers. Powerful global customers expect coverage, speed, consistent and high-quality service, and extraordinary attention from their suppliers, that reflect their buying power. These expectations require suppliers to provide a single point of contact, uniform terms of trade, and worldwide standardization of products and services.[52]

Global customers demand more uniform and transparent global prices from suppliers. In 2000, British supermarket Tesco acquired a small supermarket chain in Poland called Hit. Hit was obtaining better prices from its suppliers than was Tesco. The lack of a logical worldwide pricing structure allows global customers like Tesco to demand retrospective discounts when they discover anomalies.[53]

Global Account Management Structures

We considered earlier the challenges of managing strategic customer relationships (Chapter 7) and channel strategy (Chapter 10). However, the growth in importance of global customers has led many suppliers to develop specialized organizational units and processes

Global Account Management Strategy at Microsoft

Global Account Management (GAM) puts a single executive or team in charge of a single customer and all its global needs. This executive must be able to call on all the company's resources and be able to market all its products to the customer.

GAM involves a relationship with the customer that doesn't just find solutions for operational needs, but builds strategies for the future and develops new business.

Main tasks in initiating GAM are selecting the accounts, developing corporate structure that make GAM a distinct company operation, and recruiting account managers.

Microsoft began introducing GAM in 2000, and focuses on multi-million dollar, global corporate customers that depend heavily on information technology.

To be a Microsoft global account, candidates must have enough revenue potential to justify Microsoft's allocating significant resources. Account size is only one criterion, the candidate must:

- be willing to collaborate;
- be ready to share information for developing new products and processes;
- be willing to establish multilevel relationships with Microsoft;
- be a leader in their industry (to leverage Microsoft's reputation);
- possess superior skills and knowledge and be early adopters of new technology;
- and already have global organizational coordination.

Microsoft encourages its senior managers to develop relationships with senior decision makers in the global account and to be active in ensuring that GAM initiatives get all the resources they require from within Microsoft.

At Microsoft, account managers, called Global Business Managers, are encouraged to be innovative and have their own budgets. They work across business units, functions and organizations, and get support in marshalling resources from a headquarters team of ten, and support from a broader group of 150 people worldwide, who contribute in various ways to account planning and operational management.

Source: Adapted from Christoph Senn and Axel Thoma, "Worldy Wise: Attracting and Managing Customers Isn't the Same When Business Goes Global," *Wall Street Journal,* March 3 2007, R.5.

---

to manage their relationship. Global account management is "an organizational form and process by which the worldwide activities serving a given multi-national customer are coordinated by one person or team within the supplying company."[54]

In some companies, Global Account Managers have been developed in parallel to Strategic Account Management functions (Chapter 7). Procter & Gamble, for example, has established global customer development teams to present a single face to the global customer. P&G's global customer teams operate in parallel with the company's business units and country organizations, in the form of a matrix. The customer teams have specialists in IT, retail merchandizing, finance, sales, supply chain, marketing, and marketing research. The teams manage relationships with global retailers and develop joint plans with them, as well as working with business units and country managers to deliver against strategic goals for the customer in each product category and geographic location.

Global account management teams are multi-functional and can only operate effectively by addressing cross-functional coordination and communication around the strategy development for the global customers. Global account managers frequently report to very senior levels of the organization. Effective organizational responses to the global customer are becoming extremely important in a wide range of companies. The approach to managing global accounts at Microsoft is described in the GLOBAL FEATURE.

Increasing globalization of organizations driven by the factors we have described means that for an increasing number of marketing executives global experience will be an important step in career development. Skills in managing internationally and developing effective global customer relationships will be at a premium.

Summary

Market-driven organizations reflect customer value requirements in their design, roles and activities. This is a foundation for implementing and managing market-driven strategy. For many companies organizational change is a constant process aimed at achieving this alignment.

The market-driven organization is related in part to major trends in organization design on a broader front. Traditional structures—dominated by vertical "silos"—are increasingly inadequate to meet the requirements of new strategies in complex and turbulent environments. New organizing imperatives are driven by communications technology, the globalization of production and sales, and the transfer of responsibility to outside organizations for core business functions. Organizational designs emphasize innovation, the productivity of the knowledge worker, the management of culture in line with strategy, collaborative working inside and outside the company, informal networks, and organizational mechanisms to manage external relationships with partner organizations. The design and management of organizational processes has become a key issue in design. Organizations are being designed to achieve agility and flexibility, and to accommodate new challenges in employee engagement and motivation.

These trends in organizational design are relevant to organizing for market-driven strategy and achieving effective strategy implementation. In particular, the impact of the customer on design choices mandates consideration to the alignment of the organization with the market, and developing structures to achieve this goal. Considerable emphasis is placed on managing marketing processes that cut across traditional organizational boundaries and underline high priorities for cross-functional partnering and effective integration around the drivers of customer value.

Several important questions center on the organization of marketing resources. Design choices are faced in the centralization or decentralization of the marketing organization, and the integration of diffusion of responsibility for marketing tasks. No one way of structuring matches all situations, and important contingent factors surround this design choice. Within marketing resource groups, the major structural choices are between functional, product, market, or matrix designs. Consideration must also be given to the identification of new marketing roles and specializations as the role of marketing evolves in a company. One major issue is partnership, both internally, for example, in venture marketing organizations, but also externally in working with marketing partners. In some cases the networked organization will be an important development.

Global marketing strategy and the global customer identify several additional organizational imperatives. Global marketing frequently relies on strategic alliances. Global programs imply organizational choices regarding the international location of business functions and designing appropriate organizational forms to meet the additional challenges of international coordination and communication. The growing globalization of customers in many sectors leads to the organizational response of developing global account management structures and processes. New buyer expectations for a single point of contact with a supplier, together with uniform terms of trade and worldwide standardization of products and services frequently indicate the need for an organizational design at a global level to manage these customer relationships.

Questions for Review and Discussion

1. The chief executive of a manufacturer of direct-order personal computers is interested in establishing a marketing organization in the firm. A small sales force handles sales to mid-sized businesses and advertising is planned and executed by an advertising agency. Other than the CEO, no one inside the firm is responsible for the marketing function. What factors should the CEO consider in designing a marketing organization?

2. Of the various approaches to marketing organization design, which one(s) offers the most flexibility in coping with rapidly changing market and competitive situations? Discuss.

3. Discuss the conditions where a matrix-type marketing organization would be appropriate, indicating important considerations and potential problems in using this organizational form.

4. Assume that you have been asked by the president of a major transportation services firm to recommend a marketing organizational design. What important factors should you consider in selecting the design?

5. Discuss some of the important issues related to integrating marketing into an organization such as a regional womens' clothing chain compared to accomplishing the same task in The Limited Inc.

6. What are possible internal and external factors that may require changing the marketing organization design?

7. Is a trend toward more organic organizational forms likely in the future?

8. Summarize and chart the current and future impact of the Internet on marketing processes and organization.

9. Discuss the important organizational design issues in establishing an effective strategic alliance between organizations.

10. What are the major approaches to organizing the marketing function for international operations? Discuss the factors that may affect the choice of a particular organization design.

11. As companies begin to replace functions with processes, what are the possible effects on organizational designs?

12. What characteristics would you seek in a candidate for a Global Account Management position?

Internet Applications

A. Visit the website of the Strategic Account Management Association (www.strategicaccounts.org), and review some of the research library resources available at the site. What is the basis for suggesting that the strategic/key account manager is anything more than a senior salesperson working on major accounts—why is it any different? Where can a strategic account manager be positioned in the marketing and sales organization?

B. Go to the website of Coca-Cola Inc. (www.cocacola.com). Use the corporate information pages (Our Company, Our Brands, and Around the World) to identify the growth in brands marketed by the company and its geographic emphasis. Identify the challenges for this company in organizing marketing for a growing brand portfolio in a diverse global marketplace.

C. Consultants Booz Allen and the Association of National Advertisers have an online tool for assessing the "DNA" of marketing organizations—www.marketingprofiler.com. Visit this site and consider if the questions asked in the diagnostic provide a good basis for evaluating a marketing organization. Use the profiling diagnostic to evaluate a marketing organization that you know.

Feature Applications

A. Read the INNOVATION FEATURE "Venture Marketing Organization at Starbucks." What lessons can be learned about the organizational requirements for rapid and effective innovation?

B. Consider the STRATEGY FEATURE "The Toyota Way." Can other companies learn from the Toyota approach to managing its organization, or is the success of the approach unique to Toyota?

Notes

1. George S. Day, *Aligning the Organization with the Market,* Marketing Science Institute Report 05–003 (Cambridge, MA: Marketing Science Institute, 2005).

2. This illustration is based in part on the following sources: Patricia Van Arnum, "Procter & Gamble Moves Forward with Reorganization," *Chemical Market Reporter,* February 1, 1999, 12. John Bissell, "What Can We Learn from P&G's Troubles," *Brandweek,* July 10, 2000, 20–22. Christine

Bittar, "Cosmetic Changes," *Brandweek,* June 18, 2001, 2. Jack Neff, "P&G Outpacing Unilever in Five Year Battle," *Advertising Age,* November 3, 2003, 1–2. Jack Neff, "Well–Balanced Plan Allows P&G to Soar," *Advertising Age*, December 12 2005, 2–4.

3. Lowell L Bryan and Claudia I. Joyce, *Mobilizing Minds: Creating Wealth from Talent in the 21st-Century Organization* (New York: McGraw–Hill, 2007).

4. Peter Doyle, *Marketing Management and Strategy,* 3rd ed. (Harlow: Pearsin Education, 2002).

5. This section is adapted from *The New Organization: A Survey of the Company,* Special Report: *The Economist*, January 21, 2006.

6. Bryan and Joyce (2007), ibid.

7. Bryan and Joyce (2007), ibid.

8. Bryan and Joyce (2007), ibid.

9. George S. Day, "Aligning the Organization to the Market," in *Reflections on the Futures of Marketing,* Donald R. Lehman and Katherine E. Jocz, eds. (Cambridge MA: Marketing Science Institute, 1997), 69–72.

10. Ibid., 70–71.

11. Ibid.

12. Ibid., 72.

13. Steve Hamm, "Speed Demons," *BusinessWeek,* March 27, 2006, 68–76.

14. Kathleen Kerwin, Christopher Palmeri, and Paul Magnusson, "Can Anything Stop Toyota?" *BusinessWeek,* November 17, 2003, 62–70.

15. *Business Agility,* The Sunday Times, Special Report, February 26, 2006. *Understanding Business Agility,* Financial Times Special Report, May 8, 2003.

16. Edward Lawler and Christopher Worley, *Built to Change: How to Achieve Sustained Organizational Effectiveness* (San Francisco: Jossey-Bass, 2006).

17. This section is based on George S. Day, *Aligning the Organization with the Market,* Marketing Science Institute Report 05–003 (Cambridge MA: Marketing Science Insititute, 2005).

18. Nirmalya Kumar, *Marketing as Strategy: Understanding the CEO's Agenda for Driving Growth and Innovation* (Boston MA: Harvard Business School Press, 2004).

19. Mohan Sawney, "Five Steps That Take Marketing to the Next Level," A Microsoft and Kellogg School of Management Collaboration, www.microsoft.com/business/executive circle, 2006.

20. Elliot Maltz, William E. Souder, and Ajith Kumar, "Influencing R&D/Marketing Integration and the Use of Market Information by R&D Managers," *Journal of Business Research,* Vol. 51 No. 2, 2001, 69–82.

21. Nigel F. Piercy, *Market-Led Strategic Change: A Guide to Transforming the Process of Going to Market* (Oxford: Butterworth-Heinemann, 2002), 242.

22. James Mac Hulbert, Noel Capon, and Nigel F. Piercy, *Total Integrated Marketing: Breaking the Bounds of the Function* (New York: The Free Press, 2003).

23. Hulbert, Capon, and Piercy, 2003.

24. Elliot Maltz and Ajay Kohli, "Reducing Marketing's Conflict with Other Functions: The Differential Effects of Integrating Mechanisms," *Journal of the Academy of Marketing Science,* Fall 2000, 479–492.

25. Nick Wreden, "Marketing Organization of the Future," *www.fusionbrand.blogs.com,* June 4, 2004.

26. William Band and John Guasperi, "Creating the Customer-Engaged Organization," *Marketing Management,* July/August 2003, 35–39.

27. This section is adapted from Ajay K. Kohli and Rohit Deshpandé, *Marketing Organizations: Changing Structures and Roles, Marketing Science Institute Special Report No. 05-200* (Cambridge MA: Marketing Science Institute, 2005).

28. John P. Workman, Christian Homburg and Kjell Gruner, "Marketing Organization: An Integrative Framework of Dimensions and Determinants," *Journal of Marketing,* 62 (July) 1998, 21–41.

29. Christian Homburg, John P. Workman, and Ove Jensen, "Fundamental Changes in Marketing Organization: The Movement Toward a Customer-Focused Organizational Culture," *Journal of the Academy of Marketing Science,* 28 (Fall) 2000, 459–478.

30. Peter Doyle, *Marketing Management and Strategy,* 3rd ed. (London: Prentice-Hall, 2002).

31. Kohli and Deshpandé (2005), ibid.

32. Homburg, Workman, and Jensen (2000), ibid.

33. Workman, Homburg, and Gruner (1998), ibid.

34. Karen N. Kennedy, Felicia G. Laask, and Jerry R. Goolsby, "Customer Mind-Set of Employees Throughout the Organization," *Journal of the Academy of Marketing Science,* 30 (Spring) 2002, 159–171.

35. Quote from Robert W. Ruekert, Orville C. Walker, Jr., and Kenneth J. Roering, "The Organization of Marketing Activities: A Contingency Theory of Structure and Performance," *Journal of Marketing,* Winter 1985, 23–24.

36. Donald R. Lehmann and Russell S. Winer, *Product Management,* 4th ed. (Chicago: McGraw-Hill/Irwin, 2004).

37. "FMCG Firms Need to Focus on Category Before Brand," *Marketing,* September 27, 2001, 5.

38. Peter Doyle, *Marketing Management and Strategy,* 3rd ed. (London: Prentice-Hall, 2002).

39. Lehmann and Winer, *Product Management.*

40. Christian Homburg, John P. Workman, and Ove Jensen, "Fundamental Changes in Marketing Organization: The Movement Toward a Customer-Focused Organizational Structure," *Journal of the Academy of Marketing Science,* Vol. 28 No. 4, 2000, 459–478.

41. Russell S. Winer, "A Framework for Customer Relationship Management," *California Management Review,* Vol. 43 No. 4, 2001, 89–105.

42. Homburg, Workman, and Jensen (2000), ibid.

43. Noel Capon, *Key Account Management and Planning* (New York: The Free Press, 2001). Christian Homburg, John P. Workman, and Ove Jensen, "A Configurational Perspective on Key Account Management," *Journal of Marketing,* April 2002, 38–60.

44. Michael Porter, "Strategy and the Internet," *Harvard Business Review,* March 2001, 63–78.

45. Andrew Edgecliffe-Johnson, "Staples Brings Dotcom Back into Fold," *Financial Times,* April 4, 2001.

46. Nora A. Aufreiter, Teri L. Lawver, and Candance D. Lun, "A New Way to Market," *The McKinsey Quarterly,* Issue 2, 2000, 52–61.

47. Erin Anderson and Bob Trinkle, *Outsourcing the Sales Function: The Real Cost of Field Sales* (Mason OH: Thomson/South-Western, 2005), 55.

48. Ravi S. Achrol, "Evolution of the Marketing Organization: New Forms for Turbulent Environments," *Journal of Marketing,* October 1991, 77–93.

49. David W. Cravens, Nigel F. Piercy, and Shannon H. Shipp, "New Organization Forms for Competing in Highly Dynamic Environments, the Network Paradigm," *British Journal of Management,* Vol. 7, 1996, 203–218.

50. Morgan W. McCall and George P. Hollenbeck, *Developing Global Executives: The Lessons of International Experience* (Boston, MA.: Harvard Business School Press, 2001).

51. This discussion is based on Philip R. Cateora and John Graham, *International Marketing,* 12th ed. (Burr Ridge IL: McGraw-Hill/Irwin, 2005), 335–338.

52. Nirmalya Kumar, *Marketing as Strategy: Understanding the CEO's Agenda for Driving Growth and Innovation* (Boston MA: Harvard Business School Press, 2004).

53. Kumar (2004), ibid., 119.

54. George S. Yip and Thomas L. Madsen, "Global Account Management: The New Frontier in Relationship Marketing," *International Marketing Review,* Vol. 13 No. 3, 1996, 25.

Chapter

15

Marketing Strategy Implementation and Control

How well marketing strategy is implemented and managed on a continuing basis is the ultimate test of market targeting and positioning decisions. Putting strategy into action and making adjustments to eliminate performance gaps are essential stages in strategic marketing. Strategy and implementation are interdependent activities concerned with matching capabilities with opportunities.

The importance of effective processes for both strategy and implementation is illustrated by the strategic turnaround at carmaker Fiat in Italy. Turin saw the launch of the Fiat 500 in Europe in mid-2007—a modern mini-car designed to resemble the tiny 1957 Cinquecento that put many Italians on the road for the first time.[1] Yet when Sergio Marchionne was appointed Fiat CEO in 2004, Fiat was deeply in debt and making substantial financial losses. The reputation of Fiat vehicles was for terrible quality and reliability, considerable market share had been lost, and the Fiat Group had diversified into everything from banking and insurance to energy. In the early 2000s, Fiat actively considered leaving the auto industry altogether.

Marchionne's strategy started with a radical restructuring and dismantling of Fiat's management and bureaucracy. Young managers were taken from lower levels of the organization to take charge of new units for each of Fiat's car brands. He negotiated his way out of an alliance with General Motors, and advertisements proclaimed to customers and employees "Fiat is all-Italian again." R&D and operations were overhauled and updated—the Fiat Bravo progressed from design to production in a record eighteen months, about half the usual time.

Marchionne has launched a range of strategic relationships in cooperative ventures and technology license deals. Fiat diesel engines and transmissions are made in a joint venture with Tata in India, and used by both companies. Fiat buys petrol engines from Chinese company Chery for its cars made in China and elsewhere. A partner in Russia builds the low-cost Fiat Albea for local markets. The Fiat 500 is made alongside Ford cars at the Fiat plant in Tychy, Poland.

Strategically, Fiat is seen as a brand that has regained its sense of direction. The brand credibility does not rely on expensive cars. Fiat is succeeding with small cars, on which other manufacturers find it hard to make money, because it is very efficient at making them. Fiat is trying to position itself as a leader in cleaner cars. The new Cinquecento is a basic-segment car. The Cinquecento aims for the emotional appeal of an iconic retro brand combined with lower fuel consumption and carbon dioxide emissions.

Management has succeeded in implementing radical change in a short time period. While it is still relatively early in the change process, Fiat is back in profit, regaining market share, and is reducing its mountain of debt.

We begin by reviewing several issues relating to the development of strategic marketing plans and management of the planning process. Next, we discuss strategy implementation and building implementation effectiveness, including consideration of internal marketing approaches. Then we provide an overview of strategic evaluation and control in marketing. This is followed by an evaluation of the measurement of marketing performance, including the development of marketing metrics and the marketing management dashboard. Finally, we consider several global marketing aspects of planning, implementation and control. Marketing metrics are discussed in the Appendix.

The Strategic Marketing Planning Process

The strategic marketing plan indicates marketing objectives and the strategy and tactics for accomplishing the objectives, and guides implementation and control. The Appendix to Chapter 1 presents a step-by-step planning process. Our perspective at this stage is more on implementation and control than analysis.

The Marketing Plan Guides Implementation

The relationships between marketing strategy and the annual marketing plan are shown in Exhibit 15.1. The planning cycle is continuous. Plans are developed, implemented, evaluated, and revised to keep the marketing strategy on target. Since a strategy typically extends beyond one year, the annual plan is used to guide short-term marketing activities. An annual planning period is necessary, since several of the activities shown require action within twelve months or less and budgets also require annual planning.

A look at the marketing planning process used by a large pharmaceutical company illustrates how planning is done. Product managers are responsible for coordinating the preparation of marketing plans. A planning workshop is conducted midyear for the kickoff of the next year's plans. The workshop is attended by top management and by product, research, sales, and finance managers. The firm's advertising agency manager also participates in the workshop. The current year's plans are reviewed and each product manager presents the proposed marketing plan for next year. The workshop members critique each plan and suggest changes. Since the requested budgets may exceed available funds, priorities are placed on major budget components. Each product manager must provide strong support for requested funds. The same group meets again in ninety days and the revised plans are

EXHIBIT 15.1
Strategy and Planning Relationships

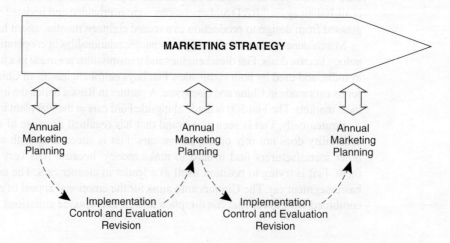

MARKETING STRATEGY

Annual Marketing Planning

Annual Marketing Planning

Annual Marketing Planning

Implementation Control and Evaluation Revision

Implementation Control and Evaluation Revision

reviewed. At this meeting the plans are finalized and approved for implementation. Each product manager is responsible for coordinating and implementing the plan. Progress is reviewed throughout the plan year and when necessary the plan is revised.

Contents of the Marketing Plan

An outline for developing the marketing plan is presented in the Appendix to Chapter 1 (Exhibit 1A-1, page 28). Many plans follow this general format. Planning activities include making a situation assessment, identifying market targets, setting objectives, developing targeting and positioning strategies, deciding on action programs for the marketing-mix components, and preparing supporting financial statements (budgets and profit-and-loss projections).

The typical planning process involves considerable coordination and interaction among functional areas. Team planning approaches like the pharmaceutical company's planning workshop are illustrative. Successful implementation of the marketing plan requires a broad consensus among various functional areas.[2] For example, a consensus is essential between product managers and sales management. Collaboration between product managers and sales managers is necessary to provide sales coverage for the product portfolio. Multiple products require negotiation in reaching agreement on the amount of sales force time devoted to various products. Recall the Chapter 14 discussion of the importance of efforts to secure the integration of marketing with other functions and units in the organization and approaches to achieving this.

Managing the Planning Process

A useful perspective is to consider planning as an organizational process in which interactions and discussions between executives shape outcomes. Examining planning as an organizational process can provide several insights into improving planning effectiveness. Planning involves more than analytical techniques and computation. Research suggests that problems faced in making marketing planning effective may be addressed by considering the behavior of executives in conducting planning and the organizational context in which planning is done, as well as by formal training in planning techniques and procedures.[3] An effective planning process is closely linked to successful implementation of plans. Exhibit 15.2 shows three dimensions of the planning process: analytical, behavioral and organizational dimensions, which should be managed consistently.

The analytical dimension of the planning process consists of the tools for systematic planning—analytical techniques, formal procedures and systems—which are needed to develop robust and tested plans and strategies. The behavioral dimension of planning is concerned with how managers perceive planning activities and the strategic assumptions

EXHIBIT 15.2
Dimensions of Marketing Planning Process

Source: Adapted from Nigel F. Piercy, *Market-Led Strategic Change: A Guide to Transforming the Process of Going to Market* (Oxford: Butterworth-Heinemann, 2002), 586.

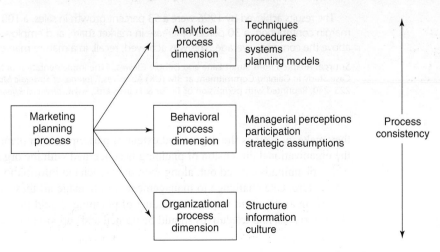

Innovation Feature

Planning for Commitment at 3M (UK)

3M is a global enterprise manufacturing more than 60,000 products from a base of 112 technology platforms, and 28 autonomous business units, of which Abrasive Systems Division (ASD) is one. ASD is 3M's original business and operates in a mature market, supplying abrasives mainly to manufacturing companies.

- At 3M (UK), the early 1990s saw ASD market share falling, accompanied by declining staff morale (compared to other company units and benchmark companies outside 3M).

- The appointment of Stuart Lane as ASD business unit manager in 1992 had three key goals: to restore sales growth to a minimum of 5 percent p.a., to return gross margin to the levels of the 1980s, and to bring the employee satisfaction level to at least the company average.

- Lane's first observations were that people felt they were not treated with respect or thanked for jobs well done; they lacked freedom to use initiative and make decisions; there was little information-sharing and too much bureaucracy.

- Lane's first decision was to double ASD's sales growth target from the 25 percent required by senior management (for 1992–1996) to 50 percent.

- In collaboration with 3M's Corporate Marketing business planners he designed what he describes as "a semi-formal, structured, iterative process" of planning for ASD.

- The new planning process started with a two-day planning workshop in spring 1992, followed by five workshops over the following three months. Lane considers the workshops as critical to developing a robust plan for ASD, but also the team-building, ownership, enthusiasm and commitment to make the plan happen, and confidence among the team members that they were going to achieve the ambitious, "stretch" goals for ASD. Lane was prepared to sacrifice some sophistication in planning in favor of simplicity and involvement to win people's support.

- The planning was linked directly to an implementation process with three key elements:

  1. A written plan, presented to management, but also reduced to an index card containing the essence of the plan in simple and memorable terms

  2. The launch of the new plan to the ASD organization at the annual sales conference, and distribution of the index cards to be kept at the front of people's diaries

  3. The introduction of Segment Action Teams (with a member of the management team as leader, but including people from sales, marketing, customer service and technical services from different levels in the organization), to take responsibility for segment-specific tactics and programmes. The Segment Action Teams have evolved into a key and permanent part of the ASD structure.

The results achieved by 1996 were a 53 percent growth in sales, a 100 percent growth in gross margin contribution, a 30 percent increase in market share, and employee satisfaction 12 percent above the company average. This was achieved, recall, in a mature market showing little growth.

Source: Adapted from Stuart Lane and Debbie Clewes, "The Implementation of Marketing Planning: A Case Study in Gaining Commitment at 3M (UK) Abrasives," *Journal of Strategic Marketing* 8, no. 3, 2000, 225–240. Reprinted with permission of Taylor & Francis Ltd., *www.tandf.co.uk/journals.*

they make, as well as the degree and extent of participation in planning. Correspondingly, the organizational dimension of planning is concerned with the organizational structure in which planning is carried out, along with the associated information resources and corporate culture. One challenge to management is to manage all these aspects of the planning process in a consistent way—the conduct of planning should fit with other organizational characteristics, and executives should be trained and supported in developing plans.

The INNOVATION FEATURE describes how a manager addresses planning process issues at an SBU of the 3M Corporation in the United Kingdom. It illustrates the advantages of linking the planning process to implementation issues.

Implementing the Strategic Marketing Plan

The effectiveness of strategy implementation determines the outcome of marketing planning. The management of the planning process may enhance implementation effectiveness, by building commitment and "ownership" of the plan and its execution. For example, actively managing the participation of different functions and executives from different specializations may improve the fit between the plan and the company's real capabilities and resources, and avoid implementation barriers. Planning and execution are interdependent parts of strategic change.[4]

Marketing managers increasingly function as boundary-spanners both internally between functional areas and externally with suppliers, organizational partners, and customers (Chapter 14). Additional efforts to make the strategy implementation process more effective are a high priority in many companies. Estimates suggest as many as 70 percent of new strategic initiatives in companies fail at the implementation stage.[5] Many companies now recognize that implementation capabilities are an important corporate capability that requires detailed management attention.[6]

Implementation Process

Research underlines the influence of two sets of factors on marketing strategy implementation: *structural* issues, including the company's marketing functions, control systems, and policy guidelines, and *behavioral* issues, concerning marketing managers' skills in bargaining and negotiation, resource allocation, and developing informal organizational arrangements.[7] We consider several organizational and interpersonal aspects of effective implementation process.

A good implementation process spells out the activities to be implemented, who is responsible for implementation, the time and location of implementation, and how implementation will be achieved (Exhibit 15.3). For example, consider the following statement from a product manager's marketing plan:

EXHIBIT 15.3
The Implementation Process

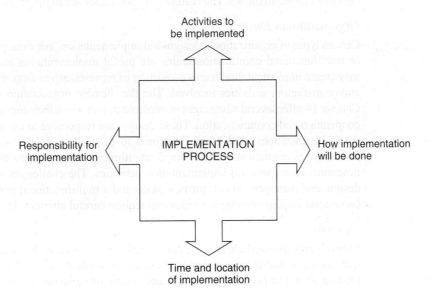

Sales representatives should target all accounts currently using a competitive product. A plan should be developed to convert 5 percent of these accounts to the company brand during the year. Account listings will be prepared and distributed by product management.

In this instance, the sales force is charged with implementation. An objective (5 percent conversion) is specified but very little information is provided as to *how* the accounts will be converted. A strategy is needed to penetrate the competitors' customer base. The sales force plan must translate the proposed actions and objective (5 percent conversion) into assigned salesperson responsibility (quotas), a timetable, and selling strategy guidelines. Training may be necessary to show the product advantages—and the competitors' product limitations—that will be useful in convincing the buyer to purchase the firm's brand.

The marketing plan can be used to identify the organizational units and managers that are responsible for implementing the various activities in the plan. Deadlines indicate the time available for implementation. In the case of the plan above, the sales manager is responsible for implementation through the sales force.

Building Implementation Effectiveness

Managers are important facilitators in the implementation process, and some are better implementers than others. Planners and implementers often have different strengths and weaknesses. An effective planner may not be good at implementing plans. Desirable implementation skills include:

- The ability to understand how others feel, and good bargaining skills.
- The strength to be tough and fair in putting people and resources where they will be most effective.
- Effectiveness in focusing on the critical aspects of performance in managing marketing activities.
- The ability to create a necessary informal organization or network to match each problem with which they are confronted.[8]

Research underlines the importance of engendering a sense of role significance among those responsible for implementation.[9] In addition to skilful implementers, several factors facilitate the implementation process. These include *organizational design, incentives,* and *effective communications.* The features of each factor are highlighted.

Organizational Design

Certain types of organizational designs aid implementation. For example, product managers or multifunctional coordination teams are useful implementation methods. Management may create implementation teams consisting of representatives from the business functions and/or marketing activities involved. The flat, flexible organization designs discussed in Chapter 14 offer several advantages in implementation, since they encourage inter-functional cooperation and communication. These designs are responsive to changing conditions.

As organizations shift from functional to process structures, the resulting changes promise to strengthen as well as complicate implementation strategies.[10] The use of cross-functional teams will aid implementation activities. The challenges of process definition, design, and management call for new skills and a multifunctional perspective, which will complicate implementation activities and require careful attention by management.

Incentives

Various rewards may help achieve successful implementation. For example, special incentives such as contests, recognition, and extra compensation are used to encourage salespeople to push a new product. Since implementation often involves teams of people, creation of team incentives may be necessary. Performance standards must be fair, and incentives should encourage something more than normal performance. Focusing incentives on the achievement of overall plan goals rather than individual efforts is particularly relevant.

Communications

Rapid and accurate movement of information through the organization is essential in implementation. Both vertical and horizontal communications are needed in linking together the people and activities involved in implementation. Meetings, status reports, and informal discussions help to transmit information throughout the organization. Computerized information and decision-support systems like corporate intranets help to improve communication' speed and effectiveness.

Problems often occur during implementation and may affect how fast and how well plans are put into action. Examples include competitors' actions, internal resistance between departments, loss of key personnel, supply chain delays affecting product availability (e.g., supply, production, and distribution problems), and changes in the business environment. Corrective actions may require appointing a person or team for trouble-shooting the problem, increasing or shifting resources, or changing the original plan.

Internal Marketing

One interesting approach to enhancing strategy implementation effectiveness is the adoption of internal marketing methods. Internal marketing involves: developing programs to win line management support for new strategies; changing the attitudes and behavior of employees working at key points of contact with customers; and gaining the commitment of those whose problem-solving skills are important to superior execution of the strategy. Research suggests that many organizations fail to deliver their planned brand experience because of insufficient internal marketing.[11] Exhibit 15.4 shows internal marketing and external marketing programs as parallel outputs from the planning process. While external marketing positions the strategy in the customer marketplace, internal marketing is aimed at the internal customer within the company. Internal marketing goals may include: promoting the external marketing strategy and how employees contribute, developing better understanding between customers and employees (regardless of whether they have direct contact), and providing superior internal customer service to support external strategy.[12]

EXHIBIT 15.4   Internal Marketing

Source: Reprinted from *Market-Led Strategic Change: A Guide to Transforming the Process of Going to Market,* Nigel F. Piercy, Copyright 2002, with permission from Elsevier.

Relationship Feature   *Nucor Corp.*

In a Rust Belt industry, Nucor has nurtured one of the most dynamic and engaged work-forces around. Nucor's flattened hierarchy and emphasis on pushing power to the front-line leads its employees to adopt the mind-set of owner-operators. Company performance in sales growth and profitability is outstanding.

Nucor Corporation's mission statement is: "Nucor Corporation is made up of 11,900 teammates whose goal is to 'Take Care of Our Customers.' We are accomplishing this by being the safest, highest quality, lowest cost, most productive and most profitable steel and steel products company in the world. We are committed to doing this while being cultural and environmental stewards in our communities where we live and work. We are succeeding by working together."

Nucor gained renown in the late 1980s for its radical pay practices, which base the majority of most workers' income on their performance. Nucor's management style is based on the belief that employees will make extraordinary efforts if you reward them richly, treat them with respect, and give them real power.

Nucor is an example of outstanding strategy execution. Managers have abandoned the command-and-control model that has dominated American business for the better part of a century. They trust their people, and do a better job of sharing corporate wealth.

Nucor places a premium on teamwork and idea-sharing between frontline workers and management, to create a highly profitable partnership.
Key elements of the Nucor approach:

- Pay for performance—even with the risks of lower income in bad times.
- Listen to the front line—the best ideas come from the factory floor.
- Push authority down in the organization.
- Protect your culture—cultural compatibility is a big focus in acquisitions.
- Try unproven technologies—it is important to take risks.

Source: Nanette Byrnes, "The Art of Motivation," *BusinessWeek,* May 1, 2006, 57–62.

An internal marketing approach involves examining each element of the external marketing program to identify what changes will be needed in the company's internal marketplace and how these changes can be achieved. If used as part of the planning process, analysis of the internal marketplace can isolate organizational change requirements (e.g., new skills, processes, organizational structures), implementation barriers (e.g., lack of support and commitment in key areas of the company), and new opportunities (by uncovering organizational capabilities otherwise overlooked).[13] Internal marketing is a promising way of identifying and resolving some of the implementation issues associated with the move from functional to process-based organizational designs (Chapter 14). The importance of gaining the buy-in of all employees and managers to strategy is illustrated in the RELATIONSHIP FEATURE, which describes the performance culture at steelmaker Nucor.

We examined market orientation as a key aspect of the market-driven company in Chapter 1. Interestingly, recent suggestions are that in addition to external market orientation of the conventional type, executives' attention should also be devoted to internal market orientation—aligning managerial behaviors with the employee behaviors and outcomes important to strategy implementation. The intention is to better align external market objectives with internal capabilities.[14]

One developing aspect of internal marketing is the opportunity to actively market plans and strategies not only inside the company, but also with partner organizations and their employees. Effective implementation may rest also on company-wide and network-wide efforts to put marketing plans and strategies into effect.

A Comprehensive Approach to Improving Implementation

One comprehensive way to deal with difficulty in the implementation of the marketing plan is to employ the balanced scorecard method.[15] This process is a formalized management control system that implements a given business unit strategy by means of activities across four areas: financial, customer, internal business process, and learning and growth (or innovation).

The balanced scorecard was created by Kaplan and Norton in reaction to the difficulties that many managers experienced when trying to implement a particular strategy. A strategy is often not defined in a manner that describes how it might be achieved. Merely communicating the strategy to employees does not provide any instruction as to what actions they must take to help achieve the strategy. More importantly, managers might even take action to the detriment of other areas in an organization when attempting to implement the strategy. The balanced scorecard provides a framework to minimize such an occurrence by encouraging implementation of a common strategy, which is communicated and coordinated across all major areas of the organization. The "balanced" component of the balanced scorecard reflects the need to consider how all areas of the organization function together to achieve a common goal of strategy implementation.

The major benefit of the balanced scorecard is that an often aggregate, broadly-defined strategy is translated to very specific actions. Through execution and monitoring of these actions, management can assess the success of the strategy and also modify and adjust the strategy if necessary. Another major benefit of the balanced scorecard methodology is that it is feasible for any business unit level strategy and provides a means to link performance evaluation to strategy implementation.

Our marketing plan outline (Exhibit 1A-1) can be adapted to the balanced scorecard format. A marketing plan is designed to achieve specific objectives through a set of strategies. Often a difficult area is determining which activities will lead to achieving market segment objectives and ensuring that activities in one area do not interfere with activities in another area. The balanced scorecard approach allows consideration of specific activities which will accomplish the objective, but also formally includes an assessment of the strategy component across all aspects of the business unit at the same time. This assessment helps to include performance measures and targets that are more long-term oriented and are not solely financially based. In this way, a consideration of activities to execute a marketing strategy would also involve how these activities affect four major areas of the company: (1) the financial perspective; (2) the customer; (3) internal business processes; and (4) learning and growth. This integrated assessment considers how the strategy would affect all major areas of the company and what performance indicators should be monitored in each of the four major areas. In this manner, it is much easier to integrate the marketing plan with the overall business strategy.

Internal Strategy-Organization Fit

It is important that the organization's competitive and marketing strategy be compatible with the internal structure of the business and its policies, procedures, and resources (Chapter 14).

Organizational Stretch

The absence of good fit between marketing strategy and organizational characteristics is likely to be a significant barrier to effective strategy implementation. "Organizational stretch" to execute strategy should be considered, that is, the degree to which structures, capabilities, systems, processes, and resource allocation may require adjustment to deliver the strategy. Marketing strategy must also be considered in the context provided by corporate strategy and business strategies being pursued by other business units, since lack of compatibility may be problematic.

The importance of internal fit is shown by Hennes and Mauritz (H&M), the largest apparel retailer in Europe and a highly successful global fashion business. H&M sells "cheap chic"—very new, very extreme, very cheap fashion clothes to younger buyers. As well as outsourcing manufacturing to a huge network of garment shops in low-wage locations, H&M is run on principles of frugality internally as well. Overheads are minimized everywhere—executives rarely fly business class; taking cabs is frowned upon; all employee cell phones were taken away in the 1990s and even now only a few key employees have them. The fit between H&M's strategy and positioning, and its internal culture and management approach may help explain its success.[16]

The Role of External Organization

The implementation of marketing strategy is affected by external organizations such as strategic alliance partners, marketing consultants, advertising and public relations firms, channel members, and other organizations participating in the marketing effort (Chapter 7). These outside organizations may present a major coordination challenge when they actively participate in marketing activities. Their efforts should be identified in the marketing plan and their roles and responsibilities clearly established and communicated. There is a potential danger in not informing outside groups of planned actions, deadlines, and other implementation requirements. For example, the organization's advertising agency account executive and other agency staff members need to be familiar with all aspects of promotion strategy as well as the major aspects of marketing strategy (e.g., market targets, positioning strategies, and marketing-mix component strategies). Withholding information from participating firms hampers their efforts in strategy planning and implementation.

The development of collaborative relationships between suppliers and producers improves implementation. Value chain management strategies encourage reducing the number of suppliers and building strong relationships (see Chapter 10). We noted earlier that internal marketing is playing a growing role in sustaining alliance and network-based organizations based on partnering. Companies that are effective in working with other organizations are likely to also do a good job with implementation inside the organization, since they have skills in developing effective working relationships. Total quality programs also encourage internal teamwork among functions.

Strategic Marketing Evaluation and Control

Marketing strategy has to be responsive to changing conditions. Evaluation and control keep the strategy on target and show when adjustments are needed. Managers need to continually monitor performance and, when necessary, revise their strategies due to changing conditions. Strategic marketing planning requires information from ongoing monitoring and evaluation of performance.

Discussion of strategic evaluation has been delayed until this stage in order to first clarify the strategic areas that require evaluation and to identify the kinds of information needed for assessing marketing performance. Thus, the first 14 chapters establish an essential foundation for building a strategic evaluation program. We now examine the impact of customer relationship management systems, give an overview of evaluation activities, and the discuss role of the strategic marketing audit.

Customer Relationship Management

Recall that the widespread adoption of customer relationship management (CRM) systems to integrate all customer data from different sources, in combination with electronic point-of-sale customer data capture, offers several new and powerful resources for strategic evaluation and control (see Chapter 4). Penetrating analysis of databases may reveal important purchasing patterns and the effect of marketing actions. The ability to identify profitability at the level of the individual customer by combining CRM and purchase data with other databases is becoming an especially important capability of strategic appraisal for marketing management. CRM systems have the potential to greatly expand the measures of performance used, and to take a more fine-grained look at marketing effectiveness related to customer acquisition and defection rates, customer tenure, customer value and worth, proportion of inactive customers, and cross-selling.[17]

Overview of Control and Evaluation Activities

Control and evaluation consumes a high proportion of marketing executives' time and energy. Evaluation may seek to (1) find new opportunities or avoid threats, (2) keep performance in line with management's expectations; and/or (3) solve specific problems that exist.

An example of a threat identified via product-market analysis for Royal Doulton, a premier brand of formal chinaware famed for its expensive dinner plates, is the move by consumers towards informal dining. This change in preferences is a major threat for Royal Doulton, which saw its sales falling at 20 percent a year in the late 1990s. An example of information to keep performance in line with management expectation is closely tracking innovation in Web applications and earnings from acquisitions at Cisco Systems Inc. Finally, evaluating the effectiveness of alternative TV commercials is an example of solving specific problems.

The major steps in establishing a strategic control and evaluation program are described in Exhibit 15.5. Strategic and annual marketing plans set the direction and guidelines for the evaluation and control process. A strategic marketing audit may be conducted when setting up an evaluation program, and periodically thereafter. Next, performance standards and metrics need to be determined, followed by obtaining and analyzing information for the purpose of performance-gap identification. Actions are initiated to pursue opportunities or avoid threats, keep performance on track, or solve a particular decision-making problem.

The Strategic Marketing Audit

A marketing audit is useful when initiating a strategic evaluation program. Since evaluation compares results with expectations, it is necessary to lay some groundwork before setting up a tracking program. The audit can be used to initiate a formal strategic marketing planning program, and it may be repeated on a periodic basis. Normally, the situation analysis is part of the annual development of marketing plans. Audits may be conducted every three to five years, or more frequently in special situations (e.g., acquisition/merger).

A guide to conducting the strategic marketing audit is shown in Exhibit 15.6. This format can be adapted to meet the needs of a particular firm. For example, if a company does not use indirect channels of distribution, this section of the audit guide will require

EXHIBIT 15.5   **Strategic Marketing Evaluation and Control**

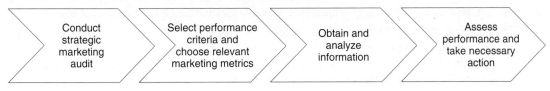

Conduct strategic marketing audit → Select performance criteria and choose relevant marketing metrics → Obtain and analyze information → Assess performance and take necessary action

EXHIBIT 15.6   **Guide to Conducting the Strategic Marketing Audit**

I. CORPORATE MISSION AND OBJECTIVES

   A. Does the mission statement offer a clear guide to the product-markets of interest to the firm?

   B. Have objectives been established for the corporation?

   C. Is information available for the review of corporate progress toward objectives, and are the reviews conducted on a regular (e.g., quarterly, monthly) basis?

   D. Has corporate strategy been successful in meeting objectives?

   E. Are opportunities or problems pending that may require altering marketing strategy?

   F. What are the responsibilities of the chief marketing executive in corporate strategic planning?

II. BUSINESS COMPOSITION AND STRATEGIES

   A. What is the composition of the business (business segments, strategic planning units, and specific product-markets)?

   B. Have business strength and product-market attractiveness analyses been conducted for each planning unit? What are the results of the analyses?

   C. What is the corporate strategy for each planning unit (e.g., develop, stabilize, turn around, or harvest)?

   D. What objectives are assigned to each planning unit?

   E. Does each unit have a strategic plan?

   F. For each unit what objectives and responsibilities have been assigned to marketing?

III. MARKETING STRATEGY (FOR EACH PLANNING UNIT)

   A. Strategic planning and marketing:

     1. Is marketing's role and responsibility in corporate strategic planning clearly specified?

     2. Are responsibility and authority for marketing strategy assigned to one executive?

     3. How well is the firm's marketing strategy working?

     4. Are changes likely to occur in the corporate/marketing environment that may affect the firm's marketing strategy?

     5. Are there major contingencies that should be included in the strategic marketing plan?

   B. Marketing planning and organizational structure:

     1. Are annual and longer-range strategic marketing plans developed, and are they being used?

     2. Are the responsibilities of the various units in the marketing organization clearly specified?

     3. What are the strengths and limitations of the key members of the marketing organization? What is being done to develop people? What gaps in experience and capabilities exist on the marketing staff?

     4. Is the organizational structure for marketing effective for implementing marketing plans?

   C. Market target strategy:

     1. Has each market target been clearly defined and its importance to the firm established?

     2. Have demand, industry, and competition in each market target been analyzed and key trends, opportunities, and threats identified?

     3. Has the proper market target strategy been adopted?

     4. Should repositioning or exit from any product-market be considered?

   D. Objectives:

     1. Are objectives established for each market target, and are these consistent with planning-unit objectives and the available resources? Are the objectives realistic?

     2. Are sales, cost, and other performance information available for monitoring the progress of planned performance against actual results?

EXHIBIT 15.6—*(continued)*

    3. Are regular appraisals made of marketing performance?

    4. Where do gaps exist between planned and actual results? What are the probable causes of the performance gaps?

  E. Marketing program positioning strategy:

    1. Does the firm have an integrated positioning strategy made up of product, channel, price, advertising, and sales force strategies? Is the role selected for each mix element consistent with the overall program objectives, and does it properly complement other mix elements?

    2. Are adequate resources available to carry out the marketing program? Are resources committed to market targets according to the importance of each?

    3. Are allocations to the various marketing mix components too low, too high, or about right in terms of what each is expected to accomplish?

    4. Is the effectiveness of the marketing program appraised on a regular basis?

IV. MARKETING PROGRAM ACTIVITIES

  A. Product strategy:

    1. Is the product mix geared to the needs and preferences that the firm wants to meet in each product-market?

    2. What branding strategy is being used?

    3. Are products properly positioned against competing brands?

    4. Does the firm have a sound approach to product planning and management, and is marketing involved in product decisions?

    5. Are additions to, modifications of, or deletions from the product mix needed to make the firm more competitive in the marketplace?

    6. Is the performance of each product evaluated on a regular basis?

  B. Channel of distribution strategy:

    1. Has the firm selected the type (conventional or vertically coordinated) and intensity of distribution appropriate for each of its product-markets?

    2. How well does each channel access its market target? Is an effective channel configuration being used?

    3. Are channel organizations carrying out their assigned functions properly?

    4. How is the channel of distribution being managed? What improvements are needed?

    5. Are desired customer service levels being reached, and are the costs of doing this acceptable?

  C. Pricing strategy:

    1. How responsive is each market target to price variations?

    2. What role and objectives does price have in the marketing mix?

    3. Should price play an active or passive role in program positioning strategy?

    4. How do the firm's pricing strategy and tactics compare to those of the competition?

    5. Is a logical approach used to establish prices?

    6. Are there indications that changes may be needed in pricing strategy or tactics?

  D. Advertising and sales promotion strategies:

    1. Have a role and objectives been established for advertising and sales promotion in the marketing mix?

    2. Is the creative strategy consistent with the positioning strategy that is being used?

    3. Is the budget adequate to carry out the objectives assigned to advertising and sales promotion?

(continued)

EXHIBIT 15.6—*(concluded)*

4. Do the media and programming strategies represent the most cost-effective means of communicating with market targets?

5. Do advertising copy and content effectively communicate the intended messages?

6. How well does the advertising program measure up in meeting its objectives?

E. Sales force strategy:

1. Are the role and objectives of personal selling in the marketing program positioning strategy clearly specified and understood by the sales organization?

2. Do the qualifications of salespeople correspond to their assigned roles?

3. Is the sales force of the proper size to carry out its function, and is it efficiently deployed?

4. Are sales force results in line with management's expectations?

5. Is each salesperson assigned performance targets, and are incentives offered to reward performance?

6. Are compensation levels and ranges competitive?

V. IMPLEMENTATION AND MANAGEMENT

A. Have the causes of all performance gaps been identified?

B. Is implementation of planned actions taking place as intended? Is implementation being hampered by marketing or other functional areas of the firm (e.g., operations, finance)?

C. Has the strategic audit revealed areas requiring additional study before action is taken?

adjustment. Likewise, if the sales force is the major part of a marketing program, then this section may be expanded to include other aspects of sales force strategy. The items included in the audit correspond to the strategic marketing plan because the main purpose of the audit is to appraise the effectiveness of strategy being followed. The audit guide includes several questions about marketing performance. The answers to these questions are incorporated into the design of the strategic tracking program.

There are other reasons besides starting an evaluation program for conducting a strategic marketing audit. Corporate restructuring may bring about a complete review of strategic marketing operations. Major shifts in business activities such as entry into new product and market areas or acquisitions may require strategic marketing audits. The growing impact of Internet-based business models may also encourage management to undertake an audit.

The results of the strategic marketing audit provide the basis for selecting performance criteria and choosing relevant marketing metrics to assess actual performance against plans and strategic intent.

Marketing Performance Measurement

As marketing plans are developed, performance criteria need to be selected to monitor performance. Specifying the information needed for marketing decision making is important and requires management's concentrated attention. In the past, marketing executives could develop and manage successful marketing strategies by relying on intuition, judgment, and experience. Successful executives in the twenty-first century need to combine judgment and experience with information and decision support systems.

The purpose of objectives is to state the results that management is seeking and also provide a basis for evaluating the strategy's success. Objectives set standards of performance. Progress toward the objectives in the strategic and short-term plans is monitored on a continuing basis. In addition to information on objectives, management requires other kinds of feedback for use in performance evaluation. Some of this information is incorporated into regular tracking activities (e.g., the effectiveness of advertising expenditures). Other information is obtained as the need arises, such as a special study of consumer preferences for different brands.

Examples of performance criteria are discussed in several chapters. Criteria should be selected for the total plan and its important components. Illustrative criteria for total performance include sales, market share, profit, expense, and customer satisfaction targets. Brand-positioning map analyses may also be useful in tracking how a brand is positioned relative to key competitors. These assessments can be used to gauge overall performance and for specific market targets. Performance criteria are also needed for the marketing mix components. For example, new-customer and lost-customer tracking is often included in sales force performance monitoring. Pricing performance monitoring may include comparisons of actual to list prices, extent of discounting, and profit contribution. Since many possible performance criteria can be selected, management must identify the key measures that will show how the firm's marketing strategy is performing in its competitive environment and point to where changes are needed. Recall that the growing impact of CRM systems offers management access to a larger number of performance measures, particularly those relating to customer retention and defection (Chapter 4).[18]

The importance of monitoring performance against objectives and demonstrating the added value achieved through marketing efforts has led many organizations to make substantial investments in systems of marketing metrics to evaluate marketing's contribution. Marketing metrics use both internal and external information sources to provide a structure for monitoring the effectiveness of marketing activities and strategies.

The Importance of Marketing Metrics

In the majority of organizations, marketing executives are under growing pressure to demonstrate their contribution to firm performance. This pressure reflects a mandate for greater accountability in the use of company resources, but also impacts the professional standing of the marketing organization within the firm. The goal is to make better causal links between marketing activities and financial returns to the business.[19] Research suggests that the ability to measure marketing performance, through appropriate systems and metrics, is significantly and positively related to company performance, profitability, stock returns, and to marketing's stature within the organization.[20]

The Use of Marketing Metrics

The quantitative measurement of marketing performance is not a simple task. Most useful marketing metrics require data from sources external to the firm. Some potentially useful measures like customer lifetime value require complex modeling and statistical analysis, which may be hard to sell to top management and other parts of the organization. Linking marketing metrics to firm performance and value has proved problematic in the past.[21]

Research from a five-country study (U.S., U.K., Germany, Japan, France) of large companies finds that the majority of companies report one or more marketing metrics to their boards of directors. Most frequently the reported measures are market share and product/service quality. Least used were more complex metrics like customer or segment lifetime value. Respondents in the study concurred that metrics reporting would increase in the near future.[22]

Critical questions to consider in developing a metrics-based reporting system related to marketing performance are:

- Does what we report to management actively probe end-user behavior (customer retention, acquisition, usage) and why consumers behave that way (awareness, satisfaction, perceived quality)?
- Are the results of end-user research routinely reported and in a format integrated with financial metrics?

- In these reports, are results compared with levels previously forecast in business plans?
- Are the results compared with the levels achieved by competitors on the same indicators?
- Is short-term performance adjusted according to the change in brand equity?[23]

Types of Marketing Metrics[24]

There are several ways of grouping marketing metrics. Some measures are associated with assessing competitive position and effectiveness with the customer, while others address product profitability, product and portfolio performance, customer profitability, sales and channel effectiveness, pricing, promotion, advertising and Web activities, and financial performance. Also, some emphasis has been placed on metrics which address brand equity as a summary measure of marketing performance. Metrics have also been developed to monitor internal market characteristics like innovation health, employee-based equity, and internal process performance. The Appendix to this chapter provides more detail concerning these different types of marketing metrics.

Selecting Relevant Metrics

The choice of the most relevant metrics is critical. Guidelines suggest that choices should be made in the light of the need to (1) measure performance relative to strategy; (2) track performance relative to competitors; (3) track performance relative to customers; (4) track performance over time; and (5) model performance (to test the impact of different elements of strategy being changed).[25]

A single performance metric is unlikely to meet these needs. The goal is to implement better ways of measuring marketing performance. Clarifying objectives and the business model (which shows the links between inputs such as financial expenditure and competitive activities and outputs in expected results) is prerequisite. Measures of these key steps, or the objectives themselves, become the metrics that should be used to monitor performance and form part of future plans. Research suggests that for a large firm eight to ten is usually about the right number of metrics, while a smaller firm will need fewer.[26]

Importantly, metrics should be chosen to reflect strategic priorities and the issues most closely linking marketing investments with profits. For example, for monitoring external market performance, footwear retailer Payless ShoeSource uses two types of marketing metrics: spending efficiency and effectiveness (e.g., ROI by advertising medium, advertising to sales spending ratios); and business building (e.g., customer traffic, ratio of loyal to new customers). On the other hand, at food company Cadbury Schweppes, in the Managing for Value program, key measures include: performance against strategic milestones, market share, advertising spending, brand and advertising awareness, average purchases, percent of total volume from new products.[27] Many major organizations are developing new sets of metrics to give top management better insight into performance against competitors and the value achieved from marketing investments.

In some cases, choice of metrics may be tied closely to specific marketing activities. For example, Shell's large expenditure on sponsoring Ferrari in Formula One motor racing underlines the need for financial justification for this expenditure. Before signing a new five-year sponsorship contract, Shell management evaluated costs and benefits in five ways:

- Comparing attitudes toward the Shell brand of those who were aware of the Ferrari link, and those who were not.
- Examining change in purchasing behavior associated with shifts in attitudes toward the brand.
- Commissioning an independent evaluation of brand value, including branding, sales, price premium, and advertising effects.

- Making country-by-country comparisons—different Shell companies had merchandized the sponsorship locally to varying extents, so if the sponsorship was profitable, those who promoted it more should have obtained more benefit.

- Surveying manager opinion and their ratings of the impact of the sponsorship on return on investment.

After top management review, Shell approved the new five-year contract for the sponsorship as an important part of the company's marketing strategy.[28]

In other situations, the selection of metrics may reflect the need to provide management with a continuous monitoring process for evaluating the effectiveness of marketing strategy.

Designing a Management Dashboard

As formal marketing performance measurement becomes more central to planning and control activities, because it documents and drives the effectiveness of marketing actions, a "dashboard" for senior managers is often becoming integral. The dashboard takes its name by comparison with the instrument panel of an automobile, which also presents key data in an easily understandable way.[29]

The dashboard may be a conventional report or a software product. The dashboard requires that senior management agree to a restricted set of key marketing metrics to communicate and evaluate the company's marketing performance. The dashboard facilitates control of short-term activities and longer-term planning. Objectives and processes should be aligned with the marketing dashboard.[30]

The attraction of the dashboard concept is to provide decision makers with a reduced set of vital measures in a form that is easy to interpret and apply. Advanced software packages can display critical information in easy-to-read graphics, assembled in real time from corporate information systems.[31]

For strategic decision makers, the marketing dashboard should contain metrics related to the main business drivers, the factors that directly and predictably affect performance, and should reflect the pipeline of growth ideas—how knowledge of customers is translated into a strategy for sustaining growth—and review the marketing talent pool. The main business drivers might include share of customer wallet, or retention, compared to competitors. The pipeline of growth section could indicate new products in the pipeline and expected revenues and profits from them. The marketing talent pool addresses the marketing skills the company needs and its inventory of talent.[32]

At an operational level, managers might choose dashboard metrics more closely related to strategy implementation. For example, Exhibit 15.7 shows the marketing dashboard for the senior managers at a manufacturer of branded luggage distributed through retail stores, over a four-year period, showing five critical measures. The brand shows strong sales growth and has maintained its margins at attractive levels, even though selling less expensive items. However, returns for the retailer have fallen dramatically, while inventory levels at the retail level have escalated. Sales per store has fallen substantially. The price premium for the brand has fallen and a growing proportion of sales are on promotional deals. The metrics underline concerns about the company's ability to maintain its distribution without reversing these trends, knowing that weaker distribution will hit future sales and margins.

Nonetheless, there remains a concern that the use of marketing dashboards should be monitored carefully. There is a danger that the dashboard contains metrics relevant to assessing past performance rather than those which give insight into present performance and future developments. The uses of marketing dashboards at several major companies are illustrated in the METRICS FEATURE.

EXHIBIT 15.7

Illustrative Marketing Dashboard for a Branded Luggage Product

Source: Paul W. Ferris, Neil T. Bendle, Philip E. Pfeifer and David J. Reibstein, *Marketing Metrics: 50+ Metrics Every Executive Should Master,* (Upper Saddle River NJ: Wharton School Publishing/Pearson Education, 2006), 332.

Revenue and Margins

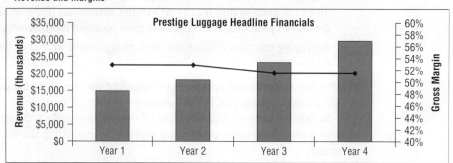

The financial metrics look healthy, revenue showing good growth while margins are almost unchanged.

Manufacturer Prices to Store Prices

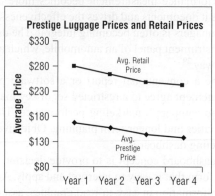

Prestige Luggage is selling less expensive items.

Store Inventory and GMROII

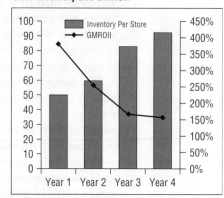

Prestige Luggage is making diminishing returns for retailer.

Distribution

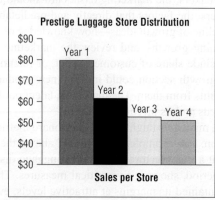

We are moving into smaller stores.

Pricing and Promotions

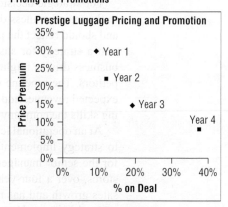

Prestige Luggage is becoming reliant on promotion.

Interpreting Performance Measurement Results

When actual results achieved are compared with planned results, if performance gaps are too large, corrective actions may be required. The process of interpretation and decision on appropriate actions is critical.

Opportunities and Performance Gaps

Strategic evaluation activities seek to identify opportunities or performance gaps and initiate actions to take advantage of the opportunities or to correct existing and pending problems.

"Dashboards are one of management's key techniques to make sure an organization is performing according to its objectives"—Kan Rau, Bay Area Consulting Group.

Steve Balmer, MICROSOFT

- Ballmer requires his top officers to bring their dashboards with them into one-to-one meetings. Ballmer zeroes in on such metrics as sales, customer satisfaction, and status of key products under development.
- More than half of Microsoft employees use dashboards.

Ivan Seidenberg, VERIZON

- Seidenberg and others can choose from 300 metrics to put on their dashboards, from broadband sales to wireless defections. Managers pick the metrics they want to track, and the dashboard flips the pages twenty-four hours a day.

Jeff Immelt, GENERAL ELECTRIC

- Many GE executives use dashboards to run their day-to-day operations, monitoring profits per product line and fill rates for orders. Immelt occasionally looks at a dashboard, but he relies on his managers to run the businesses, so he can focus on the bigger picture.

Larry Ellison, ORACLE

- A fan of dashboards, Ellison uses them to track sales activity at the end of a quarter, the ratio of sales divided by customer service requests, and the number of hours that technicians spend on the phone solving customer problems.
- Although all 20,000 of Oracle's salespeople use dashboards, some 20 percent of them refuse to enter their sales leads into the system. Salespeople don't want to be held accountable for a lead that is not converted into a sale. This makes it harder to get a true picture of the demand for Oracle's products, and Ellison has even considered refusing to pay commission on a sale if the lead is not entered into a dashboard.

Source: Spencer E Ante, "Giving the Boss The Big Picture," *BusinessWeek*, February 13, 2006, 48–51.

The real test of marketing evaluation and control approaches is whether they help management to identify performance problems early enough that remedial action is possible. In monitoring, there are two critical factors to take into account:

Problem/opportunity definition

Strategic analysis should lead to a clear explanation of an opportunity or problem since this will be needed to guide whatever strategic action may be taken. Often it is easy to confuse problem symptoms with problem causes.

Interpreting information

Management must also separate normal variations in performance from significant gaps in performance, since the latter are the ones that require strategic action. For example, how much of a drop in market share is necessary to signal a performance problem? Limits need to be set on the acceptable range of strategic performance.

No matter how extensive the information resources may be, they cannot interpret the strategic importance of the information. This is the responsibility of management.[33]

The Exhibit 15.7 illustration of a marketing dashboard provides an example of strategic problem identification. An illustration of opportunity monitoring is provided by the emergence of concerns about environmental and "green" issues in many countries. Environmental concerns are ongoing areas of strategic evaluation. Companies must identify

Ethics Feature

From Plunderer to Protector

- Ray C. Anderson is founder and now chairman of Atlanta-based Interface Inc., the world's largest manufacturer of commercial carpet tiles.
- In the mid-1990s, Interface was peppered by questions from interior designers about the dangers in the materials and processes it was using.
- Anderson convened a task force to answer his customers' questions. The members of the task force asked him for his environmental vision. Anderson comments, "But I had no vision, absolutely none . . ."
- He found his environmental vision in a book describing the need for sustainability to protect the earth's limited resources.
- Anderson pledged that by 2020 Interface would be a completely sustainable company, producing no dangerous waste, no harmful emissions, and using no oil.
- By 2004, Interface's eco-scorecard looked like this:

INTERFACE'S ECO-SCORECARD

A decade ago, Interface founder, Ray Anderson, pledged that his $924 million company would stop using the earth's natural resources, eliminate waste, and emit no harmful emissions by 2020. Reductions made so far:

Waste	Down 80%
Water intake	Down 78%
Emission of greenhouse gases	Down 46%
Energy consumption	Down 31%
Use of petroleum-based materials	Down 28%
Total Savings	$231 million

Source: Michelle Conlin, "From Plunderer to Protector," *BusinessWeek*, July 19, 2004, 62–62.

important areas of concern and implement strategies that take into account consumer, public policy, and organizational priorities. Major changes in perceptions of environmental responsibility may also create important opportunities. The change in direction at Interfaces Inc. described in the ETHICS FEATURE is an interesting example of a CEO effectively combining his environmental and ethical judgment with responsiveness to customer concerns, and measuring the results achieved.

Determining Normal and Abnormal Variability

It is important to recognize that operating results and metrics such as sales, market share, profits, order-processing time, and customer satisfaction are likely to display normal up-and down-fluctuations. The issue is determining whether these variations represent random variation or instead are due to special causes. For example, if a salesperson's sales over time remain within a normal band of variation, then the results are acceptable under the present operating conditions. Random high and low variations do not indicate unusually high or low performance. If this range of performance is *not* acceptable to management, then the system must be changed. This may require salesperson training, redesign of the territory, improvement in sales support, or other changes in the salesperson's operating system.

Statistical process-control concepts and methods are useful in determining when operating results are fluctuating normally or instead are out of control. Quality-control charts can be used to analyze and improve results in marketing performance measures such as the number of orders processed, customer complaints, and territory sales.[34] Control-chart analysis indicates when the process is experiencing normal variation and when the process is out of control.

The basic approach to control-chart analysis is to establish average and upper and lower control limits for the measure being evaluated. Examples of measures include order-processing time, district sales, customer complaints, and market share. Control boundaries are set using historical data. Future measures are plotted on the chart to determine whether the results are under control or instead fall outside the acceptable performance band determined by the upper and lower control limits. The objective is to continually improve the process that determines the results.

Deciding What Actions to Take

Many corrective actions are possible, depending on the situation. Management's actions may include exiting from a product-market, new-product planning, changing the target-market strategy, adjusting marketing strategy, or improving efficiency.

Avon Products Inc., the leading direct selling cosmetics organization, faced falling sales across the world in 2005.[35] After several years of solid growth, sales stalled in the U.S., but also at the same time in developing markets like Central Europe and Russia, which had proved very successful for Avon. Big problems for Avon around the world had remained unrecognized. The CEO, Andrea Jung, faces the challenge of turning this business around. Among the changes implemented, she has reorganized Avon's management structure, taking away much autonomy from country managers, in favor of globalized manufacturing and marketing. Previously, Avon country managers ran their own plant, developed their own new products, and created their own advertising, often relying as much on instinct as numbers. Jung has trimmed out seven layers of management, and importantly has launched return-on-investment analysis to study performance market by market in a more rigorous way. Recent recruits to Avon's management team have come from larger, more analytical consumer products companies such as Gillette, Procter & Gamble, PepsiCo, and Kraft. New approaches to data at Avon have revealed surprises: the number of products for sale in Mexico had ballooned to 13,000, and decreasing average pay for new representatives had stalled the U.S. business. Key elements of Jung's recovery strategy are a more data-centric approach to making strategic decisions, increased advertising and new product development expenditure, and opening the China market.

Progress continues in rebuilding Avon's competitive position. The company's experience underlines the importance of basing strategic realignment on rigorous analysis of evidence regarding marketing performance and the underlying drivers of performance.

Managing in a changing environment is at the center of strategic marketing. Anticipating and responding effectively to change is the essence of evaluation and control. Executives develop innovative marketing strategies and monitor their effectiveness, altering the strategies as a result of changing conditions.

Global Issues for Planning, Implementation, and Control

The coverage of strategic marketing planning, implementation, and control processes in this chapter is relevant to global marketing strategy. Nonetheless, there are several additional issues which arise regarding the international situation.

Global Marketing Planning

While the underlying process of planning is the same, international plans frequently necessarily make simplifying assumptions to cope with the additional complexity of planning for the global situation. For example, global plans often use regional identities as the planning unit. Many companies refer to "EMEA" as a global market for which plans are formed. EMEA stands for Europe, Middle East, and Africa. This region contains country-markets which are substantially different from each other in economic development, infrastructure, and culture. While regional plans may be a necessity, it is important to look in more detail at the countries and cultures within these regions to identify opportunities and trends. The same applies to designations like "PRA" (Pacific Rim and Asia) or "ROW" (Rest of World—all areas outside the domestic market).

Planning globally must also accommodate more substantial variation in marketing strategies and programs than is the case domestically. Situations will differ regarding the balance between standardizing strategy internationally and adapting to local market conditions, but it is important that the chosen level of adaptation and variability should not be obscured by the way in which plans are constructed. Strategy variation between markets may be extreme. Consider, for example, the major shift in Microsoft's business model for the China market, which is a radical departure from how the company operates elsewhere, described in the GLOBAL FEATURE.

It is also often the case that information regarding global markets is not available in the same quantity or at the same quality that would be expected in the domestic market. Many of the most promising market prospects are in areas like the developing countries, where high quality market information may be least available.

Implementation Globally

The implementation of global strategies must often address issues related to market differences in national culture, economic development, and political characteristics. The GLOBAL FEATURE case is illustrative. Particular issues concern the relationships between managers in the domestic market and executives located in overseas markets. Recall, for example, the Avon Products Inc. recovery strategy described earlier, and the company's moves to reduce local management autonomy to develop a more globally unified brand.

Performance Measurement and Control Globally

Performance measurement and control follows the same general principles but in the global market situation must additionally consider market differences—in local marketing arrangements, in product or market life cycle stage, in the availability of information, and in the strength of the relationships between local and central management. A particular risk is that measurement approaches and metrics chosen for the domestic market may not be the most relevant for international markets. If the product is in an earlier life cycle stage in international markets than at home, then the most relevant metrics may be different. Culture-based differences in attitudes towards control activities may also be a consideration.

For example, assessing global sales operations effectiveness is more complex because individual salespeoples' ability to adjust to local conditions and culture may differ significantly and impact performance. In some countries, teamwork is favored over individual accomplishment, rendering individual salesperson evaluation metrics of questionable value. In the global marketplace, cultural skills appear more relevant to evaluating sales operations than technical and managerial capabilities.[36]

The interpretation of performance, for example, against the metrics used in the domestic marketplace is extremely important. For example, consider the situation where an international market has adverse metrics on expenses, profitability, and sales—expenses metrics indicate that expenditure in this market is very high compared to other markets, and sales and profits are relatively low. These indicators could indicate (1) an international market where performance is weak, and withdrawing from the market should be considered; or (2) a market which has excellent prospects where the company is investing to build a strong competitive position. The GLOBAL FEATURE illustrates a case where conventional performance metrics would make the China market position appear

Global Feature

Microsoft's Strategy Adaptation in China

To develop its position in China, Microsoft has developed a new business model, which is radically different from how it operates elsewhere.

The problem faced in China was not brand acceptance—everyone was using Windows, but mainly counterfeit copies bought for a few dollars. China's weak intellectual property-enforcement laws meant Microsoft's usual pricing strategies were doomed to fail. Another problem for Microsoft was when Beijing's city government started installing free open-source Linux operating systems on workers' PCs.

- Microsoft entered China in 1992, but its business there was a disaster for more than a decade.
- Almost none of the policies that had made Microsoft market leader in the U.S. and Europe made sense in China. In China, Microsoft has had to become "un-Microsoft."
- Chinese prices for Microsoft products are rock-bottom. In China, instead of charging hundreds of dollars for its Windows operating system and Office applications. Microsoft sells a $3 package of Windows and Office to students. In China's back alleys, Linux often costs more than Windows, because it requires more disks.
- Microsoft's China strategy abandons the centerpiece of its public policy approach elsewhere—the protection of its intellectual property at all costs. Tolerating piracy has become part of Microsoft's long-term strategy.
- In China, Microsoft is partnering closely with the government, instead of fighting it, as it does in the U.S. and Europe—which has opened the company to criticism from human rights groups.

Source: David Kirkpatrick, "How Microsoft Conquered China," *Fortune,* July 23, 2007, 76–82.

untenable, yet for Microsoft this is a critically important long-term market prospect. Interpreting performance measures and making appropriate control decisions can only be done in the context of the strategy being pursued in a specific global market.

Increasingly, marketing strategy planning, implementation, and control will involve a global dimension for more companies. While the general approaches we have discussed are relevant, there may be additional issues to consider in the global marketing context.

Summary

Marketing strategy implementation and control are vital links in a series of strategic marketing activities. These tasks emphasize the continuing process of planning, implementing, evaluating, and adjusting marketing strategies. Market-driven strategy and implementation are interdependent activities concerned with matching a company's capabilities with market opportunities. Strategic evaluation of marketing performance is the first step in strategic marketing planning and the last step after launching a strategy. Marketing strategy planning, implementation, and control issues build on the concepts, processes, and methods developed in Chapters 1 through 14.

The strategic marketing planning process was examined earlier in the book (see Appendix to Chapter 1). The strategic marketing plan guides strategy implementation. Plans are developed, implemented, evaluated, and revised to keep the marketing strategy on target. Planning activities involve making a situation assessment, identifying market targets, setting objectives, developing targeting and positioning strategies, deciding action programs for marketing mix components, and preparing financial statements. The planning process typically involves considerable coordination and interaction between functional areas. Since planning is an organizational process, as well as analytical techniques, consideration should be given to the roles and behaviors of executives in planning, and to the organizational context in which planning is carried out. The goal is consistency between these dimensions of planning to enhance effectiveness.

The effectiveness of strategy implementation determines the outcome of marketing planning. Many strategy initiatives in organizations fail because of inadequate attention to the structural and behavioral issues surrounding implementation process. An effective implementation process spells out the activities to be implemented, who is responsible for implementation, the time and location of implementation, and how implementation will be achieved. Enhanced implementation effectiveness is related to managerial skills in execution, but also organizational design choices, providing relevant incentives and effective communications. Internal marketing programs provide a structure for addressing implementation processes. The balanced scorecard approach provides a comprehensive approach to improving implementation. The fit achieved between strategy implementation requirements and organization characteristics and external partnerships may be decisive.

Strategic marketing evaluation and control is concerned with finding new opportunities or avoiding threats, keeping performance in line with management's expectations, or solving specific problems that have been identified. Planning sets the direction and provides guidelines for evaluation and control. A strategic marketing audit may be relevant to establishing appropriate evaluation and control approaches. Performance standards and metrics need to be determined, followed by acquiring necessary information for analysis of performance gaps, leading to the choice of appropriate actions.

Measuring marketing performance compares objectives to achievement using marketing metrics of several kinds. The ability to measure marketing performance is positively related to company performance. Metrics have been developed around customer and competitor issues, profitability, products and portfolios, customer profitability, sales and channels, pricing, promotion, advertising, media and Web performance, and financial results. Particular emphasis has been placed on developing a set of metrics that assesses brand equity. Marketing metrics can also be used to evaluate internal processes like innovation and internal communications. Selecting the most relevant metrics for a particular situation has been linked to the development of management dashboards focused on the main business drivers. Interpreting performance measurement results requires careful attention to identifying performance problems that are not normal variability and require remedial action. Corrective actions may then follow.

In global marketing the general principles for planning, implementation, and control are the same. Nonetheless, there are several additional issues in considering international markets related to market diversity and differences in national cultures and stage of economic development.

Questions for Review and Discussion	1. Discuss the similarities and differences between strategic marketing *planning* and *evaluation*.
	2. What is involved in managing marketing planning as a process? What issues should be addressed in managing the planning process in a company manufacturing high-technology components for the automotive sector?
	3. Selecting the proper performance criteria for use in tracking results is a key part of a strategic evaluation program. Suggest performance criteria for use by a fast-food retail chain to monitor strategic marketing performance.
	4. What justification is there for conducting a marketing audit in a business unit whose performance has been very good? Discuss.
	5. Examination of the various areas of a strategic marketing audit shown in Exhibit 15.6 would be quite expensive and time-consuming. Are there any ways to limit the scope of the audit?
	6. Why would senior managers concerned with strategic marketing review marketing metrics concerned with internal processes?

7. One of the more difficult management control issues is determining whether a process is experiencing normal variation or is actually out of control. Discuss how management can resolve this issue.

8. What role can internal marketing play in enhancing the effectiveness of both planning and implementation?

9. How can the "balanced scorecard" methods assist managers in their implementation efforts?

10. Discuss how management control differs for a strategic alliance compared to internal operations.

11. What are the important factors that managers should take into account to improve the implementation of strategies?

12. How would the marketing dashboard differ between a business-to-business company marketing computer software and a producer of packaged consumer products?

Internet Applications

A. Visit the website for 1-800-FLOWERS (www.1800flowers.com). How does this company employ its website to adapt to a constantly changing environment?

B. Enter the phrase "marketing implementation" into your search engine and review the first twenty sites indicated. View several of those representing consultants and agencies offering products and services to support marketing implementation. Which sound likely to be effective? What role, if any, can external agencies play in developing effective marketing strategy implementation initiatives?

C. Identify suppliers of marketing dashboard software on the Web. Does this type of decision support system replace management judgment on the most appropriate performance criteria for their businesses?

Feature Applications

A. Review the ETHICS FEATURE describing the environmental strategy implemented at Interfaces Inc. List the attractions from a marketing perspective of adopting an environmentally responsible position. Discuss whether companies can undertake environmental initiatives unless there is a commercial advantage.

B. Read the RELATIONSHIP FEATURE describing Nucor Steel. Do "happy employees" always mean "happy customers"—identify and list situations where you do not believe that this is true.

C. Examine the company examples in the METRICS FEATURE concerning uses of marketing dashboards. What are the possible limitations to the dashboard concept?

Notes

1. This illustration is based on Ray Hutton, "Fiat Back from the Brink," *Sunday Times,* July 1, 2007, 3–1, 3–11. John Reed, "Fiat Paints a Picture with Rebirth of a Street Icon," *Financial Times,* Wednesday, July 4, 2007, 21.

2. James Mac Hulbert, Noel Capon, and Nigel F. Piercy, *Total Integrated Marketing: Breaking the Bounds of the Function* (New York: The Free Press, 2003).

3. Nigel F. Piercy and Neil A. Morgan, "The Marketing Planning Process: Behavioral Problems Compared to Analytical Techniques in Explaining Marketing Planning Credibility," *Journal of Business Research,* Vol. 29, 1994, 167–178.

4. Lawrence G. Hrebiniak, "Obstacles to Effective Strategy Implementation," *Organizational Dynamics,* Vol. 35 No. 1, 2006, 12–31.

5. David Miller, "Successful Change Leaders: What Makes Them?" *Journal of Change Management,* Vol. 2 No. 4, 2002, 359–368.

6. Nigel F. Piercy, "Marketing Implementation: The Implications of Marketing Paradigm Weakness for the Strategy Execution Process," *Journal of the Academy of Marketing Science,* Vol. 26, No. 3, 1998, 222–236. Nigel F. Piercy and Frank V. Cespedes, "Implementing Marketing Strategy," *Journal of Marketing Management,* Vol. 12, 1996, 135–160.

7. Charles H. Noble and Michael P. Mokwa, "Implementing Marketing Strategies: Developing and Testing a Managerial Theory," *Journal of Marketing,* October, 1999, 57–73.

8. Thomas V. Bonoma, "Making Your Marketing Strategy Work," *Harvard Business Review,* March-April 1984, 75.

9. Noble and Mokwa, ibid., 71.

10. David W. Cravens, "Implementation Strategies in the Market-Driven Strategy Era," *Journal of the Academy of Marketing Science,* Summer 1998, 237–8.

11. "Survey Reveals 'Inadequate' State of Internal Marketing," *Marketing Week,* July 3, 2003, 8.

12. Dana James, "Don't Forget Staff in Marketing Plan," *Marketing News,* March 13, 2000, 10–11.

13. Nigel F. Piercy and Neil A. Morgan, "Internal Marketing: The Missing Half of the Marketing Programme," *Long Range Planning,* Vol. 24, No. 2, 1991, 82–93.

14. Ian N. Lings and Gordon E. Greenley, "Measuring Internal Market Orientation," *Journal of Services Research,* Vol 7 No. 3, 2005, 290–305. Spiros P. Gounaris, "Internal-Market Orientation and Its Measurement," *Journal of Business Research,* Vol 59 No. 4, 2006, 432–448.

15. Robert S. Kaplan and David P. Norton, *The Strategy-Focused Organization: How Balanced Scorecard Companies Thrive in the New Business Environment* (Boston MA: Harvard Business School Press, 2001).

16. Kerry Capell and Gerry Khermouch, "Hip H&M," *BusinessWeek,* November 11, 2002, 39–42.

17. Lawrence A. Crosby and Sheree L Johnson, "High Performance Marketing in the CRM Era," *Marketing Management,* September/October 2001, 10–11.

18. Larry Yu, "Successful Customer-Relationship Management," *Sloan Management Review,* Summer, 2001, 18–29.

19. Wayne R. McCullough, "Marketing Metrics," *Marketing Management,* Spring 2000, 64.

20. Don O'Sullivan and Andrew V. Abela, "Marketing Performance Measurement Ability and Firm Performance," *Journal of Marketing,* April 2007, 79–93.

21. Donald R. Lehmann, "Linking Marketing Decisions to Financial Performance and Firm Value," *Executive Overview,* March 2002 (Cambridge MA: Marketing Science Institute).

22. Patrick Barwise and John U. Farley, *Which Marketing Metrics Are Used and Where?* Report 03–002 (Cambridge MA: Marketing Science Institute, 2003).

23. Tim Ambler, "Marketing Metrics," *Business Strategy Review,* Vol. 11 No. 2, 2000, 59–66.

24. This section is based on Paul W. Ferris, Neil T. Bendle, Philip E. Pfeifer, and David J. Reibstein, *Marketing Metrics: 50+ Metrics Every Executive Should Master* (Upper Saddle River NJ: Wharton School Publishing/Pearson Education, 2006). This book provides a definitive guide to the identification and computation of relevant metrics.

25. Bruce H. Clark, "A Summary of Thinking on Measuring the Value of Marketing," *Journal of Targeting, Measurement and Analysis for Marketing,* Vol. 9 No. 4, 2001, 357–369.

26. Tim Ambler and John Roberts, *Beware the Silver Metric: Marketing Performance Measurement Has to Be Multidimensional,* Marketing Science Institute Report 06–003 (Cambridge MA: Marketing Science Institute, 2006).

27. Tim Ambler, 2003.

28. "Marketers Still Lost in the Metrics," *Marketing,* August 10, 2000, 15–17.

29. Ferris et al. (2006), ibid., 331.

30. Bruce H. Clark, Andrew V. Abela, and Tim Ambler, "Behind the Wheel," *Marketing Management,* May/June 2006, 19–23.

31. Spencer E. Ante, "Giving the Boss the Big Picture," *BusinessWeek,* February 13, 2006, 48–51.

32. Gail J. McGovern, David Court, John A Quelch, and Blair Crawford, "Bringing Customers into the Boardroom," *Harvard Business Review,* November 2004, 70–80.

33. An interesting evaluation of providing decision makers with support in the interpretation of evidence is found in D. V. L. Smith and J. H. Fletcher, *The Art and Science of Interpreting Market Research Evidence* (Chichester: Wiley, 2004).

34. James Mac Hulbert, Noel Capon, and Nigel F. Piercy, 2003.

35. This illustration is based on: Nanette Byrnes, "Avon: More than Cosmetic Changes," *BusinessWeek,* March 12, 2007, 62–63. Dominic Rushe, "Avon Calling," *Sunday Times,* January 15, 2006, 3–5.

36. Earl D. Honeycutt, John B. Ford and Antonis C. Simintiras, *Sales Management: A Global Perspective* (London: Routledge, 2003).

Appendix **15A**

Marketing Metrics

Marketing Metrics Focusing on Marketing Operations[1]

Competitive and Customer Metrics

Measures of competitiveness include market share (in revenue and volume, and relative to competitors), though this can be deconstructed, for example, into market share with heavy users or share of customer product requirements (share of wallet). It is also possible to develop development indices for brands and categories (sales within a specified segment compared to the rest of the market), and measures of penetration (e.g., purchasers of a brand as a percentage of the total population). Consumer metrics include measures of awareness, knowledge beliefs, purchase intentions, loyalty, willingness to recommend, satisfaction, and willingness to search. By assessing the share of customer "hearts and minds," the dynamics behind market share can be explained and more valid predictions made for the future.

Profitability Metrics

Measures relating to profitability include the margin on a unit of product and on products sold through different channels. Average price per unit sold and variable and fixed costs can be included. Analyzing marketing expenditure components can be linked to contribution margins and break-even sales level calculations. Target volumes and revenues (to break-even) can be evaluated. The Appendix to Chapter 2 provides guidance on financial analysis for marketing planning and control.

Product and Portfolio Metrics

Product and portfolio related questions include what volumes can be expected from a new product; how will sales of existing products be affected by the launch of a new offering; is brand equity increasing or decreasing; what do customers really want and what are they prepared to

[1] This section is based on Paul W. Ferris, Neil T. Bendle, Philip E. Pfeifer, and David J. Reibstein, *Marketing Metrics: 50+ Metrics Every Executive Should Master* (Upper Saddle River NJ: Wharton School Publishing/Pearson Education, 2006). This book provides a definitive guide to the identification and computation of relevant metrics.

sacrifice to get it? Metrics relevant to addressing these questions include measures of the trial of a product and repeat purchases, penetration (percentage of the population buying), and volume projections. Measures also include growth rates, cannibalization rates (percentage of new product sales taken from the existing product line), and brand equity evaluation, to assess the health of the brand. Utilities-related metrics consider the relative value customers place on different attributes of the product offering—in total and by segment.

Customer Profitability Metrics

Other metrics examine the performance of individual customer relationships. These range from number counts of customers and recency of purchase and retention rates to measures of customer profit. More complex metrics evaluate customer lifetime value (the present value of future cash flows attributed to the customer relationship), prospect lifetime value (lifetime value of an acquired customer less the cost of prospecting), as well as average acquisition and retention costs.

Sales and Channel Metrics

These measures assess the adequacy and effectiveness of the systems that provide customers with reasons and opportunities to buy the product. The most common sales force metrics focus on whether sales force effort level and coverage are adequate, and the sales pipeline (number of customers at different stages of the sales cycle). Distribution metrics are concerned with measures of product distribution and availability (e.g., the percentage of potential outlets that stock the product). Logistics metrics track the operational effectiveness of the systems that service retailers and distributors—inventory turnover, out-of-stocks, service levels.

Pricing Metrics

Several metrics are relevant to evaluating pricing alternatives. There are various methods for calculating price premiums (prices relative to alternatives). Demand functions can be addressed through reservation prices metrics (e.g., the maximum an individual is prepared to pay for the product) and percent good value measures (e.g., the proportion of customers who consider the product to be good value). Price elasticity is the market response to changes in price, which may also allow for competitive reactions to price changes.

Promotion Metrics

Metrics evaluating the effectiveness of sales promotions distinguish between baseline and incremental sales, to isolate the lift achieved through the promotional activity. Metrics include the redemption rate on coupons and rebates, the costs of coupons and rebates, and the percentage of sales made using coupons and rebates. The pass-through of rebates to the consumers by retailers and distributors can also be calculated, as well as the impact on average price paid.

Advertising, Media, and Web Metrics

Media metrics reveal how many people may be exposed to an advertising campaign, how often those people have an opportunity to see the ads, and the cost of each potential impression made, e.g., cost per thousand impressions (CPM). Measures also consider frequency response function (how often an individual has to see the ad before there is a response), effective reach of the advertising, and the share of voice (compared to competitors). A variety of metrics have also been developed to track online advertising performance, such as "cost per click" (advertising costs divided by the number of clicks generated), cost per order, as well as website characteristics like number of visits and abandonment rate (rate of purchases started but not completed).

Financial Metrics

As discussed in the Chapter 2 Appendix, several measures can be used to assess the financial implications of marketing effort. These include Net Profit (sales revenue less total costs), Return on Sales (net profit as a percentage of sales revenue), Return on Investment (net profits over the investment needed to generate the profits), Economic Profit (net profit after tax, less the costs of capital), Payback (time taken to return the initial investment), Net Present Value (the value of future cash flows after accounting for the time value of money), Internal Rate of Return (the discount rate at which the net present value of an investment is zero), and Return on Marketing Investment (incremental revenue attributable to marketing over the marketing spending). It should be noted that Return on Marketing Investment remains an ambiguous concept and as a metric is addressed in several different ways.

Brand Equity Metrics

Particular attention has focused on groups of metrics indicating brand equity, as an overall indicator of marketing performance. For many companies brand equity is one of the largest and most valuable assets—for some leading organizations brand value is more than 50 percent of total market capitalization. Brand value is often as important for business-to-business companies as for consumer businesses—25 percent of the market capitalization of Microsoft is accounted for by the brand; the IBM brand accounts for 47 percent of IBM's market value.[2] The importance of brand as an intangible corporate asset underlines the importance of marketing metrics related to brand value.

Important questions regarding brand equity are: whether potential customers are aware of the brand; what proportion of the intended market has bought the brand; how do customers rate the brand's quality; how satisfied are customers with the brand experience; are customers loyal to the brand; and how easy is it to locate and buy the brand. General brand equity metrics and measures to address these questions include[3]:

Consumer metric	Measured by
• Familiarity	• Familiarity relative to other brands in the set being considered
• Penetration	• Number of customers or number of active customers as a percentage of the intended market
• What they think about the brand	• Brand preference as a percentage of preference of other brands within the set being considered, or those with intention to buy, or those with brand knowledge
• What they feel	• Customer satisfaction compared to the average for other brands
• Loyalty	• Either behavioral (repeat buying, retention) or intermediate (commitment, engagement)
• Availability	• Distribution, e.g., weighted percentage of retail outlets carrying the brand

[2] Jane Simms, "Intangible Revolution," *The Marketer,* April 2007, 20–23.
[3] Tim Ambler, *Marketing and the Bottom Line,* 2nd ed. (Harlow: Pearson, 2003).

Innovation Metrics

Other metrics are concerned with internal measurements inside the organization. One consideration is the potential for developing and reporting metrics that relate to both the quality and quantity of innovation in the organization—"innovation health"—since effective innovation in product and process is critical to marketing performance in many organizations. Metrics proposed in this area include[4]:

• Strategy	• Awareness of goals
	• Commitment to goals
	• Active innovation support
	• Perceived resource adequacy
• Culture	• Appetite for learning
	• Freedom to fail
• Outcomes	• Number of initiatives in process
	• Number of innovations launched
	• Percent of revenue due to launches in the last three years

Internal Market Metrics

There is increasing recognition of "internal branding" in organizations and consequently internal brand equity.

[4] Ibid.

These concerns reflect the link between company performance and employee attitudes. There are metrics available to assess employee-based equity[5]:

• Awareness of corporate goals.
• Perceived caliber of employer.
• Relative employee satisfaction.
• Commitment to corporate goals.
• Employee retention.
• Perceived resource adequacy.
• Appetite for learning.
• Freedom to fail.
• Customer-brand empathy.

Internal Process Metrics

When particular internal processes have been identified as critical to marketing performance, metrics can be developed to evaluate and monitor process performance and links to marketing goals. For example, internal communications have been linked to cross-functional working effectiveness, such as between marketing and sales. Metrics can be developed to monitor the quantity of cross-functional communications and their perceived quality, as a monitoring approach for this important organizational characteristic.[6]

[5] Ibid.
[6] Elliot Maltz and Ajay K. Kohli, "Reducing Marketing's Conflict with Other Functions: The Differential Effects of Integrating Mechanisms," *Journal of the Academy of Marketing Science*, Fall 2000, 479–492.

Cases for Part 5

Case 5-1

Verizon Communications Inc.

Ivan G. Seidenberg hardly looks like Old Man Telecom. The chief executive of Verizon Communications Inc. is only 56 and has the build and intensity of someone much younger. But sitting in his sun-filled, 39th-floor office in Midtown Manhattan, Seidenberg points out that he joined the company as a cable splicer's assistant in the Bronx when he was 19. He even keeps his cable splicer's shears, knife, and sheaf tucked away in his desk. "It's hard to believe, but I've been here for 37 years, more than one-third of this company's history," he says. "I feel an obligation to make sure this company is well positioned for the next 100 years."

Now Seidenberg is launching a series of sweeping initiatives to make good on his vow. From hardball pricing tactics that have knocked rivals back on their heels to a capital-spending war chest that's the largest in telecom, he's determined to transform what was once just another sleepy phone company into the pacesetter for the industry. "When you're the market leader," says Seidenberg, "part of your responsibility is to reinvent the market."

At the heart of this reinvention is the most ambitious deployment of new telecom technology in years (Exhibit 1). Verizon plans to roll out fiber-optic connections to every home and business in its 29-state territory over the next 10 to 15 years, a project that might reasonably be compared with the construction of the Roman aqueducts. It will cost $20 billion to $40 billion, depending on how fast equipment prices fall, and allow the lightning-fast transmission of everything from regular old phone service to high-definition TV. No competitor yet dares follow suit, fearing it could be their financial Waterloo. "We'll watch them closely and go to school on them if they have found something economic," says Ross Ireland, chief technology officer at SBC Communications Inc., the second-largest phone company after Verizon.

Seidenberg is being no less aggressive when it comes to the wireless technology that has consumers and companies equally abuzz—Wi-Fi. In an unprecedented move, Verizon is blanketing Manhattan with more than 1,000 Wi-Fi hotspots that will let any broadband subscriber near a Verizon telephone booth use a laptop to wirelessly tap the Net for the latest news, sports scores, or weather report. If the rollout goes well, Verizon will duplicate this wireless grid in other major cities. Next up: third-generation wireless service, known as 3G, which lets customers make speedy Net connections from their mobile phones. Verizon will begin to deploy 3G in September, at least three months before any of its major competitors. "The other guys will say they want to be the best follower. The guy on the frontier takes a lot of arrows, so they say, 'Let someone else roll out 3G and fiber-to-the-home.' Well, that someone else is Verizon," says Alex Peters, lead manager of the $200 million Franklin Global Communications Fund, which bought an undisclosed number of the company's shares last year.

Verizon is leading the way with its pricing strategies, too. In March, the company became the first Bell to slice its broadband Internet service by 30%, to $35 a month. That's typically 10% to 20% cheaper than cable players such as AOL Time Warner Inc. and Comcast Corp., which have grabbed an early lead in broadband service. Even the musty long-distance business is getting a jolt of innovation: Earlier this year, Verizon became the first Bell to offer unlimited long-distance and local calls for one flat rate, typically $55 a month. Customers loved the idea, and Verizon quickly zoomed past Sprint Corp. to become the third-largest consumer long-distance player in the country. Now, every other Bell has introduced its own flat-rate service.

What's behind Seidenberg's sudden series of audacious moves? Two major reasons: competition from cable companies and the CEO's vision of his industry's future. The cable assault is most pressing because Comcast and its brethren are cutting into Verizon's cash-cow local-phone business and swiping most of the customers in broadband, the fastest-growing segment of telecom. To compete, Verizon plans to use its fiber-optic lines to offer Net access that's 20 times as fast as today's broadband—and bundle that with local phone service.

EXHIBIT 1   Telecom's New Leader

Three years ago, Verizon looked like just another big phone company. But this year it has emerged as the industry pacesetter. Here's how:

Optics

Verizon is spending billions on blazingly fast optical lines to nearly every home and business in its territory over the next 10 to 15 years. This will challenge cable players in offering video, speedy Net access, and other services.

Impact   Not only will the initiative result in new services for Verizon customers, but phone rivals will follow suit. That could spark a new round of capital investment.

Wireless Data

In September, Verizon Wireless will roll out third-generation (3G) technology in Washington and San Diego. This will let users tap the Net directly from a cell phone or from a laptop at speeds faster than a DSL connection.

Impact   Verizon will be first to market, pressing rivals like Cingular to keep pace. Customers will get more service for about the same price.

Broadband

Cable-TV companies claim two-thirds of the 18 million U.S. broadband customers. In March, Verizon went on the attack, slashing the price of its rival DSL service by 30%, to $34.95. That's typically 10% to 20% cheaper than cable broadband.

Impact   More customers will snap up broadband. That helps new band-width-gobbling Net services, like Apple's iTunes music service.

Research

As others cut back, Verizon's scientists are focusing more on novel products. One example: the Digital Companion, which next year will let you log on to a Web page from anywhere to see calls as they come in to your home, so you can route them elsewhere.

Impact   By going beyond basic phone service, the company hopes to build consumer loyalty and add new revenue streams.

Wi-Fi

Verizon is blanketing Manhattan with 1,000 Wi-Fi hotspots, which let customers connect to the Net wirelessly within a range of several hundred feet. Verizon's DSL customers will get the service for free.

Impact   Customers are the winners. They'll get a bargain on Wi-Fi in New York and maybe elsewhere. It will be tough for cable rivals to match the deal.

Long Distance

In January, Verizon became the first Bell to introduce unlimited local and long-distance calling for a flat fee. And it has displaced Sprint as the third-largest consumer long-distance company.

Impact   All of the other major local-phone companies have followed Verizon's lead in offering flat-rate phone-service packages. Now Verizon can compete on an equal basis with rivals such as AT&T.

Just as important is Seidenberg's conviction that telecom as we know it is history. In its place will emerge what he calls a "broadband industry" that will use the new, superfast Net links and high-capacity networks to deliver video and voice communications services with all the extras, like software for security. If he's right, other companies will follow Verizon's lead and the communications industry will be remade. Seidenberg thinks ubiquitous broadband will transform broad swaths of the economy. High school students, for instance, could download the video of a biology lecture they missed. Doctors could use crystal-clear video-conferencing to examine patients in hard-to-reach rural areas. "The cable industry focuses on entertainment and games. The broadband industry will focus on education, health care, financial services, and essential

government services," he says. "I think over the next five to 10 years, you will see five, six, seven [segments of the economy] reordering the way they think about providing services."

Over the long term, the strategy will put Verizon into completely new businesses. Though video may not be its primary focus, the company says that within five years it expects to distribute video services, which could include TV programming and movies on demand, so it can compete directly with cable companies. "I think it's terrific. . . . It could definitely work," says Sumner M. Redstone, chairman and CEO of Viacom Inc., whose holdings include MTV Networks and Paramount Pictures, and where Seidenberg is a director.

There are plenty of people, however, who think all that time spent up on the 39th floor has left Seidenberg a bit light-headed. Can any company afford to do what Verizon is attempting? The company says it will pump $12.5 billion to $13.5 billion into capital expenditures this year, the third-largest capital budget in the world after DaimlerChrysler and General Electric Co. (Exhibit 2). That's on top of the $3 billion a year it's paying in yearly interest because of its $54 billion debt load. How can Verizon pay for all this? Its business is one of the great cash machines of Corporate America. The largest local-phone operator and the largest wireless company, Verizon generates about $22 billion a year in cash from operations. That's 50% more than SBC, twice as much as BellSouth, and nearly three times as much as AT&T. More than any company in the industry, Verizon can make enormous bets and pay for them out of its own pocket. Seidenberg expects to cover the fiber-optic initiative without raising the capital budget above the current level, while he continues to reduce the company's debt. "Funding is not an issue," he says.

Still, plenty of critics question whether Seidenberg is leading the industry in the right direction. SBC and Qwest Communications International ventured onto a different path when they announced partnerships with satellite-TV service EchoStar Communications on July 21. The deal will allow them to combine voice, video, and data on a single bill—sooner than Verizon and at a fraction of the cost. And rather than a massive fiber roll-out to offer broadband Net service, SBC is focused on DSL, where it has a big lead on Verizon. Other industry experts think Verizon's plan may not make financial sense. "Frankly, I'm skeptical," says former Federal Communications Commission Chairman William E. Kennard, managing director of investment company Carlyle Group.

The skepticism stems in part from history. Verizon was formed from the merger of Nynex and Bell Atlantic in 1997 and the melding of the combined companies and GTE in 2000. The predecessor companies

EXHIBIT 2 Verizon's Obstacle Course

Its ambitious agenda won't be easy to achieve. Here are the main hurdles and prospects for overcoming them:

Phone Business	Debt	Cable	Costs
Revenue from Verizon's local-phone business declined 4.2% during the first quarter, as wireless rivals and resellers like AT&T ate into its business.	Verizon has managed to cut debt to $54 billion from $64 billion, but that's still high relative to rivals. Its ratio of net debt to earnings is 1.6, compared with 0.8 for SBC and 1.1 for BellSouth.	Although cable companies have only 2% of the U.S. phone market, that will probably grow to 30% of the U.S. phone market over 10 years.	With a big union workforce and lots of older technology, Verizon's cost structure is higher than its younger rivals'. Its 228,000 workers each generate $294,000 in revenues, among the lowest in the industry.
Outlook The trend can't be reversed, but Verizon can slow the losses by offering bundled services.	**Outlook** While Verizon has plenty of cash to cover debt payments and other obligations, it will need to keep reducing its debt to free up cash for new investments. That may require the sale of some assets, such as its international holdings.	**Outlook** Verizon's investments in fiber should make it more competitive because the technology will allow it to offer TV service.	**Outlook** Verizon is in contract talks with its unions and hopes to extract cost-saving concessions. Talks are tense, however, and a strike is becoming a real possibility.

Losing Local-Phone Revenues

▲ Percentage Decline, from Year-Earlier Quarter
Data: UBS Warburg

Cable on the Rise

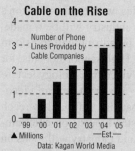

Number of Phone Lines Provided by Cable Companies

▲ Millions   —Est.—
Data: Kagan World Media

tried, and failed, several times in the 1990s to capitalize on the convergence of television and communications. Bell Atlantic and Nynex helped launch Tele-TV in 1994 to develop interactive-TV programming, but the project folded after several years. Bell Atlantic also announced a merger with cable-TV powerhouse Tele-Communications Inc. in 1994, only to see the deal fall apart a few months later.

Now Verizon faces cable companies that are spoiling for a fight. The cable industry has spent more than $75 billion since 1995 to upgrade their networks for high-definition TV, fast Internet access, and telephone service. The phone companies "have to make sizable investments to catch up," says David N. Watson, executive vice-president for marketing at Comcast, the nation's largest cable operator. "And we won't be standing still." In fact, Comcast and the other cable companies are hell-bent on torpedoing Seidenberg's plans by destroying Verizon's profits before it can use them to get into the video business. Cable players are expected to nab 3.7 million phone lines nationwide by 2005, up from 2.2 million last year, according to market researcher Kagan World Media. That, along with competition from AT&T Corp. and wireless companies, caused Verizon to lose 3.7% of its local-phone lines in 2002.

The competitive threat is compounded by Verizon's labor situation. The company is locked in intense negotiations with its two main unions over a new contract for 75,000 of its 228,000 employees. Far apart over issues of health-care costs, work-rule flexibility, and organizing in the wireless unit, the two sides may very well be headed for a strike when the current contract expires on Aug. 2. Verizon has trained tens of thousands of managers to assume union duties should the talks fail. "There is no clear break. Sometimes you can see it in advance. This time, we can't," says George Kohl, director of research for the Communications Workers of America.

Verizon's labor issues won't disappear even if a strike is averted. More than half of its workers belong to a union, while rival cable companies are typically nonunion shops. Verizon has what it says are the highest costs in telecom, with union workers in New York earning an average salary of $62,000, plus overtime and benefits. More important, Verizon has less flexibility than competitors when it comes to laying people off or reassigning them to high-growth units. On July 11, a labor mediator in New York ordered Verizon to rehire 2,300 workers the company had thought it had the right to lay off. It quickly announced it would rehire an additional 1,100 workers who were making similar claims in mediation.

Asked about all the skepticism, the understated Seidenberg responds with a wry smile. "People that watch our industry tend to be skeptical when there's hard work involved, but we've shown the resolve to get up every morning and do what it takes," he says.

Seidenberg and other execs insist much has changed at Verizon since the miscues of the '90s. In February, the FCC changed the regulations so that Verizon and other Bells won't have to share their new networks with rivals at government-controlled prices. Although final details have yet to be released, the decision strengthens the business case for building the networks. At the same time, the price of rolling out fiber to homes and offices has dropped by 50% over the past five years, and it will likely decline another 50% over the next few. "This is not a trial. It's a deployment," says Bruce S. Gordon, president of Verizon's consumer division. "The decision has been made, and it will happen. There's no going back."

If Seidenberg is right, he's positioning Verizon to thrive in the coming decades. Short-term, the deterioration in the core local-phone business probably will cancel out growth in new services. Analyst Simon Flannery of Morgan Stanley expects revenues to stay flat at $67 billion this year while net income declines 10%, to $7.5 billion, not including a $3 billion noncash charge for an accounting change and a write-down from international operations. Profits could even shrink again in 2004, to $7.2 billion. After that, Verizon's prospects look better. As broadband services are rolled out to more of its customers, Flannery estimates that the company's revenues will hit $70 billion in 2005 and net income will recover to $7.6 billion. "They are definitely the industry's future," says Brian Adamik, chief executive of market researcher Yankee Group.

Leave it to Seidenberg to do what others think impossible. The son of an air-conditioning repairman, he grew up in the working-class Gun Hill section of the Bronx. If he had potential for greatness, it was well hidden. Without the money for college, he started working for New York Telephone splicing cables in 1966. He was quickly drafted into the U.S. Army and wounded in Vietnam. After he returned to his old employer in 1968, his raw determination emerged. With his company helping to foot the bill, he earned a BA in mathematics from Lehman College, of the City University of New York, and an MBA at Pace University. He married his high school sweetheart, Phyllis, and they now have two children. During this time, he spent 12 straight years going to night school.

He worked hard on the job, too. As the youngest person on a work team laying cables at Co-op City in the Bronx, Ike, as he was called at the time, would remeasure the cable lines of other workers to see if they were the right length. Perhaps most surprising, he did it without getting throttled by more-senior workers. How? He never tried to take credit for the extra work from supervisors. He simply told the other workers so they could correct any errors as a team. Plus, he was a likable guy who played in the regular lunchtime football games. Seidenberg worked in operations and engineering before moving to Washington to handle regulatory affairs. In 1995, he became chairman and CEO of Nynex Corp.

It could have been a brief, shining moment of glory. When the local-telephone industry was deregulated in 1996, Nynex looked like takeover bait: too small to determine its own fate. Still, Seidenberg figured out a way to get the necessary scale by cutting savvy deals and sharing the spotlight. First, after the Bell Atlantic merger, he let Bell Atlantic Corp. CEO Raymond W. Smith run the combined companies for a couple of years before taking over. Then he waited his turn while GTE Corp. CEO Charles R. Lee ran the show, taking full control only after Lee stepped down as co-CEO last year, at the age of 62. "He's a master boardroom player," says Kennard.

Even now, Seidenberg is eager to let his lieutenants take the limelight. He often has Vice-Chairman Lawrence T. Babbio Jr., who runs the traditional phone business, and Verizon Wireless Services CEO Dennis F. Strigl represent the company in public forums. "All of these people could be CEOs in their own right. They are warriors, and they are on a mission," says Seidenberg. Yet they profess fierce loyalty to him and Verizon, which has been an island of stability in a churning sea.

The commander will need all the warriors he can get. Within two years, the cable-TV companies are expected to be in the phone business big time. They already have 15% of the market in a handful of Verizon neighborhoods where they offer phone service. Cable companies like Comcast, Cablevision Systems, and Cox Communications are planning to expand their phone operations in 2004 using Internet technology that's cheaper and packed with features like inexpensive second and third phone lines. At the current pace,

the cable companies will probably have 30% of the phone market over the next decade, says telecom analyst John Hodulik of UBS.

The fiber strategy will help Verizon defend itself. By offering TV, superfast Web access, and feature-rich Internet-based phone services, Verizon could reduce potential customer churn by 50%, Hodulik estimates. Assuming fiber is deployed, he thinks the company will have 2007 net income of $7.9 billion on revenues of $79.7 billion. Those numbers are 2.5% and 5.7% higher than his forecasts before the fiber strategy was outlined.

Although these are the early days, high-speed fiber connections are proving popular with consumers. Verizon already is installing fiber in Brambleton, a planned community in Loudoun County, Va. Only 200 homes have been built so far, but that will grow to 6,000. Liz and Steve Levy are among the early adopters. The high-speed Net connection helps them stay in touch with neighbors over the community Web site, and Liz Levy uses it to maintain a Web site for her stationery business. They get pitched by satellite-TV companies all the time, but they won't switch. "It works really well, and I like getting all the services from a single company," she says.

Still, there's no guarantee that Seidenberg's broadband vision will become a reality. No company has attempted what he is doing on such a massive scale, and even smaller initiatives have shown mixed results. Construction of a fiber network in Eugene, Ore., was cut back because the economics of the effort didn't pan out. The city had originally planned to extend its optical links into homes and businesses, but it canceled the plan in March, 2002, as the economy soured. "We just couldn't make the numbers work," says Lance Robertson, communications coordinator for the Eugene Water & Electric Board.

Whether the numbers work for Verizon will depend on its costs for the new network. Installing a fiber-optic line in a home or business has dropped to about $2,000 today from more than $4,000 five years ago, according to market researcher Render, Vanderslice & Associates. The firm expects that will fall another 50%, to $1,000, in the next five years, although that will depend on how quickly Verizon and the Bells buy equipment. Doreen Toben, Verizon's chief financial officer, says costs have just now come down enough for the initiative to make financial sense. It should be profitable if the company's expense per line comes in between $1,200 and $1,800.

Verizon has a card up its sleeve. About 45% of its customers are wired via telephone poles and other above-ground connections, according to Verizon Chief Technology Officer Mark Wegleitner. That's compared to 32% for BellSouth, 28% for SBC, and 13% for Qwest. Why is that key? It's as much as 30% cheaper to upgrade a line on a phone pole than it is to upgrade one buried beneath a sidewalk or someone's lawn.

Despite the challenges, Seidenberg has a track record of patient investing that pays off in the end. Consider the wireless business, 45%-owned by Vodafone Group PLC. In recent years, it invested more than its rivals and has reaped the reward. Today, with 33 million subscribers, it's far larger than No. 2 Cingular, a joint venture of BellSouth Corp. and SBC. And it's ahead on many financial metrics, from revenue and earnings growth to profitability. "We're trying to replicate wireless' successful model in other parts of the company, but it takes patience," says Babbio.

Verizon's wireless data plans should keep that growth engine humming. Beginning this September, it will introduce wireless systems in Washington and San Diego that let customers download data at peak speeds of 2.4 megabits a second. That's about five times faster than a DSL connection. While rivals are expected to deploy comparable technology, Verizon is ahead of the curve. Competitors won't roll out the technology until 2004 or 2005. By getting to market first, Verizon expects to maintain its above-average growth.

Rivals are skeptical. "The real question is, is the market ready for it?" says William E. Clift, Cingular's chief technical officer. Seidenberg thinks all of these investments will create something of lasting importance and have a positive impact on the overall economy. "As broadband becomes more pervasive over the next three or four years, all the 'excess capacity' in long distance will get absorbed," Seidenberg says. "Microsoft or IBM would never say there's overcapacity. They envision a world in which you always need more capacity to handle all the things they can make. The problem is, we don't have that capacity where it needs to be . . . in the home and office."

It will require near-perfect execution. But Seidenberg performs well under pressure. One afternoon in 1969, the young cable splicer and his buddies took a break for a game of touch football at Ferry Point Park in the Bronx. Pat LaScala, a cable splicer's assistant who had played high school football, told Seidenberg to go out for a pass as far as he could. "He ran right into a tree and got some big welt on his eye," LaScala recalled. "But he caught the ball." Today, he needs that poise more than ever. This time, it's no game.

With Tom Lowry in New York, Roger O. Crockett in Chicago, and Irene M. Kunii in Tokyo

Source: Steve Rosenbush, "Verizon's Gutsy Bet," *Business-Week,* August 4, 2003, 52–62.

Case 5-2

Home Depot Inc.

Don D. Ray is one tough hombre. The 39-year-old Kentucky native spent three years with the 82nd Airborne Div., one of the U.S. Army's elite units, serving at the head of a maintenance crew during the first Gulf War and an additional seven years on active duty. Then, after the September 11 terrorist attacks, Ray suited up for service again, this time as the commander of a special forces A-team that followed the U.S.-led invasion into Afghanistan. His 12-man squad of snipers, demolition experts, and communications specialists hunted renegade al-Qaeda and Taliban. Combing mountain villages, he grew a thick beard, wore traditional Afghan garb, and rode on horseback to blend in with local Muslims. Ray and his men never killed anyone, he says, but they arrested dozens of suspected militants.

Nowadays, Ray commands a different kind of operation. He has replaced crack-of-dawn physical training and green Army fatigues with sunrise store openings and an orange Home Depot apron. A store manager in Clarksville, Tenn., Ray runs a 110,000-square-foot box with 35,000 products and a 100-member staff, 30 of them former military. Many days start at 4 a.m. That's when he wakes, eats breakfast, catches some CNBC news, then heads to the store, where the doors open at 6. Although Ray's bookish round glasses and pressed khakis make him look more like a teacher than a one-time terrorist hunter, he exudes a steely confidence. Former soldiers on his staff call him "sir." "In the military, we win battles and conquer the enemy," says Ray. At Home Depot, "we do that with customers."

Military analogies are commonplace at Home Depot Inc. these days. Five years after his December, 2000, arrival, Chief Executive Robert L. Nardelli is putting his stamp on what was long a decentralized, entrepreneurial business under founders Bernie Marcus and

Arthur Blank. And if his company starts to look and feel like an army, that's the point. Nardelli loves to hire soldiers. In fact, he seems to love almost everything about the armed services. The military, to a large extent, has become the management model for his entire enterprise. Of the 1,142 people hired into Home Depot's store leadership program, a two-year training regimen for future store managers launched in 2002, almost half—528—are junior military officers. More than 100 of them now run Home Depots. Recruits such as Ray "understand the mission," says Nardelli. "It's one thing to have faced a tough customer. It's another to face the enemy shooting at you. So they probably will be pretty calm under fire."

Built like a bowling ball, Nardelli is a detail-obsessed, diamond-cut-precise manager who, in 2000, lost his shot at the top job at General Electric Co. to Jeffrey R. Immelt. He is fond of pointing out that if Home Depot were a country, it would be the fifth-largest contributor of troops in Iraq. Overall, some 13% of Home Depot's 345,000 employees have military experience, vs. 4% at Wal-Mart Stores Inc. And that doesn't even count James E. Izen, 38, a lieutenant colonel in the U.S. Marine Corps stationed outside Nardelli's door, is part of a Marine Corps Corporate Fellows program that Home Depot joined in 2002.

Importing ideas, people, and platitudes from the military is a key part of Nardelli's sweeping move to reshape Home Depot, the world's third-largest retailer, into a more centralized organization. That may be an untrendy idea in management circles, but Nardelli couldn't care less (Exhibit 1). It's a critical element of his strategy to rein in an unwieldy 2,048-store chain and prepare for its next leg of growth. "The kind of discipline and maturity that you get out of the military is something that can be very, very useful in an organization where basically you have 2,100 colonels running things," explains Craig R. Johnson, president of Customer Growth Partners Inc., a retail consulting firm.

Rivals such as Wal-Mart are plunging deeper into home improvement products, while archenemy No. 1, Lowe's Cos., is luring Home Depot customers to its 1,237 bright, airy stores. Even as other companies seek to stoke creativity and break down hierarchies, Nardelli is trying to build a disciplined corps, one predisposed to following orders, operating in high-pressure environments, and executing with high standards. Home Depot is one company that actually lives by the aggressive ideals laid out in *Hardball: Are You Playing to Play or Playing to Win?* the much discussed 2004 book co-authored by Boston Consulting Group management expert George Stalk (Exhibit 2).

EXHIBIT 1

Full Metal Apron

Nardelli is building an army at Home Depot. Here are the new marching orders for America's biggest home improvement store:

Issue Clear Commands

On Monday afternoons, Home Depot's in-house television station broadcasts *The Same Page*, a 25-minute live show emphasizing the week's top priorities.

Expel Underachievers

There's little room for error at the Home Depot. Weak managers are routinely booted. Of the top 170 executives, 98% of Nardelli's team are new to their positions since 2001.

Hire Warriors

Home Depot is on a military hiring spree. The number of former troops hired by Nardelli, who loves their discipline, has risen steadily from 10,000 in 2003 to 17,000 in 2005.

Quantify It

Home Depot now measures everything from gross margin per labor-hour for store workers to the number of "greets" at its front doors. Nardelli's predecessors, **Marcus** and **Blank**, relied more on instinct.

Centralize Control

Before Nardelli arrived, managers ran stores as individual fiefdoms. Now he is centralizing the operation, spending $1.1 billion on technology that helps to give Atlanta greater control over most tasks.

Borrow Military Ideas

What other company looks to Marine Corps literature for management wisdom? That's what Home Depot Marine Fellow **James Izen** did in helping to craft motivational messages for more than 300,000 store workers.

EXHIBIT 2

Take No Prisoners

Home Depot's cultural makeover echoes some of the guiding principles of *Hardball: Are You Playing to Play or Playing to Win?* co-authored by **George Stalk.**

Raise the costs of your competitors

Maneuver them into pursuing customers they believe are more profitable but aren't. Your competitors' costs increase, and profits decrease.

Devastate your rivals' profit sanctuaries

Influence the behavior of competitors by knowing where their most lucrative business niches are: then, when needed, use that knowledge to constrict their cash flow.

Take it and make it your own

Recognize the value of an existing idea, practice, or business model from another industry and deploy the insight to create an unassailable advantage.

Break the compromises your industry accepts

Customers rarely see past standard operating procedures. Instead, they accept them as "the way the industry works." Breaking those compromises can release huge cometitive advantages.

Unleash massive, overwhelming force

Establish a resource advantage over competitors, then engage them in wars of attrition. Warning: Can be costly to carry out.

The cultural overhaul is taking Home Depot in a markedly different direction from Lowe's, where managers describe the atmosphere as demanding—but low-profile, collaborative, and collegial. Lowe's does not have formal military-hiring programs, says a company spokeswoman, nor does it track the number of military veterans in its ranks. Observes Goldman, Sachs & Co. analyst Matthew Fassler: "Bob believes in a command-and-control organization."

In Nardelli's eyes, it's a necessary step in Home Depot's corporate evolution. Even though founders Marcus and Blank were hardly a pair of teddy bears, they allowed store managers immense autonomy. "Whether it was an aisle, department, or store, you were truly in charge of it," says former store operations manager and Navy mechanic Bryce G. Church, who now oversees 30 Ace Hardware stores. And the two relied more on instincts than analytics to build the youngest company ever to hit $40 billion in revenue, just 20 years after its 1979 founding. In the waning years of their leadership in the late 1990s, however, sales stagnated. The company "grew so fast the wheels were starting to come off," says Edward E. Lawler III, a professor of business at the University of Southern California. These days every major decision and goal at Home Depot flows down from Nardelli's office. "There's no question; Bob's the general," says Joe DeAngelo, 44, executive vice-president of Home Depot Supply and a GE veteran.

Although he has yet to win all the hearts and minds of his employees, and probably never will, Nardelli's feisty spirit is rekindling stellar financial performance

(Exhibit 3). Riding a housing and home-improvement boom, Home Depot sales have soared, from $46 billion in 2000, the year Nardelli took over, to $81.5 billion in 2005, an average annual growth rate of 12%, according to results announced on Feb. 21. By squeezing more out of each orange box through centralized purchasing and a $1.1 billion investment in technology, such as self-checkout aisles and in-store Web kiosks, profits have more than doubled in Nardelli's tenure, to $5.8 billion. Home Depot's gross margins inched up from 30% in 2000 to 33.5% last year. But fast-growing Lowe's is still Wall Street's darling, in large part because analysts are only now getting comfortable with Nardelli's strategy. Based in Mooresville, N.C., Lowe's has seen sales grow an average of 19% a year since 2000, and it has narrowed the gap in gross margins vs. Home Depot. Since the day before Nardelli's arrival on Dec. 14, 2000, Lowe's split-adjusted share price has soared 210%. Home Depot's is down 7%.

One way Nardelli plans to kick-start the stock: move beyond the core U.S. big-box business and conquer new markets, from contractor supply to convenience stores to expansion into China. On Jan. 19, Home Depot announced plans to scale back the growth of new stores from more than 180 per year to about 100. The slowdown will let him plow extra resources into beefing up Home Depot Supply (HDS), a wholesale unit hawking pipes, custom kitchens, and building materials to contractors and repairmen. It's a fragmented market worth $410 billion per year, according to Home Depot, where Wal-Mart and Lowe's are AWOL and the only

EXHIBIT 3   Work in Progress

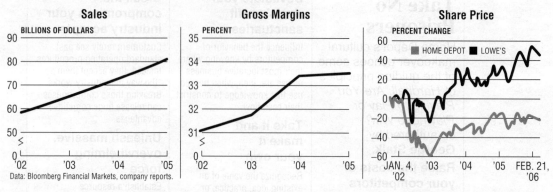

Data: Bloomberg Financial Markets, company reports.

competitors are regional companies. Already, Nardelli has spent $4.1 billion buying 35 companies to bulk up HDS, and it plans to plunk down a further $3.5 billion to buy Orlando-based Hughes Supply Inc. By 2010, HDS sales are expected to reach $23 billion, accounting for 18% of Home Depot's total, up from 5% in 2005.

The scope of the task is staggering. Nardelli, in essence, is building a whole new company—in a market twice the size of do-it-yourself retail—to service a prickly customer: professional contractors who want low prices, great quality, and instant service. Success in this field will require pinpoint execution, and Nardelli knows it. But his ambitions make some analysts nervous. "He's moving out of retail into services," says Deborah Weinswig, an analyst at Citigroup. "If it was just retail, a lot of us would be more comfortable."

"Culture of Fear"

The high stakes of Home Depot's services gambit is one of the main reasons Nardelli has pushed his cultural makeover so hard in the five years since he has been at the helm. But not all have embraced him, or his plans. *BusinessWeek* spoke with 11 former executives, a majority of whom requested anonymity lest the company sue them for violating nondisclosure agreements. Some describe a demoralized staff and say a "culture of fear" is causing customer service to wane. Nardelli's own big-time pay package, $28.5 million for the year ended Jan. 30, 2005, rubs many workers the wrong way. His guaranteed bonus, the only locked-in payout at the company, rose to $5.8 million in 2004, from $4.5 million in 2003, at a time when Home Depot's stock price finished below its yearned price in 2000, when Nardelli took over.

Before he arrived, managers ran Home Depot's stores on "tribal knowledge," based on years of experience about what sold and what didn't. Now they click nervously through Black-Berrys at the end of each week, hoping they "made plan," a combination of sales and profit targets. The once-heavy ranks of full-time Home Depot store staff have been replaced with part-timers to drive down labor costs. Underperforming executives are routinely culled from the ranks. Since 2001, 98% of Home Depot's 170 top executives are new to their positions and, at headquarters in Atlanta, 56% of job changes involved bringing new managers in from outside the company. Says one former executive: "Every single week you shuddered when you looked at e-mail because another officer was gone."

As a manager, Nardelli is relentless, demanding, and determined to prove wrong every critic of Home Depot. He treats Saturdays and Sundays as ordinary working days and often expects those around him to do the same. "He's the hardest-working guy you'll ever see," says his former boss, Jack Welch. "If I was working late at GE and wanted to feel good at 9 p.m., I would pick up the phone and call Bob. He would always be there." Privately, Nardelli admits that the move to Home Depot has sometimes been a tough slog. When he first took over—having no retail experience and replacing the beloved Bernie and Arthur—he often felt as though he were fighting a lonely, up-hill battle to convert Home Depot's legions of workers to his new vision for the company.

Nardelli's history of surrounding himself with military recruits goes back to his GE days. At GE Transportation in the 1980s, he pioneered a program of hiring junior military officers, in part because few people were willing to move to "Dreary Erie, Pa.," where the unit is headquartered. Former grunts, used to sitting in mud holes, found the locale less of a problem. William J. Conaty, senior vice-president for corporate human resources at GE, says: "Places like Erie or Fort Wayne, Ind., didn't look desolate to these guys." Welch soon expanded the program throughout GE.

Welch characterizes Nardelli as "an unusual patriot . . . a true flag-waving American." Nardelli's father, Raymond, served in Europe during World War II with the Pennsylvania Keystone unit of the National Guard. As a freshman at Rockford Auburn High School in Rockford, Ill., Nardelli joined the Reserve Officers' Training Corps (ROTC) and eventually became company commander and a member of the rifle team. He also played football. "You could either take gym class or ROTC," recalls Nardelli. "I took ROTC and enjoyed the hell out of it." When it came time for college, he applied to the U.S. Military Academy at West Point, N.Y. But the Army academy accepts applicants in part by congressional district, and the young Nardelli missed the cut by one person: He was the first alternate from his region of Illinois. Instead he attended Western Illinois University in Macomb. After graduating in 1971, his draft number was called, but, he says, he did not pass his physical. Later he went on to the University of Louisville for an MBA.

As an adult, Nardelli's passion for the military persists. At Home Depot headquarters, 1,800 "blue star banners" hang in the main hallway in honor of employees serving in Afghanistan, Iraq, and elsewhere. He is frequently shadowed by Marine Fellow Izen. During one recent project to help Home Depot hone its motivational message to 317,000 store troops, Izen consulted the *Marine Corps Doctrinal Publication 1* on "War-Fighting." MCDP *1,* as it's called in the Marines, includes a chapter on "developing subordinate leaders," which Izen found a handy guide for Home Depot workers, too. "It's about how to out-think your enemy," says Izen.

The military, says Nardelli, trains its recruits to be leaders and think on their feet, skills he wants in Home Depot stores. "Having personally been on the flight deck of an aircraft carrier where 18-year-olds are responsible for millions of dollars worth of aircraft," says Nardelli, "I just think these are folks who understand the importance of training, understand the importance of 'you're only as good as the people around you.' In their case, their life depends on it many times. In our case, our business depends on it many times."

Indeed, the Home Depot of Bob Nardelli is being run with military-style precision (Exhibit 4). These days everyone at Home Depot is ranked on the basis of four performance metrics: financial, operational, customer, and people skills. The company has placed human resources managers in every store, and all job applicants who make it through a first-round interview must then pass a role-playing exercise. Dennis M. Donovan, Home Depot's executive vice-president for human resources and a GE alumnus, measures the effectiveness of Home Depot workers by using an equation: $VA = Q \times A \times E$. Its meaning? According to Home Depot, the value-added (VA) of an employee equals the quality (Q) of what you do, multiplied by its acceptance (A) in the company, times how well you execute (E) the task. The goal is to replace the old, sometimes random management style with new rigor. "Bob's creating a second culture [at Home Depot]," says DeAngelo.

EXHIBIT 4

Buzz Words

Nardelli's cultural transformation has prompted some new lingo among Home Depot workers, some of it unflattering:

The "Aprons"
Like "troops," a term used by some senior executives to refer to Home Depot store workers (who wear aprons)

"Bob's Army"
Slang for the "store leadership program," wherein almost 50% of the 1,142 trainees hired are ex-military personnel

"Bobaganda"
The always-on Home Depot television channel, a.k.a. HD-TV, shown in rooms where employees take their breaks

"Home Despot"
For the most disenchanted workers, the moniker bestowed on the mighty home-improvement chain

"Home GEpot"
A snarky reference to the swelling ranks of General Electric alumni Nardelli has wooed

"Orange Belt"
The entry level for employees studying Six Sigma, the quality management system Nardelli imported from GE

While Nardelli is careful to say that the military is just one pipeline of talent into Home Depot—the company also recruits senior citizens through the AARP and Latinos through four Hispanic advocacy groups—he is clearly imbuing the company with "Semper Fi" spirit. If Nardelli is the four-star general, then Carl C. Liebert III is his chief of staff. A graduate of the U.S. Naval Academy at Annapolis, Md., where he played college basketball with NBA star David Robinson, Liebert, 40, stands 6 ft., 7 in. and is every bit as intense as his boss. After running Six Sigma programs at GE's Consumer Products unit, followed by a stint at Circuit City Stores Inc., he took over Home Depot's stores in the U.S. and Mexico in 2004. Now, with Lowe's and Wal-Mart picking off Home Depot's customers, Liebert is moving quickly to whip the troops into shape. "What worked 20 years ago may not work today," says Liebert. "It's as simple as warfare. We don't fight wars the way we used to."

Simple Slogans

To win the customer service war, Liebert has adjusted his tactics. At the annual store managers' meeting in Los Angeles on Mar. 8, Home Depot plans to roll out a 25-page booklet dubbed *How to Be Orange Every Day.* All store employees will be expected to keep it in their apron pocket. It contains aphorisms such as "customers cannot buy what we do not have," "we create an atmosphere of high-energy fun," and "every person, penny and product counts." Liebert hopes such simple slogans will help shore up Home Depot's once-vaunted customer service. To Liebert's mind, they recall the four basic responses to an officer's question in the Navy: "Yes, sir"; "No, sir"; "Aye, aye, sir"; and "I'll find out, sir." He calls it an effort to "align" all Home Depot workers on the same page when it comes to serving customers. "I think about that line from *A Few Good Men* when Jack Nicholson says: 'Are we clear?' and Tom Cruise says: 'Crystal,'" chuckles Liebert. "I love that."

But drilling workers in how to treat customers may not be enough. The University of Michigan's annual American Customer Satisfaction Index, released on Feb. 21, shows Home Depot slipped to dead last among major U.S. retailers. With a score of 67, down from 73 in 2004, Home Depot scored 11 points behind Lowe's and three points lower than much-maligned Kmart. "This is not competitive and too low to be sustainable. It's very serious," says Claes Fornell, professor of business

at the University of Michigan and author of the 12-year-old customer satisfaction survey, which uses a 250-person sample and an econometric model to rate companies on quality and service. Fornell believes that the drop in satisfaction is one reason why Home Depot's stock price has declined at the same time Lowe's has soared. A former executive who spoke on condition of anonymity says that Nardelli's effort to measure good customer service, instead of inspiring it, is to blame: "My perception is that the mechanics are there. The soul isn't."

Nardelli angrily disputes the survey. "It's a sham," he says, jabbing his finger in the air for emphasis. Nardelli notes that, in 2003, Fornell shorted Home Depot stock in his personal portfolio, before his survey results came out. Fornell says the trades were part of his research into a correlation between companies' customer-satisfaction scores and stock price performance. The University of Michigan banned the practice the next year. Home Depot executives add that internal polling shows customer satisfaction is improving, but they won't release complete results. They point to Harris Interactive's 2005 Reputation Quotient, an annual 600-person survey that combines a range of reputation-related categories, from customer service to social responsibility. The survey ranked Home Depot No. 12 among major companies and reported that customers appreciated Home Depot's "quality service." Still, Home Depot appears to know it has serious customer-service problems. Store chief Liebert's back-to-basics plan includes a push to improve even the "genuineness" of the greeting that customers receive at the door.

Some of the same former managers who blame Nardelli's hardball approach for corroding the service ethic at Home Depot describe a culture so paralyzed with fear that they didn't worry about whether they would be terminated, but when. One night last year, an unnamed executive in the lighting department at Home Depot headquarters left fliers on desks and in elevators containing a litany of complaints about Home Depot, including Nardelli's giant pay package and the high level of executive turnover. The rebel, say other former executives, was tracked down by security cameras and immediately fired. Citing concerns about the employee's privacy, Home Depot declined to comment on the incident. In break rooms, the company pipes in HD-TV, short for Home Depot television. But employees have mocked it as "Bobaganda," referring to Nardelli, for its constant drone of tips, warnings, and executive messages. Every Monday night, for example, store chief Liebert and Tom Taylor, executive vice-president for marketing and merchandising, host a 25-minute live broadcast for senior store staff on the week's most important priorities called *The Same Page.* "These are [their] marching orders for the week," says Liebert.

Command of Details

Still, it's hard even for Nardelli critics, including ones he has fired, not to admire his unstinting determination to follow his makeover plan in the face of scores of naysayers. They describe being "in awe" of his command of minute details. But some of them question whether the manufacturing business model that worked for him at GE Transportation and GE Power Systems—squeezing efficiencies out of the core business while buying up new business—can work in a retail environment where taking care of customers is paramount. "Bob has brought a lot of operational efficiencies that Home Depot needed," says Steve Mahurin, chief merchandising officer at True Value Co. and a former senior vice-president for merchandising at Home Depot. "But he failed to keep the orange-blooded, entrepreneurial spirit alive. Home Depot is now a factory."

Can his plan work? "Ab-so-lute-ly," says Nardelli. "This is the third time this business model has been successful." He rejects the idea that he has created a culture of fear. "The only reason you should be fearful is if you personally don't want to make the commitment," says Nardelli. "Or there's a bolt of reality that you're in a position, based on the growth of the company, that you can't deliver on those commitments." He says Home Depot is dealing with the challenges of being a more centralized company just fine. And he makes no apologies for laying off the ranks of underperforming store workers and executives to achieve aggressive financial objectives. "We couldn't have done this by saying, 'Run slower, jump lower, and just kind of get by,' " insists Nardelli, hardening his gaze. "So I will never apologize for setting the bar high."

John N. Pistone, 35, is on the elite team. A graduate of West Point and former company commander in the Army's First Cavalry Div., he served in Kuwait in 2000 and was an ROTC instructor at Boston College. Now a district manager running eight Home Depot stores on the east side of Atlanta, with 1,200 staffers, he's on the fast track, in part because of his cool demeanor and always-on smile that endears him to employees. "A private in the Army is a lot like an $8-an-hour cashier," he says. But there's another reason Pistone is on the rise: As he clicks through his BlackBerry on a Monday morning, he remarks, with a sigh of relief, that his eight stores "made plan" the previous week. "This is a quarterly business that we worry about hourly," he says. As Bob Nardelli builds his new army at Home Depot, that's a sentiment he loves to hear.

A Lab in a Secure, Undisclosed Spot

In a bland office park not far from Home Depot Inc.'s Atlanta headquarters lies a squat, unmarked building. It could easily be mistaken for the uninspiring home of an insurance firm. That's fine by the steady stream of spit-and-polish Home Depot executives who file through the entrance, many of whom don orange aprons once safely inside. What they don't want you to know is that behind this unassuming facade is Home Depot's secret weapon: an 88,000-square-foot Innovation Center, where the chain tests everything from riding lawn mowers to displays for patio furniture sets before they hit stores.

Since it opened quietly in September, 2004, the Innovation Center has become a key command center in Chief Executive Robert L. Nardelli's push to overhaul the giant retailer. "This is our working laboratory," says Thomas V. Taylor Jr., Home Depot's executive vice-president for marketing and merchandising. Bringing new and better products to its 2,048 stores is critical for Home Depot, in its battle to out-innovate archrival Lowe's Cos., which has its own product testing center on its Mooresville (N.C.) campus, and voracious juggernaut Wal-Mart Stores Inc.

So sensitive is this Home Depot-owned site that reporters are requested not to disclose its address. Hard-nosed Nardelli boasts about how outsiders must pass through a metal detector that scans for camera phones. Once you get past a burly guard stationed at the front door, the Innovation Center emerges as a kind of ersatz, unfinished Home Depot store. Amid soft lighting and wide aisles, 16-ft. racks display vacuum cleaners, power tools, and oven hoods in an effort to learn how they'll look in the real stores. Super-secret projects, in which Home Depot is testing radically new product categories with scant relation to hammers and nails, are watched separately by security personnel and covered with huge tarpaulins.

When Nardelli arrived in 2000, Home Depot had precious little elbow room to experiment. It was risky for executives to tinker with new tools or test-run different types of displays in existing stores, lest they tip their hand to spies from competitors, who are constantly walking the aisles. As a result, they would do demos in the bottom level of a parking garage at Home Depot's headquarters—but the cramped, nine-ft. ceilings made it hard to duplicate the cavernous space of the actual stores.

Now, Taylor and his team have a full-blown Home Depot mock-up to explore new product segments, frequently at blitzkrieg speed. Company officials say they can go from an Innovation Center product test to an in-store pilot project in as little as 30 days. One of the projects soon to make its way out of the Innovation Center: In late March, Home Depot will roll out a special section in 10 stores in Jacksonville, Fla., targeting car buffs with a diverse selection of new products such as Rain-X wiper blades in seven sizes, Master Lock EZ mount towing kits, and Castrol motor oil.

The Innovation Center is also a venue for experimentation. In his relentless drive for "laser execution" at Home Depot, Nardelli has pushed executives to come up with new ways to beat competitors on price, displays, and product assortment. That's why a wall in one aisle at the center is covered, floor to ceiling, with boring white lightbulbs. Each horizontal row of bulbs is set off with tape and labeled with names and price tags: Home Depot, Target, Wal-Mart, Sam's Club, Menard's, and Costco. It's Taylor's marketwide view of what Home Depot is up against—and how, down to the tiniest detail, he can innovate for an advantage.

Source: Didne Brady, Michael Arndt, and Brian Grow, "Renovating Home Depot," *BusinessWeek,* March 6, 2006, 50–58.

Case 5-3

Yahoo! Inc.

When Terry S. Semel walked into the Sunnyvale (Calif.) headquarters of Yahoo! Inc. for his first day as chief executive on May 1, 2001, he faced an unenviable task. Ad sales at the Internet icon were plummeting, and the new CEO was replacing the well-liked Timothy Koogle, who had been pushed aside by the company's board. Worse, leery employees quickly saw that Semel, a retired Hollywood exec, didn't know Internet technology and looked stiffly out of place at Yahoo's playful, egalitarian headquarters. Would this guy tour the Valley in the purple Yahoo car, as Koogle did, or play a Yahoo kazoo? Fat chance. And instead of bunking in nearby Atherton or Palo Alto, like other Silicon Valley execs, he rode off every evening in a chauffeured SUV to a luxury suite at San Francisco's Four Seasons Hotel.

Two years after taking control as chairman and CEO, Semel has silenced the doubters. By imposing his buttoned-down management approach on Yahoo, the 60-year-old has engineered one of the most remarkable revivals of a beleaguered dot-com. Once paralyzed by management gridlock and written off as another overhyped has-been, Yahoo is roaring back. The company earned $43 million on revenues of $953 million in 2002, compared with a $93 million loss in 2001 on $717 million in sales. And Yahoo's momentum is growing. Net income hit $47 million in this year's first quarter as revenues powered ahead 47%. Analysts predict that this year's profits will quadruple, to more than $200 million, while sales climb 33%, to $1.3 billion. "What he has done is just phenomenal," says Hollywood pal Barry Diller, CEO of USA Interactive Inc., a Yahoo competitor.

Semel has done nothing less than remake the culture of the quintessential Internet company. The new Yahoo is grounded by a host of Old Economy principles that Semel lugged up the coast from Los Angeles. The contrast with Yahoo's go-go days is stark. At Terry Semel's Yahoo, spontaneity is out. Order is in. New initiatives used to roll ahead following free-form brainstorming and a gut check. Now, they wind their way through a rugged gauntlet of tests and analysis. Only a few make the grade. It's a wrenching change. But Semel's self-effacing style, honed over years of navigating through the towering egos of Hollywood, helps soften the shock.

Yahoo's newfound success does, too. Semel has used the dealmaking skills that made him a legend in the movie business to land crucial acquisitions and partnerships that are producing rich new revenues for Yahoo (Exhibit 1). A deal with phone giant SBC Communications Inc. launched Yahoo into the business of selling broadband access to millions of American homes—which should add $70 million in revenue this year. The buyout of HotJobs.com last year put Yahoo into the online job-hunting business, adding $80 million in revenue. Most important, a partnership with Overture Services Inc. to carry ads on Yahoo's search-results pages is gushing some $230 million in revenue this year. The upshot? Semel's new businesses should make up half

EXHIBIT 1   Yahoo's Game Plan

Can CEO Semel lift Yahoo to greatness? The nine-year-old company is poised to notch its best-ever sales and profits in 2003. But Semel must accomplish even more to justify Yahoo's nosebleed market valuation, including a p-e of 79. Here are his biggest bets:

Paid Search

Revenues for selling links on its search-results pages rocketed from zilch to $130 million in 2002. With the overall paid-search market expected to grow 40% to 50% annually, paid search may be Yahoo!'s jet fuel in coming years.
2003 Projected Revenue
$230 million ▲ 77%
Outlook
Excellent This is the Internet's growth market, and few are positioned as well as Yahoo. Possible spoiler: Google.

Internet Advertising

Life is creeping back into Yahoo's longtime mainstay, traditional online advertising, which should top $600 million in 2003 sales. Yahoo expects to double the industry growth rate, with annual growth of at least 5% to 10% for the next several years.
2003 Projected Revenue
$615 million ▲ 18%
Outlook
Good The market is coming back, and Yahoo! has learned the hard way what works.

Paid Subscriptions

Only 1% of Yahoo's 232 million online users pay the company for services. Yahoo is working to bring in more cash outlays by offering a host of premium services, including online personals and supersize e-mail accounts.

2003 Projected Revenue
$251 million ▲ 25%
Outlook
Fair This is Yahoo's Achilles' heel. The potential is rich, but turning free Web surfers into paying subscribers is proving tough.

Broadband Access

A partnership with SBC Communications makes Yahoo a broadband player, generating fees and establishing Yahoo as a high-speed home page. But its failure to link up with other telecoms limits the offering, for now, to SBC's region.
2003 Projected Revenue
$70 million ▲ 900%
Outlook
Good Yahoo can grow with broadband, which is gaining 30% annually. The risk: It hinges on partnerships that could prove fragile.

Online Careers

Yahoo acquired Hotjobs.com in late 2001, which contributed $80 million to Yahoo's top line in 2002. But growth is slow in the stagnant U.S. employment market, and Yahoo trails job-search leader Monster.com.
2003 Projected Revenue
$80 million ▲ 0%
Outlook
Good Online recruiting is expected to grow 18% a year for the next five years. Yahoo should grab a growing share.

of Yahoo's top line in 2003. "We planted a lot of seeds a year and a half ago, and some are beginning to grow," he says (Exhibit 2).

Semel's strategy is gaining fans on Wall Street—and stoking new fears of a mini-Internet bubble. The company's shares have soared 200% in the past eight months, to $26. Sure, Yahoo's market capitalization is a mere 13% of its giddy all-time high of $127 billion in early 2000. But today's price-earnings ratio of 79 is triple that of heavyweight Microsoft Corp. and more than eBay Inc.'s 67, despite the online auctioneer's heftier revenues, profits, and growth projections. "Yahoo's valuation is a tough case to make," concedes Firsthand Funds Chief Investment Officer Kevin Landis,

who nonetheless has bought 50,000 Yahoo shares in the past eight months based on the portal's turnaround and brighter industry trends.

Investors are betting on Semel to follow up his bold debut with a sizzling encore. Call it Act Two. For this next stage of growth, Semel envisions building Yahoo into a digital Disneyland, a souped-up theme park for the Internet Age. The idea is that Web surfers logging on to Yahoo's site, like customers squeezing through the turnstiles in Anaheim, will find themselves in a self-contained world full of irresistible offerings.

In the past, Yahoo attracted visitors with free services such as stock quotes and headlines and drew 90% of its revenue from online ads. Now, Semel is trying to

EXHIBIT 2 Yahoo's Turnaround

While Online Advertising Hit the Skids . . .

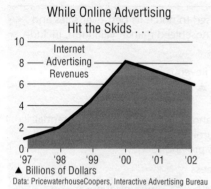

Internet Advertising Revenues

▲ Billions of Dollars
Data: PricewaterhouseCoopers, Interactive Advertising Bureau

. . . Yahoo Rekindled Sales by Diversifying . . .

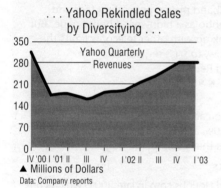

Yahoo Quarterly Revenues

▲ Millions of Dollars
Data: Company reports

. . . Giving Investors Reason to Applaud

Stock Price

▲ Dollars
Data: Yahoo!

charge for many services, coaxing Web surfers to spend hard cash on everything from digital music and online games to job listings and premium e-mail accounts with loads of extra storage. Already, he pulls in one-third of revenue from such offerings and hopes to drive it up to 50% by 2004. To do that, analysts say, he's likely to cut deals to add online travel and classified ads for cars.

But nothing is more key to Semel's strategy than his push into broadband. Lots of the services he's banking on, such as music and interactive games, are data hogs that appeal mostly to customers with high-speed

links. Plus, broadband is always on, so many of Yahoo's customers will be lingering in Semel's theme park for hours on end, day after day. "The more time you spend on Yahoo, the more apt you are to sample both free and paid services," he says.

If Semel can pull it off, the new Yahoo could become one of the few enduring powerhouses on the Net. Customers who pay for its services could more than triple, to 10 million in 2005 from 2.9 million now, analysts predict. Profits could soar 75% over the next two years, to $350 million, and sales could surge 30%, to $1.7 billion, analysts say. "Yahoo has emerged as a durable digital franchise," says Alberto W. Vilar, president of Amerindo Investment Advisors Inc., which has an undisclosed stake. "If you take the long view, this stock could still double or triple."

But Semel doesn't have a monopoly on digital theme parks. AOL Time Warner Inc. and Microsoft's MSN are pushing nearly identical agendas—and both boast advantages over Yahoo. AOL, despite its merger headaches, can tap into popular content from the world's largest media company, from CNN to Warner Music. MSN benefits from the software muscle and cash hoard of Microsoft, as well as broadband partnerships that cover 27% more lines into homes and businesses than Yahoo's SBC deal. It also may have an easier time getting Web surfers to pay for new offerings. "Yahoo's brand is built on free information services," says MSN Group Product Manager Lisa Gurry. She says coaxing Yahoo customers to pull out their wallets will be "very challenging."

An even greater challenge is coming from a newer competitor, Google Inc. In just four years, Google has turned into a global sensation and is now widely regarded as the preeminent search engine on earth. The risk to Yahoo is that the search king will give birth to a more potent business model. Instead of flocking to flashy theme parks such as Yahoo's, consumers are already starting to rely on Google's uncluttered search to find everything they need. Already, some online advertisers are moving their ad dollars to search engines. "We're shifting our emphasis away from portals [such as Yahoo, AOL, and MSN]," says Alan Rimm Kaufman, vice-president for marketing at electronics retailer Crutchfield Corp. "The people stealing these ad dollars are [companies] like Google."

Hot competition in the search business could force Semel's next big move. His partnership with Overture, a company that delivers Internet advertising, is producing some 20% of Yahoo's revenues. Microsoft's MSN has a similar deal with Overture that also is paying off richly. Analysts say Semel could make an offer for Overture—if he thinks it's necessary to preempt a Microsoft acquisition. He is already sitting on $2.2 billion in cash, 50% more than the likely price tag for Overture. Still, Semel likely won't make a bid unless he's pushed into it because of the distractions of such a large merger. Yahoo and Overture declined comment on a possible deal.

Distraction is something Yahoo can ill afford as it adapts to the changes ahead. To date, Semel has honed the company's execution—cutting costs, filtering out iffy ideas, pursuing sure things, and making money. It's the perfect model for today's sickly market. But when the slump ends, new ideas will likely make a dramatic comeback. These could define the next generation of the Internet. The question is whether Yahoo, with its careful and laborious vetting process for new projects, risks losing out to Google or getting blindsided by a nimble newcomer.

Can Semel innovate, beat back the rising tide of competition, and live up to the latest round of great expectations for Yahoo? If he plays his cards right, yes. Despite the advantages of AOL and MSN, Yahoo has kept its position as the most popular site on the Web, according to Nielsen/Net Ratings. Yahoo claims 232 million monthly visitors. Semel is demonstrating the skills to turn this large chunk of humanity into paying customers, boosting the customer count eightfold, from 375,000 when he arrived two years ago. To combat Google, Semel is hurrying to beef up Yahoo's search capabilities. He closed a $290 million deal for search company Inktomi in March, and the marketing campaign to promote it blasted off in New York's Times Square on May 19. "Yahoo has reemerged as a potent force," says Derek Brown, an analyst at Pacific Growth Equities. "It's well-positioned to leverage its massive global user base and dominant brand."

The CEO's low-key approach has worked quiet magic through a 40-year career. When Brooklyn-born Semel arrived as a sales trainee at Warner Bros. in 1965, the 22-year-old accountant had little relevant experience but an understated confidence in himself. In an industry brimming with ego, Semel stayed offstage and worked to shine the light on others. It paid dividends. As he moved from Warner Bros. to Buena Vista and back again, Semel rose to the top on a vast network of friends and allies. He used these, along with his formidable negotiating skills, to create a giant. In a two-decade partnership as co-CEO with Bob Daly, Semel turned Warner Bros. from a $1 billion studio to an $11 billion behemoth, producing megahits such as *The Matrix*.

Through his retirement in 1999, Semel kept up the winning formula, making friends and minting millions.

He says that in their two decades together, he and Daly never fought. If such a smooth track record is rare in high tech, it's even more uncommon in Hollywood. "When you're releasing 20 or 25 movies a year, you're navigating a minefield every weekend," says Barry M. Meyer, chairman and CEO of Warner Bros. Entertainment Inc. and a longtime Semel colleague. "His success at Yahoo does not surprise me at all."

It was Yahoo co-founder Jerry Yang who nudged Semel toward Yahoo in 2001. The two had met two years earlier at a media conference and had hit it off. By the spring of 2001, Yahoo was reeling from the falloff in Net advertising and needed a major overhaul. The question was whether the wealthy Semel, who was already dabbling in online entertainment companies, would dive into one of the biggest of them all at a time of crisis. Semel signed on with the proviso that Koogle step down as chairman.

When the new chief arrived, he ran into a few troubling surprises. Semel was shocked early on to learn that Yahoo did not have the technology in place to handle surging demand for services such as online personals, say two former executives. That spelled months of delay before Semel could push premium offerings.

Then there were the cultural challenges. Initially, Semel balked at the company's "cubicles only" policy, finally settling into a cube adjacent to a conference room so he could make phone calls in private. He stayed free of the Valley social scene, spending weeknights at the hotel in San Francisco and flying his private jet home to his swanky Los Angeles neighborhood of Bel Air on weekends.

Morale was also an issue. Compared with his predecessor, the relaxed and chatty Koogle, known by the troops at T.K., Semel came off at first as cold and rough. He chopped down the 44 business units he inherited to 5, stripping many execs of pet projects. Veteran Yahoo execs prodded Semel to mingle more with the rank and file and pushed him into grabbing lunch more often at the campus cafeteria. Still, such forays often fell flat. "T.K. was just one of the guys," says a former Yahoo manager. "When Semel talked to you, it felt like he was consciously making an effort to talk to employees."

Soon, Semel's strengths started to shine through. With his focus and dealmaking savvy, he appeared to have the tools to rescue Yahoo. Employees, with loads of underwater stock options, increasingly cheered him on. "People don't always agree with the direction they're getting, but they're happy the direction is there," says a current Yahoo manager who requested anonymity.

Walk through Yahoo's headquarters, past the purple cow in the lobby, the acres of cubicles, the workers in jeans, and you might think T.K. was still running the place. But sitting across from Semel, the change is evident. His voice quiet and steady, his language cordial yet deliberate, Semel seems incapable of the hype that once vaulted companies such as Yahoo into the stratosphere. This is the voice of post-dot-com era. He steers attention to his colleagues. "I love [my managers] to do their homework," he says. "I love them to help make decisions, and they do. Somewhere in that process, I'll include myself—or they'll include me."

Semel's not kidding about the homework. In the old days, Yahoo execs would brainstorm for hours, often following hunches with new initiatives. Those days are long gone. Under Semel, managers must prepare exhaustively before bringing up a new idea if it's to have a chance to survive.

It's a Darwinian drama that takes place in near-weekly meetings of a group called the Product Council. Dreamed up by a couple of vice-presidents and championed by Semel and his chief operating officer, Daniel Rosensweig, a former president of CNET Networks Inc., the group typically includes nine managers from all corners of the company. It's chaired by Geoff Ralston and often includes key lieutenants such as Jeff Weiner and Jim Brock, all senior vice-presidents. The group sizes up business plans to make sure all new projects bring benefits to Yahoo's existing businesses. "We need to work within a framework," says Semel. "If it's a free-for-all . . . we won't take advantage of the strengths of our company."

For years, managers built up their own niches around the main Yahoo site. No one, say former and current execs, appeared to be thinking about the portal as a whole, much less how the various bits and pieces could work together. "Managers would beg, borrow, and steal from the network to help their own properties," says Greg Coleman, Yahoo's executive vice-president for media and sales.

Semel wants to stitch it all together. He calls the concept "network optimization" and says it's a key goal for 2003. The idea is that every initiative should not only make money but also feed Yahoo's other businesses. It's the painstaking job of establishing these interconnections that eats up much of the time at council meetings. And the winnowing process is brutal. Of the 79 current ideas for premium services at some stage of planning inside Yahoo, only a few will launch in 2003, predicts Rosensweig.

Although some critics worry that innovative ideas may never see the light of day under Semel's tight control, he dismisses the prospect. Semel stresses instead the potential payoff: less clutter and a handful of high-performance services that feed each other. For a success story, he points to the company's recently relaunched search capabilities. Search for "pizza" and type in your area code, and Yahoo culls its Yellow Pages site to return addresses and driving maps to nearby pizza joints. Yahoo is the only heavyweight portal that integrates content this deeply with its search features.

Such smart execution was in dangerously short supply at Yahoo in the past. At the height of the Net bubble, Yahoo came off as arrogant. Its attitude, recalls Jeff Bell, a marketing vice-president at DaimlerChrysler Corp., was "Buy our stuff, and shut up." Semel has turned that around, hiring traditional media sales veterans and introducing more flexibility. The payoff: As the online ad market has recovered, advertisers are flocking back to Yahoo. Daimler's Bell says his Yahoo ad budget has doubled over the past two years.

Entertainment companies are joining the rush to buy key Yahoo ad space. Some 42 movies advertised on Yahoo in the first quarter, up from zilch in the first quarter of 2001. "Getting a presence on Yahoo's home page is huge," says Sarah Beatty, a senior marketing vice-president at USA Network, which is running seven ad campaigns on Yahoo in 2003.

Semel has supplemented Yahoo's ad revenues with dealmaking in other businesses. Consider the SBC pact to market broadband Net access. SBC pays Yahoo about $5 out of the $40 to $60 customers pay each month for service. Revenues from the deal should jump from $70 million this year to $125 million in 2004.

Still, Yahoo remains vulnerable in broadband. MSN has cut similar deals with Verizon Communications and Qwest Communications International Inc., which have 75 million lines to homes and businesses, vs. SBC's 59 million. Semel's efforts to land other broadband deals have come up short. More worrisome is the fragile nature of these partnerships. If SBC concludes that the Yahoo brand isn't a big draw, it could cut Yahoo out and save itself millions. An SBC spokesman says it is "happy" with Yahoo.

Of all Semel's deals, none shines brighter than the partnership with Overture Services. The companies team up to sell ads near Yahoo's search results, a business known as "paid search." If a user searches for "cook-ware," for instance, advertisers from Macy's to Sur La Table can bid to showcase their links near the results. Overture delivers the advertisers and forks over roughly two-thirds of the revenue. While Yahoo had debated such a partnership for years under Koogle, Semel drove it through in a hurry.

Just in time for paid search to blossom into the latest Web sensation. The partnership notched Yahoo more than $130 million in revenues last year—14% of its business. Analysts expect revenues from the partnership to increase 75% in 2003, accounting for nearly 20% of Yahoo's revenues.

That assumes that Google won't spoil Yahoo's fun. The wildly popular search engine has emerged as the fourth-most-trafficked site on the Internet, with an estimated $700 million in 2003 revenues. And the world may be heading Google's way. Industry analysts say that as Web surfers gain expertise, they visit general-interest sites such as Yahoo less and instead cut to the chase by typing in keywords on a search engine. According to analytics firm WebSideStory, the percentage of Web site visitors arriving via search engines doubled in the past year, to 13%.

Google's strength puts Semel in a bind. He licenses Google's search engine, which is popular among Yahoo's users. Trouble is, by keeping Google on Yahoo, he publicly endorses a rival. His likely goal, say analysts, is to replace Google soon with Inktomi, the search engine he acquired in March. That would save $13 million a year in licensing and pull the plug on Yahoo's apparent backing of Google. The danger? If Yahoo's Google-loving customers balk at switching to Inktomi, they could ditch Yahoo and surf straight to the Google site.

His answer is a national marketing campaign to boost Yahoo as a search brand. It kicked off on May 19 in New York's Times Square with the unveiling of a huge computer-screen ad featuring live searches on the Yahoo site. At street level in New York, teams of Yahoo's costumed "searchers" paraded among the crowds waving five-foot-long search bars.

It's all part of the growing buzz at Yahoo. Using his mix of discipline, sales, and dealmaking, Terry Semel has pulled off a stunning revival. But can he pull off Act Two and build Yahoo into the digital theme park of his dreams? If he does, Semel will be one of the biggest winners: When he took the helm, he bought 1 million shares of Yahoo at $17 apiece. Those shares are up 60%. The fact that Yahoo shares are banging on the ceiling and not the floor is a vivid sign that Semel's turnaround may be just getting started.

By Ben Elgin in Sunnyvale, Calif., with Ronald Grover in Los Angeles

Source: "Yahoo! Act Two," *BusinessWeek*, June 2, 2003, 70–76.

Case 5-4

Nissan Motor Co.

Carlos Ghosn is flat out the hottest automotive talent on the planet right now, and he enjoys the kind of street cred that execs from Detroit to Stuttgart can only dream about. In Japan, a full five years after arriving from France's Renault to run Nissan Motor Co., CEO Ghosn is still feted in *manga* comic books, mobbed for autographs during plant tours, and generally heaped with national adulation for saving a car company once given up for dead (Exhibit 1). At glitzy auto shows from Paris to Beijing, his cosmopolitan air—Ghosn speaks five languages—and sterling track record for turnarounds make him a star attraction. He's as smooth as Thai silk in public, and his colleagues marvel at his personal magnetism, his 24/7 work ethic, and his rigorous attachment to benchmarks and targets. Heck, in Lebanon, where he is a citizen, Ghosn's name was floated a few weeks back as a potential candidate for President.

But Nissan insiders will also tell you there is another side to the 50-year-old car exec: If you miss a number or blindside the boss with a nasty development, watch out. "To people who don't accept that performance is what is at stake, he can be ruthless," says Dominique Thormann, a senior vice-president with Nissan Europe. Just ask managers at Nissan's 16-month-old, $1.4 billion assembly plant in Canton, Miss., where sloppy craftsmanship marred the launch of the 2004 Quest minivan, the Titan full-sized pickup, and the Armada sport-utility vehicle. Car enthusiast websites are full of rants about loose moldings, water leaks, and noisy cabins. This spring, Nissan dropped from 6th to 11th in an annual quality survey by J.D. Power & Associates Inc. that tracks complaints in the first 90 days of ownership. Consumers quickly got wind of the troubles, and Nissan will have a tough time meeting its sales target of 80,000 Quests this year. In the first half, fewer than 26,000 moved off dealer lots. In July the company mailed recall letters offering to fix any defects for free. "We've been surprised by the level of degradation," concedes Ghosn, whose own stress on speedy execution contributed to the quality woes. "We recognize it is a problem, and we will fix it."

Ghosn is fixing the Canton debacle in his characteristic fashion—that is, with the subtlety of a chain saw. In

EXHIBIT 1

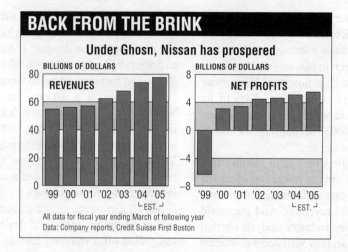

BACK FROM THE BRINK

Under Ghosn, Nissan has prospered

BILLIONS OF DOLLARS — REVENUES

BILLIONS OF DOLLARS — NET PROFITS

All data for fiscal year ending March of following year
Data: Company reports, Credit Suisse First Boston

May, he flew in 220 engineers from Japan and Nissan's older Smyrna (Tenn.) plant. The damage-control team searched every inch of the assembly line for flaws. Some were obvious: Factory hands, many of them new-comers to carmaking, wore rings and studded jeans that scratched freshly painted trucks. Other glitches were maddening: Power window switches and reading lights on the Quest often seemed possessed by gremlins, and its sliding doors didn't close quite right. So the team worked with suppliers to reengineer parts, while robots were reprogrammed to weld car bodies more tightly, and better insulation was added to the roof of the Armada. Then Ghosn shook up management, even raiding archrival Toyota to hire troubleshooter Douglas G. Betts as his new vice-president for assembly quality. As the 2005 Nissans enter dealerships this fall, buyers will learn first-hand whether Ghosn's personal inter-vention has paid off.

Lofty Targets

It's the Ghosn way: detailed planning, speedy execu-tion, and a laser focus on what needs fixing. Since 1999, when Renault paid $5.4 billion for a controlling stake in Nissan and dispatched Ghosn to Tokyo to run it, he has set—and met—sales and profit targets that have stretched the auto maker to the limit. That pattern appeared in 1990, when Ghosn turned around Michelin's North American division, and in 1996, when as chief operating officer of Renault he kicked off a program to cut $3.6 billion in annual expenses. Such acts earned Ghosn the overused sobriquet *le cost killer.* It is a name he loathes and hopes to banish for good by building an enduring car company based on product excellence, not

painful restructuring. The question is whether Ghosn is going too far, too fast. Today, he runs Nissan in Japan, where executives are battling for share in a soft market by launching six new models, and where preparations for a major expansion into China are under way. Since last spring, Ghosn has also taken charge of North America. And in April he starts his new job—replacing his men-tor Louis Schweitzer as CEO of Renault, a $46 billion giant in its own right and the controlling shareholder in Nissan, with a 44% stake. Incredibly, Ghosn will con-tinue to run Nissan from Tokyo headquarters even as he maintains oversight of U.S. operations.

Will this guy have to clone himself? Running two such complex organizations is a fiendishly difficult task, but Ghosn insists that he's ready—and that he needs to stay on at Nissan to keep the company headed in the right direction. "I won't be a part-timer, but one CEO with two hats," he says.

One CEO, as well, with an audacious plan to create what Daimler Benz and Chrysler Corp. could not—a successful global auto group from two very distinct companies. Renault and Nissan have been quietly cooperating on technology and parts buying for years. But this Franco-Japanese collaboration is set to expand significantly shortly after Ghosn arrives in Paris, in everything from parts purchasing to wholesale platform-sharing to engine design. Already, Nissan and Renault sell a combined 5.4 million vehicles a year and control 9.3% of the global market. If they were one company, it would be the fourth-largest auto maker on earth, ahead of DaimlerChrysler and right behind Ford. Ghosn says no full-fledged merger is coming—but his accession to the double thrones of Renault and Nissan signals that far deeper ties lie ahead.

Top Speed

At this crucial moment, when Ghosn can't afford a slipup, the Canton problems highlight the perils of his turbocharged management style. Carmakers know that doing too many new things at once is risky, so new plants typically make tried-and-true models, while fresh designs are usually built by seasoned workers at established factories. In Canton, though, Nissan launched five new models in less than eight months. "There was a need to get the products to market as soon as possible," says Dave Boyer, vice-president in charge of Nissan's U.S. manufacturing operations and head of the Canton plant. Ghosn today acknowledges that he may have stretched too far. And one Nissan executive, who asked not to be named, grouses that the company's cost crackdown on suppliers may have aggravated the problems. "So much effort was spent getting costs down that the quality issue went unnoticed—until it was too late," this manager says.

Ghosn says he's starting to get a handle on the quality woes. Yet at the same time he's upping the ante for Nissan's U.S. operations, which continue to grow thanks to the revamped Altima sedan and Pathfinder SUV. "I can already commit that our [quality] scores will be much better," he says. On Sept. 2, he boosted his 2004 sales target for the U.S. to make up for soft results in Japan and Europe. Ambitious, yes, but necessary if Ghosn is to reach a goal he set two years ago of annually selling 1 million more cars—an increase of 38% over three years—by September, 2005. And forget about goosing sales with rebates. "We spent five years reining in incentives, and we're not going to give it back in five months," says Jed Connelly, chief of U.S. sales. Indeed, Nissan

incentives in August averaged $1,559 a vehicle, compared with nearly $4,000 at Ford and General Motors Corp., according to auto data website Edmunds.com.

Can even a superstar such as Ghosn stay on top of industrial operations as vast as Nissan and Renault? Plenty in the industry would love to see the brash Ghosn stumble. The truth is, though, Ghosn has built a powerful machine. "It's tough to keep" a turnaround going, says GM boss G. Richard Wagoner Jr. "But it would be foolhardy to underestimate Nissan."

As turnarounds go, the Nissan saga is in a class by itself. In 1999 the company was straining under $19 billion in debt and shedding market share in both Japan and the U.S. (Exhibit 2). Ghosn was also being undermined by Nissan insiders who wanted his reforms to fail. So when he was about to announce the closing of five factories, he didn't tell his own board of directors until the night before, recalls Jason Vines, who served as Nissan's North American public-relations chief early in Ghosn's tenure and now heads PR for Chrysler Group. And to ensure those in the know wouldn't spill the beans, Ghosn threatened: " 'If this leaks out, I'll close seven plants, not five,' " Vines says. That boldness—and the factory shutdowns—led to menacing hate mail, and Ghosn began to travel with a bodyguard.

These days, though, Ghosn is more hero than target. Last year, Nissan reported profits of $4.6 billion on $68 billion in revenues, up 8%. It looks set to boost earnings by another 6% and sales by 9% this year, brokerage Morgan Stanley says. Nissan's $49.7 billion market capitalization is the second biggest in the industry, after Toyota's. It has overtaken Honda as No. 2 inside Japan. And Nissan leads the global pack in operating margins (11.1%).

EXHIBIT 2

Ghosn's Report Card

Key to Ghosn's management style is laying out ambitious goals in multiyear plans with catchy names. Here are his three big initiatives—and how he has fared.	"REVIVAL PLAN" GHOSN'S INITIAL BID TO SAVE THE CAR MAKER 2000-03	"180 PLAN" INITIATIVE AIMED AT MAKING NISSAN A GLOBAL PLAYER 2002-05	"VALUE UP" PLAN TO KEEP NISSAN IN THE PASSING LANE 2005-08
	■ Cut purchasing costs 20% and halve number of supplier's ACHIEVED, 2002	■ Increase annual sales by 1 million vehicles, to 3.0 million 3.0 MILLION SOLD, 2003	■ Maintain return on invested capital of 20%
	■ Trim workforce by 14%, to 127,000 ACHIEVED, 2002	■ Operating profit margin of 8% ACHIEVED 10.8%, 2003	■ Increase sales to 4.2 million cars and trucks by 2008
	■ Shutter three car and two engine plants ACHIEVED, 2002	■ Zero net debt ACHIEVED, 2003	■ Maintain 10% or better operating margin

Despite the problems with Canton, the brand is hot again. Nissan is turning out daring designs such as its sleek-but-muscular 350Z sports coupe, the curvaceous Altima sedan, and the round-backed Murano crossover. And in Japan, stylish numbers such as the March subcompact and the boxy Cube micro-van are driving sales. That's part of Ghosn's push to create what he calls "segment-defining" models. "Consumers either like a car or they don't, but that is O.K.," says Nissan design chief Shiro Nakamura. As long as a model isn't a bore and hits profit goals along the way, Ghosn gives his designers pretty free rein.

Yet the detail work needs to come up. The quality problems at Canton aren't the only difficulties the company has faced. Take the Quest minivan. First, Nissan underestimated demand for popular features such as snazzy skylights. What's more, the beige interior on the entry model turned off family buyers fearing spills from toddlers. Now, the Quest is getting big design changes, including darker interiors and sunroofs even in the cheapest versions. "You will see incredibly different results this fall," says Walt Niziolek, manager of Visteon's Mississippi plant, which makes many Quest cockpit parts.

Nissan still has some gaps in its lineup, too. It won't have a sub-$15,000 compact—a growing segment critical to brand loyalty that Toyota has exploited with its Gen Y Scion brand—until 2007. Ghosn continues to be skeptical of environment-friendly hybrid cars. So Nissan's first hybrid, a gasoline-electric Altima, won't hit showrooms until 2006. And even where it's filling gaps, Nissan needs to work out some kinks: The Titan, the first full-size pickup truck out of Japan, has been a disappointment. Consumers haven't been flocking to this monster as Detroit's Big Three kick in incentives on their models that are worth roughly twice the $1,500 Nissan offers on the Titan.

Ghosn, though, isn't postponing his return to the CEO's job in Paris. One factor in his favor is that Schweitzer —who will remain chairman of Renault—has done a good job spiffing up the French auto maker (Exhibit 3). Renault is now the top-selling brand in Europe and, after tough restructuring, is light years away from its days as an industrial basket case. Quality still needs to come up. But thanks to rising profits and a deserved reputation for inspired design, Renault is on the offensive. It plans to hire 10,000 workers in 2005 to raise production in emerging markets such as Turkey, Slovenia, Russia, and Romania, where it has opened a plant to build a $6,000 sedan called the Dacia Logan. Renault has profited handsomely from Nissan, too: Its initial $5 billion stake has more than tripled in value.

More important for the company's global ambitions, Schweitzer and Ghosn have a stealth vehicle to drive integration. Early on, Schweitzer set up an Amsterdam-based company, Renault-Nissan BV, as a neutral forum where both sides could map out a common strategy for product engineering, model development, and computer systems, and leverage their combined size to squeeze suppliers for better deals. Once a month, Renault-Nissan's eight board members—four from each side—meet to make medium- and long-term decisions based on proposals by a dozen cross-company teams. Already, about 70% of the parts used by the two auto makers are jointly purchased by the alliance.

The integration has been surprisingly smooth—in sharp contrast to the tumultuous marriage of Daimler and Chrysler. Renault today builds its Clio compact and Scenic minivan at Nissan plants in Mexico, while Nissan makes its Frontier pickup at a Renault factory in Brazil. The ultimate goal is to reduce the number of platforms, or chassis, the group uses to 10 in 2010 from the 34 it had in 2000. The goal is in sight: Nissan had 24 individual platforms in 1999, but uses only 15 today. That's important, because every shared platform can add $500 million-plus in annual savings for each carmaker, estimates Commerzbank. Renault will also share eight engine designs with Nissan.

When conflicts do arise, Schweitzer and Ghosn usually hash things out before alliance board meetings. After Renault acquired South Korea's Samsung Motors in 2001, the French company wanted Nissan to design the next large 4×4 sport utility for the Korean company. Ghosn resisted, but was finally swayed by Schweitzer's logic: Nissan had the best know-how in SUVs, so it should take the lead. It wasn't altruism on Ghosn's part, mind you: Nissan will get a royalty from Renault on each of the SUVs that is sold when it launches in 2007. "Every time there was a difficult decision," says Renault CFO Thierry Moulonguet, "Schweitzer and Ghosn worked out the right balance."

That's remarkable, given how different the two men are. Schweitzer, an intellectual who persuades with logic and nuance, prefers to lead from above. Ghosn, on the other hand, is in-your-face and reaches deep into an organization by constant—and often unannounced— visits to dealerships, test tracks, assembly plants, and parts suppliers. And he isn't shy about setting sky-high targets. Toshiyuki Shiga, a senior vice-president in charge of emerging markets for Nissan, recalls getting a call from Ghosn in early 2000. First the good news: Shiga had been promoted. Then the zinger: "He told me to make a clear strategy for Nissan in China, and

EXHIBIT 3   Smoothest Combo On the Road

Two Heads Of A Global Giant

Nissan and Renault combined would be the world's fourth-largest auto maker

NISSAN	RENAULT
Revenues	Revenues
$68.0 BILLION	**$46.1** BILLION
Net profit	Net profit
$4.6 BILLION	**$3.1** BILLION
Operating Margin **11.1%**	Operating Margin **3.3%**
Stock Appreciation* **267%**	Stock Appreciation* **105%**
Sales **3.0** MILLION VEHICLES	Sales **2.4** MILLION VEHICLES
Market Cap **$49.7** BILLION	Market Cap **$23.7** BILLION

*Since Jan 1, 1999, after reinvesting dividends
Nissan data (except sales) for fiscal year ended March 2004.
Nissan sales end all Renault data for calendar 2003
Data: Bloomberg Financial Markets

When Renault nabbed a controlling stake in Nissan in 1999, skeptics howled that the $5.4 billion investment would bankrupt the French carmaker. But Renault

Chief Executive Louis Schweitzer had a grand vision. Nissan, he believed, could become a pillar of a globe-spanning alliance that would help boost Renault from a regional player to one of the world's top carmakers. "In the short term, Nissan needed Renault. In the long term, Renault needed Nissan," says Philippe Lasserre, professor of strategy at INSEAD management school in Fontainebleau.

Against all odds—just ask the managers of the Daimler Chrysler-Mitsubishi alliance—Schweitzer's vision has become a reality. Together, Renault and Nissan sold 5.4 million cars in 2003, placing them fourth behind General Motors, Toyota, and Ford. Nissan already enjoys the fattest margins of any big industry player, while Renault is Europe's No. 1 brand and is expanding rapidly into developing markets. Now, Schweitzer—together with his designated successor, Nissan CEO Carlos Ghosn—is ready to hit the accelerator. "I don't feel we have reached the potential of what this alliance can achieve," Schweitzer says.

That's a big change from 1999, when neither Nissan nor Renault struck anyone as a global contender. But while Ghosn was slashing costs and dismantling supplier *keiretsu,* Schweitzer was putting the French giant through its own paces—with a helping hand from Tokyo. Schweitzer sent dozens of Renault managers and hundreds of factory hands to Nissan plants to bone up on everything from the most efficient way to hold screw guns to strategies for flattening management hierarchy. Then in 2003, Renault imported 100 Nissan employees to help oversee the launch of the Megane compact sedan, which helped trim both launch and warranty costs (the company declines to say by how much).

Schweitzer also shook off Renault's parochial French management culture and began pushing his global strategy. He set up assembly lines in Russia, Turkey, Iran, and Brazil. In 1999 he snapped up

(continued)

he gave me two months to do it," laughs Shiga. Back then, Nissan sold just a few thousand vehicles in China annually, mostly imported from Japan. Shiga, though, jumped into motion and hatched a plan that led to a 50-50 joint venture with China's Dongfeng Motors. The duo just opened a plant in Guangzhou that will roll out six new models next year. Although Nissan is far behind market leaders Volkswagen and GM, the venture

hopes to sell some 620,000 cars and trucks in China by 2007, double last year's level.

It's those surprise visits that really seem to energize Ghosn. On a recent swing through Nissan's Iwaki engine plant, 110 miles north of Tokyo, he was mobbed by eager factory hands. He doubtless enjoyed the attention, but at each stop it was evident he was looking for nuggets that would help him squeeze

EXHIBIT 3—*(concluded)*

Romania's hapless Dacia brand, investing a total of $1.5 billion over five years. The goal: Use Romania's cheap but skilled workforce to make a $6,000 car for developing markets. That push bore fruit on Sept. 9, when Dacia launched its no-frills Logan sedan. By 2010, Renault expects to sell as many as 700,000 Logans annually from Bucharest to Bombay. "While we were making the technological move to cooperate with Nissan, Renault went global," says Pierre-Alain De Smedt, Renault's engineering chief.

La plus grande surprise: To get the global message across, English is now the lingua franca at Renault's Paris headquarters—and top managers must pass tests to make sure their language skills are up to snuff. English is also the language of the 12 cross-company teams from Nissan and Renault that meet once a week by phone or in person to hammer out collaboration in everything from anticorrosion solutions to engine technology. The process can be laborious, but it pays off in harmony. In a recent deadlocked debate about which powertrain to use on a common platform, De Smedt and his Japanese colleagues needed six months to sort out a decision. "We don't force issues," says De Smedt.

Another big Schweitzer push: safety. Renault now ranks No. 1 in Europe in crash tests performed by London-based Euro N-Cap, and all five of its major model lines have earned five stars, the top score. Toyota ranks No. 2 with three models fetching five stars. "Renault has become the new Volvo," says Commerzbank analyst Adam Collins.

Revved Up The first major cost savings from sharing engines and components with Nissan will hit Renault's bottom line next year.

True, Renault's foray into new markets has squeezed earnings. Operating margins fell to 3.7% last year from 6% in 1999. But analysts say the company is poised for strong growth and rising profits. Sales in the first half of this year rose 11%, to $25 billion, and net profits surged 28.5%, to $1.84 billion, buoyed by a hefty dividend from Nissan, strong sales of the Megane series, and growing earnings in developing markets. And starting next year, the first real cost savings from shared components and engines will hit the bottom line, after the debut of Renault's first two models developed in conjunction with Nissan: the Logan and the Renault Modus minivan, which shares much of its genetic material with the Nissan Micra. For Renault alone, the cost savings from such sharing could reach $550 million next year and twice that in 2006, Commerzbank estimates.

Ghosn will still face challenges when he takes over as CEO next April. One thorny problem has been larger cars, an area where the French giant has been traditionally weak. Analysts say Renault will sell fewer than 10,000 of its $38,000 Vel Satis luxury sedans this year, a fraction of the initial target of 50,000. In Romania, meanwhile, Dacia is running smoothly, but the expat management team that has been in charge is now gradually handing control back to locals. Another dilemma: Ghosn will have to decide whether to bring Renault back to the fiercely competitive U.S. market. Schweitzer has said Renault aims to return to the U.S., but not before 2010, giving it time to develop new models tailored to American tastes. Finally, Ghosn will have to keep Renault's global push on the growth track, and deepen the integration between Tokyo and Paris. "There is much more to do to unlock the cost savings and economies of scale," says Garel Rhys, professor of automotive economics at Cardiff Business School at University of Wales. "Both companies have to fire on all cylinders." At least when Schweitzer hands the keys to Renault over to Ghosn, he'll have the satisfaction of knowing his grand alliance has passed more milestones than anyone thought possible five years ago.

–By Gail Edmondson in Paris

yet another ounce of productivity from the plant, which cranks out V-6 engines for such models as the 350Z and the upscale Infinity G35 luxury sedan. He worked the floor, chatting up assembly workers, drilling foremen, all to get that extra fact that would edge the company forward. Even if he got no cost-killing tips from line workers on this particular day, the visit clearly paid off for Ghosn, who knows he is nothing without an inspired workforce. "The only power that a CEO has is to motivate. The rest is nonsense," he says. As his next act begins, Ghosn's motivational powers must be stronger than ever.

–By Brian Bremner in Tokyo, Gail Edmondson in Paris, and Chester Dawson in Los Angeles, with David Welch and Kathleen Kerwin in Detroit

Source: "Nissan's Boss," *BusinessWeek*, October 4, 2004, 50–58.

Cases for Part 6

Case 6-1

Microsoft Corp (B)

When Microsoft Corp. hired computer scientist Kai-Fu Lee away from hardware maker Silicon Graphics Inc. in 1998, the move underscored how thoroughly the software giant dominated the computer industry. Not only did it monopolize PC operating systems and hold an edge in Web browsers, but it was also vacuuming up the world's brightest technologists. Lee's expertise was in speech recognition, considered one of the next big leaps in computing. With people like him flocking to Microsoft's labs, it seemed that the digital world's reigning champion had a lock on the future.

Things didn't turn out that way. In July, Lee bolted from Microsoft for Web search king Google Inc., and once again his personal journey is emblematic of a shift in computing's balance of power. These days it's Google, not Microsoft, that seems to have the most momentum. Microsoft sued to stop Lee from working for the upstart, citing his noncompete agreement. But on Sept. 13 a state judge in Seattle ruled that Lee could work for Google, with some restrictions, pending a January trial. Microsoft said it was happy the judge limited the type of work Lee could do. Yet when court adjourned, Lee smiled broadly and threw both arms in the air. "I feel great," he said outside the courtroom. "I can't wait to start work tomorrow morning."

Contrast that with how Lee felt about Microsoft. During the two-day hearing he painted a distinctly unflattering picture of the company's inner workings. Lee, who opened Microsoft's research lab in China in 1998 and moved to headquarters in Redmond, Wash, two years later, fretted over what he saw as repeated missteps. In court he detailed how the more than 20 product-development centers in China tripped over one another, duplicating efforts and even fighting over the same job candidate. Lee called the company "incompetent." After the ruling he praised Google, noting, "the culture is very supportive, collaborative, innovative, and Internet-like—and that's bottoms-up innovation rather than top-down direction."

For most of its three decades, Microsoft has faced intense criticism. But in the past it came from the outside world. Rivals complained about its heavy-handed tactics. PC makers griped that it was hogging the industry's profits.

Now much of the sharpest criticism comes from within (Exhibit 1). Dozens of current and former

EXHIBIT 1

What Ails Microsoft?

The software giant faces plenty of competition, and now some of its biggest challenges come from the inside. Here are the company's main internal problems:

▶▶ INNOVATION STAGNATION	▶▶ SLOW PRODUCT DEVELOPMENT	▶▶ BUREAUCRATIC RED TAPE	▶▶ SAGGING MORALE
Windows and Office still pay the bills, so Microsoft needs to keep improving them with new versions that increase security and make it easier for them to work with other devices. But all the focus on existing products has left it behind innovators such as Google and Apple when it comes to fresh ideas.	Microsoft's top execs have pushed a vision of "integrated innovation" meant to ensure that the company's many product groups work closely together. Sounds good, but in practice the strategy creates dependencies that saddle fast-moving groups with the problems of troubled divisions, slowing down innovation.	Employees complain about an endless string of meetings to discuss everything from product features to coordinating strategies among different groups. It's part of the pain of being a large company. But the process put in place to help workers deal with that growth takes valuable time away from creating new products.	With the company's stock trading where it was seven years ago, Microsoft is no longer minting stock-option millionaires. What's more, it has cut health benefits and trimmed vacation time for new employees. Combine this with other internal woes, and you have some of the company's most talented employees heading elsewhere.

EXHIBIT 2

Not-So-Crazy Suggestions

Last spring two Microsoft researchers sent a 12-page memo to Bill Gates titled "Ten Crazy Ideas to Shake Up Microsoft." An edited selection:

"Break Up" the company: Not really. But achieve the same effect by making businesses more independent, without as much concern for how they fit in with Microsoft's overall strategy.

Empower incubation projects: Set up and fund business incubators. Allow these independent outfits to start new businesses, so more new ideas see the light of the day.

Schedule unscheduled time: Like Google, Microsoft should set aside a slice of every employee's time so they can think creatively about new business ideas, rather than simply following orders from supervisors.

Cut back on bureaucracy: Create "bureacracy police" who investigate complaints and cut red tape. Reduce staffing of large projects: More people can mean slower progress. Move engineers off large projects and into incubators.

Encourage risk-taking: Give employees "shares" issued by individual business units and let them cash the shares in if their group tries something new and succeeds.

---

employees are criticizing—in *BusinessWeek* interviews, court testimony, and personal blogs—the way the company operates internally. This spring two researchers sent Chairman William H. Gates III a memo in which they wrote: "Everyone sees a crisis is imminent" and suggested "Ten Crazy Ideas to Shake Up Microsoft" (Exhibit 2). Many workers, like Lee, are in effect saying: "I'm outta here." More than 100 former Microsofties now work for Google, and dozens of others have scattered elsewhere.

It's not a mass exodus. Microsoft has 60,000 employees, and many of them are undoubtedly happy with their jobs and the company's culture. While Microsoft's annual attrition rate rose one percentage point from fiscal 2003 to 2004, it's still just 9%, a bit lower than the industry average. Microsoft says it receives 45,000 to 60,000 job applications a month, and over 90% of the people offered jobs accept.

Too Big to Move Fast?

Still, there's no doubt that Microsoft is losing some of its most creative managers, marketers, and software developers. Lenn Pryor, director of platform evangelism, left for Internet phone startup Skype Technologies, now being acquired by eBay. Stephen Walli, who worked in the unit set up to parry the open-source threat, split for an open-source consulting firm. A long list of talent has moved to Google, a trip made easier by the company's recent establishment of an office in nearby Kirkland, Wash. Joe Beda and Gary Burd, respected engineers, left and helped set up the instant

messaging service Google Talk. Mark Lucovsky, who had been named one of Microsoft's 16 Distinguished Engineers, defected to Google last November. He blogged that Microsoft's size is getting in its way. "I am not sure I believe anymore that Microsoft knows how to ship software," he wrote.

Employees' complaints are rooted in a number of factors. They resent cuts in compensation and benefits as profits soar. They're disappointed with the stock price, which has barely budged for three years, rendering many of their stock options out of the money. They're frustrated with what they see as swelling bureaucracy, including the many procedures and meetings Chief Executive Steven A. Ballmer has put in place to motivate them. And they're feeling trapped in an organization whose past successes seem to stifle current creativity. "There's a distinct lack of passion," says one engineer, who would talk only on condition of anonymity. "We're missing some spunk."

No question, most companies would kill to have Microsoft's problems. It's comfortably the most profitable player in the tech industry. And it's making more money than ever, with net income of $12.3 billion on revenues of $39.8 billion for the past fiscal year. Its twin monopolies, the Windows PC operating system and the Office suite of desktop applications, give it important advantages when it thrusts into adjacent markets, such as server software for corporations and instant messaging for both businesses and consumers.

Ballmer maintains that the company is in terrific shape (Exhibit 3). In an interview in a Las Vegas hotel, he says one of Microsoft's strengths has always been

EXHIBIT 3 Q&A

Steve Ballmer Shrugs Off the Critics

Steven A. Ballmer has been Microsoft Corp.'s chief executive officer for nearly five years. He has steered the company through the tech downturn and a slowdown in revenue growth. Now he's predicting an upswing. *BusinessWeek* Seattle Bureau Chief Jay Greene and Executive Editor Kathy Rebello interviewed Ballmer at the Venetian Hotel in Las Vegas. This is an edited version of their conversation:

How is morale at Microsoft?
We have as excited and engaged a team of folks as I can possibly imagine. Eighty-five percent of our people say they feel strongly that they're proud to be at Microsoft. They love their work. They're passionate about the impact they're having on customers and society. It's a real, real powerful statement about where our people are. Certainly, we continue to bring in new people. We will hire, in net, over 4,000 people this year. We attract great people to the company. I'm very bullish about the employee base and what it can accomplish.

Two researchers at Microsoft wrote a paper for [Bill Gates] called "Ten Crazy Ideas to Shake Up Microsoft." They say "a crisis is imminent" because of the growing bureaucracy and impediments to innovation. Do you agree?
I think we have a great culture at Microsoft. It's a culture that encourages and fosters criticism and constructive suggestion. People criticize everything: the way we do things, what we need to do in the marketplace, our product. That's a fantastic thing because that kind of strong culture drives self-improvement. We have the best new pipeline of innovation that we've ever had in our history over the next 12 months.

To be clear, do you think the points the authors made in that paper are valid ones that need to be addressed?
If you take a look at where we're going to with innovation, what we have in the pipeline. I'm very excited. I think the output of our innovation is great. We have a culture of self-improvement. I know we can continue

to improve. But, at the same time, our absolute level of output is fantastic.

Do you have concerns about the bureaucracy at Microsoft?
Great companies and the way they work start with great leaders. We have a fantastic leadership team in place. Our leadership team is empowered, and is pushing every day to take advantage of that empowerment, to move quickly, to act quickly, to drive, to get things done.

Does process hold them back at all?
Our company has to be a company that enables its people. I think if you were to take a look broadly through our company, we've got more empowered, innovative, creative people than any other company in the world. I think we've been very good at investing in the tools that allow people to work together in a way in which the whole is bigger than the sum of the parts.

Some of this sentiment comes out in blogs like Mini-Microsoft and others. Do you read those?
I do not.

But is information from those blogs getting to you?
I have lots of sources of information about what's going on at the company. I think I have a pretty good pulse on where we are and what people are thinking. I'm not sure blogs are necessarily the best place to get a pulse on anything. People want to blog for a variety of reasons, and that may or may not be representative.

In interviews and on blogs, some employees say that you've instituted bureaucracy that is hampering innovation so much so that they question whether you should be CEO. What's your response?
At the end of the day, the proof is in the output. Do we have the innovation output? Do we have the market share? Do we have the customer satisfaction? And do we have the talent? So you go through each one of those things and say, how are we doing? Numerically, we've grown from 18% of the profits of the top 25 companies in our industry to 23% of the profits of the top 25 companies in our industry over the last five years. Profits are up over 70%, where the industry profit is up about 35%. Pretty good.

(continued)

EXHIBIT 3—*(concluded)*

How are we doing in terms of talent? We've brought on fantastic new talent. You look at our performance in campus recruiting. We're the No. 1 choice among computer science students at U.S. universities as a place to work. You look at market share. Virtually every business we're in, our market share is up over the last five years. If you look at any of the critical dimensions, our company has performed well and I'm bullish about how we will drive that to continue.

You talk about your performance. Why has that not been better reflected in the stock price?
I think our stock is attractively priced, and we're buying our stock. That's the ultimate expression of our view. I think our stock represents such a good value that we told people we'd buy about $30 billion of it over four years on behalf of our shareholders.

its culture of self-criticism. What's different now, he says, is that the internal debate is spilling out into public view because of blogs and e-mail. He says internal surveys show that 85% of the company's employees are satisfied with their jobs, about the same level as in past years. "We have as excited and engaged a team of folks at Microsoft as I can possibly imagine," says Ballmer. "[Employees] love their work. They're passionate about the impact they're having on customers and society. [The 85% number] is a real, real powerful statement about where our people are."

Indeed, there are areas of excitement within Microsoft. One is MSN, the Internet operation, where the search group is the underdog competing against Google. Another is the Xbox group, which is racing full speed against Sony Corp.'s leading PlayStation 2 to win over the next generation of video gamers. It's launching Xbox 360 this Christmas, months ahead of PlayStation 3. "If you take a look at where we're going with innovation, what we have in the pipeline, I'm very excited. The output of our innovation is great," says Ballmer. "We won the desktop. We won the server. We will win the Web. We will move fast, we will get there. We will win the Web."

The company plans to release a series of major upgrades for most of its core products in the coming 18 months. That'll culminate late next year in the long-awaited update of Windows, called Vista. Analysts such as Drew Brosseau of SG Cowen & Co. expect it to help financial results—he's predicting that revenues will rise 12% during the next fiscal year, to $44.5 billion, as profits increase 12%, to $13.8 billion. He thinks the stock, now at $27, will follow. "It can be a mid-30s stock in 12 months," says Brosseau.

Still, Microsoft faces serious long-term challenges: the rising popularity of the Linux open-source operating system, a plague of viruses attacking its software,

and potent rivals such as Google in the consumer realm and IBM in corporate computing. It's the company's ability to respond to these challenges that current and former employees fear is being compromised by Microsoft's internal troubles. They're concerned that Ballmer and Gates aren't taking seriously enough the issues of morale and culture. "Why in the world did I start [this blog]?" writes Mini-Microsoft, an anonymous employee who writes a blog that has become a gathering place for the company's internal critics and reformers (Exhibit 4). "I love Microsoft, and I know we have the innate potential to be great again."

To many employees, Vista, the Windows update, exemplifies the company's struggles. When the project was conceived half a decade ago, it was envisioned as a breakthrough: an operating system that would transform the way users store and retrieve information. But the more revolutionary features have been dropped, and Vista will arrive three years after researcher Gartner Inc. originally predicted that it would ship. Worse yet, they say, nobody has been held accountable. "People look around and say: 'What are those clowns doing?'" says Adam Barr, a program manager in the Windows group.

In the past, when Microsoft faced an emerging threat, Gates could be depended on to lead it in a new direction. Most famously, in 1995 he belatedly recognized the importance of the Internet and led a furious charge to catch up. But in 2000 Gates passed on the chief executive job to Ballmer. When Ballmer took over, he was determined to overcome the looming challenge of corporate middle age. He pored over how-to management books such as Jim Collins' *Good to Great*. But since Ballmer took the helm, Microsoft has slipped the other way. The stock price has dropped over 40% during his tenure, and the company, whose revenue grew at an average annual clip of 36% through

EXHIBIT 4   Mystery Blogger

A Rendezvous with Microsoft's Deep Throat

I didn't have to change cabs twice and slip into the shadows of a suburban parking garage at 2 in the morning. Instead, we agreed to meet at a Starbucks at 5:45 pm. The signal: My contact would have a copy of *Microserfs,* the legendary 1995 book about employee life in the early days of Microsoft Corp. Sure enough, when I walked in the door, the book was sitting on the table to my right. My heart raced. "Mini?" I said, extending my hand. "It's great to put a face with a name."

The proprietor of the Web log called Mini-Microsoft may be the most notorious blogger on corporate life. For more than a year, Mini has been a thorn in the side of the software giant, posting a stream of anonymous critiques of the company, Mini's employer. Mini pulls no punches, calling Microsoft a "passionless, process-ridden, lumbering idiot" in a Sept. 4 posting. Yet the blog is also chock full of humor, intelligence, and earnest suggestions for fixing Microsoft.

While Mini-Microsoft (minimsft.blogspot.com) is just one among an estimated 2,000 blogs operated by Microsoft staffers, it has become a virtual water cooler for employees. Hundreds anonymously vent their frustrations there without fear of retribution. Mini has emerged as something of a folk hero. Visitors to the site and other bloggers describe Mini as both the employee most likely to save Microsoft—and most likely to be fired.

Mini provides a fascinating example of a phenomenon that's sweeping the nation. Employee bloggers are shining a bright light on the inner workings of their companies and thrusting all sorts of bottled-up frustrations out in the open. Whispered conversations suddenly become broadcast publicly. That puts a huge amount of power in the hands of employees—for good or ill. Indeed, the balance of power between employer and employee may be shifting. Analyst Charlene Li of Forrester Research advises companies not to try to suppress their bloggers. "You can keep it hidden, or get those voices out there and deal with the problem," she says.

Not surprisingly, it took some coaxing to get Mini to sit down with me. The meeting came with one condition: continued anonymity. So we started with some ground rules. "Can I at least disclose your gender?" I ask. "Sure," the soft-spoken Mini says, laughing. For the record, Mini is a man.

Mini knows, though, that he's a marked man. He might lose his job if the top brass ever figured out who he is. "They'd have to consider the bad publicity of firing me," Mini says. Still, there's that uneasy feeling that they would cut him loose anyway, if only to send a message. Prior to our meeting, he had never told anyone outside Microsoft of his double life. Not even his wife. "She has enough stress," he says.

So why risk a career to vent about his employer? "Microsoft has been wonderful to me. I really want to improve it. I really want to make a difference," he explains. Mini started posting in July, 2004, with little expectation that he would develop much of a following.

He doesn't track the number of visitors, but a recent missive about the unfairness of the employee-review system generated more than 150 replies. Most seemed to come from fellow Microsofties.

Mini sometimes worries that his posts might cause Microsoft some harm, but he believes it's more likely that he'll be a force for much-needed change. "Sometimes you have to destroy the village in order to save it," he says. He just hopes it doesn't come to that.

—By Jay Greene in Seattle, with Heather Green in New York

the 1990s, rose just 8% in the fiscal year that ended on June 30. That's good for a company of Microsoft's size, but it is the first time the software giant has had single-digit growth.

The company's performance even has some anonymous writers on the Mini-Microsoft Web site calling on Gates to ask Ballmer to step down. That's very, very unlikely. Gates urged Ballmer to become chief executive nearly six years ago in the wake of the company's antitrust battles with the Justice Dept., when the top job became too overwhelming for him. The two have been close friends since their days at Harvard University, and together they hold 12% of the company's shares. And board members say they stand firmly behind Ballmer.

"I am fully supportive of the transformation that Steve is leading the company through," James I. Cash Sr., a director and former professor at Harvard Business School, wrote in an e-mail to *BusinessWeek*. "He is one of the best leaders I've observed over the last four years. I've been on this Board, and the Board stands in full support of him and his efforts."

Ballmer says he should be judged on his overall performance. "At the end of the day the proof is in the output. If you look at any of the critical dimensions, our company has performed well and I'm bullish about how we will drive to continue."

While Microsoft's internal reformers don't directly criticize Gates, they're frustrated with the sluggish pace of product development. As the company's chief software architect, Gates bears that responsibility. He's the author of a strategy called "integrated innovation." The idea is to get Microsoft's vast product groups to work closely together to take advantage of the Windows and Office monopolies and bolster them at the same time. But with so much more effort placed on cross-group collaboration, workers spend an immense amount of time in meetings making sure products are in sync. It "translates to more dependencies among shipping products, less control of one's product destiny, and longer ship cycles," writes Dare Obasanjo, a program manager in Microsoft's MSN division, on his blog.

To shake Microsoft out of its malaise, radical surgery may be in order. "I think they should break up the company," says Raj Reddy, a professor of computer science and robotics at Carnegie Mellon University. Reddy is no passive industry observer: For the past 15 years he has served on Microsoft's Technical Advisory Board, a group of academics who help guide the company's research efforts. Reddy believes that a handful of Microsoft spin-offs, seeded with some of the company's $37.8 billion in cash, could compete more nimbly in the marketplace. Some insiders agree. Microsoft's Barr recently blogged that the company should be broken up after Gates and Ballmer retire.

There are plenty of bold thoughts floating around Microsoft. The two researchers who sent the "Ten Crazy Ideas" memo to Gates are Kentaro Toyama and Sean Blagsvedt. The 12-page document, reviewed by *BusinessWeek*, suggests giving product groups increased autonomy and calls for the creation of "bureaucracy police" with the authority to slash through red tape. "It's said that large organizations won't change their ways until a crisis really hits," the authors write.

"Everyone sees a crisis is imminent. Incremental changes aren't enough. Are we the kind of company that can dodge the crisis before it happens?"

Maintaining, Not Innovating

It's a question that echoes through the corridors in Redmond. To succeed, Microsoft needs motivated workers camping out in their offices at all hours to compete with tenacious rivals such as Google, Yahoo!, Salesforce.com, and a reborn Apple Computer. Yet current and former employees say there are many demoralized workers who are content to punch the clock and zoom out of the parking lot. "At this point there's a traffic jam at 9 o'clock in the morning and 5 o'clock at night," says ex-employee Walli.

Over its three decades of life, Microsoft has become an icon of American capitalism, a company that started with the intellectual firepower and relentless drive of Gates and his high school buddy, Paul Allen. It made billionaires out of its founders and multimillionaires out of thousands of its staff. And it created two of the most lucrative monopolies in American history—one of them, Windows, so powerful that it ultimately brought trustbusters down on the company.

Now, strange as it seems, those monopolies are at the root of the company's malaise. As Microsoft fought the federal government and litigious rivals, it developed an almost reflexive instinct to protect Windows and Office, sometimes at the expense of looking for groundbreaking innovations. "Every time Bill and Steve made a change to be more like other big companies, we lost a little bit of what made Microsoft special," says a former Microsoft vice-president.

One reason some employees say Microsoft isn't innovating enough: It's too busy upgrading Windows. With some of its key breakthrough features gone, Vista's improvements include better handling of peripheral devices, such as printers and scanners, and cutting in half the time it takes to start up. Those are needed improvements, and there's no doubt that hundreds of millions of copies will be sold as people upgrade to new PCs. But the changes are hardly the stuff of cutting-edge software engineering. "So much of what Microsoft is doing right now is maintenance," says Mike Smith, a former software architect at Microsoft who left the company in 2003 to work for a Bay Area startup.

And that leads to an even more worrisome problem: discontent among its software programmers. Instead of coming up with the next great technology, Microsoft programmers have to cater to its monopolies. But top-flight engineers want to tackle the next great challenge. "They want to create new worlds, not defend old ones," says a former senior executive at Microsoft. "They want to storm the Bastille, not live in Versailles."

If Microsoft loses too many top developers, it will be hard-pressed to succeed in the new markets on which it has pinned so much hope. Google, for example, embarrassed Microsoft in October, 2004, by coming out with software that lets users quickly search the files on their Windows desktop before Microsoft released its own version.

Adding to employee frustration is the company's bureaucracy. After Ballmer became CEO, he put in place processes he hoped would help manage a bigger organization better. But instead of liberating employees to do great work, Ballmer's moves have been stifling, some workers say. With so much effort placed on cross-group collaboration, employees spend more time in meetings making sure product strategies are in sync. The company schedules executive product reviews several times a year, and preparing for them is hugely time-consuming. That prep work cuts into the more interesting work creating new technologies and products.

Sweating the Small Stuff

To Ballmer's chagrin, some of his up-and-coming programmers have left for Google. He was apoplectic about Lucovsky's departure, according to documents made public during the Lee trial. Lucovsky said in a sworn statement that after he told Ballmer about his plans to move to Google, the beefy CEO threw a chair and cursed Google's chief executive. "F_ing Eric Schmidt is a f_ing pussy. I'm going to f_ing bury that guy. . . . I'm going to f_ing kill Google," Ballmer said, according to Lucovsky. In a statement, Ballmer calls Lucovsky's account "a gross exaggeration of what actually took place."

Some workers express frustration that Microsoft is so busy protecting its PC-based businesses that it comes up short when competing on the Web. Take the customer relationship management (CRM) market—software that companies use to track sales and customer service activities. Microsoft targeted it 2½ years ago with a traditional software package, Microsoft CRM. Today roughly 4,000 companies run the software for nearly 100,000 staff. Not bad, but Microsoft hasn't been nearly as successful as Salesforce.com Inc., a trailblazer of Web-based CRM software, with 308,000 users at 17,000 companies.

The secret to Salesforce.com's success: the speed with which it can update its software. Microsoft last updated its original CRM software in January, 2004, with plans for a new version in first quarter, 2006. Meanwhile, Salesforce is constantly fixing bugs and adds features without interruption to the customer or added expense. All customers need to do is open a Web browser to run the program. Microsoft CRM boss Brad Wilson argues that business software is complex and best sold as a package that customers run on their own computers. "This is really about business process where you've got multiple steps," Wilson says. "It is a much more extensive thing that often requires a lot of people, a lot of time, and a lot of resources."

While upstarts like Google and Salesforce have Microsoft on the defense, the biggest threat to the company may be its own moves. With revenue growth slowing, Ballmer has tried to squeeze more down to the bottom line to make the company more appealing to investors. In the past fiscal year he slashed $2.6 billion out of operating expenses. But that came at a price. Microsoft sliced health benefits, introducing, for example, a $40 copayment on some brand-name prescription drugs. Within a week of announcing the benefits proposal in May, 2004, human resources received 700 e-mails. Of those, 80% were negative, and fewer than 1% were positive, according to an internal e-mail obtained by *BusinessWeek*. One employee wrote in an e-mail: "Small things like this chip away at employee loyalty and morale and in the long run do more harm than benefit."

Even the cuts that seem trivial have dampened morale. Just whisper the word "towels" to any Microsoft employee, and eyes roll. Last year, Microsoft stopped providing a towel service for workers who used company locker rooms after bike rides or workouts. Employees who helped the company build its huge cash stockpile were furious.

And don't even mention stock options. Employees long counted on them to bolster their salaries. Microsoft minted thousands of employee millionaires as the stock climbed 61,000% from its 1986 public offering to its peak in 2001. Now shares are trading exactly were they were seven years ago. Microsoft has doubled its payroll in that time, adding more than 30,000 new employees, not including attrition. That means more than half of Microsoft's employees have received virtually no benefit from their stock holdings. Instead, they're working for a pay-check and not much else (Exhibit 5).

EXHIBIT 5

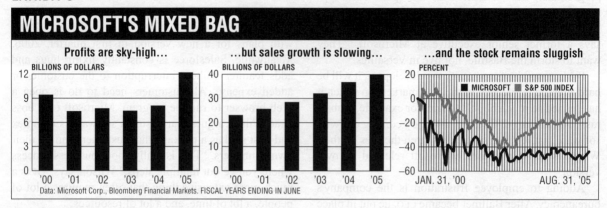

MICROSOFT'S MIXED BAG

Profits are sky-high...   ...but sales growth is slowing...   ...and the stock remains sluggish

Data: Microsoft Corp., Bloomberg Financial Markets. FISCAL YEARS ENDING IN JUNE

And even if the stock does begin to climb, employees won't hit the kind of jackpot their predecessors did. Two years ago Microsoft stopped issuing big dollops of stock options, retreating to more modest helpings of stock grants. The idea was to help retain workers by giving them a sure thing—stock with some value, since so many options were underwater. Meanwhile, 90% of the tech industry still rewards employees with stock options.

Recruiting Slack

Microsoft's compensation moves have created a haves-vs.-have-nots culture. Newbies work for comfortable but not overly generous wages, while veterans have a lucrative treasure chest of stock options. Now a new pay scheme, scheduled to go into effect this fall, threatens to make the gulf even wider. If they meet incentive goals, the 120 or so vice-presidents will receive an eye-popping $1 million in salary a year, and general managers, the next level down, will get $350,000 to $550,000, according to a high-ranking source. But the rest of the staff is paid at market rates.

The pay disparity is exacerbated by Microsoft's rating system. The company uses a bell curve to rate employees in each group, so the number of top performers is balanced by the same number of underachievers. But Microsoft has a long history of hiring top-notch computer science grads and high-quality talent from the industry. Under the rating system, if a group works hard together to release a product, someone in the group has to get a low score for every high score a manager dishes out. "It creates competition in the ranks, when people really want community," says a former Microsoft vice-president. A company

spokesman says managers don't have to apply the curve with smaller groups, where it's not statistically relevant.

Even on college campuses, long a fountain of talent for Microsoft, the tide seems to be turning. On Sept. 7, Massachusetts Institute of Technology's Science & Engineering Business Club held its annual recruiting barbecue, with about a dozen companies setting up booths to recruit as many as 1,500 students. "There was a lot of buzz around the Google table and not a lot around the Microsoft table," says Bob Richard, associate director of employer relations at MIT How much? When Richard walked through, he says, students were lined up six deep to talk to Google recruiters, while only two students stood at the Microsoft table. Carnegie Mellon's Reddy says his top students opt for Google and Yahoo ahead of Microsoft these days. Microsoft points out that in a survey conducted by market researcher Universum, the company ranks No. 1 among computer science students as employer of choice.

Microsoft is hardly the first company to struggle as it moves from adolescence to maturity. And it could learn some lessons from others that have made the transition more gracefully. Take General Electric Co. The conglomerate has long boasted an entrepreneurial culture, with hundreds of managers running fiercely independent businesses. Those leaders are given free rein yet are held accountable for their own results—meaning they can get the boot if they don't perform. "The process is transparent and rigorous and constantly reinforced," says Noel M. Tichy, a University of Michigan professor and leadership guru.

Ballmer says Microsoft is finding its way through the challenges of being a more mature company just fine and that the complaints of some employees simply reflect the kind of company Microsoft is. "We have for ourselves incredibly high expectations," he says. "And that's in some senses the greatest blessing and opportunity anybody can ever have. Our people, our shareholders, me, Bill Gates, we expect to change the world in every way, to succeed wildly in everything we touch, to have the broadest impact of any company in the world. It's great they're saying: 'Come on, we can still do better.' Great." Ballmer smacks his meaty hands together for emphasis. "We need those high expectations."

Microsoft certainly is chock-full of smart employees who want to do better. Still, many of them say that jumping through bureaucratic hoops and struggling to link products together is preventing them from being the best they can be. There's a plea for action to Gates and Ballmer to do more—slash the bureaucracy, tend to morale, and make it easier to innovate. But is anyone listening?

Source: Jay Greene, "Troubling Exits at Microsoft," *BusinessWeek*, September 26, 2005, 99–108.

Case 6-2
Samsung Electronics Co.

The office park in northern New Jersey hardly looks like a place that plays a role in cutting-edge design. Hard by a highway interchange, the two-story building is about as distinctive as white rice. But climb the stairs to the second floor, and you'll see designers from Samsung Electronics Co. studying in pains-taking detail the American consumer psyche. There, engineer Lee Byung Moo watches from behind a two-way mirror as three women and two men stuff a stainless steel refrigerator with the contents of a half-dozen bags of groceries. After the five have finished and given their opinions on several potential configurations of drawers and compartments, Lee and two others rush into the room to take photographs and note exactly where the "shoppers" have put the ice cream, chicken, beer, milk, and other food. "We want to know the tastes of American customers because we need to develop products that fit their lifestyle," says Lee.

Half a world away, Choi Won Min sits in a windowless room on the ground floor of a Seoul skyscraper—an equally unlikely spot to find the leading edge of design. He spends his days (and often his nights) in front of two piano keyboards, a phalanx of mixing consoles, and dozens of synthesizers. With his headphones on, he hits a note, listens intently, then tweaks a few settings and hits another key. His primary mission in the two-year-old lab: coming up with a suite of bells, boings, beeps, and buzzes for digital gadgets that will immediately say "Samsung" to users worldwide. In the past, "simple sounds seemed to be sufficient, but now we realize how important sounds are in user interfaces," Choi says.

Lee and Choi are foot soldiers in Samsung's continuing assault on the world of cool. In recent years, the South Korean company has begun gearing all it does, from financing to decision-making to training and labs, to make Samsung a finely tuned receptor of all the things that make its products must-haves in an increasingly competitive marketplace. Hundreds of millions of dollars have been spent spiffing up the look, feel, and function of everything from refrigerators and washing machines to cell phones and MP3 players. And the focus has been on research of the sort Lee and Choi are doing: finding out what's likely to sell before consumers even know they want it. The effort has paid off. Samsung has grown from a me-too producer of electronics and appliances into one of the world's leading brands—in large part because of its focus on design. "We want to be the Mercedes of home electronics," says Yun Jong Yong, Samsung's chief executive.

The way Samsung's moving, you'd think it wants to be the Ferrari. This year, Samsung won five citation in the Industrial Design Excellence Awards (IDEA)—making it the first Asian company to win more prizes than any European or American rival. (The competition is sponsored by *BusinessWeek*, which publishes the results, but the laureates are selected by the Industrial Designers Society.) And since 2000, Samsung has earned a total of 100 citations at top design contests in the U.S., Europe, and Asia. Brokerage Hyundai Securities expects Samsung to earn $10.3 billion on sales of $52.8 billion this year, up from profits of $5.2 billion and $39.8 billion in revenues last year. (Although much of that increase comes from the semiconductor division, the company's snazzy consumer products also helped.) "Samsung is the poster child for using design to increase brand value and market share," says Patrick Whitney, director of the Institute of Design at the Illinois Institute of Technology.

The change started in 1993, when Chairman Lee Kun Hee visited retailers in Los Angeles and saw that Samsung products were lost in the crowd, while those from Sony Corp. and and a few others stood out. So he ordered his managers to concentrate less on cost saving and more on coming up with unique products. The bottom line: Great design could catapult Samsung to the top ranks of global brands.

Decade of Determination

The boss spoke. Samsung listened. And the company's design push was under way. To attract better, younger designers, Samsung in 1994 moved its design center to Seoul from sleepy Suwon, a small city an hour south of the capital. That same year, Samsung hired U.S. design firm IDEO to help develop a computer monitor—the first of many such collaborations with IDEO and other leading consultancies. Then in 1995, the company set up the Innovative Design Lab of Samsung, an in-house school where promising designers could study under experts from the Art Center College of Design in Pasadena, Calif, one of the top U.S. design schools. Samsung designers were dispatched to Egypt and India, Paris and Frankfurt, New York and Washington to tour museums, visit icons of modern architecture, and explore ruins.

Just as important, Samsung's designers have broken through the barriers of Korea's traditional Confucian hierarchies. Although Korea has loosened up as democracy has taken hold in the last 15 years, respect for elders and a reluctance to speak out of turn are still the norm, and Samsung as a whole still holds lots of meetings where Confucian order prevails. But the design center is different. Located several minutes' walk from company headquarters, it's a place with no dress code, where some younger staffers dye their hair green or pink, and where everyone is encouraged to speak up and challenge their superiors. Designers work in three- to five-person teams, with members from various specialty areas and levels of seniority—all working as equals.

The wrenching departure from tradition has paid off. Virtually all of the 19 IDEA awards Samsung has won since 2000 are the fruit of such teams. Helped by its innovative designs and egalitarian approach, Samsung has emerged as the best-selling brand in high-end TVs in the U.S., and the world's largest LCD computer monitor producer, with 17% of the global market. And Samsung has sold more than 10 million SGHE700s—the first clamshell phone with a hidden antenna—racking up some $1.2 billion in profits since its debut 14 months ago. "Good design is the most important way to differentiate ourselves from our competitors," says CEO Yun.

Many of the new design ideas are coming from outside. Last year, Samsung started sending designers abroad to spend a few months at fashion houses, cosmetics specialists, or design consultancies to stay current with what's happening in other industries. Lee Yun Jung, a senior designer who works on colors and finishes, spent last autumn in residence at a furniture designer in Italy. While she gathered plenty of ideas for product surfaces, the real eye-opener was the relaxed culture of the place. "A 23-year-old novice could interrupt the 60-year-old master," she marvels. Since returning, Lee has tried to be more open to ideas percolating up from the bottom of her department.

Today, Samsung knows it can't afford to let up. It's the first Asian company outside of Japan to use design to vault to the first tier of global companies. But in the Digital Age it's not too hard for strivers such as Lenovo of China and BenQ to make products that approach the quality of long-standing industry giants such as Sony, Panasonic, or Philips Electronics. Samsung, of course, was an upstart itself not long ago. It was the transition from analog to digital that gave the Korean company the opening it needed. "In the analog age, Samsung devoted most of its energy trying to catch up with Japanese leaders, but the arrival of digital put everybody on the same starting line," says Chin Dae Je, Korea's Information & Communication Minister and president of Samsung Electronics before joining the Cabinet last year.

These rivals—whether newcomer or veteran—aren't standing still. The newbies often hire U.S., Japanese, or Italian design consultancies to help them shape products that won't get lost in the crush of goods at Best Buy or Circuit City Stores. And those Asian upstarts are all looking to Samsung as a role model for their own transformation into global brands. The likes of Sony and Matsushita, meanwhile, are also placing a renewed emphasis on creating stand-out products. "Sony has been losing some of its edge in design," says Makoto Kogure, head of the Japanese giant's TV division. "Now we're drastically changing and [creating a] Sony identity."

Front-Loaded Design

So Samsung must continue to reinvent itself. In the past four years, the company has doubled its design staff, to 470, adding 120 of those just in the past 12 months (Exhibit 1). And since 2000, its design budget has been increasing 20% to 30% annually. To keep an eye on trends in its most important markets, Samsung now has

EXHIBIT 1

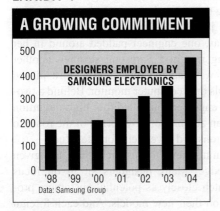

A GROWING COMMITMENT

DESIGNERS EMPLOYED BY SAMSUNG ELECTRONICS

Data: Samsung Group

design centers in London, Los Angeles, San Francisco, and Tokyo, and this year it opened one in Shanghai. More important, Samsung is changing the processes and procedures in its design department and giving designers more power to influence not just how products look but also what gets built (Exhibit 2). "Just as a lizard cuts off its own tail to move on, we will have to break with the past to move forward," says Chung Kook Hyun, the senior vice-president who runs design operations.

Samsung's designers these days no longer have to find a way to put their boxes around the devices that engineers cook up. Instead, they often give concepts to engineers, who must then build the machine inside the box dreamed up by the designers. James Choe, for instance, recently studied research showing that consumers prefer printers in which the paper lies flat rather than feeding in vertically. Engineers working on the same project, however, preferred a vertical model because it would cut the production cost of a $110 printer by about 10%. Before Choe started at Samsung three years ago, the engineers might have won. But when the desktop laser printer rolled out last year, Choe's design had prevailed. "The engineers didn't like it, but in the end management listened to us," he says.

Sometimes the designers come up with entirely new product categories. Kang Yun Je thought Samsung could do better than its rivals with a sleek, silver, rear-projection TV sporting a curved back and superthin edges, so that when viewed from an angle it looks as thin as an LCD TV. "When we first came up with the design, we had no guarantee it could be made," says Kang, a shaggy 36-year-old who sports a goatee and wears his shirt untucked. "So I went to the head of engineering, and he said that if I could give him some time and resources, he'd try to do it."

Where to get the resources? To make sure designers get heard, Samsung has created the post of chief design officer—something few other companies have bothered

EXHIBIT 2

Redesigning Samsung

Here's how Samsung is continuing to reinvent itself to keep its product designs at the leading edge

PIPELINE TO THE TOP	DESIGN-LED INNOVATION	QUESTION AUTHORITY
Designers can now go straight to top managers with ideas for new products. An award-winning rear-projection TV was developed by a designer who pitched it to the TV unit chief.	Designers no longer have to build boxes around engineers' devices. Instead, engineers now often find a way to stuff the right parts inside the designer's boxes.	Samsung is shedding its traditional Confucian hierarchy, encouraging younger designers to challenge their superiors when they think something needs to be changed.
BACK TO SCHOOL	**GLOBAL REACH**	**BEYOND HARDWARE**
Designers are sent to work at furniture, fashion, and industrial design houses to keep on top of the latest trends.	Since 2000, Samsung has opened or expanded design centers in San Francisco, London, Tokyo, Los Angeles, and this year in Shanghai.	Samsung studies everything about how consumers actually use products—from owners' manuals to packaging to the beeps, buzzes, and bells that digital devices make.

to do. And to make sure top execs stay attuned to the importance of the issue, CEO Yun holds quarterly design meetings where the chiefs of all the business units review new products and evaluate their designs. So Kang was able to simply call Choi Gee Sung, head of Samsung's TV, computer, and audio businesses and chief design officer since January, to secure backing for the TV project. A few years ago, Kang says, a designer at his level would have had to go through the marketing department and midlevel execs before reaching top management. Choi liked what he saw and gave Kang the go-ahead on the TV. Smart move: The TV, code-named L7, won a silver prize in the IDEA competition this year and is expected to be a big seller.

Samsung's design focus goes well beyond just the look and feel of its products. The company is working to improve the way people use and control gadgets, and two years ago it opened what it calls a "usability laboratory" in downtown Seoul (Exhibit 3). There, across the hall from where Choi Won Min taps away at his synthesizers in search of the perfect sound, engineers and consumers alike test everything from getting products out of the box to the icons and menus on screens. "In the past, physical design was the focal point," says Chief Design Officer Choi (no relation to the sound designer). "In the future, the user interface will be emphasized more."

The usability lab was built to provide a lifelike forum for tests. It looks like a typical living room,

with a kitchen in the corner for testing cooking appliances. Entering the room, designers and engineers kick off their shoes just as they do in a Korean home. On a recent fall day, one engineer padded around in her slippers making rice in a Samsung steamer, another checked out a washing machine, and a third played with the controls on a computer monitor. Behind a two-way mirror, an engineer controlled four high-definition cameras that can zoom in on any corner of the room to record the sessions and save them for later study.

It's that commitment to research that has given Samsung its edge. Many designers sit in on focus groups and watch closely as potential customers provide feedback on their new models. And each foreign lab has a researcher on site—unusual in the industry. Hwang Chang Hwan, Samsung's principal mobile-phone designer, faced complaints about the SPH-S2300, a three-megapixel camera phone. Techies and camera aficionados liked the optical zoom lens—a first in a camera phone—but other consumers didn't like the thickness of the lens. Most of all, young users hated the clumsy keypad, which was laid out in two rows of six keys along the bottom of the screen in order to keep the phone short enough to fit in a pocket. So when it came time to upgrade the phone, Samsung's designers listened. The new, five-megapixel successor sports a smaller lens that allows for a slimmer body, and it slides open, exposing a larger screen but leaving room for the traditional layout of three keys by four.

EXHIBIT 3

From Laggard to Leader	1969	1977	1980s
	Samsung Electronics established as maker of TVs with technology borrowed from Sanyo.	Samsung introduces its first color TV.	Focuses on undercutting Japanese rivals with me-too products. Design is an afterthought.
How Samsung ratcheted up its design emphasis	**1988** Launches first mobile phone.	**1993** Chairman Lee Kun Hee tells execs to reinvent Samsung through design.	**1994** Hires U.S. design consultancy IDEO to help develop computer monitors.
1995 Sets up in-house design school, the Innovative Design Lab of Samsung.	**1996** Lee declares "Year of Design Revolution," stressing that designers should lead in product planning.	**1998** Asian financial crisis dents Samsung's ambitions; design staff cut by 28%.	**2000** Samsung once again focuses on design, and CEO Yun Jong Yong calls for design-led management.
2001 Yun initiates quarterly design meetings for top execs; opens design labs in Los Angeles and London.	**2002** Samsung's "usability laboratory" inaugurated in downtown Seoul.	**2004** Samsung wins a total of 33 awards at top design contests in the U.S., Europe, and Asia.	

Can Samsung stay on top of its design game? Some skeptics say the company still doesn't have the breadth and depth in design of Sony, or the ingrained design culture of Apple Computer Corp. "Samsung has improved, but I don't see an identity in their design that really speaks to consumers," says Jim Wicks, Motorola Inc.'s vice-president in charge of designing cell phones. Still, few would deny that Samsung has managed to inject the importance of design into its corporate DNA. In this era of cutthroat competition, that may be just what it takes to create a lasting advantage.

Source: David Rocks and Moon Ihlwan, "Samsung Design," *BusinessWeek,* December 6, 2004, 88–96.

Case 6-2 Epilogue

Last June a group of 11 Samsung Electronics Co. employees pledged to do the last thing most people desire just as spring bursts into summer: stay inside a drab room with small, curtained windows for the bulk of the next six weeks. The product planners, designers, programmers, and engineers had recently entered Samsung's so-called Value Innovation Program (VIP) Center, just south of Seoul. They were asked to outline the features and design of the company's mainstay flat-screen TV, code-named Bordeaux. And their bosses had vowed to keep them posted there until they had completed the assignment.

After an introductory ceremony attended by senior executives of Samsung's video division, the team joined a dozen or so similar groups at the VIP Center and got down to work. The facility is a sort of boiler room where people from across the company brainstorm day after day—and often through the night. Guided by one of 50 "value innovation specialists," they study what rivals are offering, examine endless data on suppliers, components, and costs, and argue over designs and technologies. The Bordeaux team hammered out the basic look, feel, and features of the model by mid-August. Then over the next five months designers and engineers worked out the details, and by February the sets were rolling off Samsung assembly lines. They hit stores in the U.S. and South Korea this April, starting at about $1,300 for a 26-inch set. "For the first time in our company, we developed a TV appealing to customers' lifestyles," says Kim Min Suk, an official at Samsung's LCD TV Product Planning Group.

It's all part of a new mantra at Samsung: "market-driven change." In the past decade Samsung has radically improved the quality and design of its products.

Yun Jong Yong, Samsung's 62-year-old chief executive, now wants the company to rival the likes of Microsoft Corp. and IBM as a key shaper of information technology. By 2010 he aims to double sales, from $85 billion last year to $170 billion. The Korean giant, however, still isn't an innovation leader on the order of Apple Computer Inc. or Sony Corp. in its heyday. Yun says Samsung has become "a good company," but "we still have a lot of things to do before we're a great company."

Yun insists that when it comes to manufacturing, his company is second to none. Yet in the Digital Age, when mechanical parts are replaced by chips, Samsung's well-run factories are no longer enough to make it stand out. He points to MP3 players as an example. Samsung rolled out its first players two years before Apple did. But Apple gave consumers the ultimate player—the iPod—and, with the iTunes software and Web site, an easy way to fill it with music. It's time for Samsung to start developing similar products, Yun says, that better serve customers. So far, "we don't have the power to deliver total solutions."

Incubation Stage

How to make Samsung more innovative? One key initiative is the VIP Center (Exhibit 1). Yun set up the program in 1998 after concluding that as much as 80% of cost and quality is determined in the initial stages of product development. By bringing together everyone at the very beginning to thrash out differences, he believed, the company could streamline its operations and make better gadgets. In the past two years, though, the center's primary aim has shifted to "creating new value for customers," says Vice-President Lee Dong Jin, who heads the facility. Translation: Find that perfect balance of cost, innovation, and technology that makes a product great.

If it weren't such hard work, it might almost be fun. The center, at Suwon, Samsung's main manufacturing site, 20 miles from Seoul, is open 24 hours a day. Housed in a five-story former dormitory, it has 20 project rooms, 38 bedrooms for those who need to spend the night, a kitchen, a gym, traditional baths, and Ping-Pong and pool tables. Last year some 2,000 employees cycled through, completing 90 projects with names such as Rainbow, Rapido, and Rocky. Other products that have come out of the center include a notebook computer that doubles as a mobile TV, yet is thin and light enough to be carried in a handbag, and

EXHIBIT 1

Brainstorming **ABCs**

A key weapon in Samsung's success is the Value Innovation Program (VIP) Center, where the company's brightest lights dream up must-have products or streamline operations to trim costs. Here's how they do it:

LOCK 'EM UP	GUIDING HAND	MIX 'EM UP	SET A DATE	DO THE MATH
Daily routines can interrupt the flow of great ideas, so Samsung isolates its development teams in the VIP Center—and requires all members to work there for weeks on end, until the project is completed.	Some 50 specialists work at the Center, helping teams stay focused on the problems at hand, develop various alternative solutions, and reach a consensus when it's time to make a decision.	Brainstorming is most successful when a wide variety of viewpoints is represented. So Samsung gathers teams of engineers, designers, and planners from across the company to develop new products.	Deadlines force teams to make tough choices and overcome disagreements that can slow down progress. Each team is given a timetable for progress and a fixed date for the project's completion.	Team members draw "value curves," graphs that rank attributes such as a product's sound or picture quality on a scale from 1 to 5. These help the team set priorities and differentiate Samsung's product from rivals'.

the CLP-500, a color laser printer that was built at the same cost as a black-and-white model. While some teams wrap up their work within weeks, other projects drag on for months, and all division leaders sign a pledge that participants won't return to their regular jobs until they have finished the project.

The Bordeaux team shows how the VIP Center works. The goal was to create a flat-screen TV that would sell at least 1 million units. But the team members quickly discovered that they had strongly differing opinions about what consumers want in a TV. The designers proposed a sleek, heavily sculpted model. Engineers wanted to pack in plenty of functions and the best picture and sound quality. Product planners were concerned primarily with creating something that would beat the offerings of Sharp Corp., then the leader in LCD TVs.

Every step of the way, team members drew what Samsung calls "value curves." These are graphs that rank various attributes such as picture quality and design on a scale of 1 to 5, from outright bad to excellent. The graphs compared the proposed model with those of rival products and Samsung's existing TVs. The VIP Center specialists also guided the team in discussions exploring ideas and concepts from entirely different industries, picking up hints about the importance of the emotional appeal in the offerings of furniture makers and Hollywood. "We wanted a curve resembling a wine glass, and a glossy back to make the TV fit in with other furniture," says designer Lee Seung Ho, who worked on the Bordeaux project.

One challenge the team faced: Surveys showed that shoppers buy a flat-screen TV as much for its look as a piece of furniture as for its technological muscle. Some members went to furniture stores to figure out what made buyers tick, and discovered that the design of the set trumps most other considerations. So the group started shedding function in favor of form, cutting corners on high-tech features to spend more to make a TV that looks good even when it's turned off. The control buttons were placed out of sight on the side, while the speakers were tucked under the screen to create a sleek, minimalist front underlined by a flat, curving V in blue or burgundy. The back and stand got the same high-gloss coating as the front. To keep costs down (part of that quest for value), Samsung removed a sensor that automatically adjusts the brightness to the light in the room and decided not to boost resolution to accommodate the latest high-definition standards. And with the speakers under the screen, the sound quality was lowered even as the TV's silhouette improved. "We tried to make sure consumers get maximum value for an affordable price," says Kim Dong Joon, one of several senior managers at the VIP center.

The initial response is encouraging. In the last week of May, Samsung inched ahead of Sony to become the No. 1 LCD TV brand in the U.S., garnering market share (in terms of value) of 26.4%, compared with Sony's 24.6% and Sharp's 8.2%, according to researcher NPD Group. In January, Samsung was No. 3, with just 12.1%. Yun now says he wants to become the top maker of digital TVs, including those using plasma and rear-projection technologies, in the U.S. this year.

Pretty grand ambitions. But Yun has a strong record of setting stretch goals and achieving them. Under his stewardship, Samsung has transformed itself from an industry also-ran into the richest electronics maker in Asia. Now it could also become the coolest if Yun can reinvent Samsung one more time and get his engineers, designers, and marketers to dream up products such as

the Bordeaux and really fire consumers' imaginations. It just might mean spending the summer inside.

Source: Moon Ihlwan, "Camp Samsung," *BusinessWeek*, July 3, 2006, 46–48.

Case 6-3

General Electric Appliances*

Larry Barr had recently been promoted to the position of district sales manager (B.C.) for G.E Appliances, a division of Canadian Appliance Manufacturing Co. Ltd. (CAMCO). One of his more important duties in that position was the allocation of his district's sales quota among his five salesmen. Barr received his quota for 2002 in October 2001. His immediate task was to determine an equitable allocation of that quota. This was important because the company's incentive pay plan was based on the salesmen's attainment of quota. A portion of Barr's remuneration was also based on the degree to which his sales force met their quotas.

Barr graduated from the University of British Columbia in 1993 with the degree of bachelor of commerce. He was immediately hired as a product manager for a mining equipment manufacturing firm because of his summer job experience with that firm. In 1996, he joined Canadian General Electric (C.G.E) in Montreal as a product manager for refrigerators. There he was responsible for creating and merchandising a product line, as well as developing product and marketing plans. In January 1999, he was transferred to Coburg, Ontario, as a sales manager for industrial plastics. In September 2000, he became administrative manager (Western Region) and when the position of district sales manager became available, Barr was promoted to it. There his duties included development of sales strategies, supervision of salesmen, and budgeting.

Background

Canadian Appliance Manufacturing Co. Ltd (CAMCO) was created in 1998 under the joint ownership of Canadian General Electric Ltd. and General Steel Wares Ltd. (G.S.W.). CAMCO then purchased the production facilities of Westinghouse Canada Ltd. Under the purchase agreement, the Westinghouse brand name was transferred to White Consolidated Industries Ltd.,

where it became White-Westinghouse. Appliances manufactured by CAMCO in the former Westinghouse plant were branded Hotpoint (See Exhibit 1).

The G.E, G.S.W., and Hotpoint major appliance plants became divisions of CAMCO. These divisions operated independently and had their own separate management staff, although they were all ultimately accountable to CAMCO management. The divisions competed for sales, although not directly, because they each produced product lines for different price segments.

Competition

Competition in the appliance industry was vigorous. CAMCO was the largest firm in the industry, with approximately 45 percent market share, split between G.E, G.S.W. (Moffatt & McClary brands), and Hotpoint. The following three firms each had 10 to 15 percent market share: Inglis (washers and dryers only), W.C.I. (makers of White-Westinghouse, Kelvinator, and Gibson), and Admiral. These firms also produced appliances under department store brand names such as Viking, Baycrest, and Kenmore, which accounted for an additional 15 percent of the market. The remainder of the market was divided among brands such as Maytag, Roper Dishwasher, Gurney, Tappan, and Danby.

G.E marketed a full major appliance product line, including refrigerators, ranges, washers, dryers, dishwashers, and television sets. G.E appliances generally had many features and were priced at the upper end of the price range. Their major competition came from Maytag and Westinghouse.

The Budgeting Process

G.E Appliances was one of the most advanced firms in the consumer goods industry in terms of sales budgeting. Budgeting received careful analysis at all levels of management.

The budgetary process began in June of each year. The management of G.E. Appliances division assessed the economic outlook, growth trends in the industry, competitive activity, population growth, and so forth to determine a reasonable sales target for the next year. The president

*Copyright © 2002 Richard W. Pollay, John D. Claxtoan, and Rick Jenkner. Adapted with permission.

EXHIBIT 1 **Organization Chart**

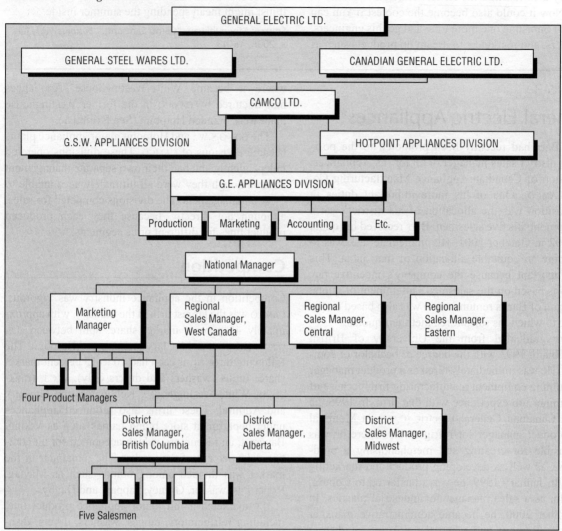

of CAMCO received this estimate, checked and revised it as necessary, and submitted it to the president of G.E. Canada. Final authorization rested with G.E. Ltd., which had a definite minimum growth target for the G.E. branch of CAMCO. G.E. Appliances was considered an "invest and grow" division, which meant it was expected to produce a healthy sales growth each year, regardless of the state of the economy. As Barr observed, "This is difficult, but meeting challenges is the job of management."

The approved budget was expressed as a desired percentage increase in sales. Once the figure had been decided, it was not subject to change. The quota was communicated back through G.E. Canada Ltd., CAMCO, and G.E. Appliances, where it was available to the district

sales managers in October. Each district was then required to meet an overall growth figure (quota), but each sales territory was not automatically expected to achieve that same growth. Barr was required to assess the situation in each territory, determine where growth potential was highest, and allocate his quota accordingly.

The Sales Incentive Plan

The sales incentive plan was a critical part of General Electric's sales force plan and an important consideration in the quota allocation of Barr. Each salesman had a portion of his earnings dependent on his performance with respect to quota. Also, Barr was awarded a bonus based on the sales performance of his district, making it advantageous to Barr and good for staff morale for all his salesmen to attain their quotas.

The sales force incentive plan was relatively simple. A bonus system is fairly typical for salesmen in any field. With G.E., each salesman agreed to a basic salary figure called "planned earnings." The planned salary varied according to experience, education, past performance, and competitive salaries. A salesman was paid 75 percent of his planned earnings on a guaranteed regular basis. The remaining 25 percent of salary was at risk, dependent on the person's sales

record. There was also the possibility of earning substantially more money by selling more than quota (see Exhibit 2).

The bonus was awarded such that total salary (base plus bonus) equaled planned earnings when the quota was just met. The greatest increase in bonus came between 101 and 110 percent of quota. The bonus was paid quarterly on the cumulative total quota. A holdback system ensured that a salesman was never required to pay back previously earned bonus because of a poor quarter. Because of this system, it was critical that each salesman's quota be fair in relation to the

EXHIBIT 2

Sales Incentive Earnings Schedule: Major Appliances and Home Entertainment Products

Sales Quota Realization (percent)	Percent of Base Salary Total	Sales Quota Realization (Percent)	Incentive Percent of Base Salary Total
70%	0 %	105%	35.00%
71	0.75	106	37.00
72	1.50	107	39.00
73	2.25	108	41.00
74	3.00	109	43.00
75	3.75	110	45.00
76	4.50	111	46.00
77	5.25	112	47.00
78	6.00	113	48.00
79	6.75	114	49.00
80	7.50	115	50.00
81	8.25	116	51.00
82	9.00	117	52.00
83	9.75	118	53.00
84	10.50	119	54.00
85	11.25	120	55.00
86	12.00	121	56.00
87	12.75	122	57.00
88	13.50	123	58.00
89	14.25	124	59.00
90	15.00	125	60.00
91	16.00	126	61.00
92	17.00	127	62.00
93	18.00	128	63.00
94	19.00	129	64.00
95	20.00	130	65.00
96	21.00	131	66.00
97	22.00	132	67.00
98	23.00	133	68.00
99	24.00	134	69.00
100	25.00	135	70.00
101	27.00	136	71.00
102	29.00	137	72.00
103	31.00	138	73.00
104	33.00	139	74.00
		140	75.00

other salesmen. Nothing was worse for morale than one person earning large bonuses while the others struggled.

Quota attainment was not the sole basis for evaluating the salesmen. They were required to fulfill a wide range of duties including service, franchising of new dealers, maintaining good relations with dealers, and maintaining a balance of sales among the different product lines. Because the bonus system was based on sales only, Barr had to ensure the salesmen did not neglect their other duties.

A formal salary review was held each year for each salesman. However, Barr preferred to give his salesmen continuous feedback on their performances. Through human relations skills, he hoped to avoid problems that could lead to dismissal of a salesman and loss of sales for the company.

Barr's incentive bonus plan was more complex than the salesmen's. He was awarded a maximum of 75 annual bonus points broken down as follows: market share, 15; total sales performance, 30; sales representative balance, 30. Each point had a specific money value. The system ensured that Barr allocate his quota carefully. For instance, if one quota was so difficult that the salesmen sold only 80 percent of it, while the other salesmen exceeded quota, Barr's bonus would be reduced, even if the overall area sales exceeded the quota. (See Appendix, "Development of a Sales Commission Plan.")

Quota Allocation

The total 2002 sales budget for G.E. Appliances division was about $100 million, a 14 percent sales increase over 1999. Barr's share of the $33 million Western Region quota was $13.3 million, also a 14 percent increase over

1999. Barr had two weeks to allocate the quota among his five territories. He needed to consider factors such as historical allocation, economic outlook, dealer changes, personnel changes, untapped potential, new franchises or store openings, and buying group activity (volume purchases by associations of independent dealers).

Sales Force

There were five sales territories within B.C. (Exhibit 3). Territories were determined on the basis of number of customers, sales volume of customers, geographic size, and experience of the salesman. Territories were altered periodically to deal with changed circumstances.

One territory was comprised entirely of contract customers. Contract sales were sales in bulk lots to builders and developers who used the appliances in housing units. Because the appliances were not resold at retail, G.E took a lower profit margin on such sales.

G.E. Appliances recruited M.B.A. graduates for their sales force. They sought bright, educated people who were willing to relocate anywhere in Canada. The company intended that these people would ultimately be promoted to managerial positions. The company also hired experienced career salesmen to get a blend of experience in the sales force. However, the typical salesman was under 30, aggressive, and upwardly mobile. G.E.'s sales training program covered only product knowledge. It was not felt necessary to train recruits in sales techniques.

Allocation Procedure

At the time Barr assumed the job of district sales manager, he had a meeting with the former sales manager, Ken Philips. Philips described to Barr the method he had used in the past to allocate the quota. As Barr understood it, the procedure was as follows.

EXHIBIT 3
G.E. Appliances—
Sales Territories

Territory Designation	Description
9961 Greater Vancouver (Garth Rizzuto)	Hudson's Bay, Firestone, Kmart, McDonald Supply, plus seven independent dealers
9962 Interior (Dan Seguin)	All customers from Quesnel to Nelson, including contract sales (50 customers)
9963 Coastal (Ken Block)	Eatons, Woodwards, plus Vancouver Island north of Duncan and upper Fraser Valley (east of Clearbrook) (20 customers)
9964 Independent and Northern (Fred Speck)	All independents in lower mainland and South Vancouver Island, plus northern B. C. and Yukon (30 customers)
9967 Contract (Jim Wiste)	Contract sales Vancouver, Victoria All contract sales outside 9962 (50–60 customers)

The quota was received in October in the form of a desired percentage sales increase. The first step was to project current sales to the end of the year. This gave a base to which the increase was added for an estimation of the next year's quota.

From this quota, the value of contract sales was allocated. Contract sales were allocated first because the market was considered the easiest to forecast. The amount of contract sales in the sales mix was constrained by the lower profit margin on such sales.

The next step was to make a preliminary allocation by simply adding the budgeted percentage increase to the year-end estimates for each territory. Although this allocation seemed fair on the surface, it did not take into account the differing situations in the territories, or the difficulty of attaining such an increase.

The next step was examination of the sales data compiled by G.E Weekly sales reports from all regions were fed into a central computer, which compiled them and printed out sales totals by product line for each customer, as well as other information. This information enabled the sales manager to check the reasonableness of his initial allocation through a careful analysis of the growth potential for each customer.

The analysis began with the largest accounts, such as Firestone, Hudson's Bay, and Eatons, which each bought over $1 million in appliances annually. Accounts that size were expected to achieve at least the budgeted growth. The main reason for this was that a shortfall of a few percentage points on such a large account would be difficult to make up elsewhere.

Next, the growth potential for medium-sized accounts was estimated. These accounts included McDonald Supply, Kmart, Federated Cooperative, and buying groups such as Volume Independent Purchasers (V.I.P.). Management expected the majority of sales growth to come from such accounts, which had annual sales of between $150,000 and $1 million.

At that point, about 70 percent of the accounts had been analyzed. The small accounts were estimated last. These had generally lower growth potential but were an important part of the company's distribution system.

Once all the accounts had been analyzed, the growth estimates were summed and the total compared to the budget. Usually, the growth estimates were well below the budget.

The next step was to gather more information. The salesmen were usually consulted to ensure that no potential trouble areas or good opportunities had been overlooked. The manager continued to revise and adjust the figures until the total estimated matched the budget. These projections were then summed by territory and compared to the preliminary territorial allocation.

Frequently, there were substantial differences between the two allocations. Historical allocations were then examined and the manager used his judgment in adjusting the figures until he was satisfied that the allocation was both equitable and attainable. Some factors that were considered at this stage included experience of the salesmen, competitive activities, potential store closures or openings, potential labor disputes in areas, and so forth.

The completed allocation was passed on to the regional sales manager for his approval. The process had usually taken one week or longer by this stage. Once the allocations had been approved, the district sales manager then divided them into sales quotas by product line. Often, the resulting average price did not match the expected mix between higher- and lower-priced units. Therefore, some additional adjusting of figures was necessary. The house account (used for sales to employees of the company) was used as the adjustment factor.

Once this breakdown had been completed, the numbers were printed on a budget sheet and given to the regional sales manager. He forwarded all the sheets for his region to the central computer, which printed out sales numbers for each product line by salesman, by month. These figures were used as the salesmen's quotas for the next year.

Current Situation

Barr recognized that he faced a difficult task. He thought he was too new to the job and the area to confidently undertake an account-by-account growth analysis. However, due to his previous experience with sales budgets, he did have some sound general ideas. He also had the records of past allocation and quota attainment (Exhibit 4), as well as the assistance of the regional sales manager, Anthony Foyt.

Barr's first step was to project the current sales figures to end-of-year totals. This task was facilitated because the former manager, Philips, had been making successive projections monthly since June. Barr then made a preliminary quota allocation by adding the budgeted sales increase of 14 percent to each territory's total (Exhibit 5).

Barr then began to assess circumstances that could cause him to alter that allocation. One major problem was the resignation, effective at the end of the year, of

EXHIBIT 4   Sales Results

Territory	1999 Budget (× 1,000)	Percent of Total Budget	1999 Actual (× 1,000)	1999 Variance from Quota (V%)
9967 (Contract)	$2,440	26.5%	$2,267	(7)%
9961 (Greater Vancouver)	1,790	19.4	1,824	2
9962 (Interior)	1,624	17.7	1,433	(11)
9963 (Coastal)	2,111	23.0	2,364	12
9964 (Ind. dealers)	1,131	12.3	1,176	4
House	84	1.1	235	—
Total	**$9,180**	**100.0%**	**$9,299**	**1%**

Territory	2000 Budget (× 1,000)	Percent of Total Budget	2000 Actual (× 1,000)	2000 Variance from Quota (V%)
9967 (Contract)	$2,587	26.2%	$ 2,845	10%
9961 (Greater Vancouver)	2,005	20.3	2,165	8%
9962 (Interior)	1,465	14.8	1,450	(1)
9963 (Coastal)	2,405	24.4	2,358	(2)
9964 (Ind. dealers)	1,334	13.5	1,494	12
House	.52	0.8	86	—
Total	**$9,848**	**100.0%**	**$10,398**	**5%**

EXHIBIT 5   Sales Projections and Quotas, 2001–2002

Projected Sales Results 2001

Territory	Oct. 2001 Year to Date	2001 Projected Total	2001 Budget	Percent of Total Budget	Projected Variance from Quota (V%)
9967	$2,447	$ 3,002	$ 2,859	25.0%	5%
9961	2,057	2,545	2,401	21.0	6
9962	1,318	1,623	1,727	15.1	(6)
9963	2,124	2,625	2,734	23.9	(4)
9964	1,394	1,720	1,578	13.8	
House	132	162	139	1.2	—
Total	**$9,474**	**$11,677**	**$11,438**	**100.0%**	**2%**

Preliminary Allocation 2002

Territory	2001 Projection	2002 Budget*	Percent of Total Budget
9967	$ 3,002	$ 3,422	25.7%
9961	2,545	2,901	21.8
9962	1,623	1,854	13.9
9963	2,625	2,992	22.5
9964	1,720	1,961	14.7
House	162	185	1.3
Total	**$11,677**	**$13,315**	**100.0%***

*2002 budget = 2001 territory projections + 14% = $13,315.

one of the company's top salesmen, Ken Block. His territory had traditionally been one of the most difficult, and Barr believed it would be unwise to replace Block with a novice salesman.

Barr considered shifting one of the more experienced salesmen into that area. However, that would have disrupted service in an additional territory, which was undesirable because it took several months for a salesman to build up a good rapport with customers. Barr's decision would affect his quota allocation because a salesman new to a territory could not be expected to immediately sell as well as the incumbent, and a novice salesman would require an even longer period of adaptation.

Barr was also concerned about territory 9961. The territory comprised two large national accounts and several major independent dealers. The buying decisions for the national accounts were made at their head offices, where G.E.'s regional salesmen had no control over the decisions. Recently, Barr had heard rumors that one of the national accounts was reviewing its purchase of G.E. Appliances. If it were to delist even some product lines, it would be a major blow to the salesman, Rizzuto, whose potential sales would be greatly reduced. Barr was unsure how to deal with that situation.

Another concern for Barr was the wide variance in buying of some accounts. Woodwards, Eatons, and McDonald Supply had large fluctuations from year to year. Also, Eatons, Hudson's Bay, and Woodwards had plans to open new stores in the Vancouver area sometime during the year. The sales increase to be generated by these events was hard to estimate.

The general economic outlook was poor. The Canadian dollar had fallen to 92 cents U.S. and unemployment was at about 8 percent. The government's anti-inflation program, which was scheduled to end in November 2002, had managed to keep inflation to the 8 percent level, but economists expected higher inflation and increased labor unrest during the postcontrol period.

The economic outlook was not the same in all areas. For instance, the Okanagan (9962) was a very depressed area. Tourism was down and fruit farmers were doing poorly despite good weather and record prices. Vancouver Island was still recovering from a 200 percent increase in ferry fares, while the lower mainland appeared to be in a relatively better position.

In the contract segment, construction had shown an increase over 2000. However, labor unrest was common. There had been a crippling eight-week strike in 2000, and there was a strong possibility of another strike in 2002.

With all of this in mind, Barr was very concerned that he allocate the quota properly because of the bonus system implications. How should he proceed? To help him in his decision, he reviewed a note on development of a sales commission plan that he had obtained while attending a seminar on sales management the previous year (see Appendix below).

Appendix: Development of a Sales Commission Plan

A series of steps are required to establish the foundation on which a sales commission plan can be built. These steps are as follows:

A. Determine Specific Sales Objectives of Positions to Be Included in Plan

For a sales commission plan to succeed, it must be designed to encourage the attainment of the business objectives of the component division. Before deciding on the specific measures of performance to be used in the plan, the component should review and define its major objectives. Typical objectives might be:

- Increase sales volume.
- Do an effective balanced selling job in a variety of product lines.
- Improve market share.
- Reduce selling expense to sales ratios.
- Develop new accounts or territories.
- Introduce new products.

Although it is probably neither desirable nor necessary to include all such objectives as specific measures of performance in the plan, they should be kept in mind, at least to the extent that the performance measures chosen for the plan are compatible with and do not work against the overall accomplishment of the component's business objectives.

Also, the relative current importance or ranking of these objectives will provide guidance in selecting the number and type of performance measures to be included in the plan.

B. Determine Quantitative Performance Measures to Be Used

Although it may be possible to include a number of measures in a particular plan, there is a drawback to using so many as to overly complicate it and fragment the impact of any one measure on the participants.

A plan that is difficult to understand will lose a great deal of its motivation force, as well as be costly to administer properly.

For those who currently have a variable sales compensation plan(s) for their salespeople, a good starting point would be to consider the measures used in those plans. Although the measurements used for sales managers need not be identical, they should at least be compatible with those used to determine their salespeople's commissions.

However, keep in mind that a performance measure that may not be appropriate for individual salespeople may be a good one to apply to their manager. Measurements involving attainment of a share of a defined market, balanced selling for a variety of products, and control of district or region expenses might fall into this category.

Listed in Exhibit 6 are a variety of measurements that might be used to emphasize specific sales objectives.

For most components, all or most of these objectives will be desirable to some extent. The point is to select those of greatest importance where it will be possible to establish measures of standard or normal

performance for individuals, or at least small groups of individuals working as a team.

If more than one performance measurement is to be used, the relative weighting of each measurement must be determined. If a measure is to be effective, it must carry enough weight to have at least some noticeable effect on the commission earnings of an individual.

As a general guide, it would be unusual for a plan to include more than two or three quantitative measures with a minimum weighting of 15 to 20 percent of planned commissions for any one measurement.

C. Establish Commission Payment Schedule for Each Performance Measure

1. Determine appropriate range of performance for each measurement. The performance range for a measurement defines the percent of standard performance (%R) at which commission earnings start to the point where they reach maximum.

The minimum point of the performance range for a given measurement should be set so that a majority of the participants can earn at least some incentive pay and the maximum set at a point that is possible

EXHIBIT 6
Tailoring Commission Plan Measurements to Fit Component Objectives

Objectives	Possible Plan Measurements
1. Increase sales/orders volume	Net sales billed or orders received against quota.
2. Increase sales of particular lines	Sales against product line quotas with weighted sales credits on individual lines.
3. Increase market share	Percent realization (%R) of shares bogey.
4. Do balanced selling job	%R of product line quotas with commissions increasing in proportion to number of lines up to quota.
5. Increase profitability	Margin realized from sales.
	Vary sales credits to emphasize profitable product lines.
	Vary sales credit in relation to amount of price discount.
6. Increase dealer sales	Pay distributor, sales people, or sales manager in relation to realization of sales quotas of assigned dealers.
7. Increase sales calls	%R of targeted calls per district or region.
8. Introduce new product	Additional sales credits on new line for limited period.
9. Control expense	%R of expense to sales or margin ratio. Adjust sales credit in proportion to variance from expense budget.
10. Sales teamwork	Share of incentive based upon group results.

of attainment by some participants. These points will vary with the type of measure used and the degree of predictability of individual budgets or other forms of measurement. In a period where overall performance is close to standard, 90 to 95 percent of the participants should fall within the performance range.

For the commission plan to be effective, most of the participants should be operating within the performance range most of the time. If a participant is either far below the minimum of this range or has reached the maximum, further improvement will not affect his or her commission earnings, and the plan will be largely inoperative as far as he or she is concerned.

Actual past experience of %R attained by participants is obviously the best indicator of what this range should be for each measure used. Lacking this, it is better to err on the side of having a wider range than one that proves to be too narrow. If some form of group measure is used, the variation from standard performance is likely to be less for the group in total than for individuals within it. For example, the performance range for total district performance would probably be narrower than the range established for individual salespeople within a district.

2. Determine appropriate reward to risk ratio for commission earnings. This refers to the relationship of commission earned at standard performance to maximum commission earnings available under the plan. A plan that pays 10 percent of base salary for normal or standard performance and pays 30 percent as a maximum commission would have a 2 to 1 ratio. In other words, the participant can earn twice as much (20 percent) for above-standard performance as he or she stands to lose for below-standard performance (10 percent).

Reward under a sales commission plan should be related to the effort involved to produce a given result. To adequately encourage above-standard results, the reward to risk ratio should generally be at least 2 to 1. The proper control of incentive plan payments lies in the proper setting of performance standards, not in the setting of a low maximum payment for outstanding results that provides a minimum variation in individual earnings. Generally, a higher percentage of base salary should be paid for each 1%R above 100 percent than has been paid for each 1%R up to 100%R to reflect the relative difficulty involved in producing above-standard results.

Once the performance range and reward to risk ratios have been determined, the schedule of payments for each performance measure can then be calculated. This will show the percentage of the participant's base salary earned for various performance results (%R) from the point at which commissions start to maximum [sic] performance. For example, for measurement paying 20 percent of salary for standard performance:

Percent Base Salary Earned		Percent of Sales Quota
1% of base salary for each + 1%R	0%	80% or below
	20%	100% (standard performance)
1.33% of base salary for each + 1%R	60%	130% or above

D. Prepare Draft of Sales Commission Plan

After completing the above steps, a draft of a sales commission plan should be prepared using the outline below as a guide.

Keys to effective commission plans

1. Get the understanding and acceptance of the commission plan by the managers who will be involved in carrying it out. They must be convinced of its effectiveness to properly explain and "sell" the plan to the salespeople.

2. In turn, be sure the plan is presented clearly to the salespeople so that they have a good understanding of how the plan will work. We find that good acceptance of a sales commission plan on the part of salespeople correlates closely with how well they understood the plan and its effect on their commission. Salespeople must be convinced that the measurements used are factors they can control by their selling efforts.

3. Be sure the measurements used in the commission plan encourage the salespeople to achieve the marketing goals of your operation. For example, if sales volume is the only performance measure, salespeople will concentrate on producing as much dollar volume as possible by spending most of their time on products with high volume potential. It will be difficult to get them to spend much time on introducing new products with relatively low volume, handling customer complaints, and so on. Even though a good portion of their compensation may still be in salary, you can be sure they will wind up doing the things they feel will maximize their commission earnings.

4. One good solution to maintaining good sales direction is to put at least a portion of the commission earnings in an "incentive pool" to be distributed by the sales manager according to his or her judgment. This "pool" can vary in size according to some qualitative measure of the sales group's performance, but the manager can set individual measurements for each salesperson and reward each person according to how well he or she fulfills the goals.

5. If at all possible, you should test the plan for a period of time, perhaps in one or two sales areas or districts. To make it a real test, you should actually pay commission earnings to the participants, but the potential risk and rewards can be limited. No matter how well a plan has been conceived, not all the potential pitfalls will be apparent until you've actually operated the plan for a period of time. The test period is a relatively painless way to get some experience.

6. Finally, after the plan is in operation, take time to analyze the results. Is the plan accomplishing what you want it to do, both in terms of business results produced and in realistically compensating salespeople for their efforts?

Case 6-4

Slendertone

Local auctioneer Eamonn McBride still remembers clearly the day in 1990 when Kevin McDonnell arrived in the truck in Bunbeg: "Kevin had asked me to organize accommodations for some employees of a new business he was setting up. I went to look for him on the industrial estate. I found him outside the factory in a big truck. He pointed to the equipment in the back of the truck and said, 'That's it there,' referring to his new business. I was totally stunned." McDonnell wanted to buy the remaining assets of a company called BMR, which had gone into liquidation. The deal included ownership of the company's brand names, NeuroTech and Slendertone. McDonnell had decided, against the advice of many, to reestablish the business in an old factory on the industrial estate outside Bunbeg. Bunbeg is a remote, windswept coastal village in the Gaeltacht (Irish-speaking) region of northwest Donegal. Within a few weeks McDonnell and five employees had begun production.

McDonnell says that he knew little about the business he was getting into when he loaded the truck in Shannon and drove north to Donegal. An accountant by training, he thought that on paper it seemed like a

This case was written by Michael J. Murphy, University College Cork. It is intended to be used as the basis for class discussion rather than to illustrate either effective or ineffective handling of a management situation. The case was made possible by the cooperation of BioMedical Research Ltd. Copyright 1999 by M. J. Murphy, University College Cork. Some of the figures, names, and other information in this case have been altered to protect company and customer confidentiality. However, all the data are representative of the actual position.

viable business. He now employs over 150 people in Ireland and another 70 in international subsidiaries of his company, BioMedical Research Ltd. Company revenue in 1998 was £22 million, £17 million of which was from sales of Slendertone, up nearly 60 percent from the previous year. The company has received a number of design, export, and enterprise awards, and McDonnell was voted Donegal Businessman of the Year in 1995. But McDonnell has little time or desire to reflect on his substantial achievement to date—not while he has still to attain one of his greatest goals: to develop Slendertone into a world-class brand.

McDonnell believes that Slendertone can be a £100 million a year business by the year 2002. He likes to relate how Slendertone now outsells popular brands such as Impulse and Diet Pepsi in the United Kingdom; or how Slendertone is now available in Selfridges, the prestigious department store in London. McDonnell is under no illusions about the arduous challenge that lies ahead. However, he believes he has the strategy to achieve his goal. He is confident that the recent marketing strategy devised by Brian O'Donohoe will enable Slendertone to achieve sales of over £100 million in two years and become a world-class brand. O'Donohoe, now managing director of Slendertone, joined the company as marketing director for Slendertone in April 1997.

According to O'Donohoe, "BioMedical Research has gone from being a product-oriented company to a market-led one." In the process O'Donohoe has had to identify and deal with a number of critical issues. He believes that the foremost issue facing the Slendertone brand is credibility. He stresses the need to get away from the "gadget" image associated with Slendertone. O'Donohoe is confident that his strategy to reposition the brand will resolve this issue successfully. Product credibility is one of a number of important issues that have arisen since Slendertone's creation over 30 years ago. O'Donohoe knows that the future of Slendertone as a world-class brand depends on how well his strategy deals with these and other issues which have arisen more recently as a result of the company's dramatic growth.

Slendertone: The Early Years

Slendertone originally was developed by a company called BMR Ltd. in 1966. The company moved from England to the tax-free zone in Shannon in 1968. BMR manufactured a range of electronic muscle stimulation (EMS) devices under the Slendertone[1] and NeuroTech brands, serving the cosmetic and medical markets, respectively. By the end of the 1980s BMR's total annual sales were £1.5 million. Around 40 percent of revenue came from the sale of NeuroTech products, which were used by medical practitioners and physiotherapists to treat conditions such as muscle atrophy. The balance came from sales of Slendertone, which was used mostly for cosmetic purposes. Ninety-five percent of Slendertone sales were to the professional (beauty salon) market, with the remaining 5 percent coming from a limited range of home use products. The home use units were very basic and had few features. They retailed for between £250 and £400. Margins on all products were high. BMR claimed that Slendertone was available in over 40 countries by the late 1980s. All international sales were being handled by small local distributors or companies with diverse product interests (including an oil importer and a garden furniture dealer).

Kevin McDonnell was a creditor of BMR at the time of its liquidation; he had been supplying the company with printed circuit boards for four years. In that time he had learned something about the company's operations. When he heard BMR was going into liquidation, he immediately saw an opportunity. In an interview with *The Financial Times* in 1995 he stated: "I thought it was a bit odd that the company could go out of business, and yet, according to its business plan, it was capable of a 20 percent return on turnover." Few shared McDonnell's belief in the future of the Slendertone business. The managing director of BMR's German office felt that Slendertone was a fad which had little future.

McDonnell was not deterred. By the end of 1990 he had notched sales of £1.4 million, producing and

[1]This case study focuses on the Slendertone division. Readers who are not familiar with EMS or Slendertone are advised to read the appendix before proceeding with the case.

selling much of the original BMR product range. With his focus initially on production, McDonnell continued to sell most of his products through distributors, many of which had previously worked with BMR. Over the next two years revenue grew gradually through increasing sales to distributors of the existing product range. McDonnell reinvested all his earnings in the business. Research into biomedical technology, with a view to developing new products, consumed much of his limited investment resources. The production facilities also were being upgraded: The company acquired a new and much larger factory in the Bunbeg industrial estate. McDonnell always believed that new product development was the key to future growth. By using distributors to develop export markets, he could focus his limited resources on developing better products.

The Gymbody 8

In late 1993 the Gymbody 8 was launched, the first "new" product produced by BioMedical Research Ltd. Designed primarily to meet the demands of a distributor in France, this "eight-pad stomach and bottom styler" was soon to outsell all the company's other products combined. Although it was much more stylish than anything else on the market at that time, initial sales of the Gymbody 8 were disappointing. Sales in general for home use products were very limited. Most sales of home use EMS-based consumer products were through mail order catalogs, small advertisements in the print media, and a very limited number of retail outlets, mainly pharmacies. After a few months of lackluster sales performance, the French distributor tried using an American-style direct response "informercial" on the national home shopping channel, M6. This 30-minute "chat show," featuring interviews with a mixture of "ordinary" and celebrity users of the Gymbody 8, produced immediate results. Between interviews and demonstrations showing how the product worked, viewers were encouraged to order a Gymbody 8 by phone. By the end of 1994 Gymbody 8 sales (ex-factory) to the French distributor totaled £3.4 million. The French promotional strategy also involved the wide use of direct response (DR) advertisements in magazines and other print media. Over time retail distribution was extended to some pharmacies and a few sports stores. The soaring sales in France indicated a large untapped market for home use EMS products, a market larger than anyone in the company had anticipated.

Other Slendertone markets were slower to grow even after the introduction of the Gymbody 8. Those markets included mainland Europe, South America, Japan, and Australia. Sales in Ireland for the Gymbody 8 began to rise but were small relative to the sales in France. The Gymbody 8 was listed in a few English mail order catalogs, but sales were low. A distributor in Colombia was the only other customer of any significance for the Gymbody 8.

Distribution

With the exception of the home market, all sales of Slendertone were through distributors. By using distributors, the company believed it could develop new markets for Slendertone (or redevelop previous markets) more cost-effectively and quickly. The company's marketing resources were very limited because of the investments being made in research and production. Some of the distributors had handled Slendertone products previously for BMR, while others were newly recruited. Most of the distributors tended to be small operators, sometimes working from their homes. Most did not have the resources to invest in large-scale market development. Efforts to attract larger distributors already in the beauty market were proving unsuccessful in spite of the potential returns indicated by the ever-growing French market. Yet management was of the view that small distributors could also generate sales quickly by using direct marketing. Without the need to secure retail distribution and with an immediate return on all promotional spending, going direct would not require the levels of investment usually associated with introducing a new product to the market. The growing sales of Slendertone in Ireland from a range of direct marketing activities was proof of this.

Along with poorly resourced and inexperienced distributors, sluggish growth in most markets was blamed on legal restrictions on DR activity and cultural factors. In Germany, DR television was not allowed.[2] Combined with a very low use of credit cards, this did not augur well for a DR-oriented strategy in Germany. Other countries also had restrictions on DR activities. With regard to cultural factors, a number of BioMedical Research personnel felt that the Germans were less likely to be interested in a product like Slendertone than were the Spanish, the French, and the South Americans. It was believed that the latter countries had a stronger "body culture" and that their people were not as conservative as those in Germany and Switzerland. Yet, it was

[2]Restrictions on DR activity in Germany, including TV broadcasts, have since been relaxed.

argued, this couldn't explain the rapidly growing sales of Slendertone in Ireland, a relatively conservative country.

Direct Response Television

In the summer of 1995 a small cable television company in Ireland agreed to broadcast a locally produced infomercial. The infomercial featured local celebrities and studio guests and adopted the French "chat show" format. Broadcast periodically throughout the summer to a potential audience of fewer than 200,000 viewers, the infomercial resulted in direct sales of almost 1,000 Gymbody 8's. Sales of Gymbody 8's also increased in a handful of retail outlets within the cable company's broadcast area. There appeared to be an increase in demand for Slendertone beauty salon treatments in this area. The success of the Irish infomercial campaign, along with the French campaign, convinced management that DR television was the best way to sell Slendertone. It was believed that if infomercials worked well in both France and Ireland, it was likely that they would work in most other countries. The focus of the sales strategy switched from developing local distributors to securing more DR television opportunities. Intensive research was undertaken to identify infomercial opportunities around the globe, from South America to the Far East. A number of opportunities were identified, but the initial costs of producing infomercials for separate far-flung markets were a constraint. It was then decided to target "home shopping" companies. These companies buy TV time in many countries and then broadcast a range of direct response programming.

By the end of 1995 a deal had been signed with Direct Shop Ltd., which was broadcasting home shopping programming in over 30 countries at that time. The advantages of using Direct Shop were that it had access to TV space across a number of markets, would handle all negotiations with the TV companies, would buy product up-front, and could handle large numbers of multilingual sales calls. BioMedical Research produced a new Slendertone infomercial exclusively for Direct Shop, using the successful chat show format. Direct Shop ran the infomercial on satellite channels such as Eurosport and Superchannel, usually late at night or early in the morning, when broadcasting time was available. The Slendertone infomercials often were broadcast alongside presentations for car care products, kitchen gadgets, fitness products and "exercisers," and various other products. Direct Shop, like all TV home shopping companies, operated on high margins. This meant that BioMedical Research would get less than 25 percent of the £120 retail price for the Gymbody 8. The company was selling this product to other distributors for around £40. Direct Shop also had a liberal customer returns policy. This resulted in return rates of product from customers as high as 35 percent. Very often the outer packaging hadn't even been opened by the purchasers. Direct Shop also returned much unsold product when TV sales were lower than expected for some countries.

Sales to Direct Shop were not as high initially as management had expected. After a few months sales began to increase, reaching monthly sales of around 3,000 Gymbody 8's. The majority of these sales were to television viewers in England.

The Direct Model

Total sales of Slendertone continued to grow rapidly. Sales (from the factory) to the French distributor totaled £5.6 million in 1995. By early 1996 it appeared that annual sales to France for that year would be considerably higher than the budgeted £7.2 million. Irish sales for 1995 were £0.4 million and were well ahead of budget in early 1996. Sales to Direct Shop were on the increase, though not by as much as management had budgeted. Sales on the order of £0.75 million were being made annually to the Colombian distributor. In early 1996 those four markets were accounting for over 90 percent of total Slendertone sales. Management continued to refine the direct model because of its success in those diverse markets.

One of the critical success factors of the direct approach was believed to be the way it allowed company representatives (either on the telephone directly to customers or through extended TV appearances) to explain clearly how the product worked. Management felt it would not be as easy to sell this product through regular retail channels. Retail sales, it was thought, required too much explanation by the sales staff, which might not be very knowledgeable about the products. Retail usually was limited to pharmacies and some sports stores. There was no definite strategy for developing retail channels. It was thought that there were some people who did not want to buy direct but who got their initial information from the infomercials, the company's telemarketing personnel, or other customers.

Going direct also allowed more targeted marketing efforts. While the target market for Slendertone was defined as "women between the ages of 25 and 55," a few niche segments also were targeted, including "prenuptials," "postnatals," and men. Postnatals were defined as women who had given birth recently and

were now eager to regain their prepregnancy shape. Customer feedback had indicated that EMS was particularly effective in retoning the stomach muscles, which normally are "stretched" during pregnancy. This segment was reached by means of direct response advertisements in magazines aimed at new mothers and the "bounty bags" which are distributed in maternity wards. Bounty bags consist of free samples from manufacturers of baby-related products. The company would include a money-off voucher along with a specially designed brochure explaining how EMS can quickly and easily retone the stomach muscles. Prenuptials, those about to get married, were reached through wedding fairs and bridal magazines. EMS would allow the bride to be to quickly and easily tone up for the big day. It also was reported that increasing numbers of men were using the home use products. As an optional accessory the company supplied nonstick rubber pads which are attached to the body with a strap. These pads are suitable for men, for whom body hair can make adhesive pads uncomfortable.

Direct response enabled the company to gauge the effectiveness of all advertising and promotions directly. Advertisements were placed in a range of media, using different copy, graphics, and selling points to identify the most effective advertising methods. Direct response also meant that every advertisement produced immediate revenue or could be pulled quickly if it wasn't generating enough sales. This approach did not require the level of investment in brand development normally associated with introducing a new product to the market. In effect, all advertising became immediately self-financing.

Another important element of the direct strategy was to allow the company to develop an extensive customer database that could be used to market other products that the company would develop in the future. It had not yet been decided what those products would be other than that they would be sold under the Slendertone brand. The database also could be used to sell other products of interest to Slendertone customers and could be traded with other companies. The personal data from customers also proved useful for research purposes, helping the company identify its market.

Finally, for some customers, buying direct provided privacy when purchasing what some considered a personal product. One Irish pharmacist with a number of retail outlets reported that some customers would buy a Slendertone product at a pharmacy far from where they lived, presumably to avoid recognition by the staff or other customers. Some users of Slendertone products were reluctant to tell others they were using the company's products even when complimented on how well they were looking. The reasons given included, "No one says they are using these gimmicks" and "Because people would say to you, 'You don't need that.'" Some customers were reluctant to tell even a spouse that they had bought or were using Slendertone.

Customer Feedback

Attitudes regarding the sensitive nature of the purchase were revealed in a focus group of Irish customers conducted in 1995. A number of favorable comments about the Gymbody 8 were recorded, such as, "It's fabulous; I lost inches around the waist, and my sister got it and she looks fantastic." Some of the comments reflected an initial doubt about the efficacy of the product but subsequent satisfaction: "It's fabulous, I'm delighted, it's wonderful—it does actually work." One user was not so satisfied: "It's not very effective. I didn't see a visible difference; no one else did—no one commented."

The majority of the participants thought it was a very good value at $99. In determining "value" they tended to compare it to the cost of EMS treatment in a salon, joining a gym, taking fitness classes, or buying exercise equipment. The research also revealed generally low long-term use of the product. One issue raised related to uncertainty about using the unit, particularly how to place the pads on the body correctly. Another issue that arose was that using the products involved a certain amount of "hassle": attaching the pads to the unit, placing the pads on the body, and actually using the product for 40 minutes and then putting it all away again. All the focus group participants had bought their unit "off the TV," having seen the Irish infomercial. Most thought that the infomercial was very effective in explaining the product and that "it looked like a good product." Some found the TV presentation interesting and even entertaining (with some people watching it a number of times), while others thought it was "a bit over the top" or "false-looking."

The findings of this research supported anecdotal evidence and customer service feedback received by company personnel: initial doubt about the product's efficacy, a certain degree of surprise that it actually worked, mixed satisfaction (though mostly very high) with the results attained, and low long-term use. The low usage levels were confirmed by the low levels of replacement sales of the adhesive pads (which are used with the home use units to apply the current to the body and need to be replaced after 35 to 40 uses).

The Competition

Slendertone was the only product of its kind being marketed on television in 1995. A number of new EMS products entered the market during the mid-1990s, using a similar direct response approach in magazines, mail order catalogs, and other media. Other products had been available for many years, sold mostly through the mail order channel. With the exception of Ultratone, an English product, the competitor products in almost all markets tended to be of much poorer quality than Slendertone (though they were not necessarily much cheaper to buy). In this very fragmented market there were no international leaders. For instance, in Italy there were at least eight products on the market, none of which was sold outside the country. Other than the occasional mail order product, there did not appear to be any EMS units for sale in Germany. Ultratone was one of the biggest players in England but did not sell in France, which then was estimated to be the largest market for EMS products. In Spain a low-quality product called the Gymshape 8 was launched; it was priced lower than the Gymbody 8.

Management saw Slendertone as being at the "top end" of the market, based on its superior quality. Although the company had by then lost most of its mail order business to lower-priced (and lower-quality) competitors, management's attitude was that the biggest and most lucrative markets lay untapped. It was felt that the company had the products and the know-how to exploit those markets, as evidenced in France and Ireland. However, the increasing competition continued to put pressure on prices; most of the cost savings being achieved through more efficient production were being passed on to the distributors. From 1993 to the beginning of 1996 the retail price of the Gymbody 8 had fallen over £40 in France. To satisfy the French distributors' demand for cheaper products for certain channels, a "low-price" range under the Minibody and Intone brands was launched by BioMedical Research. Those products did not feature the Slendertone logo anywhere.

Given the fragmented nature of the market and a complete lack of secondary data for the EMS product class, it was hard to determine what market share different companies had. Lack of data also made it difficult to determine the size of the existing market for EMS products in each country. For planning purposes the company focused on the potential market for EMS, based on the belief that most countries had a large latent demand for EMS-based cosmetic products. Potential demand for each country was calculated on the basis of the size of the target market and the niche segments in that country. As revealed in the market research findings, the competition also had to be viewed in terms of the other means to improve body shape: the gym, fitness classes, exercise equipment, diets, diet foods, and the like.

The Professional Market

The salon business in Ireland experienced a big revival in the mid-1990s. The extensive marketing for the home use products helped create new or renewed awareness among salon users of EMS treatments and the Slendertone brand. Intensive media campaigns in Ireland were run to promote the salon products. In conjunction with salons, the company placed full-page "feature" advertisements in papers such as the *Sunday Independent*. A certain amount of tension arose between the company and the salon owners because the company was simultaneously marketing salon and home use units. For the price of 15 salon treatments one could buy a Gymbody 8.

The redevelopment of the salon market in the mid-1990s attracted a number of competitors to Ireland, including Ultratone, Eurowave, CACI, and Arysis. The increased competition led to greater promotional activity, which increased the demand for salon EMS treatments. Even though Slendertone had become a generic term for salon EMS treatment in Ireland, research in early 1996 indicated that some customers thought it represented "old" technology. Ultratone had positioned itself as the product with "newer" technology, one that was more effective and more comfortable and offered faster results in spite of using very similar, if not more basic, technology. In 1996 BioMedical Research promoted the fact that Slendertone had been in existence for 30 years. A special thirtieth-anniversary logo was featured on the promotional literature for the professional market. This was done to give buyers the assurance of long-term company marketing support and technical backup in the face of many new entrants into the market. Little effort was being made by the international distributors to develop the professional market in other countries in spite of very high margins on the larger professional units, which retailed at over £4,000.

The French distributor was showing no interest in the professional market in France. It believed the size of the home use market offered much greater potential, and it did not require a sales team.

Product Development

After the success of the Gymbody 8, a number of other home use EMS products were developed by BioMedical Research before 1996, primarily to meet the requirements of the French distributor. Along with the low-cost Minibody and InTone brands, products developed under the Slendertone brand included the Bustyler (for lifting the breasts), the Face Up (a facial antiaging unit), and the Celluforme (to combat cellulite). Little market research was undertaken by the company while developing these products (the research that was done mostly consisted of prototype testing on a number of volunteers recruited locally in Galway, Ireland). The products would be developed, mostly in-house, according to criteria determined by the French distributor. The distributor also indicated the cost at which units would have to be supplied so that it could achieve certain retail price points in the targeted channels.

Rapid Growth

In March 1996 it appeared that annual Slendertone sales (from the factory) could break the £10 million barrier by year end. Sales for the Gymbody 8 represented over 70 percent of all Slendertone sales (including professional units). Over 75 percent of Gymbody 8 units being produced were for the French distributor. New employees were being recruited in a number of areas, including a large number of temporary workers in production. Many other workers chose to work overtime. There was a real sense of excitement throughout the company as orders continued to increase. The potential for Slendertone was enormous. If other countries achieved even a quarter of the per capita sales levels being attained in France or Ireland, the company would soon be a major Irish exporter. Plans were being drawn up to extend the factory and build a new headquarters in Galway. In spite of the impressive growth and the exciting potential, the board of the company was concerned about the growing dependence on one distributor.

The French distributor was becoming more demanding with regard to margins, product development, and pricing strategies. It continued to develop its own promotional material for the Slendertone range. The products were being sold as a form of "effortless exercise": "the equivalent of 240 sit-ups in just 40 minutes, while watching TV!" Some advertising featured topless models alongside sensational claims for the products' effectiveness: "the body you've always wanted in just three weeks." The distributor in France had arranged in 1996 for a well-known blond television celebrity to endorse the product. In the words of one of the Irish marketing staff, the distributor's approach was "very tacky." Still, few could argue with the ever-increasing sales. The distributor appeared to have found a large market that responded favorably to this type of promotion. Analysis of the French sales database, which was not computerized, indicated that sales were mostly to younger females; however, the distributor was very reluctant to share sales data with the company.

Developing the UK Market

A number of marketing meetings were held in April 1996 to develop a plan to reduce the company's growing dependence on this single customer. It was decided to develop the UK market directly, without any distributor involvement. This decision was made on the basis of a number of factors: the failure to attract good distributors in the past, the success of the company's direct campaign in Ireland, the reasonably successful sales to UK viewers by Direct Shop, and finally, geographic and cultural proximity to Ireland.

In May 1996 the board supported management's decision to develop the British market directly. This was going to require a substantial investment in terms of both money and management time. By the end of July an office had been established in London, with a general manager and two staff members. Direct response advertisements were soon being placed in a number of different print media, from *The Sunday Times Magazine* to the *News of the World*'s color supplement. Responses and sales were monitored closely to gauge the more likely market for the products. Sales were slow to grow; by the end of the first quarter the UK subsidiary was behind budget. The cost of maintaining an office in London also was affecting profitability. However, the Slendertone staff in both Ireland and England was optimistic about the longer-term prospects.

Slendertone in Turmoil

In late 1996 the size of the orders from the French distributor started to fall. Uncertainty about the reason for the sudden drop in French sales abounded,

particularly as it was the buildup period to the normally busy Christmas season. The company quickly went from having a healthy cash surplus to being overdrawn. The banks were putting pressure on the company to address the situation. A decision was made to lay off all the temporary production workers. The situation continued to deteriorate. Over £1.5 million of raw material and stock, mostly for the French market, had accumulated in the factory. The staff was wondering whether the company could survive. McDonnell and his management team persevered with the plan to develop the UK market while addressing the serious situation developing in France.

After the slow start, sales in the United Kingdom were beginning to grow. Most sales were coming from direct response advertisements in magazines. Also, much public relations activity was being undertaken. Limited distribution had been secured in some nationwide retail chains, mostly on a trial basis in a few stores. Sales to Direct Shop (the television home-shopping company) were still disappointing, never rising above 4,000 Gymbody 8's a month. Sales in Ireland were up more than 30 percent over the previous year. Although sales to Ireland were now the highest per capita of any market, they still accounted for less than 10 percent of total sales. Sales to Colombia were about the same, while the sales of all the other distributors were down a little from the previous year.

The market in France deteriorated rapidly in early 1997. Subsequent analysis indicated that a number of factors were contributing to the dramatic loss of business there. The distributor had lost the television slot for the Gymbody 8 to a cheaper product. Other direct response channels seemed to have become "exhausted" or were being filled by cheaper products. To compound matters, a feature on EMS products in a consumer magazine gave poor ratings to many of the home-use products in the market. Although the Slendertone product range received the highest rating, this did not protect the company. A number of the low-quality competitors suddenly pulled out of the market, leaving a bad feeling in the "trade." The trade consisted of direct marketing companies that bought products from the distributors or manufacturers to sell to their existing customer base. It also included retailers: mostly pharmacies, sports shops, and a few department stores. The sudden fall in advertising for EMS products affected market demand and left many traders with unsold product. By the time BioMedical Research had received this information, it was too late to take any action. The company terminated its relationship with the French distributor later in the year, and all Slendertone sales in France soon came to an end.

At about the same time management ended its relationship with Direct Shop. The combination of lower than expected sales, low margins, and high return rates ensured that this was never going to be a profitable undertaking for the company. Furthermore, tension with existing distributors arose when Direct Shop began to broadcast across Europe, in many cases offering a price for the Gymbody 8 that was lower than what the distributors were charging for it locally. At least the company's own sales in the United Kingdom were growing. By selling direct to customers in the United Kingdom, BioMedical Research was earning a healthy margin (though the cost of the UK office and the increasing number of promotional campaigns had to be covered).

Restructuring

There had been a widespread belief throughout the company for many years that, in the words of one manager, "more marketing was needed." Efforts in 1995 and early 1996 to recruit a "marketing manager/ marketing director designate," using advertisements in Irish and UK recruitment pages, were unsuccessful. It was suggested that the credibility issue concerning Slendertone might be having an effect on recruitment. With added urgency, the company succeeded in attracting O'Donohoe to the job of marketing director for Slendertone in April 1997. O'Donohoe had gained extensive marketing experience with Waterford Glass. He saw the opportunity to develop the Slendertone brand and welcomed the responsibility the job offered. But it was not easy at first: "When I joined in April, I had to go out to France, and everyone here in the office and factory would be waiting when I came back to see if I had gotten any new orders." Recognizing the opportunity presented by the trial placements for the Gymbody 8 in various UK stores, he immediately focused on developing the company's relationships in the retail channel.

While working on increasing retail sales, O'Donohoe initiated extensive research into the various markets for Slendertone. He started to build up a clearer picture of the markets for Slendertone and its brand positioning. His analysis of the French market identified the reasons for the drop in sales. It also revealed that Slendertone was not, nor ever had been, the market leader in France. Based on the distributor's reports, the company had been under the impression that Slendertone had had some 70 percent of the home-use EMS market. O'Donohoe's findings revealed that Slendertone's market share had been only a fraction of that figure. His analysis also revealed that sales of replacement pads had always been extremely low, indicating low customer product usage; it previously had been assumed that the French distributor was using a different supplier for the replacement pads. Focus group research in a number of countries showed that Slendertone had a very confused positioning: It was variously associated with dieting, weight loss, health, fitness, exercise, toning, and body shaping. The focus groups also reinforced the credibility issue. Many people's first thought on seeing the product being advertised was, Does it work? Secondary data showed the size of the different markets for areas such as health, fitness, and cosmetics in different countries. O'Donohoe also gathered data on consumer behaviour and motivations relating to those different markets.

The Business Defined

The next stage for O'Donohoe was to decide exactly what business the company was in. "I've read about this business being described as everything from the 'EMS business,' whatever that is, to 'passive gymnastics.' Our consumer research showed that Slendertone had a very confused message. We're in the self-confidence business," he states emphatically. "Self-confidence through improved appearance." He now defines the Slendertone brand as "the most effective and convenient appearance solutions." The new slogan for Slendertone will be "living life and loving it." In terms of people's deeper motivations with regard to health and fitness activities, O'Donohoe stresses a core need to look good. He states that most people work out to look good rather than to be healthy. Likewise, "people diet not for the sake of losing weight but to improve their appearance through their weight loss." It is this core need to look good which O'Donohoe is targeting with Slendertone. In spite of the company's involvement in the health market with its NeuroTech range of products, O'Donohoe is clear that Slendertone is about appearance, not health. He sees it as misleading to talk in terms of health and beauty, a trade category into which many products are placed. He puts a value of $170 billion on the self-confidence market in Europe; this figure includes the combined markets for cosmetics and fashion.

Also included in this market are men. Originally recognized as only a niche segment, male users now represent an important and fast-growing market for EMS cosmetic products. In late 1997 BioMedical Research modified the Gymbody 8 by adding rubber pads and redesigning the packaging and launched the Gymbody for Men. This was very successful and opened up a new market segment for Slendertone.

The company has begun extensive consumer trials at a clinic in Galway to gain a better understanding of the exact physiological benefits of Slendertone and to identify new ways to measure those benefits. According to O'Donohoe, "We want to get away from the earlier measurements of effectiveness, such as 'inch loss.'" He is conscious of the added psychological benefits that these products might offer users. BioMedical's researchers also are using these trials to identify ways to improve product convenience and comfort.

Repositioning Slendertone

By early 1999 Slendertone products were being stocked in over 2,300 retail outlets, primarily in the United Kingdom. O'Donohoe states that the increasing emphasis on retail has to be seen in terms of a complete repositioning of the Slendertone brand. "Using Direct Shop [television home shopping] was the worst thing ever for this company. And look at these [French] magazine advertisements: lots of exclamation marks, sensational product claims, very cluttered, and the models used!" he remarks, reviewing the earlier marketing of Slendertone. O'Donohoe says it is these promotional tactics which have resulted in a "gadget" positioning for Slendertone, one he is working on changing. Furthermore, he says, by making excessive product claims the company was unlikely to meet customer expectations. This was jeopardizing the opportunity for repeat purchases of Slendertone products by existing customers. Gone, says O'Donohoe, are the promises of "effortless exercise": "We are telling customers they need to work with the products to get results. This is resulting in a different type of customer for Slendertone; we want to get away from the 'gadget-freaks.'" It is this different type of customer O'Donohoe hopes will also purchase other Slendertone-branded products in the future. The target market for Slendertone now is women and men

age 20 to 60 years. The earlier niche segments, such as the "postnatals," no longer are being targeted separately. O'Donohoe believes it is important to keep the Slendertone message focused rather than having different messages for different segments of the market.

Central to O'Donohoe's strategy is the development of Slendertone into a brand in its own right. From now on O'Donohoe wants people to associate Slendertone with "effective and convenient appearance solutions" rather than EMS devices: "Slendertone will be a brand that just happens to have EMS products." The Slendertone range could in the future include many types of products. The company has just created the position of brand extensions manager to plan the development of the Slendertone range. O'Donohoe believes the company is now in a position to create an international brand: "People will tell you it takes hundreds of millions to create an international brand. We don't agree."

A priority for O'Donohoe in his goal to develop the Slendertone brand is an increased emphasis on the Slendertone name. In addition to a redesign of all the product packaging to reflect more "real" users in "real" situations (see Exhibits 1 and 2), all the product names have been changed. The original Gymbody 8 will now be marketed as the Slendertone Body, the Face Up is now the Slendertone Face, and the Celluforme has become the Slendertone Body Plus. The male products will be the Slendertone Body Profile and the Slendertone Body Profile Sports, which has been adapted from the Total Body unit. Along with the Slendertone Total Body, these products constitute the full Slendertone home-use range, reduced from some 25 products three years earlier. A new professional unit, utilizing innovative touch-screen technology and "space-age" design, is about to be launched. O'Donohoe sees the professional market playing an important role in the development of Slendertone. He does not believe that the home-use and professional markets are competing; the company's experience has been that promotions for the home-use products raise awareness (and sales) for the professional market. The company currently has four staff members dedicated to developing the professional market in the United Kingdom.

Accessing the Market

O'Donohoe continues to put greater emphasis on developing retail channels, which, he says, "still represent over 95 percent of sales for all products sold

EXHIBIT 1
The Cover of the
Gymbody 8 Case
(Used since 1994)

EXHIBIT 2
The Cover of the
'Slendertone Body'
Case (Introduced in
1999)

worldwide in spite of the current hype about direct marketing." He believes he is able to secure retail space from important multiples because he is offering them unique access to the body-shape section of the appearance market. For these retailers Slendertone represents a new category of good, with higher than average revenues. On a shop-shelf "mock-up" in a small room at the back of the office, there is a display of the new Slendertone range, alongside massagers and shavers and other personal care products. O'Donohoe is conscious of the attention Slendertone has been attracting from the big players in the personal care market. In some cases they have been losing vital shelf space to this relatively unknown company from Ireland. He believes that BioMedical Research's expertise in the marketing of EMS products, a strong brand, and greater company flexibility (because of smaller size) will enable the company to defend itself against the multinational companies now looking at the EMS market.

The focus on retail does not mean an end to the use of direct marketing. Direct sales still account for around half of all UK sales. O'Donohoe sees direct marketing continuing to play an important role in developing the UK market and newer markets. The new direct response advertisements have been changed to reflect the move toward a stronger Slendertone brand identity and away from the "oversell" of earlier years.

The company will continue to use distributors for some markets. However O'Donohoe is determined to have greater company control over the brand than was the case in the past. By maintaining "control of the message" he believes the company can avoid a recurrence of what happened in the French market. Through a strong brand identity and a carefully controlled and differentiated image, he intends to protect the Slendertone name and market from the activities of other EMS companies. He does not plan to compete on price with the lower-quality producers; he believes that by investing in the Slendertone brand the company will be able to offer the customer greater total value at a higher price. The company will develop important markets such as Germany and France directly, as it has done successfully in the United Kingdom. Slendertone offices in Frankfurt and Paris have just been opened. O'Donohoe is conscious of the cost of establishing and maintaining international operations and the need to develop those markets successfully and promptly.

Slendertone: The Future

The company views the potential for Slendertone on two fronts: the existing potential for EMS-based products (including the existing Slendertone range and new, improved EMS products) and the potential for non-EMS Slendertone products. O'Donohoe believes he can restore Slendertone's fortunes in the French market: "The need is still there." He is conscious of bad feelings which may still exist within the trade, but other companies are operating again in this market (including BioMedical's former distributor, which now sells a lower-quality EMS product). There is still a lack of published secondary data for the EMS cosmetic market in any country. It is believed that the United Kingdom is now by far the largest EMS market. Company research indicates that the other markets with significant EMS sales are Spain and Italy. There is currently little EMS sales activity being observed by the company in Germany. In light of the level of sales being attained in Ireland (which has continued to grow every year since 1991) and the phenomenal recent growth in England, combined with a universal desire to look good, O'Donohoe envisages rapid growth for the existing Slendertone range in the short term. The potential for the extended Slendertone range in the longer term is much greater. Realizing this potential will depend on how effective the marketing strategy is in addressing all the issues and how well it is implemented.

For some the question might remain, Can Kevin McDonnell succeed in offering self-confidence to millions around the world from a factory in the wilds of Donegal? Certainly the locals in Bunbeg wouldn't doubt it.

Appendix: What Is Slendertone?

Beauty salons buy electronic muscle stimulation (EMS) units such as Slendertone so that they can provide their customers with a toning/body-shaping treatment. EMS devices work by delivering a series of electrical charges to the muscle through pads placed on the skin over the muscle area. Each tiny charge "fires" the motor points in the muscle. These charges are similar to the natural charges sent by the brain, through the nervous system, to activate particular muscles and thus cause movement. EMS therefore has the effect of exercising the muscle, but without the need to move the rest of the body. Customers use the EMS treatment over a period of weeks to help tone a particular area, primarily with the aim of improving body shape. This treatment also can improve circulation and the texture of the skin. EMS gives users improved body shape through improved muscle tone rather than through weight loss. Customers typically book a series of 10 or 15 one-hour treatments that are administered once or twice weekly. A qualified beautician who is trained in the use of EMS as part of the standard professional training for beauticians administers the treatment in the salon. A series of 10 salon treatments in Ireland costs in the range of £70. An alternative salon treatment to tone muscles is a manual "toning table," which works the muscles by moving different parts of the body attached to the table. Home use EMS units allow users to treat themselves in the comfort, privacy, and convenience of their own homes. A home use unit such as the Slendertone Body currently retails for £100 in Ireland. In terms of treatment, the home use unit should offer the user similar results to a salon treatment if used correctly and consistently.

Some customers prefer to go to a salon for EMS treatment, possibly enjoying the professional attention they get in a salon environment and the break it offers from everyday life. Booking and paying for a series of treatments in a salon also encourage customers to complete the treatment. Others prefer the convenience, privacy, and economy offered by the home use units. However, the home treatment requires a certain discipline to use the unit regularly. Home users sometimes report that they are uncertain if they are using the unit correctly; this mostly involves proper pad placement. EMS has been available in salons for over 30 years, but the home use market began to develop significantly only in the last 10 years.

Is EMS/Slendertone Safe?

EMS originally was developed for medical use. A common application of EMS is the rehabilitation of a muscle after an accident or a stroke. EMS frequently is used by physiotherapists for muscle rehabilitation after sports injuries and other injuries. Slendertone was developed to enable healthy users to "exercise" muscles without having to do any exercise. By remaining seated, lying down, or even doing minor chores, users could get the benefit of a vigorous workout. The effect of EMS is similar to that of regular exercise of a muscle. For many years the company compared the effect of using EMS (as applied to the abdominal muscles) to the effect gained from doing sit-ups. With the exception of well-stated contraindications (EMS should not be used by pregnant women, on or near open wounds, on or near ulcers, by diabetics, and on or near the throat area), EMS has proved to be perfectly safe for a variety of uses. Some people wonder what might happen when one stops using EMS. Again, the effect is like regular exercise: If one stops exercising, one may regain the shape one had before starting to exercise.

The U.S. Food and Drug Administration (FDA) has classified this type of EMS-based product as a Class II device. Class II devices must be prescribed by a "licensed practitioner" and only for very specified medical purposes. The FDA regulations governing the sale and use of EMS devices are based on proven efficacy and safety. According to the FDA, there is insufficient clinical evidence to support claims such as "body shaping," "weight loss," and "cellulite removal" for EMS treatments. The FDA's decision to impose stringent controls on the use of EMS was made after a number of home use EMS users suffered minor injuries. Users of a direct-current, home use EMS unit available in the United States in the 1970s suffered skin "burns" around the pad placement area. All Slendertone products, like the other cosmetic EMS products on the market today, only use alternating current, which will not cause burns.

Case 6-5
Toyota

Yoi Kangae, Yoi Shina! that's Toyota-speak for "Good thinking means good products." The slogan is emblazoned on a giant banner hanging across the company's Takaoka assembly plant, an hour outside the city of Nagoya. Plenty of good thinking has gone into the high-tech ballet that's performed here 17 hours a day.

Six separate car models—from the Corolla compact to the new youth-oriented Scion xB—glide along on a single production line in any of a half-dozen colors. Overhead, car doors flow by on a conveyor belt that descends to floor level and drops off the right door in the correct color for each vehicle. This efficiency means Takaoka workers can build a car in just 20 hours.

The combination of speed and flexibility is world class (Exhibit 1). More important, a similar dance is happening at 30 Toyota plants worldwide, with some

EXHIBIT 1 Global Push

Data: Toyota Motor, 2002 sales figures

Toyota's on the offensive around the globe. Here's a look at its worldwide operations:

North America

SALES: 1.94 million

Toyota's products keep gaining on the Big Three's models, while Lexus is a luxury leader. Toyota employs 35,000 people and runs 10 factories in the region, and has 11.2% of the U.S. market.

Europe

SALES: 756,000

Has a 4.4% market share, led by the **Yaris** compact and a new **Avensis** with a cleaner diesel engine. Plans to boost production in Britain and France. Lexus though, is struggling.

Southwest Asia

SALES: 268,000

Builds cars in Bangladesh, India, Pakistan, and Turkey. The durable **Qualis** SUV is a big hit in India, and Toyota plans to start building transmissions there in mid-2004.

Southeast Asia

SALES: 455,000

Assembles cars in seven countries and is expanding its factories in Thailand and Indonesia. Plans to export trucks, engines, and components from the region to 80 countries.

South America

SALES: 97,000

Builds cars in Argentina, Brazil, Colombia, and Venezuela. Regionwide revenues fell 10% last year because of economic troubles in Argentina, but sales in Brazil grew after the launch of a new **Corolla**.

Africa

SALES: 140,000

Has manufacturing plants in Kenya and South Africa. Last year, it saw sales across the continent jump 10.5%, thanks to a new **Corolla** sedan and **Prado** SUV.

China

SALES: 58,000

Playing catch-up with rivals Volkswagen and GM. In April, it agreed with FAW to make the **Land Cruiser, Corolla,** and **Crown.** Share today is about 1.5%, but Toyota wants 10% by 2010.

Japan

SALES: 1.68 million

Has maintained 40%-plus market share for five years running. New models this year include the **Sienta** compact minivan, the sportier **Wish** minivan, and a revamped **Harrier** SUV.

able to make as many as eight different models on the same line. That is leading to a monster increase in productivity and market responsiveness—all part of the company's obsession with what President Fujio Cho calls "the criticality of speed."

Remember when Japan was going to take over the world? Corporate America was apoplectic at the idea that every Japanese company might be as obsessive, productive, and well-managed as Toyota Motor Corp. We

know what happened next: One of the longest crashes in business history revealed most of Japan Inc. to be debt-addicted, inefficient, and clueless. Today, 13 years after the Nikkei peaked, Japan is still struggling to avoid permanent decline. World domination? Hardly.

Except in one corner. In autos, the Japanese rule (Exhibit 2). And in Japan, one company—Toyota—combines the size, financial clout, and manufacturing excellence needed to dominate the global car industry

EXHIBIT 2 Way Ahead of the Pack

Data: Bloomberg Financial Markets, Harbour & Associates, J.D. Power & Associates, Toyo Keizai, Dresden Kleinwort, Burnham Securities. Research assistance by Susan Zegel.

	Market Cap*	Operating Profit*	Hours per Vehicle**	Defects***
Toyota	$110	$12.7	21.83	196
Nissan	54	7.5	16.83	258
Honda	40	6.1	22.27	215
DaimlerChrysler	38	5.7	28.04[†]	311
GM	24	3.8	24.44	264
Ford	22	3.6	26.14	287

*Billions
**Average assembly time (North America)
***Problems per 100 vehicles on year 2000 models
[†]Chryster only

in a way no company ever has. Sure, Toyota, with $146 billion in sales, may not be tops in every category. GM is bigger—for now. Nissan Motor Co. makes slightly more profit per vehicle in North America, and its U.S. plants are more efficient. Both Nissan and Honda have flexible assembly lines, too. But no car company is as strong as Toyota in so many areas.

Of course, the carmaker has always moved steadily forward: Its executives created the doctrine of *kaizen,* or continuous improvement (Exhibit 3). "They find a hole, and they plug it," says auto-industry consultant Maryann Keller. "They methodically study problems, and they solve them." But in the past few years, Toyota has accelerated these gains, raising the bar for the entire industry. Consider:

- Toyota is closing in on Chrysler to become the third-biggest carmaker in the U.S. Its U.S. share, rising steadily, is now above 11%.
- At its current rate of expansion, Toyota could pass Ford Motor Co. in mid-decade as the world's No. 2

auto maker. The No. 1 spot—still occupied by General Motors Corp., with 15% of the global market—would be the next target. President Cho's goal is 15% of global sales by 2010, up from 10% today. "They dominate wherever they go," says Nobuhiko Kawamoto, former president of Honda Motor Co. "They try to take over everything."

- Toyota has broken the Japanese curse of running companies simply for sales gains, not profit. Its operating margin of 8%-plus (vs. 2% in 1993) now dwarfs those of Detroit's Big Three. Even with the impact of the strong yen, estimated 2003 profits of $7.2 billion will be double 1999's level. On Nov. 5, the company reported profits of $4.8 billion on sales of $75 billion for the six months ended Sept. 30. Results like that have given Toyota a market capitalization of $110 billion—more than that of GM, Ford, and DaimlerChrysler combined (Exhibit 4).
- The company has not only rounded out its product line in the U.S., with sport-utility vehicles, trucks,

EXHIBIT 3   Kaizen in Action

Data: Toyota Motor

Data: *BusinessWeek*, Edmunds.com Inc.

Toyota stresses constant improvement, or *kaizen,* in everything it does. Here's how the company revamped the 2004 Sienna minivan after the previous generation got disappointing reviews.

- The 3.3-liter, 230 hp engine is bigger and more powerful than before, but it gets slightly better gas mileage.
- Now has five-speed transmission instead of four.
- The 2004 is nimbler with a turning diameter of 36.8 feet—3.2 feet shorter than the previous model.
- At $23,495, it's $920 cheaper than the 2003.
- Third-row seats fold flat into the floor. On the older model they had to be removed to maximize cargo space.
- The new model is longer and wider than the 2003, with more headroom, leg room, and 12% more cargo space.

Camry

Bland? Sure, as bland as the bread and butter it is to Toyota. This reliable family sedan has been America's top-selling car in five of the past six years.
$19,560–$25,920

Yaris

The snub-nosed compact is Toyota's top-seller in Europe. Its Euro-styling has made it a hit in Japan too, where it's known as the Vitz. $11,787–$14,317

Prius

A funky-looking and earth-friendly gas-electric hybrid that gets 55 mpg—but offers the power and roominess of a midsize sedan. $20,510

Tundra

This full-size pickup has built a loyal following as it has grown in bulk and power. A Double Cab model due in November will up the ante.
$16,495–$31,705*

Scion xB

An attempt to be hip and edgy included underground marketing for this new car aimed at young people. Sales have been double Toyota's forecasts.
$14,165–$14,965

Lexus RX330

The first Lexus built in North America, this luxury SUV boasts a smooth, car-like ride and nimble handling. It has been Lexus' U.S. sales leader.
$35,700–$37,500

*Doesn't include Double cab model, which isn't yet priced.

EXHIBIT 4   **Toyota's Money Machine**

Data: Toyota Motor Corp., Lehman Brothers Inc.

Fiscal year Ending in March

and a hit minivan, but it also has seized the psychological advantage in the market with the Prius, an eco-friendly gasoline-electric car. "This is going to be a real paradigm shift for the industry," says board member and top engineer Hiroyuki Watanabe. In October, when the second-generation Prius reached U.S. showrooms, dealers got 10,000 orders before the car was even available.

• Toyota has launched a joint program with its suppliers to radically cut the number of steps needed to make cars and car parts. In the past year alone, the company chopped $2.6 billion out of its $113 billion in manufacturing costs without any plant closures or layoffs. Toyota expects to cut an additional $2 billion out of its cost base this year.

• Toyota is putting the finishing touches on a plan to create an integrated, flexible, global manufacturing system. In this new network, plants from Indonesia to Argentina will be designed both to customize cars for local markets and to shift production to quickly satisfy any surges in demand from markets worldwide. By tapping, say, its South African plant to meet a need in Europe, Toyota can save itself the $1 billion normally needed to build a new factory.

If Cho gets this transformation right, he'll end up with an automotive machine that makes the Americans and Germans quake. Cost-cutting and process redesign will chop out billions in expenses. That will keep margins strong and free up cash to develop new models and technologies such as the Prius, to invest in global manufacturing, and to invade markets such as Europe and China. New models and new plants will build share, which will build more clout. And if there's a hiccup—well, there's a cash-and-securities hoard of $30 billion. "This is a company that does not fear failure," says Cho.

Roadblocks?

Can anything stop Toyota? There are some potential roadblocks. Toyota doesn't always get it right: Its early attempts at the youth market, minivans, and big pickup trucks all disappointed. It remains dependent on the U.S. business for some 70% of earnings. Its Lexus luxury sedans are losing ground to BMW, though Lexus' strong SUV sales are keeping the division in the game. The average Toyota owner is about 46, a number the company must lower or risk going the way of Buick. And most of Toyota's big sellers aren't exactly head-turners.

Meanwhile, Toyota's rivals are hardly sitting still. GM is finishing up a $4.3 billion revamp of Cadillac, and a revival is in the works: Overall GM quality is on an upswing too. "Toyota is a good competitor, but they're not unbeatable," says GM Chairman G. Richard Wagoner Jr. Over at Nissan, CEO Carlos Ghosn doubts Toyota's big bet on hybrids will pay off. "There will be no revolution," he predicts. And Detroit's Big Three are praying that a strong yen will batter Toyota. If the yen sticks at 110 to the dollar over the next 12 months, Toyota could see its pretax profits shrink by $900 million.

A strengthening yen might have hammered Toyota in the 1980s, and it will certainly have an impact next year. But today, three decades after starting its global push, Toyota can't be accused of needing a cheap yen to subsidize exports. Since starting U.S. production in 1986, Toyota has invested nearly $14 billion there. What's more, many of its costs are now set in dollars: Last year, Toyota's purchases of parts and materials from 500 North American suppliers came to $19 billion— more than the annual sales of Cisco Systems Inc. or Oracle Corp. The U.S. investment is an enormous natural hedge against the yen. "About 60% of what we sold here, we built here," Toyota Chairman Hiroshi Okuda said in a Sept. 10 speech in Washington.

Better for Toyota, those cars are also among the industry's biggest money-makers. Take SUVs: Ten years ago, Toyota had a puny 4% share. Today, it owns nearly 12% of that high-margin segment with eight models ranging from the $19,000 RAV4 to the $65,000 Lexus LX 470—and makes as much as $10,000 on each high-end model it sells. The company is steadily robbing Ford, Chrysler, and GM of their primacy in the cutthroat U.S. SUV market and has largely sat out the latest round of rebates: Toyota's average incentive per car this fall is just $647, compared with $3,812 at GM and $3,665 at Ford, according to market watcher Edmunds.com. This is one war of attrition where Detroit is clearly outgunned.

Toyota's charge into SUVs indicates a new willingness to play tough in the U.S., which it considers vital to its drive for a global 15% share. "The next era is full-size trucks and luxury, environmental, and youth cars," predicts James E. Press, chief operating officer at Toyota Motor Sales USA Inc. Toyota is already intent on boosting its 4.5% market share in pickups, the last profit refuge of the Big Three. Toyota is building an $800 million plant in San Antonio, Tex., that will allow it to more than double its Tundra output, to some 250,000 trucks a year by 2006, with rigs powerful and roomy enough to go head to head with Detroit's biggest models.

Toyota plans to extend its early lead in eco-cars by pushing the Prius and adding a hybrid Lexus RX 330 SUV next summer. The Lexus will get as much as 35 miles per gallon, compared with roughly 21 mpg for a conventional RX 330. And Toyota is vigorously attacking the youth market with the $14,500 Scion xB compact, which surprised Toyota-bashers with its angular, minimalist design. Since the Scion's U.S. launch in California in June, Toyota has sold nearly 7,700 of them, 30% better than forecast. Toyota Vice-President James Farley says three out of four buyers of the brand had no intention of buying a Toyota when they started looking. "That's exactly why we started the Scion," he says.

The Scion is evidence that Toyota's growing cash cushion gives it the means to revamp its lack-luster designs. When Cho traveled through Germany in 1994, he recalls being asked: Why are Toyota cars so poorly styled? Part of the problem, says Cho, is that too many Toyotas were designed with Japanese consumers in mind and then exported. Some worked; some flopped.

These days, design teams on the West Coast of the U.S., in southern France, and back home compete for projects. That has paid off with models such as the Yaris, Toyota's best-seller in Europe, where the company now has a 4.4% share, compared with less than 3% a decade ago. The Yaris was designed by a Greek, Sotiris Kovos, then imported successfully to Japan because of its "European" look. "Toyota has finally recognized that buyers want to feel like they have some level of style," says Wesley Brown, a consultant with auto researcher Iceology. The redesigned Solara sports coupe is getting high grades, too: A V-shape line flowing up from the grille gives it a more muscular silhouette, and its interior is 20% roomier than before.

Toyota Man

Leading Toyota to this new level of global vigor is Cho. He's Toyota Man personified: Self-effacing, ever smiling, but an executive whose radar seems to pick up every problem and opportunity. "Cho understands as much as anyone I've ever seen what's actually happening on the factory floor," says manufacturing consultant Ronald E. Harbour, whose firm's annual report on productivity is the industry bible.

That feel for the factory didn't come naturally. The 66-year-old company lifer studied law, not business, at the prestigious University of Tokyo and could have easily ended up as a faceless bureaucrat at the Ministry of Finance. But Cho learned the car business—and clearly learned it well—at the knee of Taichi Ohno, the creator of the legendary Toyota Production System, a series of in-house precepts on efficient manufacturing that changed the industry. Ohno, a brilliant but notoriously hot-headed engineer, lectured Cho about the need to be flexible and to look forward.

That advice is something Cho found invaluable when he was tapped to oversee the 1988 launch of Toyota's key U.S. plant in Georgetown, Ky., now the company's biggest U.S. factory and the maker of the Camry sedan. The good-natured and unpretentious Cho regularly worked the plant floor, making sure to shake hands with each line worker at Christmas to show his appreciation. He spoke at Rotary Club meetings and stopped to make small talk with the folks in Georgetown.

Given Toyota's booming U.S. sales in the late 1990s, few inside the company were surprised when Cho won the top job. Yet equally few had any clue that the new president was about to unleash so many powerful changes. Like his predecessor Okuda, Cho had long been frustrated by Toyota's glacial decision-making process and cultural insularity. Those had led to missed opportunities, such as when product planners at headquarters in Japan resisted calls from their U.S. colleagues to build an eight-cylinder pickup truck. Cho is rectifying that deficiency with a vengeance with the San Antonio plant.

Then three years ago, as Ghosn—"le cost killer"—was slashing billions at rival Nissan and cutting its supplier ranks in half, Cho had a revelation: If Nissan could do it, Toyota could do it better. The resulting program, called Construction of Cost Competitiveness for the 21st Century, or CCC21, taps into the company's strengths across the board to build cars more efficiently. It's also turning many operations inside out.

No Detail Too Small

Toyota has always valued frugality. It still turns down the heat at company-owned employee dormitories during working hours and labels its photocopy machines with the cost per copy to discourage overuse. But cost-cutting was often a piecemeal affair. With CCC21, Cho set a bold target of slashing prices on all key components for new models by 30%, which meant working with suppliers and Toyota's own staff to ferret out excess. "Previously, we tried to find waste here and there," says Cho. "But now there is a new dimension of proposals coming in."

In implementing CCC21, no detail is too small. For instance, Toyota designers took a close look at the grip handles mounted above the door inside most cars. By working with suppliers, they managed to cut the number of parts in these handles to five from 34, which helped cut procurement costs by 40%. As a plus, the change slashed the time needed for installation by 75%—to three seconds. "The pressure is on to cut costs at every stage," says Takashi Araki, a project manager at parts maker Aisin Seiki Co.

Just as Cho believes he can get far more out of suppliers, he thinks Toyota can make its workers vastly more productive. This is classic *kaizen,* but these days it has gone into overdrive (Exhibit 5). In the middle of the Kentucky plant, for instance, a *Kaizen* team of particularly productive employees works in a barracks-like structure. The group's sole job is coming up with ways to save time and money. Georgetown employees, for instance, recommended removing the radiator support base—the lower jaw of the car—until the last stage of assembly. That way, workers can step into the engine compartment to install parts instead of having to lean

over the front end and risk straining their backs. "We used to have to duck into the car to install something," explains Darryl Ashley, 41, a soft-spoken Kentucky native who joined Toyota nine years ago.

In Cambridge, Ont., Cho is going even further: He's determined to show the world that Toyota can meet its own highest standards of excellence anywhere in its system. It was once company doctrine that Lexus could only be made in Japan. No longer. Production of the RX 330 SUV started in Cambridge on Sept. 26. If the Canadian hands can deliver the same quality as their Japanese counterparts, Toyota will be able to chop shipping costs by shifting Lexus production to the market where the bulk of those cars are sold (Exhibit 6).

The Japanese bosses put the Canadians through their paces. The 700 workers on the RX 330 line trained for 12 weeks, including stints in Japan for 200 of them. There, the Canadians managed to beat Japanese teams in quality assessment on a mock Lexus line. Cambridge has taken Toyota's focus on *poka-yoke,* or foolproofing measures, to another level. The plant has introduced "Circle L" stations where workers must double- and triple-check parts that customers have complained about—anything from glove boxes to suspension systems. "We know that if we can get this right, we may get to build other Lexus models," says Jason Birt, a 28-year-old Lexus line worker.

The Cambridge workers are aided by a radical piece of manufacturing technology being rolled out to Toyota plants worldwide. The system, called the Global Body Line, holds vehicle frames in place while they're being welded, using just one master brace instead of the dozens of separate braces required in a standard factory. No big deal? Perhaps, but the system is half as expensive to install. Analysts say it lets Toyota save 75% of

EXHIBIT 5
Deciphering
Toyota-Speak

A handy glossary for understanding the company's vernacular.

Kaizen

Continuous improvement. Employees are given cash rewards for ferreting out glitches in production and devising solutions.

Pokayoke

Mistake-proofing. Use of sensors to detect missing parts or improper assembly. Robots alert workers to errors by flashing lights.

PDCA

Plan, do, check, action. Steps in the development cycle aimed at quick decision-making in a task such as designing a car.

CCC21

Construction of Cost Competitiveness for the 21st century. A three-year push to slash costs of 170 components that account for 90% of parts expenses.

Obeya

Literally, "big room." Regular face-to-face brainstorming sessions among engineers, designers, marketers, and suppliers.

GBL

Global Body Line. A manufacturing process that holds auto frames together for welding with one brace instead of the 50 braces previously required.

EXHIBIT 6   Lexus: Still Looking for Traction in Europe

When Dirk Lindermann was looking for a new luxury sedan last summer, he considered Mercedes and BMW before settling on a $40,000, black Audi A4. Lexus, though, didn't even enter into the game. "Lexus has no personality," says the 40-year-old Berlin advertising executive.

That's a problem for Toyota Motor Corp. The company's smooth-driving Lexus sedans sprinted from zero to luxury-market leader in the U.S. during the 1990s, overtaking German rivals Mercedes and BMW—as well as Cadillac and Lincoln—by offering better quality and service at a lower price. But Lexus is going nowhere fast in Europe: After 12 years in showrooms, last year it registered sales of just 21,156 cars—down 11% from 2001—compared with more than 234,000 in the U.S.

Toyota itself is fast shedding any *arriviste* stigma in the Old World. Since it began producing cars on the Continent in the '90s, European sales are up nearly 60%, to 734,000. Now it wants to crack the high-end with a renewed push for Lexus. The goal is to triple sales of the six Lexus models Toyota offers there by 2010, to at least 65,000 cars. "The potential in Europe for Lexus is every bit as great as in the U.S.," says Stuart McCullough, director of Lexus Europe.

To make Lexus a success, though, Toyota needs to establish it as a separate brand. Until now, the car has been sold in Europe mainly through Toyota's 250 dealerships, along with the far less lustrous Yaris, Corolla, and Avensis models. So Toyota is trying to set up dealerships that offer luxury-car buyers the kind of white-glove service they demand. "Lexus has to establish its own heritage, not just chase BMW and Mercedes," says Tadashi Arashima, president and chief executive of Toyota Motor Marketing Europe.

Will image-conscious Europeans warm up to Lexus if the cars are sold in tony showrooms? In Spain, where exclusive Lexus dealerships have been operating since 2000, sales are up 9% so far this year, though the brand sold just 969 vehicles in the country. "We've been able to show that these cars can compete with the big German brands in quality and also offer a lot more in terms of price," says Jorge Merino, head of sales at Axel, a three-year-old Lexus dealership in Madrid.

One big selling point is Lexus' six-year warranty. And the carmaker includes three years of free checkups, maintenance, and roadside assistance. That compares with a standard guarantee of two years at most luxury brands. "I like BMW and Mercedes, but I have a feeling I may get more for my money with Lexus," says Ignacio Redondo, a legal consultant in Madrid who drives a Saab 900 but is mulling a new Lexus for the first time.

Harder, though, will be conforming to the European concept of luxury. Americans love comfort, size and dependability, while Europeans think luxury means attention to detail and brand heritage. "The biggest selling point for Lexus is that it doesn't break down," says Philipp Rosengarten, analyst at Global Insight Inc.'s automotive group. That's not enough to succeed in Europe. Instead, Lexus needs to create a desire to own the car—and even with plush dealerships and extended warranties, it has kilometers to go before reaching that goal.

By Gail Edmondson in Frankfurt, and Karen Nickel Anhalt in Berlin with Paulo Prada in Madrid

the cost of refitting a production line to build a different car, and it's key to Toyota's ability to make multiple models on a single line. Better yet, the brace increases the rigidity of the car early in production, which boosts the accuracy of welds and makes for a more stable vehicle. "The end results are improved quality, shortened welding lines, reduced capital investment, and less time to launch new vehicles," says Atsushi Niimi, president of Toyota Motor Manufacturing North America.

Cho and his managers are not just reengineering how Toyota makes its cars—they want to revolutionize how it creates products. With the rise of e-mail and teleconferencing, teams of designers, engineers, product planners, workers, and suppliers rarely all convened in the same place. Under Cho, they're again required to work face to face, in a process Toyota calls obeya—literally, "big room." This cuts the time it takes to get a car from the drawing board to the showroom. It took only 19 months to develop the 2003 Solara. That's better than 22 months for the latest Sienna minivan, and 26 months for the latest Camry—well below the industry average of about three years.

If all this sounds like Toyota is riding a powerful growth wave, well, it is. While Cho is as mild-mannered and modest as they come, the revolution he has kicked off is anything but. Toyota is in the midst of a transformative makeover—and if Cho succeeds, the entire global auto industry is in for one, too.

With Kathleen Kerwin in Detroit, Christopher Palmeri in Los Angeles, and Paul Magnusson in Washington

Source: Brian Bremner and Chester Dawson, "Can Anything Stop Toyota?" *BusinessWeek* November 17, 2003, 114–122.

Case 6-6

Coca-Cola Co. (B)

Mary Minnick is not a pat-you-on-the-back kind of boss. She heads marketing, strategy, and innovation at Coca-Cola Co., and if ever there was a company that does not deserve pats on the back, Coke is it. "I tend to be quite discontented in general," she told investors last December. "It will never be fast enough or soon enough or good enough."

Minnick is blunt. She's also worldly and smart, with an acerbic sense of humor. She can be charming when she's not being stern. In her first year in the newly expanded post, she has been a shock to the sclerotic complacency that has marked Coke for the past decade. "There was a culture of politeness and consensus and talking around an issue, rather than taking it head-on," she says. If Coke employees are upset by the change, too bad: "That's one thing I won't work on."

Minnick, 46, advocates a strategy that would have been heresy to legendary ex-Chief Executive Roberto Goizueta and the old, Warren E. Buffett-backed board. They turned the company into one of the world's preeminent blue chips in the 1980s and '90s by focusing squarely on soda. To Minnick, growth means more than simply boosting sales of Coca-Cola Classic. And innovation involves more than repackaging existing beverages in slightly different flavors. Minnick is exploring new products as far afield as beauty and health care. If she accomplishes even half of what's on her drawing board, she'll usher in the greatest flowering of creativity in the company's history. And should her plan succeed, she could end up CEO, if not at Coke then

almost certainly elsewhere (Target Corp. has already put her on its board). Either way, Coke will end up a dramatically different company.

Coca-Cola is an American icon, yet it is in danger of slipping into irrelevance. Consumers are flocking to a new breed of coffees, juices, and teas—all categories where Coke has historically been weak. For the longest time, Coke seemed in denial, more fixated on reversing the stagnation in soda than investing in the alternative beverages that consumers were clamoring for. Archrival PepsiCo Inc. has eclipsed it in many important ways, including stock performance, earnings growth, talent development, and buzz. Even though Coca-Cola still racks up more annual profit than Pepsi, Pepsi now has a market value, $103 billion, virtually equal to Coke's. Just 10 years ago, Coke was three times bigger (Exhibit 1).

Now, Coke is at a turning point. On the one hand, it is still the most valuable brand in history, according to consultancy Interbrand, which measures how much a company's brand drives its sales and profits. On the other hand, the value of the Coke brand has declined 20% since 1999, to $67 billion, according to Interbrand. That's one of the largest percentage drops of any multinational during that period. The challenge of reversing this trend, of making Coke more exciting, innovative, and relevant, falls largely on Minnick's shoulders. The marketing dynamo has helped bring a new sense of urgency to everything, from how the company advertises (one of her first moves was replacing Coke's lead agency, Berlin Cameron & Partners) to how it develops new drinks. "She did not look to me like the other leaders at Coca-Cola. She looked like someone I would have met at GE," says Jeff DeGraff,

EXHIBIT 1

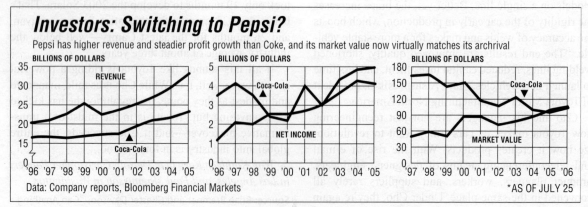

Investors: Switching to Pepsi?

Pepsi has higher revenue and steadier profit growth than Coke, and its market value now virtually matches its archrival

Data: Company reports, Bloomberg Financial Markets

*AS OF JULY 25

a University of Michigan business professor who has consulted for Coke.

Minnick's top priority has been jump-starting Coke's product development. Under her leadership, Coke has been unusually prolific, launching more than 1,000 new drinks or new variations of existing brands worldwide in the past 12 months, including a new male-oriented diet drink called Coca-Cola Zero as well as a brisk-selling coffee-flavored cola called Coca-Cola Blak. But Minnick knows that, in the long run, new flavors and brand extensions won't be enough to make Coke a growth company again. So with the solid backing of CEO E. Neville Isdell, to whom she reports, Minnick is pushing to transform Coke from a soda-centric organization that was long content to offer "me-too" products in emerging categories to one on the cutting edge of consumer trends.

At a private, mid-May meeting of Coke's top 200 global marketers in Istanbul, Minnick implored her troops to stop thinking in terms of existing drink categories and to start thinking broadly about why people consume beverages in the first place. The goal: to come to market with products that satisfy those needs before the competition. To that end, Minnick loves to talk about what she considers the 10 primal "need states" that consumers have, including "hunger and digestion," "mental renewal," and "health and beauty." Creating drinks that meet each of those need states may mean inventing entire new categories. Imagine drinks, for example, that are fortified with vitamins or nutrients and provide women the same benefits as a facial scrub or cold cream.

In the future, Minnick says, the winners will be the beverage companies that develop breakthrough products that, more often than not, cross over traditional beverage categories—just as Red Bull did when it single-handedly created the energy drink segment. "Like Henry Ford said, 'If I'd asked the consumer what they wanted, they'd have said a faster horse,'" she told her staff in Istanbul.

To be sure, some of what's currently emerging from Coke are catch-up products that finally give it an entrée into some hot categories. The Atlanta behemoth just launched a new bottled tea called Gold Peak, and in coming months it'll unveil a premium coffee drink licensed from chocolatier Godiva to compete with bottled Frappuccinos sold by Pepsi in a venture with Starbucks. And Coke is using new packaging to help reinvent some of its older brands, including the flagship Coca-Cola Classic. Earlier this year, the company began rolling out sleek, aluminum designer Coke bottles with etched, glow-in-the-dark graphics, for sale initially in a few dozen nightclubs around the world. The hope is that the designs will improve the 120-year-old brand's image with trendsetters.

Big Ambitions

But these are small victories, and Minnick knows that. At the Istanbul conference, the morning after a feel-good opening speech, she gave her staffers a cold-water wake-up call in the form of a rugged marketing critique. She was rapid-fire, speaking quickly but clearly from a dais to her 200 troops: "I don't think we've nailed the diet and light categories. I think our consumer insights are too superficial," she said. "We need to refine the Fanta vision. It's got to be more than 'Fanta fun.' It didn't grow as fast as it could last year."

Such frank appraisals are vintage Minnick. She may be brusque, but her staffers say that as a veteran of Coke, Minnick has the clout and political savvy to make sure things happen. Coke's chief creative director, Esther Lee, notes that while some previous chief marketing officers struggled to get Coke's country managers to adopt a new global ad campaign, with Minnick's backing she had no trouble getting buy-in for the new "Coke Side of Life" campaign. "I could not have done a global campaign before Mary," says Lee.

Minnick's bigger ambitions, if they take hold, would utterly redefine Coca-Cola's image as a purveyor of sugar-laden junk that you shouldn't give your kids. Based on prototypes that *BusinessWeek* saw in Istanbul, look for "nutraceutical" versions of Diet Coke, or new juices designed to help women with skin care, weight management, and detoxification. In the past year, Coke has launched 18 clinical trials to test the health benefits of different new ingredients that it hopes to use in future drinks. In Japan, Minnick's former stomping grounds, Coke is already selling some of these very products. As one of Minnick's top lieutenants, Penny McIntyre, told marketing staffers at the Istanbul summit: "It's not far away that not only can you feel better but you can look better through healthy beverages. We are going to transform our beverages and, along the way, transform the company."

That's a stirring vision, but one fraught with challenges. For one, drinks that make health claims could require government approval. An ever bigger challenge may be winning support from the company's vast network of independent bottlers. Rather than dumping finished product on the bottlers, as her predecessors did, she's engaging them as products are being conceived to ensure their input and cooperation. "There are a lot of bottlers who realize now that it's innovate or die," says Ron Wilson, president of a large Coke bottler in Philadelphia.

Minnick's role as corporate agitator may appear surprising, given that she's a Coke lifer. But she was pushing "non-carb" beverages—Coke parlance for anything that isn't a carbonated soft drink—back when doing so was career suicide. Not coincidentally, perhaps, she made her name far from Atlanta headquarters. As head of operations in Japan and, in time, all of Asia, she sold canned coffees, teas, and vitamin drinks in cultures where soda is an acquired taste.

While Minnick gets plenty of attention these days, she doesn't necessarily crave the spotlight. Minnick grew up in rural Nova, Ohio, a town so small it had no stoplight and just one stop sign. From the age of 13, she spent summers working on her father's golf course mowing fairways, raking sand traps, and flipping burgers in the clubhouse. Minnick helped pay her way through Bowling Green State University in the late '70s by slinging hash in the student cafeteria. ("There I am trying to look cool for this cute guy when I'm wearing a hairnet and an orange polyester uniform," she laughs.)

She earned an MBA from Duke University in 1983, and started her career on the bottom rung of the Coke ladder, as a sales rep in its fountain division. "My job was figuring out how to sell more beverages to a hot dog chain in Minneapolis in January, driving a car with 150,000 miles on it, living in a one-bedroom apartment in a horrible part of Atlanta, and questioning the meaning of life," she recalls.

"Wolf Sweat"

Minnick did well enough to earn a promotion into Coke's vaunted marketing department. In time she convinced management to let her lead a new team being formed to develop new drinks to counter emerging non-carb rivals such as Snapple and Gatorade, which were starting to steal customers from Coke's soft drink business. Given Coke's soda-centric culture, it was a lonely vigil. When Minnick and her team developed a clear beverage called Nordic Mist to take on a new rival drink called Clearly Canadian, some senior Coke execs derisively referred to it as "Wolf Sweat." Says Minnick: "I walked into a senior manager's office in [Coke's]

North America [division]—and I won't tell you who, but he was very senior—and he said, 'Mary, every case of Powerade and Nordic Mist I put on the truck, I have to take a case of Coke off. That doesn't pay off.'"

Similarly, when Minnick's team created Fruitopia to take on Snapple, bottlers balked at the expensive glass bottles and its more expensive brewing process. Against Minnick's wishes, management buckled, ordering a switch to plastic bottles and the same "cold fill" process used to make soda. Those two changes served to cheapen the product in the eyes of consumers and, with sales faltering, Coke eventually pulled Fruitopia from the U.S. market.

Over time, fighting battles against recalcitrant senior executives who didn't see a future outside of soda came at a cost to Minnick. "One of the senior managers of the company said to me, 'You've pushed too hard, you've alienated everyone in North America, your passion for non-carbs has gotten in the way of what's right for Coke, and nobody wants to work with you anymore,'" she remembers. Dejected, Minnick took the LSAT and applied to law school.

But her spunk and resourcefulness hadn't gone unnoticed by Sergio Zyman, who had returned to Coke in 1993 as head of marketing. He persuaded her to stay and provide marketing support to Coke's Asian operations. By 1997, Minnick found herself being shipped overseas to run the company's South Pacific group, covering Indonesia, Australia, New Zealand, and all of the Pacific Islands.

Almost immediately, the Asian economic crisis crippled the region and Coke's business there. With currencies plunging and violence rising, Coke's Indonesian bottler pleaded with Minnick to simply shut down operations in that country until after the crisis passed. But Minnick refused, opting to ride out the storm even though that meant evacuating Coke employees on two different occasions during ensuing riots. The company emerged from the crisis even stronger. "It was a great success story. We got credit from the [public] for staying," she says.

Proving Ground

As her reward, in early 2000 Minnick was named to head up all operations in Japan, which had historically generated 20% of Coke's profit until a slump in the late '90s. Minnick's full-frontal management didn't set well with the Japanese male staffers at Coke's local headquarters in Tokyo, some of whom complained privately in letters to then-CEO Douglas N. Daft in hopes of having Minnick reassigned. Daft's response to the instigators: "This woman will be there longer than you. She has my full support." Still, Minnick now admits that she had to dial back because bottlers already had begun swapping "Mary Minnick stories." "I think I started to temper my management style in Japan," she acknowledges. "Because of the culture, you have to learn patience and a certain sense of decorum. They don't appreciate anger and displays of emotion." She slashed operating costs, invested in state-of-the-art vending machines popular with Japanese teens, and after two years of flat-to-declining revenues, sales began to grow between 2% and 4% a year. That earned Minnick another promotion in 2002, to head up all of Coke's Asian operations.

Japan was a crucial period for Minnick. It was the first real test of her leadership ability. And it was the place where she realized the full potential of non-carb drinks, which are now a fundamental part of her turnaround plan for all of Coke. In most of the company's markets, Coke Classic is the cash cow. But in Japan, the company generates the bulk of its profits, surprisingly, from canned coffees and 200 or so eclectic products like Real Gold, a hangover cure sold in a small bottle, and Love Body, a tea marketed to calorie-counting women (and which contains an ingredient that some Japanese believe increases bust size). Coke's marketing team in Japan knew how to ride the trends, introducing as many as 100 new products a year, some with a life expectancy of just a few months. Thanks to constant data reports from 7-Eleven stores, "we knew within the first four weeks if we were going to be in trouble or not," she recalls.

While Minnick was helping get Asia back on track, all was not well with the rest of Coke (Exhibit 2). It had overinvested in some emerging markets, and soft drink sales had flattened. Daft (who is on the board of The McGraw-Hill Companies, *BusinessWeek*'s parent) resigned in 2004 under pressure from the board, which brought in Isdell. From the moment he arrived, Isdell preached the need for Coke to become more aggressive in selling alternative beverages. He spent an additional $400 million a year to boost marketing and fund new product development. And as he held a series of management retreats to lay out his vision, he became so impressed with Minnick's intellect that he approached her on a Friday morning in May, 2005, to become head of marketing.

"Plan, Plan, Plan"

She turned him down on the spot. "I had spent 10 years living in Asia, and I loved it—the people, the culture, the way of living." But Isdell persisted in a second meeting that same day. After she spent a weekend soul-searching, Minnick's boyfriend, Simon Cooper, who owns a fly-fishing tour service in Britain, encouraged her to take the job and "give it a year." Minnick relented, but only after Isdell assured her of his full backing to overhaul Coke's marketing. Minnick knew all too well that Coke had talked the talk about innovation but little had really happened.

Once back in the U.S., Minnick didn't bother ingratiating herself with her staff. First, she laboriously analyzed Coke's performance over each of the past 10 years and produced a "look in the mirror" report that assessed the company's marketing moves, both good

EXHIBIT 2

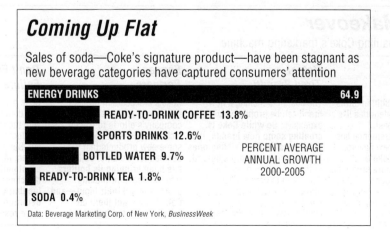

Coming Up Flat

Sales of soda—Coke's signature product—have been stagnant as new beverage categories have captured consumers' attention

ENERGY DRINKS	64.9
READY-TO-DRINK COFFEE	13.8%
SPORTS DRINKS	12.6%
BOTTLED WATER	9.7%
READY-TO-DRINK TEA	1.8%
SODA	0.4%

PERCENT AVERAGE ANNUAL GROWTH 2000–2005

Data: Beverage Marketing Corp. of New York, *BusinessWeek*

and bad, during that period. She brought in management gurus like Ram Charan and Michigan's DeGraff. Recalls DeGraff: "When I got to Coke, they liked to draw up PowerPoint slides, and they liked to plan, plan, plan. They were very slow."

In what must have been a humbling act for a company that had been considered one of the preeminent growth machines during Goizueta's glorious reign, Minnick dispatched top aides to companies like British Petroleum, Apple Computer, and Kraft to study how those companies approached innovation. "We asked ourselves, 'How can we do it in an Apple way? It's the way they did it in a 'Think Different' way." By contrast, too much of what passed for innovation at Coke over the years had been incremental line extensions that too often didn't really move the needle. "You ended up having a single flavor change—a key lime Fanta—and not transformational innovation," she says.

Culture of Candor

Coke's genteel Southern ways meant managers talked around problems, but Minnick tried to instill a culture of accountability in the marketing department and with the company's ad agencies. Minnick doesn't apologize. "Historically, we had a culture where putting the hard issue on the table made some people uncomfortable," she says. Some former Coke marketing executives praise Minnick for raising the bar. "It's a company full of belongers with not enough performers," says Zyman, who served two stints as chief marketing officer during the 1980s and '90s. "She has been right to try to shake things up" (Exhibit 3).

One of the first things that Minnick shook up was advertising. Over the decades, Coke was known for creating some of the greatest ads ever. A 1971 commercial jingle, *I'd Like to Teach the World to Sing,* became a peace anthem during the Vietnam War. But since the late '90s, Coke ads have been mostly forgettable. Within days of taking the job, Minnick began killing ads left and right, including one somber, European ad that showed angry teens clanging Coke bottles against light posts as they stormed the streets and gathered at a cliff. Before it was over, Minnick fired Coke's lead agency, Berlin Cameron & Partners, and initiated an agency "shootout" that led to the selection of Portland (Ore.)-based Wieden + Kennedy, the masterminds behind Nike Inc.'s "Just Do It" campaign. Agency President Dan Wieden, who had handled small assignments for Coke for nearly a decade, admits that he took the new assignment with some trepidation. "The layers of bureaucracy at Coke prevented you from doing good work. They had a huge reliance on [focus group] testing. And people would make decisions based not on what was in front of them, but would try to second-guess what people above them might think."

But Minnick's new team, led by creative director Lee, gave Wieden carte blanche. The result, the "Coke Side of Life" campaign unveiled earlier this year, was hailed by ad critics like *Chicago Sun-Times* columnist Lewis Lazare, who credited the spots with putting Coke advertising "gloriously back on track." Katie Bayne, a senior vice-president who oversees Coca-Cola trademark products, notes that four of the new commercials, including one where a young male

EXHIBIT 3

Mary's Makeover
How she's overhauling Coke's marketing machine

Anticipate the Customer	Retool Tired Brands	Engage Partners	Don't Fear Failure
Coke has always thought in terms of traditional drink categories like cola or juice. In the past, innovation meant incremental line extensions such as new flavors. **But Minnick wants Coke's marketers to think more creatively about consumers' needs.** That has led Coke to consider creating drinks that cater to, for example, the desire to feel healthy.	The cost of launching a new brand can be prohibitively expensive. **So while Coke is creating some new brands, it is also repositioning existing ones in categories where it's behind.** In the U.S., Coke dusted off the Tab brand to create an energy drink for women, and it's using the Sprite name for a new energy beverage in France.	Coke's independent bottlers have long resisted the company's efforts to launch niche brands, refusing to carry some new products that they deemed low volume. **So Minnick has been bringing its bottlers into the decision-making process to get their input—and, Coke hopes, get them on board—from the outset.**	Coke has a history of planning and then planning some more—with the result that many new products never made it out of the lab. But as head of a Coke in Japan, **Minnick perfected the art of putting new drinks out on the cheap and then using quick feedback from retailers to determine which new drinks were resonating with consumers.**

repeatedly steals sips from a soda fountain while the clerk isn't looking, ranked among the highest-scoring Coke commercials ever in independent consumer testing. That's good news, but people who work for Minnick know better than to bask in the momentary glory. "She's not one to celebrate," says Lee. "We don't spend a lot of time talking about why something is good."

Source: Dean Foust, "Queen of Pop," *BusinessWeek*, August 7, 2006, 44–53.

Case 6-7

Keurig Inc.

A Wednesday afternoon in February 2003 found Keurig Inc.'s president and CEO Nick Lazaris heading south on Interstate 89 back toward his Wakefield, Massachusetts, office and mulling over the day's events in preparation for a briefing with his senior management team (see Exhibit 1 on page 572). He realized that the next two weeks would be critical to the success of the company's newest product initiative in the single-cup coffee market. Lazaris had just wrapped up a presentation to the Green Mountain Coffee Roasters Inc. (GMCR) management team, one of the company's strategic partners and an investor in its business. While reviewing the company's progress toward the launch of its innovative coffee-brewing system into the at-home consumer market, GMCR had asked Keurig to reconsider its decision to use a different version of the coffee portion pack, known as a K-Cup, in the consumer market. In making its request, GMCR had offered a number of compelling reasons for using the existing commercial portion pack in both channels.

As he drove, Lazaris passed a new Starbucks and reflected on how gourmet coffeehouses had helped pave the way for Keurig's single-serve brewing system. The proliferation of soft drinks since the 1960s had caused coffee to lose its place as a central component of social gatherings, spurring a precipitous drop in coffee consumption to an all-time low of 6.1 pounds per capita in the mid-1990s from a peak of 16.5 pounds per capita in the mid-1940s.[1] The entrance of gourmet coffeehouses had reinvigorated the market, developing a distinct subculture of coffee drinkers and educating younger consumers about great traditional coffees as well as espresso and milk-based specialty beverages. As a result, by 2003 an estimated twenty million Americans were drinking gourmet coffee on a daily basis.

Keurig's launch of a single-cup brewing system in the office coffee service market in the late 1990s had benefited from coffee drinkers' increasing sophistication. Office employees could appreciate the greater variety, freshness, and convenience derived from the ability to brew a single cup of coffee on demand. Office managers recognized the advantages garnered from less coffee waste, increased employee productivity, and decreased hassle associated with tending the coffee machine.

February 2003 found Keurig poised to launch its new model B100 system in the at-home segment with hopes of repeating its success in a much larger but more competitive market. With rumors of other single-cup competitors ready to enter the market, Lazaris knew Keurig needed to move quickly in order to obtain its desired positioning in the emerging single-cup consumer market. Revisiting the decision to proceed with a two-K-Cup strategy had the potential to derail the company's launch efforts and demanded rapid attention by Lazaris and the senior management team. Reevaluation of the K-Cup decision would also force them to rethink other elements of their product plans, including pricing and marketing. With less than six months until the September launch, time was of the essence.

The Company and Its Products

Keurig Inc. had been founded to develop an innovative technique that would allow coffee lovers to brew one perfect cup of coffee at a time. Beginning with the company's inception in 1992, the word "Keurig," from the Dutch word for excellence, had been the guiding principle behind the development of its products and services. The company leveraged investments from venture capital funds to transform its concept for a single-cup brewing system into a commercially viable business with the development and patenting of a single-portion pack and a revolutionary new coffee brewer. The first brewer targeting the office coffee service market, the

[1]United States Department of Agriculture.

Source: Elizabeth L. Anderson, Keurig at Home: Managing a New Product Launch, Kellogg School of Management, January 27, 2006. One-time permission to reproduce granted by Kellogg School of Management.

EXHIBIT 1 Keurig Senior Management Team

Source: Keurig, Inc.

NICK LAZARIS: PRESIDENT, CHIEF EXECUTIVE OFFICER, AND DIRECTOR

Lazaris joined Keurig in 1997. His more than twenty years of business experience includes president/CEO- and VP-level experience in marketing, sales, finance, and business development in the home furnishings and office products industries. Prior to Keurig he was president/CEO of MW Carr, a photo frame manufacturer/marketer, and VP and divisional GM for Tech Specialists, a contract professional staffing firm. Earlier in his career, Lazaris served as chief of staff for West Virginia Governor Jay Rockefeller. In 2001 and 2003 he was a regional finalist for Ernst & Young's Entrepreneur of the Year. He received his BS from MIT and his MBA from Harvard Business School, and is a licensed CPA.

DICK SWEENEY: CO-FOUNDER AND VICE-PRESIDENT, ENGINEERING AND OPERATIONS

Sweeney co-founded Keurig in 1993 and joined the company full time as VP of engineering in 1996. He brought to Keurig more than 25 years of experience in manufacturing, product development, and consulting for industrial and consumer appliances, including espresso machines. Prior to Keurig he was VP of manufacturing for Canrad-Hanovia, a manufacturer of scientific and UV lighting. Before that he was VP of operations for V-M Industries, a consumer appliances manufacturer and importer. Sweeney received his BS from New Jersey Institute of Technology and his MBA from Fairleigh Dickinson University.

CHRIS STEVENS: VICE-PRESIDENT OF SALES

Stevens joined Keurig in 1996. He brought to Keurig more than 20 years of experience in consumer goods sales and marketing, as well as general management. After beginning his sales career with seven years at Procter & Gamble, he became president of the August A. Busch Co., a subsidiary of Anheuser-Busch. After also serving as a divisional manager with A-B, he was executive VP and general manager for United Liquors before becoming executive director of the Sports Museum of New England. Stevens received his BS from Notre Dame and completed the Executive Education program at Columbia Business School.

DAVE MANLY: VICE-PRESIDENT OF MARKETING

Manly joined Keurig in 2002. He brought to Keurig more than 20 years of experience in consumer goods sales and marketing. His experience included VP and GM positions building well-known consumer brands in the food products and consumer goods industries via innovative marketing approaches. Manly has held marketing positions at Nexus EnergyGuide, EnergyUSA, LoJack Corporation, Boston Whaler Boat Company, and Procter & Gamble (food products division). Manly received his BS from DePauw University and his MBA from Purdue University.

JOHN WHORISKEY: VICE-PRESIDENT, GENERAL MANAGER—AT-HOME DIVISION

Whoriskey joined Keurig in 2002. He brought to Keurig more than twenty years of experience that included president- and VP-level experience in marketing and sales in the home furnishings, gift, and consumer products industries. Prior to Keurig he was president of Fetco Home Décor and president of Optelec Inc. Prior to that, he worked in VP-level positions for Honeywell Consumer Products, Tucker Housewares, The First Years, and Polaroid. Whoriskey received his BS and an MBA from Boston College.

B2000, was launched in 1998. A licensing agreement allowed GMCR to pack its specialty coffees in Keurig's patented container, the K-Cup (see Exhibit 2). Eight varieties of coffee were originally available for sale to offices. Keurig continued to expand its relationships with roasters such as GMCR, using a selective but non-exclusive strategy. This ongoing effort had expanded the number of roaster partnerships to five, resulting in the largest variety of coffees available with a single-cup system in the market in 2003.

In February 2002 the ownership structure of Keurig changed through agreements with two of its roaster partners. Keurig sold stock to Van Houtte Inc. to raise nearly $10 million to support the launch of the at-home business. This investment provided Van Houtte with nearly a 28 percent ownership stake in Keurig. At

EXHIBIT 2
B2003 Commercial
Brewer and Keurig
K-Cups

Source: Keurig, Inc.

the same time, GMCR acquired and executed options to purchase a large number of Keurig shares from existing shareholders, enabling Keurig to consolidate to a smaller number of significant shareholders. GMCR obtained a 42 percent stake in Keurig. With these moves, Van Houtte and GMCR joined Memorial Drive Trust (MDT) as the three largest shareholders of Keurig. MDT, an investment advisory firm that managed a U.S.-based profit-sharing plan, had served as the lead venture investor in Keurig since 1995 and led Keurig's board of directors. As provided for in separate shareholder agreements with MDT, neither GMCR nor Van Houtte was allowed to have a seat on the board of directors. Lazaris reinforced the company's position with respect to these roaster shareholders in a letter to its authorized distributors and other roaster partners:

> We do not plan to allow any roaster or other commercial business partner to sit on our board of directors. Our core strategy remains unchanged: we are committed to a multiroaster strategy that relies on strong relationships with selected gourmet coffee roasters who take a great deal of pride in the coffee consumption experience that supports the meaning of their brand to consumers.[2]

Single-Cup Brewing Technology

Keurig's single-portion system hinged on three key elements: a coffee brewer that perfectly controlled the amount, temperature, and pressure of water to provide a consistently superior-tasting cup of coffee; a unique

portion-pack system containing ground coffee beans as well as filter paper; and a varied coffee selection to replicate the choices available in a gourmet coffeehouse.

The Keurig commercial-market brewer included an "always-on" feature, enabling it to brew a cup of coffee in less than one minute at any time of day. Plumbed to a water line, the automatically refillable water reservoir maintained up to twelve cups of water at brewing temperature. After the customer inserted a K-Cup in a drawer, positioned the 8-ounce cup to receive the brewed coffee, and pressed the "brew" button, the brewer would pierce the K-Cup, inject pressurized hot water, and brew the coffee. The K-Cup, evolved from an initial mockup design based on a modified yogurt cup, contained a built-in cone-shaped filter and the exact amount and grind of coffee to fresh-brew a single 8-ounce cup. K-Cups were impermeable to air; moisture, and light to ensure the contents stayed fresh for at least six months.

A key differentiator for Keurig's brewing system was the broad coffee selection available through licensing arrangements with a variety of gourmet coffee roasters. Coffee roasters controlled the quality of their coffee and the number of varieties available through K-Cup production lines. A production line might be owned by the coffee roaster or leased from Keurig. K-Cups were produced by five roasters with six brands and more than 75 coffee varieties.[3] Roaster partners included Green Mountain Coffee Roasters, Diedrich Coffee,

[2]Internal memo dated February 5, 2002.

[3]Currently there were three leased-production lines and an additional eight roaster-owned lines. Three additional lines were planned.

Van Houtte, Timothy's World Coffee, and Ueshima Coffee Company. For each K-Cup sold, the roaster paid Keurig a royalty of approximately $.04.

The Art of Cupping

"Cupping" was a method of tasting the finished (or brewed) coffee product used by roasters and many large retailers to evaluate the flavor profile of a coffee. Similar to wine tasting, cupping involved swishing coffee around in the mouth to evaluate elements of the flavor profile. Expert "cuppers" could taste as many as 10 to 20 varieties a day and perform an analysis that included taste, brightness (degree of acidity), fragrance and aroma, body, and finish. The process began with the roasting and grinding of a small batch of beans. Once the ground beans were placed in a cup, hot water was poured over them and the analysis process began. The cupping process could be supplemented by state-of-the-art machinery to ensure product consistency.

In the world of gourmet coffees, roasters offered a variety of coffees tailored to the different tastes of gourmet coffee drinkers. For each variety of coffee offered, cuppers had established an expected flavor profile. The process by which that profile was achieved was closely controlled by the cupper during the cupping process. However, those same controls could not always be achieved in the traditional home brewing process. The desired flavor profile could be affected by a number of factors beyond the control of the roaster or cupper: the amount of coffee or water used by the consumer, variations in the temperature throughout brewing, or the amount of time the coffee sat in the coffee pot prior to being consumed. Through close control of critical elements in the coffee brewing process, the Keurig system enabled that flavor profile to be re-created on a consistent basis and ensured that the coffee drinker had the same taste experience time after time.

Away-From-Home Market

Keurig's market included two broad target customers: office users and households.[4] Keurig chose to focus first on the away-from-home commercial segment of office users in the hopes that a successful rollout would provide a springboard for launch into the at-home segment. The groundwork for launching into the away-from-home

[4]From early trial activities, Keurig had determined its single-serve brewing system was not well aligned with the needs of food service establishments serving a large volume of coffee.

office coffee service (OCS) market was laid by Starbucks and other specialty coffee purveyors. They had successfully educated consumers about good-quality coffee and made it acceptable to pay $1.50 or more for a cup of coffee and even more for coffee-based specialty beverages. This behavior opened the door for Keurig and others to offer a single-cup system into offices, capitalizing on people's desire to have the same great taste in the office as they got at a coffeehouse.

In 2002 the OCS market reached $3.46 billion in total revenues.[5] At the same time, acceptance of the single-cup brewing technology was evident in surveys of OCS distributors. In 2000 only 14.8 percent of distributors had offered a single-cup system, but that figure had increased to 44.8 percent in 2001.[6] By 2003 total single-cup brewer placements had reached 143,200 (see Exhibit 3).

Since the launch of its first commercial brewer in 1998, Keurig had quickly moved to a leading position in the sales of single-cup brewing systems. After five years in the market at the end of 2002, Keurig had shipped more than 33,000 brewers in North America, equal to 1 percent of all OCS brewers. In comparison to the competition, Lazaris was quick to point out the speed with which Keurig had penetrated the market:

> It took Filterfresh twenty years to ship 45,000 units in North America. And in its first five years, Flavia shipped only 8,000 units in North America. In addition, our expansion into Asia at the end of 2001 provided us an added opportunity for growth. In partnership with the top Asian roaster, UCC, our initial sales in Japan and Korea had been more than 2,700 brewers.

A second measure of Keurig's achievements in the OCS market was shipment of its patented K-Cups. In 2002 Keurig's roaster partners shipped more than 125 million K-Cups, bringing total K-Cup shipments since launch to more than 340 million. Also in the works was the launch of an offering of teas in T-Cups, with the first being the "Celestial Seasonings" teas.

Away-from-Home Channel of Distribution

The office coffee market was served by a network of approximately 1,700 distributors that were responsible for placement and maintenance of office brewers and ongoing coffee supply. Keurig worked with a total of 180 Keurig authorized distributors (KADS) for

[5]International Coffee Organization, London, UK.
[6]*Automatic Merchandiser* 2002 Coffee Service Market Report.

EXHIBIT 3   U.S. Single-Cup Brewer Placements by OCS Distributors

Source: *Automatic Merchandiser,* February 2002, July 2004.

Manufacturer	Product(s)	1999/2000	2000/2001	2001/2002	2002/2003
Cafection	Avalon	7,500	11,000	13,000	16,000
Crane	Cafe System	22,500	23,000	11,000	12,000
Filterfresh	Filterfresh/Keurig	23,000	24,000	26,500[a]	30,000[b]
Flavia	Flavia	8,000	19,000	32,000	40,000
Keurig	Keurig	13,000	23,000	30,000	33,000
Newco	Gevalia	0	1,000	1,200	1,300
Progema	Venus	0	0	1,000	2,400
Unibrew	Unibrew	3,200[c]	3,200	3,200	3,200
Zanussi	Brio/Colibri	5,000	6,400	8,000	10,000
Other		1,100	1,600	516	4,600
Total		83,300	112,200	126,416	143,200

[a]Includes 1,484 Keurig units.
[b]Includes 2,300 Keurig units.
[c]Available to Filterfresh franchisees only.
Note: Table has been modified to exclude espresso machine sales.

sales throughout North America. A small number of KADS handled customers throughout the United States or North America, while the majority covered smaller regions.

The purchasing decision was handled by office managers. "Office managers are all about eliminating headaches. The variety of coffees, convenience of brewing, and negligible clean-up of the Keurig system mean fewer employee complaints and greater productivity," explained Chris Stevens, away-from-home vice-president of sales, who was responsible for managing Keurig's day-to-day relationship with its network of KADS. Customer relationships were managed by the KADS and feedback on problems or desired new features was funneled through the KADS to share with Keurig.

The KADS purchased commercial brewers from Keurig at a wholesale price that ranged from $500 to $1,000. The brewer was placed in offices free of charge or with a low monthly rental in exchange for ongoing coffee sales. Typically there was no formal contract between the KAD and the office manager, although the KAD established expected volumes based on the number of employees in the office. If volumes fell below expected levels, the KAD could remove the brewer from the office or raise the price of the K-Cups. The KAD was also responsible for ongoing repairs of the brewer.

The KAD provided a variety of coffees to offices, based on their individual consumption profiles. KADS entered into direct relationships with one or more

licensed roasters for the purchase of K-Cups. Typically, KADS paid roasters $0.25 per K-Cup and sold K-Cups to office managers for $0.40–$0.50. Roasters then paid Keurig a royalty of $0.04 per K-Cup sold.

Away-from-Home Single-Cup Competition

There were two primary competitors in the away-from-home market.

Filterfresh

Hopper-based single-cup technology was pioneered by Westwood, Massachusetts-based Filterfresh Coffee Service Inc. in the late 1980s. Filterfresh was a U.S. subsidiary of Canadian-based Van Houtte (a Keurig shareholder), a leading gourmet coffee roaster, marketer, and distributor in North America. The Filterfresh commercial single-cup system was based on the "French press" method of brewing. Ground coffee beans were loaded into a storage hopper in the machine. Once a button was pressed for a cup of coffee, an amount of ground beans would be measured from the hopper and mixed with hot water. The mixture would then be strained to remove the grounds and a single cup of coffee resulted. No brewed coffee was left to sit and become waste as was common in a traditional glass pot system, and a person enjoyed a freshly brewed cup of coffee each time. Regular tending of the coffee system was required to remove used coffee grounds and reload ground beans into the storage hopper. Filterfresh established its relationship with Keurig in October 2001 to market Keurig's commercial brewer and offer a system that could provide a greater variety of single-cup coffees and teas.

Flavia

Flavia was owned by Mars Inc. It introduced its first single-cup brewer to offices in Britain in 1985 and expanded to Europe and Japan before introducing its "Brew-by-Pack" system in the United States and Canada in 1996. Similar to the Keurig brewer, the S350 commercial brewer utilized a single-serving pack. Each Filterpack contained its own filter and the appropriate measure of ingredients, which were foil-sealed, protecting them against air and moisture. A selection of twenty-four coffee varieties was available with the system.

At-Home Market

Building on its success in the OCS market, Keurig viewed the at-home consumer market as a logical extension to its business strategy. John Whoriskey joined Keurig as general manager and vice-president of the at-home division in 2002. He brought with him more than 20 years of experience in consumer goods sales and marketing. "I fell in love with Keurig and its brewing system," he commented. "I don't consider myself a gourmet coffee drinker, but I do like a good cup of coffee. I would drive a mile out of my way to work to pick up a good cup of coffee. With a Keurig brewer, we can offer convenience benefit with taste assurance, in the comfort of your own home."

The at-home market represented an enormous opportunity for Keurig. Leading market research firms estimated the total size of the retail coffee market at approximately $18.5 billion in 2000. At-home retail consumption was a $6.9 billion market, with at-home gourmet coffee accounting for $3.1 billion (see Exhibit 4). Away-from-home gourmet coffee rep-

resented a $3.9 billion market and was typically sold by the cup at cafes such as Starbucks or in other food service venues such as restaurants. At the same time, estimates showed 157 million Americans drank coffee, with 60 percent predominantly drinking previously ground coffee and another 10 percent using freshly ground whole bean coffee.[7] Profiles of coffee drinkers varied by product type, with consumers of whole-bean coffee exhibiting an upscale profile (see Exhibit 5). In addition, about eighteen million coffee makers were purchased annually in the United States, representing about $450 million in retail sales. Coffee makers represented one of the largest-volume small appliances sold for home use.[8]

Previously the purview of upscale outlets—coffee/tea stores, gourmet/specialty stores, kitchenware stores, and coffeehouses—gourmet coffees had increasingly been sold in mass-retail outlets. At the same time, the growing popularity of whole-bean coffee had been driving the launch of a variety of roasts, blends, and flavors. Starbucks, for example, showed growth of whole-bean sales in excess of 100 percent in 2000.[9]

Coffee advertising centered on two major themes: good taste and positive stimulation. Taglines such as Maxwell House's "Good to the last drop" reflected the emphasis on the taste experience. Positive stimulation focused on the benefits caused by drinking a particular cup of coffee. As an example, the well-known tagline "The best part of waking up is Folgers in your cup" suggested that the stress and challenges in your life could be overcome by taking that first sip.

At-Home Single-Cup Market Research

Keurig commissioned a variety of market research studies on the at-home product concept from 1999 to 2001

[7]Simmons Market Research Bureau (2000).
[8]Keurig company information.
[9]*The U.S. Market for Freshly Brewed Coffee Beverages*, Packaged Facts, March 2004.

EXHIBIT 4
U.S. Retail At-Home Coffee Market

Source: *Packaged Facts Market Profile: The U.S. Coffee and Tea Market*, September 2001.

Year	Mass Market Coffee Sales ($ in Millions)	Pound Volume (in Millions)	Gourmet Coffee Sales ($ in Millions)	Pound Volume (in Millions)
2000	3,815	840	3,100	320
1999	3,800	850	3,000	310
1998	3,975	830	2,800	290
1997	4,205	845	2,500	270
1996	3,905	850	2,200	255

EXHIBIT 5
Demographic Characteristics by Product Form

Source: *Packaged Facts Market Profile: The U.S. Coffee and Tea Market,* September, 2001.

Factor	Ground	Instant	Whole Bean
Age	55–64	NS	45–54
Race	NS	Black; Hispanic	Asian; Other
Marital status	NS	Widowed	Married
Household income (in thousands)	NS	$10–$15	$75+
Education	NS	Not high school graduate	College graduate
Employment status	Retired	Homemaker	Full-time
Occupation	NS	NS	Professional/ managerial
Household size	NS	NS	NS
Region	Midwest	NS	West

Notes: U.S. adults. NS is no statistically significant differences.

prior to moving ahead with any significant development efforts. "We wanted to get an understanding of the acceptability of the single-cup approach, gain some insight into pricing of the K-Cup and the brewer, and profile our prime consumer prospects," explained Lazaris. This research was executed in a variety of formats, including intercept surveys, Internet-based surveys, surveys of current OCS users, and surveys and focus groups of home use testers.

Intercept interviews were conducted in three cities in the summer of 2000. Lazaris explained the study's focus: "We were interested in speaking with regular gourmet coffee drinkers so respondents were selected based on coffee brewing habits and coffee consumption." To qualify for the intercept survey, consumers had to drink gourmet coffee, which included coffee from freshly ground whole beans, from gourmet coffee roasters, and from premium coffee cafes such as Starbucks, Dunkin' Donuts, Seattle's Best, or Caribou Coffee. All participants had to drink at least one cup of coffee per day.

While nearly 94 percent of respondents indicated that they were satisfied with the coffee they drank at home, 88 percent expressed an interest in the product concept. Interest focused primarily on convenience, particularly quick brewing, ease of use, and minimal clean-up, sources of the most dissatisfaction with current home brewing systems. Based on explanation of the product alone, more than three-quarters of respondents said they would be likely to purchase a system like the one proposed. The product demonstration had a huge impact on this figure. More than 90 percent of respondents indicated that the demonstration increased their likelihood of buying the product. Key factors rated highest in the demonstration included the time it took to prepare coffee and the time it took to clean up.

Keurig had gained some initial insight into brewer pricing from previous market research (see Exhibit 6). It now wanted to explore product pricing with consumers who considered the system (brewer and K-Cups) and also experienced a product demonstration. Among intercept respondents, the self-reported daily consumption rate of coffee was an average of two to three cups. When asked about their willingness to pay for a cup of coffee like the one they tasted, 44 percent indicated they would pay $0.55 (see Exhibit 7 on page 578). Later in the survey, respondents were asked about their willingness to pay for both K-Cups and the brewer. More than 30 percent of respondents who were interested in the system were willing to pay $0.50 or more for a K-Cup. Before obtaining input on brewer pricing, respondents were told that high-quality

EXHIBIT 6
Initial Market Research

Source: Company-sponsored market research.

Brewer Pricing	Awares % (N = 170)	Nonawares % (N = 601)
$199	6	1
$449	9	7
$ 99	31	18

Note: Results from early street intercept testing were segmented between "Keurig-awares," people familiar with the Keurig system, and "Keurig-nonawares."

EXHIBIT 7 Intercept Testing Market Research

Source: Company-sponsored market research.

Table 7A: Willingness to Pay for Coffee

Survey respondents were asked how much they would be willing to pay for a cup of coffee like the one they tasted. Interviewers guided the respondents and started the price point inquiry at $0.55. The percentages of respondents represent the cumulative percentages of people willing to pay each price.

Initial Pricing	Percentage of Respondents (Cumulative)
$0.55	43.8
0.50	53.5
0.45	60.0
0.40	69.5
0.35	79.3
0.30	87.3
0.25	97.8

Table 7B: K-Cup Pricing Based on Coffee Consumption

Survey respondents were asked how much they would be willing to pay for a K-cup. The percentages of respondents represent the cumulative percentages of people willing to pay each price. Responses include only customers who were very or somewhat likely to purchase system.

K-Cup Pricing	1 Cup/Day[a] (N = 78) %	2+ Cup/Day[a] (N = 446) %
$0.55+	5.1	14.6
0.50–0.54	16.7	30.7
0.45–0.49	20.5	33.6
0.40–0.44	22.0	41.5
0.35–0.39	28.2	48.2
0.30–0.34	41.0	58.5
0.25–0.29	60.3	75.6

Table 7C: Brewer and K-Cup Pricing Based on Coffee Consumption

This table reflects the percentages of respondents willing to pay certain prices for the brewer. Information is segmented based on their previously stated K-cup pricing and coffee consumption. Responses include only customers who were very or somewhat likely to purchase system.

K-Cup Pricing	1 Cup/Day[a] (N = 78)%			2+ Cups/Day[a] (N = 446)%		
	< $100	$100–$129	$130+	< $100	$100–$129	$130+
< $0.30	34.1	9.4	5.9	22.2	8.9	6.3
0.30–0.39	7.1	8.2	2.4	6.2	5.3	5.2
0.40–0.49	2.4	2.4	4.7	5.7	2.5	1.9
0.50+	10.6	5.9	1.2	9.9	9.5	10.1
Don't Know	5.9			6.3		

[a]Coffee consumption per weekday.

coffee makers sold in the range of $69 to $149. Approximately one-fourth of the respondents were willing to pay more than $130 for the brewer. Consumers who drank more coffee were more willing to pay for both the K-Cup and the brewer.

An Internet-based survey used as its basis a Keurig system summary (see Exhibit 8) that was shown to people who drank coffee on a daily basis. It found that the concept had strong appeal, with 67 percent of respondents expressing interest. The main differentiating factor

EXHIBIT 8   Internet Survey Concept Description

Source: Keurig, Inc.

Introducing a Revolutionary New Home Coffee-Making System Coffee House Taste by the Cup™

Fresh
Fast
Convenient
Delicious

- *The System*—A revolutionary coffee-making system that uses individual portion packs of freshly roasted and ground coffee with a unique coffeemaker designed to brew GREAT cups of coffee, one cup at a time. Each user picks the brand and variety of coffee they want and makes a fresh, piping hot cup in just 30 seconds.
- *Delicious and Fresh*—Individual portion packs come in over 36 varieties of branded coffees from Green Mountain Coffee Roasters, Diedrich Coffee, and Gloria Jean's Coffees. The coffee is roasted, ground, and packed at the roasters' facilities into an individual portion pack where freshness is sealed in. The pack provides an oxygen, light, and moisture barrier to ensure fresh-ground quality that is guaranteed for six months. Whether you prefer light roasts, dark roasts, blends, decafs, or flavored coffees, this system serves you the coffee you prefer, brewed to perfection every time.
- *Convenient*—The entire brewing process takes place in the portion pack. There is no waste, no pot or filters to clean, and no hassle. Just discard the used portion pack after brewing.
- *Fast*—Just press a button and in 30 seconds you'll have a fresh cup of hot coffee. The machine is always plugged in and powered on with hot water ready to brew your cup of coffee.

revolved around the speed of brewing a cup of coffee. Of second highest importance was the convenience of no preparation or clean-up. As part of the study, a price point of $149.99 was tested. The 9 percent of respondents who indicated that they "definitely would buy" or "probably would buy" the coffee system at this price were classified as "core customers." These respondents tended to be younger and most were male. Follow-up survey questions revealed that the average price core customers were willing to pay for the coffee system was $125.

For the home use test, a commercial model brewer was placed in the homes of gourmet coffee drinkers. The testers were then required to purchase K-Cups at a retail price of $0.50 via fax, e-mail, or phone for their own individual coffee consumption. Subsequent interviews and focus groups found that users consistently referenced great-tasting coffee with a system that was fast and convenient. Additional attributes of the product highlighted included taste consistency, coffee variety, and cleanliness of preparation. Of particular note was the fact that coffee consumption at home increased with the presence of the Keurig brewer. On average, 2.25 cups of coffee were consumed per day at home. Not only were participants drinking more coffee in the morning, but they were purchasing less coffee outside the home. An acceptable price range for the brewer was determined to be in the $129–$199 range, with a price exceeding $200 triggering a reaction that the item would become a luxury purchase for which more consideration would be required. K-Cup pricing, however, did not appear to be an issue.

At-Home Single-Cup Competition

A key element of Keurig's strategy in the at-home market was being one of the first entrants in the product category. In establishing itself as a pioneer in the upscale single-cup brewing category, Keurig envisioned that subsequent press coverage would naturally include a reference to the Keurig system as a single-cup pioneer and enhance its visibility in the upscale market.

In the traditional consumer coffee market, Procter & Gamble (P&G) and Kraft were the market share leaders with distribution largely through grocery stores (see Exhibit 9 on page 580). In advertising expenditures, the two companies represented 84 percent of total expenditures of $163 million.[10] In the coffee maker appliance market, appliance brands targeted either upscale or mass market retailers. In the upscale segment,

[10]*Packaged Facts Market Profile: The U.S. Coffee and Tea Market,* September 2001.

EXHIBIT 9 Coffee Market Share

Source: *Packaged Facts Market Profile: The U.S. Coffee and Tea Market,* September 2001.

Company	Market Share (%)
Procter & Gamble[a]	36.9
Philip Morris/Kraft	31.8
Nestlé[b]	5.0
Starbucks	3.7
Chock Full o'Nuts[c]	3.1
Tetley[d]	2.1
Community Coffee	1.8
Private Label	7.5
Other	8.1
Total	100.0

[a]Includes sales of Folgers and Millstone ground regular.
[b]Nestlé sold its ground brands to Sara Lee in late 2000.
[c]Chock Full o'Nuts sold to Sara Lee in 2000.
[d]Tetley sold off its coffee brands in 2000.

Cuisinart, Krups, Braun, DeLonghi, and Bunn had strong distribution. In the mass channel, through which about 70 percent of all coffee makers were sold, Mr. Coffee, Black & Decker, Sunbeam, and Hamilton Beach had strong positions.

Market indicators had led Keurig to believe that a number of these large established consumer products companies were preparing to enter the emerging single-cup market. In addition to the growth of the single-cup system in the away-from-home market, recent trends in Europe were showing the adaptation of traditional espresso pod systems for American-style coffee brewing. In each case, including Keurig, the systems were proprietary, with individual brewers working only with compatible coffee pod systems.

Salton, with 2002 sales of $922 million, was a leading domestic designer, marketer, and distributor of a broad range of branded, small appliances. Under its licensed brand name, Melitta, it had formally announced plans for a May 2003 launch of a new brewing system: One:One. The One:One brewer would brew coffee utilizing Javapods, small round packets of filter paper in which the grounds were sealed. Salton's expected retail brewer pricing was $49 with pod pricing of about $0.25 per pod.

Sara Lee, a U.S.-based consumer packaged products company with sales of $17.6 billion in 2002, had been active primarily in the European coffee market, but, through a series of acquisitions completed in 2000, had become a stronger force in the U.S. market. Its two best-known brands were Chock Full o'Nuts and Hills

Brothers. Sara Lee had stated that the Senseo-Crema pod system might be in the U.S. market in the second half of 2003. Previously introduced in Europe, the Senseo Coffee Pod System used coffee pods of a different size than the Salton Javapods. The Sara Lee pods were bulk-packed in a bag made with a very thin layer of aluminum to preserve freshness. Sara Lee had placed almost two million Senseo pod systems in Europe since the product's introduction. The company's experience in the consumer market gave it the potential to be a formidable competitor. Senseo's European pricing suggested a U.S. retail price of about $70 and a pod price of about $0.20 (with two pods required to deliver an 8-ounce serving).

There were also rumors that P&G had partnered with an appliance marketer to launch its own proprietary pod system. It was expected that P&G would focus on mass channel distribution of both its pod brewers and pods, given P&G's strength in the grocery channel. P&G's pricing and distribution were expected to be similar to Salton's and Sara Lee's.

Nespresso, developed by Nestlé, was a European capsule-based single-cup espresso brewing system. It offered similar benefits to the Keurig system including taste, variety, and convenience. Since its introduction in 1987, more than 500,000 units had been sold, largely in Europe, using direct fulfillment via phone, fax, and Internet. Keurig wondered whether Nestlé would decide to enter the American-style single-cup coffee market, based on its experience with single-cup espresso.

Is the Cup Half-Full or Half-Empty?

Keurig did not have the resources to launch its B100 brewing system through the retail channel. However, it felt it could develop a direct marketing approach using an e-commerce-enabled Web site to sell both the brewer and K-Cups in conjunction with leveraging the distribution capabilities of roasters and KADs. In pursuing this strategy, Keurig had encountered a number of channel issues that could jeopardize its established business in the away-from-home OCS market. Chris Stevens explained the challenge of balancing the needs of the OCS channel with the development of the new at-home business:

> Feedback from our KADs indicated that they would interpret our entry into the at-home market with a direct sales approach as a first step towards a direct

approach in the OCS market in the long term. Concern about this would diminish the KADs' marketing efforts in both the OCS and at-home markets, resulting in erosion of our installed base and revenue stream from our core OCS segment and a less effective launch in the at-home market. At the same time, we were worried about loss of pricing control with KADs underpricing Keurig and the roasters because they had no brewer investment to recover. In addition, there was concern that the office managers would not support our at-home marketing efforts for fear of theft of K-Cups for use in the home brewer.

Given these issues, Keurig's goal had been to introduce a controlled distribution of brewers and portion packs that would maximize the launch of the at-home business while protecting the away-from-home OCS channel. Key in this strategy had been the introduction of a second portion pack as the basis for production differentiation—a new Keurig-Cup for the at-home market—and that decision had driven its development efforts to date. The K-Cup would work only in the commercial brewer, while the Keurig-Cup worked only in the at-home brewer (see Exhibit 10). Further distinction was made with the color of the two portion packs: the K-Cups were white while the Keurig-Cups were tan. These two portion packs would be manufactured on the same packaging lines. Design of the necessary tooling to thermoform the new cup bases had been completed at a cost of about $400,000. In addition, new parts for the packaging lines at licensed roasters had been manufactured by Keurig at a cost of just under $60,000 per packaging

line to enable the lines to manufacture both the Keurig-Cups and the K-Cups. While the new B100 brewer was targeted for both lower-volume OCS customers and for at-home use, different cup holder inserts and different color drawers would differentiate the brewer products in the two markets.

Building off this product differentiation, Keurig's controlled distribution strategy allowed roasters to sell Keurig-Cups in direct and indirect markets and KADS to sell them in direct markets, assuming certain volume commitments were met on sales of the associated brewer. KAD brewer volume commitments ensured that parties selling Keurig-Cups would be equally vested in brewer sales and focused on marketing an entire system. Roasters would manufacture Keurig-Cups for Keurig to resell directly to at-home users over the Internet. In addition to providing necessary assurances to KADs about Keurig's future plans, the two-portion-pack strategy eliminated office manager concerns over the potential theft of portion packs for use in home brewers, increasing the likelihood of their participation in in-office promotions of the Keurig system.

Unfortunately, the plan had reached a roadblock at that afternoon's meeting with GMCR. Lazaris later summed up GMCR's concerns to the senior management team in an e-mail, "We reviewed the controlled distribution structure with GMCR's management team. GMCR responded that it was complicated and resulted in doubling the number of portion pack products they would have to manufacture and warehouse. There could also

EXHIBIT 10
K-Cup (left) and Proposed Home Keurig-Cup (right)

Source: Keurig, Inc.

Note: Cups are shown upside down to illustrate difference in design.

be the potential for customer dissatisfaction resulting from using a portion pack in the wrong brewer. GMCR preferred the one-cup model based on long-term simplicity and the desire to move quickly because of the competitive systems coming to market. Clearly, GMCR has the same interests we do—it has the largest share of the OCS K-Cup business and can't afford to alienate the channel. It has an ownership interest in Keurig and wants to see long-term value creation. But going back to the board to discuss a major change at this point will not be easy."

At-Home Product Pricing

Another issue being wrestled with by the senior management team in early 2003 was determination of the pricing strategy for the Keurig-Cup and B100 brewer for the at-home market. A decision on the one-cup vs. two-cup approach challenged by GMCR would have a direct impact on Keurig's portion pack pricing strategy. One benefit of the controlled distribution strategy utilizing two distinct portion packs was increased control of the pricing, specifically for the Keurig-Cup. "We were interested in using a direct sales model for the at-home market," explained John Whoriskey. "With the Keurig-Cup, we could set pricing for the consumer market without having to worry about erosion of our established revenue base in the OCS market." Without the product distinction, office managers would have the opportunity to purchase portion packs from their current KAD or directly from the Keurig Web site, potentially drawing away sales from the KADs and jeopardizing their relationships with their accounts. Regardless of the one-cup vs. two-cup approach, Keurig needed to set a price for its direct sales of coffee.

Equally challenging was the pricing of the B100 brewer. Early market research suggested that consumers paid greater attention to the pricing of the brewer and it would have a direct impact on their decision to invest in the Keurig system. In price testing, upscale consumers appeared to react favorably to pricing in the $149 to $170 range, providing Keurig with the target price for its product development and business plan forecasts. With an estimated launch of September 2003, Keurig had forecasted at-home brewer shipments of about 20,000 through year-end. Just under two-thirds of those sales were expected to be through direct Keurig sales activities, with the remainder being driven by roasters and KADs either selling B100s to at-home consumers or driving leads to Keurig by referring

potential customers to the Keurig Web site. Additionally, Keurig expected KADs to buy about 3,000 B100 brewers for placement in small offices in the OCS channel. Keurig-Cup and K-Cup sales were expected to follow the same at-home/away-from-home distribution split as the brewers.

Yet another issue was the manufacturing costs of the new brewer. Development efforts on the at-home brewer were put on hold in 2002 to speed development of a smaller commercial brewer called the B1000 that was launched in December 2002. Under the leadership of Engineering Development Vice-President Dick Sweeney, development of the new B100 at-home brewer was restarted after the B1000 brewer was launched. While the B100 could also be used in offices, it was targeted at the at-home consumer market. The B1000 brewer had costs greater than $300 and some significant design issues. Sweeney explained, "Product development always has the dark cloud of unexpected consequences. What distinguishes a company is how it resolves issues and moves on. In this case, our experiences with the B1000 brewer provided valuable insight into the development of the B100 at-home brewer." Even so, the latest reports from the manufacturing partner had projected costs at $220. Additional engineering efforts were focused on reducing those costs to $200.

As a result, Keurig's senior management team and board of directors were struggling with the pricing of the B100. The three key price points being reviewed were $199, $249, and $299. The company could simply not afford to sell at the desired $149 price point and it was too late to redesign the brewer for lower costs. At $299, there would be a small profit margin to apply toward marketing and infrastructure costs. At $199, there would be a large immediate loss on brewer sales, but marketing research had shown the $199 price to be more attractive than $200 or more. While Keurig's business model allowed the recovery of losses on the brewer through the royalties on K-Cups, the degree of losses impacted cash. Lazaris wondered, "If we price high, we can always lower the price, but we may not have the time to correct the pricing, given competitive pressures."

Marketing Plan for At-Home Launch

Unlike the OCS market, the at-home market did not include a single source for both brewer and coffee sales. Traditionally, consumers made separate purchases. Brewer distribution was through small appliance retailers like department stores, mass merchants, and kitchen specialty stores, while coffee distribution was through grocery stores, gourmet food retailers, and coffee shops. Each product was promoted independently and essentially all brewers worked with all coffees. The Keurig brewer and its patented single-portion pack presented unique distribution challenges. To accomplish a Keurig system sale would require either direct distribution or a great deal of investment to develop traditional channels and to place enough brewers to pull portion packs through retail shelves. To complicate matters, market research had made it clear that the Keurig system was a "demonstration-driven product." The question was how best to demonstrate the system to the target market of gourmet coffee drinkers.

"Based on the market research and the unique challenges of the Keurig system, leveraging our current OCS penetration was a primary focus of our at-home launch strategy. We planned to target Keurig office users, people already familiar with the benefits of the Keurig system, and convert them to at-home buyers in order to build critical mass to support channel expansion," explained VP of away-from-home marketing Dave Manly. With more than 30,000 commercial brewers in place, Keurig had about one million people to focus on in its direct marketing efforts.

Critical to the success of direct marketing efforts to "Keurig-aware" coffee drinkers was the support and involvement of the Keurig authorized distributors. The KADs maintained relationships with office managers where commercial brewers were placed and had knowledge of each office's size. Keurig would not be able to market to coffee drinkers in the offices without the KADs' assistance. As a result, Keurig had designed a KAD referral program that gave them attractive incentives to support the marketing of the new brewer.

The KAD referral program was to be driven by point-of-sale (POS) advertising that had been developed for display on or near the office brewer (see Exhibit 11). In exchange for placement of the POS materials, the KAD would be compensated $15 for each home brewer sale attributed to that KAD's OCS accounts and would be paid a two-cent-per-K-Cup (or Keurig-Cup) annuity on subsequent coffee sales that Keurig made to that customer for three years. Chris Stevens outlined the company's expectations: "We anticipated that about 60 percent of our KADs would participate in our joint marketing program with sales of two brewers for each office where advertising was

EXHIBIT 11
Point-of-Sale Display

Source: Keurig, Inc.

placed. We estimated that the remaining 40 percent would already be planning their own marketing program and would want to maintain more control of their customers."

A second avenue for marketing to "Keurig-awares" would be via an Internet direct marketing campaign. Since the launch of the commercial brewer in the OCS market, Keurig had received unsolicited e-mails from more than 12,000 users of its office system who wanted to know when a similar system would be available for home use. Keurig planned to market to these people directly and expected 20 percent of them to purchase a home brewer in the first three months of the launch. Finally, a public relations campaign coupled with additional marketing activities by roasters such as placement in their retail stores, catalogs, and Web sites would provide additional avenues for sales to gourmet coffee drinkers.

Lazaris's Dilemmas

As Lazaris reflected on Keurig's strategy for the launch of its at-home brewer in preparation for the senior management meeting, he wondered:

1. How should we respond to GMCR's request to switch to the single K-Cup approach? What do we really need to know to make this decision? How will our

other roasters and the KADS respond? Can our team really implement a new game plan at this late date and still launch in six months? Can we afford the write-off on the new Keurig-Cup and packaging line tooling?

2. What is the right price for the brewer? Is there a way to afford a $149 price point on the brewer that we have not thought of?

3. How should we price the at-home portion pack? If we have one cup in all markets, what pricing is optimal? If we have both the K-Cup and the Keurig-Cup, what pricing makes sense and optimizes our market opportunity?

4. Have we taken the necessary steps for our marketing plan to succeed? Is there another avenue that we are overlooking?

Case 6-8

Dura-plast, Inc.

Tom Parker, CEO of Dura-plast-Americas, Inc (DP-A), directs the U.S. subsidiary of a profitable international equipment manufacturer, Kovner DP International (DP International). He is responsible for directing DP-A's long-term growth and welfare, as well as meeting annual sales and profitability targets. As the head of the manufacturer's largest subsidiary, Parker also has been given the task of developing and implementing sales and marketing strategies that will support the entire Dura-plast group's profitability.

It is now January, 1995, and Mr. Parker is sitting in his office at DP-A's Flint, Michigan headquarters. He is thinking about the efforts his company made and the difficulties it encountered in presenting a successful sales contract to provide Techno Plastics, Inc. with Dura-plast granulator equipment. Techno Plastics, based in France, is a major international plastics producer which had decided to build a plant in the southeastern part of the United States. The sales process was complicated by the need for coordination across DP-A's different country-based subsidiaries and because Techno Plastics was a new customer for DP-A. Parker was pleased to receive reassurance from Techno Plastics that his bid would be successful, but, realizing that more and more plastics manufacturers are setting up global manufacturing operations, Parker wondered if changes were needed to better serve global accounts.

Granulation Equipment

DP-A and its parent company are in the business of designing, manufacturing, assembling, and selling plastics granulators. A plastics granulator is used to chop plastics waste (bad parts and production rejects) into small granules for closed-loop recycling. Granulators are most commonly used in industrial shops, where excess scrap is fed into the granulator hopper for conversion through rotating knives. The small uniform bits of processing scrap and bad parts which emerge from the granulator, called the "regrind," can then be recycled.

Granulators are specified by their infeed or throat size, throughput and weight, and by the composition and chemical makeup of the plastic waste they can process within an hour. Each is fitted with an infeed hopper designed to handle various plastics dimensions. Granulators positioned next to the plastic manufacturing machine to reclaim plastic scraps immediately are known as beside-the-press (B-T-P) granulators. Other types of granulators are placed in a central location (Central) in the plant and scraps are delivered to them manually or by conveyor or sold as smaller, stand alone (Automated) units.

The granulators sold range widely in price, feature, and quality/performance tradeoffs. Because granulators can be tailored to the specific production process of the customer, both the analysis and identification of customer requirements and customization costs are figured into the price of the product.

Thorton Group and Kovner DP International

DP-A is a wholly-owned subsidiary of the Norwegian Thorton Group member, DP International. The group consists of a number of medium-sized engineering companies in the producer-goods industry, each with

EXHIBIT 1 **Organizational Structure**

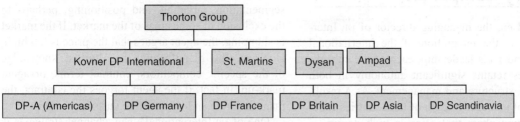

the developing medium-sized industrial companies in a particular specialty area. The Thorton Group continues to grow through expanded sales and company acquisitions. Its operational structure and tactics support the growth of individual companies operating as important market makers in focused geographic areas. While most subsidiaries hold prominent positions near their customer bases, Thorton Company Headquarters have traditionally been placed close to their representative Norwegian manufacturing plants. Thorton and DP International specifics are provided in Exhibit 1 (Organizational Structure).

DP International follows a typical Thorton company organizational system: it develops and produces its granulation equipment in Norway and conducts sales through its international subsidiaries, thereby manufacturing globally with local market support. DP International invoiced sales totaling $233 and $326 million in 1992 and 1993 with respective earnings of $11 and $47 million. The parent company had a return on capital of over 35% during this period. In 1994, approximately 2700 units were sold in Europe, 2050 in America, and 500 in Asia. There has been substantial improvement in earnings as a result of the strong volume growth. However, DP International, with its high level of sales abroad, has also benefited from a weaker Norwegian krone rate.[1]

DP International's low-noise granulators have primarily been used for granulating plastic waste in connection with the automated manufacture of plastic products. A proprietary design offers technical superiority which has allowed the company to establish a strong global market presence. Its unique, patented reversible knife design is currently produced only in Norway.

In addition to supplying all the cutting chambers to its international subsidiaries, DP International sells

a large number of complete machines because of the complexity of the electrical and drive systems. However, because products qualifying as locally made have lower costs due to lower import duties, DP International established an assembly and manufacturing plant in the US and an assembly plant in Germany. These run as autonomous P&L locations, typically assembling, customizing and adding local content to the larger granulators that are sourced from Norway for sale throughout the Americas and Europe. The small to medium-sized machines currently do not qualify as US products under NAFTA content requirements, and as such are not free from import duties.

DP International is planning further decentralization of its manufacturing operations with the establishment of a cutting chamber production facility in the US. This move will lower transportation costs, which currently add 6% or more to the final sale price of DP International units. In addition, it would enable the company to meet in-country product requirements, lessen the risk of international currency fluctuations, and lower tax and tariff duties.

DP International has responded to the cost of maintaining large product lines by developing flexibility in the manufacturing cycle. Increasingly, DP International has been able to customize its products to meet customer requirements, an important factor in DP International's low cost, high volume strategy. In fact, during 1992, DP International successfully launched a new product generation based on a modular product system, which brought about a strong volume increase in 1993. In 1994, the US subsidiary, DP-A, developed a US hopper welding cell which allowed for additional, in-house customization of the larger machines.

In order to handle market demand changes and increasing sales, DP International expanded its plant capacity in Norway this past year. When at full capacity, the new plant will allow the organization to expand sales from 5,000 to 7,000 with a substantial increase in its large-capacity machine production facilities.

---

[1]The unit of currency is the Norwegian krone, which is abbreviated NOK. NOK 1 = 100 ore. Note that all figures are in U.S. dollars unless otherwise noted. The assumed exchange rate is 7.00 NOK to $1 U.S.

Subsidiary Companies

Torger Erlandsen, the managing director of DP International, directs the integration of the international operations. Under his leadership, each of the subsidiary companies retains significant autonomy in both organizational structure and management. As a result, the operational manager in each of the countries functions in an atmosphere that offers a high degree of entrepreneurial freedom. Country managers make their own decisions with respect to sales strategy, pricing, and promotion. Erlandsen believes that granting this leadership independence is the most effective way to maximize the opportunities within the granulation equipment sales' niche marketplace.

While each of the subsidiary companies reports to the Norwegian headquarters, the subsidiary organizations do not have formal ties with each other. In a growing number of cases, however, an order may be generated from an area outside of a subsidiary's direct responsibility; the individual subsidiaries then have the responsibility to coordinate efforts which take into account specification development and business practice initiatives suitable to that business environment and culture. Final responsibility, however, and authority in decision making is given to the local subsidiary.

However, because of the interrelated nature between international marketing and manufacturing, there have been increasing problems regarding contract specification and pricing issues internationally. Some members of the DP International group, for instance, have begun to wonder if it might be a good idea to set a standard price internationally. With respect to sales strategy, some agree with the DP-A Vice President for Sales, Richard Foster, who argues that confusion in the sales cycle could be limited if the criteria for involvement in the sales relationship were more narrowly defined. His suggestion is for "involvement only when a person can enhance the sales relationship." Others suggest greater or lesser involvement across countries.

Traditionally, most countries have employed agents[2] to sell and distribute granulators. Agents buy the Dura-plast granulators and then sell them to their own customer base, setting their own price levels. Prices in some cases are higher than DP International has wanted. In this set-up, the agent decides how he wants to sell in the market, and determines his own segmentation, targeting, and positioning, perhaps to the exclusion of some areas of the market. If the market is slumping, the agent argues that the price is too high. However, the manufacturer has limited knowledge of the specific competitors, contract terms, or agent mark-up. In fact, if the agent forgoes the contract, the manufacturer can lose an entire customer base.

One of DP International's new channel strategies is its transition to Manufacturer's Representative (MR)[3] relationships in each of the DP International offices worldwide—thus standardizing part of its selling strategy. This strategy focuses on generating sales through MRS contracts instead of through sales agents. One of the primary benefits of this strategy is to help DP International to protect its current and long-term market position by getting closer to the customer. It is important for DP International to understand where its machines are being sold and to develop brand name loyalty in the market. The global program to take control of the customer has helped to clarify pricing and stabilize production. If the market is slumping, DP International's regional sales managers will be able to intensify the sales efforts or make strategic decisions, such as price reductions.

Each of DP International's subsidiaries handles the MR and other selling issues differently. The following sections provide more detail about DP International's subsidiaries in Germany, France, Britain and North America.

DP Germany (DPG)

Germany is a large market that is treated as an individual unit in DP International's international planning exercises. Germany's solo status and competitive advantage stems from its market size, homogeneity, and the location of a manufacturing plant which supplies the rest of Europe. The German market is almost as large as the US market with respect to the total number of customers.

German companies typically bid on a packaged basis. Each offer generally includes pricing and terms regarding auxiliary equipment, start-up and installation, plans,

---

[2]Agents are generally businesses that contract with original equipment manufacturers to sell their products for a given period of time. Agents take ownership of the products and usually have protected territories.

[3]Manufacturing Representatives have been employed by many original equipment manufacturers because of their knowledge and ties within a particular industry. Manufacturer's Representatives represent multiple, noncompeting manufacturers, and are generally granted exclusive territories. They represent the supplier, but are not usually involved in distribution or installation. MRS do not take possession or ownership of equipment—they only operate as agents on behalf of (usually) multiple principals (i.e., manufacturers).

and long-term spare part commitments. Each part of the bid package is important to contract acquisition.

Germany recently changed its sales organization structure by shifting from an agent driven salesforce to one which includes both agents and MRs. Under the direction of a DPG sales manager who controls a group of sales reps and one agent, the country has been divided into territories where representatives are given regional exclusivity. In addition to managing the salesforce, the sales manager develops relationships and bids for larger granulation systems, calling on original equipment manufacturers (OEMS) and the largest potential purchasers.

DP France (DPF)

In France, as with the rest of Europe, sales cycles have traditionally been much longer than those in the US. The time from initial inquiry for granulation equipment to delivery averages 12–18 months. As a result, manufacturers and their customers have a longer time to plan and delineate product quote and specifications. Tom Parker suggests that "the introduction of MRs has allowed DP France to manage its customer base more closely." Consequently, DP France has developed sales relationships with several larger firms that have plants throughout France and worldwide. France is currently the smallest DP International European subsidiary. French customers typically expect bids to be presented in the same manner that German customers do—including all details on service, spare parts and support.

DP Britain (DP-UK)

The DP International office in Britain still uses an agent system to promote and sell its products. The agent system works because it is a generally accepted practice in the market and because of the limited interaction required in the sales process. Unlike the rest of Europe, distributors in Britain do not have to delineate each of the engineering and sales support requirements in the sales contract. DP-UK is a mid-sized DP International European subsidiary.

DP-Americas (DP-A)

DP-A, the biggest company in the DP International Group, faces the challenge of marketing within the quick cycle, volatile US, Canadian, and Mexican marketplaces. Strong in the US and Canada, DP-A has not made significant inroads into the Mexican, Latin American or South American markets as yet, principally because of practically non-existent safety standards,

which allow competitors in these developing countries to build machines at a significantly lower cost.

DP-A's operations are led by a board of directors, consisting of Torger Erlandsen, a Norway-based manufacturing expert, and DP-A CEO Tom Parker. While Parker is responsible for day-to-day management of the DP-A activities, major decisions are approved by the board of directors. The board of directors currently meets on a quarterly basis with additional meetings as needed.

DP-A's domestic staff are split into three operational groups. The operations group manages the assembly and small-scale manufacturing operations in Flint, Michigan and a larger manufacturing plant just outside Knoxville, Tennessee, which will come on line in 1998. The Administration and Planning fuctions, as well as the Sales functions, are centralized in Flint.

The US bidding system is unlike Europe's. In addition to the faster selling cycle (the time from initial inquiry to final sale lasts between 2–8 months), US customers do not require the same amount of specificity and long-term price guarantees as those in Europe. DP-A, for instance, typically bids systems without the inclusion of auxiliary equipment and start-up costs. Start-up tends to be handled in-house and auxiliary equipment purchases are placed as needed. Most equipment installations are designed to be self-service— usually handled easily by in-plant engineers. DP-A does not bid for long-term spare part commitments or with detailed plant location specs either. Primarily because the market does not expect it, but also because the North American market is much more price-driven, bidding is more narrowly focused than in Europe.

DP-A's sales structure primarily relies on a network of Manufacturers Representatives. Each of DP-A's sales managers directs 4–5 MRs, spread out on a regional basis. Sales managers have responsibility for noncontiguous regions, such as a territory covering California, Canada, New England, and Texas. Richard Foster notes that noncontiguous sales areas give DP-A the ability to determine whether sales performance is a result of regional economic downturns or lackluster performance. Rising airline costs may cause DP-A to review this policy.

Currently, DP-A has exclusive, non-compete contracts with 25 MR groups, which in turn employ over 100 sales representatives. The DP-A MRs are located throughout the United States, Canada, and Mexico. MRs are the dominant distribution channel in the granulation industry because of their ability to cross-sell to the customer. A typical MR represents injection molding, blow molding, extrusion molding, vacuum systems for moving plastic, and drying systems equipment to the companies he or she visits. As such, representatives are a one-stop shop for a company's comprehensive plastic production equipment requirements.

The use of MRS allows DP-A to increase coverage while keeping full-time personnel to a minimum. MRS are not always the only contact with the end-user; however, their expertise and relationship with the buyers, built through the cross-sale of different types of plant equipment provides an effective and efficient sales strategy. MRS do not sell to all DP-A accounts. Larger sales are handled by DP-A's own marketing managers on the basis of leads generated from MRS and DP-A's direct advertising. If a lead generated by an MR generates a sale, the MR still receives the standard commission.

The best MRS generally carry the most effective and best known products because of their ability to close deals with a large group of well-established principals. MR groups have between 2–10 salespeople and close total sales in the range of 1 to 15 million dollars annually. Commissions on machines sales are generally 12% for mid-sized machines, 6% for the large-size machines, and 14% for machines under $ 10,000. If the MR and/or DP-A negotiated price discounts, these are generally split between the MR and DP-A.

MRS do not direct the installation or provide service for DP-A. Installation is not a critical sales factor for the smaller machines, because the machines arrive assembled and ready to run. For the larger central system machines, DP-A typically sends a service technician to the installation sight to check wiring and set-up specifications before the machine is first used. Service is directed from DP-A's central headquarters in Flint, Michigan.

Of DP-A sales, approximately 90% of all machines sold are used for new applications and 10% to replace outdated equipment. DP-A sales managers and MRS sell to a wide variety of individuals and companies on both a transactional and collaborative basis. DP-A classifies its current customers into the following categories.

- **Transactional accounts,** where customers purchase with both price and features in mind. In general, there are no long-term relationship or purchase commitments. Machines sold to these customers generally sell for under $10,000.

- **System accounts** are developed when MRS work with customers to define needs and establish fit.

Granulators sold to customers in this category generally sell for between $10,000 and $50,000. While the service aspect of the sale provides ground for an ongoing relationship, there are no long-term purchase commitments.

- **Key accounts** represent the top 15% of DP-A sales and include large unit volume and annual dollar sales. The DP-A employee acts as a consultant in this relationship; more technologically proficient DP-A managers discuss the company's long-term plans and project goals. Currently, there are no formal long-term purchase commitments. Machines sold to these customers often cost more than $50,000.

Customers

The plastics industry uses two types of materials—thermoplastics and thermosets—in combination with stabilizers, colorants, flame retardants, and reinforcing agents in the plastic production process. These are then shaped or molded under heat and pressure to a solid state. Thermoplastics can be re-softened to their original condition by heat; however, thermosets cannot. Thermoplastics account for almost 90% of total plastic production and nearly 100% of granulation activity.

In general, thermoplastics output takes the form of pellets, flakes, granules, powders, liquid resins, sheeting, pipe, profile, parts, or film. It can be divided into four production categories:

Type	Examples	% Total Industry
Injection molding	Automobile parts, pudding cups	50
Blow molding	Soda and milk bottles	12
Extrusion	Trash bags, plastic pipes	30
Reclaim	Post consumer recycling	7

DP International sells the largest number of its granulators to injection molding companies. Nonetheless, it generates its highest level of profit from equipment utilizing extrusion processing, because the machines in this production category are significantly larger and more complex.

Large injection molding companies include Ford, Chrysler, and GM, as well as consumer product producers such as Black and Decker. Injection molding is a versatile and quick production process, and companies relying upon it have recently taken advantage of improvements in technology to expand productivity. In 1992 and 1993, this segment's plastic purchases grew by more than 11%.

Blow molding has shown high growth in the last few years because its resulting products are less expensive and easier to design. As new technology makes blow molding more profitable, blow molding firms, which include Coke, Pepsi, Tupperware, and Rubbermaid, have continued to expand their operations.

Extrusion is a popular method of producing large quantities of both uniform and dissimilar material that can be packaged into small units and distributed easily. The demand for plastics used in extrusion grew by over 12% for both 1992 and 1993. Future projections are not so rosy; growth in some segments of the extrusion industry which are expected to drop to less than 1% in 1995, and to contract by 4.4% in 1996, due to excess capacity.

Granulator Sales

DP-A offers approximately 30 different models in four primary product groups and one secondary product group through a strategic alliance with an original equipment manufacturer (OEM). The automation product group focuses on small, automated granulators for the injection molding market segment; the B-T-P product group is geared toward mid-size granulators for the injection molding/blow molding market; the central product group concentrates mostly in central reclamation in the extrusion market, while the parts/auxiliary/service product group is directed toward all customers.

The manufacturing process for DP-A equipment is a flexible multi-step process because of the unique design needs of individual clients. Compact machines generally require less customization. These machines come with DP-A's positive feed and rotating knife systems. Specifically, the design in the cutting chamber ensures positive feed of bulky materials and high throughputs. The reversible rotating knives allow the clearance between the cutting edges of the rotating and bed knives and the screen to remain constant. Both contribute to improved efficiency by reducing energy consumption and averting heat buildup.

The heavy-duty models include the positive feed and reversible rotating knife systems, as well as engineering systems capability and special hopper availability. Specialists in the engineering department are able to design a system to fit particular production requirements.

As Tom Parker remarked, "the machines are generic but the applications are specific." Some applications require specially designed hoppers for maximum throughput and increased productivity. Energy efficiency remains a common concern in the design and purchase of both heavy-duty or compact machines.

In recent years, large global purchasers are increasingly seeking suppliers which can provide international turn-key solutions and services as opposed to sourcing from multiple suppliers for products and services. Using a single global supplier enhances negotiating power, standardizes spare parts, and allows the customer to build a closer relationship with one supplier. Global customers are asking granulator manufacturers to solve scrap recycling problems rather than simply sell them machines. This move is partly a result of the reduction in engineers at plastic manufacturer's production facilities. One customer commented that his firm wanted to focus its efforts on manufacturing, not on developing an expertise in recycling systems.

The trend is especially prevalent among European multinational firms, which traditionally have expected a high degree of supplier technical support. Additionally, rather than hiring technical expertise, purchasers are now contracting with companies which provide a centralized rather than local engineering focus.

A recent survey of DP-A customers and MRs found that they most value product performance, features, and the ability to customize the application. When asked to determine the most important attribute in the purchase decision, 41.7% of the customers chose quality/overall performance. In contrast, price was the most frequent response given by the MRs (31.4%). DP-A customers seem to view price as more of an order qualifier rather than an order winner. (Exhibit 2 provides a price/attribute comparison of DP-A customers and manufacturer representatives.)

DP-A's most recent value-added solutions include its efforts within the injection molding, blow molding and film extrusion market segments of the plastic industry. Specialized niche development includes reclaim for scrap plastic, robot-fed injection molding, hot melt resin reclamation, edge trim film/sheet, post consumer waste bottle, vinyl siding and central thermoform scrap market segments. The niche markets are highly customized and provide high gross profits with limited competition. In support of these markets, DP-A engineers have worked with the market managers to further develop product engineered systems to meet their customer's

EXHIBIT 2   Attribute Weighting

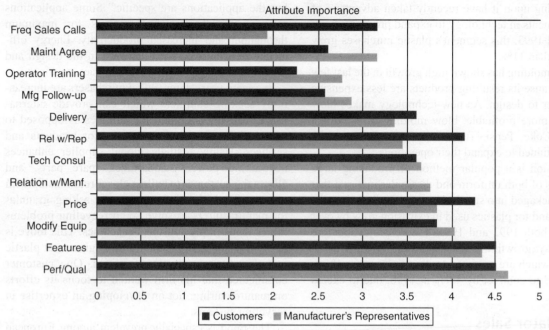

Attribute Importance

Key: 1 = "Not very important to the customer when making purchase decision"
5 = "Extremely important to the customer when making purchase decision"

application needs. Identification of these opportunities, however, continues to be a challenge.

DP-A's product portfolio overview provides information on each of the company's three major product groupings, the Automated, B-T-P, and Central. Individual components which are critical to application success and compliance include cutting chamber size, horsepower, rate screen, rotor configuration, RPM, and product features such as the tilt-back hopper and clam-shell screen cradle. Companies also have the choice of specialized features such as low infeed heights, over-sized bearings, integral soundproofing, auger in feed, and conveyor infeed.

DP International is one of the largest producers of granulators worldwide and within the United States, DP-A has grown to be the largest supplier in unit volume of granulation equipment. Serving the entire range of companies in the plastic reclamation process, DP-A's installed customer account base includes over 6000 locations across the United States.

Part of this growth comes from the addition of a new OEM client to the DP-A portfolio. DP-A's strategic alliance with Fields (Powerflow) enables it to purchase and distribute up to 500 B-T-P units a year at a percentage discount. These units are sold under Powerflow's

nameplate. DP-A is also considering the expansion of its OEM relationships to other major plastics manufacturers. Both partners benefit through these expanded relationships: DP International can increase market share and the OEMs can service their key accounts with a high quality product.

The key factors in DP-A's 1995 $21 million sales effort include the introduction of new machines, expanded service relationships, and enhanced marketing efforts, combined with further expansion of the OEM alliance with Powerflow.

For Tom Parker, DP-A volume leadership is "not a reason to be complacent." In addition to the company's drive for customer satisfaction and total quality management in the early 1990's, DP-A must now address issues related to account management and market change. Many of DP-A's larger machine segment clients now conduct business on both a domestic and international basis. Sales efforts have required significant synchronization of efforts between subsidiaries. In addition, under the goal of expanding profitability, management is working to raise the dollar volume on individual sales. Focusing on the mid- to large-size machine sales efforts has resulted in a mixed response from the salesforce. The numbers, however, continue to

EXHIBIT 3

Dura-plast, Inc.*	1993	1994
Cross Profit	$5,067,029	$6,995,259
Operating Income	$ 294,289	$1,697,332
Net Income	$ 167,055	$ 959,810

*Dura-plast, Inc. Income Statement as of December 31, 1994 and 1993.

grow, with DP-A projecting dollar bookings of 45% of the US market in 1995.

In the last year, DP-A has posted record profits, with an average profit margin of 9% per sale. Gross profit, operating income, and net income information for 1993 and 1994 are presented in Exhibit 3.

Competition

DP-A was one of 15 competitors in the US Market which contributed to the 4500 granulators orders received overall in 1989 totaling $32.7 million and 7000 granulators in 1994 totaling $120 million.

Although DP-A is the newest competitor in the US granulator sales marketplace, it is currently the leader in volume sales, primarily through the OEM relationship with Powerflow. Before the linkage, it was number three in the market, driven by a strong sales push.

DP-A's price position in relation to that of its competitors may hamper unit sales in some market segments. Some of its competitors are large conglomerates which often use granulators as loss-leaders in negotiations to close higher dollar, turn-key system orders. DP-A has traditionally had a poor record in acquiring these orders, which are generally multi-unit contracts.

DP-A credits its success in the market to outperforming competitors by delivering the highest standard of customer service. While it has created the perception of technical design superiority through marketing proprietary concepts such as the "constant flow

methodology," DP-A has traditionally viewed itself as the underdog. The company continues to resist complacency: one corporate motto states "we must provide better service than our competitors; as such, our customers are right 98% of the time."

The market leader in dollars sold is the Northway Corporation, which is owned by the Abrahams Group, a division of the German conglomerate Ludwig-Crow. It averages 35% gross margins on granulators, 60% on parts/knives, and 35% on pelletizers. Its profits last year averaged around 10%–14%.

Northway has a product management organizational structure with a vice president of Marketing and a product manager for its B-T-P/Automation, Central/Systems and Pelletizing product groups. Each product manager has an application engineer and clerical support. The company has a vice president of Sales who manages its regional sales managers, parts department and service department. The marketing group prepares their sales quotes and supports the sales group with marketing intelligence and new products. Northway recently acquired a manufacturer of screen changes and pelletizing which seems, at least in the short run, to have negatively affected the company's ability to support its granulator sales. Northway has, however, been able to use its multi-product sales to continue as a dominant force in the Central and System markets.

Northway distribution efforts have been shifted from a 20-man direct salesforce to 2 regional sales managers and 18 manufacturer representative agencies. Perhaps the two regional sales managers currently cannot provide the level of service necessary to meet customer retention requests; at any rate Northway now has the reputation of being hard to deal with and increasingly non-responsive.

Northway historically has had a wider range of products, as compared to DP-A, because of its ability to offer 20 machines in a market where DP-A has

EXHIBIT 4

	1989				1994			
Competitor	Units	Unit %	Dollars	$ %	Units	Unit %	Dollars	$ %
Northway	1200	26	$18 Million	28	1400	20	$33.5 Million	28
Grindall	150	33	16 Million	25	1650	23	27.5 Million	23
DP-A	650	14	8.5 Million	13	2050	28	30 Million	25
Fields (Powerflow)	450	10	6 Million	9	700	10	12 Million	10
Smith & Smith	400	8	5 Million	8	600	9	10 Million	8

3–4. Consequently DP-A has had to price aggressively to remain competitive, especially on granulator sales that fall into a DP-A market gap. There are times, for example, when customers want machines specified for power requirements and size that lie in between DP-A's offerings. In order to get the sale, DP-A has to bid its larger machine.

Northway currently is not advertising aggressively. In the past, however, it led the market in advertising dollars spent. The parent company, the Abrahams Group, has a cooperative advertising strategy which promotes a comprehensive turn-key organization. This reputation supplements Northway's exceptional brand awareness and solid reputation. Northway also runs a direct mail program to targeted acquisition and retention customers on a quarterly basis.

DP-A, however, is the leading advertiser in the North American market. It runs full-page color and ¼-page black and white ads in five major publications. It also attends 5–7 trade shows per year in order to exhibit its new products. DP-A has invested heavily in high-tech contemporary literature to complement its quotations.

Techno Plastics Request for Proposals

Techno Plastics, located outside of Paris, is a multinational blow molding company that specializes in the production of hardened plastic fuel tank systems for automobiles. Part of its expansion plan includes the development plan, namely, to be the largest producer of fuel tanks globally. To meet its goals, the company decided to open a new fuel tank plant in the US.

DP International has developed a strong relationship with Techno Plastics over the past 12 years and is currently servicing Techno Plastics manufacturing plants in Germany, UK, and France. Despite this relationship, Techno Plastics submitted a request for proposals (RFP) to each of the major granulator producers as part of a plan to supply the plant it was building in Lawrenceville, Georgia. What follows is a summary and timeline of events related to the RFP, which originated in France. (Exhibit 5 provides an overview of organization teams within the DP International and Techno Plastics organizations.)

August 1994

DP International's US subsidiary submitted its first quote for Techno Plastics' Georgia granulator services in August of 1994. US executives visiting Europe on a planning trip were introduced to Techno Plastics personnel at a plastics convention. The local French contact for Techno Plastics, Jean Handel, a DP France sales manager, facilitated the introduction. In private, he explained Techno Plastics' strategic importance to DP International, in part due to its annual purchases of $1,000,000 in new equipment, parts and service.

At the plastics convention, the US team members demonstrated several of DP International's latest machines to Techno Plastics and began initial strategy discussions for the upcoming RFP response. Over the next few weeks, Jean Handel followed up with information regarding the US plant's specifications and also provided recommendations with respect to pricing.

With Handel's information, the DP-A bid was developed to mirror the specifications of Techno Plastics' German Plant, currently supplied by DP-G, with slightly higher pricing than the typical US bid. These specifications included a cooling device for regrind and a conveyer system, but did not include self-cleaning capabilities because these were not currently in place at the newest Techno Plastics plant in Germany.

DP-A proposed to provide a "system to meet Techno Plastics specifications," a standard practice for US bidding. Typical of DP-A's bids to its US customers, the bid not provide specifics regarding each piece of individual equipment, formalized engineering drawings, or spare part commitments.

In addition to the bid, the US sales executives traveled to the Lawrenceville plant to meet with Michel Duval, the plant manager. Scott Millar, DP-A Regional Manager, and Richard Foster presented a sales proposal to Duval and other Techno Plastics staff. Both the presentation and bid were well received.

September 1994

At another plastics convention in Paris in late September, US and European staff met in France for a second time with Stefan Sevan, the Techno Plastics engineer responsible for the Lawrenceville, Georgia plant and Technical Director for Techno Plastics' Blow Molding Division. During this meeting, Sevan and his colleague Bill Dubois were led by Jean Handel in a discussion of the technical specification requirements for the new plant. On the basis of that discussion a new DP International product was offered to the Techno Plastics engineers. At the end of the meeting, Sevan requested that DP-A re-submit its quote for equipment and services, based on the new DP International machine and specification modifications.

EXHIBIT 5   Organizational Structures

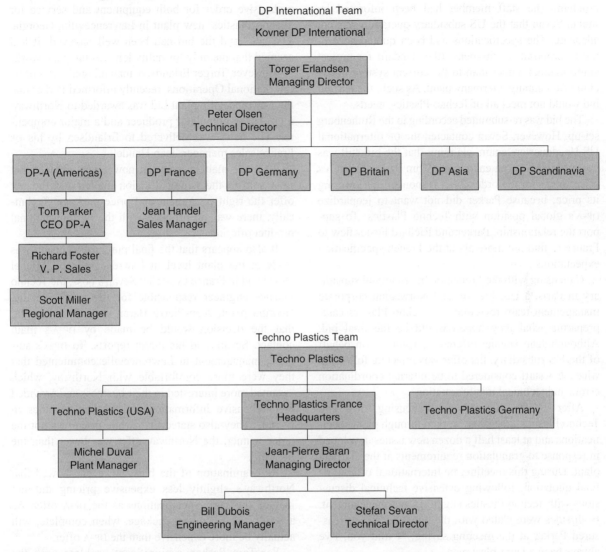

The need for outside vendor support for the new offering and associated pricing of additional conveyor and blower equipment in the revised quote forced DP-A to delay its bid resubmittal for six weeks. At the end of this period, Sevan contacted DP International's US office regarding the quote. He requested that it be forwarded as soon as possible. Additional problems surfaced, however, when Sevan contacted DP-A again, telling them he had not received the offer. Evidently it had been misdirected by office staff. Neither side admitted to the error.

During this period, Sevan also contacted Peter Olsen, Technical Director for DP International's Norwegian Headquarters team, in an attempt to gain control over the sale. Following the quote's re-transmission and review, Sevan offered a temporary approval to the sale.

Richard Foster and Scott Miller traveled again to the Lawrenceville plant, following the third quote, to meet with Michel Duval. Duval was very pleased with DP-A following rigorous technical discussions.

January 1995

Notwithstanding the previous multi-quote issues, DP International seemed well positioned to acquire Techno Plastics' granulator business. Then reports from DP International European staff member visiting the Fukuma

Plastics's trade show in Germany indicated another problem. The staff member had been informed by Stefan Sevan that the US subsidiary quotation was not adequate. The specifications had been quoted according to proposal requirements (the standard for project conformance), rather than to the current system in use at the Rothenburg, Germany plant. As such, the current bid would not meet all of Techno Plastics' needs.

The bid was re-submitted according to the Rothenburg set-up. However, Sevan contacted the DP International US Headquarters again, claiming that the bid still was not sufficient. Sevan encouraged Tom Parker to cut his price to ensure the order. DP-A responded by lowering its price, because Parker did not want to jeopardize DP-A's global position with Techno Plastics. To support the relationship, Parker and Richard Foster flew to France to find out more about the French specification expectations.

Caucusing with the French DP International subsidiary in Paris, a US, French, and Norwegian corporate management team reviewed the Techno Plastics case, preparing what they hoped would be the final bid. Although Jean Handel offered to negotiate on behalf of the US subsidiary, his offer was rejected, following what DP-A staff considered to be internal coordination errors and technical misinformation.

After lengthy intercompany caucusing, DP-A and Techno Plastics executives worked through plant specifications and at least half a dozen new issues developed in response to granulation requirements at the German plant. During this meeting, DP International offered its final quotation, following extensive technical discussions with Techno Plastics engineers and management. Both sides were elated with the outcome. Seven reassured Parker at the meeting saying, "I told you, I've always been a Dura-plast man."

Epilogue

It is June, 1995, and Tom Parker, CEO of Dura-plast, Inc. (DP-A), is reconstructing DP-A's handling of the Techno Plastics granulation equipment order. He was surprised and extremely disappointed to learn that Techno Plastics had not selected DP-A to supply granulators for their new plant.

The considerable expenditure in human and capital resources, along with meetings in both the US and France to clarify issues related to equipment specification, time frame and bid pricing, were not to be justified by first-year earnings alone. DP-A's efforts were targeted at extending the ongoing DP International-

Techno Plastics relationship in the US through a comprehensive order for both equipment and service for Techno Plastics' new plant in Lawrenceville, Georgia. The talks and the bid had been well received. It had seemed that the only formality left was the paperwork.

However, Torger Erlandsen, managing director of DP International Operations, recently informed Parker that the Lawrenceville plant bid was awarded to Northway, a US-based granulator producer and a major competitor. The news was delivered to Erlandsen by his DP France sales manager, Jean Handel.

To make matters worse, it now seems evident that DP-A sold to the wrong decision maker, and did not offer the right equipment and price package. Technically, there was no problem with the DP International product offering.

It also appears that the final purchase decision was made at the plant level in Lawrenceville by Michel Duval and in France by Stefan Sevan's boss, the Techno Plastics engineer responsible for the Lawrenceville, Georgia plant, Jean-Pierre Baran. DP-A had thought, that the decision would be made by DP-A's main contact, Sevan, and his direct reports. To DP-A's surprise, management in Lawrenceville commented that they were more comfortable with Northway, which "seemed more interested in their business and provided comprehensive information and service specifics in its bid." They also stated that, while price was not the order winner, the Northway offer was lower than the DP-A bid.

Re-examination of the bids, however, showed that Northway's slightly less expensive pricing did not include the same specifications as the DP-A offer. As a result, the Northway package, when complete, will actually be more expensive than the DP-A offer.

For Tom Parker, a significant problem with the Techno Plastics bid failure revolves around the issue of marketing coordination. As a group, Dura-plast did not understand who was the key player in charge and who was the key decision maker. While everyone intended to do the right thing, each member of the DP-A team made mistakes. Parker commented, "When Richard and I went to France and met with Stefan Sevan and his people, he assured us we had the order. We were convinced. However, we never really had the order. Sevan may have thought he could give us the order, but he was not the decision maker. It was a nightmare . . . The only solution I see is structured coordination among the DP International groups."

Global accounts are raising new issues for DP International, particularly with respect to pricing, cross-subsidiary coordination, technology and marketing strategy. These issues were brought to a head in the Techno Plastics situation. Currently, Dura-plast is trying to price at the local market, in effect, to maximize the profit potential in each subsidiary. However, there are concerns regarding this practice as a long-term policy.

Up to this point, all of Techno Plastics' granulator purchases had been through a DPI subsidiary—it was very loyal to Dura-plast. Now, however, Northway is also threatening DPG and DP-UK because of disparities between European and US pricing. Northway's inroad is a major concern because it threatens other DP International key accounts.

Known for his critical evaluation and analysis, Mr. Parker is committed to supporting the current DP-A and DP International customer bases. He is currently working on a plan to regain the US Techno Plastics account and is outspoken regarding the importance of avoiding similar situations in the future. He is also committed to supporting business expansion through appropriate corporate change and new, viable projects. Mr. Parker wonders what is the best next step for DP-A.

Case 6-9

Wal-Mart

In business, there is big, and there is Wal-Mart. With $245 billion in revenues in 2002, Wal-Mart Stores Inc. is the world's largest company. It is three times the size of the No. 2 retailer, France's Carrefour. Every week, 138 million shoppers visit Wal-Mart's 4,750 stores; last year, 82% of American households made at least one purchase at Wal-Mart. "There's nothing like Wal-Mart," says Ira Kalish, global director of Deloitte Research. "They are so much bigger than any retailer has ever been that it's not possible to compare."

At Wal-Mart, "everyday low prices" is more than a slogan; it is the fundamental tenet of a cult masquerading as a company. Over the years, Wal-Mart has relentlessly wrung tens of billions of dollars in cost efficiencies out of the retail supply chain, passing the larger part of the savings along to shoppers as bargain prices. New England Consulting estimates that Wal-Mart saved its U.S. customers $20 billion last year alone. Factor in the price cuts other retailers must make to compete, and the total annual savings approach $100 billion. It's no wonder that economists refer to a broad "Wal-Mart effect" that has suppressed inflation and rippled productivity gains through the economy year after year.

However, Wal-Mart's seemingly simple and virtuous business model is fraught with complications and perverse consequences (Exhibit 1). To cite a particularly noteworthy one, this staunchly anti-union company, America's largest private employer, is widely blamed for the sorry state of retail wages in America. On average, Wal-Mart sales clerks—"associates" in company parlance—pulled in $8.23 an hour, or $13,861 a year, in 2001, according to documents filed in a lawsuit pending against the company. At the time, the federal poverty line for a family of three was $14,630. Wal-Mart insists that it pays competitively, citing a privately commissioned survey that found that it "meets or exceeds" the total remuneration paid by rival retailers in 50 U.S. markets. "This is a good place to work," says Coleman H. Peterson, executive vice-president for personnel, citing an employee turnover rate that has fallen below 45% from 70% in 1999.

Critics counter that this is evidence not of improving morale but of a lack of employment alternatives in a slow-growth economy. "It's a ticking time bomb," says an executive at one big Wal-Mart supplier. "At some point, do the people stand up and revolt?" Indeed, the company now faces a revolt of sorts in the form of nearly 40 lawsuits charging it with forcing employees to work overtime without pay and a sex-discrimination case that could rank as the largest civil rights class action ever. On Sept. 24, a federal judge in California began considering a plaintiff's petition to include all women who have worked at Wal-Mart since late 1998–1.6 million all told—in a suit alleging that Wal-Mart systematically denies women equal pay and opportunities for promotion. Wal-Mart is vigorously contesting all of these suits.

Wal-Mart might well be both America's most admired and most hated company. "The world has never known a company with such ambition, capability, and momentum," marvels a Boston Consulting Group report. On Wall Street, Wal-Mart trades at a premium to most every other retailer. But the more size and power that "the Beast of Bentonville" amasses, the greater the backlash it is stirring among competing retailers,

EXHIBIT 1   The Long Arm of Bentonville, Ark.

For better or worse, Wal-Mart is one of the most powerful companies in history. Here's how it flexes its muscles:

The Wal-Mart Economy

It's the largest company in the world, with $245 billion in sales last year. McKinsey estimates that an eighth of the productivity gains in the late '90s came from Wal-Mart's drive for efficiency, and the discounter has been at least partly responsible for the extraordinarily low inflation rate of recent years. Its $12 billion in imports from China last year accounted for a tenth of total u.s. imports from that nation.

Lowering Wages

With a global workforce of 1.4 million, Wal-Mart plays a huge role in wages and working conditions worldwide. Its hard line on costs has forced many factories to move overseas. Its labor costs are 20% less than those at unionized supermarkets. In 2001, its sales clerks made less, on average, than the federal poverty level.

Disrupting Communities

Wal-Mart's huge advantages in buying power and efficiency force many local rivals to close. For every Wal-Mart supercenter that opens in the next five years, two other supermarkets will close. And because the chain often extracts tax breaks, some economists believe that Wal-Mart's entry into a community doesn't result in any net increase in jobs and tax revenue.

Policing the Culture

In the name of protecting customers, Wal-Mart has forced magazines to hide covers it considers racy and has booted others off its racks entirely. It won't carry music or computer games with mature ratings. Record companies sell Wal-Mart sanitized versions of CDs. Elsewhere in the store, the chain declines to sell Preven, a morning after pill. Most locations do offer inexpensive firearms.

Dominating Suppliers

In its relentless drive for lower prices, Wal-Mart homes in on every aspect of a supplier's operation—which products get developed, what they're made of, how to price them. It demands that every savings be passed on to consumers. No wonder one consultant says the second-worst thing a manufacturer can do is sign a contract with Wal-Mart. The worst? Not sign one.

---

vendors, organized labor, community activists, and cultural and political progressives. America has a long history of controversial retailers, notes James E. Hoopes, a history professor at Babson College. "What's new about Wal-Mart is the flak it's drawn from outside the world of its competition," he says. "It's become a social phenomenon that people resent and fear."

Wal-Mart's marketplace clout is hard to overstate (Exhibit 2). In household staples such as toothpaste, shampoo, and paper towels, the company commands about 30% of the U.S. market, and analysts predict that its share of many such goods could hit 50% before decade's end. Wal-Mart also is Hollywood's biggest outlet, accounting for 15% to 20% of all sales of CDs, videos, and DVDs. The mega-retailer did not add magazines to its mix until the mid-1990s, but it now makes 15% of all single-copy sales in the U.S. In books, too, Wal-Mart has quickly become a force. "They pile up best-sellers like toothpaste," says Stephen Riggio, chief executive of Barnes & Noble Inc., the world's largest bookseller.

Wal-Mart controls a large and rapidly increasing share of the business done by most every major U.S. consumer-products company: 28% of Dial's total sales, 24% of Del Monte Foods', 23% of Clorox', 23% of Revlon's, and on down the list. Suppliers' growing dependence on Wal-Mart is "a huge issue" not only for manufacturers but also for the U.S. economy, says Tom Rubel, CEO of consultant Retail Forward Inc. "If [Wal-Mart] ever stumbles, we've got a potential national

EXHIBIT 2   King Kong in Diapers

Data: A.C. Nielsen, Retail Forward, *Home Textiles Today*

Wal-Mart dominates sales in a number of categories:	
Disposable diapers	32%
Hair care	30
Toothpaste	26
Pet food	20
Home textiles	13

U.S. market share based on 2002 data; excludes Sam's Clubs

security problem on our hands. They touch almost everything. . . . If they ever really went into a tailspin, the dislocation would be significant and traumatic."

Even so, Wal-Mart appears to be in no imminent danger of running afoul of federal antitrust statutes. The Robinson-Patman Act of 1936 was passed in large part to protect mom-and-pop grocers from the Great Atlantic & Pacific Tea Co., the Wal-Mart of its day. But contemporary antitrust interpretations eschew such David-and-Goliath populism. Giants like Wal-Mart have wide latitude to do as they wish to rivals and suppliers so long as they deliver lower prices to consumers. "When Wal-Mart comes in and people desert downtown because they like the selection and the low prices, it's hard for people in the antitrust community to say we should not let them do that," says New York University law professor Harry First.

CEO H. Lee Scott Jr. and other Wal-Mart executives are aware of the rising hostility the company faces and are trying to smooth its rough edges in dealing with the outside world. But they have no intention of tampering with its shopper-centric business model. "We don't turn a deaf ear to any criticism. We're most sensitive to what the customer has to say, though," says Vice-Chairman Thomas M. Coughlin. "Your customers will tell you when you're wrong."

Wal-Mart cites customer preferences as the reason it does not stock CDs or DVDs with parental warning stickers and why it occasionally yanks items from its shelves. In May, it removed the racy "lad" magazines *Maxim, Stuff,* and *FHM.* A month later, it began obscuring the covers of *Glamour, Redbook, Marie Claire,* and *Cosmopolitan* with binders. Why did Wal-Mart censor these publications and not *Rolling Stone,* which has featured a nearly naked Britney Spears and Christina Aguilera on two of its recent covers? "There's a lot of subjectivity," concedes Gary Severson, a Wal-Mart general merchandise manager. "There's a line between provocative and pornographic. I don't know exactly where it is."

Wal-Mart was the only one of the top 10 drug chains to refuse to stock Preven when Gynetics Inc. introduced the morning-after contraceptive in 1999. Roderick L. Mackenzie, Gynetics' founder and nonexecutive chairman, says senior Wal-Mart executives told his employees that they did not want their pharmacists grappling with the "moral dilemma" of abortion. Mackenzie was incensed but tried to hide it. "When you speak to God in Bentonville, you speak in hushed tones," says Mackenzie, who explained, to no avail, that Preven did

not induce abortion but rather prevented pregnancy. Wal-Mart spokesman Jay Allen says "a number of factors were considered" in making the Preven decision, but he denies that opposition to abortion was one of them. "If anybody of any belief reads any moral decision [into] that, that's not right," he says.

Cultural Gatekeeper

There is no question that the company has the legal right to sell only what it chooses to sell, even in the case of First Amendment-protected material such as magazines. By most accounts, though, Wal-Mart's cultural gate-keeping has served to narrow the mainstream for entertainment offerings while imparting to it a rightward tilt. The big music companies have stopped grousing about Wal-Mart and are eagerly supplying the chain with the same sanitized versions of explicit CDs that they provide to radio stations. "You can't have 100% impact when you are taking an artist to a mainstream audience if you don't have the biggest player, Wal-Mart," says EMI Music North America Executive Vice-President Phil Quartararo.

This year alone, Wal-Mart hopes to open as many as 335 new stores in the U.S.: 55 discount stores, 210 supercenters, 45 Sam's Clubs, and 25 neighborhood markets. An additional 130 new stores are on the boards for foreign markets. Wal-Mart currently operates 1,309 stores in 10 countries, ranking as the largest retailer in Mexico and Canada. If the company can maintain its current 15% growth rate, it will double its revenues over the next five years and top $600 billion in 2011 (Exhibit 3).

That's a very big if—even for Wal-Mart. Vice-Chairman Coughlin's biggest worry is finding enough warm bodies to staff all those new stores. By Wal-Mart's own estimate, about 44% of its 1.4 million employees will leave in 2003, meaning the company will need to hire 616,000 workers just to stay even. In addition, from 2004 to 2008, the company wants to add 800,000 new positions, including 47,000 management slots. "That's what causes me the most sleepless nights," Coughlin says.

At the same time, Wal-Mart will have to cope with intensifying grassroots opposition. The company's hugely ambitious expansion plans hinge on continuing its move out of its stronghold in the rural South and Midwest into urban America. This year, the company opened what it describes as "one of its first truly urban stores" in Los Angeles, not far from Watts. Everyday low prices no doubt appeal to city dwellers no less

EXHIBIT 3   41 Years of Nonstop Growth

Data: Wal-Mart Stores Inc.

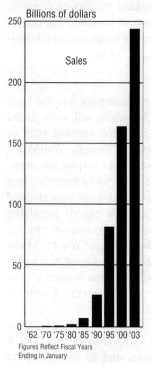

Billions of dollars

Sales

'62 '70 '75 '80 '85 '90 '95 '00 '03

Figures Reflect Fiscal Years
Ending in January

than to their country cousins. But Wal-Mart's sense of itself as definitively American ("Wal-Mart is America," boasts one top executive) is likely to be severely tested by the metropolis' high land costs, restrictive zoning codes, and combative labor unions—not to mention its greater economic and cultural diversity.

A Zero-Sum Game?

Certainly, Wal-Mart will be hard pressed to continue censoring its product lines using the justification of customer preference. The market for profanity-laced

hip-hop may be tiny in Bentonville, Ark., but it is big in Los Angeles. Overseas, the company does not presume to impose a small-town, Bible Belt moral agenda on shoppers. "We adopt local standards," says John B. Menzer, CEO of Wal-Mart's international division. Why, then, should Los Angeles be any different?

The fact is, Wal-Mart doesn't know for certain how the majority of its customers feel about *Maxim,* or any other magazine, for that matter. It appears that the company makes no scientific attempt to survey shoppers about entertainment content but responds in ad hoc fashion to complaints lodged by a relative handful of customers and by outside groups, which are usually but not always of the conservative persuasion (Exhibit 4).

On the other hand, the company seldom submits to community groups that oppose its plans to build new stores. The number of such challenges has increased steadily and is now running at about 100 a year. Wal-Mart's "biggest barrier to growth is . . . opposition at the local level," says Carl Steidtmann, Deloitte Research's retail economist. The Stop Wal-Mart movement has been bolstered of late by a series of academic studies that have debunked the notion that a new big-box store boosts employment and sales and property-tax receipts. "The net increases are minimal as the new big-box stores merely capture sales from existing business in the area," concludes a new study of Wal-Mart's impact in Mississippi. "I see it pretty much as a zero-sum game," says co-author Kenneth E. Stone, an economics professor at Iowa State University.

The most hotly contested battleground at the moment is Contra Costa County, near San Francisco. In June, county supervisors enacted an ordinance that prohibits any retail outlet larger than 90,000 square feet from devoting more than 5% of its floor space to food or other nontaxable goods. Wal-Mart promptly gathered enough signatures to force a referendum, scheduled for March. Complains County Supervisor John Gioia: "Local

EXHIBIT 4   Wal-Mart by the Numbers

The world's largest company generates some amazing statistics					
30	**44%**	**4**	**14%**	**82%**	**71%**
Supermarkets closed since Wal-Mart **saturated** Oklahoma City	**Turnover rate** for Wal-Mart's hourly workers per year	Number of Wal-Marts in Vermont, the **fewest of any state**	How much **lower** average grocery prices are where Wal-Mart competes	Percentage of **U.S. households** that made a Wal-Mart purchase last year	**Price drop** for George jeans at Britain's Asda since Wal-Mart bought it in '99
Data: Retail Forward Inc.	Data: Wal-Mart Stores Inc.	Data: Wal-Mart Stores Inc.	Data: UBS Warburg	Data: Retail Forward Inc.	Data: Wal-Mart Stores Inc.

planning should be done by our locally elected board and not by a corporate office in Bentonville, Arkansas." Robert S. McAdam, Wal-Mart's vice-president for government relations, says corporate-sponsored referenda, which Wal-Mart has promoted elsewhere in California, are "a perfectly legitimate part of the process."

Supercenter Nation

Meanwhile, the United Food & Commercial Workers union is stepping up its long-standing attempts to organize Wal-Mart stores, with current campaigns in 45 locations. For UFCW locals that represent grocery workers, the issue is nothing less than survival. The Wal-Mart supercenter—the principal vehicle of the company's expansion—is a nonunion dagger aimed at the heart of the traditional American supermarket, nearly 13,000 of which have closed since 1992.

Patterned after the European hypermarket, the supercenter is a combination supermarket and general merchandise discounter built to colossal scale. Wal-Mart didn't introduce the supercenter to America, but it has amassed a 79% share of the category since it moved into food and drug retailing by opening its first such store in 1988. Today, Wal-Mart operates 1,386 supercenters and is the nation's largest grocer, with a 19% market share, and its third-largest pharmacy, with 16%.

Wal-Mart plans to open 1,000 more supercenters in the U.S. alone over the next five years. Retail Forward estimates that this supercenter blitzkrieg will boost Wal-Mart's grocery and related revenues to $162 billion from the current $82 billion, giving it control over 35% of U.S. food sales and 25% of drugstore sales. Marketshare gains of such magnitude in a slow-growth business necessarily will come at the expense of established competitors—especially the unionized ones, which pay their workers 30% more on average than Wal-Mart does, according to the UFCW. Retail Forward predicts that for every new supercenter that Wal-Mart opens, two supermarkets will close, or 2,000 all told.

To the low-price, low-cost operator go the spoils. Isn't that how capitalism is supposed to work? Certainly, the supercentering of America can be expected to result in huge savings at the cash register. On average, a Wal-Mart supercenter offers prices 14% below its rivals', according to a 2002 study by UBS Warburg.

However, those everyday low prices come at a cost. As the number of supermarkets shrinks, more shoppers will have to travel farther from home and will find their buying increasingly restricted to merchandise that Wal-Mart chooses to sell—a growing percentage of which may be the retailer's private-label goods, which now account for nearly 20% of sales. Meanwhile, the failure of hundreds of stores will cost their owners dearly and put thousands out of work, only some of whom will find jobs at Wal-Mart, most likely at lower pay. "It will be a sad day in this country if we wake up one morning and all we find is a Wal-Mart on every corner," says Gary E. Hawkins, CEO of Green Hills, a family-owned supermarket in Syracuse, N.Y.

For suppliers, too, Wal-Mart's relentless pricing pressure is a mixed blessing. "If you are good with data, are sophisticated, and have scale, Wal-Mart should be one of your most profitable customers," says a retired consumer-products executive. Unlike many retailers, the company does not charge "slotting fees" for access to its shelves and is unusually generous in sharing sales data with manufacturers. In return, though, Wal-Mart not only dictates delivery schedules and inventory levels but also heavily influences product specifications. In the end, many suppliers have to choose between designing goods their way or the Wal-Mart way. "Wal-Mart really is about driving the cost of a product down," says James A. Wier, CEO of Simplicity Manufacturing, a lawn-mower maker that decided to stop selling to Wal-Mart last fall. "When you drive the cost of a product down, you really can't deliver the high-quality product like we have."

Critics also argue that Wal-Mart's intensifying global pursuit of low-cost goods is partly to blame for the accelerating loss of U.S. manufacturing jobs to China and other low-wage nations. "It's hard to tease out, but Wal-Mart is definitely part of the dynamic, and given its market share and power, probably a significant part," says Jared Bernstein, a labor economist at the liberal Economic Policy Institute. The $12 billion worth of Chinese goods Wal-Mart bought in 2002 represented 10% of all U.S. imports from China.

For obvious reasons, Wal-Mart has de-emphasized the "Made in America" campaign that founder Sam Walton started in the mid-1980s to great promotional effect. "Where we have the option to source domestically we do," says Ken Eaton, Wal-Mart's senior vice-president for global procurement. However, he adds, "there are certain businesses, particularly in the U.S., where you just can't buy domestically anymore to the scale and value we need." In recent years, Wal-Mart increasingly has sought additional cost advantages by bypassing middlemen and buying finished goods and raw materials from foreign manufacturers. By contracting directly with a handful of denim manufacturers in Southeast Asia, the company has driven down the retail price of the George brand jeans it sells in Britain and Germany to $7.85 from $26.67. Says Eaton: "The mindset around here is, we're agents for our customers."

"The Wal-Mart Phenomenon"

Wal-Mart's philosophy doesn't cut any ice with Wilbur L. Ross Jr., a financier and steel tycoon who soon will close on the purchase of beleaguered textile manufacturer Burlington Industries Inc. Ross contends that Wal-Mart is costing Americans jobs "not only as a business strategy, but as a lobbying strategy"—that is, by using its influence in Washington to oppose import tariffs and quotas and promote free-trade pacts with Third World countries, including the Southeast Asian countries that supply Wal-Mart with denim. "Everybody is now scurrying around trying to find the lowest price points," Ross complains. "It's the Wal-Mart phenomenon."

High on a wall inside Wal-Mart headquarters is a paper banner with a provocative question in big block letters: "Who's taking your customers?" Beneath it, "Wanted" poster style, hang photos of the CEOs of two dozen of America's largest retailers—Target, Kroger, Winn-Dixie Stores, Walgreen, and so on. None looks very happy, perhaps because they know that the only way to get off the wall is to fail utterly. Although Kmart is reorganizing under the federal bankruptcy code, a photo of its CEO continues to hang in Wal-Mart's rogues' gallery and no doubt will remain there for as long as Kmart operates even a single store.

Growth will only add to the clout that the Bentonville colossus now wields. There might well come a time, though, when Wal-Mart's size poses as much of a threat to the company itself as it does to outsiders. "Their biggest danger is just managing size," observes a longtime supplier. Adds Babson College's Hoopes: "The history of the last 150 years in retailing would say that if you don't like Wal-Mart, be patient. There will be new models eventually that will do Wal-Mart in, and Wal-Mart won't see it coming." Right now, though, Wal-Mart's day of reckoning seems a very long way off.

With Diane Brady, Mike France, Tom Lowry, Nanette Byrnes, and Susan Zegel in New York; Michael Arndt, Robert Berner, and Ann Therese Palmer in Chicago; and bureau reports

Source: Anthony Bianco and Wendy Zellner, "Is Wal-Mart Too Powerful?" *BusinessWeek,* October 6, 2003, 100–110.

Case 6-10
Blair Water Purifiers India

A pity I couldn't have stayed for Diwali," thought Rahul Chatterjee. "But anyway, it was great to be back home in Calcutta." The Diwali holiday and its festivities would begin in early November 1996, some two weeks after Chatterjee had returned to the United States. Chatterjee worked as an international market liaison for Blair Company Inc. This was his eighth year with Blair Company and easily his favorite. "Your challenge

This case was written by Professor James E. Nelson, University of Colorado at Boulder. He thanks students in the class of 1996 (batch 31), Indian Institute of Management, Calcutta, for their invaluable help in collecting all the data needed to write this case. He also thanks Professor Roger Kerin, Southern Methodist University, for his helpful comments. The case is intended for educational purposes rather than to illustrate either effective or ineffective decision making. Some data as well as the identity of the company are disguised. © 1997 by James E. Nelson. Used with permission.

will be in moving us from just dabbling in less developed countries [LDCS] to our thriving in them," his boss had said when Chatterjee was promoted to the job last January. Chatterjee had agreed and was thrilled when he was asked to visit Bombay and New Delhi in April. His purpose on that trip was to gather background data on the possibility of Blair Company entering the Indian market for home water purification devices. The initial results had been encouraging and had prompted the second trip.

Chatterjee had used his second trip primarily to study Indian cosumers in Calcutta and Bangalore and to gather information on possible competitors. The two cities represented quite different metropolitan areas in terms of location, size, language, and infrastructure, yet both cities faced similar problems in terms of the water supplied to their residents. Those problems could be found in many LDCs and were favorable to home water purification.

Information gathered on both visits would be used to make a recommendation on market entry and on the elements of an entry strategy. Executives at Blair Company would compare Chatterjee's recommendation to those from two other Blair Company liaisons who were focusing their efforts on Argentina, Brazil, and Indonesia.

Indian Market for Home Water Filtration and Purification

Like many things in India, the market for home water filtration and purification took a good deal of effort to understand. Yet despite expending this effort, Chatterjee realized that much remained either unknown or in conflict. For example, the market seemed clearly a mature one, with four or five established Indian competitors fighting for market share. Or was it? Another view portrayed the market as a fragmented one, with no large competitor having a national presence and perhaps 100 small regional manufacturers, each competing in just one or two of India's 25 states. Indeed, the market could be in its early growth stages, as reflected by the large number of product designs, materials, and performances. Perhaps with a next-generation product and a world-class marketing effort, Blair Company could consolidate the market and stimulate tremendous growth—much like the situation in the Indian market for automobiles.

Such uncertainty made it difficult to estimate market potential. However, Chatterjee had collected unit sales estimates for a 10-year period for three similar product categories: vacuum cleaners, sewing machines, and color televisions. In addition, a Delhi-based research

firm had provided him with estimates of unit sales for Aquaguard, the best-selling water purifier in several Indian states. Chatterjee had used the data in two forecasting models available at Blair Company along with three subjective scenarios—realistic, optimistic, and pessimistic—to arrive at the estimates and forecasts for water purifiers shown in Exhibit 1. "If anything," Chatterjee had explained to his boss, "my forecasts are conservative because they describe only first-time sales, not any replacement sales over the 10-year forecast horizon." He also pointed out that his forecasts applied only to industry sales in larger urban areas, which was the present industry focus.

One thing that seemed certain was that many Indians felt the need for improved water quality. Folklore, newspapers, consumer activists, and government officials regularly reinforced this need by describing the poor quality of Indian water. Quality suffered particularly during monsoons because highly polluted water entered treatment plants and because of numerous leaks and unauthorized withdrawls from water systems. Such leaks and withdrawls often polluted clean water after it had left the plants. Politicians running for national, state, and local government offices also reinforced the need for improved water quality through election campaign promises. Governments at these levels set standards for water quality, took measurements at thousands of locations throughout the nation, and advised consumers when water became unsafe.

EXHIBIT 1
Industry Sales Estimates and Forecasts for Water Purifiers in India, 1990–2005 (thousands of units)

Year	Unit Sales Estimates	Unit Sales Forecast Under		
		Realistic Scenario	Optimistic Scenario	Pessimistic Scenario
1990	60			
1991	90			
1992	150			
1993	200			
1994	220			
1995	240			
1996		250	250	250
1997		320	370	300
1998		430	540	400
1999		570	800	550
2000		800	1,200	750
2001		1,000	1,500	850
2002		1,300	1,900	900
2003		1,500	2,100	750
2004		1,600	2,100	580
2005		1,500	1,900	420

During periods of poor water quality many Indian consumers had little choice but to consume the water as they found it. However, better-educated, wealthier, and more health-conscious consumers took steps to safeguard their families' health and often continued these steps all year. A good estimate of the number of such households, Chatterjee thought, would be around 40 million. These consumers were similar in many respects to consumers in middle- and upper-middle-class households in the United States and the European Union. They valued comfort and product choice. They saw consumption of material goods as a means to a higher quality of life. They liked foreign brands and would pay a higher price for such brands as long as those products outperformed competing Indian products. Chatterjee had identified as his target market these 40 million households plus another 4 million households whose members had similar values and lifestyles but made little effort to improve water quality in their homes.

Traditional Method for Home Water Purification

The traditional method of water purification in the target market relied not on a commercially supplied product but on boiling. Each day or several times a day, a cook, maid, or family member would boil two to five liters of water for 10 minutes, allow it to cool, and then transfer it to containers for storage (often in a refrigerator). Chatterjee estimated that about 50 percent of the target market used this procedure. Boiling was seen by consumers as inexpensive, effective in terms of eliminating dangerous bacteria, and entrenched in a traditional sense. Many consumers who used this method considered it more effective than any product on the market. However, boiling affected the palatability of water, leaving the purified product somewhat "flat" tasting. Boiling also was cumbersome, time-consuming, and ineffective in removing physical impurities and unpleasant odors. Consequently, about 10 percent of the target market took a second step by filtering their boiled water through "candle filters" before storage. Many consumers took this action despite knowing that water could become recontaminated during handling and storage.

Mechanical Methods for Home Water Filtration and Purification

About 40 percent of the target market used a mechanical device to improve their water quality. Half of this group used candle filters, primarily because of their low price and ease of use. The typical candle filter contained two containers, one resting on top of the other. The upper container held one or more porous ceramic cylinders (candles) which strained the water as gravity drew it into the lower container. Containers were made of plastic, porcelain, or stainless steel and typically stored between 15 and 25 liters of filtered water. Purchase costs depended on materials and capacities, ranging from Rs. 350 for a small plastic model to Rs. 1,100 for a large stainless-steel model (35 Indian rupees was equivalent to US $1.00 in 1996). Candle filters were slow, producing 15 liters (one candle) to 45 liters (three candles) of filtered water in 24 hours. To maintain this productivity, candles regularly had to be removed, cleaned, and boiled for 20 minutes. Most manufacturers recommended that consumers replace candles (Rs. 40 each) either once a year or more frequently, depending on sediment levels.

The other half of this group used "water purifiers," devices that were considerably more sophisticated than candle filters. Water purifiers typically employed three water-processing stages. The first removed sediments, the second objectionable odors and colors, and the third harmful bacteria and viruses. Engineers at Blair Company were skeptical that most purifiers claiming the latter benefit could deliver on their promise. However, all purifiers did a better job here than candle filters. Candle filters were totally ineffective in eliminating bacteria and viruses (and might even increase this type of contamination) despite advertising claims to the contrary. Water purifiers generally used stainless-steel containers and sold at prices ranging from Rs. 2,000 to Rs. 7,000, depending on the manufacturer, features, and capacities. Common flow rates were one to two liters of purified water per minute. Simple service activities could be performed on water purifiers by consumers as needed. However, more complicated service required that units be taken to a nearby dealer or necessitated an in-home visit from a skilled technician.

The remaining 10 percent of the target market owned neither a filter nor a purifier and seldom boiled their water. Many consumers in this group were unaware of water problems and thought their water quality was acceptable. However, a few consumers in this group refused to pay for products that they believed were mostly ineffective. Overall, Chatterjee believed that only a few consumers in this group could be induced to change their habits and become customers. The most attractive segments consisted of the 90 percent of households in the target market that boiled, boiled and filtered, only filtered, or purified their water.

All the segments in the target market showed a good deal of similarity in terms of what they thought important in the purchase of a water purifier, According to Chatterjee's research, the most important factor was product performance in terms of sediment removal bacteria and virus removal, capacity (in the form of storage or flow rate), safety, and "footprint" space. Purchase price also was an important concern among consumers who boiled, boiled and filtered, or only filtered their water. The next most important factor was ease of installation and service, with style and appearance rated almost as important. The least important factor was warranty and the availability of financing for purchase. Finally, all segments expected a water purifier to be warranted against defective operation for 18 to 24 months and to perform trouble-free for 5 to 10 years.

Foreign investment in India

India appeared attractive to many foreign investors because of government actions begun in the 1980s during the administration of Prime Minister Rajiv Gandhi. The broad label applied to these actions was *liberalization*. Liberalization had opened the Indian economy to foreign investors, stemming from a recognition that protectionist policies had not worked very well and that Western economies and technologies—seen against the collapse of the Soviet Union—did. Liberalization had meant major changes in approval requirements for new commercial projects, investment policies, taxation procedures, and, most important, the attitudes of government officials. These changes had stayed in place through the two national governments that followed Gandhi's assassination in 1991.

If Blair Company entered the Indian market, it would do so in one of three ways: (1) joint working arrangement. (2) joint venture company, or (3) acquisition. In a joint working arrangement Blair Company would supply key purifier components to an Indian company, which would manufacture and market the assembled product. License fees would be remitted to Blair Company on a per-unit basis over the term of the agreement (typically five years, with an option to renew for three more). A joint venture agreement would have Blair Company partnering with an existing Indian company expressly for the purpose of manufacturing and marketing water purifiers. Profits from the joint venture operation would be split between the two

parties per the agreement, which usually contained a clause describing buy/sell procedures available to the two parties after a minimum time period. An acquisition entry would have Blair Company purchasing an existing Indian company whose operations then would be expanded to include the water purifier. Profits from the acquisition would belong to Blair Company.

Beyond understanding these basic entry possibilities, Chatterjee acknowledged that he was no expert in the legal aspects of the project. However, two days spent with a Calcutta consulting firm had produced the following information. Blair Company had to apply for market entry to the Foreign Investment Promotion Board, Secretariat for Industrial Approvals, Ministry of Industries. The proposal would go before the board for an assessment of the relevant technology and India's need for the technology. If approved by the board, the proposal then would go to the Reserve Bank of India, Ministry of Finance, for approvals of any royalties and fees, remittances of dividends and interest (if any), repatriation of profits and invested capital, and repayment of foreign loans. While the process sounded cumbersome and time-consuming, the consultant assured Chatterjee that the government usually completed its deliberations in less than six months and that his consulting firm could "virtually guarantee" final approval.

Trademarks and patents were protected by law in India. Trademarks were protected for seven years and could be renewed on the payment of a prescribed fee. Patents lasted for 14 years. On balance, Chatterjee had told his boss that Blair Company would have "no more problem protecting its intellectual property rights in India than in the United States—as long as we stay out of court." Chatterjee went on to explain that litigation in India was expensive and protracted. Litigation problems were compounded by an appeal process that could extend a case for a generation. Consequently, many foreign companies preferred arbitration, as India was a party to the Geneva Convention covering foreign arbitral awards.

Foreign companies were taxed on income arising from Indian operations. They also paid taxes on any interest, dividends, and royalties received and on any capital gains received from a sale of assets. The government offered a wide range of tax concessions to foreign investors, including liberal depreciation allowances and generous deductions. The government offered even more favorable tax treatment if foreign investors would locate in one of India's six Free Trade Zones. Overall, Chatterjee thought that corporate tax rates in India probably were somewhat higher than those in the United States. However, so were profits; the average return on assets for all Indian corporations in recent years was almost 18 percent, compared to about 11 percent for U.S. corporations.

Approval by the Reserve Bank of India was needed for the repatriation of ordinary profits. However, approval could be obtained easily if Blair Company could show that repatriated profits were being paid out of export earnings of hard currencies. Chatterjee thought that export earnings would not be difficult to realize because of India's extremely low wage rates and its central location in regard to wealthier South Asian countries. "Profit repatriation is really not much of an issue, anyway," he thought. Three years might pass before profits of any magnitude could be realized; at least five years would pass before substantial profits would be available for repatriation. Approval of repatriation by the Reserve Bank might not be required at that time, given liberalization trends. Finally, if repatriation remained difficult, Blair Company could undertake cross-trading or other actions to unblock profits.

Overall, investment and trade regulations in India in 1996 meant that business could be conducted much more easily than ever before. Hundreds of companies from the European Union, Japan, Korea, and the United States were entering India in all sectors of the country's economy. In the home appliance market, Chatterjee could identify 11 such firms: Carrier, Electrolux, General Electric, Goldstar, Matsushita, Singer, Samsung, Sanyo, Sharp, Toshiba, and Whirlpool. Many of those firms had yet to realize substantial profits, but all saw the promise of a huge market developing over the next few years.

Blair Company, Inc.

Blair Company was founded in 1975 by Eugene Blair after he left his position in research and development at Culligan International Company. Blair Company's first product was a desalinator used by mobile home parks in Florida to remove salt from the brackish well water supplied to residents. The product was a huge success, and markets quickly expanded to include nearby municipalities, smaller businesses, hospitals, and bottlers of water for sale to consumers. Geographic markets also expanded, first to other coastal regions near the company's headquarters in Tampa, Florida, and then to desert areas in the southwestern United States. New products were added rapidly as well, and by 1996

the product line included desalinators, particle filters, ozonators, ion exchange resins, and purifiers. Industry experts generally regarded the product line as superior in terms of performance and quality, with prices higher than those of many competitors.

Blair Company sales revenues for 1996 would be almost $400 million, with an expected profit close to $50 million. Annual growth in sales revenues had averaged 12 percent for the last five years. Blair Company employed over 4,000 people, with 380 having technical backgrounds and responsibilities.

Export sales of desalinators and related products began at Blair Company in 1980. Units were sold first to resorts in Mexico and Belize and later to water bottlers in Germany. Export sales grew rapidly, and Blair Company found it necessary to organize its international division in 1985. Sales in that division also grew rapidly and would reach almost $140 million in 1996. About $70 million would come from countries in Central America and South America, $30 million from Europe (including shipments to Africa), and $40 million from South Asia and Australia. The international division had sales offices, small assembly areas, and distribution facilities in Frankfurt, Germany; Tokyo, Japan; and Singapore.

The Frankfurt office had provided the impetus in 1990 for the development and marketing of Blair Company's first product targeted exclusively at consumer households—a home water filter. Sales engineers at the Frankfurt office began receiving consumer and distributor requests for a home water filter soon after the fall of the Berlin Wall in 1989. By late 1991 two models had been designed in the United States and introduced in Germany (particularly to the eastern regions), Poland, Hungary, Romania, the Czech Republic, and Slovakia.

Blair Company executives watched the success of the two water filters with great interest. The market for clean water in LDCs was huge, profitable, and attractive in a socially responsible sense. However, the quality of water in many LDCs was such that a water filter usually would not be satisfactory. Consequently, in late 1994 executives had called for the development of a water purifier that could be added to the product line. Engineers had given the final design in the project the brand name Delight. For the time being Chatterjee and the other market analysts had accepted the name, not knowing if it might infringe on an existing brand in India or in the other countries under study.

The Delight Purifier

The Delight purifier used a combination of technologies to remove four types of contaminants from potable water: sediments, organic and inorganic chemicals, microbials or cysts, and objectionable tastes and odors. The technologies were effective as long as the contaminants in the water were present at "reasonable" levels. Engineers at Blair Company had interpreted this to mean the levels described in several World Health Organization (WHO) reports on potable water and had combined the technologies to purify water to a level above WHO standards. Engineers had repeatedly assured Chatterjee that Delight's design in terms of technologies should not be a concern. Ten units operating in the company's testing laboratory showed no signs of failure or performance deterioration after some 5.000 hours of continuous use. "Still," Chatterjee thought, "we will undertake a good bit of field testing in India before entering. The risks of failure are too large to ignore. And besides, the results of our testing would be useful in persuading consumers and retailers to buy."

Chatterjee and the other market analysts still faced major design issues in configuring technologies into physical products. For example, a "point of entry" design would place the product immediately after water entry to the home, treating all water before it flowed to all water outlets. In contrast, a "point of use" design would place the product on a countertop, on a wall, or at the end of a faucet and treat only water arriving

at that location. Based on cost estimates, designs of competing products, and his understanding of Indian consumers, Chatterjee would direct the engineers to proceed only with point of use designs for that market.

Other technical details had not yet been worked out. For example, Chatterjee had to provide engineers with suggestions for filter flow rates, storage capacities (if any), unit layout, and overall dimensions, plus a number of special features. One such feature was the possibility of a small battery to operate the filter for several hours in case of a power failure (a common occurrence in India and many other LDCs). Another might be one or two "bells or whistles" to tell cooks, maids, and family members that the unit indeed was working properly. Yet another might be an "additive" feature that would permit users to add fluoride, vitamins, or even flavorings to their water.

Chatterjee knew that the Indian market eventually would require a number of models. However, at the outset of market entry, he probably could get by with just two—one with a larger capacity for houses and bungalows and the other a smaller-capacity model for flats. He thought that model styling and specific appearances should reflect a Western, high-technology design to distinguish the Delight purifier from competitors' products. To that end, he had instructed a graphics artist to develop two ideas that he had used to gauge consumer reactions on his last visit (see Exhibit 2). Consumers liked both models but preferred the countertop design to the wall-mount design.

EXHIBIT 2
Wall-Mount and Countertop Designs

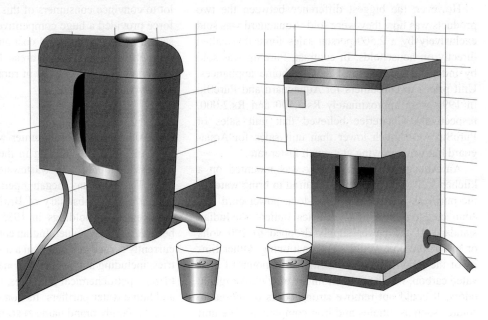

Competitors

Upward of 100 companies competed in the Indian market for home water filters and purifiers. While information on most of those companies was difficult to obtain, Chatterjee and the Indian research agencies were able to develop descriptions of three major competitors and brief profiles of several others.

Eureka Forbes

The best established competitor in the water purifier market was Eureka Forbes, a joint venture company established in 1982 between Electrolux (Sweden) and Forbes Campbell (India). The company marketed a broad line of "modern, lifestyle products," including water purifiers, vacuum cleaners, and mixers/grinders. The brand name used for its water purifiers was Aquaguard, a name so well established that many consumers used it to refer to other water purifiers or to the entire product category. Aquaguard, with its 10-year market history, was clearly the market leader and came close to being India's only national brand. However, Eureka Forbes had recently introduced a second brand of water purifier called PureSip. The PureSip model was similar to Aquaguard except in its third-stage process, which used a polyiodide resin instead of ultraviolet rays to kill bacteria and viruses. This meant that water from a PureSip purifier could be stored safely for later use. Also in contrast to Aquaguard, the PureSip model needed no electricity for its operation.

However, the biggest difference between the two products was how they were sold. Aquaguard was sold exclusively by a 2,500-person sales force that called directly on households. In contrast, PureSip was sold by independent dealers of smaller home appliances. Unit prices to consumers for Aquaguard and PureSip in 1996 were approximately Rs.5,500 and Rs.2,000, respectively. Chatterjee believed that unit sales of PureSip were much lower than unit sales for Aquaguard but were growing at a much faster rate.

An Aquaguard unit typically was mounted on a kitchen wall, with plumbing required to bring water to the purifier's inlet. A two-meter-long power cord was connected to a 230-volt AC electrical outlet—the Indian standard. If the power supply dropped to 190 volts or lower, the unit would stop functioning. Other limits of the product included a smallish amount of activated carbon, which could eliminate only weak organic odors. It could not remove strong odors or inorganic solutes such as nitrates and iron compounds. The unit

had no storage capacity, and its flow rate of one liter per minute seemed slow to some consumers. Removing water for storage or connecting the unit to a reservoir tank could affect water quality adversely.

Aquaguard's promotion strategy emphasized personal selling. Each salesperson was assigned to a specific neighborhood and was monitored by a group leader, who in turn was monitored by a supervisor. Each salesperson was expected to canvass his or her neighborhood, select prospective households (those with annual incomes exceeding Rs. 70,000), demonstrate the product, and make an intensive effort to sell the product. Repeated sales calls helped educate consumers about their water quality and reassure them that Aquaguard service was readily available. Television commercials and advertisements in magazines and newspapers (see Exhibit 3) supported the personal selling efforts. Chatterjee estimated that Eureka Forbes would spend about Rs. 120 million on all sales activities in 1996, or roughly 11 percent of its sales revenues. He estimated that about Rs. 100 million of that Rs. 120 million would be spent in the form of sales commissions. Chatterjee thought the company's total advertising expenditures for the year would be only about Rs. 1 million.

Eureka Forbes was a formidable competitor. The sales force was huge, highly motivated, and well managed. Moreover, Aquaguard was the first product to enter the water purifier market, and the name had tremendous brand equity. The product itself was probably the weakest strategic component, but it would take a lot to convince consumers of this. And while the sales force provided a huge competitive advantage, it represented an enormous fixed cost and essentially limited sales efforts to large urban areas. More than 80 percent of India's population lived in rural areas, where water quality was even lower.

Ion Exchange

Ion Exchange was the premier water treatment company in India, specializing in the treatment of water, processed liquids, and wastewater in industrial markets. The company began operations in 1964 as a wholly owned subsidiary of British Permutit. Permutit divested its holdings in 1985, and Ion Exchange became a wholly owned Indian company. The company currently served customers in a diverse group of industries, including nuclear and thermal power stations, fertilizers, petrochemical refineries, textiles, automobiles, and home water purifiers. Its home water purifiers carried the family brand name ZERO-B (Zero-Bacteria).

EXHIBIT 3
Aquaguard
Newspaper
Advertisement

ZERO-B purifiers used a halogenated resin technology as part of a three-stage purification process. The first stage removed suspended impurities with filter pads, the second eliminated bad odors and taste with activated carbon, and the third killed bacteria by using trace quantities of polyiodide (iodine). The last feature was attractive because it helped prevent iodine deficiency diseases and permitted purified water to be stored up to eight hours without fear of recontamination.

The basic purifier product for the home carried the name Puristore. A Puristore unit typically sat on a kitchen counter near the tap, with no electricity or plumbing hookup needed for its operation. The unit stored 20 liters of purified water. It sold to consumers for Rs. 2,000. Each year the user had to replace the halogenated resin at a cost of Rs. 200.

Chatterjee estimated that ZERO-B captured about 7 percent of the Indian water purifier market. Probably the biggest reason for the small share was a lack of consumer awareness. ZERO-B purifiers had been on the market for less than three years. They were not advertised heavily and did not enjoy the sales effort intensity of Aquaguard. Distribution also was limited. During Chatterjee's visit, he could find only five dealers in Calcutta carrying ZERO-B products and none in Bangalore. The dealers he contacted were of the opinion that ZERO-B's marketing efforts soon would intensify; two had heard rumors that a door-to-door sales force was planned and that consumer advertising was about to begin.

Chatterjee confirmed the latter point with a visit to a Calcutta advertising agency. A modest number of 10-second television commercials soon would be aired on the Zee TV and DD metro channels. The advertisements would focus on educating consumers with the position "It is not a filter." Instead, ZERO-B was a water purifier and was much more effective than a candle filter in preventing health problems. Apart from this advertising effort, the only form of promotion used was a point of sale brochure that dealers could give to prospective customers (see Exhibit 4).

On balance, Chatterjee thought that Ion Exchange could be a major player in the market. The company had over 30 years' experience in the field of water purification and devoted upward of Rs. 10 million each year to corporate research and development. "In fact," he thought, "all Ion Exchange really needs to do is recognize the market's potential and make it a priority within the company." However, that might be difficult to do because of the company's emphasis on industrial markets. Chatterjee estimated that ZERO-B products would account for less than 2 percent of Ion Exchange's 1996 total sales, estimated at Rs. 1 billion. He thought the total marketing expenditures for ZERO-B would be around Rs. 3 million.

Singer

The newest competitor to enter the Indian water purifier market was Singer India Ltd. Originally, Singer India was a subsidiary of the Singer Company, located in the United States, but a minority share (49 percent) was sold to Indian investors in 1982. The change in ownership led to the construction of manufacturing facilities in India for sewing machines in 1983. The facilities

EXHIBIT 4
Zero-B Sales Brochure

were expanded in 1991 to produce a broad line of home appliances. Sales revenues in 1996 for the entire product line—sewing machines, food processors, irons, mixers, toasters, water heaters, ceiling fans, cooking ranges, and color televisions—would be about Rs. 900 million.

During Chatterjee's time in Calcutta he had visited a Singer Company showroom on Park Street. Initially he had hoped that Singer might be a suitable partner to manufacture and distribute the Delight purifier. However, much to his surprise, he was told that Singer now had its own brand on the market, Aquarius. The product was not yet available in Calcutta but was being sold in Bombay and Delhi.

A marketing research agency in Delhi was able to gather some information on the Singer purifier. The product contained nine stages (!) and sold to consumers for Rs.4,000. It removed sediments, heavy metals, bad tastes, odors, and colors. It also killed bacteria and viruses, fungi, and nematodes. The purifier required water pressure (8 psi minimum) to operate but needed no electricity. It came in a single countertop model that could be moved from one room to another. The life of the device at a flow rate of 3.8 liters per minute was listed as 40,000 liters—about four to six years of use in the typical Indian household. The product's life could be extended to 70,000 liters at a somewhat slower flow rate. However, at 70,000 liters, the product had to be discarded. The agency reported a heavy advertising blitz accompanying the introduction in Delhi, emphasizing television and newspaper advertising, plus outdoor and transit advertising as support. All 10 Singer showrooms in Delhi offered vivid demonstrations of the product's operation.

Chatterjee had to admit that the photos of the Aquarius purifier shown in the Calcutta showroom looked appealing. And a trade article he found had described the product as "state of the art" in comparison to the "primitive" products now on the market. Chatterjee and Blair Company engineers tended to agree—the disinfecting resin used in Aquarius had been developed by the U.S. government's National Aeronautics and Space Administration (NASA) and had been proved to be 100 percent effective against bacteria and viruses. "If only I could have brought a unit back with me," he thought. "We could have some test results and see just how good it is." The trade article also mentioned that Singer hoped to sell 40,000 units over the next two years.

Chatterjee knew that Singer was a well-known and respected brand name in India. Further, Singer's distribution channels were superior to those of any competitor

in the market, including those of Eureka Forbes. The most prominent of Singer's three distribution channels were the 210 company-owned showrooms in major urban areas around the country. Each sold and serviced the entire line of Singer products. Each was very well kept and was staffed by knowledgeable personnel. Singer products also were sold throughout India by over 3,000 independent dealers, who received inventory from an estimated 70 Singer-appointed distributors. According to the marketing research agency in Delhi, distributors earned margins of 12 percent of the retail price for Aquarius, while dealers earned margins of 5 percent. Finally, Singer employed over 400 salespersons who sold sewing machines and food processors door to door. As with Eureka Forbes, the direct sales force sold products primarily in large urban markets.

Other Competitors

Chatterjee was aware of several other water purifiers on the Indian market. The Delta brand from S & S Industries in Madras seemed to be a carbon copy of Aquaguard except for a more eye-pleasing countertop design. According to the promotional literature, Delta offered a line of water-related products: purifiers, water softeners, iron removers, desalinators, and ozonators. Another competitor was Alfa Water Purifiers, Bombay. That company offered four purifier models at prices from Rs. 4,300 to Rs. 6,500, depending on capacity. Symphony's Spectrum brand sold well around Bombay at Rs. 4,000 each but removed only suspended sediments, not heavy metals or bacteria. The Sam Group in Coimbatore recently had launched its Water Doctor purifier at Rs. 5,200. The device used a third-stage ozonator to kill bacteria and viruses and came in two attractive countertop models with 6- and 12-liter storage, respectively. Batliboi was mentioned by the Delhi research agency as yet another competitor, although Chatterjee knew nothing else about the brand. Taken together, unit sales of all purifiers at these companies plus ZERO-B and Singer probably would account for around 60,000 units in 1996. The remaining 190,000 units would be Aquaguards and PureSips.

At least 100 Indian companies made and marketed candle filters. The largest probably was Bajaj Electrical Division, whose product line also included water heaters, irons, electric light bulbs, toasters, mixers, and grillers. Bajaj's candle filters were sold by a large number of dealers who carried the entire product line. Candle filters produced by other manufacturers were sold mostly through dealers who specialized in small household appliances and general hardware. Probably no single manufacturer of candle filters had more than 5 percent of any regional market in the country. No manufacturer attempted to satisfy a national market. Still, the candle filters market deserved serious consideration: perhaps Delight's entry strategy would attempt to "trade up" users of candle filters to a better, safer product.

Finally, Chatterjee knew that the sales of almost all purifiers in 1996 in India were in large urban areas. No manufacturer targeted rural or smaller urban areas, and at best, Chatterjee had calculated, existing manufacturers were reaching only 10 to 15 percent of the entire Indian population. An explosion in sales would come if the right product could be sold outside metropolitan areas.

Recommendations

Chatterjee decided that an Indian market entry for Blair Company was subject to three "givens," as he called them. First, he thought that a strategic focus on rural or smaller urban areas would not be wise, at least at the start. The lack of adequate distribution and communication infrastructure in rural India meant that any market entry would begin with larger cities, most likely on the west coast.

Second, market entry would require manufacturing the units in India. Because the cost of skilled labor in India was around Rs. 20 to Rs. 25 per hour (compared to $20 to $25 per hour in the United States), importing complete units was out of the question. However, importing a few key components would be necessary at the start of the operation.

Third, Blair Company should find an Indian partner. Chatterjee's visits had produced a number of promising partners: Polar Industries, Calcutta; Milton Plastics, Bombay; Videocon Appliances, Aurangabad; BPL Sanyo Utilities and Appliances, Bangalore: Onida Savak, Delhi; Hawkins India, Bombay: and Voltas, Bombay. All those companies manufactured and marketed a line of high-quality household appliances, had one or more strong brand names, and had established dealer networks (a minimum of 10,000 dealers). All were involved to greater or lesser degrees with international partners. All were medium-size firms—not so large that a partnership with Blair Company would be one-sided and not so small that they would lack managerial talent and other resources. Finally, all were profitable (15 to 27 percent return on assets in 1995) and looking to grow. However, Chatterjee had no idea if any company would find the Delight purifier and Blair Company attractive or might be persuaded to sell part or all of their operations as an acquisition.

Field Testing and Product Recommendations

The most immediate decision Chatterjee faced was whether to recommend a field test. The test would cost about $25,000, placing 20 units in Indian homes in three cities and monitoring their performance for three to six months. The decision to test really was more than it seemed; Chatterjee's boss had explained that a decision to test was really a decision to enter. It made no sense to spend this kind of time and money if India was not an attractive opportunity. The testing period also would give Blair Company representatives time to identify a suitable Indian company as a licensee, joint venture partner, or acquisition.

Fundamental to market entry was product design. Engineers at Blair Company had taken the position that the purification technologies planned for Delight could be "packaged in almost any fashion as long as we have electricity." Electricity was needed to operate the product's ozonator as well as to indicate to users that the unit was functioning properly (or improperly, as the case might be). Beyond this requirement, anything was possible.

Chatterjee thought that a modular approach would be best. The basic module would be a countertop unit much like the one shown in Exhibit 2. The module would outperform anything on the market in terms of flow rate, palatability, durability, and reliability and would store two liters of purified water. Two additional modules would remove iron, calcium, or other metallic contaminants that were specific to particular regions. For example, Calcutta and much of the surrounding area suffered from iron contamination, which no filter or purifier on the Indian market could remove to a satisfactory level. Water supplies in other areas in the country were known to contain objectionable concentrations of calcium, salt, arsenic, lead, or sulfur. Most Indian consumers would need neither of the additional modules, some would need one or the other, but very few would need both.

Market Entry and Marketing Planning Recommendations

Assuming that Chatterjee recommended proceeding with the field test, he would need to make a recommendation concerning the mode of market entry. In addition, his recommendation should include an outline of a marketing plan.

Licensee Considerations. If market entry was in the form of a joint working arrangement with a licensee, Blair Company's financial investment would be minimal. Chatterjee thought that Blair Company might risk as little as $30,000 in capital for production facilities and equipment, plus another $5,000 for office facilities and equipment. Those investments would be completely offset by the licensee's payment to Blair Company for technology transfer and personnel training. Annual fixed costs to Blair Company should not exceed $40,000 at the outset and would decrease to $15,000 as soon as an Indian national could be hired, trained, and left in charge. The duties of this individual would be to work with Blair Company personnel in the United States and with management at the licensee to see that units were produced per Blair Company's specifications. Apart from this activity, Blair Company would have no control over the licensee's operations. Chatterjee expected that the licensee would pay royalties to Blair Company of about Rs. 280 for each unit sold in the domestic market and Rs. 450 for each unit that was exported. The average royalty probably would be around Rs. 300.

Joint Venture/Acquisition Considerations. If entry was in the form of either a joint venture or an acquisition, financial investment and annual fixed costs would be much higher and would depend largely on the scope of operations. Chatterjee had roughed out some estimates for a joint venture entry, based on three levels of scope (see Exhibit 5). His estimates reflected what he thought were reasonable assumptions for all needed investments plus annual fixed expenses for sales activities, general administrative overhead, research and development, insurance, and depreciation. His estimates allowed for the Delight purifier to be sold either through dealers or through a direct, door-to-door sales force. Chatterjee thought that estimates of annual fixed expenses for market entry through acquisition would be identical to those for a joint venture. However,

estimates for the investment (purchase) might be considerably higher, the same, or lower. It depended on what was purchased.

Chatterjee's estimates of Delight's unit contribution margins reflected a number of assumptions: expected economies of scale, experience-curve effects, the costs of Indian labor and raw materials, and competitors' pricing strategies. However, the most important assumption was Delight's pricing strategy. If a skimming strategy was used and the product was sold through a dealer channel, the basic module would be priced to dealers at Rs. 5,500 and to consumers at Rs. 5,900. "This would give us about a Rs. 650 unit contribution once we got production flowing smoothly," he thought. In contrast, if a penetration strategy was used and the product was sold through a dealer channel, the basic module would be priced to dealers at Rs. 4,100 and to consumers at Rs. 4,400 and would yield a unit contribution of Rs. 300. For simplicity's sake, Chatterjee assumed that the two additional modules would be priced to dealers at Rs. 800 and to consumers at Rs. 1,000 and would yield a unit contribution of Rs. 100. Finally, he assumed that all products sold to dealers would go directly from Blair Company to the dealers (no distributors would be used).

If a direct sales force was employed instead of dealers, Chatterjee thought that the prices charged to consumers would not change from those listed above. However, sales commissions would have to be paid in addition to the fixed costs necessary to maintain and manage the sales force. Under a skimming price strategy, the sales commission would be Rs. 550 per unit and the unit contribution would be Rs. 500. Under a penetration price strategy, the sales commission would be Rs. 400 per unit and the unit contribution would be Rs. 200. These financial estimates, he would explain in his report, would apply to 1998 or 1999, the expected first year of operation.

Skimming versus penetration was more than just a pricing strategy. Product design for the skimming

EXHIBIT 5
Investments and Fixed Costs for a Joint Venture Market Entry

	Operational Scope		
	Two Regions	**Four Regions**	**National Market**
1998 market potential (units)	55,000	110,000	430,000
Initial investment (Rs. thousands)	4,000	8,000	30,000
Annual fixed overhead expenses (Rs. thousands)			
Using dealer channels	4,000	7,000	40,000
Using direct sales force	7,200	14,000	88,000

strategy would be noticeably superior, with higher performance and quality, a longer warranty period, more features, and a more attractive appearance compared with the design for the penetration strategy. Positioning also most likely would be different. Chatterjee recognized several positioning possibilities: performance and taste, value for the money/low price, safety, health, convenience, attractive styling, avoidance of diseases and health-related bills, and superior American technology. The only position he considered "taken" in the market was that occupied by Aquaguard—protect family health and service at your doorstep. While other competitors had claimed

certain positions for their products, none had devoted financial resources to a degree that prevented Delight from dislodging them. Chatterjee believed that considerable advertising and promotion expenditures would be necessary to communicate Delight's positioning. He would need estimates of those expenditures in his recommendation.

"If we go ahead with Delight, we'll have to move quickly," Chatterjee thought. "The window of opportunity is open, but if Singer's product is as good as they claim, we'll be in for a fight. Still, Aquarius seems vulnerable on the water pressure requirement and on price. We'll need a product category 'killer' to win."

Case 6-11

Murphy Brewery Ireland, Limited

Patrick Conway, marketing director for Murphy's, picked up his issue of *The Financial Times* and read the following headline on May 13: "Grand Met, Guinness to Merge." He pondered the impact on his firm. Guinness was Murphy's most formidable competitor not only in Ireland but worldwide. Since a staff meeting was already scheduled for later Tuesday morning, he decided to examine the article closely and discuss it with his team. As he read on, the £22.3 billion merger between two of the four largest distillers (Seagram's headquartered in Canada and Allied Domecq, another British company, were the other two) appeared to have much synergy. The article pointed out that the geographic and brand fits were good between the two companies. The new firm, which will be called GMG, will be approximately equal in size to such major multinationals as Unilever, Procter & Gamble, and Philip Morris.[1]

[1]John William and Ross Tieman, "Grand Met, Guinness to Merge," *Financial Times,* Tuesday, May 13, 1997, p. 1.

This case was prepared by Patrick E. Murphy, professor of marketing, University of Notre Dame, Indiana, and former visiting professor of marketing, University College Cork in Ireland, and Don O'Sullivan, lecturer in marketing, Department of Management and Marketing, University College Cork. The case was distributed by the European Case Clearinghouse.

This case is intended to serve as a basis for a class discussion rather than to illustrate either effective or ineffective handling of a business situation. The authors would like to thank Patrick Conway, David Ford, and Dan Leahy of Murphy Brewery Ireland and Michael Foley of Heineken USA for their assistance in writing this case.

During the 11 AM staff meeting, Patrick brought the merger to the attention of his colleagues. His company was in the middle of preparing its 1998 global marketing plan, and this news brought some urgency to the task ahead. Patrick stated that he felt a major assessment of Murphy's status in the worldwide market was needed He called on David Ford, his export manager, to examine Murphy's position in the British and European markets. He said he would phone Michael Foley of Heineken USA (distributor of Murphy's in the states) to report on Murphy's progress there and asked Dan Leahy to look into Murphy's status in Ireland. He asked each man to report back to him within a week.

As part of his personal preparation, Patrick decided to dig into the files and reacquaint himself with the company history, since he had joined the firm only a few years previously. He also wanted to find out more about the merger. He rang the communications department to clip and route all articles from business publications on this topic to him. Patrick considered the impact these developments would have on Murphy's brands.

In 1997 Murphy's had become a truly international brand that maintained a unique identity in Ireland. The name Murphy, the most common surname in the entire country, is recognized internationally for its Irish heritage. Exhibit 1 shows that about 85 percent of Murphy's sales came from export business in 1996 and that the company now employs 385 people. He located a report from several years earlier that provided a historical perspective on the company.

Historical Background

James J. Murphy and Company Limited was founded in 1856 in Cork City, Ireland, by the four Murphy brothers— James, William, Jerome, and Francis. In 1890 they were

EXHIBIT 1   **Export Sales versus Total Company Volumes**

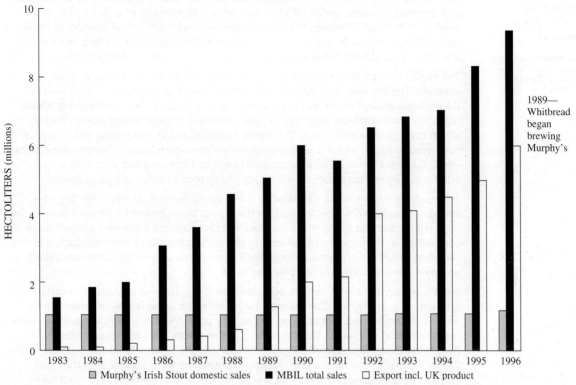

1989—
Whitbread
began
brewing
Murphy's

☐ Murphy's Irish Stout domestic sales   ■ MBIL total sales   ☐ Export incl. UK product

described as follows: "These gentlemen applied themselves with energy and enterprise to the manufacture of an article, the reputation of which now extends far beyond the South of Ireland where the firm's stout and porter have been long and favorably known and where they command a very exclusive sale."[2]

James J. Murphy inherited the family business skills. His grandfather, also called James, had founded, with his brothers, the distillery James Murphy and Company in Midleton, County Cork (15 miles to the east of Cork City), in 1825. These Murphy brothers prospered as ship owners and tea importers and had been paid quite a large sum of money before founding their distillery. This company experienced significant growth and in 1867 amalgamated with four Cork distilleries to create Cork Distilleries Company Ltd. That firm enjoyed great success over the next century and in 1966 joined with the Dublin distillery John Jameson and Son and John Power and Son to create Irish Distillers Limited.

The Murphy Brewery is located at Lady's Well in Cork, whose name derives from a celebrated well on the hill opposite of the premises. It was dedicated to

Our Lady and believed to possess miraculous properties. To the present day, pilgrimages take place to the shrine every year in the month of May. During the nineteenth century Lady's Well was one of Cork's largest breweries and was mentioned in the 1890 publication *Noted Breweries of Great Britain and Ireland,* which indicated that Murphy's Stout had become a formidable rival to Guinness in the south of Ireland.[3]

Initially, Murphy's brewed porter, but it switched exclusively to stout (the name *stout* denotes strong beers—see Exhibit 2 for a description of the product), and this remained its sole beer product until 1965. Over the years the brewery acquired a number of licensed products and developed a wholesale spirits and soft drinks bottling business.

Although Murphy's opened up trade in London, Manchester, South Wales, and other parts of England early in the twentieth century, the company began experiencing financial problems in the 1960s. There was considerable anxiety among the staff of 200 in Murphy's Brewery Cork concerning the continuity of their employment in the early 1970s. At that time they

[2]*Murphy Brewery Limited: A Profile,* undated.

[3]Company sources.

EXHIBIT 2
What Is Stout,
and How Was It
Promoted?

Source: Partially adapted from
Brendan O'Brien, *The Stout
Book* (Dublin; Anna Livia
Press, 1990).

Stout is a black beer with a thick white head. The black color is due mainly to the fact that it contains malted barley which is roasted in a similar way to coffee beans. The creamy white head is created from the "initiation" and "surging" of bubbles of nitrogen and carbon dioxide gas as the beer is poured. The gas enters the keg and forces the beer out. It is actually the nitrogen which causes the tight, creamy head.

The word *stout* has long been used to describe strong beers; it also meant stout, as in stout ale. The strength may have been in terms of taste or alcohol or both, Standard stout ranges in alcohol content from 4 percent to 5 percent. The word *stout* gradually made the transition from adjective to noun. The basic constituent of stout is barley, which consists mainly of starch. The barley becomes a malt and during this process is converted to sugar, which is fermentable. When the malt is roasted beyond the normal limits, this gives the stout its unusual dark hue. The highly roasted dark malt is 500 times darker than a pale malt and adds its distinctive color as well as flavor.

The resulting sugary liquid, called wort, is eventually formed. At this stage hops are added and boiled with wort to produce the liquid. When boiled for an hour or two, the hops release oils and resins which produce the characteristic bitterness and aroma. A comparison of the bitterness level among the leading brands of stout conducted by the European Brewery Convention found that Guinness rates 45 to 48 European units of bitterness, Beamish 40, and Murphy's 36 to 38.

Stout is synonymous with Ireland, and nowhere else is stout as popular or as intrinsically part of everyday life. The criterion by which a pub often is judged is likely to be whether it sells a good pint of stout. In the pub, pouring pints is seen as having a major impact on product quality. Stout is poured in two stages. First the glass is filled to 75 percent capacity and allowed to "settle" so that the creamy head will separate from the dark body. To top off the pint, the tap is pushed forward slightly until the head rises just below the rim. This activity takes a minute or two and results in stout taking longer to pour. Interestingly, the product is poured in one go/pull outside Ireland.

Stout has its roots in colder climates in Ireland and Scandinavia, and traditionally it has been a winter brew. Comments such as "typically consumed in the dark winter months" and "a seasonal beer brewed only in the winter" are used regularly by stout breweries worldwide. Stout is thought to be a drink suited to quiet, reflective slipping. Both in Ireland and worldwide, it is now a year-round drink.

To return to the definition, stout is often considered a strong drink. Therefore, both Murphy's and Guinness have extensively used strength in their marketing and advertising. Murphy's utilized a circus strongman who was shown lifting a horse off the ground with the label "Murphy's Stout gives strength" for many years in the late 1800s and 1900s. Guinness has utilized posters throughout Ireland depicting superhuman strength achieved by drinking Guinness with the slogan "Guinness for strength."

had an English partner (Watney and Mann), which wanted to dissolve the partnership. Colonel John J. Murphy, chairman of Murphy's, stated that "we are confident that we can satisfy" certain financial conditions to meet the demands of the creditors. The company at this time was well over 100 years old and had overcome difficult periods in the past.

In February 1975 Murphy's approached Heineken N.B. (the Amsterdam-based brewery which had been founded by Garard Adriann Heineken the same year the Murphy brothers opened their brewery in Ireland)

with a proposal to begin a licensing operation for Heineken in Ireland. Heineken examined the possibilities of the Irish market and found them favorable, and a license agreement was signed. A marketing company, Heineken Ireland Limited, was set up as a fully owned subsidiary of Heineken N.B. Heineken was well known for its lager beer, which complemented the Murphy's Irish Stout offering.

Murphy's new policy of expanding as a broad-based competitor to the leading brands (e.g., Guinness and Beamish and Crawford) worked well at first. However, the company was hit by recessionary problems, and J.J. Murphy and Company Limited went into receivership in 1982. At that time the company employed 235 people. On July 14, 1982, the *Cork Examiner* confirmed a commitment from the Dutch brewing company Heineken to invest 1.6 million pounds in the brewery.

In 1983 Heineken International purchased the assets of James J. Murphy and Company Limited, which was then in receivership. Murphy Brewery Ireland Limited became a wholly owned subsidiary of Heineken International, a move which gave a new lease on life to Murphy's Brewery. This development preserved the long and respected tradition of brewing in the Cork area and the well-known brand name. Since then Murphy Brewery Ireland Limited has continued its brewing and marketing of Murphy's Irish Stout and Heineken. The adoption of Murphy's Irish Stout by Heineken International as one of its corporate brands meant that the brand became available to drinkers worldwide.

The Heineken Era

Heineken International is the world's second largest brewer (Exhibit 3) and a private company. Its flagship Heineken lager, the world's most exported beer, and the Amstel brand are also brewed under license by third parties. They are produced in over 100 plants and sold in 170 countries on all continents. The Heineken brand is sold in the same green bottle and promoted with the same brand imagery in the same price tier in China, Spain, the United States, and elsewhere. Heineken was the first beer to be imported into the United States after Prohibition was lifted in 1933. The United States is now its largest market.

Murphy's management during the Heineken years has been led by four managing directors. Currently, Marien Kakabeeke, a native of Holland, serves in that position. He assumed the post in August 1993. Heineken has demonstrated its commitment to Murphy's by opening a new office complex in the old Malthouse at the brewery. Murphy's became accredited in 1992 with the ISO 9002 mark for all aspects of operations—the first brewery in Europe to achieve that distinction.

Murphy's Brands and Packaging

Internationally, Murphy's Irish Stout (MIS) is now available in 63 countries worldwide, up from only 20 in 1992. Export sales of the brand grew by almost 200 percent during 1996. Growth markets include the United States, where MIS sales increased 163 percent, and Germany, France, Spain, Italy, and the Netherlands, where sales volumes grew 82 percent. MIS's output has grown by 700 percent in the last decade. Most of this increase was fueled by international consumption, with sales in Ireland increasing only 10 percent over that time (Exhibit 1).

This growth is reflected in an increased turnover for MBI from Ir £125 million to Ir £140 million. The total company volume now stands at almost 950,000 hectoliters.

For most of its first 135 years Murphy's Irish Stout was available only in draft form in pubs throughout Ireland. A packaging innovation (draughtflow cans) was launched in October 1992. A plastic device (called a widget) is fitted into the bottom of the can which nitrates the liquid after the can is opened, creating the famous creamy head and giving the product a publike taste. Consumer acceptance of the can is reflected in the distribution growth of the product, which makes it available in off-licenses/liquor stores. Within Europe a 330-milliliter cream-colored can is sold, while in the United States a 14.9-ounce can is marketed. One distinguishing feature of the can in Europe is the message "Chill for at least two hours. Pour contents into glass in

EXHIBIT 3
World's Largest Brewers, 1994

Source: Havis Dawson, "Brand Brewing." *Beverage World,* October 1995, p. 52. 1994 is the latest year available.

Company	HQ	Prod./Vol.[1]	World Share	% of Sales in Exports
Anheuser-Busch	United States	105.1	9%	6%
Heineken	Netherlands	59.6	4.8	89
Miller	United States	50.1	3.9	5
Kirin	Japan	35.1	2.7	5
Foster's	Australia	34.7	2.7	73
Carlsberg	Denmark	30.4	2.3	82
Danone Group	France	27.7	2.4	65
Guinness	United Kingdom	24.2	2.1	84

[1]Production/volume is measured in hectoliters: 1 hectoliter = 26.4 gallons or .85 barrel.

one smooth action. Best before end—see base," which is reprinted in four languages on the cans.

Another packaging innovation for MIS was developed in 1995. A draughtflow bottle is now available in both the U.S. and European markets. The 500-milliliter (16.9-oz.) bottle has a long neck and is dark brown in color. It is used as a powerful unique differentiating point for the brand. The back labels acclaim the benefits of the draughtflow technology. Warning labels concerning alcoholic beverages are shown on the U.S. labels.

Murphy's Irish Amber, a traditional Irish ale, was launched in 1995 as Murphy's Irish Red Beer in Germany and France. It is brewed in Cork but is not available domestically in Ireland. In the United States Murphy's Irish Amber was introduced in both draft and a 12-ounce bottle in September 1996. The bottles are amber in color. The label's dark blue and red colors accented by gold signal a high-quality product. Compelled by the need for a stronger Murphy's portfolio due to increased interest in genuine red beers, the company believed this product would be successful. Thus far, Murphy's Irish Amber's success has far exceeded expectations.

Murphy's also offers Heineken's low-alcohol beer called Buckler. It contains 1/2 of 1 percent alcohol and about half the calorie content of normal beer. It sells in 330-milliliter bottles in bars, off-licenses, and supermarkets in the served markets.

The Competition

After returning from a business trip to the Continent a week later, Patrick Conway found on his desk a stack of articles sent to him from the communications department discussing the Guinness–Grand Met merger. Before turning his attention to them, he reflected on what he knew regarding the Guinness brand both in Ireland and elsewhere. Guinness Stout was the pioneer in this category and an even older firm than Murphy's. It was founded in 1759 by Arthur Guinness in Dublin. It was now the eighth largest brewer in the world in terms of volume, with over a 2 percent market share. Murphy's parent, Heineken, is in second place worldwide (Exhibit 3).

Guinness is brewed in almost 50 countries and sold in over 130.[4] In the stout category, it is the proverbial "500-pound gorilla" in that it commands a 70 to 90 percent share in almost all markets. When it moves, Murphy's and other competitors invariably pay close attention. The Guinness name defines the stout market

in most countries and is the "gold standard" against which all other competing brands are measured. The company's marketing prowess is well known in that Guinness Stout is positioned as "hip in the United Kingdom," "traditional in Ireland," and a source of "virility" in Africa; a special microbrew is aimed at "creating a new generation of beer snobs" in the United States. Guinness plans to continue targeting continental Europe, the United States, and Asia in a bid to expand its markets and grow its business.

Guinness has been very successful in building its stout brand around the world. The company is identified with its quirky advertising campaigns in Ireland and its high profile regarding other marketing and promotional endeavors. One significant effort involved the Irish national soccer team, which endorsed Guinness as its official beer for the 1994 World Cup. Sales of Guinness Stout rose dramatically in the United States during the World Cup finals. Another U.S.-based promotion program designed to appeal to the over 40 million Americans of Irish descent was the "Win Your Own Pub in Ireland" contest. This competition has been going on for several years and is featured in Guinness's Web page currently. Third, the huge development of the Irish pub concept around the world helped Guinness brands abroad and contributed to an increase in export sales of 10 percent in 1996. The company launched the Guinness pub concept in 1992, and there are now 1,250 "Guinness" Irish pubs in 36 countries. Four hundred more are expected to open in 1997.[5]

Patrick turned his attention to several articles about the Guinness and Grand Met merger. A rationale for the merger was that these firms could acquire new brands more easily than they may be able to find new consumers in the U.S. and European marketplace, where alcohol consumption is falling, the population is aging, and concerns about health are rising. The new firm will be a formidable force in the race to open up new markets in liquor and beer. The companies have complementary product lines and will be divided into four major divisions (Exhibit 4). The Guinness Brewery worldwide division will feature its signature stout, Harp (a lager), Kilkenny (a red ale), Cruzcampo (a Spanish beer), and Red Stripe.

The Economist noted that even though GMG will be the seventh largest company in the world, it faces major obstacles. One is that even though its brands are very well known, the combined company will lack

[4]Company fact sheet.

[5]Barry O'Keeffe, "'Black Stuff' Underpins Profit Raise at Guinness," *The Irish Times,* March 21, 1997.

EXHIBIT 4
GMG **Brands**

Source: "GMG Brands: What the Two Sides Will Contribute," *Financial Times.* May 13, 1997, p. 27.

Division	Turnover (millions)	Pretax Profit (millions)
Guinness Brewing Worldwide:	£2,262	£283
Guinness Stout, Harp, Cruzcampo (Spanish), Red Stripe		
United Distillers & Vintners (Guinness Brands)	£2,468	£791
Dewar's, Gordon's Gin, Bell's, Moet Hennessey, Johnnie Walker, Black and White, Asbach		
(Grand Met Brands)	£3,558	£502
Smirnoff, Stolichnaya, J&B (whisky), Gilbey's Gin, Jose Cuervo, Grand Marnier, Bailey's, Malibu, Absolut		
Pillsbury	£3,770	£447
Pillsbury, Green Giant, Old El Paso, Häagen-Dazs		
Burger King	£ 859	£167

Note: Turnover and pretax profit numbers denote millions of pounds sterling.

focus. Grand Met has a long history of trying its hand at different businesses but has done so with mixed success. Guinness, however, has an even longer history of not doing much besides brewing beer, and its spirits business has been a struggle for the firm. *The Economist*'s conclusion gave Mr. Conway encouragement and reflected his own impression when the magazine stated: "Unless GMG manages to show very rapidly that they can mix these ingredients into something fairly tasty, then pressure will grow on it to simplify itself."[6]

Patrick recalled that Guinness is not the only competitor of Murphy's. Beamish & Crawford, also located in Cork, was founded in 1792 and currently employs about 200 people. In 1987 the company joined the Foster's Brewing Group. The primary brands offered by the company are Beamish (stout), Foster's (lager), and Carling Black Label (lager).

Beamish stout is available in most pubs throughout the southern part of Ireland. The brand is positioned on its Irishness, the heritage of Beamish Stout, and the fact that it is the only Irish stout exclusively brewed in Ireland. In the last three years Beamish has been marketed in Europe (Italy and Spain mostly) and North America (Canada and the United States). It is distributed through the Foster's Brewing Group in those markets.

The Irish Market

Dan Leahy sent Patrick the following report on the market for Murphy's in Ireland. His memo discussed both the importance of pub life in the country and the

[6]"Master of the Bar," *The Economist,* May 17, 1997, p. 73.

competitive situation. Patrick read with interest Dan's assessment of the Irish market:

With a population of less than 4 million people, the Irish market is small in international terms. However, it is the market in which stout holds the largest share at nearly 50 percent of all beer sales. With one of the youngest populations in the developed world and one of the fastest-growing economies, it is an important and dynamic market for all stout producers. This is added to by the fact that the three competitors—Murphy's, Guinness, and Beamish—all use their Irishness as a key attribute in product positioning. A presence in the Irish market is viewed as being central to the authenticity of the Irishness claim.

Pubs have long been a central part of Irish life, particularly in rural areas, where pubs are semi-social centers. Irish pubs are regularly run by owner-operators who buy products from different breweries. This is quite different from most international markets, where pubs tend to be run by or for the breweries. For example, in the Dutch market Heineken has 52 percent of the outlets. Partly as a result of this, Irish consumers are highly brand-loyal. Also, in the Irish market, breweries engage in higher levels of promotion.

Irish pubs are perceived very positively in many parts of the world. They are seen as places which are accessible to all the family. Irish pubs are intimately linked with musical sessions and viewed as being open, friendly places to visit. This positive perception has resulted in a proliferation of Irish-themed pubs, particularly in the last decade. This development has been used extensively by Guinness and lately by Murphy's as a means of increasing distribution.

Guinness dominates the Irish stout market with an 89 percent market share. Murphy's and Beamish have roughly equal shares of the rest of the market. Guinness's dominance of the market is reflected in the fact that the term *Guinness* is synonymous with stout. In many parts of the country it is ordered without reference to its name simply by asking for "a pint." Similarly, in Britain 1 million pints of Guinness are sold every day, with 10 million glasses a day sold worldwide.

Guinness Ireland turned in a strong performance in 1996 with sales up 8 percent to 764 million pints.[7] The company began a 12-million-pound advertising campaign last year called "The Big Pint" and engaged in extensive billboard advertising emphasizing the size and strength of the brand.

In Ireland, Beamish Stout is positioned as a value for money, Irish stout selling at 20 pence (10 percent) lower than the competitors. It is slightly ahead of Murphy's currently in the race for second place in Ireland. As with Murphy's, Beamish's traditional base has been in the Cork-area market. Today, 1 in every 4 pints of stout consumed in Cork is Beamish and 1 in every 14 pints in Ireland is Beamish.

Within the lager market in Ireland, Heineken dominates with nearly 40 percent of the market, while Budweiser and Carlsberg (both distributed by Guinness) each have just over a 20 percent market share. Harp, which once held an overwhelming 80 percent share, now accounts for only 8 percent.

Murphy's is priced on a par with Guinness in all markets in the country. The average price of a pint of stout in the market is Ir £2.00.

In parts of the market where demand for the brand is low, Murphy's has begun selling the product in an innovative 3/5-keg (a keg is a barrel containing 50 liters) size. This ensures that the product reaches the customer at the desired level of quality.

Murphy's has pursued market growth through the development of export markets and development of the take-home market. The development of these markets is driven by the fact that the domestic draught market is mature with static sales over the last number of years. In 1995 pub sales fell by almost 2.5 percent, while off-license sales grew by 37 percent. The growth in the off-license business is due in part to the impact of the new stronger drunk-driving legislation and in-home summer consumption.[8]

Both of these markets rely heavily on canned and bottled packaging for the product. Traditionally this has posed a difficulty for stout products as there is a perceived deterioration in quality compared to the draught version. Murphy's is selling its product in bottles and dedicating some advertising to the superior bottled taste and using it as a differentiating feature for all of Murphy's products and using the draught bottle as a brand icon for the firm.

Conway thought about the report on the Irish market and how difficult it was to compete against Guinness and the extreme brand loyalty of the Irish consumer to it. He thought about the new three-year 5-million-pound advertising campaign launched in 1996 and hoped that the unique approach would win new customers. One memorable TV ad featured a group of Japanese samurai warriors who arrive in a line at a bar, knock back bottles of Murphy's, and leave while a Guinness drinker drums his fingers on the counter waiting for his pint to settle. Conway believed that brand awareness was growing. One successful promotional endeavor is the company's sponsorship of the Murphy's Irish Open, which was part of the PGA European Golf Tour.

He knew that strides were being made in the distribution network outside its traditional stronghold of Cork City and County. One of the inducements the company was using was a lower trade price to the pubs so that they made more on each pint sold. The company followed this philosophy internationally as well in the effort to compete with Guinness.

He also recalled two *Irish Times* articles that gave his and Kakabeeke's views on the importance of the Irish market to the company. He asked his secretary to retrieve them from the files and routed them to the marketing group. Conway was quoted as saying, "Murphy's believes it has to have an advertising spend comparable to Guinness if it is ever to achieve a critical mass in Ireland. We have to differentiate ourselves, and there's no use doing it with a whisper. A better market share in Ireland would also provide Murphy's Irish Stout with a backbone from which to grow exports."[9] Mr. Kakabeeke said that "the brewery is not happy with the 5 percent position in the Irish market and with the level of domestic growth being achieved by Murphy's Irish Stout. I feel that sales can be improved in Ireland."[10]

The UK and Continental European Markets

The United Kingdom (England, Scotland, Wales, and Northern Ireland), Ireland's closest neighbor, represents the world's largest stout market in terms of

---

[7]O'Keeffe, "'Black Stuff' Underpins Profit Raise at Guinness."

[8]Paul O'Kane, "Murphy Boosts Exports," *The Irish Times,* March 7, 1996.

[9]Paul O'Kane, "Murphy's Aims to Double Its Sales in Three Years," *The Irish Times,* June 14, 1996.

[10]O'Kane, "Murphy Boosts Exports."

consumption at 60 million hectoliters. The total population of the UK is approximately 60 million consumers. Murphy's market share stands at 15 percent, while Guinness (78 percent) and Beamish (6 percent) are the other two major competitors. MIS was launched in the UK in 1985 and has enjoyed continued growth in that market since then. Murphy's success in the UK may be attributed to several factors.

First, Heineken and Murphy's are distributed in the UK through the Whitbread Beer Company in Luton. Whitbread has an association with over 27,000 pubs in the country, which translates to an automatic distribution network for Murphy's products. Recently Whitbread has opened a series of themed bars under the banner "J.J. Murphy and Company" throughout the country. These outlets reflect the desired image for Murphy's and help raise the profile of the brand in the UK. As a point of comparison, Beamish is distributed in 10,000 outlets in Britain.

Second, Murphy's has also been successful with its advertising in the UK. Its continuing advertising theme "Like the Murphy's, I'm not bitter" campaign is a tongue-in-cheek poke at Guinness's taste. The campaign has received several awards and has resulted in a unique identity developed for the brand (see Exhibit 2 on stout). The firm has also sponsored the Murphy's English Open Golf Championship for five years.

Third, the brand has gained momentum since it was voted product of the year by the UK Vintners in 1990. Murphy's has a strong position in the minds of the British who prefer darker ales. The brand represents a viable option to those who do not like the taste of Guinness and/or seek an alternative to their favorite UK-based brands such as Thomas Hardy, Newcastle, Samuel Smith, Watney's, and Young's.

MIS is available in all Western European markets. It has excellent distribution in the Netherlands, where Heineken is headquartered. Guinness's recent Irish pub expansion program has also helped raise awareness for all entries in the Irish stout category. Murphy's experienced dramatic growth in volume and market share across Europe in 1996.

In Germany, the establishment of Murphy's Trading GmbH, a wholly owned subsidiary of Murphy Brewery Ireland, allows for greater focus and control of the Murphy's brands within this critical market. The year 1996 also saw Murphy's gain the exclusive beer rights to Paddy Murphy's, the largest chain of Irish theme pubs throughout Germany. Also, in Denmark MIS is distributed in the Paddy Go Easy chain in several Danish cities.

In 1996 new markets were developed in Eastern Europe, including Hungary and the Czech Republic. The potential of the emerging Russian market is also anticipated. With the introduction of the brand in Finland, Murphy's is now available in all the Nordic countries.

The American Market

As he reached for the phone to ring Michael Foley, current CEO of Heineken USA (Van Munching & Co. is the importer's name) and former managing director of Murphy Brewery Ireland from 1989 to 1993, Patrick thought about the United States. He knew that the United States, with its 270 million consumers and general high standard of living, represents the most lucrative beer market in the world. The $40 billion beer market in the United States is dominated by the "giants" Anheuser-Busch (10 brands and 45 percent market share), Miller (9/23 percent), and Coors (7/11 percent).[11]

Michael gave Patrick a status report on the Murphy's brand in the United States as of June 1997. Michael reiterated that the U.S. strategy is to "build slowly" and gain acceptance of Murphy's products by endorsement by customers rather than attempting to buy market share with mass advertising. The plan is to "keep off TV because it is too expensive." Murphy's is seeking a premium brand positioning aimed at the specialty imported niche rather than the mass market.

Foley indicated that he was very optimistic about the Murphy growth possibilities in the United States. "Our 1996 sales were up 180 percent, and our target is 1 million cases by mid-1998," he said. Both Murphy's Irish Stout and Irish Amber are meeting the expectations set for them by Heineken USA.

Murphy's Irish Stout has been available in the United States since 1992 and has experienced steady growth since then. MIS has been on a gradual progression, from 100,000 gallons in 1992 to 400,000 gallons in 1994 and 600,000 gallons in 1995. It is now on tap at over 5,000 bars and pubs throughout the country. The distribution tends to be concentrated in the eastern corridor running from Boston through New York City (the largest market) to Washington, D.C. Another area of intense distribution is in south Florida. The "gold coast" area running from Miami to Fort Lauderdale is a stronghold for Murphy's, partially due to its attraction to British tourists who are already familiar with the brand. Other areas of focus for MIS are the major metropolitan areas of Chicago, Los Angeles, and San Francisco.

---

[11]"Domestic Beer Shipments Drop 2.1% in '95 While Volume Dips 1.7%," *Beverage Industry,* January 1996, pp. 24–32.

For the off-premises/carryout market, MIS has been available in cans since 1993. Their size is 14.9 ounces, and they are cream colored (like the "head" of the drink) and are priced relative to domestic U.S. beers at a premium level—$1.76 versus $1.99 for Guinness in the same size can. Foley stated that cans generally signify a "down market product" and the company would like to present more of a prestige image. Therefore, in September 1996 Murphy's introduced the draughtflow bottle in the United States. While Foley believes the glass package is "more premium," the company has experienced a problem with it in the United States. The serving size of 16.9 ounces is not correct for the market since most beer glasses hold only 12 ounces. The usual price is $1.99 per bottle. The size is not that important for in-home consumption, but in bars where MIS is sold by packages rather than on draft, this is a significant issue for the company. Another issue that has arisen is that the thick brown bottle takes substantially longer to cool than does a can.

Murphy's Irish Amber was introduced into the American market in late 1996. Its on-premise penetration has exceeded company expectations, and according to Foley, "the product is doing very, very well. It is the 'real deal' and replacing nonauthentic Irish products such as Killian's in many areas." The product is available in six-packs for off-site consumption. The rich-looking green and red package makes it attractive. The company has positioned it against Bass Ale and other premium-quality ales. Its price is in the $7.50 range, which is substantially higher than many of the specialty imports, which cost $4.00 to $6.00 per six-pack. Killian's sometimes is sale priced as low as $3.99, but its regular price is in the $5.50 to $6.00 range, and Sam Adams Red and Pete's Wicked Ale are priced at $5.49 and $5.99, respectively. Bass Ale, however, carries an even higher price ($7.79) than Murphy's.

Conway thanked Foley for his update on the status of the Murphy's brands in the United States and asked if Michael could spend a few minutes discussing trends in the beer market within the country. "I know import sales are increasing about 7 percent a year in the United States and that Heineken is the leading import brand," said Conway, "But where does Guinness fall?" Foley responded that they were in tenth place, while Bass Ale held down the eighth spot and beer imports from Ireland held the sixth position among all countries (Exhibits 5 and 6).

EXHIBIT 5 Leading Imported Beer Brands in the United States (thousands of 2.25-gallon cases)

Brand	Importer	Origin	1992[1]	1993	1994[2]	% Change 1993–1994
Heineken	Van Munching & Co.	Netherlands	26,700	29,200	31,200	6.8%
Corona Extra	Barton/Gambrinus	Mexico	13,000	14,000	16,000	14.3
Molson Ice	Molson USA	Canada	–	3,000	10,000	–
Beck's	Dribeck Importers	Germany	9,650	9,700	9,720	0.2
Molson Golden	Molson USA	Canada	8,500	8,600	8,700	1.2
Amstel Light	Van Munching & Co.	Netherlands	5,500	6,000	7,500	25.0
Labatt's Blue	Labatt's USA	Canada	5,900	6,200	6,500	4.8
Bass Ale	Guinness Import Co.	United Kingdom	2,850	3,390	4,160	22.7
Tecate	Labatt's USA	Mexico	2,900	3,400	4,000	17.6
Guinness Stout	Guinness Import Co.	Ireland	3,100	3,650	3,970	8.8
Foster's Lager[3]	Molson USA	Canada	3,500	3,700	3,800	2.7
Moosehead	Guinness Import Co.	Canada	3,400	3,350	3,340	−0.3
Molson Light	Molson USA	Canada	1,900	2,000	2,200	10.0
Dos Equis	Guinness Import Co.	Mexico	1,900	2,060	2,120	2.9
St. Pauli Girl	Barton Brands	Germany	2,200	2,000	2,000	0.0
Labatt's Ice	Labatt's USA	Canada	–	845	1,910	–
Molson Canadian	Molson USA	Canada	1,640	1,690	1,710	1.2
Labatt's Light	Labatt's USA	Canada	1,100	1,020	1,100	7.8
Corona Light	Barton/Gambrinus	Mexico	1,100	1,000	1,000	0.0

[1]Revised.
[2]Estimated.
[3]The gradual production switch from Australia to Canada began in April 1992.

EXHIBIT 6 Imported Beer Market: Market Share by Supplier, 1994 (Estimated)

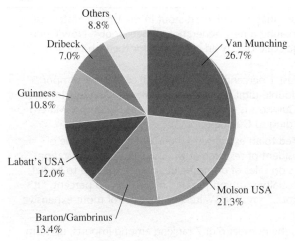

Others 8.8%

Dribeck 7.0%

Guinness 10.8%

Labatt's USA 12.0%

Barton/Gambrinus 13.4%

Van Munching 26.7%

Molson USA 21.3%

Foley said that he recalled reading that the top 20 brands (out of a total of 400 import brands) account for 90 percent of U.S. import sales.

Patrick asked about trends in the U.S. beer market. "It has been flat the last several years," said Foley. "The most significant recent trend domestically is the growth in microbreweries." Michael said he remembered seeing on a Web site that microbreweries, brewpubs, and regional specialty breweries totaled almost 1,300 in early 1997.[12] The microbrewery category has grown tenfold to 500 in 10 years. However, it still accounted for only a paltry 2 percent of the U.S. market in 1995.

Conway said good-bye and was just about to hang up when Foley said, "I almost forgot, but someone passed an article from *The Wall Street Journal* by me a few weeks ago that talked about Guinness and the microbrewery boom. I will send it to you with the other material" (Exhibit 7).

Murphy's World Market Positioning and Marketing

Dan Leahy stopped by Patrick Conway's office and handed him the information requested on Murphy's status in the world market. Patrick glanced at the statistics assembled by Dan and noticed that the specialty category (into which MIS and MIA both fell) had grown over the last few years (Exhibit 8). He was concerned that it was the second smallest of the five categories.

[12]"Craft-Brewing Industry Fact Sheet—February 1997," http://www.Beertown.org/craftbrew.html.

Dan left a revision of the Murphy's Positioning Statement on which Patrick and his colleagues had been working for several months. It read:

Murphy's is a symbol of everything authentically "Irish." Its warm history takes time to discover but its taste is easy to appreciate.

Supporting this positioning was the image of Ireland that Murphy's planned to convey in its marketing strategy (Exhibit 9). While the words in the exhibit are a bit stereotypical, they describe the perception of both the country and its people. It is in this context that Irish products are viewed by consumers in other counties. The elements of the marketing mix were summarized by Dan in several accompanying pages.

The product consists of the two brands—Murphy's Irish Stout and Murphy's Irish Amber/Red Beer (MIA/RB). It is sourced in Ireland except for the UK and New Zealand markets. Ongoing new product development continues in line with positioning, umbrella branding, and premium packaging.

The distribution objective is one of controlled distribution growth. The focus is on quality Irish bars/pubs and specialty beer outlets. Package variants are available in low-volume outlets. Dual stocking of MIS and MIA/RB will occur wherever possible. Exclusivity is a goal but not a prerequisite for stocking. The existing Heineken distribution network will continue to be used wherever possible.

The pricing strategy is one of price parity with major specialty competitors. A reasonable margin is being offered to the trade. In fact, the company prices its products slightly below the competition to the trade as an enticement to carry the products.

The promotion and communications strategy is multipronged. The brands' Irish heritage and origin continue to be reinforced. The company engages in tactical advertising and promotion rather than larger-scale strategic campaigns. For example, St. Patrick's Day and Irish music nights are exploited. The communication focus is on both brands in most markets. The company plans to use still rather than electronic media to convey the authentic Irish image of the brands.

Murphy's Future Direction

Patrick Conway assembled the reports on the Irish, UK, European, and American markets as well as the world positioning and strategy. He circulated them to the members of his group with a memo calling a meeting in early

EXHIBIT 7 **Buoyed by Boom in Microbrews, Guinness Pours Its Cash into TV**

Source: Elizabeth Jensen, *The Wall Street Journal*, February 10, 1997, p. B2.

Guinness Import Co. poured about 33 percent more of its signature dark draft stout in the United States last year as the microbrew boom helped lift import sales by creating a new generation of beer snobs. Now Guinness hopes to keep the beer taps flowing with its first large-scale U.S. TV ad campaign for the Irish-brewed brand, breaking today.

At a time when sales of all beer in the United States rose just 1 percent last year, several of Guinness Import's major brands, including Harp lager and Bass ale, posted double-digit gains. Overall, sales of Guinness Import's brands (including Moosehead, whose distribution rights Guinness is shedding, effective at the end of March) grew 20 percent to about 17 million cases last year, according to Guinness.

The company's success is one of the factors that contributed to an estimated 10 percent rise in the sale of beers last year, according to Frank Walters, senior vice president of research at M. Shanken Communications, publisher of *Impact*, which tracks beer sales. Final numbers on sales of domestic beers are expected to be flat, although it's estimated that the tiny microbrewery and specialty segment jumped more than 20 percent, "It's a good economy, and people are indulging themselves more," says Mr. Walters of the sales of more-expensive imports.

Guinness stout's fast sales pace in bars and stores lifted it to the number 6 or 7 ranking among imports, up from ninth place in 1995, according to Mr. Walter's estimates. Guinness Import, a unit of Guinness PLC of London, attributes its success to changing consumer tastes in the wake of the microbrew explosion and a more intense distribution and marketing effort. "People are getting more into beers with taste," said Sheri Roder, marketing development director for Guinness Import, "and at the same time, we've gotten behind our brands more."

There have been eye-catching promotions, such as the annual "Win Your Own Pub in Ireland" contest, now in its fourth year. A "Great Guinness Toast," on February 28, hopes to get into the *Guinness Book of World Records* for the largest number of people making a toast. And the number of outlets selling the brand jumped by 20 percent in 1996.

Even more unusual, Guinness has been sending out a force of "draft specialists" armed with thermometers and training brochures to visit bars and make sure they're serving Guinness under the best possible conditions. Brewers can't own bars, so they can't control whether tavern owners serve the product in sparkling clean glasses or how often they flush out built-up yeast in the lines that carry the beer from the keg to the tap.

With distribution and the quality program in place, Guinness decided the time was right to launch the TV campaign. "There's no point in advertising a lot when people can't find you," says Ms. Roder. "There's likelihood now that people will be able to find a pint of Guinness, poured well to our exacting standards. You don't want to get people too excited about something they can't find."

The TV ad campaign, with the tag line "Why Man Was Given Five Senses," will air through St. Patrick's Day, March 17, in 18 major markets, including New York, Los Angeles, and Atlanta. Guinness won't say what it is spending on the ad campaign, which will run in late prime-time and sports programs, but calls it a significant media buy. Chicago viewers of the Super Bowl saw the ad run twice; Guinness also has spots in NBC's high-rated Thursday prime-time lineup.

The quirky ad, which goes through the ritual of ordering a pint of Guinness, from the nod to the bartender to the long wait for the beer to settle, was created by Weiss, Stagliano of New York City. It got a five-week tryout in Chicago and Boston last fall with convincing results: Sales of Guinness in Boston were up 24 percent in December over a year earlier, compared with just an 11 percent gain for the rest of the Guinness portfolio, while in Chicago, sales are up 35 percent from a year ago, with distribution up 22 percent.

EXHIBIT 8
World Beer Market

Category	1994	1995	1996	Volume (Hectoliters)
Specialty	6.6%	7.4%	8.2%	103,000,000
Sophistication	11.9	12.4	12.9	162,000,000
Standard savings	63.5	62.7	61.0	763,000,000
Stay fit	15.9	15.5	15.8	189,000,000
Stay clear	2.1	2.0	2.1	24,000,000
Total	100	100	100	1,241,000,000

EXHIBIT 9   Image of Ireland

Perception of Country	Personality of People
Green	Relaxed
Environmentally friendly	Sociable
Natural	Friendly
Unspoiled	Different
Lost Arcadia	Humorous/witty
Underdeveloped	Pub atmosphere

June 1997. Conway indicated that he wanted to develop a long-term strategy for the Murphy's brand to take to Heineken management rather than develop a knee-jerk reaction to the Guinness–Grand Met merger.

He believed that Murphy's reputation was improving both in Ireland and throughout the world. He did not want to jeopardize the gains made in the last several years. However, he was concerned with the stagnant nature of the beer industry in Europe and North America. He called a meeting for June 10, 1997, to discuss the marketing strategy for Murphy's.

Before he met with the marketing department members, he stopped by Marien Kakabeeke's office. The managing director reminded him of the corporate goal for Murphy's, which is 20 percent of the world's stout market by the year 2000. "I know that is ambitious, Patrick, but I am confident you and your staff can achieve it."

"Do you realize that the Cork Brewery is almost at capacity now?" asked Patrick. "Even if we stimulate demand, how will we be able to meet it with production limits? Also, recall that we expanded the brewery in 1995."[13]

When Patrick, D. Ford, and Dan Leahy sat down that morning to discuss the future of Murphy's, they considered several questions:

How important is a strong showing in the Irish domestic market to Murphy's? Must it make a strong showing there to be successful worldwide?

Should Murphy's employ a global rather than local marketing strategy worldwide? The "I'm not bitter" campaign has been successful in the United Kingdom, so should several possible strategies be used, especially in the large markets of the United States and continental Europe?

Is Murphy's destined to be a "niche" product forever? Will these brands ever reach a place where they command a substantial market share?

Should the company continue to make the two brands only at the Cork brewery for the lucrative U.S. market, or should it consider making the product in that country? It worked for automobiles; why not beer?

Will Murphy's ever be able to achieve the status of other products that are famous for their Irish heritage, such as Guinness, Bailey's Irish Cream, Jameson Irish Whiskey, Waterford Crystal, and Belleek China?

[13] Paul O'Kane, "Murphy's Plans Major Expansion," *The Irish Times,* August 16, 1995.

Case 6-12
Dairyland Seed Company

The morning sun was shining brightly as Tom Strachota, Chief Executive Officer for Dairyland Seed, drove up Highway 45 in southeast Wisconsin in late February 1999. Because of the snow cover on either side of the road, it was not immediately apparent that these fields were the sites of research plots that have generated some of the most cutting-edge biotechnologies in the seed industry. Tom couldn't help but smile as he reflected on the past few years' accomplishments. He was particularly pleased with the success of their line of soybean varieties tolerant to the DuPont Chemical Company's Sulfonylurea herbicides. Dairyland had pioneered the technology—a credit to Dairyland's long-standing commitment to research and development.

"Partnering Strategies in the BioTech World: The Case of Dairyland Seed Company" by Mark P. Leach, Luiz Mesquita and W. David Downey in *Journal of Business and Industrial Marketing,* 2002. Republished with permission of the Publisher, Emerald. Copyright © 2002 MCB UP Ltd.

Dr. Mark P. Leach is Assistant Professor of Marketing, Loyola Marymount University; Mr. Luiz Mesquita is a Doctoral Student of Management, Purdue University; and Dr. W. David Downey is Professor and Director, Center for Agricultural Business, Purdue University.

The authors would like to thank Dairyland Seed for permission to develop this case around issues facing their organization. The generous contributions of information and time by Tom Strachota (CEO), John Froelich (Director of Sales), and the many others at Dairyland Seed are gratefully acknowledged. In addition, they would like to recognize the contributions of Danny Kennedy (Co-Leader for North American Markets, Monsanto Global Seed Group as of February 1999), and Tom Matya (Director of Strategic Marketing, DEKALB Genetics Corporation). Note: This case was prepared as the basis for class discussion rather than to illustrate either effective or ineffective handling of an administrative situation.

However, a lot had happened in the soybean market since the introduction of the Sulfonylurea Tolerant Soybean (STS) varieties five years ago. Competition in the STS seed market had intensified as competitors developed and promoted their own varieties. While Tom believed Dairyland still enjoyed some advantage in the expanding enhanced trait soybean seed business, other seed companies were making rapid progress in many of the same markets.

The market share growth of Round-Up® tolerant soybean varieties was one of the newest challenges. These new varieties enabled Monsanto, manufacturer of the well-known Round-Up® herbicide, to compete directly with DuPont's STS. Initially, limited amounts of Round-Up® tolerant seeds constrained growth, but Monsanto has taken major steps to ensure greater supplies in each of the past two years. As a result, Round-Up® tolerant seeds captured between 35–40 percent market share in 1998 and projections are that Round-Up® tolerant seeds will command as much as 50 percent of the market this year.

Dairyland had not been caught off guard by the Round-Up® tolerant technology, of course. In fact, Dairyland had acquired a license to develop its own Round-Up® tolerant soybean varieties. Dairyland researchers have been successful in developing several varieties that have fared extremely well in state yield trials and in the marketplace this year.

Combined, Dairyland's STS and Round-Up® tolerant varieties account for over 60 percent of Dairyland's soybean sales. This is remarkable given that STS traits entered the market in 1993, and Round-Up® in 1996. However, the growing importance of these varieties brings with it new challenges for Dairyland. By marketing both STS and Round-Up® tolerant varieties, Dairyland is in a position where Tom must manage business relationships with competitors in the chemical and biotechnology market, namely DuPont and Monsanto. With the market demands for Round-Up® tolerant technology, how closely should he establish his business relationship with Monsanto? He wondered what the impact of partnering with Monsanto might be on his carefully developed alliance with DuPont.

Adding to Tom's new challenges, agricultural chemical and biotechnology companies have chosen to become further committed to the seed industry by acquiring or establishing joint ventures with larger seed firms. Of particular interest to Tom were DuPont's 20 percent ownership position in Pioneer, and Monsanto's recent acquisitions of Asgrow and DEKALB—two major seed companies. These mergers have caused these two major technology suppliers to become more tightly allied with Dairyland's direct competitors. What might this mean to Dairyland's access to future technologies? Success had certainly brought a new set of problems, and positioning was going to be especially important for Dairyland to ensure continuity of its role as a cutting-edge seed producer.

Company Background

Simon and Andrew Strachota founded the Dairyland Seed Company in 1907. In 1920, Andrew retired, leaving his brother Simon to head the company. When Simon died unexpectedly in 1940, his son Orville left college and returned home to run the company. At 79, Orville Strachota continues to be active in the business and serves as Chairman of Dairyland's Board. However, his three sons, Steve, Tom, and John Strachota, have managed day-to-day operations of the company for over 10 years.

Dairyland began as Strachota Seeds. The company operated out of the Strachota family's general store in eastern Wisconsin. White Dutch Clover Seed was their primary product. But when the market for White Dutch Clover suddenly dropped off in 1955, Orville shifted to the production of alfalfa seed—a product with rapidly growing demand driven by Wisconsin dairy farmers searching for better forages for their cows. Dairy continued to grow in importance in their region. In 1963 Orville decided to change the name of the company to Dairyland Seed Company to reflect its commitment to the market.

Dairyland continued to respond to challenges and opportunities in the seed industry as they arose. They began to produce and market seed corn on a large scale in 1961. As soybeans began to develop in the United States in the 1960s, Dairyland also added soybean seed to their product line.

Today, Orville Strachota's three sons, Steve (President), Tom (Chief Executive Officer), and John (Vice President), jointly manage Dairyland Seed. The company is privately held, with majority stock owned by the Strachota family. Of the over 800 companies listed by the American Seed Trade Association, Dairyland is the only American family-owned seed company with proprietary research in alfalfa, corn, and soybeans.

Dairyland's board of directors, which includes family stockholders and outside directors, meets quarterly to review business strategy and plans.

The company is divided into seven functional operating areas: management, finance, research, production, distribution, marketing, and sales. Dairyland employs approximately 100 people plus seasonal help. Executive management is located at Dairyland's headquarters in West Bend, Wisconsin, while research, sales, and production employees are located throughout the company's market and production area. Dairyland's production/processing plants are in Mt. Hope and West Bend, Wisconsin. In addition, five research stations are located in Otterbein, Indiana; Sloughhouse, California; Gibson City, Illinois; Clinton, Wisconsin; and Gilbert, Iowa.

Dairyland has built its image around new product development and is well known in the upper-Midwest for innovation. Orville Strachota established a commitment to research early in the company's history. Today, over 40 percent of the company's employees work in research and development, making it the largest department in the company. Management believes Dairyland has a competitive advantage in certain markets with its continued commitment to research and development.

The Marketing Mix at Dairyland

Product

Dairyland his worked hard to build its image around quality products, its high standards of business ethics, and as a successful family-run business. This message is intentionally promoted in a myriad of ways including a highly visible commitment to research, maintaining a first-class physical plant, demonstrating employee pride in the organization, and the active involvement of Orville and three third-generation principals. Tom Strachota believes the positioning effort over the years has resulted in a positive and consistent image of Dairyland among customers and competitors alike. Tom believes that this image is very important and valuable.

The focus of Dairyland has been on high-yielding genetics rather than on specific traits. This commitment to high-performance genetics is captured in their statement of values:

1. Dairyland has a responsibility to its customers to deliver consistently high-performing products.

2. New traits are of value only if they add to the consistency of performance or bring more profit to the farmer.

3. No single genetic trait is of value by itself.

Tom Strachota puts it this way; "It is better to have high-yielding genetics with no specialty traits, than to have specialty traits with poor genetics." Guided by these values, researchers at Dairyland have developed a product mix that consists of varieties of alfalfa, corn, and soybean seed.

Alfalfa

Dairyland is especially proud of its success with alfalfa varieties. According to company executives, Dairyland has the world's largest alfalfa breeding program. Dairyland's alfalfa lineup includes several specialty alfalfa varieties from which the farmer can choose to match their particular needs (e.g., varieties suited for wet soil conditions, other varieties for high traffic fields, etc.). Strachota is quick to mention recent successful innovations Dairyland has made in the release of patented Sequential Maturity Alfalfa™ products that provide farmers with more high quality forage.

Corn

Dairyland's seed corn business has grown steadily since hybrid corn was first introduced into their product line in 1961. Seed corn now plays an important role in their overall strategy. Dairyland currently offers over 40 corn varieties that have been bred to meet the unique needs of the upper-Midwestern states. The company's "Stealth" hybrid corn breeding program (which emphasizes required growers to make increasingly more complex decisions about inputs—(seed, chemicals, and fertilizer), and the spectrum of knowledge required has grown prohibitively large. Many farmers favor retailers that can provide more technical advice to growers and maintain superior service standards. As such, a growing percentage of Dairyland's business flows through these intermediaries, and Dairyland is continuing to look for appropriate resale partners with which to license.

Promotion

Dairyland uses a wide variety of promotional programs to communicate the benefits of its soybean seed to farmers. The Dairyland Soybean Management Guide provides farmers with technical and practical advice on the best soybean production methods. Each year, the company produces a pocket-sized Dairyland seed reference guide and calendar. There is a quarterly newsletter called "The Leader" that communicates a variety of information to the customer. Other promotional efforts include tours of research and production facilities, crop management clinics, field days at Dairyland test plots, and maintenance of "show case" quality facilities.

Most of Dairyland's advertising is direct mail from an extensive database maintained on all dealers and customers. The internal database is supplemented by mailing lists from other sources. In addition, the company includes ads in state farm publications, magazines (especially Soybean Digest), agricultural newspapers, etc. Occasionally DSMs will prepare brief ads or radio announcements for local areas to promote a field day or educational program in that area.

Dealers are offered a wide range of individual and customer incentives intended to promote sales. Traditional caps, jackets, etc. are all available to dealers and their customers. In addition, dealers may work toward larger value gifts (e.g., television sets or trips to Florida are common, and even a car in the case of Dairyland's Stealth seed corn program). District sales managers are also offered sales incentives and bonus awards for achievement in increasing the sales of Dairyland's three product lines. Individual award programs depend on the specific activities that Dairyland is attempting to promote throughout the year.

Pricing

Dairyland's seed is priced slightly above the market average in all product lines (see Exhibit 1). "This is a strategy designed to encourage the premium quality image that is the core of our marketing strategy, and to generate margins necessary to support an aggressive research and development program," says Tom Strachota. "We believe farmers are willing to pay a little higher price when we deliver high quality seed, consistent performance, dependability, and cutting-edge technology." Although Dairyland seeds may not be the highest priced alternative in the market,

this philosophy generally places Dairyland's average prices at 5–10 percent above the average in market. "The idea is to realize that we can't price like the market leader, but we can deliver the best overall value," Tom argues.

Tom Strachota believes that this premium value strategy is highly successful. Dairyland has enjoyed an increase in its soybean sales for the last five years. This includes an increase in 1997 despite not having Round-Up® Ready soybeans; STS accounted for over one-third of Dairyland's soybean sales in 1997.

Channel Partners

Chemical companies like DuPont and Monsanto are using seed companies to bring their products to market. The developers of the biotechnology have sought to use a combination of seed production and distribution companies as well as licensing agreements with distributors and small seed companies in order to achieve access to growers with a high level of service. Dairyland has among its channel partners two main providers of biotechnology: DuPont and Monsanto. Among these partners, Dairyland has worked most closely in the past with DuPont. Through this relationship with DuPont, Dairyland has marketed its seed varieties of STS soybeans.

DuPont

DuPont began licensing with several larger seed companies over five years ago, giving them the right to sublicense to other smaller seed firms. While Dairyland was one of the first seed companies licensed to produce and sell STS seed, there are now nearly 100 seed companies who have been licensed to sell the STS technology These companies have developed more than 170 varieties of STS seeds. The more aggressive companies include Dairyland Seeds, Asgrow (recently purchased by Monsanto), Pioneer, Stine Seed, Countrymark and GROWMARK, and Novartis Seed. Even though Asgrow is owned by Monsanto, it still maintains a licensing contract with DuPont.

EXHIBIT 1
Estimated Industry Average Seed Prices for 1998

	Alfalfa	Corn	Soybeans
Average Retail Price—industry	$189	$99	$19.00
Average Retail Price—Dairyland	$193	$95	$18.65
Average Discounted Price—industry	$176	$78	$15.20

Based on the 1998 price list of Pioneer, Novartis, Mycogen, DEKALB, and Cargill companies.

EXHIBIT 2
Estimated Market Share for STS and Round-Up® Tolerant Soybean Seed Varieties

	1996	1997	1998	1999*	2000*
STS Varieties	7%	8–12%	10–15%	15–20%	20–25%
Round-Up Ready	3%	18–20%	35–40%	45–50%	50–60%

*The economic situation faced by producers varies widely by region. This table is based on 1998 University of Wisconsin yield trials on three varieties of Dairyland seed.

Discussions between DuPont and Dairyland were opened in the mid-80s. Acquisition of the Sulfonylureas germplasm by Dairyland occurred in the late 80s. DuPont selected Dairyland for its strong reputation in soybean development and its independent research capability. The relationship is not exclusive, however. Other companies received the germplasm and have had the opportunity to develop their own tolerant varieties.

The agreement between Dairyland and DuPont stipulates formation of a "joint-commercialization" team to review the marketing strategies for STS. Dairyland and DuPont agreed that in marketing the product, DuPont would sell herbicides and help farmers understand the benefits of STS, while Dairyland would sell seed and talk about the benefits of STS as they relate to seed selection. The joint marketing strategy was a tremendous success as the sales forces of each company were able to establish mutually supportive professional relationships. As the STS technology represents important market potential for DuPont, Dairyland anticipates continued marketing support. DuPont's efforts have clearly helped position Dairyland as one of the leading developers of Sulfonylurea Tolerant Soybeans.

DuPont has basically maintained their aggressive marketing strategy to promote the use of STS seed varieties in the market through programs that include sizable advertising and incentive programs. They have executed major herbicide launches that include TV in major markets and heavy print media advertising. DuPont sales representatives will support local agricultural chemical dealers and seed companies with educational programs in local markets and support plot tours to demonstrate the new technology. DuPont has elected not to place any premium on the Sulfonylurea herbicides.

DuPont has relied heavily on media campaigns to successfully increase its brand name and product awareness among users. However, they have recently been forced to recognize the rapid growth of Round-Up® technology, and the potential cost savings and ease of the Round-Up® system to the farmer. While most industry experts have predicted the increase of Round-Up® soybeans, almost no one expected acceptance

to be as rapid as it developed in the 1997 and 1998 markets (see Exhibit 2).[1]

DuPont has responded by increasing commitment with the seed industry substantially with the recent purchase of 20 percent of Pioneer Hybrid International stock and the holding of two seats on Pioneer's board of directors in 1997. Pioneer and DuPont also have announced the formation of a new joint venture called Optimum whose purpose is to bringing new value-added crops to market, such as high-oil corn, etc. It is clear that DuPont will be working more closely with Pioneer than with any other seed company. However, Dairyland feels that DuPont has not abandoned its STS technology or its initial seed industry partners. DuPont's relationship with other seed companies has remained the same. Time will tell whether DuPont's new relationship with Pioneer will have an impact on other seed industry firms.

In addition, DuPont made a substantial change in its pricing strategy—announcing a 75 percent price cut in August 1997 on its STS-related herbicides. This price reduction was a clear attempt to level the economics of the farmer's decision process in choosing which herbicide resistant technology to embrace. On an average basis, the farmer would pay approximately $28 per acre for Round-Up® tolerant seeds (including a $6.50 technology fee). The herbicide would cost about $15 per acre per application. With the new lower price, DuPont claims it can offer the farmer superior protection (longer weed control) for basically the same price. Dairyland believes that its STS seeds outperform most competitors' Round-Up® varieties and so it continues to be committed to the STS technology.

Monsanto and Round-Up® Ready

Monsanto's Round-Up® Ready technology has been under development for some time. From its introduction, market growth has been limited only by supply. In 1994 and 1995, Round-Up® tolerant soybeans hit the

[1]Estimation by Dairyland executives, based on reports of the American Seed Trade Association. Assuming the development of high-yielding varieties of soybean. Seeds out of the bag (does not include bin seed).

EXHIBIT 3 Alliances in the Supply Chain

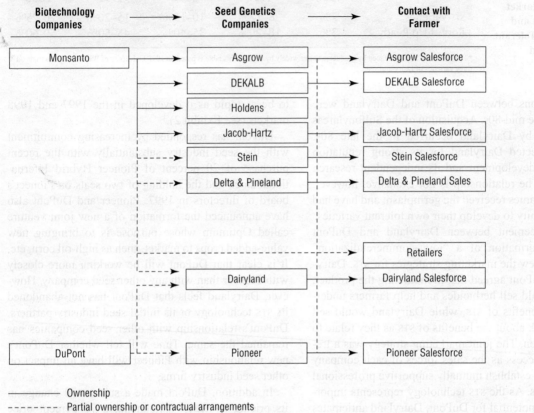

in order to assure sustainable growth for our company," says Monsanto's CEO Robert Shapiro (Monsanto Press Release, 1998).[2]

In 1996, Monsanto Company acquired Asgrow Agronomics. Asgrow is a major U.S. soybean seed company with international operations. According to Monsanto's executive vice president, Hendrik A. Verfaillie: "Asgrow's strength in soybeans is particularly important to us as we accelerate the sales of our Round-Up® soybeans and other new soybean products to farmers worldwide. The acquisition of Asgrow Agronomics strengthens our ability to quickly move our innovations into the marketplace" (Monsanto Press Release, 1998). Other examples of recent Monsanto acquisitions and alliances include:

market with limited quantity and sold out. In 1996 they sold out with a 3 percent market share. In 1997 supplies sold out, this time with approximately 20 percent market share. In 1998 Round-Up® soybeans did not sell out, but did capture nearly 40 percent of the market.

Dairyland did not have Round-Up® technology initially. In fact, Dairyland was not licensed to market Round-Up® soybeans in 1997, but it did enter into an arrangement with Monsanto in 1998. Tom attributes Dairyland's ability to license with Monsanto to Dairyland's commitment to quality, and the recognition that Dairyland receives for being the first to market with STS herbicide-resistant soybeans.

Recently Monsanto has escalated its activity in the seed industry. Through its acquisitions, partnerships, and incentive programs, Monsanto has effectively elevated its position in the seed supply chain (see Exhibit 3). These acquisitions and partnerships are part of a continuing effort of Monsanto to strengthen its position in the market for new biotechnological products. This is consistent with Monsanto's strategic vision, "to create cutting-edge environmental solutions

- In December 1997, Monsanto Company, Asgrow Seed Company, and Stine Seed Company announced a collaboration agreement. This research agreement was reportedly designed to further improve and develop soybean genetics and related technologies.

[2]Monsanto press releases are available online at http://www.monsanto.com/monsanto/media.

- On December 4, 1998, DEKALB Genetics became a wholly-owned subsidiary of Monsanto.

- Monsanto also bought Holdens in early 1997. Holdens is a major supplier of corn genetics to both large and independent seed companies.

- In June 1998 Monsanto signed an agreement to purchase Cargill's international seed operations in Latin America, Asia, Africa, and parts of Europe. This acquisition includes seed research, production, and testing facilities in 21 countries and distribution systems in 51 countries.

Through these partnerships, Monsanto has acquired a solid distribution network that should facilitate rapid seed product introduction. Also, through gearing research to complement one another, these new alliances will achieve synergies in new product development. Thus, at the same time Dairyland's initial soybean technology partner (i.e., DuPont) has become more tightly allied with one of Dairyland's key competitors (i.e., Pioneer), Monsanto has been managing its relationships with several other Dairyland competitors.

Another way that Monsanto is managing the supply-chain of its Round-Up® Ready technology is through incentive programs. Monsanto has established an incentive structure for seed manufactures, for agricultural retailing, and for growers. For example, growers who use both Round-Up® Ready soybeans and Monsanto's YieldGard Bt corn on a high percentage of acres are given a rebate.

Given the demand for Round-Up® Ready soybeans, Monsanto has been able to charge a technology fee to growers. This fee was originally $5 per 50-pound bag, but was increased to $6 for spring 1999 (the price increase was coupled with a price reduction of Round-Up® Ready herbicide so that the overall cost to a customer was essentially the same).

One incentive that Monsanto provides to seed suppliers is a special handling fee. For suppliers, Monsanto provides 10 percent of this fee back to the supplier (i.e., $0.60). In addition, if a supplier meets certain share-of-business requirements, Monsanto will rebate another 10 percent (i.e., $0.60) to the supplier. These requirements include having 90 percent of herbicide-resistant soybeans sold be Round-Up® Ready soybeans, 85 percent of herbicide-resistant corn be Round-Up® Ready corn, and 90 percent of corn borer insect-protected corn be YieldGard Bt corn. In order to obtain the additional 10 percent, all three share-of-business requirements must be met. Together, these two rebates can more than double the retail profit on a bag of seed.

For any seed company, this program can generate a lot of money. For a firm selling 100,000 bags of soybeans, meeting these requirements would mean receiving $60,000. Likewise, for a firm selling 500,000 units, this means an additional $300,000 in revenue. Given the relatively low profit margin on a bag of soybeans, this provides substantial incentive for suppliers to sell products with Monsanto technologies.

However, for companies like Dairyland who are allied with other biotechnology channel partners, Monsanto's incentive structure raises several issues. First of all, with such an attractive inducement to sell Round-Up® tolerant soybeans, should Dairyland continue to develop its relationship with DuPont? Furthermore, because this offer will shape decisions made by other genetic companies, a result may be the decrease in the number of companies providing STS technologies. Will DuPont continue to aggressively market STS even when they foresee markets becoming less attainable? Is this an opportunity for Dairyland, or a threat to its position in the market?

Another concern for Dairyland is that not all of Monsanto's business partners operate under the same set of restrictions. Due to prior contractual arrangements, neither Novartis nor Pioneer is required to pay Monsanto the $6.50/bag technology fee. However, each of these firms charges this fee to customers. This raises concerns of the equity of Monsanto business relationships, as this money may provide a source of funds for research and development that is not available to most Round-Up® tolerant soybean suppliers, or allow a significant disparity in dealer or retail pricing.

Danny Kennedy, Co-President of Asgrow Seed, believes Monsanto's success stems from its ability to add value to the farmer by capitalizing on the synergies from its portfolio of companies and technologies representing several sectors in agriculture. He states that Monsanto considers its involvement in agricultural business to be a core part of the overall technology platform. This view is consistent with the strategic actions of Monsanto. Since heading up the company in 1995, Robert Shapiro has spun off the core chemical business to focus on being the "main provider of the agricultural biotechnology. . ." (Monsanto Press Release, 1998).

With regard to herbicide-resistance technology, Monsanto executives see both seed and biotechnology as key ingredients to their long-term strategy. Danny Kennedy realizes that seed is the distribution system by which Monsanto technologies reach the farmer. He believes that seed will drive farmers' decisions in the future, and states that, "farmers will buy seed that is specialized genetically to suit their own feed stock needs, grain market needs, consumer needs, etc." Asgrow and DEKALB have competitive advantages in some regions, however, because small firms can have a strong presence in certain regions and market niches, he believes that Monsanto cannot afford not to license other seed firms with its new technologies. As an example of the commitment of Monsanto to licensing its technology to the broad market (family and small firms), as of February 1999 Monsanto has already agreed to licensing its technology to more than 200 seed firms.

Other Providers of Herbicide-Tolerant Soybean Technology

Although Dairyland has business partnerships with DuPont and Monsanto, there are several other chemical and biotechnical firms that operate in this market. AgrEvo, is the third player in the herbicide-resistant seed market. AgrEvo's herbicide, Liberty, targets a broad spectrum of broad leaf weeds. The Liberty technology was late to enter the market. Early efforts of AgrEvo to bring its herbicide-resistance technology to the seed market were through Asgrow and Holdens. This strategy has proven to be problematic, especially since Monsanto now owns both. AgrEvo has been licensing its technology to other seed companies, though it has been less successful than Monsanto and DuPont to bring its technology to the market. While pricing of the AgrEvo product is not yet clear, it appears that AgrEvo may choose a premium price strategy rather than a licensing fee as Monsanto has chosen. Liberty is fasteracting than Round-Up® but has about the same kill spectrum for weeds and grasses as Round-Up®.

American Cyanamid has maintained a significant share of the soybean herbicide market with Pursuit®, which is used with nonherbicide-tolerant soybean varieties. Recently, they have cut prices approximately 40 percent so that its use is competitively priced with Round-Up® Ultra and DuPont's Symphony. Thus, American Cyanamid continues to represent a major market challenge for DuPont/STS and Monsanto Round-Up® products. If DuPont is to be successful, it will be necessary to demonstrate a significant advantage over this and other traditional herbicide alternatives. Another relatively new release is Flexstar® by Zeneca, a formulation intended for broadleaf weed control in soybeans.

Competitive Environment in the Soybean Seed Industry

Dairyland faces a wide range of competitors in their diverse market area (see Exhibit 4). Some competitors are large international companies such as Pioneer, DEKALB, and Novartis Seeds that have broad product lines that parallel Dairyland's. Furthermore, there are a large number of regional and local seed companies who offer all or part of the seed products sold by Dairyland. Some of Dairyland's competitors develop and sell proprietary products, while others sell public varieties that are genetically identical to each other, but carry the producer's own label. Many of these smaller companies are aggressive and have strong loyalties within their own local market areas.

Competition is intense in all three product lines. Pioneer is the clear industry leader in the seed corn market with an estimated market share of about 42 percent. There is no dominant supplier in alfalfa although alfalfa has always been one of Dairyland's strengths. Pioneer has become aggressive in the soybean market with an estimated 14 percent share. Asgrow recently announced that it was the leader in soybean share with 16 percent. Accurate market share information is difficult to obtain and to interpret since many seed companies are privately held and the market is so geographically fractured. Aggregate market share information is also often

EXHIBIT 4   **Estimated 1998 National Market Share**

	Percent of Soybean Acres
Farmer-Saved Seed	32.5%
Public Varieties	15.0%
Private Varieties:	
Asgrow (Monsanto)	16.0%
Pioneer	14.0%
DEKALB (Monsanto)	≅5.0%
Novartis	≅5.0%
Stine	≅5.0%
Jacob-Hartz (Monsanto)	<5.0%
Cokers (Sandoz)	<5.0%
FS (GROWMARK)	<5.0%
Mycogen	<5.0%
Others	≅8.0%
Total Private	(52.5%)
Total	100.0%

misleading because it varies dramatically among local market areas. For example, while Dairyland Seed does not have a large market share on a national basis (i.e., less than 2 percent), in some core market areas, their market share may run as high as 30 percent.

Most soybean seed companies are marketing some STS varieties. However, these companies differ basically in their enthusiasm and commitment to the technology. Among the major players, a few of them are worth mentioning. Asgrow has had STS products developed since 1993. Asgrow has not priced their STS varieties at a premium relative to their non-STS varieties. Cenex, a major cooperative in the upper-Midwest, has introduced an STS product, and DEKALB has STS products in the market. Other seed companies, such as Stine, have introduced STS varieties but lack breadth in this product line.

A major new player in the STS market is Pioneer. Consistent with Pioneer's general pricing strategy, it is pricing its STS products at a premium relative to its non-STS products. Many in the industry expect the new relationship of DuPont and Pioneer will result in additional introductions of enhanced trait seeds.

John Froelich feels that one of Dairyland's competitive advantages continues to be their lead in the development of STS varieties. While some companies are still working to improve the performance of their STS varieties, Dairyland executives feel that their "commanding lead" allows them to concentrate on introducing enhanced traits into varieties that have already proven to be strong performers. Pursuing this strategy, Dairyland researchers have successfully bred additional traits into the STS product line. New Dairyland varieties have demonstrated resistance to a series of plant diseases, such as white mold, brown stem rot, and phytophtora. Dairyland believes these new traits will be particularly important in "niche" markets where these diseases are problematic.

Dairyland has responded to the growing market demand for Round-Up® Ready soybeans by introducing several new varieties for the '98 and '99 selling seasons. So far, over 30 percent of Dairyland's sales today come from Round-Up® Ready products. John Froelich expects this trend to continue to the end of the 1999 selling season. Research is currently underway to introduce still more Round-Up® Ready varieties in the future.

Asgrow is expected to continue the aggressive introduction of new soybean varieties. This Monsanto-affiliate is marketing a new "stacked traits" variety—one that has resistance to both STS and Round-Up® herbicides. Monsanto has not given other seed companies the legal right to offer "stacked trait" varieties. On the other hand, DuPont has announced that it will allow companies already licensed to sell (STSS) to develop and market stacked trait soybean varieties. It is unclear what Monsanto's intentions are for the future.

Dairyland's Customer Focus

Putting the customer first has always been the core of Dairyland's business philosophy. As Orville Strachota puts it, Dairyland's objective has always been to treat farmers fairly and understand their needs. If you have a good product at a fair price with good service and hold true to your word, you've got a customer and a friend for life.

However, customer buying behavior is changing. On today's large farms, more people influence decisions, and farmers are more business-oriented. Tom Matya, Director of Strategic Marketing for DEKALB Genetics Corporation, finds customers today to be more economically focused, more highly educated in germplasm and herbicides, and less brand loyal than 10 years ago. Although there is still a strong sense of loyalty, he attributes the increase in brand switching by customers today to the rapid acceleration of product innovation, and the leapfrogging of technologies.

Farmers today have been characterized as being value-driven. Farmers must justify the economics of the variety that is being purchased, and understand the mix of products that work together to provide optimal solutions. This may be one reason for the increase in sales through agricultural retailers. Through their ability to provide customers bundled packages and product expertise on everything from seeds to chemicals, agricultural retailers are providing farmers with added value through expertise, convenience, and often through creative discounting.

Farmer customers have a high level of risk aversion. Both John Froelich from Dairyland Seed and Tom Matya from DEKALB agree that farmers will be more inclined to test new technologies themselves before converting large numbers of acres to a new product. However, if the product works, adoption moves quickly.

Similarly, Tom Strachota foresees that farmers will become more focused on high-quality genetics and less driven by new specialty traits until they have been proven in the field. However, the growth

EXHIBIT 5
Percentage of
Dairyland Soybean
Sales

Year	STS Sales	Round-Up® Sales	Conventional Sales
1993	<1%	0%	99%
1994	6%	0%	94%
1995	31%	0%	69%
1996	41%	0%	59%
1997	40%	1%	59%
1998	41%	21%	38%
1999 est.	41%	32%	27%

of herbicide-tolerant varieties of soybean in general and Round-Up® Ready soybeans in particular, provides evidence that specialty traits are highly desired by today's farmers. At Dairyland, herbicide-tolerant soybeans accounted for 62 percent of total soybean sales in 1998 and are expected to increase to 73 percent in 1999 (see Exhibit 5).[3]

Dairyland has been encouraged by experiences reported by many of their key accounts who have been aggressively testing the STS and Round-Up® Ready seed on their farms. The net result has been an increase in their purchases of Dairyland STS. John Froelich believes that the sales increases further demonstrate that performance continues to be the major factor for many business-minded farmers. Yet John is quick to recognize that the differences in performance may not be enough for many farmers who simply like the convenience of Round-Up®.

John relates a Monsanto study showing approximately 95 percent of the farmers using the Round-Up® Ready system experienced "satisfaction" with the product. "That is, they got what they thought they would get with their product," John says. "I believe this means these farmers did not expect to have higher yields, but were focusing on a wider span of weed control. On the other hand," John continues, "I believe the initial impact of Round-Up® Ready will be dimmed by performance of the Round-Up® Ready varieties as farmers have more data and experience to really evaluate the results."

Dairyland believes that in many regions the STS varieties will continue to show a performance advantage over the newer Round-Up® tolerant beans. However, they believe their current advantage is temporary and the Round-Up® tolerant beans will soon equal STS varieties in performance. Further, because of all the variables involved, this performance advantage is

[3]Dairyland.

increasingly difficult to prove. John Froelich expects that most independent seed companies will continue to work with both Monsanto and DuPont in order to cover all the bases. Yet the appeal of Round-Up® Ready soybeans is unmistakable. Many farmers have had much experience with Round-Up® and are very comfortable with its use.

However, some of the economic appeal of the Round-Up® system has been reduced by recent competitive actions. Prices on both DuPont's Synchrony and American Cyanamid's Pursuit have been cut substantially, making purchase decisions less dependent on price. Dairyland believes that much of the customer demand for the Round-Up® system was the up-front cost savings that the system provided for farmer customers. If this was a major purchase motive, the virtual elimination of Round-Up® Ready's cost savings advantage may reduce the demand for Round-Up® tolerant varieties (see Exhibit 6).

A lot has changed in the soybean market in the few years since Dairyland introduced that first line of herbicide-tolerant soybean varieties. The excitement created by the advent of biotechnology has led to a rapidly changing environment where Dairyland's biotechnology suppliers are becoming more closely aligned with its competitors and where soybean seed customers are demanding the inclusion of biotechnological traits in addition to high-yielding genetics. As Tom puzzles over his current situation, and how to best manage his relationships with his technology suppliers and his customers, he is also keenly aware that herbicide tolerance is just the tip of the proverbial biotech iceberg. What will that next market-changing trait be, and when will it be developed? Will he have access to develop varieties with that trait? What types of relationships will he be managing in the future? Tom sits back from his desk and smiles. Yes, there hasn't been a more interesting time to be in the seed industry.

EXHIBIT 6
Economic Decisions
Faced by Customers*

	Yield/acre	Seed costs/acre	Herbicide costs/acre†
Dairyland Round-Up® 2341 variety			Round-Up® Ultra
One application of Herbicide	61	29.73**	35.00
Two applications of Herbicide			5.00††
Dairyland STS variety			Synchrony
One application of Herbicide	61	18.63	35.00
Two applications of Herbicide			25.00
Dairyland Conventional 256 variety			Pursuit
One application of Herbicide	64	18.63	35.00
Two applications of Herbicide			25.00

*The economic situation faced by producers varies widely by regions. This table is based on 1998 University of Wisconsin yield trials on three varieties of Dairyland seed.
**Seed costs include seed, and applicable technology fees (i.e., $19.98 + (1.5 * $6.50) = $29.73).
†Herbicide costs are based on manufacturers' suggested application rates and include a $5.00/acre application fee, and an estimated $10.00 for pre-plant and burn-down.
††The warranty for a second application of herbicide for Round-Up® customers depends on the producer following specific planting and application guidelines. Dairyland believes many farmers will not meet these requirements.

Dairyland Case Questions

Three alternative product strategies that Tom Strachota might take with Dairyland Seed are:

1. Attempt to associate more strongly with Monsanto and sell over 90 percent Round-Up® Ready herbicide-resistant seed.
2. Continue with the status quo and produce both Round-Up® Ready and STS beans letting the market dictate the level of each.
3. Attempt to associate more strongly with DuPont and focus on STS herbicide-resistant beans.

For EACH of these alternatives answer the following four questions:

1. What are the pros and cons of each strategy?
2. Are there other significantly different strategies that Dairyland should consider?
3. What would you recommend Dairyland do in the immediate future and why?
4. How can Dairyland remain family-owned and a successful seed business in the future?

Case 6-13

International Business Machines

The directors were just sitting down for the first IBM board meeting of the year on Jan. 28 when CEO Samuel J. Palmisano dropped a bombshell. For years, the board had lavished wealth upon Louis V. Gerstner Jr., keeping his pay in line with other pinstriped superstars across Corporate America. But in a surprise break from the past, Palmisano asked the board to cut his 2003 bonus and set it aside as a pool of money to be shared by about 20 top executives based on their performance as a team. Palmisano doesn't want to say how much he's pitching in, but insiders say it's $3 million to $5 million—nearly half his bonus.

A crowd-pleasing gesture? It was just his latest salvo. Five days earlier, he took aim at a bastion of power and privilege at Big Blue, the 92-year-old executive management committee. For generations, this 12-person body presiding over IBM's strategy and initiatives represented the inner sanctum for every aspiring Big Blue executive. Palmisano himself was anointed back in 1997, a promotion that signaled the shimmering possibilities ahead. But on Jan. 23, the CEO hit the send button on an e-mail to 300 senior managers announcing that this venerable committee was *finito,* kaput. Palmisano instead would work directly with three teams he had put in place the year before—they comprised people from all over the company who could bring the best ideas to the table. The old committee, with its monthly meetings, just slowed things down.

All the while, Palmisano was piecing together an audacious program to catapult IBM back to the zenith of technology (Exhibit 1). It started at an Aug. 5 strategy meeting, when he asked his team to draw up a project as epochal as the mainframe computer—IBM's big bet from 40 years ago. Through the day, the team cobbled together a vision of systems that would alter the very nature of how technology is delivered. IBM would supply computing power as if it were water or electricity. But how to tackle a project this vast? No one knew where to begin. A frustrated Palmisano abruptly cut short the meeting and gave the team 90 days to assemble and launch the megaproject. Three months later, the CEO unveiled "e-business on demand." Standing in New York's American Museum of Natural History, not far from the hulking dinosaurs whose fate IBM

narrowly skirted, Palmisano vowed to lead a new world of computing. "We have an opportunity to set the agenda in our industry," he says.

After one year on the job, Palmisano is putting his imprint on the company—and with a vengeance. Sure, IBM roared back to strength in the late '90s. But Palmisano is out to remake the company and hoist it back to greatness. Through much of the 20th century, under the leadership of Thomas J. Watson and his son, Thomas Jr., IBM not only ruled computing and defined the American multinational, it was the gold standard for corporations. From the days of tabulating machines all the way to the Space Age, when its mainframes helped chart the path to the moon, IBM was a paragon of power, prestige, and farsightedness. It was tops in technology, but also a leader in bringing women and

EXHIBIT 1
Blueprint for Big Blue: CEO Palmisano wants to bring back the days when IBM was revered as a great company. Here's how he plans to do it.

An Egalitarian Culture Palmisano has made a radical proposal to his board: Take several million dollars from his 2003 bonus and give it to his top execs based on teamwork.

Says Sam "If you say you're about a team, you have to be a team. You've got to walk the talk, right?"

Bureaucracy-Busting Big Decisions Decisions at IBM long ran through the 12-member Corporate Executive Committee. Palmisano replaced it with three teams—operating, strategy, and technology—to move more quickly.

Says Sam "Bureaucracy is an inhibiter to excellence.

A Unifying Goal IBM acted like fiefdoms: software, chips, computers. Palmisano created a unifying strategy: e-business on demand, to deliver tech like a utility. This requires all hands on deck.

Says Sam "It was about appealing to the pride of the 320,000 people to go to the next level."

Agenda Setter IBM was once the tech leader. Now, it's using R&D to leap ahead with grid computing and self-healing software.

Says Sam "IBM should be setting the industry agenda. We shouldn't let some small venture-based firm with 10 people do it. That's a joke.

Talent Magnet The company is spending $100 million to teach 30,000 employees to lead, not control their staff, so workers won't feel like cogs in a machine.

Says Sam "If you look at people's frustration, it's this inability to connect in a big place with a lot of smart people."

Squeaky-Clean Finances Palmisano is quieting criticism of IBM's accounting practices. He has allocated $4 billion to fully fund the U.S. pension plan. IBM also is paying more in taxes.

Says Sam "Write about somebody else. The pension plan is funded, the tax rate is up."

Good Works Palmisano wants IBM to give back. IBM is the leader in volunteer time. Now, he's considering more volunteers to mentor teachers and build computer systems for schools.

Says Sam "There's an attractiveness about being part of an enterprise that can make a difference."

minorities into a well-paid workforce and in creating a corporate culture that inspired lifelong loyalty. "We stood for something back then," Palmisano says.

To return IBM to greatness, the 51-year-old Palmisano is turning the company inside out. He's the first true-blue IBMer to take the reins since the company's fall from grace more than a decade ago. And while the new CEO never criticizes his predecessor, who rescued IBM and pushed many key technologies, Palmisano is quietly emerging as the antithesis of Gerstner. Where Gerstner raked in money, Palmisano makes a point of splitting the booty with his team. While Gerstner ruled IBM regally, Palmisano is egalitarian. The revolution he is leading spells the end of the imperial CEO at IBM. "Creativity in any large organization does not come from one individual, the celebrity CEO," Palmisano says. "That stuff's B.S. Creativity in an organization starts where the action is—either in the laboratory, or in R&D sites, at a customer place, in manufacturing."

If that sounds like the IBM of old, that's exactly what Palmisano is hoping for. The flattening of the organization, the lowering of CEO pay, the emphasis on teams—it's all part of his broad campaign to return to IBM's roots. Palmisano believes that core values remain in what he calls the company's DNA, waiting to be awakened. And he thinks that this message, which might have elicited chortles during the tech boom, resonates in the wake of the market crash and corporate

scandals. More important, he believes that only by returning to what made IBM great can the company rise again to assume its place of leadership in America and the world.

At the heart of Palmisano's plan is e-business on demand (Exhibit 2). The project, which is already gobbling up a third of IBM's $5 billion research and development budget, puts Big Blue in the vanguard of a massive computing shift. The company starts by helping customers standardize all of their computing needs. Then, in the course of the next 10 years, it will handle growing amounts of this work on its own massive computer grids. And this won't be just techie grunt work. The eventual goal is to imbue these systems with deep industrial expertise so that IBM is not only crunching numbers and dispatching e-mails but also delivering technology that helps companies solve thorny technical problems—from testing drugs to simulating car crashes. It's a soaring vision. But Palmisano has believers. "Sam is aiming to go where the market's going, not to where it's been," says Cisco Systems Inc. CEO John Chambers.

The obstacles he faces are immense. Start with the technology. The vision of on-demand computing is downright audacious. It proposes joining all of the thousands of computers and applications in enormous enterprises, and putting them to work seamlessly and in unison—not only in-house, but with partners and

EXHIBIT 2
The Evolution of E-Business on Demand: IBM is pushing a new strategy called e-business on demand that could cut tech users costs by 50%. But getting there could take a decade of rolling out new technologies and new ways of doing business.

STAGE 1	**Simplify** Typically, companies have different brands of gear, creating a Tower of Babel. The first step is to build a unified network. That means getting the hundreds of servers down to a dozen or so, and using open standards so all the pieces of gear speak to one another.
STAGE 2	**Efficiency** Too often, servers run idle and software sits on shelves. This phase ekes more out of the equipment through virtualization, a process by which many machines appear to be one. If one server is busy, software automatically farms out work to the others.
STAGE 3	**Grids** The technology has to be supersize. Corporations will be able to link all their networks and data centers to create a gigantic computing grid so that businesses can access information and computing power whenever they need to.
STAGE 4	**Utility** If a company runs out of capacity, it can buy computing power from a supplier on an as-needed basis instead of building a new data center. The company just flips a switch, and presto! it taps into a supplier's data center and gets billed for what it uses.
STAGE 5	**Expertise** This is the Big Kahuna: It's when customers get a new generation of Web services that speed up tasks. Take a drug company. Software that captures the myriad knowledge of researchers could be available to the entire research staff to hasten drug discovery.

customers. Assembling the pieces will require every bit of IBM's vaunted smarts, and a scrap of luck as well. IBM officials say only 10% of the technology needed for this system is ready. And many of the necessary pieces, including futuristic software programs that will heal themselves, are at the basic test stage in IBM's labs. "There are huge, huge technical challenges," says A. Richard Newton, dean of the College of Engineering at the University of California at Berkeley.

Palmisano faces an equally imposing job at home. To make good on his vision, he must turn IBM itself into a user of on-demand computing and become a prototype for its customers. This entails recharting the path of every bit of information flowing inside the company. It means not just shifting the computer systems, but redefining nearly everyone's job. And if IBM meets resistance to these changes, it could stumble in producing the new technology. This could undermine IBM's $800 million marketing campaign for e-business on demand—and scare away customers in droves. Such a failure could punish IBM financially, forcing a retreat toward fiercely competitive markets such as servers and chips. "The two most important parts of their business—services and software—are tied to the [on-demand] strategy," says Gartner analyst Tom Bittman. "They need to succeed."

Is history on Palmisano's side? Try to think of a great technology company that took a life-threatening fall and then scratched and clawed all the way back to the very top. Westinghouse? Digital Equipment? Xerox? Some have survived. But if Palmisano leads IBM back to the summit, Big Blue will be the first full-fledged round-tripper.

To get there, he must win a brutal battle raging among the titans of tech. From Hewlett-Packard Co. to Microsoft Corp., the industry's bruisers are all pushing research into next-generation computing systems that will rival IBM's. Big Blue appears to be better positioned than its foes, thanks to a wider range of offerings. But, warns Irving Wladawsky-Berger, IBM's general manager for e-business on demand: "In 1996, we had the benefit of being considered irrelevant. [Microsoft's William H.] Gates and [Steven A.] Ballmer felt pity on us. Now they are all watching us. If we don't move fast, they will pass us" (Exhibit 3).

The new initiative provides Palmisano with a prodigious tool to remake the company. Gerstner's reforms began the process, directing IBM toward software and services. But Palmisano's e-business on demand goes much further. It extends into nearly every nook of Big Blue, from its sales force and its army of systems consultants to the big brains cooking up the software code in the research and development labs. Management expert Jim Collins, author of *Good to Great,* says Palmisano's willingness to think and act boldly bodes well, and recalls earlier outsize bets in IBM's history, such as the development of the tabulating machine. "It reminds me of what Tom Watson Sr. did during the Depression," he says.

Palmisano already is banking on winning his share of the new business. Last year IBM saw revenue slip 2%, to $81.2 billion, with earnings tumbling 54% to $3.6 billion. But this year Palmisano is counting on e-business on demand to fuel the hottest sales growth at Big Blue since 1995. Analysts predict 9% revenue growth this year. And Palmisano expects 40%—nearly $3 billion—to come from new offerings in e-business on demand. These include servers running the free Linux operating system and grid software that pools the power of scores of networked computers into a virtual supercomputer.

By pursuing this plan, Palmisano is fleeing the brutish world of hardware and seeking refuge in profitable software and services businesses. He bulked up for this drive last year by spending $3.5 billion for PricewaterhouseCoopers Consulting and another $2.1 billion for Rational Software Corp., a maker of software tools to write programs. And why not? According to IBM's internal research, 60% of the profits in the $1 trillion high-tech industry will come from software and services by 2005. That's up from 45% in 2002. "We're just going where the profit is," Palmisano says.

And he's leading Big Blue in a way it has never been led before. One year before Palmisano disbanded the Executive Management Committee, he had put in place his management teams for the future. He created three of them: strategy, operations, and technology. Instead of picking only high-level executives for each team, Palmisano selected managers and engineers most familiar with the issues. "Heads are spinning," says J. Bruce Harreld, senior vice-president for strategy. "He's reaching six levels down and asking questions."

Talk to Palmisano for an hour and he'll mention teamwork 20 times. His entire on-demand strategy hinges upon it. Why? For IBM to come up with a broad array of on-demand technologies in a hurry, the whole company has to work smoothly from one far-flung cubicle to another. That means bringing researchers in touch not only with product developers, but with

EXHIBIT 3 'We Have Reinvented Ourselves Many Times'

Last year, when Sam Palmisano took the top job at IBM Corp., pundits figured he would settle in as the caretaker of former CEO Louis V. Gerstner Jr.'s strategy. Not Palmisano. He's blazing his own trail. The new CEO is streamlining management, emphasizing teamwork, and re-jiggering compensation—starting with his own. At IBM's snow-covered headquarters in Armonk, N.Y., and in an e-mail exchange, Palmisano talked with BusinessWeek *Computer Editor Spencer E. Ante about his mission to make IBM great again.*

What inspired you to try and make IBM a great company again?

IBM is one of the few companies in the world where people refer to themselves as IBMers. There's an attractiveness about being part of an institution that can do great things beyond generating financial results and paying a lot of money.

I kept thinking about an approach that would energize all the good of the past and throw out all the bad: hierarchy and bureaucracy. Get rid of all that trash. People stay at IBM for pride. It's about appealing to the pride of the people of IBM to go drive to the next level.

How are you going to measure IBM's greatness?

I think about it in four or five dimensions. If you're leading the industry agenda, you should be gaining share in your core segments. In the financials, there should be real consistency in earnings, It's about cash flows and balance sheets. It's the flexibility to fund the IBM pension fund for $4 billion. Why? Because it's the right thing to do, and you can afford to do it. It's being an employer of choice. People want to be here and want to make a big difference. So it's attrition rates. And the last dimension is being viewed as a valuable citizen. Getting people involved and using their skills to help local communities, whether that's Austin, Texas or Stuttgart.

Are you remaking IBM's core values?

No. Think about the early days of IBM. Bold moves. Diversity. I think 28 years before it was legislated, we paid equal pay for women. There was a lot that was great in the old IBM. These Watsons did not play to lose. In 1933, Thomas J. Watson Sr. gave a speech at the World's Fair, "World Peace through World Trade." We stood for something, right?

The DNA of the IBM company is what it always stood for. But get rid of the bad in the DNA, which was rigid behavior, starched white shirts, straw hats, singing company songs. I lived it. I sang the songs. That caused us to become insular, focused on ourselves. Beating up your colleagues was more important than winning in the marketplace. Lou [Gerstner] did a lot to knock all that down.

Why did you ask the board to cut your 2003 bonus?

If you say you're about a team, you have to be a team. You have to walk the talk, right? I can't have a big gap between me and my team.

We're talking about a pool of money that the board historically allocated to the chief executive. I recommended the board take the money and give it to the top officers of IBM. [There are] more than 20. The board will determine the exact size of this pool [and will determine bonuses] based on teamwork.

How do you balance your new job and family time?

It's incredibly tough to find the right balance. The workload just never lets up. On weekends I get up early and work until the kids get up. Then I go do whatever the family wants to do. People at IBM are used to getting e-mails from me early in the morning and late at night. On weekends, Sunday afternoons have pretty much become work times for me. It comes down to my family and IBM. I pretty much say no to everything else. I know it makes some people mad when I can't attend their events, but at least I'm consistent on that point.

consultants and even customers. Only by reaching across these old boundaries will IBM find out what customers are clamoring for—and produce it fast.

To head up this process, Palmisano has chosen Wladawsky-Berger, the renowned Cuban-born computer scientist who was IBM's e-biz guru in the 1990s.

Today, Wladawsky-Berger's mission is to drive the strategy across the company. In the last two months, he has assembled 28 people working in every division of IBM into what he calls a "virtual team." These are Wladawsky-Berger's on-demand agents. They nose around their areas of expertise, looking for on-demand possibilities. New servers coming out later this year, for example, will be equipped to dispatch excess work to other machines on the network.

Still, it's no easy job coaxing separate divisions to dance in unison. Clashes are common, for example, when IBM's 160,000 Global Service workers descend into the research labs. Last year, researchers were hard at work on a program for supply chains in the electronics industry. Consultants ordered up a quick version of the same program for a carmaker. The two sides battled briefly until the researchers adapted a program for cars, and then went back to work on electronics. The consultants' timeframe, says William Grey, manager of IBM's Finance Research, "is milliseconds. Ours is five years. There's a cultural gap that needs to be bridged."

The key is getting IBM itself to function as an e-business-on-demand enterprise. To drive this message through the company, Palmisano in January grabbed a star manager, Linda Sanford, and put her in charge of internal e-business on demand. Sanford, a senior vice-president, had revived IBM's storage business and was viewed as a bona fide up-and-comer at Big Blue. "I take a senior vice-president who has a great job, and say, 'O.K., you're going to make IBM on demand,'" Palmisano says. "Then, 320,000 people say, 'Holy . . . , this guy's serious."

Sanford faces an imposing job. First, she has to supervise the overhaul of IBM's massive supply chain. That means piling $44 billion of purchases into a single system. It's a slog. It means pushing IBM's engineers to switch to company-approved suppliers. Then a procurement rep is assigned to each development team, to make sure that they all use industry standard parts. It's intrusive. But like the rest of the on-demand program, it focuses the company onto a single effort. And it should pay dividends. Palmisano expects the entire initiative to yield 5% productivity gains, worth $2 billion to $3 billion a year, for the next five to 10 years.

Sanford also is working to create an online inventory of IBM's knowledge. She's turning the company's intranet into a giant collaboration portal. One feature is an "expertise locator" that helps an employee find, say, a software engineer with expertise in building databases in Linux. But at a meeting of the operations team at Armonk, N.Y. on a cold mid-February morning, a frustrated Sanford told key executives, including Palmisano, that the concept was a hard sell.

Palmisano, his face cupped in his hands, looked concerned. "There's a huge level of expectation on this portal," he said. "I just hope we can deliver." Sanford responded with a blunt message: If Palmisano wants the portal to succeed, he and his teams must lead by example, offering their own areas of expertise within a 30-day deadline. "We have to lead the way," she said.

For Palmisano, this means rallying the biggest brains and deepest thinkers in the company to the cause. In January he flew to Harvard University in Cambridge for a meeting with IBM's top computer scientists. His message was simple and straightforward: The dream of on-demand computing hinged upon their ability to produce technology breakthroughs.

While scientists are wrestling with future iterations of on-demand computing, IBM's sales team is rolling out the first products. New IBM servers include a feature called "hypervisors." These allow technicians to monitor as many as 100 servers at a time, shifting work from one machine to another. A new program from IBM's Tivoli group performs similar work, patrolling the network, constantly on the lookout for servers running short of memory. When it finds one, it automatically shifts the work to other computers. This is a key aspect of on-demand computing, and a potential money saver. Once systems can distribute work, companies will be able to run their servers at a high level, much closer to capacity. This reduces costs. And if work piles up, customers will ship excess tasks to IBM.

Many of them, IBM hopes, will eventually exit the computing business altogether and ship all their digital work to IBM. American Express likes the idea. A year ago, before Palmisano even came up with the new vision, AmEx signed a seven-year, $4 billion services contract with Big Blue. At first blush it looks like a standard outsourcing deal. The company has shifted its computers and 2,000 tech employees to IBM. But what makes it different is the economics. AmEx pays only for technology it uses every month. The advantages? AmEx is looking to save hundreds of millions of dollars over the course of the contract. And with IBM running the system, says Glen Salow, chief information officer at American Express, "they can upgrade technology five times faster."

Palmisano's vision for e-business on demand stretches beyond the technical challenges to the realm of human knowledge. In the services division, IBM has experts on industries ranging from banking to metals to autos. He wants to gather their knowhow—"deep process insights," he calls it—into the systems. Eventually, he sees IBM's on-demand offerings reinventing the company's corporate customers and shaking up entire industries.

IBM is developing 17 different industrial road maps for on demand. Pharmaceuticals is one. There, a computer grid will handle simulation and modeling to reduce the number of clinical trials needed. That, IBM says, could lead to improving the success rates of drugs, now from 5% to 10%, to 50% or better. IBM also believes it can help cut the time it takes to identify and launch a new drug to three to five years, down from 10 to 12, slicing the pre-launch cost of drug development to less than $200 million, from $800 million.

It's a splendid vision—and far too rich with opportunity for IBM alone. Microsoft has more cash than any tech company—$43 billion—and its .net Windows initiative is an effort to rule the next generation of computing every bit, as ambitious as Palmisano's. But Microsoft trails Big Blue in the upper end of the corporate computing world. Sun Microsystems, an early advocate of on demand computing, is pushing its own effort to develop software, called NI, that will more efficiently manage Sun gear. Sun claims Nl will offer superior performance—at one-tenth the cost—because the software is designed only for Sun products. "Diversity is great in your workforce," says Sun Executive Vice President Jonathan Schwartz. "It sucks in your data center." IBM software head Steven A. Mills shoots back: "Nothing they have in Nl is unique."

A stronger contender is Hewlett-Packard, thanks to its array of hardware, software, and services. Analysts say HP leads IBM in a few important niches. HP, for example, has software called Utility Data Center, that shifts work across all of a company's computers, networks, and storage devices.

For now, IBM's wide-angle vision and broader range of technology gives it the overall lead. But to keep ahead, Palmisano maintains a routine of near-constant work. Even while on a Vermont ski vacation in early March, Palmisano spent a snowy Sunday afternoon reading briefing papers while his family hit the slopes. Rest assured, Palmisano won't be getting his weekends back anytime soon. He is remaking IBM, and that's a job that could last a full decade. If he pulls it off, though, a giant of technology will be reborn.

By Spencer E. Ante in Armonk, N.Y.

Source: "The New Blue," *BusinessWeek,* March 17, 2003, 80–88.

Epilogue to Case 6-13

It was over a lunch in Cincinnati two years ago that IBM Chief Executive Samuel J. Palmisano got his first inkling of Big Blue's next act. Palmisano was talking business with A.G. Lafley, CEO of Procter & Gamble Co., one of IBM's big customers. At one point, Lafley asked Palmisano to estimate how many of P&G's 100,000 employees it truly needed to keep on its payroll. When Palmisano didn't venture a guess, Lafley stunned him by saying that P&G might be able to get by with only a quarter of its workforce. Specialized service companies might be able to handle everything else, from human resources to customer care.

For IBM's new CEO, Lafley's idea delivered a strong jolt of the future. "We saw it as an industry shift," he recalls. Palmisano was already an expert in technology services, such as running data centers and managing companies' computing operations. Working under former CEO Louis V. Gerstner Jr., he had helped rescue a struggling IBM in the '90s by building its then-modest services division into a $40 billion behemoth. But what Lafley was suggesting was far bigger. It stretched beyond revamping computer systems and stitching together new networks. If other CEOs were entertaining similar thoughts, a vast new market could emerge.

Over the past two years, Palmisano has built these concepts into a strategy that would be laughable—if it weren't so serious. His goal is to free IBM from the confines of the $1.2 trillion computer industry, which is growing at just 6% a year. Instead of merely selling and servicing technology, IBM is putting to use the immense resources it has in-house, from its software programmers to its 3,300 research scientists, to help companies like P&G rethink, remake, and even run their businesses—everything from accounting and customer service to human resources and procurement. "We're giving our clients a transformational lift," says Palmisano (Exhibit 1).

While Palmisano looks out at the world through thick glasses, he's not short on vision. He expects that within 10 years IBM could build an annual revenue stream of as much as $50 billion in business consulting and outsourcing services. If so, Palmisano will have created a second services miracle and hitched IBM to a crucial growth market. And in the process, his company will be fixing—or running—big chunks of the world's business.

No Sure Bet

Palmisano is out to transform the very nature and image of Big Blue, a nickname derived a half-century ago from the company's muscular blue mainframe computers. His goal is to carry IBM beyond that 20th

EXHIBIT 1

MAKEOVERS &
TAKEOVERS

R&D PARTNERSHIPS

IBM and **Boeing** have formed a 10-year R&D alliance to create technologies for network-centric warfare—where all the branches of the military and the intelligence services are linked via a network that allows them to share information and make battle decisions on the fly.

CORE BUSINESS PROCESSES

IBM has taken over a large part of **BP**'s finance and accounting in Europe and the Americas. Workers in remote locations such as ocean drilling platforms handle purchases of materials and parts digitally—so there's no paperwork to get lost.

RESEARCHING BIG CHALLENGES

IBM's science research arm is helping the **U.S. Postal Service** come up with a new mail processing and distribution system for its 400-plus facilities nation-wide. They'll use advanced algorithms to select the right transport—air, rail, or trucks—for each shipment.

RETHINKING WHOLE INDUSTRIES

Mayo Clinic and IBM have teamed to pool the digital information Mayo has on 4.5 million patients. Mayo researchers can now search the data for clues to better treatments. Eventually they hope to give doctors instant treatment guidance when they're talking to patients.

TECHNOLOGY-LED TRANSFORMATIONS

IBM helped **The New York Stock Exchange** rebuild its electronic trading system so it could complete on an equal footing with all-digital up-and-comers. A key piece: handheld devices for floor brokers that allow them to make and track trades.

NEW TYPES OF OUTSOURCING

IBM is experimenting with **"intelligent transportation systems"** for cities that want to ease traffic congestion. Stockholm is the laboratory. Drivers, identified electronically, pay variable tolls based on their status—commuter, tourist, taxi driver, etc.—and what time of day it is.

---

century legacy, beyond computing and, yes, beyond blue—while making IBM as indispensable to clients today as it was during the heyday of mainframes.

The change at IBM is palpable. The number of employees focused on business rather than pure technology has leaped from 3,500 in mid-2002 to more than 50,000 today—out of a total of 330,000. And that's growing at more than 10,000 a year. Meanwhile, in a painful process, other employees are exiting by the thousands—those in administration and computer repair, for instance, and from shuttered offices in Germany and Scandinavia.

Entire divisions are now in play. With the sale of the money-losing PC division to China's Lenovo Group Ltd., Palmisano cuts loose a big piece of the company's computer legacy. Meanwhile, he has snapped up more than a dozen business-service outfits in the past year, including Daksh, a 6,000-employee Indian customer-relations shop. Late last year he hired James Liang, a former Morgan Stanley mergers ace, to pick up the pace. "We're committed to completely reinventing the portfolio over the long haul," says Palmisano.

Yet getting there will be a slog—and coming out on top is no sure bet. To pull off his strategy, Palmisano must win a torturous trifecta: He must manage wrenching change inside IBM while, as a pitchman, convincing

corporate customers worldwide to hand over their operations. And he must deliver decisive results. This means turning laggards into leaders everywhere from emergency rooms to blast furnaces. "I think IBM is on the right track," says analyst Steven Milunovich of Merrill Lynch & Co. "But it's not going to be clear for two years if they're right or not."

Why has Palmisano embarked on such a risky adventure? In truth, he has little choice. The world of computing that IBM long ruled is increasingly becoming a commodity business. Ruthlessly efficient Dell Inc., fresh from its conquest of the PC market, is climbing up in servers and even tech services. Dell's services, which focus on setting up computer systems, are still small compared with IBM's $46 billion services business, but they are growing at more than 30% annually and are expected to hit $4 billion this year. "The big question is: Will services go the same way hardware has? We think it will," says Steve Meyer, a vice-president in Dell's services unit.

IBM, with its legions of PhDs and closets full of patents, is not built to duke it out with the likes of Dell. Palmisano's strategy promises a neat escape. Instead of battling in cutthroat markets, he takes advantage of all the low-cost technology by packaging it, augmenting it with sophisticated hardware and software, and selling it to customers in a slew of what he calls business transformation services. That way IBM rides atop the commodity wave—and avoids drowning in it.

The danger? Simple. An IBM stumble would spell slower growth and smaller profits, undermining its research-driven business model and its position atop the corporate tech world. Palmisano has only to reflect on IBM's sorry state in the early 1990s to taste the consequences of falling short now.

The initial challenge is to make a grand vision that can sound threatening or full of hype into a must-have. McDonald's Corp., for instance, last year decided not to hand over its accounting and finance operations after IBM promoted the idea, opting to keep everything in-house instead. Even William H. Davidow, co-author of the 1992 book *The Virtual Corporation,* which championed the idea of handing off tasks to partners, cautions execs against going too far or too fast. "It would scare me to death if all my administration and strategy functions were outsourced to one company. You become a hostage," he warns.

To win over lukewarm customers, IBM might be tempted to offer overly favorable terms for unpredictable long-term contracts. This poses another risk. Time and again, tech companies have misjudged the actual costs of running companies' ever-changing computing operations. As a result, they lose money on the deals for years. That's what happened with IBM's contract to run computing for JPMorgan Chase & Co., which the bank dissolved late last year when it took back control. That was a technology deal, not operations outsourcing, but the same uncertainties apply.

IBM faces strong competition as it forges into alien territory. The most potent rival is consultancy Accenture Ltd. The $15.6 billion services giant has been dipping a big toe into business process outsourcing. While Accenture can't match IBM's tech skills or research staff, it outguns IBM in business expertise. "IBM is genetically a technology company," says Joel P. Friedman, president of Accenture's BPO unit. "I think our history of solving business problems and our industry knowledge gives us an enormous advantage." Accenture notched $2.2 billion in BPO revenues last year, up 50%, while IBM's business outsourcing and related revenues hit $3 billion, a 45% gain.

Challenging both IBM and Accenture are aggressive Indian outsourcers, including Wipro and Tata Consultancy Services Ltd. Wipro's BPO business is going gangbusters and hiring about 1,400 employees per month. They offer customers lower costs but without the operational makeover IBM promises—which they view as risky. "We believe making changes at the customer end will be very hard," says T.K. Kurien, head of Wipro's BPO business. "Nine times out of 10 you'll fail."

Glimpses of Greatness

Still, if Palmisano and his crew fend off rivals and prove the skeptics wrong, the opportunities are enormous. Market researcher IDC estimates that in IBM's target markets, nearly half a trillion dollars are already flowing to outsourcers in everything from HR to industrial design. It expects the field to grow by 8% to 11% per year. Merrill Lynch's Milunovich figures that this new business could heat up annual growth in IBM Global Services from less than 5% a year over the next few years to as much as 9%, excluding currency effects. Business services promise to pretty up profits, too. Analysts haven't made estimates yet, but IBM's senior vice-president for strategy, J. Bruce Harreld, says the company will be able to achieve 20% operating-profit margins—double the margins in traditional tech services.

IBM's commitment to Wall Street is to deliver single-digit revenue gains and double-digit profit gains. Analysts expect the $96 billion company to expand revenues 7% this year, not counting the spun-off PC unit. They project a 12.5% gain in earnings per share, so Palmisano is good for now. But analysts are nervous about a 7.5% decline in IBM's overall outsourcing backlog last year, as the average length of IT deals declines. Palmisano is counting on gains from his new initiatives to sustain growth.

Investors, it appears, need more convincing. IBM's stock has been trading recently at about $90 a share, after briefly reaching $126 in 2002. The trouble? Palmisano is selling visions that can seem a bit vaporous to investors grounded in mainframes and tech services. With his business-services push, Palmisano is building on top of the "On Demand Business" campaign he launched 2½ years ago. The idea there: to use advanced computer and software technologies to quicken the flow of knowledge within corporations so executives can react instantly to changes. That's still a work in progress. Now, with business services, it's as if he's building a big addition onto a house that's still under construction.

But Palmisano has gotten glimpses from early IBM deals of the magic that business outsourcing can work (Exhibit 2). In 2002, Marathon Oil Corp. wanted to trim costs in its finance department and at the same

EXHIBIT 2

HOW IBM'S
BUSINESS-SERVICES STRATEGY WORKS
Big Blue's methodology isn't set in stone, but here's how it played out with Marathon Oil

A PUSH FOR CHANGE	IBM RESPONDS	THE PATH FORKS	IBM CREATES NEW PRODUCTS
In 2002, Marathon Oil's executives want to trim costs in the finance department and put in place monitoring tools so that managers can follow daily operations and make quick adjustments. They call in IBM consultants and researchers to talk it over.	Big Blue's consultants and software developers analyze Marathon's business processes. They suggest ways to reduce accounts payable and other processes from 18 days to eight. They build a "dashboard" on execs' PCs to help monitor the business.	While some clients keep control of their business processes and technology supplied by IBM, Marathon hands much of its finance operations directly to Big Blue. Other customers go further, having IBM manage human resources and customer service.	IBM builds businesses around the know how it develops for early customers, such as Marathon. Already, IBM has sold the business-analysis dashboard it created for Marathon to more than a dozen other clients—and has installed it within IBM itself.

time give top execs an up-to-the-minute view into how the company was performing. IBM's consultants analyzed Marathon's business processes and suggested fixes. The average time to complete financial processes, such as accounts payable, shrank from 18 days to eight. They also built a "dashboard" on execs' PCs to help monitor the business. When the consulting project was complete, Marathon handed much of its finance operations directly to IBM in a seven-year, $100 million to $200 million outsourcing contract. "IBM is changing its definition from international business machines to international business models," says analyst David Cearley of researcher META Group.

IBM's early wins include groundbreaking contracts with some two dozen large companies and government agencies. Dun & Bradstreet Corp., for instance, just handed over some of its essential credit report data-processing operations to IBM. This is work that companies in the past would rarely entrust to outsiders. For the U.S. Postal Service, IBM is using complex algorithms from its research scientists to optimize mail handling and shipping. Then there's the unprecedented partnership with Boeing Co. The two companies are teaming up to create and market technologies for network-centric warfare.

Such joint projects call for a new type of IBMer—people like Saul J. Berman, a business consultant who came to the company with Price-WaterhouseCoopers Consulting, which IBM bought in 2002 for $3.5 billion. Berman's résumé includes stints as a management professor and a retail executive. IBM used to sell machines. Now, in a way, it sells well-connected teammates. Berman identifies so deeply with one of his clients, Virgin Megastores, where he's helping reorganize the handling of merchandise, that he seems like a staffer.

When he travels, he invariably stops in at the local Virgin outlet and prowls the aisles looking for surprises or things that are amiss. If a CD is in the wrong spot, he'll move it back. It's like he owns the place.

Team Players

On a recent rainy night in Los Angeles, Berman gives a guided tour of the Virgin store on the Sunset Strip. Pleased that several dozen shoppers turned out in spite of the deluge, he ambles through the store pointing out newer types of merchandise, including cell phones and Ben Sherman designer clothing. He's trying to get Virgin to hire IBM to devise a strategy to help the retailer diversify to avoid being undercut by rampant Internet music pirating and steep discounting by Wal-Mart Stores Inc. "The question I ask the Virgin people is, 'Are you a music store or a lifestyle store? What are you?'" he says.

As IBM morphs from computer company into business expert, the blue-suited computer salesman of the past is being symbolically elbowed aside by people like Berman—who tours Virgin dressed in black. But this makeover isn't as easy as hiring a batch of new employees to add new gloss. IBM is also overhauling its workforce by retraining and redeploying many longtime staffers, even some at the very top. For the past six years, IBM Research manager William Pulleyblank ran the company's Blue Gene project, creating the world's most powerful computer. Now he has a very different role—as a business consultant. Late last year, IBM set up a Center for Business Optimization and put him in charge. Pulleyblank's task is to harness mathematics to solve the thorniest conundrums involving inventory management, pricing optimization, and the routing of shipments.

Even the vaunted 38,000-person sales force is undergoing a painful overhaul. In the 1990s, salespeople representing the various IBM business units were essentially on their own—looking for hot opportunities to sell individual products or services. But Palmisano is busy "reintegrating" IBM in front of customers by bringing together specialists from computers, software, consulting, and even research. That's tougher than it sounds. People who don't play well with others get replaced. These teams gather with customers, which often leads to discussions about business problems and strategies.

In its pursuit of vital industry experience, IBM—much like an eager college intern—is sometimes willing to work for free. IBM's unpaid partnership with the Mayo Clinic dates back to a cocktail party in 2000 in Mayo's hometown of Rochester, Minn., where IBM has a computer factory. A Mayo employee and an IBMer realized that scientists at both companies were working on genomics research. This soon led to joint projects on gene profiling of leukemia cells, and a published paper in a scientific journal in 2003. This is not the kind of connection that Dell, Accenture, or Wipro is likely to make.

IBM and Mayo quickly moved on to a more ambitious project: changing the way medical research is done. They set out to gather data on 4.5 million patients and to make it easily searchable by researchers—but without compromising patients' privacy. A research task that used to take five people a year can now be done by one person in 15 seconds. Eventually, Mayo and IBM believe, physicians will tap into a vast storehouse of data, real-time, when they're diagnosing patients. "This is the way to transform the way we practice medicine," says Dr. Nina M. Schwenk, chairperson of Mayo's Information Technology Committee. And for IBM, it's a foot in the door of the $1.4 trillion health-care business.

While IBM had plenty of skilled engineers in Rochester, they practically needed brain transplants if they were to do breakthrough work for Mayo. So the company sent some of its brightest engineers back to school. Working with the University of Minnesota, the company arranged in 2003 for a series of three-day crash courses in everything from molecular biology to protein sequence analysis. So far, 50 people have taken the classes. Nothing illustrates more starkly the gyrations at IBM: Engineers who once worked on a fading family of main-frame-style computers are now helping to chart the future of medicine. "Part of your job is to be a visionary," says Jeffrey Tenner, one of the engineers.

Now IBM is directing part of its Rochester staff toward bioinformatics, privacy, and regulation compliance—all skills learned through the Mayo alliance.

Leveraging Success

While IBM has forged cozy ties with Mayo, the business payoff is still unclear. IBM's goal with this alliance and others is to take lessons and turn them into products and services to sell within the industry. The Mayo work has led to a new software product for medical research. Other health-care products are on the way. And IBM is hoping one day to manage patient databases or networks of health-care organizations.

The Mayo alliance is now a model for forging research and development linkups with clients. Late last year, in quick succession, it struck up R&D alliances with Honeywell International Inc. and Boeing. The 10-year Boeing deal teams Boeing's military command systems expertise with IBM's facility with databases and collaboration. "This alliance with IBM is unique in the industry," says Roger F. Roberts, head of Boeing's Space & Intelligence Systems business. "We share our strategies, we share our R&D, and we offer joint solutions for customers."

IBM doesn't wait around for clients to come to it with R&D projects. Engineers are encouraged to dream up products and peddle them to potential customers. IBM engineer and cycling enthusiast Bryan Streimer, for example, rigged up a wireless heart-rate system to alert family members if a cyclist has a heart attack on the road. IBM channeled Streimer's invention into an electric pill dispenser, which it's developing for Danish electronic device maker Bang & Olufsen. If patients forget to take a pill on schedule, the device calls their cell phone. Now IBM is helping a British mobile-phone carrier build a new business offering wireless medical alert systems.

While the product design deals are nice one-offs, IBM's strategy hinges on winning broad long-term contracts. The seven-year, $180 million contract with D&B that was announced last October shows how it's done. For D&B, IBM not only pulls together credit information on 63 million companies but also handles customer support, telemarketing, electronic credit-report distribution, and crucial finance operations. IBM uses advanced analytics software to size up D&B's customers and identify good prospects for additional services for the telemarketing staff.

A lot of these newfangled service deals haven't been around long enough to show results—but a few have.

EXHIBIT 3

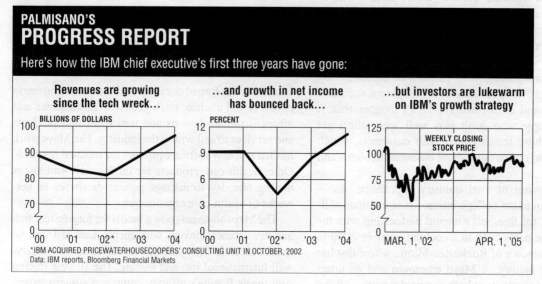

PALMISANO'S
PROGRESS REPORT
Here's how the IBM chief executive's first three years have gone:

Revenues are growing since the tech wreck...

...and growth in net income has bounced back...

...but investors are lukewarm on IBM's growth strategy

*IBM ACQUIRED PRICEWATERHOUSECOOPERS' CONSULTING UNIT IN OCTOBER, 2002
Data: IBM reports, Bloomberg Financial Markets

At Nextel, for instance, IBM's takeover of the company's customer-service operations helped improve its customer satisfaction ratings from also-ran to top of the heap. P&G is another success story. In January, 2004, IBM took over part of P&G's human resources in a 10-year deal valued at $400 million. P&G has so far outsourced 3,500 jobs, including some in computing and customer relations. In HR, it had set 21 standards for speed and accuracy in such categories as payroll and expense management. The IBM-run operations met them all. In the month before IBM took over, P&G had met only nine of the goals, according to market researcher Gartner Inc.

With those victories under its belt, IBM is scrounging for new markets. In addition to its four original businesses—accounting, HR, customer service, and procurement—it is now plowing into six others. They include after-sales service for consumer electronics, insurance-claims processing, and supply-chain

optimization. The old IBM would have studied for many months before deciding whether to enter these new businesses. This time, it has set up small SWAT teams to work with a handful of initial clients and launch businesses. This is in some cases a tough sell. "These are markets we're making. A client may not have thought of doing this before," says Ginni Rometty, managing partner of IBM Business Consulting Services.

Plenty of pitfalls lie ahead. But for companies like IBM that bank on innovation, there's little choice but to create new markets and exploit them. "In the past, IBM defended the mainframe against client-server computing and PCs," Palmisano says. "We're not defending the past anymore" (Exhibit 3). No, IBM is off and running into a new world of business, beyond computers. So long, Big Blue.

Source: Steve Hamm, "Beyond Blue," *BusinessWeek,* April 18, 2005, 68–76.

Case 6-14
L'Oréal Nederland B.V.

Yolanda van der Zande, director of the Netherlands L'Oréal subsidiary, faced two tough decisions and was discussing them with Mike Rourke, her market manager for cosmetics and toiletries. "We have to decide whether to introduce the Synergie skin care line and Belle Couleur permanent hair colorants," she told him.

Synergie had recently been introduced successfully in France, the home country for L'Oréal. Belle Couleur

This case was prepared by Frederick W. Langrehr, Valparaiso University; Lee Dahringer, Butler University; and Anne Stöcker. This case was written with the cooperation of management solely for the purpose of stimulating student discussion. All events and individuals are real, but names have been disguised. We appreciate the help of J. B. Wilkinson and V. B. Langrehr on earlier drafts of this case. Copyright © 1994 by the *Case Research Journal* and the authors.

had been marketed successfully in France for two decades. Mr. Rourke responded:

> Yes, and if we decide to go ahead with an introduction, we'll also need to develop marketing programs for the product lines. Fortunately, we only need to think about marketing, since the products will still be manufactured in France.

Ms. van der Zande replied:

> Right, but remember that the marketing decisions on these lines are critical. Both of these lines are part of the Garnier family brand name. Currently Ambre Solaire (a sun screen) is the only product we distribute with the Garnier name in the Netherlands. But headquarters would like us to introduce more Garnier product lines into our market over the next few years, and it's critical that our first product launches in this line be successful.

Mr. Rourke interjected, "But we already sell other brands of L'Oréal products in our market. If we introduce Garnier, what will happen to them?" After some more discussion, Ms. van der Zande suggested:

> Why don't you review what we know about the Dutch market. We've already done extensive marketing research on consumer reactions to Synergie and Belle Couleur. Why don't you look at it and get back to me with your recommendations in two weeks.

Background

In 1992 the L'Oréal Group was the largest cosmetics manufacturer in the world. Headquartered in Paris, it had subsidiaries in over 100 countries. In 1992, its sales were $6.8 billion (a 12 percent increase over 1991) and net profits were $417 million (a 14 percent increase). France contributed 24 percent of total worldwide sales, Europe (both western and eastern countries, excluding France) provided 42 percent, and the United States and Canada together accounted for 20 percent; the rest of the world accounted for the remaining 14 percent. L'Oréal's European subsidiaries were in one of two groups: (1) major countries (England, France, Germany, and Italy) or (2) minor countries (the Netherlands and nine others).

The company believed that innovation was its critical success factor. It thus invested heavily in research and development and recovered its investment through global introductions of its new products. All research was centered in France. As finished products were developed, they were offered to subsidiaries around the world. Because brand life cycles for cosmetics could be very short, L'Oréal tried to introduce one or

two new products per year in each of its worldwide markets. International subsidiaries could make go/no go decisions on products, but they generally did not have direct input into the R&D process. In established markets such as the Netherlands, any new product line introduction had to be financed by the current operations in that country.

L'Oréal marketed products under its own name as well as under a number of other individual and family brand names. For example, it marketed Anaïs Anaïs perfume, the high-end Lancôme line of cosmetics, and L'Oréal brand hair care products. In the 1970s it acquired Laboratoires Garnier, and this group was one of L'Oréal's largest divisions. In France, with a population of about 60 million people, Garnier was a completely separate division, and its sales force competed against the L'Oréal division. In the Netherlands, however, the market was much smaller (about 15 million people), and Garnier and L'Oréal products would be marketed by the same sales force.

Dutch consumers had little, if any, awareness or knowledge of Garnier and had not formed a brand image. The Garnier sunscreen was a new product, and few Dutch women knew about the brand. It was therefore very important that any new Garnier products launched in the Netherlands have a strong concept and high market potential. To accomplish this, the products needed to offer unique, desired, and identifiable differential advantages to Dutch consumers. Products without such an edge were at a competitive disadvantage and would be likely not only to fail but to create a negative association with the Garnier name, causing potential problems for future Garnier product introductions.

The Dutch Market

In the late 1980s, 40 percent of the Dutch population (about the same percentage as in France) was under 25 years old. Consumers in this age group were the heaviest users of cosmetics and toiletries. But as in the rest of Europe, the Dutch population was aging and the fastest-growing population segments were the 25-or-older groups.

Other demographic trends included the increasing number of Dutch women working outside the home. The labor force participation rate of women in the Netherlands was 29 percent. That was much lower than the 50 percent or above in the United Kingdom or the United States, but the number of women working outside the home was increasing faster in the Netherlands than it was in those countries. Dutch women were also delaying childbirth. As a result of these trends, women in the Netherlands were exhibiting greater self-confidence and independence; women had more disposable income, and more of them were using it to buy cosmetics for use on a daily basis.

Despite their rising incomes, Dutch women still shopped for value, especially in cosmetics and toiletries. In the European Union (EU), the Netherlands ranked fourth in per capita income, but it was only sixth in per capita spending on cosmetics and toiletries. Thus, Dutch per capita spending on personal care products was only 60 percent of the amount spent per capita in France or Germany. As a result of both a small population (15 million Dutch to 350 million EU residents) and lower per capita consumption, the Dutch market accounted for only 4 percent of total EU sales of cosmetics and toiletries.

Synergie

Synergie was a line of facial skin care products that consisted of moisturizing cream, antiaging day cream, antiwrinkle cream, cleansing milk, mask, and cleansing gel. It was made with natural ingredients, and its advertising slogan in France was "The alliance of science and nature to prolong the youth of your skin."

Skin Care Market

The skin care market was the second largest sector of the Dutch cosmetics and toiletries market. For the past five quarters unit volume had been growing at an annual rate of 12 percent, and dollar sales at a rate of 16 percent. This category consisted of hand creams, body lotions, all-purpose creams, and facial products. Products in this category were classified by price and product type. Skin care products produced by institutes such as Shisedo and Estée Lauder were targeted at the high end of the market. These lines were expensive and were sold through personal service perfumeries that specialized in custom sales of cosmetics and toiletries. At the other end of the price scale were mass-market products such as Ponds, which were sold in drugstores and supermarkets. In the last couple of years a number of companies, including L'Oréal, had begun to offer products in the midprice range. For example its Plénitude line was promoted as a high-quality, higher-priced—but still mass-market—product.

Skin care products also could be divided into care and cleansing products. Care products consisted of day and

EXHIBIT 1 Usage of Skin Care Products by Dutch Women

Product	Percentage of Women Using
Day cream	46%
Cleansers	40
Mask	30
Tonic	26
Antiaging cream	3

night creams; cleansing products were milks and tonics. The current trend in the industry was to stretch the lines by adding specific products targeted at skin types, such as sensitive, greasy, or dry. An especially fast-growing category consisted of antiaging and antiwrinkling creams. Complementing this trend was the emphasis on scientific development and natural ingredients.

Almost 50 percent of the 5 million Dutch women between the ages of 15 and 65 used traditional skin care products. The newer specialized products had a much lower penetration, as shown in Exhibit 1.

The sales breakdown by type of retailer for the middle- and lower-priced brands is shown in Exhibits 2 and 3.

Competition

There were numerous competitors. Some product lines, such as Oil of Olaz (Oil of Olay in the United States) by Procter & Gamble and Plénitude by L'Oréal, were offered by large multinational companies; other brands, for example, Dr. vd Hoog and Rocher, were offered by

EXHIBIT 2 Sales Breakdown for Skin Care Products in Supermarkets and Drugstores

Type of Store	Unit Sales (%)	Dollar Sales (%)
Supermarkets	18%	11%
Drugstores	82	89
	100	100

EXHIBIT 3 Sales Breakdown for Skin Care Products by Type of Drugstore

Type of Drugstore	Unit Sales (%)	Dollar Sales (%)
Chains	57%	37%
Large independent	31	39
Small independent	12	24
	100	100

EXHIBIT 4   Competitive Product Lines of Cosmetics

	Price Range (Guilders)*	Positioning
Lower End		
Nivea Visage†	9.50–11.50	Mild, modest price, complete line
Ponds	5.95–12.95	Antiwrinkle
Middle		
Dr. vd Hoog	10–11.95	Sober, nonglamorous, no illusions, but real help, natural, efficient, relatively inexpensive
Oil of Olaz (Procter & Gamble)	12 (day cream only)	Moisturizing, antiaging
Plénitude (L'Oréal)	10.95–19.95	Delay the signs of aging
Synergie	11.95–21.95	The alliance of science and nature to prolong the youth of your skin
Upper End		
Yves Rocher	10–26.95	Different products for different skins, natural ingredients
Ellen Betrix (Estée Lauder)	12.95–43.50	Institute line with reasonable prices, luxury products at nonluxury prices

*One dollar = 1.8 guilders; one British pound = 2.8 guilders; 1 deutschmark = 1.1 guilders.
†Although Nivea Visage had a similar price range to Dr. vd Hoog, consumers perceived Nivea as a lower-end product.

regional companies. Some companies offered a complete line, while others, such as Oil of Olaz, offered one or two products. Exhibit 4 lists a few of the available lines along with the price ranges and positioning statements.

The Dutch market was especially competitive for new brands such as Oil of Olaz and Plénitude. The rule of thumb in the industry was that share of voice for a brand (the percentage of total industry advertising spent by the company) should be about the same as its market share. Thus, a company with a 10 percent market share should have had advertising expenditures around 10 percent of total industry advertising expenditures. But there were deviations from this rule. Ponds, an established and well-known company with loyal customers, had about 9 percent share of the market (units) but accounted for only about 2.5 percent of total industry ad expenditures. Alternatively, new brands such as Oil of Olaz (10 percent market share, 26 percent share of voice) and Plénitude (5 percent market share, 13 percent share of voice) spent much more. The higher ad spending for these brands was necessary to develop brand awareness and, ideally, brand preference.

Any innovative products or new product variations in a line could be quickly copied. Retailers could develop and introduce their own private labels in four months; manufacturers could develop a competing product and

advertising campaign in six months. Manufacturers looked for new product ideas in other countries and then transferred the product concept or positioning strategy across national borders. They also monitored competitors' test markets. Since a test market typically lasted nine months, a competitor could introduce a product before a test market was completed.

Consumer Behavior

Consumers tended to be loyal to their current brands. This loyalty resulted from the possible allergic reaction to a new product. Also, facial care products were heavily advertised and sold on the basis of brand image. Thus, users linked self-concept with a brand image, and this increased the resistance to switching. While all consumers had some loyalty, the strength of this attachment to a brand increased with the age of the user. Finally, establishing a new brand was especially difficult since Dutch women typically purchased facial creams only once or twice a year. Dutch women were showing an increasing interest in products with "natural" ingredients, but they were not as familiar as the French were with technical product descriptions and terms.

Market Research Information

Earlier, Mike Rourke had directed his internal research department to conduct some concept and use tests for

EXHIBIT 5 Buying Intentions for Synergie Products

	All Participants	Plénitude Users	Dr. vd Hoog Users	Other Brand Users
Price Not Known				
Antiaging daycream				
After trial	5.37*	5.63	5.00	5.42
After use	5.26	5.55	5.08	5.17
Moisturizing cream				
After trial	5.34	5.60	5.38	5.11
After use	5.51	5.74	5.56	5.22
Price Known				
Antiaging daycream				
After trial	3.75	4.13	3.82	3.44
After use	3.60	3.76	3.54	3.54
Certainly buy†	24%	21%	23%	27%
Moisturizing cream				
After trial	4.08	4.36	4.17	3.77
After use	4.06	4.26	4.13	3.78
Certainly buy	39%	52%	38%	30%

*Seven-point scale with 7 being most likely to buy.
†Response to a separate question asking about certainty of buying with "certainly buy" as the highest choice.

the Synergie products. The researchers had sampled 200 women between the ages of 18 and 55 who used skin care products three or more times per week. They sampled 55 Plénitude users, 65 Dr. vd Hoog users, and 80 users of other brands.

The participants reacted positively to Synergie concept boards containing the positioning statement and the terminology associated with the total product line. On a seven-point scale with 7 being the most positive, the mean score for the Synergic line for all the women in the sample was 4.94. The evaluations of the women who used the competing brands, Plénitude and Dr. vd Hoog, were similar at 4.97 and 4.88, respectively.

The researchers then conducted an in-depth analysis of two major products in the line: antiaging day cream and moisturizing cream. Participants reported their buying intentions after they tried the Synergie product once and again after they used it for a week. Some participants were told the price, and others did not know the price. The results of this analysis are shown in Exhibit 5.

Belle Couleur

Belle Couleur was a line of permanent hair coloring products. It had been sold in France for about two decades and was the market leader. In France the line had 22 shades that were mostly natural shades and a few strong red or very bright light shades. It was positioned

as reliably providing natural colors with the advertising line "natural colors, covers all gray."

Hair Coloring Market

There were two types of hair coloring: semipermanent and permanent. Semipermanent colors washed out after five or six shampooings. Permanent colors disappeared only as the hair grew out from the roots. Nearly three-quarters (73 percent) of Dutch women who colored their hair used a permanent colorant. Over the past four years, however, the trend had been toward semipermanent colorants, with an increase from 12 percent to 27 percent of the market. Growth in unit volume during those years for both types of colorant had been about 15 percent per annum. The majority of unit sales in the category were in chain drugstores (57 percent), with 40 percent equally split between large and small independent drugstores. Food retailers accounted for the remaining 3 percent.

Competition

In the Netherlands 4 of 10 total brands accounted for 80 percent of the sales of permanent hair colorants, compared to 2 brands in France. Exhibit 6 gives the market share of the leading permanent color brands in the period 1987–1989. Interestingly, none of them had a clear advertising positioning statement describing customer benefits. By default, then, Belle Couleur could be positioned as "covering gray with natural colors."

EXHIBIT 6 **Major Brands of Hair Colorant**

Market Shares of	1987	1988	1989
Upper end (14.95 guilders)			
Recital (L'Oréal brand)	35%	34%	33%
Cuhl	9	12	14
Belle Couleur (12.95 guilders)	—	—	—
Lower-priced (9.95 guilders)			
Andrelon	12	14	17
Poly Couleur	24	23	21
Others	20	17	15
Total	100	100	100

Hair salons were indirect competitors in the hair coloring market. The percentage of women who had a hairstylist color their hair was not known, nor were the trends in the usage of this method known. It was projected that as more women worked outside the home, home coloring probably would increase because it was more convenient.

L'Oréal's current market entry (Recital) was the leading seller, although its share was declining. Guhl's and Andrelon's increases in shares between 1986 and 1989 reflected the general trend toward using warmer shades, and these two brands were perceived as giving quality red tones. In the late 1980s Guhl had changed its distribution strategy and started selling the brand through drug chains. In 1987 less than 1 percent of sales were through drug outlets; in the first quarter of 1990 drug-outlet sales had reached nearly 12 percent. Guhl also had become more aggressive in its marketing through large independents, with its share in those outlets climbing from 16 to 24 percent over the same period. Both the increasing shares of the smaller brands and the decreasing shares of the leaders sparked a 60 percent increase in advertising in 1989 for all brands of hair coloring.

Consumer Behavior

Consumers perceived permanent hair color as a technical product and believed its use was very risky. As a result, users had strong brand loyalty and avoided impulse purchasing. When considering a new brand, both first-time users and current users carefully read package information and asked store personnel for advice.

Traditionally, hair colorants had been used primarily to cover gray hair. Recently, however, coloring hair had become more of a fashion statement. This partially accounted for the increased popularity of semipermanent hair coloring. In one study the most frequently

cited reason (33 percent) for coloring hair was to achieve warm/red tones; another 17 percent reported wanting to lighten their hair color, and covering gray was cited by 29 percent. It was likely that the trend toward using colorants more for fashion and less for covering gray reflected the increase in hair coloring by consumers less than 35 years old. In 1989, 46 percent of Dutch women (up from 27 percent in 1986) colored their hair with either semipermanent or permanent hair colorants. Exhibit 7 contains a breakdown of usage by age of user.

Hair coloring was purchased almost exclusively in drugstores; only 3 percent of sales were through supermarkets. The percentage of sales for drug outlets was chains, 58 percent; large independents, 22 percent; and small independents, 20 percent.

Market Research

As with Synergie, Mr. Rourke had the L'Oréal market researchers contact consumers about their reactions to Belle Couleur. Four hundred twelve Dutch women between the ages of 25 and 64 who had used hair colorant in the last four months were part of a concept test, and 265 of those women participated in a use test. A little over 25 percent of the participants colored their hair every six weeks or more often, while another 47 percent did it every two to three months. (The average French user colored her hair every three weeks.) Nearly 60 percent used hair color to cover gray, while the remainder did it for other reasons.

After being introduced to the concept and being shown some sample ads, participants were asked their buying intentions. The question was asked three times—before and after the price was given and after Belle Couleur was used. The results are shown in Exhibit 8.

In most product concept tests (as with the Synergie line) buying intentions declined once the price was revealed. For Belle Couleur, buying intentions increased after the price was given but decreased after actual use. As the exhibit shows, the percentage of participants who

EXHIBIT 7 **Hair Coloring by Age (%)**

	1986	1989
Less than 25 years	35%	50%
25–34	24	54
35–49	32	55
50–64	24	33
65 and over	15	19

EXHIBIT 8
Buying Intentions

	Price-Unaware	Price-Aware	After Use
Certainly buy (5)	18%	26%	29%
Probably buy (4)	60	57	30
Don't know (3)	12	5	9
Probably not (2)	7	7	11
Certainly not (1)	3	6	21
Total	100%	100%	100%
Mean score	3.85	3.92	3.35

EXHIBIT 9   Purchase Intentions and Evaluation of Belle Couleur by Brand Currently Used

	Brand Currently Used				
	Total Sample	Andrelon	Poly Couleur	Guhl	Recital (L'Oréal)
After-Use Purchase Intentions of Belle Couleur					
Probably not (2)	11%	12%	12%	14%	5%
Certainly not (1)	21	24	29	20	5
	32%	36%	41%	34%	10%
Overall mean score	3.35	3.4	3.1	3.4	3.95
Evaluation of Final Color of Belle Couleur					
Very good (1)	25%	24%	31%	22%	35%
Good (2)	43	40	31	44	49
Neither good or bad (3)	10	10	14	6	8
Bad (4)	12	14	5	18	8
Very bad (5)	9	12	19	10	. . .
Mean	2.37	2.5	2.5	2.5	1.89
Comparison to Expectations					
Much better (1)	11%	12%	14%	14%	14%
Better (2)	26	12	21	24	38
The same (3)	29	38	26	28	32
Worse (4)	19	24	19	18	11
Much worse (5)	15	14	19	16	5
Mean	3.0	3.17	3.07	2.98	2.57
Compared with Own Brand					
Much better (1)		17%	17%	24%	14%
Better (2)		21	19	24	32
The same (3)		21	31	14	30
Worse (4)		21	12	16	16
Much worse (5)		19	21	22	8
Mean		3.05	3.02	2.88	2.73

Note: Data for total sample not available.

would probably or certainly not buy the product after using it increased from 13 to 32 percent. In Exhibit 9 only participants who gave negative after-use evaluations of Belle Couleur are included, and they are grouped according to the brands they were using at the time.

To try to determine why some users didn't like the product, the dissatisfied women were asked to state why they disliked Belle Couleur. The results are shown in Exhibit 10.

Many of the women thought that their hair was too dark after using Belle Couleur and said it "didn't cover gray." Those who thought Belle Couleur was different from expected were primarily using the blond and chestnut brown shades of colorant. This was expected,

EXHIBIT 10
Reasons for Negative
Evaluations of Belle
Couleur by Brand
Currently Used

	Brand Currently Used				
	Total Sample	Andrelon	Poly Couleur	Guhl	Recital (L'Oréal)
Hair got dark/darker instead of lighter	13%	14%	17%	14%	5%
irritates skin	8	10	7	2	11
Ammonia smell	5	7	–	2	–
Didn't cover gray	5	12	2	4	3
Color not beautiful	5	7	5	6	3
Color different from expected	5	5	10	4	3

Note: Some of the cell sizes are very small, and caution should be used when comparing entries of less than 10 percent.

since in France Belle Couleur was formulated to give a classical, conservative dark blond color without extra reflections or lightening effects and the product had not been modified for the Dutch test. The competing Dutch-manufactured hair colorant competitors, by contrast, were formulated to give stronger lightening effects. Thus, some of the negative evaluations of Belle Couleur were due to the fact that Dutch women tended toward naturally lighter hair colors, and the French toward darker shades.

Role of Distributors

Distributors' acceptance of the two product lines was critical for L'Oréal's successful launch of both Synergie and Belle Couleur. At one time, manufacturers had more control in the channel of distribution than did retailers. Retailers, however, had been gaining power as a result of the increasing size of retailers, the development of chains with their central buying offices, and the proliferation of new brands with little differentiation from brands currently on the market. Retailers had also increasingly been offering their own private-label products, since they earned a higher-percentage profit margin on their own brands.

Following are the criteria, listed in order of importance (3 being "most important"), that retailers used to evaluate new products:

1. Evidence of consumer acceptance   2.5
2. Manufacturer advertising and promotion 2.2
3. Introductory monetary allowances   2.0
4. Rationale for product development   1.9
5. Merchandising recommendations   1.8

L'Oréal's goal for developing new products was to introduce only products that had a differential advantage

with evidence of consumer acceptance. It did not want to gain distribution with excessive reliance on trade deals or higher than normal retail gross margins. L'Oréal also wanted to have its Garnier product lines extensively distributed in as many different types of retailers and outlets as possible. This approach to new product introduction had been effective for L'Oréal, and it currently had a positive image with Dutch retailers. L'Oréal was perceived as offering high-quality, innovative products supported with good in-store merchandising.

For L'Oréal's current products, 35 percent of sales came from independent drugstores, 40 percent from drug chains, and 25 percent from food stores. For all manufacturers, drug chains and supermarkets were increasing in importance. These stores required a brand with high customer awareness and some brand preference. The brands needed to be presold since, unlike independent drugstores, there was no sales assistance.

Introducing a line of products rather than just a product or two resulted in a greater need for retail shelf space. Although the number of new products and brands competing for retail shelf space frequently appeared unlimited, the space itself was a limited resource. With Belle Couleur, L'Oréal had already addressed this issue by reducing the number of Belle Couleur colorants it planned to offer in the Netherlands. Although 22 shades were available in France, L'Oréal had reduced the line to 15 variations for the Netherlands. As a result, 1.5 meters (about five linear feet) of retail shelf space was needed to display the 15 shades of Belle Couleur. Synergie required about half this shelf space.

Decision Time

After reviewing the information on the market research on the two product lines, Ms. van der Zande summarized the situation. L'Oréal Netherlands could leverage its advertising of the Garnier name by promoting two lines at once. Consumers would hear and see the Garnier name twice, not just once. As a result, Dutch consumers might see Garnier as a major supplier of cosmetics and toiletries. But she was concerned about the selling effort that would be needed to sell the L'Oréal brands that were already in the Dutch market and at the same time introduce not just one but two new brand name product *lines*. The Dutch L'Oréal sales force would have to handle both family brands, since the much lower market potential of the Netherlands market could not support a separate Garnier sales force, as in France. She was also concerned about retailer reaction to a sales pitch for two product lines.

Ms. van der Zande reflected that she was facing three decision areas. First, she had to decide if she should introduce one or both product lines, and she had to make this decision knowing that L'Oréal would not reformulate the products just for the Dutch market. Second, if she decided to introduce either one or both of the product lines, she needed to develop a marketing program. This meant she had to make decisions on the promotion of the product line(s) to both retailers and consumers as well as the pricing and distribution of the line(s). Third, given that the Garnier product introductions might negatively affect the sales of her current product lines, she needed tactical marketing plans for those products.

Case 6-15

ESPN

On Sept. 19, millions of fans tuned in to a rare Monday night pro football doubleheader. Interlaced with plays were cutaways to a telethon to help victims of Hurricane Katrina. Viewers of ESPN and ABC saw some of the biggest legends in sports fielding calls from a studio in Manhattan's Times Square: Frank Gifford, Bart Starr, Gale Sayers, John Elway, Eric Dickerson, Donovan McNabb, George Bodenheimer . . . huh? George Boden-who?

What most folks watching didn't realize was that the stiff-looking guy with the phone in his ear is perhaps the single most influential person in all things sports. As president of the ESPN Networks and ABC Sports, George W. Bodenheimer runs one of the most successful and envied franchises in entertainment, the jewel of Walt Disney Co., and among the most powerful brands of the last quarter-century. While his round-the-clock networks are all about being brash and in-your-face, Bodenheimer is the rare media mogul who is adamant about staying behind the scenes. ESPN's top public-relations executive had to practically drag Bodenheimer out of a production booth and push him in front of the cameras to make an appearance at the Katrina telethon, which he helped pull together with the National Football League in a matter of days. "It's just not about me," he could be heard mumbling as the PR chief made sure his tie was straight.

That modesty has worked well for the 47-year-old Bodenheimer, and ESPN has flourished in his seven years at the helm. Sure, the ESPN he inherited had already extended itself from TV to print, the Internet, and other platforms. And its smart-aleck, testosterone-laden culture was already a trademark. But Bodenheimer's vision of his company, where he started in the mailroom, is as a ubiquitous sports network—and more. To really understand ESPN, you need to see it as a cluster of feisty, creative enterprises under one killer brand (Exhibit 1). Its units, spread out mostly over offices in Connecticut, New York, and Los Angeles, act like startups, full of passionate staffers who are given the freedom to drive forward but always with a mission to keep the customers (rabid and tech-savvy fans like themselves) happy. Bodenheimer "realizes ESPN has to be fast-paced," says Simon Williams, CEO of consultant Sterling Branding. "In his realm, if you stand still you're dead."

So, through 50 different businesses, Bodenheimer has pushed ESPN into broadband, on-demand video, wireless, high-definition, even books. His company has the X Games. It has burgers and fries at ESPN Zone restaurants. Video games are coming soon. All the while, the daily news and highlights show, *SportsCenter,* is as much must-see TV for millions of Americans as the nightly news shows were a generation ago. Put it all together, and Bodenheimer's competitors can't help but express awe. So ESPN has become a model for a wide range of companies, media and others, struggling to make their brands work in new markets. "They have always had a halo to do things like a *SportsCenter* really well," says Jeff Price, chief marketing officer at *Sports Illustrated.* "Nobody has created those touchpoints with consumers like they have." Adds Adam Silver, the top TV executive at the National Basketball Assn.: "George lets others shine, but don't be fooled

EXHIBIT 1
ESPN The Empire

ESPN The Empire

First, a TV channel, and now.....

MORE CHANNELS Nine TV outlets, including ESPN2, ESPN HD, ESPN Deportes, and ESPN Classic.

ORIGINAL PROGRAMMING ESPN develops its own shows and movies, including ESPN2's *ESPN Hollywood, Cold Pizza*, and the new *Bound For Glory* high school football reality series featuring Dick Butkus.

RADIO The largest U.S. sports-radio network, with more than 700 affiliate stations, features hit shows *Mike & Mike in The Morning* and *The Dan Patrick Show.*

ONLINE ESPN.com gets more than 16 million unique users a month. Includes ESPN Motion, an online video service, and ESPN360, offered via broadband; Verizon is one carrier.

PUBLISHING The biweekly *ESPN The Magazine* won a National Magazine Award for general excellence in 2003. It launched a China edition in the fall of 2004.

WIRELESS Mobile ESPN is an ESPN-branded phone and customized service that rolls out in February.

GAMING Video game leader Electronic Arts has a 15-year deal to be the sole licensee of the ESPN brand in sports games, which will include console, handled, PC, and wireless games.

X GAMES Annual extreme sports competition features motocross, bike stunts, and skateboarding.

ESPY AWARDS Athletes and celebs recognize top achievements in sports and to support The V Foundation for Cancer Research founded by ESPN and late college coach Jim Valvano.

ESPN ZONES Eight sports-themed restaurants operate nationally, with a new one set to open in ESPN's planned $100 million studio facility near the Staples Center in Los Angeles.

INTERNATIONAL The world's largest distributor of sports, ESPN makes its programming available in 11 languages in more than 180 countries.

---

by the aw-shucks manner. He's an extremely effective manager who has put his company at the cutting edge of the digital revolution." (Exhibit 2).

Remember to Have Fun

Never one to gloat about the successes, the understated Bodenheimer confesses that the track he has been pounding is getting a whole lot steeper lately. At his back is a slew of rivals gaining momentum. First among them is Comcast Corp., the No. 1 U.S. cable operator. Looking to build a cable sports network to rival ESPN's, Comcast is also ESPN's biggest distributor, so its plans could aggravate what's already a delicate relationship. Right about now, Bodenheimer is placing a hefty bet on an ESPN-branded cell phone and has said that making the new business a winner will be one of his biggest challenges of the year. The cell phone is a move into an alluring market—delivering sports data and images to insatiable fans at all hours. But the payoff is uncertain at best, and the venture, announced on Sept. 27, could ultimately dent earnings and tarnish the brand. Bodenheimer's angst was turned up a notch

or two higher when a key executive, Mark Shapiro, resigned in August. As head of programming and production, Shapiro was seen as a driven ideas guy who kept new shows flowing and viewers tuning in. He was also an effective bad cop to Bodenheimer's good cop at the negotiating table.

Shapiro is often compared with Bodenheimer's high-energy predecessor, Steve Bornstein, ESPN's president during much of the 1990s. The 26-year-old network's initial blast of growth came under Bornstein, whose swagger infused the place with the cocky culture so strong today (Exhibit 3). Bodenheimer's core strength, say longtime staffers, has been to preserve and encourage that vibe without making it all about George. His message to the staff is something like: ESPN isn't mine, it's yours, so run with it. And remember to have fun.

Bodenheimer is in Brooks Brothers most days, but his operation is anything but buttoned-down. It's more about hoodies and DC skateboarding shoes, which is to say it's all about being young. When *ESPN The Magazine* launched in 1998, designer F. Darrin Perry gave its pages a bold look with bright colors and unconventional type. That high-octane feel extends even to

EXHIBIT 2

Branding, By George

George Bodenheimer, oversees one of the great brands not only in sports but in all of Corporate America. Here are his tips for nurturing a top brand:

 1 **DEFINE YOUR MISSION** "Serve the fans. That's why we are launching our new cell phone and service, to be able to reach fans wherever they are."

 2 **KNOW WHAT YOUR BRAND IS** "We view ourselves as the world's biggest sports fan. Be fun. That's why we try to keep our programming lively without taking ourselves too seriously."

 3 **CULTIVATE RELATIONSHIPS WITH YOUR CUSTOMERS** "Talk to fans, not at them. We try to do that with our award-winning ad campaigns."

 4 **DEVELOP AN INCLUSIVE CULTURE** "I came up from the mailroom, so I had managers who were listening to me. You need to let everyone contribute."

 5 **CONTINUALLY ENHANCE YOUR PRODUCT** "We have launched three new channels in the past two years, a broadband service, and a cell-phone service. And we are always tweaking our franchise show, *SportsCenter.* We've added more music and highlights recently."

the magazine's offices in midtown Manhattan, which are designed to look like a gym, complete with an old school scoreboard. On any given day at the main ESPN campus in Bristol, Conn., now encompassing 100 acres dotted with dozens of satellite dishes, you might find former All-Star second baseman and *Baseball Tonight* host Harold Reynolds waiting in line for brick-oven pizza in the fancy staff cafe, or *SportsCenter* anchor Stuart Scott looking for someone to spot him on the bench press in the state-of-the-art gym. A new $160 million digital center and studio, crammed with robotic cameras and lighting rigs, is ringed with flat screen TVs beaming sports in crisp hi-def. A central control room houses producers at computers editing a constant stream of digital-video game feeds.

The whole scene is NASA meets the bleacher creatures. "People have a passion for sports," says Rich Weinstein, the ESPN account director at ad agency Wieden + Kennedy, which has captured the spirit of ESPN through its award-winning spots for the network. "If your job is your passion, it brings a new perspective to the creative process. George was here when this was a startup, and he has preserved that feeling." True to form, at a strategy session this summer for the new phone, the boss rolled up his sleeves, snapped open a Diet Coke, and burrowed down into every marketing idea the team pitched. Un-mogul-like, he never checked his BlackBerry or cut off discussion. Then he took the group out to a swanky trattoria.

Bodenheimer, who squeezes in a golf game when he can, loves to break the ice by talking about—what else?—sports. He tries to stay engaged with workers across the company without micro-managing. "The great thing about George is that he can stand back and let his managers create," says Gary Hoenig, editor-in-chief of *ESPN The Magazine.* Going up against venerable *Sports Illustrated,* ESPN's seven-year-old biweekly has made great strides. Since 1999, circulation has grown by about 1 million, to 1.8 million, while *SI* has held steady at 3.3 million, according to the Audit Bureau of Circulations (Exhibit 4). Hoenig also credits Bodenheimer with granting him the freedom to develop lucrative specialty newsstand magazines like one on fantasy football.

Tanya Van Court, whom Bodenheimer hired from Cablevision in April, 2004, to oversee a revamp of broadband service, insists, too, that the boss never meddles. During the eight months that the new product ESPN360 was in development, "he would send hand-written notes with suggestions every week and a half or so," she says. "He would offer up [notes like], 'make it the ultimate on demand product for the sports fan and one that is as flexible as possible.'" When ESPN360 launched last January with programming tailored for broadband—including short clips recapping Sunday games—it just may have hit on a new model (Exhibit 5). ESPN insiders liken it to cable TV in its infancy in the 1970s. So far, ESPN360 is available to nearly 5 million users through 14 different broadband providers.

Irresistible Economics

Can Bodenheimer the delegator and his decentralized, free-thinking culture keep up the winning streak? "The next two years will be a real big test for George," says

EXHIBIT 3   **Mr. Touchdown for NFL TV Deals**

If you want to beat the other team, what better way than to put someone in charge who knows their plays? No surprise, then, that when National Football League Commissioner Paul Tagliabue was looking for an executive to renegotiate the league's TV contracts and expand its media presence, he drafted former ESPN President Steve Bornstein.

A 22-year veteran of ESPN and ABC, Bornstein knew every network exec's head fakes and stutter steps. The payoff has been tremendous for the NFL at the bargaining table as well as with the launch of its own cable channel, the NFL Network. Since his arrival at the league in late 2002, Bornstein, 53, has negotiated $24 billion worth of new rights contracts—resulting in a 53% hike over earlier deals. "He's a great auctioneer," says Stephen B. Burke, president of cable operator Comcast. "The NFL has tremendous value. He gives it more."

The Bornstein process isn't always pretty. To be sure, the tough-talking New Jersey native who learned to use sharp elbows to get his shot as a sports cameraman while at the University of Wisconsin, plays hard. He dangles games before competitors and applies pressure like a blitzing strong safety.

Both CBS and Fox agreed to hefty increases last year after Bornstein began talking to NBC, which had dropped broadcasting football but got back in this spring. And heading into talks with his old employer, he knew how much ESPN needed football. If it lost the NFL, the network would have had to pay a 35¢ monthly fee per subscriber back to cable operators, or about $370 million annually. The result: ESPN offered $8.8 billion for a new Monday night package.

What's more, Bornstein is building up the potential competition against his successor, ESPN President George Bodenheimer. He oversees the NFL Network, a cable channel the league launched two years ago. It is seen in 35 million homes, which is still less than half of all cable and satellite households. "He brought a perspective we didn't have," says NFL Executive Vice-President Roger Goodell. The NFL's channel doesn't air regular season games yet, but its shows, like *NFL Total Access,* have that ESPN feel.

What's more, the NFL Network is a strategic asset. The NFL can simply threaten to put its own games on its own channel if it is not getting high enough offers from others. It's also a great way to boost distribution. Satellite operator Direc TV Group, for instance, agreed to distribute the channel to help it negotiate its new $700 million-a-year deal for the Sunday Ticket telecasts.

Bornstein, who lives in the former Fred Astaire mansion in Beverly Hills, shuttles between the NFL's West Coast offices and its Park Avenue digs in New York. "He's still got the entrepreneurial spirit that ESPN had in the '80s and '90s," says NASCAR Vice-President Dick Glover, who worked with Bornstein in the 1990s. Bornstein earned a reputation as a no-nonsense taskmaster who would shoot down underlings by pointing to a "bull-****" meter on a blackboard.

His ability to make ESPN into a money spinner earned Bornstein a ticket upward at parent Walt Disney Co., but his thankless task was to turn around ABC and jump-start Disney's woeful Go.net. "I told him not to take the Internet job, but he really didn't have a choice," says former Cap Cities Chairman Thomas S. Murphy, a Disney board member. "Michael [Eisner] wanted him to do it." But after CEO Eisner picked Robert A. lger as Disney president, Bornstein resigned.

Within months he had joined the NFL. "It was fun getting back to my roots, starting a cable channel," says Bornstein. Spoken like a guy who's back in the lineup.

—*By Ronald Grover in Los Angeles*

Sean McManus, head of competing CBS Sports and a friend of Bodenheimer's. All around it, companies are imitating ESPN's cool and edgy packaging of sports. And if live sports is the last great mass market to lure advertisers, then how long can ESPN expect to dominate? Throw in a sports-crazed, often-elusive audience of young men bordering on the fanatic, and the economics are irresistible. That's why so many players are pushing into Bodenheimer's domain, from teams and leagues

launching their own channels to cable and satellite operators creating new offerings. "ESPN listens to its audience very closely," says Sterling's Williams. "If it keeps doing that, [that] should be the glue that holds it together."

Even so, the ESPN chief these days finds himself playing more defense than offense to keep games out of competitors' hands. One sign of the times: big hikes in the prices ESPN is paying to lock up new pro football and Major League Baseball rights contracts. The

EXHIBIT 4
Youth Rules

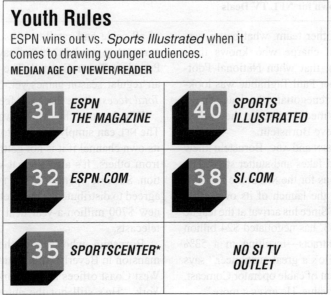

Youth Rules

ESPN wins out vs. *Sports Illustrated* when it comes to drawing younger audiences.

MEDIAN AGE OF VIEWER/READER

31	ESPN THE MAGAZINE	40	SPORTS ILLUSTRATED
32	ESPN.COM	38	SI.COM
35	SPORTSCENTER*		NO SI TV OUTLET

*11 p.m. show   Data: ESPN *Sports Illustrated*

EXHIBIT 5   **ESPN.Com: Guys and Dollars**

The ESPN cable channel, seen in 90 million households, is a must-stop for any channel surfer. But espn.com is the real boys' club. Young men don't show up *en masse* to anything very often, but where they do, advertisers will spend. That's what makes espn.com, with its devoted audience of guys 18 to 34, a coveted spot.

But luring Web users with hot commentators (*Sports Guy* columnist Bill Simmons), cool streaming video (ESPN Motion), the latest scores, and top-notch fantasy-league services, ESPN can use in-house promos to send them back out to its other platforms. "We look at our Web site as being like a bazaar with something always going on," says John Kosner, a senior vice-president.

The 10-year-old site is the biggest Internet draw for sports. In August, espn.com had 16.6 million unique visitors, says ComScore Media Metrix. That's far more than its closest rivals, Fox Sports on MSN (with 12.6 million uniques), nfl.com (12.6 million),

and Yahoo! Sports (12.3 million). SI.com, the Web site of ESPN's magazine rival *Sports Illustrated,* trails at 5 million. The median age of an espn.com user is 32 vs. 38 for Net users in general.

ESPN doesn't disclose revenues, but Kosner says the Web site makes most of its money from ads. "It offers the big three," says Tim Hanlon, a senior vice-president at media-buyer Starcom MediaVest. "Young guys. Sports. And a powerhouse media brand. That's just a home run for advertisers." Subscription revenues at espn.com are growing, too, through its $6.95-a-month Insider and with fantasy services. Broadband's rise will accelerate offerings. And espn360, a customizable high-speed service, showcases super-sharp video and behind-the-scenes coverage. As for rivals, such as a revamped CBS SportsLine. ESPN's Kosner says: Bring it on. "I'd rather be where we are sitting." No kidding.

—By Tom Lowry in New York

$2.4 billion, eight-year MLB deal announced on Sept. 14 represents a 50% annual increase in fees. And in April, ESPN ponied up $8.8 billion for a new eight-year *Monday Night Football* deal with the NFL for only one night of football. ABC will no longer broadcast games, including the lucrative Super Bowl; NBC grabbed ESPN's

old Sunday night spot. The bottom line: ESPN will pay nearly twice as much a year than it did last time around, though other goodies were included, such as wireless rights that will allow ESPN for the first time to deliver Monday night highlights to cell phones. "You have to ask yourself how much growth will be left if they keep spending like this," says Richard Greenfield, an analyst at Fulcrum Global Partners LLC. Counters Bodenheimer: "Look, we are a sports-media company, and we program sports. It's like saying a seafood restaurant is being defensive when it reorders lobsters."

Bodenheimer, of course, lives in a world that's not totally of his own making. His ESPN is part of a tempest-rocked ship known as Disney. For years, ESPN has been able to do its own thing for one reason: It was the outfit former CEO Michael D. Eisner could count on for the numbers. Now, with Eisner gone, Bodenheimer will work closely with an old friend, new CEO Robert A. Iger, a onetime exec at ABC Sports. The bond between Bodenheimer and Iger is strong, one pro league executive suggests, because they see themselves in each other—"two executives who have always been underestimated." Says Iger: "People sometimes mistake being polite for being easy. That's not the case with George. He's a man of great integrity, but he can be tough." Some speculate that Iger might bring Bodenheimer to Burbank, but for now he needs his friend to stay put, keeping ESPN the financial bulwark it is to counterbalance the fickle businesses of theme parks and hit-driven TV and movies.

Indeed, ESPN revenues alone this year could be about $5 billion, with operating earnings of nearly $2 billion, according to projections from various analysts. The revenues—about 60% from distribution fees and 40% from advertising—would represent about 15% of Disney's total. Analysts estimate that revenues could grow to nearly $6.8 billion in 2008. More important, ESPN is so central to cable menus that it gives Disney bargaining power with distributors to pick up other Disney channels, be they SOAPnet or the ABC Family Channel. Emblematic of ESPN's clout, its longtime head of affiliate sales, Sean R.H. Bratches, was promoted a year ago to oversee distribution for all of Disney's cable channels and broadband services. Using ESPN's leverage was a favorite tactic of Eisner's. So precious was ESPN to the Mouse House that the former CEO told investors several years ago: "We bought the ABC media network and ESPN for $19 billion in 1995. ESPN is worth substantially more than we paid for the entire acquisition."

Muscles Flexed

It's all the more remarkable, then, that ESPN was created with such modest intentions. It was founded in 1979 by former Hartford Whalers play-by-play man Bill Rasmussen on a patch of mud in the blue-collar central Connecticut town of Bristol by putting $9,000 on several credit cards. Rasmussen started the Entertainment and Sports Programming Network (ESPN) as a way to beam University of Connecticut Huskies games to a larger audience using satellite dishes. But it soon became clear to Rasmussen and his son, Scott, that they were on to something with national potential. Getty Oil would kick in $100 million a year after Rasmussen put on the first shows. Five years later, ABC bought out Getty's position (then owned by Texaco Inc.) and in 1988, Hearst Corp. bought a 20% position that was held at the time by RJR Nabisco. Hearst still has a 20% stake, but Disney is the active manager. "Nobody could have anticipated how much of a financial juggernaut ESPN would become," says Fulcrum analyst Greenfield.

Over the years, ESPN began to flex its muscles like the jocks it had helped turn into celebrities. It charged its cable and satellite distributors nearly twice as much for its service than any other channel fetches. (Today, ESPN gets an estimated $2.80 per subscriber per month, vs. about 40¢ for CNN, according to Morgan Stanley.) Double-digit hikes each year created a lot of ill will, culminating in a showdown two years ago that erupted in the halls of Congress. The battle pitted Bodenheimer against James O. Robbins, the outspoken CEO of cable operator Cox Communications Inc., who, acting on behalf of his industry, complained to lawmakers about the steep fees.

The brawl put Bodenheimer in an unwelcome spotlight, where he defended ESPN's pricing by blaming the high cost of rights deals with the leagues. Eventually Cox won lower annual fee increases, down from about 20% to about 7%. But ESPN claimed victory, too: New agreements included the operators' carriage of the latest ESPN channels, such as its Spanish-language outlet ESPN Deportes. "We achieved everything we wanted in that negotiation," says Ed Durso, ESPN's top executive for government and public affairs. "George rose to the occasion."

Bodenheimer knows the next battle is the big one. News Corp. founder Rupert Murdoch, with 15 regional sports channels, is only making noises about a national sports channel. Comcast is making plans. It has held several meetings in recent weeks to talk strategy and has even contacted ESPN executives about jumping ship, say sources close to both companies. Comcast already owns the Philadelphia 76ers, the Philadelphia Flyers, and a bunch of regional sports networks in cities from Philadelphia to Chicago to San Francisco. And it's no secret that Comcast CEO Brian L. Roberts and President Stephen B. Burke, a former Disney executive, want a piece of the ESPN business model. When the Philadelphia-based cable operator made its unsolicited $54 billion bid for Disney in February, 2004, it was driven in part by a desire to capture ESPN.

Having its own hot sports channel would give Comcast ESPN-like leverage, amplifying its powerful 22 million subscriber base—even if its expertise is largely that of a distributor, not a programmer. For now, it's sticking to plans to convert its relatively unknown Outdoor Life Network, available in 64 million homes, into an ESPN for the new millennium. OLN got some buzz by airing Lance Armstrong's cycling feats every summer from the Tour de France. The rest of the channel's programming, from bull-riding to fishing shows, has niche appeal at best.

But Comcast is moving fast. It signed a $300 million, five-year deal in August to broadcast National Hockey League games on OLN starting this fall, with an option to bail out after two years. (ESPN ditched the sport after its contract expired this year following the acrimonious lockout.) Now, Comcast needs to cinch some of the remaining 60 games available from MLB and win a package of Thursday and Saturday games from the NFL, which draws the largest TV audiences in sports. "Without the NFL, I don't see anybody being a threat to ESPN," says John Mansell, a senior analyst at Kagan Research LLC.

Games in Your Pocket

Even as he fends off rivals, Bodenheimer is about to lead his troops into ESPN's trickiest brand extension so far. The idea is that ESPN could be missing the chance to stay in touch with fans who get off the sofa or walk away from their computer screens. Says Bodenheimer: "We want fans to know you don't have to let the rest of your life get in the way of being a sports fan. You can take it with you." In the past year he has met frequently with the Mobile ESPN development team to sign off on everything from the phone's black-and-red design on a Sanyo handset to the special displays constructed for big retailers. ESPN is leasing network time from Sprint Nextel Corp. and will outsource billing, messaging, and customer service (its price is yet to be announced). The opportunity to partner with ESPN was a no-brainer for Sprint Nextel CEO Gary Forsee. "As proud as we are of our brand, we'd be hard pressed to say Sprint can successfully go after the segments that ESPN [does]," he says. "But ESPN is the world leader, right?"

Still, the risk for ESPN is that if the phone bugs out, users won't be cursing some wireless outfit—they'll be blaming ESPN. "Content providers need to focus on what they do best," says one TV executive. "Hardware plays are fraught with problems." And the venture will require patience. "Sometimes it is up to two years with this kind of business before you reach enough scale with subscribers to be able to turn a profit," says Marina Amoroso, a wireless analyst with researcher Yankee Group. Bodenheimer says he's aware of the perils, "but it is a riskier move not to do this."

The last thing Bodenheimer needs now is to worry about top talent. Yet shortly before programming whiz Shapiro quit, Chief Marketing Executive Lee Ann Daly resigned as well. Losing Shapiro, who quit to join Washington Redskins owner Dan Snyder in remaking Six Flags Inc., is the most problematic. Shapiro's handiwork is all over the network. ESPN Original Entertainment, the cable network's venture into movies, episodic dramas, and talk shows, was his creation. He gave juice to *Sports Century,* the Emmy Award-winning series of profiles of top athletes (and a horse, Secretariat).

In June, Disney heaped new responsibility on Shapiro, promoting him to executive vice-president, overseeing programming at both ESPN and ABC Sports. To all the world it looked as if his next step would be into headquarters. Then, in early August, Shapiro met with Bodenheimer to tell him he was thinking about leaving. He'd had a feeler to head news operations at NBC. A few weeks later he accepted the offer from Snyder. "I knew at some point I was going to go entrepreneurial. It was just a question of when," says Shapiro.

Questions remain about why Bodenheimer and Iger waited so long to lock Shapiro into a new contract. But it is known that top executives at ESPN had been fielding complaints from the brass at pro sports leagues for some time that they could no longer work with Shapiro. Several league officials said they had never dealt with a negotiator as aggressive or as eager to pass himself off as the smartest guy at the table. "ESPN had just had tough relations with their customers, the cable guys," says one TV executive. "They could ill-afford to have bad relations with their suppliers, too. They need the leagues." Shapiro shakes off such criticism. "Of course I'm going to be tough in negotiations. That's my job . . . not to say to [the leagues]: 'Here's a check, fill out how much you want.' " Still, by the end of Shapiro's tenure at ESPN, officials in at least two leagues refused to deal with him unless Bodenheimer was in on the talks.

"Minute-to-Minute Battle"

Shapiro may have also ticked off Disney top brass when he turned down an offer last year to become president of ABC Entertainment, the No. 2 job under then-ABC executive Susan Lyne, who would have become chairman, say sources within the company. The plan was to eventually move out Lyne and put Shapiro in charge, those sources say. Shapiro told Iger he was excited about running prime time—but ultimately turned him down flat. Bodenheimer denies that there was any ill will toward Shapiro at Disney.

Bodenheimer says he is confident that the culture he has fostered, one of tapping ESPN's inner strengths, will ultimately make Shapiro's departure less of a blow. "Mark was obviously a significant contributor," says Bodenheimer. "He's a great talent, but we have a tremendous reservoir of talent here." In fact, Bodenheimer used Shapiro's departure to realign top management in early October into new segments: content, technology,

sales and affiliates, and international. John Skipper, the much-admired senior executive who oversaw advertising and new media, will now run content, assuming much of Shapiro's programming mantle.

How Bodenheimer leads will go a long way in determining whether ESPN remains preeminent, especially as competitors zoom in on niches like volleyball, tennis, you name it. "ESPN will always be a general store of sports," says Brian Bedol, co-founder of college sports channel CSTV, "but it may have to learn to coexist with the leagues and new media companies [that] want to reach fans with very special interests. Technology today is allowing for a direct relationship with those fans."

Nobody wants to understand fans more than Bodenheimer, who will often leave the luxury boxes at games and walk through arenas studying the crowds—unrecognized, of course. "It's a minute-to-minute battle to retain viewers in today's media world," says Bodenheimer. "That's why I want to know what fans are saying—about sports, about ESPN." It's also why the most powerful man in sports needs to stay at the top of his game.

Source: Tom Lowry, "In the Zone," *BusinessWeek,* October 17, 2005, 66–78

Case 6-16
Cowgirl Chocolates

Marilyn looked at the advertisement—a beautiful woman wearing a cowboy hat in a watering trough full of hot and spicy Cowgirl Chocolate truffles (see Exhibit 1). The ad would appear next month in the March/April edition of *Chile Pepper* magazine, the leading magazine for people who liked fiery foods. The ad, the first ever for the business, cost $3,000 to run and Marilyn wondered if it would be her big mistake for 2001. Marilyn allowed herself one $3,000–$6,000 mistake a year in trying to get her now four-year-old business to profitability. Two years ago, it was the pursuit of an opportunity to get her product into Great Britain on the recommendation of the owner of a British biscuit company who loved her chocolates.

John J. Lawrence, University of Idaho; Linda J. Morris University of Idaho; Joseph J. Geiger University of Idaho.

Reprinted by permission from the *Case Research Journal,* Copyright 2002 by John L. Lawrence, Linda J. Morris, Joseph J. Geiger, and the North American Case Research Association. All rights reserved. John J. Lawrence, et al., "Cowgirl Chocolates" *Case Research Journal,* Volume 22, issue 1, 2002.

Despite significant effort and expense, she could not convince anyone in Great Britain to carry her chocolates. Last year it was her attempt to use a distributor for the first time. It was a small, regional distributor, and she had provided them with $5,000 worth of product and had never gotten paid. She eventually got half her product back, but by the time she did it had limited remaining shelf life and she already had enough new stock on hand to cover demand. She ended up giving most of what she got back away.

Marilyn knew it took time to make money at something. She was now an internationally celebrated ceramicist, but it had taken 20 years for her ceramic art to turn a profit. She also knew, however, that she could not wait 20 years for her foray into chocolates to make money, especially not at the rate that she was currently losing money. Last year, despite not paying herself a salary and occasionally bartering her art for services, the small business's revenues of $30,000 did not come close to covering her $50,000+ in expenses. While her art for a long time did not make money, it did not lose that kind of money either. Her savings account was slowly being depleted as she loaned the company money. She knew that the product was

EXHIBIT 1 Cowgirl Chocolate Ad to Appear in *Chile Pepper* Magazine

excellent—it had won numerous awards from the two main fiery food competitions in the U.S.—and her packaging was also excellent and had won awards itself. She just was not sure how to turn her award winning products into a profitable business.

Company History

Cowgirl Chocolates was started in Moscow, Idaho, in 1997 by Marilyn Lysohir and her husband, Ross Coates. Marilyn and Ross were both artists. Marilyn was an internationally known ceramicist and lecturer; Ross was also a sculptor and a professor of fine arts at a nearby university. They had started publishing a once a year arts magazine in 1995 called *High Ground.* *High Ground* was really a multimedia product—each edition contained more than simply printed words and pictures. For example, past editions had included such things as vials of Mount St. Helen's ash, cassette tapes, seeds, fabric art, and chocolate bunnies in addition to articles and stories. One edition was even packaged in a motion picture canister. With a total production of about 600 copies, however, *High Ground* simply would not pay for itself. But the magazine was a labor of love for Marilyn and Ross, and so they sought creative ways to fund the endeavor. One of the ways they tried was selling hot and spicy chocolate truffles.

The fact that Marilyn and Ross turned to chocolate was no random event. Marilyn's first job, at age 16, was at Daffin's Candies in Sharon, Pennsylvania. The business's owner, Pete Daffin, had been an early mentor of Marilyn's and had encouraged her creativity. He even let her carve a set of animals, including an 8-foot tall chocolate bunny, for display. Her sculptures proved irresistible to visiting youngsters, who would take small bites out of the sculptures. It was at this point that Marilyn realized the power of chocolate.

In addition to loving chocolate, Marilyn loved things hot and spicy. She also was aware that cayenne and other chilies had wonderful health properties for the heart. But it was her brother who originally gave her the idea of combining hot and spicy with chocolate. Marilyn considered her brother's idea for a while, and could see it had possibilities, so she started experimenting in her kitchen. She recruited neighbors, friends and acquaintances to try out her creations. While a few people who tried those early chocolates were not so sure that combining hot and spicy with chocolate made sense, many thought the chocolates were great. Encouraged, and still searching for fund-ing for *High Ground,* Marilyn found a local candy company to produce the chocolates in quantity, and she and her husband established Cowgirl Chocolates.

The name itself came from one friend's reaction the first time she tasted the chocolates—the friend exclaimed "these are cowboy chocolates!" Marilyn agreed that there was a certain ruggedness to the concept of hot and spicy chocolates that matched the cowboy image, but thought that *Cowgirl* Chocolates was a more appropriate name for her company. Marilyn found the picture of May Lillie that would become the Cowgirl Chocolate logo in a book about cowgirls. May Lillie was a turn of the century, pistol-packing cowgirl, and Marilyn loved the picture of May looking down the barrel of a pistol because May looked so tough. And it certainly was not hard to envision May adopting the Cowgirl Chocolate motto—Sissies Stay Away. That motto had come to Marilyn when a group of friends told her that they really did not like her hot and spicy chocolates. Marilyn was a little disappointed and hurt, and thought to herself 'well, sissies stay away, if you don't like them, don't eat them.'

The Product

Cowgirl chocolate sold its hot and spicy creations in three basic forms: individually wrapped truffles, chocolate bars, and a hot caramel dessert sauce. The individually wrapped truffles were available in a variety of packaging options, with most of the packaging designed to set Cowgirl Chocolates apart. The truffles could be purchased in gift boxes, in drawstring muslin bags, and in a collectible tin. According to Marilyn, this packaging made them "more than a candy—they become an idea, an experience, a gift." The truffles were also available in a plain plastic bag over Cowgirl Chocolate's website for customers who just wanted the chocolate and did not care about the fancy packaging. The chocolate bars and truffles were offered in several flavors. The chocolate bars were available in either orange espresso or lime tequila crunch. The truffles were available in plain chocolate, mint, orange, lime tequila and espresso. The plain chocolate, mint, and orange truffles were packaged in gold wrappers, while the lime tequila truffles were packaged in green wrappers. The espresso truffles were the hottest, about twice as hot as the other varieties, and were wrapped in a special red foil to give customers some clue that these were extra hot. Cowgirl Chocolates' full line of product offerings are described in Exhibit 2 and are shown in Exhibit 3.

EXHIBIT 2   Cowgirl Chocolate Product Offerings with Price and Cost Figures

Item	Approximate Percentage of Total Revenues	Suggested Retail Price[1]	Wholesale Price[1]	Total Item Cost (a + b)	Cost of Chocolate or Sauce (a)	Cost of Product Packaging[2] (b)
Spicy Chocolate Truffle Bars (available in 2 flavors: orange-espresso or lime tequila crunch)	50%	$2.99	$1.50	$1.16	$1.04	$0.12
1/4 pound Muslin Bag (13 truffles in a drawstring muslin bag—available in 3 flavors: assorted hot, lime-tequila, and mild-mannered)	16%	$6.95	$3.50	$2.35	$1.69	$0.66
1/2 pound Tin (assorted hot & spicy truffles in a collectable tin)	12%	$14.95	$7.50	$4.78[3]	$3.25	$1.53
Hot Caramel Dessert Sauce (9.5 oz. Jar)	10%	$5.95	$3.50	$2.50	$2.00	$0.50
Sampler Bag (4 assorted hot truffles in a small drawstring muslin bag)	7%	$2.95	$1.50	$0.97	$0.52	$0.45
1/4 pound Gift Box (assorted hot truffles or mild-mannered truffles in a fancy gift box with gift card)	1%	$8.95	$4.50	$2.95	$1.69	$1.26
1 pound Gift Box (assorted hot truffles or mild-mannered truffles in a fancy gift box with gift card)	1%	$24.95	$12.95	$9.05	$6.37	$2.68
Gift Bucket (tin bucket containing 1/4 pound gift box, 2 truffle bars and 1 jar of caramel sauce)	1%	$39.95	$20.95	$11.02	$5.77	$5.25
Gift Basket (made of wire and branches and containing 1/2 pound tin, 2 truffle bars, 1 jar of caramel sauce and a T-shirt)	1%	$59.95	$30.95	$23.06	$15.29[3]	$7.77
Nothing Fancy (one pound assorted hot truffles or mild-mannered truffles in a plastic bag)	1%	$19.50	N.A.	$7.42	$6.37	$1.05

[1]Approximately 1/3 of sales were retail over the Cowgirl Chocolate website, the remaining 2/3 of sales were to wholesale accounts (i.e., to other retailers).
[2]Packaging cost includes costs of container (bags, tins, or boxes), labels, and individual truffle wrapping. Packaging cost assumes Marilyn packs the items and does not include the packing & labeling fee charged by Seattle Chocolates if they do the packing ($1.00 per 1/2 pound tin or 1 pound box; $0.75 per 1/4 pound box; $0.25 per 1/4 pound bag; $0.20 per sampler bag).
[3]This cost includes the cost of the T-shirt.

EXHIBIT 3
Picture of Cowgirl
Chocolate Products
& Packaging

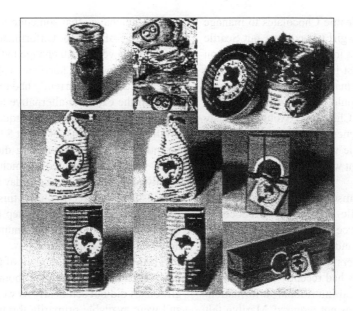

Marilyn was also in the process of introducing "mild-mannered" truffles. Mild-mannered truffles were simply the same fine German chocolate that Marilyn started with to produce all of her chocolates, but without the spice. Marilyn had chosen silver as the wrapper color for the mild-mannered truffles. While she took kidding from friends about how this did not fit with the company's motto—Sissies Stay Away—which was integrated into the company's logo and printed on the back of company t-shirts and hats, she had decided that even the sissies deserved excellent chocolate. Further, she thought that having the mild-mannered chocolate might allow her to get her product placed in retail locations that had previously rejected her chocolates as being too spicy. Marilyn was the first to admit that her chocolates packed a pretty good kick that not everybody found to their liking. She had developed the hot and spicy chocolates based primarily on her own tastes and the input of friends and acquaintances. She had observed many peoples' reactions upon trying her hot and spicy chocolates at trade shows and at new retail locations, and while many people liked her chocolates, the majority found at least some of the varieties to be too hot. In general, men tended to like the hotter truffles much more than women did. Marilyn knew her observations were consistent with what information was available on the fiery foods industry—only approximately 15% of American consumers were currently eating hot and spicy foods and

men were much more inclined to eat hot and spicy foods than were women. In addition to introducing "mild-mannered" chocolates, Marilyn was also thinking about introducing a chocolate with a calcium supplement aimed at woman concerned about their calcium intake.

All of Cowgirl Chocolate's chocolate products were sourced from Seattle Chocolates, a Seattle-based company that specialized in producing European-style chocolate confections wrapped in an elegant package fit for gift giving. Seattle Chocolates obtained all of its raw chocolate from world-renowned chocolate producer Schokinag of Germany. Seattle Chocolates sold its own retail brand plus provided private label chocolate products for a variety of companies including upscale retailers like Nieman Marcus and Nordstroms. Seattle Chocolates was, at least relative to Cowgirl Chocolates, a large company with annual sales in excess of $5,000,000. Seattle Chocolates took Cowgirl Chocolates on as a private label customer because they liked and were intrigued by the company's product and owners, and they had made some efforts to help Cowgirl Chocolates along the way. Seattle Chocolates provided Cowgirl Chocolates with a small amount of its table space at several important trade shows and produced in half batches for them. A half batch still consisted of 150 pounds of a given variety of chocolate, which was enough to last Cowgirl Chocolates for six months at 2000 sales rates. Marilyn hoped that she could one day convince Seattle Chocolates to manage the wholesale side of Cowgirl Chocolates, but Seattle Chocolates simply was not interested in taking this on at the present time, at least in part because they were not really sure where the market was for the product. Marilyn also knew she would need to grow sales significantly before Seattle Chocolates would seriously consider such an arrangement, although she was not sure exactly how much she would have to grow sales before such an arrangement would become attractive to Seattle Chocolates.

The chocolate bars themselves cost Cowgirl Chocolates $1.04 per bar while the individual chocolate truffles cost $0.13 per piece. Seattle Chocolates also performed the wrapping and packing of the product. The chocolate bar wrappers cost $0.06 per bar. The wrapper design of the bars had recently been changed to incorporate dietary and nutritional information. While such information was not required, Marilyn felt it helped convey a better image of her chocolates. The change had cost $35 to prepare the new printing plates. Including the materials, wrapping the individual truffles cost $0.02 per piece.

The distinctive muslin bags, collector tins and gift boxes also added to the final product cost. The muslin bags cost $0.35 each for the quarter-pound size and $0.32 each for the sampler size. The tamperproof seals for the bags cost an additional $0.05/bag. The minimum size bag order was 500 bags. As with the chocolate bar wrappers, Cowgirl Chocolate had to buy the printing plates to print the bags. The plates to print the bags, however, cost $250 per plate. Each color of each design required a separate plate. Each of her three quarter-pound bag styles (assorted, lime-tequila, and mild-mannered) had a three-color design. One plate that was used to produce the background design was common to all three styles of bags, but each bag required two additional unique plates. There was also a separate plate for printing the sampler bags. Marilyn was planning to discontinue the separate lime-tequila bag, and just include lime-tequila truffles in the assorted bag as a way to cut packaging costs. The lime-tequila bags had been introduced a year ago, and while they sold reasonably well, they also appeared to mostly cannibalize sales of the assorted bags.

The collectible tins cost $0.80 each, and the labels for these tins cost $0.19 per tin. The tape used to seal the tins cost $0.04 per tin. The minimum order for the tins was for 800 units. The company that produced the tins had recently modified the tin design slightly to reduce the chance that someone might cut themselves on the edge of the can. Unfortunately, this change had resulted in a very small change to the height of the can, which left Cowgirl Chocolate with labels too big for the can. Each label currently had to be trimmed slightly to fit on the can. The alternative to this was to switch to a smaller label. This would require purchasing a new printing plate at a cost of about $35 and might require the purchase of a new printing die (the die holds the label while it is printed), which would cost $360. Marilyn also had hopes of one day being able to get her designs printed directly on the tins. It would make for even nicer tins and save the step of having to adhere the labels to the tins. The minimum order for such tins, however, was 15,000 units.

The gift boxes, including all of the associated wrapping, ribbon, and labels, cost about $1.70 per box. The gift boxes did not sell nearly as well as the tins or bags and were available primarily through Cowgirl Chocolates website. Marilyn was still using and had a reasonable inventory of boxes from a box order she had placed three years ago.

Marilyn currently had more packaging in inventory than she normally would because she had ordered $5,000 worth in anticipation of the possibility of having her product placed in military PX stores at the end of 2000. Seattle Chocolates had been negotiating to get their product into these stores, and there had been some interest on the part of the PX stores in also having Cowgirl Chocolate products. Given the six- to eight-week lead-time on packaging, Marilyn had wanted to be positioned to quickly take advantage of this opportunity if it materialized. While Marilyn was still hopeful this deal might come about, she was less optimistic than she had been at the time she placed the packaging order.

Marilyn was concerned that the actual packing step was not always performed with the care it should be. In particular, she was concerned that not enough or too many truffles ended up in the bags and tins, and that the seals on these containers, which made the packages more tamper resistant, were not always applied correctly. Each quarter-pound bag and gift box was supposed to contain 13 individual truffles, each half-pound tin was supposed to contain 25 individual truffles, and each one-pound gift box was supposed to contain 49 individual truffles. The tins, in particular, had to be packed pretty tightly to get 25 truffles into them. Marilyn had done some of the packing herself at times, and wondered if she would not be better off hiring local college or high school students to do the packing for her to insure that the job was done to her satisfaction. It could also save her some money, as Seattle Chocolates charged her extra for packing the tins and bags. The tins, in particular, were expensive because of the time it took to apply the labels to the top and side of the tin and because of the extra care it took to get all 25 truffles into the tin. Seattle Chocolates charged $1.00 per tin for this step.

Marilyn made the caramel sauce herself with the help of the staff in a commercial kitchen in Sandpoint, Idaho, about a 2½-hour drive north of Moscow. She could make 21 cases of 12 jars each in one day, but including the drive it took all day to do. As with the chocolate, she used only the best ingredients, including fresh cream from a local Moscow dairy. Marilyn figured her costs for the caramel sauce at about $2.50 per jar, which included the cost of the ingredients, the jars, the labeling and the cost of using the Sandpoint kitchen. That figure did not include any allowance for the time it took her to make the sauce or put the labels on the jars. She was considering dropping the caramel sauce from her product line because it was a lot of work to produce and she was not sure she really made any money on it after her own time was factored in. She had sold 70 cases of the sauce in 2000, however, so she knew there was some demand for the product. She was considering the possibility of only offering it at Christmas time as a special seasonal product. She was also looking into the possibility of having a sauce company in Montana make it for her. The company produced caramel, chocolate, and chocolate-caramel sauces that had won awards from the fancy food industry trade association. Marilyn thought the sauces were quite good, although she did not like their caramel sauce as much as her own. The company would sell her 11 oz. jars of any of the sauces, spiced up to Marilyn's standards, for $2.75 per jar. Marilyn would have to provide the labels, for which she would need to have new label designs made to match the jar style the company was set up for, and she would also have to pay a shipping cost of $70–$90 per delivery. The company requested a minimum order size of 72 cases, although the company's owner had hinted that they might be willing to produce in half batches initially.

All of Cowgirl Chocolate's products had won awards, either in the annual Fiery Food Challenges sponsored by *Chile Pepper* magazine or the Scovie Award Competitions sponsored by *Fiery Foods* magazine

(the Scovie awards are named after the Scovie measure of heat). All in all, Cowgirl Chocolates had won eleven awards in these two annual competitions. Further, the truffles had won first place in the latest Fiery Food Challenge and the caramel sauce won first place in the latest Scovie competition. The packaging, as distinctive as the chocolate itself, had also won several awards, including the 2000 Award for Excellence for Package Design from American Corporate Identity.

Distribution and Pricing

Marilyn's attempts to get her chocolates into the retail market had met with varying degrees of success. She clearly had been very successful in placing her product in her hometown of Moscow, Idaho. The Moscow Food Co-op was her single best wholesale customer, accounting for 10%–15% of her annual sales. The Co-op sold a wide variety of natural and/ or organic products and produce. Many of its products, like Cowgirl Chocolates, were made or grown locally. The Co-op did a nice job of placing her product in a visible shelf location and generally priced her product less than any other retail outlet. The Co-op sold primarily the chocolate bars, which it priced at $2.35, and the quarter-pound muslin bags of truffles, which it priced at $5.50. This compared to the suggested retail prices of $2.99 for the bars and $6.99 for the bags. The product was also available at three other locations in downtown Moscow: Wild Women Traders, a store that described itself as a 'lifestyle outfitter' and that sold high-end women's clothing and antiques; Northwest Showcase, a store that sold locally produced arts and crafts; and Bookpeople, an independent bookstore that catered to customers who liked to spend time browsing an eclectic offering of books and drinking espresso before making a book purchase.

Marilyn was unsure how many of these local sales were to repeat purchasers who really liked the product and how many were to individuals who wanted to buy a locally made product to give as a gift. She was also unsure how much the Co-op's lower prices boosted the sales of her product at that location. At the Co-op, her product was displayed with other premium chocolates from several competitors, including Seattle Chocolates' own branded chocolate bars, which were priced at $2.99. Marilyn knew the Seattle Chocolate bars were clearly comparable in chocolate quality (although without the spice and cowgirl image). Some of the other competitors' comparably sized bars were priced lower, at $1.99, and some smaller bars were priced at $1.49. While these products were clearly higher in quality than the inexpensive chocolate bars sold in vending machines and at the average supermarket checkout aisle, they were made with a less expensive chocolate than she used and were simply not as good as her chocolates. Marilyn wondered how the price and size of the chocolate bar affected the consumer's purchase decision, and how consumers evaluated the quality of each of the competing chocolate bars when making their purchase.

Outside of Moscow, Marilyn had a harder time getting her product placed onto store shelves and getting her product to move through these locations. One other Co-op, the Boise Food Co-op, carried her products, and they sold pretty well there. Boise was the capital of Idaho and the state's largest city. The Boise Museum of Fine Arts gift shop also carried her product in Boise, although the product did not turn over at this location nearly as well as it did at the Boise Co-op. Other fine art museums, gift shops in places like Missoula, Montana, Portland, Oregon, and Columbus, Ohio, carried Cowgirl Chocolates and Marilyn liked having her product in these outlets. She felt that her reputation as an artist helped her get her product placed in such locations, and the product generally sold well in these locations. She thought her biggest distribution coup was getting her product sold in the world-renowned Whitney Museum in New York City. She felt that the fact that it was sold there added to the product's panache. Unfortunately, the product did not sell there particularly well and it was dropped by the museum. The museum buyer had told Marilyn that she simply thought it was too hot for their customers. Another location in New York City, the Kitchen Market, did much better. The Kitchen Market was an upscale restaurant and gourmet food take-out business. The Kitchen Market was probably her steadiest wholesale customer other than the Moscow Co-op. The product also sold pretty well at the few similar gourmet markets where she had gotten her product placed, like Rainbow Groceries in Seattle and the Culinary Institute of America in San Francisco.

Marilyn had also gotten her product placed in a handful of specialty food stores that focused on hot and spicy foods. Surprisingly, she found, the product had never sold well in these locations. Despite the fact that

the product had won the major fiery food awards, customers in these shops did not seem to be willing to pay the premium price for her product. She had concluded that if her product was located with similarly priced goods, like at the Kitchen Market in New York City, it would sell, but that if it stood out in price then it did not sell as well. Marilyn was not sure, however, just how similarly her product needed to be priced compared to other products the store sold. It seemed clear to her that her $14.95 half-pound tins were standing out in price too much in the hot and spicy specialty stores that thrived on selling jars of hot sauce that typically retailed for $2.99 to $5.99. Marilyn wondered how her product might do at department stores that often sold half pound boxes of "premium" chocolates for as little as $9.95. She knew her half pound tins contained better chocolate, offered more unique packaging and logo design, and did not give that "empty-feeling" that the competitor's oversized boxes did, but wondered if her product would stand out too much in price in such retail locations.

Several online retailers also carried Cowgirl Chocolates, including companies like Salmon River Specialty Foods and Sam McGee's Hot Sauces, although sales from such sites were not very significant. Marilyn had also had her product available through Amazon.com for a short time, but few customers purchased her product from this site during the time it was listed. Marilyn concluded that customers searching the site for music or books simply were not finding her product, and those who did simply were not shopping for chocolates.

Marilyn also sold her products retail through her own website. The website accounted for about one-third of her sales. She liked Web-based sales, despite the extra work of having to process all the small orders, because she was able to capture both the wholesale and retail profits associated with the sale. She also liked the direct contact with the retail customers, and frequently tossed a few extra truffles into a customer's order and enclosed a note that said "a little extra bonus from the head cowgirl." Marilyn allowed customers to return the chocolate for a full refund if they found it not to their liking. Most of her sales growth from 1999 to 2000 had come from her website.

The website itself was created and maintained for her by a small local Internet service provider. It was a fairly simple site. It had pages that described the company and its products and allowed customers to place orders. It did not have any of the sophisticated features that would allow her to use it to capture information to track customers. Although she did not know for sure, she suspected that many of her Internet sales were from repeat customers who were familiar with her product. She included her website address on all of her packaging and had listed her site on several other sites, like saucemall.com and worldmall.com that would link shoppers at these sites to her site. Listing on some of these sites, like saucemall.com, was free. Listing on some other sites cost a small monthly fee—for the worldmall.com listing, for example, she paid $25/month. Some sites simply provided links to her site on their own. For example, one customer had told her she had found the Cowgirl Chocolate site off of an upscale shopping site called Style365.com. She was not sure how much traffic these various sites were generating on her site, and was unsure how best to attract new customers to her website aside from these efforts.

Marilyn had attempted to get her product into a number of bigger name, upscale retailers, like Dean & Delucca and Coldwater Creek. Dean and Delucca was known for its high-end specialty foods, and the buyers for the company had seemed interested in carrying Cowgirl Chocolates, but the owner had nixed the idea because he found the chocolates too spicy. One of the buyers had also told Marilyn that the owner was more of a chocolate purist or traditionalist who did not really like the idea of adding cayenne pepper to chocolate. Marilyn had also tried hard to get her product sold through Coldwater Creek, one of the largest catalog and online retailers in the country that sold high-end women's apparel and gifts for the home. Coldwater Creek was headquartered just a couple of hours north of Moscow in Sandpoint, Idaho. Like Dean & Delucca, Coldwater Creek had decided that the chocolate was too spicy. Coldwater Creek had also expressed some reservations about carrying food products other than at its retail outlet in Sandpoint. Marilyn hoped that the introduction of mild-mannered Cowgirl Chocolates would help get her product into sites like these two.

Promotion

Marilyn was unsure how best to promote her product to potential customers given her limited resources. The ad that would appear in *Chile Pepper* magazine was her first attempt at really advertising her product. The ad itself was designed to grab readers' attention and pique their curiosity about Cowgirl Chocolates. Most of the ads in the magazine were fairly standard in format. They provided a lot of information and images of the product packed into a fairly small space. Her ad was different—it had very little product information and utilized the single image of the woman in the watering trough. It was to appear in a special section of the magazine that focused on celebrity musicians like Willie Nelson and The Dixie Chicks.

Other than the upcoming ad, Marilyn's promotional efforts were focused on trade shows and creating publicity opportunities. She attended a handful of trade shows each year. Some of these were focused on the hot and spicy food market, and it was at these events that she had won all of her awards. Other trade shows were more in the gourmet food market, and she typically shared table space at these events with Seattle Chocolates. She always gave away a lot of product samples at these trade shows, and had clearly won over some fans to her chocolate. But while these shows occasionally had led to placement of her product in retail locations, at least on a trial basis, they had as yet failed to land her what she would consider to be a really high volume wholesale account.

Marilyn also sought ways to generate publicity for her company and products. Several local newspapers had carried stories on her company in the last couple of years, and each time something like that would happen, she would see a brief jump in sales on her website. The *New York Times* had also carried a short article about her and her company. The day after that article ran, she generated sales of $1,000 through her website. More publicity like the *New York Times* article would clearly help. The recently released movie *Chocolat* about a woman who brings spicy chocolate with somewhat magical powers to a small French town was also generating some interest in her product. A number of customers had inquired if she used the same pepper in her chocolates as was used in the movie. Marilyn wondered how she might best capitalize on the interest the movie was creating in spicy chocolates. She thought that perhaps she could convince specialty magazines like *Art & Antiques* or regional magazines like *Sunset Magazine* or even national magazines like *Good Housekeeping* to run stories on her, her art and her chocolates. But she only had so much time to divide between her various efforts. She had looked into hiring a public relations firm, but had discovered that this would cost something on the order of $2,000/month. She did not expect that any publicity a public relations firm could create would generate sufficient sales to offset this cost, particularly given the limited number of locations where people could buy her chocolates. Marilyn was considering trying to write a cookbook as a way to generate greater publicity for Cowgirl Chocolates. She always talked a little about Cowgirl Chocolates when she gave seminars and presentations about her art, and thought that promoting a cookbook would create similar opportunities. The cookbook would also feature several recipes using Cowgirl Chocolate products.

In addition to being unsure how best to promote her product to potential customers, Marilyn also wondered what she should do to better tap into the seasonal opportunities that presented themselves to sellers of chocolate. Demand for her product was somewhat seasonal, with peak retail demand being at Christmas and Valentine's Day. But she was clearly not seeing the Christmas and Valentine sales of other chocolate companies. Seattle Chocolates, for example, had around three-quarters of its annual sales in the fourth quarter, whereas Cowgirl Chocolate sales in the second half of 2000 were actually less than in the first half. Likewise, while Cowgirl Chocolates experienced a small increase in demand around Valentine's Day, it was nowhere near the increase in demand that other chocolate companies experienced. Marilyn did sell some gift buckets and baskets through her website, and these were more popular at Christmas and Valentine's Day. The Moscow Co-op had also sold some of these gift baskets and buckets during the 2000 Christmas season. Marilyn knew that the gift basket industry in the U.S. was pretty large, and that the industry even had its own trade publication called the *Gift Basket Review*. But she was not sure if gift baskets were the best way to generate sales at these two big holidays and thought that she could probably be doing more. One other approach to spur these seasonal sales that she was planning to try was to buy lists of e-mail addresses, that would allow her to send out several e-mails promoting her products right before Valentine's Day and Christmas. She had talked to the owners of a jewelry store about sharing the expense of this endeavor and they had tentative plans to purchase 10,000 e-mail addresses for $300.

What Next?

Marilyn looked again at the advertisement that would be appearing soon in *Chile Pepper* Magazine. The same friend who had helped her with her award winning package design had helped produce the ad. It would clearly grab people's attention, but would it bring customers to her products in the numbers she needed?

Next to the ad sat the folder with what financial information she had. Despite having little training in small business accounting and financial management, Marilyn knew it was important to keep good records. She had kept track of revenues and expenses for the year, and she had summarized these in a table (see Exhibit 4). Marilyn had shared this revenue and cost information with a friend with some experience in small business financial management, and the result was an estimated income statement for the year 2000 based upon the unaudited information in Exhibit 4. The estimated income statement, shown in Exhibit 5, revealed that Cowgirl had lost approximately $6,175 on operations before taxes. Combining the information in Exhibits 4 and 5, it appeared that the inventory had built up to approximately $16,848 by December 31, 2000. Marilyn had initially guessed she had $10,000 worth of product and packaging inventory, about twice her normal level of inventory, between what was stored in her garage turned art studio turned chocolate warehouse and what was stored for her at Seattle Chocolates. But the financial analysis indicated that she either had more inventory than she thought or that she had given away more product than she originally thought. Either way, this represented a significant additional drain on her resources—in effect cash expended to cover both the operational loss and the inventory buildup was approximately $23,000 in total (see note 5 of Exhibit 4 for a more detailed explanation). When Marilyn looked at the Exhibits, she could see better why she had to loan the firm money. She also recognized that the bottom line was that the numbers did not look good, and she wondered if the ad would help turn things around for 2001.

If the ad did not have its desired affect, she wondered what she should do next. She clearly had limited resources to work with. She had already pretty much decided that if this ad did not work, she would not run another one in the near future. She was also pretty wary of working with distributors. In addition to her own bad experience, she knew of others in the industry that had bad experiences with distributors, and she did not think

EXHIBIT 4
Summary of
2000 Financial
Information
(unaudited)

Revenues:	
Product Sales	$ 26,000
Revenue from Shipping	4,046 (see Note 1)
Total Revenues	**$ 30,046**
Expenses: (related to cost of sales)	
Chocolate (raw material)	$ 16,508
Caramel (raw material)	2,647
Packaging (bags, boxes, tins)	9,120
Printing (labels, cards, etc)	3,148
Subtotal	$ 31,423 (see Note 2)
Other Expenses	
Shipping and Postage	$ 4,046
Brokers	540
Travel (airfare, lodging, meals, gas)	5,786
Trade shows (promotions, etc.)	6,423
Website	1,390
Phone	981
Office Supplies	759
Photography	356
Insurance, Lawyers, Memberships	437
Charitable Contributions	200
Miscellaneous Other Expenses	1,071
State Taxes	35
Subtotal	$ 22,024
Total Expenses	**$ 53,447**
Cash needed to sustain operations	**$ 23,023** (see Note 3)
Estimated year-end inventory (12/31/00):	
Product Inventory	$ 9,848
Extra Packaging and Labels	7,000
Total Inventory	**$ 16,848**

Notes
(1) The $4,046 Revenue from Shipping represents income received from customers who are charged shipping and postage up front as part of the order. Cowgirl then pays the shipping and postage when the order is delivered. The offsetting operating expense is noted in "Other Expenses."
(2) Of this amount, $14,575 is attributed to product actually sold and shipped. The remaining $16,848 represents leftover inventory and related supplies (i.e., $16848 + $14575 = $31,423).
(3) Marilyn made a personal loan to the firm in the year 2000 for approximately $23,000 to sustain the business's operations.

she could afford to take another gamble on a distributor. She wondered if she should focus more attention on her online retail sales or on expanding her wholesale business to include more retailers. If she focused more on her own online sales, what exactly should she do? If she focused on expanding her wholesale business, where should she put her emphasis? Should she continue to pursue retailers that specialized in hot and spicy foods, try to get her product placed in more Co-ops, expand her efforts to get the product positioned as a gift in museum gift shops and similar outlets, or focus her efforts on large, high-end retailers like Cold-water Creek and Dean & Delucca now that she had a nonspicy chocolate in her product mix? Or should she try to do something else entirely new? And what more should she do to create publicity for her product? Was the cookbook idea worth pursuing? As she thought about it, she began to wonder if things were beginning to spin out of control. Here she was, contemplating writing a cookbook to generate publicity for her chocolate company that she started to raise money to publish her arts magazine. Where would this end?

EXHIBIT 5   Cowgirl Chocolates Income Statement (accountant's unaudited estimate for Year 2000)

			% of Sales
Revenues:			
Product Sales	$26,000		
Miscellaneous Income	$ 4,046		
Total Net Sales		**$30,046**	100%
Cost of Sales (shipped portion of chocolate, caramel, packaging, and printing)		$14,197	47%
Gross Margin		**$15,849**	53%
Operating Expenses:			
Advertising & Promotions:			
Trade Shows	6,423		
Website	1,390		
Charitable Contributions	200		
Subtotal		8,013	27%
Travel		5,786	19%
Miscellaneous		1,071	4%
Payroll Expense/Benefits @ 20%	(no personnel charges)	—	0%
Depreciation on Plant and Equipment	(no current ownership of PPE)	—	0%
Continuing Inventory (finished and unfinished)	(not included in income statement)	—	
Shipping & Postage		4,046	13%
Insurance, Lawyers, Professional			
Memberships		437	1.5%
Brokers		540	1.8%
Office Expenses (phone, supplies, photography, taxes)		2,131	7%
Total Operating Expenses		**22,024**	
Grand Total: All expenses		**$36,221**	
Profit before Interest & Taxes		**($6,175) [see note]**	
Interest Expense (short term)		—	
Interest Expense (long term)		—	
Taxes Incurred (Credit @ 18%, approximate tax rate)		($1,124)	
Net Profit After Taxes		**($5,051.15)**	
Net Profit After Taxes/Sales			−17%

Note: The ($6,175) loss plus the $16,848 in inventory build-up approximates the cash needed ($23,023—see Exhibit 4) to cover the total expenses for year 2000.

Case 6-17

Procter & Gamble Co.

It's Mother's Day, and Alan G. "A.G." Lafley, chief executive of Procter & Gamble Co., is meeting with the person he shares time with every Sunday evening—Richard L. Antoine, the company's head of human resources. Lafley doesn't invite the chief financial officer of the $43 billion business, nor does he ask the executive in charge of marketing at the world's largest consumer-products company. He doesn't invite friends over to watch *The Sopranos,* either. No, on most Sunday nights it's just Lafley, Antoine, and stacks of reports on the performance of the company's 200 most senior executives. This is the boss's signature gesture. It shows his determination to nurture talent and serves notice that little escapes his attention. If you worked for P&G, you would have to be both impressed and slightly intimidated by that kind of diligence.

On this May evening, the two executives sit at the dining-room table in Antoine's Cincinnati home hashing over the work of a manager who distinguished himself on one major assignment but hasn't quite lived up to that since. "We need to get him in a position where we can stretch him," Lafley says. Then he rises from his chair and stands next to Antoine to peer more closely at a spreadsheet detailing P&G's seven management layers. Lafley points to one group while tapping an empty water bottle against his leg. "It's not being felt strongly enough in the middle of the company," he says in his slightly high-pitched voice. "They don't feel the hot breath of the consumer."

If they don't feel it yet, they will. Lafley, who took over when Durk I. Jager was pressured to resign in June, 2000, is in the midst of engineering a remarkable turn-around. The first thing Lafley told his managers when he took the job was just what they wanted to hear: Focus on what you do well—selling the company's major brands such as Tide, Pampers, and Crest—instead of trying to develop the next big thing.

Now, those old reliable products have gained so much market share that they are again the envy of the industry. So is the company's stock price, which has climbed 58%, to $92 a share, since Lafley started, while the Standard & Poor's 500-stock index has declined 32%. Banc of America analyst William H. Steele forecasts that P&G's profits for its current fiscal year, which ended June 30, will rise by 13%, to $5.57 billion, on an 8% increase in sales, to $43.23 billion. That exceeds most rivals'. Volume growth has averaged 7% over the past six quarters, excluding acquisitions, well above Lafley's goal and the industry average.

The conventional thinking is that the soft-spoken Lafley was exactly the antidote P&G needed after Jager. After all, Jager had charged into office determined to rip apart P&G's insular culture and remake it from the bottom up. Instead of pushing P&G to excel, however, the torrent of proclamations and initiatives during Jager's 17-month reign nearly brought the venerable company to a grinding halt.

Enter Lafley. A 23-year P&G veteran, he wasn't supposed to bring fundamental change; he was asked simply to restore the company's equilibrium. In fact, he came in warning that Jager had tried to implement too many changes too quickly (which Jager readily admits now). Since then, the mild-mannered 56-year-old chief executive has worked to revive both urgency and hope: urgency because, in the previous 15 years, P&G had developed exactly one successful new brand, the Swiffer dust mop; and hope because, after Jager, employees needed reassurance that the old ways still had value. Clearly, Lafley has undone the damage at P&G.

What's less obvious is that, in his quiet way, Lafley has proved to be even more of a revolutionary than the flamboyant Jager. Lafley is leading the most sweeping transformation of the company since it was founded by William Procter and James Gamble in 1837 as a maker of soap and candles (Exhibit 1). Long before he became CEO, Lafley had been pondering how to make P&G relevant in the 21st century, when speed and agility would matter more than heft. As president of North American operations, he even spoke with Jager about the need to remake the company.

So how has Lafley succeeded where Jager so spectacularly failed? In a word, style. Where Jager was gruff, Lafley is soothing. Where Jager bullied, Lafley persuades. He listens more than he talks. He is living proof that the messenger is just as important as the message. As he says, "I'm not a screamer, not a yeller. But don't get confused by my style. I am very decisive." Or as Robert A. McDonald, president of P&G's global fabric and home-care division, says, "people want to follow him. I frankly love him like my brother."

Indeed, Lafley's charm offensive has so disarmed most P&Gers that he has been able to change the company profoundly (Exhibit 2). He is responsible for P&G's

EXHIBIT 1
Lafley's Vision

Outsourcing If it's not a core function the new P&G won't do it. Info tech and bar-soap manufacturing have already been contracted out. Other jobs will follow.

Acquisitions Not everything has to be invented in company labs. Lafley wants half of all new-product ideas to come from the outside.

Building Staff Managers are under much closer scrutiny, as Lafley scans the ranks for the best and the brightest and singles them out for development.

Brand Expansion The Crest line now includes an electric toothbrush and tooth-whitening products along with toothpaste. Lafley is making similar moves elsewhere.

Pricing P&G isn't just the premium-priced brand. It will go to the lower end if that's where opportunity lies.

EXHIBIT 2   P&G Turning the Tide

Data: Banc America securities.

Fabric and Home Care	Beauty Care	Baby and Family Care	Health Care	Snacks and Beverages
Lafley has aggressively cut costs in the company's largest division. But Tide in particular faces intense competition from lower-priced rivals. To compensate, Lafley is introducing high-margin products, such as the Swiffer Duster.	Lafley has quickly expanded this business by acquiring Clairol and Wella. But the company has less expertise here and still has to prove it can grow internally.	P&G now vies with Kimberly-Clark to dominate the disposable-diaper market. But competition has pushed prices down, which is why this division has the slowest profit-margin growth.	With its SpinBrush and tooth-whitening products, P&G has regained the lead in oral care from Colgate. The division will get a lift from distributing heart-burn drug Prilosec over the counter. But the pharmaceutical business depends on one big seller, Actonel for osteoporosis.	Because the division generates the company's lowest profit margins many expect Lafley to continue to extricate P&G from these businesses. He has already sold Crisco and Jiff to J.M. Smuckers.
Sales* 29%	Sales 28%	Sales 23%	Sales 13%	Sales 7%
Operating Profit Margin 25%	Operating Profit Margin 23%	Operating Profit Margin 17%	Operating Profit Margin 18%	Operating Profit Margin 15%
Outlook Very Good	Outlook Good	Outlook Good	Outlook Mixed	Outlook Weak

*Share of total sales. Estimates for fiscal year ending June 30, 2003

largest acquisitions ever, buying Clairol in 2001 for $5 billion and agreeing to purchase Germany's Wella in March for a price that now reaches $7 billion. He has replaced more than half of the company's top 30 officers, more than any P&G boss in memory, and cut 9,600 jobs. And he has moved more women into senior positions. Lafley skipped over 78 general managers with more seniority to name 42-year-old Deborah A. Henretta to head P&G's then-troubled North American baby-care division. "The speed at which A.G. has gotten results is five years ahead of the time I expected," says Scott Cook, founder of software maker Intuit Inc., who joined P&G's board shortly after Lafley's appointment.

Still, the Lafley revolution is far from over. Precisely because of his achievements, Lafley is now under enormous pressure to return P&G to what it considers its rightful place in Corporate America: a company that is admired, imitated, and uncommonly profitable. Nowhere are those expectations more apparent than on the second floor of headquarters, where three former chief executives still keep offices. John Pepper, a popular former boss who returned briefly as chairman when Jager left but gave up the post to Lafley last year, leans forward in his chair as he says: "It's now clear to me that A.G. is going to be one of the great CEOs in this company's history."

But here's the rub: What Lafley envisions may be far more radical than what Pepper has in mind. Consider a confidential memo that circulated among P&G's top brass in late 2001 and angered Pepper for its audacity. It argued that P&G could be cut to 25,000 employees, a quarter of its current size. Acknowledging the memo, Lafley admits: "It terrified our organization."

Lafley didn't write the infamous memo, but he may as well have. It reflects the central tenet of his vision—that P&G should do only what it does best, nothing more. Lafley wants a more outwardly focused, flexible company. That has implications for every facet of the business, from manufacturing to innovation. For example, in April he turned over all bar-soap manufacturing, including Ivory, P&G's oldest surviving brand, to a Canadian contractor. In May, he outsourced P&G's information-technology operation to Hewlett-Packard Co.

No bastion has been more challenged than P&G's research and development operations. Lafley has confronted head-on the stubbornly held notion that everything must be invented within P&G, asserting that half of its new products should come from the outside. (P&G now gets about 20% of its ideas externally—up from about 10% when he took over.) "He's absolutely breaking many well-set molds at P&G," says eBay Inc.'s CEO, Margaret C. "Meg" Whitman, whom Lafley appointed to the board.

Lafley's quest to remake P&G could still come to grief. As any scientist will attest, buying innovation is tricky. Picking the winners from other labs is notoriously difficult and often expensive. And P&G will remain uncomfortably reliant on Wal-Mart Stores Inc., which accounts for nearly a fifth of its sales. Lafley is looking to pharmaceuticals and beauty care for growth, where the margins are high but where P&G has considerably less experience than rivals.

The biggest risk, though, is that Lafley will lose the P&Gers themselves. Theirs is a culture famously resistant to new ideas. To call the company insular may not do it justice. Employees aren't kidding when they say they're a family. They often start out there and grow up together at P&G, which only promotes from within. Cincinnati itself is a small town: Employees live near one another, they go to the same health clubs and restaurants. They are today's company men and women—and proud of it.

Lafley is well aware of his predicament. On a June evening, as he sits on the patio behind his home, he muses about just that. The house, which resembles a Tuscan villa and overlooks the Ohio River and downtown Cincinnati, is infused with P&G history. Lafley bought it from former CEO John G. Smale three years before he was named chief executive. A black-and-gold stray cat the family feeds sits a few feet away and watches Lafley as he sips a Beck's beer. The clouds threaten rain. "I am worried that I will ask the organization to change ahead of its understanding, capability, and commitment," Lafley admits.

For most of its 166 years, P&G was one of America's preeminent companies. Its brands are icons: It launched Tide in 1946 and Pampers, the first disposable diaper, in 1961. Its marketing was innovative: In the 1880s, P&G was one of the first companies to advertise nationally. Fifty years later, P&G invented the soap opera by sponsoring the *Ma Perkins* radio show and, later, *Guiding Light*.

Its management techniques, meanwhile, became the gold standard: In the 1930s, P&G developed the idea of brand management—setting up marketing teams for each brand and urging them to compete against each other. P&G has long been the business world's finest training ground. General Electric Co.'s Jeffrey R. Immelt and 3M's W. James McNerney Jr. both started out on Ivory. Meg Whitman and Steven M. Case were in toilet goods, while Steven A. Ballmer was an assistant product manager for Duncan Hines cake mix, among other goods. They, of course, went on to lead eBay, AOL Time Warner and Microsoft (Exhibit 3).

But by the 1990s, P&G was in danger of becoming another Eastman Kodak Co. or Xerox Corp., a once great company that had lost its way. Sales on most of its 18 top brands were slowing; the company was being outhustled by more focused rivals such as Kimberly-Clark Corp. and Colgate-Palmolive Co. The only way P&G kept profits growing was by cutting costs, hardly a strategy for the long term. At the same time, the dynamics of the industry were changing as power shifted from manufacturers to massive retailers. Through all of this, much of senior management was in denial. "Nobody wanted to talk about it," Lafley says. "Without a doubt, Durk and I and a few others were in the camp of 'We need a much bigger change.'"

When Jager took over in January, 1999, he was hell-bent on providing just that—with disastrous results. He introduced expensive new products that never caught on while letting existing brands drift. He wanted to buy two huge pharmaceutical companies, a plan that threatened P&G's identity but never was carried out. And he put in place a companywide reorganization that left many employees perplexed and preoccupied. Soaring

EXHIBIT 3 **P&G's Family Tree**

The CEOs who preceded Lafley launched ambitious projects but also oversaw a gradual erosion of P&G's core brands.

1981–90	1990–95	1995–99	1999–2000
John Smale moves P&G into the health-care and beauty business, which becomes central to the company. His decision to expand its food and beverage division doesn't amount to nearly as much.	Edwin Artzt helps bring P&G to the world, and cosmetics to P&G, through the purchase of Max Factor and Cover Girl. But sales of major brands slow—as international expansion and new-product launches take precedence.	John Pepper pushes into developing markets such as China and Russia and starts to revamp the company's international structure. But sales remain weak, and much of P&G's profit gains come from cost-cutting.	Durk Jager tries to jump-start innovation by launching expensive new products, which flop, and by trying to shake up P&G's stodgy culture, which quickly demoralizes many employees.

commodity prices, unfavorable currency trends, and a techcrazed stock market didn't help either. At a company prized for consistent earnings, Jager missed forecasts twice in six months. In his first and last full fiscal year, earnings per share rose by just 3.5% instead of an estimated 13%. And during that time, the share price slid 52%, cutting P&G's total market capitalization by $85 billion. Employees and retirees hold about 20% of the stock. The family began to turn against its leader.

But Jager's greatest failing was his scorn for the family. Jager, a Dutchman who had joined P&G overseas and worked his way to corporate headquarters, pitted himself against the P&G culture, contending that it was burdensome and insufferable, says Susan E. Arnold, president of P&G's beauty and feminine care division. Some go-ahead employees even wore buttons that read "Old World/New World" to express disdain for P&G's past. "I never wore one," Arnold sneers. "'The old Procter is bad, and the new world is good.' That didn't work."

On June 6, 2000, his 30th wedding anniversary, Lafley was in San Francisco when he received a call from Pepper, then a board member: Would he become CEO? Back in Cincinnati, a boardroom coup unprecedented in P&G's history had taken place.

As Lafley steps into the small study in his house three years later, a Japanese drawing on the wall reminds him of what it was like to become CEO. The room, with its painting of a samurai warrior and red elephant-motif wallpaper, alludes to his stint running P&G's Asian operations. Bookshelves hold leather-bound volumes of Joseph Conrad and Mark Twain. A simple wooden desk faces the window. Lafley focuses on the drawing, which depicts a man caught in a spider's

web; it was given to him by the elder of his two sons, Patrick. "In the first few days, you are just trying to figure out what kind of web it is," he says.

In a sense, Lafley had been preparing for this job his entire adult life. He never hid the fact that he wanted to run P&G one day. Or if not the company, then a company. That itself is unusual since, like almost all P&Gers, Lafley has never worked anywhere else. After graduating from Hamilton College in 1969, Lafley decided to pursue a doctorate in medieval and Renaissance history at the University of Virginia. But he dropped out in his first year to join the Navy (and avoid being drafted into the Army). He served in Japan, where he got his first experience as a merchandiser, supplying Navy retail stores. When his tour of duty ended in 1975, he enrolled in the MBA program at Harvard Business School. And from there, he went directly to Cincinnati.

When he was hired as a brand assistant for Joy dish detergent in 1977 at age 29, he was older than most of his colleagues and he worried that his late start might hinder his rise at P&G. Twice within a year in the early 1980s, Lafley quit. "Each time, I talked him back in only after drinking vast amounts of Drambuie," says Thomas A. Moore, his boss at the time, who now runs biotech company Biopure Corp. On the second occasion, then-CEO John Smale met with Lafley, who had accepted a job as a consultant in Connecticut. Without making any promises, Smale says he told Lafley that "we thought there was no limit on where he was going to go."

Sure enough, Lafley climbed quickly to head P&G's soap and detergent business, where he introduced Liquid Tide in 1984. A decade later, he was promoted to head the Asian division. Lafley returned from Kobe,

Japan, to Cincinnati in 1998 to run the company's entire North American operations. To ease the transition home, he and his younger son, Alex, who was then 12, studied guitar together. Two years later, Lafley was named CEO.

Along the way, he developed a reputation as a boss who stepped back to give his staff plenty of responsibility and helped shape decisions by asking a series of keen questions—a process he calls "peeling the onion." And he retained a certain humility. He still collects baseball cards, comic books, and rock 'n' roll 45s. Whereas some executives might have a garage full of antique cars or Harley-Davidsons; Lafley keeps two Vespa motor scooters. "People wanted him to succeed," says Virginia Lee, a former P&Ger who worked for Lafley at headquarters and overseas.

As CEO, Lafley hasn't made grand pronouncements on the future of P&G. Instead, he has spent an inordinate amount of time patiently communicating how he wants P&G to change. In a company famed for requiring employees to describe every new course of action in a one-page memo, Lafley's preferred approach is the slogan. For example, he felt that P&G was letting technology rather than consumer needs dictate new products. Ergo: "The consumer is boss." P&G wasn't working closely enough with retailers, the place where consumers first see the product on the shelf: "The first moment of truth." P&G wasn't concerned enough with the consumer's experience at home: "The second moment of truth."

Lafley uses these phrases constantly, and they are echoed throughout the organization. At the end of a three-day leadership seminar, 30 young marketing managers from around the world present what they have learned to Lafley. First on the list: "We are the voice of the consumer within P&G, and they are the heart of all we do." Lafley, dressed in a suit, sits on a stool in front of the group and beams. "I love the first one," he laughs as the room erupts in applause.

When he talks about his choice of words later, Lafley is a tad self-conscious. "It's *Sesame Street* language—I admit that," he says. "A lot of what we have done is make things simple because the difficulty is making sure everybody knows what the goal is and how to get there."

Lafley has also mastered the art of the symbolic gesture. The 11th floor at corporate headquarters had been the redoubt of senior executives since the 1950s. Lafley did away with it, moving all five division presidents to the same floors as their staff. Then he turned

some of the space into a leadership training center. On the rest of the floor, he knocked down the walls so that the remaining executives, including himself, share open offices. Lafley sits next to the two people he talks to the most, which, in true P&G style, was officially established by a flow study: HR head Antoine and Vice-Chairman Bruce Byrnes. As if the Sunday night meetings with Antoine weren't proof enough of Lafley's determination to make sure the best people rise to the top. And Byrnes, whom Lafley refers to as "Yoda"—the sage-like *Star Wars* character—gets a lot of face time because of his marketing expertise. As Lafley says, "the assets at P&G are what? Our people and our brands."

Just as emblematic of the Lafley era is the floor's new conference room, where he and P&G's 12 other top executives meet every Monday at 8 a.m. to review results, plan strategy, and set the drumbeat for the week. The table used to be rectangular; now it's round. The execs used to sit where they were told; now they sit where they like. At one of those meetings, an outsider might have trouble distinguishing the CEO: He occasionally joins in the discussion, but most of the time the executives talk as much to each other as to Lafley. "I am more like a coach," Lafley says afterward. "I am always looking for different combinations that will get better results." Jeff Immelt, who asked Lafley to join GE's board in 2002, describes him as "an excellent listener. He's a sponge."

And now, Lafley is carefully using this information to reshape the company's approach to just about everything it does. When Lafley describes the P&G of the future, he says: "We're in the business of creating and building brands." Notice, as P&Gers certainly have, that he makes no mention of manufacturing. While Lafley shies away from saying just how much of the company's factory and back-office operations he may hand over to someone else, he does admit that facing up to the realities of the marketplace "won't always be fun." Of P&G's 102,000 employees, nearly one-half work in its plants. So far, "Lafley has deftly handled the outsourcing deals, which has lessened fear within P&G," says Roger Martin, a close adviser of Lafley's who is dean of the University of Toronto's Joseph L. Rotman School of Management. All 2,000 of the information-technology workers were moved over to HP. At the bar-soap operations, based entirely in Cincinnati, 200 of the 250 employees went to work for the Canadian contractor.

Lafley's approach to selling P&G products is unprecedented at the company, too: He argues that P&G doesn't have to produce just premium-priced goods. So now there's a cheaper formulation for Crest in China. The Clairol deal gave P&G bargain shampoos such as Daily Defense. And with Lafley's encouragement, managers have looked at their most expensive products to make sure they aren't too costly. In many cases, they've actually lowered the prices.

And Lafley is pushing P&G to approach its brands more creatively. Crest, for example, isn't just about toothpaste anymore: There's also an electric toothbrush, SpinBrush, which P&G acquired in January, 2001 (see Appendix). P&G is also willing to license its own technologies to get them to the marketplace faster. It joined with Clorox Co., maker of Glad Bags, last October to share a food-wrap technology it had developed. It was unprecedented for P&G to work with a competitor, says licensing head Jeffrey Weedman. The overall effect is undeniable. "Lafley has made P&G far more flexible," says Banc of America's Steele.

But Lafley still faces daunting challenges. Keeping up the earnings growth, for example, will get tougher as competitors fight back and as P&G winds down a large restructuring program—started under Jager but accelerated under Lafley. Furthermore, some of the gains in profit have resulted from cuts in capital and R&D spending, which Lafley has pared back to the levels of the company's rivals. And already, P&G has missed a big opportunity: It passed up the chance to buy watersoluble strips that contain mouthwash. Now, Listerine is making a bundle on the product.

Nor are all investors comfortable with growth through acquisitions. The deals make it harder for investors to decipher earnings growth from existing operations. Then there's the risk of fumbling the integration, notes Arthur B. Cecil, an analyst at T. Rowe Price Group Inc., which holds 1.74 million P&G shares. "I would prefer they not make acquisitions," he says. Already, Clairol hair color, the most important product in P&G's recent purchase, has lost five points of market share to L'Oréal in the U.S., according to ACNeilsen Corp.

Making deals, however, could be the only way to balance P&G's growing reliance on Wal-Mart. Former and current P&G employees say the discounter could account for one-third of P&G's global sales by the end of the decade. Meanwhile, the pressure from consumers and competitors to keep prices low will only increase. "P&G has improved its ability to take on those challenges, but those challenges are still there," says Lehman analyst Ann Gillin.

Still, Lafley may be uniquely suited to creating a new and improved P&G. Even Jager agrees that Lafley was just what the company needed. "He has calmed down the confusion that happened while I was there," says the former CEO. Jager left a letter on Lafley's desk the day he resigned telling his successor not to feel responsible for his fall. "You earned it," he recalls writing. "Don't start out with guilt."

Lafley says he learned from Jager's biggest mistake. "I avoided saying P&G people were bad," he says. "I enrolled them in change." Lafley, a company man through and through, just can't resist trying out a new slogan.

Source: Robert Berner, "P&G", *BusinessWeek,* July 7, 2003, 52–63.

Appendix to Case 6-17

Darin S. Yates had watched many consumer focus groups at Procter & Gamble Co., but he had never witnessed a response like this. Out of a panel of 24 consumers evaluating a new electric toothbrush, 23 raved about the product, begging to take it home. "We were just blown away," the 36-year-old brand manager recalls.

But Yates, team leader on the new toothbrush, never imagined how successful the Crest SpinBrush would be. While most electric brushes cost more than $50, SpinBrush works on batteries and sells for just $5. Since that focus group in October 2000, it has become the nation's best-selling toothbrush, manual or electric. In P&G's last fiscal year, it posted more than $200 million in global sales, helping Crest become the consumer-product maker's 12th billion-dollar brand. It has also helped Crest reclaim the title as No. 1 oral-care brand in the U.S., a position it lost to Colgate-Palmolive's Colgate brand in 1998. "It's hard for P&G's business models to conceive of a business growing as quickly as SpinBrush," Yates says.

One reason is that P&G didn't conceive SpinBrush to begin with. Four Cleveland-area entrepreneurs developed the gizmo in 1998 with the idea of selling it to P&G. They parlayed a $1.5 million investment into a $475 million payout. Three of them even went on the P&G payroll for a year and a half to shepherd the product—something unheard of at the insular company. Says John Osher, the lead entrepreneur behind SpinBrush: "My job was to not allow P&G to screw it up."

SpinBrush marks a dramatic departure for the 165-year-old company. For once, P&G didn't insist on controlling every step, from product development to pricing. Instead, it harnessed its greatest strength—the ability to market and distribute products—to the innovation and risk-taking ability of a tiny startup that wasn't constrained by the culture inside P&G's Cincinnati headquarters. The strategy is not without risks or cultural challenges. P&G had to bend on how it packaged, manufactured, shipped, and worked its mighty marketing machine. And the story isn't over: The SpinBrush founders question if the product will reach its potential once it is fully enveloped in P&G's big-company culture. "I'm not sure you can teach an elephant to dance," Osher says.

Even so, the acquisition of SpinBrush says a lot about the leadership of Alan G. Lafley, who became chief executive in June 2000, when predecessor Durk I. Jager was ousted. Jager, a combative change agent, had pushed P&G to ramp up development of new products. He shook P&G's identity with proposals to buy two large pharmaceutical companies. In the end he overreached, missing earnings forecasts.

Lafley has been more deft. He has refocused the company on the big brands that drive earnings, including Pampers, Tide, and Crest. Like Jager, he has made acquisitions. But the $4.9 billion purchase of Clairol, P&G's largest ever, and SpinBrush have been closer to P&G's core strengths in hair and oral care than Jager's forays with Iams pet food and PUR water-filter systems.

Those moves have helped Lafley find a balance between sales and profit growth—something that eluded his predecessor. P&G has exceeded Wall Street's earnings estimates in the last three reported quarters, while at the same time increasing share in its markets through higher promotional and ad spending. For the fiscal year ended June 30, analysts expect P&G's operating earnings to climb 9% to $5 billion, reversing a prior-year decline. Such gains will get harder, though, as savings from a $6 billion restructuring started under Jager start to wind down.

Still, Lafley is proving to be a radical strategic thinker by P&G standards. When Kimberly-Clark Corp. launched a moist toilet paper last year, he went against P&G's make-it-here mentality by acquiring a manufacturer of a similar product. That let him parry Kimberly more quickly and tied up less money in the capital-intensive business. Recent negotiations to outsource P&G's 6,000-employee, back-office operations would also have been unlikely at the old P&G. The move reflects Lafley's efforts to focus the company on its core strengths and suggests further payroll cuts ahead.

The SpinBrush saga also shows a new recognition that not all great ideas originate at P&G (Exhibit 4). Lafley has made clear that as many as a third of P&G's new product ideas may come from outside, and he has stepped up efforts to identify and acquire other small companies. But perhaps the biggest change for P&G was in SpinBrush's pricing. P&G usually prices its goods at a premium, based on the cost of technology. But competitors now follow new products more quickly, eroding P&G's pricing power. With SpinBrush, P&G reversed its usual thinking. It started with an aggressive price, then found a way to make a profit. If P&G had conceived SpinBrush, admits Yates, "my gut tells me we would not have priced it where we did."

That's just the opportunity John Osher and his three colleagues saw when they had the SpinBrush brainstorm back in 1998. Osher, 55, had spent most of his career inventing things and selling them to big companies. His latest creation had been the Spin Pop, a lollipop attached to a battery-powered plastic handle, in which the candy spun at the press of a button. He had teamed up on the Spin Pop with John R. Nottingham and John W. Spirk, the principals of a Cleveland industrial design firm, and their in-house patent lawyer, Lawrence A. Blaustein. The Spin Pop had recently sold to Hasbro for millions and the men were looking for another way to utilize the technology.

EXHIBIT 4 Different Strokes for P&G

The marketing giant broke a lot of its own rules when it launched the SpinBrush. Here's what it did:

Looked Outside	Empowered the Inventors	Got Aggressive on Price
SpinBrush wasn't invented at P&G. Instead, the company bought it from a group of entrepreneurs.	To make sure the new toothbrush didn't get smothered by the P&G bureaucracy, the inventors were hired for the first year to help with everything from packaging to logistics.	Instead of starting at the high end and cutting prices as competitors moved in, P&G started low and made it harder for newcomers to steal market share.

They can't remember who came up with the concept, but they know it came from their group walks through the aisles of their local Wal-Mart, where they went for inspiration. They saw that electric toothbrushes, from Sonicare to Interplak, cost more than $50 and for that reason held a fraction of the overall toothbrush market. They reasoned: Why not create a $5 electric brush using the Spin Pop technology? At just $1 more than the most expensive manual brushes, they figured many consumers would trade up. They spent 18 months designing and sourcing a high-quality brush that wouldn't cost more than $5, batteries included. "If it had cost $7.99, we wouldn't have gone forward," Osher says.

They also formulated an exit strategy: Sell it to P&G. In 1998, they saw that Colgate toothpaste was dethroning Crest, the market champ since the early 1960s. Colgate edged out Crest by launching Total and pitching it around the new theme of whitening. P&G, meanwhile, clung to its cavity-fighting message. Colgate gained 5.6 percentage points of market share in 1998, giving the company 29.6% of the market, vs. P&G's 25.6%. "We knew that P&G would be very hungry," says Nottingham.

But first they had to prove the product could sell. They couldn't afford to advertise and sell SpinBrush at that low price. So they resorted to the marketing ploy they used with Spin Pop: packaging that said, "Try Me" and that allowed the consumer to turn the brush on in the store. They also hired a former Clorox salesman, Joseph A. O'Connor, who had years of experience selling to Wal-Mart and other big chains.

When they tested SpinBrush in Meijer Inc., a Midwest discount chain, in October 1999, it outsold the leading manual brush nearly 3 to 1, convincing Meijer to carry it. Using that sales data, they cracked drugstore chain Walgreen Co. and caught the interest of Wal-Mart in early 2000. To help close that deal, O'Connor persuaded a health and beauty aid manager at a Phoenix Wal-Mart to buy 240 SpinBrushes. "They sold out over the weekend," he recalls.

In 2000, the entrepreneurs sold 10 million SpinBrush units, more than triple the existing 3 million U.S. electric toothbrush market. With that record, it wasn't hard for Osher to get an appointment at P&G in July. The company had another reason to take notice: Colgate's recently launched ActiBrush electric toothbrush, at $19.95, was off to a fast start, too.

Yates, a financial manager on the Crest brand, headed a team to evaluate SpinBrush. P&G code-named the project Julius, after basketball great Julius Erving. With approval to negotiate a purchase and focus group reactions off the charts, Yates moved fast. A deal to buy the startup closed in January, 2001, six months after the first meeting with Osher.

The deal's structure was unprecedented for P&G. Instead of paying a lump sum, P&G would pay $165 million up-front with an "earn-out" payment in three years based on a formula pegged to financial results. The up-front payment alone—nearly four times SpinBrush's prior year sales of $43 million—was rich by P&G's standards. The company paid three times sales for Clairol. But P&G was banking on faster sales growth from SpinBrush.

The deal had another unique feature: Osher, Blaustein, and O'Connor agreed to join the company for the three-year earn-out period with a mandate of keeping the business entrepreneurial. They would become part of a 27-person team headed by Yates that would have authority to bend any P&G rules that interfered with the business. The entrepreneurs would guide the team and had carte blanche to go higher within P&G to resolve conflicts.

And there were conflicts aplenty. Some P&Gers questioned the "Try Me" feature, fearing the batteries would wear out. Others wanted to stop store deliveries for three months so P&G could build inventories. Still others worried about having more automated factories in China. In the end, though, "they would listen to us and fight their own bureaucracy," says Osher.

Yates broke the biggest rule of all for a company whose heritage is in marketing—he didn't advertise SpinBrush for the first seven months. The traditional P&G model for a launch calls for heavy TV advertising from the outset and a high enough price to help carry that cost. But Yates didn't want the ad expense, which could force him to raise prices, until sales could support it. "I didn't want to mess up the economic structure of the business," he says.

P&G now sells SpinBrush in about 35 countries, marking its quickest global rollout ever. And it's added a multitude of models, including ones with replaceable heads. Colgate earlier this year launched Motion, a SpinBrush look-alike, at the same price. In a recent earnings conference call, Colgate CEO Reuben Mark admitted that the company had cut the price of ActiBrush from $19 to $12 because of the competition.

P&G and the SpinBrush founders agreed to an early payout in March, 21 months ahead of schedule. Osher's employment contract ended that month, and O'Connor's and Blaustein's ended in June. P&G pushed for the deal because SpinBrush's sales so far exceeded plans that the company faced the prospect of a much bigger payout if it waited, Osher says. The founders settled on a final payment of $310 million. The total price of $475 million was about 2.3 times last fiscal year's sales, a price some analysts consider a steal.

But Osher and his partners had their own reason for getting out early—they wanted to hedge their bets.

They're uncertain whether SpinBrush will live up to its potential as it is further folded into P&G. Osher had an exit interview with Lafley in May in which the CEO vowed to keep SpinBrush on course. Osher has no doubt about Lafley's sincerity. It's just that he is still not sure an elephant can learn to dance.

By Robert Berner in Chicago

Source: "Why P&G's Smile Is So Bright," *BusinessWeek*, August 12, 2002, 58–60.

Case 6-18
Amazon.com Inc.

It was one of the web's typical flash frenzies, a gaggle of geeks seeking the new, new thing. At 2 a.m. on Aug. 24, a new venture called Elastic Compute Cloud quietly launched in test mode. Its service: cheap, raw computing power that could be tapped on demand over the Internet just like electricity. In less than five hours, hundreds of programmers, hoping to use the service to power their MySpace and Google wannabes, snapped up all the test slots. One desperate latecomer instant-messaged a $10,000 offer for a slot to a lucky winner, who declined to give it up. "It's really cool," enthuses entrepreneur Luke Matkins, who will run his soon-to-launch music site on the service. The creator of this *très* cool service: Amazon.com Inc.

Yes, Amazon founder and Chief Executive Jeffrey P. Bezos, the onetime Internet poster boy who quickly became a post-dot-com piñata, is back with yet another

new idea. Many people continue to wonder if the world's largest online store will ever fulfill its original promise to revolutionize retailing. But now Bezos is plotting another new direction for his 12-year-old company, which he will lay out on Nov. 8 at San Francisco's Web 2.0 Conference, the annual gathering of the digerati crème. Judging from an advance look he gave *BusinessWeek* on one recent gray day at Amazon's Seattle headquarters, it's so far from Amazon's retail core that you may well wonder if he has finally slipped off the deep end.

Bezos wants Amazon to run your business, at least the messy technical and logistical parts of it, using those same technologies and operations that power his $10 billion online store. In the process, Bezos aims to transform Amazon into a kind of 21st century digital utility (Exhibit 1). It's as if Wal-Mart Stores Inc. had decided to turn itself inside out, offering its industry-leading supply chain and logistics systems to any and all outsiders, even rival retailers. Except Amazon is starting to rent out just about everything it uses to

EXHIBIT 1 Out of the Jungle

OUT OF THE JUNGLE

Amazon has quietly launched a flurry of new businesses, many in the past years, that are seemingly unrelated to its core retail store. Here's a sampling:

COMPUTING	CROWDSOURCING	MEDIA
Amazon's Simple Storage Service and its Elastic Compute Cloud offer startups such as photo-sharing site SmugMug a way to store data and run their programs on Amazon's computers over the Internet.	Amazon Mechanical Turk is a marketplace for piecework. CastingWords pays "Turkers" to transcribe snippets of podcasts that it then assembles for clients. Amazon takes a 10% commission.	Launched in September, Amazon Unbox is software that lets customers download and play movies and TV shows. Amazon.com is also hosting a show with Bill Maher and buying a movie option on a book.
SEARCH	**DISTRIBUTION**	**WEB MEASUREMENT**
After watching Google quickly become a dominant force on the Web, Amazon launched its own search site, A9.com, in 2003. But it never caught on, and Amazon recently cut many of its novel features.	For years, Amazon has run e-commerce operations for the likes of Target and Borders. In September it launched a test of Fulfillment By Amazon. Smaller merchants plug their products into Amazon's distribution system.	Alexa Internet Services provides free Web traffic rankings and other paid services, such as detailed reports on specific sites for 15¢ per 1,000 requests. It is becoming a popular alternative to other measurement services.

run its own business, from rack space in its 10 million square feet of warehouses worldwide to spare computing capacity on its thousands of servers, data storage on its disk drives, and even some of the millions of lines of software code it has written to coordinate all that.

Another big idea from Jeff Bezos? Go ahead and groan. It's fine with him. Even after all these years spent battling back claims that his company would be "Amazon.toast," he's still bounding up and down stairs two at a time to exhort his band of nerds on to the Next Big Thing. And now, more than ever, he's determined to keep going for the big score, even if people think he's crazy. In fact, Bezos, 42, sounds downright eager to confound a new generation of skeptics. "We're very comfortable being misunderstood," he says, letting loose one of his famously thunderous laughs. "We've had lots of practice."

But if techies are wowed by Bezos' grand plan, it's not likely to win many converts on Wall Street. To many observers, it conjures up the ghost of Amazon past. During the dot-com boom, Bezos spent hundreds of millions of dollars to build distribution centers and computer systems in the promise that they eventually would pay off with outsize returns. That helped set the stage for the world's biggest Web retail operation, with expected sales of $10.5 billion this year.

What it didn't translate into was the consistent profit growth many investors had expected by now. Lately profits have fallen, dragged down by spending on new technology projects and on free-shipping offers that Amazon considers marketing in place of TV ads. Analysts expect full-year net income this year to come in at about $180 million, or half of last year's total. Most worrisome to investors is Amazon's three-year-plus binge on new technologies. So far this year its spending on technology and content, including hiring hundreds of engineers and programmers to produce all these new services and buy more servers to run them, is up 52%, to $485 million. As a result, operating margins, at 4.1% for the past four quarters, now come in at less than Wal-Mart's 5.9%. Even Barnes & Noble Inc., that doughty bricks-and-mortar book chain that many expected to get remaindered by the Web, has higher margins, at 5.4%. "I have yet to see how these investments are producing any profit," gripes Piper Jaffray & Co. analyst Safa Rashtchy. "They're probably more of a distraction than anything else."

All that has investors restless and many analysts throwing up their hands wondering if Bezos is merely flailing around for an alternative to his retail operation.

Eleven of 27 analysts who follow the company have underperform or sell ratings on the stock—a stunning vote of no confidence. That number of sell recommendations is matched among large companies only by Qwest Communications International Inc., according to investment consultant StarMine Corp. It's more than even the eight sell opinions on struggling Ford Motor Co.

Neither analysts nor investors think Amazon's business is in danger of collapse. It's just that they're slowly losing confidence in Bezos' promises. The company's 2007 price-to-earnings ratio of 54 is much higher than its peers', even than high-flying Google Inc. at 35. But Amazon's stock is down 20% since the start of the year. A 12% one-day jump on Oct. 24 reflected slightly better-than-expected third-quarter results, but also investor relief that Bezos plans to slow the growth of new tech spending (Exhibit 2).

What's more, at the same time Bezos is thinking big thoughts, Amazon's retail business faces new threats. Its 25% sales growth tracks a little above the pace of overall e-commerce expansion and nearly double its own pace way back in 2001. But other sites are fast becoming preferred first stops on the Web. Google, for one, has replaced retail sites such as Amazon as the place where many people start their shopping. And more personalized and social upstarts such as News Corp.'s MySpace and YouTube, which Google is buying, have become the prime places for many people to gather online—and eventually shop. It's a trend Amazon could have trouble catching up to. Says consultant Andreas Weigend, Amazon's chief scientist until 2004: "The world has shifted from e-business to me-business."

With all those problems, some might view Bezos' latest tech toys as an attempt to take their eye off the ball. But spend some time with Bezos, and it becomes clear there may well be a method to his madness. Amazon has spent 12 years and $2 billion perfecting many of the pieces behind its online store. By most accounts, those operations are now among the biggest and most reliable in the world. "All the kinds of things you need to build great Web-scale applications are already in the guts of Amazon," says Bezos. "The only difference is, we're now exposing the guts, making [them] available to others."

And, he hopes, making money. With its Simple Storage Service, or S3, Amazon charges 15¢ per gigabyte per month for businesses to store data and programs on Amazon's vast array of disk drives. It's also

EXHIBIT 2
Where's the Payoff?

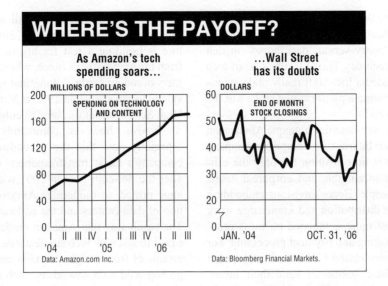

WHERE'S THE PAYOFF?

As Amazon's tech spending soars...
MILLIONS OF DOLLARS

SPENDING ON TECHNOLOGY AND CONTENT

200
160
120
80
40
0

I II III IV | I II III IV | I II III
'04   '05   '06

Data: Amazon.com Inc.

...Wall Street has its doubts
DOLLARS

END OF MONTH STOCK CLOSINGS

60
50
40
30
20
0

JAN. '04   OCT. 31, '06

Data: Bloomberg Financial Markets.

charging other merchants about 45¢ a square foot per month for real space in its warehouses. Through its Elastic Compute Cloud service, or EC2, it's renting out computing power, starting at 10¢ an hour for the equivalent of a basic server computer. And it has set up a semi-automated global marketplace for online piecework, such as transcribing snippets of podcasts, called Amazon Mechanical Turk. Amazon takes a 10% commission on those jobs.

Bezos is initially aiming these services at startups and other small companies with a little tech savvy. But it's clear that businesses of all kinds are the ultimate target market. Already, Amazon has attracted some high-powered customers. Microsoft Corp. is using the storage service to help speed software downloads, for instance, and the service is helping Linden Lab handle the crush of software downloads for its fast-growing Second Life online virtual world. Highly anticipated search upstart Powerset Inc. plans to use the Amazon computing service, even though it's still in test mode, to supplement its own computers when it launches in mid-November. And the search engine marketing firm Efficient Frontier uses Mechanical Turk to determine the most effective keywords that drive traffic to Web sites.

By all accounts, Amazon's new businesses bring in a minuscule amount of revenue. Although its direct cost of providing them appears relatively low because the hardware and software are in place, Stifel Nicolaus & Co. analyst Scott W. Devitt notes: "There's not going to be any economic return from any of these projects for the foreseeable future." Bezos himself admits as much. But with several years of heavy spending already, he's

making this a priority for the long haul. "We think it's going to be a very meaningful business for us one day," he says. "What we've historically seen is that the seeds we plant can take anywhere from three, five, seven years."

A Dark Horse in a High-Stakes Race

Sooner than that, those initiatives may provide a boost for Amazon's retail side. For one, they potentially make a profit center out of idle computing capacity needed for that retail operation. Like most computer networks, Amazon's uses as little as 10% of its capacity at any one time just to leave room for occasional spikes. It's the same story in the company's distribution centers. Keeping them humming at higher capacity means they operate more efficiently, besides giving customers a much broader selection of products. And the more stuff Amazon ships, both its own inventory or others', the better deals it can cut with shippers.

But there's much more at stake for Bezos than making a few extra bucks selling services that his online store is already providing for itself. This is nothing less than a bid to lead the next wave of the Internet. A dozen years in the making, the economy that has grown up with the Internet by most accounts remains in its infancy. And leadership of that burgeoning economy remains up for grabs.

Google and Microsoft, in particular, are each angling to be the Net's kingpins: Just as Microsoft ruled the PC world (and its profits) with Windows software, so Google and Microsoft want to build what techies call the "platform" for the Web—the powerful layer of basic services on top of which everyone else builds their Web sites. "Amazon's a pretty serious dark horse" in that race, says Internet visionary Tim O'Reilly, CEO of tech publisher O'Reilly Media Inc. "Jeff really understands that if he doesn't become a platform player, he's at the mercy of those who do."

Bezos believes he has identified a unique Amazonian edge: Like no other Internet or computer company today, the e-retailer is in a position to apply the efficiencies of the Net to tangible and corporeal assets like products and people. Bezos envisions embedding the tasks of product distribution and knowledge work right into the flow of more automated business processes such as order taking and payment processing. For instance, a new service called Fulfillment by Amazon lets small and midsize businesses send their inventory to Amazon warehouses. Then when a customer places an order, Amazon gets an automated signal to ship it out—no muss, no fuss, no servers or software or garages full of stuff. "Amazon's in the business of managing complexity," says Amazon director John Doerr of the venture firm Kleiner Perkins Caufield & Byers. "There's no other e-commerce player that does that."

Mundane as these business-focused services may sound, the implications for the economy at large are startling. Google, MySpace, and YouTube cracked open for the masses the means to produce media and the advertising that sustains it, creating tens of billions of dollars in market value and billions more in new revenues. Now, by sharing Amazon's infrastructure on the cheap, Bezos is taking that same idea into the realm of physical goods and human talent, potentially empowering a whole new swath of businesses beyond the Internet itself.

The upshot: While Wall Street yawns, Bezos' pioneering dot-com is actually starting to look almost hip again, at least to the all-important Web 2.0 geek gods who set the Net agenda today. More importantly, some venture capitalists have noticed, and they're encouraging their startups to consider using Amazon services to save money and get to market faster. "Amazon is becoming a very interesting company," says Crosslink Capital general partner Peter Rip. "They're taking their store in the sky and unbundling it."

In any case, this looks like Bezos' biggest bet since he and his wife, MacKenzie, drove west in 1994 to seek fame and fortune on the Net. Since then he has survived the dot-com boom and bust with his ambitions intact. Now with three sons, and a daughter recently

adopted from China, Bezos still has managed to find time to start a rocket company, Blue Origin. The venture is building a test facility in West Texas not far from his grandfather's ranch, where he once spent summers branding cattle. A longtime space nut, he made a valedictorian speech in 1982 at Miami Palmetto Senior High School about the need to colonize space.

Amazon, however, commands his full attention, especially now that the groundwork is laid for the company's latest transformation. He began not long after the dot-com bust in 2001 with—big surprise—a huge project to modernize Amazon's massive collection of data centers and the software running on them. The result was that Amazon made it much faster and easier to add new Web site features. Small, fast-moving groups of five to eight Amazon employees now could go hog wild with new ideas, such as customer discussion boards on each product page and software to play music and videos on the site. Since then these "two-pizza teams," which Bezos calls them because each team can be fed with two large pies, have become Amazon's prime innovation engines. "There's a huge value in this small, nimble team approach," says tech consultant and author John Hagel III. "But you can't do that without this kind of computer architecture."

Next came an epiphany: If the new computer setup allowed folks inside to be more creative and independent, why not open it up to outsiders, too? So in 2002, Amazon began offering outside software and Web site developers access to selected Amazon data such as pricing trends, gradually adding more and more until this year. Now it's basically getting free help from more than 200,000 outside Web developers, up 60% from a year ago. They're building new services on top of Amazon technology, further feeding back into Amazon's core retail business. One service, Scanbuy, lets people check Amazon prices on their cell phones to see if they're better than prices in a retail store.

Starting a few months ago, Amazon upped the ante. It began offering not just data but computing power, storage, and more, all intended to turn even more of its internal operations into salable services. One of the most interesting is Amazon Mechanical Turk. A couple of years ago, Amazon needed to make sure photos it took of thousands of businesses for the online Yellow Pages on its A9 search site actually matched the right business. Computers are bad at recognizing and sorting images, but people can do so very quickly. So Amazon set up a Web site where it could farm out the sorting to people for a penny or two per photo, clearly more for fun than for big pay. Last November, it launched the site, naming it after an 18th century chess-playing machine that actually had a real chess master hidden inside it.

New Spark Plugs for Startups

Since its debut, the service has attracted thousands of "Turkers" working for dozens of companies. They're doing jobs that Mechanical Turk Director Peter Cohen says "couldn't be done at all before," because there was no economical way to gather people for these tiny, often ephemeral tasks. Efficient Frontier has used the service to analyze tens of thousands of search keywords to see which best attract potential shoppers to particular Web sites. "There have not been any other services like Mechanical Turk that can do this so efficiently," says software engineer Zachary Mason.

Forget for a moment whether this will eventually turn us all into low-paid piece workers. The important thing is that the service is nurturing startups. Casting-Words co-founder Nathan McFarland uses Turkers—who he says are largely the "bored and nothing-on-TV" set who treat the tasks like crossword puzzles—not only to transcribe 10-minute podcast segments but also to assemble them into full transcriptions and to check the quality. Eighteen-year-old Eric Cranston, a onetime Turker living with his parents in Visalia, Calif., plans to use the service for a company he's starting that will retouch photos for Web sites. Essentially, Bezos sees the thousands of people from all over the world working inside Mechanical Turk's online marketplace as a big "human computer."

Amazon's other new services are getting even more serious attention. Last March, Amazon introduced its Simple Storage Service, which offers cheap space on its disk drives for any programmer or business to use to store data. Right away, Amazon approached an online photo-sharing startup called SmugMug Inc. Ironic choice: President and co-founder Chris MacAskill had fiercely battled Amazon in an earlier startup, an online bookstore called Fatbrain, later bought by BarnesandNoble.com. But his son Don, SmugMug's co-founder and CEO, says that when he heard how easily and cheaply SmugMug could back up its photos on S3, "my eyes got all big." Now, by zapping customers' photos to Amazon to store on its servers, he's avoiding the need to buy more storage devices of his own—and saving $500,000 a year. "Everything we can get Amazon to do, we will get Amazon to do,"

says Chris MacAskill. "You're going to see all kinds of startups get a much better and faster start" by using Amazon's services.

They already are. Consider Powerset, the secretive search startup backed by A-list angel investors, including PayPal Inc. co-founder Peter Thiel and veteran tech analyst Esther Dyson. Co-founder and CEO Barney Pell harbors ambitions of out-Googling Google with technology that he says would let people use more natural language than terse keywords to do their searches. By analyzing the underlying meaning of search queries and documents on the Web, Powerset aims to produce much more relevant results than the current search king's.

Problem is, Powerset's technology eats computing power like a child munches Halloween candy. The little 22-person company would have to spend more than $1 million on computer hardware, two-thirds of that just to handle occasional spikes in visitor traffic, plus a bunch of people to staff a massive data center and write software to run it. That's when Pell heard about Elastic Compute Cloud. He was sold. Based on tests so far, using the Amazon site for part of the company's computing power could cut its first-year capital costs alone by more than half.

Not least, Amazon is now opening its vast network of more than 20 distribution centers worldwide to all comers. For years it has handled distribution and even Web site operations for the likes of Target Stores Corp. and Borders Group. Recently it has started providing customized handling, packing, and customer service people for upscale retailers and manufacturers such as fashion boutique Bebe. And with Fulfillment By Amazon, it's opening all that up to small and midsize businesses.

With all these initiatives, Amazon empowers new startups, which are hungry to knock off Internet leaders that happen to be . . . Amazon competitors. Has Bezos thought about how he may be creating an army of allies to fight his rivals? His answer: "Absolutely!"

It's hard to dismiss another possibility, though: Amazon is biting off more than it can chew. Some of the new tech projects have come out with a thud. Compared with Google's, Amazon's A9.com search site never got traction, and its features were recently downsized. The new Amazon Unbox Video downloading service struck many early reviewers as clunky and slow.

Mostly, it's unclear whether Bezos can escape his and Amazon's linoleum-floor image. Amazon's mission to be the place where "customers can find and discover

EXHIBIT 3   Playbook: Best-Practice Ideas

SURFING THE AMAZON

Jeff Bezos keeps innovation flowing by following these rules:

MEASURE EVERYTHING.	KEEP PRODUCT DEVELOPMENT TEAMS SMALL.	DON'T BE AFRAID OF WEIRD IDEAS.	OPEN UP TO OUTSIDERS.	WATCH CUSTOMERS NOT COMPETITORS.
Decisions are easy when you measure things. Amazon wasn't sure if its TV ads paid off, so it ran a 16-month test in two cities. Result: Bezos nixed the ads and spent the money instead on free-shipping offers.	That forces you to break up projects into doable, measurable chunks. Now most of Amazon's new features and services come from employee teams that can fed on two large pizzas.	It breaks you out of either-or thinking. Publishers said Bezos was nuts to let customers post negative product reviews. Now the reviews, which presaged the social Web craze, are one of the most popular features.	They often will do your innovation for you. Starting in 2002, Amazon began letting outside programmers use its pricing and product data. They've created new services that feed back into Amazon's business.	Customer needs change more slowly, requiring less effort than chasing competitors. By constantly lowering prices, Amazon loses near-term revenue but believes customers will spend more later.

anything they might want to buy online" doesn't especially mesh with the goal to be the prime source of services needed to run an Internet Age business. By contrast, nearly all of Google's services are clearly aimed at building the dominant digital utility. Likewise, IBM is much better known as a provider not only of technology services but also of expertise in automating a wider range of business processes, from inventory management to sales tracking. Can Bezos manage a company that simultaneously sells the most routine stuff to consumers and the most demanding business services to entrepreneurs and corporations?

So it is that Jeff Bezos faces a managerial moment of truth. Having saved Amazon from oblivion years ago, he still must prove his latest big bet can help transform the company into something truly enduring. Not only does he make no apologies for such wagers, he revels in them. Every year in his annual letter to shareholders he resurrects his 1997 letter, which reads in part: "We will make bold rather than timid investment decisions where we see a sufficient probability of gaining market leadership advantages" (Exhibit 3).

Today, it's just the same. "We are willing to go down a bunch of dark passageways," he says, "and occasionally we find something that really works." As always, investing in Bezos and his company will require faith that there's light at the end of his newest tunnel—not just a money pit.

Source: Robert D. Hof, "Jeff Bezos' Risky Bet," *BusinessWeek*, November 13, 2006, 52–58.

Case 6-19

Nanophase Technologies Corporation

The 2001 business year was finished and **Nanophase Technologies Corporation,** the industry leader in commercializing nanotechnology, had just reported financial results to shareholders. It was a discouraging year for the Romeoville, Illinois company, with revenues declining to $4.04 million from $4.27 million in 2000. The year was disappointing in other respects as well. **Nanophase** reported a loss of $5.74 million for 2001, even though management had been optimistic about achieving operating profitability. Reflecting on the Statement of Operations shown in Appendix Table 1

and the Balance Sheet in Appendix Table 2, the company's President and CEO, stated:

> "2001 was disappointing in terms of revenue growth due to the economic recession, especially in the manufacturing sector that represents our primary customer and business development market, and the events in September, which lingered through the end

Nanophase Technologies Corporation was prepared by Dr. Lawrence M. Lamont, Professor Emeritus of Management, Washington and Lee University. Case material is prepared as a basis for class discussion and not designed to present illustrations of either effective or ineffective handling of administrative problems. Used by permission of the author.

The author gratefully acknowledges Nanophase Technologies Corporation for reviewing the accuracy of the case study and granting permission to reproduce certain materials used in the preparation. Copyright 2002.

of the year," stated Joseph Cross, President and CEO. "However we believe that the company had several outstanding accomplishments that provide a solid basis for future revenue growth." (Nanophase Technologies Corporation, Press Release, February 20, 2002)

Later, Cross expanded on the operating results and future prospects when Nanophase hosted a quarterly conference call for investors which was broadcast over the Internet and posted on the company Web site (www.nanophase.com). In the transcript of his prepared remarks, Cross said:

> "Entering 2002, we believe that the company is stronger and better positioned than at any time in its history. We have established the vital delivery capabilities to succeed with our enlarged platform of nanoengineering technologies and delivery capability investments, our market attack is broader and at the same time better focused, the infrastructure - people and equipment are ready to deliver, our processes have been proven demonstrably scalable and robust, and we have strengthened the company's supply chain." (Nanophase Technologies Corporation, Fourth Quarter Conference Call, February 21, 2002)

While Cross was encouraged about the future, there were reasons to be cautious. After all, the company had been in business since 1989 and had not yet earned a profit. Questions arose about 2002, because the U.S. economy was only beginning to emerge from a significant manufacturing recession. Nanophase management remembered that in 2001, after its largest customer had expanded and extended its supply agreement, a weak economy had caused the customer to delay receipt of shipments of zinc oxide powder during the year to adjust inventory. Given the short notice provided by the

customer, Cross had indicated that the company would not be able to find additional business to fill the revenue shortfall. Later in 2001, a UK company, Celox, Ltd., failed to fulfill a purchase contract for a catalytic fuel additive which resulted in a substantial loss of revenues and a nonrecurring inventory adjustment. In late November, Nanophase announced a temporary hourly manufacturing furlough until January 7, 2002 to enable the company to reduce existing inventory and lower its cost of operations during the holiday period (Nanophase Technologies Corporation, Press Releases: October 25 and November 14, 2001 and February 20, 2002).

Transition times from start-up to commercialization exceeding ten years were not unusual for companies developing emerging technologies. Typically new high technology firms struggled with product development, experienced set-backs in bringing products to market and were slow to earn profits. Nanophase experienced some of these problems, but the company had managed to achieve a solid record of revenue growth since introducing it's first commercial products in 1997. Exhibit 1 summarizes the revenues, profit (loss) and cost of revenues for the 1993–2001 time period.

Nanophase records revenue when products are shipped, when milestones are met regarding development arrangements or when the company licenses its technology and transfers proprietary information. Cost of revenue generally includes costs associated with commercial production, customer development arrangements, the transfer of technology and licensing fees. It does not include all of the costs incurred by the company. Gross margin, a useful indicator of a businesses move toward profitability, can be calculated as revenue minus cost of revenue divided by revenue.

EXHIBIT 1   **Revenue, Costs and Profit (Loss), 1993–2001**

Source: SEC form 10-K, 1997 and 2002.

Year	Revenues	Net Profit (Loss)	Cost of Revenues
2001	$4,039,469	$(5,740,243)	$4,890,697
2000	4,273,353	(4,518,327)	4,754,485
1999	1,424,847	(5,117,067)	2,610,667
1998	1,303,789	(5,633,880)	3,221,996
1997	3,723,492	(3,072,470)	3,935,766
1996	595,806	(5,557,688)	4,019,484
1995	121,586	(1,959,874)	532,124
1994	95,159	(1,287,772)	167,746
1993	25,625	(729,669)	61,978

What Is Nanotechnology?

Nanotechnology is the science and technology of materials at the nanometer scale—the world of atoms and molecules. It is a multi-disciplinary science drawing on chemistry, biology, engineering materials, mathematics and physics. Scientists use nanotechnology to create materials, devices and systems that have unusual properties and functions because of the small scale of their structures. Nanophase uses the technology in its patented manufacturing processes to produce nanocrystalline materials, like microfine zinc oxide powder, sold as a component material to producers of industrial and consumer products, such as cosmetics. See Appendix Table 3 for additional description.

Over the next 20–30 years, it is expected that nanotechnology will find applications in chemicals and engineering materials, optical networking, memory chips for electronic devices, thin film molecular structures and biotechnology. Experts predict that the technology could spawn a new industrial revolution. According to Mihail Roco, senior advisor for nanotechnology at the National Science Foundation's Directorate for Engineering: "This is a technology that promises to change the way we live, the way we combat disease, the way we manufacture products, and even the way we explore the universe. Simply put, nanoscale manufacturing allows us to work with the fundamental building blocks of matter, at the atomic and molecular levels. This enables the creation of systems that are so small that we could only dream about their application years ago." "Because of nanotechnology, we'll see more changes in the next 30 years than we saw in all of the last century." (Roco, 2001)

Because nanotechnology promises to impact so many different industries, the National Nanotechnology Initiative has received the financial support of the United States government. The annual letter sent by the Office of Science and Technology Policy and the Office of Management and Budget to all agencies put nanotechnology at the top of R&D priorities for fiscal year 2001. The expenditures have reflected the priority, and in fiscal 2001 actual federal expenditures for nanotechnology were $463.85 million. In 2002, Congress enacted a fiscal year nanotechnology appropriation of $604.4 million. The 2003 budget request was set at $710.2 million, another substantial increase reflecting the continuing interest and commitment to the commercial potential of the technology. (www.nano.gov)

History of Nanophase Technologies Corporation

Nanophase Technologies Corporation traces its beginnings to the mid-1980's and the research of Richard Siegel, who developed the "physical-vapor synthesis" (PVS) method for producing nanocrystalline materials at the Argonne National Laboratory, southwest of Chicago. Siegel, an internationally known scientist, co-founded the company in 1989 after receiving funding from the Argonne National Laboratory-University of Chicago Development Corporation. The mission of Nanophase was to produce nanostructured materials by developing and applying the PVS process. For several years, the company was located in Burr Ridge, Illinois. In 2000, Nanophase expanded its manufacturing capabilities and moved its headquarters to a facility in Romeoville, Illinois. The original Burr Ridge manufacturing facility was also retained and is currently the main source of PVS production. The Romeoville addition enables the company to increase its manufacturing operations and expand its customer application technology to meet future demand. (Stebbins, 2000; www.nanotechinvesting.com; Nanophase Technologies Corporation, 2000 Annual Report)

Developing the Technology

From its beginning as a 1989 start-up, Nanophase emphasized the development of technology, the pursuit of patents and the design of manufacturing processes to transition the company from R&D to a commercial enterprise. Through 1995, the majority of the company's revenues resulted from government research contracts. From this research, the company developed an operating capacity to produce significant quantities of nanocrystalline materials for commercial use. At the same time, Nanophase was involved with potential customers to facilitate the development of products that would utilize the capabilities of the PVS process. During 1996, Nanophase began emerging from product development and in 1997, the first complete year of commercial operations, the company significantly increased its revenues from sales to businesses.

Protecting Intellectual Property

Nanophase was also successful in protecting its technology, equipment and processes with patents. Early in 2002, the company had 38 U.S. and foreign patents, patent applications, or licenses covering core technologies and manufacturing processes. (Nanophase

Technologies Corporation, Fourth Quarter Conference Call, February 21, 2002) Intellectual property such as patents and trade secrets are valuable because they protect many of the scientific and technological aspects of the company's business and result in a competitive advantage.

Reducing Manufacturing Costs

Nanophase placed importance on research and technology development to reduce manufacturing costs. Although the company de-emphasized the pursuit of revenue from government research contracts in 1995, research was funded by the company to improve manufacturing processes for commercial production. For example, in 2001, Nanophase made expenditures to improve PVS manufacturing technology in product quality and output quantity. Nanophase was successful in reducing variable manufacturing cost by 40 to 65% (including a 25% reduction in manufacturing staff) and increased reactor output by 100 to 200% depending on the material. The company was also successful in commercializing a new, lower-cost manufacturing process, trademarked NanoArc Synthesis (TM). The new process promises to further cut some production costs by an estimated 50 to 90%, increase production output rates by estimated factors of 2 to 10 times, and permit the use of less expensive raw materials. The process also will allow Nanophase to increase the variety of nanocrystalline products available for sale and address the needs of potential customers who need nanoparticles in liquid solutions and dispersions. (Nanophase Technologies Corporation, Press Release, February 20, 2002; Fourth Quarter Conference Call, February 21, 2002)

Financing Operations

To date, Nanophase has financed operations from a private offering of approximately $19,558,069 of equity securities and an initial public offering in 1997 of 4,000,000 common shares at $8.00 a share to raise $28,837,936 for continued development of the company. (SEC form 10-K405, 1997) In 2000, Nanophase entered into an agreement with BASF (its largest customer) to borrow $1.3 million to finance the purchase and installation of new equipment to meet the customer's requirements during 2001–2002. (Nanophase Technologies Corporation, Press Release, December 8, 2000)

Nanophase will need additional financing to complete another year of operations. At the end of 2001,

the balance sheet indicated that about $7.4 million was available from cash and investments. Nanophase has reported cumulative losses of $34,754,188 from inception through December 31, 2001. (Nanophase Technologies Corporation, 2001 Annual Report)

Transition and Changes in Management

To speed the transition to a commercial venture, executives with experience in developing hightechnology businesses were hired. According to critics, Nanophase had too many development projects under way and did not have enough products and customers to generate a dependable revenue stream. As a result, the company lost its focus and progress fell behind expectations.

Joseph E. Cross came to Nanophase in November 1998 as a Director and President and Chief Operating Officer. In December 1998, Cross was promoted to CEO and he continues to serve in that capacity. Cross brings a background of directing high-technology start-ups and managing rapid growth and turnaround operations. His biography is in Appendix Table 4.

According to Cross, Nanophase was focused more on pure research than on finding practical applications for nanoengineered materials and making money. Cross stated: "We had a bunch of scientists but didn't have any engineers or a sales distribution or manufacturing system." (Stebbins, 2001) Since his appointment, Cross and his management team have been concentrating on six major areas:

1. Emphasizing new business development to expand revenues.

2. Achieving a positive gross margin on products.

3. Increasing the technology and intellectual property base by developing new manufacturing processes and establishing patents and trademarks.

4. Reducing manufacturing costs by using less expensive raw materials, increasing output rates and yields and reducing supply chain costs.

5. Increasing manufacturing skills and the capability to produce products to address current and new market opportunities.

6. And, strategically positioning the company for economic recovery.

Following his appointment to CEO, Cross moved quickly to expand and strengthen the management team in the

EXHIBIT 2   **Profile of Executive Officers**

Company Officer	Title	Joined	Previous Experience
Joseph Cross	Pres. and CEO	1998	Senior Management
Daniel Billicki	VP Sales and Mkt.	1999	Senior Management
Dr. Richard Brotzman	VP R&D	1994	Research Director
Dr. Donald Freed	VP Bus. Development	1995	Senior Marketing
Jess Jankowski	VP and Controller	1995	Controller
Dr. Gina Kritchevsky	Chief Technology Officer	1999	Business Development
Robert Haines	VP Operations	2000	Manufacturing

areas of marketing, manufacturing, technology and engineering. Exhibit 2 shows the executive officers of the company, including their title, year of appointment and previous business experience. At the end of 2001, Nanophase had approximately 51 full-time employees.

Nanophase also attracted an impressive outside Board of Directors to provide management and technical advice to the Company. In addition to Cross, the Board included Donald Perkins, retired Chairman of the Board of Jewel Companies, a Chicago retail supermarket and drug chain; James A. Henderson, former Chairman and CEO of Cummins Engine Company; Richard Siegel, co-founder and internationally known scientist; Jerry Pearlman, retired Chairman of Zenith Electronics Corporation and James McClung, a Senior Vice President and a corporate officer for FMC Corporation. Donald Perkins currently serves as Chairman of the Nanophase Board of Directors. (www.nanophase.com)

The Science of Nanotechnology at Nanophase

Nanotechnology is used to produce nanocrystalline particles in powder form using metallic materials such as aluminum, cerium, copper, iron and zinc. The extremely small size of the particles, combined with the properties of surface atoms gives nanoparticles unusual chemical, mechanical, electrical and optical properties that often exceed those of the original raw materials.

Different technologies are used to achieve these results, but two of the most important are Physical Vapor Synthesis (PVS) and Discrete Particle Encapsulation (DPE). Exhibit 3 illustrates the PVS process patented and used by Nanophase.

The PVS process uses a solid metallic wire or rod which is heated in a reactor to high temperatures (about 3000 F) using jets of thermal energy. The metal atoms boil off, creating a vapor. A reactive gas is introduced to cool the vapor, which condenses into liquid molecular clusters. As the cooling process continues, the molecular clusters are frozen into solid nanoparticles. The metal atoms in the molecular clusters mix with reactive gas (e.g., oxygen atoms), forming metal oxides such as zinc and aluminum oxide. The nanocrystalline particles are near-atomic size. For example, about nine hundred million zinc oxide crystals could be spread across the head of a pin in a single layer. (Nanophase Technologies Corporation, 2000 Annual Report)

Because of the PVS process, Nanophase is able to produce nanoparticles with properties that are highly

EXHIBIT 3   **Nanophase Patented PVS Process**

Source: www.nanophase.com

Thermal Energy Is Applied → **Reactive Gas Is Added** → **Vapor and Gas Are Cooled**

Solid Metal ⟹ **Vapor Is Formed** ⟹ **Molecular Clusters Are Formed** → **Nanoparticles Are Formed**

desirable to customers. These product features include spherical, nonporous particles of uniform size and large surface area, particles virtually free of chemical residues and particles that flow freely without clustering together. The company is also able to use the PVS process and NanoArc Synthesis (TM) to custom-size the particles for a customer's application.

In some applications, the nanoparticles created by the PVS process require additional surface engineering to meet customer requirements. Nanophase has developed a variety of surface treatment technologies to stabilize, alter or enhance the performance of nanocrystalline particles. At the core of these surface treatment technologies is the patented Discrete Particle Encapsulation (DPE) process. DPE uses selected chemicals to form a thin durable coating around nanoparticles produced by the PVS process to provide a specific characteristic such as preventing the particles from sticking together or enabling them to be dispersed in a fluid or polymer to meet specific customer needs. (SEC form 10-K405, 1997)

Product Markets and Customer Applications

Substantial commercial interest has developed in nanotechnology because of its broad application. Although most companies refuse to disclose their work with the technology, it is likely that materials science, biotechnology and electronics will see much of the initial market development. Nanotechnology has already attracted the interest of large companies like IBM (using the technology to develop magnetic sensors for hard disk heads); Hewlett-Packard (using the technology to develop more powerful semiconductors); 3M (producing nanostructured thin film technologies); Mobil Oil (synthesizing nanostructured catalysts for chemical plants) and Merck (producing nanoparticle medicines). In other applications, Toyota has fabricated nanoparticle reinforced polymeric materials for cars in Japan and Samsung Electronics is working on a flat panel display with carbon nanotubes in Korea. (Roco, 2001)

Nanophase is not active in all of the areas. Instead, the company focuses selectively on products and market opportunities in materials science that can be developed within 12–18 months. Longer range product applications in the 18–36 month time frame were also of interest, but they were pursued mainly to give the company a pipeline of new, future opportunities. Nanophase evaluated markets by using criteria such as

revenue potential, time-to-market and whether or not a product developed for one application could be successfully modified for sale in other markets.

Dr. Donald Freed, Vice President of business development, explained the company's strategy for commercializing nanotechnology: "Opportunities for nano-materials will mature at different rates, and there are substantial opportunities in the near term—those with a not too demanding level of technical complexity. There are truly different problems in nanotechnology, such as those falling into the realm of human genetics or biotechnology. So we are successfully pursuing a staged approach to developing products for our customers." Freed further explained that this staged approach to developing customer applications enables the company to build product-related revenues while also expanding its foundations for developing more complicated applications. Nanophase was established in six product markets and was developing one potential market that met its time-to-market criteria of 12 to 18 months. (Nanophase Technologies Corporation, Press Release, October 31, 2000; Nanophase Technologies Corporation, 2000 Annual Report; Analyst Presentation, 2000)

Healthcare and Personal Products

The largest product market for Nanophase was zinc-oxide powder used as an inorganic ingredient in sunscreens, cosmetics and other health care products produced by the BASF cosmetic chemicals group. In early 2001, BASF signed an exclusive long-term purchase contract in which Nanophase agreed to supply a product that met technical and FDA regulatory requirements for active cosmetic ingredients. When added to a sunscreen the specially designed particles are small enough to allow harmless light to pass through the sunscreen while the ultraviolet light bounces off the particles and never makes it to the skin. Zinc-oxide formulations also eliminate the white-nose appearance on the user's skin without a loss of effectiveness. BASF Corporation is a diversified $30 billion global corporation and the third largest producer of chemicals and related products in the United States, Mexico and Canada. Sales to this company accounted for 75.5 percent of Nanophase revenues in 2001. (SEC form 10-Q, May 15, 2002)

In another healthcare application, Schering-Plough Corporation uses Nanophase zinc oxide as an ingredient in Dr. Scholl's foot spray to act as a fungicide and prevent the nozzle from clogging. (Stebbins, 2000) The unique properties of nanoparticles has also enabled their use in antifungal ointments and as odor and wetness absorbents. Both customers continue to explore opportunities for Nanophase products in other areas. The company estimated the market potential for its products in the healthcare and cosmetics market at approximately $45 million. (Nanophase Technologies Corporation, Press Release, October 31, 2000; Nanophase Technologies Corporation, 2000 Annual Report; SEC form 10-K, 2000; Stebbins, 2000)

Environmental and Chemical Catalysts

Nanophase was beginning to sell cerium dioxide to a manufacturing company that supplied one of the three largest automobile companies in the U.S. with catalytic converters for installation on a new car model. The product replaced expensive palladium, which was used in the converters to reduce exhaust emissions. Because a pound of nano-size particles has a surface area of 5.5 acres, less active material was needed to produce comparable emission results saving the customer money and space. Catalysts promised to be a rapidly growing market for Nanophase. Opportunities in industry for new types of nanoparticles to catalyze chemical and petroleum processes and for other environmental applications offered the potential to generate $30–$60 million in revenues. (Nanophase Technologies Corporation, Press Release, October 31, 2000; Nanophase Technologies Corporation, 2000 Annual Report)

Ceramics and Thermal Spray Applications

Nanoparticles were sold for the fabrication of structural ceramic parts and components used in corrosive and thermal environments. The properties of the company's materials enabled the rapid fabrication of ceramic parts with improved hardness, strength and inertness. Fabrication costs were lower because nanoparticles reduced the need for high temperatures and pressures and costly machining during the manufacturing process. Nanophase worked with parts fabricators to design and develop ceramic parts and components using its technologies and materials. (SEC form 10-K405, 1997)

Nanophase products were also used in thermal spray materials to repair worn or eroded metal parts on naval vessels and replace conventional ceramic coatings where properties such as abrasion and corrosion resistance and tensile strength were needed for longer service life. For example, the U.S. Navy uses thermal

sprays incorporating aluminum and titanium oxides to recondition worn steering mechanisms in ships and submarines. With less wear and barnacle growth on the bow planes used to steer, the Navy expects to save $100 million a year when the program is fully implemented. Nanophase sells its products to U.S. Navy approved contractors who formulate the spray with nanoparticles and then apply it to critical parts. In addition to the Navy, Nanophase has several development programs with industrial companies involving similar applications. According to Dr. Donald Freed, Vice President of Business Development, "Our materials are being evaluated in such diverse applications as improving wear resistance in the plastics molding industry and in protective coatings for industrial equipment, gas turbine and aircraft engines." The company estimates the potential market for these and similar applications to be in the range of $25 million. (Nanophase Technologies Corporation, Press Release, October 31, 2000)

Transparent Functional Coatings

Nanophase has translated the technology used to make transparent sunscreens into ingredients for coatings designed to improve the scratch resistance of high gloss floor coatings, vinyl flooring and counter tops. Apparently, nanoparticles fit so tightly together that they make vinyl flooring up to five times more scratch resistant than existing products. Additionally, Nanophase is pursuing a number of opportunities for abrasion resistant coatings. Eventually the products may end up in automobile and appliance finishes, eyeglass lense coatings, fabrics and medical products. According to management, the opportunity in transparent functional coatings is estimated at $50–$60 million. (Nanophase Technologies Corporation, Press Release, October 31, 2000; Nanophase Technologies Corporation, 2000 Annual Report)

Conductive and Anti-static Coatings

Nanophase produces indium/tin oxide and antimony/tin oxide formulations for use as conductive and antistatic coatings for electronic products. The nanoparticle coatings are stored and used at room temperatures, which is an economic advantage to manufacturers. Indium/tin oxide is used primarily as a conductive coating to shield computer monitors and television screens from electromagnetic radiation. The world market for indium/tin oxide conductive coatings is estimated at $10–$20 million.

Antimony/tin oxide materials are used for transparent anti-static coatings in electronic component packaging. Nanophase replaced coatings based on carbon black and/or evaporated metals. The key advantage of nanoparticles in this market is that the transparent coatings maintained anti-static protection while enabling end-users to see the contents inside a package. (Nanophase Technologies Corporation, 2000 Annual Report)

Ultrafine Polishing

The newest application for Nanophase was the use of nanoparticles to create ultra smooth, high quality polished surfaces on optical components. The company provided NanoTek (R) metal oxides engineered specifically for polishing semiconductors, memory disks, glass photo masks and optical lenses. The application was made possible because of the 2001 technology advances in the core PVS process, commercialization of the new NanoArc Synthesis (TM) process, and the improved technology for preparation of stable dispersions of nanocrystalline metal oxides. Nanophase received orders of $100,000 and $200,000 for the materials in early 2002 and expected the application to quickly grow to annual revenues of approximately $500,000. (Nanophase Technologies Corporation, Press Release, February 21, 2002)

Nanofibers—A Developing Market

In a developing market called Nanofibers, engineered nanoparticles that could be incorporated directly into fibers for better wear properties and ultraviolet resistance were being developed. It was expected that the customer solution would result in a more stain and wear-resistant fiber with a high level of permanence. The products were being co-developed with leading companies producing nylon, polyester and polypropylene fibers for industrial carpets and textiles. Nanophase estimated that the applications could be commercialized in about 18 months with a potential market opportunity of several million dollars. (Nanophase Technologies Corporation, Fourth Quarter Conference Call, February 21, 2002)

Business Model and Marketing Strategy

Business Model

For most of its revenues, the Nanophase business model used direct marketing to customers. Teams worked collaboratively with prospective customers to identify an unsatisfied need and apply the company's proprietary technology and products to solve a problem. In most cases, the nanocrystalline materials were custom engineered to the customer's application. International and some domestic sales were made through trained agents and distributors that served selected markets. Nanophase was also engaged in on-going research, technology licensing and strategic alliances to expand revenues. The markets served were those where the technology and nanocrystalline materials promised to add the most value by improving the functional performance of a customer's product or the economic efficiency of a process.

Marketing Strategy

The marketing strategy used a business development team to work on nanotechnology applications with new customers. Business development activities included evaluation and qualification of potential markets, identification of the lead customers in each market and the development of a strategy to successfully penetrate the market. Nanophase then formed a technical/marketing team to provide an engineered solution to meet the customer's needs. Since one-third of the company staff had a masters or doctorate in materials-related fields, including chemistry, engineering, physics, ceramics and metallurgy, Nanophase had the expertise to understand the customer's problem, determine the functions needed and apply nanocrystalline technology. The team formed a partnership with the customer to create a solution that delivered exceptional value. After a satisfactory solution was achieved, application engineering and customer management staff were moved to a sales team organized along market lines. The sales team was expected to increase revenue by selling product and process solutions and broadening the customer base in the target market. Customers and applications were carefully selected so the science and materials would represent a technology breakthrough thus enabling the customer to add substantial value to its business, while at the same time making Nanophase a profitable long-term supplier. (Nanophase Technologies Corporation, 2001 Annual Report)

Although Nanophase focused its strategy in the markets previously mentioned, applications existed in related markets where the performance of products could be improved using similar technologies without extensive re-engineering. Based on market research, these included applications in fibers, footwear and apparel, plastics and polymers, paper, pigments and other specialty markets. The company strategy in these instances was to pursue only those applications which fit its primary business strategy and were strongly supported by a significant prospective customer.

Nanophase permitted prospective customers to experiment with small research samples of nanoparticles. About eight different products, branded Nano-Tek (R), were available for sale in quantities ranging from 25 grams to 1 kilogram. The samples included Aluminum Oxide, Antimony/ Tin Oxide, Cerium Oxide, Copper Oxide, Indium/ Tin Oxide, Iron Oxide, Yttrium Oxide and Zinc Oxide. They were sold by customer inquiry and on the Nanophase web site in different particle sizes and physical properties. Prices for research materials ranged from $0.80 to $10.00 per gram depending on the product and the quantity desired. (www.nanophase.com)

Customer inquiries were initiated by a variety of methods including the Nanophase web page, trade journal advertising, telephone inquiries, attendance and participation at trade shows, presentations and published papers, sponsorship of symposia and technical conferences and customer referrals. Management and staff followed-up on inquiries from prospective customers to determine their needs and qualify the customer and application as appropriate for a nanotechnology solution. Cross described the process as developing a collaborative relationship with the customer. "Our particular sort of chemistry enables people to do things they can't do any other way. To make that happen, you have to have a close relationship with a customer. You have to make it work in their process or their product. So it is indeed providing a solution; not just the powder that we make, which is nanocrystalline in nature. Its formulating the powder to work in a given application." (CNBC Dow Jones Business Video, 1999)

Using management and staff to build collaborative relationships with customers was time consuming and expensive. Exhibit 4 provides the annual selling, general and administrative expenses for the years 1993–2001. While not all of the expenses can be attributed to personal selling, the expenditures are indicative of the substantial growth of the expense category as Nanophase built the business development and marketing capability to commercialize its business. Management expected that these expenses would decrease or stabilize as the markets for the company's products developed.

EXHIBIT 4 Selling, General and Administrative Expense, 1993–2001

Source: www.nanophase.com; Nanophase 2001 Annual Report; SEC form 10-K405, 1997.

Year	Expenditures
2001	$3,798,543
2000	3,388,758
1999	3,641,736
1998	3,594,946
1997	2,074,728
1996	1,661,504
1995	1,150,853
1994	799,558
1993	556,616

In a few instances, Nanophase leveraged its resources through partnerships with organizations and individuals focused on market-specific or geographic-specific areas. For example, licensees and agents were used to increase manufacturing, engineering and sales representation. The agents were specialized by geographic region and the types of products they were permitted to sell. Ian Roberts, Director of U.S. and International Sales stated: "The use of experienced sales agents in selected markets is a fast and cost effective way to multiply the Nanophase sales strategy. The agents bring years of industry experience and contacts to the task of introducing nanoparticles to potential customers. We intend to form close partnerships with selected agents for specific products to speed product introduction and horizontal applications." (Nanophase Technologies Corporation, Press Release, November 27, 2000)

In November 2000, Nanophase appointed Wise Technical Marketing, specialists in the coatings industry, to represent the line of NanoEngineered Products (TM) in the Midwest and the Gillen Company LLC to promote the NanoTek (R) metal oxides in Pennsylvania and surrounding areas. Nanophase also announced the appointment of Macro Materials Inc., specialists in thermal spray materials and technology, as its global, nonexclusive agent for marketing and sales of the company's line of NanoClad (TM) metal oxides for thermal spray ceramic coatings.

Nanophase retained international representation in Asia through associations with C.I. Kasei Ltd. and Kemco International of Japan. C.I. Kasei was the second largest customer, accounting for 9.4 percent of

Nanophase revenues in 2001. Kasei was licensed to manufacture and distribute the Company's NanoTek (R) nanocrystalline products, while Kemco represented conductive coatings. Nanophase was also working with customers in Europe and intended to expand its European presence as part of its future marketing strategy. (Nanophase Technologies Corporation, Press Release, November 27, 2000; Nanophase Technologies Corporation, 2000 Annual Report; SEC form 10-Q, May 15, 2002)

Competition

Competition in nanomaterials is not well-defined because the technology is new and several potential competitors are start-up businesses. However, the situation is temporary and eventually Nanophase could face competition from large chemical companies, new start-ups and other industry participants. Five types of industry participation seem to exist.

First, there were several large chemical companies located in the United States, Europe and Asia already involved in manufacturing and marketing of silica, carbon black and iron oxide nanoparticles sold as commodities to large volume users. The companies have a global presence and include prestigious names such as Bayer AG, Cabot Corporation, Dupont, DeGusa Corporation, Showa Denka and Sumitoma Corporation. All of these companies are larger and more diversified than Nanophase and pose a significant threat because they have substantially greater financial and technical resources, larger research and development staffs and greater manufacturing and marketing capabilities.

Second, there are OEMs making nanoparticles for use in their proprietary processes and products. For example,

Eastman Kodak makes nanoparticles for use in photographic film. Similarly, the technology attracted the interest of other large OEM's like IBM, Intel, Lucent Technologies, Hitachi, Mitsubishi, Samsung, NEC, Thermo Electron, Micron Technology, Dow Chemical, Philips Electronics and Hewlett-Packard. They are pursuing applications that involve optical switching, biotechnology, petroleum and chemical processing, computing and microelectronics. These companies are potential competitors in the sense that they could sell nanoparticles not needed in their own operations to outside customers, putting them into competition with Nanophase.

Third, is the group of start-up companies shown in Exhibit 5 that will compete directly with Nanophase. These competitors, funded by venture capital or other private sources, are located in the United States, Canada, Europe and the Middle East. Most were founded in the 1990's after nanotechnology began to gain attention. For example, Oxonica Ltd., Nanopowder Enterprises Inc. and TAL Materials are spin-off firms out of university and government research laboratories. They were founded by scientists and engineers attempting to commercialize a nanotechnology developed while they were employed in a research organization. Richard Laine, a scientist at the University of Michigan, was a driving force behind the founding of TAL Materials. TAL was incorporated to commercialize the nanotechnologies developed in the Science and Engineering Department at the University. (Spurgeon, 2001) Most of the firms listed in Exhibit 5 have not yet reached commercial production. Nanophase is presently the only firm capable of producing substantial quantities of nanoparticles to rigid quality standards. The company is acknowledged by industry peers as the world leader in the commercialization of nanomaterials.

EXHIBIT 5 **Summary of Potential Nanophase Competitors**

Source: Company Internet Web sites.

Company	Location	Year Founded	Public/Private
Lightyear Technologies Inc.	Vancouver	1996	Private
Argonide Corporation	Florida	1994	Private
TAL Materials Inc.	Michigan	1996	Private
Altair Nanotechnologies Inc.	Wyoming	1999	Private
Nanomat	Ireland	1995	Private
Oxonica Ltd.	England	1999	Private
Nanopowders Industries	Israel	1997	Private
Nanopowder Enterprises, Inc.	New Jersey	1997	Private
Nanosource Technologies, Inc.	Oklahoma	Unknown	Private

Fourth, there are firms that hold process patents or supply commercial equipment to nanotechnology firms, but also have the capability to produce nanomaterials in small quantities using an alternative manufacturing process. These companies, while not competitors at present, could enter the nanocrystalline materials market and compete with Nanophase in the future. Plasma Quench Technologies is an example. This company, which holds a process patent, recently spun out two small development companies, NanoBlok and Idaho Titanium Technologies, to produce titanium powders using the company's patented plasma quench manufacturing process.

Finally, Altair Nanotechnologies is an emerging competitor that has a natural resource position in titanium mineral deposits. Altair is developing the technology to produce nanoparticles such as titanium dioxide in commercial quantities. The company is completing a manufacturing plant and offering its products for sale on an Internet Web site. (www.altairtechnologies.com)

Recent Developments

As the U.S. economy dramatically slowed during 2001, companies around the world delayed the receipt of shipments and rescheduled purchase orders for future delivery. Nanophase was impacted by the slowdown, but the company continued to aggressively pursue applications of nanoparticles with selected customers in each of its product markets. Fortunately, the interest level in nanotechnology remained and some customers continued to move forward on the business development projects already initiated. Despite some setbacks, the results of Nanophase's R&D and intensified business development activities slowly began to show results.

April 24, 2002

On April 24, Joseph Cross, President and Chief Executive Officer, offered some observations about the position of the company:

> Cross said that the company entered 2002 with a wider array of improved technology applications tools than it entered 2001 with, and has significantly increased momentum in business development in several markets. "The improvement in our core PVS Technology, commercialization of our new NanoArc Synthesis (TM) process technology, and multiple application developments during the last half of 2001 and this far into 2002,

provide an integrated platform of nanotechnologies that should allow the company to engineer solutions across more markets," explained Cross. (Nanophase Technologies Corporation, Press Release, April 24, 2002)

May 29, 2002

Nanophase completed a private placement of 1.37 million newly issued shares of common stock for a gross equity investment of $6.85 million. Nanophase plans to use the net proceeds to fund the continued development and capacity expansion of its NanoArc Synthesis (TM) process technology, expand marketing and business development activities, increase process capability and capacity in the PVS process and for general corporate purposes. (Nanophase Technologies Corporation, Press Release, May 29, 2002)

June 26, 2002

Nanophase announced a strategic alliance with Rodel, Inc., a part of the Rohm and Haas Electronic Materials Group. Rodel is a global leader in polishing technology for semiconductors, silicon wafers and electronic storage materials. The company will combine its patented technology with Nanophase's new nanoparticle technology to develop and market new polishing products for the semiconductor industry. The alliance is a five-year partnership and supply agreement with appreciable revenues targeted for 2003 and a planned ramp in volume through 2005 and beyond. Nanophase believes that the revenue opportunities approach the size of the Company's personal care and sunscreen markets. Rodel, headquartered in Phoenix, Arizona, has operations throughout the United States, Asia and Europe. (Nanophase Technologies Corporation, Press Releases, June 26 and June 28, 2002)

July 24, 2002

Nanophase announced financial results for the first two quarters of 2002. Revenues were $3.07 million compared with first half 2001 revenues of $2.12 million for a revenue growth of 45% year-over-year. Gross margin for the first half of 2002 averaged a positive 12% of revenues versus the annual 2001 average of a negative 21%. The company reported a net loss for the first half of 2002 of $2.72 million, or $0.20 per share, compared with a net loss for the first half of 2001 of $2.38 million, or $0.18 per share. Appendix Table 5 shows the comparative results for the first two quarters of operations.

Commenting on the balance of 2002, President Cross noted:

> While we are somewhat concerned with general market conditions and the normal market slowness that we expect during the summer, we remain cautiously positive about 2002. Based on information from current and prospective customers, we currently believe additional orders will be received during July through September toward our annual revenue target. Although orders are always subject to cancellation or change, and these estimates are based on various product mix, pricing, and other normal assumptions, we are maintaining our 2002 revenue target of $7.00 million or an anticipated revenue growth of approximately 75% compared to 2001. (Nanophase Technologies Corporation, Press Release, July 24, 2002)

Synopsis

The 2001 business year had proven to be difficult for Nanophase. The economic recession in the manufacturing sector of the economy had impacted the company's primary customer base; the manufacturing firms using nanomaterials in their processes and products. While interest continued to remain strong in the potential of nanotechnology, it was still difficult to stimulate interest among prospective customers who were also facing economic challenges and declining business activity. Finally, as the third quarter of 2002 rolled in, a slowly improving economic environment was on the horizon. Maybe 2002 and the years that followed would be the breakout years management was planning for.

APPENDIX TABLE 1   Statements of Operations (Years ended December 31)

Source: Nanophase Technologies Corporation, 2001 Annual Report.

	2000	2001
Revenue		
Product revenue	$ 3,824,159	$ 3,650,914
Other revenue	449,194	388,555
Total revenue	4,273,353	4,039,469
Operating Expense		
Cost of revenue	4,754,485	4,890,697
R&D expense	1,837,036	1,601,671
Selling, general and administrative expense	3,388,758	3,798,543
Total operating expense	9,980,279	10,290,911
Loss from operations	(5,706,926)	(6,251,442)
Interest income	1,188,599	511,199
Loss before provision for income taxes	(4,518,327)	(5,740,243)
Provision for income taxes	—	—
Net loss	$(4,518,327)	$(5,740,243)
Net loss per share	$ (0.34)	$ (0.42)
Common shares outstanding	13,390,741	13,667,062

APPENDIX TABLE 2   Balance Sheets (Years ended December 31)

Source: Nanophase Technologies Corporation, 2001 Annual Report.

	2000	2001
Assets		
Current Assets:		
Cash and cash equivalents	$ 473,036	$ 582,579
Investments	16,831,721	6,842,956
Accounts receivable	1,238,334	1,112,952
Other receivables, net	144,818	67,449
Inventories, net	892,674	956,268
Prepaid expenses and other current assets	770,200	381,696
Total current assets	20,350,783	9,943,900
Equipment and leasehold improvements, net	3,266,245	8,914,745
Other assets, net	213,135	325,743
Total Assets	$23,830,163	$19,184,388
Liabilities and Stockholders Equity		
Current Liabilities		
Current portion of long-term debts	$ 285,316	$ 714,135
Current portion of capital lease obligations		48,352
Accounts Payable	824,338	1,233,466
Accrued Expenses	884,780	732,427
Total Current Liabilities	1,994,434	2,728,380
Long-term debt	827,984	758,490
Long-term portion of capital lease obligations		53,900
Stockholders' equity		
Preferred stock, $.01 par value; 24,088 authorized and none issued	—	—
Common stock, $.01 par value; 25,000,000 shares authorized and 13,593,914 shares issued and outstanding at December 31, 2000; 12,764,058 shares issued and outstanding at December 31, 1999	135,939	137,059
Additional paid-in capital	49,885,751	50,260,747
Accumulated deficit	(29,013,945)	(34,754,188)
Total stockholders' equity	21,007,745	15,643,618
Total liabilities and stockholders' equity	$23,830,163	$19,184,388

APPENDIX TABLE 3   Nanocrystalline Materials (Nanoparticles)

Source: SEC from 10-K. 2001.

Nanocrystalline materials generally are made of particles that are less than 100 nanometers (billionths of a meter) in diameter. They contain only 1,000s or 10,000s of atoms, rather than the millions or billions of atoms found in larger size particles. The properties of nanocrystalline materials depend upon the composition, size, shape, structure, and surface of the individual particles. Nanophase's methods for engineering and manufacturing nanocrystalline materials results in particles with a controlled size and shape, and surface characteristics that behave differently from conventionally produced larger-sized materials.

APPENDIX TABLE 4   Biographical Profile of Joseph E. Cross, Chief Executive Officer

Source: The Wall Street Transcript, January 22, 2001.

Joseph E. Cross is CEO of Nanophase Technologies Corporation. Mr. Cross has been a Director since November 1998 when he joined Nanophase as President and Chief Operating Officer. He was promoted to Chief Executive Officer in December 1998. From 1993–1998, Mr. Cross served as President and CEO of APTECH, Inc, an original equipment manufacturer of metering and control devices for the utility industry and as President of Aegis Technologies, an interactive telecommunications company. He holds a BS in Chemistry and attended the MBA program at Southwest Missouri University. He brings a background of successfully directing several high-technology start-ups, rapid growth and turnaround operations.

APPENDIX TABLE 5 Statements of Operations (Six months ended June 30)

Source: Nanophase Technologies Corporation, Press Release, July 24, 2002.

	June 30, 2001	June 30, 2002
Revenue		
Product revenue	$ 1,937,489	$ 2,829,773
Other revenue	183,815	239,755
Total revenue	2,121,304	3,069,528
Operating Expense		
Cost of revenue	1,857,122	2,696,720
R&D expense	800,189	1,003,726
Selling, general and administrative, expense	2,226,949	2,091,319
Total operating expense	4,884,260	5,791,765
Loss from operations	(2,762,956)	(2,722,237)
Interest Income	416,616	61,177
Interest Expense	(17,664)	(56,282)
Other, net	(12,000)	(50)
Loss before provision for income taxes	(2,376,004)	(2,717,392)
Provision for income taxes	(30,000)	(30,000)
Net loss	(2,406,004)	(2,747,392)
Net loss per share	$ (0.18)	$ (0.20)
Common shares outstanding	13,628,562	13,980,694

References

Nanophase Technologies Corporation—Press Releases

Nanophase Announces Second Quarter and First Half 2002 Results, July 24, 2002. PRNewswire.

Nanophase Technologies Provides Additional Information at Annual Shareholder Meeting, June 28, 2002. PRNewswire.

Rodel Partners with Nanophase Technologies to Develop and Market Nanoparticles in CMP Slurries for Semiconductor Applications, June 26, 2002. PRNewswire.

Nanophase Technologies Completes Private Equity Financing, May 29, 2002. PRNewswire.

Nanophase Technologies Announces First Quarter 2002 Results, April 24, 2002. PRNewswire.

Nanophase Receives Order for Ultrafine Optical Polishing Application, February 21, 2002. PRNewswire.

Nanophase Technologies Announces Fourth Quarter and 2001 Results, February 20, 2002. PRNewswire.

Nanophase Announces Temporary Hourly Manufacturing Furlough, November 14, 2001. PRNewswire.

Nanophase Technologies Announces Third Quarter 2001 Results, October 25, 2001. PRNewswire.

Nanophase Technologies Announces Capital Investment, December 8, 2000. PRNewswire.

Nanophase Technologies Increases Sales Representation, November 27, 2000. PRNewswire.

Experts From Nanophase Elaborate on New Technology Opportunities, October 31, 2000. PRNewswire.

Online Magazine and Newspaper Articles

Spurgeon, Brad, "Nanotechnology Firms Start Small in Building Big Future," January 29, 2001. *International Herald Tribune.* www.iht.com.

CEO Interview with Joseph E. Cross, January 22, 2001. Reprinted from The Wall Street Transcript. Roco, Mihail C. "A Frontier for Engineering," January, 2001. www.memagazine.org. Stebbins, John, "Nanophase Expects to Turn Tiniest Particles into Bigger Profits," November 5, 2000. www.bloomberg.com

Transcripts of On-line Conference Calls, Analyst Presentations and Personal Interviews

An Interview with Joseph Cross, President and CEO of Nanophase Technologies Corporation, January 2002. www.nanophase.com.

Fourth Quarter Conference Call, February 21, 2002. www.nanophase.com Analyst Presentation, 2000. www.nanophase.com.

CNBC/Dow Jones Business Video, February 9, 1999.

SEC Documents

SEC form 10-K, 2002.
SEC form 10-Q, May 15, 2002.
SEC form 10-K, 2001.
SEC form 10-K, 2000.
SEC form 10-K405, 1997.

Annual Reports

Nanophase Technologies Corporation, 2001 Annual Report.
Nanophase Technologies Corporation, 2000 Annual Report.

Web Sites

www.altairtechnologies.com

www.argonide.com
www.ltyr.com
www.nano.gov
www.nanomat.com
www.nanophase.com
www.nanopowders.com
www.nanopowderenterprises.com
www.nanosourcetech.com
www.nanotechinvesting.com
www.oxonica.com
www.plasmachem.de
www.talmaterials.com

Case 6-20
Cola Wars in China

IVEY

Richard Ivey School of Business
The University of Western Ontario

On July 7, 2002, Zong Qinghou, the general manager of the Wahaha Group (Wahaha), China's largest soft drink producer, was reviewing market data on Wahaha's Future Cola brand in his office in Hangzhou, Zhejiang Province. Wahaha Future Cola had been launched four years earlier to compete with products from Coca Cola and PepsiCo, the dominant players in the category. At the launch, Zong and his management team had been tremendously energized by the opportunity to compete with some of the world's best companies. Four years later, despite the failure of several other domestic colas, Wahaha Future Cola and other Future Series carbonated drinks had achieved an impressive 18 percent of the carbonated drinks market in the first half of 2002. However, as Future Cola's share grew, Zong was preoccupied with how his multinational competitors would respond, how Wahaha should prepare for these responses, and how it should continue to increase its market share. Competition for share in the high-stakes market of the world's most populated country was intensifying.

Wahaha Group

Company Profile

With 2001 sales revenue of RMB6.23 billion, and profits of RMB914 million,[1] the Wahaha Hangzhou Group Co. Ltd. consisted of more than 40 wholly-owned

[1] An exchange rate of US$1 = RMB8.27 applied in 2002.

subsidiaries and majority holding companies in 23 provinces, autonomous regions and cities. With total assets of RMB6 billion and 14,000 employees, the group operated more than 68 advanced automated production lines at various locations. Unlike many other Chinese companies of its size, the group had a solid cash position and no long-term bank debt. Wahaha's 2002 target was to achieve sales revenues of RMB8 billion, and a profit of RMB1.3 billion. In the longer term, the Wahaha Group aimed to become a truly national, and even international, player. Specifically, it was working on establishing subsidiaries in most provinces,

Nancy Dai prepared this case under the supervision of Professor Niraj Dawar solely to provide material for class discussion. The authors do not intend to illustrate either effective or ineffective handling of a managerial situation. The authors may have disguised certain names and other identifying information to protect confidentiality.

maintaining its leading position in water, milk drinks and mixed congee, and on increasing its market share in carbonated beverages, tea and juice drinks.

In 2002, Wahaha competed in six major product categories: milk drinks, packaged water, carbonated drinks, tea and juice drinks, canned food and healthcare products. For several years, its milk drink, packaged water and canned mixed congee had been leaders in their respective categories. For the first half of 2002, the total soft drink output for Wahaha was 1.83 million tons (1.66 billion litres), while its closest competitors—Coca Cola and PepsiCo—sold 1.61 million tons (1.461 billion litres) and 0.76 million tons (0.689 billion litres), respectively. This was the first time that a domestic company's soft drink output had exceeded that of Coca Cola in China. It was also an unusual situation for Coca Cola that a local competitor had seemingly come out of nowhere to upstage the global giant. In a nation of 1.3 billion people, per capita consumption of Wahaha beverages in China was more than 10 bottles a year.

Wahaha's Development

Wahaha was founded in 1987, when it began selling bottled soda water, ice cream and stationery to the children in Hangzhou, Zhejiang Province. Founder Zong Qinghou and two employees discovered in 1988 that although there were 38 companies nationwide producing nutritional drinks, none was specifically targeted toward children. The one-child policy had created a whole generation of "little emperors" who, due to their parents' and grandparents' indulgences, were fastidious with food, and presented a potentially huge opportunity. By some estimates there were 200 million such children in China. The company developed a nutritious drink called the Wahaha Natrient Beverage for Children and aggressively pursued the children's market. (The brand Wahaha means "to make children happy.") The product was supported with the slogan "Drinking Wahaha boosts appetite." The product was an instant success, propelling corporate revenues to RMB400 million and profits to RMB70 million by 1990.

Management quickly realized that it was not easy to sustain growth with a single product that had low entry barriers and low technical content. Competitors followed close on the heels of Wahaha. Between 1992 and 1994, 3,000 companies entered the market for children's beverages. Zong decided to expand the product range, entering the fruit-flavored milk drinks market. At the time, a couple of companies had already launched fruit-flavored milk drinks, and the product had won market acceptance. Zong felt this was the best time to enter. In what was to become a pattern in several product categories, Wahaha was a fast follower that quickly ramped up production and achieved high retail coverage with its nationwide production facilities, well-known brand, and well-established distribution network. Its wide range of products made it competitive relative to other domestic producers who tended to have a narrow product line. By the end of 1991, Wahaha launched its fruit-flavored milk drink, followed quickly by Wahaha Milk enriched with vitamins A and D, and calcium. Its catchy advertising jingles rolled off the tongues of tots in many provinces. In 1996, amidst concerns over polluted tap water in several provinces, the company launched Wahaha purified water, which rapidly achieved leading market share, contributing to corporate sales revenues of over RMB1 billion in that year.

Wahaha's brand extensions had aroused much debate among industry observers who held that Wahaha was mainly a children's brand and extending it to categories such as mixed congee and purified water would either not work, or would dilute the brand. Zong, while admitting the advantages of launching different brands for different product categories, held that it would spread the limited financial resources of most Chinese enterprises too thin. Wahaha's logic had been to continue to extend the brand into food and beverage categories in which there was no dominant player. For consumers, the connotation of the Wahaha brand broadened and came to represent health, wholesomeness, happiness, quality and reliability, and not just a brand for children's nutritious drinks. Results from the market rewarded and justified Wahaha's approach. After a series of brand extensions, Wahaha's sales revenue exceeded RMB2 billion in 1997, and the revenue of Wahaha purified water and mixed congee exceeded RMB500 million and 100 million, respectively. This was a rare achievement, even in China's rapidly growing food and beverage industry. In 1998, spurred by its success in other beverage categories, Wahaha decided to tackle the prize: the carbonated drinks market. Industry observers were skeptical and predicted that it would last no more than a few months on the market.

Corporate growth was powered not just by the launch of new products, but also through acquisitions, such as loss-making companies that were several times larger, but poorly managed. Acquisitions supported geographic expansion and allowed Wahaha to produce locally in various provincial markets, as well as to increase its market share and brand awareness in other provinces. By 2002, over a third of Wahaha's output was produced outside its home province.

Wahaha's Joint Ventures with Danone

In 1996, despite Wahaha's excellent performance, management realized that it needed to scale its operations quickly and obtain world-class production technology if it was to survive competition from both local and multinational competitors. After careful consideration, it chose to partner with the giant French food company, Groupe Danone. The two companies established several production-oriented joint ventures. While Danone eventually held a 51 percent share of the joint ventures, Wahaha retained control of management and marketing. In 2002, among Wahaha Group's 42 companies and RMB3.5 billion registered capital, Danone's investment was 32 percent. With the injection of capital from Danone, Wahaha launched Wahaha Future Cola and introduced advanced production lines for bottling water, milk and tea. Prior to the joint venture, the annual increase in revenues and profits was about RMB100 million and RMB10 million, respectively. Since 1996, both revenue and profit had grown even more rapidly (see Exhibit 1).

Zong Qinghou's Management Style

Founder and general manager Zong Qinghou was a charismatic leader who liked to "put his eggs in the baskets he knew best." Like most of his generation of the Cultural Revolution, he spent 15 years in the countryside after finishing junior school. This experience taught him a lot about rural China. When he came back to his hometown, Hangzhou, he worked in a factory, first as a worker and then in sales. During this period, he traveled extensively throughout China, deepening his knowledge of markets and consumers in various regions. He was 42 when he began his career as sales manager of the two person sales team at the factory. His job included delivering goods to retailers on his cycle.

When asked what made Wahaha so successful, Zong responded that the company understood the Chinese market well:

Market research reports in China are not reliable. You pay the market research firms large amounts of money and you don't know where the money was spent. However, our own marketing people are our market research staff since we are always collecting information about the market, and we make decisions based on their understanding of the market.

Now in his late 50s, Zong worked long hours and still traveled more than 200 days every year "to keep a finger on the pulse of the market." He hosted most of the marketing meetings at Wahaha and participated in every product launch and marketing planning activity.

Wahaha's Marketing

Marketing, research and development (R&D) and logistics management were centralized at headquarters, while the subsidiaries were engaged in production. Wahaha's marketing was clearly homegrown.

Wahaha's Advertising

A typical new product launch followed a pattern established early on in Wahaha's history. In an early launch of Wahaha Natrient Beverage, Zong signed advertising deals worth several hundred thousand RMB with local television stations, exceeding even the company's cash reserves at the time. In its advertisement, Wahaha highlighted data from reports about children's malnutrition and endorsements from experts about Wahaha Natrient Beverage's nutritional benefits for children. On the strength of the advertising, Wahaha would convince the local government-controlled distribution companies to carry the product. If distributors hesitated, Wahaha's marketing staff would call every retailer and smaller distributor in the local yellow pages to inquire if they carried Wahaha Natrient Beverage. This created a buzz that usually resulted in the product being listed with the distribution companies.

In 2001, Wahaha was among the top 10 advertisers in China's US$11.2 billion advertising market, and the only beverage company in the group.[2] Wahaha's total advertising expenditures amounted to more than

[2]"China Market racks up largest ad spending in Asia-Pacific," www1.chinadaily.com.cn/bw/2002-03-05/60571.html, March 12, 2002.

EXHIBIT 1 Wahaha Group Sales Revenue and Profit 1996 to 2001 (in RMB million)

Source: Company files.

	1996	1997	1998	1999	2000	2001
Sales revenue	1,110	2,110	2,870	4,510	5,440	6,230
Profit	155	334	501	875	906	914
Profit margin	14%	16%	17%	19%	17%	15%

RMB500 million, with media buys accounting for 80 percent. Comparatively, Coca Cola's 2001 media expense in China (including cinema, TV, radio, print, and outdoor) was US$19 million. Wahaha's television advertising was mainly intended to build brand awareness and recognition, while print advertising elaborated on product benefits and promotions. Wahaha spent 75 percent of its marketing budget on television advertising, and half of that was on CCTV Channel 1 (the national news channel). The remainder was spent on print media (5 percent), promotion (10 percent) and outdoor advertising (10 percent). Wahaha's advertising targeted the mass market, and not just the wealthier urban consumers. The prices of its products were usually lower than those of comparable products from its multinational competitors.

In addition to Wahaha's advertising, its sponsorship activities had helped build positive associations for its brand. Wahaha established Wahaha elementary school, Wahaha Children's Palace (a recreation center for children), Wahaha Children's Art Troupe and Wahaha Summer Camps to underscore its involvement in child development. In 2001, Wahaha held a campaign to celebrate Children's Day and Beijing's application to host the 2008 Summer Olympic Games.

Wahaha was also the first among Chinese companies to use celebrity product endorsement for its products. In 1996, Jinggangshan, a pop singer, was signed to endorse Wahaha purified water. Celebrity endorsement was also used for Wahaha Future Cola and Wahaha Tea series.

Wahaha's Distribution

Key success factors for Wahaha were the unique relationships developed with distributors over the previous 10 years. In a vast country where logistics are notoriously difficult, Wahaha's network was able to quickly deliver its products, reaching even remote corners of China within days. Unlike many multinational and domestic companies which preferred to establish their own distribution networks, Wahaha focused on partnering with local distributors, and its initial promotional efforts on entry into a region included distributors rather than end-consumers alone.

Partnerships with local distributors were not without problems. In particular, accounts receivable and bad debts were a perennial headache and the main reason why multinationals shunned this mode of distribution. In 1994, Wahaha concluded that the problem of accounts receivable was serious enough to jeopardize its growth and success. The company tackled the issue head-on by developing a radical new policy that ensured compliance and on-time payment by introducing incentives for channel members to play for long-term gain: distributors were required to pay an annual security deposit in advance and operate according to Wahaha's payment policy. In return, Wahaha would pay a higher-than-bank interest rate on the security deposit and offered discounts for early payment. At the end of the year, bonuses were awarded to distributors making prompt payments. The policy was replicated down the chain as distributors, in turn, developed secondary wholesalers, some of whom enjoyed preferential policies by paying security deposits to the distributors. It took Wahaha two years to implement the policy. In the process, a number of distributors that had low credibility dropped out of the system. Those that remained were more committed than ever to Wahaha.

Wahaha established offices in more than 30 provinces with sales staff coordinating operations with the distributors. Distributors were in charge of carrying inventory, providing funds and delivering to the retailers, and Wahaha's local offices supported them in retail coverage, inventory management, advertising and promotion. Wahaha established coordination teams to monitor prices in different areas to protect the interests of local distributors. Wahaha's staff collected information from the market and provided feedback to headquarters, which enabled the company to adjust its sales strategy and develop new products. Today, Wahaha's 2,000 sales staff work closely with more than 1,000 influential distributors that have the credibility and infrastructure to sell large volumes. Loyalty and stability of the distributors are key, and bad debts have decreased substantially. In 2002, Wahaha began implementing an information system that would enable distributors and Wahaha to exchange information in real time.

The World Soft-Drink Industry

The term "soft drinks" refers to beverages that do not contain alcohol, and includes packaged water, carbonated drinks, juices and juice drinks, ready-to-drink tea, as well as sports and energy drinks.

In 2000, global soft drink consumption reached 320.2 billion litres. That total was split into 170 billion litres (53 percent) of carbonated drinks, 77 billion litres (24 percent) of packaged water, and the "other" category which included juices, ready-to-drink tea, sports and energy drinks, and miscellaneous drinks accounting for 73.2 billion litres (23 percent). Worldwide, the growth of

EXHIBIT 2
World Soft Drink
Average Annual
Growth Rate
1994 to 2003

Source: Canadean Ltd.

Category	1994–2000	2001–2003
Carbonated drinks	4%	2%
Packaged water	8%	6%
Other*	5.70%	5.30%
Juice and nectars	4.10%	4.20%
Non-carbonated drinks	4.90%	6.30%
Iced tea	11.70%	5.80%
Sports and energy drinks	6.40%	5.90%

'Other' category includes juice and nectars, still drinks, iced tea, sports and energy drinks.

GLOBAL SOFT DRINK CATEGORY DEVELOPMENT
(billions of litres)

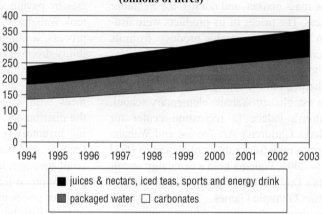

carbonated drinks had been slowing in recent years from an average annual rate of four percent between 1994 and 2000 to a predicted rate of only two percent in 2003 (see Exhibit 2). These numbers masked fast growth in countries such as China and India, which compensated for declines in the more mature markets of North America and Europe. Packaged water was growing worldwide, in some markets due to consumer trends toward a healthier lifestyle, and in others due to the poor quality of tap water. The "other" category had great growth potential due to increased demand for more healthy, nutritious and tasty drinks. The size of this category had rapidly grown from 52.7 billion litres in 1994 to 73.2 billion litres in 2000. By 2003 volumes were forecast to reach 85.6 billion litres. Within this category, "ready-to-drink tea" had had the fastest growth since 1994, with an annual increase of over 11 percent and industry observers believed it still had plenty of untapped potential.

The Players in China

The leading soft drink producers in the world included Coca Cola, PepsiCo, Nestlé and Danone, and all four were also present in China. Globally, the first two were dominant in the carbonated category with more than 70 percent combined market share, while the latter two were strong in the ready-to-drink tea and water categories.

Coca Cola

Coca Cola was the world's largest soft-drink company, and the fifth-largest food and beverage company. Its 2001 revenues were US$20.092 billion, with a net income of US$3.969 billion. The firm sold about 300 drink brands, including coffees, juices, sports drinks and teas in 200 nations. Its major brands included Coca Cola Classic, Diet Coke, Sprite, Fanta (carbonated drinks), Minute Maid (juice), POWERade (sports drink) and Dasani (water). It distributed Danone's Evian water in North America and Danone's spring water brands in the United States. Beverage Partner Worldwide, its joint venture with Nestlé, S.A., marketed ready-to-drink coffee and tea. More than 60 per cent of its sales revenues came from outside the United States. Coca Cola's stated aim was to become an all-around beverage company. In 2001, water was the second largest contributor to its growth after carbonated drinks. Coca Cola had recently instituted a "think local, act local, but leverage global" mandate to empower local decision-makers, in recognition of the need to both respond to local preferences and react to local competitors. In response, its local subsidiaries had launched a wide variety of drinks aimed at local needs.

Coca Cola first opened bottling plants in Shanghai and Tianjin in 1927, which were shut after the communist revolution in 1949. In 1979, when Coca Cola reentered China, following the re-establishment of relations between China and the United States, it became the first American consumer product to return to China. In 2000, it moved its marketing headquarters for China from Hong Kong to Shanghai. By 2002, Coca Cola had a total of 28 bottling plants in China, with a total investment of US$1.1 billion. In most of these joint ventures, Coca Cola didn't have majority shareholding. Its soft-drink output in China was 16 per cent of the national total in 2001 and its carbonated drink output was about 35 per cent of total carbonated drink output. China was the sixth largest market for the company worldwide. In addition to its global carbonated drink brands such as Coca Cola, Diet Coke, Fanta and Sprite, the company also developed local brands such as Heaven and Earth (non-carbonated fruit juice, tea, water), Jinmeile (tea), Smart (fruit-flavored carbonated drink), Lanfeng (honey green tea) and Qoo (juice drink). In 2001, it launched its water brand "Sensation" (at the remarkably low wholesale price point of RMB0.50, while the market leader Wahaha water was selling at RMB0.90). In its advertising, the company included Chinese cultural icons such as windmills and dragons. Local film and sports stars were engaged as endorsers, including diver Fu Mingxia, the three-time Olympic gold medalist. It also sponsored the Coca Cola Cup National Youth Soccer Tournament and the China national soccer teams at all levels. Coca Cola also extended its sponsorship contracts with the International Olympic Committee up to 2008, which included US$1 billion in funding for the Beijing Games. In 2001, the total revenue for Coca Cola China was about US$189 million and revenue from carbonated drinks was about US$186 million. However, the annual per capita consumption of Coca Cola products in China was a meager eight servings (about 0.2268 litre per serving). Consumption was still a far cry from the average 415 servings consumed in the United States, 163 in Japan, 98 in Europe and 68 in South Korea.

PepsiCo

After the merger with Quaker in 2001, PepsiCo became the fourth-largest food and beverage company in the world. Its 2001 total sales revenue of US$26.935 billion included beverage revenue and profit of US$10.44 billion and US$1.678 billion, respectively. Forty-two per cent of its sales were outside the United States. Its powerful soft drink brands included Pepsi-Cola, Diet Pepsi, Mountain Dew, 7Up, Miranda, Gatorade (sports drink), Tropicana (juice), Lipton teas and Aquafina (water).

In 1981, PepsiCo signed a deal with the Chinese government to establish a joint-venture bottling plant in Shenzhen. By 2002, the company had invested a total of US$500 million in China on 14 bottling plants and employed close to 10,000 people. Unlike Coca Cola, PepsiCo sought a majority share in the joint ventures. Its flagship carbonated drink brands in China were Pepsi-Cola, Pepsi Light, Pepsi Twist, 7Up, Miranda and Mountain Dew. It also owned local brands such as Asia, Arctic and Tianfu. Its non-carbonated drink brands in China included Gatorade and Dole (fruit juice). Its non-beverage brands included Lay's potato chips, Doritos and Cheetos. Its soft-drink output in China was about eight per cent of the national total in 2001. According to A.C. Nielsen's market data in Asia, Pepsi-Cola was the most popular soft drink brand for young consumers, a reflection of its positioning for that demographic market. In its advertising in China, PepsiCo used popular entertainers such as Faye Wang, Guo Fuchen and Chen Huiling as endorsers. Despite its marketing efforts and popularity among China's youth, PepsiCo China had not been profitable during its 20 years in China: high marketing costs and conflicts with joint venture partners were holding the company back.[3]

Nestlé S.A.

With revenues of CHF84.698 billion[4] (approximately US$56 billion) and profit of CHF6.681 billion (approx. US$4 billion) in 2001, Nestlé was the world's largest food and beverage company. Its major products included coffee, water, dairy products, breakfast cereals, culinary products, ice cream, frozen food, chocolate and confectionary, and pet care. Its major water brands included Nestlé Pure Life, Nestlé Aquarel, Perrier and Vittel. Other beverage brands included Nestea,

---

[3]Yan Shi, "Pepsi's Business Model Encountering Trust Crisis in China," *Economic Observation,* April 24, 2002.

[4]1 U.S. dollar (US$) = 1.35 Swiss Francs (CHF).

Nesquik, Nescau, Milo, Carnation, Libby's and Caro. In 2001, Nestlé was the world leader in bottled water with a market share of 16.3 per cent. Nestlé owned four of the top six water brands in the world.

Nestlé came to China in 1979. By 2002 it had established 14 fully owned enterprises, 19 joint ventures and one R&D center for a total investment of US$72 million. Its 2001 sales in China amounted to US$570 million. Due to the growth of packaged water and its profitability, Nestlé China aimed to be the market leader in this category. It established plants for producing packaged water in Tianjin and Shanghai and was expanding its own sales network to co-operate with distributors.

Groupe Danone

The French company ranked sixth in the global food and beverage industry. In 2001, it had revenues of € 14.470 billion (approximately US$14 billion), with net income of € 132 million (approximately US$127.7 million). It operated in three core businesses: fresh dairy products, beverages and cereal biscuits and snacks. Its major brands included Danone and Dannon for fresh dairy products, Evian, Volvic and Aqua for mineral water, and LU for biscuits. Its leading position worldwide was based on a portfolio of major international brands and a solid presence in local markets (about 70 percent of global sales came from brands that were local market leaders in which Danone had shares). As part of a recent push toward globalization, the company had made about 40 acquisitions in Asia, Latin America, Central Europe, Africa and the Middle East.

Danone's major products in China included biscuits, water, yogurt and milk. Most of these products were sold under the Danone brand. In 1987, the company had begun operations in China by establishing the Guangzhou Danone Yogurt Company. This was followed in 1992 by the Shanghai Danone Biscuit Company. Since then, it had acquired a number of companies: in 1996 it purchased 63.2 per cent of Haomen Beer, 54.2 per cent of Wuhan Donghu Beer and its stake in the five joint ventures with Wahaha. In 1998 it owned 54.2 per cent of Shenzhen Danone Yili Beverages Co. Ltd., and in 2000 it purchased 92 per cent of Robust Group, one of the top 10 Chinese soft-drink producers. In December 2000, it had acquired a five per cent stake in Shanghai Bright Dairy, one of the top milk producers in China. It also purchased 50 per cent of Meilin-Zhengguanghe Water Company and 10 percent of Zhengguanghe Online Shopping Company.

China's Soft-Drink Industry

With the entry of multinationals into the Chinese market in the 1980s, marketing, advanced production technology and cutting-edge management expertise were injected into China's soft-drink industry, spurring its development. Over the past 20 years, the industry had grown at an annual rate of over 21 per cent, and annual output had increased from 0.288 million tons (261 million litres) in 1980 to 16.69 million tons (15.141 billion litres) in 2001 (see Exhibit 3). Per capita consumption increased from 0.3 litre per annum in 1982 to eight litres per annum in 2001, 27 times that of 1982. Total revenues exceeded RMB40 billion in 2000. In urban areas, soft drinks were no longer seen as an occasional luxury to be consumed only in restaurants and hotels, but a regularly consumed product. Drink package formats diversified to meet new consumption patterns, and now included cans, polyethylene terephtalate (PET) and paper packs.

China's soft-drink industry had sped through three major development stages in a short time: the rise of carbonated drinks in the 1980s, packaged water in the

EXHIBIT 3 China's Soft Drink Output

Source: The beverage industry.

Year	Soft Drinks output (in millions of tons)	Carbonated Drinks output (in millions of tons)	Carbonated Drinks as a percentage of total Soft Drinks
1994	6.29	3.14	50%
1995	9.82	5.21	53%
1996	8.84	4.29	49%
1997	10.69	4.92	46%
1998	12.00	5.40	45%
1999	11.86	4.27	36%
2000	14.91	4.62	31%
2001	16.69	4.57	27%

1990s and tea in the 2000s. In 2001, packaged water accounted for 40.6 per cent of total sales, carbonated drinks for 27 per cent and the "other" category for 32.4 per cent. The fastest growing product was bottled tea because of its low-calorie, low-fat and low-sugar content, and convenience. It had a share of about 12 per cent and an annual growth of 85 per cent. It was predicted that juice and milk drinks would become the catalyst for growth in the next phase of development. Despite rapid growth, China's national per capita consumption was still only 20 per cent of the world average and 33 per cent of the United States average. Growth potential for all categories remained high. It was predicted that over the next 10 to 15 years, industry output would grow at an annual rate of about 10 per cent, reaching 22.65 million tons (20.548 billion litres) in 2005, and 37 million tons (33.566 billion litres) by 2015. With China's entry into World Trade Organization (WTO) in 2001, China's soft-drink industry was expected to develop even more rapidly and competition was already intensifying as restrictions on foreign investment were lifted.

A number of large companies and brands were present on the national stage, yet the industry remained fragmented in comparison to developed markets. In 2001, the combined output of the top 10 domestic soft-drink producers in China (see Exhibit 4) accounted for 40 per cent of the national total.[5] With Coca Cola China and PepsiCo China, the total output of the top players represented 63 per cent of national output. In the 2000s, several of the top 10 companies were undergoing major changes: Jianlibao, a large domestic player, was in crisis; Danone invested in Wahaha, Robust and

[5]Data from China Soft Drink Industry Association.

Meilin-Zhengguanghe; Xuri Group, the largest tea producer, failed in its competition with two iced-tea brands from Taiwan (named Mr. Kon and President), which now held 75 per cent share, with combined revenues of RMB3.5 billion. Nestlé, despite its leading position in the global tea market, did not do as well in China. Robust, in which Danone had a majority share, had its own problems. Five of its top executives resigned due to the company's failure to meet growth targets and because of differences of opinion on the future strategy of the company with Danone. Danone China's CEO took over the management role.

Consumers

According to research conducted in 2001, the target customers for soft drinks were people in the 11 to 40 age group. Income and education level were positively related to soft drink purchase. When purchasing soft drinks, taste was a key criterion. In addition, young consumers were concerned with brand, lifestyle and fashion. Older consumers cared more about health and nutrition. Women and children preferred sweeter drinks, men and young consumers preferred a crisp taste, while older consumers preferred a light taste. Most consumers purchased soft drinks in supermarkets for reasons of price, choice, and the quality assurance the retailer provided. Drinks were also sold through convenience stores, ice cream shops and roadside stalls, especially those near residential areas and schools.

Marketing in the soft drink industry had changed in recent years. Prior to 1997, the emphasis had been on brand-building, and companies had spent heavily on advertising. However, with brand proliferation and

EXHIBIT 4   **Top Ten Domestic Soft Drink Producers in China**

Source: China Soft Drink Industry Association.

Company	Major Soft Drink	Major Brand
Robust (Guangdong) Food & Beverage Co., Ltd.	non-carbonated drink	Robust
Guangdong Jianlibao Beverage Co., Ltd.	sport drink	Jianlibao
Shanghai Maling Aquarius (Group) Corporation	canned food, packaged water	Zhengguanghe
Beijing Huiyuan Juice Group Corporation	juice	Huiyuan
Hebei Xurishen Co. Ltd.	tea	Xurishen
Hebei Lolo Co. Ltd.	almond drink	Lolo
Hangzhou Wahaha Group Corporation	packaged water, carbonated drinks, tea, dairy drink	Wahaha, Future
Hainan Coconut Palm Group Corporation	coconut milk	Coconut Palm
Shenzhen Danone Yili Beverage Co., Ltd.	mineral water	Yili
Cestbon Food & Beverage (shenzhen) Co., Ltd	distilled water	Cestbon

several companies adopting similar positioning, distribution had become a key battleground for gaining competitive advantage.

Cola in China

Thanks to Coca Cola and PepsiCo, cola was the most popular soft drink worldwide, with consumption amounting to 70 billion litres, and accounting for 20 per cent of all soft-drink sales. Cola sales were still on the rise, though its role in the overall soft-drinks mix was diminishing.

In the early 1980s, before Coca Cola and PepsiCo entered China, more than 10 domestic cola manufacturers produced cola, but with little marketing, revenues remained small. With the arrival of the two multinational giants, the local producers found it hard to compete, and gradually withdrew from the market or established joint bottling ventures with the two giants.

Coca Cola and PepsiCo's sales volumes rose in line with overall sales of cola until they dominated China's carbonated drink market. The two companies had replicated their global rivalry in China and were initially determined to seize market share from domestic cola producers, even at the cost of profitability. The headquarters of both companies in China co-ordinated the marketing efforts of the bottling plants. Both used heavy advertising and sponsoring to support their cola brands. By 2000, Coca Cola had an average of 85 per cent distribution penetration in cities, while PepsiCo stood at about 65 per cent but was growing faster (3.7 per cent growth rate versus Coca Cola's 1.3 per cent).[6] Coca Cola expanded its sales nationwide: it first targeted the 150 cities with a population greater than one million by establishing sales channels there. Next, it continued to roll out into cities with populations greater than 0.5 million, and so on. In comparison, PepsiCo focused on key markets and in cities such as Shanghai, Chongqing, Chengdu, Wuhan and Shenzhen, where it had a higher share than its rival.

In 1998 some domestic soft-drink producers, attracted by the rapidly growing market, launched their own cola brands. Among them were Wahaha Future Cola from Wahaha, and Fenhuang Cola from Guangzhou Fenhuang Food Company. Both advertised

heavily on CCTV. Wahaha launched its Wahaha Future Cola brand during the soccer World Cup and utilized its well-established distribution channels. Fenhuang Cola signed up the famous martial arts actor Jackie Chan to endorse its brand. Both brands emphasized a "China's own cola" positioning, and were targeting smaller cities and the rural market where the two big foreign cola producers were comparatively weak. This revitalization of domestic cola brought other competitors into the fray, including Alishan Zhonghua Cola and Yanjing Cola in 2000, as well as Jianlibao's Huating Cola in 2001.

Wahaha Future Cola

By 1998, Wahaha had firmly established its production and distribution system, and its dominant position in non-carbonated drinks was secure. Wahaha could not, for long, neglect the carbonates market which represented almost half of the volume of the soft-drink industry. Entering the market would provide a much better utilization of its distribution network, and leverage its marketing skills. But it would also mean direct competition with Coca Cola and PepsiCo. In 1997, the total cola output in China was 1.36 million tons (1.234 billion litres) and Coca Cola and PepsiCo held a combined market share of 80 per cent. In 1998, Coca Cola's total beverage output in China was two million tons and PepsiCo 0.8 million tons. Wahaha, despite its number one position among domestic producers, had a total output of 0.93 million tons. Coca Cola and PepsiCo's success against the domestic cola producers in the early stages and their strong brand name and sales network in big cities formed a high entry barrier for new competitors.

Zong firmly believed local companies were capable of competing with the multinational players. He pointed to the computer industry, where domestic companies such as Legend were dominating the local market, and even building global brands. He pointed out that in the food and beverage industry where the technical requirements were relatively low and an understanding of domestic preferences was a distinct advantage, domestic companies had an edge. He concluded that the failure of domestic colas in the early stages was due to their lack of marketing and brand management skills, and that Wahaha had proven that it had these skills. As well, he believed some domestic producers did not want to compete with the multinationals because they lacked the confidence to compete against the giants. Confidence was not lacking at Wahaha.

[6]"An Analysis of the Competition Between Coca Cola and PepsiCo in China," *China Business,* October 16, 2001. Market penetration refers to the percentage of consumers of a certain cola brand among total cola consumers.

EXHIBIT 5
Comparison of Urban Residents' and Rural Residents' Disposable Income in China

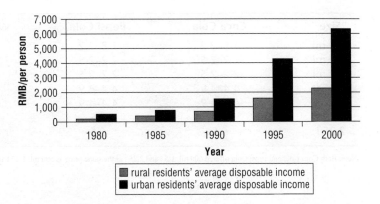

rural residents' average disposable income
urban residents' average disposable income

Zong decided to target the rural market first because he knew and understood this market, and because it was not the focus of Coca Cola and PepsiCo. He reasoned that cola had the potential to be a mass-market product, and the rural areas were where the mass market resided. The 1.1 billion people in the rural market were impossible to ignore. Over the years, China's rural population had become wealthier. In 2000, rural residents' average income was 36 per cent of that of an urban resident (see Exhibit 5), but due to their large numbers, they accounted for two-thirds of national spending. A rural resident's spending on food and beverage totaled RMB820.52 a year, 42 per cent that of an urban resident. Meanwhile, the development of mass communication had made the rural population more accessible, and exposed it to the outside world. Zong believed these trends represented an unparalleled and untapped opportunity.

To develop the product, Wahaha co-operated with R&D institutes and leading domestic flavor producers. To ensure that its cola would be of a high quality, Wahaha sought the advice of global beverage experts and conducted thousands of taste tests worldwide. Its taste was designed to be close to international colas, but a little bit sweeter and stronger to cater to the Chinese consumers' taste. In domestic blind taste tests, consumers preferred Wahaha Future Cola to other colas.

The name Wahaha Future Cola was put forward by Wahaha's employees. The Chinese characters of the brand meant "unusual," a reference to the unusual move of launching against entrenched and strong competitive rivals.

Wahaha did not intend to start a price war in the cola category, but it prepared to win such a war if one broke out. At launch, Wahaha offered three pack sizes, the same as Coca Cola and PepsiCo: 355 ml, 500 ml and 1.25 litres. A standard unit case (12 bottles of 500 ml) of Wahaha Future Cola was priced at RMB19 (wholesale), RMB7 lower than Coca Cola and Pepsi-Cola. This translated into a price difference of approximately RMB0.50 per bottle at retail. One reason for the lower price, Wahaha executives explained, was that Future Cola was aimed at the rural market which was more price-sensitive than the urban markets where the international competitors focused. Assessing potential competitive responses, Zong said:

> It is possible that Coca Cola might reduce its price. But if it lowers the price per bottle of cola by RMB0.10, it will probably lose profit of about RMB0.5 billion; if it cuts price by RM0.50 it stands to lose RMB2.5 billion. If it is willing to do so, we are willing to follow.

Wahaha reasoned that its revenues from other products could support Future Cola through a price war. As it happened, Wahaha maintained the price difference with Coca Cola and PepsiCo over the years despite the launch of new pack sizes (see Exhibit 6).

Wahaha supported the launch with an RMB33.9-million TV campaign, including RMB12.44 million spent on CCTV during the soccer World Cup. Simultaneously, Wahaha greatly increased its brand-building efforts. In 1998, total TV advertising of Wahaha reached RMB368.7 million, of which RMB65.18 million was devoted to Future Cola. CCTV's coverage (national, including rural areas) and credibility (as a domestic national voice) among consumers made it an excellent channel to convey Wahaha Future Cola's brand image. According to a national survey, 61 per cent of rural consumers said TV was their most important source of information and 33.8 per cent said CCTV Channel 1 was the most frequently viewed channel. Favorite programs for rural residents included films, TV series and CCTV

EXHIBIT 6
Retail Price
Comparison of
Various Pack Sizes
in 2002 (in RMB)

Source: Company files.

Size	Coca Cola	Pepsi Cola	Wahaha Future Cola
355 ml	1.8–2.2	1.8–2.2	1.7–2.0
500 ml	2.2–2.5	2.2–2.5	1.9–2.2
600 ml	2.2–2.5	2.2–2.5	none
1.25 l	4.4–4.9	4.4–4.9	3.8
1.5 l	4.4–4.9	4.4–4.9	none
2 l	6.5	6.5	6.0–6.5
2.25 l	6.5	6.5	none

Note: Both Coca Cola and Pepsi Cola offered 600 ml, 1.5 l and 2.25 l at the same price as 500 ml, 1.25 l and 2 l as promotion prices.

news. Prime advertising time was 7 p.m. to 10 p.m. It helped that Wahaha had been advertising on CCTV for 10 years and already had high brand awareness among rural consumers.

Wahaha relied on its nationwide distribution network to get the product to rural consumers. While Coca Cola and PepsiCo had the advantage in large cities where chain stores and supermarkets accounted for half the grocery trade, Wahaha played on its strength in the countryside where the trade was fragmented, and reachable primarily through multi-layered wholesale markets. Distributors who had been working with Wahaha for years and who had benefited from Wahaha's remarkable growth supported the launch of the cola.

The initial success of the cola surprised even Wahaha. The company could not meet demand using its own bottling facilities and even resorted to outsourcing bottling to other bottlers. When Coca Cola bottlers were approached, the answer was a firm "no." At the same time, many of Coca Cola's distributors noticed that if they sold Wahaha Future Cola, Coca Cola would stop supplying them and refuse end-of-year bonuses.[7]

On average, advertising expenses of Wahaha Future Cola comprised about 20 to 30 per cent of the company's total advertising expenditure, adjusted for seasonal and promotional focus. Besides advertising on CCTV and other local TV channels, Wahaha used outdoor advertising and point-of-sale advertising. In particular, to tackle the rural market, it used "wall advertising"— painting walls with advertising slogans—a cost-effective way to promote brand awareness. At busy roads and fairs, Wahaha set up large brand and slogan banners. It also sponsored traveling troupes that performed in rural markets and at fairs. In villages where there was no cinema, Wahaha sponsored traveling film shows. These activities catered to the needs of rural

[7]Wu Xiaobo and Hu Honwei, *Extraordinary Marketing Strategy,* Zhejiang People's Publishing House, 2002, pp. 230–231.

customers and quickly increased Wahaha Future Cola's awareness in the rural market.

In 2000, Yu Chen Qing, a pop singer from Taiwan, was signed on to endorse Wahaha Future Cola, while Coco Li Wen, another pop singer from Taiwan, endorsed the Future Lemon carbonated drink. In 2000 and 2001, Wahaha was the exclusive sponsor for CCTV's spring festival party, a program that attracted a mass audience, building national brand awareness.

In 2001, Wahaha Future Cola launched a new advertising slogan "Future Cola, the choice for happy occasions." To support this association, Wahaha provided free cola to wedding parties in some key markets. A co-promotion with liquor producers further reinforced the association.

Before the spring festival in 2002, Zong noticed that Coca Cola changed its original paper case packaging to plastic wrap to save costs. Zong saw this as an opportunity to promote Wahaha Future Cola's paper packaging, which was easier to carry and looked better than plastic wrap. Sales staff promoted the paper case as a gift item for the festival, inserting posters of the image of the god of fortune in each case.

Wahaha Future Cola's focus on rural markets meant that 60 per cent to 70 per cent of total sales came from rural areas. In 2002, Wahaha launched carbonated drinks with fresh apple juice and orange juice. With the wider product range, it increased its sales efforts in supermarkets and big stores, and in larger cities.

During the same period, Coca Cola and PepsiCo began to notice and respond to the domestic upstart, while continuing to compete with each other. In a few markets they offered their cola products at a lower price than Wahaha Future Cola. Meanwhile, they further localized their marketing. For example, Coca Cola adjusted its advertising strategy and increased its advertising on CCTV. It also signed on pop singers from Taiwan and Hong Kong, Zhang Huimei and Xie

Tingfeng, to endorse its brand. In 2001, to celebrate Beijing's victory in its bid to host the 2008 Olympics Games, Coca Cola announced a new thematic pack design just 22 minutes after the news announcement. The following day the new design (in gold, integrating various architectural and sports themes in Beijing) was launched in key markets. In 2001 during the Spring Festival, Coca Cola packs carried a picture of a traditional Chinese clay doll "A Fu" (a symbol of luck).

Coca Cola and PepsiCo also began to actively develop the non-carbonated drink market while continuing to promote their carbonate products. Pepsi promoted non carbonate drinks such as Dole (100 per cent fruit juice) and Gatorade. Coca Cola launched "Sensation" water in 2001 without any advertising support, and with a wholesale price that was 40 per cent lower than Wahaha purified water in some regions. In 2002, it launched new 600 ml, 1.5 litre and 2.25 litre packages for its cola without increases in price over the 500 ml, 1.25 litre and two litre, respectively. Coca Cola also announced its intention to increase the number of bottling plants to 34 from 28 within five years, growing especially in the mainly rural western region.

Both Coca Cola and PepsiCo were also working on their distribution policy, according to a report in *China Business*.[8] Coca Cola and PepsiCo had never been directly involved in the sales of their products. Instead, their bottlers managed sales in their assigned territory, relying on distributors to cover areas their own systems

[8]Ma Qiang, "Comments on Banning the Association of PepsiCo's Bottlers," *China Business,* August 1, 2002.

could not serve. The two companies' practice was to set stringent sales targets for bottlers, and in turn bottlers would set targets for distributors. Bonuses were contingent on reaching these goals. Distributors paid upfront for goods and couldn't return unsold merchandise. However, different wholesale prices in different regions and the incentive of the bonus resulted in distributors selling across provinces to achieve their sales targets, even though both companies had strict policies against cross-territory sales. Recognizing the problems of the current system, the two companies had recently redefined the roles of bottlers and distributors: distributors were in charge of carrying inventory and delivering to the retailer and their profit would come from the volume handled, but they no longer had any discretion over selling prices; bottlers were responsible for order taking, promotion and product display at the retail end, and retained ownership of the product until the retailer bought it. In comparison, Wahaha's sales company bought the products from its wholly-owned bottling subsidiaries and then co-ordinated sales and marketing on a national scale. Its sales company directly dealt with the distributors (see Exhibit 7). Coca Cola and PepsiCo both made money from the sales of concentrate, thus limiting the potential profitability (and price flexibility) of third-party bottlers. Wahaha made money from the sales of the final product, as the production of concentrate and the final product was handled by its own subsidiaries. This gave Wahaha greater pricing flexibility in the field.

In 2002, PepsiCo encountered some problems with a local joint-venture partner. PepsiCo was applying to

EXHIBIT 7   Comparison of Product Flow and Revenue Flow

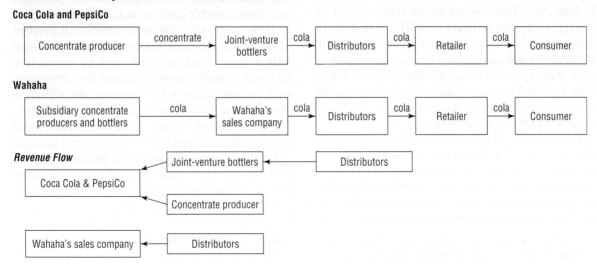

EXHIBIT 8   **Comparison of Coca Cola, PepsiCo and Wahaha's Carbonate Sales**

	1998		1999		2000		2001	
	Total (in tons)	Market Share	Total	Market Share	Total	Market Share	Total	Market Share
Coca Cola	1,940.0	36%	2,040.0	48%	2,180.0	47%	1,920.0	42%
PepsiCo	760.0	14%	910.0	21%	1,090.0	24%	1,066.7	23%
Wahaha	73.8	1%	399.0	9%	480.0	10%	640.0	14%
China's total carbonated drink sales	5,400.0	100%	4,273.8	100%	4,620.0	100%	4,571.4	100%

a commercial arbitration court in Stockholm to cancel its contracts with the joint-venture partner in Chengdu, Sichuan Province—a key Pepsi-Cola market. PepsiCo contended that it had been prevented from exercising its rights under the joint-venture contract, and alleged that there were major financial irregularities within the local company, while the latter accused PepsiCo China of bugging its phones. This was unprecedented in PepsiCo's 20 years in China. While PepsiCo was distracted by these internal problems, Coca Cola was launching a campaign to seize market share in Sichuan and Chongqing—other key markets for PepsiCo.

In the meantime, Wahaha steadily increased sales and market share of Future Cola. Between 1998 and 2001, Wahaha Future series' sales volume increased from 73,800 tons (66.95 million litres) to 0.64 million tons (580 million litres), a share of 14 percent of the carbonated drink market (see Exhibit 8). In comparison, 2001 carbonated-drink sales for Coca Cola and PepsiCo were 1.9 million tons (1.724 billion litres) and 1.07 million tons (971 million litres), respectively. In June 2002, Future series market share reached 18 percent, with sales revenues of RMB930 million. In some provinces such as Hunan, Xinjiang, Jiangxi and the three provinces in northern China, Future's market share was higher than that of Coca Cola and Pepsi-Cola. In some provinces, Wahaha Future Cola was the only cola brand carried by retailers. In 2001, the Future brand was extended to tea drinks.

Coca Cola now admitted that it faced competition from domestic companies. According to a *Wall Street Journal* article, Coca Cola had been aggressively ramping up its sales efforts and "by opening more bottling plants and using recyclable bottles, it has brought the price down to one yuan for a single serving in remote towns."

During the past three years, Coke and its bottlers have been trying to map every supermarket, restaurant,

barbershop or market stall where a can of soda might be consumed throughout much of China. Their army of more than 10,000 sales representatives makes regular visits, often on bicycle or foot, to each outlet to ensure there is enough in stock and to record how much was sold. All the information goes into a central database, updated daily, that gives Coke some of the most accurate consumer profiles available in China. Those data help Coke get closer to its customers, whether they are in large hypermarkets, spartan noodle shops or schools . . . . And in a strategy proven in markets such as Africa and India, Coke lets local distributors gradually own their own assets, whether these be tricycles used for deliveries or small refrigeration units.[9]

Wahaha, in the meantime, was planning on expanding its sales and marketing staff from 2,000 to 8,000 in 2002.

As Zong Qinghou reviewed the progress of Wahaha Future Cola, he knew that his strategy had allowed Wahaha to quickly become a player in the soft-drink business in China. As Coca Cola and PepsiCo realized the threat from Chinese domestic cola producers and the vast market potential in the countryside, they would certainly take action to protect their position in the carbonated-drink market and tackle the rural market. Zong wondered what steps he should take next with Wahaha Future Cola and the carbonated-drink market. Meanwhile, changes in the soft-drink industry also posed challenges for all participants. The rapid growth of new drink categories offered both opportunities and risks. As the general manager of China's number one soft-drink producer, he also needed to consider competition in the rapidly growing non-carbonated drink market and the future growth of Wahaha.

[9]Gabriel Kahn, "Coke Works Harder at Being The Real Thing in Hinterland," *Wall Street Journal*, November 26, 2002.

Case 6-21
Smith & Nephew—Innovex

At the beginning of March 2000, James Brown, CEO of Smith & Nephew, S.A. (S&N), was in a meeting with Josep Serra, Director of the Medical Division.

Almost six months earlier, on September 29, 1999, they had signed an agency contract with Innovex whereby Innovex employees would promote S&N's moist wound healing (MWH) products Allevyn®, Intrasite® Gel and Opsite®[1] to primary care centres[2] in Galicia and Asturias. It was the first time S&N had used the services of a contract or outsourced sales force in Spain.

Among other things, the contract specified that the agreement would expire on March 29, 2000.

Brown and Serra had to assess the results of their collaboration with Innovex and decide not only what to do in Galicia and Asturias but also, more generally, what their policy should be with respect to the sales personnel who promoted the company's MWH products in the rest of Spain.

Smith & Nephew, S.A. (S&N)

Smith & Nephew, S.A. (S&N) was the Spanish subsidiary of the Smith & Nephew group (for information on the group, see Exhibit 1).

Founded in Spain in 1963, S&N sold in Spain the healthcare products manufactured by the Smith & Nephew group in various countries, mainly the United Kingdom and the United States, though it also imported products from France, Germany and South Africa, among others.

With annual sales of more than 4,000 million pesetas, the Spanish subsidiary had two commercial divisions: a medical division, and a surgical division. Between them these two sold all of the group's product ranges and families except consumer healthcare

products, which were sold almost exclusively in the United Kingdom and some former Commonwealth countries. The company also had an administrative and finance division.

At the beginning of the year 2000, James Brown had been with the Smith & Nephew group for 18 years. He had been appointed CEO of the Spanish subsidiary in 1993. He reported to the Managing Director for Continental Europe, who was responsible for various countries in the north and south of continental Europe. The Managing Director for Continental Europe, in turn, reported to the Group Commercial Director, who was a member of the Group Executive Committee, along with the chief executive, the three presidents of the group's Global Business Units, and other senior executives.

The Spanish subsidiary had been the official supplier of certain healthcare products during the 1992 Barcelona Olympics. It had had ISO 9002 certification for several years and had almost finished computerising its entire sales network.

Since November 1998 S&N had been using the services of a specialized shipping and logistics company, which, under contract, took care of the reception of imported goods, storage, stock control, order preparation, and transport and delivery to the customer's address. Given its small workforce of fewer than 100 people, S&N also outsourced certain other services, such as payroll administration and social security paperwork, legal and tax advice, design and execution of advertising materials, organization of sales conventions, etc.

And yet the company had an uneven profit record, and its management faced certain challenges. For example, throughout 1998 and 1999 the pound sterling had steadily appreciated against the peseta, giving rise to a steady increase in the peseta cost of the products sold in Spain, most of which were imported from the United States and the United Kingdom.

Selling prices in the Spanish market for healthcare products were significantly lower than in other European countries. Also, in Spain it was more difficult to raise prices because the Social Security Administration often did its purchasing by a system of open bidding, and because other competitors were less affected by the strength of the dollar and sterling.

---

[1] Allevyn®, Opsite® and Intrasite® Gel are registered trademarks of T. S. Smith & Nephew Ltd. Innovex™ and Quintiles™ are registered trademarks of Quintiles Transnational Corporation.

[2] Also known as health centres, basic health areas, or, previously, outpatient clinics. They delivered primary care services to the population covered by Spanish Social Security. There were some 3,000 primary care centres in the country as a whole, each tied to a referral hospital. A hospital and the group of primary care centres tied to it made up what was known as a health management area.

Lluis G. Renart, "Smith & Nephew - Innovex," Case of the Research Department at IESE, May 2000. (M-1092-E). Reprinted by permission of IESE PUBLISHING. To order copies or request permission to reproduce materials, call 34 93 2536558, send an e-mail to: iesp@iesp.com or go to http://www.iesp.com.

EXHIBIT 1 The Smith & Nephew Group

This global medical device company, headquartered in London, traced its origins back to 1856, when Thomas James Smith founded a pharmacy in Hull in the United Kingdom.[1]

In 1896, the founder brought his nephew Horatio Nelson Smith into the business as a partner, giving rise to the name Smith & Nephew. The company grew rapidly with the addition of products such as elastic adhesive bandages (Elastoplast), plaster casts (Gypsona), and sanitary towels (Lilia), often through acquisitions.

In 1999, the group reported worldwide sales of 1,120 million pounds sterling[2], with earnings of 171 million pounds[3] before tax and extraordinary income. In that year the group had activities in 90 countries. Geographically, the sales revenues were distributed as follows: 19 percent in the UK, 20 percent in continental Europe, 43 percent in America, and the remaining 18 percent in Africa, Asia and Oceania.

The main product ranges or families sold worldwide were: orthopaedics and trauma (mainly hip and knee prostheses, and trauma implants, 26 percent of worldwide sales); endoscopy (particularly knee and shoulder arthroscopy, 18 percent); wound management (e.g., Allevyn®, Opsite®, and Intrasite® Gel, 21 percent); orthosis and rehabilitation, casting and bandaging (bandages and plaster casts), and otology (prostheses and instrumentation for microsurgery of the inner ear) (together, 18 percent); and consumer healthcare (17 percent).

In the 1999 Annual Report, Chris O'Donnell, Chief executive, declared:

> We are concentrating our strategic investment on the three markets of orthopaedics [implants and trauma procedures], endoscopy, and wound management.

Each of these three Global Business Units was headed by a president.

In these three specialities, or in some of their subspecialties, the Smith & Nephew group held first or second place in the global ranking. In its three priority business units it expected to grow both organically and through acquisitions, whereas growth in its other businesses would be basically organic.

The group invested 4 percent of its sales revenue in research and development. One of its latest developments, precisely in the Wound Management GBU, was Dermagraft, a dressing of human tissue developed through bioengineering processes, which made it possible to heal certain types of chronic ulcers, such as diabetic foot ulcers, in just a few weeks. Although at the beginning of the year 2000 it was already being sold in some countries, Dermagraft was not yet available in Spain.

To summarize, starting from the British parent company, the group had evolved to the point where it had a broad range of ever more high-tech healthcare products that were sold around the globe.

[1]In fact, Thomas Southall had founded a pharmacy in Birmingham as early as 1820, and Southalls (Birmingham) Ltd. had been acquired by Smith & Nephew in 1958. So the roots of the company could be said to stretch back even further, to 1820.

[2]Equivalent to approximately 1,800 million dollars or euros, or almost 300,000 million pesetas, at the exchange rates prevailing at the beginning of March 2000. On January 1, 1999, the exchange rate of the peseta had been irrevocably fixed at a rate of 166.386 pesetas per euro. At the beginning of 1999, the euro had traded at 1.18 dollars, but over the year had steadily slipped against the dollar until by the end of February 2000 one euro was practically equal to one dollar. Thus, the peseta was quoted at 166 pesetas per dollar, and 267 pesetas per pound sterling. At the beginning of the year 2000 the pound sterling, the Greek drachma, the Swedish krona and the Danish krone had not joined the euro.

[3]Data about the group are taken from the Smith & Nephew plc "1999 Annual Report and Accounts." For more information, go to <http://www.smith-nephew.com>.

Commercialization of Healthcare Products in Spain

According to EC directives, before a healthcare product could be commercialized, it first had to obtain the "CE marking" from an authorized body in any EU member country. In addition to this, in Spain the company commercializing the product had to submit, generally to the Ministry of Health or the regional government, a "market introduction report." Once these requirements had been met, the product could be marketed and sold.

However, given the way Social Security operated in Spain, the second key requirement for a product to achieve widespread use was for the product to gain approval from the Social Security Administration as a reimbursable product. Reimbursable products were identified by what was known as the *cupón precinto* or "Social Security coupon."[3] As is explained in greater detail later on, obtaining reimbursable status as certified by the Social Security coupon was critical for sales of a particular product through pharmacies, though not strictly necessary for its use in hospitals.

[3]Only products classed as "medical accessories" (under Royal Decree Legislative 9/1996 of January 15, which regulates the selection of medical accessories, their financing from Social Security funds or government funds earmarked for healthcare, and the basis on which they may be supplied and dispensed to outpatients) could apply for reimbursement.

The Social Security coupon was a rectangle printed on the packaging of each unit of product, with perforated edges to allow it to be detached. On it were printed the initials A.S.S.S. ("Social Security healthcare"), the commercial name of the product, certain data about the product and manufacturer, and the price.

Healthcare Products Sold in Pharmacies

In the case of drugs and healthcare products sold in pharmacies, patients covered by Social Security had to obtain a prescription from their Social Security physician, who would usually have her office in a primary care centre. They could then take the prescription to any pharmacy to obtain the medicine. At the time of purchase, the patient would have to pay 40 percent of the retail price (except for pensioners and the chronically ill, for whom prescriptions were completely free). Before handing over the product, the pharmacist would cut out the Social Security coupon and staple it to the prescription, so as later to be able to obtain reimbursement of the remaining 60 percent (or 100 percent if sold to a pensioner or chronic patient) from the Social Security Administration.

If a drug or healthcare product was authorized for sale but did not have the Social Security coupon, a patient could still apply to the Social Security Administration's own medical inspection service for reimbursement as an exceptional case, but this was a very laborious procedure with no guarantee of success. The alternative was to pay the full 100 percent of the retail price. In either case use of the product was seriously inhibited, above all if there were alternative healthcare products on the market that had similar therapeutic qualities and were reimbursable.

Given the pressure to contain health spending in the Spanish state budget, it was quite possible for a more modern and more efficient yet more expensive drug or healthcare product not to obtain Social Security approval because an alternative product was available which, while not so advanced from a therapeutic point of view and possibly less efficient, could cover the same need.

Healthcare Products Used in Hospitals and Primary Care Centres

In hospitals, whether a healthcare product was reimbursable or not had no direct impact on sales (though it did affect them indirectly, as we shall see later). Private hospitals and clinics purchased healthcare products in the normal way, paying the price freely agreed with the manufacturer or distributor.

Hospitals and primary care centres belonging to the Social Security Administration, in contrast, used a system of procurement by public bidding. Usually, an individual hospital or primary care centre, or all of the hospitals and primary care centres in a particular geographical area, would issue an invitation to tender once a year, specifying the quantity and characteristics of the products they wanted to purchase. All of this would be set out in a bidding document, which would also specify the information and other things required of prospective bidders, the bid closing date, the selection criteria, etc.

Healthcare Products for Ulcer and Wound Care

Traditionally, the main wound care products were elastic adhesive bandages, gauzes, and the classic dressings. These constituted what was known as the wet-to-dry method. In the year 2000, wet-to-dry dressings were still commonly used in the management of acute wounds, where it was possible to predict the duration of the healing process. They were products with a low unit value, and so whether they were reimbursable or not was practically irrelevant, as hardly anybody went to the doctor to get a prescription for a roll of plaster.

From the early 80s onward, however, a new method, known as moist wound healing, began to be adopted in the treatment of chronic ulcers.[4] It was found that wounds healed more quickly if they were kept moist and protected from infection, allowing the passage of moisture vapour and maintaining the physiological temperature.

Over the years a variety of products for moist wound healing (MWH) came onto the market, such as polyurethane dressings, hydrocolloids, alginates, hydrocellular dressings, and carbon moist wound dressings.

In Spain, in 1999, the total market for MWH products was worth around 3,200 million pesetas at manufacturer's prices. Of this total, around 1,870 million was sold through pharmacies and around 1,300, to hospitals and clinics. A large proportion of the total MWH market consisted of hydrocolloids.

---

[4]Chronic ulcers are ulcers of unpredictable duration. The healing process can easily go on for several months. The most common causes of chronic ulcers are continuous pressure on a particular part of the body (e.g., bedsores) or vascular or circulatory problems. A chronic ulcer can be shallow or deep, and in serious cases can lead to necrosis, gangrene, and may even require amputation of the affected part.

The main competitors in the MWH product category were C.S. (with a market share of around 35 percent), Danplast (22 percent), and Smith & Nephew (9 percent).[5]

The Medical Division of Smith & Nephew, S.A. (S&N)

Under the overall management of Josep Serra, the medical division's sales and marketing activities were carried out by a sales team and a marketing team. In 1999 the division had total sales in the region of 3,000 million pesetas, shared between three product families: wound care (1,000 million); casting and bandaging; and orthosis, rehabilitation and aids for everyday living (2,000 million between these last two families).

Of the 1,000 million pesetas in wound care, around 600 million were wet-to-dry and around 400 million, moist wound healing (MWH) products.

At the beginning of the year 2000, S&N competed in only three categories of MWH products (in various sizes and varieties):

- Intrasite® Gel, a cleansing hydrogel that regenerated the ulcer, debriding and absorptive, sold in packs of five 15g units (see Exhibit 5). It had the Social Security coupon. In 1999, S&N had sold 130 million pesetas of the product and had a market share in this subcategory in the order of 40 percent of sales through pharmacies.
- The Allevyn® range, a controlled absorption hydrocellular dressing (see Exhibit 6). Three sizes of the range had the Social Security coupon. In 1999, S&N had sold 170 million pesetas of the product and had a market share in this subcategory in the order of 50 percent of sales through pharmacies.
- The Opsite® range, a transparent polyurethane dressing. Six sizes of the range had the Social Security coupon. In 1999, S&N had sold 100 million pesetas of the product and had a market share in this subcategory in the order of 90 percent of sales through pharmacies.

These products had various technical advantages that made the healing of an ulcer or wound faster, safer and less painful.

[5]Throughout the case, unless stated otherwise, the market shares of specific products refer to the pharmacies channel, which was monitored by IMS, a market research services company. Market share data for hospitals were difficult to estimate, as they depended on the outcome of the bidding process.

However, the correct prescription, use and application of MWH products required certain knowledge that only doctors and nurses were likely to have. This meant that patients and their relatives very rarely influenced the type of product used.

Nevertheless, a significant volume of MWH products was sold through pharmacies. It was true that it was always a doctor who prescribed the use of a particular product. But, often, a relative of a housebound chronically ill patient would go to the pharmacy, obtain the product free of charge, and then give it to the nurse who, in the course of a home visit, would apply the dressing.

The management of S&N's medical division estimated that slightly over 50 percent of their MWH products were sold through pharmacies.

Almost all the remainder, just under 50 percent, was used in hospitals and primary care centres belonging to the Social Security administration.

S&N Medical Division's Sales and Promotional Activities

The division's *sales* efforts, strictly speaking (i.e., activities undertaken to generate orders and invoices), were conducted in three channels:

1. Sales to Social Security hospitals and primary care centres were made by bidding in yearly auctions.[6] Products that won a contract would be supplied and billed over the course of the year, and were used either in the hospital or primary care centre itself, or during home visits.
2. Sales to pharmacies were accomplished through pharmaceutical wholesalers or cooperatives, which replenished their stocks at regular intervals without S&N having to make hardly any effort to sell to them.
3. Lastly, the medical division's own sales representatives sold directly to private hospitals and large private clinics, or indirectly, through healthcare product wholesalers/distributors, to other private hospitals and clinics, geriatric homes and the private practices of doctors and vets.

The division's *promotional* efforts were targeted at doctors and, above all, nurses. The aim was to bring the products to their attention, explain their advantages and how to use them, give the doctors and nurses an opportunity to try them out, and explain to them the differential therapeutic advantages of the company's products compared with older or competing alternatives.

[6]In 1999, S&N had bid in almost 500 auctions.

When dealing with healthcare professionals working in the public health system, the sales representatives' mission was also to persuade doctors and nurses to issue favourable reports on S&N's products.

Lastly, an important goal of the promotional effort was to ensure, once a contract had been won and the S&N product was in use in a given healthcare facility, that the product was always at hand for any doctor or nurse who needed it.

As Josep Serra remarked:

> It's a major training and "merchandising" challenge seeing to it that the products we sell are available on every floor, in every consulting room, on every trolley, and that they are used correctly.

Promotional Tasks Carried Out in the Field by the Medical Division's Own Sales Representatives

The national sales manager supervised two regional sales managers. Between them the two regional sales managers had 18 sales representatives and three commission agents, who did all the sales and promotional work for all the division's products (Exhibit 7).

This sales team's coverage of the Spanish market as a whole was considered poor, particularly compared with the division's main competitors. It was estimated that it covered almost 100 percent of the hospitals but only 20 percent of the primary care centres. In contrast, Danplast, S.A. was thought to have around 50 sales representatives, and another major competitor, C.S., S.A., more than 40.

S&N's marketing manager estimated that to be able to provide a satisfactory level of promotional and sales service for the medical division's products throughout Spain, they would need about 40 sales representatives. Without that number it would be impossible to visit all the primary care centres.

One of the division's sales representatives nominally covered the area of Galicia. But given the size of the region,[7] in practice he only ever had time to visit hospitals and clinics and healthcare product wholesalers.

In 1999 the medical division's full-time sales representatives had sold an average of 150 million pesetas each, at an average cost per representative of 8.5 million

---

[7]Galicia has an area of 29,575 km² and is almost square in shape. In 1998 its population was approximately 2,716,000. Asturias is elongated and narrow in shape, with an area of 10,604 km² (approx. 200 × 50 km), and in 1998 had 1,060,000 inhabitants.

pesetas, including salary, incentives, Social Security, vacations, travelling expenses, etc.

The division's three remaining commission agents (previously it had had five or six of them) had between them sold 150 million pesetas. The agent for the region of Extremadura was a company that had been working with S&N for about eight years. The other two agents were individuals. One covered the islands of Majorca and Ibiza, selling only S&N products. The other covered the island of Menorca, offering a very wide range of products by different companies, exclusively to hospitals. Both had been working with S&N for around 20 years, and in both cases the relationship was considered stable.

The commission agents had agency contracts. They visited only hospitals, that is to say, they did not promote the products to primary care centres. According to Serra, "They go for the guaranteed sales, what I mean is, they try to sell the products for which there's already a demand. They don't make much effort to introduce new products. They're undoubtedly more profitable than having full-time representatives of our own in those territories. That would be too expensive, in the case of Extremadura because its so extensive, and in the other cases because they're islands."

When they made a sale without going through a bidding process, the commission agents would close the deal and pass the order on to S&N, which would serve the goods, invoice the customers and collect payment. The commission agents were only responsible for collecting debts from private (nonpublic) customers, and earned a commission of between 7 percent and 10 percent. When there was an auction, the commission agents would gather the necessary information, so that S&N executives could prepare the documentation and put in a bid.

Other Promotional Activities Carried Out by the Marketing Department: Advertising, Seminars, "Study Days"

In addition to the sales and promotional activities carried out by the medical division's sales team, the marketing department, consisting of a marketing manager and two product managers, carried out a number of complementary activities.

These consisted mainly of:

- Advertising the division's products through inserts in medical journals and through special brochures.
- Attending nursing conferences organized by the professional associations of nurses for particular

medical specialities. For example, in 1999 S&N had attended four conferences, including one in Bilbao on gerontological nursing. Attending a medium-sized conference could cost S&N around 3 million pesetas. A conference could be attended and sponsored by some 15–20 companies.

- Study days: These were meetings, organized entirely by S&N and generally held in a hotel, with a specific scientific interest provided by a guest speaker. Following the guest speaker's lecture, an S&N product manager would present the company's products for the application in question. The meeting would end with a colloquium and aperitifs.

In 1999 23 study days had been held, each of which had been attended by around 65 specially invited nurses. The average cost per study day had been around 300,000 pesetas. To make the most of these occasions, it was vital to carry out close personal follow-up.

Social Security Approval for the Allevyn® Range and First Contacts with Innovex

Up until April 1998, only two of Smith & Nephew, SA.'s MWH products had the Social Security coupon and were therefore reimbursable: Intrasite® Gel and Opsite®. In fact, hardly any other medical division product had the coupon.

In April 1998, after a long wait, S&N's Allevyn® product was finally granted the right to carry the prized coupon. This was an important development, as Allevyn® was potentially a similarly priced but functionally superior substitute for hydrocolloids, which accounted for a large proportion of the total market for MWH products.

Allevyn® was already sold by bidding to hospitals and primary care centres. Now, with the Social Security coupon, it seemed set to achieve a significant volume of sales through the pharmacy channel. With sales potential to hospitals and primary care centres currently in the order of 1,100 million pesetas, its potential market could therefore be considered to be augmented by a further 1,600 million or so, in the pharmacy channel, despite the fact that only some of the sizes in which the product was sold were reimbursable by Social Security.

As we said earlier, in order to bid in Social Security procurement auctions, a product did not have to be reimbursable. However, doctors and nurses preferred, when starting treatment of a wound or ulcer in hospital, to use products that *were* reimbursable because that made it much easier for the patient to continue the treatment at home, using the same products as in hospital.

Conversely, if a particular product was *not* reimbursable, doctors and nurses were sometimes reluctant to use it, even in hospital, so as not to have to change the patient's prescription on discharge and prescribe a different product that *was* reimbursable and would therefore be free of charge for the patient.

First Fruitless Contact with Innovex

In March 1998, with approval of Allevyn® now imminent, the medical division's top executives contacted Innovex, an international company already established in Spain that specialized in providing contract sales teams for the pharmaceutical and medical devices industry (see Exhibit 2 for information on Quintiles Transnational Corporation and its Innovex division.)

They were keen to explore the possibility of contracting a team of Innovex sales representatives to reinforce the efforts being made by the medical division's own sales team to promote its MWH products to primary care centres.

Smith & Nephew's Spanish subsidiary had never worked with Innovex previously, nor with any other company that offered this kind of contract sales services. But they knew that it was a fairly common practice among their competitors in the healthcare industry, particularly when launching new products onto the market.

Also, colleagues in the group's United Kingdom offices confirmed that they had worked with Innovex and thought highly of the company. One or two other companies that provided services similar to those of Innovex were contacted for the purpose of comparison.

In the end, however, the idea of working with Innovex was dropped for fear that the necessary level of sales and profitability might not be attained.

Developments in the Period April 1998 to February 1999

Between April and June 1998, sales of Allevyn® rose sharply, only to flatten out again in the following months.

By February 1999, the management of the medical division were concerned that if they did not take decisive action, Allevyn® was in danger of being sidelined, with a share of only 2 percent or 3 percent of the total MWH market in Spain.

In this situation, they decided that the only course of action was, on the one hand, to intensify and extend the promotional activities aimed at customers already covered by the company's sales team; and on the other, to achieve

EXHIBIT 2   **The Quintiles Transnational Group and Its Innovex Division**

Innovex Spain, S.L. was the Spanish subsidiary of Innovex Inc., which in turn was a division of Quintiles Transnational Corp. Both had their headquarters in North Carolina, United States.[1]

At the end of 1998 the Quintiles group had more than 18,000 employees in 31 countries and that year reported net revenue of 1,188 million dollars. Of this total, 583 million had been generated in the United States and 340 million in the United Kingdom.

The Quintiles group provided full, outsourced research, sales, marketing, healthcare policy consulting and information management services to pharmaceutical, biotechnology, medical devices and healthcare companies throughout the world.

For example, a pharmaceutical laboratory could turn to the Quintiles group to take care of anything from the basic research needed to synthesize a new molecule or active substance (Phase 1), plus any of the intermediate phases of research and development, clinical trials by physicians and hospitals, data compilation, etc., to the management of the new drug approval and registration process (Phase 4). Then, if it wanted, the laboratory could also hire the Quintiles group to do all the marketing and actually bring the product to market.

Innovex Inc. was a division of the Quintiles group that specialized in sales and marketing services for third parties.

In 1998, Innovex Inc. was present in 19 countries and had more than 7,000 sales representatives, sales managers and marketing directors. In that year its sales teams had made an average of almost two million product presentations per month.

Innovex had been present in Spain since 1996, when it had acquired an existing Spanish company that was already active in the business of providing contract sales teams. Subsequently it had extended, or intended to extend, its services to other areas connected with the commercialization of drugs or medical devices, such as marketing and sales strategy consulting, training, communication, resource optimization, etc.

As Jesus Polanco, CEO of Innovex's Spanish subsidiary, pointed out:

> "It's not just a matter of 'getting people out knocking on doors'. In line with the group's general approach, we aim to create value by carefully managing each sales territory, monitoring the costs and results of our actions, collecting and compiling the valuable commercial information generated in each territory, and so on."

See Exhibit 3 for various examples of Innovex's more recent projects in Spain.

At the end of 1999, Innovex's Spanish subsidiary had a team of 152 people. Of these, 17 belonged to the management team, while the remaining 135 made up the sales force that went out 'knocking on doors'. Seventy-seven of the sales representatives were full-time Innovex employees, with open-ended contracts, while the remaining 58 had temporary contracts linked to a particular job for a client.

[1]Data are taken from Quintiles Transnational Corp.'s "Annual Report 1998." For further details, go to <http://www.corporate.quintiles.com> and <http://www.innovexglobal.com>.

fuller coverage of primary care centres in the underserved regions of Valencia, Andalusia, Galicia and Asturias.

The medical division's managers were in a tight spot: there seemed to be a potentially profitable opportunity to promote Allevyn® to primary care centres, but CEO James Brown and his superiors would be reluctant to add to the company's workforce.

Steps towards an Agreement with Innovex

In March 1999 the management of S&N's medical division got back in touch with Innovex to explore the feasibility of contracting a team of medical sales representatives to promote the products of the Opsite®, Intrasite® Gel and Allevyn® ranges in the regions of Spain hitherto least well covered by the company's own sales staff and commission agents.

In all, they considered the possibility of contracting from Innovex a team of 10 sales representatives and an area manager to serve Galicia [3], Asturias [1], Andalusia [3] and Valencia [3].

Ideally, S&N's management would have preferred to contract a sales team that would devote only 50 percent of its time to promoting S&N's products.

Unfortunately, at that time they were unable to find any other company in the healthcare sector that needed Innovex sales representatives working half-time for precisely the hours that would fit in with S&N's requirements, in the same geographical areas and for the six-month period S&N envisaged.

EXHIBIT 3   Examples of Recent Projects Carried Out by Innovex in Spain in the Field of Contract Sales Teams

Zeneca

Before Zeneca merged with Astra to form Astra-Zeneca, it planned to launch two new products in the same year. To do this, Zeneca's sales force required reinforcement in the form of 65 people hired from Innovex for a period of two years to carry out visits to cardiologists, neurologists, psychiatrists and general practitioners.

The main goal was rapid market share gain to block the entry of competitors.

However, it would have been too expensive to keep the 65 people on for a second phase focused on maintaining the products' market presence.

Géminis

Géminis was the new generic Pharmaceuticals division of Novartis, which marketed out-of-patent products.

As it was a new division, the company did not want to hire extra sales representatives until they had seen what results the new division was capable of achieving. Note that promoting generics requires a different sales approach, both when selling to doctors and when selling to pharmacies.

The task Innovex undertook between 1998 and 2000 initially required a team of 12 promotors, later expanded to 17.

Pierre Fabre

Pierre Fabre contracted a team of seven "beautician" promotors from Innovex to persuade and educate pharmacists to recommend, for each individual customer, the most appropriate Klorane® product from among a wide range of shampoos and hair creams.

Cardionetics

At the beginning of the year 2000, Innovex was preparing to set up a "virtual" company, i.e. using only temporary employees, to commercialize in Spain an innovative portable ECG device for monitoring and diagnosing abnormal heart rhythms as a person went about his normal daily activities.

It would be responsible for all the functional areas involved in commercialization, including, among other activities, the deployment of a contract sales team.

[1]Data are taken from Quintiles Transnational Corp.'s "Annual Report 1998." For further details, go to <http://www.corporate.quintiles.com> and <http://www.innovexglobal.com>.

It was therefore agreed that the sales team contracted from Innovex should devote 100 percent of its time to promoting S&N's MWH products to primary care centres.

In view of the cost this would represent, S&N's management asked Innovex to submit a formal offer for the provision of just two sales representatives to promote S&N's MWH products to primary care centres in Galicia and Asturias. At that time, Arturo, the company's only sales representative in Galicia, only had time to visit the region's hospitals, so the primary care centres were more or less neglected.

If Innovex's offer was accepted, it would be very much an experiment. After six months, they would decide whether the system should be extended to other areas of Spain where the primary care centres were also relatively poorly served, such as Valencia and Andalusia.

S&N's management chose to conduct the trial in Galicia and Asturias because, of all the poorly covered areas, Galicia was the most suitable.

On July 2, 1999, Jesus Polanco, for Innovex, presented the project to the top managers of S&N's medical division (see Exhibit 4 for a summary of his presentation).

On September 29, 1999, after clarifying and discussing certain details without making any substantial changes, James Brown and Jesus Polanco signed the contract for a term of 6 months, i.e. to March 29, 2000. Besides the operational details, the contract included clauses regulating confidentiality, contract termination in the event of non-compliance by either of the parties, etc.

Lastly, S&N undertook not to hire any of the Innovex employees involved in the project, and agreed to pay Innovex compensation equal to a percentage of the employees' base salary if it did. In the case of the sales representatives, the compensation would be equal to 20 percent of 2.8 million pesetas per sales representative per year.

Execution of the Contract

As soon as the contract was signed, Innovex proceeded to select the two sales representatives. S&N gave its approval to the candidates chosen:

- Isabel, the person selected for Galicia, to be based in Vigo, already had some experience of medical sales visits. The S&N products she would have to

EXHIBIT 4   Summary of the Presentation Given on July 2, 1999 by Innovex's Jesus Polanco to the Top Management of Smith & Nephew, A.A.'s Medical Division

- The plan was to conduct a trial campaign to promote the products Opsite®, Intrasite® Gel and Allevyn® in the four provinces of Galicia and in Asturias using a team hired from Innovex, whose target contacts would be nurses. If the trial objectives were achieved, the scheme would be extended to other geographical areas.
- The contract would have a term of six months.
- The team contracted from Innovex would consist of two sales representatives, a project manager, and a clerical assistant. The latter two would devote two days a month to the project. The sales representatives would receive five days' training.
- The sales representatives would devote their efforts exclusively to promoting the above mentioned S&N products.
- The fee per sales representative would be 35,102 pesetas per day actually worked, i.e. neither sick leave nor vacations would be billed.

The daily cost given above would include:

- Salary and social security.
- Health insurance and accident and third party cover.
- Monthly food + travel expenses, including the sales representatives' travelling, parking and telephone expenses up to a maximum of 80,000 pesetas per person per month.
- Vacations.
- All expenses deriving from the vehicles used by Innovex personnel in providing the contracted services.
- Costs of personnel selection by Innovex (in particular the cost of press adverts, costs associated with the selection interview, and the costs of hiring). Innovex would only select people who matched the profile and culture required by S&N.
- All aspects of payroll and associated costs, company cars, and the telephone expenses of the project manager.
- The costs of the administration department.

The following items were not included in the price per day previously given:

- Incentives for the sales representatives.[1]
- Promotions aimed at doctors and customers.
- Promotional materials, samples, etc., which would have to be provided by S&N.
- Trips and field visits by S&N executives.
- Training costs. S&N would be responsible for all training in products, therapeutic areas and customers.
- Innovex would be responsible for managing the sales team. The two companies would agree on the kind of reporting and information S&N thought necessary in order to monitor the team's activities.

In an appendix, Jesus Polanco's presentation also described:

- The recommended profile for the sales representatives.
- The selection process.
- The functions of the Innovex project manager, who would liaise between the two companies.
- The responsibilities of Innovex's human resources department.
- The responsibilities of Innovex's finance department.

Finally, the presentation included a page stressing the advantages of using a sales team contracted from Innovex as opposed to a company-employed sales team.

[1]In the end no incentives were established.

promote were already known and used in the region, thanks to the hospital work done by Arturo, the local representative, who lived in Corunna. This meant that the new sales representative would have some local support.

- The person chosen for Asturias, Federico, had little experience but the right profile and plenty of enthusiasm. Asturias had the added disadvantage of having been neglected during the previous two years following the death of S&N's previous sales representative, who had not been replaced. Because of this, in Asturias there had not even been the momentary surge in sales registered in other parts of Spain after Allevyn® got the Social Security coupon; and the products Federico would have to promote were practically unknown in the region.

Both the Innovex sales representatives were given two weeks' training. In the first week they had three days' instruction on the products they would be promoting (given by S&N), and one day on sales techniques (given by Innovex). The second week was given over to on-the-job training, accompanied by one of S&N's regional sales managers.

Following this, towards the middle of October 1999, they took up their posts in their respective sales territories and started to visit customers, using a list of primary care centres provided by Innovex and approved by S&N. The centres were ranked on an ABC basis according to their purchasing potential.

The regional sales manager for the central-northern area of S&N's medical division approved the sales routes proposed by Innovex, and after the first week started to accompany the two new representatives on their rounds.

According to the medical division sales manager, "We treated them as if they were our own employees."

It should be said, however, that about two weeks after Isabel, the representative for Galicia, had taken up her post, the marketing department held two study days in Vigo and Corunna, which had already been scheduled from earlier. This gave Isabel a chance to make contacts much more quickly than she could have done without the study days.

In Galicia, Isabel's promotional activities were concentrated in the provinces of Orense (342,000 inhabitants) and Pontevedra (904,000 inhabitants).

Both sales representatives took about three months to adapt to the normal pace of work.

Evaluation of the Results

At the end of February 2000, the director of S&N's medical division, together with his sales manager and marketing manager, analysed the results on the basis of the data available at the time.

With regard to costs, the average amount billed by Innovex to S&N had been 810,000 pesetas per sales representative per month.

EXHIBIT 5 Intrasite® Gel Range

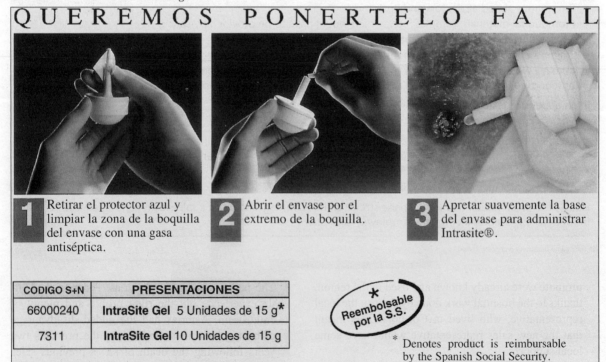

EXHIBIT 6   Allevyn® Range

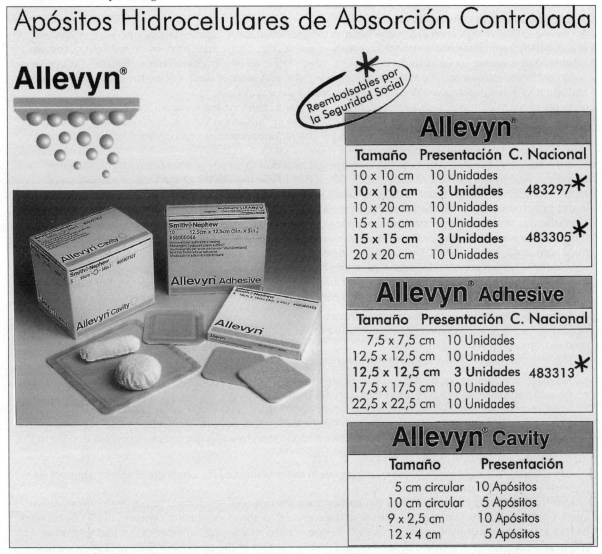

Apósitos Hidrocelulares de Absorción Controlada

Allevyn®

Reembolsables por la Seguridad Social

Allevyn®

Tamaño	Presentación	C. Nacional
10 x 10 cm	10 Unidades	
10 x 10 cm	**3 Unidades**	**483297** *
10 x 20 cm	10 Unidades	
15 x 15 cm	10 Unidades	
15 x 15 cm	**3 Unidades**	**483305** *
20 x 20 cm	10 Unidades	

Allevyn® Adhesive

Tamaño	Presentación	C. Nacional
7,5 x 7,5 cm	10 Unidades	
12,5 x 12,5 cm	10 Unidades	
12,5 x 12,5 cm	**3 Unidades**	**483313** *
17,5 x 17,5 cm	10 Unidades	
22,5 x 22,5 cm	10 Unidades	

Allevyn® Cavity

Tamaño	Presentación
5 cm circular	10 Apósitos
10 cm circular	5 Apósitos
9 x 2,5 cm	10 Apósitos
12 x 4 cm	5 Apósitos

With regard to sales, they had data from the territorial sales analysis (ATV)[8] for the last quarter of 1999, and internal billing data up to January 2000.

Everybody agreed that the results had been very different in the two areas:

In Galicia:

According to the October–December ATV report, the market share of Allevyn®, Intrasite® Gel and Opsite®, in pesetas, for the whole of Galicia had increased from 3.3 percent to 6.4 percent of the total value of MWH products sold. In Orense and in Pontevedra, the increase had been from 5.4 percent to 12 percent.

The additional sales revenue (on top of the minimal revenue obtained previously in the region) amounted to around 5,133,000 pesetas in four months (October 1999–January 2000 inclusive).[9] The gross margin had been 1,540,000 pesetas, i.e. 30 percent on average.

[8]The company IMS conducted a panel study of pharmaceutical retailers. Usually, it only provided aggregate data for the whole of Spain. The territorial sales analysis *(análisis territorial de ventas, ATV)* was a special service that IMS provided, offering the same data broken down by geographical areas similar in size to postal districts.

[9]606,000 pesetas. in October; 1,042,000 in November; 1,779,000 in December 1999; and 1,706,000 in January 2000.

EXHIBIT 7   Sales Representatives' Legal Status

1. Salaried sales representatives
According to labour legislation in force in Spain in the year 2000, sales representatives who were integrated in a company's workforce had a "labour" contract of employment with that company. In the light of certain court rulings, a worker could be understood to be integrated in a company's workforce when he was unable to organize his professional activity at his own discretion, when his place of work was on the company's premises, and when he was subject to working hours stipulated by the company.

In the event of dismissal, such a sales representative could challenge the company's decision before the labour courts and require them to decide on the "fairness" or "unfairness" of the dismissal. If the dismissal was declared unfair, the company had to pay the worker severance payment or compensation equal to 45 days' salary per year of service up to a maximum of 42 months' salary.

If the company chose to terminate the employment relationship on any of the objective grounds for dismissal specified by the Workers' Statute (Article 52), it had to pay the worker, at the time of notification of termination, compensation equal to 20 days' salary per year of service up to a limit of 12 months' salary. Again in this case, the worker could challenge the dismissal and ask the court to declare it unfair. If in the end the company was unable to demonstrate the existence of objective grounds and the dismissal was declared unfair, the company would have to pay the worker compensation equal to 45 days' salary per year of service up to a maximum of 42 months' salary. Exceptionally, however, if the dismissed worker was hired under the terms of Law 63/1997, which provided for urgent measures to improve the labour market and promote stable employment, the above did not apply. Instead, in such cases, if the dismissal was found to be unfair, the company was obliged to pay compensation equal to 33 days' salary per year of service up to a maximum of 24 months' salary.

2. Sales representatives with an agency contract
According to the Agency Contract Law (Law 12/92 of May 27), a company could decide to establish a commercial relationship with a sales agent.

The features that defined a sales agent's commercial relationship with the company were:

- His place of work was not on the company's premises.
- He was not subject to working hours that were set by the company.
- In his professional activities he acted independently and organized his work as he saw fit.
- He could assume the business risk of the activities he performed, but this circumstance was not considered a defining feature of a commercial agency relationship and therefore was not sufficient by itself to prevent the relationship from being declared one of employment.

Any disputes that might arise between the parties in the execution of the commercial agency contract were resolved by the civil courts.

Unless otherwise expressly agreed by the parties, the company was not obliged to pay any compensation upon termination of the contract. Nevertheless, the commercial agent could claim compensation if by his work he had added new customers to the company's customer base. In any case, whether or not this right arose, and in what circumstances, would depend on the specific content of the agreement between by the parties.

Given that the relationship was not one of employment, the company was not obliged to pay Social Security contributions for the sales agent.

In Asturias:

The market share of the three products, in the last quarter of 1999, had increased from 0.9 percent to 2.36 percent of total sales, in pesetas, of all MWH products sold by all companies in Asturias.

The additional sales revenue amounted to only 1,484,000 ptas. in four months (October 1999–January 2000 inclusive),[10] with a gross margin of 371,000 pesetas (25 percent).

[10]134,000 pesetas in October: 252,000 in November; 528,000 in December 1999; and 570,000 in January 2000.

The difference in gross margin was due to the fact that the sales representative in Asturias had sold more products that had a lower gross margin. S&N's sales representatives did not know the gross margin of the products they sold. Only indirectly, through marketing actions, were they encouraged to sell higher gross margin products. Essentially, the difference in gross margin between Galicia and Asturias could be said to be due to chance factors.

In response to the low sales in Asturias, the regional sales manager felt that Federico would have to improve his sales technique, in particular his closing abilities.

Sales Projection

In view of the actual results achieved, the medical division's marketing manager estimated that, if new Innovex sales representatives were introduced in other geographical areas, each one of them could be expected to generate roughly the following sales:

Month 1	**450,000 pesetas.**
Month 2	**900,000** "
Month 3	**1,650,000** "
Month 4	**2,225,000** "
Month 5	**2,700,000** "
Month 6	**3,000,000** "
Month 7 onward	**3,000,000 pesetas each month.**

Assuming a gross margin of 30 percent and average Innovex billing steady at 810,000 pesetas per representative per month, breakeven for a representative would be reached in the fifth month (2,700,000 × 30% = 810,000 pesetas of gross margin).

If these sales and margin forecasts were accurate, from month 6 onward the company would generate new gross income of 90,000 pesetas per month (gross margin less the amount billed by Innovex).

Other Considerations

The following are comments made by the director of the medical division and his sales and marketing managers, during their meeting, as they analyzed the facts and figures:

- "Innovex gives us a chance to try things out, to start working with new people and new regions, with a controlled level of risk. Then we can decide whether or not we want to actually hire the people once they've proved they can work profitably."
- "You have to remember that Innovex takes over a whole range of management tasks. During the trial period in Galicia and Asturias all we had to do was approve a bill of 1.6 million pesetas each month. And monitor sales as we wanted. Everything else (payroll, checking the expense sheets, mileage, and so on) was taken care of by Innovex."
- "If the Asturias salesman doesn't perform as well as expected, we can ask Innovex to replace him. And it'll be up to them to carry out the selection, hiring, sales training, etc."
- "Before we replace the salesman, though, we need to be sure it's him who's letting us down, rather than the sales potential of the territory itself, or lack of support on our part."

- "I suspect that Innovex doesn't pay its salespeople very highly. Take our sales representative in Galicia, for example. I'm already starting to worry that one of our competitors will notice our sudden gain of market share, realise that this person is worth her salt, or at least has potential, and offer her a permanent job with better pay."
- "Is it feasible to use Innovex sales representatives in the medium and long term? Or do companies just use them for tactical sales drives that never last more than 6 or 9 months?"

The Decision

Given the results of the trial, Brown and Serra now faced a set of alternatives deriving from the possible combinations of three variables:

1. To use salaried sales representatives or to use contract sales representatives employed by Innovex
2. Level of geographical coverage
3. Timing: when would be best to do one thing or another?

For example, without trying to be exhaustive, the above three variables could be combined in different ways to generate at least the following possible courses of action:

1. Terminate the contract with Innovex and leave the areas of Galicia and Asturias as they were before, i.e., with a single representative, Arturo, visiting hospitals.
2. Renew the contract with Innovex for another six months, only for Galicia and Asturias, in order to prolong the trial and so obtain more reliable data on sales trends and to verify whether the sales and financial performance could be consolidated.
3. Terminate the contract with Innovex and proceed immediately to hire:
   a. One salaried sales representative for Galicia.
   b. Two salaried sales representatives, one for Galicia and one for Asturias.
   c. Two or three salaried sales representatives for Galicia and one for Asturias, as in the original plan.

And in the rest of Spain:

4. Sign a new agreement with Innovex to establish contract sales representatives in all or some of the regions currently lacking coverage: Valencia (2 or 3 representatives) and Andalusia (2 or 3 representatives).

The contract could be for six months or one year. Following that, introduce own salaried sales representatives in all or some of those regions, depending on the level of sales and profitability attained in each one.

5. Directly hire a certain number of salaried sales representatives for those same underserved regions.

Finally, if they decided to hire new salaried sales representatives, they would have to decide whether it was better for the representatives to work in tandem, as Isabel and Arturo had done in Galicia, i.e., with Arturo visiting mainly hospitals and Isabel visiting primary care centres; or whether it would be better to divide up the territory and for each representative to visit both

hospitals and primary care centres in the part of the territory assigned to him or her.

Obviously, for each of these options they would have to weigh up the costs and the benefits, both in strictly financial terms and in terms of sales and marketing strategy.

In this latter respect, CEO James Brown was starting to get excited at the thought of the strategic possibilities that would be opened up if he ever reached the position of having a sales team fully deployed throughout Spain.

At the same time, however, he needed to make sure that the Smith & Nephew group's Spanish subsidiary reported a profit, as he personally desired and as the company's year 2000 budget demanded.

Case 6-22
Sun Microsystems

Scott G. McNealy looks mighty calm for a man running a company whose stock has cratered. In the past two years, shares in Sun Microsystems Inc. have plunged from $64 to a lowly $3.28. A cool $195.1 billion in market cap has evaporated. Subtract Sun's cash from the equation, and investors value the company at barely $1.63 per share, less than they'd pay for a slice of pizza. Now, from the coffee bars to the research and development labs of Silicon Valley, the buzz is that Sun, long a symbol of ingenuity and dynamism, is looking more and more like a relic of a free-spending era that's long gone.

McNealy, Sun's chairman and chief executive, says he's not fazed. Throughout Sun's 20-year history, he has grappled with crises before, struggling to convince skeptical investors, customers, and employees that Sun could transform itself. Each time, he pulled it off. In the early 1990s, tech pundits said Sun should ditch its workstation business and jump on the cheap Intel-Microsoft Windows bandwagon. McNealy wouldn't listen. He went the other direction and built bigger and more powerful machines, setting up Sun to take advantage of the Internet boom. These days, the 48-year-old CEO, dressed in his trademark jeans and sneakers, says matter-of-factly that he understands why investors are treating his stock so poorly. "We're not making money."

Worse, sales have taken a nosedive, down 32%, to $12.5 billion, from a high of $18.3 billion two years ago, as net losses over the past five quarters, excluding

special charges, have mounted to $307 million (Exhibit 1). In the past two years, gross profit margins have skidded by 20%. Top managers, including highly regarded President Edward J. Zander, have jumped ship. And yet McNealy clings tightly to the formula that has worked for him before. It calls for stubbornness, hard work, and faith that the research and innovation that have kept Sun at the head of the industry through the years will come to the rescue.

There's no time to waste. A fearsome posse of competitors, from Dell Computer to Microsoft and Intel, is battering its way into Sun's core market for computer servers, selling low-cost machines at a fraction of Sun's price. A few years ago, servers powered by Microsoft Windows software and Intel chips couldn't perform in the same league with Sun. Now they can. Worse, Linux' open-source software is making inroads into McNealy's market. It's created by legions of volunteers, and it's free—a price that's hard to beat. McNealy finds himself selling the tech equivalent of a Mercedes in a market of Honda buyers. "Sun will need to reinvent its business model," says Henry W. Chesbrough, a management professor at Harvard Business School.

Try saying that to McNealy. He maintains there's a home for Sun at the very top of the industry, safely above the Linux- and Microsoft-powered hoi polloi. He fiercely resists the notion that Sun's sophisticated servers could ever follow the brutal course of a commodity market. At the mention of the word "commodity," McNealy's eyes flash, and the Harvard alum growls that "a hammer is a commodity, a nail is a commodity. A computer is not a commodity."

EXHIBIT 1
**The Problem: Rivals
and Technologies
Are Undermining
Prices . . .**

LINUX This free operating software undermines Sun's Solaris. Linux servers are expected to triple to $6.5 billion by 2005.

MICROSOFT WINDOWS Sales of Windows servers, which sell at a fraction of Sun's, are expected to rise 36%, to $19 billion, by 2005—three times faster than Sun's market.

INTEL The chipmaker is selling microprocessors to work with Linux or Windows in low-priced machines as powerful as Sun's.

DELL With its low-priced servers, Dell has leapt to No. 2 in unit sales in the server market, with a 19.2% share, vs. Sun's 6.2%.

IBM Big Blue is a leader in Linux servers, and its software has grabbed 33% of the market for Internet infrastructure programs, vs. 9% for Sun.

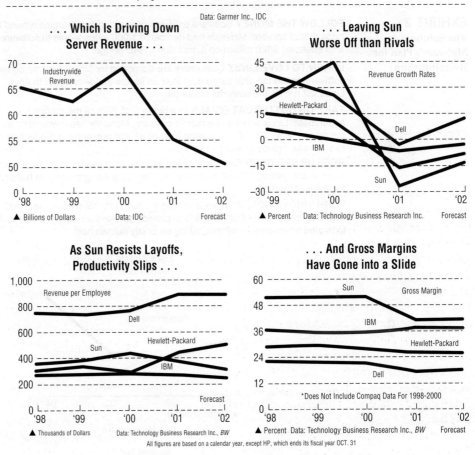

Data: Garmer Inc., IDC

**. . . Which Is Driving Down
Server Revenue . . .**

▲ Billions of Dollars   Data: IDC   Forecast

**. . . Leaving Sun
Worse Off than Rivals**

▲ Percent   Data: Technology Business Research Inc.   Forecast

**As Sun Resists Layoffs,
Productivity Slips . . .**

▲ Thousands of Dollars   Data: Technology Business Research Inc., *BW*   Forecast

**. . . And Gross Margins
Have Gone into a Slide**

*Does Not Include Compaq Data For 1998-2000

▲ Percent Data: Technology Business Research Inc., *BW*   Forecast

All figures are based on a calendar year, except HP, which ends its fiscal year OCT. 31

But if those $4,000 boxes rolling off the assembly lines at Dell Computer Corp. aren't technically commodities, they behave very much like them, pummeling prices in Sun's core business. Consider Sun customer E*Trade Group Inc. In August, the $1.3 billion online financial-services company finished yanking out 60 Sun servers that cost $250,000 apiece and replaced them with 80 Intel-powered Dell servers running Linux that cost just $4,000 each. That took a huge bite out of expenses, including a one-time depreciation of the

Sun gear and big maintenance fees. The savings so far: Nearly $13 million—and the company expects to shave another $11 million annually from its $220 million tech budget. "It wasn't a hard decision," says Joshua S. Levine, chief technology officer at E*Trade. And here's the really painful part: When the Intel-powered machines break, E*Trade doesn't bother calling a repairman. It just junks the server and plugs in a new one.

McNealy is battling disposable computers. And even when he looks away from the cheap Dells, he finds little relief. In the pricey side of the business, IBM, with its horde of consultants, is swooping into Corporate America offering the ultimate in no-headache computing: It will take over the entire burden of running corporate computer systems for clients. Says Microsoft Corp. Chairman William H. Gates III: "In terms of products that meet the market's needs, [McNealy's] in tough shape."

Yet McNealy has a plan, one that he says will lift Sun not only back to profits but to the apex of the Information Economy (Exhibit 2). At the heart of the plan is Sun's classic franchise: heavy research and top-of-the-line computer systems. In a world of specialty players, Sun is a rare bird that designs its own chips and writes its own server software and computer chips. And McNealy's sticking to his integrated model. He's pouring research dollars into network software. His goal, stunningly ambitious, is to have Sun servers and Sun software running superefficient networks of the future—marvels that run virtually free of human

EXHIBIT 2
The Solution:
McNealy's Plan for
Reigniting Sun

FOLLOW THE MONEY Software products generate gross margins around 80%, twice that of servers. McNealy had dedicated 1,000 salespeople to software. He's also spending $900 million on it, half Sun's R&D budget.

LEARN TO LOVE LINUX Customers are clamoring for Linux, the free operating software. In the fall, Sun rolled out Linux on its low-end servers. With time, Linux will run on the powerful boxes too.

TAKE ON CUTTHROAT RIVALS In a bid to grab 30% of the market for supercheap Linux servers in a couple of years, McNealy has unveiled new servers priced as low as $2,700. He's using Intel chips and outsourcing production in an effort to still make money at that price.

BEEF UP SERVICES Sun has doubled its force of consultants, to 13,000, over the past three years, getting 32% of revenues from services. Longer term, he hopes to offer more lucrative consulting.

PUSH INNOVATION McNealy is betting the farm that his outsize R&D budget will help Sun become the first company to provide software for smart networks that look after themselves—without calling on costly human help.

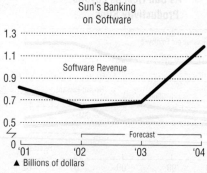

Sun's Banking
on Software

Software Revenue

Forecast

▲ Billions of dollars

Data: Merrill Lynch & Co.

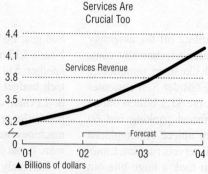

Services Are
Crucial Too

Services Revenue

Forecast

▲ Billions of dollars

Data: Merrill Lynch & Co.

attention. In other words, while investors worry about Sun's very survival, McNealy, ever the contrarian, is plotting a path to supremacy.

And he has certain strengths to build on. By hacking costs, McNealy has stanched much of the bleeding and says Sun will break even by next year's second quarter. Net income has taken a beating, but Sun has generated cash in every quarter of the downturn. In the fiscal quarter that ended in September, Sun's cash total was $2.6 billion, up $140 million from the kitty in the fall of 2000. Tack on $2.6 billion in marketable securities, and McNealy has $5.2 billion to play with. He's using that money to tidy up the books and spice up Sun's image. In the most recent quarter, Sun also bought back $500 million worth of stock and paid off $200 million in debt, bringing debt levels down to $1.5 billion. And he's spending $70 million on a worldwide ad blitz.

But the clock's ticking. Analysts say McNealy has only two years before low-end technologies in operating systems and chips catch up to his own. That's precious little time to defend the company from the onslaught—and to broaden his high-margin beachhead in software. It's fears about Sun's business model that are giving investors the willies. And financial worries are on the rise. On Oct. 16, Standard & Poor's lowered Sun's credit rating from a BBB+ to BBB, saying that Sun's profits would be too unpredictable in the coming year.

McNealy recognizes that hardware is unlikely to produce fat boom-level profits again. He's hoping that higher-margin software, which now makes up only 5% of Sun's revenue and an estimated 9% of profits, will pick up the slack. He won't predict when, but a bullish report from Merrill Lynch & Co. says that within two years Sun could generate up to 9% of revenues from software. That would tack on an estimated $417 million in gross profits.

To reach that target, McNealy needs faultless execution and more than a little luck. He must come up with new network software that matches the best in the business, from IBM's to Microsoft's. It's a tough challenge for a box maker. Indeed, McNealy can only hope the company learned from its failure in the late '90s when it treated software as an ugly stepchild to its booming server business—and blew a golden chance to run away with the market for e-business software.

McNealy must also plow into services, but without disrupting relationships with consulting partners, such as Electronic Data Systems Corp., that install Sun systems. Perhaps most difficult, he must convince workers, many of whom hold stock options that are deep under water, to bust their gut for a company many in the tech world are writing off. And they must hurry: If the cheap servers climbing up the food chain catch up to Sun's top line before McNealy's plan has traction, he's in trouble.

As McNealy leads his company up this steep slope, he'll doubtless face some tough choices. Like the pioneers who tossed their beloved pianos and rocking chairs before crossing the raging Missouri, he'll likely be forced to let loose a few of his precious technologies. High on the list are Sun's proprietary Sparc chips and Solaris server software, which together eat up more than $200 million of R&D investment annually, according to analysts. But even here McNealy faces a dilemma. First, he has lots of customers who rely on maintenance and upgrades for these proprietary components. Cutting back R&D could cripple an important source of revenue. What's more, if he ditches the very pieces that make Sun special, he runs the risk of tumbling into the cutthroat commodity world below.

Will McNealy hoist Sun back to the top? More likely is a Sun that settles into a specialty niche, providing high-margin servers with all the bells and whistles built in, a path similar to the one trod by Apple Computer Inc. in the consumer market. A drearier possibility: Sun could follow the footsteps of Digital Equipment Co., which failed to keep up with cost-saving changes in the computer industry and was eventually bought by Compaq Computer Corp. in 1998 for $9.6 billion. "In a couple of years, if Sun can't turn it around, it could be acquired for its installed base and technology," says Steven Milunovich, a managing director at Merrill Lynch.

If McNealy comes up short, the effects will be felt far and wide. The ideas pouring out of Sun's labs have made the midsize computer maker into an outsize thought leader. Indeed, Sun has been strong enough to take on mighty Microsoft. Its Java programming language, which works on any operating system, remains an alternative to a windows-dominated world. And many in the computer industry maintain that integrated manufacturers, like Sun and Apple, which focus on entire systems, generate far more creativity than the component-based champions such as Microsoft, Intel, and Dell.

Yet creativity doesn't always win the day. And as Sun struggles, Microsoft grows stronger. On Nov. 1, when U.S. District Judge Colleen Kollar-Kotelly upheld a settlement among Microsoft, the Bush Administration, and nine states, the software giant emerged virtually unscathed from a four-year antitrust case, which Sun actively supported. McNealy refuses to talk about the settlement. "I don't get paid to get aggravated," he says.

Still, McNealy has long enjoyed a parallel career as the industry's anti-Microsoft ringleader. But now he barely has time for Bill-baiting. He has a company to rescue. Friends say it's times like these that get McNealy fired up. Tony Scott, chief information officer at General Motors Co., who worked at Sun in the late 1980s and played club ice hockey with McNealy, says McNealy is doing his job with the intensity he always brought to the ice. "He'll put his body on the line to get the job done," says Scott, now a Sun customer.

McNealy is gripping the reins tighter than ever. He's working to put in place the management controls and succession planning learned at the side of the man he considers his mentor, former General Electric Co. Chairman and CEO Jack Welch. McNealy has cut a layer of management that kept him from execs on the front lines. He's acting like a battlefield sergeant, making sure his managers are following his strategy for facing the low-cost onslaught. In October, McNealy even moved his office from Sun's headquarters in Santa Clara, Calif.—a landmark building constructed in 1888—to Menlo Park so he could be closer to a customer center where he's spending most of his time these days.

When he's not meeting with customers, McNealy is making needed repairs to his company. In July, he created an executive vice-president position for software for the first time, organized all of Sun's consulting under one person, and assigned 1,000 salespeople to hawk Sun software.

But McNealy's first big management changes didn't come off as hoped. About 18 months ago, he started work on a succession plan patterned after what he had learned while sitting on the board at GE. McNealy believed the timing was perfect. Several longtime execs, including Zander, wanted to leave the company. By last spring, McNealy had his plan in place.

When Zander left, McNealy would eliminate the president's position. When John Shoemaker, head of Sun's computer unit, retired, McNealy would ax that position, too. This would cut out two layers of management, and more execs would report directly to the CEO. Just like Welch at GE, McNealy planned to evaluate and train a new generation of leaders. At an April, 2002, powwow for Sun's 200 vice-presidents, he unveiled his plan.

Then it blew up in his face. Instead of presenting a cohesive management plan, McNealy, over the course of a month, dribbled out separate announcements for each of the five executives leaving the company, culminating with Zander. Coupled with the downturn in Sun's business, it looked as though the top people were jumping ship—or McNealy was forcing them out. "When they said Ed was leaving, that's when I said to myself, 'Maybe I should think about looking for another job,'" says one former Sun employee. Sun's stock dropped 10% the week after Zander announced he was leaving. McNealy was so flabbergasted by the debacle he called Welch to ask what he did wrong. "Jack said, 'Don't worry about it. They'll forget about it soon enough,'" says McNealy.

Other concerns promptly leaped to the fore, led by Sun's plunging stock. For months, as Sun shares descended into single figures, McNealy turned a deaf ear to Wall Street and resisted further layoffs. He wanted to keep positioning the company, he said, to cash in on the tech recovery. But to a skeptical market he looked less like a determined visionary than a CEO in dangerous denial. On Oct. 17, with Sun's stock wallowing around $3, McNealy finally bowed to the market and announced a second round of layoffs. Combined with last year's cuts, he will have slashed 20% of the company's 43,700 workers.

Now he's hurrying to save money in operations. This year, Sun has shaved $600 million in costs from its supply chain. That has saved five points on its gross margins. "If we hadn't done that, we'd be dead," says Marissa Peterson, executive vice-president of worldwide operations at Sun.

To kick-start business in the low end, McNealy is making a tactical retreat in servers (Exhibit 3). He has opened up a place for the commodity components, Linux and Intel chips, in his economy offerings. To proclaim his newfound love of Linux, McNealy showed up at a Feb. 7 conference in San Francisco in the costume of a penguin, the Linux mascot. The challenge for McNealy is to crack open a door to low-cost business without encouraging high-end customers to swarm through and switch to the cheaper fare.

McNealy has aggressive goals for the Linux servers. He's not airing them publicly, but several Sun executives say McNealy has told them that within the next two years he wants to grab 30% of what will then be a $6.5 billion market, according to researcher IDC. To take on cutthroat rivals, McNealy is keeping costs low and outsourcing production of Sun's Linux machines,

EXHIBIT 3 Tough Decisions for Sun

Data: *BusinessWeek*

McNealy faces challenges. Here's what experts say he should do:

The Dilemma	The Fix
CHIPS Sun must decide if it can afford to spend $200 million a year designing its own microprocessor, the Sparc, when it and Fujitsu are the only two major companies using the chip.	• McNealy can phase Intel chips into most of Sun's servers over time. Power-hungry users will still pay a premium for high-end Sparc machines—at least until Intel crashes the party.
LINUX Customers want choices, and that's what they get with the open-standard Linux operating system.	• Phase in Linux on Sun servers, starting with the low end. As Linux improves, cut back Solaris.
EXPENSES If sales continue to slide, McNealy may have to tighten expenses even more than the 20% payroll cuts he has made so far.	• At 14% of sales, Sun's R&D budget needs reduction surgery. And McNealy may have to proceed with further job cuts.
MICROSOFT-BAITING Does Sun really stand a chance taking on Microsoft with StarOffice, a low-cost knockoff of the software giant's popular Office program?	• McNealy has to pick his fights with Microsoft. Give this one up. It's a distraction.

which start at $2,700. That's a highly ambitious goal, given that Sun has no market share today. But if McNealy can hit his target, the low-end gear could add $400 million in gross profits in 2004.

That may be just enough to cover the slide in sales of Sun's midrange Solaris machines. The trouble with such calculations is that Dell and its low-cost collaborators represent a fast-moving target—one that slashes prices to woo new business. Merrill Lynch estimates that from 2001 to 2004, revenue in Sun's midrange will fall 60%, to $1.7 billion. That translates into an estimated $500 million hit on profits.

McNealy's bid hinges on his ability to focus the company on a handful of key initiatives. One is services. As Sun extends its business from the boxes to the broader network, it will be up to the service staff to help customers install the full gamut of Sun offerings. IBM has mastered this approach. And McNealy, who long denigrated the industry's march toward services, is now following suit. Sun has 13,000 service consultants, double three years ago. And while they're dwarfed by IBM's 180,000 consultants and HP's 65,000-member force, they appear to be gaining traction. In the most recent quarter ended Sept. 30, service revenues were up 9%, to $879 million. Patricia C. Sueltz, Sun's executive vice-president in charge of consulting, targets $1 billion in quarterly services revenue by next year.

Equally vital for McNealy is software. While Sun has been a bold software innovator, coming up with

such advances as Java, software has remained a niche business marked by Sun's failure to turn leading-edge technology into sales and profits. Now McNealy needs it more than ever. Software is at the center of his vision of a Sun-driven networked world—and it delivers gross profit margins of 80%. It's little surprise that McNealy is plowing more than half of his R&D budget into software, much of it for Web applications.

Again, Sun risks new battles with old friends as the company plunges into different businesses. For years, Net software maker BEA Systems Inc. was an enthusiastic Sun partner. It created software to run on Sun's Solaris servers that let customers deliver applications effortlessly via the Web. Now, Sun's assault on the Web-software business has pushed BEA into the arms of chip giant Intel. Why? Unlike Sun, Intel isn't likely to compete in software. Now BEA is shipping a Linux version of its software to run on Intel chips, and sales are taking off. In the last year, Sun's share of the BEA installed base has tumbled from 75% to 55%.

At the heart of McNealy's vision is an ambitious software project called N1 (Exhibit 4). Sun's software developers have been working on the technology for two years, tucked away in a space-age data center at Sun's Sunnyvale (Calif.) facility. The idea is to create vast networks in which the software administers itself. If one computer runs out of memory, the software seeks spare capacity elsewhere on the network. If the software develops a glitch, the program itself will work

EXHIBIT 4

Data: Sun Microsystems Inc.

SUN'S ELDORADO

Sun is staking its software future on a vast project to automate the work in complex data networks. In September, Sun unveiled its nascent effort, called N1. Here's what it aims to do by mid-decade:

ONE SYSTEM Think of N1, as one huge operating system for the network. The software will automatically manage all of the computers, storage, and switches, making them work together as one giant machine.

VIRTUAL RESOURCES The software views all the tech gear in a corporate data center as one virtual pool of resources. If a big project taps out the supercomputer, N1 will automatically route the work to other computers.

LOW-COST COMPUTING By running computers close to capacity, the system will reduce the need for new machines. The software also will manage and update software installations. That will eliminate many of the tasks now handled by squadrons of systems administrators.

to fix it, without calling on costly human administrators. Sun will be releasing the first components of the program by the end of the year.

The trouble is, McNealy must invest heavily in N1 just to stay in step with competitors. IBM and HP are hard at work on very similar systems. On Oct. 30, IBM

CEO Samuel J. Palmisano told customers that he was betting the future of his company on a vast, N1-type project called "on-demand computing." He's investing billions to develop new products and will spend $800 million on the marketing. And although HP CEO Carleton S. Fiorina keeps it quiet, HP's version of N1, called Utility Data Center, already has 450 engineers behind it and 10 customers in pilot projects.

With all these challenges, it might make sense for McNealy to shelve his ongoing war with Microsoft. But he has trouble letting it rest. Since May, he's been offering a low-cost office-applications package to battle Microsoft's ubiquitous Office desktop suite. This is David taking on Goliath without the slingshot. McNealy's colleagues urge him to focus on more pressing threats. Before a Sept. 18 speech to Sun customers at San Francisco's Moscone Center, his vice-president for software, Jonathan Schwartz, bet his boss $2 that he couldn't avoid mentioning Microsoft during his speech. McNealy took the bet—and collected his money after his talk.

At the event, Sun's first big customer conference in seven years, dreadlocked drummers on stage were pounding a beat when McNealy jumped up, beating on a drum of his own. He promptly launched into a 45-minute stump speech defending Sun, one of the last of the integrated computer makers. "There is no automobile-integration industry," he says. "You get a car fully assembled. They even wash it for you." Jokes and debating points aside, McNealy has to get Sun making money again. Only then will he convince the world that Sun can shine anew.

By Jim Kerstetter in Menlo Park, Calif., with Jay Greene in Seattle and bureau reports

Source: "Will Sun Rise Again?" *BusinessWeek*, November 25, 2002, 120–130.

Case 6-23
Telus Mobility—What to Do with Mike

In early 2001, Wade Oosterman reflected on TELUS Corporation's recent acquisition of Clearnet Communications Inc. As executive vice-president of sales and marketing at the new TELUS Mobility, Oosterman was eager to realize the synergies from merging the two compatible personal communications services (PCS) networks of TELUS and Clearnet to achieve a stronger

IVEY

Richard Ivey School of Business
The University of Western Ontario

competitive position in the Canadian consumer wireless market. However, his attention soon turned to Mike, a completely separate digital wireless network that was extremely important to TELUS.

What implications did the recent changes have for Mike? From a broader perspective, given the continued advancement in wireless technology and the increasingly competitive industry climate, what changes, if any, would need to be made to TELUS's short-medium term strategy for Mike? New risks and potential opportunities that needed to be considered. For example, Mike was tied to one handset manufacturer, competition was making aggressive moves, and new technology platforms and migration paths to these needed to be considered. Mike had been incredibly successful within the high revenue commercial market, but Oosterman knew that it would be a challenge to defend that position and continue to grow the business. He started by reviewing the broad landscape of the industry.

The Canadian Wireless Communications Industry

Cellular phone service was first introduced in Canada in 1985. Since then, the industry has experienced unprecedented growth. In 2000 alone, a record 5.9 percent of Canadians adopted wireless, representing a net addition of 1.8 million users. This brought the penetration of wireless services across the Canadian population to 28.4 percent. To put this in perspective, it took over 10 years for the Canadian wireless industry to add its first 1.8 million customers.

Canadian Wireless Penetration Rates

	Net Additions (#) (million)	Net Additions (%)	Total Penetration (%)
2000	1.8	5.9	28.4
1999	1.5	5.0	22.5
1998	1.1		17.5

Jack Wong prepared this case under the supervision of Professor Don Barclay solely to provide material for class discussion. The authors do not intend to illustrate either effective or ineffective handling of a managerial situation. The authors may have disguised certain names and other identifying information to protect confidentiality.

Industry analysts expected robust growth in the wireless sector to continue over the next five years. Current estimates for wireless penetration in 2005 range from 57 percent to 70 percent. These forecasts translate into gains of between 8.8 million and 12.8 million new wireless subscriptions over this period. Experience overseas illustrates that these forecasts are reasonable. Already in Finland and Italy, over 70 percent of the population was using wireless phones.

It is widely believed that wireless subscriptions will eventually reach, or possibly even exceed, 100 percent of the population. In spite of the fact that the addressable market is in the range of 80 percent to 85 percent of the population (excluding the very young and elderly), it is believed that many customers will utilize two or even more wireless devices. While a majority of wireless users communicate through digital PCS phones, new devices such as personal digital assistants (PDAS) manufactured by companies like Palm and Handspring have been gaining popularity.

Consumer demand for freedom, mobility and "anywhere, anytime" access to information has fuelled the development of wireless telemetry applications and user-relevant mobile Internet services. Also, advanced second and third generations of wireless technology (2.5G, 3G) bring the promise of broadband, which will allow for high-speed data transmissions and the introduction of more robust features and services. The convergence of wireless technology and the Internet makes such high penetration increasingly possible.

Economics

In an immensely capital-intensive industry, network operators invest billions in building wireless infrastructure. Wireless phones use radio waves to transmit and receive sound through a wideband radio frequency or channel. A network requires numerous cell sites to be deployed throughout its coverage area. Cell sites are radio antenna towers that transmit signals to and from wireless handsets. Also, switches are required to co-ordinate call traffic, interconnect calls with local and long distance landline telephone companies, and compile billing information. The final significant capital expenditure for operators consists of fees paid to the federal government for spectrum licences that are awarded through an auction process. As the spectrum of radio frequencies is a valuable finite resource, spectrum assignment is regulated and controlled by federal government agencies, such as Industry Canada.

EXHIBIT 1
Historical
Performance of
Major Wireless
Industry Players

	2000*	1999	1998	1997
Subscribers				
Mike	–	210,121	114,095	44,549
Clearnet PCS	–	349,210	194,374	50,676
TELUS PCS	2,156,000	1,099,000	963,000	823,000
Bell Mobility	2,340,000	1,797,000	1,475,000	
Rogers AT&T	2,514,000	2,153,100	1,737,600	1,552,100
Microcell	922,500	484,487	282,174	n/a
ARPU				
Mike	–	68.91	73.32	72.28
Clearnet PCS	–	46.97	49.60	44.24
TELUS PCS	59.00	60.00	70.00	76.00
Bell Mobility	46.00	51.00	60.00	
Rogers AT&T	46.00	49.00	54.00	59.00
Microcell	43.55	47.08	58.40	n/a
Churn				
Mike	–	1.64%	1.28%	1.50%
Clearnet PCS	–	1.87%	1.54%	0.47%
TELUS PCS	n/a	1.40%	1.30%	1.20%
Bell Mobility	1.50%	1.80%	n/a	n/a
Rogers AT&T	2.36%	1.86%	1.90%	1.63%
Microcell	2.20%	2.10%	2.10%	n/a
COA				
Mike	–	$578	$619	$603
Clearnet PCS	–	$544	$662	$1,107
TELUS PCS	537	360	412	338
Bell Mobility	n/a	n/a	n/a	n/a
Rogers AT&T	$441	$391	$525	$ 623
Microcell	$388	$421	$687	n/a
MOU				
Mike	–	378	358	315
Clearnet PCS	–	249	202	182
TELUS PCS	271	218	219	200
Bell Mobility	n/a	n/a	n/a	n/a
Rogers AT&T	263	216	202	213
Microcell	185	190	257	n/a

*2000 numbers for TELUS PCS are adjusted figures to reflect acquisitions.

Given the high level of fixed costs in the industry, considerable attention is paid to particular metrics once a network is established and operational. In particular, there are four key elements in the profit dynamic in the wireless industry (see Exhibit 1 for historical performance of major industry players):

Subscribers

Currently, industry success is primarily measured by subscriber growth. Network operators generate revenue from subscribers who use their service. Naturally, this means that the acquisition of new users is a foremost objective in order to recover the heavy fixed investment. In Canada, the major industry players have been aggressively targeting new entrants to the market as opposed to focusing on converting subscribers from competitors.

Cost of Acquisition (COA)

COA refers to the cost of acquiring a network subscriber. While wireless handsets typically cost consumers from $50 to $250, in most cases the handset costs have been subsidized by network operators to encourage greater adoption by users. Industry research has shown that, in the consumer market, up-front handset costs are the largest inhibitor for potential new subscribers. This has led many network operators to subsidize the cost of handsets in an effort to boost subscriber additions. A common tactic in the industry involves offering customers free handsets while tying them to long-term contracts, ensuring that the initial handset costs would be recovered over time.

Handset manufacturers such as Ericsson, Nokia, Motorola and Samsung decrease the wholesale price of their handsets as they realize economies of scale, learning curve effects in production, and advances in component technology (semiconductor, screen, battery). However, because wireless networks operate on different technology platforms, some more established than others, certain operators benefit from a substantial handset cost advantage.

Additional costs that are considered in the calculation of COA are sales, marketing and advertising costs that include commissions, gifts with purchase, and rebates.

Average Revenue per Subscriber Unit *(APRU)*

Not surprisingly, the average revenue per subscriber unit per month is an important target, one that operators would logically seek to maximize. However, over the past few years, APRU has been decreasing within the industry. Despite Canada's relatively low wireless penetration rate among developed nations, Canadian airtime prices are among the least expensive in the world. The aggressive pricing strategies of some players, eager to gain new users, have led to a highly competitive market. A multitude of airtime packages now exists to meet the needs of a variety of users. Business customers continue to represent the most lucrative segment of the wireless market. Many believe that the introduction of new services, such as wireless Internet, will have a positive impact on APRU in the future.

Churn

Churn refers to the rate at which clients leave an operator's network. Given the substantial costs incurred in acquiring a subscriber, customer retention is critical. Every network operator wants to realize a payback on COA before losing a customer, especially wireless service providers with a high handset subsidy structure and no-contract policies. Unfortunately, this is not always achievable and churn is unavoidable. Customers leave for a number of reasons including relocation, insufficient network coverage and poor customer service. Industry churn in 2000 was approximately two percent, indicating that an average network operator lost two percent of its subscriber base each month of the year.

Year 2000 Key Metrics of Industry Players

	TELUS Mobility	Bell Mobility	Rogers AT&T	Micro-cell
Subscribers	2,156,000	2,340,000	2,514,000	922,500
COA	$537	n/a	$441	$388
ARPU/month	$ 59	$46	$ 46	$ 44
Churn/month	1.95%	1.5%	2.36%	2.20%

Company Background

In setting the strategic direction for Mike, Oosterman had to consider that two companies with distinct histories had just come together—Clearnet and TELUS.

Clearnet

Clearnet was founded in 1984 as a subsidiary of Lenbrook Inc., a private Canadian company specializing in electronics marketing and distribution. Clearnet was created to give Lenbrook a foothold in the specialized mobile radio (SMR) service industry. SMR systems allow for radio conversations between users through simple walkie-talkie devices that operate in a push-to-talk mode in which a user cannot hear the other(s) while transmitting. Clearnet's SMR business targeted dispatch companies like taxi fleets, fire departments, paramedic squads, police departments, construction services and parcel delivery companies.

Headquartered in Pickering, Ontario (and later Scarborough), Clearnet became the first and largest licensed SMR operator in Canada. The company attained its Canadian leadership position in SMR by increasing its 800 megahertz (MHZ) spectrum position, securing smaller regional operators, and acquiring Motorola's Canadian SMR business. Clearnet also operated a wholly owned dealership division, Clearnet Business Communication Centres, that sold and serviced the company's range of wireless technologies.

In 1996, Clearnet introduced the digital Mike network, becoming the first and only Canadian wireless communications company to provide fully integrated two-way radio, mobile telephone, and alphanumeric paging services in a single handset on a single network. Mike was targeted primarily at business workgroup users.

In 1997, Clearnet launched digital PCS in Canada's largest urban centres, becoming the first Canadian company to operate two digital wireless networks. Compared to existing wireless analog phone technology, PCS offered consumers superior call clarity, lighter handsets, longer battery life and enhanced security. As PCS was intended for the growing individual consumer market, Clearnet expanded its distribution network to include flagship stores in major Canadian cities, a wide variety of retailers, and eventually corporate-owned in-mall stores.

The company's success was attributable to its industry foresight, strategic partnerships and unique supplier relationships. Clearnet saw the advantage of accumulating radio spectrum in the expectation of emerging digital technologies that would utilize radio frequencies more efficiently and creatively. Initially, the spectrum was used for two-way dispatch radio services. However, Clearnet understood that owning spectrum was like owning precious real estate. As cellular technology developed, Clearnet was well positioned because it owned the right to offer high revenue cellular/PCS services on those radio frequencies that other companies, at the time, did not see value in. The company was successful at raising the capital necessary to construct its digital networks. Clearnet's initial public offering in 1994 resulted in $121 million. Also, strategic alliances with wireless giants Motorola and Nextel Communications gave Clearnet cutting-edge technology and research and development (R&D) capability, while exclusive alliances with leading industry suppliers, such as Lucent Technologies Canada, provided vendor financing arrangements and industrywide recognition.

Telus

TELUS Corporation is one of Canada's leading telecommunications companies, providing a full range of communications products and services. Originally Alberta's provincial telephone service provider, TELUS merged with BC Tel, its counterpart in British Columbia, in 1999, retaining the TELUS name. Since then, TELUS has aggressively pursued Eastern Canadian markets in an effort to become a national telecommunications service provider. Through expansion and acquisitions (e.g., Quebec Tel purchase), TELUS soon began to provide voice, data, Internet, advertising and wireless services to Central and Eastern Canada, in addition to servicing its home markets in Western Canada.

In 2000, TELUS acquired Clearnet in what was the largest transaction in Canadian telecommunications history. This move allowed TELUS to create a national wireless company with an industry leadership position in overall revenue, revenue growth, revenue per subscriber and wireless spectrum position. Technological synergies were apparent, as Clearnet's digital PCS network operated on the same CDMA technology platform as that of TELUS. To otherwise realize its national ambition, TELUS would have had to brave the risks and time-to-market delays associated with building its own greenfield digital network in Central-Eastern Canada. Additionally, Clearnet offered an extensive national retail and dealer distribution system.

The newly combined company, under the name TELUS Mobility, ended 2000 with more than 2.1 million subscribers across Canada, pro forma annual revenue of more than $1.7 billion, more than 4,000 employees, and digital coverage of 22.6 million of the 31 million total Canadian population that TELUS had licences to cover. TELUS had inherited Mike from Clearnet as one of its key offerings.

The Mike Network

The Mike network is an enhanced specialized mobile radio (ESMR) system based on iDEN (integrated digital enhanced network), a proprietary technology of Motorola. To date, it is the only technology in the world with the ability to integrate four distinct services in a single portable phone: digital telephone, dispatch radio (Mike's Direct Connect), alphanumeric paging and data transmission. iDEN networks have been deployed worldwide in countries such as Canada, the United States, Argentina, Brazil, China, Colombia, Israel, Japan, Korea, Mexico, the Philippines and Singapore.

In Canada, TELUS is the sole operator of iDEN and offers service in British Columbia, Alberta, Ontario and Quebec. These four provinces represent 85 percent of the Canadian population. In the United States, iDEN is operated by Nextel, with whom TELUS enjoys a strong partnership. This has allowed for the introduction of value-added features for Mike clients. For example, Mike users are able to use their handsets in the United States, at local Canadian rates, without paying any roaming fees.

Target Customers

Clearnet's initial marketing strategy for Mike was directed at existing dispatch and two-way radio users. The appeal to these users was obvious. Mike's digital technology gives users higher quality transmission and greater geographic coverage than SMR systems. Since a considerable number of dispatch subscribers also use cellular phones and paging services, Mike would eliminate the need for businesses to subscribe to multiple services. Clearnet began converting its existing SMR client base to its ESMR system, Mike. The other primary target market consisted of commercial users with a mobile work force, such as real estate firms and other sales-driven companies.

As Mike possessed all the capabilities of PCS, along with additional functionality, its target market broadened to include traditional "white collar" businesses. Over time, Mike users would include airlines, film and television companies, government agencies and utilities. Mike's positioning evolved to that of "a universal communication tool designed to save businesses time and money." It became clear that Mike had incredible market potential, much of which still remains untapped.

Products and Services

All Mike handsets are manufactured by Motorola. See Exhibit 2 for descriptions of TELUS Mobility's Mike product line. Since its launch, Motorola has regularly introduced new handsets, continually incorporating improvements in features and design. For example, the palm-sized iDEN i1000 handset offered sophisticated buyers the first phone with a built-in speaker phone, while still satisfying their demand for handsets featuring sleek "form factor." The latest Mike handsets are "dot-com ready," built with microbrowsers to allow users to connect with wireless Internet services. Internet services are the same on Mike as on TELUS PCS, enabling users to access news, directories, restaurant and movie listings, and other entertainment-related information. Also, Mike handsets support mobile computing by acting as a modem that can connect to laptop computers.

Mike's Direct Connect

Mike's competitive advantage lies in its Direct Connect feature. While cellular phones can now offer features such as digital clarity, secure calling, text messaging and longer battery life, they have not been able to duplicate the digital two-way radio feature of iDEN. Mike's Direct Connect allows users to contact each other instantly at the touch of a button. Unlike telephones, Direct Connect does not require any dialing or ringing, eliminating the delay and frustration from waiting for connections and playing "telephone tag." Direct Connect allows users to talk to one person at a time (private mode) or to many (group mode).

Mike Networks

Clearnet recognized the growing value that Mike created in certain industries and capitalized on this opportunity to foster loyalty among Mike customers.

In 1998, Clearnet introduced Mike Networks, expanding the functionality of Direct Connect to allow instant contact, not only within one's own organization of Mike users, but also with other groups of Mike users. Without Mike Networks, only an organization's own Mike users can communicate with one another using Direct Connect.

Construction Net, the first Mike Network, was embraced by the construction sector, which realized the value of instant contact with industry partners. In Eastern Canada, Construction Net grew to include more than 650 construction businesses, 4,000 subscribers, and associations such as the Ontario Road Builders Association and the Greater Toronto Home Builders Association. It became evident that construction companies looking to operate at peak efficiency would have to be a part of Construction Net.

Each of the Mike Networks was designed around specific communities to give users efficient and cost-effective access to business partners. Mike Networks now exists in Professional Services, Construction, Media and Entertainment, Health and Social Services, Transportation and Automotive, Friends and Family, and Hospitality and Travel services.

Pricing

Unlike the consumer segment of the market, commercial users demonstrate less sensitivity to the price of handsets. Their purchase decisions are more influenced by the cost effectiveness of a service's rate plans. TELUS currently prices Mike handsets between $49.99 and $249.99. To respond to varying business communication needs, TELUS offers 11 monthly rate plans designed for individual users, small teams or larger businesses that start at $30 per user. Available plans offer flexible features and add-ons, such as unlimited local evening calling and long distance, designed for travellers and heavy business users. See Exhibit 3 for Mike Service Plans. Mike also offers a cost saving Account Pooling feature that allows a user's unused dollars to be applied to the excess minutes of another user in the organization (see Exhibit 4).

Distribution

Initially, Mike was sold through two competing channels of distribution: Clearnet Business Communication Centers and an independent dealer network. As the sales process for Mike simplified, distribution grew to include Clearnet stores and national retailers with a wireless category focus. Because Mike sales typically

EXHIBIT 2   **Mike Handsets—Product Descriptions**

Features					
Weight - Phone plus std Battery (g)	170	204	243.5	170	170
Size	11.5cm × 5.6cm × 3cm	13.2cm × 5.4cm × 3.6cm	13.4cm × 5.4cm × 3.6cm	11.5cm × 5.6cm × 3cm	11.5cm × 5.6cm × 3cm
Talktime (minutes)	180	330	330	180	180
Standby Time (hours)	28hrs	85	85	50	50
Display	Large 4-line backlit display	Large 4-line backlit display	Large 4-line backlit display	Large 8-line backlit display	Large 8-line backlit display
Multi-language support	English, French, Portuguese, and Spanish	English, French, Portuguese, and Spanish	English, French, Portuguese, and Spanish	English, French, Portuguese, and Spanish	English, French, Portuguese, and Spanish
Phone					
Speed Dial	100 entries	100 entries	100 entries	250 consolidated phone book entries	250 consolidated phone book entries
Speakerphone	Yes	No	No	Yes	Yes
Phone Only Mode	Yes	Yes	Yes	Yes	Yes
Name and Number Scrolling Display	Yes	Yes	Yes	Yes	Yes
Consolidated Directory Programming	Yes	Yes	Yes	Yes	Yes
Call Waiting/Call Hold	Yes	Yes	Yes	Yes	Yes
Call Forwarding	Yes	Yes	Yes	Yes	Yes
Vibra Call	Yes	No	Yes	Yes	Yes
Any Key Answer	Yes	Yes	Yes	Yes	Yes
Keypad Lockout	Yes	Yes	Yes	Yes	Yes
Selectable Ring Styles	Yes	Yes	Yes	Yes	Yes
One-touch Emergency Dial	Yes	Yes	Yes	Yes	Yes
Last 10 Calls Sent/ Received	Yes	Yes	Yes	Yes	Yes
Missed Call Indicator	Yes	Yes	Yes	Yes	Yes
Quickstore of Phone Numbers	Yes	Yes	Yes	Yes	Yes
Quickstore of Private IDs	Yes	Yes	Yes	Yes	Yes
Wireless Modem	Yes	Yes	Yes	Yes	Yes
Dot Com Ready	Yes	Yes	Yes	Yes	Yes
Mike Smart Card Enabled	No	No	No	Yes	Yes
Certified to Military Standard 810 C/D/E for Mechanical Shock and Vibration	No	No	Yes	No	Yes
Java 2 Micro Edition™ (J2ME) Ready	No	No	No	Yes	Yes

EXHIBIT 2—*(concluded)*

Direct Connect (Private Call)					
Directory	100	100	100	250 consolidated phone book entries	250 consolidated phone book entries
Call Alert Stacking	Yes	Yes	Yes	Yes	Yes
Caller ID / Name Display	Yes	Yes	Yes	Yes	Yes
Vibra Alert	Yes	No	Yes	Yes	Yes
Direct Connect (Group Call)					
Programming Talkgroups	30	30	30	30	30
Message Mail Slots	16	16	16	16	16

involve multiple users and handsets, its sales cycle still remains longer than that of PCS. Also, it remains a challenge for sales representatives to clearly articulate the benefits of Mike's Direct Connect without a live demonstration of the feature. Even then, it is often not until a customer is personally using Direct Connect that they understand and appreciate the utility it provides.

Communication

Clearnet launched iDEN services under the brand name Mike to create a brand that is simple to say, easy to remember and bilingual. Mike also allowed Clearnet to differentiate itself from the brands of competitors, which at the time of Mike's introduction were geared primarily towards consumers (e.g., Liberti, Amigo, Fido). In addition, Mike was clearly positioned for business users while Clearnet's other digital network, PCS, was focused on the mass consumer market. Mike existed in a very formidable and dynamic competitive context.

Competition

Bell Mobility

Bell Mobility, a division of Bell Canada, offers analog cellular and digital PCS, paging, two-way messaging and data services to customers in Ontario and Quebec. In a competitive market, Bell Mobility has chosen to focus its efforts on value as opposed to aggressive pricing. The company was the first in Canada to offer a mobile browser service on PCS, allowing users to access the Internet from their phones. Similar to Mike's data capabilities, its Digital Data to Go service allows digital PCS phones to send and receive e-mail, surf

the Internet, and send and receive faxes. Bell Mobility offers a solid product mix backed by an extensive network of dealers, established customer service and financial stability. The company also continues to leverage its connection to other Bell Canada Enterprises (BCE) companies through service bundling.

In 2000, Bell Mobility launched wireless e-mail services through handheld devices manufactured by Research In Motion (RIM). Driving the appeal of RIM wireless handhelds are features such as alphanumeric keyboards, thumb-operated trackwheels, and integrated e-mail/organizer software. The devices can also be synchronized with laptops and desktops. Users can send and receive e-mail; forward attachments; update schedules, contacts and task lists; and access traditional paging services.

While PCS phones and Mike handsets allow for basic access to e-mail, their current design and size limit effectiveness, as the screens are small and data must be entered using numeric keypads (e.g., the letter "L" is entered by pressing the "5" key three times). Additionally, wireless phones currently require users to retrieve e-mail. RIM handhelds are designed to remain on and continuously connected to the wireless network, automatically notifying users when e-mail is received. Users save time because they do not have to initiate routine connections to check for messages.

RIM has been an industry success story and its Blackberry handhelds have been extremely popular among professional business users. However, its current lack of voice calling capability limits its ability to act as a complete communications solution. RIM handsets are sold by Bell Mobility's corporate sales force and its retail and dealer networks. Also, RIM has its own corporate sales force tasked with selling wireless e-mail solutions to corporate customers.

EXHIBIT 3 Mike Service Plans

Rate Plan	Phone 40	Dispatch 40	Work 40	Work 65	Work 100	Work 150	Travel 75	Travel 150	Travel 250
Monthly Fee	$40	$40	$40	$65	$100	$150	$75	$150	$250
Target Audience	Phone Users	Heavy Dispatch Users	Multi-function Users	Multi-function Users	Multi-function Users	Heavy multi-function Users	Travelers	Travelers	Travelers
Total combined minutes or messages									
	Up to 400	Unlimited + Unlimited Direct Connect	267	650	1000 + Unlimited Message Mail	1500 + Unlimited Message Mail and Direct Connect	250 + Unlimited Message Mail	600 + Unlimited Message Mail and Direct Connect	1250 + Unlimited Message Mail and Direct Connect
Anytime rate									
Phone	10c/min (up to 400 mins)	n/a	15c/min	10c/min	10c/min	10c/min	30c/min	25c/min	20c/min
Direct Connect (private and group)	20c/min (up to 200 mins)	Unlimited (private), 20c/min (group)	15c/min	10c/min	10c/min	Unlimited (private), 10c/min (group)	30c/min	Unlimited (private)	Unlimited (private)
Message Mail	20c/message (up to 200 messages)	n/a	15c/message	10c/message	Unlimited	Unlimited	Unlimited	Unlimited	Unlimited
Additional Airtime									
Phone	20c/min	20c/min	20c/min	20c/min	20c/min	10c/min	30c/min	25c/min	20c/min
Direct Connect	20c/min	20c/min (group)	20c/min	20c/min	20c/min	10c/min (group)	30c/min	Unlimited	Unlimited
Message Mail	20c/message	20c/message	15c/message	10c/message	Unlimited	Unlimited	Unlimited	Unlimited	Unlimited

EXHIBIT 3—*(concluded)*

Rate Plan	Phone 40	Dispatch 40	Work 40	Work 65	Work 100	Work 150	Travel 75	Travel 150	Travel 250
Unlimited Add-ons									
Unlimited evenings and weekends (phone)	$15	$25	$15	$15	$10	Included	n/a	n/a	n/a
Unlimited Direct Connect	n/a	Included	$20	$15	$10	Included	$10	Included	Included
Unlimited Message Mail	$5	$5	$5	$5	Included	Included	Included	Included	Included
Unlimited Surf	$10	$10	$10	$10	$10	$10	$10	$10	$10
Unlimited Surf-A-Lot	$15	$15	$15	$15	$15	$15	$15	$15	$15
Optional Add-on									
Mike Online (mobile computing)	$5 (+ airtime)	$5 (+ airtime)	$5 (+ airtime)	$5 (+ airtime)	$5 (+ airtime)	$5 (+ airtime)	$5 (+ airtime)	$5 (+ airtime)	$5 (+ airtime)
Included Features	Basic voice, mail, caller ID, call waiting, call forwarding		Basic voice mail, caller ID, call waiting, call forwarding		Advanced voice mail, caller ID call waiting, call forwarding		Direct Connect wide area, voice mail, caller ID, call waiting, call forwarding		Wide area, advanced voice mail, caller ID, call waiting, call forwarding

EXHIBIT 4 Mike Account Pooling

Account pooling allows individuals belonging to a particular account to make use of the unspent dollars from the monthly plan(s) of other individuals within the same account. Those unused dollars are automatically applied to other users' excess minutes at their per-minute rate. At the time of this case, no other provider provided such service. Below is an example of account pooling:

Example	Bill	Sue	John	Account Total
Monthly Rate	$40 +	$100 +	$100	= $240
Actual Usage	$40 +	$ 55 +	$150	= $245
Additional Usage	$ 0 +	($ 45) +	$ 50	= $ 5
Amount Due (greater of total monthly rates and total actual usage)				$245
Charges from other companies	$40 +	$100 +	$150	= $290

Savings under account pooling: $45

Rogers AT&T Wireless

Rogers AT&T Wireless is one of Canada's largest national wireless communications service providers, offering subscribers a wide selection of products and services. With extensive network coverage and over 6,000 points of distribution, it provides analog cellular, digital PCS, paging, and wireless data services nationwide. Rogers also offers RIM handsets, which complement its line of communication products. The company intends to compete vigorously for all customer segments and in all markets based on the strengths of its broad digital service coverage and extensive distribution network.

Like Bell Mobility, Rogers's wireless business unit leverages the capabilities of other Rogers companies. Consumers benefit from the bundling of core cable TV, digital TV, high-speed Internet access, and wireless communication services. Research has shown that over 60 per cent of U.S. customers are interested in receiving all their communication services from one provider on one bill. This can be an effective retention tool provided that services delivered meet the expectations of consumers.

In 2001, Rogers launched a wireless product specifically targeted at the youth market under a completely separate brand called iD. Analysts predict that the wireless penetration rate among 14-year-olds to 19-year-olds will grow from 1.2 million to 3.8 million in two years. Fuelling the growth and high adoption rates is the availability of Internet services. In Europe, short message services (SMS) is an incredibly popular form of communicating, where users send short text messages to and from wireless phones. Instant messaging is a low-latency, short form of Internet messaging that is used by large communities of users, allowing participants to identify "buddies" and see when members of their "buddy list" are online to chat. Rogers intends to build a similar community among users aged 14 to 24.

Microcell

Microcell Telecom first launched PCS in November 1996, under the brand Fido. Fido was positioned as an everyday communications tool, and its consumer proposition was based primarily on price, with a focus on fairness and simplicity. Service was marketed in communities where 56 percent of the Canadian population resides. Distribution was initially achieved through corporate flagship stores in major city centres and has since expanded to include major electronics retailers. In 1999, the company introduced two data products, Fido E-Mail and FidoData. Together, these products delivered mobile e-mail and wireless connectivity to the customer's data environment, including the Internet and corporate intranets. At the end of 2000, Microcell reported 922,527 customers on Fido postpaid and Fidomatic prepaid services.

Microcell's PCS network is based on the global system for mobile communications (GSM). GSM is an older technology platform for PCS and is the prevalent standard in Europe. In North America, a majority of PCS providers selected the more technologically advanced CDMA standard for PCS. While CDMA offers superior call clarity, soft call handoffs, and more efficient use of wireless spectrum, these differences are not easily discernible by consumers. GSM allows Microcell to enjoy a significant cost advantage in the procurement of handsets, as there are many manufacturers and models to choose from.

Fido has experienced considerable success in the youth market. Approximately 70 percent of its sales are to youth. However, unlike Rogers's iD, Microcell has positioned its pre-paid service, Fidomatic, to this segment. Traditionally, pre-paid churn is higher than that of post-paid, while APRU is typically lower.

As Oosterman worked through the above scenario, a number of risks and opportunities surfaced.

The Current Situation—Risks

Highly Competitive and Uncertain Wireless Communications Industry

The ability of a service provider to compete successfully is based on factors such as pricing, distribution, services and features, ease of use, quality of geographic and in-building coverage, image and brand recognition, customer service, reliability of service, and customer satisfaction. With five major digital networks, including Mike, in the Canadian wireless market, new pricing, aggressive advertising and innovative marketing approaches are anticipated. The increase in demand for wireless Internet communication device options could bring new competitors to the market (e.g., mobile satellite). Also, the Canadian government has actively encouraged more competition in the industry.

Dependency on Motorola

To date, Mike has relied on one handset manufacturer, Motorola. The presence of multiple manufacturers in the PCS market has allowed competitors to choose from a wider selection of economically priced handsets. The cost of iDEN handsets is higher than the cost of those used on networks of certain competing technologies and is subsidized by TELUS. In the absence of competitive supply, there is no assurance that the cost of iDEN handsets will remain competitive vis-à-vis the cost of others or that they will be available in sufficient quantities, on a timely basis, to satisfy demand.

iDEN's Future

The wireless industry is in the process of adopting advanced second (2.5G) and third generation (3G) technologies that are expected to deliver high-speed wireless IP and data services. Various operators are announcing plans to permit existing wireless protocols to migrate to 2.5G in 2001 and subsequently 3G over the next two to three years. TELUS Mobility's CDMA protocol has a reasonable and cost-effective migration path to 2.5G and 3G (W-CDMA), as does Microcell's GSM protocol (UMTS).

TELUS's Mike service uses an iDEN technology protocol that already has packet data capability, a primary feature of 2.5G. However, iDEN is not compatible with any other digital protocol. It has not yet been determined how it will migrate to 3G. iDEN may become obsolete or provide no cost-effective migration path to allow for the competitive provision of 3G service.

In addition, there can be no assurance that the Direct Connect technology that is now unique to iDEN will not become available on other technology platforms, especially with the emergence of 3G technologies. Oosterman knew that while his immediate concern was Mike's short- to medium-term strategy, any actions would have to be consistent with TELUS's overall long-term vision.

The Current Situation—Opportunities

Virtual Private Networks

Virtual private networks (VPN) are a growing aspect of the Mike business. Mike VPNs deliver dedicated coverage, customized handset services and high-volume airtime packages, allowing clients to incorporate Mike on a very broad scale. Mike's greatest VPN success to date is a 10-year contract with General Motors of Canada Ltd. for its 14-million-square-foot Autoplex in Oshawa, Ontario, the largest auto plant in North America. The VPN concept has also been employed in other sectors. In the area of public safety, the Durham Regional Police Service has employed Mike as a digital communications solution. There are many potential areas where the customized services of VPNs could be deployed (e.g., university campuses). However, the institutional sales process requires a significant investment of time. In order for VPNs to be economically viable, customers must be organizations with user bases large enough to warrant the development of customized solutions.

New Products

In spring of 2001, Motorola announced the introduction of the first Java technology-enabled handsets in North America, which will be available for iDEN. Positioned by Motorola as a digital personal companion, the handsets enable users to download and run applications that meet individual user needs. For example, a handset could be customized to allow a particular user to schedule meetings in a datebook, submit expense reports remotely and play the latest Sega games. This is in addition to the existing features available through iDEN.

To allow for personal handheld computing, the handsets are equipped with flash memory, which permits the storage of several applications. Motorola plans to pre-install applications such as productivity tools and a Sega game. The handsets can retrieve information using the phone's "always on" Internet access, without the need to establish a dial-up connection, and its offline capabilities allow applications to be run even when disconnected from the network. The handsets will also feature interchangeable faceplates in a variety of colors.

New Segments

The powerful functionality offered by iDEN, coupled with demand trends in the wireless industry, makes it clear that businesses are not the only ones who could benefit from the services of Mike. For example, basic two-way radios have been gaining popularity among everyday users. The radios are limited to communication over short distances (four to 10 kilometres) and, as they do not require a cellular network, users are not required to pay any service fees. The devices are used by families to keep in touch in shopping malls, amusement parks and while hiking.

Mike's strategy could be altered to focus more heavily on additional market segments. For example, Mike handsets could be bundled in two to target consumers who would benefit from PCS handsets integrated with Direct Connect capability. However, expanding Mike's target market to explicitly include consumer segments is not without risk. To date, Mike has been clearly positioned to business users, who have very different needs from everyday consumers. PCS handsets have been marketed and designed with consumers in mind. For example TELUS offers PCS handsets with features such as color screens and integrated MP3 player capability. While iDEN may offer some distinct feature advantages over PCS, a considerable investment has been made to build TELUS's consumer PCS brand. A key objective for TELUS Mobility is to minimize market confusion, while optimizing performance on key wireless industry metrics (subscribers, APRU, COA and churn). Any decision to enter new segments would therefore require additional consideration.

Conclusion

Oosterman knew that with TELUS's acquisition of Clearnet now complete, he must reevaluate the strategy for Mike. However, he was concerned about what criteria to use to make this decision. He also realized that he didn't have a lot of time to gather more information before he made this strategic choice. Things were moving too quickly to do more extensive analysis. What was the best course to take for Mike in the competitive wireless market that would result in future success for TELUS Mobility?

GLOSSARY

AMPS	Advanced Mobile Phone Service. The North American analog cellular phone standard
Analog	An older method of wireless transmission that uses a continuous electrical signal (sound waves), which is easily intercepted or scanned, leading to the possibility of eavesdropping and fraud. Used in traditional cellular (AMPS) service.
ARPU	Average Revenue Per User. Total monthly revenue generated, divided by the average subscriber base in the period examined.
Broadband	Broadband refers to telecommunication in which a wideband of frequencies is available to transmit information, allowing more information to be transmitted in a given amount of time (much as more lanes on a highway allow more cars to travel on it at the same time).
CDMA	Code Division Multiple Access. A digital technology used by PCS providers. The newest PCS standard prevalent in North America.
Cellular Network	Any mobile communications network with overlapping radio cells. Common term describing older, analog networks.
Churn	Typically expressed as a rate per month for a given measurement period, equal to the number of subscribers disconnected divided by the average number of the entire installed base of subscribers.

Digital	The newer method of wireless transmission (versus analog) in which speech is converted into binary digits (various combinations of 0 and 1). These digits are transmitted to a receiver and converted back into speech within a fraction of a second. Comparing analog to digital is like comparing a vinyl record to a CD. Because computer data is already in digital form, digital transmission also facilitates data-based services on a PCS network.
Dual-mode Handset	A wireless phone capable of supporting both digital and analog communications.
ESMR	Enhanced Specialized Mobile Radio.
GSM	Global System for Mobile Communications. A digital technology used by PCS providers. The prevalent standard in Europe.
Handset	The device (phone) with which a subscriber accesses a wireless network.
iDEN	Integrated Digital Enhanced Network. A digital technology that integrates the services of PCS with digital two-way radio communications.
Licence	The right to exclusive use of a particular block or blocks of spectrum. Industry Canada awards radio communication licenses in Canada. In 1995, Industry Canada awarded four national PCS licences in the 1.9 GHz spectrum band to encourage competition in the mobile wireless marketplace. Microcell and Clearnet were both awarded national licences of 30 MHz of spectrum.
MOU	Minutes of Usage. The amount of time a user spends connected to the network. An average of this, measured monthly, is often used to compare usage on different wireless networks.
PCS	Personal Communications Services. Digital mobile wireless service that offers voice communication plus a number of other capabilities, such as e-mail, fax and text messaging. PCS also offers subscribers improved voice quality and security. The term PCS distinguishes this type of wireless service from older analog technology.
PDA	Personal Digital Assistant. Term for any small mobile hand-held device that provides computing and information storage and retrieval capabilities for personal or business use, often for keeping schedule calendars and address book information at hand.
Postpaid PCS	A form of PCS in which the customer opens a wireless account and receives a monthly invoice. The alternative is prepaid PCS.
Prepaid PCS	A form of PCS in which customers do not receive a monthly invoice from their wireless service provider. Rather, they buy increments of airtime as required. Prepaid PCS services have airtime rates that are higher than traditional postpaid services. They are more appropriate for occasional users or for customers who want to closely control their wireless costs. Also, because there is no credit risk for the network operator, prepaid customers do not have to submit to a credit check.
Roaming	The ability to travel freely between compatible wireless networks.
SMR	Specialized Mobile Radio. Two-way radio system typically used by dispatch companies (e.g., taxi fleets, construction services).
SMS	Short Message Service. A feature available on handsets that allows customers to send and receive short alphanumeric messages.
Single-mode Handset	A wireless phone capable of supporting only one type of communication (e.g., digital only).
TDMA	Time Division Multiple Access. A digital technology used by PCS providers.
3G	Third Generation. A generic name for mobile systems that will offer high-speed data and voice services. First Generation = analog cellular, Second Generation = digital PCS.
2.5G	2.5G describes the state of wireless technology and capability between the second and third generations of wireless technology. The term describes services of a higher data rate than PCS, though not as advanced as those promised by 3G.

*From www.microcell.ca and whatisit.techtarget.com.

Resource List

1. 3gnewsroom.com

2. anywhereyougo.com

3. Bruno, L. 2000. Broadband Unwired. Red Herring, 83: 280–282.

4. Diamond, R. What's Up at Palm. Wireless Business and Technology, 1(1): 68–71.

5. Drummond, M. 2001. Wireless at Work. Business 2.0, 3.6.2001: 68–83.

6. Girard, K. 2001. The Palm Phenom. Business 2.0, 4.3.2001: 74–80.

7. Neil, K., & Hibbard, J. 2000. Spectrum Shortage. Red Herring, 83: 284–290.

8. Phan, S. 2000. Who Needs a PC? Business 2.0, 11.14.2000: 52–57.

9. Smith, W. 2001. Surviving the Wireless Disruption. Wireless Business and Technology, 1(1): 64–66.

10. Splevin, G. 2001. Product Roundup—Wireless Devices. Wireless Business and Technology, 1(1): 86–87.

11. whatisit.techtarget.com

12. Williamson, A. 2001. What Does It All Mean? Wireless Business and Technology, 1(1): 72.

13. www.3g-generation.com

14. www.bce.ca

15. www.bellmobility.ca

16. www.clearnet.com

17. www.fido.ca

18. www.mformobile.com

19. www.microcell.ca

20. www.motorola.com

21. www.nextel.com

22. www.rim.net

23. www.rogers.com

24. www.TELUS.com

25. www.wbt2.com

26. Young, L. 2001. Tapping into Youth Wireless Market. Marketing Magazine, 4.9.2001: 2.

27. Zeichick, A. 2000. 3G Wireless Explained. Red Herring, 83: 314–317.

Case 6-24

Tri-Cities Community Bank*

Case A: Balanced Scorecard Development

Tri-Cities Community Bank (TCCB) is located in the Midwest U.S. and has a total of 10 branches grouped into two divisions, the southern division (SD) and the northern division (ND). Each division consists of five branches; each branch employs a branch president, branch vice-president/chief loan officer, customer service representatives, loan representatives, mortgage loan originators, head tellers, tellers, and administrative assistants. All branches are located within a 60-mile radius.

TCCB has enjoyed strong financial success over the past few years but continues to look for ways to improve its performance. The strategic direction of the bank is reviewed annually at a meeting of top bank officials and outside consultants. The purpose of the meeting is to outline the vision and mission of the bank and to ensure all top managers understand and agree on the

*By Tom Albright, Stan Davis, and Aleecia Hibbets. Used by permission.

direction of the organization. In 1997, TCCB management adopted the master strategy of balancing profits with growth to ensure the bank remains an independent entity existing to provide quality service and products to an increasingly diverse customer base.

Chris Billings recently was promoted from marketing director to SD president. The promotion came just as Chris finished her evening Master of Business Administration (MBA) degree in December 1999. As part of her graduate studies, she was introduced to the balanced scorecard (BSC), a performance measurement system that directs decision makers toward long-term value-creating activities. Chris thought the BSC could be used to improve the financial performance of TCCB. In late December 1999, she approached the chief executive officer (CEO) and requested permission to implement the new program.

TCCB's CEO was apprehensive about the new program. His reluctance stemmed from his own unfamiliarity with the BSC and Chris's short tenure as SD president. The CEO also was concerned about whether Chris's ideas would be accepted by the ND president and ND branch employees. Finally, he was uncertain about the BSC's benefits. At the same time, however, the CEO didn't want to respond negatively to Chris's first efforts as SD president. To appease Chris without totally committing the bank to implement the BSC, the CEO agreed to allow Chris to begin the process of developing the BSC in the five branches of her division. In turn, Chris agreed to make a presentation to the CEO and the bank's Board of Directors in three months. In this meeting, Chris would present BSC concepts and how she planned to use the program to improve the financial performance of her branches. Given the short period of time to design a pilot study, Chris wondered how she could convince the Board of Directors to give her permission to implement the BSC. She knew she must convince the SD branch presidents of its value.

On January 7th, 2000, Chris met with her branch presidents to discuss the BSC program and enlist their help in developing balanced scorecards for their branches. She began the meeting by distributing a handout (Exhibit A1) highlighting the key objectives of the BSC. She used the handout to inform the branch presidents of the four business "perspectives" (categories of measures to be included on the BSC). The example measures she included on the handout were from a hospital that had implemented the BSC. Because she didn't have example measures from a bank using the BSC, she wanted to show measures from another service industry for the branch presidents to consider. As the handout shows, the hospital uses operating margin and cost per case as their primary financial measures, recommendation ratings from outgoing patients and discharge timeliness information as customer measures, length of stay

EXHIBIT A1 Key Business Perspectives and Lead/Lag Indicators

Source: Adapted from Kaplan and Norton's 1996 *Translating Strategy into Action: The Balanced Scorecard* (1996) and *The Strategy-Focused Organization* (2001).

Key Business Perspectives

- **Financial Perspective**—*How do we look to our shareholders?*
  - The financial objectives of the organization serve as the focus of all activities. Every measure selected for a balanced scorecard should be part of a causal chain that results in improved performance on financial objectives.
  - Some examples of financial perspective objectives in the hospital industry include operating margins, cost per case, and capital fund-raising.

- **Customer Perspective**—*How do customers view us?*
  - In the customer perspective, organizations must identify key customers and market segments. Organizations must also determine how they add value for customers and seek to deliver better products and services that are tailored to specific customer needs.
  - Some examples of customer perspective objectives in the hospital industry include improved recommendation ratings and discharge timeliness.

- **Internal Business Perspective**—*At what must we excel?*
  - For the internal business perspective, organizations identify those processes that must be improved or created in order to reach the objectives of the customer and financial perspectives.
  - Some examples of internal business perspective objectives in the hospital industry include reducing the readmission rate (for the same medical condition) and increasing the doctor-to-patient contact time.

- **Learning and Growth Perspective**—*How do we continue to improve and create value?*
  - To achieve the lofty standards set in the previous three objectives, organizations must invest in their people and infrastructure. For this perspective, organizations identify where resources are needed and craft a plan to enable its employees to achieve the objectives of the other perspectives.
  - Some examples of learning and growth perspective objectives in the hospital industry include increased employee training and retention, improved information technology systems, and adequate staffing for all shifts.

Lead and Lag Indicators

Nonfinancial measures (NFMS) selected in the customer, internal business process, and learning and growth perspectives serve as *lead indicators* of improvement in financial objectives because improvement in these NFMS often "lead" or precede the improvement observed in financial measures. Likewise, the financial measures selected in the financial perspective are often called *lag indicators* because improvement in these financial measures often "lags" or comes after the improvement in the NFMS.

and readmission rate (patients being admitted again for the same injury or illness) for the internal business measures, and employee training and retention measures in the learning and growth perspective. She then instructed the branch presidents to work together to develop meaningful measures to be included on branch BSCs. While each branch would eventually develop a branch-specific scorecard, she believed the branches were similar enough to allow branch presidents to work together initially. The group was to meet again in six weeks to discuss their progress in developing branch BSCs.

The group meeting on February 25th did not go as well as Chris had hoped. While the branch presidents had done a good job of identifying areas that needed attention within each branch, the information presented could, at best, only be considered as raw materials necessary to build a BSC program. Much work was needed prior to implementing the program.

With time running out, Chris grew concerned about the scheduled meeting with the Board of Directors on March 31st. She had nothing concrete to present at the meeting and worried she might not receive permission to pursue the program if she did not make a solid presentation to the Board. Chris's goal is to present a group

of quantifiable measures that are linked through causal relationships and that lead to improvement of key financial measures.

One of the primary benefits of the BSC comes through mapping causal relationships from nonfinancial performance measures to financial measures. Nonfinancial measures are categorized into three perspectives: Learning and Growth, Internal Business Processes, and Customer Focus. The cause and effect linkages in the BSC will occur in the following manner: If *learning* improves, then *internal processes* will improve. If *internal processes* improve, then *customer value* will increase. If *customer value* increases, *financial performance* will improve. Financial performance is the ultimate evaluation of a firm's strategy. If financial performance improves significantly, the firm's strategy is successful. Thus, if the strategy is good, the measures of the nonfinancial perspectives will be lead indicators of increasing value that will ultimately be proven by improved financial measures.

Exhibit A2 provides a list of performance measures developed by the branch presidents and notes Chris took during meetings with them. Exhibit A3 illustrates a sample cause-and-effect chain. For example,

EXHIBIT A2 **Performance Measures for TCCB Balanced Scorecards**

- Outstanding Loan Balances
- Deposit Balances
- Number of Products per Customer
- Number of New Customers
- Non-Interest Income-income earned from fees on services and products provided by the bank. NII includes fees associated with CDs, ATM cards, insurance policies, lock boxes, annuities, brokerage accounts, checking accounts, and travelers' checks.
- New Loans Created
- New Accounts
- New Products Introduced

- Employee Training Hours
- Customer Satisfaction
- Customer Retention
- Employee Satisfaction
- Sales Calls to Potential Customers
- Thank-You Calls/Cards to New & Existing Customers
- Employee Turnover
- Referrals-referrals occur when an employee suggests a customer see another branch employee for more information about a product
- Cross-Sells-selling multiple products to a customer when the customer comes in for only one product

Notes from Branch Presidents' Meetings
The most important financial measures are loan balances, deposit balances, and noninterest income. Everything we do should be aimed toward improving these three financial measures.

Customer satisfaction must be improved. Because we are a small community bank, we rely on delivering quality services with a "hometown" feel. We rely on word-of-mouth advertising as much as we do radio and newspaper ads.

Our employees must have training in several different areas, including sales techniques, customer service, and product knowledge/profitability. This type of training would improve the interactions between our employees and customers, allowing tellers and Customer Sales Representatives to recognize customer needs and make more effective referrals and new product offerings.

EXHIBIT A3   **Cause-and-Effect Chain Illustration for TCCB**

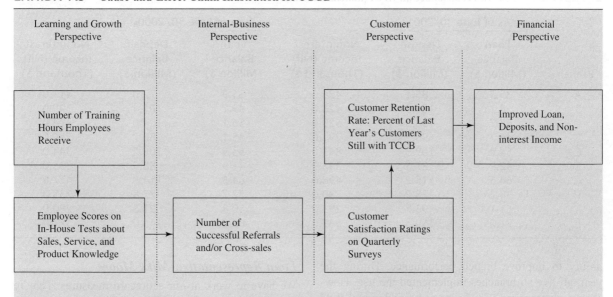

Causal Chain Explanation

If employees receive training in sales effectiveness, customer service, product profitability and local bank knowledge, then better customer service and higher quality interactions with existing clients can take place. TCCB employees will be better able to ascertain the needs of customers, thereby making higher quality referrals and cross-sell proposals to customers, and customers will be more satisfied and choose to continue banking with TCCB. Increased referrals or cross-sales increase non-interest income and provide the basis for growth in deposit and loan balances.

as shown in Exhibit A3, if employees receive training in sales effectiveness, customer service, product profitability, and local bank knowledge, they will be better equipped to provide customers with higher-quality service. TCCB measures the effectiveness of the training programs by having employees take in-house tests on various training topics. By increasing employee knowledge and skills, higher-quality referrals and cross-sell proposals will take place, leading to higher customer satisfaction and greater customer retention. Maintaining the current customer base provides the basis for growth in deposit and loan balances, while a greater number of successful referrals and cross-sells increase noninterest income.

Chris wants to prepare a series of cause-and-effect chains to illustrate to the Board of Directors how the BSC can be used to improve performance on three key financial measures: loan balances, deposit balances, and noninterest income. She knows that any program emphasizing improvement in these three measures has a strong chance of receiving approval. An example of a cause-and-effect chain appears in Exhibit A3.

Assignment

Prepare a presentation for the Board of Directors that explains how the BSC may be used to help TCCB achieve its strategic goals. Include in your presentation the following:

1. A table that categorizes each of the measures in Exhibit A2 into one of the four BSC perspectives. State why you placed a measure in a particular perspective.

2. Two cause-and-effect chains similar to the one shown in Exhibit A3. Use the measures listed in Exhibit A2, or suggest other measures you feel are appropriate. *Be sure to include a Causal Chain Explanation with your answer.*

Case B: Assessing Financial Improvement

The presentation to the Board of Directors was well received and Chris secured permission for a pilot study of the BSC in the five SD branches. She had one year to convince the CEO and Board of Directors of the BSC's

EXHIBIT B1 Branch Performance on Key Financial Indicators

	As of June 30, 2001			As of June 30, 2000		
Branch	Loan Balance (Million $)	Deposit Balance (Million $)	Noninterest Income (NII) (Thousand $)	Loan Balance (Million $)	Deposit Balance (Million $)	Noninterest Income (NII) (Thousand $)
A	39.3	85.1	476.0	35.9	77.0	411.0
B	58.1	104.5	428.0	49.7	101.4	399.0
C	63.7	136.3	529.0	56.1	124.0	474.0
D	46.7	93.1	291.0	45.1	86.7	276.0
E	54.4	109.3	343.0	53.9	108.2	344.0
F	42.9	87.5	345.0	41.9	88.5	335.0
G	64.5	115.2	498.0	64.5	114.8	477.0
H	33.2	78.2	230.0	32.7	77.8	233.0
I	51.1	93.7	293.0	50.8	91.6	280.0
J	71.2	150.8	589.0	68.0	145.0	571.0

ability to improve branch performance. During the year, all five SD branches implemented the BSC. However, each manager brought his or her individual style to the implementation process.

Now, the one-year trial period is over, and Chris has collected data to determine whether the program was successful. Because no unusual business situations occurred during the year, Chris believes any changes in performance among the adopting branches can be attributed to the BSC. Exhibit B1 reports financial data on loan balances, deposit balances, and noninterest income for the years ended June 30, 2001, and June 30, 2000, respectively. The SD branches, Branches A–E in Exhibit B1, began their BSC programs on July 1, 2000.

As part of her program assessment, Chris interviewed several employees at each branch.[1] Turnover of tellers has always been a significant issue for the branches. In the past, the tellers would leave the bank if they could find a job that paid as little as $.25 more per hour. The interviews are summarized below.

Branch A

Customer Service Representative–Mary Richards

One reason for implementing the BSC is to help us reach our branch goals. Everyone understands that our strategy is to balance loans, deposits, and Certificates of Deposit, with growth. For example, to create greater loan volume, we are willing to accept a lower profit margin on each loan. The BSC helps clarify our strategy.

[1] Most excerpts are actual comments gathered from interviews assessing a balanced scorecard implementation.

Loan Representative–Mike Moore

We have to work at our scorecard measures. They're not easy, but they are realistic. The process seems fair because my measures are just as hard as the other scorecards I've seen. Of course, the measures on my co-workers' scorecards may be different from mine, but everyone has to work hard.

Head Teller–Paul Franks

If we meet or exceed our targets, we are eligible to earn cash bonuses. Each month the top performers are recognized and rewarded. There's also a $1,000 reward per quarter to the individual who performs the best on his or her scorecard.

Branch B

Loan Representative–Pamela Wise

As I understand it, the BSC is a tool to measure our progress in achieving the goals established by management. In our case, we want to meet the financial needs of a growing community, yet keep a small-town feeling to our services.

Teller–Glenda Smalley

Some of my scorecard measures are challenging, but no more so than the other scorecards I have seen. The measures are difficult but not unattainable. I think the BSC is being used to encourage us to do better. We are rewarded when we improve. For example, our performance on the BSC helps to determine our year-end bonuses, as well as promotions and raises.

Branch C

Customer Service Representative–Bill Sorensen

Sure, I understand why we implemented the balanced scorecard. Its purpose is to promote teamwork among tellers, loan officers, and customer service representatives. Also, it helps everyone understand our goals and how to reach them.

Mortgage Loan Originator–Debbie Hansen

The scorecard taught us how everyone has a part in achieving branch goals by selling, cross-selling, serving as a communication port, and making customers feel welcome. Management wanted a lot of employee feedback when we were deciding to start the BSC. They wanted to be sure we knew about the program.

Administrative Assistant–Lou Martin

When we reach our BSC goals as a branch on a quarterly basis, we throw a big party. Individually, we can earn time off, up to a day every two months, if we do well on the BSC. Unfortunately, some of my scorecard measures are next to impossible to achieve.

Branch D

Loan Representative–Gary Smith

As I understand it, the BSC is for charting growth. We had to determine which measures were important to the company. Thus, our branch manager asked a few questions when we were deciding which measures to include on the scorecards. I think she helped focus our ideas.

Customer Service Representative–Al Taylor

My scorecard measures are not impossible; they are fair. All of our measures are probably about the same difficulty. There are some incentives to achieve our goals. For example, we can earn $50 each month if we meet our individual BSC goals. Our branch president is always looking for better ways to reward us for good BSC performance.

Branch E

Loan Representative–Ann Stone

In our branch, the BSC is to keep track of what we're doing and to compare our performance with others. I don't see it as a big deal. I reached all of my goals within two months of starting the program.

Teller–Pete Jones

I think the scorecard is used just to keep up with people's activities. I'm not sure any tangible rewards are associated with my performance on the BSC. If I do poorly, I'll probably be fired, however. On the other hand, keeping my job may be considered a tangible reward.

Administrative Assistant–Daniel Hughes

We didn't get to participate very much in developing our scorecards. Management just came in one day and told us about the new performance measurement system.

Loan Representative–Tim Vines

I've read that the scorecard is supposed to help companies with their strategy. It's difficult to get an idea of our strategy from management. Maybe what I do helps us achieve our strategic goals—who knows? Chris believed the BSC had been a success. She expressed her confidence to the CEO about winning Board approval for her plan to expand the BSC to all branches. However, she understood the board would require hard evidence before approving a plan. Chris also understood she must be prepared to answer questions about what went right and what went wrong during the pilot study in the SD branches.

Assignment

1. Prepare an analysis to determine whether the BSC appears to have had an effect.

2. Summarize your results in a presentation appropriate for the Board of Directors.

3. Identify differences in implementation quality that may explain variation in performance among branches A-E. What implementation recommendations would you make to ND managers who are considering adopting the balanced scorecard?

Source: Tom Albright is the J. Reese Phifer Faculty Fellow at the Culverhouse School of Accountancy, University of Alabama, Tuscaloosa, AL. He can be reached at (205) 348-2908 or Talbrigh@cba.ua.edu.

Stan Davis is an assistant professor at the Babcock Graduate School of Management, Wake Forest University, Winston-Salem, NC. He can be reached at (336) 758-4492 or stan.davis@mba.wfu.edu.

Aleecia Hibbets is a doctoral student at the Culverhouse School of Accountancy, University of Alabama. Tuscaloosa, AL. She can be reached at (205) 348-0149 or ahibbets @cba.ua.edu.

Reprinted with permission from the Institute of Management Accountants, Montvale, NJ, www.imanet.org.

Case 6-25

Cima Mountaineering, Inc.

"What a great hike," exclaimed Anthony Simon as he tossed his Summit HX 350 hiking boots into his car. He had just finished hiking the challenging Cascade Canyon Trail in the Tetons north of Jackson, Wyoming. Anthony hiked often because it was a great way to test the hiking boots made by Cima Mountaineering, Inc., the business he inherited from his parents and owned with his sister, Margaret. As he drove back to Jackson, he began thinking about next week's meeting with Margaret, the president of Cima. During the past month they had been discussing marketing strategies for increasing the sales and profits of the company. No decisions had been made, but the preferences of each owner were becoming clear.

As illustrated in Exhibit 1, sales and profits had grown steadily for Cima, and by most measures the company was successful. However, growth was beginning to slow as a result of foreign competition and a changing market. Margaret observed that the market had shifted to a more casual, stylish hiking boot that

appealed to hikers interested in a boot for a variety of uses. She favored a strategy of diversifying the company by marketing a new line of boots for the less experienced weekend hiker. Anthony also recognized that the market had changed, but he supported expanding the existing lines of boots for mountaineers and hikers. The company had been successful with those boots, and Anthony had some ideas about how to extend the lines and expand distribution. "This is a better way to grow," he thought. "I'm concerned about the risk in Margaret's recommendation. If we move to a more casual boot, then we have to resolve a new set of marketing and competitive issues and finance a new line. I'm not sure we can do it."

When he returned to Jackson that evening, Anthony stopped by his office to check his messages. The financial statements shown in Exhibits 2 and 3 were on his

Lawrence M. Lamont is professor of management at Washington and Lee University, and Eva Cid and Wade Drew Hammond are seniors in the class of 1995 at Washington and Lee, majoring in management and accounting, respectively. Case material was prepared as a basis for class discussion and not designed to prevent illustrations of either effective or ineffective handling of administrative problems. Some names, locations, and financial information have been disguised. Copyright © 1995, Washington and Lee University.

EXHIBIT 1
Cima Mountainee ring, Inc., Revenues and Net Income, 1990–95

Year	Revenues	Net Income	Profit Margin (%)
1995	$20,091,450	$857,134	4.27%
1994	18,738,529	809,505	4.32
1993	17,281,683	838,162	4.85
1992	15,614,803	776,056	4.97
1991	14,221,132	602,976	4.24
1990	13,034,562	522,606	4.01

EXHIBIT 2
Cima Mountaine ering, Inc., Income Statement, Years Ended December 31, 1995, and December 31, 1994

	1995	1994
Net sales	$20,091,450	$18,738,529
Cost of goods sold	14,381,460	13,426,156
Gross margin	5,709,990	5,312,373
Selling and admin. expenses	4,285,730	3,973,419
Operating income	1,424,260	1,338,954
Other income (expenses)		
Interest expense	(160,733)	(131,170)
Interest income	35,161	18,739
Total other income (net)	(125,572)	(112,431)
Earnings before income taxes	1,298,688	1,226,523
Income taxes	441,554	417,018
Net income	$ 857,134	$ 809,505

EXHIBIT 3

Cima Mountaineering, Inc., Balance Sheet, Years Ending December 31, 1995, and December 31, 1994

	1995	1994
Assets		
Current assets		
Cash and equivalents	$ 1,571,441	$ 1,228,296
Accounts receivable	4,696,260	3,976,608
Inventory	6,195,450	5,327,733
Other	270,938	276,367
Total	12,734,089	10,809,004
Fixed assets		
Property, plant, and equipment	3,899,568	2,961,667
Less: accumulated depreciation	(1,117,937)	(858,210)
Total fixed assets (net)	2,781,631	2,103,457
Other assets		
Intangibles	379,313	568,087
Other long-term assets	2,167,504	1,873,151
Total fixed assets (net)	$18,062,537	$15,353,699
Liabilities and shareholder equity		
Current liabilities		
Accounts payable	$ 4,280,821	$ 4,097,595
Notes payable	1,083,752	951,929
Current maturities of long-term debt	496,720	303,236
Accrued liabilities		
Expenses	2,754,537	2,360,631
Salaries and wages	1,408,878	1,259,003
Other	1,137,940	991,235
Total current liabilities	11,162,648	9,963,629
Long-term liabilities		
Long-term debt	3,070,631	2,303,055
Lease obligations	90,313	31,629
Total long-term liabilities	3,702,820	2,334,684
Other liabilities		
Deferred taxes	36,125	92,122
Other noncurrent liabilities	312,326	429,904
Total liabilities	14,672,043	12,820,339
Owner's equity		
Retained earnings	3,390,494	2,533,360
Total liabilities and owner's equity	$18,062,537	$15,353,699

desk, along with a marketing study from a Denver consulting firm. Harris Fleming, vice president of marketing, had commissioned a study of the hiking boot market several months earlier to help the company plan for the future. As Anthony paged through the report, two figures caught his eye. One was a segmentation of the hiking boot market (Exhibit 4), and the other was a summary of market competition (Exhibit 5). "This is interesting," he mused. "I hope Margaret reads it before our meeting."

History of Cima Mountaineering

As children, Anthony and Margaret Simon had watched their parents make western boots at the Hoback Boot Company, a small business they owned in Jackson, Wyoming. They learned the craft as they grew up and joined the company after college.

In the late 1960s the demand for western boots began to decline, and the Hoback Boot Company struggled to survive. By 1975 the parents were close to retirement

EXHIBIT 4 Segmentation of the Hiking Boot Market

	Mountaineers	Serious Hikers	Weekenders	Practical Users	Children	Fashion Seekers
Benefits	Durability/ruggedness Stability/support Dryness/warmth Grip/traction	Stability Durability Traction Comfort/protection	Lightweight Comfort Durability Versatility	Lightweight Durability Good value Versatility	Durability Protection Lightweight Traction	Fashion/style Appearance Lightweight Inexpensive
Demographics	Young Primarily male Shops in specialty stores and specialized catalogs	Young, middle-aged Male and female Shops in specialty stores and outdoor catalogs	Young, middle-aged Male and female Shops in shoe retailers, sporting goods stores, and mail order catalogs	Young, middle-aged Primarily male Shops in shoe retailers and department stores	Young marrieds Male and female Shops in department stores and outdoor catalogs	Young Male and female Shops in shoe retailers, department stores, and catalogs
Lifestyle	Adventuresome Independent Risk taker Enjoys challenges	Nature lover Outdoorsman Sportsman Backpacker	Recreational hiker Social, spends time with family and friends Enjoys the outdoors	Practical Sociable Outdoors for work and recreation	Enjoys family activities Enjoys outdoors and hiking Children are active and play outdoors Parents are value-conscious	Materialistic Trendy Socially conscious Nonhikers Brand name shoppers Price-conscious
Examples of brands	Asolo Cliff Raichle Mt. Blanc Salomon Adventure 9	Raichle Explorer Vasque Clarion Tecnica Pegasus Dry Hi-Tec Piramide	Reebok R-Evolution Timberland Topozoic Merrell Acadia Nike Air Mada, Zion Vasque Alpha	Merrell Eagle Nike Air Khyber Tecnica Volcano	Vasque Kids Klimber Nike Merrell Caribou	Nike Espirit Reebok Telos Hi-Tec Magnum
Estimated market share	5%	17%	25%	20%	5%	28%
	Slow growth	Moderate growth	High growth	Stable growth	Slow growth	At peak of rapid growth cycle
Price range	$210–$450	$120–$215	$70–$125	$40–$80	Up to $40	$65–$100

EXHIBIT 5 Summary of Competitors

Source: Published literature and company product brochures, 1995.

Company	Location	Mountaineering (Styles)	Hiking (Styles)	Men's	Women's	Children's	Price Range
Raichle	Switzerland	Yes (7)	Yes (16)	Yes	Yes	Yes	High
Salomon	France	Yes (1)	Yes (9)	Yes	Yes	No	Mid
Asolo	Italy	Yes (4)	Yes (26)	Yes	Yes	No	High
Tecnica	Italy	Yes (3)	Yes (9)	Yes	Yes	No	Mid/high
Hi-Tec	United Kingdom	Yes (2)	Yes (29)	Yes	Yes	Yes	Mid/low
Vasque	Minnesota	Yes (4)	Yes (18)	Yes	Yes	Yes	Mid/high
Merrell	Vermont	Yes (5)	Yes (31)	Yes	Yes	Yes	Mid
Timberland	New Hampshire	No	Yes (4)	Yes	No	No	Mid
Nike	Oregon	No	Yes (5)	Yes	Yes	Yes	Low
Reebok	Massachusetts	No	Yes (3)	Yes	Yes	Yes	Low
Cima	Wyoming	Yes (3)	Yes (5)	Yes	Yes	No	High

and seemed content to close the business, but Margaret and Anthony decided to try to salvage the company. Margaret, the older sibling, became the president, and Anthony became the executive vice president. By the end of 1976, sales had declined to $1.5 million and the company earned profits of only $45,000. It became clear that to survive, the business would have to refocus on products with a more promising future.

Refocusing the Business

As a college student, Anthony attended a mountaineering school north of Jackson in Teton National Park. As he learned to climb and hike, he became aware of the growing popularity of the sport and the boots being used. Because of his experience with western boots, he also noticed their limitations. Although the boots had good traction, they were heavy and uncomfortable and had little resistance to the snow and water always present in the mountains. He convinced Margaret that Hoback should explore the possibility of developing boots for mountaineering and hiking.

In 1977 Anthony and Margaret began 12 months of marketing research. They investigated the market, the competition, and the extent to which Hoback's existing equipment could be used to produce the new boots. By the summer of 1978 Hoback had developed a mountaineering boot and a hiking boot that were ready for testing. Several instructors from the mountaineering school tested the boots and gave them excellent reviews.

The Transition

By 1981 Hoback was ready to enter the market with two styles of boots: one for the mountaineer who wanted a boot for all-weather climbing and the other for men and women who were advanced hikers. Both styles had water-repellent leather uppers and cleated soles for superior traction. Distribution was secured through mountaineering shops in Wyoming and Colorado.

Hoback continued to manufacture western boots for its loyal customers, but Margaret planned to phase them out as the hiking boot business developed. However, because they did not completely understand the needs of the market, they hired Harris Fleming, a mountaineering instructor, to help them with product design and marketing.

A New Company

During the 1980s Hoback prospered as the market expanded along with the popularity of outdoor recreation. The company slowly increased its product line and achieved success by focusing on classic boots that were relatively insensitive to fashion trends. By 1986 sales of Hoback Boots had reached $3.5 million.

Over the next several years distribution was steadily expanded. In 1987 Hoback employed independent sales representatives to handle the sales and service. Before long, Hoback boots were sold throughout Wyoming, Colorado, and Montana by retailers specializing in mountaineering and hiking equipment. Margaret decided to discontinue western boots to make room for the growing hiking boot business. To reflect the new direction of the company, the name was changed to Cima Mountaineering, Inc.

Cima Boots Take Off

The late 1980s was a period of exceptional growth. Demand for Cima boots grew quickly as consumers caught the trend toward healthy, active lifestyles. The company expanded its line for advanced hikers and improved the performance of its boots. By 1990, sales had reached $13 million and the company earned profits of $522,606. Margaret was satisfied with the growth but was concerned about low profitability as a result of foreign competition. She challenged the company to find new ways to design and manufacture boots at a lower cost.

Growth and Innovation

The next five years were marked by growth, innovation, and increasing foreign and domestic competition. Market growth continued as hiking boots became popular for casual wear in addition to hiking in mountains and on trails. Cima and its competitors began to make boots with molded footbeds and utilize materials that reduced weight.[1] Fashion also became a factor, and companies such as Nike and Reebok marketed lightweight boots in a variety of materials and colors to meet the demand for styling in addition to performance. Cima implemented a computer-aided design (CAD) system in 1993 to shorten product development and devote more attention to design. Late in 1994, Cima restructured its facilities and implemented a modular approach to manufacturing. The company switched from a production line to a system in which a work team applied multiple processes to each pair of boots. Significant cost savings were achieved as the new approach improved the profit and quality of the company's boots.

The Situation in 1995

As the company ended 1995, sales had grown to $20.0 million, up 7.2 percent from the previous year. Employment was at 425, and the facility was operating at 85 percent of capacity, producing several styles of mountaineering and hiking boots. Time-saving innovations and cost reduction also had worked, and profits reached an all-time high. Margaret, now 57, was still president, and Anthony remained executive vice president.

Cima Marketing Strategy

According to estimates, 1994 was a record year for sales of hiking and mountaineering boots in the United

[1]Two processes are used to attach the uppers to the soles of boots. In classic welt construction, the uppers and soles are stitched. In the more contemporary method, a molded polyurethane footbed (including a one-piece heel and sole) is cemented to the upper with a waterproof adhesive. Many mountaineering boots use classic welt construction because it provides outstanding stability, while the contemporary method often is used with hiking boots to achieve lightweight construction. Cima used the classic method of construction for mountaineering boots and the contemporary method for hiking boots.

States. Retail sales exceeded $600 million, and about 15 million pairs of boots were sold. Consumers wore the boots for activities ranging from mountaineering to casual social events. In recent years, changes were beginning to occur in the market. Inexpensive, lightweight hiking boots were becoming increasingly popular for day hikes and trail walking, and a new category of comfortable, light "trekking" shoes was being marketed by manufacturers of athletic shoes.

Only a part of the market was targeted by Cima. Most of its customers were serious outdoor enthusiasts. They included mountaineers who climbed in rugged terrain and advanced hikers who used the boots on challenging trails and extended backpacking trips. The demand for Cima boots was seasonal, and most of the purchases were made during the summer months, when the mountains and trails were most accessible.

Positioning

Cima boots were positioned as the best available for their intended purpose. Consumers saw them as durable and comfortable with exceptional performance. Retailers viewed the company as quick to adopt innovative construction techniques but conservative in styling. Cima intentionally used traditional styling to avoid fashion obsolescence and the need for frequent design changes. Some of the most popular styles had been in the market for several years without any significant modifications. The Glacier MX 350 shown in Exhibit 6 and the Summit HX 350 boot shown in Exhibit 7 are good examples. The MX 350, priced at $219.00, was positioned as a classic boot for men and had a unique tread design for beginning mountaineers. The Summit HX 350 was priced at $159.00 and was a boot for men

EXHIBIT 6   The Glacier MX 350 Mountaineering Boot

EXHIBIT 7   The Summit HX 350 Hiking Boot

and women hiking rough trails. Exhibit 8 describes the items in the mountaineering and hiking boot lines, and Exhibit 9 provides a sales history for Cima boots.

Product Lines

Corporate branding was used, and "Cima" was embossed on the leather on the side of the boot to enhance consumer recognition. Product lines were also branded, and alphabetic letters and numbers were used to differentiate items in the line. Each line had different styles and features to cover many of the important uses in the market. However, all the boots had features that the company believed were essential to positioning. Standard features included water-repellent leather uppers and high-traction soles and heels. The hardware for the boots was plated steel, and the laces were made of tough, durable nylon. Quality was emphasized throughout the product lines.

Glacier Boots for Mountaineering

The Glacier line featured three boots for men. The MX 550 was designed for expert all-weather climbers looking for the ultimate in traction, protection, and warmth. The MX 450 was for experienced climbers taking extended excursions, while the MX 350 met the needs of less-skilled individuals beginning climbing in moderate terrain and climates.

Summit Boots for Hiking

The Summit line featured five styles for men and women. The HX 550 was preferred by experienced hikers who demanded the best possible performance.

The boot featured water-repellent leather uppers, a waterproof inner liner, a cushioned midsole, a nylon shank for rigidity, and a sole designed for high traction. It was available in gray and brown with different types of leather.[2] The Summit HX 150 was the least expensive boot in the line, designed for individuals who were beginning to take more than the occasional "weekend hike." It was a versatile boot for all kinds of excursions and featured a water-repellent leather upper, a cushioned midsole, and excellent traction. The HX 150 was popular as an entry-level boot for outdoor enthusiasts.

Distribution

Cima boots were distributed in Arizona, California, Colorado, Idaho, Montana, Nevada, New Mexico, Oregon, Washington, Wyoming, and western Canada through specialty retailers selling mountaineering, back-packing, and hiking equipment. Occasionally, Cima was approached by mail order catalog companies and chain sporting goods stores offering to sell its boots. The company considered the proposals but had not used those channels.

Promotion

The Cima sales and marketing office was located in Jackson. It was managed by Harris Fleming and staffed with several marketing personnel. Promotion was an important aspect of the marketing strategy, and advertising, personal selling, and sales promotion were used to gain exposure for Cima branded boots. Promotion was directed toward consumers and to retailers that stocked Cima mountaineering and hiking boots.

Personal Selling

Cima used 10 independent sales representatives to sell its boots in the Western states and Canada. Representatives did not sell competing boots, but they

[2]Different types of leather are used to make hiking boots. *Full grain:* High-quality, durable, upper layer of the hide. It has a natural finish and is strong and breathable. *Split grain:* Underside of the hide after the full-grain leather has been removed from the top. Light weight and comfort are the primary characteristics. *Suede:* A very fine split-grain leather. *Nubuk:* Brushed full-grain leather. *Waxed:* A process in which leather is coated with wax to help shed water. Most Cima boots were available in two or more types of leather.

Mountaineering and hiking boots are made water-repellent by treating the uppers with wax or chemical coatings. To make the boots waterproof, a fabric inner liner is built into the boot to provide waterproof protection and breathability. All Cima boots were water-repellent, but only styles with an inner liner were waterproof.

EXHIBIT 8
Cima
Mountaineering, Inc.,
Mountaineering and
Hiking Boot Lines

Product Line	Description
Glacier	
MX 550	For expert mountaineers climbing challenging mountains. Made for use on rocks, ice, and snow. Features welt construction, superior stability and support, reinforced heel and toe, padded ankle and tongue, step-in crampon insert, thermal insulation, and waterproof inner liner. Retails for $299.
MX 450	For proficient mountaineers engaging in rigorous, high-altitude hiking. Offers long-term comfort and stability on rough terrain. Features welt construction, deep cleated soles and heels, reinforced heel and toe, padded ankle and tongue, step-in crampon insert, and waterproof inner liner. Retails for $249.
MX 350	For beginning mountaineers climbing in moderate terrain and temperate climates. Features welt construction, unique tread design for traction, padded ankle and tongue, good stability and support, and a quick-dry lining. Retails for $219.
Summit	
HX 550	For experienced hikers who require uncompromising performance. Features nylon shank for stability and rigidity, waterproof inner liner, cushioned mid-sole, high-traction outsole, and padded ankle and tongue. Retails for $197.
HX 450	For backpackers who carry heavy loads on extended trips. Features thermal insulation, cushioned midsole, waterproof inner liner, excellent foot protection, and high-traction outsole. Retails for $179.
HX 350	For hikers who travel rough trails and a variety of backcountry terrain. Features extra cushioning, good stability and support, waterproof inner liner, and high-traction outsole for good grip in muddy and sloping surfaces. Retails for $159.
HX 250	For hikers who hike developed trails. Made with only the necessary technical features, including cushioning, foot and ankle support, waterproof inner liner, and high-traction outsole. Retails for $139.
HX 150	For individuals taking more than day and weekend hikes. Versatile boot for all kinds of excursions. Features cushioning, good support, waterproof inner liner, and high-traction outsoles for use on a variety of surfaces. Retails for $129.

EXHIBIT 9
Cima
Mountaineering, Inc.,
Product Line Sales

	Unit Sales (%)		Sales Revenue	
Year	Mountaineering	Hiking	Mountaineering	Hiking
1995	15.00%	85.00%	21.74%	78.26%
1994	15.90	84.10	22.93	77.07
1993	17.20	82.80	24.64	75.36
1992	18.00	82.00	25.68	74.32
1991	18.80	81.20	26.71	73.29
1990	19.70	80.30	27.86	72.14

sold complementary products such as outdoor apparel and equipment for mountaineering, hiking, and backpacking. They were paid a commission and handled customer service in addition to sales. Management also was involved in personal selling. Harris Fleming trained the independent sales representatives and often accompanied them on sales calls.

Advertising and Sales Promotion

Advertising and sales promotion also were important promotional methods. Print advertising was used to increase brand awareness and assist retailers with promotion. Advertising was placed in leading magazines such as *Summit, Outside,* and *Backpacker* to reach mountaineers and hikers with the message that Cima boots were functional and durable and had classic styling. In addition, cooperative advertising was offered to encourage retailers to advertise Cima boots and identify their locations.

Sales promotion was an important part of the promotion program. Along with the focus on brand name recognition, Cima provided product literature and point of sale display materials to assist retailers in promoting the boots. In addition, the company regularly Exhibited at industry trade shows. The exhibits, staffed by marketing personnel and the company's independent sales representatives, were effective for maintaining relationships with retailers and presenting the company's products.

Pricing

Cima selling prices to retailers ranged from $64.50 to $149.50 a pair, depending on the style. Mountaineering boots were more expensive because of their construction and features, while hiking boots were priced lower. Retailers were encouraged to take a 50 percent margin on the retail selling price, and so the retail prices shown in Exhibit 8 should be divided by two to get the Cima selling price. Cima priced its boots higher than competitors did, supporting the positioning of the boots as the top-quality product at each price point. Payment terms were net 30 days (similar to competitors), and boots were shipped to retailers from a warehouse in Jackson, Wyoming.

Segmentation of the Hiking Boot Market

As Anthony reviewed the marketing study commissioned by Harris Fleming, his attention focused on the market segmentation shown in Exhibit 4. It was interesting, because management had never seriously thought about the segmentation in the market. Of course, Anthony was aware that not everyone was a potential customer for Cima boots, but he was surprised to see how well the product lines met the needs of mountaineers and serious hikers. As he reviewed the market segmentation, he read the descriptions for mountaineers, serious hikers, and weekenders carefully because Cima was trying to decide which of these segments to target for expansion.

Mountaineers

Mountain climbers and high-altitude hikers are in this segment. They are serious about climbing and enjoy risk and adventure. Because mountaineers' safety may depend on their boots, they need maximum stability and support, traction for a variety of climbing conditions, and protection from wet and cold weather.

Serious Hikers

Outdoorsmen, who love nature and have a strong interest in health and fitness, are the serious hikers. They hike rough trails and take extended backpacking or hiking excursions. Serious hikers are brand-conscious and look for durable, high-performance boots with good support, a comfortable fit, and good traction.

Weekenders

Consumers in this segment are recreational hikers who enjoy casual weekend and day hikes with family and friends. They are interested in light, comfortable boots that provide a good fit, protection, and traction on a variety of surfaces. Weekenders prefer versatile boots that can be worn for a variety of activities.

Foreign and Domestic Competition

The second part of the marketing study that caught Anthony's attention was the analysis of competition. Although Anthony and Margaret were aware that competition had increased, they had overlooked the extent to which foreign bootmakers had entered the market. Apparently, foreign competitors had noticed the market growth and were exporting their boots aggressively into the United States. They had established sales offices and independent sales agents to compete for the customers served by Cima. The leading foreign brands, such as Asolo, Hi-Tec, Salomon, and Raichle, were marketed on performance and reputation, usually to the mountaineering, serious hiker, and weekender segments of the market.

The study also summarized the most important domestic competitors. Vasque and Merrell marketed boots that competed with Cima, but others were offering products for segments of the market where the prospects for growth were better. As Anthony examined Exhibit 5, he realized that the entry of Reebok and Nike into the hiking boot market was quite logical. They had entered the market as consumer preference shifted from wearing athletic shoes for casual outdoor activities to wearing a more rugged shoe. Each was marketing footwear that combined the appearance and durability of hiking boots with the lightness and fit of athletic shoes. The result was a line of fashionable hiking boots that appealed to brand and style-conscious teens and young adults. Both firms were expanding their product lines and moving into segments of the market that demanded lower levels of performance.

Margaret and Anthony Discuss Marketing Strategy

A few days after hiking in Cascade Canyon, Anthony met with Margaret and Harris Fleming to discuss marketing strategy. Each had read the consultant's report and studied the market segmentation and competitive summary. As the meeting opened, the conversation went as follows:

Margaret: It looks like we will have another record year. The economy is growing, and consumers seem confident and eager to buy. Yet I'm concerned about the future. The foreign bootmakers are providing some stiff competition. Their boots have outstanding performance and attractive prices. The improvements we made in manufacturing helped control costs and maintain margins, but it looks like the competition and slow growth in our markets will make it difficult to improve profits. We need to be thinking about new opportunities.

Harris: I agree, Margaret. Just this past week we lost Rocky Mountain Sports in Boulder, Colorado. John Kline, the sales manager, decided to drop us and pick up Asolo. We were doing $70,000 a year with them, and they carried our entire line. We also lost Great Western Outfitters in Colorado Springs. They replaced us with Merrell. The sales manager said that the college students there had been asking for the lower-priced Merrell boots. They bought $60,000 last year.

Anthony: Rocky Mountain and Great Western were good customers. I guess I'm not surprised, though. Our Glacier line needs another boot, and the Summit line is just not deep enough to cover the price points. We need to have some styles at lower prices to compete with Merrell and Asolo. I'm in favor of extending our existing lines to broaden their market appeal. It seems to me that the best way to compete is to stick with what we do best, making boots for mountaineers and serious hikers.

Margaret: Not so fast, Anthony. The problem is that our markets are small and not growing fast enough to support the foreign competitors that have entered with excellent products. We can probably hold our own, but I doubt if we can do much better. I think the future of this company is to move with the market. Consumers are demanding more style, lower prices, and a lightweight hiking boot that can be worn for a variety of uses. Look at the segmentation again. The "Weekender" segment is large and growing. That's where we need to go with some stylish new boots that depart from our classic leather lines.

Anthony: Maybe so, but we don't have much experience working with the leather and nylon combinations that are being used in these lighter boots. Besides, I'm not sure we can finance the product development and marketing for a new market that already has plenty of competition. And I'm concerned about the brand image that we have worked so hard to establish over the past 20 years. A line of inexpensive, casual boots just doesn't seem to fit with the perception consumers have of our products.

Harris: I can see advantages to each strategy. I do know that we don't have the time and resources to do both, so we had better make a thoughtful choice. Also, I think we should reconsider selling to the mail order catalog companies that specialize in mountaineering and hiking equipment. Last week I received another call from REI requesting us to sell them some of the boots in our Summit line for the 1997 season. This might be a good source of revenue and a way to expand our geographic market.

Margaret: You're right, Harris. We need to rethink our position on the mail order companies. Most of them have good market penetration in the East, where we don't have distribution. I noticed that Gander Mountain is carrying some of the Timberland line and that L.L. Bean is carrying some Vasque styles along with its own line of branded boots.

Anthony: I agree. Why don't we each put together a proposal that summarizes our recommendations, and then we can get back together to continue the discussion.

Harris: Good idea. Eventually we will need a sales forecast and some cost data. Send me your proposals, and I'll call the consulting firm and have them prepare some forecasts. I think we already have some cost information. Give me a few days, and then we can get together again.

The Meeting to Review the Proposals

The following week, the discussion continued. Margaret presented her proposal, which is summarized in Exhibit 10. She proposed moving Cima into the "Weekender" segment by marketing two new hiking boots. Anthony countered with the proposal summarized in Exhibit 11. He favored extending the existing lines by adding a new mountaineering boot and two new Summit hiking boots at lower price points. Harris presented sales forecasts for each proposal, and after some discussion and modification, they were finalized as shown in Exhibit 12. Cost information was gathered by Harris from the vice president of manufacturing and is presented in Exhibit 13. After a lengthy discussion in which Margaret and Anthony were unable to agree on a course of action, Harris Fleming suggested that each proposal be explored further by conducting marketing research. He proposed the formation of teams from the Cima marketing staff to research each proposal and present it to Margaret and Anthony at a later date. Harris presented his directions to the teams in the memorandum shown in Exhibit 14. The discussion between Margaret and Anthony continued as follows:

Margaret: Once the marketing research is completed and we can read the reports and listen to the presentations, we should have a better idea of which strategy makes the best sense. Hopefully, a clear direction will emerge and we can move ahead with one of the proposals. In either case, I'm still intrigued with the possibility of moving into the mail order catalogs, since we really haven't developed these companies as customers. I just wish we knew how much business we could expect from them.

Anthony: We should seriously consider them, Margaret. Companies like L.L. Bean, Gander Mountain, and REI have been carrying a selection of hiking boots for several years. However, there may be a problem for us. Eventually the catalog companies expect their boot suppliers to make them a private brand. I'm not sure this is something we want to do, since we built the company on a strategy of marketing our own brands that are made in the U.S.A. Also, I'm concerned about the reaction of our retailers when they discover we are selling to the catalog companies. It could create some problems.

Harris: That is a strategy issue we will have to address. However, I'm not even sure what percentage of sales the typical footwear company makes through the mail order catalogs. If we were to solicit the catalog business, we would need an answer to this question to avoid exceeding our capacity. In the proposals I asked each of the teams to provide an estimate for us. I have to catch an early flight to Denver in the morning. It's 6:30; why don't we call it a day.

The meeting was adjourned at 6:35 P.M. Soon thereafter, the marketing teams were formed, with a leader assigned to each team.

EXHIBIT 10   Margaret's Marketing Proposal

MEMORANDUM

TO: Anthony Simon, Executive Vice President
      Harris Fleming, Vice President of Marketing
FROM: Margaret Simon, President
RE: Marketing Proposal

I believe we have an excellent opportunity to expand the sales and profits of Cima by entering the "Weekender" segment of the hiking boot market. The segment's estimated share of the market is 25 percent, and according to the consultant's report, it is growing quite rapidly. I propose that we begin immediately to develop two new products and prepare a marketing strategy as discussed below.

Target Market and Positioning

Male and female recreational hikers looking for a comfortable, lightweight boot that is attractively priced and acceptable for short hikes and casual wear. Weekenders enjoy the outdoors and a day or weekend hike with family and friends.

The new boots would be positioned with magazine advertising as hiking boots that deliver performance and style for the demands of light hiking and casual outdoor wear.

Product

Two boots in men's and women's sizes. The boots would be constructed of leather and nylon uppers with a molded rubber outsole. A new branded line would be created to meet the needs of the market segment. The boots (designated WX 550 and WX 450) would have the following features:

	WX 550	WX 450
Leather and nylon uppers	X	X
Molded rubber outsole	X	X
Cushioned midsole	X	X
Padded collar and tongue	X	X
Durable hardware and laces	X	X
Waterproof inner liner	X	

Uppers: To be designed. Options include brown full-grain, split-grain, or suede leather combined with durable nylon in two of the following colors: beige, black, blue, gray, green, and slate.
Boot design and brand name: To be decided.

Retail Outlets

Specialty shoe retailers carrying hiking boots and casual shoes and sporting goods stores. Eventually mail order catalogs carrying outdoor apparel and hiking, backpacking, and camping equipment.

Promotion

Independent sales representatives   Point of sale display materials
Magazine advertising   Product brochures
Co-op advertising   Trade shows

Suggested Retail Pricing

WX 550: $89.00
WX 450: $69.00

Competitors

Timberland, Hi-Tec, Vasque, Merrell, Asolo, Nike, and Reebok.

Product Development and Required Investment

We should allow about one year for the necessary product development and testing. I estimate these costs to be $350,000. Additionally, we will need to make a capital expenditure of $150,000 for new equipment.

EXHIBIT 11   Anthony's Marketing Proposal

MEMORANDUM

TO: Margaret Simon, President
        Harris Fleming, Vice President of Marketing
FROM: Anthony Simon, Executive Vice President
RE: Marketing Proposal

We have been successful with boots for mountaineers and serious hikers for years, and this is where our strengths seem to be. I recommend extending our Glacier and Summit lines instead of venturing into a new, unfamiliar market. My recommendations are summarized below:

Product Development

Introduce two new boots in the Summit line (designated HX 100 and HX 50) and market the Glacier MX 350 in a style for women with the same features as the boot for men. The new women's Glacier boot would have a suggested retail price of $219.00, while the suggested retail prices for the HX 100 and the HX 50 would be $119.00 and $89.00, respectively, to provide price points at the low end of the line. The new Summit boots for men and women would be the first in the line to have leather and nylon uppers as well as the following features:

	HX 100	HX 50
Leather and nylon uppers	X	X
Molded rubber outsole	X	X
Cushioned midsole	X	X
Padded collar and tongue	X	X
Quick-dry lining	X	X
Waterproof inner liner	X	

The leather used in the uppers will have to be determined. We should consider full-grain, suede, and nubuck since they are all popular with users in this segment. We need to select one for the initial introduction. The nylon fabric for the uppers should be available in two colors, selected from among the following: beige, brown, green, slate, maroon, and navy blue. Additional colors can be offered as sales develop and we gain a better understanding of consumer preferences.

Product Development and Required Investment

Product design and development costs of $400,000 for the MX 350, HX 100, and HX 50 styles and a capital investment of $150,000 to acquire equipment to cut and stitch the nylon/leather uppers. One year will be needed for product development and testing.

Positioning

The additions to the Summit line will be positioned as boots for serious hikers who want a quality hiking boot at a reasonable price. The boots will also be attractive to casual hikers who are looking to move up to a better boot as they gain experience in hiking and outdoor activity.

Retail Outlets

We can use our existing retail outlets. Additionally, the lower price points on the new styles will make these boots attractive to catalog shoppers. I recommend that we consider making the Summit boots available to consumers through mail order catalog companies.

Promotion

We will need to revise our product brochures and develop new advertising for the additions to the Summit line. The balance of the promotion program should remain as it is since it is working quite well. I believe the sales representatives and retailers selling our lines will welcome the new boots since they broaden the consumer appeal of our lines.

Suggested Retail Pricing

MX 350 for women: $219.99
HX 100: $119.00
HX 50: $ 89.00

Competitors

Asolo, Hi-Tec, Merrell, Raichle, Salomon, Tecnica, and Vasque.

EXHIBIT 12
Cima
Mountaineering,
Inc., Sales Forecasts
for Proposed New
Products (Pairs of
Boots)

	Project 1		Project 2		
Year	WX 550	WX 450	MX 350	HX 100	HX 50
2001–02	16,420	24,590	2,249	15,420	12,897
2000–01	14,104	21,115	1,778	13,285	11,733
1999–2000	8,420	12,605	897	10,078	9,169
1998–99	5,590	8,430	538	5,470	5,049
1997–98	4,050	6,160	414	4,049	3,813

Note: Sales forecasts are expected values derived from minimum and maximum estimates.
Some cannibalization of existing boots will occur when the new styles are introduced. The sales forecasts provided above have taken into account the impact of sales losses on existing boots. No additional adjustments need to be made.
Forecasts for WX 550, WX 450, HX 100, and HX 50 include sales of both men's and women's boots.

EXHIBIT 13
Cima
Mountaineering, Inc.,
Cost Information for
Mountaineering and
Hiking Boots

	Inner Linear	No Inner Linear
Retail margin	50%	50%
Marketing and Manufacturing costs		
Sales commissions	10	10
Advertising and sales promotion	5	5
Materials	42	35
Labor, overhead, and transportation	28	35

Cost information for 1997–98 only. Sales commissions, advertising and sales promotion, materials, labor, overhead, and transportation costs are based on Cima selling prices. After 1997–98, annual increases of 3.0 percent apply to marketing and manufacturing costs and increases of 4.0 percent apply to Cima selling prices.

EXHIBIT 14 Harris Fleming's Memorandum to the Marketing Staff

MEMORANDUM

TO:	Marketing Staff
CC:	Margaret Simon, President
	Anthony Simon, Executive Vice President
FROM:	Harris Fleming, Vice President of Marketing
SUBJECT:	Marketing Research Projects

Attached to this memorandum are two marketing proposals (see case Exhibits 10 and 11) under consideration by our company. Each proposal is a guide for additional marketing research. You have been selected to serve on a project team to investigate one of the proposals and report your conclusions and recommendations to management. At your earliest convenience, please complete the following.

Project Team 1: Proposal to enter the "Weekender" segment of the hiking boot market.

Review the market segmentation and summary of competition in Exhibits 4 and 5. Identify consumers who would match the profile described in the market segment and conduct field research using a focus group, a survey, or both. You may also visit retailers carrying hiking boots to examine displays and product brochures. Using the information in the proposal, supplemented with your research, prepare the following:

1. A design for the hiking boots (WX 550 and WX 450). Please prepare a sketch that shows the styling for the uppers. We propose to use the same design for each boot, the only difference being the waterproof inner liner on the WX 550 boot. On your design, list the features that your proposed boot would have, considering additions or deletions to those listed in the proposal.

2. Recommend a type of leather (from among those proposed) and two colors for the nylon to be used in the panels of the uppers. We plan to make two styles, one in each color for each boot.

3. Recommend a brand name for the product line. Include a rationale for your choice.

EXHIBIT 14—*(concluded)*

4. Verify the acceptability of the suggested retail pricing.

5. Prepare a magazine advertisement for the hiking boot. Provide a rationale for the advertisement in the report.

6. Convert the suggested retail prices *in the proposal* to the Cima selling price and use the sales forecasts and costs (shown in Exhibits 12 and 13) to prepare an estimate of before-tax profits for the new product line, covering a five-year period starting in 1997–98. Assume annual cost increases of 3.0 percent and price increases of 4.0 percent beginning in 1998–99. Discount the future profits to present value, using a cost of capital of 15.0 percent. Use 1996–97 as the base year for all discounting.

7. Determine the payback period for the proposal. Assume product development and investment occur in 1996–97.

8. Provide your conclusions on the attractiveness of these styles to mail order catalog companies and their customers. You may wish to review current mail order catalogs to observe the hiking boots featured. Assuming that Cima is successful selling to mail order catalog companies, estimate the percentage of our sales that could be expected from these customers.

9. Prepare a report that summarizes the recommendations of your project team, including the advantages and disadvantages of the proposal. Be prepared to present your product design, branding, pro forma projections, payback period, and recommendations to management shortly after completion of this assignment.

10. Summarize your research and list the sources of information used to prepare the report.

Project Team 2: Proposal to extend the existing lines of boots for mountaineers and hikers.

Review the market segmentation and summary of competition in Exhibits 4 and 5. Identify consumers who match the profile described in the market segment and conduct field research using a focus group, a survey, or both. You also may visit retailers carrying hiking boots to examine displays and product brochures. Using the information in the proposal, supplemented with your research, prepare the following.

1. Designs for the hiking boots (HX 100 and HX 50). Please prepare sketches showing the styling for the uppers. We propose to use a different design for each boot, so you should provide a sketch for each. On each sketch, list the features that your proposed boots would have, considering additions or deletions to those listed in the proposal. No sketch is necessary for the mountaineering boot, MX 350, since we will use the same design as the men's boot and build it on a women's last.

2. Recommend one type of leather (from among those proposed) and two colors for the nylon to be used in the panels of the uppers. We plan to make two styles, one in each color for each boot.

3. Verify the market acceptability of the suggested retail pricing.

4. Prepare a magazine advertisement for your hiking boots. Include a rationale for the advertisement in the report.

5. Using the suggested retail prices *in the proposal,* convert them to the Cima selling prices and use the sales forecasts and costs (shown in Exhibits 12 and 13) to prepare an estimate of before-tax profits for the new products covering a five-year period starting in 1997–98. Assume annual cost increases of 3.0 percent and price increases of 4.0 percent beginning in 1998–99. Discount the profits to present value using a cost of capital of 15.0 percent. Use 1996–97 as the base year for all discounting.

6. Determine the payback period for the proposal. Assume product development and investment occur in 1996–97.

7. Provide your conclusions on the attractiveness of these styles to mail order catalog companies and their customers. You may wish to review current mail order catalogs to observe the hiking boots featured. Assuming that Cima is successful selling to mail order catalog companies, estimate the percentage of our sales that could be expected from these customers.

8. Prepare a report that summarizes the recommendations of your project team, including the advantages and disadvantages of the proposal. Be prepared to present your product design, pro forma projections, payback period, and recommendations to management shortly after completion of this assignment.

9. Summarize your research and list the sources of information used to prepare the report.

Name Index

Note: Page numbers followed by *n* indicate material in source notes, footnotes, and endnotes.

A

Aaker, David A., 205n14, 205n16, 307n, 310n, 312, 316n7, 316n9, 316n14, 317n31, 317n48
Abary, Mik, 279
Abela, Andrew V., 498n20, 498n30
Abell, Derek F., 73n11
Abramson, Michael L., 202n
Achrol, Ravi S., 204n3, 232n4, 472n48
Adamik, Brian, 505
Adams, Richard, 283
Ahlberg, Erik, 417n8
Allen, Herbert A., 44, 46
Allen, Paul, 530
Allen-Mills, Tony, 51n
Allison, Kevin, 9n, 97n, 344n1
Alpert, Mark I., 73n9
Alsop, Ronald, 317n27
Ambler, Tim, 498n23, 498n26, 498n30, 500n
Amelio, Gil, 269–270
Anderson, Chris, 116n
Anderson, Erin, 345n15, 345n32, 472n47
Anderson, James C., 345n30
Anderson, Ray C., 492
Anhalt, Karen Nickel, 32n
Ante, Spencer E., 154n39, 425n, 491n, 498n31
Anthony, Scott D., 154n24
Araki, Takashi, 564
Arens, William F., 383n, 387n, 395n14
Arndt, Michael, 284n, 514n
Arnold, Catherine J., 145n, 154n31, 158, 160
Arrington, Michael, 234n46
Arruñada, Benito, 233n27
Arthur, Douglas, 34
Ashley, Darryl, 564
Assael, Henry, 111n12
Aufreiter, Nora A., 465n, 472n46

B

Babbio, Lawrence T., 506–507
Bagchi, Subroto, 177
Baker, Stephen, 375n
Baldauf, Artur, 73n3
Baldwin, Carliss Y., 232n2

Ball, Deborah, 391n12
Ballmer, Steven A., 419–423, 425, 454, 491, 526, 527–531, 533
Balmer, John M. T., 233n11
Bamford, James D., 233n14, 234n42, 234n48, 234n57
Band, William, 471n26
Barr, Adam, 528
Barr, Larry, 539–545
Barrett, Amy, 162n, 181n, 182n
Barrett, Craig R., 186, 275, 279, 280
Bartlett, Christopher A., 167
Barwise, Patrick, 498n22
Battelle, John, 40
Beatty, Sarah, 518
Beda, Joe, 526
Bedbury, Scott, 427
Beebe, Matthew G., 161, 162
Belch, George E., 395n10, 395n13, 417n17
Belch, Michael A., 395n10, 395n13, 417n17
Bell, Charles, 281
Bell, Genevieve, 276
Bell, Jeff, 518
Belluzzo, Richard E., 421
Bendle, Neil T., 490n, 498n24, 499n
Benedict, Jan, 317n24
Benioff, Marc, 404
Berelson, Bernard, 111n18
Berkowitz, Eric N., 95n, 111n19
Berner, Robert, 305n, 358n, 371n13, 378n, 394n8
Berry, D., 345n22
Berry, Leonard L., 111n10
Berthon, Pierre, 316n4
Betts, Douglas G., 520
Bezos, Jeff, 11
Bharat, Krishna, 168
Bhargava, Mukesh, 127n1
Bianco, Anthony, 40n, 94n, 111n2, 112n21, 204n2, 386n
Birchall, Jonathan, 115n, 132n, 154n26, 154n41, 234n37, 338n, 340n, 345n14, 417n29
Bird, Laura, 371n7
Birt, Jason, 564
Bissell, John, 470–471n2
Bittar, Christine, 470–471n2
Blackett, Tom, 312
Blagsvedt, Sean, 530
Blair, Donald W., 428–430
Blair, Jayson, 34, 36
Blank, Arthur, 508
Blumenstein, Rebecca, 371n12

Bodoff, Russ, 277
Bond, Andy, 286
Bonoma, Thomas V., 497n8
Boudette, Neal E., 316n6
Bounds, Wendy, 395n12
Bowerman, Bill, 427, 428
Boyd, Gerald, 36
Boyd, Harper W., Jr., 339n
Boyer, Dave, 521
Boyle, Matthew, 111n1, 135n
Brady, Diane, 73n2, 112n25, 193n, 249n, 514n
Braithwaite, Tom, 338n, 370n1
Branson, Richard, 311
Bremner, Brian, 524n, 565n
Brooker, Katrina, 316n1
Brooks, Rick, 417n7
Brosseau, Drew, 528
Brown, Derek, 517
Brown, Shona L., 268n33
Brown, Stephen, 193n
Bryan, Lowell L., 471n3
Bryant, Chris, 87n
Bryant, Kobe, 269, 273
Brynjolfsson, Erik, 437
Buckley, Neil, 112n22, 153n4
Buffett, Warren, 46
Bulkeley, William M., 73n1, 155n59
Burd, Gary, 526
Burgum, Douglas J., 424
Burke, Raymond R., 155n48
Burrows, Peter, 274n, 344n1, 371n4
Bush, George W., 37–38
Bush, Jason, 19n, 68n, 73n16, 112n22
Busky, James, 361
Byrnes, Nanette, 92n, 136n, 305n, 317n30, 344n1, 480n, 498n35

C

Cacciotti, Jerry, 179
Calvert, Gemma, 155n64
Cameron, Doug, 5n
Campbell, Andrew, 234n50
Cantalupo, James R., 281–283
Capell, Kerry, 87n, 132n, 168n, 345n11, 498n16
Capon, Noel, 112n37, 154n46, 234n35, 317n18, 471n22, 472n43, 497n2, 498n34
Carlton, Jim, 316n11
Carstedt, Goran, 166

Carter, Adrienne, 112*n*20
Carter, Meg, 111*n*15
Cash, James I., Sr., 530
Cateora, Philip R., 204*n*11, 341*n*, 346*n*34, 467*n*, 472*n*51
Catmull, Edwin, 269, 270
Cespedes, Frank V., 345*n*28, 497*n*6
Cha, Ariana Eunjung, 111*n*1, 125*n*
Chandler, Brue, 181
Chandy, Rajesh K., 267*n*13
Chen Xiaoyue, 174
Chiagouris, Larry, 317*n*51
Chin Dae Je, 534
Cho, Fujio, 560, 562–565
Choe, James, 535
Choi, Thomas Y., 233*n*21
Choi Won Min, 533, 536
Chon, Gina, 316*n*3
Christensen, Clayton M., 73*n*4, 111*n*7, 154*n*24, 204*n*6, 241–242, 267*n*9
Christopher, Martin, 345*n*17, 345*n*21, 345*n*23
Chung Kook Hyun, 535
Church, Bryce G., 509
Church, Jonathan, 286
Ciachella, John, 168–169
Ciskowski, Edwin C., 159
Clark, Bruce H., 498*n*25, 498*n*30
Clark, Kim B., 232*n*2
Clarke, Jeff, 439
Clarke, Thomas E., 429
Claxtoan, John D., 548*n*
Clewes, Debbie, 476*n*
Clift, William E., 507
Clinton, Bill, 35
Close, Wendy S., 128*n*18
Cohen, Jack, 285
Coleman, Greg, 518
Collins, Adam, 524
Collins, Jim, 528
Collins, Lance, 45
Collis, David J., 25*n*24
Colvin, G., 128*n*25
Comstock, Beth, 249
Conaty, William J., 511
Conigliaro, Laura, 437
Conlin, Michelle, 313*n*, 492*n*
Connelly, Jed, 521
Cook, Scott, 111*n*7
Cooper, Donald R., 205*n*21, 268*n*35
Cooper, Robert, 267*n*12, 316*n*12
Cornwell, Lisa, 153*n*4
Coughlin, Anne, 345*n*32
Court, David, 498*n*32
Crary, John, 440
Cravens, David W., 25*n*21, 73*n*3, 205*n*20, 233*n*30, 234*n*54, 417*n*9, 417*n*11, 417*n*14, 472*n*49, 498*n*10
Cravens, Karen S., 80*n*, 234*n*54

Crawford, Blair, 498*n*32
Crawford, C. Merle, 261*n*, 268*n*23
Crawford, Shawn, 426
Cressman, George E., Jr., 361*n*, 371*n*6, 371*n*15
Croce, Robert W., 180, 181
Crockett, Roger O., 344*n*2, 507*n*
Crosby, Lawrence A., 498*n*17
Cruise, Tom, 512
Curry, Bruce, 155*n*48
Cusamano, Michael A., 419

D

Daft, Douglas N., 43–46
Dahlgren, Lennert, 166
Dahlvig, Anders, 162, 163, 165, 167
Daly, Bob, 517
Darby, Gavin, 46
Davey, Jenny, 132*n*
Davidson, Andrew, 153*n*4
Davies, Fiona, 155*n*48
Dawson, Chester, 524*n*, 565*n*
Day, George S., 6*n*, 25*n*1, 25*n*5, 25*n*16, 73*n*10, 73*n*14, 127*n*5, 153*n*1, 153*n*7, 153*n*8, 153*n*10, 154*n*23, 154*n*27, 155*n*52, 204*n*5, 246*n*, 449*n*, 453*n*, 470*n*1, 471*n*9, 471*n*17
DeAngelo, Joe, 509, 511
Dearborn, Barbara, 182
Delios, Andrew, 235*n*58
Dell, Michael S., 23*n*, 270, 433–439
Denninghof, Albrecht, 32
Denson, Charles D., 429
Deshpandé, Rohit, 25*n*9, 155*n*50, 155*n*58, 471*n*27
De Smedt, Pierre-Alain, 524
Desrosiers, Julie, 166
Di Benedetto, Anthony, 261*n*, 268*n*23
DiBona, Charles, 423–424
Dickenson, Larry, 401
Dickson, Peter R., 111*n*8, 112*n*24
Diller, Barry, 514
Dillon, William R., 154*n*29, 256*n*, 268*n*27
Disney, Roy E., 274
Ditucci, Richard, 441–442
Dolan, Robert J., 371*n*8
Done, Kevin, 87*n*
Donovan, Dennis M., 511
Downes, L., 317*n*40
Doyle, Peter, 25*n*2, 471*n*4, 472*n*30, 472*n*38
Dreves, Frank, 32
Drucker, Peter F., 13, 26*n*26, 26*n*32, 148, 155*n*51
Duke, Mike, 286
Duncan, Tim, 430
Dunn, Edwina, 286
Dyer, Jeffrey H., 234*n*53

E

Eckert, Robert A., 46
Eden, Schmuel "Mooly," 280
Edgecliffe-Johnson, Andrew, 472*n*45
Edison, Thomas, 249
Edmondson, Gail, 32*n*, 88*n*, 233*n*26, 325*n*, 524*n*
Edmunds, Marian, 117
Edwards, Cliff, 16*n*, 186*n*, 280, 281*n*, 344*n*3
Egan, Robert W., 425
Eidam, Michael, 88*n*
Einhorn, Bruce, 26*n*37, 205*n*18, 233*n*25
Eisenhardt, Kathleen M., 268*n*33
Eisner, Michael D., 269, 271, 272, 274
Eitel, Maria S., 430
El-Ansary, Adel I., 345*n*15, 345*n*32
Elgin, Ben, 145*n*, 519*n*
El Guerrouj, Hicham, 426
Eliashberg, Jehoshua, 155*n*48
Ellison, Lawrence J., 435, 491
Engardio, Pete, 26*n*36, 26*n*39, 120*n*, 177*n*, 233*n*25, 251*n*, 348*n*
Engman, Lars, 164
Enright, Allison, 21*n*, 153*n*5, 154*n*25, 154*n*42, 313*n*, 395*n*17
Eppinger, Stephen D., 248*n*, 265*n*
Eriksen, Rolf, 195
Ernst, David, 234*n*42, 234*n*48, 234*n*57
Evans, B., 345*n*24
Evans, Philip B., 153*n*19
Evans, Richard T., 160
Everett, G. Carl, 438
Ewing, Jack, 325*n*

F

Farley, James, 563
Farley, John U., 498*n*22
Farley, John V., 25*n*9
Faroult, Bertille, 165
Farris, James E., 441–442
Fassler, Matthew, 509
Feldman, Alan, 284
Fenby, Jonathan, 345*n*26
Fenton, Ben, 193*n*
Ferris, Paul W., 490*n*, 498*n*24, 499*n*
Fiala, Adele, 286
Fidler, Stephen, 346*n*39
Fielding, Michael, 153*n*15, 154*n*38
Fine, John, 361
Fine, Jon, 417*n*29
Fiorina, Carleton S. "Carly," 437, 440
Firtle, Neil H., 256*n*, 268*n*27
Flannery, Simon, 505
Fletcher, J. H., 498*n*33
Fletcher, Richard, 132*n*

Ford, John B., 498n36
Fornell, Claes, 512
Foster, George, 80n
Foster, Norman, 168
Foust, Dean, 46n
Freeman, Hadley, 111n4
Fritz, Mary, 361–362
Frow, Pennie, 121, 123n, 127n3
Fruit, Charles B. "Chuck," 45
Fubrini, David G., 234n48
Fullerton, Mark, 33

G

Galbraith, Jay R., 277
Gandhi, Sonia, 176
Ganesan, Shankar, 416n1
Gapper, John, 346n36
Garahan, Matthew, 26n41, 395n17
Garnett, Kevin, 430
Garone, Stephen J., 312n
Gary, Loren, 234n44
Gates, William H., III, 23n, 420–423, 425,
    437, 526, 527, 529–530, 533
Gensler, Art, 281
Ghosn, Carlos, 519–524, 562, 563
Gilmore, James H., 268n33
Ginter, James L., 111n8, 112n24
Gogoi, Pallavi, 284n
Goizueta, Roberto C., 40–46
Gold, Stanley P., 274
Golden, Michael, 39
Goldin, Robert S., 284
Goldman, Emanuel, 41
Gomes-Casseres, Benjamin, 233n14, 233n15
Goolsby, Jerry R., 472n34
Gordon, Bruce S., 505
Gounaris, Spiros P., 498n14
Graham, John L., 204n11, 341n, 346n34,
    467n, 472n51
Grande, Carlos, 26n47, 26n48, 154n44
Grant, Jeremy, 26n35, 234n38
Grant, Peter, 73n15
Gray, Steven, 279
Green, Heather, 16n
Greenberg, Jack M., 281–284
Greene, Jay, 344n2, 527, 529n, 533n
Greenley, Gordon E., 25n21, 498n14
Grossman, Mindy F., 429–430
Grove, Andrew S., 274–275, 279, 280
Grover, Ronald, 274n, 394n3
Groves, Randall D., 434–435
Grow, Brian, 390n, 514n
Gruner, Kjell, 471n28
Guasperi, John, 471n26
Guerrera, Francesco, 153n3, 264n
Guilding, Chris, 80n
Gulati, Ranjay, 235n59

Gundry, Lisa, 464n
Gunther, Marc, 297n
Gupta, Mahendra, 80n
Gurry, Lisa, 516
Gurumurthy, Ragu, 275
Gutierrez, Carlos M., 46

H

Hagel, John, III, 228, 233n24, 235n63
Hainer, Herbert, 431
Hall, James N., 30, 31
Hall, Taddy, 111n7
Hamel, Gary, 25n23, 70–71, 73n18
Hamilton, Joan O'C., 151n
Hamm, Mia, 425
Hamm, Steve, 153n14, 195n, 210n, 242n,
    251n, 268n31, 342n, 425n, 471n13
Hansen, Eric J., 154n43
Harbour, Ronald E., 563
Harlow, John, 132n
Harris, Thomas, 385
Hartley, Steven W., 59n, 95n, 111n19,
    371n19
Harvey, Fiona, 264n
Hatfield, Tinker, 426
Hayward, Martin, 287
He, Hong-Wei, 233n11
Heckman, James, 317n39
Heinzl, Mark, 371n12
Heitz, Jean-Francois, 421
Hemerling, Jim, 174–175
Hemp, Paul, 21n
Hempel, Jessi, 97n, 251n, 452n
Henderson, John C., 233n13, 234n45
Hensley, Scott, 408n, 417n15
Heyer, Steven J., 45
Hindo, Brian, 26n51
Hira, Nadira A., 452n
Hiserman, Christopher, 234n56
Hobbs, Matt, 345n31
Hodulik, John, 506
Hoehn, Bill, 33
Hof, Robert D., 21n, 26n25, 26n42, 51n,
    394n1, 417n27
Holahan, Catherine, 67n
Holden, Reed K., 359n, 371n17, 371n22
Holland, Brian, 42
Holland, Charles H., 205n20
Holland, John, 438
Holland, Nick, 84
Hollenbeck, George P., 472n50
Holmes, Stanley, 222n, 344n2, 401n, 417n5,
    428n, 433n
Holt, Douglas B., 112n28
Holveck, David P., 181
Homburg, Christian, 471n28, 472n29,
    472n40, 472n43

Honeycutt, Earl D., 498n36
Honomichi, Jack, 154n30
Hooley, Graham J., 205n23
Horch, August, 32
Houlder, Vanessa, 155n56
Howes, Stephen, 175
Hoyas, Carola, 235n68
Hrebiniak, Lawrence G., 497n4
Hughes, Jonathan, 234n55
Hulbert, James M., 112n37, 154n46, 316n4,
    317n18, 471n22, 497n2, 498n34
Humby, Clive, 285
Hunt, Ben, 16n
Hunt, Shelby D., 26n31
Hunter, Dick, 438
Hurd, Mark, 12, 294, 439–441
Husson, Leon, 173
Hutton, Ray, 497n1
Hwang Chang Hwan, 536

I

Iger, Robert A., 269–270, 273, 274, 293
Ihlwan, Moon, 235n64, 537n, 539n
Ikenberry, Stanley O., 156
Immelt, Jeffrey, 264, 438, 454, 491
Ingram, Thomas M., 417n11
Ingrassia, Lawrence, 267n14
Inkpen, Andrew C., 235n58
Ireland, Ross, 502
Isdell, E. Neville, 40, 42–46
Ivester, M. Douglas, 42–43, 45

J

Jackson, Tony, 116n
James, Dana, 317n38, 498n12
James, LeBron, 427
Jaworski, Bernard J., 205n13, 371n21,
    417n18, 417n21
Jenkner, Rick, 548n
Jensen, Jakob, 167
Jensen, Nina Leth, 167
Jensen, Ove, 472n29, 472n40, 472n43
Joachimsthaler, Erich, 312, 317n48
Jobs, Steve, 269–274, 279
Jocz, Katherine E., 25n14, 417n18,
    449n, 471n9
Johnson, Craig R., 508
Johnson, Sheree L., 498n17
Johnson, William, 46
Johnston, Mark W., 69n, 394n4, 398n,
    405n, 417n3
Johnston, Zachary T., 267n2
Jones, Alex S., 35
Jones, Daniel T., 344n8, 345n19, 345n20
Jordan, Michael, 428, 435

Joseph, Stephanie R., 431
Joy, Bill, 32
Joyce, Claudia I., 471n3
Juan Carlos, King of Spain, 30
Jung, Andrea, 493
Jung-A, Song, 229n

K

Kahn, Barbara E., 112n32
Kale, Prashant, 234n53
Kale, Sudhir, 127n4
Kamprad, Ingvar, 162, 165–167
Kang Yun Je, 535, 536
Kanter, Steen, 166
Kaplan, Robert S., 316n12, 481, 498n15
Kara, Ali, 112n31
Karlkjell, Mattias, 163
Katen, Karen L., 159, 160
Kawamoto, Nobuhiko, 561
Kaynak, Erdener, 112n31
Kean, Danuta, 395n17
Keenan, Faith, 344n2
Keene, Dennis, 161
Keller, Bill, 34, 36–37
Keller, Kevin Lane, 154n45, 316n15,
  316n16, 344n5, 345n9
Keller, Maryann, 561
Kennard, William E., 504
Kennedy, Donald, 151
Kennedy, John F., 181
Kennedy, Karen N., 472n34
Keough, Donald R., 42, 46
Kerin, Roger A., 59n, 95n, 111n19, 371n19
Kerstetter, Jim, 425n
Kerwin, Kathleen, 32n, 471n14,
  524n, 565n
Khermouch, Gerry, 498n16
Kickul, Jill, 464n
Kiley, David, 162, 394n1
Killgren, Lucy, 338n
Kilts, James M. "Jim," 46
Kim, Eric B., 274–279
Kim, W. Chan, 52, 73n6, 370n3
Kim Dong Joon, 538
Kim Min Suk, 537
Kirchgaessner, Stephanie, 19n, 155n60
Kirkpatrick, David, 232n1, 495
Klick, Howard, 182
Kliman, Stuart, 234n56
Knight, Philip H., 426–429, 431–433
Knight, Rebecca, 26n45
Knox, Simon D., 127n8, 128n20
Kogure, Makato, 534
Kohl, George, 505
Kohli, Ajay K., 471n24, 471n27, 501n
Komivaram, Hideki, 297
Koogle, Timothy, 514
Koselka, Rita, 205n20

Kotler, Philip, 25n15, 154n45, 344n5, 345n9
Kovos, Sotiris, 563
Krakauer, Jon, 116
Kramer, Mark R., 22, 26n49
Kranhold, Kathryn, 122n, 128n28
Krauss, Michael, 317n50
Kripalani, Manjeet, 342n
Kruger, Irwin, 284
Kuczmarski, Thomas D., 267n2
Kumar, Ajith, 471n20
Kumar, Nirmalya, 303, 317n24, 345n12,
  471n18, 472n52
Kumar, V., 118n, 119n, 128n9, 128n15
Kunii, Irene M., 507n

L

Laask, Felicia G., 472n34
Lafley, A. G., 46, 129
LaForge, Raymond W., 417n11
Lagnado, Lucette, 371n20
Lakshman, Nandini, 205n18
LaMattina, John L., 160
Lamb, Charles W., Jr., 205n20
Lambert, Michael D., 438–439
Lambkin, Mary, 204n5
Lamont, James, 344n4
Lanchester, John, 155n62
Landis, Kevin, 515
Lane, Douglas C., 43
Lane, Nikala, 153n17, 154n28, 234n34
Lane, Stuart, 476, 476n
lang, k. d., 30
Langston, Edward L., 160
Larréché, Jean-Claude, 339n
Larsen, Peter Thal, 233n10
Larsen, Ralph S., 178
Larsson, Anders, 167
LaScala, Pat, 507
Lasserre, Philippe, 523
Lasseter, John, 269–271
Lassk, Felicia G., 417n14
Latour, Almar, 73n15, 268n30, 371n14
Laudon, Jane Price, 154n33
Laudon, Kenneth C., 154n33
Laughlin, Jay L., 111n13
Laurence, Ben, 447n
Lawler, Edward E., III, 471n16, 509
Lawver, Teri L., 465n, 472n46
Leahy, Joe, 19n
Leahy, Terry, 286
Lederhausen, Mats, 281–282
Lee, Charles R., 506
Lee, Kai-Fu, 525, 531
Lee, Louise, 371n4, 417n31
Lee Byung Moo, 533
Lee Dong Jin, 537
Lee Kun Hee, 533–534
Lee Seung Ho, 538

Lee Yun Jung, 534
Lehmann, Donald R., 25n14, 62n, 449n,
  460n, 471n9, 472n36, 498n21
Lenehan, James T., 179–180
Lennon, John, 271
Leopold, Jordan, 163
Lesser, Eric, 155n57
Lester, Tom, 234n51
Levine, Daniel S., 111n14
Levy, Liz, 506
Levy, Steve, 506
Lewis, Nicole, 464n
Lewis, Russell T., 34, 38
Li, Charlene, 529
Li, Josh, 173
Liebert, Carl C., III, 512–513
Liker, Jeffrey K., 233n21
Lilien, Gary L., 205n22
Lim, Kevin, 233n29
Lindberg, Sanna, 195
Linehan, John, 423
Lings, Ian N., 498n14
Livermore, Ann, 439, 442
London, Simon, 26n28
Lorange, Peter, 154n22
Lothson, David, 178
Loveman, Gary, 154n34
Low, George S., 417n9, 417n14
Lowry, Tom, 507n
Lublin, Joanne S., 155n63
Lucas, George, 270
Lucovsky, Mark, 526, 531
Ludeman, Kate, 436
Lun, Candance D., 465n, 472n46
Lusch, Robert E., 316n2
Lynn, Gary S., 267n6
Lynn, Matthew, 317n32
Lyons, Teena, 233n18

M

MacDonald, Elizabeth, 155n63
Macinnis, Deborah J., 205n13
Mackintosh, James, 234n40
Madden, Thomas J., 256n, 268n27
Madsen, Thomas L., 472n54
Magnusson, Paul, 471n14, 565n
Mahurin, Steve, 513
Maitland, Alison, 26n44, 345n33
Maklan, Stan, 127n8, 128n20
Maloney, Sean M., 277, 279
Malter, Alan J., 416n1
Maltz, Elliot, 471n20, 471n24, 501n
Mandel, Michael J., 417n27
Marchionne, Sergio, 473
Marcus, Bernie, 507
Maremont, Mark, 371n5
Markey, Rob, 112n23

Marsh, Peter, 153*n*6, 233*n*23
Marshall, Greg W., 69*n,* 394*n*4, 398*n,* 405*n,* 417*n*3, 417*n*14
Martin, Chris, 166
Martin, Roger L., 26*n*43
Masek, Karen, 287
Maslow, A. H., 111*n*16
Mathers, John, 312
Matlock, Carol, 235*n*65, 314*n*
Matsatsinis, Nikolaos F., 154*n*47
Matschullat, Robert W., 274
Mauborgne, Renee, 52, 73*n*6, 370*n*3
Mayer, Marissa, 239, 240, 272
Mazur, Laura, 25*n*18
McBride, Eamonn, 548
McCall, Morgan W., 472*n*50
McCaslin, Mark, 166
McCluney, Jim, 269
McConnon, Aili, 151*n*
McCullough, Wayne R., 498*n*19
McDonald, William J., 417*n*30
McDonnell, Kevin, 548, 549, 558
McGovern, Gail J., 498*n*32
McGrady, Tracy, 430
McGregor, Jena, 238*n,* 267*n*1
McGregor, Richard, 19*n*
McIntyre, Shelby H., 155*n*58
McKinnell, Henry A. "Hank," 156–161
McNealy, Scott G., 437
McQuarrie, Edward F., 155*n*58
Meehan, Robert, 345*n*25
Meer, David, 111*n*5
Mehrotra, Parth, 235*n*59
Meichtry, Stacy, 325*n*
Melligeri, Aravind, 174
Merrick, Amy, 309*n*
Messinger, Trevor, 43
Meyer, Barry M., 517
Meyer, Russ, 278
Miller, David, 497*n*5
Miller, Judith, 38
Miller, Kerry, 120*n*
Miller, Steve, 428
Mills, Lauren, 338*n*
Milunovich, Steven, 435, 439
Mishra, Devendra, 135*n*
Mitchell, Adrian, 53*n*
Mitchell, Alan, 153*n*4
Mitchell, George J., 274
Mokwa, Michael P., 497*n*7
Moncrief, William C., III, 205*n*20
Monroe, Kent B., 355*n,* 368*n,* 371*n*11
Monroe, Marilyn, 181
Montgomery, Cynthia A., 25*n*24
Moore, Michael, 37
Morgan, Neil A., 112*n*36, 497*n*3, 498*n*13
Morgan, Robert M., 26*n*31
Moriarity, Rowland T., 112*n*29
Morone, Joseph G., 267*n*6
Morrison, Scott, 234*n*41

Morrow, Keith, 442
Moulonguet, Thierry, 522
Moutinho, Luiz, 155*n*48
Mui, C., 317*n*40
Mullaney, Timothy J., 417*n*28
Mundel, David, 155*n*57
Mundie, Craig, 174
Murphy, Dan, 242
Murphy, Michael J., 559*n*
Murray, Sarah, 230*n*
Murry, Shailagh, 371*n*20

N

Nagel, David, 424
Nagle, Thomas T., 355*n,* 359*n,* 370*n*2, 371*n*6, 371*n*9, 371*n*17, 371*n*22
Naim, M. M., 345*n*22
Nakamura, Shiro, 522
Nardelli, Robert L., 507–514
Narus, James A., 345*n*30
Narver, John C., 25*n*4, 153*n*9, 153*n*16
Nash, John M., 46
Naylor, J. B., 345*n*22
Neff, Jack, 470–471*n*2
Newell, Claire, 370*n*1
Newing, Rod, 233*n*7, 233*n*12
Nicholson, Jack, 512
Niimi, Atsushi, 565
Nilekani, Nandan M., 171, 175
Nilsson, Mats, 166
Nilsson, Pia, 167
Nishida, Atsutoshi, 270
Niziolek, Walt, 522
Noble, Charles H., 497*n*7
Norton, David P., 481, 498*n*15
Novak, David C., 284
Novak, Robert, 38
Nunes, Paul F., 345*n*28
Nussbaum, Bruce, 243*n,* 249*n,* 259*n,* 267*n*11
Nuttall, Chris, 9*n,* 344*n*1
Nysschen, Johan de, 31, 33

O

Obasanjo, Dare, 530
O'Brien, Thomas, 167
O'Donohoe, Brian, 548, 555–558
Ohmae, Kenichi, 175
Ohno, Taichi, 563
Okrent, Daniel, 37
Okuda, Hiroshi, 562, 563
Olins, Rufus, 317*n*32
Olsen, Eric M., 268*n*17
Olsen, Ken, 437
Olson, Sally, 361
O'Sullivan, Don, 498*n*20

Otellini, Paul S., 275–280
Overell, Stephen, 65*n*
Owen, Glen, 108*n*
Owen, Jon, 286

P

Pacofsky, Nina, 361
Palmer, Maija, 9*n,* 314*n,* 344*n*1
Palmer, Nick, 233*n*16
Palmeri, Christopher, 317*n*30, 471*n*14
Palmisano, Samuel J., 227–228, 235*n*62
Panke, Helmut, 30
Parise, Salvatore, 233*n*13, 234*n*45
Park, Andrew, 439
Park, C. Whan, 205*n*13, 205*n*15
Parker, Chance, 31
Parker, Mark G., 429, 431, 433
Parks, Rosa, 271
Parloff, Roger, 210*n,* 233*n*28
Parsons, A. J., 317*n*49
Passariello, Christina, 325*n*
Patrick, Aaron O., 395*n*19
Paulson, Albert S., 267*n*6
Payne, Adrian, 121, 123*n,* 127*n*3, 128*n*20
Pecoriello, William P., 43
Pei, I. M., 168
Peltz, Nelson, 447
Peng, Mike W., 235*n*69
Penguino, Roger, 162
Peppard, Joe, 128*n*20
Peppers, Don, 111*n*3, 124, 127*n*6
Perez, William D., 431–433
Perkins, Wendell L., 282–283
Peters, Alex, 502
Peters, Tim, 438
Peterson, Joe, 418, 424–425
Peterson, Per A., 177, 180
Peterson, Robin T., 145*n*
Pfeffer, Philip E., 490*n*
Pfeifer, Philip E., 498*n*24, 499*n*
Philips, Ken, 542–543
Picasso, Pablo, 271
Piëch, Ferdinand, 32
Piercy, Niall C., 345*n*16
Piercy, Nigel F., 25*n*21, 25*n*22, 73*n*3, 112*n*36, 153*n*17, 154*n*28, 205*n*23, 234*n*34, 234*n*54, 345*n*18, 417*n*9, 471*n*21, 471*n*22, 472*n*49, 475*n,* 479*n,* 497*n*2, 497*n*3, 497*n*6, 498*n*13, 498*n*34
Pine, Joseph, II, 268*n*33
Piper, Jeff, 38
Pirko, Tom, 41
Pischetsrieder, Bernd, 32
Pistone, John N., 513
Pitt, Leyland F., 316*n*4
Plame, Valerie, 38
Plattner, Hasso, 425

Pollay, Richard W., 548n
Polmisano, Samuel J., 236
Pomerantz, Dorothy, 395n22
Pooch, Bernd, 30
Poon, Christine A., 182
Porter, Michael E., 6, 22, 25n11, 26n40,
    26n49, 63, 73n13, 472n44
Powell, M., 345n24
Prahalad, C. K., 70–71, 73n17, 73n18,
    168–169, 233n30
Press, James E., 563
Pritchard, Stephen, 16n
Pryor, Lee, 526

Q

Quattrone, Frank P., 438
Quelch, John A., 112n28, 498n32
Quinlan, Michael R., 284

R

Raines, Howell, 34–37
Raja, Jay, 46
Raman, Anand P., 448n
Ramaswami, Sridhar N., 127n1
Ramaswamy, Venkat, 233n30
Ramstad, Evan, 204n4
Ranga, V. Kasturi, 112n29
Rangaswamy, Arvind, 155n48, 205n22
Rattner, Steven L., 36
Rau, Kan, 491
Ray, Don D., 507
Raynor, Michael E., 73n4, 204n6,
    241–242, 267n9
Rayport, Jeffrey F., 371n21, 417n21
Rebello, Kathy, 527
Reddy, Raj, 530, 532
Redstone, Sumner M., 503
Reed, John, 88n, 497n1
Reed, Stanley, 25n3
Reibstein, David J., 490n, 498n24, 499n
Reichheld, Frederick F., 127n7, 128n14
Reinartz, Werner J., 118n, 119n,
    128n9, 128n15
Reinemund, Steven S., 44
Revall, Janice, 371n23
Rhys, Garel, 524
Richard, Bob, 532
Rigby, Darrell K., 127n7, 268n19
Rigby, Elizabeth, 234n36, 340n, 346n37
RimmKaufman, Alan, 516
Rita, Paulo, 155n48
Rizzuto, Phil, 545
Roberts, Bryan, 164
Roberts, Dan, 19n
Roberts, Dexter, 235n64, 348n
Roberts, John, 498n26

Robertson, Lance, 506
Robinson, David, 512
Robinson, Janet L., 34, 38
Robinson, Michael S., 233n14
Rocks, David, 26n38, 537n
Rockwell, Norman, 45
Roering, Kenneth J., 458n, 472n35
Rogers, Martha, 111n3, 127n6
Rohwedder, Cecilie, 287n, 317n29
Rollins, Kevin B., 433, 437–438
Romanelli, Elaine, 204n8
Rosenbush, Steve, 507n
Rosensweig, Daniel, 518
Ross, Jerry, 235n58
Rossant, John, 40n
Roth, Erik A., 154n24
Rovit, Sam, 283
Rowling, J. K., 193
Royal, Weld, 345n27
Rubens, Paul, 123n, 125n
Ruckert, Robert W., 458n
Rudelius, William, 59n, 95n, 111n19,
    371n19
Ruekert, Robert W., 268n17, 472n35
Ruiz, Hector J. de, 277
Rushe, Dominic, 116n, 345n10, 498n35
Ruskin, Gary, 151
Ryals, Lynette, 127n8, 128n20
Rydberg-Dumont, Josephine, 166

S

Saber, Paul, 283
Saldana, Alma, 195
Sanchanta, Mariko, 344n7
Sanchez, Ron, 232n3
Sanzo, Richard, 74n
Sauder, William E., 471n20
Saunders, John A., 205n23
Sawney, Mohan, 471n19
Scala, Stephen M., 159
Schafter, Phil, 127n7
Scheinman, Dan, 168, 171
Schell, Orville, 34
Schifrin, Matthew, 234n47
Schindler, Pamela S., 205n21, 268n35
Schine, Eric, 314n
Schneider, Peter, 270
Schultz, Don E., 317n21
Schuster, Timothy, 161–162
Schwartz, Nelson D., 235n66
Schweitzer, Louis, 520, 522–524
Seamon, Erica B., 267n2
Seely-Brown, John, 228, 235n63
Segrest, Jen, 167–168
Seid, Michael, 284
Seidenberg, Ivan G., 491, 502–507
Selden, Larry, 122, 128n25
Semel, Terry K., 514–519

Senn, Christoph, 468n
Shanley, John J., 428
Shansby, J. Gary, 205n14
Sharma, Amit, 174
Shedlarz, David L., 159
Shiga, Toshiyuki, 522–523
Shiling, Zheng, 168
Shipp, Shannon H., 472n49
Shirouzu, Norihiko, 268n41
Shocker, Allan D., 73n9
Shoemaker, Paul J. H., 154n23, 154n27
Shorenstein, Joan, 35
Silva, Walter Maria de, 32
Silverman, Gary, 395n18
Simintiras, Antonis C., 498n36
Simmonds, K., 80n
Simms, Jane, 500n
Simon, Bernard, 16n, 234n40,
    316n13, 395n21
Simonian, Haig, 323n
Simons, Andrew, 268n34
Simpson, Joe, 116
Singh, Harbir, 234n53
Siskos, Y., 154n47
Slater, Stanley F., 25n4, 25n21,
    153n9, 153n16
Slywotzky, Adrian J., 26n30,
    153n11, 153n18
Smith, D. V. L., 498n33
Smith, Gerald E., 355n, 371n9
Smith, Mike, 530
Smith, Peter, 370n1
Smith, Raymond W., 506
Soble, Jonathan, 235n67
Solomon, Deborah, 371n12
South, Gill, 233n8
Soutus, Sonya H., 46
Spagat, Elliot, 268n26
Spiers-Lopez, Pernille, 167
Spilotro, Kathryn W., 267n2
Srivastava, Rajendra K., 73n9, 127n1
Stadler, Rupert, 32
Stalk, George, 508
Steenkamp, E. M., 303, 317n24
Steere, William C., Jr., 159
Steiner, Gary A., 111n18
Steiner, Rupert, 154n37
Steinig, Richard, 281
Stern, Louis W., 345n15, 345n32
Stern, Stefan, 317n23
Stewart, Thomas A., 155n49, 155n53, 448n
Stibel, Gary M., 46
Strickland, A. J., III, 75n
Strigl, Dennis, 506
Stringer, Howard, 297
Sull, Donald, 134, 154n21
Sullivan, Alanna, 101n, 112n26
Sulzberger, Arthur, Jr., 35–40
Sulzberger, Arthur Ochs "Punch," 34–35
Sutcliffe, Kathleen M., 153n2

Swain, Gill, 108*n*
Swartz, Gordon S., 112*n*29
Symonds, William C., 305*n*
Sytch, Maxim, 235*n*59

T

Tait, Nikki, 111*n*9
Tam, Pui-Wing, 73*n*7, 416*n*2, 442*n*
Taylor, Andrew, 26*n*46, 340*n*
Taylor, Charles R., 111*n*13
Taylor, Earl L., 112*n*28
Taylor, Paul, 16*n*, 25*n*17, 344*n*6
Taylor, Thomas V., Jr., 513
Tellis, Gerald J., 267*n*13
Thoma, Axel, 468*n*
Thomas, Kim, 154*n*40
Thomke, Stefan H., 268*n*20
Thompson, Arthur A., 75*n*
Thompson, Stephanie, 317*n*45
Thormann, Dominique, 519
Tichy, Noel M., 532
Tomkins, Richard, 128*n*29, 317*n*47
Toomey, Robert, 427
Topfer, Martin L., 439
Towill, Denis R., 345*n*23
Toyama, Kentaro, 530
Toyoda, Sakichi, 448
Trahan, Marc, 30, 33
Treville, Suzanne, 267*n*4
Trinkle, Bob, 472*n*47
Tucker, Sundeep, 19*n*

U

Ulrich, Karl T., 248*n*, 265*n*
Ungood-Thomas, Jon, 155*n*61
Urban, Glen L., 268*n*28, 417*n*22, 417*n*26
Urry, Maggie, 87*n*

V

Valeriani, Nick, 180
Välikangas, Liisa, 25*n*23
Van Arnum, Patricia, 470–471*n*2
van Bruggen, Gerrit, 154*n*47

van den Bosch, Margareta, 195
van Duyn, Aline, 417*n*29
Van Horne, James, 74, 74*n*
Vargo, Stephen L., 316*n*2
Vásquez, Xosé H., 233*n*27
Vence, Deborah L., 154*n*32
Viemeister, Tucker, 259
Vilar, Alberto W., 516
Vines, Jason, 521
von Hippel, Eric, 268*n*20

W

Wagoner, G. Richard, Jr., 521, 562
Walker, Orville C., Jr., 268*n*17, 339*n*, 458*n*, 472*n*35
Walli, Stephen, 526
Walton, Sam, 165, 435
Wansley, Brant, 317*n*51
Watanabe, Hiroyuki, 562
Waters, Richard, 9*n*, 51*n*, 97*n*, 208*n*, 234*n*41
Watson, David N., 505
Weaver, Bill, 441
Webb, Reggie, 283
Weber, Joseph, 65*n*, 345*n*33
Weber, Karl, 153*n*11
Weber, Klaus, 153*n*2
Webster, Frederick E., Jr., 13, 25*n*14, 26*n*33, 233*n*7, 233*n*20, 416*n*1
Wegleitner, Mark, 507
Weinstein, Michael, 182
Weinswig, Deborah, 510
Weitzer, Dorothy L., 185
Welch, Andrew, 312
Welch, David, 268*n*29, 524*n*
Welch, Jack, 454, 510–511
Weldon, William C., 177–182
Wensley, Robin, 25*n*16, 73*n*14
Westwood, Vivienne, 84
Whitehead, Mark, 345*n*24
Whitman, Meg, 274
Wicks, Jim, 537
Wiecha, Charles, 155*n*57
Wierenga, Berend, 154*n*47
Wiggins, Jenny, 108*n*, 233*n*9, 234*n*36, 323*n*, 447*n*
Wild, Anthony H., 160
Wilding, Richard, 234*n*49

Wildstrom, Stephen H., 97*n*
Williams, Serena, 430
Willman, John, 26*n*52
Wilson, Gary L., 274
Wilson, Hugh, 345*n*31
Wilson, William T., 173
Wind, Jerry, 155*n*48
Winer, Russell S., 62*n*, 128*n*10, 460*n*, 462*n*, 472*n*36, 472*n*41
Winnett, Robert, 370*n*1
Winterkorn, Martin, 30–32
Witzel, Morgan, 234*n*52
Womack, James P., 344*n*8, 345*n*19
Wood, Brian, 433
Woodruff, David, 317*n*32
Woodruff, Robert, 44, 73*n*8, 112*n*35
Woolard, Edgar S., Jr., 270
Workman, John P., 471*n*28, 472*n*29, 472*n*40, 472*n*43
Worley, Christopher, 471*n*16
Wozniak, Stephen, 271, 272
Wreden, Nick, 471*n*25
Wright, Robert, 230*n*
Wurster, Thomas S., 153*n*19

Y

Yang, Zhilin, 145*n*
Yankelovich, Daniel, 111*n*5
Yip, George S., 472*n*54
Yoffie, David B., 418
Young, Clifford E., 417*n*11
Young, D., 112*n*38
Young, Shawn, 371*n*12
Yu, Larry, 498*n*18
Yun Jong Yong, 533–534, 536, 537–538
Yustein, Tony, 425

Z

Zaltman, Gerald, 154*n*36, 205*n*15
Zander, Edward J., 437
Zeitler, William M., 437
Zellner, Wendy, 5*n*, 192*n*, 222*n*, 305*n*
Zimmerman, Ann, 204*n*10
Zook, Chris, 268*n*19

Subject Index

A

Abbott Laboratories, 182
ABG Sundal Collier, 163
Accessible memory, 134
Accor, 116, 117
Ace Hardware, 509
AC Nielsen, 303
Actionable segments, 97
Activity-Based Costing (ABC), 81, 356
Activity-Based Management (ABM), 356
Activity ratios, 76
Ad hoc issue groups, 137
Adidas, 21, 92, 430, 431
Administered vertical marketing systems
    (VMS), 326
Adria Airways, 212
Advanced Micro Devices, 277
Advertising agencies, 386–388
    agency relationship, 386–387
    compensation, 387
    evaluating, 387
    industry composition, 387–388
Advertising metrics, 500
Advertising strategy, 196, 381–389
    budget determination, 382–384
    creative, 384
    in distribution process, 319
    impact on profits, 140
    implementing, 388
    marketing information and, 134
    market segmentation and, 85
    measuring effectiveness, 388, 389
    media/scheduling decisions, 384–386
    objectives, 382, 383
    in promotion strategy, 373, 376
    role of advertising agency, 386–388
    targeting children, 108
    television and fewer ads watched, 94
    vanishing mass market, 386
    Web 2.0 and, 20
Adware, 145
Aer Lingus, 212
Aeroflot, 212
AeroMexico, 212
Agentrics, 337
Agile supply chains, 335
Ahold, 467
AirAsia, 87
Air Canada, 212
Air China Limited, 212
Air Deccan, 87

Air Europa, 212
Air France, 212
Air New Zealand, 212
Aldi, 467
Alfa Romeo, 32
Alitalia, 212
All Nippon Airways, 212
Alza Corp., 182
Amazon.com Inc., 11, 116, 238, 241, 408
AMD, 9, 23, 293
American Airlines, 64, 87, 185, 212, 217,
    300, 366, 367
American Apparel Inc., 21
American Express, 294, 412
American Fit, 84
American Marketing Association,
    291, 413
America Online, 208, 375, 423–424
Amerindo Investment Advisors Inc., 516
Amgen Inc., 182
Anheuser-Busch Companies, 304, 311, 466
Ansett Airlines, 212
Antiglobal segment, 102
AOL Time Warner Inc., 502, 516, 517
AppExchange, 404
Apple Computer Inc., 9, 135, 162, 213, 219,
    236, 237, 258, 269–274, 277, 279,
    293, 298–299, 322, 324, 338, 421,
    503, 530, 537
Arbitron Inc., 139
Arcelor Mittall Steel, 2–3, 6–8, 18, 130
Arysis, 553
Asda Sainsbury, 341
Asiana Airlines, 212
Assembly activities, in distribution
    process, 319
Astra/Merck, 91–92
Astron Clinica, 211
A.T. Kearney, 168–169
AT&T Corp., 213, 214, 220, 225, 503,
    504, 505
Attitudes, in market segmentation, 93
Attribute costing, 81
Auchan, 467
Audi AG, 30–33, 191, 216
Audits
    channel, 333
    strategic marketing, 483–486
AU Electronics, 229
Austrian Airlines Group, 212
Autodesk, 185
Avon Products Corp., 332, 377, 407, 410,
    493, 494

B

Bain & Co., 98, 114, 119, 121, 122, 283,
    432–433, 438
Bait and switch, 364
Balanced scorecard approach, 226, 481
Banana Republic, 336
Bath & Body Works, 309
Bay Area Consulting Group, 491
Bayer, 162
Bean (L.L.), 413, 415
BehaviorScan system, 261
Beiersdorf, 92
Bell Atlantic Corp., 504–505, 506
BellSouth Corp., 504, 507
Belo Corp., 254
Benchmarking, 81
Benetton, 325
Benjamin (F J) Holdings, 216
Ben & Jerry's, 145
Berkshire Hathaway, 349
Best Buy Co., 83–85, 89, 135, 279, 358, 534
BevMark LLC, 41
Beyond Fleece, 84
Bharat Forge Ltd., 174
BIOC, 229
BioMedical Research Ltd., 548–550, 553,
    555–556
BJ's Wholesale Club, 222
Blackberry, 16, 279–281, 438
Bloomsbury, 193
Blue1, 212
bmi British Midland, 212
BMW, 30, 31, 32, 33, 88, 196, 216, 238,
    292, 294, 295, 303, 310
Boeing Co., 91, 130, 168, 213, 216, 217,
    236, 238, 400, 401
Boise Cascade Corp., 425
BoKlok, 167
Bon Marché, 84
Booz, Allen & Hamilton, 451
Borders, 306
Boston Consulting Group, 174–175, 236,
    296, 433, 446, 448, 449–450, 508
Boston Market, 284
Boyd Watterson Asset Management LLC, 42
Brain scanning technology, 150
Brand(s). *See also* Brand management
    defined, 291
    global brand scorecard, 293–294
    strategic role of, 291–292
Brand analysis, 297, 298–301
    positioning analysis, 301

product life cycle analysis, 300
product performance analysis, 300–301
tracking brand performance, 299–300
Brand Asset Valuator (BAV), 301
Brand building
  Internet strategy in, 410
  in promotion strategy, 377
  strategies, 308
Brand equity measurement and management, 298, 301–302
Brand equity metrics, 500
Brand extension
  example, 312
  nature of, 311
Brand health reports, 301–302
Brand identity strategy, 298, 302–304
  alternatives for brand identification, 302–303
  brand focus, 303
  identity implementation, 304
Brand leveraging, 310–314
  brand extension, 311, 312
  brand theft, 313–314
  co-branding, 311
  global branding, 293–294, 311–312
  Internet brands, 312–313
  licensing, 311
  line extension, 310
Brand management, 290–315
  brand analysis, 297, 298–301
  brand equity measurement and management, 298, 301–302
  brand identity strategy, 298, 302–304
  brand leveraging strategy, 310–314
  brand portfolio, 295, 298, 306–309
  challenges, 292–296
  components, 291, 296–298
  global brand scorecard, 293–294
  improving product performance, 304–306
  nature of, 17
  responsibility, 296
  strategic role of brands, 291–292
Brand portfolios
  brand strength, 307–308
  brand vulnerabilities, 308–309
  managing, 298, 306–309
  roles of brands, 307
  sample, 295
Brand revitalization, 308
Brand theft, 313–314
Brand valuation, 81
Break-even analysis, 77–79, 365–366
Bristol-Myers Squibb Co., 182
British Airways, 87, 124, 212
British Petroleum (BP), 229
British Telecom (BT), 214, 225
Broadview Advisors, 159

Brooks and Dunn, 389
Brooks Brothers, 84
Budgets
  advertising, 382–384
  promotion, 311, 378–380
Budweiser, 304, 466
Burberry PLC, 304
Burger King, 92, 283
Bush Boake Allen (BBA), 251
Business analysis, 255–257
Business and marketing strategy, 12–18
  components, 13
  defined, 9
  marketing strategy process, 13–18
  relationships, 13
Business composition, in corporate strategy, 11–12
Business needs analysis, in Customer Relationship Management (CRM), 119
Business Performance Management Forum, 129
Business segments, in corporate strategy, 11–12
Buyer(s)
  choices of, 59
  defining, 58
  describing, 58
  stages in consumer and organizational purchases, 59
Buyer considerations, direct distribution by manufacturers, 321
Buyer diversity
  in emerging markets, 188
  in mature markets, 190–191
Buying activities, in distribution process, 319
BuzzLogic, 313

C

Cablevision Systems, 506
CACI, 553
Cadbury Schweppes, 446, 447, 488
Call center technologies, 120, 125
Canadian Airlines, 212
Canadian Appliance Manufacturing Co. Ltd. (CAMCO), 539
Canadian General Electric (C.G.E.), 539
Cannibalization, 244
Canon, 136
Capabilities
  in emerging markets, 189
  in growth markets, 190
  matching to value opportunities, 240–241
  in mature markets, 191
  partnering, 225
Carat Press, 38

Carrefour, 163, 218, 340, 341, 467
Carreman, 392
Catalogs, 413
Category management, 460
Caterpillar Inc., 22, 197
Cathay Pacific Airways, 212, 401
Censorship, 313
Centocor Inc., 181
Centralization, of marketing department, 456
Centrica, 19
Cerberus, 225
Change agents, 444–445
Channel audits, 333
Channel configuration, 328–329
Channel globalization, 336–337, 340–343
Channel hopping, 338
Channel leadership, 334
Channel maps, 329–330
Channel metrics, 499
Channel migration, 332–333
Channel performance, 338
Channels for services, 321
Channels of distribution
  channel strategy, 323–333
  distribution function, 319–321
  nature of, 318
Channel strategy, 323–333
  changing, 331–333
  channel configuration, 328–329
  channel maps, 329–330
  distribution intensity, 327–328
  selecting, 330–331
  types of channels, 324–327
Chevron, 229
Chick-fil-A Inc., 283
Chief knowledge officers, 148
Children, advertising to, 108
Chi Mei, 229
China, 168–177
  collaboration with state-owned enterprises, 230
  customer markets, 218
  globalization process and, 18, 19, 133
  income variations, 58
  market access, 211
  marketing research on, 139
  Microsoft strategy adaptation in, 495
  pricing strategy, 347, 348, 350
  technology innovation in, 20
China National Offshore Oil Corporation, 19
China Southern Airlines, 212
China Standard Software Co., 425
Chipotle Mexican Grill, 284
Christian Dior, 314
Chrysler Corp., 148–149, 216, 225, 520, 521, 561
Cingular, 503, 507
Circuit City Stores Inc., 338, 358, 534

Cisco Systems Inc., 168, 238, 294, 439, 562
Citigroup, 293, 342, 510
Clayton Act, 364
ClearChannel, 51
Client satisfaction, Customer Relationship
    Management (CRM) and, 124
Close customer relationships, 105
Cluster analysis, 103
CNET Networks Inc., 518
CNPC, 229
Coach, 100, 131
Co-branding, 311
Coca-Cola Co., 21, 40–46, 61, 64, 191, 221,
    239, 285, 290, 293, 329
Colgate-Palmolive, 42, 129, 305, 352
Collaboration. *See also* Strategic
        relationships
    in channel relationships, 336
    costs of, 213–214
    new organization, 448–449
    new product teams, 460–461
    partnering with other organizations,
        463–464
Combination branding, 303
Comcast Corp., 502, 505, 506
Commercialization, 263–264
Commerzbank, 522
Commitment
    in channel relationships, 336
    planning for, 476
Commodization, 51–52, 242
Communication
    in distribution process, 320
    in global marketing strategies, 466–467
    implementation effectiveness, 479
    in promotion strategy, 376–378
Compaq Computer Corp., 435, 440
Competencies, strategic relationships
    and, 223
Competition-oriented pricing, 351,
    352–353, 365
Competitive advantage
    competitive differentiation and, 126
    in corporate strategy, 11
    cost analysis, 357
    information-based, 126
    learning and, 130, 132–133
    in marketing program, 198–199
    sustaining and building, 48
Competitive considerations, direct distribu-
    tion by manufacturers, 321–322
Competitive differentiation, in strategic
    marketing, 124–126
Competitive forces, 63–64
Competitive metrics, 499
Competitive parity, in promotion strategy,
    379–380
Competitive position monitoring, 81
Competitive space, 14

Competitive strategy, strategic relationships
    and, 209
Competitor analysis, 61–67
    anticipating competitors' actions, 66–67
    competitive forces, 63–64
    industry analysis, 61–62
    key competitor, 64–66
    levels of competition, 62
    of market segments, 107
    phases of competition, 70
    in positioning evaluation, 199, 200
    in pricing strategy, 357–359
    value-added chain analysis, 62–63
Competitor intelligence
    gathering, 65
    in market orientation, 4
Competitor performance appraisal, 81
Competitor ratings, 65–66
Complex systems development process, 265
Concentration, 91
Concept evaluation, 254–255
Concept tests, 254–255
Conflict, in relationship management, 224
Conflict resolution, 337–338
Confused positioning, 201
Conjoint analysis, 122
Consultative selling, 400
Consumer-focused assessments, 66
Consumer Goods Pricing Act, 364
Consumer markets
    characteristics of, 90–91
    male shoppers, 92
Consumer metrics, 500
Consumer needs, in market segmentation, 93
Continental Airlines, 212
Continuous learning, about markets, 15
Contractual vertical marketing systems
    (VMS), 326
Contribution analysis, 77
Control
    in channel strategy, 331
    in commercialization process, 263–264
    over costs, 357
    direct distribution by manufacturers,
        322–323
    in marketing strategy process, 17–18
    in relationship management, 226
    strategic marketing planning, 483
Conventional channels, 324
Copa Airlines, 212
Copycat brands, 303
Corning, 219
Corporate branding, 303
Corporate culture
    for innovation, 245
    managing, 447–448
    strategic relationships and, 214
Corporate Social Responsibility (CSR), 2
    government regulation, 230

    nature of, 20–23
    One Laptop Per Child program, 22, 23
Corporate strategy
    components of, 10–12
    defined, 9, 10
    framework for, 10–12
Corus, 19
Corvis Corp., 438
Cosi, 282
Cost analysis
    competitive advantage, 357
    pricing situation, 356–357
    sales organization, 402–403
Cost/benefits of segmentation, 98
Costco Wholesale, 135, 163, 222, 303,
    305, 455, 514
Cost estimation, new-product, 257
Cost-oriented pricing, 356–357, 365–366
Cost reduction
    in managing brand strategy, 305
    strategic relationships and, 224
Counterfeiting, 313–314
Cowen (SG) & Co., 528
Cowen Securities Corp., 159
Cox Communications, 506
Creative strategy, 384
Credit Suisse First Boston, 158, 160, 438
CRM. *See* Customer Relationship
    Management (CRM)
Croatia Airlines, 212
Crompco Corp., 21
Cross classification analysis, 100
Cross-functional participation, 4
    aligning structure and processes, 8
    cross-functional teams, 133
    marketing as cross-functional
        process, 454–455
    in marketing program, 199
    in market orientation, 4–5
Crutchfield Corp., 516
CSA Czech Airlines, 212
Cultural differences
    global marketing plan, 494–495
    in relationship management, 225
Cummins Inc., 174
Customer analysis
    of market segments, 106–107
    in positioning evaluation, 199, 200
Customer base analysis centers, 65
Customer contacts, in database
    marketing, 115
Customer focus, in market orientation, 4
Customer function, product-market, 56
Customer group identification, 99–102
    cross classification analyses, 100
    data mining for segmentation, 100–101
    management insight and available
        information, 99–100
    segmentation illustrations, 101–102

Customer Growth Partners Inc., 508
Customer knowledge, leveraging, 148–149
Customer lifetime value (CLV),
    115–116, 122
Customer linking, 8
Customer metrics, 499
Customer price sensitivity, 353–356
Customer profiles, 60
Customer profitability metrics, 499
Customer Relationship Management
    (CRM), 113–127, 454, 464
  customer lifetime value, 115–116, 122
  and database marketing, 114–115
  deselecting customers through, 125
  developing, 116–121
  estimating segment attractiveness,
    107–108
  implementation, 119–121, 123–124
  integration through, 84
  levels, 116–118
  marketing strategy process, 14–15, 84,
    89, 94–95
  nature of, 113–114
  new marketing roles, 462–464
  in perspective, 114
  purchase behavior, 94–95
  segment attractiveness, 107–108
  strategic marketing and, 123–126
  strategic marketing planning, 483
  strategic perspective, 14–15
  strategy development, 118–119
  value creation process, 121–123
  Website resources, 121
Customer relationships
  end-user, 217
  intermediate, 216
  strategic customers, 217–219
Customer retention, in promotion strategy,
    377–378
Customer satisfaction, 87
Customer segment, product-market, 56
Customer service, Internet strategy in, 410
Customer value
  direct marketing strategies, 412–413
  distinctive capabilities and, 7
  finding opportunities for, 239
  Internet strategy, 410–411
  market segmentation and, 86–87
  nature of, 7
  objectives of customer value analysis, 239
  providing, 7
  strategic relationships and, 208–209
  in value creation process, 121–122
Customer Value Mapping (CVM), 354–356
Customization, 91, 92, 104–105, 259, 321
Customized product development process,
    265
Cutco, 377
Cypher, 180

D

Dad segment, 92
Daimler-Benz, 225, 520
DaimlerChrysler, 504, 518, 522, 523, 561
Database marketing
  Customer Relationship Management
    (CRM) and, 114–115
  database components, 115
  direct marketing strategies, 412
  privacy and, 149–150
Data mining, for segmentation, 100–101
Datamonitor PLC, 156
Data warehouses, 120
DeBeers, 326
Decentralization, of marketing
    department, 456
Deceptive pricing, 364
Decisions
  in market segmentation, 89
  pricing, responsibility for, 350, 361
  in promotion strategy, 377
Declining markets, 187
Dell Inc., 9, 16, 22, 23, 215, 230, 238, 270,
    271, 279, 294, 313, 318–319, 331,
    333, 350, 415, 433–439, 440
Deloitte Consulting, 115–116
Delphi technique, 69
Delta, 212
Demand-oriented pricing, 365, 366
Demand stimulation, price in, 352
Demographic variables, 90–91
Dentsu, 387
Dependence, in channel relationships, 336
Descriptive information, in database
    marketing, 115
Designing market-driven organizations, 17,
    444–469. *See also* Market-driven
    strategy
  marketing departments, 456–458
  organizing for global marketing and
    global customers, 465–469
  organizing for market-driven strategy,
    452–455
  structuring marketing resources,
    459–465
  trends in organization design, 445–452
"Devil customers," 125
Diageo, 385–386
Diesel, 430
Digital channels, 327
Digital Convergence Corp., 254
Digital Equipment Corp., 437
Direct mail, 413
Direct marketing strategies, 321–323,
    407, 412–415
  advantages, 414
  marketing strategy and, 415
  methods, 413–414

  in promotion strategy, 374, 378
  reasons for using, 412–413
Direct response media, 413–414
Direct Shop Ltd., 550, 554–555
Discounting cash flows, 79
Discovery Communications Inc., 39
Disney (Walt) Co., 237, 269–274, 293, 311
Disruptive innovation, 50–51
Distinctive capabilities
  classifying, 6–7
  customer value and, 7
  determining, 5–6
  types of, 6
Distribution function, 319–321
Distribution intensity, 327–328
Distribution strategy, 349–350
Diverse customer base, 105
Divisions, in corporate strategy, 11–12
dMarc, 51
Dogster.com, 97
Dollar General Stores, 363
Dominant customers, 218
Doubtful positioning, 201
Dow Jones & Co., 35
Dreyer's Grand Ice Cream, 465
Dun & Bradstreet, 74
DuPont, 270, 455
Dyson, 92

E

Eastman Kodak Co., 7, 46, 48–49, 135,
    136, 190, 236
Eatons, 543, 545
eBay Inc., 2, 66, 67, 208, 238, 274, 515
EchoStar Communications, 504
E-commerce strategy, 410
Economic Value Modeling (EVM), 354–356
Efficient Consumer Response (ECR),
    334–335, 460
Electronic shopping, 414
Eli Lilly & Co., 161, 162, 216, 225
EMC Corp., 215, 437, 439
Emerging markets, 18, 187, 188–189
Emulex Corp., 269
Encyclopedia Britannica, 308
End-users, 57–59
  buyer choices, 59
  considerations for, 328
  customer profiles, 60
  customer relationships, 217
  describing buyers, 58
  direct marketing strategies, 321–323,
    407, 412–415
  environmental influences, 60
  identifying buyers, 58
  price elasticity, 354
  stages in consumer and organizational
    purchases, 59

Enron Corp., 42
Environment. *See also* Market environments
    effects of products on, 306
    influence on buyers, 60
    strategic relationships and, 209
Eos, 87
Epinions.com, 145
E-procurement, 335
Ernst & Young, 148
Estée Lauder, 328
E-tailing, 409
Ethicon Endo-Surgery Inc., 180–181
Ethics
    brand theft, 313–314
    channel relationships, 338–340
    collecting and using customer
        information, 149–151
    competitor intelligence gathering, 65
    CRM tools in deselecting customers, 125
    ethical consumerism, 22
    ethical standards, 2
    information on, 150
    nature of, 20–23
    neuromarketing, 150, 151
    pricing strategy, 363–365
    in selling and sales management, 398
    targeting children, 108
Ethnographic studies, 143–144
Eurowave, 553
Exane, 32
Exclusive distribution, 327
Existing functional groups, 137
Exiting from alliance, 226–227
Experience effect, 357
Express, 125
Extended warranties, 358
External information resources,
    138–140, 252
External organization, 482
External partnering, 463–464
Extranets, 414
ExxonMobil, 229

F

Facebook.com, 97, 385
Federal Express, 241, 249
Federal Trade Commission (FTC), 364
Federated, 333
Federated Cooperative, 543
FedEx Corp., 401
Fiat Group, 471–472
Filene's Basement, 125
Financial analysis, 74–80
    alternative units, 74
    in channel strategy, 331
    evaluating alternatives, 77–79
    financial planning, 79
    financial ratio analysis, 74–76, 500

financial situation analysis, 74–77
    model for, 77
    supplemental, 79–80, 81–82
    unit of, 74
Financial considerations, direct distribution
        by manufacturers, 322–323
Financial constraints, and strategic
        relationships, 210–211
Financial metrics, 74–76, 500
Financial performance, price in, 351, 352
Financial planning, 79
Financial ratio analysis, 74–76
Financial situation analysis, 74–77
Financing activities, in distribution
        process, 319
Finer segmentation strategies, 104–106
    logic of finer market segments, 104–105
    types of, 105–106
Finnair, 212
Firestone, 543
F J Benjamin Holdings, 216
Flexibility
    in channel strategy, 331
    organizational, 451
    in pricing strategy, 360–362, 368
    in relationship management, 224
Ford Motor Co., 53, 90, 149, 161, 218,
        521, 523, 561
Forecasting
    advantages and disadvantages of
        techniques, 69
    estimating market segment attractive-
        ness, 107–108
    future strategies of competitors, 66
    market opportunity, 68–70
    market potential, 67
    market share, 68
    in pricing strategy, 356
    revenue, 255
    sales, 68, 69
    strategic vision about future in, 70–71
Forrester Research Inc., 170, 337, 464, 529
Franklin Global Communications Fund, 502
Fresh & Easy, 132
Friedman, Billings, Ramsey & Co., 159
Frito-Lay Inc., 45, 290
Fuji Xerox Co., 219, 221
Functional organizational design, 459
Functional positioning concepts, 196
Fuze Beverage LLC, 45

G

Game theory, 359
Gannett Co., 35
Gap Inc., 195, 202, 216, 310, 336
Gartner Inc., 119, 424, 528
Gatorade, 290
Gazprom, 19, 229

Genentech, 238
General Electric Appliances, 539–548
General Electric Company (GE), 122, 130,
        143–144, 174, 197, 237, 249, 264,
        292, 293, 342, 418, 434, 438, 454,
        491, 504, 508, 510–511, 532
General Motors Corp., 63, 89, 160, 168,
        185, 191–192, 252, 253, 291, 389,
        391, 448, 457, 521, 523, 561
General Steel Wares Ltd. (G.S.W.), 539
Generation F3 segment, 101
Generation Y, 452, 453
Generic (market pull) development
        process, 265
Generic product-markets, 53–54
GfK AG, 139
GfK NOP, 22
Gillette, 18, 96, 191, 218, 294, 305, 352, 493
GlaxoSmithKline PLC, 161, 162, 216
Global Account Management (GAM),
        217–218, 467–469
Global Agnostic segment, 102
Global branding, 293–294, 311–312
Global Citizen segment, 102
Global customers, 467–469
Global Dreamer segment, 102
Global Exchange Network, 337
Global Growth Group, 283
Globally integrated enterprise (GIE), 227–228
Global marketing planning, 493–494
Global marketing strategies, 466–467
Global markets
    airline alliances, 212
    BMW mini, 88
    Chinese income variations, 58
    escalating globalization, 18–19
    expansion from emerging markets, 19
    Harry Potter books, 193
    international call centers, 120
    market sensing at Tesco, 132
    nature of, 192–193
    organizing for, 465–469
Gol, 87
Goldman, Sachs & Co., 175, 437, 509
Good Technology, 16
Google Inc., 2, 7, 9, 20, 48, 51, 97, 134–136,
        142, 145–146, 150, 168, 208, 236,
        237, 239, 240, 245, 272, 279, 292,
        293, 294, 314, 372, 375, 381, 420,
        421, 515, 516, 517, 519, 525–526,
        528, 530–532
Gore Company, 252
GoreTex, 11
Government, 228–230
    collaborating with state-owned
        enterprises, 229–230
    competing with state-owned
        enterprises, 229
    interventions, 228–229
    regulation, 230

Green products, 340
Grey Global Group, 173
Grocery Works, 213–214
Groups, in corporate strategy, 11–12
Growth markets, 187, 189–190
GTE Corp., 506
Guidant Corp., 179

H

Haier, 19
Hansen Transmissions, 19
Harley-Davidson, 202, 217
Harrah's Entertainment, 141–142
Harris Interactive, 512
Harrods, 84
Harry Potter books, 193
Hasbro, 230
HCL, 216
Hedonistic Grazer segment, 101
Heineken, 322, 323
Heinz (H.J.), 46, 341
Henley Center, 143
Hennes & Mauritz (H&M), 132–133, 136,
        195, 324, 482
Hero-Honda, 342
Hershey, 304
Hewlett-Packard Co., 12, 16, 168, 213, 225,
        230, 292, 294, 333, 350, 351, 396,
        397, 435, 439–442
High-active pricing strategy, 362–363
High-passive pricing strategy, 363
High-risk product development process, 265
Hindustan Lever, 342
HIS Energy, 142
H&M, 132–133, 136, 195, 324, 482
Homebody segment, 101
Home Depot Inc., 313, 336, 363, 389,
        507–514
Honda Motor, 219, 237, 294, 521, 561
Hong Kong Disneyland, 219
Horizontal marketing systems, 326–327
Horizontal price fixing, 364
Horizontal relationships, 214–215
HotJobs.com, 514
Hudson's Bay, 543, 545
Hughes Supply Inc., 510
Hypo- und Vereinsbank, 32
Hyundai Securities, 533

I

Iberia, 212
IBM, 19, 20, 21, 52, 136, 137, 148, 149,
        206, 209, 210, 219, 227–228, 230,
        236, 237, 251, 293, 303, 304, 333,
        434, 440, 446, 448–449, 451,
        500, 507

IC3D (Interactive Custom Clothes Company
        Designs), 84
Icos Corp., 161
Idea generation, 249–253
    methods of, 251–253
    sources of ideas, 249–251
Identifiable market segments, 97
Identity implementation, 304
IDEO, 258, 259
IKEA, 162–168, 303
IMI, 218
Implementation
    of advertising strategy, 388
    comprehensive approach to
        improving, 481
    of Customer Relationship Management
        (CRM), 119–121, 123–124
    effectiveness, 478–479
    global marketing plan, 494
    identity, 304
    in marketing strategy process, 17–18
    process, 477–478
    of promotion strategy, 380–381
    of strategic marketing plan, 474–475,
        477–482
IMS Health Inc., 139
Incentives, implementation effectiveness,
        478–479
In-company marketing information
        resources, 141
Incremental innovations, 239
India, 168–177
    customer markets, 218
    distribution channels, 342
    globalization process and, 18, 19
    international call centers, 120
    market access, 211
    marketing research on, 139
Industrial design, 258
Industrial targets, sales promotion to, 392
Industry analysis, 61–62
Informal networks, new organization, 449
Information-based competitive
        advantage, 126
Information distribution for synergy, in
        learning organization, 133
Information Resources, Inc., 64, 100,
        139, 261
Information technology, strategic
        relationships and, 211
Infosys Technologies Ltd., 171, 175
In-N-Out, 284
Innovation, 236–244. *See also* New product
        strategy
    characteristics of successful innovators,
        243–244
    customer knowledge-based strategy at
        Best Buy, 135
    customer needs, 53
    customer value opportunities, 239

in designing market-driven strategies, 16
    disruptive, 50–51
    initiatives of successful innovators,
        242–243
    most innovative companies, 237–238
    new product opportunities, 239–242
    open source software, 210
    organization design, 446
    product cannibalization, 244
    risk and, 246
    types of innovations, 239
    value, 303
Innovation metrics, 501
Inside-out capabilities, 6–7
InsightExpress, 144–145
Integrated performance measurements, 82
Integration
    challenge of, 454–455
    global enterprise, 227–228
    of global markets, 192
    of marketing department, 456–457
    of promotion strategy, 380–381
Intel Corp., 9, 23, 144, 185, 186, 238,
        274–281, 293, 304, 352–353,
        367–368, 463
Intensive distribution, 327
Interactive/Internet marketing, in promotion
        strategy, 374, 375
Interbrand, 292
Interface Inc., 492
Intermediate customer relationships, 216
Internal analysis, in positioning
        evaluation, 199
Internal information resources, 138, 252
Internal marketing, 479–480
Internal market metrics, 501
Internal partnering, 221–222, 463
Internal process metrics, 501
International distribution channels,
        336–337, 340–343
    factors affecting, 342
    multichannel strategies, 342–343
    nature of, 341–342
International Monetary Fund (IMF), 176
Inter-nation collaborations, 228
Internet, 408–411
    advertising based on, 385
    channel hopping, 338
    e-commerce strategy, 410
    e-procurement, 335
    e-tailing, 409
    future of, 411
    impact on organization design, 464
    Internet-based channels, 463
    Internet-based marketing research,
        144–146
    managing unfavorable customer
        behavior, 123
    measuring Internet effectiveness, 411
    objectives, 409–410

Internet—*Cont.*
   reach of the Web, 97
   sales promotion and, 392
   strategy development, 409
   value opportunities and risks, 410–411
   Web metrics, 500
Internet brands, 312–313
Internet chat-rooms, 150
Interorganizational relationships. *See*
   Strategic relationships
Intranets, 414
Ipos Group SA, 139
iTunes, 327, 503

J

Jaman, 97
Japan Airlines, 212
JCPenney, 333
J.D. Power & Associates Inc., 31, 33, 519
Jeep, 216
jetBlue, 241, 455
Johnson Asset Management, 282–283
Johnson & Johnson, 159, 177–182, 197
Johnson (S.C.) & Son, 431, 432
Joint ventures, 221
J.P. Morgan Securities, 182
Jury of executive opinion, 69

K

Kagan World Media, 505
Kantar Group, 139
Kanter International, 166
Kao and Lion, 263
Kearney (A.T.), 169
Kellogg Co., 46, 311
Kentucky Fried Chicken (KFC), 284
Kenya Airways, 212
Key competitor analysis, 64–66
Kimberly-Clark Corp., 239, 285, 287
Kiosk shopping, 414
Kleiner Perkins Caufield & Byers, 32
KLM, 212
Kmart, 12–13, 135, 167, 298, 439, 512, 543
Knight-Ridder Inc., 35
Knowledge-based workers, 447
Knowledge-intensity, 131
Knowledge management, 148–149
Kohl's, 192, 333
Koogle, 517, 519
Korea, globalization process and, 18
Korean Airlines, 212
Kraft Foods Inc., 44, 341, 450–451, 493
Kroger Inc., 286, 326–327
Krogers, 303
K-Swiss, 428, 430
Kurant/Pro, 67

L

LAN Airlines, 212
Landor Associates, 278, 312
Leadership structure, in relationship
   management, 224
Lean supply chains, 334–335
Lear Corp., 440
Learning organization, 131–134
   competitive advantage and, 132–133
   learning about markets, 133–134
Learning process, 129–152
   barriers to, 134
   continuous learning about markets, 15
   ethical issues, 149–151
   learning organization, 131–134
   marketing information and knowledge
      resources, 134–147
   marketing intelligence and knowledge
      management, 147–149
   market sensing, 130–131
Legal issues
   channel relationships, 338–340
   government regulation, 230
   pricing strategy, 363–364
Leica, 49
Lenovo, 19, 52, 293, 313
Level 3 Communications Inc., 357–358
Leverage ratios, 76
Leveraging strategy
   brand, 310–314
   customer knowledge, 148–149
Levi Strauss & Co., 84, 191, 192, 466
Lexmark International, 437
LG Electronics, 229
LG Group, 229
Licensing, 311
Life cycle costing, 82
Lifestyle variables, 91
Li & Fung, 228
Limited Brands, 309
Line extension
   nature of, 310
   vertical, 310
Linens 'n Things, 336
Linux, 422, 425, 448, 528
Lipton, 311
Liquidity ratios, 75–76
Liz Claiborne Inc., 333, 430
L.L. Bean, 413, 415
Lockheed Martin, 213
Loctite Corporation, 355
"Long tail," theory of, 116
Long-term value, in strategic
   marketing, 124
Louis Vuitton, 294, 306, 314
Low-active pricing strategy, 363
Lowe's Cos., 508, 509, 512, 513
Low-passive pricing strategy, 363
Lufthansa, 212

M

Magna Steyr, 216
Magnetic resonance imaging (MRI), in
   neuromarketing, 150, 151
Mail-in rebates, 390
Malev, 212
Management dashboard, 489–490, 491
Management information systems (MIS),
   146–147
Managerial segmentation, 85
Manufacturers
   capabilities and resources, 329
   direct distribution by, 321–323
Mapping networks, 449
Market(s), 48–60. *See also* Competitor
   analysis
   challenges in, 50–52
   defining, 14, 52–53
   fast-changing, 52
   interlinkage with strategies, 49
   matching needs with product
      benefits, 52–53
   product-. *See* Product-markets
   thinking outside "competitive box," 50
Market access
   and channel strategy, 330–331
   and strategic relationships, 211
Market-driven management, 296
Market-driven organizations, 8–9, 129.
   See also Designing market-driven
   organizations
Market-driven program development, 16–17
Market-driven strategy, 2–24
   aligning organization with market,
      452–453
   becoming market driven, 7–8
   business and marketing, 9, 12–18
   characteristics, 3
   classifying capabilities, 6–7
   corporate, 9, 10–12
   customer value creation, 7
   determining distinctive capabilities, 5–6
   marketing as cross-functional process,
      454–455
   marketing functions versus marketing
      processes, 453–454
   market orientation, 4–5
   market segmentation and, 86–89
   market sensing and learning
      processes, 130–134
   new era for strategic marketing, 18–23
   organizing for, 452–455
   strategic marketing and, 452
Market environments, 187–193
   declining, 187
   emerging, 18, 187, 188–189
   global, 192–193
   growing, 187, 189–190
   mature, 187, 190–192

Market-focused design, 461
Marketing decision-support systems
  (MDSS), 147
Marketing departments, 456–458
  centralization versus decentralization, 456
  contingencies for organizing, 457
  evaluating organization designs,
    457–458
  integration versus diffusion, 456–457
Marketing information, 134–147
  advertising strategy, 134
  creating new, 143–146
  existing sources, 141–142
  external information resources, 138–140
  internal information resources, 138, 252
  management information systems,
    146–147
  marketing decision-support systems, 147
  marketing information systems, 146
  marketing research studies, 138, 252
  relationship with external marketing
    research providers, 139–140
  scanning processes, 136–138
Marketing information systems, 146
Marketing intelligence, 147–148
Marketing performance measurement,
    486–493
  designing management dashboard,
    489–490, 491
  importance of, 487
  interpreting results, 490–493
  selecting relevant metrics, 488–489
  types of marketing metrics, 488
  use of marketing metrics, 487–488
Marketing plan(s)
  in commercialization process, 263
  contents, 475
  in implementation process, 474–475
  planning. *See* Marketing planning
    process
  preliminary, 255–257
Marketing planning process, 474–482
  evaluation and control, 482–486
  global issues, 493–495
  implementation, 474–475, 477–482
  managing planning process, 475–477
  marketing performance measurement,
    486–493
  marketing plan contents, 475
  overview, 475
Marketing program, 197–199
Marketing research studies, 138, 252
Marketing strategy process, 13–18
  Customer Relationship Management
    (CRM), 14–15, 84, 89, 94–95
  decisions in, 260
  designing market-driven strategies, 15–16
  implementing market-driven
    strategy, 17–18
  managing market-driven strategy, 17–18

market-driven program development,
    16–17
  markets, 14
  segments, 14
Market niche, 86, 87
Market orientation, in market-driven
    strategy, 4–5
Market position
  pricing objectives and, 352
  strategic relationships and, 223
Market potential, estimating, 67
Market segmentation, 83–110
  activities in, 89
  decisions in, 89
  defining market to be segmented, 89–90
  finer segmentation strategies, 104–106
  forming market segments, 96–104
  identifying market segments, 90–95, 97–99
  levels of, 85
  market-driven, 86–89
  nature of, 14, 84
  requirements for, 96–98
  role of, 85
  selecting segmentation strategy, 106–109
Market segment structure, 453
Market selectivity, strategic relationships
    and, 223
Market sensing, 8, 130–131
  example, 132
  nature of, 130
  processes, 131
Market share, estimating, 68
Market size estimation
  evaluating market opportunity, 68–70
  market potential, 67
  market share, 68
  sales forecasts, 68, 69
Market targeting strategy, 185–193, 260
  in designing market-driven strategies, 15
  in different marketing environments,
    187–193
  factors influencing targeting decisions,
    186–187
  market segmentation and, 87–89
  nature of, 15
  targeting alternatives, 185–186
Market targets, 65
Market testing, 69, 260–263
Marlboro, 294
Marriott Courtyard, 99
Marriott International, 143, 217, 310
Mars, 321–322
Mary Kay, 407
Mass customization, 92, 105, 259
Material Martyr segment, 102
Matrix design, 453, 461–462
Matsushita Electric Industrial, 229, 534
Mattel, 230, 347, 455
Mature markets, 187, 190–192
Maturiteen segment, 92

Maxjet, 87
May's, 333
Maytag, 19
McDonald's Corp., 42, 55, 281–284, 293, 373
McDonald Supply, 543, 545
McGraw-Hill Cos., 43
McKinsey & Co., 21, 118, 368, 432–433
McKinsey Global Institute, 171
McNeil Pharmaceutical, 182
MEA, 212
Media metrics, 500
Media/scheduling decisions, 384–386
Medpointe Inc., 160
Menard's, 514
Mercedes-Benz, 30, 31, 32, 33, 216, 293,
    306–307
Mercer, 113
Merck & Co., 19, 156, 160–161
Merrill Lynch & Co., 294, 425, 435, 436, 439
Metrics. *See* Performance metrics
METRO, 340, 467
Metrosexual segment, 92
Mexicana Airlines, 212
Micro-segmentation strategy, 84, 105, 185
Microsoft Corp., 9, 16, 20, 22, 23, 51, 52,
    174, 208, 210, 237, 251, 252, 270,
    275, 279, 293, 308, 313, 340,
    418–425, 434, 454, 468, 491, 495,
    500, 507, 515, 516, 517, 525–533
Midas Inc., 284
Miller Brewing, 96
MindTree Consulting Ltd., 177
Missionary selling, 399–400, 405
Mitsubishi Heavy Industries, 229
Mittal Steel, 2–3, 6–8, 18, 130
Mobil, 101–102
Modal Targeting, 143
Modern Man segment, 92
Modularity, 51–52, 259
Monitoring
  in commercialization process, 263–264
  competitive position, 81
Monster.com, 313
Morgan (J.P.) Securities, 182
Morgan Stanley, 32, 34, 43, 505, 521
Morrisons, 341
Mothercare, 338
Motivation
  new organization employees, 451
  sales force, 467–468
  sales organization, 406
Motorola Inc., 64, 168, 174, 236, 257, 271,
    272, 424, 437, 537
Multichanneling
  global issues, 342–343
  nature of, 337
Multivariate testing (MVT), 200
Mutually informed interpretations,
    133–134
MySpace, 20, 51, 97, 208, 385, 452

N

National Association of Corporate
    Directors, 46
NCR, 441
Needs of buyers
    in market segmentation, 90, 93–94
    matching with product benefits, 52–53
    in promotion strategy, 376
Neiman-Marcus, 192
Nescafe, 294
Nestlé, 192, 221, 251, 307, 312, 322, 323
NetJets, 349
Networked organizations, 464
Neuromarketing, 150, 151
New Balance, 428
New business selling, 399, 405
New competitors, 66–67
Newell Rubbermaid Inc., 402
New England Consulting Group, 46
New marketing information, 143–146
New markets
    new market space, 52
    strategic relationships and, 223
New market space, 86–87
New organization, 445–449
    collaboration, 448–449
    external relationships, 449
    informal networks, 449
    innovation, 446
    knowledge-based worker, 447
    managing culture, 447–448
    new marketing roles, 462–464
    organizational design shifts, 446
    organizational diversity, 449
    traditional structures, 445–446
New product lines, 308
New product strategy. *See also* Innovation
    business analysis, 255–257
    commercialization, 263–264
    concept evaluation, 254–255
    in designing market-driven strategies, 16
    finding new product opportunities,
        239–242
    idea generation, 249–253
    marketing strategy decisions, 260
    market testing, 260–263
    need recognition, 376
    new-product planning, 244–249,
        264–265
    new product teams, 460–461
    process development, 259
    product development, 257–259, 265
    screening, 253, 256
News Corporation, 20, 51, 208
New York Telephone, 505
New York Times Co., 34–40
New York Times Digital, 39
NEXT Software Inc., 269
Niche strategy, 86, 87

Nielsen Media Research, 64, 142, 388
Nike Inc., 42, 64, 84, 197, 302, 311, 322,
    384, 425–433
Nissan Motor Co., 257, 277, 519–524,
    561, 562
Nitori Co., 167
Nokia Corporation, 16, 64, 140, 173, 174,
    197–199, 201, 236, 237, 257, 279,
    292, 293, 342, 422, 424
Nonprice factors, 354–356
Nordstrom, 192
Northwest Airlines, 212
NPD Group, 538
Nucor Corporation, 480
Nynex Corp., 504–506

O

Objective(s)
    advertising, 382, 383
    in corporate strategy, 10, 11
    of customer value analysis, 239
    Internet, 409–410
    pricing, 352–353, 359
    in promotion strategy, 376–378, 379
    of strategic relationships, 223–224
Objective inquiry, in learning
    organization, 133
Observation, 143–144
Office Depot, 363, 399
Ogilvy & Mather, 381
One Laptop Per Child program, 22, 23
One-size-fits-all marketing, 84
One-to-one marketing, 84
Oneworld, 212
Online surveys, 145
Open source marketing information
    resources, 142
Operational segmentation, 85
Oracle Corp., 225, 404, 422, 437, 441,
    491, 562
Organizational change, 444–445, 452
Organizational commitment, to Customer
    Relationship Management
    (CRM), 118
Organizational diversity, new
    organization, 449
Organizational markets, characteristics of, 91
Organizational process, 449–451
Organizational relationships. *See* Strategic
    relationships
Organizational stretch, 481–482
Organization design. *See also* Designing
    market-driven organizations
    employee motivation, 451
    evaluating, 457–458
    functional, 459
    implementation effectiveness, 478
    Internet impact on, 464

    managing organizational process,
        449–451
    market-focused, 461
    marketing versus hierarchical
        organization, 458
    matrix, 453, 461–462
    new organization, 445–449
    organizational agility and flexibility, 451
    product-focused, 459–461
    sales organization, 402–403
Organization structure
    for marketing resources, 459–465
    in organizing for market-driven
        strategy, 452, 453
Organization value, 122
Outside-in processes, 6–7
Outsourcing, 63, 137, 216
    international call centers, 120
    new organization, 449
    partnering with other organizations, 463
Overpositioning, 201
Ownership vertical marketing systems
    (VMS), 325–326

P

Pacific Growth Equities, 517
Palm, 16
palmOne, 322, 324
Palm Pilot, 298–299
Panasonic, 534
Parle, 46
Patek Philippe, 92
Pay by Touch, 115
Payless ShoeSource, 488
PayPal, 67, 208
PDVSA, 229
PeopleSoft, 404
PepsiCo Inc., 41–43, 49, 64, 118, 264,
    290, 294, 329, 391, 399, 428–429,
    465, 493
Percent of sales, in promotion strategy, 379
Perceptions, in market segmentation, 93–94
Perceptual mapping, 94, 103–104
Performance gaps, in marketing perfor-
    mance measurement, 490–491
Performance implications, in market
    orientation, 5
Performance metrics
    advertising strategy, 388, 389
    brand equity, 298, 301–302
    channel objectives, 339
    Customer Relationship Management
        (CRM), 122, 124
    Internet strategy, 411
    marketing, 486–493, 499–501
    in relationship management, 226
    sales organization, 407–408
Personal digital assistants (PDAs), 16

Personal selling, 320, 373–374, 376, 378
Petrobas, 229
Petronas of Malaysia, 229
Pfizer, 156–162, 185, 397
Pharmacia Corp., 160, 225
Philips Electronics, 534
Philips Norelco, 92, 446
Physical distribution management, 334–335
    e-procurement, 335
    impact of supply chain management on
        marketing, 335
    supply chain strategy, 334–335, 460
Pier 1 Imports, 163
Piggly Wiggly, 115
Pitney-Bowes, 250
Pixar Animation Studios, 269, 270–272, 293
Planet Retail, 164
Planning
    financial, 79
    marketing. *See* Marketing planning
        process
    new-product, 244–249, 264–265
    in relationship management, 224
    strategic marketing, 474–482
Platform development process, 265
Pohang Iron & Steel Co., 174
Point-of-purchase promotion, 390
Polaroid, 4
Polish Airlines, 212
Polo Ralph Lauren Corp., 92, 429
Portfolio management
    brand, 295, 298, 306–309
    product, 296
Portfolio metrics, 499
Portugalia Airlines, 212
Positioning analysis
    brand, 301
    of market segments, 107
Positioning concept, 195–196
Positioning decision, 196
Positioning effectiveness, 199–202
    analytical positioning techniques, 201
    competitor research, 200
    components of, 199
    customer research, 200
    determining, 201
    errors and, 201
    nature of, 194
    positioning strategies, 202
    targeting strategies, 202
    testing marketing, 200–201
Positioning strategy, 193–202, 260
    defined, 194
    in designing market-driven strategies, 15
    developing, 196–199
    marketing program decisions, 197–199
    market segmentation and, 87–89
    nature of, 15, 193–195
    positioning effectiveness, 194, 199–202
    price in, 349–350, 352, 362

scope of, 197
    selecting positioning concept, 195–196
Power, in channel relationships, 336
Power (J.D.) & Associates Inc., 31, 33, 519
Predatory pricing, 364
Preferences of buyers, in market
        segmentation, 90, 93–94
Preliminary marketing plans, 255–257
Premium store brands, 303
Price discrimination, 364
Price elasticity, 354
Price fixing, 364
Price segmentation, 367–368
Price Shopper segment, 101
Pricing activities, in distribution process, 319
Pricing management, 367–369
Pricing metrics, 499
Pricing policy, 367
Pricing situation, 353–359
    competitor analysis, 357–359
    cost analysis, 356–357
    customer price sensitivity, 353–356
    nature of, 350
    pricing objectives, 359
Pricing strategy, 198, 347–369
    competitor analysis, 357–359
    cost analysis, 356–357
    customer price sensitivity, 353–356
    determining specific prices, 365–366
    establishing pricing policy and
        structure, 367
    examples, 362–363
    legal and ethical considerations,
        363–364
    nature of, 17, 351–352
    objectives, 352–353, 359
    in positioning strategy, 349–350, 362
    pricing management, 367–369
    pricing situations, 350, 353–359
    roles of pricing, 350–351
    selecting, 360–365
    strategic role of price, 348–353
Pricing structure, 367
Prisoner's dilemma, 359
Privacy, 149–150
Private branding, 303
Process development, 259
Processes, in corporate strategy, 12
Processing activities, in distribution
        process, 319
Process-intensive development process, 265
Procter and Gamble Company (P&G), 18,
        46, 92, 129–130, 160, 197, 209, 211,
        218, 236, 237, 244, 249, 252, 262,
        263, 285, 304, 305, 308, 353–354,
        356, 360, 376, 377, 378, 384, 389,
        444–445, 446, 456, 468, 493
Product(s), defined, 291
Product/brand management, 296, 459–460
Product characteristics, 322, 329

Product cost, 356
Product customization, 91
Product development process, 257–259, 265
Product differentiation, 98
Product-focused organizational design,
        459–461
Product group/marketing management, 296
Product improvement, 305–306
Product life cycle (PLC), 187, 188
    brand strategies, 300
    marketing strategy alteration, 306
    pricing based on, 369
    rate of change, 300
Product line branding, 303, 304
Product-markets
    changing composition of, 56
    composition of, 54–55
    defining, 54–55
    end-users, 57–59
    extent of complexity, 56
    forming, 55–56
    illustrative, 57
    market environments, 187–193
    matching needs with product benefits,
        52–53
    nature of, 52–53
    new products. *See* New product strategy
    product life cycle, 187, 188, 300, 306, 369
    segmentation. *See* Market segmentation
Product-market structure, 53–54
    in emerging markets, 188
    in growth markets, 189–190
    in mature markets, 191
Product metrics, 499
Product performance analysis
    nature of, 300–301
    strategies for improving product
        performance, 304–306
Product performance evaluation, 407
Product placement, 391
Product portfolios, 296
Product positioning, price in, 352
Product specifications, 258
Product strategy, 197, 199, 349
Product-type product markets, 54
Product use situation segmentation, 91–94
Product-variants, 54
Profitability metrics, 499
Profitability ratios, 75
Profit projections, new-product, 257
Pro forma income statements, 79
Progressive Insurance, 53
Promotion metrics, 500
Promotion strategy, 198, 199, 373–381
    communication objectives, 376–378
    composition of, 373–375
    designing, 375–376
    effectiveness of, 381
    implementing, 380–381
    integrating, 380–381

Promotion strategy—*Cont.*
  nature of, 17
  promotion budget, 311, 378–380
  promotion component strategies, 380
  role of promotion components, 378
Prototypes, 258
PS Ellan, 166
Psychographic variables, 90
Public relations, in promotion strategy,
  374–375, 379
Public Services Broadcasting (PBS),
  136–137
Puma, 430
Purchase behavior, 94–95
Purchase-behavior variables, 90

Q

Qantas Airways Ltd., 212, 401
Quaker Oats Co., 41, 46, 290
Quality-control charts, 492–493
Quality costing, 82
Quanta Computer, 23
Quantum Corp., 421
QuEST, 174
Quick-build product development
  process, 265
Quintiles Transnational, 8
Quizno's, 282
Qwest Communications International Inc.,
  357–358, 504, 507, 518

R

Radio Frequency Identification (RFID), 150
Radio Shack, 254
Ranbaxy Laboratories Ltd., 19, 159–160
Random House, 116, 385
Rateitall.com, 145
Ratio analysis, 74–76, 500
Ray-Ban, 91
Rebates, mail-in, 390
Reebok International Ltd., 64, 430
Relationship management, 224–225, 226
Relationship vertical marketing systems
  (VMS), 326
Renault, 520–524
Render, Vanderslice & Associates, 506
Rent.com, 67
Resale price maintenance, 364
Research agency marketing information
  resources, 142
Research in Motion Ltd. (RIM), 16, 279–280
Research surveys, 144, 145
Resource gaps, strategic relationships and,
  209–211
Resources
  in corporate strategy, 11

in emerging markets, 189
in growth markets, 190
in mature markets, 191
structuring marketing, 459–465
Response differences
  forming groups based on, 102–103
  nature of, 96–97
Response to marketing stimuli, in database
  marketing, 115
Restructuring, strategic relationships and, 224
Retrosexual segment, 92
Return Exchange, 123
Revenue analysis, sales organization, 402–403
Revenue forecasts, 255
Reverse auction pricing, 366
Revlon, 328
Rewe, 467
Road Warrior segment, 101
Robert Morris Associates, 74
Robinson-Patman Act, 364
Royal Dutch Shell, 229
Royal Jordanian, 212
Russia
  globalization process and, 18, 19
  marketing research on, 139
  market potential and, 67–68
  market segmentation in, 96–97
Ryanair, 87

S

Saatchi and Saatchi, 377
Safeway, 213–214
Sales and effort response models, 404
Sales channels, 401–402
Salesforce.com, 241, 403, 404, 530, 531
Sales force composite, 69
Sales force strategy, 196, 199, 392, 397–408
  defining selling process, 400–401
  designing sales organization, 402–406
  role of selling in, 398–399
  sales channels, 401–402
  sales force evaluation and control,
    407–408
  types of sales jobs, 399–400, 405
Sales forecasts, 68, 69
Sales jobs, 399–400, 405
Sales metrics, 499
Sales organization, 402–408
  finding and selecting salespeople,
    405–406
  organizational design, 402–403
  sales force deployment, 403–405
  sales force evaluation and control,
    467–468
  supervision and motivation, 406
  training, 406
Sales promotion strategy, 389–393
  activities, 390–392

advantages and limitations, 392–393
developing, 393
in distribution process, 319
nature and scope of sales promotion,
  389–390
in promotion strategy, 374
selling in, 398–399
Sampson Tyrrell Enterprise, 312
Sam's Club, 222, 305, 514
Samsung Electronics Co., 64, 238, 241,
  242, 248–249, 533–539
Samsung Group, 131, 173, 197, 219, 229,
  277, 279, 294
Samsung Motors, 522
Sandelman & Associates Inc., 284
Sanford C. Bernstein & Co.,
  160, 386, 423–424
Sara Lee Corp., 197, 426
SAS-Scandinavian Airlines, 212
Saudi Aramco, 229
SBC, 507
S.C. Johnson & Son, 431, 432
Scanned based tests, 261
Scanning processes, 136–138
Schering-Plough Corp., 162
Scholastic Corp., 193
Scope, in corporate strategy, 10
Screening, of new-product ideas, 253, 256
Search process, for new ideas, 250, 251
Sears, 137, 303
Second Life, 20, 21
Segmentation "fit," 108
Segmentation variables, 90–91. *See also*
  Market segmentation
Segment attractiveness analysis
  estimating segment attrac-
    tiveness, 107–108
  nature of, 108–109
Selective distribution, 327–328
Self-interest, in relationship
  management, 224
Selling activities, in distribution
  process, 319
Selling process, 400–401
Servicing and repairs, in distribution
  process, 320
7-11 Inc., 442
SG Cowen & Co., 528
Shanghai Airlines, 212
Shareholder value creation, product-markets
  and, 52–53
Sharp Corp., 229, 538
Shell Oil, 148, 488–489
Sherman Act, 364
Short-term value, in strategic marketing, 124
Siebel Systems, 404
Siemens, 210
Sierra Mist, 264
Signal, price as, 351
Signode Corporation, 102

Silicon Graphics, 525
Silverjet, 87
Simulated tests, 261
Singapore Airlines Ltd., 212, 376, 401
Single-factor models, 404
Situation variables, 90
Skechers, 428
Skills
    in distribution channel, 329
    strategic relationships and, 209–211
Skoda, 308
Skype Technologies, 20, 67, 526
SkyTeam, 212
Slendertone, 548–559
SoBe Beverages, 49
Society of Competitive Intelligence, 65
Socioeconomic trends, 412
Sofres plc, 139, 285
SoftCom Technology Consulting, 425
Sony Corp., 92, 206, 237, 244, 260, 270,
    278, 297, 327, 411, 422, 453, 528,
    533–534, 537
Sony Electronics, 322, 324
Sony Ericsson Mobile Communications, 424
South African Airways, 212
South Beach Beverage Co., 44
Southwest Airlines, 5–6, 7, 64, 313, 363
Spanair, 212
Specialization, 185–186, 462–463
Springtime USA, 259
Sprint Corp., 502
Spyware, 145
Stability over time, 98
Standard Chartered Bank, 211
Standard & Poor's 500-stock index, 178
Standard Rates and Data Services, 385
Staples, 336, 441–442
Star Alliance, 212
Starbucks, 45, 162, 237, 258, 302, 465, 529
Starwood Hotels, 21
State-owned enterprises
    government collaboration with, 229–230
    government competition with, 229
Statistical demand analysis, 69
Steady Builder segment, 102
Storage activities, in distribution
    process, 319
Strategic account management
    (SAM), 218–219
Strategic alliances, 219–221, 230, 466
Strategic analysis, of market segments,
    106–109
Strategic Business Units (SBUs),
    12, 296, 298
Strategic costing, 82
Strategic customers, 217–219
Strategic Decisions Group, 179
Strategic/Key Account Management, 217–218
Strategic marketing
    audits, 483–486

competitive differentiation, 124–126
Customer Relationship Management
    (CRM) and, 123–126, 483
new era, 18–23
in organizing for market-driven
    strategy, 452
performance metrics, 124
planning for. See Marketing planning
    process
short- versus long-term value, 124
Strategic market segmentation. See Market
    segmentation
Strategic pricing, 82
Strategic relationships, 206–231
    control and evaluation, 226
    in designing market-driven strategies, 15
    drivers of, 207
    end-user customer relationships, 217
    exiting from alliance, 226–227
    intermediate customer relationships, 216
    internal partnering, 221–222
    joint ventures, 221
    nature of, 15
    new organization, 449
    objective of relationship, 223–224
    partnering capabilities and, 225
    rationale for, 207–214
    relationship management, 224–225, 226
    strategic alliances, 219–221, 230, 466
    strategic customers, 217–219
    supplier relationships, 215–216
Strategic segmentation, 85
Strategic suppliers, 215–216
Strategic vision, 70–71
Strategies
    in corporate strategy, 10
    creating new market space, 52
    for fast-changing markets, 52
    interlinkage with markets, 49
Structure
    channel, 334
    in corporate strategy, 12
Stubhub, 67
Stumbleupon, 67
Substantial innovation, 239
Sumerset Houseboats Inc., 217
Sun Microsystems Inc., 21, 32, 209, 210,
    423, 437
Supervision, sales organization, 406
Supplemental financial analysis,
    79–80, 81–82
Supplier Relationship Management
    (SRM), 464
Supplier relationships, 215–216
Supply chain strategy, 334–335, 460
SurveyMonkey, 145
Susquehanna Financial Group, 428
Suzlon Energy, 19
Suzuki, 342
Swatch, 215–216

Swiss International Airlines, 212
Symbolic positioning concepts, 196
Synergistic distribution of information, 133
Synovate, 139
Syntex Corporation, 353–354
Systems, in corporate strategy, 12

T

Taco Bell, 284
Taiwan, international call centers, 120
TAP Air Portugal, 212
Target Corp., 163, 167, 192, 238, 298,
    303, 306, 333, 349, 514
Target costing, 82
Targeting strategy
    in global markets, 192–193
    in growth markets, 190
    in mature markets, 191–192
Tarom, 212
Tata Steel, 19, 174
Taylor Nelson Sofres, 139, 285
Team selling, 399
Technical selling, 400, 405
Technology. See also Internet
    to build customer profiles, 115
    diversity of, 19–20
    product-market, 56
    strategic relationships and, 223
    uncertainty and, 19–20
Technology constraints, and strategic
    relationships, 210
Technology-push development process, 265
Technology transfer, in relationship
    management, 225
Technomic Inc., 284
Telemarketing, 402, 413
Tesco International, 131, 132, 146, 193,
    213–214, 218, 340, 341, 467
Tesco plc, 285–287
Test marketing, in positioning evaluation,
    200–201
Texas Instruments, 270, 277
Thai Airways International, 212
Thailand, globalization process and, 18
Thomson First Call, 418
3M, 237, 244, 249, 476
Threshold levels, 402
Time-series analysis, 68, 69
Time Warner, 160
Timex, 91
TNS Media Intelligence, 161
Toshiba, 206, 260
Toyota Motor Corp., 30, 63, 123, 131, 173,
    236, 237, 292, 293, 301, 306, 338,
    367, 389, 447–448, 451, 455, 520,
    523, 559–565
Toys 'R' Us, 336
Trader Joe's, 341

Trade selling, 399, 405
Trade shows, 392
Traditional market tests, 262
Training, sales organization, 406
Transactional selling, 399
Transactions, in database marketing, 115
Transformational innovation, 239, 241–242
Transportation activities, in distribution
      process, 319
T. Rowe Price Value Fund, 423
True Blue segment, 101
True Value Co., 513
Trust
    in channel relationships, 336
    in relationship management, 224
Turkish Airlines, 212
Tyco Healthcare Group L.P., 240

U

Ultratone, 553
Umbria Inc., 136–137
Underpositioning, 201
Unilever, 92, 129, 146, 385
United Airlines, 87, 212
United Parcel Service, 133
United States Automobile Association
    (USAA), 90
U.S. Central Intelligence Agency (CIA), 142
U.S. Commerce Department, 255
U.S. Food and Drug Administration (FDA),
    156, 162, 178
U.S. Surgical Corporation (USS),
    180, 239–241
Unit of financial analysis, 74
Unocal, 19
Upjohn, 225
USA Interactive Inc., 514
US Airways, 212
USA Network, 518
User expectations, 69
Use tests, 258–259

V

Vaio, 279
Value-added chain, 62–63
Value-added competencies, 331
Value-chain analysis, 107
Value-chain costing, 82
Value-chain pricing, 368
Value-chain strategy, 318–343
    channel strategy, 323–333
    ethical and social responsibility
        imperatives, 340

international channels, 340–343
    Internet, 409
    managing the channel, 333–340
    nature of, 17
    in positioning strategy, 197–198, 199
    relationships, 216
    sales promotion in, 392
    strategic role of value chain, 319–323
    value creation process, 123
Value creation process, 121–123
    customer value, 121–122
    value-chain strategy, 123
    value received by organization, 122
Value innovators, 303
Value proposition, 22
Vanguard Group, 186
Variability, in marketing performance
    measurement, 492–493
Variety-seeking strategy, 105
VARIG Brazilian Airlines, 212
Venture Marketing Organizations
    (VMOs), 463, 465
Venture teams, 460
Verizon Communications Inc., 491,
    502–507, 518
Vertical line extension, 310
Vertical marketing systems (VMS), 324–326
Vertical markets, 91
Vertical price fixing, 364
Vertical relationships, 214–215, 216
Victoria's Secret, 303, 309, 336, 413
Viral marketing, 385–386
Virgin Airways, 124
Virgin Atlantic, 87
Virgin Group, 162, 238, 311, 312
Virtual innovation teams, 445
Virtual reality, 20, 21
Vision
    in corporate strategy, 11
    strategic, 70–71
    in strategic marketing, 13
VNU NV, 139, 142
Vodafone Group, 342, 507
Voice-Over Internet Protocol (VOIP), 66, 189
Volkswagen, 30, 31, 32, 216, 310, 385
Volume, effect on cost, 357

W

Walgreens, 463
Wal-Mart Stores Inc., 9, 12–13, 18, 64, 132,
    135, 144, 163, 165, 190–191, 192,
    193, 218, 222, 237, 279, 285, 286,
    303, 305, 319, 340, 341, 342, 348,
    349, 358, 363, 411, 434, 439, 467,
    508, 512, 513, 514

Walt Disney Co., 237, 269–274, 293, 311
Warner Bros. Entertainment Inc., 517
Warner-Lambert Co., 160
Warner Music, 516
Warranties, 358
Warren Kade, 210
Washington Post Co., 35
WD-40, 143
Web 1.0, 2, 20
Web 2.0, 2, 20, 208
Web-enabled tests, 262
Web metrics, 500
Wells Fargo, 21
Wendy's, 283
Westat Inc., 139
White Consolidated Industries Ltd., 539
White-Westinghouse Appliances, 539
Whole Foods Market Inc., 184, 185, 341
Wikipedia, 20, 142
Williams Sonoma, 337
Woodwards, 545
Woolworths, 135
World Bank, 142, 148
Worldwide Retail Exchange, 337
World Wrestling Entertainments
    (WWE), 314
Wrigley's, 191
Wyeth, 407, 408

X

X14, 143
Xerox, 22, 135, 136, 148, 221
XM Satellite Radio, 241, 242, 248–249

Y

Yahoo! Inc., 142, 145–146, 208, 220,
    375, 514–519, 530
Yankee Group, 505
Young & Rubicam, 254, 301, 387
YouTube, 20, 51, 385
Yum! Brands Inc., 284

Z

Zara, 136, 324, 451, 455
Zoomerang, 145